OXFORD HISTORY OF MODERN EUROPE

General Editors

LORD BULLOCK *and* SIR WILLIAM DEAKIN

Oxford History of Modern Europe

A PEOPLE APART

A POLITICAL HISTORY OF
THE JEWS IN EUROPE
1789–1939

BY

DAVID VITAL

OXFORD
UNIVERSITY PRESS

OXFORD

UNIVERSITY PRESS

Great Clarendon Street, Oxford OX2 6DP

Oxford University Press is a department of the University of Oxford.
It furthers the University's objective of excellence in research, scholarship,
and education by publishing worldwide in

Oxford New York

Athens Auckland Bangkok Bogotá Buenos Aires
Cape Town Chennai Dar es Salaam Delhi Florence Hong Kong Istanbul
Karachi Kolkata Kuala Lumpur Madrid Melbourne Mexico City Mumbai
Nairobi Paris São Paulo Singapore Taipei Tokyo Toronto Warsaw
and associated companies in Berlin Ibadan

Oxford is a registered trade mark of Oxford University Press
in the UK and certain other countries

Published in the United States
by Oxford University Press Inc., New York

British Library Cataloguing in Publication Data

Data available

Library of Congress Cataloging in Publication Data

Vital, David.
A people apart : a political history of the Jews in Europe, 1789–1939 / by David Vital.
p. cm.—(Oxford history of modern Europe)
Includes bibliographical references and index.
1. Jews—Europe—History. 2. Jews—History—1789–1945. 3. Jews—
Europe—Politics and government. 4. Holocaust, Jewish (1939–1945)—
Causes. 5. Antisemitism—Europe—History. 6. Europe—Ethnic
relations. I. Title. II. Series.
DS135.E83V58 1999 940'.04924—dc21 98-51332

ISBN 0–19–821980–6 (hbk.)
ISBN 0–19–924681–5 (pbk.)

1 3 5 7 9 10 8 6 4 2

Typeset in Monotype Bembo
by Jayvee, Trivandrum, India
Printed in Great Britain
on acid-free paper by
Bookcraft Ltd., Midsomer Norton
Nr. Bath, Somerset

לעליזה

PREFACE

> Real or fancied grievances are in themselves [in]sufficient to produce, however strongly they may favour, the emergence of active hostility against a social order. For such an atmosphere to develop it is necessary that there be groups to whose interest it is to work up and organize resentment, to nurse it, to voice it, and to lead it. . . . The mass of people never develops definite opinions on its own initiative. Still less is it able to articulate them and to turn them into consistent attitudes and actions. All it can do is to follow or refuse to follow such group leadership as may offer itself.
>
> Joseph Schumpeter[1]

This is a political history.

There is, of course, a great deal more to public and private life than politics and much that is infinitely more agreeable to contemplate. The study of power and authority and the men and women who wield them draws us, like it or not, to an examination of what is harshest, ugliest, and most dangerous in human conduct—besides which, of all spheres of public activity, that which entails social control is the one most likely to be touched by pathology.

But there is more than a little truth in Lenin's infamous, yet penetrating remark that much—he himself thought everything—boils down to the question who rules whom.[2] For indeed, when all is said and done, the realm in which the ultimately crucial affairs of society evolve is the power-political. There life touches most closely upon death. There the siren calls to conflict are sweetest. There cowardice vies most successfully with courage, cruelty with enterprise, and overweening personal ambition with infinite despair. Thus for all peoples at one time or another. Thus for the Jewish people throughout their history—but with quite exceptional intensity in Europe during the period with which this book deals.

While it has been difficult, therefore, to avoid writing this book in any other spirit than that which Jonathan Swift termed 'savage indignation',

---

[1] *Capitalism, Socialism and Democracy*, 5th edn. (London, 1976), 145.

[2] 'Novaya ekonomicheskaya politika', report to the Second All-Russian Congress of Political Education Departments, 17 Oct. 1921. V. I. Lenin, *Polnoe Sobranie Sochionenii*, 5th edn., xliv (Moscow, 1964), 161.

the effort has been made. How successful the effort to write with an appropriate measure of restraint has been I leave, needless to say, to others to judge—although, that said, I have not thought that restraint should deter one from asking the deeper questions raised by the grim fate that overtook the Jews of Europe; or that an attempt to answer them, if only in part, could be in any other than political terms; or again that, with that being the intention, the account could fail to be anything other than rigorously selective.

Much in the recent social, cultural, theological, and literary history of the Jews that is by any ordinary reckoning of surpassing interest has, accordingly, been set aside. It is to the sourer, harsher matters that lay at the centre of the political evolution and travails of European Jewry between the French Revolution and the outbreak of the Second World War that attention has been paid almost exclusively. The present account is selective too in that it was not, and could not have been, part of my intention to construct a full, which is to say geographically and demographically comprehensive, account even of the *politics* of the Jews of Europe in the period chosen, let alone of their social, cultural, and religious life. Many ancient and distinguished communities will be found to be absent, or virtually so, from these pages. But then if the absolute essentials of the Jewish condition were not to recede from view it had to be those whose affairs had demonstrable consequences for the Jewish people in Europe as a whole and in the longest of runs, or whose affairs serve to illustrate the main continent-wide lines of overall development with special clarity, that would have to speak for all.

This was not a happy course to follow nor, having regard for past distinction and achievement, could it be an altogether just one. But to have proceeded otherwise, namely to have given all communities their due, let alone attempt to treat all communities in all their aspects, would have been to compile a study of an essentially encyclopaedic character, besides increasing the size of the book beyond the tolerance of even the most generous of publishers—and, of course, beyond that of any readily conceivable potential reader as well. And it would have vitiated the one basis on which, as it seemed to me, it might be worth while to attempt a study of this kind in the first place: that of interpretation. Strict chronology and an attempt at comprehensiveness had to give way to the exploration of themes. The function of what it has become customary to call anecdotal detail had to be limited to the support and elucidation of argument. Description had never to be more than the handmaiden of analysis.

Some may think that it would, none the less, have been braver to seek to deal with the entirety of European Jewry in the relevant period come what may. Perhaps. My view has been that coherence depended before all else on setting a limit to the questions to be dealt with and on being as clear as possible in one's own mind about the terms on which answers were to be sought and formulated. Above all, both questions and answers had to be geared to what were plainly the final determinants of the Jews' situation, to the manner and degree to which those who presumed to lead them sought—or failed—to cope with successive onslaughts upon their people, and to the ease and rapidity with which so great a segment of this ancient nation could be made (but equally, was allowed) to founder.

However one were to proceed it was inevitable that great debts would be incurred. That has certainly been so in my case: in the first instance to the very many authors of scholarly studies on which I found myself relying, few of them known to me personally, but whose names, number, and variety are attested to in the Bibliography and the footnotes.

A debt of a direct and more personal order is owed to the Editors of this series, Lord Bullock and Sir William Deakin: for their very great patience over rather more than a decade while the book was in the making, for the constant, quiet, and indispensable encouragement repeatedly afforded me, and for the advice they gave me when it was most needed.

My old friend Professor [Lord] Max Beloff was kind enough to scrutinize the manuscript and save me from many errors. Michel Opatowski gave generously of his time to prepare the maps. The International Institute of Social History at Amsterdam provided me with hospitality for a season and invaluable assistance in the location of important material. I am most grateful too to Dr Sylviane Colombo, Dr Oleg Gorelov, Mrs Ayala Laron, Dr Dina Porat, Ms Svetlana Pererozin, Dr Gerhart Riegner, Mrs Liora Sonshine, and the librarians at Tel Aviv and Northwestern Universities, all of whom were helpful to me in one way or another, in some cases over very long periods, while this book was in preparation.

As it is usual but always proper to say, the faults of the book and all remaining errors in it are, of course, mine alone.

D.V.

April 1998

CONTENTS

Part II. Aspirations and Equivocations

Part III. New Dispensations

LIST OF MAPS

LIST OF TABLES

A NOTE ON TRANSLITERATION
AND TRANSLATION

Hebrew terms have been rendered phonetically, so far as possible, rather than according to strict scholarly convention. No distinction has been drawn between *tav* and *tet*, for example; both are rendered as *t*. The (soft) *pe refuya* is rendered as *f*, the (hard) *pe degusha* as *p*. The gutturals *het* and *khaf* (both of which are approximately the *ch* in 'loch') have been transliterated as *ḥ* and *kh* respectively; the *ẓaddi* (roughly the *ts* in 'pits') as *ẓ*; the guttural *'ayin* as *'*; the *alef* (where transliteration might otherwise suggest a diphthong) as *'*.

Names have been given in the form preferred or employed by the person in question, if known, or in the form by which he or she is best known. In case of doubt the *Encyclopaedia Judaica* has been consulted. Where English equivalents for place-names are sufficiently familiar they have been used: Jerusalem, therefore, not Yerushalayyim; Moscow not Moskva. In a very few cases it seemed appropriate to refer to the Jewish or the Julian calendars (the latter indicated by the addition of 'O[ld]. S[tyle].' Otherwise, dates are according to the usual western or Gregorian calendar.

Unless otherwise indicated, English translations of source material are the author's.

ABBREVIATIONS

AE	French Foreign Ministry Archives
AIU	Alliance Israélite Universelle
AJA	Anglo-Jewish Association
BoD	Board of Deputies of British Jews (Archives)
Bund	Algemeyner yidisher arbeter Bund in Lite, Poyln, un Rusland (General Jewish Workers' Party of Lithuania, Poland, and Russia)
CAHJP	Central Archives of the History of the Jewish People
CZA	Central Zionist Archives
DGFP	Documents on German Foreign Policy
Diaries	Theodor Herzl, *The Complete Diaries*, ed. Raphael Patai, English trans. Harry Zohn, 5 vols. (New York, 1960)
EAC	Smaller Actions Committee (Executive) of the World Zionist Organization
FRUS	*Foreign Relations of the United States*
GAC	Greater Actions Committee of the World Zionist Organization
HaBaD	Hokhma Bina Da'at (Hasidic movement founded by Shne'ur Zalman of Lyadi)
HLRO	House of Lords Record Office
ICA	Jewish Colonial Association
IOLR	India Office Library and Records
ITO	Jewish Territorial Organization
JFC	Joint Foreign Committee of the Board of Deputies of British Jews and the Anglo-Jewish Association
JSS	*Jewish Social Studies*
Kolo	Koło Żydowskie (Jewish caucus in the Polish parliament)
KPD	Kommunistische Partei Deutschlands (German Communist Party)
KPP	Komunistyczna Partia Polska (Communist Party of Poland)
LBIYB	*Leo Baeck Institute Year Book*
Mapai	Mifleget Po'alei Erez Yisrael (Palestine Workers' Party)
OZON	Oboz Zjednoczenia Narodowego (Camp of National Unity in Poland)
PPS	Polska Partia Socjalistyczna (Polish Socialist Party)
PRO	Public Record Office
RSA	Russian State Archives
RSDWP	Rosiiskaya sotsial-demokraticheskaya rabochaya partiya (Russian Social Democratic Workers' Party)

SHAT	Service Historique de l'Armée de Terre
SPD	Sozialdemokratische Partei Deutschlands (German Social Democratic Party)
SRO	Scottish Record Office
WA	Weizmann Archives
WJC	World Jewish Congress
WZO	World Zionist Organization

INTRODUCTION
The Old Dispensation

I

O N 18 December 1744, in the wake of the siege and occupation of Prague in the course of the War of the Austrian Succession and the suspicion (unfounded, as it later turned out) that the Jews of Prague had given aid and support to the Prussians, Maria Theresa of Austria decreed the total and immediate expulsion of the distinguished and long-settled Jewish community of Prague. It was to be carried out almost immediately. It was to be followed in short order by the expulsion of all Jews from all of Bohemia and Moravia. *Gzeirot* (punitive decrees) of this and other kinds were familiar enough to Jews everywhere throughout their history. The fortunate knew them as a permanent possibility. The less fortunate knew them as a palpable menace. The rule was to do whatever could be done to have them revoked; if not revoked postponed; if not postponed watered down; and if that could not be managed then so far as possible circumvented. What was understood by all, high and low, was that if all else failed, the Jews upon whom the *gzeira* fell would have to learn to live with it if it was possible to do so and to move on to other lands if it was not. There were no real choices. Outright (for example, armed) resistance was out of the question. *Gzeirot*, it was necessary to recognize, were characteristic, and in the long term unchanging and unchangeable features of the Exile itself. They might take the form of an increase in the burden of taxation so sudden, steep, and extortionate as to be barely sustainable, or fresh restrictions on—or, worse, an absolute prohibition of—residence in, or temporary entry into, a designated town or territory. They might be measures regulating the dress of Jewish men and women, or laying down rules for the external or even internal furnishing of their synagogues or homes. They could be the establishment of a constraint so severe as to amount to a *de facto* or even *de jure* prohibition of the right to marry and raise a family, or to bear arms, or to employ non-Jews, or to be employed by non-Jews, or to bury one's dead in a communal cemetery—and therefore, in effect, to maintain a community of any kind at all. Commonest of all was the institution of some additional restriction on what was almost invariably highly restricted freedom to engage in particular trades, crafts, or professions.

However, all this said, while the repertoire from which a sovereign ruler or city corporation or the Church (in Rome itself, notably) had long been free to draw their material (and, for the most part, public) advantage was a large one, recourse to it had been declining since the end of the seventeenth century. Certain items had dropped entirely from view. Forced religious confrontations and disputations—in which Jews well knew they dared not have the better of the official representatives of Christianity—had gone out of fashion. The forced attendance of entire communities at sessions in which representatives of the Church were free to harangue them on the merits of Christianity and the evils and errors of Judaism were now virtually unknown. The much harsher—from the ruler's point of view less profitable, although, in the eyes of many faithful Christians, more meritorious—*gzeira* of banishment had become quite rare. By the eighteenth century, in western and central Europe such celebrated and dramatic cases of expulsion as that from England in 1290, from France in 1306, from Germany in 1348, from Lithuania in 1445, from Spain in 1492, from Portugal in 1497, and from countless cities and minor territories (Cracow, Magdeburg, Trent, and Paris among them) at one time or another had begun to seem to all, Jews and non-Jews alike, to belong to a truly benighted and fortunately (or, as some still thought, unfortunately) irrecoverable past.

In these circumstances, Maria Theresa's revival of so brutal a sanction in the mid-eighteenth century struck a nerve throughout European Jewry. Implemented in full it would have put an entire population on to the roads of Europe to march through lands in which they were unlikely to be allowed to settle in search of one in which they might. It was to condemn very many thousands to months, conceivably years, of homelessness, uncertainty, pauperization, sickness, and the high probability of unspeakable depredations *en route* at the hands of those inhabiting the territories through which the travellers would have to pass. The further consequences might be larger still. Would the Empress's decree set a precedent? Would there be reason to fear, as a Jewish notable in Amsterdam wrote to a correspondent in Venice, that 'the fire would spread to other kingdoms and states and to the remotest of corners, . . . wherever [the people of] Israel were to be found'?[1] When leading figures in communities within the Habsburg domains and in Holland were alerted by the elders of Prague to what was impending, and as the news passed by letter and by word of mouth from community to community throughout central and western Europe, and to a limited extent in eastern Europe as well, the response was electric. Every ruler, minister, parliamentary assembly, or prelate thought likely to be willing to intercede with the empress in Vienna and plead for mercy for her Jewish subjects was approached: the Dutch States-General, the king of England, the king of

---

[1] B. Mevorah, 'Ma'asei ha-hishtadlut be-eiropa li-meni'at geirusham shel yehudei bohemiya u-moraviya, 1744–1745', *Zion*, 28, 3–4 (1963), 136–7.

Denmark, the Senate of the Venetian Republic and the rulers of other Italian states, numerous bishops and archbishops, those of Bamberg-Würzburg and Mainz among them, the Pope himself, the Sultan of Turkey—some directly, some indirectly, as each case was thought to warrant. Remarkably, the response was gratifying. The Dutch representative at Vienna was told to point out that, while it was true that the issue was a domestic one, the economic ruin of Bohemian Jewry was certain to have serious financial consequences for Holland. His English colleague was instructed to convey to the empress that King George II, having received a Jewish delegation and heard of what was impending, 'does extremely commiserate the terrible circumstances of distress . . . [and] is most . . . earnestly desirous of procuring the repeal of it by His Royal intercession'. The ambassador was further instructed to co-operate with his Dutch colleague, as was the Danish minister in Vienna as well. It is true, that none of these representations, nor any of the many others that followed, produced immediate results. Always profoundly hostile to Jewry on a priori theological grounds, the empress was adamant in her refusal to entertain pleas of any kind on behalf of the Jews of Bohemia and Moravia and resented the pressure being exerted upon her. Her ministers, most of whom, on reflection, regretted the decree, learned to be circumspect about discussing it with her. The few Jews privileged to reside in Vienna itself (there was no *community* to speak of at this point), their privileges normally extending to access (limited, to be sure) to the court, were warned of dire penalties if they so much as dared to raise the issue. When George II of England (and Elector of Hanover) ordered a second approach to the empress and had his ambassador make clear his view, that 'Her persevering in that severe and merciless resolution could not but be esteemed by all mankind as an indelible stain both in point of justice and clemency upon her hitherto moderate and equitable Government',[2] Maria Theresa was infuriated. But, bit by bit, the stings went home and the wind changed. Three Jewish notables were allowed at long last to kneel in the dust before the empress's carriage and submit a petition for mercy to her. The full expulsion from all Bohemia and Moravia was first postponed, then, in effect, rescinded. After a decent interval, those Jews of Prague whose exodus had already begun were allowed to return to their city and to their homes.

A century would pass before those who were accepted as leaders in European Jewry would again be roused to such a spurt of integrated and purposeful activity in a cause of this kind. Another century would pass before the fate of the Jews of Prague, along with those of all Bohemia and Moravia and indeed those of the rest of Europe, would again be in question. But what the affair of Maria Theresa's decree of banishment calls

[2] Citations in Mevorah, 'Ma'asei', 148–9, 156.

attention to most precisely is the fragility of the balance between the new,
civilizing impact of the Enlightenment on the approach of some among
the prominent European princes and governments to the matter of the
Jews, and the older, more deeply rooted, countervailing considerations
that governed the conduct of others. It calls attention too to the degree
to which public action on behalf of a segment of the Jewish people still
turned in the mid-eighteenth century on the contingency of *personal*
access to the governing lay and ecclesiastical authorities in the lands of
their Dispersion; and indirectly to the fact that the system of governance
which lay at the heart of the matter of power and authority under the Old
Dispensation was a dual one: sovereign power on the one hand, largely
autonomous internal governance on the other.

II

The contrast between the two levels of authority to which the Jews of
Europe were subject was striking. While the exercise of power and
authority *within* Jewry was limited in degree and variable in scope, power
over Jewry, meaning that wielded by others, was generally firm, enduring,
and, for all practical purposes, absolute. It was absolute in the sense that
the circumstances of the Jews through the centuries of their presence in
Europe were such that life in a particular place, and what they were
allowed to make of it, was, ultimately, the gift of others to grant or to
withdraw. And yet, while absolute and virtually irresistible, the power of
the sovereign was never comprehensive. Each communal authority—and
all supra-communal institutions too where their establishment was permitted[3]—had indeed to operate in its shadow. But it was always an open
question how far and in what precise respects the higher, sovereign power

---

[3] The most famous of such supra-communal institutions was the Council of the Four
Lands (*Va'ad arb'a arazot*), founded at the end of the sixteenth century, suppressed by the
Polish Sejm in 1764. At its peak, in the seventeenth century, it operated as the central,
oligarchic regulator of Jewish life in Poland and Lithuania, the forum in which serious
internal disputes could be settled without recourse to alien authority, and as Jewry's established, institutional representative *vis-à-vis* king, Sejm, and Church for a great range of
subjects, among them, typically, the buying-off of authorities where the banishment of
entire communities had been ordered, the ransoming of prisoners, and, in one celebrated
instance, the dispatch of an emissary to appeal to the Pope to intervene in the case of an
accusation of ritual murder (an ancient, monstrous, but not infrequent charge laid against
Jews, on which see below, pp. 233 ff). The Council's value to the kingdom and its institutions lay elsewhere, of course: chiefly in its uses as a tax-gathering machine. Its suppression in the middle of the eighteenth century owed something to the winds of modernism
and efficient state administration that had begun to enter eastern Europe from the west,
but a good deal more to both king and Sejm having concluded that the Jews had been
milked dry and that the Council was effectively bankrupt. It followed, they believed, that
its days as a tax-farming institution were over and that the republic would do better to
subject its Jewish inhabitants to direct taxation.

would wish or be able to encroach upon the community's internal affairs and in what circumstances the community was prepared to acquiesce or, on the contrary, likely to try to stand its ground. All concerned, rulers and ruled, non-Jews and Jews, high and low, learned and unschooled, were agreed that the law of the land—in practice the law of the alien ruler— was, generally speaking, law for Jews no less than for the ruler's other subjects. The matter of its intrinsic legitimacy so far as the Jews were concerned remained problematic, however. The famous, endlessly repeated Talmudic doctrine of *dina de-malkhuta—dina*[4] ('the law of the kingdom [is] law') could be understood as laying down a formal, perhaps even a moral, obligation to respect and obey the alien ruler of the day and place. It could be taken too as recommending no more than a pragmatic accommodation to the reality of superior power. In the Talmudic way of things, no final and definitive teaching on this score ever emerged; and if Jews did commonly conceive of the law of the land as binding upon them, in practice it was mostly as a matter of general, day-to-day necessity rather than as a consequence of full moral and political obligation. The prevailing view was that it was for themselves, not for others, to determine what true obedience they owed the sovereign, if any at all.

It needs to be noted, however, that this limited and conditional acceptance of the ruler's authority (as opposed to power) over them was mirrored in the status they themselves were accorded by their political masters. The governing view of Jewry in the Christian world was of a people who were deeply alien and antagonistic to, and therefore, if only by their presence within it, subversive of, the *res publica christiana*.[5] But as, regrettably, they had come to be embedded physically within Christendom, it was necessary to ensure that formally, legally, morally, and socially they needed in some way to be excluded from it. It followed, too, that nothing was owed them, at all events not as a matter of principle or fundamental law; and that on the contrary, again as a matter of principle, much was to be denied them. They might be granted specific privileges: the right of residence, the right to worship after their own fashion, the right to bury their dead in a cemetery of their own, the right to trade in, for example, old clothes and old coins and other suchlike debased and debasing lines of commerce. They had also, of course, the celebrated freedom to lend money against interest. There was a distant sense, therefore, in which, the Roman system of public, universally applicable law having died away, the Jews, taken community by community, assumed a form that was analogous to that of other social or economic collectivities and organisms allowed to operate on the basis of the specific privileges

[4] Nashim: Nedarim 28.

[5] Matters were somewhat different in the Islamic world, although the rule that the Jews were to be kept explicitly and visibly in a subordinate social and political position was never in question there either.

granted them by (or successfully wrested from) the sovereigns in question. Still, the case of the Jews was conceived of as fundamentally different from that of the guilds, the universities, the city corporations, the orders of knighthood, and, moving from medieval times to the age of the Reformation and beyond, the dissident Christian sects. The difference was moral and ideological and, by extension, political. Both the rights and privileges granted them from time to time and the consequences for the Jews themselves in the event of their being subsequently withdrawn were different in kind. In general, the open, arbitrary revocation of rights solemnly granted by a European sovereign was rare and tended very commonly to be perceived as improper, even illegitimate. The Revocation of the Edict of Nantes by Louis XIV reverberates to this day—in history books, at all events—as an immensely dishonourable, and, many would say, misguided act of state. No such judgement was accorded the revocation of rights formally granted to Jews. It was the actual granting of rights or privileges that rendered the ruler liable to public (by no means exclusively churchly) censure. By the same token, the cancellation of such privileges was likely to be met with approval, contemporary or retrospective. With the possible exception of the wholesale expulsion of their Jewish subjects by the Catholic monarchs of Spain no great and irreversible act of state directed against the Jewish people in pre-modern times ever attained anything like the notoriety that accrued to the Revocation of the Edict of Nantes. And even then 1492 came to be seen by those who ventured to disapprove of it as a blunder,[6] rather than a wrongdoing or a betrayal. In this sense the protests Maria Theresa brought upon herself in 1744 indicated a certain (although not, as we shall see, final and decisive) shift in the prevailing wind.

Underlying everything was the central fact that under the old regime no Jew was, or could be, a member of (civil) society. No matter how learned or wealthy or contingently influential he might be within or without Jewry itself, a Jew was held to belong to a moral and, of course, theological category inferior to that of the meanest peasant. Dealings with him and his kind were therefore in a class apart from all other social and economic and *a fortiori* political relations. Of admitting the Jews collectively or by community to a legitimate and established place and status in the state and in society as an *estate* there was no question. They were alien. They were tainted. They were therefore removable. Arrangements respecting them could not and need not be other than *de facto* and *ad hoc*, functions, most commonly, of anticipated material advantage, as opposed to justice or equity. Even where matters were somewhat otherwise, in the sense that considerations of a humane nature did operate to some degree,

---

[6] Prescott, it may be recalled, took the milder view that the expulsion of the Jews (and of the Muslims) from Spain was dictated by intelligible considerations of *raison d'état*.

it was still the essentially arbitrary nature of the relevant ruling that was uppermost. What a liberally minded seventeenth-century king of Denmark was pleased to allow, his jealous and bigoted neighbour, the corporation of Hamburg, was intent on denying. But the king of Denmark was still free to change his mind—as, of course, was (and, in the course of time, did) the City of Hamburg. But in one important respect, the vast power and seemingly untrammelled freedom of action that accrued to the sovereign was less simple. The exclusion of the Jews from the main formal structures of the realm, and their consignment *en bloc* to what Max Weber correctly termed pariah status, served to reduce, not enhance, the sovereign's ability to rule their daily lives.

The precedents for accepting that for certain purposes and within certain limits the Jews remained subject to laws of their own were of great antiquity and it had always been beyond the wit of anyone to devise a means by which the law of the land and the Law of the Jews could be rendered compatible. The penalties Jews incurred for crossing the wishes and ignoring the predilections of the alien temporal or ecclesiastical power could be very severe. It did not matter how large or small their community, how prosperous or indigent its members, whether they were mild or pugnacious in their habits of mind and speech, and what the restrictions were that they were expected to labour under. So long as their presence in the form of a structured community was permitted—or 'tolerated', as the cant term had it—their governance invariably rested on a working arrangement between the wielders of the two varieties and levels of authority and power, the internal and the external. However stringent and oppressive the conditions laid down by the superordinate, external sovereign power in the land, there had still to be room for the community's own leaders to manage its essential, internal affairs in their own way. Which of its affairs fell within their remit and what conditions and reservations, if any, attached to their management were questions to which very diverse answers were given at various times and places. In all cases, however, so far as the Jews themselves were concerned, it was before all else by the degree and quality of self-government allowed them that the alien regime would ultimately be judged. Where the constraints laid upon Jewish self-government were minimal, there the pull of Jews into the territory in question was likely to be great. Where they were heavy and difficult or even impossible to sustain, there the effect was to encourage, if not to compel, emigration, even flight. What was decisive and invariable was that observance of the Law was predicated absolutely on a regularly functioning community and that this in turn was predicated on a structure of authority and management within it. Whatever constraints happened to be placed upon its individual members, however difficult people's day-to-day existence might be rendered, it was the degree to which the community as such was able to maintain its essential,

continuous internal autonomy that was decisive. And since no community (as traditionally conceived) could function on the basis of total subjection to the law of the land, namely to the law of the gentiles, there had
to be some minimal satisfaction of the Jews' uncompromising view that
they must be free to live their own lives in their own way and for their
own reasons if there was to be a Jewish presence in the land at all. Church
and state alike had to accept that attempts to incorporate the Jews into an
alien society either collectively or individually would be resisted; that
whatever could be done to block the erosion of their internal solidarity
and cohesion would be done; and, in sum, that it was a fundamental article of faith and outlook among the Jews that they were, and were
required by the Almighty to continue to be, a nation apart.

It was entirely characteristic, therefore, that the once great Jewish concentration in Poland began, famously, with the laying down of the principle—established and made effective in parts of the land as early as the
thirteenth century under the terms of the *privilegium* (Statute of Kalisz,
1264[7]) decreed by Prince Boleslaw the Pious and extended by later
rulers—that Jews were not to be subject to ordinary judicial jurisdiction
and procedures. A century later Casimir the Great extended it to virtually all of Poland as then constituted. The same principle entailed, as a
central element, the withdrawal of the rights of the Church, the urban
patriciate, and (at least for a time) of the nobility as well to judge the
Jews—most notably in cases where charges had been brought against
them by non-Jews—and the formal entitlement of Jewish rabbinical
courts to try all civil cases in which all parties to the dispute were Jewish.
Considering that in Old Poland, as elsewhere in the Middle Ages, judicial authority was a prime symbol of government as well as one of its
major instruments, these were remarkable concessions. They highlighted
the formal separation of the Jews from the rest of the body politic. They
signalled recognition of the fact that a Jew had no reason to expect that
justice would be done him in an ordinary court where the plaintiff was a
Christian, still less where the alleged victim was one. Where the rabbinical court to which Jews would normally have recourse proved unable to
settle the dispute, or one or other of the Jewish disputants sought to
appeal its decision, or it was a civil case in which both Jews and Christians
were involved, or where a criminal case had been brought against a
Jewish defendant, there a specially appointed *judex Judaeorum* would try
the case under the authority of the prince's (later the king's) lord lieutenant, the *wojewoda*.[8]

In time, as power shifted from the supreme ruler to the nobility and the

---

[7] But see Sh. A. Cygielman, 'Le-'inyan kevi'at ha-ta'arikh le-matan ha-privilegia
ha-kelalit li-hudei polin-gadol (1264)', *Zion*, 44, 3 (1984), 289–2.

[8] Later, in certain parts of Poland, a competing royal official, the *starosta*, claimed
authority in this, as in other spheres.

wojewoda came to function less as the man who spoke for the king and more as the nobility's own representative before the sovereign, so the nobility's ability to exert control over the Jews inhabiting their estates and privately owned towns increased and this special and separate judicial system began to erode—before finally being swept away upon the partitioning of Poland towards the end of the eighteenth century and the effort by each one of the new sovereign powers to assert a new, ostensibly more rational system of government.[9] But while it lasted it was a useful and in many ways comfortable arrangement for the Jews themselves. It articulated their separate and—within what had become well understood and more or less acceptable limits—their autonomous corporate status. It helped, as intended, to protect them from much, although never all, of the harassment that was their lot. It confirmed the authority of their own rabbinical courts and so the legitimacy and prestige of the rabbinical half of their own half-lay, half-clerical system of internal government. Less deliberately, but equally effectively, it served to strengthen that same system's other half: that of the *parnassim*, the lay leaders of the communities in whose hands the day-to-day management of each community was placed—and to some extent the lives and destinies of each of its members too—by whom, to no small extent, even the rabbis' own ability to function was determined. Contrariwise, where Jews were tempted, or obliged, to bring their disputes before an alien judicial authority, there the dual system of government may be said to have broken down.

III

But as to the questions who the Jews' leaders might be, how they were to be selected, how it might be proper for given individuals to rise to communal, or supra-communal office and position, and under what terms and subject to what limits they were to exercise such powers as the community or communities allowed them, no clear and binding, let alone universal, answers were ever established. In this regard, as in many others, traditional Jewish public law was shot through with uncertainties and ambivalences that derived in the first instance from the sheer antiquity of its origins. Much public law (as opposed to the law of personal status) was necessarily inapplicable to the circumstances of exile and to the varying sets of social and political conditions that had obtained in Europe and elsewhere in the course of the fifteen or so centuries that had elapsed since the completion of the Talmud and the consolidation of the Exile. It was the case too that much of what the Sages held to be relevant to

---

[9] Binyamin Cohen, 'Ha-voivoda be-torat shofet ha-yehudim be-polin ha-yeshana', *Gal-'ed*, 1 (1973), 1–12; and 'Ha-rashut ha-voivodit ve-ha-kehilla ha-yehudit ba-me'ot ha-16–18', *Gal-'ed*, 3 (1976), 9–32.

communal governance, the law of property, the administration of justice, and the like, is best read as a compendium of references to a utopian state such as neither the Jews nor any other people have ever possessed. The Sages were concerned both with what was intrinsically right and proper and what could, at one and the same time, be worked out in the course of exegesis and amplification of the relevant sacred texts. What emerged from their labours was a conception of government that was in some respects as fanciful as it was morally admirable.[10] It is true that the Law of the Jews is of great complexity. It comprises, in addition to the fundamental 'Written', Biblical Law of Moses the 'Oral' Law, the latter being the accumulated interpretations and elaborations of the Written Law as promulgated by the Talmudic Sages, passed on, further reinterpreted, and modified by later commentators and masters on the basis of minutely scholastical, casuistical argument. Many seemingly contradictory things can be read in it and it has indeed been one of the functions of the rabbis to squeeze out the actual rules by which this non-sovereign people, dispersed in countless, widely scattered communities, might order its public and private affairs. Still, it was never in doubt (until the modern age) that, taken as a whole, despite the immensity of the relevant texts and their burden of real or apparent internal contradictions, the Law was fundamental to the life of the Jews. To question its truth, validity, or sacred quality was regarded as silly and impudent at best, wicked and heretical at worst, the really determined questioner being *ipso facto* in the wrong and beyond the communal pale.

On the other hand, not being a territorial people and not being an estate of any of the realms which they inhabited, the boundaries enclosing the Jews as members of the various communities were in important respects porous. Subject to the exigencies of time and place and allowing for the general conditions of the age—the incidence of war, plague, banditry, the difficulties of, and the obstacles to, travel, and so forth—movement from one community to another was always possible in theory and law, and to a great extent in practice too. Beyond the licence to mobility, there was the unique nature of their semi-contractual relationship with the relevant governing power. Jews might be in debt to this or that magnate or corporation—typically to city burghers and to members of the hierarchy of the Church. But they were not serfs, nor were they, in the

---

[10] For example: Talmudic criminal law, very properly, it may be thought, lays down multiple safeguards against the undoubted horror of judicial error and the wrongful conviction and condemnation of the innocent. Alas for practicality, these include the virtual unacceptability of circumstantial evidence; the requirement that at least *two* adult, male, socially respectable eyewitnesses of the alleged offence be produced before the court; an assurance that the alleged offender had been explicitly warned beforehand against committing the crime of which he was to be charged; and, in the event of all other conditions being satisfied, a very large bench of judges voting unanimously for conviction.

accepted sense, vassals. Having no established rights within any territory, they were generally free of overriding obligations: military service, for example. Nor was the internal socio-political structure of any Jewish community of such a nature as to bind one man or woman within it to another on any basis other than that of free contract.

The problem of social control in Jewry was therefore acute and compounded by the absence in Exilic Jewry of an established aristocracy or of any other form of clearly defined governing class. The Jews had long been without an Exilarch and had no bishops or regular, continent-wide, let alone worldwide, synods. High moral and legal authority accrued to particular rabbinical figures from time to time as a function of their reputation for very great learning and integrity; and their status relative to lesser colleagues can loosely—but only loosely and informally—be considered hierarchical. But towering figures such as Gershom Me'or ha-Golah of Mainz (960–1028), Levi ben Gershom of Orange (Gersonides, 1288–1344), and perhaps greatest of all Moshe ben Maimon of Cordoba, Fez, and Cairo (Maimonides, 1135–1204) were rare at all times. In the period closer to our own age only Eliyahu ben Shelomo Zalman, the so-called Ga'on of Vilna (1720–97), may reasonably, if still distantly and to some extent retrospectively, be compared with the luminaries of the medieval period. And there were intrinsic difficulties about rabbinical (or theocratic) governance anyway.

In Jewish orthodoxy's remote, heroic past the rule had been that rabbinic learning, no matter how great, implied neither office nor livelihood. The Sages of antiquity were artisans and cultivators. Maimonides, the greatest of mediaeval Jewish scholars, was a practising physician. But if this ideal was not forgotten, as the embodiment of a rule of conduct that it was incumbent upon all to follow, it fell into disuse. By early modern times the usual pattern was for rabbi-scholars to devote themselves to their religious-communal functions exclusively; and therefore for all but the most prestigious, or the independently wealthy, or the most ascetic and undemanding, to be in some degree dependent upon—in certain cases at the mercy of—the leading *lay* members of the community they were called upon to serve and guide. The tendency—evident even in antiquity—to consider that especially devout and pious men did well to refrain from dealing with mundane affairs may have played a role as well. By the end of the eighteenth century, in any event, it was the case almost everywhere that the effective leadership of European Jewish communities was either in the hands of lay members and rabbis jointly or had devolved on to laymen alone. Thus, at least for public purposes, the rabbis (except in matters of a strict moral or ritual nature) retained little more than a residual moral influence in matters that were thought to be of particularly great moment and upon which they, for their part, were prepared to go so far as to define a clear position. In brief, the effective day-to-day leadership of Jewry, especially in times of distress and crisis and actual or impending conflict, had virtually everywhere fallen into the hands of the man of material substance, the *gevir*.

IV

The special force in old regime Jewry of authority and influence derived from the accumulation of wealth lay first and foremost in the fact that, apart from rabbinic learning and (more doubtfully) craftsmanship of certain kinds, no other path to significant, *public* personal achievement existed. That apart, a man who had accumulated wealth was held *ipso facto* to be of proven ability. The successful accumulation of wealth suggested a battle with alien forces that had been fought and won; and further, that having done such battle the man of substance was necessarily a man with access of some kind—and if of great substance then substantial access—to the men who really made the weather in his world: the territorial magnates, the sovereign's ministers and lesser servants, perhaps the sovereign himself. It followed that his own community would look to the *gevir* for more than the simple material, philanthropic support of its institutions that he and they knew he owed it. The interdependency between personal wealth and personal access to the centres of power in the land led naturally to the expectation that he would perform the additional pious duty of *shtadlanut* (intercession on the community's behalf). The actual economic roles and achievements of the various *gevirim-shtadlanim*, the grandees of Jewry, differed greatly, of course, in kind and degree, much as did the political and social status and the economic resources of their respective political masters. Still, in their significance to their communities, the duties of the Jewish bailiff managing a Polish landowner's estates, the organizer and purveyor of supplies to an eighteenth-century military commander in the field, and the 'court Jew' (*Hofjude*) serving the ruler of a petty German state as personal financial adviser and operator, were all of a kind.

Two men who were especially remarkable for having known how to seize their opportunities and achieve personal wealth and political connections in the manner that was for some three centuries the commonest of all bases on which the prestige and power of lay leadership in Jewry rested were Sir Solomon de Medina (*c.*1650–1730) and Samuel Oppenheimer (1630–1703). Both were military provisioners to European armies in the field, an important class of Jewish entrepreneurs whose strength lay in the connections and trust in which they held each other and their unrivalled ability to locate and purchase the supplies demanded and deliver them to military commanders with (by the standards of the times) extraordinary speed and reliability. Medina was a Dutch Jew of

Portuguese origin settled in England who made a name and a fortune for himself as a leading member of an entire syndicate of Dutch-Portuguese Jews who operated as military provisioners and financiers (*providiteurs*) first to William III's forces in Flanders and later to those of the Duke of Marlborough during the War of the Spanish Succession. Typically, upon his arrival in London he was elected to a position of authority in the local Jewish (Spanish and Portuguese) community as a matter of course. The community was small and on the whole untroubled and little was required of him beyond regular contributions to the upkeep of the synagogue and to the usual charitable and educational purposes. Still, the potential for intercession in case of need was there and it was taken for granted in his community that he would serve it and that, in one way or another, something of his glory would be reflected to the benefit of its members.

Medina's career was not without its share of scandal. He was accused at one point of having bribed Marlborough to enter into a contractual relationship with him, although how far the charges against him (as opposed to the parallel charges against Marlborough himself) were fair in the circumstances is open to question. He seems to have overreached himself financially too. Nevertheless, the treatment accorded him by his masters in King William's and then Queen Anne's England—the key to his position—was remarkable and quite unlike that which was meted out to Oppenheimer in late seventeenth-century Habsburg Vienna. When Medina, with all his 'goods and merchandise', was admitted to England in 1672 he and his family were formally and without discernible fuss or opposition granted 'all privileges and freedoms of a natural born subject'. By the end of the century his position was such that the king himself was prepared to pay him a visit at his home in Richmond. A year later, in June 1700, he was awarded a knighthood, the first professing Jew to be so honoured. This in turn did something to establish if not a binding precedent at any rate a new way of thinking about the status of the Jews in British society. When in 1712 a Scottish court of law was faced with a plea to disallow the evidence of a Jew on the grounds that Jews were 'inhabile in law, considering the rooted hatred they bear all Christians', the judge, with Medina in mind, held that if 'a Jew trading in London' could be knighted and so manifestly rated 'capable of honours', there was no evident reason why the witness or any other Jew should be thought of as incapable of bearing testimony.[11]

Samuel Oppenheimer was a man of greater substance than Medina, but his strength too rested before all else on his capacity to lead and co-ordinate lesser men of his own kind.[12] He was a native of Heidelberg. His

---

[11] Oskar K. Rabinowicz, *Sir Solomon Medina* (London, 1974), 2, 20.
[12] 'Anat Peri, 'Pe'ilutam shel sapakei zava yehudiim be-mamlekhet hungaria ba-mahazit ha-rishona shel ha-me'ah ha-18', *Zion*, 57, 2 (1992).

commercial and financial career began with service as a military purveyor to the Elector of the Palatinate. It then progressed, by stages, to the position of principal, at certain times virtually sole, officially designated purveyor to the entire Austrian army in its wars against the French and the Turks. The sheer, virtually continent-wide scale of the financial and logistic operations which he undertook to see through either alone or with carefully chosen partners was staggering. By 1694 the Austrian state debt to Oppenheimer alone amounted to no less than 3 million florins. At his death, by his son Emmanuel's estimate, it had reached double that figure. But it needs to be said too that Oppenheimer's case demonstrates much more closely than Medina's, and in ways more characteristic of his class, that while the material and social rewards that accrued to men who conducted enterprises on such a scale could not fail to be very real, the penalties for failure or loss of favour were correspondingly severe. Oppenheimer was granted the then exceedingly rare right of residence in Vienna. His wealth and (fluctuating) access to high quarters enabled him to pursue his interests with diligence and at the same time do something to protect and re-settle Jews who had fallen on evil times in consequence of the central European wars, to ransom Jewish captives in the time-honoured manner prescribed by tradition, and to obtain for at least some of his brethren the same prize of residence in Vienna that had been granted him. But the award of the bureaucratic (non-noble) title of *Oberkriegsfaktor* was a step taken, like all moves favouring him, in the teeth of great opposition, especially from clerical quarters. He had continually to cope with intrigues and vilification of a nastily anti-Jewish kind. There was no compunction when he was at one point out of favour about expelling the great man (and great servant of the Habsburg crown) from Vienna along with the rest of the small collection (hardly a community) of Jews who had at one time or another been privileged to reside there.

Towards the end of his life he suffered the still greater indignity of the mob being allowed to sack his unprotected mansion in Vienna. And while the imperial authorities were ready enough to use him from time to time, they made repeated attempts to repudiate the enormous debts they owed him both in his lifetime and, later, beyond the grave—on the grounds that Oppenheimer had cooked his books and was guilty of other fraudulent and underhand manipulations. The charges were never substantiated; and it does not seem that anyone of great consequence ever believed the allegations to be true. Moreover, the chief and most interesting result of the government's repudiation of its debt to Oppenheimer was the major financial crisis that erupted throughout central Europe and the subsequent damage done to the financial credit of the Habsburg Empire.[13] But the intrinsic fragility of a Jewish grandee's position cannot

[13] Jonathan I. Israel, *European Jewry in the Age of Mercantilism 1550–1750* (Oxford, 1985), 124–7; and Henry Wasserman, *Encyclopaedia Judaica*, xii, cols. 1431–3.

be better demonstrated. For all its brilliance, Oppenheimer's career was almost fatally shot through with insecurity and uncertainty of status and clearly showed up the advantages that accrued to the *employer* of an agent, factor, bailiff, purveyor, or any other kind of middle man who was a Jew. Such a man was always less likely to obtain justice than another, or even dare demand it. In the event of a dispute or of the relevant operation going sour, he was ideally suited for the role of the party on to whom criticism could most easily be deflected.

A classic example of this precarious position was that key figure in contemporary eastern Europe's peasant economy: the manager—bailiff or *arendar* (leaseholder)—of the Polish nobleman's estates, a man caught perpetually between his landowner-master's unremitting demands for rent and profit and the dark and equally dangerous hostility of the peasantry on whose labour all and everything ultimately turned. For those successful in such an enterprise there was a living to be had—no small thing in increasingly impoverished Polish Jewry. For the unsuccessful there could be dire punishment. On the very great estates the position of the Jewish leaseholder might be, indeed needed to be if any good was to come of it to anyone, one of extraordinary power—over the lesser Jews inhabiting the landowner's towns and villages no less than over the peasants. But it was a position inexorably marked and damned at every level by tyranny, fear, manipulation, and resentment. The brothers Shemuel and Gedaliya Izakowicz, leaseholders and factors on the immense estates of Hieronim Radziwill, were notorious both for their managerial efficiency and economic good sense and for the hatred and the fear they inspired in serfs and lesser Jews alike. Their efficacy as factors owed everything to their figurative and literal ability to whip everyone into an unprecedented frenzy of labour, productivity, and profit. They did so at the behest and on the authority of their Radziwill master; they did so, of course, on their own behalf as well. Unsurprisingly, they were nearly brought down by the wave of peasant rebellion and accompanying pogroms that extended sporadically over the years 1739-44,[14] that was as much a reaction against them personally as against the Radziwills themselves. But if their ability to control the peasants and, indirectly, the minor noblemen caught up in the effort to rationalize the management of the Radziwill estates was shaky for a time, their absolute mastery of the equally resentful Jewish population over whom they had, in effect, been placed in authority was never in question. But nor, as it needs to be said too, was there any question of their perfectly genuine, active concern for the safety of their own people so far as it was in their power to ensure it.

---

[14] Known in Polish-Jewish annals as 'Gzeirat Woszczylo', on which see I. Halpern, 'Gzeirat Woszczylo', *Zion*, 22, 1 (1957), 56–67; and Hillel Levine, *Economic Origins of Antisemitism: Poland and its Jews in the Early Modern Period* (New Haven, 1991), 157–8.

Another large figure, comparable to Oppenheimer and Medina but no less illustrative than the brothers Izakowicz of the savage and unsettled conditions that obtained in eastern Europe, especially in independent Poland during its decline, was Shemu'el Zbitkower (173?–1801). Notable as a purveyor to the Polish, Russian, and Polish-insurgent armies in succession, he was a man with a finger in a great many other commercial pies—with trade in meat, hides, and horses among them.[15] Of great wealth, immense energy, a very sharp eye for business, and few scruples, Zbitkower, crucially, had friends and protectors in very high places, the corrupt royal minister Adam Poninski and King Stanislaw Augustus Poniatowski himself (to whom he was formally appointed 'crown servant') among them. He further conformed to the pattern of the *gevir* in that he insisted on a role of power and influence in the world of Jewry as well. He had himself appointed *parnas* (elder) of Warsaw Jewry and functioned for a time as its tax-farmer. He sought and obtained the right to establish a cemetery in Warsaw—a fine achievement had it not been followed by his asserting personal control of its use and exploiting even this small increment of influence for private profit. Yet, like the equally awful brothers Izakowicz half a century earlier, Zbitkower made great efforts and expended much private wealth to protect the Jews of the Praga suburb of Warsaw when the Cossacks were let loose upon them in the course of the Russians' suppression of the Kosciuszko rising in 1794.[16]

The advent of the *gevir* or grandee as the dominant oligarch in Jewry during the final centuries of the old regime introduced an active factor within it that had hitherto been relatively rare. Thirsty for status and privileges and for avenues of influence that were not only beyond the access and the ken, but also, by and large, the imagining of lesser folk in Jewry, the *gevir* would be associated, as we shall see, with the first stirrings of such demand as there was from *within* Jewry for a lasting solution to the problem of civil and political status. The question he needed to face was whether the demand should be on behalf of Jews of all classes and categories indiscriminately or limited to improvement in the status of his own kind alone. No clear, let alone definitive and agreed, answer was forthcoming, but a petition submitted to the Prussian government in 1787 by Jewish representatives, in the semi-mercantilist terms that, as they rightly judged, the authorities were most likely to digest, argued the latter case.

If one of our co-religionists was the one who founded the first silk factory in our country . . . and if others followed his example and founded a very respectable number [*eine ansehnliche Menge*] of factories of all kinds in the land; if as a result of their industry and application thousands of Christian families

---

[15] And Henri Bergson's great-grandfather.
[16] On Zbitkower's career see especially Emanuel Ringelblum, 'Shemu'el Zbitkover; 'askan ẓiburi-kalkali be-folin bi-imei ḥalukata', *Ẓion*, 3, 3 and 4 (1938)—one of the last articles by that much lamented scholar to be published in his lifetime (1900–44).

earn *their* living, why then surely they [the Jewish entrepreneurs] are not idle or useless, or a burden on the State, but subjects who contribute to its true prosperity. . . . In which case, [is it just that] they or their descendants be treated as foreigners?[17]

What was ominous about this, from the point of view of the Jewish community in question, but also, by extension, any Jewish community, was the identification of the long-term interests of those for whom, legitimately or otherwise, the spokesmen were determined to speak with what were patently their own private material interests. Where the accepted spokesmen for the community had once been men who could, it was commonly thought, be relied upon by reason of their close observance of the rules of piety and religion and their *active* membership in what were still, even in western and central Europe, traditionalist communities, it would now, increasingly, be on men who were likely to be ever more remote socially and mentally from the commonalty of Jewry that all would have to rely: a circumstance that would unfailingly breed new forms of dissension and distrust.

V

While the structure and patterns of the political life of the Jews in the final stages of the old regime were especially marked by the clerical leadership of Jewry giving way to leadership by plutocracy, the fundamental principles of public action—and, rather more famously, inaction—that had been so great a part of the legacy of the Sages had in no sense faded from Jewish minds. Least of all was this the case in respect of the most deeply inculcated and the most powerful of all ancient precepts, the rule of political self-abnegation.

At its most basic this took the simple form encapsulated in the Talmudic Sages' injunction to eschew the political and keep a proper distance from the power in the land, the *rashut*. It was their teaching that the affairs and, indeed, the very vicinity of the *rashut* were fraught with danger, moral confusion, and corruption. To frequent it was to be deflected from man's proper business—this being the study of, and obedience to, the Law. 'Love labour and hate mastery, and seek not acquaintance with the ruling power' (Shemaiah). 'A name made great is a name destroyed . . . and he that studies not is worthy of death' (Hillel). 'Be heedful of the ruling power for they bring no man nigh to them save for their own need: they seem to be friends such time as it is to their gain, but they stand not

---

[17] Quoted in M. Bodian, 'Ha-yazamim ha-yehudiim be-Berlin, ha-medina ha-absolutistit, ve-"shipur maẓavam ha-ezraḥi shel ha-yehudim" ba-maḥaẓit ha-sheniya shel ha-me'ah ha-18', *Ẓion*, 49, 2 (1984), 181–2. Emphasis added.

with a man in his time of stress' (Rabban Gamaliel).[18] The philosophic resignation proper in men and women who believed themselves to be in the hands of a personal god dictated no less.

But if political quietism was taught as the acme of both prudence and piety, its remoter, deeper implications, namely that to avoid political thought, *a fortiori* political action, was to eschew the proper investigation and assessment of one's own resources as well as those of one's opponents, were rarely examined. There was thus a conspicuous lack of practical seriousness and system in Jewish thinking on public affairs, a tendency too to refrain from a large and comprehensive view of things, to cleave to the immediate, the limited, the palpable, and, especially in moments of crisis, to think insistently in terms of the tactical rather than the long term and the strategic. None of this was unconnected with the doctrine that the history of the Jewish people was one of reward and punishment: that it needed to be interpreted in terms of Jewry's putative cosmological, chiliastic role; that the Exile being divinely ordained punishment, the eventual, redemptory Return would be in the nature of a pardon and a rehabilitation; that all hinged in any case on divine intervention; and that, in the long meanwhile, good and strict behaviour was all. Where such a view of the world lies at the root of social vision a tendency to avoid rather than engage in the political is probably inevitable—in which connection there needs again to be recalled the compensatory merit traditionally attached in Jewry to the close study of the Law. For apart from its many intrinsic merits, it offered the finest minds in Jewry the surest of all means of escape from the vulgar, the mundane, and so, by natural extension, from the public-political as well.

There was, however, an aspect of this negativism which may be termed proto-anarchistic. The state that held ultimate power over the Jews was perceived, correctly of course, as alien and, as a general rule, hostile, unjust, and threatening as well. The Jews' own internal structures of government, in telling contrast, were, as we shall see, intrinsically weak, uncertain, often bullying, or all three together; but above all, even with the best of intentions, they were incapable of according their people the protection against the predators preying upon them that they so urgently required. It followed that while obedience was the prevailing rule, the European Jew, in his heart of hearts, by the circumstances of his birth, and by the impact upon him of his own people's accumulated experience, had reason to be deeply sceptical of civil authority of *all* kinds, internal as well as external, and that the lasting effect of such scepticism was to leave him peculiarly independent in mind and social outlook. Having no earthly masters to whom he thought he owed unquestioning political obedience (the special case of the Hasidic *rebbe* or *zaddik* and his devotees aside), his

---

[18] Nezikin, Avot 1: 9, 13; 2: 3.

was therefore a spirit that, for his times, was remarkably free. Permitted no land, he had no territorial lord. Admitted to no guild, he was free of the authority of established master-craftsmen. Not being a Christian, he had neither bishop nor priest to direct him. And while he could be charged and punished for insubordination to state or sovereign, he could not properly be charged with disloyalty. Betrayal only entered into the life of the Jews in regard to their own community or, more broadly, to Jewry as a whole. It was to their own nation alone that they accepted that they owed undeviating loyalty.

For their enduring cohesion and continuity, the individual communities scattered through Christian Europe[19] relied in part on the internalization of specific doctrine and historical experience handed down from generation to generation, on the constant, daily reinforcing effect of ritual, and on the real, often bitter circumstances of membership in a pariah community. But they relied no less on a general assumption of social compact and on the acceptance all round of a high degree of mutual responsibility famously encapsulated in the Talmudic maxim *kol Yisrael 'arevin zeh ba-zeh* (in literal translation from the Hebrew: 'all [members of] Israel are responsible one for the other').[20] What this specially articulated was the obligation of collectivities, institutions, and private individuals alike to give whatever aid and protection they might be able to muster to any member or segment of the Jewish people that might be in distress—notably, although not solely, distress caused by gentile agency. To this doctrine of positive, mutual responsibility there needs to be added, however, the darker gloss that it was the way of the world anyway for Jews to be held responsible for the deeds, real or alleged, of other Jews. In both its high moral and its more pragmatic and defensive aspect, the doctrine of mutual responsibility drew therefore on the deepest possible

---

[19] Once again the case and circumstances of the Jewish communities in the Islamic world, notably in the Ottoman Empire, were somewhat different in this respect—as in many others with which this study is especially concerned. An instructive borderline case is that of the governance of the Jews in the Danubian Principalities, Moldavia and Wallachia, *prior* to independence. There, in the Ottoman manner, Jews were organized corporatively, with very considerable internal fiscal, administrative, and judicial autonomy and led and largely ruled by a *ḥakham bashi* (chief rabbi) in Moldavia, appointed by the prince, but operating in Wallachia too through a lay deputy. The Jews, wrote two Scottish observers, 'are regarded by the Government as a separate community, and the capitation tax is not levied on them individually, but from their chief men, who are left to gather the sum from their brethren in the way they think equal and fair. . . . The way in which the rulers of the Jews levy the tax is as follows: They lay it not on the provisions of the poor, but on the articles of luxury. For example, a goose is sold for about a *zwanzig*, but they put a tax on it of half a *zwanzig* and eight *paras*. Thus the rich, who wish luxuries, pay a high price for them; while the poor, who are content with the necessities of life, escape' (Andrew A. Bonar and Robert Murray M'Cheyne, *Narrative of a Mission of Inquiry to the Jews from the Church of Scotland in 1839* (Edinburgh, 1844), 409).
[20] From the Talmud, Nezikin: Shevu'ot 39a.

roots of sentiment and precedent, an obligation never to be shrugged off by those in a position to fulfil it, and powerfully reinforced by the common, generally well-founded assumption that, in a largely hostile and alien world, help would indeed be forthcoming. In her famous auto-biography, Glückel of Hameln (1645–1724) relates how

Night had fallen when we landed at Delfzijl and it was too late to find lodging in an inn or even a Jew's house. It was still stormy and we feared that nothing remained for us but to spend the night in the street. But the following day was the fast before the New Year, we had not eaten a bite all day while on shipboard, and we were still faint from our sea-sickness. So we did not relish lying in the street all night without food or drink.

But presently my husband came to the house of a Jew whose brother had married the daughter of Chaim Fürst of Hamburg and begged a night's shelter for us and our children, so that we might have a roof over our heads at least. The man's immediate response was, 'Enter, in God's name, my house is yours. I can give you a good bed, although food there is none;' (for it was already late and his wife was away in Emden).[21]

At a more exalted and more urgent level than that applicable to Glückel and her family's need for a night's lodging, but stemming from the same source, there was the specific rule of *pidyon shevuyim*—the duty to ransom captives. In antiquity and down to early modern times this was conceived of, typically, in terms of the rescue of people unlucky enough to have been seized and held by robbers, pirates, slavers, or, as needs hardly be added, local tyrants. By extension, it came to be accepted as a duty to seek the release of any Jew thought to have been unjustly treated or detained. This was a matter on which the Talmudic Sages and later commentators had laid down precise priorities: the ransoming of women preceded that of men, the rescue of one's teacher came before that of one's father, the ransoming of captives of any category came before the otherwise primary duty of dispensing charity to the poor; and to delay performance of the duty of *pidyon shevuyim*, let alone avoid it, was to be guilty of a wickedness as great and unforgivable as that of the spilling of blood. The obligation to attempt the relief of an entire community in distress was of course doubly and trebly compelling, as the speed and energy with which all those who could do so proceeded to contribute their mite of influence to save the Jews of Bohemia and Moravia from the threatened horrors of Maria Theresa's decree of banishment served to illustrate. It followed, of course, that to fail in the performance of such a well-defined social duty was to incur the great displeasure and disapproval of the community. So too in respect of other obligations.

In general, the greater the failure to abide by accepted norms, the greater the displeasure, naturally enough, and the greater too the urge to

---

[21] Glückel of Hameln, *Memoirs*, trans. Marvin Lowenthal (New York, 1977), 102–3.

inflict condign punishment. In extreme cases the punishment inflicted would be equally extreme—and none greater than that meted out to the *malshin*: the delator or informer, the carrier of tales to the alien authority. True or false, straight or crooked, ostensibly plausible or obvious fabrication—a story of any kind, but the darker the better provided it had emanated from within the closed (and to the alien mind ominous) world of the Jews, was always grist to the perpetually revolving mills of mis- and dis-information about them. There was no knowing what report or rumour or evident piece of nonsense might be brought before, and pounced upon by, prince or bishop or landowning magnate or mere policeman, or city burgher or village priest, or indeed by anyone who had a doctrinal or material interest in the dispossession or expulsion or simple liquidation of the Jews as the enemies of God and man; or had a quarrel with any actual Jew whom he or she faced day to day, whose property he or she coveted; or whose supposed influence on innocent Christian folk he or she resented; or whom, for deeper reasons of ineradicable prejudice and psychological need, he or she was intent on holding responsible for the ills of society at large. The hatred, contempt, and fear in which the *malshin* was held by his own people were therefore boundless and the vengeance to which he rendered himself liable correspondingly implacable. He and all like renegades were consigned not only popularly but textually and *ex cathedra* to eternal damnation. The prayer 'And let the delators despair' remains (to this day, it may be added) an integral part of the Eighteen Benedictions, the observant Jew's regular morning prayer. Exceptionally, moreover, in the otherwise profoundly quietistic and pacific culture of exilic Jewry, violent revenge was liable to follow verbal condemnation. Delation was authoritatively seen as one of the rare forms of villainy that called for execution, death being not only right and proper in such a case, but expedient.[22] No other form of social or religious dissidence was treated with such ferocity, although the penalties for lesser, but still serious instances of dissidence could be severe enough.

It needs to be borne in mind in this connection that members of a traditional community were bound to one another not only by religious faith and practice, birth and situation, but by general culture. Until quite modern times, few Jews in any part of Europe had more than such limited knowledge of the language of a country, namely the language of their gentile neighbours, as might be necessary to conduct commercial

---

[22] In the nature of things, documented case-histories of *malshinim* who were put to death are rare, although not so rare, in relatively modern times at any rate, as to leave in doubt the actual practice of punitive execution. See, for example, the account of executions done in Ushitz (now Novaya Ushitsa, in the Ukraine) in 1836, and the corresponding efforts of the Russian authorities to uncover the affair, in David Assaf, *Derekh ha-malkhut: R. Yisrael me-Ruzhin u-mekomo be-toledot ha-ḥasidut* (Jerusalem, 1997), 163–75.

transactions with them. Even this rarely extended to the ability to read and write in the vernacular. Fewer still had direct experience—and therefore correct and reasonably detailed knowledge—of non-Jewish society as such, of its forms and rules, its mores, or indeed anything at all of social and cultural importance about it, except what, at the most superficial level, they might have gained in the course of daily commercial or administrative dealings. Least of all did Jews, through the long stretch of time in which general culture was closely intertwined and interdependent with religion, have more than the vaguest glimmerings of the content of Christianity, or indeed any interest in it. Even the barriers to professional and strictly secular association between Jews and non-Jews, set, for example, by the universal refusal to admit Jews to the guilds, tended to be virtually impenetrable, the more so as Jews were commonly limited to trades and professions in which they had perforce to operate alone or exclusively in the company of other Jews. Finally the workings of the ghetto system of physical enclosure in what can fairly be termed locked and barred night-time urban cages, while never universal in Europe, had profound socio-psychological consequences for all as the most vivid articulation of how Christendom regarded them. Except for the rarest and boldest and most rebellious of spirits, a clear departure from the community, a venture out into the wider, unfamiliar, intimidating world of the gentiles, especially if, as was so often the case, it was in some way interlocked with the prospect or obligation of apostasy, was thus not only fraught with immense practical difficulties, but was for the overwhelming majority no less than unthinkable. The loyalty of Jews to their own people might seem to some outsiders, and here and there, in their heart of hearts, to some Jews as well, to be incomprehensible. But it was the Archimedean point on which virtually all else in their private and collective life turned. Outright rebellion was exceedingly rare. When it occurred, it could, as often as not, even in the face of countervailing external support for the rebel, be made to collapse.

Consider the case of Yiẓḥak Rofeh, called to order in 1732 by the elders of the Amtchislav (Mstislavl) community in Byelorussia, then under Polish rule, for his 'evil' conduct. Rofeh had aroused his leaders' wrath by frequenting members of the local Polish nobility and, horrible to recount, going so far, with his *wife* in tow, as to dance with them. Summoned before the elders to be rebuked he had further transgressed by failing to treat them with the respect they believed to be their due. On the contrary, he had been so bold as to appear before them in the company of his Polish patron and, as the communal minute book recorded, speak 'wickedly and rudely' to them—in his Polish protector's hearing and for his benefit, moreover, and slanderously too. Yiẓḥak Rofeh and his wife, 'may her name be wiped out', were thereupon proscribed. No Jew was to enter their dwelling place. None was to break bread with them. Their sons were to be removed from school. Their property was for the taking. They were, in effect, placed without the law and beyond the pale so far as all of Jewry was concerned; and like penalties were imposed on any Jew who was so presumptuous as to violate the terms of the ban in the villain's favour. The Amtchislav communal minute book records that Yiẓḥak responded ferociously to the judgement meted out to him, that he expressed himself in 'words that cannot be put in writing', and that he went on to compound his original fault and his very great sins by complaining to unnamed 'rulers who were established enemies of the Jews' (local landowners or churchmen, in all probability), bearing false tales to them. At that point the advantage passed to Yiẓḥak who so worked on his Polish protectors that one of their number, having ordered an elder of the community to appear before him, set upon the poor man, and flogged him 'near to death and before all'. But Yiẓḥak did not hold the advantage for long, nor was this the end of the story, or, as Simon Dubnov observed of the case, where its interest lies. Despite the support and protection accorded him by his Polish patrons, despite, as it appears, their having half accepted him socially along with his wife, and despite what must have been the fury and indignation of the communal leadership faced with one who, over and above his improper social behaviour, had been prepared so flagrantly to violate the rules of group loyalty on which Jewish society had relied from time immemorial, the ban on Yiẓḥak and his wife was eventually rescinded. When or on what grounds this was done, or even whether it was in the lifetime of the rebellious couple or later, at the behest of their children, remains unclear. What is known, because duly noted in the communal minute book, is that an act of repentance of some sort was performed and accepted.[23] What can be presumed is that the disgrace proved unbearable even to the 'evil' and unruly Yiẓḥak Rofeh. It can be presumed too that this was very well understood by the communal authorities and accounts at least in part for what they themselves must have regarded as an appropriate display of lenience.

Life under ban of excommunication for one who would not or could not bring himself to apostatize was indeed intolerable and in many ways impossible. There could be no marriage, divorce, schooling for his children, burial of the family's dead, or effective observance of the dietary laws by the living. There could be no professional or economic relations with other Jews. To be under the ban was to be cast out, condemned to a terrible loneliness, and in all likelihood to poverty too, in a world that had become doubly hostile. The power to place its members, however well placed and protected, under the ban was therefore power enough to induce all but the most determined rebels to knuckle under to those who held what all others in the community accepted as legitimate authority. It

[23] S. M. Dubnov, 'Fun mayn arkhiv', *YIVO Bletter*, 1 (Jan.–May 1931), 405–7.

was the sharpest of the disciplinary weapons ordinarily available to the communal authorities. In some ways it remains the most instructive. There were others, however: fines, withdrawal of social privileges, and, as we shall see, in the special case of Russia under Nicholas I, the preferential drafting of young men and boys for lifetime military service. Corporal punishment, while rare, was not unknown.

VI

Sporadic rebellion apart, communal self-government faced the difficulty that it needed to be more than merely virtuous to be effective. It could not be populist. It could not, strictly speaking, be popular. There was no way in which it could model itself on the patterns of government and authority, country-wide or local, that were common in the world outside Jewry. Given the general prohibition on ownership of land by Jews and their exclusion from the estates of the realm under the old regime it could not in any ordinary and regularized sense be aristocratic or hereditary. It could not be theocratic in anything like the sense associated with the Christian churches: rabbis were not priests serving as the indispensable mediators between man and God; they were no more than judges and experts in the Law. It is true that in principle a rabbi is free and independent in his judgement, bound only by the Law and that, as a Master of the Law, his moral authority is in principle immeasurable. Of course, the Law itself can be variously interpreted, as we have seen. Pressures of time and place and circumstance may induce the rabbi to soften or deflect its impact. Not all rabbis are of equal calibre. Few among them are of independent means. The lay members of the community who elect the rabbi to his office and whose duty it is to sustain him materially are capable of bringing pressures of their own to bear upon him. And beyond the risk of malleable mediocrity, there is the danger the rabbis themselves are the first to recognize, that incompatible interpretations of the Law lead inexorably to loss of rigour, precisely that feature of the Law that they were trained to hold in reverence and protect with special zeal.

The overwhelming tendency of the rabbinate has therefore been to seek safety in consensus. The governing rule of conduct and articulated judgement has been to refrain from straying from what is acceptable to one's fellows, to keep to whatever passes for the mainstream of opinion, to avoid, at almost any cost, the marginal, the eccentric, and the minoritarian. Wisdom, in short, is encapsulated in the Mishnaic injunction *aḥarei rabim lehatot* (which, somewhat roughly and removed from its immediate context, has been taken to mean 'follow the majority').[24] Some, to be sure, may think that there may be discerned in this dictum at least a hint of what in our own times is thought of as the democratic duty to have a decent regard for opinion at large. In practice, the chief operative, long-term result of obeisance to it has been further consolidation of the (orthodox) rabbinate as deeply conformist and intellectually and theologically unadventurous—although, to be sure, a class of men who by and large are united on essentials and, with the rarest of exceptions, high-minded and incorruptible. That it has only been by the exercise of great judgemental rigour that the coherence of Judaism as a doctrine and as a pattern of conduct, and the cohesion of the Jews themselves as a people, has been maintained came to be held on both the rabbinic and the lay sides of Jewry as a social doctrine that admitted no question or qualification. What it did nothing to help determine was the answer to another fundamental question. Who in practice was to lead Jewry when the issues confronting it were not bound up in the petty details of ritual, private conduct, and personal status, but were those concerning the welfare and safety of entire living communities?

[24] Nezikin: Sanhedrin, 1: 6. However, as has long been noted, the same phrase is employed in the Book of Exodus (23: 2) to imply the opposite, namely as a warning against mere numbers—effectively the majority opinion—being allowed to determine judgement and leave the way open to the perversion of justice.

PART I

Integration and Fragmentation

THE principal engine of change in the modern history of the Jews of Europe was the revolutionary idea that it might after all be right and proper for them to enjoy full and equal civil and political rights with all other subjects of the several realms that they inhabited. All turned, therefore, in the final analysis on the matter of emancipation: on where and on what terms it was offered to them; on where and with what consequences it was, on the contrary, denied; and on where and how and with what implications, having first been granted, it would later be withdrawn. But in all cases, it sufficed for the question of emancipation to have been posed to call the ancient structure of relations between the Jews and the state and between the Jews and their neighbours into question— to most lasting effect on the Jews themselves. No other factor operating upon them in modern times would serve so powerfully to precipitate such revolutionary changes in their mores, their culture, their internal social structure, and, more generally and loosely, their private and collective concerns and expectations. The introduction of the simple notion that their political circumstances not only could, but perhaps should, be otherwise was to leave them in the course of little more than a single century transformed. Some within Jewry welcomed the prospect of radical internal and external change. Others were profoundly repelled by it. But like it or not, all would consistently and at an ever higher level of intensity be confronted by choices of a kind for which no precedents were to be found either in their history or in their Law. And in important cases the problem posed was the more difficult to deal with by reason of the ambiguity of what was offered them and the accompanying obscurity of ultimate intention. Where formal, open, and explicit legislative determination of their status was the case they were apt to find actual implementation patchy and reluctant. Where a frank and clear-cut reordering of their position was denied them—on grounds of high Christian principle, for example—there, in contrast, it was not impossible to find that a somewhat shadowy approximation to an outright grant of a decent place in civil society had been granted them after all. Where state and society were both firmly against civil equality and sought to subject the Jews and their affairs to an order founded essentially on the same repressive basis as that of old, there Jews, some of them, at all events, would be moved— unprecedentedly, and to some minds belatedly—to rebellion. It would be a very long time, and not until the end of the fourth decade of the twentieth century, that these mixed, contradictory, always deeply controversial results would be swept away, and clarity, albeit of a kind that relatively few on either side of the divide had originally anticipated, would be restored.

1
Proposals

I

I T can be said of the Jews of Europe that as late as the final decades of the eighteenth century they all displayed substantially similar political, social, and economic features. For this reason among others, the question of their admission to civil society appeared to lend itself to being cast—and at any rate debated—in terms of universal application. Where it was so conceived, there, as we shall see, it appeared to admit of correspondingly clear and unambiguous answers. Initially, such were the terms on which the Jews themselves tended to approach the question and the relatively simple operative conclusions they were apt to draw depended on whether they judged the prospect of emancipation a blessing or a curse. However, what the Jews thought of the matter counted for very little. At least a century would pass before Jews of any standing anywhere in Europe were in a position to play a role of some import in those political arenas, large or small, in which their fate, and the matter of their emancipation in particular, was the subject of debate. Even then the influence they were able to bring to bear in their own cause would prove to be exceedingly limited. The power to bestow the gift (if gift it was) of emancipation or, contrariwise, to withhold it lay exclusively with others—with the governments of the day in the first instance, of course, but no less fundamentally, if less directly, with those elements of society to which those who held formal power were inclined to lend an ear. In general, the approach to the matter of the emancipation of the Jews tended to correspond to the favoured approach to other major aspects of political and constitutional policy. Where the balance of opinion (and eventual policy) tended towards decisions being founded on principled, a priori, moral, and therefore, in a loose sense, philosophical considerations, the question of the Jews was likely to be taken up in a similar spirit. Where social and political debate leaned towards the pragmatic, the specific, the local, and the historical—and therefore the idiosyncratic— there the approach to the Jews was likely to be of a similar nature. In all cases it was a question of balance. No state or society dealt with the matter of the Jews in one exclusive mode. All tended very strongly to mix considerations of interest with what were at any rate thought of as matters of principle. Only the proportions varied.

From the end of the eighteenth century, the tendency in all the major continental states of Europe was to aspire to a powerfully centralizing, rationalized, internal ordering of society. One largely incidental consequence was to encourage government to take a fresh look at its country's Jewish population. The purpose, typically, was to formulate an attitude, even a policy, towards the Jews that was in keeping with whatever were considered to be the broad and binding principles on which government and the social order as a whole ought properly to be based. While the specific rules and considerations thought applicable in each case varied, the central, underlying intention was everywhere much the same. All strove for coherence. The one social value none were prepared to eschew was order. The difficulty about the Jews was that, over and above all the old objections to their presence, they seemed to present an insuperable obstacle to the establishment of just such a coherent, smoothly operating, centrally directed social order as was striven for. Here and there the question whether they were likely, in significant numbers and in some foreseeable future, to abandon their faith and convert without equivocation to Christianity would be posed. But underlying the old insistence on the truth of Christianity and the corresponding errors of Judaism was the secular, socio-political conviction that the Jews could no longer be allowed—for their own good, but more especially for the good of society at large—to continue in their set and ancient manner. To be sure, there was nothing new in the notion that they were a profoundly anomalous people. What was new, what would now gather force and lie close to the heart of the matter of their eventual emancipation, was the view that an anomaly of the kind they represented, and continued so very wilfully to perpetuate, needed finally to be done away with. This alien, apparently indigestible element in society was always and everywhere *in* society and *in* the state, but never properly *of* either one or the other. The problem it presented must therefore be addressed first and foremost in political terms as one of the aspects of society that needed to be tidied up. For some of the statesmen and for many administrators concerned, tidiness was indeed all.

There was therefore something in this approach that was simplistic, brutal, and proto-totalitarian. And, in general, it was certainly the case that the light in which the matter of the Jews was chiefly seen was defined much less by considerations of their welfare than by *raison d'état*. Expediency, efficacy of administration, economic and, as it were, military mercantilism, and, above all, social control—these were the decisive criteria. The spirit in which the Jews' affairs were discussed, when discussed at all, by those who were in a position to decide upon them was étatist and rationalist. The dominant considerations were the welfare and efficiency of the state itself: the state as structure and as machine, the state as one of a number of competing states. Pragmatism boiled down therefore to rulers and administrators reluctantly conceding that awkward and regrettable though it might be to have Jews present among them, it was neither possible nor, in fact, desirable not to bear them in mind. On the contrary, a defined, fixed, and intelligible place had to be found for them. They too had to render the state the services that were its due. They had to be allowed—rather, they had to be encouraged and if necessary compelled—to move towards social uniformity with all the other subjects of the realm. In a word, the Jews needed to be brought at long last within the orbit of central administration. Social (and of course fiscal and military) control of the Jews themselves would be enhanced thereby; but so would the general structure of society and its overall amenability to rational and efficacious government.

But if an ostensibly rational, value-free, étatist approach informed the governing circles of the major European states in their approach to the matter of the Jews from the middle of the eighteenth century until the dying days of all three surviving continental empires early in the twentieth century, it will be found to have been shot through and through with certain set convictions about them. Again and again in the reports of district governors and policemen, in discussion papers, in the comments superior officials noted on the margins of documents submitted by their inferiors, in travellers' accounts, in the literary delineation of Jewish characters, and in the course of general conversation on those not too frequent occasions when the Jews and their affairs cropped up, Jews tended overwhelmingly to be regarded—and, in effect, dismissed—as an incorrigibly inferior lot. Nothing was rarer than for those who for one reason or another addressed themselves, however briefly, to the matter of the Jews than to begin, at least implicitly—and as often as not explicitly—with the proposition that they were not only hopelessly stubborn and difficult to deal with, but in many ways depraved, ignorant, and unclean. Their religious convictions and conduct were held to be vitiated by hideous error. Their Talmud was regarded as a rag-bag of obscurities and sophisms. Whether there was more to be said for their rabbis none could rightly know, but there was little doubt that they did batten on a credulous and superstitious people and that these, in turn, taken as a whole, were sickly, unproductive, in large measure parasitical, and therefore as undesirable socially as they were culturally and intellectually and, of course, morally and spiritually. They might conceivably have had other, meritorious features in the past. It was admitted by the well informed that towards the end of the tenth century there had been great numbers of Jewish physicians in Europe and that, as the director of the faculty of medicine in Vienna, Gerhart van Swieten, put it authoritatively to the Empress Maria Theresa in 1753, 'there were even popes who availed themselves of their services.' Although that, he then went on to explain, was in the age of barbarism and ignorance, when Greek and Roman medicine had been forgotten, and Arab medicine was in vogue, and the

Jews, knowing oriental languages, had had a linguistic advantage which they proceeded to misuse by presenting themselves as more knowledgeable than they were in fact. Now, in practice, except where 'rabbinic and cabbalistic superstition' worked on the credulous and the vulgar, they could no longer sustain the façade. Even in Holland, where their synagogues were regrettably 'public' and they were in certain circumstances treated more favourably than Catholics, they had never been allowed to enter any of the medical professions. And that, so van Swieten explained to the empress, was because Jewish surgeons were known to be incompetent and because no Dutch surgeon would take a Jew as his apprentice. Nor did he think it right to let Jews practise as mere apothecaries. 'A nation that seeks constantly to deceive' would take advantage of the opportunity 'to commit innumerable and most likely undetectable acts of fraud and duplicity'.[1]

Attempts at a strict and systematic formulation of what, in the course of time, would be thought of as 'the problem' of the Jews[2] were still rare in the latter half of the eighteenth century. Attitudes were loose and as often as not flippant, as much among men of influence and power as among mere observers—and their emotive content might still count for more than the empirical. Rejection, charity, revulsion, and what happened to be thought of by the people in question as right and proper and in the public spirit were all intermingled. The one common point of departure for those who claimed to know a thing or two about the Jews and sought—or were duty bound—to deal with them, was that they were a backward, unproductive, and (this was especially telling) militarily useless people. The one thread running through all such attitudes as chanced to be struck by the truly literate and/or the truly powerful was condescension. The conventional wisdom on the Jews even at the governmental level being negative, critical, restrictive, and minatory, it was natural that a collective, blanket, and free admission of the Jewish segment of the population into whatever it was that passed for civil society was unthinkable.

For all these reasons, what the periodic flurries of official interest in the matter tended to produce was a series of awkward compromises between what seemed to rulers and officials to be dictated by new wave étatist and pragmatic notions of government and what had been carried over from older times: between ancient but still powerful, often implacably hostile sentiments and judgements on the Jews and the new tendency

---

[1] 'Gutachten Van Swietens an Maria Theresia', 20 Aug. 1753, in A. F. Pribram (ed.), *Urkunden und Akten zur Geschichte der Juden in Wien, Erste Abteilung, Allgemeiner Teil 1526–1847 (1849)*, i (Vienna and Leipzig, 1918), No. 162, 347–8. The queen's response to the physician's opinion was a royal instruction on 8 Sept. *extending* the ban on medical practice by Jews: 'Den jüdischen Ärzten, Chirurgen, Apothekern, Bädern und Hebammen wird die Ausübung ihres Berufes auch unter Juden verboten' (ibid. 348).

[2] See below, Chapter 3.

to look at them in a clinical light and to therapeutic purpose. The difference in tone, terminology, and content between Empress Maria Theresa's *Judenordnung* of 5 May 1764 and her son and successor's *Toleranzpatent* of 2 January 1782 will serve to mark the transition.

The *Judenordnung* was concerned in all its forty-five clauses to instruct those few Jews who had been permitted to reside in Vienna on the terms on which they might earn their living, maintain a family, run a household, marry their children, and employ servants; when they were to refrain from being seen in the street (on Sundays and holidays before noon) and what they were to do if they chanced to be outside their homes when the Host was carried past. The tone was threatening, the terminology uncompromising. The 'privileged Jew' (*privilegirter Jud*) was insistently distinguished from the 'foreign Jew' (*fremder Jud*). What was 'authorized' (*befugt*) was distinguished from what was 'unauthorized' (*unbefugt*). What forms of conduct were 'indictable' (*belangend*), what misdeeds would be 'punished' (*gestrafet*), and whether by fines or by expulsion, were laid down. Throughout the text of the *Ordnung*, the commonest word was the negative *kein*. In its bureaucratic thoroughness and as an articulation of the martinet policeman's mind it remains a very modern document. In its inner concept of what was desirable in society it was of a piece with—and did indeed anticipate—Pope Pius VI's still more degrading edict on the Jews of Rome (*Editto sopra gli ebrei*) of 1775.

What Emperor Joseph II's own rescript on toleration had in common with his mother's ordinance was that it too had been most meticulously formulated in the course of extended, close discussion within the Vienna bureaucracy and that many drafts were prepared before the definitive version was reached. Otherwise, albeit in a limited and unadventurous way, it was much more plainly the first fruit of the European Enlightenment: an act of government intended *inter alia* to demonstrate what a calm, rational, mildly benevolent examination of the real structure and the real needs of society led one to recognize as its, i.e. society's, requirements. The spirit and the tone of the whole is set out in the preamble which speaks of 'Our pre-eminent attention [*Unser vorzüglichsten Augenmerke*]' being directed

to the end that all Our subjects without distinction of nationality and religion, once they have been admitted and tolerated in our States, shall participate in common in public welfare, . . . shall enjoy legal freedom, and encounter no obstacles to any honest way of gaining their livelihood and of increasing general industriousness.

The new departure, it was asserted, followed from the fact that 'existing laws pertaining to the Jewish nation [*die jüdische Nazion*] . . . are not always compatible with these Our most gracious intentions'. In future, the government would be guided by the goal of making the Jews 'useful and serviceable to the State [*dem Staate nützlicher und brauchbarer zu machen*], mainly through better education and enlightenment of its youth and by directing them to the sciences, the arts and the crafts.' 'Tolerated Jews' [*tolerirten Juden*] would therefore be allowed under certain circumstances to send their children to Christian schools; free entry to universities was confirmed. 'All kinds of crafts or trades' could henceforth be learned from Christian masters. The Jewish nation as a whole would be granted 'a general licence to carry on all kinds of trade' and its individual members would be free to apply for the right to engage in wholesale trade on the same basis as Christians. 'Tolerated' Jews would be entitled to employ as many servants, Jewish *or* Christian, as they might require. Restrictions on housing would be allowed to lapse. The capitation tax on foreign Jews entering Vienna would be abolished, as were certain other tiresome or demeaning impositions. Jews of a certain commercial standing would be allowed to carry swords, as would their sons. The rescript concludes, however, with an admonition.

Since by these favours We almost [*beynahe*] place the Jewish nation on an equal level with adherents of other alien religious associations [*andern fremden Religionsverwandten*] in respect of trade and enjoyment of civil and domestic facilities, We earnestly advise them to observe scrupulously all political, civil, and judicial laws of the country to which they are bound in the manner incumbent on all other inhabitants.[3]

All this was far removed from the spirit and the letter of the older *Judenordnung*. But it was not emancipation. The emperor's rescript specifically laid down that the right of admission to certain occupations and institutions did *not* carry with it the right of citizenship and craft mastership. From these the Jews 'remained excluded' [*wovon sie ausgeschlossen bleiben*]'. Tucked away in clause fifteen was the requirement that the Jews themselves, in the interests of 'maintaining common confidence [*für die Aufrechthaltung des gemeinschaftlichen Zutrauens*]', cease to employ Hebrew and Yiddish. And while the central idea on which the rescript turned, toleration, signified broadmindedness, its corollary, the distinction repeatedly drawn between the Jews who were to be tolerated and improved and those of their alien and unimprovable brethren, did not. Finally, running through it all, was the patronizing idea of improvement, the notion that what the imperial government in Vienna would now be about was an effort to bring the Jews up to scratch in the light of some never very clearly defined model of ethnic German, but especially Christian, goodness and civic worth. It was characteristic of the governing spirit in which the enterprise had been approached that a later decree that dealt specifically with the employment of young Jewish people by

[3] Pribram, *Urkunden*, i, No. 205, XVI, 494–500.

Christian master craftsmen, and was designed to encourage such link-ages, was frankly entitled *Verbesserung der Judenmoral*—the 'Improvement of Jewish Morals'.[4]

How much of this was cant? Jewry and Judaism in their complexity would continue to be rejected out of hand: not so ruthlessly and mind-lessly as before, somewhat more thoughtfully, somewhat less irritably, and ostensibly to better purpose. But if the social and cultural features of the Jews continued to puzzle their masters, there was no evidence of any interest in exploring them beyond what was reckoned to be strictly rele-vant to the good order and prosperity of the empire. The thought that they might be dealing with an authentic, living, unquestionably anom-alous and tormented, but in the final analysis legitimately discrete social organism with profoundly rooted views, sentiments, and purposes of its own did not much enter the minds or calculations of the officials con-cerned. It had been settled, on imperial authority, that the Jews needed to be reformed. And that being the case, and things being what they were in the lands of the Habsburgs, plainly they would indeed have to be reformed. But from above. It followed, therefore, once again in quite striking contrast to what had obtained under the older regime, that the general thrust of the new approach was towards the *future*. A later edict issued in 1797 (in the wake of the French Revolution, therefore, rather than in any sense in conscious or unconscious anticipation of it) went so far as to concede explicitly that if all went well the general legal inequal-ity of the Jews might eventually be entirely abolished—in Bohemia at any rate, not, so far as anyone could see, elsewhere. Even so, it was clear that if that were to happen it would be in consequence, first and foremost, of what the Jews themselves had made of the great new effort to bring them into line with the rest of the emperor's subjects.

II

The imperial Austrian approach embodied a distinct effort to accommo-date the teachings of the Enlightenment to an unwavering insistence on absolutist government. In one form or another, wittingly or otherwise, its example would be followed throughout central and eastern Europe, with, as we shall see, far-reaching consequences for much the greater part of Jewry. Crucially, however, in determining the way in which European Jewry as a whole evolved, matters were otherwise in western Europe. The methods and principles by which Great Britain, France, and the Low Countries were governed brought about, in the course of time, changes

---

[4] Decree of 4 Apr. 1786, ibid., No. 239, 575–6.

in the condition and outlook of the Jewish inhabitants of those countries of a kind that were unprecedented in themselves and would long be unknown in any of the lands that lay east of the Rhine.

The salient characteristic of the British approach to the matter of the Jews was that there was little or no interest in *reform*. The drive towards social control, social uniformity, and meticulous social regulation that was so prominent on the continent was absent in Britain as much in society as in government. There were, however, other roots to what might be thought of as British idiosyncrasy in this respect. It was in Great Britain, curiously, that the 'Jewish Question' had first been seriously posed and to some extent debated in a major European state in modern times. When Cromwell resolved to rescind King Edward I's edict of expulsion of 1290 in the interests of allowing London's very small colony of crypto-Jews to surface and permit other Jews, mostly from Holland, to join them, he did so primarily because he had his eye on the advantages Spanish and Portuguese Jews with their worldwide connections might bring to English commerce, the information on foreign affairs with which they could supply him, and the political services they could perform for him on the continent. What is of greatest interest, because, unwittingly, it set a pattern of sorts, was that Cromwell had begun by considering a more open and comprehensive policy than the one that his administration was eventually to implement. When it became apparent, however, that by formally revoking the thirteenth-century edict of expulsion a noisy and troublesome opposition would be aroused, the plan was abandoned.[5] The resettlement of Jews in England was allowed to take place, but on a *de facto* basis and Edward I's edict left to pass into history.

A century later there would be a new attempt to settle the matter of the status, rights, and privileges of Jews in England by formal legislation, and so, presumably, once and for all. This was the Jewish Naturalization Bill, or 'Jew Bill' so-called, introduced by the Pelham ministry and passed into law by Parliament in 1753. It was not a radical measure. It provided for little more than specific procedures whereby foreign-born Jews might be naturalized and so allowed to acquire rights already possessed by their own native-born children under the principle of *jus soli*. Nevertheless, it failed. The implications of the bill were correctly understood to be wider and the lesson that Oliver Cromwell had had to learn was rehearsed by the government of the day. To the opposition's charge that 'Nothing could be more absurd in its Nature, or more contrary to the Maxims of our own Policy, than to allow the natural Enemies of the Christian

---

[5] Lucien Wolf, 'Cromwell's Jewish Intelligencers', *Essays in Jewish History* (London, 1934), 93–114. Cf. D. S. Katz, *Philosemitism and the Readmission of the Jews into England 1603–1655* (Oxford, 1982), *passim*; and Avrom Saltman, *The Jewish Question in 1655: Studies in Prynne's Demurrer* (Ramat-Gan, 1995).

Religion to be the natural subjects of the Christian State',[6] the government was incapable of formulating an effective answer—for all that the authorized spokesmen for Christian England, the senior bishops of the Anglican Church, viewed the matter with indulgence. Their position was that the Church, having the interests of the state at heart, had no reason to object to a limited measure of toleration. It was at the popular level that opposition to the measure was strong. Still, the government took the accusations of impiety heaped against it to heart and a mere seven months after its original passage through Parliament had the act repealed, reinforcing the Cromwellian precedent.

From that time on British governments, when called upon to take any position at all, were content to sanction (or ignore) piecemeal lifting of what had been, as in all other European states, an entire series of restrictions or prohibitions on the entry and presence of Jews into the country, on the occupations they might engage in, on the public bodies they might join, on the role they might play in public affairs, and, not least, their freedom to form and maintain an organized community, to worship, to marry, to care for their own, and to bury their dead. It was a slow and irregular process, mostly rather offhand. Where specific restrictions on personal freedom and on communal activity had not explicitly been lifted they were allowed to fall into desuetude by default. Perhaps, as a procedure, it was no more than was to be expected of an increasingly commercial nation, the more so as the tendency had grown, somewhat in the manner that it had long since taken root in the Low Countries, to regard the Jews as allies in Britain's economic enterprise. By the early years of the eighteenth century, political interest in the Jews of the kind that had initially drawn the Cromwellian government to favour them had largely faded. But English conventional wisdom was firm in holding them to be of worldwide commercial significance. They

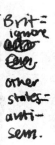

Brit = ignore as in other states = anti-sem.

are, indeed, so disseminated through all the trading Parts of the World, [wrote Addison in 1712] that they are become the Instruments by which the most distant Nations converse with one another, and by which Mankind are knit together in general Correspondence. They are like the Pegs and Nails in a great Building, which, though they are but little valued in themselves, are absolutely necessary to keep the whole Frame together.[7]

By the end of the eighteenth century the Jews of England had little to complain of. Those who had been born in Great Britain became British subjects as a matter of course. The grant of civil and commercial liberties to individual Jews, native or foreign-born, met with few difficulties. Jews

[6] *An Answer to a Pamphlet, entitled, Considerations on the Bill to permit persons professing the Jewish Religion to be naturalized* (London, 1753), 11. Cited in A. E. Vital, 'The Jew Bill of 1753 and English National Consciousness' (New Haven, 1986, unpub.), 11.

[7] *Spectator*, 27 Sept. 1712.

continued to be excluded from the Guilds of the City of London for a considerable period. But it was not long before they were admitted as brokers in the Royal Exchange. Whether ancient legislation prohibiting ownership of land by Jews retained its force was unclear technically, but in practice no obstacle to freehold possession was raised. The oaths that certain elected and appointed officials, and which junior and senior members of the universities were obliged to take, operated against Jews, although they had been formulated with the exclusion of Roman Catholics and Protestant dissenters rather than Jews in mind. The phrase 'on the true faith of a Christian' automatically prevented any Jew at all, observant or otherwise, from taking them. But the ancient, and for the Jews themselves vastly more sensitive, issue of the legal force and validity of an oath taken by a Jew in court—when serving as a witness, for example—had effectively been disposed of as early as 1667; and the swearing of Jews on the Old Testament as matter of routine was confirmed in a formal judgment in 1744 when Lord Chief Justice Willes held that to deny the swearing (and therefore the evidence) of a witness who was not a Christian, but did acknowledge a Supreme Being, was 'contrary not only to the scripture but to common sense and common humanity'. It was 'a most impolitic notion,' said the judge, 'and would at once destroy all that trade and commerce from which this nation reaps such great benefits'. Besides, 'It is a little mean, narrow notion to suppose that no one but a Christian can be an honest man'.[8] The matter of the swearing-in of Jewish trial witnesses, and the associated question of the validity of whatever evidence they gave, took very much longer to settle on the continent of Europe, even in post-revolutionary France, as we shall see.[9]

While generally humane, this *ad hoc* approach to the matter of the Jews and their emancipation was unquestionably untidy. This had something to do with the Jewish community in Great Britain being a very small one at least until the final decades of the nineteenth century. As late as the middle of the nineteenth century it numbered no more than 30–40,000 members of all ages and conditions throughout the British Isles. Moreover, virtually all were city-dwellers and of these most (some 25,000) lived in the single, but already immense city of London. England's Jews were therefore sufficiently inconspicuous for such anti-Jewish militants as there were in eighteenth- and early nineteenth-century London to be unable to make much of a meal of their presence there. And the fact that British Jews were concentrated in London (and Bristol and a few other cities) and therefore almost entirely unknown in the countryside—

----

[8] In *Omichund* v. *Barker*, 23 Feb. 1744, *Cases argued and determined in the Court of Common Pleas. Reports of Chief Justice Willes, 1737–60*, ed. C. Durnford, 538–54. Cited in M. C. N. Salbstein, *The Emancipation of the Jews in Britain: The Question of the Admission of the Jews to Parliament* (East Brunswick, 1982), 46–7.

[9] See below, pp. 231–2.

except, and then very marginally, as pedlars travelling through it—was a further, unintended contribution to their presence in the country being seen, at any rate at the time, as raising issues of no great urgency or public importance. In this respect, as in so many others, their situation was therefore strikingly unlike that of most Jews on the continent of Europe, still overwhelmingly a rural people. British Jews had the further advantage of being totally free of the primal curse of being ground between lord and peasant as in eastern Europe, especially Poland. They were not engaged in moneylending to anything like the same extent as were the Jews of eastern France. The economic roles for which they were best known were stock-jobbing and wholesale and foreign commerce— spheres which were favoured by the government in London—and trades and crafts of the middle-lower rank: silversmithery, shopkeeping, diamond polishing, tailoring, watchmaking, and the like. Those who could not set up shop on their own account engaged in peddling and trading in old clothes as did many Jews in Germany, but among these the driving tendency to escape from the lower levels of the economy was evident and likely to be approved of. That United Kingdom citizenship was determined primarily by *jus soli* was another boon; and those who had not been born on British soil found that it could be granted them quite freely by a process of naturalization. Possessed of citizenship, provided they met the appropriate property qualifications, they were entitled to vote in local and parliamentary elections and serve as magistrates and city aldermen. Admission to Oxford and Cambridge was barred to them, but so it was to Dissenters and Catholics. In sum, as would be repeatedly and correctly claimed in the course of the sole great formal and politically binding public debate on the integration of the Jews into the body politic of England to be held in the nineteenth century, there were virtually no hurdles left for them to overcome apart from that which occasioned that debate: the admission of Jews to membership of parliament itself.[10]

In the light of the experience elsewhere in Europe it remains an oddity that a century would pass between the fiasco of the 'Jew Bill' and the next full-dress public and parliamentary debate on the matter of the Jews in England and that, in the interim, virtually all the questions that had troubled the political classes respecting the Jews were resolved. This had much to do, no doubt, with the fact that the norms of British politics and administration both encouraged and facilitated an incremental and ameliorative treatment of any issue in which ideology and interest were intermixed. But the generally mild approach to the renewed presence of Jews in England and to the question of their legal status in it—a mildness that was only sporadically distinguishable from lack of concern—is perhaps better accounted for by factors of another category altogether. The

[10] On the parliamentary debate of 1847, see below, pp. 177–80.

English had long experience of the presence among themselves of members of other nations and religious denominations. The Scots, the Irish, and the Welsh were considered by the English, as they were, of course, by themselves, to possess a separate and distinctive nationality. But 'nationality' in the context of the British Isles had long had something less than the usual ring. The Scots, the Irish, and the Welsh were not in the ordinary sense of the term, if in any sense at all, *foreign*. Religion, to be sure, was another matter. But where religion was at issue, and where it related to the Jews, and to their emancipation in particular, the questions it raised tended to be assimilated into, or, more commonly still, to fall into line behind, the much more immediate, politically weightier questions of the political rights and liberties to be accorded (or denied) to Protestant Dissenters, to Unitarians, and, above all, to Roman Catholics. Elsewhere in Europe the terms and significance in which matters of religion and nationality were perceived were of another order, and this was most dramatically so in France. And there were other ways in which France and Britain were not at one in these respects and in which the differences between revolutionary France and the absolutist regimes to the east were subtle rather than decisive.

III

A double note, benevolent and severe, charitable and demanding (but ominous too, as we, with hindsight, are in a position to detect), was sounded in the first and very remarkable debate on the subject in the French National Assembly on 23 December 1789—relatively early therefore in the life of the country's new revolutionary parliament.[11] There had been a few earlier calls for a fresh look at the matter of the Jews. Just prior to the Revolution, when in the wake of the edict of toleration issued in the Protestants' favour the question whether it might or might not be extended to the Jews first arose, the royal minister Chrétien de Malesherbes was instructed by the Conseil d'État to look into it. At a less exalted level, when in 1777 two Jewish merchants of Metz asked permission to trade in Thionville (a bare 25 kilometres away), and were turned down on the grounds that they were only allowed to settle and operate in 'authorized locations', their case was taken up by the distinguished jurist Pierre Louis de Lacretelle. Lacretelle spoke in court of the need to 'soften' (*adoucir*) the condition of the Jews. They deserved better of the French. 'Their ways are simple and religious; an impoverished people, living secluded lives, they often find in close family union the

---

[11] *Archives parlementaires de 1787 à 1860, premières séries (1787–1799)* (Paris, 1878; repr. Lichtenstein, 1969), x. 752–60.

happiness that their political condition seemingly denies them.'[12] He lost his case and there was no follow-up to his ideas before 1789, any more than there had been to those of Malesherbes—not, at all events, in the decisive realm of government and administration.

The debate in the National Assembly was, of course, of an entirely different order in that it took place as a preliminary to a sovereign decision. The immediate issue before the Assembly was the admission of certain semi-pariah classes—among them actors and public executioners—to what came to be termed 'active citizenship'. It was soon apparent, however, that the issues presented by the Jews were very different. It was apparent, too, that it would make no better sense to examine the Jews' case in tandem with that of the Protestants. The latter, like the Jews, were non-Catholics, but their *national* identity was not in doubt, nor, therefore, their right to the new liberties being decreed for all. Whatever else they were, they were Frenchmen. No one in the National Assembly thought otherwise. But were the Jews Frenchmen? If they were not, could they become citizens? The contention of the lead speaker in the debate, Count Stanislaw de Clermont-Tonnerre, was that the argument for granting them full rights of citizenship needed to be founded on the most general principles. Religion was a private affair. The law of the state need not and ought not to impinge upon it. So long as religious obligations were compatible with the law of the state and contravened it in no particular it was wrong to deprive a person, whose conscience required him to assume such religious obligations, of those rights which it was the duty of all citizen *qua* citizens to assume. One either imposed a national religion by main force, so erasing the relevant clause of the Declaration of the Rights of Man and the Citizen to which all now subscribed. Or else one allowed everyone the freedom to profess the religious opinion of his choice. Mere *tolerance* was unacceptable. 'The system of tolerance, coupled [as it is invariably] to degrading distinctions, is so vicious in itself, that he who is compelled to tolerate remains as dissatisfied with the law as is he whom it has granted no more than such a form of tolerance.' There was no middle way. The enemies of the Jews attacked them, and attacked him, Clermont-Tonnerre, on the grounds that they were deficient morally. It was also held of the Jews that they were unsociable, that their laws prescribed usury, that they were forbidden to mix with the French by marriage or at table or join them in defence of the country or in any other common enterprise. But these reproaches were either unjust or specious. Usury was blameworthy beyond a doubt, but it was the laws of France that had compelled the Jews to practise it. And so with most of

---

[12] P. L. de Lacretelle, 'Mémoire pour deux Juifs de Metz', *Œuvres*, i (Paris, 1823), 213–35. I am grateful to Professor Sara Maza for calling my attention to the episode and providing me with the source.

the other charges. Once the Jews had title to land and a country of their own the practice of usury would cease. So would the unsociability that was held against them. So would much of their religious eccentricity [*ces travers religieux*]. As for the further argument, that they had judges and laws of their own, why so they did, and on this matter he, Clermont-Tonnerre, would say to his critics (coming to the passage in his address to the Assembly that would be quoted over and over again in the course of the two centuries that followed), that that indeed was impermissible.

As a nation the Jews must be denied everything, as individuals they must be granted everything; their judges can no longer be recognized; their recourse must be to our own exclusively; legal protection for the doubtful laws by which Jewish corporate existence is maintained must end; they cannot be allowed to create a political body or a separate order within the state; it is necessary that they be citizens individually.

There remained the question, what if, as some argued, it was the case that the Jews themselves had no interest in citizenship? Why in that case, he went on, 'if they do not want it, let them say so, in which case expel them [*s'ils veulent ne l'être pas, qu'ils le disent, et alors, qu'on les bannisse*]'. The idea of a society of non-citizens within the state and a nation within a nation was repugnant to him.[13] But in fact, the speaker concluded, that was not at all what the Jews wanted. The evidence was to the contrary. They wished to be incorporated into the nation of France.

Clermont-Tonnerre was promptly contradicted on this last, vital point by the abbé Maury. The term *Jew*, said the abbé did not denote a religious sect, but a nation, one which had laws which it had always followed and by which it wished to continue to abide. 'To proclaim the Jews citizens would be as if to say that, without letters of naturalization and without ceasing to be English or Danish, Englishmen and Danes could become Frenchmen.' But Maury's chief argument was of a moral and social order. The Jews were inherently undesirable, socially as well as economically. They had been chased out of France, and then recalled, no less than seven times—chased out by avarice, as Voltaire had rightly put it, readmitted by avarice once more, but in foolishness as well.

The Jews have passed seventeen centuries without mingling with the other nations. They have never engaged in anything but trade in money; they have been the plague of the agricultural provinces; not one of them has ever dignified [*su ennoblir*] his hands by driving a plough. Their laws leave them no time for agriculture; the Sabbath apart, they celebrate fifty-six more festivals than the Christians in each year. In Poland they possess an entire province. Well, then! while the sweat of Christian slaves waters the furrows in which the Jews' opulence germinates they themselves, as their fields are cultivated, engage in

[13] *Archives parlementaires*, x. 755–6.

weighing their ducats and calculating how much they can shave off the coinage without exposing themselves to legal penalties.

They had never been labourers, Maury continued, not even under David and Solomon. And even then they were notorious for their laziness. Their sole concern was commerce. Would you make soldiers of them, the abbé asked. If you did, you would derive small benefit from them: they have a horror of celibacy and they marry young. He knew of no general who would wish to command an army of Jews either on the Sabbath—a day on which they never gave battle—or indeed at any other time. Or did the Assembly imagine that they could make craftsmen of them when their many festivals and sabbath days presented an insurmountable obstacle to such an enterprise. The Jews held 12 million mortgages in Alsace alone, he informed his colleagues. Within a month of their being granted citizenship they would own half the province outright. In ten years' time they would have 'conquered' all of it, reducing it to nothing more than a Jewish colony—upon which the hatred the people of Alsace already bore for the Jews would explode.

It was not that he, Maury, wished the Jews to be persecuted. 'They are men, they are our brothers; anathema on whoever speaks of intolerance!' Nor need their religious opinions disturb anyone. He joined all others in agreeing that they were to be protected. But that did not mean that they could be citizens. It was as individuals that they were entitled to protection, not as Frenchmen.[14]

Robespierre took the opposite line, supporting Clermont-Tonnerre. All who fulfilled the *generally* applicable conditions of eligibility to citizenship were entitled to the rights that derived from it, he argued, including the right to hold public office. And so far as the facts were concerned, much of what Maury had said about the Jews was 'infinitely exaggerated' and contrary to known history. Moreover, to charge the Jews themselves with responsibility for their own persecution at the hands of others, was absurd.

Vices are imputed to them. . . . But to whom should these vices be imputed if not to ourselves for our injustice? . . . Let us restore them to happiness, to country [*patrie*], and to virtue by restoring them to the dignity of men and citizens; let us reflect that it can never be politic, whatever anyone might say, to condemn a multitude of men who live among us to degradation and oppression.[15]

Mgr. de Lafarre, bishop of Nancy, rallied to his clerical colleague Maury. He claimed, not implausibly, that, as bishop of Nancy, he knew the real situation in the eastern provinces of France at first hand. He repeated—albeit in somewhat more generous terms—the abbé Maury's strictures on the Jews and his characterization of them as members of a separate and distinct nation. And he introduced an element of his own

---

[14] Ibid. 756–7.   [15] Ibid. 757.

into the debate. He had, it was true, been delegated by his constituency to plead against the motion that lay before the Assembly. But it needed to be said that it was plain to him that it was equally in the Jews' own interests that it be defeated. For if the motion were passed, if the Jews were released from the constraints under which they had functioned socially and economically virtually from time immemorial, they themselves would be the first to suffer:

The people hate them; they are frequent victims of popular movements in Alsace. Four months ago there was an attempt to pillage their homes. I travelled to where the rebellion was taking place. I asked what the complaints were. Some claimed that the Jews had monopolized the wheat trade; others that they had gone too far, that they had bought the finest houses, that they would soon possess the entire city. One of the rioters added: 'Yes, sir, if it ever came to our losing you we should see a Jew as our bishop—they are capable of taking over everything.' A decree granting the Jews the rights of citizenship would ignite a conflagration.[16]

The issue thus defined, the National Assembly was asked to choose between two courses, the central distinction between them having as much to do with the general logic by which public business had now to be conducted as with the Jews themselves. One was the application to the specific matter of the Jews of the universal, first (and therefore necessarily unprovable) principles that the new leaders of French society were now all assumed to be agreed upon. The other was an insistence on a hard (and, as it happened, generally uncharitable and in some respects false or misleading[17]) look at the real, particular, and peculiar case the Jews actually presented French society and government—and by implication society and government elsewhere as well. The dilemma was a real one. Its reach and implications extended beyond the immediate issue under debate. When the motion was put to a formal vote the Assembly proved to be almost equally divided. All that could immediately be agreed upon was postponement. And when the matter was taken up once more a month later—with remarkable dispatch, therefore, considering the doubts and hesitation, not to say ill will, that had rapidly clouded the entire question—the results were still equivocal. On this second occasion, the motion to decree emancipation was put before the Assembly by Talleyrand, still a bishop (of Autun), but otherwise with little in common with the bishop of Nancy. Talleyrand limited his argument, however, to the special cases of the so-called Portuguese Jews of Bordeaux and the small Jewish communities of the Avignonnais and the Comtat Venaissin. Unlike the much more numerous Jews of Alsace, the Jews of Bordeaux had explicitly asked to be granted full citizenship. They were long settled

---

[16] *Archives parlementaires*, 758.
[17] Typically, the number of festivals and fast days ascribed to the Jews was inflated by a factor of three or four (there being marginally different criteria for calculating them).

in France. They had the advantage that, historically and legally, as well as socially, they could be presented as being in a category of their own—a very different one, by implication, from that in which the Jews of Alsace had been said, on the whole with good reason, to fall.[18] They were substantially acculturated. They had long been free to possess all forms of property. They were already on an equal footing with all other Frenchmen so far as taxes, participation in local government, service in the militia, and other such civic duties were concerned; and they performed all relevant functions regardless of the day of the week on which their duties might fall. And finally, it was claimed on their behalf by Talleyrand (inaccurately) that they had no laws or tribunals of their own. In brief, and having regard to long-standing custom and past formal legislation and ordinances,

What they ask, gentlemen, is not to be granted the rights of citizens, but rather to be confirmed in their enjoyment of those rights. Their demand has seemed to us to be a perfectly just one. You have in no way wanted—nor could you have done—to deprive a person of the honourable quality of citizen short of his having lost his right to it in the eyes of the nation; and it is evident that not to recognize the Jews of Bordeaux['s right to citizenship] at this juncture would be to deprive them of it.[19]

The debate that followed was an angry and noisy one on this occasion. It revolved chiefly around the question whether the case of the 'Portuguese', 'Spanish', and Avignonnais Jews could in fact be treated separately from that of the 'German', i.e. Alsatian, Jews. The abbé Maury argued that a decree in favour of the former, formulated in the terms proposed by Talleyrand and his committee, would be 'eternal'. A precedent would have been established and when similar arguments in favour of the Jews of Alsace were submitted, as was bound to be the case, it would prove irresistible. Others argued that the two cases were wholly distinct. The Jews of Bordeaux had asked for no more than a reaffirmation of their present status. The case of the Alsatian Jews had to do with the grant of rights which they did not as yet possess. A roll-call vote was taken. Talleyrand's motion passed by a substantial majority (374 to 224).[20] The relatively uncontroversial matter of the small communities in south-west France and the still smaller ones in the Avignonnais and the Comtat Venaissin having been settled, the larger, unquestionably more complex and far-reaching one of the Jews of Alsace and Lorraine was then set aside

---

[18] Exceptionally, under the *ancien régime*, a few wealthy Jews of Alsace-Lorraine, among them Cerf-Berr, purveyor and contractor to the king, had been granted *lettres de naturalisation* which allowed them to live and trade and purchase land anywhere in France. This had placed them on a footing that approximated to that of the Bordeaux Jews or even improved upon it.

[19] 28 Jan. 1790, *Archives parlementaires*, xi. 364.

[20] Ibid. 365.

once more. Clearly, the Assembly had wearied of the subject. Besides, it had much other business to deal with. To the proposal by the duke de Llancourt some weeks later that it be taken up once more, another deputy, a M. Target replied, that

The question concerning the Jews is doubtless very important, but we have other, more important ones to deal with. Whatever it is we decide in respect of the Jews will be of concern to very few; to set the terms under which the judicial power is to operate, to set the size and quality of the French army, and to establish how the finances are to be regulated—these, evidently, are three matters which concern the entire kingdom and which require all your attention. I demand the adjournment of the question of the Jews.[21]

However, when the question of the Jews inhabiting the eastern provinces was brought before the Assembly a little less than two years later, on 28 September 1791, it was dealt with very quickly. All special decrees and 'privileges' relating specifically to Jews were rescinded. The right of all Jews who had taken the 'civic oath' to full French citizenship as provided by the Constitution was affirmed. Those who had maintained their opposition to the reform, and continued to warn of trouble ahead in Alsace if it were passed,[22] were to be mollified, to be sure, by a thorough survey of indebtedness to Jews in the Departments of Haut and Bas-Rhin being conducted and the means to liquidate it being sought for.[23] But for the rest, the reformers' a priori argument had proved to be compelling. The offer of citizenship to all the Jews of France was to be made in the shape of a reform based on abstract principles and applied as a matter of universal propriety and justice, but not justice long denied to the Jews specifically nor any other special consideration that might be their due. The standpoint of the revolutionaries in Paris both on questions relating to the largish community of Jews in Alsace and on those relating to the much smaller communities elsewhere in France was that if these matters merited treatment it was only in terms dictated by an agreed conception of how society *as a whole* needed to be organized and governed. It is noteworthy, too, that none of those who had argued on the Jews' behalf had troubled to deny the allegations of faults and misbehaviour levelled at them. Such speakers had confined themselves to offering excuses and to advancing the claim that a new deal for the Jews was

[21]   26 Feb. 1790, *Archives parlementaires*, xi. 710.
[22]   Prince Victor de Broglie spoke ominously of the danger of 'mauvais effets en Alsace' (ibid. 441); and not unreasonably so. News of the taking of the Bastille had been greeted in Alsace with an extensive pogrom perpetrated by peasants. It was put down by troops in short order, but injury to person and property was widespread and many hundreds of Alsatian Jews fled to Basel, Mulhouse, and Dijon. Verbal agitation against the grant of emancipation to the Jews continued steadily thereafter, as did periodic threats of renewed violence. See Zosa Szajkowski, 'Pera'ot be-alzas be-'et ha-mahapekhot shel 1789, 1830, ve-1848', *Zion*, 20, 1–2 (1955), 82–9.
[23]   Ibid, 21. 441–2.

precisely what a newly benevolent society needed to do in order to bring this very unsatisfactory, but neither hopelessly nor wholly wicked, people into line with the rest of the population. In this respect, then, the position taken by the masters of the new revolutionary France differed little from that of the masters of legitimist and absolutist Austria. The underlying logic and thrust of the offer of emancipation lay in the fact that virtually all—moderates no less than radicals, Dantonists no less than Robespierrists, Christians as well as deists, pantheists, and atheists—held that equality of status in the state they were in their various ways intent on establishing was bound up of necessity with the elimination of all groups, classes, or corporations intermediate (and therefore mediating) between the state itself and the citizen. *All* social classes and categories, therefore, however they might be defined, whatever their specific nature, and regardless of their purpose, had now to be shorn of such special rights, prerogatives, status, or duties as they had at some point in the past been endowed with. This applied to the aristocracy and to the guilds, as a matter of course. It applied to the established Roman Catholic Church and to non-Catholic religious groups and sects, notably the Protestants. And it applied *a fortiori* to all alien national or ethnic groups whose members had now to decide, therefore, whether they wished to become Frenchmen or to remain foreigners—people whose presence would still be tolerated, quite possibly, but who would have to remain wholly outside the circle of recognized citizenship and political participation. It was an immense departure from all that had gone before in respect of such groups. It was underlined and, so to speak, endorsed, by the choice—somewhat as in Austria—being theirs to make. Indeed, the kinship with Austria and, as we shall see, with the other absolutist regimes went further.

The uncertainty about the nature and quality of Jewry and what could or should be done about it, if anything at all, remained unresolved by the decree of emancipation. The Jews, seen as a collective, were evidently a 'church'. But the grounds for regarding them as members of an alien nation were almost equally strong. And there was the question, what did the Jews themselves intend? Did all want to be citizens? Did all want to be Frenchmen? Were the Jews prepared, as part of the promised release from their long-standing disabilities, to give up what was seen by all, by the Jews themselves as well as by non-Jews, as their ancient propensity to isolation, to social organization in self-contained communities, to the settling of their affairs and disputes among themselves and by themselves, and to marrying exclusively within the community and the faith? It was evident that what might be true of the Jews of Bordeaux and Paris was unlikely to be true, at any rate not equally true, of the Jews of Metz or Altkirch. Representations to the Assembly on the part of the former spoke, effectively, of a desire for incorporation into the body politic of France, the single reservation being continued personal loyalty to the ancient religion.

Representations submitted on behalf of the Jews of Lorraine and Alsace, always more timid in language and approach, emphasized the need and wish to retain a firm communal structure in all circumstances.

The logic that had moved the French revolutionaries to resolve on an emancipation of the Jews posed, not solved, the question of their continued identity as a distinct people; and its urgency was reinforced by the circumstance that the idea of the Nation lay at the very foundation of the revolutionaries' own political and social outlook. If the sovereign, unitary Nation was to replace the king under God as the fundamental social and political entity and it was to be in *its* terms that the highest public good would be determined henceforth and all legitimate authority derived, it followed that there could be no room for other, distinct, separable peoples with distinct and separate rules of behaviour—not, that is, within a single nation-state, least of all within their own French Republic. There could certainly be no room at all in France for closed groups that positively rejoiced in their social and to some extent economic, perhaps even political, isolation, but certainly in their own mental and cultural particularity. It was conceivable that such groups might be tolerated as strangers. It was inconceivable that they be admitted to full membership in society and to regular membership in the Republic as free and equal citizens. It followed, in practice, that what the revolutionaries were calling for was not only equality of official treatment of the individual by the state and its institutions, but a high degree of uniformity within the citizenry itself as well. France was no longer to be an untidy complex of estates, guilds, classes, and corporations, all quite loosely supervised from above, if at all, none totally devoid of autonomy and the capacity to go its own way. There was now to be a strictly defined, sovereign, central, secular authority fit to represent all and to govern all without encountering entrenched or inalienable or special and peculiar prerogatives of any kind—a central authority that was therefore capable of assuming virtually untrammelled power. To the question whether this was a system in which room for Jewry as traditionally constituted could be found, the answer, manifestly, was: no. Thus in theory; but thus in practice too, as would soon be apparent in Alsace and to some extent in Lorraine as well, these being the only provinces in France in which Jews formed more than a negligible fraction of the population and in which, by no means coincidentally, as we have seen, Jews were commonly thought of as presenting a socio-economic problem that required especially firm action.

Alsace and Lorraine, acquired by France under the terms of the Treaty of Westphalia in 1648, contained the westernmost segment of Ashkenazi, Yiddish-speaking Jewry. On the eve of the Revolution the some 20,000 Jews of Alsace whose economic role, social characteristics, and sheer presence in the province were at the centre of the debate accounted for approximately half the entire Jewish population of France. (In Paris at the time there were less than a thousand souls all told.) Like their brethren in the Germanies, the Alsatian Jews inhabited small towns and villages, partly because they were explicitly prohibited from taking up residence in the cities of Strasbourg, Colmar, and Mulhouse, although visits for commercial purposes by daytime were tolerated. Four-fifths of the lesser localities in the province were similarly (although unlike the cities, not necessarily) without Jewish residents. In the 183 communes which Jews did inhabit, they typically constituted a minority of 5–10 per cent; in some (about a score) they accounted for 15–25 per cent. All told, they formed just under 3 per cent of Alsace's total population of 684,000. Nevertheless, and characteristically of the terms in which their affairs were almost invariably viewed, the authorities in the period immediately prior to the Revolution had been much worried lest they be multiplying too rapidly. To an inquiry by de la Galazière, the *Intendant* of the province, one *bailli* reported 'a nation that propagated as hurriedly as rabbits' [*la propagation hâtive de cette nation rivale des lapins*]' and another that in the course of time the Christian population of the province would be reduced to a minority. It had been laid down by letters patent in 1784, therefore, that Jews might not marry without royal authorization. In fact, there had been no basis for such panic in high places. Jewish girls did tend to marry somewhat earlier than was the norm in France and the records of eleven localities in Alsace did show that there were 2.96 children in the average Jewish family compared with 2.6 children in the average Christian family. But it needs to be recalled in this connection that celibacy was much rarer among Jews of both sexes than among Christians, there being no priests, monks, nuns, or long-serving soldiers among them and even Jewish domestic servants, unlike many Christian servants, tending to be married.

But in any event, the enduring complaints against the Jews, over and above the fundamental objection to their actual presence in the province, had to do with their occupations. These, principally, were peddling and dealing in second-hand clothing and merchandise apart from the more fortunate and successful among them who were dealers in grain, cattle, and horses—a circumstance that had opened the road to their serving as purveyors to the king's armies, as we have seen. And there was money-lending. It was mostly on a petty scale and, contrary to the common supposition, it was a trade in which it was very far from easy to build up a fortune no matter how assiduously one went about it. It was, besides, a difficult, risky, and, of course, exceedingly unpopular business. Debt collection was invariably hard and doubtful and rendered especially difficult by the prohibition on Jews' owning land, the consequence of which was that land acquired upon default of a loan had to be sold within a year. [24]

[24] Paula E. Hyman, *The Emancipation of the Jews of Alsace* (New Haven, 1991), 11–29;

That numbers of local Jews were engaged in this always and inevitably bitter, not to say nasty and dangerous, business of extending financial credit was not in dispute. There was no disputing either, that on the eve of the Revolution one-third of all mortgages in the province were in the hands of Jews, nor, of course, that the credit they extended was against interest, thus exposing them to the charge thought to be peculiarly applicable to them: usury.

The roots of usury as a Jewish occupation and as a charge to be levelled against them are traceable to medieval Christendom's insistent repression and humiliation of the Jews. Forced out of virtually all socially acceptable occupations, they were thereupon damned and despised for taking up what was left to them: peddling, dealing in second-hand clothing, pawn-broking, and the making of straightforward money loans against interest. All these retained their negative emotive force for many centuries and go part of the way to explain the continuing hostility towards Jews—either on the ground, as in Alsace, or in the abstract, as in Paris, well after the new norms set by the Revolution had sunk in. For then, remarkably, where the Jews were concerned, the otherwise strict and insistent athe-ism—or at best, deism—of the republicans can be seen to have been admixed with a good many of what had always been distinctly Christian, especially Roman Catholic, dislikes, prejudices, and pieces of mischie-vously inculcated ignorance. A demand issued by the authorities in Nancy on the 23 of Brumaire of the Year Two of the new revolutionary calendar (13 November 1793), calling on 'philosophers of the former Jewish religion' to hasten and intensify the process of accommodation to the new regime, required them to hand over 'their mystical charters as well as . . . all objects of gold or silver, furniture, ornaments, [and other artefacts and] emblems serving a ritual purpose'.[25] On the first of Frimaire (21 November) of the same year the district procurator took up the matter for himself to denounce the Jews of Lorraine for their contin-ued religiosity. They had, he declared, continued wickedly to observe the Sabbath, engage in the ritual slaughter of animals, wear distinctive cloth-ing, and, worst of all, circumcise their infant sons. Notionally and chronologically this form of denigration accorded with the movement to 'de-Christianize' France and the systematic desecration and destruction of Christian icons, the abdication of the archbishop of Paris, the renam-ing of Notre Dame, and other such actions. Still, the procurator's lan-guage is revealing:

It is the inhumane law of these people that the new-born male infant is to be bloodily operated upon as if nature herself were imperfect. They wear long

Rina Neher-Bernheim, *Documents inédits sur l'entrée des Juifs dans la société française (1750–1850)*, i (Tel-Aviv, 1977), 61–5, 75–8.

[25] Cited in Robert Anchel, *Napoléon et les Juifs* (Paris, 1928), 16.

beards with ostentation, mimicing the patriarchs whose virtues they themselves have failed to inherit. They employ a language of which they are ignorant and which has long since fallen into disuse. In consequence, I do require of the provisional commission that it forbid them such practices and arrange for an *auto da fé* [*sic*] to Truth of all Hebrew books and of the Talmud most especially, the author of which was so mischievous as to permit them to make usurious loans to men who are not of their faith.[26]

In fact, numbers of Jews had gone far to accommodate themselves to the new regime. Torah scrolls had been put away, synagogues closed, ritual candelabra handed over to municipal authorities, beards shaven off, dress revised. Some of this was voluntary; some of it was in the nature of passive surrender to a new *gzeira*. And if there was still much disquiet and silent resistance to the effort to secularize and in effect dissolve Jewry, helped by the fact that in the early, dangerous, and tumultuous years of revolutionary and republican France the matter of the Jews was not one to which great and consistent attention was ever paid, the trend towards acculturation which the new regime had precipitated would continue to gather force. It was only with the rise of Napoleon and the remarkable effort to establish a fresh and coherent social and political order for all of France to which he and his entourage were to devote so much energy that the affairs of the Jews were given something like serious attention overall: serious and systematic, if not substantially different in spirit.

The administrators of the Napoleonic Empire saw three difficulties about the Jews. The first was constitutional. Once the revolutionary and ideology-intensive approach to government and politics had at least partly been superseded by Napoleonic opportunism, relations with the Roman Catholic Church and the French Reformed Church could be put on an orderly basis. The new, tidily minded Bonapartist administrators recognized that by the same token the Jews too would have to be dealt with: disputes within the Jewish community that had boiled over and come before them from time to time periodically reminding them of the fact. In one case the authorities found themselves having to contend with a conflict between the rabbi and the elders of an Alsatian community on the one hand and a man whom they were determined to expel from their midst on the other. When the excommunicant and his family found themselves denied the traditional communal services of *shoḥet* (ritual slaughterer) and *mikva* (ritual bath), they lodged an appeal against the judgment with the civil authorities. Such recourse to extra-communal authority ran wholly against the grain of traditional Jewish practice, as we have seen, and by the same token had always been rare. What was relatively new was not so much that it landed the authorities with an issue of which they had had no prior experience, no machinery to deal with, and

---

[26] Ibid. 18.

no precedents to rely upon, but one for which the criteria by which to decide it were unclear. Whom was the departmental prefect to support: the private citizen with a seemingly legitimate grievance? or the established communal leaders through whom a regime that was reluctant to leave any part of the social fabric of the country wholly alone, even so obscure a segment as the Jewish, believed it was best able to effect its control and impose its wishes?

The second difficulty arose from the fact that the makers and legatees of the French Revolution, all in their way children of the Enlightenment, approached the needs and problems of society in fundamentally ahistorical terms. It was on the universal, not the particular, that their minds were set. They tended to see things and to define issues in relatively abstract terms—in terms of models, as we would now say. Reason, not revelation, or faith, or grace, or, least of all, ancient authority was the proper determinant of social questions. If the world was to be built anew—a better, cleaner, neater, above all more rational world, a world from first principles—much of the past and its incongruities had necessarily to be sloughed off. Could this, therefore, continue to be a world in which the Jews, always, to many European minds, the most peculiar and, at the same time, most irritating and offensive social category of all, had a place?

But however irritated by Jewish particularism and anxious to stamp it out, there was the third, countervailing difficulty facing the Bonapartists that stemmed from the loosely mercantilist principles to which, by and large, they were equally wedded. Believing that increase of population led normally to an increase of national wealth, and that this was as much the case where commerce and industry, as opposed to agriculture, were concerned, they were reluctant to deal with the Jews in the drastic and peremptory manner of their medieval forebears, namely by expulsion or worse. If the Jews contributed to commerce and industry, and generally to the wealth and the civil and military power of the state, it was expedient, they reasoned, to keep them. If it was found that they did not contribute, or that they contributed insufficiently, might it not be possible to compel them to do a great deal more? Either way, the result of such exploratory reasoning was their recourse to the now ever commoner habit of distinguishing between those Jews who were indeed 'useful' to the state and the economy (or thought capable of being so) and those who were not. How 'usefulness' was to be defined, how the 'useful' were to be identified, and, of course, what was to be done with those who failed the relevant tests were all exceedingly tricky questions to which the Bonapartists had no better answers than anyone else. True, where the injection of these and similar elements of the intellectual and politico-theoretical baggage of the Enlightenment into the administration of the state had been attempted very sparingly and the problem presented by a Jewish presence in civil society was not thought to be so significant or serious as to demand drastic and systematic treatment, none of this much mattered. Such was the case, by and large, in eighteenth- and nineteenth-century England, as we have seen. But where matters were otherwise—as they were, and as they will further be shown to be, in most other parts of Europe—and where those who ruled the Jews sought actively to compose and apply a working distinction between those who were useful to them and worth retaining and those who were not, there the impact on Jewry itself, both structurally and materially, would be significant—and in some respects disastrous. The prosperous members of Jewry, the 'useful' ones by most criteria, would tend to grow in prosperity. The indigent, the 'useless', and the 'superfluous' would tend to lapse into deeper indigence. The line drawn between the privileged and the under-privileged in Jewry would steadily sharpen and within the various Jewish communities it would be the privileged, increasingly, who called the tune for all. As the impact of the Enlightenment began to wear off in the course of the nineteenth century a reversion to ancient, more brutal, less intellectualized forms of dealing with the Jews would gain in strength. But in all cases it would be the application of ideas born of the Enlightenment that paved the way both conceptually and administratively.

Something of this can already be detected in the forms in which Napoleon finally took up the matter of the Jews. Napoleon's basic decree on Jewish affairs of 30 May 1806 began, in traditional, pre-revolutionary style, with a denunciation of 'certain Jews, whose sole occupation is that of usury'. These, by their most 'immoderate' insistence on high rates of interest, had reduced a great many French peasants to a 'condition of great distress'; and the emperor, for his part, was determined to come to the aid of those of his subjects whose circumstances had been so drastic-ally reduced by the Jews' 'unjust avidity'. So far, so familiar. But it was equally urgent, the emperor declared, to go to the root of the matter. It was necessary to seek to revive active 'sentiments of civic morality' among the Jews themselves for such sentiments, unfortunately, 'had slackened [amortis] among far too many of them in consequence of the condition of abasement and humiliation in which they had long lan-guished'. This too was a condition which he, Napoleon, promised not to tolerate and with these considerations and purposes in mind an Assembly of Jewish Notables would be convoked, its duty being to consider the relevant issues systematically and make specific proposals for the precise basis on which the condition of this people might be subject to cor-rection and their admittance to civil society allowed.[27]

The intensely critical and emotive language apart, there was little in

---

[27] 'Décret impérial portant sursis à l'exécution de jugements rendus en faveur de juifs contre cultivateurs non négociants de plusieurs départements de l'empire', 30 mai 1806, in A. E. Halphen (ed.), *Recueil des lois . . . concernant les Israélites depuis la révolution de 1789* (Paris, 1851), 18–19.

these last, operative clauses of the decree, or so it could be argued, that was not in the spirit of the age, the more so as the decree was in accord with the underlying thrust of two of the best known and most widely publicized contemporary tracts on the subject. One of these was French, the abbé Grégoire's celebrated prize submission to a competition held by the Royal Society for Arts and Sciences of Metz (in Lorraine) in 1787. The subject set the competitors had been: 'Est-il des moyens de rendre les juifs plus heureux et plus utiles en France?' ('Are there ways and means of rendering the Jews [both] happier and more useful in France?'). Grégoire's own essay was entitled, equally characteristically: 'Essai sur la régénération physique, morale, et politique des Juifs' ('An essay on the physical, moral, and political regeneration of the Jews').[28] The other tract was German: Christian Wilhelm von Dohm's 'Über die bürgerliche Verbesserung der Juden' ('On the Civic Improvement of the Jews'), begun at the instigation of Moses Mendelssohn,[29] published in 1781. Grégoire, who became a prime mover in the campaign to grant the Jews civil rights, had argued that the moral and social failings of the Jews were due to the conditions to which they had been subject and that their political emancipation, besides releasing them from subjection, would rid them of their superstitions and of their tendency to separatism as well. Dohm's argument was on roughly the same lines, except that he, for his part, had a somewhat higher regard for the Jews' religion and culture than Grégoire and was better informed about both. Dohm placed particular emphasis on the need to couple emancipation with education. But what counted in either case was the two men's common denominator neatly encapsulated in the key terms in each man's title: Grégoire's 'régénération' and Dohm's 'Verbesserung'. The Jews were an unsatisfactory lot; they needed to be, and fortunately could be, remade and brought up to the mark.

Napoleon's lay Assembly of Jewish Notables, chosen by the government itself, mostly on the recommendation of the departmental *préfets* rather than by the communities themselves, convened in Paris in July 1806. In February of the following year it was followed in turn, as planned, by the somewhat better known, quasi-ecclesiastical, but presumptuously entitled 'Sanhedrin'. The Sanhedrin's function was to provide a form of rabbinic sanction for the notables' recommendations. Neither the Assembly nor the Sanhedrin were genuine deliberative bodies, however. The notables were to respond to a series of precise questions formulated and presented to them by Napoleon's commissioners.

---

[28] Published in its original form in 1789; published in London in English translation two years later. Grégoire, it needs to be added, *shared* his prize with Adolphe Thièry, a Protestant attorney practising at the *parlement* of Nancy, and Zalkind Hourwitz, a Polish Jew with original and radical ideas of his own on the entire subject of the condition of his people. On Zalkind Hourvitz see below, pp. 99–102.

[29] On Mendelssohn see below, pp. 141–4.

Their answers, taken together, were to serve as the basis for a lasting definition of the position of the Jews in respect of the questions the emancipation had evoked and, as all could agree, were still largely hanging fire. It was, of course, these questions that shaped the form and content of the proceedings, defined the issues considered, set the very narrow framework in which such discussions as were conducted took place, and largely determined the terms in which first the notables, then the rabbis, were—according to the nature of each topic—either free or under some compulsion to make their case. Was a Jew permitted to take more than one wife? Did the Jewish religion sanction divorce? What precisely was the nature of rabbinical authority? Was it permissible for Jews to intermarry with Christians? Were Frenchmen brethren or strangers in Jewish eyes? Did a Jew born in France and treated as a citizen consider France to be his own country, one that he was bound to defend and whose laws he was bound to obey? Did Jewish law distinguish between usurious loans to Jews, presumably forbidden, and usurious loans to others, presumably permitted?

Ostensibly requests for authoritative information, all the questions put to the notables by the commissioners touched on the terms on which the Jews would be seen, or proposed to see themselves, as actual or future citizens of France and members of the French nation. Some were simple enough and easily answered, others were embarrassing. The questions about marriage outside the faith and usury—the latter, in plain language, meaning the legitimacy of extending credit to non-Jews against interest—were especially tricky. Jewish Law being clear on both counts (negative in the former case, positive in the latter, as the commissioners seem to have known), the notables could only prevaricate. But it was their response to the questions bearing directly on their loyalty and patriotic sentiment that was most revealing and was to be of most lasting consequence.

Men who have adopted a country [they told the commissioners], who have resided in it these many generations—who, even under the restraint of particular laws which abridged their civil rights, were so attached to it that they preferred being debarred from the advantages common to all other citizens rather than leave it—cannot but consider themselves Frenchmen in France; and they consider as equally sacred and honourable the bounden duty of defending their country. . . . Love of country is in the heart of Jews a sentiment so natural, so powerful, and so consonant with their religious opinions, that a French Jew considers himself in England, as among strangers, although he may be among Jews; and the case is the same with English Jews in France. To such a pitch is this sentiment carried among them, that during the last war, French Jews were fighting desperately against other Jews, the subjects of countries then at war with France.[30]

There is in all this more than a hint of an overawed and somewhat frightened people's anxiety to please. Anxiety was no doubt at the root

[30] D. Tama (ed.), *Transactions of the Parisian Sanhedrin*, English trans. F. D. Kirwan (London, 1807), 149–56 [slightly amended].

too of one of the better known and longest lasting 'reforms' associated with the Assembly of Notables, the reclassification of the Jews of France as 'Israélites' on the grounds that, over and above the 'unhappy prejudices' evoked by the term 'Jew', it connotes a nation, not a religion. But the dilemma in which the notables had found themselves was real and harsh enough. They had no precedent before them for dealing with the questions with which the imperial commissioners had chosen to confront them. They had not been required to apostatize, as Jews had so often been asked or required to do in the past, as the price of simple survival, let alone admittance to civil society. They had not even been asked whether they were prepared to do so. The issues they were required to pronounce upon were political and cultural, not religious. What the commissioners most wanted to know was whether *they* understood the meaning of Jewish nationhood (or peoplehood) to be compatible with effective membership in the French nation? And if it was not, were they then prepared to modify the former to suit the terms and needs of the latter? Napoleon and his ministers ended by accepting the declaration of unequivocal national adherence and loyalty offered them at the conclusion of the proceedings as satisfactory. Whether their doubts about the validity of the answers given them were fully removed is less certain. The commissioners' doubts about the Jews and their hostility to them had been much in evidence throughout these transactions. And, indeed, in the event, the upshot for French Jewry was less clear-cut than the notables and rabbis assembled in Paris seem to have anticipated and a good many among them had hoped for. French Jewry would now be officially treated as a purely religious denomination and incorporated into a typically Napoleonic framework modelled after those established for the governance of other religious bodies. But Napoleon's decision to follow up the meetings of the Assembly of Notables and the rabbinic Sanhedrin with the institutional and social reorganization of French Jewry was combined, very much at his personal insistence, with a partial, but by no means insignificant, rolling-back of the emancipatory process itself.

On 17 March 1808 three decrees were promulgated in the emperor's name and over his signature. Two followed directly from the deliberations and recommendations of the Assembly and the Sanhedrin. These laid down the outline for the new institutions, principally the *consistoires*, through which Jewish religious and educational services would now be administered and controlled, and the plan to rehabilitate the Jews morally and culturally carried forward. The third decree was of another order. It was explicitly hostile. It hit a large segment of the Jews of France very hard. And it was, indeed, soon to be known—as much for the spirit which informed it as for its content—as the 'infamous decree' (*décret infâme*). Its chief stated purpose was to stamp out usury and to relieve the peasants of the eastern provinces of France, Alsace in particular, of their indebtedness to Jewish moneylenders and to that end existing debts to Jews were to be heavily and arbitrarily reduced. But the stipulations of the decree went a great deal further. Restrictions were to be levelled on the freedom of Jews to engage in a trade of their choice and to move from one part of the country to another without special permission.[31] They were to submit to special commercial registration. They were not to employ the Hebrew language in their commercial transactions. Unlike all other citizens, they were to be forbidden to offer substitutes in case of conscription for military service. And the entry of foreign Jews into France was to be conditional either on military performance or on satisfaction of specified property qualifications. Unquestionably, the *décret infâme* bore the stamp of Napoleon's barely governable personal aversion to the Jews—linked, to be sure, to his determination to stamp out the social and economic plague of usury in which, as was undeniable, great numbers of Jews in eastern France were involved.[32] These would now, inexorably, be reduced to bankruptcy and in many cases indigence. And they would be set still further apart from other citizens as a pariah class by the exemption from the stipulations of the decree that were granted the Jews of south-west France and other, specified departments of the country. The distinction drawn between the acceptable, because relatively assimilated, Jews of south-west France and the unacceptable, because manifestly unassimilated, Jews of Alsace and Lorraine was thus formally renewed and reinforced. If it was by no means a complete and definitive reversal of the emancipatory process, it was certainly a flat, albeit implicit denial of the principles on which it had been founded.[33]

---

[31] Clause 16 of the third decree, Halphen, *Recueil des lois*, 46.

[32] Although substantially less, playing a smaller economic role, than was commonly claimed. It was characteristic of the turn that the image of the Jews in France would take with special force after the Revolution, that it was a charge that the emperor accepted without further question as entirely valid. The notion that Jews played a major role in the business of moneylending and that, as a consequence of bad debts owing to them, vast holdings of land had come, or were likely to come, into their possession, continued to be generally accepted under the Restoration. It has, indeed, been almost as easily accepted by ostensibly disinterested observers, not excluding reputable historians, in retrospect. The facts were otherwise. Examining the registers of mortgages in the five eastern departments of Haut Rhin, Bas Rhin, Moselle, Meuse, and Vosges for the years 1799 to 1850, Zosa Szajkowski found that of 62,000 mortgages for a total value of 105,500,000 francs, only 9,000 (14.5 per cent) for a total value of 7,400,000 francs (7 per cent) had Jews as their beneficiaries. A far greater participant in the business of moneylending turned out to be the Church (Szajkowski, 'Pera'ot be-alzas', 97). None the less, it was the myth of assiduous Jewish skullduggery, not the ascertainable facts, that then, as always, caught the imagination and carried greatest conviction. Thus in matters that were open to systematic inquiry; thus, doubly so, as we shall see repeatedly, in matters that were not susceptible to proof at all or, most dramatically and fatefully of all, were demonstrably fictitious. Thus in revolutionary and post-revolutionary France; thus throughout the entire European continent.

[33] The bitter taste which the *décrêt infâme* left in Jewish mouths would be sweetened somewhat when, Napoleon's decree having run the ten-year course specified for it, the

It was true, of course, that emancipation had come to the Jews of France as a gift. If it was in some sense a victory, it was not one that they had won for themselves. Nor could it have been. The Jews of France were devoid both of the structure of internal leadership and authority and of the political and material resources that would all have been necessary for them to have embarked on such an enterprise either by themselves or with allies. There had been neither the possibility nor any question of agreed collective needs and interests—as opposed to some very limited, uncoordinated lobbying by a handful of well-placed individuals, some acting for the Jews of Bordeaux and their analogues, others for the Jews of the eastern provinces. It was as a function of the philosophical and political ideas on which the French revolutionary state had been founded and to which its true founders, with rare exceptions, held with all their hearts that emancipation had been awarded them, along with permission to apply for membership in society at large. It had everything to do, therefore, both with the dramatic changes that had occurred in France's governing circumstances and in the climate of opinion in French society—to which there needs to be added the revolutionaries' unbending conviction that it was necessary and proper to apply their chosen social political principles universally. Emancipation so conceived and so promulgated had, that is to say, very little, if anything at all, to do directly with the specific condition, or needs, or history, of the Jews themselves.

But the lasting significance of the French revolutionary decree of 1791 lay less in its impact on French Jewry than in its having established an example for government, society, and Jewry itself in the rest of Europe to follow or to reject or to avoid altogether. What none could do from this time on was to ignore it totally: not while French political and military power was at its peak, but not later, either, when it had been radically diminished and the *French* origins of the idea of Jewish emancipation had largely faded from view. The gift of emancipation beyond the borders of France was never entirely for the French to grant. In the duchy of Warsaw, distant to be sure, but wholly dependent on French goodwill, the

Restoration regime refrained from renewing it. So doing, it fell in line, curiously, in this respect at least, with the strict revolutionaries of 1789 and 1791. However, it was not forgotten and along with other questions relating to late eighteenth- and early nineteenth-century French opinion on Judaism and the Jews revolutionary and Napoleonic treatment of the Jews would become a topic of fierce debate among some historians. The classic instance was the ferociously hostile reception accorded Robert Anchel's meticulous doctoral study (published as *Napoléon et les Juifs* (Paris, 1928)) by the then senior Marxist specialist on French revolutionary history, Albert Mathiez. Mathiez, who would brook no criticism of his heroes, savaged Anchel both in the course of Anchel's viva at the Sorbonne and in a long review article published in *Annales historique de la Révolution française: Organe de la société des études Robespierristes*, 5, 4 (July–Aug. 1928), 371–83. Anchel's academic career suffered devastating injury.

resistance of France's Polish allies to the prospect of Jewish emancipation
was absolute and French acquiescence in their obstruction virtually total,
as we shall see. In the Netherlands matters were otherwise, but only to a
limited degree for reasons of geographical proximity and the very much
tighter incorporation into the Napoleonic system that had been
imposed. The real key lay with the Dutch themselves, then and later. The
Jewish communities had enjoyed a famous degree of freedom in much (if
not all) of the country since early in the seventeenth century. What the
patriotic 'Batavian Republic' established under French auspices in 1795
would put through was less a dramatic change than a regularization of
their status by comprehensive legislation—in much the manner it had
settled the more difficult and, for the Dutch, substantially more important question of the status and rights of the country's Roman Catholics.
The pattern was indeed analogous to the French. In March 1796 the
Dutch Reformed Church was disestablished. On 2 September of that
year the Batavian National Assembly proclaimed 'the equality of Jews
with all other citizens', article one of the decree stipulating that 'No Jew
shall be debarred from any rights or privileges that are enshrined in the
Batavian Constitution'. Later, under the brief reign of the emperor's
brother, Louis Napoleon, the communal structure of Dutch Jewry was
reorganized and a central *consistoire* established to regulate religious
appointments, observance, and teaching. And as in France in 1789, the
fundamental plan of emancipation was contested. The Jews, it was
argued, saw their true fatherland in their ancestral Palestine. Even in exile
they maintained a system of law and governance of their own. While
civic rights were in order, political rights were not—unless the Jews
themselves explicitly opted for Dutch citizenship rather than it being
imposed upon them wholesale and from above. The debate was longer
than the one in the French National Assembly. A note was struck that
would never have been heard in Paris: to grant the Jews political rights
here and now would be to divert them from their true path as they
awaited the Messiah. And the nastiness of tone and reference that had so
rapidly surfaced in Paris were absent. There was no talk at all of commercial and financial avidity or of endemic involvement in usury. And after
the withdrawal of the French all these reforms were allowed to stand
without serious questions being raised.

Where, however, unlike Holland, the pre-revolutionary and pre-
Napoleonic rules by which the Jews had been governed stood in absolute
contrast to the idea of emancipation, there matters were otherwise. There
there would be no question of allowing Jewish emancipation to stand—
if indeed it had been granted. The only issue would be whether the old
restrictive regime was to be reimposed in its entirety. In Italy, where
French rule and influence, while it lasted, had been particularly marked,
the determination of rulers to restore the *status quo ante*, once their

armies had gone, was unmistakable, although not everywhere of the same intensity. In the States of the Church it was unbending: under the reinstated Pope Pius VII the gates of the Roman ghetto were firmly shut upon its Jewish community once more.[34] In Ferrara the ghetto chains were put back; but left unlocked and unused, on display, so to speak, perhaps as some kind of ill-defined warning. In Ancona the chains were not restored at all.

It was in Germany, however, in all its geo-political complexity, that matters became most fraught. In the greatest political event of the era, at the Congress of Vienna itself, it had been resolved formally on 8 June 1815 that it was incumbent on the members of the German Confederation to consider an 'amelioration' of the civil status of all those who 'confessed the Jewish faith in Germany'. But, as the architects of the Legitimist Restoration themselves may well have anticipated, the resolution remained a dead letter. In Frankfurt there would be a concerted effort to force the Jews back into the city's notorious ghetto. In other German states and cities too, notably in the Hansa towns of Bremen and Lübeck, the right of residence was cut down to approximately the old proportions and fresh expulsions instituted. True, the fact that the Congress should have agreed to formulate a resolution in favour of the Jews— 'in the Name of the Most Holy and Indivisible Trinity', it may be added—was in itself a sign that the climate of the times was not, after all, as before. And indeed, much the commonest tendency in the Germanies was not so much totally to annul such reforms as had already been promulgated, willingly or otherwise, as to slow down and limit their application. The long-term result was that official minds everywhere were painfully divided. On the one hand, the thesis that the material interests of the state required it to proceed to the emancipation of the Jews now seemed to all to be undeniable. On the other, few doubted that to proceed to emancipation was to engender social and political changes which, as members of the governing class, they were among the least willing to swallow. Like so many other dilemmas of contemporary government, there was in this a reflection of the great caesura that now separated the age that had ended in 1789 from the one which may reasonably be said to have begun in 1815. As a source of intellectual and moral irritation it would for some time be especially on view in Prussia— perhaps because the bureaucratic rigour with which that kingdom's rulers and officials applied themselves to the matter of the Jews in the early decades of the century was of much the same order as that with which they applied themselves to other, and to their minds weightier, topics.

---

[34] And were to remain so until 1870.

IV

Compared with Austria, the lines along which policy on the Jews was made to move in the other German states were generally stiff, narrow, and, if anything, more deeply etched in acid. An edict promulgated by the duchess of Sachsen-Meiningen in 1811 to consolidate and reorder the multiple restrictions governing the private, communal, and economic lives of Jews who had been allowed to reside in the duchy, begins, to be sure, very much in the proper spirit of the times, with the affirmation, that she is 'At all times moved by the wish to concede and grant the greatest possible equality of rights to my trusted subjects without discrimination between religions'.[35] And, as in the Josephine *Toleranzpatent*, one of the principal notes struck is that of improvement and education. 'The spread of common beneficial knowledge missing from the education of indigenous Jews' is to be encouraged, all schools are to be opened to them without restriction and on the same basis of entitlement as other children, and, 'to prevent all misunderstanding, they are expressly exempted from those specific lectures that are devoted to instruction in [the Christian] religion'. Moreover, 'all poor Jewish boys who show talent for the sciences' will be assured of support as will be those who show 'exceptional talent for the arts'.[36] The edict was drawn up with some care. The ducal official instructed to prepare a draft took the trouble to study contemporary legislation on the Jews that had been promulgated in France (specifying the special attention he had paid to the Napoleonic decrees of 1806, 1807, and 1808), in Frankfurt, and in the grand duchy of Baden.[37] Austria is not mentioned in his report, but it is unlikely that he and his colleagues, or the duchess herself, were unaware of what had been decided in Vienna long before and had been in the process of (gradual) implementation for several decades since. But in any event, what marked the edict, apart from the Josephine emphasis on education, improvement, and the implicit distinction between 'useful' and dispensable Jews, was the insistence on their being subject to a regime of stringent social control. Their lives as private individuals would be constrained by a string of social, administrative, and economic rules designed to propel them into predetermined 'useful' and appropriate crafts and commercial channels. But in their communal affairs too they would be subject to the higher will of their ruler as never before. Internal communal arrangements, rabbinical (especially judicial) authority, the qualities required of *parnassim*—all these were meticulously laid down. Above all,

---

[35] Ducal Edict of 5 Jan. 1811. Staatsarchiv Meiningen, Inneres Alt, 42, 1373. I am grateful to Mr Franz Levi for providing me with this and related documents.

[36] Ibid., clause 20.

[37] Memorandum by Schwendler, 4 Mar. 1810. Thüringer Staatschiv, Inneres Alt, 42, 1393.

their community would not be allowed to grow. Other than in exceptional circumstances foreign Jews would not be allowed to settle. And those who had now, under the terms of the edict, been recognized at last as subjects of the duchy, would be prevented from increasing in number by the simple rule that no more than one son from each family would be allowed to marry and raise a family of his own.[38]

Sachsen-Meiningen, however typical, was politically and in every other way, a negligible quantity. It was Prussia, where Frederick II's *Revidiertes Generalprivilegium und Reglement* of 1750 set the tone in all matters relating to its Jewish population for at least a century, that would count for most in Germany from this time on *pari passu* with the steady growth of Prussian power, influence, and territory. In spirit and purpose the Prussian *Generalreglement* was closer kin to Maria Theresa's legislation than to her heir's edict of toleration in that it consolidated a long-established regime in a particularly strict, uncompromising, and onerous manner. Prussian Jews, like those of virtually all other German states, had long been heavily policed with a view, on the one hand, to the severe limitation—and, if possible, reduction—of their numbers[39] (on the grounds that Jews were intrinsically undesirable) and, on the other hand, to the squeezing of the highest possible return in taxes from them consistent with maintaining them as a source of revenue. To these ends the key to the regulations of 1750 was the continuing division of the Jewish population into those who might, and those who might not, aspire to the blessed condition of *Schutzjuden* ('protected' Jews). This was a category derived from the thirteenth-century classification of Jews as 'serfs of the chamber' (rather than of particular territorial lords) who, while taxed by the emperor, were entitled to his protection. In practice, the privilege of taxing them and the corresponding duty of protecting them came generally to be farmed out from time to time, or sold outright, to the territorial princes and to the free cities. In Prussia, at all events, the relevant taxes were numerous, heavy, and arbitrary. They included simple capitation taxes, taxes on passage, taxes on temporary residence, taxes on entry into specific occupations, taxes on changes in personal status. They could be humiliating and mean-spirited and they could be ingenious. Marriage, for example, was heavily restricted and regulated, ostensibly in pursuit of the general purpose of keeping the Jewish population down. But matters were eased somewhat for certain classes of Jews on condition that the

---

[38] Edict of 5 Jan. 1811, clause 2.

[39] The best measure of the Jewish population of Prussia proper is the census return for 1811 (after the loss of Polish territories under the Treaty of Tilsit of 1807, therefore, and before the recuperation of Posen and the annexation of the Rhineland by the terms of the 1815 settlement). Some 32,000 Jews were counted out of a total population of about 6 million or a little over one-half of 1 per cent. It is to be noted that 50 per cent of all who might at this time be reasonably categorized as German Jews lived in Prussia.

ruler's thirst for state revenue was slaked somewhat by purchase of fixed quantities of the inferior goods produced at the royal porcelain factory.

While the policy of seeking to reduce the number of Jews in the kingdom by all possible means was, of course, an ancient one with ancient roots, in practice it too had tended increasingly to be geared to the now all but universal distinction—but drawn especially sharply in Prussia—between 'useful' and 'useless' or 'unproductive' Jews. But however sharp the distinction between 'useful' and 'useless' might be in theory, everything depended in practice on how the bureaucracy chose to apply it; and, too, to what extent, if at all, those lucky enough to be classed as privileged *Schutzjuden* were prepared (or were sufficiently audacious) to protest and fight an expulsion order on behalf of brethren who were less fortunate. Beggars, pedlars, and vagrants fell so clearly into the category of the 'useless' that it was generally conceded in Jewish circles that there was nothing to be done for them. Yet from the state's point of view, communal functionaries—rabbis, cantors, teachers, ritual slaughterers, and the like—were equally 'useless'. What of them? How were the settled, privileged Jews to deal with their cases? Harshest of all the elements of the Prussian system, but exceedingly revealing of the logic underlying the network of obligations and prohibitions in which its Jewish subjects were enveloped, was the rule that the organized community—consisting for all practical purposes of the high-grade, especially privileged, and necessarily affluent *Schutzjuden* who led it—was to be held responsible for the conduct of *all* members of the community. This, it needs to be stressed, was no mere matter of general understanding. It was a formal, legally established responsibility. It covered all points at which the interests of the state touched on the affairs of the individual: full and prompt payment of taxes, as might be expected, but also bankruptcies and similar financial or economic failures and delinquencies and common law crimes and misdemeanours as well. This holding of the community's leaders to account for the conduct of all their people reflected the persistence into modern times of the classic basis on which the alien sovereign power was likely, if at all, to acquiescence in the existence of an autonomous Jewish community within its territory: an equally ancient, deeply rooted, a priori distrust of Jews as such and a lack of confidence in the state's ability to police the Jews except through the instrumentality of the Jews' own institutions. It meant, however, that the elders of each community were held in perpetual hostage for the good behaviour of their flock and that, these being the principles on which their community was policed, they themselves had little choice but to seek the fullest possible control over their social and economic inferiors. By the end of the eighteenth century, however, not least in view of what had occurred west of the Rhine, it had become obvious to all that the entire system was intolerably vexatious and anachronistic. When in 1800, after repeated applications by the *parnassim* of the Prussian communities and thirteen years of internal debate within the Berlin bureaucracy itself, the principle of collective responsibility was abolished, a new order for Prussian Jewry began. However, while the abolition of the rule went far to dismantle the invisible, legal ghetto in which the Jews had been confined, it did not in itself establish their formal equality with others in the kingdom. Nor did the vastly more comprehensive and far-reaching Edict on the Civil Status of the Jews in the State of Prussia issued by King Frederick William on 11 March 1812, even though that, ostensibly, was what it provided for.

The Prussian edict laid down the primary and crucial rule, that Jews domiciled in Prussia were henceforth to be considered natives (*Einländer*) and citizens of Prussia and that as such they were to 'enjoy equal civil rights and liberties with Christians'. The category of *Schutzjuden* was abolished. Jews were no longer to be burdened with special taxes. They would be free to settle in towns as well as in the country. They would require no special permission to marry. Even peddling by Jews was to be subject to the same police regulations as peddling by non-Jews. For their part, Jews would be obliged to adopt surnames and to employ the German language in their business records and transactions. They would be liable for military service on the same basis as other citizens. The judicial functions of their rabbis were to come to an end.

Although this was not as sweeping as the full emancipation decreed in Paris, it went far beyond the Austrian *Toleranzpatent* of 1782 and so set Prussia ahead of all other German states, at least until 1848. It was the creation of an officialdom that not only tended exceedingly strongly to see itself as the faithful guardian of the interests of the state, but, remarkably, had good cause to do so. But the edict has to be understood too as part— a small part—of the general inclination to contemplate reform of government and society that followed in the wake of Prussia's military defeat at the hands of Napoleon at Jena, the drastic amputatory terms of the Peace of Tilsit of 1807, the cumulative impact of French political and constitutional ideas, and the concrete examples offered by France itself and by France's satellites in other parts of Germany. The Prussian king and bureaucracy were determined to think hard about the structure and quality of their state; and in their anxiety to clear away as much as possible of what were recognized as the inefficiencies of the *ancien régime* and to learn from their enemies, many of the specific reforms introduced turned out to be analogous, if not identical, with those that had been decreed in revolutionary and then Napoleonic Paris. Serfdom was abolished, the power of the guilds was reduced almost to a nullity, freedom to take up previously restricted crafts and occupations was granted and other (although not all) impediments to free trade removed, the officer corps was opened (to some extent) to commoners, the basis for a mass army was laid, the army's disciplinary system was humanized, the school system was reorganized and rationalized, a proper statistical bureau was set up, and, finally, some progress towards orderly, cabinet government at the centre was made as well. The special edict on the Jews took longer than most to work its way through the machine, but it was certainly of a piece with the other reforms. It too followed from a recognition that the old regulatory system was anachronistic and injurious to the state; that it was one among many other impediments to the effort to maximize economic perform-ance; and that it was a potential source of political disaffection. If Jews were treated badly, and knew they were likely to be treated better else-where, what grounds were there for expecting them to be loyal to the state? What was the point of applauding the fact that the treatment meted out to them encouraged them to emigrate if, in the real world, it was the 'useful' Jews who were the first to leave?

But if the post-Jena, post-Tilsit reforms shared with those legislated in France, and those imposed directly by the French in the Rhineland, the same centralist and rational spirit, there was a respect in which they were fundamentally different. In Prussia they were not derived, and did not purport to be derived, from first political and moral, let alone universal, principles. Prussian reforms were pragmatic and opportunistic.[40] They were intended to maximize and mobilize the resources of the state and were governed by what its master and his loyal servants considered expe-dient, not virtuous. They were therefore rarely clear-cut. The nobility was required to serve the state in ways and to a degree that were without precedent in Prussian history. It was not deprived of all its rights and priv-ileges, nor was it wholly subordinated to the crown. The peasantry was liberated—by stages—but neither fully provided for nor totally freed of its feudal obligations. So too in the case of the Jews.

Of the issues that remained unsettled in their regard two were salient. One was ostensibly formal. The other ran very deep. The Edict referred to the possibility of Jews being admitted to the public service. But it did not prescribe it, nor did it explicitly authorize it. Would they then be admitted to the ranks of government officials, to the judiciary, to the offi-cer corps after all? Would they be allowed to serve, say, as school and uni-versity teachers? All that was promised was that the question would be taken up 'in the course of time'. The other issue was that of the Jews' social fate. This was an older, still thornier issue, views on which would be propounded from this point on, as we shall see, with steadily mount-ing stridency and bitterness. The Prussian bureaucrats, for their part, did wonder, however. What was to become of these people? Would they 'forget Palestine' when they were at long last permitted to be fully natur-alized in Europe? Would they 'perhaps go on to believe that Jesus was the

---

[40] Except, perhaps, but then only in part, in the case of the educational reforms associ-ated with Wilhelm von Humboldt.

Messiah once they were no longer under any sort of compulsion to await another?'[41] Official thinking at this stage turned chiefly on Dohm's concept of *bürgerliche Verbesserung* (civil improvement), the notion that they were as they were because of the way they had long been treated, the corollary of which was that if they were treated differently they would behave differently. Since 'for the better' was understood to amount to being like everyone else, few doubted that in the event of 'improvement' being achieved, the state, at any rate, would stand to benefit. Social coherence would increase, a not unimportant source of social tension would be eliminated, a substantial addition to the sum total of 'useful' citizens would have been made. All, therefore, would be for the best in the near-Panglossian world to which the masters of the state aspired and in which, ultimately, the foundation of policy remained, as always, *raison d'état*. However, not all in Prussia, even in the administration itself, could bring themselves to subscribe to so functional and culturally neutral a view of the matter. Even granted that freedom for the Jews, not excluding the non-political freedom to prosper, would have to be contingent on their acceptance and internalization of Prussian requirements, it was much less clear precisely what those requirements might be. Besides, a look at opinion among the Jews themselves revealed that there was no unanimity there either on any of the issues, least of all on the matter of social integration. The Jews who tended to accept the idea of *bürgerliche Verbesserung* as indeed representing the condition they would be happy to aim for tended, in the first instance, to be those who had a great deal to gain economically and politically from what it seemed to offer. These, typically, were of the class of *parnassim* and *Schutzjuden* who, by virtue of their *de facto* or *de jure* leadership of their respective communities, had long regarded themselves as bearing a disproportionately heavy communal burden of which they were anxious to be rid. By and large, they were those who, in their private affairs too, were most impeded by anti-Jewish regulations.[42] Whatever their case, they were therefore very far from being representative of their brethren, the more so as there were other, conflicting schools of thought. There were those, well represented in Berlin itself, as it happened, who were prepared to go only part of the way towards the kind of 'improvement' Dohm and his school had had in mind, because they wished to preserve a distinctive Jewish way of life, and believed that there were ways and means of doing so that were compatible with the grant (and acceptance) of civil rights and the satisfaction

---

[41] J. W. Süvern, a specialist in education serving in the Ministry of Religions and an associate of Wilhelm von Humboldt. Cited in Raphael Mahler, *Divrei yemei yisrael: dorot aḥaronim*, ii (Merḥavia, 1954), 129.

[42] Miriam Bodian, 'Ha-yazamim ha-yehudiim be-Berlin, ha-medina ha-absolutistit, ve-"shipur maẓavam ha-ezraḥi shel ha-yehudim" ba-maḥaẓit ha-sheniya shel ha-me'ah ha-18', *Ẓion*, 49, 2 (1984), 159–84.

of the demands the modern state normally made on its citizens. A third school took a wholly opposite course, rejecting what it considered to be the poisoned gift of civil liberty on the grounds that, if accepted, it would inexorably undermine all that the Jews had traditionally stood for and all that it, at any rate, wished to maintain. The members of this school had no interest in *bürgerliche Verbesserung* in any way that Christian Dohm or Wilhelm von Humboldt or Karl von Hardenberg (Prussian Chancellor at the time the Edict was issued) or anyone else in Berlin might understood the term. But while these differences within German Jewry, much magnified and deepened and in the process too, as we shall see, of spreading with fair rapidity throughout the Jewish population of the continent, were due to become of first importance for the internal social and political development of the Jews themselves, they were of negligible interest to the Prussian political class. Its approach to the matter of the Jews was dictated less by direct observation and accumulated knowledge than by its own, idiosyncratic, internally generated, exceedingly inflexible views on society, state, and nation and an underlying, if somewhat less than universal, hostility to Jewry *per se*. Promptly after its promulgation in France, Napoleon's distinctly and viscerally anti-Jewish 'infamous decree' had been extended to the then French-controlled Rhineland. Ten years later, as we have seen,[43] it was allowed to become a dead letter—without much fuss or discussion. In the Rhineland itself, now under Prussian control, this particular Napoleonic decree was kept in force for another three decades. But it is to developments much further to the east, in Poland, where the true centre of gravity of European Jewry lay, that closest attention is due.

V

Jews had long been tolerated by the kings of Poland and, for the most part, by the magnates, the real rulers of the country, as well. Much less so by the Church, however, and not at all by the urban classes who saw them as competitors in commerce and crafts. The peasants, especially those whom magnates and lesser landowners had placed under the supervision of Jewish bailiffs and leaseholders and who were encouraged by all, king, nobility, Church, and city burghers, to regard the Jews as their greatest enemies, loathed them. The weakness of the Jews, but in some ways their strength as well, lay in the fact that their function and influence hinged on their role as sources of income, on their being susceptible, that is to say, to being regularly milked by whoever held political authority over them: king, elders in the royal towns, magnates, lower nobility, the Church.

[43] See n. 33.

They were not perceived, however, as a wholly foreign or illegitimate component of society—as were their cousins in the Germanies, for example. Nor, in so far as such matters lend themselves to judgement, were they. They were not recent arrivals. Set against the burghers' right to limit their presence in particular towns or to exclude them totally, were a host of formal charters and licences according them countervailing 'privileges' of one kind or another, the sum total of which could be seen as confirming Polish Jewry as *virtually* one of the established estates of the realm. Yet, privileges notwithstanding, they were forever vulnerable to an arbitrary exercise of authority that bordered on, and at times had positive recourse to, outright persecution—a vulnerability tempered only by the degree to which, as individuals or as members of particular communities, they were perceived as useful to whoever was in power nationally or locally as objects of extortion. In this sense, their position and status and the terms in which these were perceived were not, in the final analysis, radically different from those of their brethren in central Europe except, as we shall see, that the consequences were if anything more poignant. It was the condition of the state that differed. Poland, towards the end of the eighteenth century, was teetering on the brink of final dissolution. With the Russians at the gates and the other dangers facing what had been left of Greater Poland after the Second Partition looming, minds in the court of King Stanislaw Augustus Poniatowski and in the Commonwealth's last parliament, the so-called Quadrennial Sejm (1788–92), turned, as rarely before, to the idea of putting some order into the country's affairs—at which point the idea of taking up the matter of the Jews met, as had so rarely been the case before, with a not wholly negative response. This was true of the king, of some of the more far-sighted members of the magnate and gentry classes—and therefore of the Sejm—and to some extent of Polish intellectuals and publicists as well. As in the west, a small body of literature developed in which the problem of the Jews was discussed in some detail, often with considerable penetration, and with a view to how this awkward, but to some minds potentially very useful, people might be integrated into Polish society and made to bring greater benefit to the much battered Polish state.[44]

The immediate problem lay in the fact that, for the most part, the Jews of Poland were deeply impoverished and, as a body, heavily in debt—to the magnates, to the city burghers, and to a high degree to the Church. But although their uses as a source of revenue to the men of power were therefore judged, probably correctly, to have diminished beyond the

---

[44] Mayir Vereté, 'Haza'ot polaniyot le-fitron teritoriali shel "she'elat ha-yehudim" ', *Zion*, 6, 3 (1941), 148–55; Adolf Haber, 'Ha-pundekaim ha-yehudiim ba-publizistika ha-polanit shel "Ha-seim ha-gadol" (1788–1792)', *Gal-'Ed*, 2 (1975), 1–24; Hillel Levine, *Economic Origins of Antisemitism: Poland and its Jews in the Early Modern Period* (New Haven, 1991), ch. 5.

point of recuperation, they continued to be subject to a host of overlapping imposts, prohibitions, quotas, and sundry other burdens and humiliations—all of which were rendered the more untenable by reason of the inefficacy of central government. It was only as a consequence of action from the centre, in practice by the king, that these matters stood any chance at all of being sorted out: more specifically, that an initiative to add the matter of the Jews to the list of constitutional and social reforms that were being put before the Sejm was likely or indeed possible. In the terms in which the plan of reform was conceived, there may be discerned, however, some of the threads in which the affairs and prospects of the Jews of Poland were fatally entangled—and some of the consequent causes of failure.

The question of what to do about the Jews had been brought up in the Sejm before. In 1775, when the poll tax to which they were liable was raised, the measure was condemned by some members as a fiscal absurdity, given the steadily deepening pauperization and the vagrancy that were known to be afflicting Polish Jewry. To which other members retorted with the old charges: that Jews played too great a role in certain trades anyway, that they competed commercially and, what is more, dishonestly with the burghers and the guild craftsmen to the latter's great detriment and to the detriment of the Polish urban population generally. To the practical question, what then was to be done about them, a popular response was that they needed to be settled on the land—to which the countercharge was that the idea did not bear examination. Where, precisely, were they to be settled? Was it the *impoverished* among them—the obvious candidates for agricultural settlement—who were seriously expected to set themselves up as farmers on the basis of their own resources, namely without public assistance? If so, were they to be allowed to own the land allotted them? And what was to be their civil status? Were they to be enserfed? If so, were Jews expected to *agree* to that? It was pointed out in an anonymous paper prepared for the Quadrennial Sejm, that as it was the peasants, in their misery and poverty, bore

the stigma of eternal disgrace, of eternal serfdom. . . . If we want to encourage [other] people to till the soil, we must show them imminent advantage. Our laws forbid the Jew to inherit land. What then is left to them? Only to become peasants and work for somebody else, not for themselves. Reason and experience have taught us that it will never come to this.[45]

The Quadrennial Sejm was thus the occasion for the first more or less serious debate on the matter of the Jews to be held in Poland. And if, as such, it prompted a host of questions to which no answers, authoritative or persuasive, were forthcoming, it was less because of unfamiliarity with

[45] Cited in Artur Eisenbach, *The Emancipation of the Jews in Poland, 1780–1870* (Oxford, 1991), 46.

the subject than because no genuine, really far-reaching socio-political revolution was ever envisaged by more than a tiny handful of the participants. Were the Jews finally to be incorporated into the burgher class, for example? Were they to be liable for military service? Some voices did argue for reform somewhat along the lines of Dohm's *bürgerliche Verbesserung*: the Jews had been treated unjustly; they had been deprived through no fault of their own of the means of making an honest living and in sundry other ways had been prevented from improving themselves and from providing Poland with a loyal and potentially valuable segment of the population, instead of the embittered and harmful one that they had become. Civic rights were therefore to be granted them—always provided that the existing feudal estate structure of the Commonwealth remained intact. The counterarguments (in the press and in pamphlet form) were in a more familiar vein: let the Jews first prove themselves; to release them of the obligation to do so would be to put the cart before the horse; Jews were inherently unsuitable for military service; the essential thing, in any event, was to change *their* socio-economic structure, not that of Poland as a whole. It was consistent with the dominant outlook that the reforms introduced in Austria by Joseph II received more attention as models for possible application in Poland than those recently decreed by the French National Assembly. The Declaration of the Rights of Man did arouse some interest, although commonly and comfortably judged remote from, and therefore inapplicable to, Polish circumstances. The emancipation of the Jews of France two years later received only the barest notice in the Warsaw press and was largely ignored.[46]

But that was not the whole of the sad, brief story of the handling of the matter of the emancipation of the Jews in the twilight years of the old Polish Commonwealth, nor of the impact, however marginal, of distant, foreign examples. Tellingly, the man who played the central role in the attempt, such as it was, to introduce order into all that related to the presence of the Jews in Poland with a view to establishing a rational basis on which they might co-habit peacefully with its other inhabitants, was not a Pole. He was an Italian clergyman of exceptional curiosity, talent, and energy who had chanced in 1783 to find a political role for himself in Poland, Scipione Piattoli (1749–1809), counsellor and secretary to King Stanislaw Augustus.

On a visit to France in 1789, it is believed, he became interested in Malesherbes's views (on which more below) on the need to improve the social and economic condition of Jews in Alsace who, he noted, unlike the Jews of south-west France and the Avignonnais, had much in common culturally and socio-economically with the Jews of Poland. On his return to Poland in 1790 and his entry into politics as an active and diligent

[46] Eisenbach, *Emancipation*, 63–6.

participant in the constitution-making of the period, he set out to devise and then promote a plan that comprised two interlocked components: a detailed blueprint for a consolidated and rationalized legal system that would enable the Jews not merely to live, but to prosper, in the constitutional monarchy-to-be; and the setting out of the financial terms under which all those who had a material interest in the perpetuation of the *status quo*—or whose approval was needed if any such reform was to be implemented—were to be squared. Briefly put, a bargain was to be struck. The Jews were to be granted virtually all civil rights, released from all specific constraints and 'privileges', and permitted to purchase and own land and housing. They would retain a degree of juridical autonomy amounting effectively (or so, in Piattoli's view, it could be argued) to their having the status of a distinct estate. There would be special, but reasonably tolerant, concessions regarding the perpetually vexed matter of their dress, their beards, and all else that helped to distinguish them visibly and publicly from everyone else.[47] Finally and crucially, the money by which the nobility, the Church, and the burghers—and the crown itself—were to be paid off in exchange for their acquiescence in this radical change would come from the Jews themselves. Piattoli, and those who served as his interlocutors on behalf of Polish Jewry,[48] believed 20 million zlotys, payable in ten annual instalments as a gift to the crown, would go as far as was needed to compensate those for whom the proposed emancipation meant immediate financial loss. And thus, as Piattoli put it, 'if our plan succeeds we will do an unfortunate nation a necessary good deed and obtain a very substantial annual subvention for the Treasury of the Republic'.[49] In pursuit of these two ends, the latter especially, he had the somewhat hesitant support of his master, the king. 'The essential thing is that Your Majesty's debts be paid, regardless of whether it takes fifteen or twenty years,' he wrote to Stanislaw Augustus. Twenty million zlotys was a tremendous sum and Piattoli was right to think that money counted for

[47] Piattoli's exceedingly elaborate 'Plan pour les Juifs' will be found in Artur Eisenbach, *et al.* (eds.), *Materialy do dziejów Sejmu Czteroletniego*, Institut Historii Polskiej Akademii Nauk (Wroclaw, Warsaw, and Cracow, 1969), vi. 350–72.

[48] As any go-between would have done, Piattoli tended to portray the king to the Jews as hugely benevolent, and the Jews to the king as infinitely appreciative and grateful. After one of his talks with a Jewish interlocutor, he reported to Stanislaw Augustus that only good could result from action that accorded with the king's views and was taken under his auspices. That way 'one was sure . . . that we were guided by no private interest, that the Father of the country, the guardian angel of Poland, has turned his attention to the unhappy Jewish nation and that he intends to ease its condition and provide it with a tranquil and decent existence in the Republic'. Upon which, Piattoli told the king, 'My man had tears in his eyes and left me to give a full account to his mistress', the context suggesting that the 'mistress' in the case was the woman landowner to whom the Jew was bound in some way. On the common Jewish response to these proposals for constitutional change, see below, pp. 107 ff.

[49] Piattoli to Kollataj, 29 Nov. 1791, in Eisenbach, *Materialy*, 299, no. 8.

a great deal in this affair: 'If the Jews fail to find the means to pay their debts and compensate the hereditary lords, the bill will never pass the Diet and, in that case, all will be lost for Your Majesty.'[50] Twenty million zlotys may in fact have been too small a sum to be persuasive. But the chief consideration fuelling the opposition was most probably objection to change as such—which, while not absolute, was effectively overwhelming. In a 'nobleman's republic' in which the nobility, apart from all its other privileges, had virtually exclusive right to ownership of land, even noted 'liberals' and 'reformers' were opposed to anything that might seriously undermine the established constitutional structure. Andrzej Zamoyski, sometime Crown Chancellor of Poland, leader of the more liberal strain among the landed nobility, and one who had sought to set an example by freeing his serfs, opposed the grant of civic rights to Jews. His view was that they should have the status of tolerated foreigners. Hugo Kollataj, another noted reformer, was an ally of Piattoli's; but he wanted to preserve the privileges of nobility, the town burghers' corporate privileges, the estate system, and the established inequality of the various classes and estates before the law as well. He was even opposed to the abolition of serfdom. The nobility, it may be recalled, had been overwhelmingly opposed to giving non-Roman Catholic Christians (the Orthodox, the Lutherans, and the Calvinists) political rights until well into the eighteenth century. Only in 1768 did 'dissidents' get 'partial equality'. They were admitted to municipal citizenship in 1775. They lost it again two years later. Opposition to the abolition of serfdom and the corvée was still more intense. As for the Jews, to the vast majority of minds there could be no question at all of emancipating them. Some thought any Jewish cause and any one who supported it were *ipso facto* ridiculous. 'Good Christians, my dear Piattoli, are infinitely pained by your passion for the Israelite,' Ignacy Potocki wrote to the king's adviser, suggesting they meet to discuss it. 'Would you, as the new Moses, have a moment in the morning for a gentile?'[51] But Piattoli seems to have been convinced that if the magnates were well compensated for the loss of certain rights—rights which he did not doubt were, in themselves, 'abusifs à la vérité'—they would eventually succumb.[52]

The stiffest opposition of all to change in the status of the Jews was voiced by the middle-class burgher estate. After repeated and tedious haggling over the precise terms on which certain prohibitions were to be lifted, and a surprise demand at one point that the entire agreement be revised, the Italian cleric was reduced to despair. 'They quibbled about almost every word, one of the burghers dealing with the religious clause

[50] Piattoli to Stanislaw Augustus, 2 Jan. 1792, in Eisenbach, *Materialy*, 305–6, no. 19.
[51] 4 Jan. [1792], ibid. 310, no. 25.
[52] Piattoli to Stanislaw Augustus, 10 Jan. 1792, ibid. 314–15, no. 37.

like an inquisitor of the most inflexible kind,' he complained to the king. They insisted on 'endless corrections and amendments, all of which were dictated by prejudice, hatred, and, in one word, by ancient ideas'.[53] But the burghers, the small middle or upper-middle class in Poland, had long experience in pressing for what they regarded as their rights. Most towns in Poland were private, belonging either to noble landowners or to the Church (to monastic orders, for example). Only a minority were royal towns, the practical meaning of which was that their inhabitants possessed all civic freedoms including the right to own land; and this was the segment of the burgher estate that was most determined and vociferous of all in its opposition to a relaxation of the regime to which the Jews were subject. Townsfolk of all categories are commonly estimated to have formed about a sixth of the country's population at the time. Of these some two-thirds were Jews and a third Christians (about 10 per cent and 5 per cent of the total population respectively). In effect, because different laws applied to them, Jews and Christians constituted two separate but exceedingly unequal classes. To be domiciled in a city or town was one thing, to be admitted to formal 'citizenship' was another. But it was urban citizenship that was the indispensable condition of economic activity at every level except the very lowest. Without it there could be no membership of a guild, no right to exercise an artisan craft, no access to a confraternity of merchants entitled to carry on a particular trade, no political or even semi-political rights such as participation in the making of municipal law, voting in elections, or holding of public office. Not being members of the burgher estate, Jews were excluded from political rights even in towns which they were permitted to inhabit and they were excluded again, with no less serious consequences, from the economic benefits that citizenship provided as well. Even their right to own town plots of land on which to build their homes was heavily restricted— limited, in effect, to a few 'private towns' belonging to well-disposed magnates.[54] When the burghers proved to be immovable in their refusal to countenance any real relaxation of these rules, Piattoli's plan was fated to fail.

In the long term, the effect of this intermingling of watered-down, but not inauthentic *post*-1789 ideas with ideas of a much older, distinctly feudal and medieval origin and content was fatally to box together the related, but still separable subjects, of reform of the Jewish condition, relations between Jews and non-Jews, the political status of the Jews, the political constitution of the Polish state, and the general structure and quality of Polish society. It continued to be thought entirely reasonable to expect the Jews to pay—and pay very heavily—in exchange for being

---

[53] Piattoli to Stanisław Augustus, 10 Jan. 1792, ibid. 321, no. 44.
[54] Eisenbach, *Emancipation*, 24–30.

freed of burdens arbitrarily placed upon them and the harassment to which they were perpetually subject. It was thought proper and reasonable that the heirs of those who had placed those burdens upon the Jews should be compensated for the effect the cancellation of these impositions was likely to have on their pockets. It was believed that the liberators of the Jews, for their part, were entitled to compensation too. But it was at least as commonly accepted that a plan to alter the condition of the Jews for the better must in some way be illegitimate—an illegitimacy demonstrated by the provision that the Jews *buy* their release from the rulers of Poland. It appears almost natural therefore that on the Polish side only so bizarre a figure as a displaced Italian clergyman could have made a serious move to bring the emancipation of the Jews in pre-partition Poland at least into the realm of speculative discussion. Although, that said, for reasons which will be gone into in some detail in due course, there was always—or would have been had anything come of Piattoli's efforts—Jewish reluctance to envisage change to contend with. Certainly, for an individual Jew to think and act for himself in these matters was to swim against the immensely powerful tide of Jewish conservatism and was exceedingly difficult and in practice very much rarer than in western Europe. One such very rare being was Shelomo (or Salomon) Polonus of Vilna, a doctor of medicine, physician to the king, and a man of general culture as well. He was well acquainted with the political writings and events of the day. He was privy to the proposals on the status of the Jews that the abbé Piattoli had prepared for submission to the king and to the Sejm. And he had a plan of his own which the grant of full emancipation in 1791 by the French National Assembly had evidently encouraged him to work on. Its general tenor is indicated by his references to developments in France and the arguments advanced by the abbé Grégoire:

If 50,000 Jews have convinced the French nation, this refined and enlightened nation of Europe, that . . . they will help their country with the wealth of their life, if these Jews have been granted civic rights and have been put on an equal footing with any Frenchman, then there are even fewer reasons to doubt whether the nearly one million Jews in the Polish state will through enlightenment become happy and useful to their country.

However, the content of Polonus's scheme, after necessary adjustment to Polish circumstances, was more modest. He wanted Jews to be allowed to live in all towns without exception and without hindrance, to engage in any form of trade, craft, and industry they chose, to be admitted to the guilds, to be called up with other citizens for active military service, and at least gradually to be granted civic rights as well—by which, however, Polonus meant no more than municipal rights. Full political rights in contemporary, feudal Poland were too obviously out of the question and were not referred to. And even then, such civic rights as were granted would be limited either by the social category of the candidates or by time. They were to be granted to those who had opened, or had undertaken to open, a factory and to soldiers who had completed five years' military service, for example. They would be granted to other Jews only after a lapse of twenty years. Exceptionally, persons who had 'distinguished themselves by their enlightenment and [were] using it to improve the nation' were to be 'adorned' with citizenship immediately.[55]

But in any event, the differences between the Polish Commonwealth and revolutionary France—or France under the *ancien régime*, for that matter—were, of course, far too great to be overcome, even marginally and symbolically by the enactment of such modest reforms as either Polonus or Piattoli had in mind, even if there had been the will among the greater and lesser nobility to consider such a step. There was never any contact or dialogue between representative Jews and representative members of the Polish nobility that was, or could be, conducted on a basis that was remotely analogous to that on which Malesherbes had been prepared to conduct his discussions with the delegates from Bordeaux. There were no Grégoires in the Polish branch of the Roman Catholic Church. No group of burghers in Poland were prepared to take up a position in respect of their Jewish neighbours analogous to that taken by the civic leaders of Bordeaux in respect of theirs. And there was no substantial group within Polish Jewry itself whose status was analogous to that of the Jews of Bordeaux, let alone one that was willing, as they were, to move into the half-way house of Jewish emancipation.

Meanwhile, with the Russians at the gates of Warsaw and poised for invasion, the attention of those who sought both to lead the country in the short term and to make it effectively governable in the longer term passed to other matters. In 1792 the Sejm was dissolved. Three years later what was left of independent Poland was snuffed out. The issue of the Jewish presence in Poland as a distinctly *Polish* responsibility and problem was not to arise for another century and a quarter. And what was most remarkable, and central to the Jewish experience in the country, was that in this long interim the refusal of indigenous Polish centres of influence to countenance any really substantial reordering of the legal and economic strait-jacket in which the Jews of their country were confined changed hardly at all. Even under the impermanent French puppet regime, the duchy of Warsaw (1807–15), the Polish ministers responsible

---

[55] Shelomo Polonus, 'Projekt wzgledem reformy Zydow', cited in Eisenbach, *Emancipation*, 89; Israel Bartal, ' "Ha-model ha-mishni"—ẓarfat ke-mekor hashpaʿah be-tahalikhei ha-modernizaẓiya shel yehudei mizraḥ eiropa (1772–1863)', in Yeraḥmiel Cohen (ed.), *Ha-mahapekha ha-ẓarfatit ve-rishuma* (Jerusalem, 1991), 272–5.

for daily government were quite as firmly set on preventing Jews from being granted civic and political rights as any of their predecessors had been. They had the advantage, moreover, that their new, non-resident ruler, King Frederick Augustus of Saxony, was considerably less sympathetic to reform in this domain than their own King Stanislaw Augustus had been. In July 1808 the king went so far as to ask Paris for special authority to suspend for ten years the electoral rights that the new French model legislation promulgated in the duchy appeared to grant to the Jews. His stated grounds were that it was 'beyond doubt' that even the numerous class of ostensibly useful Jews living in the duchy of Warsaw as merchants and industrialists were without a claim to the rights and privileges the constitution accorded citizens who were not of the nobility. As, in the event, no formal decision was taken one way or the other in Paris, in Warsaw itself, as the elections drew near, a decree depriving the Jews of electoral rights was promulgated (7 September 1808) by the king on his own authority and on the following day the duchy's minister of the interior instructed the prefects confidentially not to include Jews in the register of citizens. Should Jews go so far as to claim the right to be included on the roll and to vote, they were to be told that no instructions from higher authority permitting registration had been received. A little later, on 17 October, a decree *explicitly* suspending Jews' civil and political rights was issued, but perhaps the real interest in this last step lies less in its formal, if to be sure all-embracing, content, than in the attempt made to sweeten it somewhat and reduce its blatant incompatibility with the new constitution. It was to be in force for ten years only, it was announced; and the decree was glossed with an expression of 'the hope that within this period they [the Jews] will eradicate those traits which have so divided them from all others'.

It follows that beside the unmistakable evidence of the Polish nobility's intention to obstruct the extension of political and economic liberties beyond the narrow circle to which they were accustomed to limit them, there were some signs none the less of a certain awkwardness and a reflection too, however pale and distant, of the *Zeitgeist*. It was accepted that a matter of general principle was involved, that the principle in question was one that civilized nations were expected to abide by, and that if they did not do so they were, at any rate, under an obligation to explain themselves. Jan Luszczewski, the duchy's minister of the interior, did indeed feel called upon to argue that while 'nobody will probably deny the Jews the right of civil liberty and equality before the law', it was the case, on the other hand, that 'everybody must admit that these rights may be restricted by police measures . . .' Everybody, the minister went on to say, 'receives an equitable share of rights and freedoms in society according to the age, civilization, customs and even religion that he brings in'. Alas, Polish Jews were of a lower level of civilization than Jews in the western

European countries. Laws restricting their access to civic rights were therefore, in his considered opinion, fully justifiable.[56]

In the post-Napoleonic settlement of the new European state system, the greater part of the territory of what had been the French-sponsored duchy of Warsaw was reincorporated into the Russian Empire as the semi-autonomous kingdom of Poland—soon to be known most commonly as 'Congress Poland'. The Tsar of Russia was king, represented in Warsaw by a viceroy and other officials. But the ordinary administration of this rump of the old Polish Republic[57] was left, by design, in the hands of Poles, more specifically much the same class of Poles—major landowners chosen from among the higher nobility—as before. Their domination of the Council of State in Warsaw was absolute, it was they who had the ears of their new, Russian overlords, and in all matters of day-to-day administration it was they and their kind who continued to make the running. So they did too, to some extent, so far as the tone and content of such public and published debate on matters of public interest as took place. The brief period of French overlordship had produced little more than a technical emancipation of the serfs. In practice, their lot had hardly changed: they were bound to the soil as before, as firmly ruled as ever by the owners of the estates on which they lived and for whom they laboured, and, being landless, they remained as fatally dependent on their masters for their livelihood as they were subordinate to them politically and legally. The situation of the burghers is generally held to have improved somewhat. The new semi-autonomous Polish army contained patriotic elements that, in their thirst for rebellion, would prove to be imperfectly controlled by those magnates who, having made a peace of sorts with the Russians, were now set on a course of prudent inactivity. But all in all, initially, matters in Congress Poland (as opposed to the Prussian and Austrian bits of the old Republic) were to be much as they had been a generation and more earlier.

This was certainly the case so far as the Jews were concerned. As with the serfs, so with them, all moves towards emancipation were arrested. The application of such provisions of the Napoleonic civil code as might, on the one hand, have impaired the nobility's monopoly of the ownership of land and, on the other hand, have enabled some Jews materially to improve both their formal status and their economic elbow-room— those relating to rights of property, freedom to purchase and transfer property, and freedom of contract, for example—were either aborted or severely watered down. With the return of the Russians, the notion of granting the Jews civic and political rights by, for example, incorporating

[56] Eisenbach, *Emancipation*, 137–8.
[57] The Lithuanian territories had been incorporated into Russia proper. Prussia and Austria retained, with some changes, those portions of the Republic that they had seized in the course of the late eighteenth-century partitions.

them into the burgher estate, faded totally away. The right of the burghers of certain towns, under their ancient freedom to invoke the *de non tolerandis Judaeis* privilege, to expel Jews who inhabited them was restored. The power to set aside a specific quarter (*revir*) in which Jews who were allowed to remain were compelled to reside, was maintained. A blanket prohibition on residence anywhere that was less than 20 versts (about 20 kilometres) from the Austrian and Prussian borders and a multitude of other such legal and administrative restrictions and taxes directed at the Jews exclusively were instituted or refurbished or repromulgated. The question of the Jews of Poland would be looked into from time to time by the Russian authorities, but would undergo no substantial change until, in the wake of the dismal failure of the 1830 rebellion against Russian rule, the process of incorporation of Russian-ruled Poland into the Russian administrative system began in earnest. The decisive engine of policy for the kingdom, as for all the other domains of the Tsar, would be none other henceforth than the one over which the Tsar exercised his own direct control in St Petersburg. The result, coupled to the long-term effects of the punishment meted out to the rebels of 1830, was a further weakening of the authority and prestige and, above all, the power of Poland's traditional landowning ruling class. The Jews, with some notable but still very rare exceptions, had taken no part in the rebellion. It had done them no good, but nor had it done them palpable harm. In its aftermath, however, there were as good and sufficient reasons for Jews in Warsaw and Lublin, as there had been previously in Kovno and Minsk—in so far to be sure, as their eyes were not wholly in their books and averted from the world outside their study halls—to begin to look to St Petersburg for relief, if relief there was ever to be.

VI

Austria, Prussia, and Russia, all absolutist, centralizing, and bureaucratizing states governed by opinionated rulers and administrators, had this in common too, that they were the promoters and beneficiaries of the destruction and partition of Poland. And this had the result, among many others, that at the end of the process of partition and the seemingly final distribution of territory under the terms of the Vienna settlement, each found itself lumbered with an unprecedentedly large and, from their point of view, deeply undesirable and problematic Jewish population. There were, however, immediate and striking differences between Prussia and Austria on the one hand and Russia on the other. The successive partitions of Poland left Russia with ever larger segments of the country and also much the largest segment of Polish-Lithuanian Jewry specifically. From the Russian point of view, this was a particularly unintended, unwished-for, and in important respects quite bitterly resented and vexatious consequence of Russia's successes as an expanding, imperial power. Alone of all the major European powers, the Russian Autocracy founded its approach to everything that touched upon Judaism as a faith and as a culture, and upon the Jews as a people, upon a fundamentally religious hatred. This was all the more powerful for its being extraordinarily simplistic and shot through at the same time with a deep, instinctive, and so to speak generalized xenophobia in which fear, contempt, and suspicion of the alien were all combined. Now and again, at various levels of government, an effort to reconsider policy on the Jews in a spirit of calm and objectivity would occur. On several such occasions, as we shall see, a limited mitigation of its rigours was conceded. But in its fundamentals it was never reversed. On the contrary: it was cleaved to—with remarkable tenacity, it must be said—to the end. And the result was that, in contrast to what happened in the other major states of the old Europe, an emancipation of the Jews was never decreed; and on the exceedingly rare and fleeting occasions when the uses of a move towards it were raised it was promptly and authoritatively rejected.

It needs to be said that the Jews of what was once Greater Poland were overwhelmingly of a type and a class and a culture that, even as early as the end of the eighteenth century, had begun to diminish in parts at least of central Europe and in a marked and accelerating fashion in the west. They were at one and the same time in much poorer, meaner, and humiliating circumstances and, by virtue of their greater numbers and the fact that they lived, typically, in denser and more coherent communities than any in the west, much more distinctively and unselfconsciously a people apart than their brethren elsewhere. Members of the western and to some extent the central European communities too had by this time begun to adopt the vernacular for everyday use and some were already well versed in it. Overwhelmingly, the Jews in independent Poland had not done so. Not until well into the nineteenth century did substantial numbers—still a minority—speak Polish or Russian or German. Great numbers (not all) read and wrote Hebrew. Greater numbers still read, wrote, and, most important of all, spoke Yiddish, having carried this essentially German tongue to Poland (much as the Iberian Jews had carried their Spanish tongue to the Balkans). They were generally more observant of the niceties of Jewish ritual than were their brethren in the west, more respectful of their rabbis, more inward looking. They were, for these reasons, very much more obviously alien, a feature that was the more marked for their belonging almost exclusively to the lower economic orders. Here and there in Poland there were, as we have seen, a handful of men who had achieved power and influence in Jewry by virtue, ultimately, of the services they performed for great men outside it. But unlike, say, the Jews of medieval Spain—with whom in some respects they bear comparison—there were none among them who were in any serious sense great men themselves. Still, broadly speaking, the Polish Jews of Galicia and Poznania were not of a category that the Austrians and Prussians found entirely unfamiliar when these provinces were annexed. For the Russians, in contrast, the incorporation into the empire of substantial numbers of Jews as part of the settled population of what would later be termed 'Congress Poland' presented a problem of which the Autocracy had no experience and which it would prove singularly ill-equipped to tackle.

Unlike the Austrian and Prussian bureaucracies and police, the Russian state had neither volumes of established rules and regulations nor any philosophy of government, ready-made or under discussion, that could reasonably be considered applicable to the Jewish case. Prior to the First Partition of Poland, Russia, by long and jealously maintained tradition, had to all intents and purposes been—to use a term that would be notorious a century and a half later, but is appropriate here despite the anachronism—*Judenfrei*. Tsar Peter I had permitted a handful of crypto-Jews to settle in Russia to serve him. But even the great modernizer himself had allowed no significant, let alone visible, deviation from the rule. A papal delegate who had asked him to permit the free passage through Russia of Catholic missionaries bound for Persia and China was given the famous answer, that both Jews *and* Jesuits were banned from his kingdom as a matter of course.[58] His daughter Elizabeth was as firm or firmer on this score during her reign (1740–61). Rejecting mercantilist arguments favouring the admission of 'useful' Jews to her lands, the Tsarina declared, in equally well-known terms, that she wished to derive no profit from 'the enemies of Christ'. In short, prior to the partitions of Poland, Russia, as far as Jews were concerned, was a prohibited land to be entered, if at all, only by the occasional, especially intrepid trader or physician who came prepared to face the very real dangers consequent on discovery. Nevertheless, to present the pattern of official behaviour established after the partitions as turning entirely on a sort of hankering for the *status quo ante* is to oversimplify it.

It was among the peculiarities of the Russian Empire, as we shall see, that, through the workings of the harsh political and administrative logic which the Autocracy had made its own since the time of Peter the Great, many of the effects and even some of the explicit rules and instruments that had defined 'toleration' (and even 'emancipation') elsewhere, notably in Central Europe, came *in practice* to be detectable and operative in the course of time in Russia as well. This owed a good deal to the nature of the Russian state itself: it was one in which such traces of

---

[58] 'Judeos et Jesuitas habemus proscriptos e regnis nostris.' Cited in Shmu'el Ettinger, 'Medinat moskva be-yaḥasa el ha-yehudim', *Zion*, 18, 3–4 (1953), 148 n.

independent nobility or Church or city government as there once were had long since been wiped clean, in which the classes into which society was divided were defined with respect to each other with unparalleled rigour, and in which all subjects without any exception at all were subordinated, not to say enslaved, to the person of the Tsar-despot as absolute owner and master of all he (or she) surveyed. There was therefore no way, for example, in which the feudal, landowning, and traditionally independent, not to say ungovernable, nobility and gentry of Poland (to which the Jews of Greater Poland had been subject in their time) could be fitted into such a system except, as would eventually prove to be the case, by main force and at the cost, to both Poles and Russians, of repeated rebellion. But in their case there was at least the compensating factor that the serfs who served the Polish nobility and gentry as a class could be more or less assimilated into the Russian system without real difficulty. In contrast, the Jews, being unassimilable—so far as anyone could see—into any of the categories, classes, estates, and hierarchies of which the Russian social and political order had been constructed, presented a problem that was rapidly recognized as insuperable short of drastic reforms of some not easily imaginable kind.

It was therefore as good as inevitable, and at the same time wholly characteristic of the Russian style of government, that the history of Russo-Polish Jews should be heavily marked—and very heavily scarred—by periodic attempts to examine the issues they presented and to grapple with them with a measure of application and ruthlessness that remains without parallel elsewhere in Europe until the twentieth century. In practice, upon Catherine II's accession to the Russian throne and the dissolution of Poland as a sovereign state that followed shortly after, the matter of the Jews was instantly transformed from a topic that had been only of the most marginal interest to Russian officialdom into one that would occupy its collective mind and draw its close attention for years to come and to a degree that, in retrospect, is ever harder to credit. At a single blow in 1772, and twice again and with still larger consequences, in 1793 and 1795, the Autocracy was confronted on its own ground with the largest, most sharply defined, least acculturated—and therefore plainly least digestible—segment of the very people it had been at such pains to keep out and away. However, Catherine the Great was a woman of very different character and political outlook from Elizabeth—let alone her more distant predecessors. And it is safe to say that the spirit of the times alone would have sufficed to inhibit her and the men who served her from following past example. No one in authority in St Petersburg, that is to say, seriously considered ordering a mass expulsion of the Jews from the Tsarina's new domains. No one proposed attempting their forcible conversion. The contradiction between settled, age-old Russian policy and the actual presence of a very large Jewish population on what was now Russian territory in an age when few at the centre of what purported to be enlightened government were likely to hold, and fewer still actually to proclaim, such beliefs about the Jews as Ivan the Terrible had held (that among the wickednesses of the Jews had been the introduction of poisons into Russia) was evident.

The forthright methods Ivan had chosen to tackle the awkward presence of Jews whom he came across in the course of his territorial conquests,[59] or those chosen by his successors—Tsar Alexei Mikhailovich, for example, in similar circumstances[60]—could not be employed as freely in the eighteenth century as had been possible in the sixteenth and the seventeenth. Already, earlier in the eighteenth century, the advance of Peter the Great's forces into areas populated by Jews (no more than thinly, be it said) was not accompanied by the horrors that his predecessors had set as virtually the norm, although by and large the principle that Russia should be *Judenfrei* was still carefully adhered to. On the other hand there could be no question of following the example set by Joseph II of Austria, still less—after the third and last of the eighteenth-century Polish partitions in 1795—that of revolutionary France. The old precedents concerning the Jews continued to exert a sort of moral force which was not unconnected with the fact that all in Russia at this time hinged on St Petersburg's absolute refusal to relax the autocratic system itself. In the event, the initial approach of the Russian administration to the Jews they encountered in the new western territories was, by contemporary Russian standards, liberal. It was proclaimed upon the entry of Russian troops into Byelorussia in 1772, that all such rights and privileges—property rights and freedom of religious worship among them—as her new subjects had possessed under Polish rule would be preserved under the empress's new rule. And the Jews, remarkably, were specifically, if somewhat apologetically, included in the sweep of Catherine's benevolence in the generous language and civilized terms which the 'enlightened despots' of the age had made their own throughout Europe. 'Her Imperial Majesty's love of her fellow men [*chelovekolyubie*]' did not permit her to exclude the Jews from the favour with which she treated all her subjects, provided they, for their part, were loyal, obedient, and engaged in occupations that were appropriate to their status (*zvanie*).[61]

What ensued, however, was a long period of ambivalence. In 1785 and again in 1795 (on the occasion of the Third Partition) the principle that Jewish town-dwellers and merchants were entitled to treatment on an equal footing with all other town-dwellers and merchants was

---

[59] In 1563, on the arrival of his army at Polotsk on the river Dvina, Ivan ordered the forcible conversion of the town's Jews. Those who refused to apostatize were put to death.

[60] At the conquest of Mogilev and Smolensk in 1654. See especially Ettinger, 'Medinat moskva', 141–2.

[61] N. D. Gradovsky, *Torgoviye i drugiya prava evreev v rossii* (St Petersburg, 1885), 45–6.

authoritatively restated. Allowance was even made for Jews of the appropriate class to serve as electors to municipal office and to be elected themselves. But precisely what social class or classes Jews should be permitted to belong to was (and would remain) a vexed question. Clearly, they were not peasants (*krestyaniny*). They were certainly not serfs (*krepostnye*). They were not of the gentry (*dvoryanstvo*). They might be merchants (*kuptsy*), but membership of the guilds of merchants, especially the higher guilds, was a costly affair and few Jews were of the requisite wealth and standing to join them; and, in any event, such membership entailed rights to which the 'native' or 'indigenous' people (*korennoye naseleniye*), namely the ethnic Russian (and of course the Polish) merchants, objected. That left the class of town-dwellers (*meshchantsvo*); but the fact was that the great majority of the Jews of Russia and Poland at this point were *not* town-dwellers. They lived in, and were very much a people of, the countryside: on the large, Polish-owned estates whose masters they served directly and indirectly as leaseholders, bailiffs, rent-collectors, suppliers, and general factotums; as inn-, tavern-, and shop-keepers; as millers and distillers of alcohol from surplus grain; and as cobblers, tailors, carpenters, and members of other, similar crafts. Most typically, they inhabited their own little hamlets, the *shtetls*, which were in every economic and social sense a well-established feature of the Byelorussian, Ukrainian, and Polish countryside and formed a distinct, but none the less integral segment of the overall socio-economic and socio-political structure intermediate between the peasants and the landowners who ruled them.

In sum, it cannot be overly stressed that, while the Jews (with rare exceptions) had long been deprived of the privilege of ownership of land on their own account, they had, on the other hand, escaped enslavement as serfs; and that in an almost exclusively agricultural economy their established function was to provide the other classes, the one situated above them no less than the other situated beneath them, with the commercial and artisanal services the gentry were unwilling and the peasants unable to provide for themselves. The Jews' only real economic competitors were therefore the genuine, at this stage overwhelmingly non-Jewish, town and city folk. So long as they kept to the countryside, where they had the backing of the gentry and the nobility in return for the services they performed and ventured into the larger commercial world in which the city merchants were dominant only sporadically or even exceptionally, a balance of sorts between them and Russia's and Poland's urban and commercial classes could be maintained. But it had been evident when the idea of their political, and by extension economic, emancipation was brought up for consideration on the occasion of the Quadrennial Sejm, that this balance was becoming difficult to maintain by reason of the resistance of the Polish burghers to any and every sign of Jews—even in quite small numbers—breaking out of the territorial and functional limits in which they had long been locked. When it turned out that among the new, Russian provincial governors there were some who thought it proper to insist on the new non-discriminatory rules being observed to the letter, matters became urgent in the eyes of the Polish merchant, the indigenous merchants of 'inner' Russia following closely in the Polish wake.[62] They became more urgent still when what would take shape as one of the major purposes of overall Russian policy towards the Jews was revealed: the desire of the Autocracy to remove the Jews from the countryside—altogether, if that were possible. The idea was radically to reduce, preferably to eliminate, what was taken to be the moral and economic harm Jews were considered to be inflicting on the truly indigenous population, the ignorant, unthinking, Christian, essentially innocent *peasant* people who, of all classes of the empire, were most in need of the Tsar's benevolent protection.

It cannot be said of any of the states of Europe (apart from the lands still ruled by the Ottomans and in a narrow, formal sense, and then very briefly, Jacobin France) that they were other than *Christian*. But nor, apart from the special case of the States of the Church in pre-*Risorgimento* Italy, can it be said that in any of them the Church, regardless of denomination and however influential it might be, was other than subordinate ultimately to the temporal power. This was certainly the case in Russia where the Church had not only long been the political captive of the state to a degree unknown in the west, but had long since resigned itself to that condition. There were differences, however, between Russia and the other European states not only in the political relationship between state and Church, but in respect of the place of religion generally and what were taken to be the teachings of religion on what were unquestionably the state's affairs. It was not merely that in principle Russia continued to be held by its Autocrat and his minions to be a Christian state with a particular duty to uphold its own Orthodox Church. It was that, far from the matter of the state's specifically Christian duty slowly wasting away, as in the west, it continued actively to exercise the minds of Russia's rulers as one of the central criteria by which questions of public policy were to be judged and decided. The continuous search for an effective definition of the role, quality, and ultimate purposes of the Autocracy itself was an enterprise which, considering the energy and seriousness with which it was pursued, sufficed in itself to distinguish Russia from its contemporaries. The programmes to which the state was committed and all its structures were under obligation to promote varied somewhat over time. But in no instance was there serious deviation from the rule that Russian Orthodoxy was and needed to remain a central and indispensable

---

[62] See for example the 1790 memorandum on the subject by Count A. R. Vorontsov, President of the Commercial Collegium Council, in *Istoricheskii arkhiv*, 6 (1993), 197–200.

component of the ruling ethos. Nineteenth-century imperial Russia was therefore an ideological state in a manner and to a degree that had become so rare as to be virtually unknown in Europe and would not be familiar again for at least a century. And the fact that its ideology was among other things distinctly and very strongly Christian—and Christian in a mode that was substantially less tolerant and theologically sophisticated than almost any of the other major European branches of Christendom—necessarily carried with it direct and unfortunate consequences for the country's Jews. That, and one other central pillar of what was in the process of becoming the state's programme: nationality. This was not a simple matter of recognizing the Russian nation as the largest of the many ethnic groups inhabiting the empire to which, therefore, it was obligatory to pay special attention and with which the Autocracy would be naturally inclined to associate itself and build upon as one of the foundations of the state. It was a conception of the Russians as a people uniquely possessed of the very highest moral, spiritual, and social qualities; and of the Russian nation alone being legitimately and indissolubly congruent with the state. It was therefore the one into which all the Tsar's subjects were properly encouraged—if not actually forced—to assimilate. It would not be until the reign of Nicholas I (1825–55) that these threads of belief and ideology would, as we shall see, be clearly formulated and a deliberate effort made to move the state and its inhabitants in the requisite direction. But their roots were detectable much earlier—much, indeed, as their fruit would be evident long afterwards.

While, as is the nature of such things, formally established policy crystallized slowly and somewhat unsteadily, measures that with hindsight can be seen as indicating the underlying thrust of official Russian thinking on questions relating to the Jews were enacted virtually from the first. Among them were a series of frankly discriminatory measures in the spheres of taxation and the occupations and trades in which Jews might continue to engage; listing the parts of Russia in which Jews were *not* to enjoy such rights as, initially, they had been said to possess; a considerable and continuing effort to deprive them of their long-standing right to distil alcohol and trade in it—with calamitous consequences for the many individuals concerned; and an imperial edict that laid down the rule that Jews were forbidden to register as merchants in the towns of 'inner Russia', or in Russia's port cities, although in White Russia, exceptionally, they might have the benefit of the rights of citizens by special authorization—a privilege that was extended later to Yekaterinoslav and the Crimea. These measures and others like them were handed down *ad hoc*, in no particular order, and fairly quickly, before the century had ended. They were not as yet components of a considered scheme. In some cases, they were dictated by no more than immediate administrative and fiscal convenience. In others, they were responses to protest and pressure by rapidly organized groups of merchants in 'inner Russia' who were sure that they had much to fear from the commercial competition Jews were likely to offer them if ever given a chance to do so; and by Poles of the noble and gentry classes who were soon adept at instilling their own settled views, hatreds, and jealousies in the minds of their new rulers—partly out of conviction, partly by way of advancing their own economic interests, but as a way too of laying responsibility for the misery, poverty, and drunkenness of their own peasantry on the shoulders of others.[63] To such factors as these there must be added the government's own separate search for a means of shunting potential settlers into the sparsely populated new Russian territories to the south and east: Jews, an eminently landless people, were rated by unthinking officials as likely candidates for the task. But it is probable that the reversal of the initial promise of equal or near-equal treatment owed something too to St Petersburg's mounting desire to rid itself of its own confusion of mind as it took stock of the sheer demographic magnitude and the real, which is to say ineradicably alien socio-economic, character of that great segment of Polish (and, indeed, European) Jewry it had unwittingly incorporated into its dominions. The element of shock in the response of the Tsarina's officials to what confronted them is, indeed, unmistakable. So was their instinct to explain what struck them as impossibly foreign and unreasonably resistant to incorporation into the Russian scheme of things as being rooted in backwardness and immorality. The probability is that, native prejudice apart, they tended very strongly to accept, virtually without question, what they were told about the Jews by members of the one class with which they were likely to have more than mere administrative contact: the Polish gentry. True, the Jews did not drink to excess, the first Russian governor of Mogilev province, reported,

but they are lazy, inclined to deceive, sleepy, superstitious, unclean, and poorly housed; they are all new arrivals [in the province], and they multiply where government is weak and law and justice are not enforced. They live by fraud and off the fruit of the labour of the peasants; they live on the credit extended to them by local and foreign residents; they are in debt to whomever they can borrow from; and they end by going into fraudulent bankruptcy.[64]

Mogilev had fallen to Russia under the terms of the First Partition of Poland (1772). By Russian calculation,[65] the Jewish population incorporated into the empire at that point was of the order of 30,000. On the completion of the Third Partition (1795) the total Jewish population the

---

[63] Shmu'el Ettinger, 'Ha-yesodot ve-ha-megamot be-'izuv mediniyuto shel ha-shilton ha-rusi klapei ha-yehudim 'im halukat polin', He-'Avar, 19 (1972), 7–10.

[64] Memorandum by Mikhail Kokhovsky, in 'Le-toledot ha-yehudim be-rusiya be-sof ha-me'ah ha-18 (shalosh te'udot)', He-'Avar, 19 (1972), 74–8.

[65] Ibid. 78.

Autocracy had to deal with was at least ten times that number and may have been as high as 400,000.[66] But if there was a sense growing in Russian officialdom that something needed to be done about these people, there was also a suspicion that the regime might never be able to work its will on the Jews except at a cost in time, effort, resources, and reputation that would be beyond what it was disposed—and perhaps even able—to pay. All that was certain was that no Russian government would find it in its heart to leave them alone.

VII

The first serious moves towards a comprehensive approach by the Russian regime to the multiple problems it considered its Jewish subjects to have forced upon it were taken by a handful of especially strong-minded, totally loyal, senior servants of the Autocracy itself. These were men of much the same culture and cast of mind, and in some cases of the same social and ethnic background, as their analogues in the higher reaches of the Austrian and Prussian bureaucracies. In common with the Austrians and the Prussians they too viewed the Jews as a people sunk in a state of social and spiritual disorder from which they needed to be redeemed. It was only when the common people of Jewry had been protected from the fallacious teachings and the material exploitation with which their betters in Jewry itself oppressed them that there would be a prospect of rendering them useful to the state. The Russian contribution to this simple doctrine was, indeed, to emphasize the role of the state. Far-reaching reform was indispensable, it was argued by the governor of Lithuania, I. G. Frizel (or Friesel); but if anything of value was to be achieved it would be by an enterprise that the state itself directed. Lithuania was a province very heavily populated by Jews and Governor Frizel was a man of great energy who had acquired decided, if not particularly accurate, views on the state of contemporary Russo-Polish Jewry, not excluding the theological and social divisions dividing it. He was noted too for his fierce dislike of the *kahal*, the communal governing body, which he charged, not without cause, with keeping the poorer classes of Jews in thrall. But his great object was less the reform of Jewish practices and institutions than the bringing of the Jews in their entirety into line with the Christian subjects of the Tsar. It was to this end that he wanted the autonomous Jewish school system revamped and the Jews redirected to the land and, generally, to harder, heavier, but supposedly more salubrious (morally speaking) trades and crafts—blacksmithing, for example, rather

[66] John D. Klier, *Russia Gathers her Jews: The Origins of the Jewish Question in Russia* (De Kalb, IL., 1986), 55–6.

than tailoring. He proposed that the practice of early marriage be ended and the autonomous Jewish judicial system sharply restricted in its authority. And like all administrators who found the standing difficulty of placing the Jews in any of the recognized social classes a permanent irritant, he wished to place them in three specially established *Jewish* classes: merchants, craftsmen, and free peasants.[67] It was Frizel's belief, too, that at the heart of the trouble lay the Jews' religion, more precisely, perhaps, the encrustations in which its original and not unworthy simplicities had come to be enveloped over many centuries. One way or another it too needed to be dealt with. Frizel's ideas were therefore harsh. They spoke too of exaggerated confidence in the ability of a government—the Russian or any other—to implement so ambitious a programme of social engineering. But there may be detected in his views and in those of some of his colleagues and epigoni a certain benevolence too, at least so far as the common people of Jewry were concerned. Certainly, he does not seem to have doubted that, with firmness all round, something could be made of them after all. He did not think their case hopeless. Nor did he think them depraved.[68]

The next, and much more influential Russian official to pronounce on the problem of the Jewish presence in Russia, Gavriil Romanovich Derzhavin (1743–1816), *did* see them as depraved. Sent to Byelorussia in June 1799 and then again in April 1800 to investigate the famine that had afflicted the province and the causes of the poverty and misery of the peasants generally, Derzhavin went well beyond his original remit. Rather than touching on the fundamental matters of serfdom or the agrarian regime as such, or the role and responsibility of the gentry for the condition of their peasants, he took up the matter of the Jews. It was the easier course, the more so as others before him had held the Jews responsible both for the peasants' hunger and for their endemic drunkenness. Some scholars have detected a deep, a priori hostility to Judaism and Jewry in Derzhavin's outlook. What is not in question is that he knew next to nothing about either before making his two brief visits to Byelorussia. Elements of traditional Christian thinking on the subject are certainly prominent in his thinking. For the rest, he appears to have relied on existing official reports, on what he had been told by members of the local nobility and gentry, much of it hearsay spiced with malignant and ignorant gossip, and on ideas he had gleaned from one or two maverick Jewish critics of the internal Jewish scene whom he had chanced to come across.[69] There is no evidence that he sought out anyone of genuine standing and authority in the relevant Jewish communities to hear what

---

[67] The Jews, having never been enserfed, were rated a 'free people' (*vol'niye liudi*).
[68] Ettinger, 'Ha-yesodot', 11.
[69] Among them Nota Kh. Notkin.

they might have to tell him. But, in any case, what he lacked in knowledge of his subject he made up for in personal status. Frizel had been a hard-working, journeyman-official, fated to be lost to sight upon the assassination of his master, Tsar Paul, and the (dubious) accession to the throne of his son, Alexander I. Derzhavin was a man of parts, a pillar of the Russian establishment, and a poet of genuine distinction. He had served the state as a provincial governor. He was a member of the Senate. For a time he was Tsar Alexander's minister of justice. His views received—and by virtue of his standing still deserve—attention.

The gist of Derzhavin's view of the Jews, as submitted to the Tsar in a long, formal 'Opinion' (*Mnenie*),[70] was that almost everything about them was deplorable. They were hopelessly corrupt and corrupting and very badly in need of correction and surveillance. It was necessary too, so far as possible, to keep them apart from the indigenous, Christian subjects of the empire—most urgently of all from the commendably God-fearing, hard-working, essentially innocent Russian peasant-serfs. Some or all of this had been said before. Derzhavin himself referred approvingly to the views of the sometime governor of Mogilev, Kokhovsky, when, like his predecessor, he pronounced the Jews an indolent and deceitful people, liable to criminal association and to counterfeiting, whose presence and activities led directly to the demoralization, impoverishment, and criminalization of the peasantry. It was, indeed, because the Jews had bought up the crops to distil alcohol, therefore raising the price of bread beyond the peasants' means, that the peasants of Byelorussia had starved. Where Derzhavin was more daring and original than Frizel or any of the others was in the plan of action which he outlined for the Tsar's attention, a scheme of breathtaking sweep, comprehensiveness, and inhumanity. He envisaged the reform of virtually every aspect of Jewish life, public and private. The Jews would retain their freedom to profess their religious beliefs. But other promises and guarantees made to them were to be withdrawn. All Jews in the Tsar's domains were to be counted, supplied with surnames, and divided up into four, specifically and exclusively Jewish classes or estates: merchants, artisans, farmers, and labourers. Merchants and a certain category of artisans would, under certain conditions, retain their existing rights to urban residence. Exceptionally, a limited number of lesser folk would be allowed to remain in the Byelorussian countryside, although on terms amounting to the condition of indentured labourers, care being taken, moreover, to separate them physically, street by street, from their Christian neighbours. But the rest, the overwhelming majority, would either have to move to the new Russian territories as agricultural settlers or leave Russia entirely. The *kahal* was to be

---

[70] *Mnenie ob otvrashchenii v Belorussii goloda i ustroistve byita evreev*, in Ya. Grot (ed.), *Sochineniya Derzhavina* (St Petersburg, 1878), vii. 274–355.

abolished on the grounds that it usurped functions that belonged properly to the government and served to reinforce and perpetuate the isolation of the Jews. Like Frizel, Derzhavin regarded it as the instrument whereby the elders of the Jews controlled and exploited the commonalty and the rabbis were enabled to maintain their people in a state of credulity, fanaticism, and backwardness.

Why the good Lord had put this 'dangerous' (*opasnyi*) people on the face of the earth was a puzzle to him, he wrote. But, if they had to be 'suffered' (*terpet'*), it was necessary to make them useful—useful to themselves, but useful to the societies in which they were embedded as well.[71] To that end, and in the interests of improved governance and social control generally, he wanted Russian Jewry, once the essential changes had been pushed through, to be reorganized on an entirely new, countrywide basis. They were to be ruled by a non-Jewish procurator who would be advised (but no more) by a Jewish Sanhedrin. The procurator alone would bear responsibility for the Jews' welfare and the right to represent his wards *vis-à-vis* the authorities, the Jews themselves losing the privilege of direct petition to, and negotiation with, the central or provincial authorities on their own behalf. A sort of Jewish protectorate would thus be formed, its advantage to the state lying in its possibilities: the revamping of the Jewish school system, for example; the provision that while Jewish religious teaching would still be allowed it would be systematically offset by the rabbis themselves having to offer their pupils unprejudiced accounts of other religions as well. Similarly, Jewish books, religious and secular, could be made subject to rigorous censorship and, the importation of Jewish religious books from abroad being prohibited totally, a carefully supervised, special Jewish publishing house could be established to fill the gap. Derzhavin envisaged proper and punctual private and public behaviour being sedulously inculcated into the entire Jewish population by subjecting them and their homes to regular inspection. They would, of course, be required to abandon their traditional style of clothing and to dress according 'to their station and calling' instead, although rabbis, in application of the same logic, would be entitled to clothe themselves as before. Only members of the procurator's Sanhedrin would, when in St Petersburg, be required to wear 'German-style frock coats'.[72]

Derzhavin's aim, in sum, was the complete and irreversible social and economic transmogrification of the Jews, a purpose to which their redeployment within the territories of the empire was, it seems, no more

---

[71] *Mnenie*, 277.

[72] *Mnenie, passim*. S. Dubnov, 'Sudby evreev Rossii v epokhu zapadnoi "pervoi emansipatsii" (1789–1815)', *Evreiskaya Starina*, 5 (St Petersburg, 1912), 3–25, 113–43; and Arnold Springer, 'Gavriil Derzhavin's Jewish Reform Project of 1800', *Canadian-American Slavic Studies*, 10, 1 (1976), 1–23.

than of secondary interest to him. In its inner spirit his plan had something in common therefore with that of the Josephine *Toleranzpatent*. It also had it in common with the Austrian measures of reform that it was not immediate results that were seriously to be expected, but rather, over several generations, a sea-change of an essentially cultural kind. Again, like the Austrians and the Prussians, Derzhavin (and his epigoni) sought always to distinguish useful Jews from others and to find a means of harnessing the immediately useful and the potentially useful to the purposes of the state. Where he differed from them, from the Prussians particularly, was in his being less intent on the expulsion of undesirables and in the confidence with which he envisaged the social and moral re-education of Russia's Jews. But then his blueprint relied on a totally new form of governance being imposed on them, one that would provide, as none ever had before, for a degree of social control that was not far short of total.

Derzhavin's 'opinion' was submitted to the Senate in December 1800. But it was not until November 1802, under the new Emperor Alexander, that it was acted upon. A special committee of inquiry entitled Committee on the Improvement of the Jews (Komitet o blagoustroistve evreev) was formed to look into the entire question of the status of the Jews and the regulation—and regularizing—of their lives within the lands of the Autocracy. Derzhavin's report and proposals were among the materials put before it. So it seems was a separate, very much shorter memorandum composed by N. P. Rumyantsev, minister of commerce at the time, later to be minister for foreign affairs. Rumyantsev's ideas were not especially original, but the intention to be realistic before all else was evident. His point of departure was the obvious if rarely stated one that the twin policies of keeping the Jews out of Russia and Russian life and allowing them, at the same time, to participate in the commercial life of the country were mutually contradictory. To resolve the contradiction, it was necessary to look at the condition of the Jews directly and consider what needed to be done about them. One could only go so far. Care should certainly be taken to avoid the sort of embarrassment the British government had had to face in 1753.[73] But consideration should be given too to the possibility of borrowing something from the 'prudent regulations [*ot blagorazum-nykh pravil*]' of Joseph II. The Jews' 'vile [*gnusnoe*]' commercial practices should be suppressed. But the main thing was positive action to move them into useful occupations, agriculture especially. If that was done successfully, then, all appropriate precautionary measures being taken, it would be reasonable to allow them to live in all parts of Russia. On the other hand, until that was the case, namely until they had changed their ways, they would have to remain under the existing special regime and the laws prohibiting their entry into inner Russia maintained—although

---

[73] A reference to the Pelham government's abortive 'Jew Bill'. See above, pp. 38 f.

again, that said, the Jews were nevertheless to be treated fairly, as the laws of the empire prescribed.[74]

The Committee on the Improvement of the Jews itself was of a high level. The minister of the interior, V. P. Kochubey, presided. Derzhavin, now the recognized authority on the subject in high places, and M. M. Speransky, the rising star among the new Tsar Alexander's advisers, were members. So were two Polish noblemen of the first rank, Adam Czartoryski[75] and Seweryn Potocki. Despite the cumulative influence of such men on the spot as Frizel and the other governors of the western territories, not to speak of that of Derzhavin himself, everything suggests that its members were expected to have views of their own. And this indeed proved to be the case. In the Committee's minutes (for 20 September 1803) there were recorded, for example, the remarkable observations that 'reforms brought about by the state are, as a rule, unstable [*preobrazovaniya proizvodimyya vlastiyu pravitel'stva, voobshche ne prochny*]' and that it was best to 'guide' the Jews to 'perfection [*k sovershenstvu*]' from a certain distance. It was therefore better to remove those obstacles that were likely to divert the Jews from following the course the state wished them to travel, rather than to seek to shunt them along it by force. Generally, it was thought that in the case of the Jews compulsion was to be avoided. The most efficacious of operative principles, the Committee believed, was that there should be as few prohibitions and as much liberty as possible (*skol' mozhno menshe zapreshchenii, skol' mozhno bol'she svobody*). These, after all, were no more than the elements of every social order. What was really needed in dealing with the Jews was 'quiet encouragement'. It was this that would serve the interests of the state best.[76] All this was far removed from Derzhavin's *mnenie*.

The tone in which the Committee's final paper was written was equally mild, which may have had something to do with the fact that Derzhavin himself had retired from the Committee before its work was completed and that it was Speransky who was in the ascendant. The religious ferocity that had informed Derzhavin's original report (his assertion that the Jews, as the enemies of Christianity, *deserved* punishment, for example) was absent, as was the idea of subjecting Russo-Polish Jewry to a wholly restructured internal hierarchy of the Autocracy's own design. On the

---

[74] N. P. Rumyantsev, 'Evrei', in D. E. Feldman (ed.), 'Trebuyutsya spravedlivye ogranicheniya', *Istoricheskii Arkhiv*, 5 (1994), 205–8.

[75] Fourteen years earlier, at the age of 18, Czartoryski had been a pupil of Scipione Piattoli (W. H. Zawadzki, 'Prince Adam Czartoryski and Napoleonic France, 1801–1805: A Study in Political Attitudes', *Historical Journal*, 18, 2 (1975), 257 n. 75). How far the Polish prince's contribution to the St Petersburg committee was governed by what (if anything) Piattoli had taught him is of course a matter for speculation alone.

[76] Dubnov, 'Sudby evreev', 18–22; Yu. I. Gessen, *Evrei v Rossii* (St Petersburg, 1906), i. 75–6.

other hand, in much of its substance and in the general thrust of the
working philosophy on which it was based, the Committee's completed
report, submitted to Tsar Alexander in October 1804, displayed something of Derzhavin's imprint after all—which, when all is said and done,
was itself no more than a close reflection of the political principles on
which the Autocracy always and ultimately relied. A high degree of compulsion was to be the order of the day, despite what had been said in the
course of discussion. The Jews were to be subject to re-education and
'improvement', like it or not. They were to cease to employ Hebrew in
their documents. And, most tellingly, they were to be removed bodily
and forcibly from the countryside and an effort made to resettle them
elsewhere in large numbers. Just how far the terms of the final recommendations were determined by the Committee's desire to ensure a good
reception on their submission to the Autocrat, or actually anticipate his
wishes, is unclear. It remains, that the Committee's recommendations
proved acceptable to him and that appropriate regulations were promulgated as a Statute for the Jews *Polozhenie dlya evreev* on 9 December
1804.[77]

Looking both back and forward in time, the Statute for the Jews was,
in its way, a remarkable document. Much attention (no less than eight of
the fifty-four clauses) was paid to the prominence of the Jews both in the
distilling industry and in the retailing of spirits to the peasantry in the
thousands of tiny taverns in what had once been Polish domains. Everything was to be done to eliminate them. This, of course, was a perennial
issue and to be expected: Frizel, Derzhavin, and virtually all the other
observers and would-be social engineers who had applied their minds to
the newly annexed territories before and after the promulgation of the
Statute, had duly commented on the endemic drunkenness of the peasantry and on the prominence of Jews in the trade. All had then gone on
to link the latter to the former as cause and effect. That Jews were no
more than *lessors* of the nobility's established monopoly of the right to distil alcohol and trade in it and that there was no reason to suppose that if
the Jews were eliminated from the chain others would not take their
place were aspects of the problem that were, as usual, ignored. The absurd
thesis that to remove the Jews was to cure the peasants continued to be
relied upon, at least notionally: how seriously it was ever really taken by
people in the field there is no way of knowing. But in any event, severe
penalties, up to and including penal servitude for life in Siberia, were
provided in case of violation of the new regulations. There was to be no
relaxation of the ancient rule that Jews (negligible exceptions apart) were
to be prevented from penetrating into 'inner Russia'. Provision was made

---

[77] *Polnoe sobranie zakonov rossiskoi imperii*, xxviii ([St Petersburg], 1830), No. 21547,
731–7.

for an eventual, but determined, attack on the rabbinate's ancient—but in the government's view presumptuous and unacceptable—practice of adjudicating cases that went beyond the strict limits of the religious (as opposed to the civil and criminal) domain, but also on rabbinical independence and authority generally. Somewhat in the spirit, although far from the actual letter, of Derzhavin's recommendations, vastly closer official supervision of the rabbis was to be instituted. Procedures for appointment to rabbinical office and rules governing the emoluments to which rabbis might (or, in the official view, might not) be entitled were to be laid down. Finally, in the general interests of administrative order and convenience Jews were to assume surnames; and

No Jew, in any part of Russia whatsoever, shall be tolerated so long as he remains unregistered in any one of the established . . . classes. Jews who fail to provide [on demand, for inspection] an appropriate certificate, written and issued in due form, will be treated with all the severity of the law as vagrants. (Clause 30)

But the Jews themselves could take some comfort in it being expressly stated that there was to be no question of forcible conversion to Christianity; that they were not to be oppressed or harassed in the observance of their faith and in their general social activities; that the private property of the Jews remained inviolable; and that Jews were not to be exploited or enserfed. They were, on the contrary, to enjoy the same, presumably full protection of the law that was accorded other subjects of the realm. They were not to be subject to the legal jurisdiction of the landowners on whose estates they might happen to be resident. And they were to be encouraged in every way the Committee could imagine—by fiscal and other economic incentives, for example, by the grant of land and loans to develop it, by permission to move to the New Russian Territories in the south—to undergo decisive and (so it was presumed) irreversible change in the two central respects which both Frizel and Derzhavin had indeed, and perfectly reasonably, regarded as vital: education and employment. In this they were to be encouraged very strongly; but they were not to be forced.

In regard to their principal concern, the authors of the Statute were generally confident, optimistic, and, all things considered, not wholly illiberal. This, as in the case of Joseph of Austria's *Toleranzpatent* of 1782, was education. The first three of the Statute's fifty-four clauses laid down that all Jewish young people were to be entitled to admission to all elementary schools, high schools, and universities in Russia on an equal basis with all other young people; that under no circumstances was advantage to be taken of their presence in Russian schools to procure their apostasy; that they were not to be compelled to study matters that were contrary to, or even merely incompatible with, their religion; and, surprisingly (considering the constant harping on the supposedly unattractive, insalubrious, and generally anomalous and hateful style in which Jews were held to be generally dressed), children in elementary schools might continue to wear their 'Jewish clothing [*plat'e evreiskoe*]'. Only those attending high school would be obliged to wear German or Polish dress—'in the interests of uniformity and good manners [*dlya edinobraziya i blagopristoinosti*]'.[78] The consequences of these provisions would be slow to mature. But eventually they would prove, much as the Tsar's Committee on the Improvement of the Jews had hoped, of capital importance.

Of more immediate concern were the provisions setting down the means by which the Jews were to earn their living, the role they were to play in the economy, the linked matters of their civil status and, especially, the territories in which they would be at liberty to reside. The Jews were indeed to be divided into four classes: farmers (free, it was emphasized, not enserfed), artisans, merchants, and miscellaneous city-dwellers. In certain stated provinces Jewish agriculturists would be entitled both to purchase land or lease it and to hire labour to help them work it. Government land (up to 30,000 *desyatiny*[79] in the first instance) would be set aside for them in the new territories. Loans would be available to those who were unable to raise the purchase money or afford the initial costs of settlement and there would be an extended release from taxation. Those taking up agriculture within the existing areas of Jewish settlement would be relieved of the customary double taxation. Jewish entrepreneurs moving into industries favoured by the state would enjoy similar financial and fiscal encouragement. All crafts not specifically forbidden them by law would now to be open to Jewish artisans. And finally, Jewish industrialists, artisans, and merchants would be allowed to travel to the 'inner provinces and even to the capital cities'[80] at any rate on a *temporary* basis, on their legitimate business, or for training, or for demonstration of their skills and achievements, provided they had the authorization of the provincial governors concerned who, in turn, were required to report to the minister of the interior on the grant of such travel documents on a monthly basis.

Such Jews, [it was laid down] on arriving [in inner Russia] for brief periods, would, however, be under an obligation to wear German clothing, as would their wives and children, so as not to differ from others. Should they wear their own [traditional Jewish] clothing, they were not to be tolerated at all and were immediately to be expelled by the police.[81]

---

[78] The obligation to wear 'Russian' or 'German' or 'Polish' clothing applied to certain categories of adult Jews as well, for example, as to those who had been elected to municipal office.

[79] Roughly 81,000 acres or 328 sq. kilometres.

[80] i.e. St Petersburg and Moscow.

[81] Clause 28.

However, the Statute of 1804, the Jewish constitution, as some called it, was never fully implemented. The will to do so was not lacking. It was rather that in the course of the decade that followed other, greater matters (the Napoleonic wars among them) supervened and attitudes to the Jews—and to what *they* might feel about the Statute's provisions—varied with the vicissitudes of Franco-Russian relations. Tsar Alexander's own changes of mind about the principles appropriate to the governance of Russia as a whole had their effect as well. So did the dawning by stages within the administration itself of a somewhat deeper understanding of what might really be involved in a scheme to transplant very substantial numbers of Jews from the western provinces to the new territories, what its cost to the Treasury might amount to, and what social consequences were likely to flow from it if its aims were ever actually achieved. Did the Tsar and his ministers and advisers really want to facilitate the entry of the Jews into the Russian body politic even in the attenuated, not to say sterilized, manner the Statute envisaged? And finally and in the event decisively, there was the government's recognition that the first and perhaps only sure result of a determined effort to effect the changes in Jewry that it held to be desirable would be the irreversible pauperization and embitterment of a vast, admittedly unwanted, but hitherto politically harmless population.

A generation would pass before a tougher, somewhat more carefully thought-out, by intention more radical, and in practice very much harsher set of measures for the regularization of the lives of the emperor's Jewish subjects would be drawn up and a really powerful attempt to implement them made. In the interim, certain important formal precedents had none the less been established, ideas had crystallized, approaches frozen, and a series of minor moves of an openly restrictive kind launched on the ground—to be only very marginally mitigated by occasional flurries of good intentions. Not the least of these was a substantial contribution to the rapid consolidation of what would later become the officially demarcated Pale of Jewish Settlement (*Cherta postoyannoi evreiskoi osedlosti*).[82] But in sum, both the broad outlines of the problem of the Jews as it would long be perceived at the pinnacle of government in St Petersburg and the general terms in which it was thought proper to approach it, had, by the end of Alexander I's reign, been quite firmly established.

[82] For a map of the Pale of Settlement, see below, pp. 300–1.

2

Disjunctions

I

FEW in Jewry anywhere in Europe had anticipated emancipation. All that was certain about it when it was first enacted in France and as the prospect of its enactment elsewhere began to loom, was that it augured unprecedented but also irreversible change in the structure and character of the Jewish people. From this point on, the questions on which virtually everything of importance in the lives of the Jews of Europe would turn was whether, if only as a hypothesis, such change was to be welcomed or rejected; and whether the welcome—or rejection—was to be flat or qualified. Upon these issues Jews in all parts of the continent would now begin to be deeply and, in the course of time, irreparably divided.

It is useful to recall that in France itself no Jews had gone so far as to ask for emancipation before the revolutionary summer of 1789. And those who, after July of that year, had been encouraged to do so by the revolutionaries' evident disposition to attend to the matter were all either eccentric in their persons or unrepresentative in some other way of the Jews of France in their majority: men whose place was on the social and ideological margins of their people, if not beyond. Zalkind Hourwitz (1740–1812),[1] a notable example, was not a native of France at all, but a displaced Polish Jew who had rather more in common with Shelomo Polonus of Vilna[2] as far as the matter of emancipation was concerned than with the common run of Jewish contemporaries in his adopted country. In France itself Hourwitz had gone very far towards breaking with his original, hugely restricted circumstances. By dint of painful self-instruction he had acquired sufficient command of the French and German languages and the secular learning of the day to find employment in the oriental department of the Bibliothèque Royale. He had launched himself with some success in pre-revolutionary Paris as a free-floating intellectual and on the eve of the Revolution cut a minor figure in Paris as a publicist and political activist. And that he was a man of irrepressibly independent views and comportment was demonstrated

---

[1] On Hourwitz's career, see especially Frances Malino, *A Jew in the French Revolution: The Life of Zalkind Hourwitz* (Oxford, 1996).

[2] See above, pp. 76–7.

impressively not only in the parallel position that he insistently claimed for himself as a self-appointed spokesman for Jewish interests, but in his being at one and the same time intensely and genuinely loyal to his people and deeply and openly critical of Jewry's actual social arrangements and leaders. Hourwitz had first staked out a position for himself in this latter sphere by entering what was to be the celebrated essay competition launched by the Royal Society for Arts and Sciences at Metz in 1787 on the subject 'Are there ways and means of rendering the Jews happier and more useful in France?'[3] He did well, sharing the prize with the abbé Grégoire and the Protestant lawyer Adolphe Thièry. But, an altogether obscurer figure than Grégoire and totally without private means, he had to wait until the year of the Revolution itself before finding the funds to get his essay published[4]—a delay that must have contributed to his analysis of the Jewish condition and to his prescription for its improvement failing to leave more than a limited mark on contemporary opinion,[5] and hardly any at all on posterity. But the greater weakness of his essay as a contribution to public debate was that in its general thrust Hourwitz's 'Apologie des Juifs' did not, on the face of things, differ all that drastically from Grégoire's. Both wrote as men of the Enlightenment. Both denounced society for subjecting the Jews to an intolerable system of multiple social and economic constraints. Both were critical of Jewry's own internal regime and of the precedents and mores on which that regime relied. Most of Hourwitz's specific recommendations—release from special, restrictive laws and regulations, admission of Jewish children to the general school system, military service (subject to safeguards for Sabbath observance), use of French for all commercial purposes, and so forth—were, when taken together, quite close to the now well-established Josephine notion of what counted as a policy and plan of 'toleration'. In sum, like Grégoire and Dohm and the rest, Hourwitz had been intent, before all else, on there being laid the groundwork from which it would in due course be possible to move the Jews forward to modernization and *aggiornamento*. Certainly, he voiced no demand for full and explicit civil and political emancipation, least of all in anything like the terms that would eventually be decreed by the National Assembly four years later. If he considered doing so, it is probable that he judged the time—two years before the Revolution—unpropitious. Besides, he thought radical legislation unnecessary. When a royal edict of toleration in favour of the Protestants was issued in November 1787, Hourwitz added a gloss to the original text of his essay, arguing that what he proposed was the 'more

[3] See above, p. 56.

[4] As *Apologie des Juifs en réponse à la question: Est-il des moyens de rendre les Juifs plus heureux et plus utiles en France?* (Metz, 1789).

[5] Although Shelomo Polonus of Vilna is known to have read an abridged version of Hourwitz's essay.

practicable for it being unnecessary to make new laws on the matter of the Jews and that it would suffice if His Majesty deigned to proclaim that they were included in the category of non-Catholics'.[6]

Yet all this said, the difference between Hourwitz and his competitors was profound. Being a Jew—one who had emerged, moreover, out of the fastnesses of the ancient Jewish Tradition itself—he was vastly better informed about Jewry in general and the actual content of traditional Jewish theology and law in particular than Dohm or Grégoire or Thiéry and their like were ever likely to be. There was, moreover, no thought in Hourwitz's mind, as there was in Grégoire's and Domb's, of the liberation and modernization of the Jews leading them eventually into the Christian fold. There is no suggestion in his plan of the Jews having to undergo a form of triage: of their being divided actually or even conceptually into the privileged and the non-privileged, the useful and the useless, the native and the foreign. His subject was undifferentiated Jewry, Jewry as a whole; and it is especially when he turned inward, speaking as a Jew and with the authority of a man of substantial traditional learning himself, that he struck his most authentic, individual, and, at moments, even passionate notes. For finally at the heart of his argument lay his criticism of the Talmudic corpus and of the rabbinate whose business it was to expound it and whose social and moral authority turned, of course, on its command of the Talmud's content and method. Hourwitz was careful to defend both Jewish learning and the rabbis themselves from the sweeping, vulgar accusations commonly levelled against them by the men of the Enlightenment, Voltaire among them. But he made no bones about his view of the internal constraints to which Jews in all parts were subject through the workings of the rabbinical–Talmudic system: of the limits it set upon their worldly freedom, of the manner in which it effectively barred their entry into society on a basis of equality. The social liberation of the Jews was conditional, he believed, on the power that the rabbis and the *parnassim* jointly exercised over ordinary people in their daily lives being terminated—in great matters as in small.

Their rabbis and syndics [i.e. *parnassim*] must be strictly forbidden to assume the least authority over their fellows outside the synagogue, or refuse honours to those who have shaved off their beards, or curled their hair, or who dress like Christians, go to the theatre, or observe other customs that bear no actual relation to their religion, but derive from superstition alone as a means of distinguishing them from other peoples.[7]

---

[6] *Apologie*, 68–9, 70.

[7] Ibid. 38–9. Hourwitz's essentially irreligious approach set him apart from an otherwise somewhat analogous figure, Menaḥem Mendel Lefin of Satanov, like himself a learned Polish Jew with advanced opinions in which he had been confirmed in the course of an extended stay in Berlin. Lefin strongly favoured secular learning, was intensely critical of what he took to be an obscurantist rabbinate, and was exceedingly dismissive of all that smacked of mysticism, Hasidism (a school that relied on charismatic leaders and emphasized the joys rather than the rules of Judaism) included. But he had no doubt that

This was an argument for which the leaders of Jewish orthodoxy in France never forgave Hourwitz, his ideological sins being compounded in their eyes by his Polish origins—of which, it needs to be said, he was far from making a secret. When, later, under the Napoleonic regime, it was proposed that he attend the Assembly of Jewish Notables a number of rabbis threatened to leave if he so much as appeared among them. And a full century and a half later, when it was proposed that his arrival in France be marked by a modest academic celebration, the most distinguished historian of French Jewry of the day, in an article entitled 'Un Juif polonais en France', took the trouble to sniff: 'It is is not enough to come from the East to be a source of illumination.'[8]

The leaders of the small communities in south-west France known colloquially as 'Portugais' (and in pre-revolutionary official jargon as 'les Anciens de la Nation Portugaise') were marginal men of another kind. The 'Portugais' were the highly self-conscious descendants of people of *converso* (or crypto-Jewish) origin who had been allowed to settle in Bordeaux and Bayonne and a few other localities upon their flight from the Iberian peninsula and who had gradually and rather circumspectly returned to an open profession of their faith. But it was not their antecedents alone that distinguished them from the much more numerous and, in the long term, more important communities of eastern France. As would be pointed out in the National Assembly, they were already largely free of the restrictive regulations that still bore heavily on the Alsatians and Lorrainers. They were already profoundly acculturated. And their very Judaism was selective and, in a sense, of their own devising. A contemporary noted, that

The Jews of Bordeaux and Bayonne, far from making the Mishna and the Talmud, like all other Jews, the fundamental basis of their discipline, reject that within it which they find contrary or inconsistent with common sense and a literal reading of the Bible on which they rely for the dogmas to which they subscribe.[9]

Chrétien de Malesherbes, the royal minister, instructed by the Conseil d'État to look into the question of the Jews just prior to the Revolution, was a staunch enough royalist, but a man of liberal views. He turned out to be sympathetic to the idea of emancipation and, unusually among European statesmen set by their masters to deal with the matter, prepared to inquire into the opinions of the Jews themselves. An informal committee of inquiry was established. A series of what seem to have been

religion was the motor force of Jewry and was not to be circumvented or thrown overboard. Lefin was a protégé of Prince Czartoryski and played a small role in the abortive negotiations on a form of limited emancipation of the Jews at the time of the Four-Year Sejm.

    [8] Robert Anchel, 'Un Juif polonais en France. Zalkind Hourwitz', *Univers israélite*, 92, 38 (1936/7), 505–6.
    [9] Cited in Z. Szajkowski, 'Hitnagshuyot ha-ortodoxim ve-ha-reformim be-zarfat', *Horeb*, 14–15 (1960), 257 n. 16.

fairly discreet talks were held with small groups of Jewish notables, the one really formidable delegation among them being that which the Jews of Bordeaux had dispatched to Paris to represent them. There, the 'Portugais', explained that their main concern was to ensure that they should continue to enjoy their unique condition of *de facto* toleration.[10] Their particular and, in the circumstances, not unreasonable fear was that a formal redetermination of policy on the Jews of France in their entirety, while it might carry some benefits for all, would in practice work against them. That the government was likely to demand that it be generously compensated for granting the Jews of Bordeaux liberties which, for all practical purposes, they already enjoyed worried them as well. But above all, they were desperate to keep their case apart from that of the Alsatian Jews. It was only in the following year, when the matter of full emancipation for all Jews had already been raised in the new National Assembly by others, that they proceeded to demand full and *formal* equality of status with other Frenchmen, upon which the Assembly, in the event, as we have seen, was quick to decree their absolute emancipation, leaving the much more controversial case of the Alsatian Jews in abeyance.[11] As for the Alsatian Jews themselves, they had been slower still to ask for liberation. There is no evidence of their authorized representatives pressing for anything remotely of the kind before the Revolution; and when they made their own first approach to the new National Assembly it was to ask for no more than an end to the special taxes laid upon them and the abolition of the residential, and travel restrictions to which they were subject. The greatest anxiety of the Alsatians was to retain their own internal communal autonomy—to which end, with only rare exceptions, they (at all events, their authorized representatives) were prepared to forgo emancipation altogether. Only when they learned that other branches of French Jewry, the small community in Paris among them, were prepared to yield to the demand that they give up their ancient corporate status did the Alsatians and Lorrainers fall, reluctantly, into line.

II

None of this should have been unexpected. Jewish orthodoxy in its pristine form had always been deeply conservative, profoundly interested in beating back all that signified social, cultural, and intellectual change and

[10] In which plea, it may be said, they had the support of the city authorities of Bordeaux who were happy to confirm that they, for their part, saw no cause not to include the 'Portugais' in the newly tolerated category of 'non-Catholics'.

[11] For the reports of delegations sent to Paris by the Jews of Bordeaux, see Z. Szajkowski, 'Mishlaḥoteihem shel yehudei bordo el va'adat malzerb (1788) ve-el ha-aseifa ha-le'umit (1790)', *Zion*, 18, 1–2 (1953).

diversion, immensely resistant to the idea of accommodation to altered circumstances. This is not to say that it permitted itself the intellectual and moral luxury of total withdrawal from the world around it. It was rather that the initial primary division of opinion within the communities would therefore be between those whose instinct it was to resolve on total rejection of what their political and alien masters seemed to wish of them and those who were drawn to the prospect of new opportunities despite an anxiety to retain a foothold or more in their old, closed world as they proceeded to tread with varying degrees of enthusiasm, caution, and trepidation in the unfamiliar waters of the new. The two invariable obstacles to any such halfway house, however, were the intensely alien character of the world without and the view upon which, on reflection, the primary moral and intellectual leaders of orthodoxy were to settle, namely that a halfway house of any kind was fundamentally incompatible with authentic Judaism and the survival of the Jewish people as they understood both the one and the other.

On few subjects were the traditional and most authoritative leaders and spokesmen for European Jewry so circumspect as on Christianity itself and, by extension, the Christian Churches: the Roman Catholic and the Russian Orthodox before all others. In the safety of twelfth-century Muslim Egypt Maimonides had been free to write that

With regard also to 'that certain man' [i.e. Jesus] who imagined that he would be the Messiah and was executed by order of the Court, Daniel already prophesied concerning him, as it is said, 'and the men of violence among your own people shall lift themselves up in order to fulfil the vision; but they shall fail.' Is there then a greater failure than this? For all the prophets foretold that the Messiah would redeem Israel and deliver them and gather their exiles and strengthen their observance of the precepts. Whereas *he* [Jesus] caused Israel to be put to the sword, their remnant to be scattered and humiliated, the Torah to be displaced, and the greater part of the world to be misled into serving a god other than the Lord.[12]

No Jew in Christian Europe who ventured to reflect on the subject thought otherwise of the intrinsic validity of Christianity or of the incalculable injury it had caused his people. But comment of so dangerous an order would be subject to routine internal censorship. Even private, unwritten comment was dangerous if reported, doubly and trebly so if, as was always possible, it was misreported, torn out of context, or ascribed to the rabbis with deliberately injurious intent by apostates, *provocateurs*, and *malshinim* (delators). But reference to Christianity was rare for a more fundamental reason than fear. It was a central and telling fact of Jewish life and learning that neither the people nor their rabbis took much interest

---

[12]   *Ha-yad ha-ḥazaka*, 'Hilkhot melakhim', xi. Cited in English translation in H. H. Ben-Sasson, 'The Reformation in Contemporary Jewish Eyes', Israel Academy of Sciences and Humanities, *Proceedings*, 4, 12 (1970). Maimonides's reference is to the Book of Daniel 11: 14.

in other religious systems *per se* and where any thought at all was given to Christianity specifically it was as to a religion that to a Jewish mind unfailingly verged on the idolatrous. The doctrines that most obviously separated it from Judaism (the Messianic status of Jesus, the Trinity, the Virgin Birth, the Resurrection) were, in so far as they were known about, apt to be dismissed as rubbishy paganism. Many of the commonest of Christian practices (adoration of Saints, for example) struck Jews as pantheistic. The grounds for concluding that Christians, whether they knew it or not, indulged in the idolatrous worship of images were all around them and seemed overwhelming. This is not to say that none in Jewry, notably among the learned, ever raised his eyes from the sacred literature that was his proper object of study to observe his neighbours, nor that some of those who did were not led in due course to accord a cautious, if silent welcome to certain aspects of the Protestant Reformation, for example. The Reformation did seem to some Jews to signal a move away from those practices in the Roman Church which struck them as especially idolatrous and a mark of progress therefore towards somewhat more explicit reliance on what Christians termed the Old Testament. If it marked the beginning of a reversion to Judaism's absolutely central prohibition on graven images,[13] and perhaps to Judaism generally then, perhaps, there was some small reason to be hopeful after all: some reason—but not much, as the turn taken in the Lutheran camp especially soon demonstrated. But, in any event, the Jews' abhorrence of Christianity, the intensely negative light in which non-Jewish society had always been regarded, and the deeply ingrained suspicion and fear in which all forms of non-Jewish authority were commonly held all went beyond the theological.

The Christian world in which the Jews of the greater part of Europe were embedded struck them as barbarous and hypocritical beyond repair. Secular and clerical authorities spoke repeatedly of peace and loving kindness. Their actual conduct, so far as most Jews could see and judge for themselves, was shot through and through with violence and cruelty: thus in the Christians' own treatment of each other, certainly so in their treatment of the Jews themselves. The lesson of Exile in Europe was that as much by sword as by word the masters of Christendom had sought to bring about if not the death of Jewry, at any rate its decimation; and that failing that, they had sought to ensure that Jews lived out their lives in the greatest possible moral and material squalor and degradation. There had been a time, to be sure, when Christian theologians were anxious to challenge the rabbis to engage in ostensibly even-handed formal debate. But such debates were never even-handed in practice. They were not debates that Jews were ever allowed to win, nor such as any possible good could ever come to them. If it appeared to authority that the churchmen, as was

---

[13] See Ben-Sasson, 'Reformation', *passim*.

hoped, had the better of the argument, pressure on the Jews to follow through and apostatize would intensify, perhaps insuperably. If it was the rabbis who appeared to be having the upper dialectical hand, the Christian response was likely to be vengeful and doubly devastating. Success, even so much as a demonstrably good defence of the Jewish position (there was no question ever of a direct attack on the *Christian* position itself), could only be a source of fleeting, private satisfaction. This the rabbis were glad to forgo. For at bottom there remained the certain knowledge that the more serious and open-minded the theological debate the greater the danger of the old spectre of Judaism as a living threat to the Church rising anew; and with it the suspicion that the Jews, or at all events their rabbis, continued to harbour secret proselytizing (so-called Judaizing) ambitions. In fact, the Jews of Christian Europe (like the Jews of the Islamic lands) had learned to shun missionary activity and, generally, high and low, were all aware of the danger of crossing or provoking the gentiles in the crucially delicate realms of faith and religion. There was some satisfaction therefore in noting that in more recent times the Christian urge to confront the Jews theologically, common enough in medieval, and not unknown in Renaissance Europe, had largely faded away. Such, at all events, had been the conventional wisdom for some time. It therefore followed, by the same token, that to the learned and conventional mind in Jewry plans and proposals directed explicitly at the ordering and reordering of the Jews' internal social affairs could not fail to be alarming in the extreme. Thus it was when the intentions of authority were ostensibly well-meaning, even benevolent. Doubly so, of course, when its benevolence was in doubt. The closer one's attachment to ancient Jewish tradition and practice, the stronger would be one's inclination to fend off such proposals; and, when the pressure to accommodate oneself to them grew, to temporize. It was true and plain that the offer of improvement in the civil status of the Jews was nowhere linked in any overt, obvious, and explicit way—in France, indeed, in any way at all— to the demand that the Jews, as private individuals, abandon their faith. Even in Russia where, once the Autocracy had made up its mind on the matter of the Jews, official thinking was to go a good deal further, there was no serious question of force being employed frankly and openly to such an end. But the hope that eventually, as the Jews entered what was, of course, a *Christian* society, and as they discovered the truths and beauties on which it was held to be founded, they would be drawn to it in religious terms as well was at least implicit in the measures adopted in Austria and Prussia, and in Russia all but explicit. Such, at all events, was the ultimate purpose. The teachings and terminology of the Enlightenment were manifest, to be sure, almost everywhere in the details and language of the various edicts of toleration and decrees of partial emancipation. But to the informed, thoughtful, and devout Jew this in itself was cold comfort. For while it might be the case that the demand that the Jews accept baptism as the price of freedom had been abandoned, the provisions of the various laws and edicts—to say nothing of the thinking that lay behind them—struck unmistakably and with deliberately injurious intent at the traditional *conduct* of the Jews. In Judaism, unlike Christianity, the decisive emphasis had always been on behaviour, rather than on belief. Faith and belief were of the utmost importance, but they were not ordinarily matters for discussion, least of all for regular examination. Nor, more generally, were the secular and religious realms regarded as distinguishable from each other. The lives of the Jews might not be seamless webs in practice, but the thrust of the teaching was that they should strive to make them so. It followed, therefore, that even ostensibly innocent and benevolent measures to encourage the entry of Jewish children into schools which catered to the general population and wean Jews away from the use of their own languages and script for mundane purposes signalled nothing but danger to the devout. The promise—*a fortiori* the threat—of state education being extended to the Jews even on a voluntary basis horrified and frightened them. What could state education of the young mean except a paving of the way to eventual de-Judaization? What could consent to the state's assumption of responsibility for schooling signify except a reduction of the realm of the Law—whence a narrowing of rabbinical jurisdiction and rabbinical authority and a surrender of a central function of the Jewish community itself from time immemorial? The more closely those who remained wedded to the old forms and principles of Judaism considered what appeared to be on offer, the readier they were, therefore, to forgo its presumed advantages, the more so as in eastern Europe especially there were additional reasons for caution. For while the issue of emancipation was fated to remain no more than hypothetical there for very many years to come, all knew that its origins were French and revolutionary.

There was some general, non-specific awareness even in Poland and the western provinces of Russia that the French bore a promise of political and, perhaps, economic liberty too in their knapsacks. And something too was known of Napoleon's retreat from the originally unambiguous position of the French revolutionaries articulated in the decree of 1791. The sobering impact of the conjunction of these contradictory signals served to reinforce the ancient Jewish instinct to keep out of the quarrels of the gentiles so far as possible; and Jewish calm stood in sharp contrast, therefore, to the relative warmth with which some, though by no means all, ethnic Poles received those they hoped would be their deliverers. But then the prospect, followed by the brief experience, of renewed Polish rule under French patronage held little attraction for most of the Jews concerned, some scattered exceptions to the contrary, the models (or model) for the character of Jankiel, the patriotic Jewish innkeeper in

Mickiewicz's epic poem *Pan Tadeusz* among them. The ancient argument against Jews in any way risking a quarrel with whoever held the actual power in the land could and did marginally work the other way, notably in Lithuania where members of the Polish nobility lent their support to the French and many of those Jews who were politically and economically dependent upon their Polish masters went a good part of the way with them willy-nilly.[14] None the less, by and large, where it was necessary and politic to make a stand one way or the other and the choice was to some extent a free one, it was the Russians who had the support of the Jewish inhabitants of the domains over which they ruled or to which they laid claim. For in general, the Russian *status quo* had come in the course of a decade or so to be seen as preferable to the Polish *status quo ante*; and the Russian authorities had noted and encouraged this tendency by taking the precautionary step of issuing vague, but encouraging promises of good things to come for the Jews once the war was over and by granting minor immediate improvements—some easing of the tax burden, for example. Still, more important than any such considerations was the conviction held by the traditional leaders of Jewish opinion and the traditional wielders of communal authority that the Autocracy was firm at any rate in its wish to maintain the authority of the rabbis—clipped, no doubt, and subordinate to state interests, but at any rate in place, as was consistent with its insistence on organized religion of any kind as a primary instrument of social control all round. The French, in contrast, were suspected, not without reason, of course, of being intent on eroding it. 'It has been put to me,' wrote the influential Hasidic leader, R. Shne'ur Zalman of Lyady, as the French invasion of Russia began in 1812 and all-round political change seemed for once to be in serious prospect, 'that, if Bonaparte were victorious, happiness in Israel would increase and the dignity of the Jewish people magnified.' But to believe that, he informed his people, would be a very gross error of judgement. To maintain loyalty to Russia was not only a matter of simple prudence. It was vital to Jewry itself *per se*. For whereas Napoleon was godless, the Tsar was not. If the French were victorious the Jews would be stripped not merely of their worldly goods, but of Judaism itself. The consequence of liberation would be a

parting and estrangement of the hearts of the Jews from their Father in heaven. If, on the other hand, our sovereign Alexander were victorious, the poverty of Israel would [doubtless] increase, and the dignity of Israel would [as before] be downtrodden. But the hearts of the Jews would be bound and attached and joined [more strongly than ever] to their Father in heaven.[15]

[14] I. Bartal, ' "Ha-model ha-mishni"—ẓarfat ke-mekor hashpa'a be-tahalikhei ha-modernizaẓiya shel yehudei mizraḥ eiropa (1772–1863)', in Y. Cohen (ed.), *Ha-mahapekha ha-ẓarfatit ve-rishuma* (Jerusalem, 1991), 276–9 and *passim*.
[15] Cited in B. Mevoraḥ (ed.), *Napoleon u-tekufato* (Jerusalem, 1968), 181–3. Cf. S. S. Deutsch, 'Milḥemet ha-ADMOR ha-zaken mul napoleon', *Kefar Ḥabad*, 556, 14 Jan. 1993.

How far R. Shne'ur Zalman had been rendered at one and the same
time fearful of the Russians and yet drawn to them by the discovery of
common concerns upon his arrest, incarceration, and interrogation some
fourteen years earlier there is no knowing. But the affair of his arrest, profoundly reflective of both the fissures in European Jewry and of the ambiguities of Russian–Jewish relations, must have left its mark. It had begun
with an anonymous letter emanating from Vilna in May 1798 and
addressed to the Tsar Paul, the writer charging Shne'ur Zalman with
being a political conspirator. He was engaged, it was said, in 'drawing up
lists [of militants] with intent to assist the French Revolution' and of having a hand in the organization of a group of idle, pleasure loving, thieving, and dissolute young Jews who had shaken off the authority of their
elders and were a standing disgrace to their families. While justice clearly
required that the *rebbe* and his followers be drafted into the ranks of the
Tsar's army and sent to the battlefield, or failing that, into distant exile, his
friends and disciples and his protectors in St Petersburg itself had ensured,
so it was claimed, that nothing of the kind be done. When two more such
letters arrived in the capital and the Procurator-General, P. V. Lopukhin,
conveyed their contents to the Tsar, Shne'ur Zalman's arrest and investigation were ordered. The Governor-General of Lithuania, Y. I. Bulgakov,
was instructed to look into the affair, more particularly into the nature of
the Hasidic 'sect' generally. The investigation revealed that the charges
against Shne'ur Zalman were false, but note was taken of the fact that the
view of the Hasidim taken by the more reputable Jews of Vilna was an
exceedingly unfavourable one, that great efforts had been made to
prevent them from establishing themselves in that city, and that some in
Vilna had gone so far as to liken them, provocatively, to the Free Masons.
The governor of Byelorussia, who knew rather more about Shne'ur
Zalman and his people than did his colleague in Vilna, pointed out for his
part that while *his* information was that Shne'ur Zalman's conduct was
free of corruption, that in itself only made him and his circle more dangerous to the state. For under the *rebbe's* modest demeanour, said the governor, there was evidence of great and fully conscious *authority*. His
followers, totally obedient to him, were, as a group, unruly, and not easily controlled by others, if at all. 'Much benefit and profit would accrue
to Jewish society' therefore if the Procurator-General were to recommend the total abolition of this sect to the Tsar. The Procurator-General
followed the governor's advice, recommending on 16 November 1798
that the 'sect' be dissolved, stating, however, that there were no grounds
for continuing to hold Shne'ur Zalman himself under arrest. In the event,
only the latter half of his recommendation was accepted, although with
the proviso, by special instruction of the Tsar, that the *rebbe* and his
people be subject thenceforward to surveillance. The 'sect' itself was not
to be dissolved, however, and to that extent the delation may be said to

have failed. None the less, the incident struck sensitive nerves on both sides, as may be seen from the record of Shne'ur Zalman's interrogation.

QUESTION. What foreign connections do you have; with whom; and where?

ANSWER. I have no connection with foreign Jews except for such as are in Jerusalem and apart from those with whom the community [here] is in correspondence by means of such messengers as have been sent from there [Jerusalem], from time immemorial, to various places in Poland, Lithuania and places in Germany on the other side of the [Russian] frontier [for the collection of funds] on behalf of Jews in Jerusalem.

QUESTION. Who recruited you into the secret associations [or plots], and was it long ago?

ANSWER. [I am] not involved in any secret plots or special associations. [I] only write [to the people in Jerusalem] to encourage them to pray to God—as do many others.

Closely interrogated on the difference between his 'sect' and other segments of Jewry, Shne'ur Zalman was at pains to deny that his HaBaD[16] following was a 'sect' at all or that its teachings and order of prayer differed in any way from what was accepted and practised by 'all Israel'. It was indeed the case, that they sang psalms and suchlike where others perhaps might not do so. But there was no question of theirs being a new religion, as the Russians had been told and as the Russians seemed to fear. Where the HaBaD Hasidim did differ from some Jews was in their insistence on purity of heart and full sincerity and intensity in prayer. His interrogators needed to understand that among the matters at issue was that of the corruption of the regular rabbinate that had occurred under Polish rule: the system whereby official sanction for a rabbi's appointment and the grant and assumption of authority over his people were for purchase. The king of Poland, in his time, had refused to intervene or even pay adequate attention to the abuse. Such had been the state of affairs 'until, by God's grace and His having brought about an extension of Russian Imperial government into all Poland . . . the aforementioned system of [corrupt] rabbinical rule was dissolved, especially in White Russia . . . and all the people were made free men in our land of Russia and all had the right and the possibility to pray in any way or place or company they might wish'.[17]

To be sure, the servility of Russian Jewry in the early years of the Tsar's rule in the new western provinces—prayers being regularly offered up in places of public worship for his safety and well-being, for example[18]—has

[16] The common acronym for *Hokhma, Binah, Da'at* (Wisdom, Understanding, Knowledge) by which Shne'ur Zalman's following, and that of his successors in the Lubawitsch line of Hasidim, have wished to be known, emphasizing their stress on intellectuality.

[17] Record of interrogation and Shne'ur Zalman's signed statement (in Hebrew) in Yehoshu'a Mundschein (ed.), *Kerem HaBaD: 'Iyun ve-Heker be-Mishnat HaBaD: Divrei Yemei ha-Hasidut ve-Darkei ha-Hasidim*, iv, 1 (Kefar Habad, 1992), 43–53.

[18] For a statement of the grounds for loyalty to Russia generally and to the Tsar specifically—effusive in language, but not uncharacteristic of the optimistic mood which swept

to be seen in its context, which is to say as not much more than the external casing in which the deeply considered position and desires of virtually
all who mattered in Russo-Polish Jewry at the time customarily wrapped
their primary concerns. What was presented to the public at large—admittedly with a weather eye out for the authorities—was no more than what
short- but also long-term considerations did seem to dictate. It was the firm
view that the political liberation of the Jews on something like the French
model, if ever it was to take place, would prove disastrous for Jewry as
traditionally—which is to say, historically, spiritually, and, so to speak, rabbinically—conceived. Better by far further servitude to earthly rulers than
disruption of the service Israel owed to God. If, as seemed ever more clearly
to be the case, proper and wholehearted devotion to the latter was conditional upon continued servile acquiescence in the former, so be it. For all
these reasons, it followed that in the Tsar's domain the question whether
there was a socially and morally but, especially, a doctrinally tenable position that fell short of absolute fidelity to the old forms and the old sources
of communal authority *without* entailing abandonment of them would not
be high on the Jewish social agenda for the time being. In central and western Europe, where the still moderate reordering of the affairs of the Jews
was already precipitating autonomous processes of internal change, matters
were otherwise. The traditionalist and orthodox party's need to mark out a
position for itself and resolve how to defend it had become overwhelming.

The established rabbinical position on conduct had always been that
while egregious human appetites were not to be countenanced, they
could be—and at times needed to be—understood. By and large, in the
fullness of time, they could be passed over. Consider the matter of the
Sabbath and the absolute, biblical injunction to keep it under all circumstances short of what might urgently be required to save life (and, but
somewhat more doubtfully, limb). To profane the Sabbath privately, *a fortiori* publicly, was to commit an unforgivable offence that fell short, if
short at all, only of intermarriage or apostasy. On the other hand, the difficulties of Sabbath observance had always been great and could now, in
the new commercial and technological circumstances of early nineteenth-
century Europe, be expected to multiply. The question how an anxious
orthodox rabbinate was to deal with its profanation was therefore urgent.
Was it to take the view that profanation was not to be tolerated under any
circumstances at all? Were there instances that could reasonably, even
if not entirely legitimately, be passed over in disapproving silence? The
prohibition on writing on the Sabbath was absolute.

through much of Russian Jewry, but most powerfully among those who, by virtue of their
mildly modernist tendency, might have been expected to welcome the French—see the
speech delivered by one Hillel Aharon Markievich in a synagogue in Dorpat late in Aug.
1812 (two months after the crossing of the Niemen), reported in 'Evrei v voine 1812
goda', *Evreiskaya starina*, 5 (1912), 87–8.

But might there be a way out and around it? The question arose in a case that came before the rabbinate in Germany whether, in place of a signature, it might be proper to do no more than affix one's personal seal to a document? Would that constitute *writing*? A man of affairs had been called to a government office to sign and seal papers on the Sabbath. Unable either to refuse to appear or to postpone the summons he wished to employ a gentile to affix his seal for him. Would that constitute a transgression? The rabbi called to pass judgement passed over the matter of the actual transaction of business on the Sabbath in what one supposes was diplomatic silence. An official summons to officialdom could be judged an instance of *force majeure* and the relative tolerance accorded the questioner can be read, moreover, as implicit recognition of the compelling force of economic necessity and of the reluctance of rabbis, in central Europe at all events, to contribute to what might be the ruin of their parishioners or, worse, their departure from the fold entirely. But on the narrow and specific issue of the employment of a seal and its actual use by the gentile in the Jew's name, the rabbi refused to budge, pleading an absence of authority for any such obvious manipulation of the Talmudic sources.[19] Here therefore, by extension, was a secondary issue, duly accompanied by a large corpus of rabbinical discussion and (divided) judgement. The most ancient authorities seem to have forbidden vicarious profanation altogether: the original biblical injunction applies explicitly to all within the Jew's household regardless of ethnic or religious identity or gender or civic status or even species: therefore to male and female servants, to bondsmen and bondswomen, and to beasts of burden as well. Later authorities took the view, however, that while the Sabbath injunction did certainly apply to Jews absolutely and regardless of condition and situation, it was not applicable to gentiles *per se*. It was not, that is to say, in a class with the so-called Noachide Laws that posited an absolute prohibition applicable to all human kind of such major crimes as incest and the shedding of blood. On the matter of Sabbath observance by non-Jews in Jewish service, the masters of the Talmud were if anything somewhat ambivalent and their successors tended positively towards the pragmatic. The kindling of fire on the Sabbath was 'labour' and therefore, ostensibly, forbidden. But it was plain that what could be demanded of Jews inhabiting the warm lands of the Mediterranean could not as reasonably be demanded of those who needed to survive a north European winter. It was conceded, for example, that it was legitimate for Jews to venture on a long sea voyage, it being obviously impossible to disembark on each Sabbath and the seamen in any case being gentiles. But was what was applicable to a journey by sea equally applicable to Jews setting out on a journey by inland waterway?

---

[19] The case is recounted in Jacob Katz, *Goy shel Shabbat* (Jerusalem, 1983), 99–100.

The biblical injunction aside, the social importance of the issue of rigorous observance of the Sabbath lay in the fact that in daily practice no issue arising out of the full code of 613 injunctions which it was incumbent upon an adult male Jew to observe cut so closely and directly and regularly to the bone of Jewish unity and identity. It enjoined forms of uniform private and public conduct by all; and these in a form that necessarily drew the sharpest, most frequent, and most visible of behavioural distinctions between Jew and non-Jew. Where and when Jews lived apart, observance was part of the natural order of things. In the new condition of enhanced freedom within civil society, it served as a perpetual reminder of Jewish distinctiveness. The dilemma was plain. Where the rabbis and established secular leaders of the community insisted on strict observance, either on simple principle or because they explicitly valued it for its cohesive value, there they now faced the danger of being ignored or rejected. The Jewish magnates who had purchased great estates and town houses and maintained entire households which were intended from the first to be managed and worked by non-Jews tended increasingly not to be troubled by *halakhic* (i.e. legal-behavioural) questions of any kind, the more so as the underlying purpose of the exercise on which most of them were embarked was in any case their own closer social integration into the highest society in the land. But the lesser folk who had done no more than take advantage of their new freedom to exchange old homes, trades, and occupations for new were apt to find that their new circumstances were only with difficulty compatible with rigorous observance of the *halakha*, and of the Sabbath in particular. Farming presented obstacles that were especially difficult, if not impossible, to overcome. But many urban trades and crafts presented great difficulties too. There were skills, along with licence to exercise them that could only be acquired by a process of apprenticeship to non-Jewish masters. These were likely to make demands of their own, beside catering to a clientele that expected service on Saturdays. But where the enterprise was in Jewish hands and gentiles were especially employed to deal with clients on the Sabbath, there was still the awkward—and from a traditional Jewish-rabbinical point of view intolerable—problem of a Jewish proprietor living over his shop while others, Jews or gentiles, worked below.[20] The result, inexorably, was a slowly rising, increasingly open call for a general loosening of the chains, although, that said, it seems to have been the parallel, more systematic attack on religious worship and ritual itself, rather than the phenomenon of illicit and individually determined private and public non-observance, that was to strike most painfully at orthodoxy's vital nerve.

The first serious, public, and therefore especially notorious attempt to

[20] Ibid. 104–5, 107–22.

institutionalize a reform of the strictly religious practices and rituals of Judaism was undertaken by an independently minded branch of the Jewish community in Hamburg late in 1817. A private synagogue run on what were thought of at the time as shockingly revolutionary lines (men and women seated together, the Torah read in Sephardi Hebrew, hymns sung in the German vernacular) had been established in Berlin three years earlier by the radical Westphalian rabbi, Israel Jacobson. The organized community in Berlin limited itself to silent disapproval. It was King Frederick William III and his officials who, for reasons of their own, among them their fear that a bright new form of Judaism might prove attractive to Christians, insisted on it being closed down.[21] There were no such official objections to Hamburg's new synagogue, however, for all that the radicals' reordering of the service was intended to cut deeper. It was to be more decorous than was usual: in effect, more like a service in a German church. The eighteen daily morning benedictions and prayers that expressed a longing for a Return to the Holy Land and for national Redemption were deleted from the service. The Sabbath service was heavily altered too and then rendered doubly scandalous by the installation of an organ and the employment of a non-Jew musician to play it. The preponderant, although not exclusive, language of prayer was German. All in all, it was a case of dissidence that could not fail to seem to embody almost everything—outright apostasy excepted—that might excite orthodoxy's loathing and contempt as imitative of the gentiles, disloyal to the Jewish people, deeply heretical, and shamelessly public into the bargain. When the outraged Hamburg conservatives appealed to a panel comprising some of the most distinguished rabbis of the day in central Europe the response, as anticipated, was immediate and their ferocious statements of condemnation were promptly gathered together and published for all to read.[22]

It says something about the fear and urgency with which Jewish orthodoxy[23] at its most rigorous sought to confront the situation that this should be one of the rare occasions on which it found a leader. Moshe Sofer (1762–1839), more commonly known as 'the Ḥatam Sofer', was in most ways a prototypical member of his class of prodigious scholars which, given its ancient prestige, its continuing influence over ordinary people, and the extreme difficulty of ignoring or circumventing its authority once it had seized on an issue, may be regarded as a learned

---

[21] Michael A. Meyer, *Response to Modernity* (New York, 1988), 30–46.

[22] *Eleh divrei ha-berit* [*These are the words of the Covenant*] (Altona, AM 5579 [1818/19]).

[23] Or perhaps more precisely: 'Jewish ultra-conservatism'. Professor Jacob Katz has pointed out that 'orthodox' is a borrowing from Christian usage and something of a misnomer when applied to Jews. In Jewish usage it has less to do with theological doctrine than with the practices which Jew are expected to observe and the rules of behaviour to which they are to conform.

aristocracy, a sort of *noblesse de robe*—and a near-hereditary one at that. The respect, not to say awe, in which Sofer, as a great Talmudic and moral authority, came to be held was to be extended almost as a matter of course to the dynastic line of which he was a beneficiary and at the same time a founder. He himself was the son-in-law of one of the greatest of the Talmudic luminaries of the age, Rabbi 'Akiva Eiger. His own son, son-in-law, and grandson went on to partake of the prestige that was his legacy. It was of course an aristocracy of piety and learning. It relied ultimately on merit and virtue, never on material power. It was an aristocracy, therefore, in the literal sense of the term, founded on what counted as 'best' in the Jewish world as then constituted. By the same token, it stood in starkest possible contrast to the inauthentic, because plutocratic 'aristocracy' that had begun to evolve at great speed and with a steadily deepening impact of its own on the society and values of the Jews of Europe in the course of the formative years of the period with which this study deals. Where the Ḥatam Sofer was uncommon was in his ability—and his readiness— to articulate both scholarly judgement and social opinion not only with great force, but with singular clarity.

Sofer's early years were passed in Frankfurt where the teacher who is believed to have influenced him most deeply was Nathan Adler, an exceedingly controversial and independently minded rabbi himself, unbending in his demand for stringent observance of *halakhic* minutiae, but, unusually, inclined to take more interest in *kabbalah* mysticism and cosmology than the nineteenth-century central European rabbinate considered respectable. When Adler was forced out of Frankfurt by the communal notables, clerical and lay (backed by the city's civil authorities) on the grounds that he was exceeding his authority, Sofer, loyally, went with him, settling eventually, in 1806, in Pressburg (Bratislava). There, in the course of time, he established, and for thirty years headed, a *yeshiva* (or Talmudic seminary) of considerable renown, achieving personal recognition as one of the most eminent rabbinic authorities of the day, and emerging in due course as the leading figure in the central European branch of the party of uncompromising and immovable ultraconservatism.

The heart of Sofer's philosophy on the combined matters of doctrine and behaviour was summed up in his famously uncompromising exposition of the Talmudic dictum that 'the Torah forbids innovation' (*ḥadash asur min ha-torah*). He took this literally. Modification of any kind and in any degree of what had long been established could not fail to be incompatible with *halakha* and that the rule itself was absolute and all-embracing. There could be no question of drawing distinctions, fine or rough, between greater and lesser matters, between greater and lesser precepts and injunctions. Innovation, whatever its form and context, was unacceptable. All who cleaved to religious orthodoxy and to the principles of behavioural propriety long since laid down by accepted authority were enjoined to reject it.[24]

Should hunger and misery lead you into temptation . . . resist [it, ran his message] and do not turn to the idols or to some god of your own making! . . . Be warned not to change your Jewish names, speech, clothing. . . . Never say: 'Times have changed!' We have an old Father—praised be His name—who has never changed and never will change. . . . The order of prayer and synagogue shall remain forever as it has been up to now, and no one may presume to change anything of its structure.[25]

To the question whether there was a middle way between strict and uncompromising observance of the *halakha* and its abandonment the reply of orthodoxy at its most unbending was that there was none and that the dilemma was indeed stark and unforgiving. The position laid down by the Ḥatam Sofer and his school was that the attempt to subject the fundamentals of Judaism to reconsideration was itself damnable: in that it was designed finally to draw off the independently modernizing Jews from the body of the faithful it was divisive; in that it was evidently intended to gain the approval of those non-Jewish reference groups to whose voices the ears of the modernists within Jewry were now increasingly cocked it was reprehensible; in that it was founded on the assumption that the intellectual and conceptual conventions of the day had indeed to be accommodated was intrinsically flawed. The notion that the ground Judaism was supposed to hold in *common* with other faiths and cultures might be relevant to the question was therefore fit only to be rejected out of hand as an immense and unpardonable deviation from ancient doctrine, precedent, and the Jewish people's own self-definition.

Characteristically, Sofer's response to the 'bitter news' of the doings of 'evil men' in Hamburg was to recall ancient authority. 'It is very well known,' he wrote, 'that in [his] exile, the splendid Daniel [*Daniel ish ḥamudot*] knelt down three times a day, and prayed, and gave thanks before his God, just as he had done before.'[26] He then went on to assert the absolute unacceptability of any breach whatsoever in the 'wall' or 'fence' the Sages had set around the Law—and, by extension and with deliberate intent, about the Jewish people—for its and their protection. As for those who presumed to destroy that fence, who refused to submit to the 'yoke of heaven', and who sought to nullify the Covenant into which their forefathers had entered with the Almighty, 'let them seek to be

---

[24] Famously codified by Yosef Caro in the sixteenth century in his compendium *Shulḥan Arukh*. Dedicated and meticulous observance of the *halakhic* prescriptions specified in Caro's guide remains to this day the ultimate criterion by which true (orthodox) piety will be measured: the corollary being that the more meticulous the observance, the more pious the individual.
[25] Cited in W. Gunther Plaut, *The Rise of Reform Judaism: A Sourcebook of its European Origins* (New York, 1963), 256 f.
[26] Sofer in *Eleh divrei ha-berit*, 7.

counted and compared with the sages of our own times if that is their claim'. If their response was that they were not of a mind to accept the teachings of the Sages, why then, he wrote, they fell under Maimonidean ruling, that 'He who repudiates the Oral Law . . . [i.e. the Talmud] is to be classed [and condemned] with atheists', following which nothing more needed, in his view, to be said.[27]

The specific justifications the reformers were bold enough to advance were to be dismissed as unworthy. The argument that prayers for the advent of the Messiah and the Restoration of Israel to its Land need no longer be said on the grounds that the Jews had already found 'tranquillity and goodness among the gentiles' and no longer required the Land of Israel was blasphemous. The Jews continued to be what they had long been: a people in exile awaiting deliverance—deliverance *and* Redemption. It was not illusory material tranquillity that they sought and pined for. It was the privilege of once again

dwelling in the presence of God in the place designated for his service and for the observance of his Law. Nor was there anything in this that implied deprecation of the king and high officers of state whose protection we [currently] enjoy. . . . Neḥemia . . . served his king as viceroy in honour and in riches; yet at the sight of the ruined city [of Jerusalem] he grieved. . . . We [too, for our part] are as captives of the war of the destruction [of the city and the Temple]. . . . while yet duty bound to seek and pray for the welfare of our kings.[28]

Sofer conceded that it was incumbent upon the Jews to be grateful for the 'many great kindnesses' bestowed upon them by 'the kings and ministers of the nations' under whom they lived and to pray for their safety. It did not follow, however, in his view, that they should cease to pine for their true patrimony. There was no reason why this or any other of the wishes and beliefs of the Jews should vex 'the nations'. The reformers, possibly, thought otherwise. But then they themselves neither anticipated a Return nor believed the words of the prophets who foretold the building of the Third Temple and the coming of the Messiah. In sum, writing in 1819, his position was that nothing had occurred to justify a change in the Jews' own long-established conception of their destiny as a people and the set view of the duties it was incumbent upon them to perform as private individuals. Nor had the fundamentals of their relations with the gentiles and of their condition among them altered. Those who held otherwise were wrong. Those who believed otherwise were simple-minded.

It is to be noted, that his views—and the views of his rabbinical colleagues generally—were mediated as a matter of course through the language of the Law. They tended therefore to be cast in severe and uncompromising terms. Language, tone, and purpose all conspired to ensure that dialogue with the reformers, were it ever attempted, would

[27] Ibid. 8–9.   [28] Ibid. 9.

be a dialogue of the deaf. So too did the conceptual difference between the schools and what was held by each of the parties to constitute a valid argument. Whereas modernizers and reformers of all persuasions had it in common, that they appealed to what they held to be universal categories and to the rights and still more the needs of contemporary man, Sofer and his kind assumed the sanctity of divine law as handed down at Sinai and authoritatively interpreted thereafter. They did not think, much less argue, in universal categories. Universal categories were precisely what they rejected, at any rate so far as these might be thought applicable to the Jews. This held true of political as well as other obligations. Sofer was as well aware as any of the new men that the Jews were vulnerable. His gratitude to those 'kings and ministers' who were prepared to allow the Jews to live in peace and in their own way need not be thought of as other than genuine. But the duty to pray for the ruler's welfare and, by implication, to obey him, was wholly distinct in his mind from that quite different wish to identify with the governing power which he detected, correctly, among the reformers. In his view, obedience to the ruler was a temporary requirement. The true and unvarying obligation was to divine, not earthly, authority. Least of all was it one which they were free to determine in accordance with their private, necessarily ill-informed understanding of their current needs.

Yet there may be detected in this great master of anachronism something that was distinctly of his place and time after all: a view that bore traces of the influence of the romantic movement and that therefore, in one or two respects, were not far removed from those who were sharpest in their criticism of the place and function of his own people. Sofer placed great value on agriculture. By virtue of its evident contribution to the most fundamental of the needs of humankind, it was superior, in his eyes, to commerce and industry. It was superior too in its being the true and ultimate source of a country's wealth and prosperity. But, above all, it was morally superior. Commerce, industry, and finance were all sources of much that was evil and fearful in society. They were inseparable from man's sad propensity to employ his energies in the search for luxury, property, and the opportunity to preen himself before his fellows and set himself above them, as opposed to being content with the little he really needed to satisfy his material wants and ensure some freedom to devote time and energy to higher things. No doubt, the merchant did play an important role in the economy; but it was not, Sofer thought, a productive role. Nor was that of the bankers: necessary, perhaps, but not productive. It was participation in the production of goods that earned a man an honourable place in human society, not the competitive accumulation of capital. For *that* way lay moral corruption, social and international conflict, the mad pursuit of profit and prestige, and the creation of whole classes of fearful and obsequious inferiors—in brief, the entire, ghastly structure of power and wealth organized and presided over inexorably by selfish, violent, and extortionate regimes.[29]

A second respect in which Sofer will be found to have been not unobservant of the world around him, and perhaps for that reason perhaps marginally more liberal in some of his views than were many of his colleagues (and even some of his disciples), was his relative tolerance of the study of secular subjects. Where others ruled them out totally, Sofer, wiser and, perhaps, more confident of his authority, was prepared to allow them provided only that the empirical investigation of the world proceeded selectively and could be shown to serve, if only indirectly, the higher purpose and the infinitely more meritorious activity of the one form of study which it was the undoubted business of Jews (the men of Jewry at all events) to engage in unreservedly: the study of the Law. Sofer is generally believed to have had a command of the German language (not an attribute to be assumed of the majority of men of his class in his time, even when natives of Germany) and to have delved fairly deeply himself into mathematics and the physical sciences. He saw no objection to the translation of classic Jewish texts into German on a limited basis and for carefully defined purposes. He said of Rabbi David Sintzheim,[30] with whom he was for many years in friendly correspondence, that among his Alsatian colleague's distinguishing and praiseworthy qualities was his command of both Jewish *and* secular learning—to which he, Sintzheim, owed his special standing and prestige among 'the king and his ministers' of France. But Sofer drew back from the kind of large-scale translation of Jewish texts into the vernacular and the general intermingling and mutual fertilization of Jewish and general scholarship that the modernist *maskilim* (of whom more below) seemed to him to have in mind. The fundamental question, for him, was not balance and proportion, but primacy. He viewed both reliance (by Jews) on alien philosophies as a basis for the interpretation of their own Jewish texts and the use (even the innocent use) of Jewish learning as a vehicle for the inculcation of alien ideas and doctrines as impermissible. Such had been the outcome historically of the original translation of the Bible into Greek (the Septuagint); such, he believed, would be the consequence of the *maskilim's* ambitious projects of translation of Jewish texts into German. But he does not seem to have been fully consistent in this respect. It is recorded that at one stage a project for the translation of the Talmud itself gained his approval, later to be withdrawn when the results dissatisfied him.[31]

---

[29] Eli'ezer Katz, *He-Ḥatam Sofer: Rabbi Moshe Sofer, ḥayyav vi-ẓirato* (Jerusalem, 1960), 118–23.

[30] Presiding member of the Napoleonic Sanhedrin.

[31] Katz, *He-Ḥatam Sofer*, 103; Shelomo Sofer (ed.), *Sefer Igrot Sofrim* (Vienna, 1929), part 2, 70–1.

Where Sofer was entirely unbending was in his objection to the move-ment for emancipation. This he regarded with the deepest distrust. He saw it as leading ineluctably to religious reform, thence to assimilation, and finally to the collapse of the structure and integrity of the Jewish people as a whole. Such material liberties as the gentiles were prepared to grant the Jews needed to be measured, he thought, against the loss of spiritual free-dom the Jews themselves would unfailingly suffer. The price of civil rights would be the loss of soul, the cost of personal freedom the loss of national freedom. It was true that an enslaved and persecuted Jewry, quite apart from the suffering to which it was subjected, was a people unable to worship and do God's bidding. But there was another form of enslavement.

The source of the affliction could be the contrary: it could be the liberty granted Israel by the kingdom and the privileges and attention bestowed upon [its members] . . . Whence in practice a greater calamity than the other would befall the Jews in that, on this earth [i.e. as is the way of the world], the Jews would tend to move ever closer towards the king's men and imitate their manners and abandon Torah and its duties, all of their own free will. But this too is in the nature of an enslavement, for while they would be free [in the civic sense], in fact it would be the abomination of the land that would rule them.[32]

Sofer was not an isolated figure. What he expressed, in much clearer and more confident terms than was usual, were the immediate responses and concerns of what would for some time to come be the greater part of European Jewry. And in much of what he said he did unquestionably touch a nerve that was likely to be present in the make-up even of those who, in practice, were disinclined to follow his injunctions. The great strength of orthodoxy was only nominally in the realm of ideas. Its true appeal was to the emotive and the irrational: to loyalty, to fear of the unknown and the unfamiliar, to concern for dignity and self-respect, and to doctrines and dogmas which, in turn, owed their special force to their having been inculcated and internalized and regularly transmitted from father to son over centuries as well, of course, as simple faith and confi-dence in the divine—strong in some, no more than residual in others. In the long term, therefore, what he and the other masters of orthodoxy had now to contend with was not theological opposition, but social action and social processes. The critics of orthodoxy from within Jewry had ideas of their own, as we shall see. But these too derived their force less from their intrinsic cogency than from the needs and desires of men and women whose impatience for change was growing mightily and would grow still further and faster as liberation from the social system to which absolute loyalty to orthodoxy had once bound them took root. What would prove irrefutable in what was presented as *religious* reform was, in fact, its *social* logic. It would appear to ever greater numbers of western

[32] Moshe Sofer, *Derashot*, ii. 500b. Cited in Katz, *He-Ḥatam Sofer*, 87.

and central European Jews, that to maintain the old norms of conduct and the old communal structure would be to fix the Jews' presence at the very margins of both contemporary society and the economy forever. It would be to do so, moreover, at the very point in the general evolution of Europe—western and west-central Europe, at all events—when all was manifestly in flux and progress of a hitherto inconceivable kind was being made on all social, economic, and political fronts. To reject this new Europe in the spirit demanded of them by the Ḥatam Sofer and his school was, for a rapidly growing number of people, to evoke a prospect of stasis and entrenchment that was too anomalous and too disheartening to be bearable.

III

As a class, the first to break out of the old shell of conformity and submission to internal authority was the new plutocracy. To be sure, it may be regarded as the old eighteenth-century class of court Jews and military purveyors triumphantly enriched and expanded. The revolutionary and Napoleonic wars had lasted longer than any that had occurred in the previous century, the armies had been incomparably larger, the military and political arena had been virtually congruent with Europe in its entirety, and larger numbers of Jewish entrepreneurs than ever before were called upon to serve. Their reward, as before, was the grant of those formal privileges and marks of esteem that set them apart from their brethren for all to see and marvel at: the right of residence where it had formerly been denied and was still otherwise restricted (in Vienna and St Petersburg, for example), the cancellation of the badges and taxes that at once identified and exploited Jews as such, and ennoblement. Most decisive and reflective of the new age, however, was the circumstance that the grant of status and privilege, together with the security of accumulated wealth, had ceased to be reversible.

Consider Alsatian Jewry, the first substantial, fully traditional European community to enjoy formal emancipation. Deeply impoverished before the Revolution, its general condition changed only slowly in the aftermath. Just prior to the convening of the Assembly of the Notables in Paris in 1807, the *préfet* of the Bas-Rhin department reported to Paris that of the 600 highest tax payers in the Bas-Rhin, only two were Jews. (Since there were then all of 22,000 Jews in the department as opposed to 455,000 non-Jews, this was nominally disproportionate by a factor of 15.) Most Jews, he informed his superiors, were in the business of second-hand goods and small loans, as before.[33] On the other hand, what was true

---

[33] R. Neher-Bernheim, *Documents inédits sur l'entrée des Juifs dans la société française 1750–1850*, i (Tel Aviv, 1977), 324–8.

of most of the Jewish population was not true of all; and the mechanics of
the rise to great affluence of some among them are instructive.[34] The
pre-revolutionary precedents for Jews in Alsace and elsewhere to serve as
purveyors to the French armies were firm, as has been noted. What
changed was the scale of the demand for food, clothing, and horses and
the immensely steep rise in monetary reward that followed. In the winter of 1794/5 Zachariah Cerf of Metz took it upon himself to supply the
French Rhine army with no less than 12,000 tons of wheat for which, in
June 1795, he was paid 3 million francs. The brothers Cerfberr, in February 1795, at the behest of the Committee of Public Safety, undertook
to supply the revolutionary army with 40,000 horses within six months
of the signing of the contract, earning a similarly large sum. Where payment was in paper money, the purveyors learned to invest their receipts
in real estate before the inevitable inflation took its toll. Paid 3.6 million
francs in 1795 for supplying the army with food, cloth, and iron, Léon
Fould (with one other), promptly purchased 230 hectares of state land
with the proceeds. Five years later Fould was among the two hundred
principal shareholders of the new Napoleonic Bank of France and both
the shift from the provision of food and horses to that of money and the
conversion of purveyor to financier was complete. But it needs to be said,
too, that such success was contingent on each major provisioner being
able to build up an entire network of subcontractors to serve him. The
brothers Cerfberr maintained commercial relations with no less than 67
lesser suppliers, purveyors, and provisioners, all Jews. In the years in question, by Michael Graetz's calculation, the heads of over a quarter of all
Jewish households in Alsace were engaged in some way in the provision-
ing of the French armies and in some small rural communities as many as
half the local Jewish population might be involved. In their essentials,
therefore, these were so many replications of the method whereby
Oberkriegsfaktor Samuel Oppenheimer, purveyor to the Habsburg armies,
and others of his class had operated a century earlier. And it is interesting
to note that something of the same reliance on ethno-familial connections would be maintained by the sometime purveyors upon their entry
into the more exalted realm of banking. Much like the families of eminent rabbinical dynasties, they tended—at first quite strongly, later less
so—to consolidate their connections and ensure mutual support by
marriage. When Ber Léon Fould was in financial trouble during the
1810–11 economic crisis the Oppenheim bank of Cologne came to his
aid: Fould's son Baruch (Benoît) was married to Helena, Avraham
Oppenheim's daughter. The result, notably when viewed from without,
was the arrival on the periphery of the very highest circles of society in

---

[34] Closely examined by M. Graetz, ' 'Aliyato vishki'ato shel sapak ha-zava ha-yehudi
be-'itot milhama', *Zion*, 56, 3 (1991), 255–73.

Europe's major capitals of a wholly new class of Jewish men, and women too, who had rapidly and somewhat spectacularly coalesced into a sort of supra-communal, all-European, but in any case readily identifiable category of grandees. Viewed from within Jewry itself, its members duly took on the meretricious lustre that habitually accrued to people who were thought to have been granted free entrée into the non-Jewish world. But if such a rise and consequent notoriety were rapid and without precedent, decline would follow. The children and grandchildren of the founding members of this new élite tended to remove themselves. Marriages (and the dowries the brides brought with them) ceased to be treated as matters of material significance, sought for and arranged with the consolidation and perpetuation of financial connections in mind. Exogenous marriage and religious conversion would register ever more frequently as the surer, in some societies indispensable, staging-posts along the route towards the true summits of society, on the conquest of which a high proportion of the members this class were embarked.[35]

There are ambiguities about apostasy by Jews which have served to make the full meaning of what might seem a simple and clear-cut step uncertain. On the Christian side of the divide the tendency (at least since the invention in Spain of the term 'new Christian' and the concept of 'purity of blood'—*limpieza de sangre*) to distinguish between the formal religious significance of baptism as a Jew's entry into the Christian world and its social significance, the terms on which he or she is likely to be received into that world in actual practice, has been a strong one, strongest of all in modern times. Judaism has always regarded it, needless to say, as a major and unpardonable sin. But all sinners, even the apostates, remained in some sense or other members of the Jewish people: Jews of a very inferior and so to speak damaged sort, but Jews none the less—the more so as, except where the conversion took place under duress or the motives were crassly opportunistic, apostasy remained fundamentally incomprehensible to the Jewish mind and at least as much a source of

[35] The proliferation of new style Jewish grandees in nineteenth-century Jewry was too extensive a phenomenon for a representative list to be compiled and incorporated into the present study. But any such list, however short, would have to include the Arnsteins of Vienna, notably Nathan Adam von Arnstein (1748–1838) and his brother-in-law and partner Bernhard von Eskeles (1753–1839), who were among the Jewish notables who petitioned the Congress of Vienna for a general grant of civil rights to the Jews; the French banking dynasty founded by Ber Léon Fould (1767–1855); the banking family founded in Baden by Salomon Haber (1764–1839); the Kaulla family of Württemberg financiers, led, unusually, by a woman, Caroline Raphael (1739–1809), with her brother and successor Jacob Raphael (1750–1810); the Cologne banking house founded by Solomon Oppenheim (1772–1828); the Speyer family of bankers of Frankfurt whose activities were later extended to the United States, as were those of the Warburgs, originally of Hamburg; the Rothschilds, originally of Frankfurt, later of Paris, London, Vienna, and Naples as well; the de Worms dynasty, originally of Frankfurt, domiciled in England, connected by marriage and business to the Rothschilds, ennobled by both Austria and Britain; and in eastern Europe the Guenzburgs.

bewilderment and distrust as anger. To the secular Jewish mind no less than to that of the believer, to apostatize is not simply to transgress, it is to betray. In any event, precise measurement of the phenomenon has never been possible, partly for the reasons that have rendered the collection of statistics on the Jews difficult at all times: shifting frontiers, continual migration, rising populations overall, census figures of doubtful reliability in many cases, and a total absence of figures in others; and partly because in many cases the Jewish origins of the baptized and their descendents have been kept secret. The difficulty of comparing one moving target (the number of conversions at any one time) with another (the entirety of the Jewish population in question) is immense.[36] What is certain, however, is that while in absolute terms and in terms relative to the total Jewish population formal conversions to Christianity in nineteenth-century Europe were few in all parts, the difference between eastern Europe and western and central Europe is striking. The Jewish population of eastern and south-eastern Europe rose from about 2 million to 7.4 million in the course of the century. The number of conversions taking place in this period has been estimated at no more than approximately 85,000 which suggests a notional annual rate of less than a thousand souls, or not much more than 0.01 per cent of the total Jewish population in those parts, in an average year. 'That about six million persecuted and miserable wretches remain steadfastly faithful to a religion that causes their life to be changed into a fiery furnace without the angel to keep it cool,' wrote an English observer in 1900, 'is the nearest approach to a grandiose miracle that has been vouchsafed to this unbelieving generation.' Were any of the measures employed against the Russian Jews applied to their neighbours they would suffice, he thought, to convert three-fourths of Christian Russia to Shamanism or Buddhism within 'a week'.[37] In western and central Europe, the total number of conversions in the course of the entire nineteenth century was only slightly larger— an estimated 100,000—than in the east. But since the Jewish population of western and central Europe was very much smaller, rising from about 0.4 million early in the century to about 1.3 million towards the century's end, the rate of conversion was a good deal higher, probably ten times as high. It was, besides, a preponderantly urban phenomenon: almost unknown in small towns and villages, commoner in cities, commonest of all in the very largest cities. It has been estimated that in Berlin alone, between 1800 and 1924, 5,250 Jews were converted to Protestant Christianity (always more common in Germany than conversion to Roman

---

[36] But see, for example, N. Samter, *Judentaufen im neunzehnten Jahrhundert* (Berlin, 1906); and among recent studies T. M. Endelman (ed.), *Jewish Apostasy in the Modern World* (New York, 1987).

[37] E. B. Lanin, 'The Jews in Russia', *Fortnightly Review*, 54 (1900), 498, cited in Carl Cohen, 'The Road to Conversion', *LBIYB* 6 (1961), 260.

Catholicism). And slow at first, the rate of conversion rose steadily both absolutely and proportionately in the last two decades of the nineteenth century: 43 (0.8 per cent of the city's Jewish population) in 1880; 146 (0.18 per cent) in 1890; 160 (0.16 per cent) in 1900.[38] In Vienna the numbers were greater and the rise was steeper: 39 Jews converted to Christianity in 1870, 110 in 1880, 302 in 1890, and 559 in 1900.[39] In the course of the eight years 1898–1907 4 per cent of the total Jewish population of Vienna apostatized. Even in the somewhat more settled Jewish populations of urban Bohemia and Moravia the rates were higher than in Berlin, although lower than in Vienna: 2.25 per cent in Prague in the same period, 2.5 per cent in Brno.[40]

On the face of things, then, a paradox. In the illiberal east (where in all relevant respects Romania was soon to move alongside imperial Russia), where pressure to apostatize was still practised sporadically, as we will shortly see, the numbers of apostates as a proportion of the Jewish population were negligible, as before. In the partially liberalized west, where public, but more especially state, pressure on Jews to convert to Christianity had ended and the condition of the Jews had greatly eased in other ways, apostasy had at any rate ceased to be uncommon. But the paradox is resolved when it is noted that the apostate in the west was almost invariably the man or woman who had already gone some way, often a very considerable way, into the non-Jewish world, ambition—often very high ambition—providing the final, powerful push out of Jewry altogether.

Ambition in its gross form is well illustrated by the case of Karl Marx's father Heinrich. Heinrich Marx's life plan was twice altered out of all recognition: first by the entry of French revolutionary troops into the Rhineland in 1792, then by their withdrawal almost two decades later. Soon after their entry the French decreed emancipation for the Jews. But although they followed up their original measures by imposing the limitations set upon them by Napoleon's *décret infâme* of 1808, even a limited form of Jewish emancipation was an event of a genuinely revolutionary kind for all concerned in this part of Germany: for the Jews certainly, but for the non-Jews as well. The history of Rhineland Jewry had been a long and unhappy one, an exceptionally dismal chronicle of persecution, massacre, mob violence, expulsion, and extortion. The community in the city of Cologne itself dated from Roman times and was the oldest in Germany, but its story culminated in 1424 in what was intended to be a final, irredeemable expulsion—to be rescinded only three and three-quarters

---

[38] Based on Samter, *Judentaufen*, 146–7. For additional, later figures and for figures of intermarriage, see below, pp. 315 ff.

[39] Figures collated by Jakob Thon, cited in Marsha L. Rozenblit, *The Jews of Vienna, 1867–1914: Assimilation and Identity* (Albany, NY, 1983), 132.

[40] M. A. Riff, 'Assimilation and Conversion in Bohemia: Secession from the Jewish Community in Prague 1868–1917', in *LBIYB* 26 (1981), 78.

centuries later under the French. Heinrich Marx had been among the beneficiaries of the French regime, having been allowed to study law. Unfortunately for him, he had just been about to begin a practice of his own at the low legal rank of *avoué* when the French were replaced by the Prussians in 1814. Would he be allowed to proceed to the German legal rank of *Rechtsanwalt*? His application for permission to do so was passed to Berlin. The answer, when it came down after two years of deliberation, was negative. No Jew could be endowed with authority (as the rank of *Rechtsanwalt* would have provided) over Christians. And the blow to his aspirations was the more painful for Heinrich Marx who, throughout the years of the French, had been careful to display his own unquestioned and obsequious loyalty to the Prussians. Like the Rothschilds in Frankfurt, he had, that is to say, in his very minor way, gambled on the eventual downfall of Napoleon. But the authorities were unmoved and it was clear to him that, if he were not to abandon his professional ambitions altogether, the only remaining course was baptism. There is some evidence that he was reluctant to take the step. It is known that when he took it he resolved on Lutheranism, totally unrepresented in Trier, as opposed to the dominant Catholicism, and likely therefore to spare him regular church attendance. The ceremony itself was conducted in semi-secrecy by a chaplain to one of the Prussian regiments on Rhineland occupation duties. The rest of his family remained Jewish for some time. Still, within the decade, all in Heinrich Marx's immediate family had followed him to the font— although how authentic their Christianity might ever have been remains an open question. What is certain is that little residual loyalty to Jews and Judaism remained: none at all, on the evidence, in the case of the man who has been the cause of such interest as has been taken in Heinrich Marx himself.[41] It was Heinrich, it seems probable, who determined that Karl, born a Jew in 1818, should not be circumcised,[42] and, it is certain, should be baptized in his childhood (in 1824 or 1825). It is beyond question, too, that despite Karl's uncle, one Shemu 'el Marx, officiating as a rabbi in Trier, the boy was brought up with nothing of an authentically Jewish nature being taught him. Of there being an historically important connection between these circumstances and Karl Marx's own considered views on matters Jewish (of which more later) there can be little doubt.

Social ambition when unadulterated by grosser, material purposes, is of another order. Its springs lie deeper. It seeks justification or rationalization. It is likely to be a good deal more fraught. Rahel Varnhagen, née Levin (1771–1833), a woman who fought her way desperately, by sheer grit, but also by apostasy and intermarriage, out of her run-of-the-mill,

[41] Shelomo Na'aman, 'Heinrich Marx, Karl Marx ve-Eleanor Marx: shelosha dorot nokhaḥ etgar ha-shivyon ha-ezraḥi', *Zion*, 57, 4 (1992), 395–427.
[42] Ibid. 408.

orthodox, commercial middle-class origins and into the glittering reaches of Berlin's high society, provides a celebrated, effectively proto-typical case in point. That hers was a journey that she was capable of pur-suing to its end was remarkable. The unremitting despair of this gifted woman at her having been born a Jewess, even upon safe arrival at her destination, even when presiding over her famous salon, is still more interesting and telling. Of its kind, her inconsolably bitter, passionate, but well-considered view of her 'disgrace', her 'infamous birth', and her true place in the social order is memorable:

How loathsome it is always having to establish one's identity first. That alone is enough to make it so repulsive to be a Jew. . . . I really do not understand *at all* what can be done for and with the Jews. . . . Hitherto it has not been possible to do anything for the scattered, neglected, and more than all that, deservedly despised nation. . . . People like us [she concluded] cannot be Jews. . . . The Jew must be extirpated from us, that is the sacred truth, and it must be done even if life itself were uprooted in the process.[43]

But it is the case of Heinrich Heine (1797–1856) that excites the great-est interest and, in the present context, is of most importance precisely because he was, arguably, the greatest lyric poet in the German language and certainly the greatest of Jewish figures to have emerged in Germany in modern times. If it verges on the absurd to link so complex, honest, self-deprecating, critical, and certainly more ironic observer of both society and self with Rahel Varnhagen the social climber, let alone with Heinrich Marx the obscure Rhineland attorney, it remains that he stands to this day as the best known of all early nineteenth-century German-Jewish apostates, as he himself seems to have been at least half aware. And there is, after all, the sobering fact that Heine, a man of infinitely greater worth than either Varnhagen or Marx, had this in common with them—that he had responded to the bite of worldly ambition in much the same way as they had. But finally it is of the highest importance in this con-nection, that Heine, as we shall see, was both a close observer of, and for some time an active participant in, Jewish affairs as was his sometime friend and partner in apostasy, Eduard Gans (1798–1839). Both had grown up in the age of Napoleon, Heine in the Rhineland city of Düs-seldorf, Gans in Berlin. Both were sons of commercial families of mod-erate standing. Both had had non-Jewish schooling. Both had gone on to university. Both aspired mightily to academic, or, if not academic, then official distinction and appointments. Gans was among the founders of a society devoted to a secularly minded, academically rigorous study of Judaism (on which more below), one of the declared purposes of which was to teach other Germans something about the Jews, heighten the

---

[43] Cited in H. Arendt, *Rahel Varnhagen: The Life of a Jewess* (London, 1957), 102, 105, 178–80. Emphasis in original.

regard in which they were held, and so facilitate their integration into German society. Heine had been the group's first secretary. However, when each in his turn was halted at the first, formal obstacle to an academic or official career, each chose to circumvent the obstacle by conversion. Denied a regular academic post at the University of Berlin to which none doubted that he was eminently qualified, Gans agreed fairly readily to baptism. 'If the state is so stupid,' he is reported as saying, 'as to forbid me to serve it in a capacity which suits my particular talents unless I profess something I do not believe—and something the responsible minister *knows* I do not believe: all right then, it shall have its wish.'[44] Heine, more sensitive than his friend Gans, thereupon composed (although never published) a bitter denunciatory poem (to which Professor S. S. Prawer has drawn attention). It runs in part:

> Und du hast dich, kühlern Blutes,
> Mit den lieben Herrn verständigt.
>
> Und du bist zu Kreuz gekrochen,
> Zu dem Kreuz, das du verachtest,
> Das du noch nur wenig Wochen
> in den Staub zu treten dachtest![45]

But the truth was that Heine had preceded Gans along that path; and that there were two real differences between the two young men. Unlike Gans and others, Heine believed to the end of his life that he had disgraced himself; and Heine, as is well known, was never rewarded for the step he had taken. Gans, in contrast, did well. He was duly appointed to a university chair and proved to be immensely successful as a professor of jurisprudence, enjoying his glory as an *ordinarius* for a decade until his death at the early age of 42. Curiously, he was succeeded by another Jewish apostate, Friedrich Julius Stahl (né Joel Jolson, 1802–61). Stahl's background was similar to that of Heine and Gans except for his conversion to Lutheranism coming at an earlier age and being most probably the consequence of a genuine reconsideration of religious and social, but also, unusually, political values as well. In further contrast to the liberal Gans (and, needless to say, to the politically radical Heine), Stahl would evolve as one of the great legal-philosophical defenders of Prussian conservatism and, very particularly, of Prussia itself as a Christian state. His view of the matter of Jewish emancipation, over and above his jaundiced view of 'the Jewish tribe' itself, was firmly negative. The Jews, he thought, needed to be kept legally and politically apart from the general

---

[44] Cited in S. S. Prawer, *Heine's Jewish Comedy* (Oxford, 1985), 12.

[45] Ibid. 15, where the following translation of half of the first verse and all of the second is offered: 'Now [that] your blood has cooled somewhat, you have | come to an arrangement with the gracious lords. | You have humbled yourself before the cross, | the very cross that you despised, | that only a few short weeks ago | you sought to tread into the dust!'

German *Volkstum*. They should not be allowed to be more than second-class citizens. Whereas all citizens, regardless of religious faith, were entitled to civil rights (*bürgerliche Rechte*), political rights (*politische Rechte*) must, in a Christian state, be limited to members of recognized Christian churches only.[46]

It needs to be said, however, that the path along which most apostates resolved to tread differed only marginally, in the final analysis, from that which all others who sought to venture out of the old, closed Jewish community were prepared to take. Brute professional and social ambition aside, it was a journey whose attraction lay in its being thought of as leading inexorably to a broader, braver, freer, nobler, altogether more cultivated world, a world untouched, or only negligibly so, by the provinciality and vulgarity that marked, so the travellers were inclined to believe, the one in which they had previously been confined. It was in all cases, that is to say, a matter of anticipating great delights at journey's end: in the great, rapidly growing capital cities which it had now begun to be possible for Jews to enter, to establish themselves, and to prosper in. The exceptionally talented, energetic, and ambitious hoped to be able at last to slake their new-found thirst for the full individual freedom they believed they would enjoy. For some it was the novelty or advantages or the simple glory of playing a role in great affairs that drew them. Others, still looking inward, saw the dismantling of the ghetto in material form, but more especially in its figurative sense, as the opening of a road to internal change. All such aspiration constituted rebellion against the old Jewish regime, however, a means of establishing social, economic, but above all mental and ideological, distance from the community as it was still constituted and from those who still ruled and sustained it. Otherwise the rebels had little in common. Their purposes were too disparate, if not totally incompatible. The very attempt to group and categorize them tends to distort a social scene of which the dominant features were disorder, mixed and conflicting motives, incoherence, uncertainty, and, to be sure, much vulgar material opportunism as well. In no case was what was on offer to the rebels in practice straightforward progress onward and upward to their goals. It was rather an endless series of choices at a succession of countless crossroads, a perpetual need to overcome obstacles of one kind or another and periodically to retreat as well as advance. Many stages along the journey were emotionally fraught. None was easy to calculate ahead of time. Only the fact of movement out of the confines of the community being contingent upon acculturation was constant. Language in the first instance, internalized patterns of thought, behaviour, and social values and those stores of common knowledge that serve to

---

[46] F. J. Stahl, *Der christliche Staat und sein Verhältnis zu Deismus und Judenthum* (Berlin, 1847), 31.

denote the native and, in their absence, reveal the alien—these were the indispensable items of travelling equipment. In principle, of course, it was here, in the realm of culture, that the final promise and purpose of liberation, toleration, and emancipation were generally considered to lie.

IV

In the early decades of the century it was still commonly the case that Jews in all parts of Europe had a system of education of their own. It was inefficient in many ways, narrowly focused, deeply in need of reform, by western standards hopelessly inadequate, but in eastern Europe capable of assuring the Jews a degree of literacy virtually unknown at the time among their gentile neighbours. A senior official of the Russian-controlled kingdom of Poland believed in 1818 that

Almost every one of their families hires a tutor to teach its children. There are undoubtedly 25,000 tutors per 100,000 families. We [i.e. the non-Jewish population] do not have more than 868 schools in towns and villages and 27,985 pupils in all. They [the Jews] probably have the same number of pupils because their entire population studies. Girls too can read, even the girls of the poorest families. Every family, be it in the most modest circumstances, buys books, because there will be at least ten books in every household. Most of those inhabiting the huts in our [non-Jewish] villages have only recently heard of an alphabet book and of books of religion and morals that console one in times of pain and affliction.[47]

In its unorganized and informal way it was no less therefore than a comprehensive system of general education. The majority of Jewish children acquired at least some knowledge of basic biblical and religious texts and learned to read and write in Hebrew and in their Yiddish vernacular. The results satisfied neither the authorities nor the modernists among the Jews themselves, but in any case there was no alternative. Attempts to enter Jewish children into schools serving the general Catholic population in Poland tended to fail in the face of Catholic resentment and equally strong objections by most Jews. The Lublin district education committee reported to the central State Committee for Religions and Public Education in December 1817, that

The committee was of the opinion that it was impossible to persuade the [Jewish] population to send their children to schools serving Catholic children jointly. The Jews, being unenlightened and sunk in superstitions, do not dare, despite our many rebukes, to dress their children in non-traditional clothing. They do not dare remove their skullcaps nor cut off their side-curls. Although

---

[47] Quoted in Sabina Lewin, 'Batei-ha-sefer ha-elementariim ha-rishonim li-ladim benei dat Moshe be-Varsha, ba-shanim 1818-1830', *Gal-'Ed*, 1. (1973), 68.

the Jews in Lublin did approach [us] and expressed a desire to send their children to the elementary schools, when they learned of the terms of admission they stated that they were unable to fulfil those conditions.[48]

In the west resistance to the modernization of Jewish schooling with all its likely social consequences was weaker, but not negligible. Alsace, its Jewish population being initially closest of any in the west to that of eastern European Jewry, but subject from the first to the strongest of modernizing influences by revolutionary, Napoleonic, Restoration, and Second Empire France, and Second Reich Germany in succession, provides particularly abundant evidence of traditionalist Jews being pulled both ways.[49] As late as the early 1830s, nine-tenths of all Jewish children of primary school age in the department of the Bas-Rhin were receiving no modern education worthy of the name. In the country areas especially, children continued to be subject to inferior instruction at the hands of untrained and incompetent traditional teachers (*melamdim*) in crowded, unsanitary, dark, and generally intolerable physical conditions. As in Poland, this was partly due to the still very common refusal to send children to what were to all intents and purposes Christian schools, partly to the Jews' insistence on maintaining and running schools of their own however inadequate they might be, and partly to there being no state-supported system of education that was both fully compulsory and secular until late in the century.[50]

Still, even in the country villages, the signs of a slow process of acculturation were evident, the declining presence of Hebrew signatures on marriage documents attesting to the diffusion of the French language through the Alsatian countryside. As late as the 1820s and 1830s a quarter of the males and half of all females were still unable to sign their names on official documents in Latin script despite their having lived all their lives in the post-emancipatory period. Not until the 1860s had the proportions dropped to one-tenth and one-sixth respectively. The rate at

---

[48] Quoted ibid. 70.

[49] See especially Paula E. Hyman in her *The Emancipation of the Jews of Alsace* (New Haven, 1991); and Neher-Bernheim, *Documents inédits*, i, ii, as well.

[50] Hyman, *Emancipation*, 101–3; 66. An indicator of progress made under the Third Republic towards the end of the century and beyond is provided by what were found to be the educational qualifications of Jewish recruits to the French army, as follows:

	Primary	Post-primary and higher	Professional
	%	%	%
1867–9	—	—	11
1885–7	47	9	15
1905–7	66	13	17

Source: Doris Bensimon-Donath, *Socio-demographique des Juifs de France et d'Algerie: 1867–1907* (Paris, 1976).

which French names and Gallicized biblical names (e.g. Rachelle for Rachel, Jacques for Jacob) replaced Hebrew and traditional Jewish (i.e. Yiddish) names in the Alsatian countryside was similarly slow. In the communes examined by Paula Hyman, traditional Jewish names were given to 76 per cent of the males and 29 per cent of the females of the cohorts born in 1770–89, the proportions falling to 64 per cent and 11 per cent respectively for the cohorts born in the 1850s.[51] However, matters were otherwise in the cities of Alsace, which in the mid-century accounted for about a fifth of the total Jewish population of the province. Jews whose families had taken up residence in Strasbourg after the Revolution, but had themselves been born before it, bore French and German names, as opposed to Hebrew or Jewish ones, in approximately the same proportions as country Jews. Permanent residence in Strasbourg having been forbidden Jews before the emancipation, they would have been of similar background to those of their contemporaries who were still in the countryside. After the Revolution, all changed (see Table 2.1).[52]

TABLE 2.1. *French and German (as opposed to Hebrew and Jewish) names borne by Jews in Strasbourg*

Date of birth	Males %	Females %
Pre-revolution	33	70
1820s	46	88
1850s	82	93

Equally telling are the data on secondary school (*lycée* and *collège*) students in Alsace collated in the course of a government survey conducted in 1864. While the Jewish population of the province remained a fairly steady fraction of the total population (3 per cent in 1784; 3.5 per cent in 1861), the Jewish fraction of the student body had grown from zero to 8 per cent. Jewish and non-Jewish students were found to be aspiring to middle-class occupations in commerce, industry, and the professions in roughly the same proportions; and these, broadly, were the occupations which Jewish and non-Jewish students ended by taking up equally. The particular novelty in the case of the Jews was their desire, in almost exactly the same proportions as the gentiles (slightly over a quarter), to be admitted to a military academy or to one of the *grandes écoles*. No less significantly, success rates in each case were almost identical (at *c.*10 per cent).[53]

---

[51] Hyman, *Emancipation*, 66–9.
[52] Ibid. 123. The fact that there was a stronger tendency to give women rather than men non-Jewish names both before and after 1789 is worth noting.
[53] Allowance has been made, however, for the fact that while 5 per cent of the Jewish students wished to be admitted to the École Polytechnique and the Ponts et Chaussées

All in all, the *préfet* for the Alsatian department of Bas-Rhin had some reason to report to the minister of the interior in Paris in 1843, with evident satisfaction, that the effect of the emancipation on 'the civil and private lives' of the Jews had been commendable. There had been created among them a middle class which, in externals at any rate, has shed 'the flaws [*du vice*] for which members of this religion were rightly blamed'. Unlike Alsatian Jewry's lower classes, its middle class was fully disposed to make the most of its opportunities for social and intellectual progress.[54]

Similar trends, displacement from country to town, from autonomous Jewish to general public education, and of aspiration to, and actual entry into, occupations and professions of a higher status, can be identified in all parts of Europe. Most spectacular, and contributing most profoundly to the process of acculturation throughout the continent, was the huge influx of Jews into the major, especially capital cities of central Europe. The Jewish population of Berlin was 3,300 in 1816 (1.2 per cent of the total); 12,700 in 1855 (2.9 per cent); 36,300 in 1871 (4.15 per cent); 94,391 in 1895 (4.5 per cent). The rise of the Jewish population in the two capitals of the Habsburg Empire was faster yet, as can be seen in Table 2.2.[55] And much the same occurred in those areas of the Russian Empire and within those areas, in the cities—in which Jews were allowed to reside, Warsaw, the capital of Russian-ruled Poland (from which, after 1807 Jews were no longer barred) and the industrial city of Lodz among them (see Table 2.3).[56]

Leaving aside for the moment the supremely important case of Russia proper, admission to schools, universities, entry into the professions, and, in the unique case of the Austro-Hungarian Empire, admission to the officer corps as well, followed suit. By 1851 there were 1,251 Jewish students in Austrian secondary schools, by 1903/4 the number had risen by a factor of 12.5 to 15,880 (that of non-Jewish students had risen by a factor of only 4.5 in the same period). On average, in the Habsburg domains, Jewish students accounted for 13 to 14 per cent of the total student body.[57]

(3 per cent being admitted), none applied to St Cyr or to the Naval College to which no less than 8.6 of the non-Jewish students applied (and 4.6 were admitted) (see Hyman, *Emancipation*, 117–19).

[54] Neher-Bernheim, *Documents inédits*, ii. 358–9.

[55] See Wolfdieter Bihl, 'Die Juden', in *Die Habsburgermonarchie 1848–1918*, iii. *Die Völker des Reiches* (Vienna, 1980), 884–5. Or, to inverse the figures, whereas 97.8 per cent of all Jews in 'Cisleithanian' Austria in 1846 were to be found in Galicia, Bohemia, and Moravia and only 0.9 per cent in Lower Austria, by 1910 the proportion in Lower Austria had risen to 14.07 per cent and that for the other three provinces had fallen to 76.03 per cent (ibid. 889).

[56] Lucjan Dobroszycki, 'The Fertility of Modern Polish Jewry', in Paul Ritterband (ed.), *Modern Jewish Fertility* (Leiden, 1981), 67.

[57] High average figures should not obscure differences. In Vienna, from the 1870s onwards, Jews comprised some 30 per cent of all *gymnasium* (or academic secondary school) students, a very high proportion that may be equally well expressed by parallel figures for the total population: in 1881 0.6 per cent of all Viennese attended gymnasia, but

TABLE 2.2. *Jewish population of Vienna and Budapest in absolute numbers and as a proportion of the cities' total population*

	1784		1806		1838		1848		1857		1870		1880		1890		1900	
	No.	%	No.	%	No.	%	No.	%	No.	%	No.	%	No.	%	No.	%	No.	%
Vienna	230	—	290	—	2010	—	c.4,000	—	6217	2.16	—	—	72,588	10.06	118,495	8.69	146,926	8.77
Budapest	—	—	—	—	—	—	—	—	—	—	44,747	16.6	70,277	19.7	102,377	21.0	166,198	23.6

TABLE 2.3. *Jewish population of Warsaw and Lodz in absolute numbers and as a proportion of the cities' total population*

	1781		1808		1810		1846		1857		1882		1897	
	No.	%	No.	%	No.	%	No.	%	No.	%	No.	%	No.	%
Warsaw	3,532	4.5	—	—	14,061	18.1	44,149	26.7	—	—	127,917	33.1	219,128	32.0
Lodz	—	—	58	13.4	—	—	—	—	2,886	11.7	—	—	98,671	31.4

In the exceptional case of Bukovina they accounted for 44.2 per cent; and in the *Staatsgymnasium* of the capital city of Czernowitz, to which Jewish students were first admitted in 1820, no less than 664 of a total student body of 870 by 1905 were Jews. The pattern in Austrian universities and technical colleges was similar: 641 students in 1851, 4,485 (15.6 per cent of the total student body) in 1904. The precise number of Jewish officers in the Austro-Hungarian armed forces is uncertain, but by the end of the century (when neither in Germany nor in Russia was it possible for a professing Jew to hold a commission at all) it was very probably over 2,000 in a total army and naval officer corps of 27,000. In all these cases, the indispensable condition of admission to the schools, institutions, and established professions of the major states of western and central Europe was, of course, language. In multinational and multilingual Austria-Hungary alone, by 1910, well over a quarter of the Jews of Cisleithania had acquired German at least as a working language (*Umgangsprache*). In the Hungarian domains of Transleithania, where the matter of language and national identity carried greater weight still, the mother tongue of 57 per cent of all Jews was Magyar as early as the 1880s.[58]

Finally, to these revolutionary and on the whole irreversible changes there need to be added the long-lasting effects of the discovery of new, distinctive, and in important respects incompatible interests between Jewry's social classes. The older, eighteenth-century distinctions between the privileged and the non-privileged, the *Schutzjuden* and the *fremde*, the Portuguese and the Alsatians, the 'useful' and the 'useless' or the 'non-productive', between those with a seemingly firm foot in the general economy and those subsisting on its margins—all these survived. Rather than fading, they had been granted new life, taking on a sharper, less fluid, more permanent form by virtue of their being ever more firmly and visibly correlated with acculturation—or *per contra* with resistance to it. Material (commercial and political) pragmatism and opportunism would now be reinforced—and in the process transformed—by cultural loyalties, ambitions, and achievements. For those who considered that they had escaped from the 'ghetto', the horror of being dragged back into it, with huge consequent loss of status, rights, general welfare, and of course political freedom too, was likely to be compounded by fear lest a forced retreat from what had been accomplished bring in its wake a loss of linguistic, social, and cultural identity as well.

2.2 per cent of the total Jewish population of Vienna. Later, with the accelerated influx of eastern European Jews, the figure for Jewish students as a proportion of all Jews in Vienna was to fall: to 1.3 per cent in 1910. On the other hand, at the elite Theresianische Akademie the relative and absolute number of Jewish students was consistently very low indeed: 4 students (1.2 per cent of the student body) in 1881/2, 2 students (0.5 per cent) in 1910. See Rozenblit, *Jews of Vienna*, 103–6.

[58] Bihl, 'Die Juden', 924, 944, 905–7.

V

The drives towards religious reform and acculturation had it in common that each was compatible with a third impulsion, the drive to de-nationalize Jewry: to reconceive and restructure the Jewish people as an exclusively religious denomination, in effect to remake it as a church. This, of course, was one of the principal charges the traditionalists laid against all programmes of reform. They could point to the fact that where there was no question of the Jews being seen by themselves or by anyone else in other than national terms—as, for different reasons, was the case in the Russian and the Ottoman Empires—there religious reform on the western (principally German) model was failing to take root. Observance and attendance might be less assiduous than before. A certain secular tendency could be seen to be gathering strength. But observance and ritual remained in the old mould exclusively. Where, on the contrary, the de-nationalization of the Jews was thought feasible and people of influence judged it necessary and desirable, there religious reform could be seen to flourish. Only where Germanization or Magyarization or whatever other form the de-nationalization of the Jews was expected to take was the order of the day, did a reworking of the Tradition seem to substantial, as opposed to entirely negligible, numbers to be indispensable. But while all this was true, as a reflection of the several broad directions in which European Jewry was moving, it was incomplete. For where insistence on renewal went hand in hand with an objection to total integration into other nations and a reluctance to jettison more of the baggage of the Tradition than proved to be absolutely necessary, there a search for an accommodation of another kind was in progress. It is at this point that the movement for *haskalah* (enlightenment) comes into its own, veering away from the movements for religious reform and social integration as strictly understood, but unalterably opposed to social and cultural stasis as well.

The *haskalah* can best be understood as the (belated) analogue of the general European Enlightenment. The principal elements of the latter—rationalism, intellectualism, scepticism, humanism, huge suspicion of, if not contempt for, dogma and authority, a corresponding confidence in the power of the human mind to distinguish between false and true problems and, dismissing the former, to proceed to the solution of the latter—all these were to be found within it. In part, it was a function—or by-product—of the European Enlightenment in its specifically German manifestation, the *Aufklärung*. In part, especially in its early years, it represented a brave, to some extent forlorn, attempt by a handful of scholarly Jews who had had access to the larger movement, and been much influenced by it, to construct a bridge between European civilization in its new, universalistic dress and that of the Jews. It was brave because they had in mind a bridge capable of carrying traffic in both directions. It was forlorn because the response on the other side of the divide was fated never to be greater than negligible. Still its deepest roots were internal: the slow, ultimately inexorable percolation of new ideas into segments of Jewish society which objective circumstances, private ambition, and great physical distance from the great east European heartland all permitted, when they did not actually require, a high degree of freedom of thought and action. All these combined to render a certain class of western and central European Jews, in Germany especially, both receptive to what was new and sufficiently independent intellectually and psychologically to allow their new convictions to begin to determine their private and public behaviour.

What the *haskalah* had especially borrowed from the European Enlightenment proper was a mode of thought that subjected virtually all matters of contention to the test of universal quality, content, application, and significance. Its thrust was therefore towards the discounting of differences, real or supposed, between nations, cultures, and, of course, religions as well. The European Enlightenment had tended therefore to neglect the specific and be drawn towards the secular. There were difficulties about this for the adepts of the *haskalah*, the *maskilim*. Anxious to draw from the great store of ideas, attitudes, programmes, and techniques on which the doors of the Enlightenment proper had opened, they were never sure what they might decently adopt and apply to the largely hermetic culture of the Jews themselves. Demoting Christianity from its previously unquestioned role in European culture as sole—certainly ultimate—source of moral truth, the Enlightenment had simultaneously inaugurated a fresh approach to Judaism, now susceptible of examination as one religion among others rather than, crudely as before, as the supreme enemy of the one which alone was true. And if, in some cases, the inquiry into Judaism was neutral or even friendly, in others it was fraught, as before, with hostility and contempt. Judaism, some would now argue, was trebly flawed: in that it was a religion, because it was (was it not?) a particularly absurd one, but, worst of all, and as strongest evidence of its flaws, because it was the *fons et origo* of Christianity itself. Nothing in any of this was likely to trouble the orthodox in Jewry. Their moral and intellectual sustenance was drawn from sources of their own. But there was much in it to trouble those for whom the European Enlightenment had set the cultural and intellectual standards governing the corpus of ordered knowledge into which they sought to integrate their own scholarly findings and, more generally, in the world in which they wished in some sense to be included themselves. Voltaire had famously and contemptuously dismissed the 'philosophy of the Hebrews' as non-existent and the Jews themselves, 'nos maîtres et nos ennemis',[59] as

---

[59] *Dictionnaire philosophique portatif* (London, 1756), 1.

'an ignorant and barbarous people, who have long united the most sordid avarice with the most detestable superstition and the most invincible hatred for every people by whom they are tolerated and enriched'. He did add, magnanimously, that 'Still, we ought not to burn them',[60] but the anguish with which the very early adherents of the Enlightenment in western Jewry responded was extreme. 'Would it be just to impute responsibility for the torment of Charles I to the entire English nation or to all Frenchmen in Charles IX's day responsibility for the St Bartholomew massacre?' was the well-known protest of Isaac de Pinto of Amsterdam. Are there crimes for which an entire nation can be charged? All universal propositions, said Pinto, were *ipso facto* suspect and liable to error, most especially when they referred to the general character of a nation and were subject necessarily to variations of station, rank, temperament, and profession.[61] But, in itself, the question how far it was proper and decent for Jews to go in Voltaire's and others' footsteps was unanswerable. The operative question was how far adherents of the *haskalah* might be willing to bring themselves to go. All believed that the cultural and intellectual heritage of the Jews was ripe for careful, rational, perhaps even radical, but certainly scientific-historical re-examination. None doubted that to some extent the tools had to be borrowed from the world outside. But they were wary. If the heritage was to be rethought, it was by no means to be diminished. Least of all was it to be reduced and distorted by a procrustean effort to shape it to an alien model.

Eventually, the *haskalah* would prove to be not only an intellectual and academic enterprise, but, most notably of all perhaps, a literary one. In its early years, however, its most important and long-lasting manifestations were two: a most successful effort to draw fresh attention to the Hebrew language and the establishment of an entirely new model for Jewish scholarship and learning generally. Hebrew, to be sure, had never been a 'dead' language in the sense that Latin and classical Greek might be so rated. Apart from its being the language of daily prayer, of the Bible, and, with Aramaic, the language of the Jews' sacred and essential legal texts, old and new, it had for centuries been the language of choice for written correspondence between Jews, especially, but not exclusively, between the learned among them. In the Middle Ages Hebrew had been the language in which some of the finest poetry in the Jewish literary canon was written. True, it was not much spoken. And its employment for correspondence on profane subjects (in commerce, for example) had begun to

---

[60] *Œuvres complètes*, vii (Geneva, 1756), ch. 1, cited in Paul R. Mendes-Flohr and Jehuda Reinharz (eds.), *The Jew in the Modern World: A Documentary History* (New York and Oxford, 1980), 252–3.

[61] Isaac de Pinto, *Apologie pour la nation juive, ou réflexions critiques sur le premier chapitre du VIIᵉ tome des œuvres de M. de Voltaire au sujet des Juifs* (Amsterdam, 1762), cited in J. S. Wijler, *Isaac de Pinto, sa vie et ses œuvres* (Apeldoorn, 1923), 45 ff.

die out—not least in consequence of the freer entry of Jews into the general commercial and industrial world and the objection of governments to the records and transactions of Jewish merchants, bankers, and so forth being kept in a form that rendered them inaccessible to official inspection. But this had to do with the latter-day traditionalists' objection to the use of Hebrew for any purpose other than such as might be termed rabbinic. *Per contra*, the move to foster wider employment of Hebrew was inseparable from the very earliest stirrings of *secular* nationalist feeling among Jews and the influence upon the *maskilim* of examples set by their neighbours. 'The nations around us, far and near, [do] not cease and [do] not rest from making books without end', wrote one of the forerunners of the *haskalah*, Mordechai Schnaber. 'Everyone speaks and creates in the language of his people so as to broaden it; and why should we be deprived of the inheritance of our forefathers by forsaking our holy tongue? But indeed we are lazy.'[62]

The other direction in which the *haskalah* moved, initially much the more important one, was that of the new (because essentially secular) Jewish scholarship. This was the celebrated *Wissenschaft des Judentums* (the science or learning of Judaism—or Jewry), conceived as a mighty effort to apply the highest standards of systematic, academic, and so far as possible objective (and therefore *wissenschaftlich* or 'scientific') research and analysis to all that pertained to the intellectual and cultural heritage of the Jews and—the most revolutionary step of all—their history as well. Its accomplishments were indeed to be considerable: Moses Mendelssohn's biblical and philosophical work; the first serious Hebrew-language scholarly and literary periodical (the *Ha-Me'assef* quarterly established in 1783); the path-breaking ventures of Leopold Zunz (1794–1886) into close analysis of great parts of the Jewish literary corpus, but especially his inauguration of modern Jewish historiography; and the first, and in some ways still unsurpassed, work of comprehensive history by Heinrich Graetz (1817–91), his *Geschichte der Juden* intended as no less than, in the author's own words, 'a survey of the entire history of the Jewish nation'. These were among the peaks of an entire range of scholarly endeavour which would gather force and prestige among all Jews who were of a literate *and* a modernist turn of mind throughout the nineteenth century and beyond into the twentieth. Having regard for the sheer novelty of the enterprise and its deliberate departure from the old scholarly-rabbinical tradition, its importance for determining the direction Jewish scholarship would take from Mendelssohn's day on can hardly be overstated. But the *Wissenschaft des Judentums* had social purposes as well. Its proponents believed that what they were about was the easing of the acceptance of Jewry and

---

[62] Mordechai Schnaber, *Ma'amar ha-tora ve-ha-ḥokhma* (London, 1771), 5. Cited in Moshe Pelli, *The Age of Haskalah* (Leiden, 1979), 76–7.

Judaism by state and society, virtually *in toto* and more or less on their own terms. Once mediated in universal terms and categories, the exposition and transmission of Jewish learning, with everything, or almost everything,[63] being looked at with a fresh and critical (but not servile) eye, would unfailingly have a benign effect on the status of the Jews and on the approach to them all round. 'Through larger intellectual culture and more thorough knowledge of their own affairs,' wrote Leopold Zunz, the Jews would gain 'a higher degree of recognition, and thus of rights'. Many of the failures to improve those rights, much of the prejudice against Jewish ancient history, and the condemnation of the Jews' new aspirations, were he thought, no less than the direct result of the state in which, especially in Germany, Jewish literature and the study of Judaism had fallen.[64]

Plainly, then, whatever their intentions, the purposes of the *maskilim* could not in all respects be compatible. Their desire to reanimate Hebrew and greatly extend its use as part of the more general intention of revivifying all that could be usefully and successfully retrieved from the great storehouse of Jewish civilization was beyond question. Yet one of the telling characteristics of the new Jewish learning in its early years in Germany (and elsewhere in the course of time) was that the greater part of its product was presented to the public not in Hebrew, but in the language of the country. The audience to which the Jewish *Wissenschaftler* addressed themselves in the ever more numerous books, articles, and independent journals devoted to scholarly revision and analysis of texts, early attempts at chronological history, probing discussions of points in Jewish law, and the like, was at least as much the non-Jewish as the Jewish, if indeed it was not the world of non-Jewish scholarship that was uppermost in their minds. Hebrew as a subject was one thing. Hebrew as a vehicle was another. The desire to normalize Jewish learning and scholarship, to make it available to a larger world, to demonstrate its intrinsic importance and value *sub specie aeternitatis*, to make it an integral part of humane learning as a whole, and, not least, to bring its own expert scholars shoulder to shoulder with their German (and, later, Russian) analogues both in terms of standards and, of course, repute—all these were central to the enterprise.

It followed that there was more than enough in the *haskalah* to establish it as a movement whose internal logic and implicit purposes were secular, although some time would pass before its secular and—to borrow

---

[63] A common question was how far to press the rule of free inquiry. Some, but not all, while having no objection to the Talmud and even the Bible in general being subjected to 'higher' criticism and textual analysis drew back in the case of the Pentateuch.

[64] Leopold Zunz, *Die gottesdienstlichen Vorträge der Juden* (Berlin, 1832), p. vii. Cited in Michael A. Meyer, 'Jewish Religious Reform and Wissenschaft des Judentums', *LBIYB* 16 (1971), 24.

a term from the non-Jewish context—anticlerical style and drive would be explicit. But while the traditionalists were quick to grasp its inner significance and to condemn it from the start, the general tendency among the *maskilim* themselves, at all events in the movement's early years, was to avoid collision. They tended equally to avoid an outright resolution of the consequent ambiguities in their own position. Their first foothold in the world they sought to penetrate owed a good deal therefore to the man whom they accepted as their *primus inter pares* having been able to position himself with great dexterity astride the divide between the Tradition and the rebellion against it as well as astride the cultural and intellectual divide between the Jews and their neighbours. Strictly speaking, the career of Moses Mendelssohn (1729–86) precedes the chronological bounds of this study. But his influence so greatly outlived the man himself that to most minds he remains the *haskalah*'s primary representative, if not supreme progenitor. Famously, he had been bold enough to lead a team of Jewish scholars in a translation of the Hebrew Bible into the German vernacular—his caution evident in his having the German text printed in Hebrew characters, however. That Mendelssohn frequented non-Jewish literary and scholarly circles of a liberal and deistic disposition in late eighteenth-century Berlin on a basis of intellectual and even social equality was in itself, of course, a remarkable tribute to his distinction as a philosopher in the then accepted academic mode. Indeed, his standing in fashionable intellectual circles in Berlin was strong enough for it to be proposed that he be elected to the Prussian Academy of Sciences. The attempt failed, to be sure, his sponsors (and Mendelssohn himself) being reminded that no Jew was as yet sufficiently emancipated for such an election to be confirmed, as was required, by the king. But he remained at ease in non-Jewish society (despite a crippling deformity of the spine), thoroughly acculturated in German terms, and at the same time a stout defender of Judaism and of the Jews when necessary, a profoundly learned man by traditional Jewish standards, and, most remarkably of all in these circumstances, an orthodox, observant Jew to the end of his life.[65] In combination, these features were immensely rare at the time, leaving Mendelssohn in retrospect as in some ways an ambiguous figure: an intermediate between the old internal Jewish regime and the still imperfectly defined new. He favoured the inculcation of universal and civic values into Jews. But he was opposed to the requirement that citizens conform to a single set pattern or model of good citizenship. He believed it possible and legitimate for Jews to retain a measure of social distinctiveness

---

[65] There is a view, held by Heinrich Heine among others, that in his heart of hearts Mendelssohn was a deist. This is disputed, but the least that may be said of the thesis is that it is not wholly improbable. For a brief discussion of the issue, see Pelli, *Haskalah*, 18 ff. and n. 63.

not only in the world of affairs, but even in the armed forces where, while he recognized the evident contradictions between the exigencies of military service and the *halakha*, he took the view that they were soluble. On the other hand, if the demands of citizenship, when granted, were to prove irreconcilable with those of the *halakha*, why then, in Mendelssohn's view, it was the Jew's duty to remain faithful to the *halakha* after all.[66] But, in general, he was optimistic and forward-looking, as may be seen in the role he played in a characteristically heated contemporary debate that turned on just those issues which were rapidly dividing the arch-traditionalists from even the most cautious and accommodating of early modernists.

A *halakhic* rule—of great antiquity and of absolute textual clarity—lays down that the dead are not to be left unburied overnight.[67] In February 1772, however, Duke Frederick, sovereign ruler of Mecklenburg Schwerin, was persuaded by one Olaf Gerhard Tychsen, professor of oriental languages at Bützow and Rostock, that an end should be put to this 'inhuman' practice on the grounds that the Jews, in their haste, might be burying the living. The duke ordered his Jewish subjects to institute a waiting period of three days.[68] The Jewish community, placed under a compulsion to transgress the Law, appealed. So did the duke's own cabinet which pressed him to reconsider his decision. Their argument was that the Jews were entitled to manage their own affairs according to their own laws and customs without interference, besides which, the rules prescribing the cleansing of the body prior to burial effectively eliminated the alleged danger of burial alive. The duke refused to withdraw his decree, but did agree to the eliciting of an authoritative answer to the jurisprudential question whether the practice of almost immediate burial was indeed of central significance in the Jewish scheme of things. When the Jewish convert to Christianity to whom the ducal government addressed its inquiry asserted that it was *not* of great significance, the community in its distress asked for time to apply to experts who were of unquestioned repute and of its own choosing; and they were permitted to do so. They wrote to Mendelssohn and they sent a delegation to Rabbi Jacob Emden of Altona, a much older man than Mendelssohn (who, as it happens, had been Emden's pupil) and was noted amongst other things for his protracted battle against the followers of Sabbetai Zevi and for his pitiless denunciation of all whom he suspected of harbouring residual attachment to that or any other form of (manifestly) false messianism. He was, however, a man of great independence of mind and many esteemed him as the foremost Talmudic scholar of the day in Germany: rabbinical

---

[66] Miriam Bodian, 'Ha-yazamim ha-yehudiim be-Berlin', *Zion*, 49, 2 (1984), 179.

[67] The Talmud. Sanhedrin 6: 5.

[68] The account that follows relies chiefly on the late Professor Alexander Altmann's meticulous *Moses Mendelssohn* (London, 1973), 288–95.

authority personified. Emden agreed to consider the question, but was slow to formulate his ruling. Mendelssohn was quicker off the mark and, in the circumstances, more adroit. He took a practical and so to speak diplomatic line, preparing a carefully worded draft of a memorandum to be submitted by the community elders to the duke, written, as is worth noting, in just that proper German literary style of which he was a master, but that none in Schwerin, and very few Jews anywhere else in Germany at the time, could command. The duke was thanked for his attention to his subjects' welfare. The terms of the formal conflict between his edict and relevant Jewish law as handed down from antiquity were restated. It was admitted that the actual biblical authority for the injunction was open to debate, but the fundamental assertion that it was rabbinical authority that was binding on the Jews in actual practice and that it was the Law as laid down by the rabbis to which the duke's own established guarantees to his Jewish subjects applied was firmly stated. The duke was assured that no burial ever took place until certainty of death had been established and that, in consequence, he had no cause for concern. However, to remove such doubt as might still linger, the Jewish community of Schwerin undertook in future to insist on a formal medical death certificate being obtained prior to burial. Mendelssohn's draft was gladly accepted and sent forward. The new arrangement proved satisfactory to the duke. So far as he was concerned, the matter was closed. Not so, however, in its internal Jewish ramifications.

Mendelssohn had attached a covering letter to his draft memorandum in which he explained that he had done what he could to help the good Jews of Mecklenburg-Schwerin, but that he could not see what the original fuss had been about. In the first place, they had their own, perfectly competent rabbi. Why had they not relied on him? Secondly, while the old rabbinical injunction on not deferring the burial of the dead (*halanat ha-met*) was clear enough, it was equally the case that the rabbis had always permitted delay under certain special circumstances. Had not these been special circumstances? Thirdly, the ancient rule against postponing burial had been formulated in an age when the dead were placed in caves and watched over for three full days. In more recent times, when, on the one hand, the practice was to bury them underground and, on the other hand, medical science had as yet no clear criterion for establishing death, there was surely something to be said in favour of the duke's original edict after all. For all these reasons, his own view was that if the duke should decide to stick to his original decision the community should acquiesce.

There were several respects in which this was daring. Mendelssohn was suggesting that an established Talmudic injunction might be reconsidered in the light of changed historical (and topographical) circumstances. In so doing, he introduced into a classic *halakhic* dispute considerations that were logically—given the rules by which Talmudic discourse proceeded—extraneous. There was too an aspect of the Mendelssohnian argument that was in essence opportunistic since it had to do with how it would be most politic for the community to deal with a ducal edict. And then there was the reference to contemporary medical science. When Mendelssohn's advice to the community was brought to Emden's attention his sometime master was horrified. The older man dismissed the point about the very ancient practice of burial in caves as incorrect and in any case irrelevant. Equally irrelevant to his mind was what modern medical practitioners were or were not capable of establishing. The Torah had its solution for this, as for all other problems, and to it alone did one apply. What disturbed Emden most of all, however, was the fact that his former pupil had taken it upon himself to question the validity of ancient practice and an established ruling of the Sages. No less grave and impermissible was the example he had set: that of Jews being advised by one of their own to adjust, if not entirely abandon, an age-old custom founded, as all knew, on impeccable Talmudic authority. And to what purpose? In the interests of accommodation to the gentiles.

Even as late as the end of the eighteenth century and on into the nineteenth, it was almost exclusively to their own people that religious and ideological leaders of Jewish orthodoxy, Emden and Ḥatam Sofer and their analogues among them, addressed themselves. Only in extreme circumstances, and then with great reluctance and foreboding and mostly under great public pressure and moral duress, did they undertake to speak to non-Jews on matters touching on the norms by which Jews were expected to govern themselves and live out their lives. Of what they conceived to be the rationale underlying those norms they were still less inclined to speak. Partly, it was wariness of the danger of venturing on to *terra incognita*. But it appears to have had rather more to do with the fact that, by and large, they not only knew very little about the prevailing intellectual climate in which they might have to explain their position, but that they had little interest in whatever and whoever its constituents might be. And finally, as has already been suggested, they had been schooled in the belief (well founded, historically) that little was to be gained, and much damage might be incurred, by an attempt to articulate the foundations of the Law before an alien audience. Everything then, not least the fact that in any case few had an adequate command of the vernacular, bolstered their natural tendency to look inwards and to concern themselves chiefly, even exclusively, with those of their followers and pupils who remained devoted to what they themselves stood for. There was, they thought, more than enough in the vast body of Jewish law and philosophy, and in the accumulated commentaries of some four score generations of scholars upon it, to occupy the brightest and busiest of minds. But the consequence of abstention from social action was that the perennial duty of intercession and direct representation of the

organized community before rulers and their minions was one that genuinely scholarly Jews tended to forgo and leave to others. And the others,
in this case, were most commonly lay people whose prominence, such as
it was, stemmed from mundane sources. Thus, by default, the moral and
intellectual defence of Jewry and Judaism *per se* was left to the profane to
take up as best they were able; or worse, left without any defenders at all.
Not the least of the early indicators of the changes of outlook, structure,
and discourse that were about to sweep the Jews of Europe in the period
with which this study deals was indeed the emergence of new, necessarily
untested classes of champions. Some, as we shall see, would be revealed as
immensely dedicated to the task and exceedingly impressive and articulate
in its performance. But the more impressive and articulate they were, the
more likely were their specifically religious beliefs and philosophical opinions to be at variance with those of the traditionalists. There was no knowing as yet what the cumulative impact of the new men upon the inner life
of the people they sought to instruct and to speak for would amount to. All
that they themselves had in common was that they were self-appointed. It
would soon be clear, however, that they presented a challenge of an
unprecedented kind to the moral and intellectual leaders of traditionalist
Jewry and that while, until very late in the day, it was a challenge that would
be declined, there could be no real meeting of minds between them.

Taken together, then, the effects of half a century or so of movement
on the matter of the Jews by most of the major and some of the minor
states of Europe had been remarkable. It is true, and worth re-emphasizing,
that this did not mean that the Jews had been accorded social equality or
unimpeded access to all the professions or, in all parts, full and formal civil
rights. Only France and Holland had gone so far as to grant their Jews
unqualified legal, political emancipation. But progress of some kind in
that general direction had been made everywhere and the changes that
had been instituted were sufficiently real for there to be quite solid
grounds for thinking—or fearing, depending upon one's point of view—
that further progress in much the same direction was, or would soon be,
the order of the day. To this rough rule there were four exceptions
worthy of attention. Two of these were the curious, if now intrinsically
unimportant, exceptions of Spain and Portugal. There the decrees of
total exclusion and expulsion promulgated at the end of the fifteenth
century in Spain and extended to Portugal early in the sixteenth century
were in force and maintained by the authorities as a matter that was
beyond public dispute. There was the special, historically and politically
instructive, but demographically marginal case of the States of the
Church. And there was Russia.[69]

[69] The Muslim-ruled territories of Turkey-in-Europe constitute a separate category
that lies beyond the scope of this study, although as the Ottomans retreated, so the

VI

It needs to be recalled that Russia was a despotism in which the regulation of the Jews as a nation apart was an established matter of principle. To the end of its time in 1917, the Autocracy would cleave conscientiously to an approach to everything that touched upon Judaism as a faith and as a culture and upon the Jews as a people that, by the standards of its far from philo-Semitic western contemporaries, was archaic. Being, as already suggested, a policy fed by, indeed very largely founded upon, a fundamentally *religious* hostility, it was therefore particularly complacent and self-righteous. But it was shot through too with that tendency, common in Russia at all levels of society, to succumb to fear and contempt of all that was perceived as alien. Efforts to look afresh at existing rules for the treatment and regulation of the Jews and consider what their advantages or otherwise to the state might be would recur. Occasions when some mitigation of their rigour was conceded would be registered. But in their fundamentals neither the underlying approach nor the policy that was its fruit were ever reversed. And if the ideas which informed the Autocracy in its dealings with its Jewish subjects were no better than commonplace, the consistency and tenacity with which it stuck to them remained remarkable. This is not to say that either the formulation or the implementation of state policy on the Jews was ever straightforward. Some at least of the practical effects, and even some of the explicit rules that elsewhere in Europe, notably in central Europe, had come to define 'toleration' (and even 'emancipation' in watered-down form), came to be operative in the course of time in Russia as well. While imperial Russia was a despotism it was in important respects, in the sense that not all was arbitrary, a *Rechtsstaat*. Land and inhabitants were chattels of its ruler; but the daily administration of things and people was carried out by an administrative bureaucracy, a police machinery, and in due course by a judicial system which tended increasingly over time to operate according to established procedures and regulations. Nineteenth-century Romanov Russia was therefore somewhat closer kin to Hohenzollern Prussia and Habsburg Austria than to its nominal analogues Kajar Persia and Manchu China. However, while the 'enlightened' monarchies of central Europe, in so far as they were not already in retreat before the waves of liberalization and democratization and nationalism that were now besetting them, were at any rate on the defensive, the role the Autocracy had devised for itself, notably after the Napoleonic fiasco of 1812, was that of arch counter-revolutionary. Thus abroad and thus at home—at home above all. The notorious dependence of all classes in

condition of the Jews underwent change and the important case of the Danubian Principalities will, at a later stage, be integrated into the present discussion.

Russia—not excluding the nobility and the higher reaches of the governmental bureaucracy—on the personal will and favour of the Tsar consistently tipped the *effective* balance of public opinion heavily in his favour and increased the weight of whatever particular and idiosyncratic views he himself might hold on matters of state and policy. And if this personal dominance of the social and political scene went far to ensure the rise and coalescence of countervailing, mostly secret, circles, parties, juntas, cabals, and other kinds of subversive factions, it served greatly to undermine their prospect of achieving some success. The Decembrist rebellion of 1825 (on which more in the next chapter) sent an unforgettable shock through the autocratic system. But the relative ease with which it was crushed was the supreme illustration of the regime's near-impregnability. Under Nicholas I the uncertainties that had marked the reign of Alexander I—the alternating hopes and disappointments, the shifts from a benign mood to a near-tyrannical one and back again, the presence in the higher reaches of government of men of a genuine liberal disposition side by side with others who were devotees of the established autocratic system—would be forgotten, giving way to something clearer, more coherent, more consistent, but also grimmer. The central purpose of government would now be the re-formation of state and society by fiat, an army on its drill ground being the model: uniformed, disciplined, rationally organized, imbued with a single spirit and a single loyalty, and obedient to a single master. It was intended to be and was in fact 'that prison without leisure, that is called Russia (*cette prison sans loisir, qu'on appelle la Russie*)' which the marquis de Custine famously examined and reported upon, a land, as this most observant of Frenchmen wrote, in which 'the government dominates everything and invigorates nothing; . . . where a man has two coffins, the cradle and the tomb'; where 'mothers have better reason to weep upon the birth of their children than upon their death'; and in which 'one man alone in all the Empire has the right to a will, and therefore to a life of his own'.[70]

Summing up his achievements after a decade in office, Count S. S. Uvarov, Tsar Nicholas's foremost ideologue and for sixteen years his minister of education, considered what he viewed as 'the rapid collapse in Europe of religious and civil institutions' and 'the general spread of destructive ideas' and set out the 'firm foundations' on which he and his master believed the Russian fatherland needed to be established:

It was necessary to gather into one whole the sacred remnants of Russian nationality and to fasten to them the anchor of our salvation. Fortunately, Russia had retained a warm faith in the sacred principles without which she cannot prosper, gain in strength, live. Sincerely and deeply attached to the church of his fathers, the Russian has of old considered it the guarantee of social and family happiness.

⁷⁰ A. L. L., marquis de Custine, *La Russie en 1839* (Paris, 1843), iv. 489, 418, 423.

Without a love for the faith of its ancestors a people, as well as an individual, must perish. A Russian, devoted to his fatherland, will agree as little to the loss of a single dogma of our *Orthodoxy* as to the theft of a single pearl from the Tsar's crown. *Autocracy* constituted the main condition of the political existence of Russia. The Russian giant stands on it as the cornerstone of his greatness. An innumerable majority of the subjects of *Your Majesty* feel this truth: they feel it in full measure although they are placed on different rungs of civil life and although they vary in education and in their relations to the government. The saving conviction that Russia lives and is protected by the spirit of a strong, humane, and enlightened autocracy must permeate popular education and develop with it. Together with these two national principles there is a third, no less important, no less powerful: *nationality*.[71]

But while the theory might be that the Autocrat was the ruler of what was—or at any rate ought to be—an ethnic-Russian and Russian-Orthodox state and that it was precisely therein that its distinctive merit lay, the indigestible fact was that the empire of the Romanovs was nothing of the kind. It was multinational, multicultural, and multireligious. And as its rule was extended westwards, to the recognition of the plain facts of the case there had been added, as we have seen, a positive undertaking to respect the integrity and to some extent the autonomy of the Tsar's non-Russian and non-Orthodox subjects, provided only his political authority as Autocrat was accepted. However, if the contradiction was there for all to see, it was not for that reason more tolerable. In the eyes of the Tsar and many of his chief functionaries it was not tolerable at all. It was notably intolerable in the case of the Jews, as we have seen. And it is in the light of what would now be this supremely self-regarding regime's most serious and intrusive effort ever to correct the anomaly that the further evolution of Russian Jewry must be seen. This would not be the case primarily because of the actual impact of state policy on Jewish society, although the wounds it would leave would be deep and long-lasting. It was rather because it would be established, once and for all, that the direction taken by this vast network of communities would be contingent in great measure on its dialectical relationship with the Russian state.

In the view of the Autocracy as Uvarov had defined it for the ruler, the Jews of Russia failed all three of the relevant tests. They were not Russians or even remotely kin to them. They were not Christians of *any* kind. And regardless of whether they paid lip-service to the Autocracy or not, the salient fact was that they were subject to it only incompletely. They maintained a working system of internal self-government of their own to which the state bureaucracy had no effective access, over which it had no influence to speak of, and which it was prudent, therefore, to regard with suspicion. The Russia to which the regime was striving was therefore

---

[71] S. S. Uvarov, *Desyatiletie ministerstva narodnogo prosveshcheniya 1833–43*, 2–3. Cited by N. V. Riasanovsky, *Nicholas I and Official Nationality in Russia, 1825–1855* (Berkeley, 1967), 74–5. Emphases in the original.

manifestly not one into which the Jews could be fitted. They were unacceptable as candidates for the service nobility. They could, at a pinch, be taken into the ranks of the army, but under no circumstances could they be allowed to enter the officer class. They could not, with the rarest of exceptions, be allowed to become landowners in their own right or masters of serfs. But nor could they themselves be enslaved. In a society conceived, but also, for the most part, actually functioning as an immense pyramid of slaves who differed one from the other only in the degree of conditional liberty permitted them and in which the sole, wholly free spirit was, as Custine had so clearly seen, the man at the apex, their master the Tsar, the Jews could not be other than an exceedingly irritating anomaly. If they were ever to be integrated they had first to be transformed.

All this was understood by Nicholas and his ministers; and it was indeed the transformation of the Jews that they intended, much as Derzhavin and his contemporaries had done a generation earlier. What they were slower to realize was that such a transformation would fail unless it extended beyond even such fundamental matters as religion, communal organization, culture, behaviour, and language. The Jews would have to accustom themselves to changes of ethos in matters so deeply ingrained in their tradition and their psyche as hardly ever to serve them as topics for discussion, let alone debate or open controversy. They would have to accept, for example, the notion that the Tsar ruled by divine right and spoke with god-like authority. In his first circular to regional officials in 1833, Uvarov had laid down that 'Our common obligation consists in this, that the education of the people be conducted according to the supreme intention of our August Monarch, in the joint spirit of Orthodoxy, autocracy and nationality'. Accordingly, he expected 'every professor and teacher [to be] permeated by one and the same feeling of devotion to throne and fatherland, [and to] use all his resources to become a worthy tool of the government and earn its complete confidence'.[72] But nothing could be more remote from a scheme of things in which the central element was God's Covenant with the People of Israel in its entirety, for whom to acquiesce in a political relationship conceived in such terms was to accept a form of slavery that, being essentially blasphemous, was doubly repugnant. The ethos of Jewry had been deeply antithetical to slavery from the first. It was with the great escape from slavery in Egypt (mythical or otherwise) that the history of the Jewish people had always been held to have begun. As Lord Acton put it with great eloquence:

In the midst of an invincible despotism, among paternal, military, and sacerdotal monarchies, the dawn rises with the deliverance of Israel out of bondage, and with the covenant which began their political, life. . . . They governed themselves without a central authority, a legislature, or a dominant priesthood; and

[72] Ibid.

this polity, which, under forms of primitive society, realised some aspirations of developed democracy, resisted for above three hundred years the constant peril of anarchy and subjugation.[73]

And while it was the case that slavery was not forbidden under ancient Jewish law, few sets of biblical prescriptions are clearer than those relating to the rights of slaves, to the corresponding obligations of masters towards them, and most specially to the master's duty to manumit his bondsmen after a fixed period—all of which were exceptional for their times. The contempt with which the biblical legislators regarded a Hebrew slave who none the less *wished* to remain enslaved to his master beyond the time laid down for his release is equally exceptional and perhaps clearest of all.[74]

   Unlike the peasants of Russia, Poland, and the Ukraine—or indeed the peasants of any other part of Europe in earlier times—the Jews, as has already been observed, had never been enserfed. However heavily the ruler or landowner pressed down upon them, formally they remained free men. So they were in fact, and so they thought of themselves. Where they found themselves *bound* in some way to an overlord—prince, bishop, landowner—they conceived the bond as a free (if unequal) contract or simply the product of illegitimate duress. In the latter event, they would wait with greater or lesser patience for the evil to fade away or for an opportunity to shake it off, being, in this sense, much like a modern businessman subject to criminal extortion. If some were inclined to regret the onset and, more than anything, the likely further implications of emancipation, it was not because they looked back to what they perceived as the warm and protected irresponsibility of bondage to benevolent masters. Theirs was in no sense a view analogous to that of the old servant Firs in Chekhov's *The Cherry Orchard* who thought the emancipation of the serfs a disaster. They did not think of their long, undoubted exclusion from civil society as slavery at all. Here then was a further reason for Nicholas's bureaucracy, as it moved ponderously but purposefully towards the realization of its goal of a faithful, docile, and homogeneous society, to attempt to do something about the Jews. The nub of the problem was that in the view of their political masters the only real and lasting cure for the Jews' condition was the oldest of all—conversion and dispersal among the general population. What was unclear was how this was to be achieved. What techniques of social engineering were applicable and available? By what stages and at what speed was it best to proceed? What force was to be applied and at what targets precisely? Official Russia never doubted the propriety and even, to some extent, the benevolence of its

---

[73] 'Sir Erskine May's "Democracy in Europe" ' (1878), *Essays on Freedom and Power* (Boston, 1949), 132.
   [74] The biblical text (Exodus 21: 6) prescribes for such a case the deliberately humiliating ceremony of nailing the slave's earlobe to a doorpost to signify for all to see his indignity and moral inferiority.

ultimate intentions in respect of the Jews—at all events, the ordinary Jewish man in the street, as we have seen. Nor did it much doubt the validity of its overall judgement upon Jewry and what it believed it knew of Jewish laws, practices, and beliefs. It is this self-confidence, arrogance, and brutality of mind that goes furthest to explain the fact that both the thinking behind its plans and the steps actually taken to realize them would be more ambitious and far-reaching than anything imagined, let alone achieved, anywhere else in Europe. Joseph II of Austria, for example, to whose ideas on the matter of the Jews those of Nicholas I bore some resemblance, and earlier rulers of Russia itself went no way so far. And yet, arrogance and brutality were not exclusively the rule in their handling of the problem. If, overall, the legacy of Nicholas's reign for the Jews was an evil one, it was not entirely so; and there was one sphere in which the general effort to undermine the cohesion and integrity of Russian Jewry was pursued without recourse to force at all and less by fiat than in an effort to be cunning.

Uvarov, in his role of minister of education rather than ideologist, was of all the major figures in Nicholas's court the one most directly and personally concerned to push policy on the Jews forward. He had ideas. He had the talent to formulate them in such a manner as to gain their acceptance. In this respect his role was somewhat like that of Derzhavin under Nicholas's father Paul and his elder brother Alexander. But Uvarov's actual thoughts on, and approach to, the Jews differed from Derzhavin's. They were less bilious, less suspicious, and were at one and the same time more liberal and more realistic. A further, more important difference between the two lay in the fact that it was Uvarov's assignment (and opportunity) not merely to imagine and to design, but to operate the instrument, or so it was hoped in St Petersburg, that would do more than anything any one else could think of to precipitate that irreversible transformation of the Jews the Autocracy had always had in mind. Under Nicholas and Uvarov the plan was to strike with great force, but also with deliberation in the sphere which all concerned, Jews and non-Jews, recognized as potentially decisive: education. It would do so, moreover, by enlisting the *willing* co-operation of at least some of the Jews themselves: the still very small, but now steadily growing, class of Jewish modernizers who, having failed to get very far on their own, would be glad to have the government (and its resources) behind them. These were 'enlightened' Jews, *maskilim*, who (at this stage) were still much under the influence of their more numerous, more distinguished, and far better entrenched analogues in the west, notably in Germany. The German example was not one that could be followed in Russia, however, even in the realm of schooling. Except in places that were socially and geographically on the outer margins of the Pale—in Odessa, for example, or beyond it altogether in Riga, namely where life was freer and commerce (in all senses of the term) unashamedly of more concern to people than spirit—the eastern European Jewish public was far too deeply traditionalist and so too instinctively hostile to what the *maskilim* represented to co-operate. And, by and large, they were too poor to sustain the institutions needed. A partial exception to this rule was Vilna, but then Vilna was unique among centres of Jewish population in the Russian domain, for many reasons. It was a fortress of the Tradition at its most rigorous intellectually. By the same token it was the greatest of all centres of opposition to the Hasidic movement. But since it was the Hasidim who of all traditionalist trends were most implacably and vociferously hostile to the *haskalah*, it happened that such voices as might be found to speak for a measure of careful tolerance of at least some aspects of the *haskalah* (the systematic study of the Hebrew language, for example) were likely to be found in Vilna. So while Vilna as the prime centre of Jewish learning and intellectual and cultural activity in eastern Europe, a capital of sorts, was not in itself an especially free and liberal place, it was not one in which all were deaf a priori to all whose opinions differed from their own. There the *maskilim* had at least been able to make a very modest start. Elsewhere, they most commonly found themselves badly harassed, alienated, and lonely. And the triumph of the traditionalists over them was compounded by the Russian provincial governors and policemen, accustomed to the convenience of collaboration with the (orthodox) Jewish establishment on the basis of a common interest in maintaining discipline among ordinary Jewish people, having little use for them either. Uvarov, however, wiser than the governors and policemen on the spot, grasped how they might serve his purposes: Jewish society in eastern Europe being so very heavily opposed to everything the *haskalah* stood for, the *maskilim* having almost nowhere to go in search of really decisive support within Russian Jewry itself, and the underlying thrust of their enterprise being change and modernization, the logic of their predicament might move them to take the historically unprecedented step of being receptive to what the state had to offer them. On the face of things it was not unreasonable on either side to think that they could make common cause. If eventually it was to prove an uncertain and ultimately an abortive alliance, that was because it had been based from the start on a fundamental misunderstanding.

An early landmark along the road towards such co-operation was the decision taken in 1826, some years before Uvarov came on the scene, to subsidize the publication of a book, *Te'uda be-Yisrael*.[75] The author, Itzhak Baer Levinsohn (1788–1860), one of the very first *maskilim* of note in Russia, argued for a new occupational structure for Jewry—more manual, especially agricultural labour, less trading—but, most especially, for a thorough revamping of the institutions and content of Jewish

---

[75] Published in Vilna in 1828.

education. He wanted Hebrew and major European languages taught systematically, the lower tier of the Jewish autonomous school system, the *hadarim* (literally 'rooms' which he called *hadrei mavet* ('rooms of death'), done away with, proper schools run by qualified personnel established, an end to corporal punishment, and in place of a curriculum that centred on the Talmud one that was altogether broader and in great part modern and secular. Neither the terms in which he condemned the existing system nor his recommendations for its reform were notably original. They followed lines that were already familiar outside Russia and which, in any event, would soon be part of the common currency of the *haskalah* movement within Russia as well. But for his time and his milieu they were shocking. Levinsohn had difficulty getting his book printed. When it was finally published the response, as expected, was for the most part violently hostile. But what was remarkable about the incident was that Levinsohn had appealed to the government for help and that, more remarkably still, it was decided in St Petersburg to reward him. A friendly gesture towards Jews of any kind from on high was rare enough for those to whom it was addressed to be encouraged, but the *maskilim* seem to have read into this small gesture a deal more sympathy for their cause than was warranted. Some went so far as to imagine that it would now be possible to persuade the Autocracy to establish an official, empire-wide consistory on something like the French model through which the religious and social affairs of the Jews would all be channelled and in which they themselves would play the dominant role. But, more than anything, they wanted to believe both that the Enlightenment held the key to their troubles and that it had indeed successfully penetrated Russia. Results similar to those they had witnessed in the west were now to be expected there too. In Levinsohn's own fanciful language:

All the nations of Europe, great and small, are [now] devoted to moral improvement and seek man's love regardless of his nation and religion. In some European lands the Jews have already been granted liberty; and in this country, in particular, in the kingdom of Russia, . . . from the day we came under its wings . . . the kingdom has been sworn to good and mercy and seeks with all its might and main to improve our name and condition and ensure our happiness and welfare.[76]

But the St Petersburg officialdom too was in error. An admittedly robust critique of the rabbinical establishment for its extreme narrowness of vision and the hugely obsolete methods by which it continued to instruct the young by an entirely loyal son of his people was read as an intentionally subversive, broadside attack on Judaism *per se*. Still, in the common failure to take each other's true measure lay the germ of a form of co-operation that would prove useful to both sides.

[76] Cited in E. Etkes, 'Parashat ha-"haskalah mi-ta'am" ve-ha-temura be-ma'amad tenu'at ha-haskalah be-rusiya', *Zion*, 43, 3–4 (1978), 273–4.

A second, much more substantial and lasting, landmark in the process whereby the state ventured to extend a cautious welcome to the services and enthusiasm of the *maskilim*, and the *maskilim* for their part were moved to welcome the support of the state, was the establishment in the 1840s of a network of Jewish primary and secondary schools crowned by two state-sponsored and state-maintained rabbinical seminaries. Jews had been admitted to Russian (state) schools and universities since the beginning of the century, as we have seen. Few among them had the requisite preliminary academic qualifications to take advantage of the opportunity, however; and the social and doctrinal obstacles and objections to the acquisition of such qualifications by submitting to a full course of primary and secondary education in an intensely Christian environment were immense. The numbers were therefore exceedingly small: not much over one hundred young Jewish people in all state academic secondary schools (*gimnazii*) in the early 1840s;[77] less than two score in the universities. A major ambition of the *maskilim* was therefore to establish modern schools of their own which would open the path to further, higher education, but in which, none the less, the essentials of Jewish civilization (Bible, Talmud, Hebrew) would be properly taught in tandem with equally proper, up-to-date instruction in the sciences, modern European languages, mathematics, history, general literature, geography, and the like. There could, of course, be no greater threat to the traditionalists than this on every possible count: doctrine, the integrity of their own all but monopolistic system of schooling, employment, social and moral authority. The campaign against all such projects was therefore exceedingly vehement: threats of excommunication, verbal and physical harassment of potential pupils and their parents, denunciation before provincial governors who, when faced with such disputes and such clamour tended, as already suggested, to side with their tried and true associates among the traditionalists. In the short term, the pool from which a student population might be drawn was therefore not much larger than that formed by the *maskilim* themselves and their immediate sympathizers; and these, taken together, were too few and too scattered for more than a mere handful of schools to be even marginally viable. It was only when Uvarov perceived the use he might make of the *maskilim's* intense desire to set up modern, if still explicitly Jewish, schooling and when a German rabbi, Dr Max Lilienthal, who had been invited to run a small German-language Jewish school in Riga in 1839, came briefly on stage

---

[77] By 1863 the number had risen to 552 (or 3.1 per cent of the entire Russian secondary school student population of 17,320. Yu. I. Gessen, *Istoriya evreiskogo naroda v Rossii* (revised edn., Moscow and Jerusalem, 1993), ii. 179. A fifth of the Jewish students attended school in Odessa alone (S. J. Zipperstein, 'Jewish Enlightenment in Odessa: Cultural Characteristics, 1794–1871', *JSS* (Winter 1982), 19–36). Zipperstein (p. 29) gives a slightly different figure for the all-Russian Jewish student population.

and to the minister's attention, that matters changed and prospects brightened.

The story of Lilienthal's meetings with Uvarov, his official appointment as Russia's first 'learned Jew' (*uchënyi evrei*),[78] his services as Uvarov's agent for the promotion of the minister's ideas and plans among influential members of Russian Jewry, and his subsequent sudden, imperfectly explained decision to leave Russia for the greener fields of the United States is a staple of Russian Jewish historiography.[79] Lilienthal was not a man of great scholarly attainments, although as a graduate of the University of Munich he was well above the ruck. He was very young, exceedingly ambitious, and probably very vain; and besides having neither Russian nor Yiddish, he proved to be too insensitive (or too inexperienced) to make useful and friendly contact with the Jewish notables he needed to work with if he was to get anywhere at all in so vast a community. It was not until Uvarov made Lilienthal a government official (almost certainly the first Jew to be formally incorporated into the bureaucracy) and made it absolutely clear to all concerned that he was determined to proceed to the establishment of an entire Jewish school system of (his and Lilienthal's own) modern design that the clamour precipitated by his appointment died down somewhat. Even so, it was hard going. The rabbinical members of the commission of Jewish notables appointed to consider the Jewish content of the curriculum and underwrite its legitimacy rebelled and were first threatened with punishment and then ignored. Popular resistance was continuous and it was necessary to show that Lilienthal personally and schools, staff, and pupils all had the firm backing of the state (and its police) and that no interference would be tolerated. It took until 1847, three years after the law authorizing the establishment of the primary and secondary schools for the first such institutions to be established in Minsk and Vilna and for the rabbinical seminaries to be opened in Zhitomir and Vilna. Eight years later, when Jewish state schools had been established in almost every major town within the Pale, seventy institutions in all, the entire student body still numbered no more than *c*.2,500—a minute segment of the Jewish school-age population.[80] And had it not been known that attendance at Uvarov's schools provided a virtual guarantee of exemption from military

---

[78] Lilienthal was succeeded by Leib (Leon) Mandelstamm, the first Jew to be admitted (in 1840) as a student to a Russian university. Mandelstamm himself had no successor in the Ministry of Education, but 'learned Jews' of lesser standing were regularly appointed by the Ministry of the Interior to advise its officials and provincial governors serving in the Pale of Settlement on matters concerning the customs, laws, and rituals of the Jews.

[79] Admirably summed up in Etkes, 'Parashat ha-"haskalah mi-ta'am" '; and M. Stanislawski, *Tsar Nicholas I and the Jews: The Transformation of Jewish Society in Russia 1825–1855* (Philadelphia, 1983), 69–96.

[80] Gessen, *Istoriya*, 161; Stanislawski, *Tsar Nicholas* I, 106.

service it is more than probable that the schools' population would have been smaller yet. In sum, the victory of the Jewish modernists was a limited one and the system Uvarov and his *maskilim* had devised would prove to be no more than a halfway house at best on the road to a truly lasting accommodation with modernity.

The network of schools and the two rabbinical seminaries Uvarov had founded were closed in 1873. While they operated they contributed something to the consolidation of the Russian version of the *haskalah* movement itself in that they provided an institutional and economic base for some of its leading lights who were happy to serve as instructors, inculcating a hitherto unknown, because more liberal, form of Judaism in their pupils, notably among the graduates of the rabbinical seminaries established in Vilna and Zhitomir. The only flaw in the system, so far as the more rigorously minded *haskalah* sectarians were concerned, was its appeal to private self-interest no less, if not more, than to concern for a Jewish national cultural revival. But in any case, as would be clear in the course of time, it was the more prestigious regular state *gimnazii* that attracted most young Jewish people in search of a formal academic education. As for the government, it is likely that Uvarov's eccentric reliance on volunteers, on persuasion, and on the goodwill of at least part of Jewry was regarded, if not with displeasure, then at any rate with embarrassment, heightened, to be sure, by the undeniable failure of the scheme. The numbers were always far too small for anyone to speak seriously of success. And the only conclusion to be drawn was that it was not in the nature of such a project as the provision of a special school system to contribute anything of substance to the purposes in which the regime was really interested, the dismantling of the barriers to the Jews' integration into the general population and their eventual absorption within it. In this matter of legislating and administering social change, the special taxes levied on the traditional dress of the Jews in 1839 and the total ban upon them promulgated in 1851 were more in character. And it was certainly the attention the regime was determined to pay, schools or no schools, to the key matters of Jewish self-government and to the regular conscription of Jews into the Russian army that were to leave the deeper marks on the fabric of Jewish life and society in the empire.

VII

The Autocracy had always greatly disliked what it saw, correctly, as a barrier to its own unobstructed control of its Jewish subjects and the corresponding diminution of the individual Jew's need for, and subordination to, its own institutions, among them the judiciary. It had long recognized in the local institution of communal self-rule, the *kahal*, a rival for the Jewish subject's loyalty to the Autocracy and moral dependence on the state. It saw it as encapsulating—and, what was worse, promoting—that tendency among the Jews of which the 1804 Committee[81] and all Russian administrators before and since complained: 'Alienating themselves from general laws and the respect due them, they are part of the state organization in matters of police only, while in internal matters one may say that they remain outside of it.'[82] The upshot was that all those in St Petersburg who gave any thought at all to the matter sought to do away with the *kahal*, some going so far as to employ the falsely benevolent, self-serving, although not entirely unfounded, argument that it had destroyed the influence of the rabbis and 'held the people in such servility [*podobostrastiye*] that the poor Jews, fearing revenge, dare not reveal how they secretly did wish to order their own lives'.[83] But the rulers of Russia were perpetually torn between the desire to abolish the *kahal* outright and enjoy the administrative convenience of using it as a much more effective instrument of government over the Jews than any that they themselves could devise for ruling so difficult and recalcitrant a people.

The negative considerations gained special force under Nicholas I and finally and formally the *kahal* was abolished in 1844.[84] Some of the functions that had previously been laid upon it by the state devolved on the regular police and municipal administrations—some completely, but some half-heartedly. The immensely important power to determine who was and who was not eligible for an internal passport or other necessary official papers was withdrawn, but only in part: to obtain them from the police or municipal authorities the Jewish subject needed a certificate of good conduct which it was the function of community officials to issue at their discretion. For while the *kahal* was abolished, the 'community' (*obshchestvo*)—ill-defined, but consisting essentially of the communal *parnassim* and constituted therefore on much the same basis as the *kahal* had been—remained the body through which the state chose to operate in the spheres that concerned it most. The rule by which the Jewish population was to be kept subject to the state's control remained that of collective responsibility. To that end the duties of the community, despite the abolition of the *kahal*, were no more than marginally respecified. In some respects they were rendered more onerous and the *de facto* powers

---

[81] See above, pp. 93–5.

[82] N. N. Golitsyn, *Istoriya russkago zakonodatel'stva o evreiakh 1649–1825* (St Petersburg, 1886), p. 436. Cited in I. Levitats, *The Jewish Community in Russia, 1772–1844* (New York, 1943), 31.

[83] Count Kisselev, chairman of the committee on Jewish affairs to Vorontsov, governor-general of New Russia and Bessarabia, 13 Feb. 1841 (OS). Cited in A. Shohat, 'Ha-hanhaga bi-kehilot rusiya 'im bitul ha-"kahal"', *Zion*, 43, 3–4 (1977), 156 n. 28.

[84] Strictly speaking, the decree of 1844 did no more than implement a law providing for the abolition of Jewish self-government that had been promulgated in 1786.

they required to perform those duties were substantially increased.[85] In sum, while continuing to object as a matter of principle to the Jews having semi-autonomous instruments of communal government of their own the Autocracy continued to rely upon them to do its will in all realms to which it attached some importance. Of these the most notable, not least because they impinged directly on the Jewish man and woman in the street, were taxation and military service.

For fiscal purposes Jewish communities had long been held to be coherent and separate units. The taxes laid upon them were different in kind from those laid upon other subjects of the empire and, generally speaking, heavier. The original justification for such differentiation was the community's need to maintain its institutions, pay its functionaries, and provide for charitable services of its own. As a corollary and to some extent as a concession, the task of collecting taxes was left to the community itself. It had never worked well or fairly, however. Certain classes of Jews were exempt from taxation by virtue of their economic standing. The communities' control over the *use* made of the money they collected diminished in the course of time in favour of the central government. The impoverishment of Russo-Polish Jewry steadily reduced the Jews' capacity to sustain the economic burden the state laid upon them. And the result was that tax arrears mounted steadily: it has been calculated that by the mid-1830s arrears in four of Russia's western provinces had reached the equivalent of a two-year levy.[86] As for social justice, the broad result was a system in which those who were best able to pay taxes were entrusted with the duty and power to extract them from those least able to do so.

But it was the decision to conscript Jews into the Russian army that more than any other governmental measure affecting Jews during Nicholas's long rule served to mark it in their minds. Jews had not been called up previously. The conventional wisdom—throughout Europe, of course—was that Jewish menfolk were a feeble, cowardly, and untrustworthy lot—therefore useless to the army, perhaps even damaging to it if ever admitted to its ranks. But to Nicholas this blanket exemption was unacceptable; and, given his belief in the unique merits and uses of military service in the general effort to homogenize and discipline his subjects, his objection to it was doubly unyielding. Ostensibly, what would now be enacted in Russia was a measure, the formal rationale of which was comparable to what had long since been established thinking in France, Prussia, and the Habsburg Empire: that the Jews both deserved and owed the state equal treatment; and equal treatment in this sphere particularly would benefit the Jews as a class and hasten their emancipation and integration into society at large. But if the conditions

---

[85] All meticulously discussed and analysed in Shoḥat, 'Ha-hanhaga bi-kehilot rusiya'.
[86] Levitats, *The Jewish Community*, 56.

of service in the ranks of all early nineteenth-century armies were harsh, those of the Russian army were notably so. And the terms under which Jews were to be recruited were uniquely and peculiarly cruel even by Russian standards. It was laid down (on 26 August 1827), that Jews would be conscripted on the same proportionate basis as all other subjects: so many young, single males per thousand,[87] and for the same period of twenty-five years. But it was further enacted that in the Jews' case specifically the minimal age would fall from the usual 18 or 20 to 12. The boys were to be separated from the men. Their service would be passed in the special, so-called cantonist, youth battalions before posting to regular military units upon their reaching their majority. Their full twenty-five-year term of military service would then begin in earnest.

It is true that there were other categories of child recruits to the Russian armed forces, much as there were (drummer and bugle boys and naval midshipmen, for example) in other European armies and navies. What was peculiar to Russia was the recruitment of boys as a punitive or, in the best of cases, as a social measure. The ranks of the cantonist battalions were filled with abandoned children, the sons of political and common law prisoners, and young offenders. Even so, there were at least four ways in which the decision to incorporate Jewish children into these battalions was exceptional. In no other case was the cantonist format applied— applied compulsorily, it needs to be said—to an entire ethnically (i.e. not criminally or politically) defined segment of the population. The purpose was devoid of military significance or calculation. It was not conceived of as punitive. And the chosen instrument on which the duty to implement it devolved (along with the recruitment of able-bodied young adults in the normal way as well) was the Jewish community itself. The elders of each community were informed of the quota for the year. It was then their function and their responsibility, by no means that of the army or the police or the civil authorities, both to select the recruits and to deliver them bodily to the military authorities.

Long-term military service in the Russian army was contemplated with horror and fear by almost all subjects of the Tsar. 'The peasants treated induction as a sentence of death', writes Richard Pipes.[88] But it paled before the particular horror with which a parent—or any other decent person[89]—was likely to contemplate the fate of a Jewish child so

---

[87] The precise number varied from year to year. It could be as low as four. It seems never to have reached ten.

[88] R. Pipes, *Russia under the Old Regime* (New York, 1974), 150.

[89] There is a famous passage in which Alexander Herzen, in his memoirs, recounts his seeing a convoy of Jewish boys, 'little fellows of eight and ten' being marched to Kazan to serve in a cantonist battalion, 'sick children, uncared for and uncomforted, exposed to the wind which blows straight from the Arctic sea, . . . marching to their graves' (*Byloe i Dumy* (Leningrad, 1946), 124).

unlucky as to be pressed into service in a cantonist battalion. There is abundant evidence of the extraordinary harshness of the demands made on the children (who in practice, and in crass violation of the rules, were as likely as not to be substantially *younger* than 12 years of age), of beatings for the slightest of offences, of filthy quarters, inadequate food, an exceedingly high mortality and sickness rate, frequent (in many cases invariable) refusal to allow them the performance of their religious duties (despite the formal requirement to permit it), and the consistent pressure—physical pressure for the most part—to submit to baptism. Beyond the immediate cruelty of the system and the manner in which the law was implemented, there was too the intense and unremitting pain suffered by all Jews in the Russian army, young men no less than children, even when, as was frequently the case, they did finally succumb and agree to baptism. They found themselves isolated in an alien and hostile society. Contact with other Jews in their place of service was made deliberately difficult or in fact virtually impossible (when the posting was to places outside the Pale of Settlement). The consequence of long military service was therefore always a degree of psychic confusion, and often total loss of social identity. To have been recruited for twenty-five years (in some cases twenty years, in the case of the cantonists many more) was to be torn from family and people, very likely never to return. That was how all understood it. So, with fairly rare exceptions, it turned out to be. 'I shall not describe my meeting with my mother, my brother, my sisters and with others of my relatives who were still alive', wrote a certain Ilya Isayevich Itskovich, sent to a cantonist battalion at the age of 7 (!) in 1853, but lucky enough to see his family again nineteen years later. 'They had long since buried me; and even I did not believe that I would emerge alive from the cantonist [battalions].'[90] But therein, of course, lay the rationale of the scheme and its attraction for the regime. While there are no fully reliable and precise figures, there is sufficient evidence to show that the majority of Jews recruited during Nicholas's thirty-year reign were indeed minors, that their number did not fall far short of 50,000 and may have been higher, that half or more of them were induced to apostatize, and that one way or another it was the cantonist system specifically that accounts for most of the cases of Jews converting to Russian Orthodoxy in the course of the nineteenth century.[91] These were not numbers that could have been attained in any other way, the more so as the social class most grievously touched was the one that was otherwise least penetrable by the cultural and religious agents of the Russian state.

But the cantonist system of boy recruitment ate into foundations of

[90] I. I. Itskovich, 'Vospominaniya arkhangel'skago kantonista', *Evreiskaya Starina*, 5 (1912), 63–4.
[91] Samter, *Judentaufen*, 40–2, 72–3; Stanislawski, *Tsar Nicholas I*, 22–5.

Russian Jewry in more subtle ways as well. It created a small, but not insignificant, class of Jews who, while remaining technically of their ancestral faith and people, had grown away from both. Their language, and to some extent their ways as well, were now Russian. Even those who had managed secretly or even openly to stick to their Judaism, were likely to have acquired an outlook that was loosely secular or marginally receptive to Christianity—having been exposed to it for so long—in ways that to other Jews were normally foreign. That they had been *soldiers*—rarest of all occupations for a traditionalist Jew—set them still further apart from their original class and brought them closer to gentiles. Privileged upon release to live outside the Pale of Settlement, and therefore in conditions of tenuous ties to a Jewish community, or no ties at all, it is not surprising that many chose to do so. Still, the deepest wound upon the body politic of Russian Jewry delivered by the cantonist system—and indeed by the military recruitment system generally—was to the cohesion of the communities themselves and to the fabric of trust and obligation on which its cohesion and integrity necessarily depended.

The initial, instinctive Jewish perception of the plan to recruit Jews into the army was that of a new, if especially monstrous *gzeira*. Thereupon, in traditional style, great efforts were made by Jewish notables to induce officials at the highest level of government (by argument if possible, by massive bribery if necessary) to scuttle it, or water it down in some way, or at least delay its promulgation.[92] They failed. The emperor was adamant. But the deeper and far bitterer failure was internal. That the hatred and fear of what might be in store for their loved ones would lead people to be willing to do anything to allow their sons and brothers to escape the levy was inevitable. That the authorities were not much concerned (or could easily be deflected from noticing) whether the very loose rules that were supposed to ensure equitable treatment of all were observed in practice was equally inevitable. That certain social and occupational categories were totally exempt from service (rabbis, guild merchants, students at government schools, for example) meant that the burden tended to fall disproportionately on the poor and the ill-educated in all circumstances. And that those who were well placed economically and socially were better able to evade service where they were liable for it was bound further to exacerbate the inequalities: the difference between those who could raise bribe money, pay for a substitute (who had to be another Jew, however), or be informed of the movements of the communal press-gang in time to take their son to safety and those who could manage none of these things was of course crucial. On the other hand, the powers granted the communal officials to facilitate their task and

---

[92] S. Dubnov, 'Kak byla vvedena rekrutskaya povinnost' dlya evreev v 1827 g.', *Evreiskaya Starina*, 2 (1909), 256–65.

generally to impose their will were immense. The law provided that 'the community may at any time draft by verdict any Jew who is guilty of irregularity in the payment of his taxes, or of vagrancy, or of any offence not tolerated by the community'.[93] And since the punishment the state was prepared to mete out to the communal officials themselves should they fail in their duty to deliver the quota set them (or to any one at all who interfered with the relevant procedures) could be severe—heavy fines, Siberian exile, penal servitude, or their own induction into the army—those who assumed the task and the power tended very strongly to use it. It was an evil system. None thought otherwise. Some ended by being resigned to the evil. 'It stands to reason [*samo soboyu razumeetsya*],' wrote Ilya Isayevich Itskovich, 'that among the Jews, as among the other peoples in Russia, the rich or the educated did what they could to avoid the recruitment of their children.'[94] Some rebelled. In some communities the elders went out of their way to avoid the office. Here and there, a braver rabbi than most stood up publicly and denounced those who had assumed it. Very occasionally, courageous spirits at the very bottom of the social ladder submitted complaints of favouritism to the authorities despite the vengeance likely to be exacted of them from above. And, unusually for the Jews in their exile, there was some violence. Communal officials were beaten or stoned. Press-gangs were forced to release their victims. Convoys were ambushed and recruits freed. How widespread such resistance may have been has not been established. The evidence is almost entirely anecdotal. By the standards to which periodic peasant rebellions had accustomed successive Russian governments it was certainly negligible. And while the authorities seem to have expected some trouble, they were unconcerned by the prospect: Jews were known to be too cowed a people to mutiny.[95] It is, indeed, the fact that there was any resistance at all that deserves attention. It suggests the beginning of a change of mood in Russian Jewry, some loss of ancient patience, a certain deep disquiet, evidence that there was a point beyond which these people could no longer be pushed and punished either by the state or—most especially—by their own leaders without their ancient docility being subject to evaporation. But, in general, the fact was that one class of Jews had been set to hound another and that, exceptions apart and despite misgivings in many cases, one cannot speak of a coherent, let alone a widespread, attempt to avoid the duty or so much as seriously consider doing

---

[93] Levitats, *The Jewish Community*, 60.

[94] Itskovich, 'Vospominaniya', 54.

[95] Shoḥat, 'Ha-hanhaga bi-kehilot rusiya', 181–4 and *passim*; E. Tcherikower, 'Hehamon ha-yehudi, ha-maskilim ve-ha-memshala bi-mei Nikolai I', *Ẓion*, 4, 2 (1939), 150–69; Stanislawski, *Tsar Nicholas I*, 127–37. For an apologia on behalf of the mostly silent and embarrassed orthodox rabbinate, see Yaʻakov Halevi Lifshitz, *Zikhron yaʻakov: historiya yehudit be-rusiya u-folin*, i (2nd edn., Benei Berak, 1968), 106–17.

so. In a society in which internal class distinctions had always been fluid, differences of status, privilege, means, and power would now be tightened, consolidated, and exposed as never before for all to see, and for all to reflect upon. Few phenomena in living memory, if any at all, were so corruptive of Jewish society as the duty laid upon communal elders first to select and then to deliver—by force if necessary—the quota of recruits that had been laid upon them. There would be nothing like it anywhere else in Europe for a century to come.

The scars left by the *rekrutchina* were therefore to be lasting.[96] It destroyed what was left of the moral authority of the *kahal* and its lineal successors. It did much to introduce into the public life and the private calculations of Russian Jews the socially destructive, heretofore largely alien, principle of *sauve qui peut*. It contributed to the growing class of semi- or entirely secularized Jews, barely represented until now in eastern Europe. And all this, it is to be noted in final analysis, was the work, directly and indirectly, of the state. It was the state that had resolved to employ the organized community in a purpose and in a manner that could not fail to be both destructive and corruptive of it. At the same time the effect was paradoxical. The uses of the community as an effective sub-contracting intermediary between the state and the Jewish public was reduced. The public itself was rendered somewhat more self-reliant, not less, somewhat less docile, not more. And as a class, so far as the Jews of the empire were concerned there was to be less question than ever of their taking the place for which they had been designated in Nicholas's parade-ground society. The age of Jews as rebels and insurgents was about to begin.

VIII

What was in process of being lost in the course of the post-Napoleonic years was consensus. None of the slowly consolidating new schools of thought was equipped socially and intellectually, nor perhaps psychologically, to formulate a view of the modern matter of Jewry that was at one and the same time fresh, comprehensive, and acceptable beyond the circle in which it had originated. The traditionalists, while manifestly losing ground, were capable of responding to the threat—or reality—of change only by rearguard action and general denunciation of anything that smacked of innovation, reappraisal, or an impairment of established sources of authority. There was no question of their retaking ground. The process of erosion that had overtaken them at the outer margins of

---

[96] The forced recruitment of minors was abolished shortly after Alexander II's accession to the throne in 1855. There was no recruitment at all between 1856 and 1863.

the heartland of European Jewry, namely in western, northern, and southern Europe, in the great cities of central Europe, and in such small modernist communities as had been permitted *ad hoc* to drop anchor and perpetuate themselves just outside the limits of the Russo-Polish Pale of Settlement, was proceeding too rapidly to be arrested. And if within the eastern European heartland itself the mass of Jewry was held firm for the time being, it was none the less the case that steadily expanding chinks of alien light were plainly visible and that moderate *de facto* and, so to speak, technical and external bits and pieces of compromise on a strictly private, individual, often shamefaced basis were ever more common: beards shaven off, dress changed, heads uncovered as people went about their daily business, and multiple concessions made to the ever more pressing need for secular, theologically neutral learning. Thus at all events in the middle and educated classes, most notably of all with deepest consequences among those who, within Russian Jewry, would form the analogue to the Russian intelligentsia.

Where, on the other hand, innovation was positively favoured, where emancipation and the connected challenges of integration and accultur-ation were the rage—there, of course, the logic of the situation did not call for thoughts on a comprehensive reconstitution of the Jewish people and its governing ethos at all. There everything pointed if not to the definitive dissolution of Jewry, at all events to a reworking of the Jews' nature, quality, and status to accord with what was likely to be acceptable to the societies in which the Jews were embedded. Some would now argue that Jews were to be regarded primarily, even exclusively, as mem-bers of a religious denomination; that they needed so to reshape them-selves that they were no more (if admittedly no less) distinguishable from their non-Jewish fellow citizens than Protestants of one kind were distin-guishable from Protestants of another kind, and all Protestants taken together from Roman Catholics. Others took the view, steadily gather-ing force, but its implications still imperfectly understood, that the Jews were now, or ought now to be, divided permanently according to the political nations to which geography, history, diplomacy, sheer chance, and, in some cases, private preference had assigned them. Had there not always been a loose identification of Jewish communities with the land in which they found themselves? Was it not the case, over time, that quite distinctive communal traditions of one kind or another—each with read-ily identifiable linguistic, occupational, culinary, and to a moderate extent even ritual components—had evolved? It might be true, it would be argued, that ultimate social and political loyalties had once been owed to the Jewish nation and not, except in a limited and pragmatic way and on a contractual basis, so to speak, to the ruler of the land in question, still less to the nation, if such there was, over which he or she actually ruled. But that was in the past and in very different circumstances. The issue of political loyalty in the modern sense could no longer be avoided. Napoleon's commissioners had put it plainly to the Assembly of Jewish Notables in Paris in 1806 and the notables' response had been equally clear-cut. They were Frenchmen now, much, so they said, as the Jews in England were Englishmen. Could it be otherwise elsewhere? This was another genie that could under no circumstances be put back into its bottle.

The fragmentation of Jewry and Jewish opinion was the deeper for there being no machinery for continent-wide deliberation on what had occurred and what might be in store. That there was no authority capable of establishing a compelling and binding ruling for all was not new. What was new, or relatively so, was that this was a condition for which there were no ancestral precedents to evoke and rely upon. The terms and general spirit in which Jews in the course of their exile had been accustomed to debate and determine how it might be wisest to approach a new and unfamiliar ruler, for example, or respond to a threat of fresh proscriptions, or weigh the balance of advantages and disadvantages where an offer of privileges was conditional on specific obligations—none of these offered guidance. A hundred different answers to the interconnected questions of what was right and what was politic to do in present circumstances were on offer. But the central, fateful characteristic of the era ushered in by the Enlightenment, the Great French Revolution, the final partition of Poland, and the first stirrings of political nationalism in all parts, was that the Jews were now irreparably divided in their social purposes, privately and as groups. External constraints and a deeply internalized low profile had long since rendered them incapable of effective concerted action. But if unity of action had been beyond their capability, they had, by and large, enjoyed the minor benefit of unity of opinion and approach. That unity was crumbling.

3
Questions from Without and Within

I N its modern, secular, and political form the notion that the Jews,
collectively, presented a threat to the other European peoples was in
the main the invention of men of letters—scholars, philosophers,
publicists—and serious political dissidents. So was its corollary: that the
role the Jews played in society and in the economy was at once an acutely
representative symbol of the times and one of its governing factors. In
certain interesting ways the idea had roots in ancient, especially Christian,
theses and sentiment. In other ways it constituted a departure from them,
reflecting changes in social and political conditions at all levels of European society and the common thinking on public affairs. However, the
rapidity and avidity with which it was taken up and propagated cannot be
fully accounted for except in the light of the advance of the process of
Jewish emancipation and of its twin, the admittedly incomplete, but still
noticeable and continuing integration of the Jews in society at large. Such
was the case where emancipation had been decreed and embarked upon.
Such too was the case where it was contemplated from afar and denied.
Some of the early formulations of the conceit dated from just before the
collapse of the *ancien régime*, elements being present in the minds both of
those who had decreed measures of emancipation and those who had
sought actively to obstruct it, the entire process, as we have seen, being
shot through therefore with reservations and internal contradictions.
Still, in its full and explicit form it remained fundamentally incompatible
with the general thinking of the effective social and political leaders of the
western and central (as opposed to the eastern) states of nineteenth-
century Europe whose principal concern, as always, lay elsewhere: the
preservation of the structures of government and the established order.
The incumbent rulers, administrators, and bureaucrats were not immune
to new ideas of this or any other kind. But they tended to absorb them, if
at all, with something less than clarity and without translating them
firmly and confidently into current policy. Most retained a certain basic
loyalty to their predecessors, the men of the Enlightenment who had first
allowed Jews to tiptoe into the socio-political space from which they had
been excluded in the past. All were at one with their fathers at least in
their *dirigiste* and self-confident approach to matters social and political,
unafraid of what the Jews themselves might make of their new possibilities

provided they themselves were not faced with too many disturbing or even merely irritating contradictions.

Of this school Metternich, for all that he was the supreme champion of the post–Napoleonic order in his role as defender of whatever could be salvaged from the pre–revolutionary age, was as good a representative as any. He did not hesitate to maintain good relations with Jews when he found it interesting or profitable to do so. He rarely gave overt expression to anti-Jewish sentiments. He had (as his wife's journal tells us) as little difficulty meeting the Vienna Rothschilds on what was virtually a basis of social equality as in making sure that they contributed substantially to his system. At the Congress of Vienna, he had joined the Prussian minister Hardenberg in taking a largely sympathetic line on the Jewish question, at any rate in so far as their situation in the Hansa cities and certain other German towns were concerned. And he lent something of his influence—measured out in teaspoons, to be sure—in the furtherance of other Jewish causes, that of the Damascus affair (of which more later), for example. He was consistent, however, in his cleaving to the *status quo*. For the mass of Jews in Austria itself he would do nothing and was explicit on the subject. Joseph II's *Toleranzpatent* was still 'en pleine vigueur', at any rate in the German parts of Austria: the schools were open to, and attended by, numerous Jewish children; Jews served in the army on a basis of equality with others and could rise to all ranks including staff appointments. Except for such very special cases as the orders of chivalry, admission to which required specifically Christian oaths, no position, title, or office was now denied them. The measured terms of the memorandum 'Über die Judenfrage in Oesterreich' prepared for the international conference at Aix-la-Chapelle in 1818 in which all this was laid out set the balance as he understood it and was determined to maintain it. So on the one hand it was the case, he argued, that 'those [Jews] who had most distinguished themselves by their civic virtues and their honourable condition had gone so far as to acquire titles of nobility which put them on an equal footing with Christian noblemen'. On the other hand, certain 'measures of precaution' had to be taken 'in view of the abusive advantage Jews had taken of the concessions made to them. Devoted to trade, generation after generation, supporting one another with immense capital resources, they prefer to seek profit in legal or illegal commerce rather than by means that would require of them greater attention and effort.'[1] In none of this was there any real deviation from the spirit that had informed the carefully limited reforms initiated a generation earlier. Metternich's language, being self-congratulatory, can irritate. But his carefully indirect reference to the evolving difference for the Jews

---

[1] *Aus Metternich's nachgelassenen Papieren*, ed. Richard Metternich-Winneburg, iii (Vienna, 1881), 181–2.

themselves between the admittedly very mildly liberal approach of the Habsburgs and the consistent hostility displayed them by the Romanovs was not without merit: 'The laws of the Emperor Joseph had led to one very real benefit exemplified . . . in the difference between the Jews of [Austrian-ruled] Galicia and those of the old Poland.'[2]

Still, while it was indeed the case, that within the Habsburg Empire the forces generated by the original emancipatory approach could not now be entirely arrested even where there was the will to do so, it was equally the case that, in the course of maintaining the Metternichian balance, the rate of progress—manifestly, a linear form of progress—had been lowered. Some of the specifics of the original Austrian *Toleranzpatent* had been approached very gingerly from the start. Some were abandoned almost immediately. The plan to bring Jews fully into the general school system was dropped on the stated grounds that the benefit Jewish children would derive from access to it would be offset by the harm done Christian children by their having been brought into close contact with Jews. When in 1816, moved by the not unreasonable belief that the post-Napoleonic reaction was sure to soften, the leaders of the Jewish community of Vienna asked for an easing of the framework of restrictions by which all the Jews of the empire continued to be bound, they were systematically put off. It availed them nothing that they had drafted their petition in the servile terms custom still dictated. Nor had the ostensibly countervailing fact that the content of their memorandum was comparatively bold done them any good either. Did not Jews and Christians pray to the same god, they asked, the former relying on the Old Testament, the latter on the New? Was it not the true function of government to establish (equal) civil rights and obligations for all the emperor's subjects? Was it not unjust and anomalous for a people that had been settled in the lands of the Habsburgs for eight centuries to be denied rights freely accorded to absolute foreigners? If it *was* the case that not all Jews met the standards required of them, did not the source of the evil lie in the system of segregation and discrimination imposed upon them? Was it not known that none of those states that had followed the example of the present emperor's illustrious predecessor but one (Joseph II) and had then gone further and accorded their Jewish citizens full rights regretted doing so? And was it not understood that if their petition was rejected and envy and ancient prejudices did triumph over

experience, truth and the loud voice of the present century; and if indeed the [Jews] of the empire are fated to be regarded in the future [as in the past] as worse than the helots in ancient Sparta . . . then those of the religion of Moses inhabiting his imperial majesty's fortunate lands will see themselves and themselves

---

[2] *Aus Metternich's nachgelassenen Papieren*, 181–2.

alone as abandoned to sacrifice and despair and fated by their very existence to be a burden both to themselves and to the state.[3]

But two full years passed before their case was so much as brought up for serious discussion in official Vienna; and even then it was only when a further petition (26 February 1818) reminded the bureaucracy that an explicit promise to abolish discriminatory legislation had been made in 1787, thirty-one years earlier, by the emperor himself. This piece of impertinence was then softened slightly by the admission that no date had been set for the *fulfilment* of Emperor Joseph's promise and that in any case it had been addressed specifically (and therefore, so it could be argued, exclusively) to the Jews of Bohemia. It was softened further by the petitioners' admission that the labour entailed by a serious reformist effort to revise legislation on the Jews throughout the empire might prove too great and complex a task to be undertaken as a single, comprehensive enterprise. And in the end, the petitioners reduced their request almost to a nullity by limiting it to their own very specific case, that of the Jews of Vienna alone, on the self-justificatory, but not unreasonable, grounds that results in Vienna would serve as a model for reform elsewhere. None of this made the desired impression, however. The imperial bureaucracy at its highest reaches refused to go beyond the operative conclusion that far too many contradictory considerations and interests ran through the matter of the Jews for it to be dealt with in a reforming spirit. The emperor himself did note that there was a lack of logic and some injustice too in the requirement that Jews serve in the imperial army on a basis of equality with everyone else while continuing to suffer a greater burden of taxes than others. But the counter-consideration, part fiscal, part political, carried greater weight. The state, it was decided, could not afford to dispense with the revenue raised through the various special taxes laid upon the Jews. If the burden on the Jews was to be eased, an increased burden would have to be levelled—indiscriminately—on the population as a whole. That would imply that improvement in the condition of the Jews had to be at the cost of the non-Jewish subjects of the empire, which would make a very bad impression all round and was therefore out of the question. In contrast, the inverse proposition, namely that an improvement in the condition of the non-Jewish subjects might be at the cost of the Jews, was always acceptable—except among the Jews themselves to be sure, but their views hardly mattered. On the linked issue of the method whereby taxes were collected, the Austrian bureaucracy, like the Russian, recognized that the effect of holding the Jewish communal organizations responsible for their collection was to strengthen their authority and reinforce the internal self-government and political

[3] Raphael Mahler, *Divrei yemei yisrael: dorot aḥaronim*, vi (Tel Aviv, 1976), 180.

cohesion of the Jewish communities. This was intrinsically undesirable, besides running counter to the larger political and social purposes of the state. Alas, it was admitted privately in Vienna, were those great socio-political purposes ever achieved and, more concretely, if a majority of Jews were actually to abandon their religion for one of the three Christian faiths, 'as we would all dearly wish them to', the imperial treasury would find it more difficult than ever to cover its deficit. It was an awkward dilemma out of which the Habsburg bureaucracy saw no escape. Raphael Mahler's dictum, that 'as a defenceless national and religious minority, [the Jews] served both as an object of special and unrestrained fiscal exploitation and as a scapegoat to mollify the bitterness of a Christian population burdened as it was with ordinary taxes',[4] could not have been more starkly confirmed.

It is true, that *proposals* for the reform of the system of Jewish disabilities were never lacking in Vienna. There was a suggestion that the Jews be permitted at long last to purchase land for cultivation. The rationale was the familiar one: they would then be free to perform those useful functions in society and in the economy that had long been demanded of them; the improvement in their economic standing would render them a better source of tax-derived state income than the one they now provided; closer contact with the general, Christian population would bring them closer to Christianity itself; and hard labour in the fields, salutary in itself, would have the added happy result of raising their death rate. Still, in *Vormärz* (i.e. pre-1848) Austria, this was too radical an idea to be adopted. When, after the Napoleonic wars, imperial policy on the Jews was finally reformulated and promulgated (22 January 1822) it was laid down that there was to be no increase either of Jewish numbers or of areas of permitted settlement and that existing laws and ordinances were all to continue to be complied with meticulously. The sole concession to those pressing for change was an instruction to prepare a province-by-province survey of all legislation applicable to Jews carrying the explanatory proviso that the purpose of the operation was 'to render the morality, way of life, and occupations of the Jews unharmful' and to accommodate them, little by little, and so far as possible, to those spheres in civil society into which they will be permitted to enter. Some minor easing of the tax burden did follow in Bohemia and Hungary when it was realized that the communities concerned were incapable of raising the funds demanded of them. An attempt to Germanize Jewish ritual and prayer services was made, but failed when it was borne in upon the authorities that the partly acculturated, still tiny community in Vienna was hopelessly unrepresentative of the deeply orthodox mass of Jewry in the rest of the empire. And the ever less certain and coherent approach of the Habsburg bureaucracy

---

[4] Raphael Mahler, *Divrei yemei yisrael: dorot aharonim*, 181.

prior to 1848 and for years thereafter is perhaps best illustrated by its response to pressure from Vienna's Roman Catholic archdiocese in 1833 for a rule prohibiting Jewish midwives from tending to Christian women in confinement except in the presence of another Christian woman. The government caved in, but indecisively so, the demand ran too blatantly counter to the general thrust of its policy which, all in all, was one of reducing, if not totally eliminating, restrictions of this nature: the ordinance was approved and promulgated, later it was withdrawn as impracticable, later still it was promulgated anew in modified form. The final requirement was that Jewish midwives were indeed to be watched over by Christian women; but it was laid down too that in the event of no qualified Christian observer being available to watch over her, the Jewish midwife was entitled nevertheless to proceed alone.[5] There was a brief moment when, under the terms of the liberal constitution of 4 March 1849, civil and political rights ceased entirely to be dependent on religion. But that constitution was abrogated at the end of 1851. Not until the 1860s was the legal equality of all the Jews of Austria finally resolved upon and mean-mindedness of this order done away with.

In the Germanies the reservations of the reformers were closer to the surface and somewhat more to the forefront of the official mind. In Bavaria, a Registration Law (1813) designed to keep the numbers of Jews down and subsidiary rules making their emancipation conditional on individual occupation, education, and property remained in force until 1848. The right of fully free movement within the kingdom was not granted until 1861. In Prussia, the reforming minister Karl vom Stein, having gone some distance towards legislating emancipation, ended by changing his mind. The Jews were not true Germans, he decided. Their influence on society was pernicious and corruptive, notably in respect of the peasantry. The rights extended to them had been extended prematurely. They could be improved somewhat, he thought, some of them anyway. But best of all would be to have them removed from Germany altogether.[6] Stein was not alone among Prussian statesmen of the first order in his feelings on the subject. Wilhelm von Humboldt, more liberal, more inclined to a universalistic outlook, a man who had favoured the immediate grant of political rights to Jews, wished none the less to do so on the basis of a clear restriction of their numbers,[7] especially of *citizen* Jews as opposed to resident *alien* Jews. This was the spirit in which the Prussian Edict of Toleration of 1812 was applied in practice, restricting it solely to the old Prussia, namely that which had been contained within the borders as they stood in 1812 in contrast to the enlarged post-1815

[5] Ibid. 185.
[6] Alfred D. Low, *Jews in the Eyes of the Germans* (Philadelphia, 1979), 120–3.
[7] P. L. Rose, *Revolutionary Antisemitism* (Princeton, 1990), 79 ff.

Prussian state. In re-annexed Posen, where a full 40 per cent of all the Jewish subjects of the new, enlarged Prussian state resided and Jews formed 6.5 per cent of the total population, it was firm policy to keep them confined within the province and so far as possible deprived of formal citizenship. As late as 1846, 80 per cent of Posen Jews were still without citizenship.

Within Prussia in its entirety, the specific article of the original Edict of Toleration that provided for Jews' eligibility (under certain conditions) to state office had been suspended indefinitely. In 1818 Jews were excluded from academic positions. In 1819 Jewish officials in the Rhineland (appointed under the French) were sacked. And as an odd, but seemingly logical, consequence of the Edict of 1812 the sphere of governmental regulation of matters Jewish was extended. If the Jews—certain categories of Jews, at all events—were to be members of the body politic, Prussian officialdom was obliged to pay not less, but more attention to them. A range of topics to which no more than summary attention, or none at all, had been paid in the past were now being looked into: the education of Jewish children, the dress of the rabbis, the precise degree to which Jews were entering the professions, especially that of the law, or, in contrast and rather more in the old spirit, their continued presence or otherwise in certain sectors of the criminal classes (illicit peddling, smuggling, horse thievery, for example). But it was all more complicated than in the past. While there had been nothing like the clean regulatory and administrative sweep as, when all is said and done, had been the case in France, it was evident that the Jews themselves were changing. It had now to be accepted that they were of more than one kind. Those who were still in the traditional mould continued to evoke the old stereotypical responses in the official mind and in official conduct. But what of the others, the new men and women?

Under the terms of the *Judenordnung* of 1750, still in force despite its harking back quite openly to medieval rules and practices, Jews were disqualified from bearing witness in criminal cases, cases of homicide especially. In circumstances where Jewish testimony was absolutely indispensable it had been customary for the oath to be taken in an ancient and peculiarly grotesque and humiliating form: a variation on the notorious 'Jewish oath' (*more judaïco*).[8] This was deeply resented by Jews as an affront

---

[8] The origins of the Jewish oath have been traced to the Dark Ages. It took a variety of forms, some exceedingly and deliberately demeaning, many bizarre. All were founded on the notion that unless a Jew was in some way tied down by a multitude of self-imposed, religiously ordained, specifically Jewish sanctions that he himself believed would operate against him in the event of his uttering a falsehood his evidence was worthless. Where his testimony was indispensable, however, so that some use might be made of it after all, the witness would be compelled to swear his oath in some unique, generally grotesque form: wearing special dress or headgear for the occasion, having it administered to him by a rabbi

and an obvious denial of equality before the law. And it had become too anomalous in a self-respecting *Rechtsstaat* for some judges to swallow. It was pointed out on one occasion that as the law stood Jews could be openly murdered in their synagogues and the murderers remain unpunished on the grounds that Jewish testimony, all that would be available, was unreliable a priori. Courts in Posen went so far as to refuse to deal with criminal cases until the disability had been removed.[9] And the same tidy-mindedness worked in the Jews' favour in other spheres of government too to some extent. Where Jews were manifestly reform minded, accul-turated, comparatively comfortable in their circumstances, and able—by the Prussian ruling class's own standards—to pass muster, there, increas-ingly, it was almost impossible for officials not to find themselves regard-ing them with something akin to favour. Here after all was evidence that acculturation and 'de-nationalization' had had precisely the effect that had been hoped for. The rise amongst the Jews of manifestly 'respectable businessmen' of 'unblemished record and behaviour' was even likely, so some believed, to put an end not only to much of what had always been objectively undesirable about them, but also to that socially disturbing envy and disregard which the wealth of the Jews and their economic hyperactivity (*Betriebsamkeit*)[10] tended to provoke in others. In the early years of Frederick William IV's reign (1840–61) there was a reversal: a plan to restructure Prussian Jewry from top to bottom all over again, remaking it as a legal socio-economic corporation on what was con-ceived to be more like the original medieval model, was put forward. By 1847 matters had gone so far that a new, distinctive constitution for Jews was passed into law. Whether so anachronistic a plan could ever have been made to work is questionable. And in the event, the proclamation of reli-gious freedom issued in the revolutionary year of 1848 rendered it inop-erative anyway. On the whole, it was uncertainty and fluidity of attitude that defined the period.

In the long term, therefore, it was a matter of choice and judgement whether one placed one's emphasis on the evident progress towards full emancipation or on the equally evident limits set upon it. Discrimination against Jews in the state bureaucracy, the academy, the judiciary, and the armed forces was very carefully maintained, firmest of all in the army where discrimination amounted to total prohibition. It was impossible for a Jew to be commissioned in a Prussian regiment even as an officer in

---

rather than an officer of the court, probably in a synagogue rather than the courtroom, holding or confronting a scroll of the Law rather than a printed Bible, and very likely hold-ing a lighted candle in his hand. On the issue of the oath *more judaïco* in contemporary France, see below, pp. 231 f.

[9] Herbert Strauss, 'Pre-Emancipation Prussian Policies towards the Jews 1815–1847', *LBIYB* 11 (1966), 123–4.

[10] Ibid. 118–20.

the reserves. For a baptized Jew it was virtually impossible to be admitted (as an officer) into a 'good' regiment. But there were respects in which military rules, practices, and the rationale of overall policy were as untidy and contradictory as the civilian. The oath of loyalty and obedience was administered to Jewish army recruits in a simple and dignified form and phrased so as to cause them neither offence nor humiliation. On the other hand, over and above the particular issue of commissioned rank, the actual incorporation of Jews into the ranks of the Prussian army continually raised questions which neither the military authorities nor the sovereign himself either in the original Prussian state or in the post-1870 Reich that followed it could ever bring themselves to deal with in the forthright manner they sometimes privately thought its due. Should Jews be enlisted at all? No one seriously denied that in practice they had proved to be apt for service. And their time in the army was thought, not unreasonably, to move them still further along towards their 'denationalization'. Besides, to go so far as to exclude them entirely would be implicitly, but unmistakably, to express 'unwarranted lack of confidence in the Jewish population'. And that was surely undesirable. But were Jewish soldiers, once enlisted, to be allowed the rights and privileges accorded all other servicemen and ex-servicemen? Were they to be allowed to rise in the ranks to a degree consistent with their abilities and qualifications, for example? Were they to be allowed to take up appropriate posts in the state bureaucracy upon release? None of these questions was ever answered unequivocally. All caused sufficient discomfort in the higher circles of government for the king himself[11] at one point to consider ending military service for the Jews altogether rather than perpetuate what he himself recognized as the injustice being done them.[12] It was characteristic of the ambiguity in which the matter of the Jews as a whole was enveloped, long after their civil emancipation had been agreed upon, that while Jews continued to be subject to conscription, their inequality of status went uncorrected until the upheaval of the Great (or First World) War and the unprecedentedly dire needs it generated led to a general, if still reluctant, limited, and temporary loosening of the old restrictions. In contrast, it is worth noting, in the Austro-Hungarian Joint Army[13] and, of course, in France matters were entirely otherwise. A

---

[11] Frederick William IV.

[12] Strauss, 'Pre-Emancipation Prussian Policies', 125–6.

[13] Jews were admitted to the Austro-Hungarian officer corps mostly as reservists, but some as career officers—not, with rare exceptions, to serve in the best (e.g. cavalry) regiments, but at any rate on a basis that allowed a small number to rise to field and even general rank. In 1911 3 per cent of the Joint Army's rank and file, 17 per cent (!) of all reserve officers, and 0.6 per cent of all career officers were Jews. The Jewish share of the total population at this time was 4.4 per cent (István Deák, *Beyond Nationalism: A Social and Political History of the Habsburg Officer Corps, 1848–1918* (New York, 1990), 171).

French traveller to Germany c.1860 noted with very considerable surprise that Jews were regarded as unsuited to military service there and that it was said of them that they had 'great repugnance' for it. In France, he remarked, out of 4,000 pupils admitted in the previous thirty years to the finest military academy of them all, the École Polytechnique, over a hundred were Jews. 'Thus while the Israelite population forms barely a four-hundredth part of our population, its members figure in the military schools in the proportion of a fortieth' (or ten times what might have been thought the proportion due).[14]

By and large, therefore, under the terms of the rather more severe Prussian version of what might be termed the Metternichian balance, the freedoms that had been accorded the Jews as individuals were retained; and the administrative establishment, whatever its members may have thought privately of the Jews and their emancipation, stuck to its emancipatory guns. There was, that is to say, no *retreat*. For the modernists among the Jews and for the strong-minded liberals in the general population this was still unsatisfactory, of course. But the process of liberalization had moved slowly forward and the Jews themselves had learned to rely on the workings of the *Rechtsstaat* into which, with whatever reservations, they had been admitted. The state, as they could perceive, while in many ways unfriendly, was generally correct in its treatment of them. The abortive effort to reconstitute Prussian Jewry as a separate and separable corporation in 1847 could be dismissed as an aberration—in the precipitation of which the king's personal idiosyncratic and anachronistic role counted for more than that of the bureaucrats who served him. In any event, no more was heard *authoritatively* from within the official establishment of putting the process of emancipation and integration into reverse. Discordant notes were sounded from time to time, however.

In 1826 the governor (*Oberpräsident*) of the Prussian-ruled province of Westphalia proposed to the minister of the interior in 1826 that all Jews in the kingdom of Prussia be given the choice of either accepting baptism within ten years or being unconditionally expelled. In 1847, in the United Prussian Diet, the Prussian Minister Ludwig von Thile declared that it was inconsistent with Christianity to grant political rights to Jews: their fatherland was Zion, not Prussia. In Baden, State Councillor Johann Ludwig Kübler declared that Jews were 'a fully closed, hereditarily conspiratorial society for specific political principles and commandments . . . which excludes any gradual progress towards higher culture'.[15] In the course of the rare occasion of an open debate in the Prussian *Landtag* on

---

[14] Dr Gallavardin, *Voyage médical en Allemagne* (Paris, 1860), 125. Cited by Léon Poliakov, *The History of Anti-Semitism*, iii. *From Voltaire to Wagner* (New York, 1975), 539 n. 3.
[15] Peter Pulzer, *Jews and the German State* (Oxford, 1992), 17–18; and Helmut Berding, *Moderner Antisemitismus in Deutschland* (Frankfurt-on-Main, 1988), 63, cited ibid.

the matter of the Jews and their emancipation held on 15 June 1847, Bismarck took the line that Prussia was indeed a Christian state and that Jews could not expect equality within it, only a subordinate position. That might not be perfectly Christian, he said. But admitting the Jews into Prussia would not make Prussia itself more Christian. What the Jews most wanted, Bismarck continued, was to become military and civilian officers of the state. That *had* to be out of the question. He would only favour their complete emancipation if they, for their part, brought down the barriers by which they separated themselves from the Germans. Ten days later, when a motion to award the Jews full emancipation was put before the house, Bismarck's concluding position was that it was unclear whether full emancipation was desirable and whether it amounted to *progress*.[16]

It was under Bismarck, nevertheless, twenty-two years later, in 1869, that (virtually) full emancipation was decreed. His famously unsentimental approach to politics had been to the forefront for some time. In 1853 he had opposed an attempt by the citizens of Frankfurt to deprive the Jews of recently achieved civic rights—although this was at least in part because he judged the Frankfurters pro-Austrian.[17] When on 3 July 1869 he led the *Bundestag* of the North German Confederation (only the Mecklenburgers opposing) to pass a law stating that 'All existing limitations of the . . . civic rights which are rooted in differences of religious faith are hereby annulled. In particular, the capacity for participation in representation on the community and state level and in serving in public office shall be independent from religious faith.' On this occasion Bismarck's intention, ostensibly, was to settle the matter of the Jews' civil rights once and for all. They were to be accorded *Staatsbürgertum*, not mere *Bürgertum*: effectively full political, rather than mere civic, rights. Once again, however, while the principle of full equality was conceded in principle it was only grudgingly and incompletely accorded in practice: the unwritten, but almost total, ban on the inclusion of Jews into the official civil and military hierarchies (with the partial exception of the lower judiciary) was retained. This owed much to the continuing ambivalence of sentiment on the subject in the governing classes of contemporary Germany. It probably owed a good deal too to Bismarck's robust, unworried, and generally realistic approach to the Jews and their affairs: his refusal to take them quite as seriously as many of the people around him were accustomed to do and—so rare in the present context—the light touch he was capable of bringing to this, as to other public issues. In the 1847 *Landtag* debate he had expressed his flat opposition

---

[16] Low, *Jews in the Eyes of the Germans*, 295–6, citing Preussische Versammlung, 32nd sitting, 14 and 15 June 1847; ibid. 25 June 1847.
[17] Low, *Jews in the Eyes of the Germans*, 313.

to the legalization of mixed marriages between Jews and Christians. Years later he was reported to have spoken of them approvingly, at any rate in private. It was true, he affirmed, that there was a sense in which Jews had 'no real home, that they are *generally* European, cosmopolitan, nomads. . . . [But] there are good honest people among them' who had the virtues of respect for parents, marital fidelity, and charitableness. They were, he said on another occasion, diligent, frugal, sober, enterprising, abstemious.[18] What really needed to be done was to render them 'innocuous through marriage'. The results of such marriages were known to be good, involving as they did 'quite intelligent, nice people'. The fairly numerous marriages transacted between German baronesses and wealthy and talented Jews would serve as examples. But better still, Bismarck thought, were marriages between 'Christian stallion[s] of German upbringing with Jewish mare[s]. Money must [be made to recirculate]; there is no such thing as an evil race.'[19]

In Great Britain the governing classes were, on the whole, disinclined to take either so dark or so cynical a view of the Jews. The nature of the state, the normal methods and purposes of government and official decision-making, and the still very small dimensions of the Jewish community in Great Britain all combined to spare the political establishment—and the Jews themselves—from systematic consideration of anything that might reasonably be identified as a Jewish Question. With the salient exception of membership in the Houses of Parliament political rights had long been conceded them. When this too was demanded in the form of the repeated election of a Jew to the House of Commons—making it a demand that could not be dismissed on the grounds that it came from Jews alone—there was, eventually, no choice but to deal with it. The result was a full dress, public debate on the matter of the Jews closely interconnected with issues of general social and political principle of a kind and quality that had occurred nowhere else in Europe since the celebrated debate in the French National Assembly in 1789. Its eccentricity alone would suffice to render it worthy of attention.

The issue had arisen earlier on several occasions, but it was not until 1847, in the wake of the general election that had led to the formation of a new, Liberal government under Lord John Russell and the election of Lionel de Rothschild as one of the four members for the City of London (one of whom, as it happened, was Lord John Russell himself) that the matter finally came to a head. The formal propriety of Rothschild's *election* was not in question. The sticking-point, as before, was the oath required of all Members of Parliament before taking their seats. Changes

---

[18] Speaking to Moritz Busch, a prominent anti-Semite himself, in 1870 and again in 1892. Cited by Low, *Jews in the Eyes of the Germans*, 361.

[19] Ibid.

in the wording had already been made to accommodate those who were not members of the established Church, but the phrase 'on the true faith of a Christian' remained. Decades earlier, as would soon be pointed out, Edward Gibbon, a deist rather than a Christian, had sworn the oath and taken his seat. Nor had the oath presented a problem for Unitarians whose denial of the validity of the central tenet of the Christian religion, the Trinity, was in its way as firm as that of the Jews. On the other hand, no one seriously questioned the proposition that a Jew could not, and should not be expected to, take such an oath. The formal proposal to change the rules put to the House of Commons by the new Prime Minister, Russell, on 16 December 1847 was cast in sweeping terms: 'It is expedient to remove all civil disabilities at present existing, affecting Her Majesty's subjects of the Jewish religion, with the like exceptions as are provided for Her Majesty's subjects professing the Roman Catholic religion.' A long, intense, often learned, and on the whole unacrimonious debate followed on 16 and 17 December 1847, the nub of which was whether England was and should remain, and if so in what precise sense, a Christian country.[20] Some Members did think the question an irrelevance, alternatively of negligible importance: the principle of the admission of Jews to society and to quite important offices of state had long since been conceded. But others thought that, on the contrary, the matter of admission to Parliament was unique and that the Bar of the House of Commons was one that no non-Christian—Jew or Hindu, Muslim or pagan, for that matter—should be allowed to cross if the religious, moral, and historic foundations of the state were not to be irreversibly compromised. For some the overriding question for Parliament to consider and to affirm was whether Christianity was or was not the true religion. If the answer was in the affirmative (as all were presumed to agree that it was), was it not unreasonable to assert, merely because some who were 'infidels in their lives and writings' had none the less found seats in this House, 'that the national profession of Christianity on the part of the supreme Legislature of the country ought to be withdrawn?'[21] In this sense, though never fully explicitly, the basic division of opinion revealed by the debate was between those whose conception of the state was traditionalist and conservative (therefore, in party terms, Tory) and those whose view was liberal, if in fact not fully secular, progressive, and open-minded (and therefore Liberal). All in all, the great strength and authenticity of the religious convictions of the great majority of the participants in the debate in the House of Commons were unmistakable—wherein the

[20] Hansard, 3rd series, lccccv, cols. 1233–1401.
[21] Sir R. H. Inglis, Member for Oxford University, the leading opponent of the measure, ibid., col. 1259. W. E. Gladstone, the other member for Oxford University, although a member of the opposition, took the opposite line, supporting Russell.

salient differences between it and the revolutionary National Assembly in France in 1789 and 1791.[22] There the debates had by no means been devoid of reference to Christian values and the articulation of long-established Christian views and judgements upon Judaism and Jewry. But the central concerns had been socio-economic and political and, in a broad sense, philosophical. It is true that in London, as in Paris in 1789, and fairly regularly elsewhere from that time on, the question of the *national* character of Jewry along with that of the Jews' continued belief in messianic redemption and eventual migration to Palestine and a nation-state of their own were raised in the course of the debate. But they were not raised with special force. Nor was much time and energy devoted to them. Gladstone's very carefully phrased denial of 'the supposition that the Jews are a separate nation in such a sense as to be disqualified from the performance of civil duties' prevailed.[23] This single, never to be repeated, full-scale public debate on the matter of Jewish emancipation in London differed from its analogues on the continent in the further respect that it was almost entirely devoid of anti-Jewish animus. Not all went so far as to assert with Lord Ashley, the future Lord Shaftesbury, as he agonized over his inability to support the motion, that

The Jews were a people of very powerful intellect, of cultivated minds, and with habits of study that would defy the competition of the most indefatigable German. Their literature extended in an unbroken chain from the days of our Lord down to the present time. . . . [And] he (Lord Ashley) was speaking not of the old Jews in their palmy days, but of the Jews oppressed and despised in their days of dispersion. Even thus, their literature embraced every subject of science and learning, of secular and religious knowledge. . . . They took the lead in grammar and lexicography. . . . [T]heir labours . . . formed the basis of everything that had been done since by Christian doctors . . .

But none directly contested him.

[T]he Jews [Ashley went on to say] presented . . . in our day, in proportion to their numbers, a far larger list of men of genius and learning than could be exhibited by any Gentile country. Music, poetry, medicine, astronomy, occupied their attention, and in all they were more than a match for their competitors. . . . They had discarded very many of their extravagant and anti-social doctrines. Their hatreds and their suspicions were subdued, and undoubtedly they exhibited a greater desire and a greater fitness [*sic*] to re-enter the general family of mankind.

So while Ashley could not bring himself to agree to anything that implied a separation of politics from religion and was, for that reason, unwilling to have words that 'asserted the truth and maintained the

---

[22] See above, Chapter 1.
[23] Hansard, 3rd series, lccccv, col. 1285.

supremacy of the Gospel' struck from the parliamentary oath, he was firmly of the view that the Jews merited 'every [other] concession that could contribute to their honour and comfort'.[24]

To the view that the Jews merited a 'concession' that could contribute to their 'honour and comfort' there was, in fact, no opposition at all. Gladstone, once again, helped to set the tone of the debate by being prominent among those who restated and reaffirmed Ashley's high opinion of the Jews. Speaking of their 'indefatigable diligence, which outstrips even German assiduity' he, for his part, drew the conclusion that to exclude them from privileges that they had good reason to claim was to instil a justifiable grievance: justifiable and needless—as if the presence of a few Jews in the House of Commons could have any effect on the way in which it conducted its business or impinge, for that matter, on its essentially Christian character.[25] Disraeli, with his flair for paradox and provocation, sided with those who, unlike Lord John Russell, Gladstone, and his own political partner Lord George Bentinck, but like Ashley, thought everything must turn ultimately on the principle that Britain was a Christian state. But he turned that argument on its head. There was, he agreed, a matter of principle at stake. But he disagreed with those who asserted that it was the principle of religious liberty. On the contrary, just as the opponents of the measure had argued, it was a matter of religious truth, except that he, for his part, drew the opposite conclusion. It was precisely because Britain was a Christian state and Christianity was the true religion that the government's measure should be supported. The Jews, Disraeli told the House,

humanly speaking, were the authors of your religion. They are unquestionably those to whom you are indebted for no inconsiderable portion of your known religion, and for the whole of your divine knowledge.

As for the matter of conduct,

Well, then I say that if religion is a security for righteous conduct, you have that security in the instance of the Jews who profess a true religion. It may not be in your more comprehensive form. I do not say it is the true religion; but although they do not profess all that we profess, all that they do profess is true.[26]

Disraeli's contribution to the debate was not taken very seriously. Nor, one suspects, did he himself expect it to be. It can serve, of course, as yet another (if minor) illustration of the fact that matters of religious principle continued to count for a good deal in Victorian England. Nothing remotely like the open repudiation of Christianity and organized religion generally that, as everyone knew, was possible in France and, in certain circumstances and circles both popular and politically useful there, was

---

[24] Hansard, 3rd series, lccccv, cols. 1281–2.
[25] Ibid., cols. 1284–90.   [26] Ibid., cols. 1323–5.

acceptable as yet in Great Britain, certainly not in open debate in Parliament. There were indeed references in the course of the debate to ways in which the French had dealt with the issue—more especially to what were supposed to have been the larger consequences of the full emancipation of the Jews in France. An opponent of the measure argued that the Roman Catholic Church's 'deserting the Government that had cast it off' and its adoption of 'the Ultramontane system of entire dependence upon the See of Rome' should serve as a warning against any move in England towards the separation of Church and State.[27] A supporter of the measure replied that in fact the results had been all to the good: 'There is more vital religion at present in France, both in the Protestant and Catholic sections, than has been known before.' He added, for good measure, that 'the Church of France . . . enjoys increasing power over the people'.[28]

On the whole, therefore, it was a mild and civilized debate: supporting evidence, it could be argued, for Lord George Bentinck's contention that 'there is no longer that deep feeling even of prejudice in the country against the Jews, which ought to prevent us from listening to their just demands, backed by the voice of the city of London'.[29] To which further supporting evidence was supplied by the results: a firm majority in favour of the measure (253 ayes; 186 noes) that was well in excess of the government's nominal strength, many of the Peelites and two of the fiercest of all the opponents of the government, Bentinck and Disraeli, having supported Russell on this special occasion. And there is no good reason to suppose that the outcome was not a fair reflection of opinion in the more sophisticated reaches of English society. Opinion elsewhere, however, was less easygoing. Bentinck paid for his independence of mind by being driven from the leadership of his own parliamentary faction: mostly Tories of the old school, a class of people, country gentlemen prominent among them, whose view of the matter of the Jews was at once more abstract and less friendly than that of the worldly Whigs and the practical and in many cases intellectually inclined Peelites.[30] And the consequence was that in real terms nothing changed for the time being. The unreformed House of Lords, its Bench of Bishops playing a prominent role in its debates, rejected the Bill and continued systematically to reject all subsequent Bills passed to it by the Commons that were designed to make it possible for a Jew (more specifically, for Lionel Rothschild) to take a seat in Parliament once elected to it. Only in 1858 did Rothschild finally gain admittance on the basis of an agreement that each House would be free

---

[27] C. G. Newdegate, ibid., col. 1370.
[28] Viscount Morpeth, ibid., col. 1373.
[29] Ibid., col. 1385.
[30] Oddly, when Bentinck died a year later, it was Benjamin Disraeli, whose position had been identical with that of Bentinck's, and who was of course a Jew himself (although a baptized member of the Church of England), who was chosen to replace him.

to determine for itself the wording of the oath it required its members to take. Not until 1866, in response, as it happened, to Catholic pressure, was a wholly new oath drawn up, one that contained neither the pledge to abjure the intention to subvert the established Church of England (which the Catholics found offensive) nor the words 'on the true faith of a Christian' which the Jews could under no circumstances affirm. And not until the Promissory Oaths Act of 1871 were the last impediments to Jews holding public office swept wholly away.[31]

In general, however, it was not the more dramatic and easily isolated stages—the set-piece battles, as it were—in the process by which the formal, legal liberation of the Jews unfolded in western and central Europe that attracted consistent comment and, over time, precipitated the sharpest reactions in the wider public. It was the continuing spectacle of Jews intermingling relatively freely with others socially, penetrating places of business and academic study and the world of letters, proposing themselves and being proposed by others as candidates for office and social position of all kinds, and beginning to expect and even positively and independently *claiming* equality of status and opportunity with men and women of the established governing classes that excited comment and left a wake of comment, displeasure, and opposition. For these were all phenomena that ran counter to previous experience, *a fortiori* to notions of conventional propriety. More disturbing still for those who viewed the scene with disquiet, in some cases with distress, the mounting, demonstrable ability of Jews to meet acceptable standards of language, dress, deportment, and culture increasingly deprived those who would deny them access to the inner arenas of society and the economy of the arguments that had long been the established grounds for doing so. But it would be men of ideas, not men of power, still less the merely angered but mostly passive observers of the scene, who would give voice to this still commonly unfocused irritation. Broadly these were of two kinds. The milder formulations of the general notion that the presence of the Jews in European society struck not merely at their actual or potential commercial and professional rivals and, in somewhat new and subtle ways at Christendom, but at the very fundaments of European society tended to emerge from among those who, on the whole, wished to maintain the established social and political order. The stronger formulations were the work of those who wished to demolish it. It was the latter too who would do most to cause their case against the Jews to percolate into the public arena to greatest effect. Their weakness, to be sure, lay in the fact that in the nature of things they operated on the margin of the relevant circles of power and social control or, more likely still, entirely beyond them. Their strength— and the latent danger of their ideas for the Jews themselves—lay in what

---

[31] With, it seems, the single exception of the office of Lord Chancellor.

they were really about: a grand attempt at one and the same time to explain the contemporary political universe and to vindicate the effort to destroy it.

II

Looking back upon the course of the emancipatory process this was a very remarkable development. To those of the preceding generation who had sought to promote, or at any rate allow the emancipation of the Jews and their integration on terms of one kind or another into general society the placing of the matter of the Jews in any of its aspects anywhere except on the distant rim of public consciousness—or beyond it altogether—could not have failed to be seen as odd, if not perverse. Those who had taken up the issue of emancipation at the end of the eighteenth century had approached it, as we have seen, with fairly clear, but very general principles in mind. These had to do with efficacious government, natural justice, a certain view of human nature and the human condition as a whole, a strong belief in what in our own times would be called social engineering, and an equally firm conviction that social singularities and eccentricities that stood in the way of society's refoundation on a rational and coherent basis should and could be done away with. But except to a certain degree in Russia and Poland none regarded the matter of the Jews as one of central and abiding social concern. Nor was there much interest in Jewry as a society or civilization. The view taken of them was patronizing rather than sympathetic. And it tended to be dismissive of their culture and ethos in very much the style of those major central European intellectual figures, Goethe among them, who were hostile to the entire exercise and saw the Jews much as did the rest of the society of which they were members, namely in accepted stereotypical terms: a race of vulgar and by and large unscrupulous traders and moneylenders. It cannot be said that there was much fire in Goethe's belly about the issue. The Jews of antiquity impressed him; those who were his contemporaries did not. But he thought that while the Jews could be suppressed they could not so easily be annihilated—in which regard they were much like the Germans themselves—and that once certain concessions had been made to them it would be hard to rescind them. What Goethe opposed very strongly was the legalization of mixed marriages on the old-fashioned, rational grounds—grounds that any orthodox Jew would have understood and approved of—that it made a nonsense of established religion. To marry 'a Jewess in the name of the Holy Trinity [demonstrated] contempt for religious feeling,' he said; adding, 'But I do not hate Jews.'[32]

---

[32] Mark Waldmann, *Goethe and the Jews: A Challenge to Hitlerism* (New York, 1934), 246 ff. and *passim*; and Low, *Jews in the Eyes of the Germans*, 67–86.

Kant, for his part, thought very little of ancient and traditional Jewry, so far as he ventured to study it, which was not in fact very far. His view of the 'Palestinians who live among us' was harsher still. They were inclined to usury and fraud and other unproductive and nefarious activities, 'a nation of cheaters of which by far the greatest part does not seek any civil honours, which is held together by an old superstition recognized by the state in which they live, and which seeks the advantages of tricking the people among whom they find protection and cheating each other'.[33] But Kant does not seem to have thought that there was anything that was irremediably wrong about the Jews. And given his insistence on equality for all and on differences of origin and religion being irrelevant to the duties of one man to another, he saw no reason to oppose their being granted civil rights and equality before the law. He thought that the adoption of Christianity would help clear the way to it. So would education. So too would a general cleaning-up of Jewish ritual—an idea he may have borrowed from 'progressive' or reformist Jews whom he had come to know. Hegel took no more interest in the matter of contemporary Jewry than Kant and where he touched upon it his thoughts were primarily on their improvement, their moral improvement above all. Freedom and morality were always intertwined and interdependent, certainly so in the case of the Jews. They had therefore to be rendered *worthy* of life within the superior European society into which they had come to be embedded. To provide for the Jews' emancipation would be to set them on the road to eventual moral and social improvement. But emancipation had to be conditional in turn upon their moral and social improvement. The tone is patronizing rather than critical.[34]

These quite mild views on the subject of contemporary Jewry accorded fairly well with what the central European governments were actually about. And in a general way they accorded too with the views expressed by the very much smaller figure of Christian Wilhelm Dohm[35] who knew (or who certainly presumed to know) rather more about the Jews than Goethe or Hegel or Kant and counted for a good deal more in the present context. Yes, wrote Dohm, the Jews were corrupt, in fact rather more corrupt than other nations. Yes, they were aliens: their origins were in Asia. No, there could be no question of conferring full Prussian citizenship upon them or of admitting them to public office, not for a very long while, at any rate. Nor would it be in their own deeper interest for them to be allowed to do so. The hugely regrettable

---

[33] Probably from *Anthropologie in pragmatischer Hinsicht abgefasst* (Königsberg, 1798). Cited by Low, *Jews in the Eyes of the Germans*, 94.

[34] G. W. F. Hegel, *Grundlinien der Philosophie des Rechts*, ed. Johannes Hoffmeister, 4th edn. (Hamburg, 1955), 225–6 n. Cf. Shelomo Avineri, 'Le-birur 'emdato shel Hegel li-she'elat ha-emanzipazia', *Zion*, 25, 2 (1960), 134–6.

[35] See Chapter 1.

commercial spirit with which most Jews were infused was more likely to
be broken by heavy physical labour than by sedentary work as public servants. But, alas, the idea of settling them on the land was a doubtful one.
There was little uncultivated land left in Europe to allot to them. The
Jews were unused to 'the interminable industry [*unausgesetzten Fleiβ*] and
hard work that farming demands. Their minds are too restless [*unruhig*]
and they lack the necessary physical strength. . . . [And] how will the Jew
feed his farmhands if he is not allowed to give them pork?'[36] Still, the nub
of the matter, so far as Dohm was concerned, lay elsewhere. While the
Jews were corrupt, they were not wholly corrupt. If their nation's exaggerated love of every kind of profit, usury, and crooked practice competed incessantly with the finer traits of Jewish character, why these
were faults that had been nourished on the one hand by the Jews' religious
principles and the sophistries of their rabbis and, on the other hand, by
Christian oppression. Like so many other protagonists of 'amelioration'
or even eventual emancipation Dohm had scarcely a good word to say
about the Jews themselves as he knew (or thought he knew) them.
The difference between him and those who, in the final analysis,
would do most to formulate the Jewish Question as it came to be most
widely accepted and understood in the course of the nineteenth century
lay not in either party's assessment of the Jews as they were, but in
their belief or disbelief in the Jews susceptibility to change and
improvement.

III

A world away from the compliments paid the Jews in the House of Commons in 1847 was the popular image of 'the Jew': old clothes' man,
tailor, petty usurer, occasional thief, hook-nosed, pot-bellied, lisping,
obsequious, unclean, alien, absurd. *Punch*, faithful reflecting mirror of
English middle-class views, was generally favourable to the effort to gain
admittance to Parliament for the Jews. But it chose to report on it from
time to time in terms such as these:

> My name is MO SAMUEL, a poor little Jew;
> Tro de Shety I trampsh it, de Commonsh in view;
> But though I am shent dere, 'tis bootlesh to go,
> For de Lordsh sets deir face agin poor little Mo'!
>
> My constituensh often have chose me in vain,
> And shent me to Parliament over again,

[36] C.W. Dohm, *Über die bürgerliche Vebesserung der Juden*, Part Two (Berlin and Stettin, 1783), 246–7.

Determined the shpirit of Britonsh to show;
But de Lordsh sets deir face agin poor little Mo'![37]

But more important, because more powerfully and emotively put, and
more revealing of deeper strains of anti-Jewish opinion in English society,
were the dissident voices on the ultra-radical left. The Chartists favoured
Jewish emancipation as a matter of principle and they did not hesitate to
condemn oppression of the Jews by the government of Russia. But in
general they lumped Jews with other parasitical and oppressive enemies
of the working class. 'We do not live in a Christian country,' wrote
'Anonymous' in the *Poor Man's Guardian*, 'we live in a country of Jews,
and usurers, and parsons, and plunderers, and hangmen, and lawyers, and
shopcrats, and vampires, and soldiers, and "statesmen", and blood-
hounds.'[38] For William Cobbett (1763–1835), on the other hand, successively copying clerk, soldier, traveller, journalist, farmer, convict (for
attacking the brutal forms of punishment employed in the British army),
fugitive for fear of imprisonment for seditious libel, author of a famous
account of journeys through contemporary England, and finally Member
of Parliament himself, the matter of the entry of Jews into English life
was a capital one. He fought the first substantial steps to dissolve Jewish
disabilities in the harshest terms he could muster. '*Jew*,' he wrote, 'has
always been synonymous with sharper, *cheat*, *rogue*. This has been the case
with no *other race* of mankind. Rothschild married his own niece. They
will flock in upon us from all countries.'[39] It is worth recalling that Cobbett was a man of very modest origins born in a land still ruled for all practical purposes by an immensely affluent landed aristocracy. To the end of
his life he was an outsider and an eccentric. Hugely radical and xenophobic
in his views, he was also a reactionary in the strict sense of favouring a
return to a pre-industrial agrarian economy and its supposed, associated
virtues. He was famously cantankerous and abusive. But he was a man
whose finger was on the pulse of his country as Britain moved to the
summit of its time as the most modern, liberal, technically accomplished
and wealthy of major European states. Cobbett denounced the Jews as
murderers of Christ and blasphemers of his Gospel. The 'murder of Jesus
Christ by the Jews, had been a

savage murder, committed after long premeditation, effected by hypocrisy and
bribery and perjury; accompanied with scorn and mockery of the innocent suf-
ferer; and proceeding from motives of the basest and blackest that ever disgraced

[37] *Punch*, 1853. Cited in Anne and Roger Cowen, *Victorian Jews through British Eyes*
(Oxford, 1986), 26.
[38] 16 Mar. 1833. Cited in E. Silberner, 'British Socialism and the Jews', *Historia Judaica*,
14 (1952), 33.
[39] Lewis Melville, *The Life and Letters of William Cobbett in England and America*, 2 vols.
(London, 1913), 21. Emphases in original.

the hearts of even that reprobate people whom God, by the mouth of the prophets, has appropriately denominated '*filth* and *dross* and *scum*' and who he has doomed, as in the words of my text, to be '*dispersed* in the countries', and to have no inheritance except in their own bodies, on which also he has set his mark of reprobation making them 'a *mocking* to all countries'.[40]

But he denounced them too as parasites who in their persons epitomized the new world of urban living and finance capital in which, unlike in earlier golden, more generous times, Mammon and materialism were supreme; and this was of a piece with the rest of his thinking and writing. Cobbett's vision of his country was of 'England' rather than of England: Constable's England, one might say, rather than Turner's. It was, in any event, an England to which the Jews, he had no doubt, contributed nothing. To the claim (made in the early debates in Parliament on the removal of Jewish disabilities and in the later ones as well) that the Jews were among the most industrious of British subjects, Cobbett's response was to challenge anyone to 'produce a Jew who ever dug, who went to the plough, or who ever made his own coat or his own shoes, or who did anything at all, except get all the money he could from the pockets of the people'.[41] In any event, they were 'on the side of oppression, assisting tyranny . . . bitter foes of . . . popular rights and liberties, . . . it is amongst masses of debts and misery that they thrive as birds and beast get fat in times of pestilence . . . instruments in the hands of tyrants for plundering their subjects. . . . [In sum] the enemies of all Christians',[42] not so much a principal enemy, then, more one intolerable manifestation among others of a general, evil phenomenon. In this Cobbett had something in common with writers of other kinds, other social classes, later generations, and, politically speaking, less radical opinions, Dickens among them, whose portrayal of the Jew Fagin as a monster of criminality remains unforgettable.

The walls and ceiling of the room were perfectly bleak with age and dirt. There was a deal table before the fire: upon which were a candle, stuck in a ginger-beer bottle, two or three pewter pots, a loaf and butter, and a plate. In a frying pan, which was on the fire, and which was secured to the mantel-shelf by a string, some sausages were cooking; and standing over them, with a toasting fork in his hand, was a very old shrivelled Jew, whose villainous-looking and repulsive face was obscured by a quantity of matted red hair. He was dressed in a greasy flannel gown, with his throat bare . . . 'This is him, Fagin,' said Jack Dawkins: 'my friend Oliver Twist.' The Jew grinned; and making a low obeisance to Oliver, took him by the hand, and hoped he should have the honour of his intimate acquaintance.[43]

In Anthony Trollope's novels, however, 'the Jew' moves on from being

---

[40]   *Good Friday; or, the Murder of Jesus Christ by the Jews* (London, 1830), 4, 17.
[41]   Hansard, 3rd series, xvi, 22 Mar. 1833, cols. 973–5.
[42]   *Good Friday*, 17.
[43]   Charles Dickens's *Oliver Twist* was first published in 1838.

merely alien and nasty and a symbol of a world gone wrong towards the more advanced position that he was not merely sign but cause as well. In his novel *The Landleaguers*, the Jewish music master, Mahomet Moss, is given what Trollope presumably thought was his (and his people's) due: professionally punctilious and effective, even indispensable. At the same time, like all his kind, forever and incurably 'greasy'.[44] The ancient fear of falling into the Jews' debt is much harped upon. And his alien character is driven home in close parallel with Trollope's separate, rather grave discussion of the matter of individuals of any kind passing from one society to another (the boy Florian, of Protestant family, by conversion to Catholicism becomes in Irish eyes 'one of us' both conceptually and literally to his cost and everyone else's). Here Trollope, as close an observer of the upper classes of Victorian society as was Dickens of the lower and middle classes, reflects the image of the Jews as it would appear and reappear and be repeatedly refined in the upper reaches of society and in the literature of his times and well into the twentieth century. There were exceptions to what was virtually the rule, George Eliot offering the crowning example. But it was the rule that counted: the Jew as alien, vulgar, anything but socially acceptable, and . . . greasy. Whereas the poorly imagined Mahomet (*sic*) Moss and his people are incidental to *The Landleaguers*, in Trollope's much more serious and heartfelt discussion of middling to late Victorian society, written well before his Irish novel, but when he had already succumbed (prematurely) to the old man's disease of bitterness and disappointment, matters are otherwise. In *The Way We Live Now* Jews are indeed offered up as primary, unmistakable symbols, but also as the makers of a very great deal of what is evil and intolerable in a world in which honour and decency have been lost, in which material gain and appetite are all, and in which society from top to bottom has been corrupted. All the clichés are there. The Jewish businessman, Mr Brehgert is described twice on alternate pages as 'a fat, greasy man of fifty, conspicuous for hair-dye'. The Christian girl who is about to marry this perfectly decent man wonders how she can ever tell her parents, 'that she was engaged to marry a man who at the present moment went to the synagogue on a Saturday and carried out every other filthy abomination common to the despised people'. But it is as corrupters of a society that is already disposed to corruption—by Jews or by anyone or anything else—that they chiefly signify, their evil function being inseparable, to be sure, from their alien origins. It is Augustus Melmotte of uncertain provenance, who claims to be an Englishman, but clearly isn't—the more

---

[44] 'At any rate he's not a greasy Jew' (ch. 6). 'He's a nasty, stuck-up, greasy Jew' (ch. 7). Speaking of her horror at having been courted by a Jew, the heroine explains to her listener: 'If you know the sort of feeling I have for him—such as you would have if you found a cockroach in your dressing-case' (ch. 8). *The Landleaguers* was published, unfinished, in 1883, the year after Trollope's death.

so as his wife is identified firmly as a Bohemian Jewess—who bestrides the book. Melmotte gathers simple-minded but venal noblemen into his pocket, uses them for his criminal schemes, and ruins them. In so doing—and this is the gravamen of Trollope's charge—the depth to which the ancient ruling class of England and indeed England as a whole have fallen stands revealed. The old marquis tries to talk his son into marrying the Jew's daughter despite strong suspicions about Melmotte's honesty and even his resources. 'I don't believe in the money,' the son finally objects. The marquis tries another tack.

'They tell me,' said the old man, 'that one of those Goldsheiner girls will have a lot of money.'
'A Jewess,' suggested [Lord] Nidderdale.
'What difference does that make?'
'Oh no;—not in the least;—if the money's really there.'

The story is studded with lesser indicators of Trollope's views. Regarding the admission of Jews to Parliament, one respectable character was 'certain' that 'when that had been done . . . the glory of England was sunk for ever'. 'It's only since those nasty Radicals came up that they have been able to sit in Parliament,' a proper mother tells her rebellious daughter. 'One of the greatest judges in the land is a Jew,' the daughter retorts. The mother is not to be moved: 'Nothing that the Radicals can do can make them [i.e. the Jews] anything else but what they are.'[45] What is absent in Trollope, however, or in Dickens for that matter, or any other writer of the day who touched on the subject in this spirit is anything approaching close, to say nothing of systematic, study of the Jews themselves. Trollope's complacent ignorance of Jewry and Judaism, epitomized in the absurdly impossible name (*Mahomet* Moss) he gave the Jewish music master in *The Landleaguers*, is at least as telling as his dislike of them. But while his dislike of the Jews is unmistakable and his bitterness about what he perceives to be the social and moral decline of his country is affirmed with something like passion, there is no serious suggestion of what might be done to deal with either the one or the other. On the continent, as so often, the inter-play between 'opinion' and political action was generally a great deal closer and the tendency to knead the former into a system of ideas of one kind or another in the interests of the latter always very much stronger.

IV

One of the ironies of the position of the modernists in Jewry and one of the reasons why the form and stridency of the campaign that was

---

[45] *The Way We Live Now*, chs. 60, 85, 78. The book was conceived in 1873 and pub-lished in 1875.

beginning to be mounted against them struck so sensitive a nerve was that it was precisely that feature of mid-nineteenth-century political society that had encouraged them to hope for the best that threatened to undermine so much of what they had achieved. The general, if unequal movement in all central and western states towards a liberalization of the regime, the lifting of censorship on books and newspapers in whole or in part, the establishment of party-parliamentary systems, and the outright legitimization of organized political opposition to the structures of power all favoured them. But equally, and in the end disastrously, it facilitated the marshalling of forces against them as well. This was the case in varying degrees throughout Europe. As in Britain, so in continental Europe, it was not overt political action against them that they had reason to fear at this stage. It was the insertion of the matter of Jewry into the public agenda and the creation of a substantially new climate of received opinions that would begin to unnerve them. Whole ranges of disconnected and unsupported—and therefore, when taken together, unanswerable—assertions, isolated facts, half- and quarter-truths, and simple fictions began to be gathered together in ever more compact and orderly form under the general rubric of 'The Jewish Question', shot through in turn with all manner of global, interpretative hypotheses and attempts—some highly pretentious and patently absurd, some that were intellectually quite subtle—to deal with the matter of the Jews systematically and, as it were, philosophically. Versions of the past and the present, warnings of the future, references to history, philosophy, sociology, and religion, themes in ethics, law, and aesthetics—all these would be called into play and beaten together as a case for the prosecution.

It was characteristic of the genre, that Bruno Bauer (1809–82) who has some claim to be among the first to have given wide currency to the term 'The Jewish Question' by publishing a fiercely hostile book of that title in 1843,[46] should have begun his essay in an ostensibly learned manner with antiquity. Judaism, his thesis ran, was the lowest stage of a long process of religious development which, after passing through the Roman-Greek stage, culminated in Christianity. It was because at the lower (Jewish) stage God stood well beyond Man, whereas at the highest (the Christian) stage Man had raised himself to the level of God that he, Bauer, while intensely critical of Christianity, affirmed its superiority over Judaism. Christianity was the religious expression of Man's emancipation. Among the Jews no such emancipation had taken place, nor was any envisaged. In the world of action the Jew continued to act in total subjugation to what he himself perceived and accepted as an external power. The rules under which he and his fellows pursued their lives were therefore arbitrary. More

---

[46] *Die Judenfrage* (Braunschweig, 1843). Cf. Bruno Bauer, *Die Fähigkeit der heitigen Juden und Christen frei zu werden* (Zurich and Winterthur, 1843).

unfortunately still they were all-embracing. *All* was in the service of religion in the Jewish scheme of things. And because at the foundation of Judaism lay a body of Law which was held to be unchangeable, the very essence of the life of the Jews was immobilism. But immobilism was incompatible with liberty; and so while it might be necessary to give the Jews their due—they had paid heavily for their stubborn refusal to move with the times—it must be recognized that it was they themselves who needed to be held responsible for the oppression meted out to them. In any case, the real and most immediate point was that the Jews' contemporary demand for emancipation was misplaced and unwarranted. Their desire to be emancipated was perverse and self-contradictory for they were an 'unhistoric' people. They were uninvolved in the general stream of world history. They did not participate in it. They did not form part of its overall pattern. They bore no responsibility for it. They remained as they had always been: unaware of their own potential as free agents and rational beings. It followed, Bauer argued, that there could be no question of their integration into society at large—the integration at which emancipation aimed and which constituted its *raison d'être*—short of total abandonment of their separate identity, their self-willed segregation, and of the absolute distinction between themselves and their neighbours to which they had always cleaved. If they really did wish to be integrated, it was for them to make the appropriate sacrifice and the relevant concessions. They had to choose, finally and irrevocably, between their Jewishness and their humanity. 'History wants development, new creations, progress, and transformations [*Entwicklung, neue Gestaltungen, Fortschritt und Umänderungen*]; Jews, fighting this first Law of History, want to stay the same, perpetually.' If great pressures had been exerted against them in the past it was because they themselves had been the first to press 'against the Wheel of History' [*gegen das Rad der Geschichte*]'.[47]

All this went far beyond Dohm and his kind, let alone Cobbett. Bauer himself was a man of parts, moreover, a serious and for some years a reputable academic student of theology, history, and philosophy, and of his time intellectually in the particular sense that he had been much influenced by Hegel. Principally and notoriously, he was an academic student of what would now be termed comparative religion—the notoriety lying in the fact that he had had the temerity to look more closely than was customary in Germany at the origins of Christianity itself, to proceed to sharp criticism of much that he held it to embody, and to arrive finally at a frank and (for his day) scandalous atheism. This cost him his university appointment, even though in his politics he remained conservative. It was Bauer's study of the foundations of Christianity, however, that had led

[47] *Die Judenfrage*, 5.

him, not unnaturally, to Judaism. And it is at least likely that it was his jaundiced view of the former that was the origin of what would be his still more hostile outlook on the latter. Like Voltaire before him, but more especially in the spirit of the fiercely anti-Jewish eighteenth-century German atheist Johann Christian Edelmann,[48] Bauer regarded Judaism as the source of much that was wrong with Christianity, for all that it remained vastly inferior to it. The Jews themselves he perceived as a benighted and socially harmful people. Even their wholesale conversion to Christianity, if ever they agreed to it, would fail to advance matters in his view: it would amount to no more than the substitution of member-ship in one special group for membership in another, the abandonment of one set of privileges and their replacement by others. The question of the emancipation of the Jews needed to be seen as part of the larger prob-lem of the emancipation of all men. So far as the *question* of the Jews was concerned, the crux was their willingness or otherwise to give up their claim to, and their belief in, their own special world role, their 'war against mankind as a whole' for ultimate world mastery and domination, the war in which, so Bauer argued, lay the real 'truth and fulfilment of Judaism'.

All assurances, even when sincerely meant, even by the most enlightened of Jews, that he does not think of 'his people' as an independent nationality, are illusory. Articulating them, he necessarily and instantaneously revokes and renounces them with the very same words that he employs to utter them. So long as he wishes to be a Jew he can not and may not disown his nature, [his] exclusivity, the idea of his special destiny, the autocratic mastery [*Alleinherrschaft*], in short the chimera of colossal privilege [*die Chimäre des ungeheuersten Priv-ilegiums*].[49]

Some of this—the allegation that Jewry was engaged in a 'war against mankind', for example—while following Edelmann, was of still earlier lineage. Bauer refers very favourably to Johann Eisenmenger's scurrilous 1699 compilation of allegations against Jewry and Judaism *Das Entdeckte Judenthum und Christenthum* (*Judaism Unmasked and Christianity*).[50] But, in any case, the placing of Judaism at the bottom of a sort of hierarchy of religions and states of spiritual being and the notion that the Jewish people were outside history partook of long-established Christian criticism of Judaism. His account of what those Jews who actively desired emancipa-tion were or were not prepared to sacrifice to achieve it was not without foundation although grossly overstated. But the emphasis on Jewish

---

[48] The degree to which Bauer's views were derived from Edelmann's is cogently argued in Zevi Rosen, 'Hashkafotav ha-anti-yehudiyot shel Bruno Bauer (1838–1843), mekorot yenikatan u-mashma'utan', *Zion*, 33, 1–2 (1968), 57–76.

[49] *Die Judenfrage*, 29–30.

[50] Ibid. 84.

exclusiveness and immobilism was not to be dismissed and, given the author's purpose, was shrewd. The implicit charge that the Jews were either unwilling or unable entirely to shake off their origins was well-founded, if too sweeping. Applied to the strict traditionalists, *their* interest in emancipation being in any event either minimal and wholly instrumental or non-existent, it was no more than the truth. Applied to those at whom Bauer's charges were chiefly directed, namely those who did actively seek social, political, and cultural integration into German society, it at any rate struck home and Bauer's pamphlet unfailingly caused the pain, concern, and uncertainty it was clearly designed to induce. What was more important, however, relatively new, and more ominous, was the demonological sting at the end of Bauer's long, pretentious, historiographical-philosophical-theological-anthropological tail. The *immediate* issue to which the Jews gave rise, and therefore the real 'Jewish Question' was not really emancipation at all, he argued. In theory 'the Jew' might be without political rights. In fact, he was possessed of immense power (*eine ungeheure Gewalt*); and though his political influence was curtailed in small matters, in large matters he was able to wield it to very great effect. 'The Jew in Vienna, for example, who is no more than tolerated, decides by his money-power [*seine Geldmacht*] the destinies of the entire Empire. The Jew who may be without rights in the smallest of German states, determines the fate of Europe [*entscheidet über das Schicksal Europa's*].'[51]

Bauer's originality and importance as a model for others lay partly in his articulation of the radical thesis that emancipation was a useless and hopeless exercise: that it could not succeed; that it would not be to the advantage of society if it did; and that it did not even promise to be of real benefit to the Jews themselves *qua* Jews since it was incompatible with what he, Bauer, claimed to be the 'essences' of Judaism. But the impact of his ideas owed most to that central element in his thesis that harked back to the pre-Enlightenment approach to the matter of the Jews while at the same time anticipating what would soon be a central feature of the anti-Jewish (and, as it would soon be termed, anti-Semitic) outlook in its principal modern variations. This was the casting of the issue in rigorously *collective* terms. The case and interests of the individual as a free agent and independent member of society were diminished or wholly eliminated from the discussion. The customary distinctions between good and bad Jews, between the useful and the useless, between the productive and the parasitical, were rendered irrelevant. Everything of significance in this context was raised, as Bauer claimed it needed to be, to the level of generalities. It was the Jews as a collective and Judaism as the ethos of that collective that mattered because it was they that determined

[51] Ibid. 114.

the common and indelible characteristics, motives, functions, and relationships of which no Jewish individual could ever free himself however
genuinely and strongly he might (of his own volition or at the behest of
others) wish to do so.

Finally, while Bauer made what use he could of well-established
Christian teachings on Judaism and the Jews, the fundamental thrust of
his essays was secular. The real problem, the real objections to the presence of the Jews in German (and, by implication, any other European)
society, and to their legal and political emancipation in particular, were
not such as could be overcome by their religious conversion. It was not
the *Christian* character of society that needed to be protected from an
unwarranted penetration of non-believers. It was society *tout court* that
needed to be protected from injury. And, indeed, while the religious
objection to the entry of unconverted Jews into society—certainly to
positions of influence within it—never seriously faded in western and
central Europe, and here and there a certain objection in religious circles
to the entry of the converted as well remained in force (on something like
the Iberian principle of *limpieza de sangre*), it was this general, societal
approach that would now be gathering force. The balance between religious or theological considerations and secular and societal ones would
vary from country to country, as did, of course, the salience of the, or a,
'Jewish Question' conceived in either set of terms or as a mixture of
both. What counted, at all events, was that in all cases where the shift to
the latter, secular set was strong, there the way was opened and the indispensable basis provided for the barbarisms that were to follow. There is
therefore much to be said for the obituary comment on Bauer in the
Allgemeine Zeitung des Judentums in 1882, that he had been 'the true father
of anti-Semitism [*der eigentliche Vater des Antisemitismus*]' because his 'essay
Die Judenfrage contained *in nuce* everything inimical to the Jews that has
developed in Germany'.[52] And it is very precisely indicative of the nature
of the generally accelerating departure from older frameworks and
starting-points for any discussion of the Jews, that Bauer's sharpest critic
was not a spokesman for any of the Churches or an established academic
figure, let alone one who was a frank (non-Jewish) proponent of Jewish
emancipation and integration, but his contemporary and fellow dissident
Karl Marx with whom he had, in fact, a good deal in common.

Bauer, Marx contended, had been quite right to single out the Jews as
a threat to society, but he had misinterpreted the nature of the evil and
had understated its scope. It was not 'the Jew of the Sabbath' that needed
to be looked at, but 'the real Jew of our time . . . the Jew of everyday life'.
It was not on account of religious and philosophical problems that they

[52] Ludwig Philippson in *Allgemeine Zeitung des Judentums*, 1882, 282, cited by Jacob
Toury, ' "The Jewish Question"—A Semantic Approach', *LBIYB* 11 (1966), 99–100.

and their emancipation were at issue. It was as matters that had to do with the general economic and social organization of society in its entirety. For what *was* the nature of the Jews' religion? It was a religion of egotism, not altruism; it sought to meet practical, not spiritual needs. And what did the Jew worship? Usury. Once society had abolished usury the Jew's religion, and therefore the Jew himself, would be impossible.

Money is the zealous one god of Israel, beside which no other god may stand. Money degrades all the gods of mankind and turns them into commodities. Money is the universal and self-constituted value set upon all things. It has therefore robbed the whole world of both nature and man of its original value. Money is the essence of man's life and work which have become alienated from him. This alien monster rules him and he worships it. [It is thus, that] the God of the Jews has become secularized and is now a worldly god. The bill of exchange is the Jew's real god. . . . What Bauer held to be a function of the religion of the Jews, namely contempt for theory, art and history and man-as-an-end-in-himself, is an actual and conscious point of view held to be virtuous by the man of money. Even the relations between the sexes, between man and woman, become an object of commerce. The woman is auctioned off. . . . The law of the Jew, lacking all foundation, is only a religious caricature of morality and law in general, but it provides the formal rites in which the world of property clothes its transactions.

It followed that the values and functions which Jewry embodied merged infallibly with those of bourgeois society. But while it was the case that

Jewry reaches its peak with the perfection of bourgeois society . . . bourgeois society reaches perfection only in the Christian world. Christianity is the sublime thought of Judaism, Judaism is the everyday practical application of Christianity. But this application could become universal only after Christianity had been theoretically perfected as the religion of self-alienation of man from himself and from nature.

It was therefore not so much Jewry that needed to be emancipated within society, Marx concluded, as society itself that needed to be emancipated from Jewry.[53]

The violence of Marx's language and his desire to wound are evident even though (as is generally believed) he may originally have taken up the subject as a stick with which to beat Bauer, rather than out of any great interest in the Jews and their Question as such. But as had often been the case, so in this instance, the attempt to deal with the matter of the Jews for an oblique purpose and as a topic that was incidental to a greater concern, released much dammed-up bile. Equally characteristic of the quality of the discourse that the matter of the Jews has tended to evoke is the fact that Marx's venom failed to spare him from being denounced as a Jew

---

[53] Karl Marx, *A World without Jews*, trans. and ed. D. D. Runes (New York, 1959). Cf. Z. Rosen, *Bruno Bauer and Karl Marx* (The Hague, 1977), 171–9 and *passim*.

himself in terms that were fully as venomous in some cases as those he himself was apt to employ, and not merely by obvious enemies of his cause, but by his nominal colleagues from within the general revolutionary fellowship of the day.

You may note that all our enemies, all these dogs snarling against us are Jews [Bakunin wrote to Albert Richard]. Marx, Hess, Borkheim, Liebknecht, Jacoby, Weiss, Kohn, Outine, and many others are Jews; all belong to that same restless, scheming, exploitative, and by tradition and instinct bourgeois nationality. Marx, the most distinguished of the lot, is of great intelligence, all the others are no more than retailers of his ideas. Marx has rendered great service to socialism. But it needs to be admitted at the same time that he is a very unpleasant customer: detestable, vain, irascible, jealous, touchy, sly, and perfidious, a man capable of great villainy and intrigues, as, by the way, all Jews are.[54]

The general point about the fatally alien, aberrant, and generally undesirable character of the Jews could of course be made less biliously (if less memorably) and in a cooler and ostensibly more disinterested spirit, as by F. K. von Savigny (1779–1861), for example. Savigny, the leading academic legal authority in Germany of his day, was, as it happens, the man who more than any other had opposed Eduard Gans's election to a chair in law alongside his own at the University of Berlin, maintaining his objections even after Gans's apostasy and admission to the university as a colleague.[55] This may have had something to do with Savigny's (well-founded) suspicion that Gans's conversion was morally dishonest. It probably had something to do with Gans's liberal politics as well. But it is likely to have derived principally from Savigny's firm conviction that Jews, taken as the clear-cut socio-historical category—or better still, caste—he judged them to be, were immiscible in German society. They were best regarded, he wrote, as comparable to the *peregrini* in ancient Rome—subjects, but not citizens, and therefore under special legal jurisdiction. Moreover,

Jews are and will be strangers to us [by virtue of] their inner nature, and only the most unfortunate confusion of political notions could mislead us into failing to recognize this: not to bear in mind, that even if this civic and political equalization is intended kindly and philanthropically [*menschenfreundlich*], it will . . . serve only to preserve the unfortunate national existence of the Jews [*die unglückselige Nationalexistenz der Juden*] and even extend it where possible.[56]

---

[54] 1 Apr. 1870. *Michel Bakounine sur la guerre franco-allemande et la révolution sociale en France 1870–1871*, ed. Arthur Lehning (Leiden, 1977), 278. Liebknecht, as it happened, was not a Jew; but as a term of abuse 'Jew' was very serviceable. Bakunin made something of a habit of attacking Marx (and others) as Jews, closely interconnected members therefore—along with 'Rothschild' himself—of a nation of leeches and greedy parasites. 'Persönliche Beziehungen zu Marx', *Gesammelte Werke*, iii (West Berlin, 1975), 208–9.

[55] S. S. Prawer, *Heine's Jewish Comedy* (Oxford, 1985), 20.

[56] F. C. von Savigny, *Vom Beruf unserer Zeit* (Heidelberg, 1840), 175.

This was a loftier view of the matter of the presence of the Jews in society than Cobbett's or Marx's or Bakunin's and of most others whose arguments were furiously and fundamentally ideological in form in the sense that they sought to integrate their reading of the Jewish Question into a broader critical and denunciatory analysis of the condition of society and the direction in which it was travelling. And, indeed, where no operative political conclusions in respect of society in general or of the Jews in particular were at issue, there the tone was apt to be relatively calm no matter how sharp the critique. Where criticism and dissatisfaction boiled over into a call for action, notably revolutionary action, there, as we shall see repeatedly, the tone and language tended to be ferocious. The Jews, wrote Paul Pfitzer, a lawyer and publicist who was to make a minor name for himself in the revolutionary year 1848, were the primary agents of Germany's current (1836) moral decay, the 'inner sickness', the 'hatred of sacrifices', the 'enthusiasm for the sensual, the piquant, the lecherous' with which it was afflicted. Pfitzer could in no way be compared with Savigny for legal eminence, social position, or intellectual merit. His views derived such importance as they may have had from the fact that where Savigny was a pillar of the established order Pfitzer was not unrepresentative of *Vormärz* radicalism in Germany and it is firmly to the future that the tone of his writing points.

They are in possession of great means, thanks to their diabolic instinct for precious metals and most lately their magical gift for creating gold out of paper. But the Jew lives in the clearest awareness that he can acquire only the means and never the essence of any race [*Nationalität*] other than his own. And he can pursue his policy of conquest not through iron, which is available to true men, but only through the smuggling of moral frauds of all kinds. To the Jew without a fatherland, love of fatherland must seem foolishness. . . . It was told in darker times how the Jews poisoned the wells and how thousands of Jews consequently fell victim to the revenge of the people. Such lies have become truth.[57]

The operative implications of the thesis were left unstated: a common, although not universal practice. In the Germanies, as in the lands of the Habsburgs, it still tended to be very widely accepted that it was for the state to deal with the matter of the Jews, that it was officially defined and sanctioned policy that would have to be determinant. In this sense, matters were somewhat as in Russia, although the results at this stage were less brutal and bloody-minded and reflective of a residual disposition to treat Jews according to their presumed usefulness and, at a pinch, their individual merit. The result, in sum, was that in the Germanies and the Habsburg Empire successive attempts to keep the affairs of the Jews in what were deemed acceptable channels were never so inconsistent and

---

[57] Paul Pfitzer (but published anonymously), *Die Jeune Allemagne in Deutschland* (Stuttgart, 1836), 15–27. Cited in Rose, *Revolutionary Antisemitism*, 178–9.

self-contradictory as totally to extinguish the promise of that eventual, total regularization of their status that they, for their part, believed to have been held out to them. Nor in the meantime, was their ability to advance culturally and economically seriously hindered. What had grown was the discrepancy between the *pays légal* and the *pays réel*.

V

Unlike the Germanies and Austria, the French state as such had no policy on the Jews that deviated significantly from the position sanctified in 1791. Apart from the sole and justly considered aberrant exception of Napoleon's *décret infâme* of 1808, this would continue to be the case for the full century and a half that followed the Revolution. Questions relating to the role of the Jews in society and the economy, and in the management of the state itself, were raised from time to time by ministers, deputies, and civil servants in the privacy of their confidential discussions and correspondence. But at no point under either the restored monarchy, Bourbon or Orleanist, or the Second Empire, or under the Second and the Third Republics, was the *principle* of full citizenship for French Jews placed seriously in doubt so far as the working and inner purposes of the machinery of state were concerned. When vestiges of the old restrictive regime were found to be operative and were duly challenged, invariably, if with some delay, they were removed. Here then was one respect in which the revolutionary heritage was preserved; and it is therefore one of the ironies with which the modern history of the Jews is so plentifully shot through that the origins of much the sharpest, most effective and— from the Jews' own point of view—most dangerous modern formulations of the Jewish Question lay with that wing of the world of French politics that chose to see itself as the Revolution's faithful and uncompromising heirs. It was equally ironic, that ideas formulated with the utmost force on the left should in the course of time be adopted almost *in toto* and with little or no reservation by those who abhorred the Revolution and fought to restore as much of the *ancien régime* as they believed was capable of resuscitation. And this, no doubt, speaks as much for the depth of the particular roots in French society tapped by these ideas as for the intrinsic power of the ideas themselves.

On a journey to Frankfurt in 1842, Jules Michelet, France's preeminent nineteenth-century historian, then in his prime, paid a visit to Amschel Rothschild, eldest son of Mayer Amschel, the founder of the dynasty, whom he described in his diary as a

Dark mediator between the nations who speaks the language common to all: gold, and so compels them to come to terms with each other better than they would do so on their own. . . . Mr Rothschild knows Europe prince by prince and the Stock Exchange broker by broker. . . . There is only one thing [he and his like] fail to provide for and that is sacrifice. It will not occur to them that in Paris there are ten thousand men ready to die for an idea. July [the Revolution] surprised them.[58]

Michelet's considered view of the Jews is to be found most clearly articulated, however, in his *Bible de l'Humanité*,[59] where his point of departure is the proposition that 'Humanity is continually in process of putting its soul in a common Bible. Each great people inscribes a verse of its own within it.' He discusses India, ancient Persia, and ancient Greece in some detail. Ancient Israel is discussed in summary terms and the Jews' unalterable characteristics are laid down with Michelet's customary confidence in the precision of his judgement.

The Jew has always been a man of peace, a man of business. His ideal is not the warrior, the labourer, or the farmer. A nomadic shepherd in days of yore, he later reverted to his nomadic life as pedlar, as banker, as dealer in second-hand goods. . . . Art and industry (and agriculture) stand condemned [in his eyes] in the shape of Tubal-Cain.[60] Builders are stigmatized and jeered at for achieving nothing but the hollow enterprise of Babel. The true Jew, the patriarch, is the *shepherd-speculator* who knows how to increase his flocks by careful and intelligent acquisition and calculation. . . . The great and true glory of the Jews they owe to their wretchedness, namely that they alone among the peoples have given voice—a penetrating, eternal voice—to the sigh of the slave.[61]

As Michelet proceeds with his biblical-historical-anthropological analysis, the revulsion he feels for contemporary Jewry becomes more explicit.

God preferred to manifest his glory among the chosen people by choosing the *weak rather than the strong, the small rather than the large,* the junior rather than the senior. He preferred Joseph to the proud Judah; Jacob, delicate and soft as a woman, to the valiant Ishmael and to the strong Esau. He had little David slay the giant Goliath. He loves, and had therefore chosen for himself, a single, small people. Humankind is rejected. . . . The Jew settles early on the politics of a slave: infallible in [royal] courts, *secretly giving and giving again.* The Jew will be favoured by the kings. There is no better, more docile, more intelligent slave.[62]

The Jews, he goes on to tell his readers (echoing Marx, probably unknowingly), are distinguished by their having put their faith in profit (*gain*) and in money. They were taught, and did most profoundly believe,

---

[58] Jules Michelet, *Journal*, i (1828–48), entry for 21 July 1842, 2nd edn. (Paris, 1959), 458.

[59] Jules Michelet, *Bible de l'Humanité* (Paris, 1864).

[60] In fact, the Jewish Sages damned Tubal-Cain not as a mere craftsmen, but specifically as a smith and a maker of cutting tools (Genesis 4: 22), so equipping mankind with the means of repeating his ancestor Cain's act and sin of murder.

[61] Michelet, *Bible de l'Humanité*, 366–7. Emphasis in text.

[62] Ibid. 374–80. Emphases in text.

that it was in riches that their security lay—a doctrine encapsulated, he argues, in the biblical verse 'The rich man's wealth is his strong city' (Proverbs 18 : 11).[63] In practice, so far as the Jews were concerned, riches *were* gold—the form in which wealth could be rendered most mobile, although gold in its 'invisible' guise was better still: 'If the Phoenicians, as they say, invented writing, the Jews, almost immediately invented the bill of exchange.'[64]

It is not without interest and significance that so practised and eminent a historian should indulge in an attempt to construct a bridge between the semi-mythical ancestry of the Jews and the people he had in view in his own day and to do so out of such poor material and in such superficial terms. It brings him closer to Cobbett, Bauer, and Marx than to the more austere Savigny. But it brings him closest of all to the several principal fathers of French socialism. Led by Fourier and Proudhon, writing in language as stripped of niceties as Cobbett's and Marx's, but going well beyond them in the scope of their theses, they would provide the most powerful of all articulations of left-wing political opinion on the matter of the Jews for at least a century to come.

Of all the recent evils of the times, wrote Charles Fourier, the emancipation of the Jews ('l'admission des Juifs au droit de cité') was the most shameful. They were not a civilized nation, they were a 'patriarchal' one. They had no ruler. They believed any piece of knavery ('fourberie') to be praiseworthy so long as it was not one of their own religion who was deceived. They gave themselves up 'exclusively' to trade ('trafic'), to

---

[63] This is curious. The thrust of the passage is diametrically opposed to the meaning with which Michelet invests it, as a plain reading of verses 10 to 12 of Chapter 18 of the Book of Proverbs even in the (Christian) Authorized Version will show: 'The name of the Lord is a strong tower: the righteous runneth into it and is safe. The rich man's wealth is his strong city, and as an high wall in his own conceit. Before destruction the heart of man is haughty and before honour is humility.' The rich man, in other words, is contrasted with he who is the righteous and held up to ridicule in the bargain. Certainly, this has always been the Jewish reading of the text and traditional Jewish teaching in general. Michelet's point might have been the perfectly valid, but (for so eminent a historian) utterly banal one that in practice individual Jews have gone their own way and failed to follow biblical, Talmudic, and rabbinical teaching. But that does not seem to be the case, perhaps because in that event, the conclusion would have had to be that they were much like other people, whereas what Michelet was concerned to assert was that they were nothing of the kind, nor ever had been. This poses the secondary question of his knowledge—or even his interest—in the precise text to which he was alluding. The translation quoted here is that of the Authorized Version. It corresponds very fairly both to the original Hebrew and, it may be added, to such standard French translations as the present writer is acquainted with. There is, of course, no way of knowing what text (if any) Michelet himself may have had before him. And, no doubt, it all adds up to an issue of very little weight in itself (apart from such interest as it might hold for Michelet's biographers). What it does serve to illustrate and epitomize is the extreme lack of intellectual rigour with which even the most illustrious of men of letters have permitted themselves to approach, and to pronounce upon, the matter of Jewry when it pleased them to do so.

[64] Michelet, *Bible de l'Humanité*, 379.

usury, to commercial depravities. In France, fortunately, they were not yet present in great numbers. Otherwise

France would be nothing more than one vast synagogue, for if the Jews held no more than a quarter of all properties they would, by reason of their being in secret and indissoluble league with each other, be in a position to wield the greatest influence. This particular danger is [only] one of a thousand symptoms that attest to social degradation, the defective nature of the industrial system, and the need to reconstruct it on a new basis if Civilization is to last any longer contrary to God's pleasure.[65]

Commerce was an evil, Fourier believed. It was a universal method of exchange whereby sellers might deceive buyers with impunity and the good of all was sacrificed to the individual's love of gain. The heart of the matter of the Jews was that they were nothing less than the embodiment of the commercial spirit; and were, by the same token, *incorrigibly dishonest.*

They will reform, say the philosophers. Not at all: They will pervert our morals without altering theirs. Besides, when will they reform? Will it take a century for them to do so? . . . The Jews, with their commercial morality, are they not the leprosy and perdition of the body politic? . . . Let the Jews remain in France for a century and they . . . will become in France what they are in Poland and end by taking commercial industry away from the nationals who have managed it without the Jews thus far. . . . Wherever they are conspicuous, it is at the expense of the nationals. . . . The Jew millionaire lives on potatoes. Squalidly avaricious, he will sell at 5 per cent less than the Christian and increase his profit by the same amount. That is how the Jews crush the Christians. . . . Has it not been demonstrated politically that were all property-owner squalid and greedy the peoples' means of subsistence would be totally wiped out. Greed can be as ruinous as profligacy. In short, the Jews, politically, are a parasitical sect that tend to invade commerce at the expense of the nationals of the states in question without identifying themselves with the fate of any single fatherland.[66]

A government concerned to ensure propriety of public and private conduct was therefore under an obligation to constrain them; to force them into productive labour; to prohibit their free entry into France or free movement within it; to disperse those already domiciled in the country in villages; and then to keep them well away from frontier areas lest the temptation to engage in smuggling prove irresistible. In the long term they needed to be removed—at any rate encouraged to remove themselves. In a curious (and admittedly exceptional) flight of fancy, Fourier imagined the head of the Paris House of Rothschild leading his people to

---

[65] Charles Fourier, *Le Nouveau Monde industriel et sociétaire* (1829), 2nd edn. (Paris, 1845), 421; id., *Théorie des quatre mouvements et des destinées générales* (1808), 3rd edn. (Paris, 1846), 252–3.

[66] Written in 1804. *Publication des manuscrits de Charles Fourier* (Paris, 1856), 34–7.

a land of their own beyond Europe altogether, the pleasures of anticipated power having finally outweighed those of the stock exchange.

It is said that there was a time when he [Rothschild] had the intention of emancipating and reconstituting the Jewish nation; restoring Jerusalem to a Jewish monarch with his own flag, consuls, diplomatic standing. He [himself] would obtain the post of king of Judaea without negotiation; for within the Chaldaean empire one of the royal divisions, Judaea or Lebanon, extended over all of Phoenicia and Palestine as far as the Red Sea and all that part of Syria that is watered by the Orontes as well. . . . There are more enticing speculations than those [limited] to the play of government stock, more secure too![67]

One notes the evocation of antiquity; and one may note it again in Pierre-Joseph Proudhon (1809–65)—of whom it may at least be said that he had taken the trouble to study ancient Jewry a deal more assiduously than had Fourier—and a deal more assiduously too than he himself ever bothered to study his own Jewish contemporaries. Like Voltaire, Cobbett, Bauer, Michelet, and countless others, Proudhon had no doubt at all that deep and continual connections subsisted between the Jews of antiquity and the Jews of his own day and that these bore directly on what he took to be the evident fact that they were central figures in the evil world surrounding him. They were and always had been, an 'unsociable, obstinate, infernal race', he wrote, 'the first authors of that evil superstition called Catholicism in which the furious, intolerant Jewish element consistently overwhelmed the other Greek, Latin, barbarian, etc. elements and served to torture humankind for so long.'[68] And treading (like Voltaire) in the well-worn footsteps of a Church of which in all other respects he was hugely critical, Proudhon was at pains to assert that the religious message conveyed by the Jews was a false and distorted one and that their claims to religious and theological originality were of a piece with the rest of the wickedness that they embodied. 'One is tempted to believe in the Jewish people being subject to a special grace, an illumination, a revelation. Examined closely, the phenomenon dissolves into nothing.' For all peoples were monotheistic: each people had its particular god. The idea of a universal god was as foreign to the Jews as to others at least until the Babylonian captivity 'which caused them to *dream ambitiously* for Jehovah'.[69] Whereupon, as was characteristic of them, they went much further than was warranted and, in their 'messianic obstinacy', they placed themselves entirely 'beyond the bounds of the human conscience. . . . The charge brought against Jesus by the Jews was entirely specious, proof only of their own decline, their bad faith,

---

[67] *La fausse industrie, morcelée, répugnante, mensongère*, ii (Paris, 1835), 224.

[68] *Carnets*, ii, ed. Pierre Haubtmann (Paris, 1961), entry for 1847, 23.

[69] P.-J. Proudhon, *Jésus et les origines du Christianisme*, ed. Clement Rochet, 2nd edn. (Paris, 1896), 19–20. Emphasis in the original.

their unfitness. They were finished. The success of Paul's mission shows that.[70]

To the question what was to be done with this vagabond nation which he so loathed, whose 'natural condition' it was to live dispersed and parasitically on others, Proudhon offered firm, if moderately self-contradictory, answers. 'Voltaire's wish to send them back to Jerusalem must be carried out.'[71] They must be expelled from France—all of them, except perhaps those married to Frenchwomen. They must be refused all employment. Their synagogues must be abolished. And an end must be put to the practice of their religion. For

There was good reason for the Christians to call them deicides. The Jew is the enemy of humankind. The race must either be sent back to Asia or extermin-ated. . . . By the sword, by amalgamation, or by expulsion the Jew must be made to disappear. . . . [Il faut renvoyer cette race en Asie, ou l'exterminer. . . . Par le fer, ou par la fusion, ou par l'expulsion, il faut que le juif disparaisse.] Those whom the peoples of the Middle Ages loathed by instinct I loathe upon reflection, irrevocably. Hatred of the Jew, as of the Englishman, needs to be an article of our faith.[72]

But it was Alphonse Toussenel (1803–85), a lesser figure than either Fourier or Proudhon, who articulated most vehemently of all, but also most successfully (in a book which rapidly went through several edi-tions), the reasons for a Frenchman to detest the Jew and, as it happened, the Englishman as well. Commercial capitalism and Jewry were intim-ately and wickedly involved one with the other to the immense detri-ment of decent, ordinary men and women and in defiance of all established moral principles. So was capitalism and the English. A self-declared pupil of Fourier,[73] and in the matter of the Jews, at any rate, one who is considered to have had some influence on Proudhon, Toussenel's particular distinction lay in his having had the talent to devise what for decades would remain among the most pungent formulations of the thesis in question—a talent well represented by the brilliance of the title he had devised for the book on which his notoriety rests: Les Juifs, rois de l'époque: histoire de la féodalité financière (The Jews, kings of the age: a history of financial feudalism).[74] The themes Fourier had adumbrated laboriously and Proudhon semi-privately are tied together in Toussenel with the vigour and impertinence of argument that are the true hallmarks of effective demagogy. They are applied in the first instance to the France that had so mistakenly emancipated the Jews. They are then extended with special emphasis to other nations that, like the Jews themselves, are commercial. The wickedness of the Jews, Toussenel told his readers, is

[70] Ibid. 122.   [71] Carnets, ii. 150.   [72] Ibid. 337–9.
[73] Described by Toussenel as 'le plus puissants des génies de ce siècle'. (Les Juifs, rois de l'époque: histoire de la féodalité financière, i (2nd edn., Paris, 1847), p. xi.)
[74] First published in Paris, 1845.

portrayed for all to read in the Bible from which they themselves continue to draw nourishment. But neither in their wickedness nor in the nourishment they draw from the Old Testament are they alone. 'To say Jew is to say Protestant. . . . The Englishman, the Dutchman, and the Genevan who learned to read the will of God in the same book as the Jew profess the same contempt for the laws of equity and the rights of workers.' What all these peoples had in common was greed and an absolute devotion to commerce. 'The talmudist of Frankfurt, the old Jew of usurious blood and circumcision, is no more fervently attached to the letter of the Bible and to the cult of the golden calf than the puritan of Geneva whose ancestors burned Servetus or the Methodist of England or the pietist of Germany. They are all children of the same father.'[75] As for the French themselves, it was to be recognized sadly that, 'freed supposedly of the yoke of nobiliar feudalism by the revolution of '89, in fact they had done no more than change masters'.[76]

Some four decades would pass before a book of comparable tendentiousness, brilliance, and unscrupulous exposition would be written, published, and accorded a public response to match.[77] But a style and a format for the genre had been set. So had a position. The working classes and the Jews were to be understood as being placed on opposite sides of the class struggle divide. The Jews, regardless of their real circumstances, were to be found alongside the exploiting bourgeoisie.[78] There was a set posture too: a false defensiveness—as if it were exceedingly courageous to have ventured to speak the truth about the Jews publicly. And there was the implication, but more often than not the assertion, that there was here a matter of inherited and inalienable characteristics; not so much as a hint therefore (in what might be termed the Montesquieu spirit) that there might after all be other values in play, other interpretations of the circumstances past or present, or even, say, of the Jews' own Bible. Above all, and most curiously, it was a phenomenon of retrogression by these politically radical, socially dissident, secularly minded people back to a deep, essentially Christian, as much Byzantine as Roman Catholic, hatred of

[75] Les Juifs, rois de l'époque, p. iv.
[76] Ibid. 256.
[77] On Edouard Drumont's La France juive, see below, pp. 103f. But Toussenel was not forgotten. Louis Thomas, Alphonse Toussenel: socialiste national antisémite (1803–1885) is a study of the man and his work by one who admired Toussenel for his loathing of the English as strongly as he admired him for his loathing of the Jews and advanced the one and the other as evidence of National Socialism avant la lettre. The book was published in Paris by Mercure de France in 1941 and went into six editions almost immediately.
[78] The interpenetration of western European, but especially French socialism and what in the course of time would be termed anti-Semitism is most authoritatively and cogently dealt with in the late Edmund Silberner's Ha-sozialism ha-maʿaravi u-sheʾelat ha-yehudim (Jerusalem, 1955) of which regrettably, so far as I know, no English language translation has ever been prepared.

the Jews: the Jews as deicides—and unrepentant ones at that; the Jews as deicides *because* they were and have remained evil; the Jews as a people to whom no form of differentiation—between rich and poor, male and female, adult and children, or even 'useful' and 'useless'—need be or can be applied. The best in generosity Proudhon could manage, once he had finally determined in his own mind that they had all, most probably, to be exterminated was the afterthought that perhaps the very old might be spared. After all, they would have no progeny.[79]

VI

Set against such a standard as this it would not have been difficult to find a fair number of senior policemen and bureaucrats in Alexander I's, and even Nicholas I's, Russia who shone—not by reason of an especially kindly disposition to the Jews to be sure, but at least by the measure of decent restraint they were apt to display. But then the objective differences between eastern Europe and western and central Europe in respect of all issues relating to the Jews, qualitative as well as quantitative, were continually widening. Unlike the situation in Russia, occasional, hugely exaggerated claims to the contrary apart, it was never the brute numbers of the Jews in mid-nineteenth-century Great Britain, France, the Italian States, the Low Countries, the several German states, or even the German parts of the Habsburg Empire that were seriously at issue. The question how they were to be policed did not seem to anyone in power to be especially grave, let alone insuperable. The Jews' place, actually or potentially, but at any rate collectively, as one people or nation among the others, did not trouble anyone in authority. They were fast ceasing to be thought of—except in the popular mind to some extent and the minds of demagogues—as a distinctive socio-economic caste identified with very specific trades and crafts. In brief, in the western half of the continent it was not as a problem of day-to-day *government* that the Jews presented themselves to the official or, by and large, even the legislative mind. Some administrators were entirely indifferent to them. Others, as we have seen, thought they posed problems of principle that touched on the inner nature of the state, but of a general, long-term, hardly an urgent nature. Most people in government, whatever they happened to think of the Jewish population, if and when they thought of it at all, were at any rate unworried. Thus in the west. In eastern Europe, in contrast, and most notably in the Russian Empire, very little of this applied. As we have seen, no one either in St Petersburg or in the provinces who had taken the trouble to consider the Jewish segment of the population in real and immediate, as opposed to detached and abstract, terms doubted for one moment that by reason of its very nature and its presence within the Tsar's domains it posed a socio-economic problem, possibly a political problem too, and that both the one and the other were of very considerable dimensions and acute difficulty.

In themselves, the actual terms in which the question of the Jews was most commonly raised in public and in the (censored) press, as opposed to government circles, were unremarkable. In most respects they corresponded fairly closely *mutatis mutandis* to those that were in the process of being made familiar in central and western Europe. 'Rothschild' was in no sense an exceptional figure in Jewry, wrote a leading figure in the Slavophil movement, A. S. Khomyakov, in 1847. He owed his 'seven hundred millions' and his position as a financial power in the land neither to circumstances nor to personal ability. His financial power was no more than an echo of the history and ancient faith of his 'tribe': a people without a fatherland driven as always by 'ancient Palestine's commercial spirit' and imbued with the same love of the pleasures of this world as had 'prevented them in ancient times from recognizing the Messiah in his poverty and humiliation'.[80] The ordinary exploitation of the worker or peasant by landowner or factory-owner was bad enough, wrote Ivan Aksakov. It was not to be compared, however, with the Jews' exploitation of the population in the western provinces of Russia. Like a boa constrictor, it strangled the people, drained them of their blood, kept them in fetters. 'It is an old oppression, an arrogant oppression. . . . [And] it is the more insulting by reason of the exploiters belonging to another race and another creed.'[81] Every man for himself, all personal relations reduced to the opportunistic—such was the spirit of the age, wrote Dostoevsky. And *that* was why the Jews were able to exercise their absolute rule in the stock exchanges and the international political arena. As for the future, the Jews knew what it would be, for 'Their rule was nigh, their total rule! [*Blizit'sya ikh tsarstvo, polnoe ikh tsarstvo!*]'[82]

On the other hand, much that was apt to be passed off in the west fairly simplistically was recognized as complex in eastern Europe. If 'Rothschild' as a figure representing both the Jews and the age passed muster of a kind in the west, it required at least some modification and amendment in the east where it was so abundantly obvious that the overwhelming majority of Jews were deeply, painfully impoverished—in fact, that poverty and squalor were among their defining external characteristics.

---

[80] Cited in Shemu'el Ettinger, 'Ha-rek'a ha-idiologi le-hofa'ata shel ha-sifrut ha-antishemit ha-ḥadasha be-rusiya', *Ẓion*, 35, 1–4 (1970), 194.

[81] I. S. Aksakov, *Sochineniia*, iii (Moscow, 1886), 723. Cited in S. Lukashevich, *Ivan Aksakov* (Cambridge, Mass., 1965), 97.

[82] 'Status in statu. Sorok vekov bytiya', *Dnevnik pisatelya za 1877 g.*, reprinted in R. Kh. Shakirzyanov (ed.), *Taina Izrailya* (St Petersburg, 1993), 16.

The theme of the Jews as a nation (or caste) wedded to the commercial exploitation of their neighbours was a mandatory one. But if their portrayal as a people of wealth and power was to carry conviction, it had to be squared with what any child could actually observe. This may go some distance to explain Russian reluctance to delve into the real socio-economic circumstances of the Jews, more especially into their causes. It owed something too to the fact that the centres of intellectual, academic, and journalistic activity were mostly in 'inner' Russia, far from the western provinces and therefore well away from the mass of ordinary Jews. Still, the questions as to how the Jewish urban and village lower classes were finally to be fitted into efforts to pull together a systematic account and interpretation of the condition of contemporary Russia as a whole and whether the empire's Jewish subjects were likely at some point to be approached politically by dissident forces, and if so how and with what consequences, would not go entirely away no matter how awkward the results of an honest examination of their circumstances were likely to be. The view of M. P. Dragomanov, a hostile observer, but a closer one than most and a socialist, a Ukrainian nationalist and a historian as well, was that the Jews were indeed a commercial, unproductive, exploitative, insular, superstitious, and above all profoundly alien people. But while the effort to control and restrict them had failed to put an end to their systematic exploitation of the peasants, they themselves, in the mass, were quite as badly in need of liberation from their own plutocrats and from their own Hasidic *zaddikim* as were the Christians from the Jews. Emancipation would do no more than free wealthy Jews to suck poorer Jews dry. The case of the Jews of the Ukraine was therefore a pathological one and needed to be seen in *all* its aspects if ever it was to be properly dealt with.[83]

It is probable that the language employed and the judgement commonly handed down would have been as harsh even if the Russian state had been differently constituted and motivated and had refrained from forever seeking to alter the internal order of Jewish society and the structure and quality of the Jews' relations with the other peoples of the empire. The dimensions of the problem of the Jews were such that no Russian regime, no matter how composed and regardless of the principles of government informing it, would have been inclined to act otherwise. In this respect, the case of the Decembrists, closest of any dissident force to seizing power and unique among nineteenth-century rebels against the state in that they had devised detailed plans for the reconstitution of Russia along lines that were almost diametrically opposed to those of the Autocracy, is instructive. Like successive Tsars and

---

[83] M. P. Dragomanov, 'Evrei i Polyaki v yugo-zapadnom krae', *Vestnik Evropy*, 7 (July 1875), 133–79.

their minions, the Decembrists, the most nearly successful of nineteenth-century oppositional movements, believed in the validity and uses of master-plans for society. They looked at all the obvious topics—government, army, society, and foreign relations—and they made a remarkable attempt to grasp the nettle of the 'tribes in the Russian population' too: the problem posed the Russian state and the Russian people proper by the massive presence and disparate cultures and purposes of a host of non-Russian peoples. The Poles, they thought, should be allowed independence—in close alliance, to be sure, with the new Russian state whose borders would then be drawn so as to exclude not only Warsaw, Vilna, and Bialystok, but even Minsk. Lesser (presumably less dangerous) 'tribes'—Finns, Letts, Moldavians, Tatars, and Cossacks, and the peoples of the Caucasus and Siberia—were to be absorbed into a single Russian nation: absorbed and, so to speak, lost forever, culture, identity, folk memories, and all. There were lacunae in their plans, one of them immense: it proved impossible to bring the officers who formed the insurrectionary move-ment, many of whom were landowners, some of whom were members of great noble families, to agree on what was to be done about the serfs. But there was no attempt, contrary to what might have been expected, to avoid the problem of the Jews. And their outline of a solution to it is interesting for two reasons. One is that the careful wording of the chapter on 'the Jewish people' (narod)[84] in Russkaya Pravda (Russian Justice, the encompassing plan for a new Russian state drawn up by the most important of the leaders of the conspiracy, Colonel Pavel Ivanovich Pestel) makes it very clear that the Decembrists' outlook on the Jews differed hardly at all from what had long been the conventional judgement upon them in high places in Russia for many decades. The Jews, that is to say, were too closely knit a people to be penetrated by others. They settled their affairs among themselves. They were ruled, to all intents and purposes, by their rabbis rather than by the state on the false—or at least doubtful—authority of the Talmud. Their interests ran counter to those of the peasants. And, most fundamental of all, while awaiting the Messiah, they saw themselves as no more than temporary inhabitants of whatever coun-try they happened to find themselves in. The difference between the Autocracy's established outlook and that which was implied in Pestel's prescription for a solution to the Problem of the Jews lay in his remarkable combination of such entirely conventional elements with something that was a great deal more imaginative, not to say fantastic. The endemic conflict between Jews and Christians and, by extension, the consequent damage done to the Christian population by the Jews, must be brought

---

[84] Where the Finns, the Letts, the other Baltic peoples, the Tatars, and the Moldavians were all defined as 'tribes' (plemena), the Siberians (Kalmuks, for example), the Caucasians, and the Jews were all defined as 'peoples' (narody).

to an end, he thought. That needed to be the principal consideration. But there were two quite distinct ways in which this might be accomplished. One was for the Jews' social order to undergo total change (*v sovershennom izmenenii sego poryadka*) in the interests of their final assimilation into the Russian *narod*. True, this was no more than the Autocracy's own, ultimate purpose. But where the Autocracy had not—and would not—finally make up its mind as to whether it was attainable, the Decembrists were not far from concluding that in fact it was not. The emphasis was therefore on what they (or at any rate Pestel himself) conceived as the alternative: radical in nature, vastly more promising. The idea, plainly the product of a brisk military mind, was that it would be best for all concerned if the Jews left Russia entirely. They were to do so peacefully. They would so with Russian help. Given the right (unspecified) international circumstances *and* the goodwill of the Jewish people itself on whom it was incumbent, of course, to make the primary decision to leave, there could be established for them, Pestel had no doubt, 'somewhere in Asia Minor [*kakoi libo chasti Maloi Azii*]' an independent Jewish state which they would form and to which they would proceed. A massive trek to the south and east would be set afoot. An initial point of assembly would be fixed. Some Russian military forces would be deployed (on a temporary basis) for reinforcement and protection— although the Jews themselves would constitute a very substantial force of their own. When all the Jews of Russia and Poland had gathered together their numbers would exceed 2 million souls; and so great a mass should have no difficulty overcoming whatever obstacles the Turks chose to put in their way as they passed through European and Asiatic Turkey on to their final destination. Once arrived there would certainly be room and land enough for all and the basis on which to establish their own 'special Jewish state [*osobennoye evreiskoe gosudarstvo*]'.[85]

After the collapse of the Decembrist conspiracy the carefully packed committee of inquiry appointed to investigate its origins and purposes declared *Russkaya Pravda* to have been 'conceived in a spirit that was entirely republican'. It noted the passages devoted to the Jews and summarized them in its report, but it refrained from commenting on them directly, being content, presumably, to offer them to the Tsar as so much additional, dismaying proof of the 'total ignorance of the interests and needs of the country'[86] displayed by the conspirators. There was certainly no question of the Autocracy taking any part at all of Pestel's overall plan for a new Russia seriously, not even the idea—probably not unwelcome in itself—that it would be best for all concerned if the Jews were

[85] Glavnoe Arkhivnoe Upravlenie, Vosstanie Dekabristov: Dokumenty, vii, *Russkaya Pravda P. I. Pestelya* (Moscow, 1958), 146–8.
[86] *Rapport de la commission d'enquête* (St Petersburg, 1826), 42 n.

evacuated totally from the Tsar's dominions. *Russkaya Pravda* was far too deeply subversive of the regime in intent and spirit for anyone to consider what might be learned from it—with the incidental result that Pestel himself was among the very few conspirators to be hanged and his pro-gramme kept out of the public domain until after the revolution of 1905. There was no question therefore of a *public* response of any kind to so extraordinarily ambitious a project. Indeed, Pestel himself had observed that, considering the necessarily 'gigantic' *(ispolinskoe)* nature of the undertaking, it was too early to suggest that a firm decision on the mat-ter be taken by the Decembrists' own provisional government-to-be. He offered the idea, he explained, as food for further—and, as he evidently hoped, serious—thought. Least of all could there have been a comment from Jewish quarters. There was only one (converted) Jew among the Decembrists themselves, albeit only on the outer margins of the conspir-acy, Grigorii Abramovich Perets. Perets seems to have been privy to Pestel's thinking and to have disliked it.[87] In any event, after 1825, as before, the all-powerful regime would continue to arrogate to itself the absolute lead in examining, seeking to define, and actually attempting to deal in practice and in detail with the Problem of the Jews. There was no ques-tion then or later of entertaining ideas emanating from other quarters. It followed, that the role Russian men of letters might play in the definition and ventilation of the Problem or Question of the Jews could never be of the same order of importance as that played by their analogues in the west. The famous moral prestige enjoyed by those Russian writers, poets, publicists, and even academics whom the public was prepared to perceive as genuinely free and independent spirits did count for something in this sphere, as in others. But it was the regime itself, in its controlled but unmistakable hostility to Jewry and Judaism, that most effectively reflected and concretized popular anti-Jewish sentiment. And there is no reason to think that the harsh, intensely visible policing of the Jews did not count for more in the shaping of the public mind than did even such profoundly hostile and derisive, not to say venomous, portraits of them as happened to be evoked here and there in Russian literature, even in the pages of so talented, widely read, and prestigious a writer as Gogol.

In any event, far from resisting the demands of such individuals and special interest groups as objected to an easing of the policy of restriction and coercion to which the Jews were traditionally subject, the Autocracy was inclined to respond to them with sympathy and good will. Certainly, the Russian government was not one that could be faulted for favouring the Jews unduly, let alone for being hand in glove with them. It was in no need of lessons in what in Russia was widely defined as 'Judaeophobia' from the multitude of eminent publicists, university professors, and great

---

[87] Vl. N. and L. N. Perets, *Dekabrist Grigorii Abramovich Perets* (Leningrad, 1926), 25–7.

and good figures among men of letters generally who held negative views on the Jews and regarded their presence on Russian soil as, if not an outright offence, certainly a source of danger and corruption to be neutralized and so far as possible got rid of. In sum, the Autocracy was as dedicated as any to ensuring that *pays réel* and *pays légal* corresponded very closely to one another so far as the Jews were concerned, whence the almost unique circumstance in Europe that there was no way of separating the question of the Jews as such from the still larger question of the regime itself. It followed that no argument, hostile or friendly, on the affairs of the Jews could fail to hinge on an implicit—or even explicit—appraisal of the framework of governmental regulations under which they were constrained to live. And no matter what one thought of the constraints and afflictions imposed upon the Jews specifically, there was no way of avoiding the intricately connected, parallel matter of the constraints and afflictions imposed by the Autocracy on its other subjects. To argue publicly for the emancipation of the Jews was to take up an unpopular cause. To be perceived as friendly to them was to render oneself vulnerable to abuse. But it bordered on the dangerous as well, necessarily so, since it was to take up a position that was implicitly, if not explicitly, critical of the government as well. Finally, it was to beg the very large question indeed whether in Russian circumstances the lot of the Jews was worse than that of others. The Jews, wrote Dostoevsky, complained continually that they were not free to live where they liked. 'But was the native Russian person [*russkii 'korennoi' chelovek*] free to choose his [place of] residence?' Were not the constraints imposed on the serfs in earlier times still operative to a considerable extent on ordinary people today? They might say what they liked, but the Jews' freedom to choose where they might live had been mightily extended in the course of the past twenty years. Yet they complain, continually. Whether they have the right to do so is a question in itself. But even if they have the right, they are not alone in having it. They 'scream' (*krichat*) about the persecution and oppression they have suffered for centuries. But what of the Russians? Haven't they suffered oppression and persecution over very many centuries too? 'Can it really be affirmed that the Russian people has endured fewer calamities and less evil [*men'she bed i zol*] than the Jews?'[88]

VII

The internal political history of the Jews themselves in modern times hardly begins with politics proper. There is no set and delineated

---

[88] 'Evreisky vopros' and 'No da zdravstvuyet bratstvo!', in *Dnevnik pisatelya za 1877 g.*, 13–14, 22.

struggle for internal power and authority, no competitive organizing of influence, support, and opinion, no driven personalities, no real attempt to crystallize the issues with a view to eventual, purposeful collective action. But there can be discerned, by the middle of the nineteenth century—in the western half of Europe, at any rate—a good deal of that fluidity of attitude of mind and those signs of dissatisfaction, unease, and in certain cases anger that form the necessary groundwork of political debate and political action. For the time being, then, all is response—to the new circumstances in general, but more particularly to the ever more vehement terms in which the Question of the Jews had come to be posed outside the still quite easily detectable borders that separated the Jews from their neighbours. It is a defensive response, often an indignant one, in some cases intensely personal, in others out of calmer, but reasoned concern for the community as a whole. Here it will be articulated by individuals who are devoted heart and soul to Jewish causes, there by others who have become isolated from their fellows or have cut themselves off from them entirely. All is somewhat patchy and shadowy, more easily detectable to the beholder in retrospect than to participants floundering in indecision and dubiety at the time. And everything in the invertebrate and increasingly fragmented structure of Jewish society continues as before to militate against ideas, reflections, and programmes being pulled together as a basis for coherent and co-ordinated action or even the very simple declarations of common purpose and intention on which the least of political acts is necessarily contingent. Certainly, it was in the nature of the processes of emancipation and social liberation that beside hope and expectation they should breed uncertainty. That it had been borne in upon modernists in western Jewry that a strong, growing, potentially powerful body of opinion was opposed to their peaceful admission to civil society on any terms whatsoever was initially and inevitably a source of palpable shock and dismay. But it rarely sufficed to disperse set views and expectations altogether. It only added something to the confusion of mind and social judgement that now prevailed among them—itself a function of Jewry's ancient inability to relate needs and purposes to the actual political and mental topography in which fate, repeatedly and to its cost, had placed it. Even the wave of anti-Jewish riots that erupted in 1819 did nothing to clear minds to the extent of setting people in motion in what was discernibly a fresh direction.

The so-called Hep! Hep![89] riots of 1819 broke out initially in the city of Würzburg, spread rapidly through much of southern and west-central Germany, then to the north as far as Hamburg and Copenhagen and to

---

[89] 'Hep! Hep!' was the rioters' rallying call. Its origins remain obscure. Some have believed that 'Hep' stood for 'Hierolyma est perdita', others that it was no more than a goatherd's cry common in south Germany.

the east to Danzig and Cracow. They took the form of violent mob attacks on the persons and property of Jews, falling short, however, of the standard of brutality that would be set in eastern Europe later in the century: rape and murder were virtually unknown. In Würzburg itself the trouble had been precipitated by a quarrel between those who favoured and those who opposed the abolition of the civil and commercial freedoms granted the Jews in the course of the brief period of Habsburg rule between 1804 and 1814. Tension built up through the summer of 1819. Rioting began on the evening of 2 August 1819. Within three days not a Jew was to be seen anywhere in the city. All had either found a hiding place within it or escaped to one of the outlying villages. And there the matter rested for a week while the local authorities debated what to do. When they had mustered up the courage to decide that it might after all be best for *everyone* if the violence were stopped the city fathers discovered to their dismay that it was beyond their power to do so and troops had to be sent in by the central government in Munich.

The stakes in Würzberg were small. The Jewish community that so enraged the local commercial classes by pressing their right to reside and trade freely in the city and had thereupon been judged by rivals and enemies to have reached intolerably high numbers amounted to no more than thirty families in all—or about 1 per cent of Würzburg's total population of about 20,000. But an example had been set and when news of the rioting reached Frankfurt several days later a similarly bitter, but considerably more extensive, and—by reason of the prominence of both the city itself and its Jewish population—more serious wave of violent disorder was sparked off. From Frankfurt the plague spread in other directions although, on the whole, with steadily diminishing force. The actual scale, duration, and intensity of the rioting in each case was before all else a function of the speed and vigour with which the local authorities set themselves to deal with it. But the general impression was grim. As late as September of that year the French ambassador in Munich reported home that there was no place in all of Germany where Jews were now secure;[90] and bodies and property did indeed seem to be at risk in ways and to a degree unknown for very many years. Moreover, if the mobs themselves, as might be expected, were preponderantly composed of members of the lower orders of society—workmen, apprentices, discharged soldiers, petty criminals, and other marginal folk—educated and socially established people were to be found among the *agitators*. Heine, caught up in Hamburg in September 1830 in a second wave of rioting, smaller in scope, but of much the same kind and origins as that of 1819, observed that 'It was not only the mob, but that respectable bourgeoisie

[90] Jacob Katz, 'Pera'ot hep-hep shel shenat 1819 be-germaniya 'al rik'an ha-histori', *Zion*, 38, 1–4 (1973), 103.

which in Paris too played such an active part: the shopkeepers who stand in the doorways in their slippers and conduct business in comfort.'[91] On the other hand, in so far as state was distinguishable from society in these circumstances, it was plain in retrospect that official will and official machinery remained decisive and that, in general, a commendable effort had been made to damp the riots down (to speak of their being *crushed* would be to employ too strong a term). What had been totally lacking (except to some degree in Hamburg and the Grand Duchy of Baden) was regard for the welfare and safety of Jewish citizens themselves—as opposed, that is to say, to regard for visible law and order in the streets. In Frankfurt the city government's eventual decision to quell the mob owed most to the Senate's fear that its newly re-won, but fragile, political independence would be imperilled if it did not finally climb down on the law and order, alas ostensibly pro-Jewish, side of the fence.

So long as this was the pattern in central Europe and it was held to, the impact on the Jewish rank and file of the riots of 1819 and subsequent protests against them in the streets and elsewhere was limited. The burghers of Würzburg, Frankfurt, Danzig, and other towns where the mob had been active in pillage, arson, and physical violence against individuals had ended by being alarmed at what had transpired so very near their own doors and wished not to see it repeated. Further encouragement could be drawn from the tendency at all levels of government to put the unpleasantness of these years behind it and so far as possible to play it down. It was true that, where this proved difficult, there to be sure the municipal authorities sought to extend blame for what had happened to the Jews themselves, taking the opportunity to remind them that if they wished to avoid similar trouble in the future they needed first to mend their manners. Thus even in Hamburg. The city's relatively liberal city government had published its finding that, contrary to allegations made, the Jews had in no way provoked the local outbreak of rioting and had added nothing of their own to the friction once it had erupted. The city fathers had then gone on to affirm that they would tolerate no further attempt to harass the Jewish population either physically or by word of mouth. Duty done, however, they turned to rap the Jews on their knuckles. The Jews may have been blameless in the past, but they would be wise to refrain from immodest and discourteous behaviour in public places in the future. They would be equally well advised, they were told, to abstain from demands upon the state that could be shown to be incompatible with their own true sentiment towards it. It was true, the Senate of Hamburg declared, that the leaders of the community were to be

---

[91] Prawer, *Heine's Jewish Comedy*, 222–3. Cf. Eleonore O. Sterling, 'Anti-Jewish Riots in Germany in 1819: A Displacement of Social Protest', *Historia Judaica*, 12 (1950), 105–42.

complimented on their good intentions and on the beneficial influence they were known to exert on their constituents and were deserving, therefore, of the city's protection. But there would now be no question, they were informed (in veiled language), of full, formally legislated civic rights being granted them, not in the foreseeable future at any rate.[92] But again, comfort could be taken from the fact that, whatever the reason and however belatedly, there was a sense in which Hamburg and virtually all other states had all ended by coming down—if with some embarrassment—on the side that effectively was that of the Jews after all.

Assured of protection from the mob and, on the whole, of non-demeaning treatment at the hands of the authorities, the Jews of Germany and its periphery could continue, not without reason, to judge themselves beneficiaries of the *Rechtsstaat*—the more so as what had occurred accorded with historical experience. Where it was the state itself—the sovereign power—that had set about their persecution, expulsion, or simple annihilation, there indubitably all was lost and all had to be abandoned. But in the central Europe of 1819 or 1830 and its immediate periphery, this very plainly had not been the case. On the whole, therefore, the response to the riots of 1819 was mild. The prevailing tendency was to be patient and to fall in with the evident wish of authority to put the ugliness of mob violence behind it. The editors of *Sulamith*, the first—and for some time the leading German-language Jewish periodical—did not go quite so far as wholly to ignore the violence; but they were careful to pay no more than minimal attention to it, for fear, as they were frank enough to explain to their readers, lest 'our co-religionists' love for our Christian fellow citizens' be weakened.[93] Among the wealthier merchants and bankers who had been hit or openly threatened by the rioters, the Frankfurt Rothschilds among them, there were some who took a stronger stand; and not without results. As far as they were concerned, there was to be no question at all of going back to the pre-emancipatory state of affairs. The Rothschilds gave out, therefore, that they were contemplating departure from Frankfurt if their security there could not be guaranteed and this was reported to Vienna by the Austrian Legation in the city as a matter of urgency. The sensation, Metternich was assured, would be 'enormous' if they left, and the 'splendour of Frankfurt . . . considerably dimmed'.[94] In the event, the Rothschilds did not abandon Frankfurt. They chose instead, having been given the opportunity, to strengthen their foothold in Vienna itself; and the authorities there, despite their generally hostile policy to Jewry as a whole, and to the entry and settlement of Jews in Vienna in particular, went out of their way to

[92] Katz, 'Pera'ot', 97.

[93] *Sulamith*, 6, 1 (1819), 34.

[94] Count Egon Caesar Corti, *The Rise of the House of Rothschild* (New York, 1928), 209–10.

facilitate the consolidation of their presence. Considered from the Austrian angle, this relaxation of long-standing Habsburg policy was less a sign of the transitional and generally fluid character of the period immediately subsequent to the Napoleonic wars than a throw-back to the *ancien régime* in its final, 'Enlightened' stage. It accorded very well, that is to say, with the now well-established rule that where 'useful' Jews could be identified it was politic to distinguish them from their lesser brethren and to afford them (on a rigorously selective and minimalist basis) the facilities of which they stood in need. It had the advantage too of compatibility with the equally popular thesis that in the matter of emancipation and the integration of the Jews into civil society the eventual outcome depended on the Jews themselves. Such, as we have seen, had commonly been the view from without. But now, increasingly, it would be the view from within as well: theses that were being rapidly picked up and applied by an entirely new class of Jews to their own affairs and indeed to themselves in person and who, no less than the Rothschilds, were determined never to return to the Frankfurt ghetto or any of its analogues. The ghetto in Frankfurt, wrote Ludwig Börne, was 'probably the most densely populated spot on earth' in which the Jews

enjoyed the most loving care on the part of the government. On Sundays they were not allowed to leave their street lest they be beaten up by drunkards. They were not allowed to marry before reaching the age of 25 to ensure the strength and health of their children. On holidays they were only allowed to pass through the [ghetto] gate after six in the evening lest the excessive heat of the sun harm them. The public footpaths were closed to them; and they were compelled to walk in the open country to stimulate their interest in agriculture. If a Christian called out to a Jew who passed him by, 'Mach Mores Jud', the Jew had to doff his hat. It was a courtesy intended to strengthen the bonds of affection between the two religions. . . . The Jews of Frankfurt enjoyed many other privileges.[95]

It was difficult therefore for anyone who had made some progress in what was held on all sides (except that of orthodox and traditionalist Jewry itself) to be the right direction, and who had been led by ever greater command of the language of the country, growing involvement in its affairs, and, most critical of all, exposure to what was actually said privately and publicly *about* the Jews, not to accept that they did indeed have to meet their opponents and critics halfway at the very least. To take a generally optimistic view of the future was necessarily to accept that by and large the Jews of western and central Europe had not done so, or at any rate not as thoroughly as had been expected of them, and that in this matter of integration and acculturation the Jews did therefore have a case

---

[95] Ludwig Börne, *Sämtliche Werke*, iii (New York, 1858), 23. Quoted in slightly different form in Eleonore Sterling, 'Jewish Reaction to Jew-Hatred in the First Half of the Nineteenth Century', *LBIYB* 3 (London, 1958), 107 n.

to answer. In sum, to continue to put heart and soul in the emancipatory movement as the engine of social and political advance was to incline one to the argument that the 1819 riots needed to be seen as a regrettable, but inexorable stage in a dialectical process that was leading, ultimately, in the right direction after all. The violence it had engendered had to be accepted with as much good grace as could be mustered, the more so as no clear alternative, other than return to an actual or notional ghetto, was on offer.

The predicament was not peculiar to German Jews. Anti-Jewish mob violence of the kind displayed in Germany in 1819 and sporadically thereafter was, if anything, more of a plague in France—at any rate in Alsace where it was sufficiently frequent in the first half of the nineteenth century to be regarded as endemic.[96] The pattern and the causes—real and alleged—had something in common with those that had formed the background to the disturbances in Germany. And both the French prefectoral authorities and Jewish observers were moved to ascribe the outbreak of anti-Jewish riots in 1819 and 1820 in the departments of Bas- and Haut Rhin and in the adjoining department of the Moselle in Lorraine to the German example.[97] The basic social and economic features of Alsatian Jewry were, of course, quite similar to those of Jews east of the Rhine in the early years of the century and the major sources and forms of opposition in word and deed encountered were essentially of the same kind. Their long established role as providers of objectively important, but subjectively despised and resented services to the peasantry as pedlars, horse- and cattle-dealers, and minor moneylenders had yet to be entirely shaken off. Their new residential, and therefore much strengthened commercial presence in the cities had already brought them into conflict with the merchant classes of Strasbourg, Colmar, and the other cities of the province from which they had been legally excluded under the old regime. To the still more ancient, essentially ineradicable theological anti-Judaism of the Church there had been added the circumstance that the Jews in one way or another were among the moral and legal beneficiaries of the hated, godless Revolution—even to the extent that from 1831 onwards their rabbis had their salaries paid by the state on a basis of strict equality with Protestant ministers and Roman Catholic priests. And there were the separate objections to Jewish particularism of those who were still devoted to the principles for which the Revolution was held to stand in their sharpest, least compromising, Jacobin form. Each group or class on the grounds peculiar to it, allowed itself to be periodically infuriated by the fact that great numbers of Jews in the eastern

---

[96] Z. Szajkowski, 'Pera'ot be-alzas be-'et ha-mahapekhot shel 1789, 1830, ve-1848', *Zion*, 20, 1–2 (1955), 82–102; Paula E. Hyman, *The Emancipation of the Jews of Alsace* (New Haven, 1991), 20–7.

[97] Szajkowski, 'Pera'ot', 98–9.

provinces of France continued to dress, behave, and generally adhere to what the overwhelming majority of non-Jews were convinced were unpardonably ignorant and superstitious religious and social practices. Both sides of the great political divide within France regarded the Jews as having been incomprehensibly slow and reluctant to make the most of the opportunities so very generously offered them. There was therefore much that rankled in the various sectors of Alsatian society besides the nastiest issue of all, usury. The power Jewish moneylenders were supposed to have gained over the peasantry by obtaining mortgages on peasant land as security for the loans they had granted was very greatly exaggerated.[98] But the charge was an old one, ever lively, always effective, and one that lent itself to be combined with other charges to very great effect. In modern ears, when adduced as evidence of the cause of the impoverishment of the peasantry, the consequent ruin of traditional country life, and the assumption of hidden and, because ultimately political, illegitimate and unacceptable power by the Jews as an entire class, it rang with especially great power.

How deeply all those who were determined to keep their heads down in such circumstances through force of habit, or by choice, or, commonest of all, because it was the burdens of daily life that most preoccupied them, were touched in their innermost beings by the change for the worse in the climate surrounding them remains an open question. Certainly, an abiding confidence in the state did much to encourage German Jews to continue to 'assimilate themselves to German servility', as Ludwig Börne put it in characteristically cruel language, and to follow the advice of the editors of Sulamith to remain loyal to the state whether or not their loyalty and respect for authority was recognized and rewarded as it surely deserved to be. 'For the sake of the tranquillity and welfare of your native land of birth (despite the many unchristian Christians who refuse to have you name it *your* Fatherland), wherever you may be, whatever your position, seek in every way to carry out the Prophet Jeremiah's . . . teaching during the Exile in Babylon which was namely to be mindful of the words of Solomon the Wise: Fear God and the king!'[99] And as in Germany, so *mutatis mutandis* elsewhere. If all else failed, time and good sense could be relied upon to peel prejudice away and smooth the path to full and final emancipation. 'It is my belief, that just as the force of habit is immense in all things,' wrote Israel Schwarz, a 20-year-old student at Heidelberg, in a petition to the Frankfurt Assembly in 1848, 'so it is in the case of the emancipation of the Jews. It is because people are accustomed to see the Jew as unfree, unemancipated, and, on the contrary, invariably oppressed and subservient that its implementation is so

---

[98] On the ascertainable facts, see above, p. 52 n. 32.
[99] *Sulamith*, 8, 1 (1820), 38 n.

difficult.'[100] Of course, for those who were still under the sway of the Tradition in its established form none of this was of much moral or social significance in any case. In no way could *their* moral armour be touched by the conduct of the gentiles no matter how offensive the tone or damaging the practice. It was upon detachment from the Tradition that concern for personal dignity in the specific context of relations with the non-Jews bore a potential for personal distress. As the years passed, however, the dominant (but never universal) social feature of western and central European Jewry came to be its dissociation from most of what had determined the mental and behavioural lives of earlier generations, and the incidence of such distress did incessantly rise. To have joined the 'respectable' socio-economic classes, as more than half of all Jews in Prussia alone had done by the middle of the century, was to have been brought into contact with non-Jews on a regular and nominally equal footing to a degree and in ways that had hitherto been unknown. It was also to have had the cohesive power of the community over one reduced, if not dissolved.

The result was that the individual Jew needed increasingly to make his way alone.[101] But again, so long as he was careful not to set his sights too high, so long as his professional purposes were modest and limited to well-established channels, so long as he kept his head down in society and avoided downright notoriety of a literary, intellectual, political, or any other kind—matters were generally tolerable. So at any rate it could reasonably be argued; and comfort and support for such a view could be derived from the fact that in central and western Europe especially, but even in eastern Europe to some extent, with the rise in acculturation and the fading of the old, immediately visible and aural distinctiveness of the individual Jew, the incidence of petty harassment was tending to decline. In sum, very great caution and propriety, zeal in attending to the wider public interest, and a strong measure of good luck could carry one quite far, it was thought, in the requisite direction. Exceptional diligence and exemplary citizenship might take one very far indeed. Hirsch Oppenheimer (1805–83) of Gronau in the kingdom of Hanover had had no more than a traditional elementary Jewish education. He had begun to make his way as a pedlar. Later he managed to set himself up as a trader with a shop of his own. He then went on to achieve regular citizenship in Gronau (against payment of the necessary fee) and to move into the iron business first in a small way, then into large-scale trading in scrap metal in Hamburg. Finally, he took up insurance and banking, his standing with

---

[100] *Sendschreiben an das teutsche Parlament in Frankfurt . . . von Israel Schwarz stud. theol. Heidelberg.* Text in R. Moldenhauer, 'Jewish Petitions to the German National Assembly in Frankfurt 1848/49', *LBIYB* 16 (London, 1971), Appendix, 199.

[101] On this complex matter see especially Jacob Toury, *Kavim le-ḥeker knisat ha-yehudim la-ḥayyim ha-ezraḥiim be-germaniya* (Tel-Aviv, 1972), *passim*.

the authorities improving all the while. In the revolutionary year of 1848 he emerged as a public figure in his own right by taking it upon himself to appear before the insurrectionary crowd in the market-place of Gronau, promising to represent them and to see their just complaints dealt with, and managing, to the great relief of a thoroughly frightened municipal council, to induce them to disperse. The wording of the formal declaration of appreciation issued to Hirsch Oppenheimer by the city fathers of Gronau upon his definitive departure for Hanover in 1865 says all that a man of his kind and very probably most German Jews of his generation with him would want to hear: 'We make out this testimonial with the addition that it is with reluctance that we see Mr Banker Hirsch Oppenheimer and his family, associated with the most respected among us, leave our midst.'[102] So surely there was room for the hard-working bourgeois after all.

The more difficult and unsettling cases were those of men (and here and there some women) whose inclinations went beyond the solidly commercial and professional. The especially ambitious, the intellectually talented, the very sensitive, those who had taken what appeared to be the boundless prospects that had opened for all in these times, for Jews surely among all others, to mind and to heart—these had to swim against stronger tides. Hardest of all were the obstacles before those who had been touched by the language, literature, history, presumed destiny, and general national fervour of the land in which they lived and with which they had come to associate and ultimately to identify themselves in just the manner demanded of them. What their social equals, but intellectual and cultural inferiors, within Jewry itself were inclined to put out of their minds could not fail to appal and torment them and to lead either to heroic efforts to square an evident circle or to retreat and evasion.

The founder-members of the *Verein für Kultur und Wissenschaft des Judenthums* assembled in Berlin at the end of the riot year of 1819 to consider what their leader Eduard Gans called the 'terrible scenes in many cities of the German Fatherland that had led some to suppose that an unforeseen return to the Middle Ages had occurred'. They asked themselves what they could bring to bear on the problem and decided upon scholarship: the scholarly study of Judaism and Jewry conducted, however, in such a spirit and by such methods as would restore the intellectual freedom and independence of which, so they held, the rabbis had deprived the Jews by their insistence on separation and isolation from the world in general and from the wider world of intellect in particular. It would be their purpose too, they would add later, to demonstrate that there were ways of investigating the history and literary and cultural

---

[102] Monika Richarz (ed.), *Jüdisches Leben in Deutschland. Selbstzeugnisse zur Sozialgeschichte, 1780–1871* (Stuttgart, 1976), 148.

heritage of the Jewish people other than by intellectual and scholarly sub-ordination to the dictates of Christian theology and the purposes of the Church.[103] But over and beyond the tasks the Society set itself was its members' belief that it was incumbent upon Jews of all classes to find a way—honourable and dignified, but effective and convincing—to move *towards* gentile society. This was its motor force and this is what provided an internal logic for its activities. Gans and his colleagues had chosen to do what they could—plainly, to their minds, it was all they could do—in the field which they believed they were best equipped to operate. But the implication was clear: something of this sort was required of other, per-haps most, sectors of the Jewish public. It was not enough for the Jews to ask for civil rights even if these were no more than their due. They had themselves to participate in the preparation of the ground. They needed to move of their own volition, under their own steam, towards such internal changes as would lead in turn to a reformulation of the terms in which they, Jews *and* Judaism, were perceived. Only thus would the feasi-bility and validity of the very notion of their integration into society be demonstrated and irreversible progress towards its realization made. Theirs was therefore a social, not merely academic, purpose, much as David Friedländer, one of Mendelssohn's leading followers, had defined it for his associates over a generation earlier: 'I must endeavour to join my fellow citizens, to approach them in custom and habit, to enter with them into social and personal connections; for the bonds of sociability and love bind more closely and strongly than the law itself. Only through these bonds can I achieve the aim of living with my fellow citizens in harmony, peace and friendship.'[104] If that were achieved, the tacit assumption was that the mob and its violence could be dismissed as a negligible and wasting force and authority itself encouraged still further to oppose it.

In this view, the real question concerned the educated, the *gebildete*. It was upon them, necessarily, that the hopes of Friedländer and Gans and their like necessarily rested. Yet it was increasingly plain that it was from among the educated, the professionally trained, the philosophically-minded, the academics, and in due course the students—not from the mob at all, that is to say not from the men and women in the street—that the loudest, most articulate, and most insistent voices hostile to Jewry in general, and to the modernist, ever more equally *gebildete* Jews in particu-lar, were to be heard. While on the other hand, and not unnaturally, however ironically, it would as often as not be the most talented of their own number who, besides going furthest of all in cutting themselves adrift from Jewry and speaking from its outer margin or beyond, would give sharpest expression to the uncertainties of their condition and the insuperable difficulty of accommodating Jewry and Judaism as they knew it to what most modernist Jews hoped to find on the other shore. Gans himself, as we have already seen, would shortly abandon *Wissenschaft des Judenthums* as a worthy but, so far as he was concerned, hopeless enterprise and opt for conversion and absorption into the Prussian academic system. And within this class of the disaffected and the sharp-eyed there were others, equally desperate for acceptance and accommodation, and equally clearly above the ruck.

Ludwig Börne (1786–1837), one of the most prolific and best-known critics and essayists in early nineteenth-century Germany, was born Loeb Baruch in the Frankfurt *Judengasse*, son of a communal worthy who operated as a money changer and dealer in coins on something like the original Rothschild model, but of substantially less wealth and standing. Börne broke the mould by acquiring a university education, and while the Napoleonic system lasted became one of the beneficiaries of the new age and the new regime by serving in Frankfurt as a local official. At the Restoration he lost his office, but refused his father's demand that he follow an established profession and turned to journalism. When he discovered that he was unable to escape either the minor, but still painful, humiliations that were the lot of Jews of his class in post-Napoleonic Germany or the more serious obstacles to progress in his chosen career he sought relief in conversion as Gans and Heine had done. Börne was to make his mark eventually as an exceedingly well-known man of letters, but also as a German patriot of a loosely socialist kind and as a figure of influence and standing among the revolutionary-minded German students of the 1830s. But he was to carry the scars inflicted upon him by his origins to the end of his life and his thoughts on Jewry itself—much influenced, if not determined, by what he knew of it at close quarters in the Frankfurt *Judengasse*—were pitiless. The Jewish people, in Börne's view, was no more and no better than a survival from an earlier age, society, and civilization. It was a people that had long since accomplished its mission, yet refused to die, cursed by the commerce in which it engaged and afflicted by the money that was at the centre of its being and which both alienated it from other peoples and consoled it for the consequences of that alienation. Richard Wagner was to pay Börne what he, Wagner, evidently considered signal tribute as a true writer and a true 'human being' and for having 'ceased to be a Jew'.[105] But it is fair to say that Börne's dislike of things Jewish and his corresponding admiration for things German were tempered by an eye that was as sharp for the failings of the Germans and the absurdity of their claim to virtues that were

---

exclusively theirs as for the flaws and inadequacies of Judaism. Tempered by wit as well: 'Were I not a Jew myself,' he wrote on one occasion, 'I would say something in praise of the Jews. As it is, German vanity obliges me to affect modesty.'[106] Like others of his class he can be seen to be perpetually seeking to square the identity determined for him by his birth with the identity he had chosen to adopt: in practice to escape the double alienation from Jewry as a renegade and from *Deutschtum* as a Jew after all. He argued on one occasion that it was because he was a Jew that he was able to be a better German than most: having been a slave he understood freedom better than did other Germans. His striving for his country was the more ardent, he said, for his having been born without one. And anyway, the Germans had a good deal more in common with the Jews than they might think. They too needed badly to be liberated: 'Is not Germany the ghetto of Europe? . . . Are not all citizens of Frankfurt, my former masters, like the Jews of former times? Are not the Austrians and the Prussians *their* Christians? And the insult which they, poor and rich, young and old, by day and by night, shouted at every Jew: "Mach Mores, Jew!" [get manners!], are they not obliged hear this themselves now?'[107]

This runs close to Heine's argument for the integration of the matter of the Jews into the matter of the Germans, and beyond that into that of all mankind: all are entitled to attention, none has a special claim to it. And Börne and Heine were at one too in their contempt for any Jew who failed his own people by undignified conduct. Commenting on a loan the Rothschilds had granted the Holy See in 1832, Börne observed that now that Rothschild has kissed the Pope's hand 'the order God first intended when he created the world has been restored. . . . If Rothschild had only kept [the interest on] his Roman loan at 60 instead of 65 per cent and so been able to spend more than ten thousand ducats on the Cardinal-Chamberlain, he would have been allowed to fall on the Holy Father's neck.'[108]

What Börne lacked was pity and a sense of the tragic. Heine had both in abundance. Celebrating the endowment of a Jewish hospital in Hamburg, Heine saw the ironic side of the worthy enterprise, but his comment was gentler, that of a man who had been moved by what he regarded as the pathos of the occasion:

---

[106] 'Wenn ich nicht selbst ein Jude wäre, so wollte ich manches zum Lobe der Juden sagen; aber die deutsche Eitelkeit zwingt mich, Bescheidenheit zu affektieren.' Cited in Orlando Figes, 'Ludwig Börne and the Formation of a Radical Critique of Judaism', *LBIYB* 29 (London, 1984), 367.

[107] From *Menzel der Franzosenfresser*, an attack on the ultra-nationalist Wolfgang Menzel who took the position that there was an unhealthy Franco-Jewish nexus and that a German writer who went so far as to actually and openly to admire French culture was *ipso facto* a 'Jew'. Inge and Peter Rippmann (eds.), *Ludwig Börne, Sämtliche Schriften* (Dreieich, 1977), iii. 889.

[108] 'Briefe aus Paris 1830–33', 72nd letter (28 Jan. 1832), ibid. 482.

Ein Hospital für arme, kranke Juden,
Für Menschenkinder, welche dreifach elend,
Behaftet mit den bösen drei Gebresten,
Mit Armut, Körperschmerz und Judentume!

Das schlimmste von den dreien ist das letzte,
Das Tausendjährige Familienübel,
Die aus dem Nilthal mitgeschleppte Plage,
Der altägyptisch ungesunde Glauben.

Unheilbar tiefes Leid! Dagegen helfen
Nicht Dampfbad, Douche, nicht die Apparate
Der Chirurgie, noch all die Arzneien,
Die dieses Haus den siechen Gästen bietet.[109]

But then Heine, unlike Börne who had ceased to have any use at all for the Jews ('The Jewish nation,' Börne wrote, 'is like an Egyptian mummy that has the glow of life without life itself and as a corpse resists decomposition.'[110]), never lost a certain fellow-feeling for them. His respect for his forebears and for those of his contemporaries who were akin to them—still untouched and seemingly unspoiled—was ungrudging. After visiting Poland in 1822 he pronounced the Polish Jews altogether superior to their German brethren. 'We no longer have the strength to wear a beard, to fast, to hate, and to put up with hatred; that is what is at the bottom of our Reformation.'[111] He wrote to his brother Maximilian on one occasion:

Our fathers were tough. They humbled themselves before God and were therefore so obstinate and defiant towards men, towards the powers of this world. As for me, I was brazen towards Heaven and humble and cringing towards men—and that is why I now lie underfoot like a crushed worm. Glory and honour to God in the highest![112]

[109] 'Das neue Israelitische Hospital zu Hamburg' (1842), *Sämtliche Werke*, ed. Ernst Elster, i (Leipzig and Vienna, 1893), p. 309. The gist of the poem is that of the three maladies afflicting the Jews, poverty, bodily pain, and Judaism, the third is the most ancient and the hardest to bear, besides being one which no such hospital is capable of curing. It was Heine's uncle, Solomon Heine (1766–1844), a banker and a philanthropist who had served the city of Hamburg well, notably after the 1842 fire, but who was denied citizenship and admission to the Chamber of Commerce, who established the hospital. He did so with the proviso that it be open to gentiles only when Hamburg Jews had been granted civil rights. The condition was not met until 1864, twenty years after the philanthropist's death (Prawer, *Heine's Jewish Comedy*, 433).

[110] *Sämtliche Schriften*, i (Düsseldorf-Darmstadt, 1964–8), 163. Cited by Figes, 'Ludwig Börne', 368.

[111] Letter to Immanuel Wohlwihl, 1 Apr. 1823, in Friedrich Hirth (ed.), *Heinrich Heine: Briefe*, i (Mainz, 1950), no. 41, 62.

[112] 'Unsere Väter waren wackere Leute: sie demüthigten sich vor Gott und waren deshalb so störrig und trotzig den Menschen, den irdischen Mächten, Gegenüber; ich dagegen, ich bot dem Himmel frech die Stirne und war demüthig und kriechend vor den Menschen—und deswegen liege ich jetzt am Boden wie ein zertretener Wurm. Ruhm und Ehre dem Gott in der Höhe!' 3 May 1849, ibid., iii, no. 1011, 180. English trans. in Poliakov, *History of Anti-Semitism*, iii. 552 n. 70.

Heine was correct, of course, in thinking that in western and central Europe the old, deeply inculcated Jewish rejection of the alien world—or, in milder instances, simple indifference to it—was weakening. In part this was in consequence of the western Jews' own newly afforded access to that world. More fundamentally, it was because its aspect had softened, its norms and mores had become more familiar and—but this was (and remains) in dispute on all sides—better understood. Above all, however, it was because the norms and mores of what had once been a firmly alien world had in one degree or another, consciously or otherwise, been internalized. If in the eyes of Börne and Heine and thousands upon thousands like them much had been gained, the old armour had been lost, leaving the acculturated Jews painfully vulnerable to attack from without on the validity or otherwise of the positions they had adopted. Their dignity and pride, if not indeed the very fibres of their being, were exposed. The question each man and woman among them had to face was not only whether he or she had the ability and the inner resources to establish him or herself peacefully and permanently in what had hitherto been an entirely alien human environment. It was whether, and if so on what terms, he or she would be allowed by others to do so. Once again, it was a person who had gone as far beyond the normal bounds of Jewry as it was possible for anyone anywhere at all to go and whose ambitions in the world outside it were incomparably high, literally so, who would articulate the dilemma most clearly, while working hardest at devising a personal solution to it.

I am not in a condition to have had hereditary opinions carved out for me, and all my opinions, therefore, have been the result of reading and thought. I never was a follower of either of the two great aristocratic parties in this country. My sympathies and feelings have always been with the people, from whom I spring; and when obliged as a Member of this House to join a party, I joined that party with which I believed the people sympathise.[113]

Thus Benjamin Disraeli in 1846 at precisely the point in the evolving course of British parliamentary politics at which an opportunity for this otherwise improbable and hugely foreign figure to find a central place for himself presented itself. As a credo it was astute. His politics, Paul Smith has pointed out, were unavoidably those of 'denization, of settlement,' founded on the need to find a home for himself, 'the politics of a stranger, a sojourner, whose attitudes and responses could not be the predictable outgrowth of a settled position and the unstudied inheritance of a native tradition.'[114] His solution to the problem, totally unlike that of Börne, had been to embrace his predicament, not to run away from it. It was not

---

[113] 8 May 1846. Hansard, 3rd series, lxxxvi, col. 279.
[114] Paul Smith, 'Disraeli's Politics', *Transactions of the Royal Historical Society*, 5th series, 37 (1987), 73–4.

to minimize his origins—an exercise in which he was wise enough to see that he would never succeed. Least of all was it to denigrate the Jewish people, to reduce it in historical terms, or to deny it a future. On the contrary, Disraeli set himself to *celebrate* the Jews. He made all that he could of the hermetic quality of their society and the mystery of their survival. He demanded general admiration and respect. And if he did so in the interests of presenting himself specifically as a man of ancient and aristocratic lineage by virtue of his having been born one of their number, the performance was not the less brilliant, nor the impact on the terms in which other Jews were perceived in England the more harmful. Most of what Disraeli claimed for himself, and much of what he claimed for the Jews as a people, was no better than fantasy.[115] To the end of his life, people who were close and loyal to him were unsure how much of it he believed himself. What was important was that, however improbably, he had hit on a way out of the modernist Jew's new moral and intellectual dilemma. Equality of esteem for himself as an individual would be attained by inverting the assumptions that underlay the Jews' emancipation as the men of the Enlightenment had conceived it and which great numbers of modernizing Jews had accepted as their own. It was the superior qualities of Jewry that entitled its individual members to fair and equal treatment, not its failings, still less the will of some of their number to escape from it or, at a pinch, improve it.

    Had the Tory party not been in dire straits in the mid-1840s, had Disraeli himself not been a man whose genius rendered him extraordinarily apt for the theatre of politics, and had Victorian England at its higher social reaches not been, as we have seen, in several, contradictory minds about the Jews, he could hardly have succeeded in establishing himself as a major public figure, let alone as Gladstone's one real rival not only at Westminster but in the country at large. And certainly none of this juggling with images and aspirations would have worked on the continent at all. No role such as Disraeli had devised for himself could have been conceived and put on any other contemporary political stage with the remotest expectation of success. Ferdinand Lassalle in Germany and Adolphe Crémieux in France had it in common with Disraeli that they were highly political men of action, that their respective political positions were wholly public ones, of their own making, and owed nothing at all to personal wealth or financial power or private connections. All three were therefore of a class that was as far away from that of the court Jews of the previous century as it was from that of the notables of the Jewish *haute finance*, the Rothschilds and their analogues, in their own. All

[115] On Disraeli's Jewish fantasies see Isaiah Berlin, 'Benjamin Disraeli, Karl Marx, and the Search for Identity', in Jewish Historical Society of England, *Transactions*, 22, 1968–9 (London, 1970), 1–20.

three were obvious beneficiaries too of the shift in all the lands that lay to the west of Congress Poland away from dynastic and aristocratic-oligarchic rule and towards constitutional-parliamentary regimes. But that said, the differences in the speed and quality of the shift in each case were to be reflected in the role each man was finally able to play in the political world into which he was determined to enter.

Ferdinand Lassalle (1825–64) had much in common with Disraeli. He was flamboyant, theatrical, and exceedingly eloquent. His rise to fame was justly rated meteoric. It was his ambition to shine in the world of letters as well as in that of politics (although in the realm of academic philosophy and jurisprudence, rather than, as in Disraeli's case, political fiction). His desire to cut a figure in society was as intense, his social romanticism would be translated politically into something like the same contempt for the bourgeoisie and belief in the possibility of an alliance with the landowning aristocracy from which the working class would stand to benefit. And there was in him a strong nationalist streak too—Lassalle's Germanism being loosely comparable to Disraeli's glorification of England and its empire. Yet too much should not be made of these similarities. They counted for less than the evident contrast between Disraeli's deep conservatism and Lassalle's revolutionary purposes. Where Disraeli became the willing favourite of Queen Victoria Lassalle's ideological proclivities led him to association with, and to (largely unreciprocated) admiration for, Marx and in 1848 and later to repeated trials and imprisonment as a rebel. What these similarities and analogies do suggest are brilliant parvenus who were determined to drive a path for themselves through the socio-political thicket in which they happened to find themselves entrapped. Disraeli was more fortunate in not having to cope, as had Lassalle, with a state of affairs in which a man of his class and origins knew himself to be excluded a priori from participation in actual government: these being the iron rules of the game as it was played in the Germanies of his day. There being no entry for him into the existing structure of politics, at all events not one with any prospect of leadership within, let alone over, it, he set about creating a power base of a novel sort to which his genuine socialist tendencies would contribute the spirit and the substance would be fashioned by its being all his own. Lassalle's creation, the Allgemeiner Deutscher Arbeiterverein—the General German Workers' Association—would outlast him as the seed from which the mighty German Social Democratic Party, pride of the Socialist International and major repository of the hopes of virtually the entire European 'hard' Left (at least until 1914), would grow. But it is as an indication of his grasp of the nature of political life as well as of his own native talent for it that his determination to construct a movement of which he himself would be fully and exclusively in control is most remarkable. In his classic analysis of the structure of political parties, Robert Michels offers him as his prime example of a leader whose distinguishing quality was that he knew what was needed.

The modern party is a fighting organization in the political sense of the term, and must as such conform to the laws of tactics. Now the first article of these laws is facility of mobilization. Ferdinand Lassalle, the founder of a revolutionary labour party, recognized this long ago, contending that the dictatorship which existed in fact in the society over which he presided was as thoroughly justified in theory as it was indispensable in practice. The rank and file, he said, must follow their chief blindly, and the whole organization must be like a hammer in the hands of its president.[116]

It was indeed precisely as a man of marked political ability as well as ambition that he appealed to Bismarck, as fine a judge of the species as any. Bismarck found him a worthy rival and just possibly a potential partner. 'Lassalle was greedy for honours [*ehrgeizig*] in the grand manner,' he told the Reichstag many years after Lassalle's death; 'and whether the German Empire should end up with a Hohenzollern dynasty or a Lassalle dynasty was perhaps an open question so far as he was concerned, but he was a convinced monarchist through and through.'[117]

Where Lassalle differed entirely from Disraeli—and, as we shall see, from Crémieux as well—was in his handling of the matter of his origins and what could and should be done on behalf of the people from which he sprang. Born in Breslau, the son of a local Jewish merchant of some means, brought up in a mildly traditionalist manner, he was given in his childhood and youth to dreams of revenge on the tormentors of his people, reform of their religion, and a search for a way finally to square Judaism with Germanism. By early manhood, however, he had put such notions behind him. He changed his surname from Loslau to the Frenchified Lassalle; and he turned an intensely critical eye on Judaism on the philosophic and aesthetic grounds that he is commonly judged to have derived from Hegel. Judaism, he decided, was both theologically and philosophically inferior to Christianity. And its historic mission over and done with, he, for his part, need have no further interest in it. He refused to apostatize, explaining to a girl with whom he had become infatuated on one of the rare occasions on which he referred to the matter, that he thought it would be an undignified and dishonourable thing to do, a concession to prejudice and bigotry quite incompatible with his position as a political leader, and the more hypocritical for his having no more sympathy for Christianity than he had for Judaism.[118] And unlike

---

[116] *Political Parties* (New York, 1962), 78.

[117] *Stenographische Berichte über die Verhandlungen des Deutschen Reichstages*, 4. Legislaturperiode, I. Session 1878, vol. i, 17 Sept. 1878, 68.

[118] Letter to Sofya Sontzev, 1860. Cited by Silberner, *Ha-sozialism ha-maʿaravi*, appendix no. 21, 331–3.

Marx (who habitually referred to Lassalle as 'Itzig') or his future biographer, the thoroughly assimilated Danish-Jewish critic Georg Brandes, (who traced Lassalle's 'chutzpah' to his 'racial' origins[119]), he refrained from saying or writing anything negative about the Jews in public. But his thoughts and private observations remained harsh. Observing Jews (and other 'Semites') in Constantinople, he judged 'the Jew' as a man 'intoxicated and consumed by the sense of his nullity, his worm-like being, and his abnegation before his transcendental master [*berauschte und verzehrte im Gefühl seines Nichts, seiner Wurmheit, seiner Verworfenheit, vor seinem transzendentalen Gebieter*]'.[120] For the rest, the Jews remained external and irrelevant to his thinking on public affairs. It is true that Lassalle was not noted for his intellectual and ideological contributions to socialism. Marx, always rather disdainful of him personally and strongly disapproving of the political direction he had taken, dismissed him as a theoretician who was as pretentious as his work was derivative. The best he could do was to give Lassalle (posthumous) credit for awakening the German proletariat to the socialist cause. There was never any question, however, of Lassalle employing his undoubted political talents to rouse the Jewish proletariat, or the Jews generally, to their needs and to the advantages that might accrue to them if they were organized in the modern manner of which he was himself a master. There is no trace of an attempt to consider the matter or Question of the Jews in the socialist terms that determined his general outlook on society. But then he refused to pay them close attention of any kind and to any serious purpose. And he would be followed in this by virtually all the major figures on the European left, 'soft' no less than 'hard', whose origins were Jewish, most notably by those who aspired to a substantial political role for themselves within the states of which they were, or in which they sought to be, citizens.

Adolphe (Isaac Moïse) Crémieux (1796–1880), a man of the 'soft' left, to be sure, remains a remarkable exception to this rule. Born in Nîmes into the class of Jews whose immensely long settlement in France and relatively high degree of acculturation before the Revolution had assured them candidature for full emancipation from the first, Crémieux was in every respect their worthy representative as the complete Jewish Frenchman. Step by step this totally acculturated, non-observant but non-apostatizing, Jew rose to hitherto unprecedented heights: pupil at the prestigious lycée Louis-le-Grand, student at the University of Aix, practising lawyer in Nîmes and (from 1830 onwards) before the Court of Appeal in Paris, parliamentary deputy from 1842 to 1851, minister of

---

[119] Georg Brandes, *Ferdinand Lassalle: eine kritische Darstellung seines Lebens und seiner Werke* (Leipzig and Berlin, 1900), 10–11.

[120] Letter to Countess Sophie von Hatzfeldt, 21 Oct. 1856, from Constantinople, in Gustav Meyer (ed.), *Ferdinand Lassalle: Nachgelassene Briefe und Schriften*, vi (Stuttgart-Berlin, 1925), 219.

justice in the provisional government of 1848, briefly a supporter, then an opponent of, Louis Napoleon (which cost him a spell of imprisonment and forced retirement from active politics), deputy again in 1869, and minister of justice once more in the government of National Defence of 1870. Throughout this long and distinguished career as attorney and politician Crémieux was recognizably a man of the liberal left, a noted defender in the courts of victims of persecution and prosecution by the government, Proudhon, whom he defended in 1850 and again in 1858, among them.[121] Crémieux was noted equally for doing what he could to further general libertarian causes on those brief occasions when he was in power: extension of freedom of the press, abolition of the death sentence for political offences, security of tenure for judges. In sum, his was by any standard a public career of distinction and this alone would have assured him his status as the most eminent Jew in nineteenth-century France, the pride of the community, an example to all of what modern France allowed its Jewish citizens to make of their native abilities and energy. In straightforward political terms, Crémieux never went and, as seems likely, never aspired to go as far as Disraeli. He did not seek to carve out a role for himself as leader of a social class and founder of a distinct party after the manner of Lassalle. Nor would it have been feasible for a man of his views and convictions to do so in either Restoration or Second Empire France. In any case, he was not as theatrical and imaginative as Disraeli or as self-absorbed and as liable to ill-considered, but fateful decisions as Lassalle. In most ways, while he stood somewhere to the left of the middle of the road, he was, perhaps, before all else, the wise, experienced, and principled attorney in whom formal training and professional habit had inculcated an aversion to lapses into fantasy and posture. Everything in his role as lawyer-statesman and in his approach to matters Jewish too spoke of sobriety and carefully constructed arguments, but also, at times, of courage and daring when confronting the powers-that-be. Only in his unremitting demand for equity and justice does there seem to have been the authentic glint of passion. And if this was evident in the general causes he took up, it was doubly so in the case of Jewish causes. His services to his community were in fact never ending, leading him, much as did his activities in the general public arena, to a succession of offices: membership, then chairmanship, of the constitutionally established communal government of French Jewry, the Consistoire Central in Paris, and later to the leadership of the Alliance Israélite Universelle.[122]

---

[121] On the second occasion, he was initially reluctant to take up Proudhon's case, agreeing to do so only after receiving a long, impassioned letter begging him to oblige. 'Whom shall I turn to if not to you, my old defender, my saviour?' Proudhon wrote to him on 12 May 1858, in 'Lettre inédite de Proudhon à Adolphe Crémieux', *Revue Bleue*, 8 (Feb. 1896), 171–3.

[122] See below, Chs. 4, 7, and 8 *passim*.

And it is precisely this, his double role as French lawyer-statesman and public champion of the Jews of France and, in case of need, of Jews else-where, that marks him as a figure of the very first importance—but also of very great potential—in the slowly evolving political history of the Jewish people at this stage. By the same token, far more than Disraeli's career or Lassalle's—or, at a lesser level of prominence and ambition, that of Gabriel Riesser[123]—it was Crémieux's that encapsulated most acutely the ambivalences and contrarieties with which Jewish life in western and central Europe in all its *public* aspects was now enmeshed. For if in obvious respects Crémieux's public life was one of rare distinction and achievement, in others, as will be argued, it suggests a role aborted, an opportunity passed over. Half a century would elapse before a compar-able, potential man of the hour would appear in a somewhat similar com-bination of circumstances. Once again, the opportunity would be passed over.

Initially, Crémieux's defence of the position of the Jews as full and equal citizens of France was compatible with what he conceived to be—and what in principle government and courts were prepared to accept—as the ideological and legal bases of the regime. His long campaign, beginning in 1827, to achieve the final abolition of the special oath *more judaïco* that Jews were still commonly required to swear on giving evi-dence in court will illustrate this. The issue was not peculiar to France, as we have seen. But that it should have survived the Revolution was, on the face of things, extraordinary.[124] When as a very young lawyer, at the cere-mony of his formal admission to the bar, Crémieux first encountered the issue in one of its many variations, he insisted on taking the set (secular) oath required of all other candidates. He had his way. Later, in the course of preparing his pleas in court, initially at Nîmes, but elsewhere from time to time wherever and whenever the issue arose, and then on appeal, he

---

[123] See below, p. 251.

[124] The issue was different from the one that had arisen in Great Britain where a new Member of Parliament was required (until 1858) to swear on his 'true faith as a Christian'. It differed too from the parallel question that had arisen in Prussia. While the Prussian con-stitution (Article 12) guaranteed freedom of religion and freedom from discrimination, oaths in courts of law were specifically of a Christian character. Jews were not required to take them, but there was then the question of the value that was to be set on their testi-mony and the separate question whether Jewish court officials were entitled to administer an oath in its standard, *Christian* form. Elsewhere, in the course of an attempt to determine whether any Dutch city still discriminated against Jews, the central government of the Netherlands discovered in 1808 that the Groningen Town Council continued to impose special oaths of Jews and required certificates of good behaviour and payment of special fees by any Jew who wished to settle in their city. This was in line, however, with other petty restrictions: the presence of (city-appointed) tax officials at Jewish communal meet-ings and a prohibition on the presence of Christians at Jewish weddings after eight o'clock in the evening (M. H. Gans (ed.), *Memorbook: History of Dutch Jewry from the Renaissance to 1940*, English trans. A. J. Pomerans (Baarn, 1977), 293).

developed systematic arguments on the subject of a kind none could easily contest even under the last of the Bourbons, still less under the July Monarchy of Louis Philippe, at any rate not directly. The law recognized only citizens, he claimed. It did not recognize their division into religious classes. Mirabeau himself had laid down that 'the relationship of man with the Being on high is independent of any public institution'. The very meaning of equality was the absence of official distinctions between men. Religion was a private matter, it was not for the courts to inquire into it. In any event it was not for the courts to determine what was and what was not a valid religious act for Jews.[125] Crémieux's pleas were successful eventually and the modernists in French Jewry, led by Crémieux (with the somewhat wavering support of the rabbinate), could congratulate themselves on having had someone to fight the good fight for them and reinforce the validity of their membership in the French nation. But it is important that his quarrel with the state was, after all, a minor one, a matter of variant symbols, never a dispute over clear-cut freedoms and rights. At no time were these seriously in question, so far as he was concerned. The Jewish cause in which Crémieux would play a very much greater role and which would finally consolidate his fame as a champion of the Jews, their very own *chevalier sans peur et sans reproche,* would be of a very different order: graver, more complex, at first sight remote from the concerns of French Jewry itself, on further examination such as to induce palpable tremors of nervousness among the more alert and better informed members of French Jewry, as well as among their analogues in the rest of Europe.

VIII

The 'Damascus Affair', as it would be known, arose out of the disappearance in February 1840 of a Father Thomas, superior of the Capuchin house in Damascus, and reports of his death at the hands of local Jews. The precise circumstances were unclear at the time—as to some extent they remain to this day. Non-Jewish witnesses testified that he had last been seen in the Jewish quarter of the city. Such evidence was unreliable by its very nature, but even had it been otherwise it would have implied nothing specific about his death there or anywhere else in Damascus or outside it. The only direct 'evidence' of Jewish involvement and criminality were confessions extracted from members of the Jewish community who had been pounced on by the local police and severely tortured, several unfortunates dying in the process. The small, but ancient Jewish

---

[125] Phyllis Cohen Albert, *The Jewish Oath in Nineteenth-Century France* (Tel-Aviv, 1982), 23–5.

community of Damascus had long been the object of intolerant, often mindless brutality at the hands of the Muslim majority and latterly at the hands of the substantial, but exceedingly hostile Christian population as well. That members of communities hostile to the Jews should fling charges at them was in itself, therefore, neither new nor surprising. Had the inquiry into Father Thomas's disappearance launched by the Egyptian authorities (Syria was briefly under the rule of the Pasha of Egypt at the time) been in any way a serious one it would have been discovered that Father Thomas himself was not of an especially savoury character or reputation and several other lines of inquiry would almost certainly have suggested themselves. What gave the affair its special character, however, were two aspects of it that went far beyond ordinary intercommunal bullying and tensions and sloppy and dishonest police work.

The first was that the charge laid against the Jews, raised in the first instance by Christian sources, but accepted without much trouble by the authorities as valid, was not one of ordinary felony: murder for revenge, or murder in the course of robbery, for example. It was of ritual murder. It was alleged, that is to say, that Father Thomas had been killed by agents of the Jewish community to procure blood for the celebration of the feast of Passover. This horrible accusation, unfamiliar in the Islamic universe until its recent importation from Europe, was in fact a twelfth-century invention of the Christian world; and of all the many false charges laid at the doorstep of Jewry over many centuries, from the systematic poisoning of wells to the desecration of the Host, it was the one that evoked the greatest revulsion among the Jews themselves. Thus in the very distant past, but now too, almost halfway through the nineteenth century, when it did more than anything to bring the events in Damascus to the agitated attention of leading members of Jewish communities elsewhere. The upshot was a rapidly organized effort of unprecedented dimensions and character in which, as we shall see, some of the most prominent Jewish figures in Europe were involved, to secure the release of those Damascus Jews who had been charged with the crime and were still known to be alive; but also, and equally urgently, to do whatever was possible to scotch the blood libel once and for all. The first stages were unpromising. Representative members of the Jewish community in Constantinople had immediately written to Solomon Rothschild in Vienna to seek his intervention—in itself a sign of the new times and of the enormous prestige of the Rothschilds. He, in turn, approached his good friend Prince Metternich. Nothing much came of Metternich's feeble messages to the Vatican and to Mohamed Ali, the Pasha of Egypt and technically, but only technically, the Sultan's vassal. But other influential people were soon involved, other Rothschilds and, most important of all, the leading British Jew of the day, Sir Moses Montefiore. By early spring the general press in western Europe had taken up the story and the Jewish press in

Germany, Britain, and France had followed in its wake. It was not long before in one way or another the story had reached every Jewish household and the fever of concern in most communities was running very high.

The speed and thoroughness with which the news had spread was a novel and instructive feature of mid-nineteenth-century Jewish public life in itself. The rise and rapid growth of a periodical press addressed to a specifically Jewish readership in most parts of western and central Europe, especially in Germany, and published in the language of the country in question was a function (and measure) of the inroads of acculturation, but also of a growing, critical interest in the general problems of Jewry as these had now begun to emerge. The new Jewish press served both to stimulate that interest and to feed it. Eighteen European-language Jewish periodicals were published in five countries in the years 1835–40. Fifty-three periodicals were published in thirteen countries, among them Prussia, Bavaria, Austria, Great Britain, Holland, and France in the years 1841–6—monthlies and fortnightlies for the most part, a few in the form of yearbooks. Some folded almost as rapidly as they were founded. Many lasted for years.[126] The most famous of all, if only by virtue of its longevity, was (and remains) the *Jewish Chronicle* of London, founded as a weekly in 1841, initially unable to keep its head above water for much more than a year, reissued in 1844 as a fortnightly, later still reconverted into its definitive format, as a weekly. The *Jewish Chronicle's* strength lay in its detailed, extensive, and generally authoritative coverage of affairs throughout the Jewish world. And while it enjoyed the (mixed) blessing of strongly independent and opinionated editors, some for very long periods, neither the role it achieved for itself as the chief organ of British Jewry nor its duty to provide extensive local reporting was ever neglected. However, where the Jews of Great Britain and their affairs were on the margin of the main developments in European Jewry throughout the nineteenth century, those of the Germanies were not. German, moreover, was the European language with which the Jews of the continent tended to be most familiar and the principal German Jewish weekly newspaper of the day, the *Allgemeine Zeitung des Judenthums* was long the more influential and the more widely read. Its founder and editor for over fifty years from its foundation in 1837 to his death in 1889 was Ludwig Philippson, a prototypical leading figure in the movement that pressed for thoroughgoing emancipation by the authorities and (moderate) religious reform by the Jews themselves. A graduate of the University of Berlin and rabbi of a congregation in Magdeburg before whom he customarily preached in German, Philippson sought a middle

---

[126] B. Mevorah, ''Ikvoteiha shel 'alilat damesek be-hitpathuta shel ha-'itonut ha-yehudit ba-shanim 1840-1846', *Zion*, 23–4, 1–2 (1958–9), 46–65.

road between wholesale acculturation on the one hand and the (somewhat selective) preservation of the Jewish intellectual and cultural heritage on the other. Unlike the editors of the *Jewish Chronicle* who were generally careful to keep out of strictly religious and rabbinical affairs, Philippson was long and heavily involved in the effort to bring some institutional and ritual order into German-Jewish communal life. Like them, however, the spirit in which he edited his newspaper to the end of his long life was one of continuing concern for the well-being of all Jewry. The *Allgemeine Zeitung des Judenthums* was conceived therefore as a journal addressed to an audience that extended well beyond the confines of Germany proper and whose columns had necessarily to be open to a variety of conflicting views. But while room would be found for those who were critical of Philippson's own school of moderate religious reform, there was less tolerance for voices critical or sceptical of the progress and prospects of Jewish integration into German society itself.

The proximate, rather pale analogue of the *Jewish Chronicle* and the *Allgemeine Zeitung des Judenthums* in Paris was the *Archives Israélites de France*. It was founded in January 1840 by the biblical scholar Samuel Cahen, a man whose ideological temperament and intellectual attainments were somewhat like Philippson's. But it was a more limited enterprise than the *Allgemeine* or the *Chronicle*. It was a monthly, not a weekly. It catered to the requirements of a limited list of subscribers: a few hundred at its launch, about one thousand three years later—or roughly 1.5 per cent of the total Jewish population of France at the time. The ideological position of the *Archives* was one of cautious modernism in matters of religion and absolute belief in the validity of the integration of the Jews into the French nation ('Religion in no way detracts from patriotism').[127] However, when the Damascus Affair broke, shortly after its foundation as it happened, and the journal was propelled willy-nilly into a position of importance in the Jewish world, the line it took was relatively strong. The space set aside for straight reporting on general Jewish matters was increased, often to as much as a quarter of a given issue of which the greater part was devoted to the affair.[128] And the role of the French government and French opinion being crucially important in the evolution of the affair itself, as we shall see, the *Archives* became a primary source of information for other Jewish periodicals in other countries, the *Allgemeine Zeitung des Judenthums* among them.

All told, the distinctive features of this new Jewish press were generous, but none the less carefully selective, respect for the Jewish cultural,

---

[127] Béatrice Philippe, 'Les Archives Israélites de France de leur création en 1840 à février 1848; ou un journal juif sous Louis-Philippe: études de mentalité', Mémoire de maîtrise, University of Paris IV, 1974–5, p. x.

[128] Mevorah, ' 'Ikvoteiha', 52.

religious, and social tradition in its classic form; an evident desire to establish a place for Jewry, most particularly for the Jewish community directly in question, that was acceptable to all, Jews and non-Jews, as reasonable, dignified, and legitimate; and unhesitating adherence to the view that a middle way between the full assimilation of the Jews into the host society on the one hand and a separate existence on something like the old model on the other could in fact be achieved. But the most telling—and in the eyes of the traditionalists most immediately suspect—aspect of these ventures was the bare fact of Jewish journalism being conducted in European languages. This rendered the matters dealt with *public* in ways for which there was no real precedent, while subjecting them, necessarily, to a certain constant, if often subtle and unconscious, reinterpretation. The process whereby the modernist Jewish public was being introduced to a parallel, somewhat foreign mode of discourse and to wholly new frames of reference for old, familiar topics was much accelerated, as was the passage from what had been an intimate mode of debate and reporting to a more formal and alien one.

What both the general press and the Jewish press had made abundantly clear to their readers was that there was a further aspect of the affair in Damascus that was propelling it out of the ordinary. This was the steadily deepening and widening involvement of foreign consular officials serving in the Near East itself as well as, by natural extension, their home-based principals. What might otherwise have been no more than another obscure, cruel, but by no means unusual, illustration of the vulnerability of the weak to persecution by the strong and the ease with which the judicial murder of representatives of the oppressed can be accomplished by whoever happened to hold political power over them was taking shape as a many-sided scandal involving not only local and foreign Jews, Christians, and Muslims, but the governments and officials of France, Great Britain, Austria, Egypt, and the Ottoman Empire as well.

The diplomatic and military crisis occasioned by the rise of Mohamed Ali, the Ottoman Sultan's rebellious vassal in Egypt, was at its height in the years 1839–41. He had invaded and occupied Syria. He was thought to threaten the Sultanate in Constantinople itself and the major European powers, divided in their attitudes, were now engaged in complex manœuvres of their own. The French had established a special relationship with Mohamed Ali. The British, the Austrians, and the Russians feared France would end by controlling the entire area lying south and east of the Mediterranean Sea. Besides these matters of high politics, almost all important European states were busy establishing competitive local footholds in the Near East, a favoured method being the assumption of a loose form of political and judicial responsibility for one or more of the minority populations of the Ottoman Empire over and above their already well-established role as protectors of their own missionaries, pilgrims, and resident regular and secular clergy. The British had recently resolved that the Jews were a people in which it would be useful to take an interest. The French, more assiduous than others in this sphere (as they were in the matter of establishing ties with Mohamed Ali), were paying particular attention to their traditional protégés, the Roman Catholics. They were, besides, more alert than the others to evidence of competition. It was therefore neither out of character for the French consul in Damascus, Count Ratti-Menton, nor beyond the call of his official duty, once he had decided (whether in haste or out of genuine conviction or for private reasons of his own has never been clear) to back the charge of ritual murder against the Jews of Damascus, to explain repeatedly to his principals in Paris that attempts by his British and Austrian colleagues to come to the aid of the Jews were politically motivated. Early in the unfolding of the affair he had reported flatly to his superiors in Paris that the murder of the Capuchin was a case of 'fiendish sacrifices' to be understood not only as an 'outrage to human society' but as a deliberate 'challenge [by the Jews] to the tutelary action of [the French] government'. It was therefore 'advisable,' he wrote, 'to impose a salutary terror upon the Jews'.[129] It was virtually inevitable too that what he had to say on the subject should be taken at face value, acted upon, and, perhaps, even seriously believed. Neither the idea of 'fiendish sacrifices' nor that of the need to impose 'salutary terror upon the Jews' caused anyone of importance in official Paris to rustle his papers despite the fact that the consul, it soon turned out, had taken much more than a passive, observer's role in the affair even at its initial stage. He had joined the local police in the search for the presumed murderers. He had incarcerated and interrogated in his own consulate building one of the men whom he decided was a prime suspect. And satisfied with the results he then took it upon himself to press the local authorities to put him on trial. But the trial court in question would have had to be a local court and Ratti-Menton's chosen victim, Isaac Picciotto, besides being one of the notables of the community, happened to be under Austrian protection because his father had once served as Austrian consul in Aleppo. This brought the Austrian consul in Damascus into play as well and obliged him to go into the matter a good deal more carefully than he would otherwise have intended. He had especially to ensure that his own jurisdiction over Picciotto was respected. From the Austrian point of view there could be no question at all of Picciotto being judged by other than Austrian judicial authorities and happily for Picciotto, when he had examined the dossier, the

---

[129] Ratti-Menton to the duc de Dalmatie, 29 Feb. 1840. Affaires Etrangéres, Correspondance commerciale, Damas, no. 16. Cited in Tudor Parfitt, ' "The Year of the Pride of Israel"—Montefiore and the Damascus Blood Libel of 1840', in Sonia and V. D. Lipman (eds.), *The Century of Moses Montefiore* (Oxford, 1985), 142.

Austrian consul pronounced the charges drawn up by his French colleague to be baseless. He duly reported his findings both to the embassy
in Constantinople in the normal way and to his own opposite number in
France who, as it happened, was James de Rothschild (appointed to the
post by Metternich). There was now no way of disentangling the question of what had actually happened in Damascus from the wider repercussions of the affair. To the murky police aspects of the case and the
conduct of the French consul there had been added the gently bubbling
diplomatic quarrel between the French on one side and the Austrians and
the British on the other. The French consul in Damascus called the attention of his masters in Paris to what he claimed was the tendency of the
cabinet in Vienna to exploit 'the Jewish affair' to its own advantage. The
protection it proposed to grant to the defendant 'would have the immediate effect of rallying the Jews of Asia to Austria', thus providing it with
'an incontestable means of influence'. A 'subsequent result would be to
assure the Austrian Government of the gratitude of European Jews and
consequently to facilitate loans'.[130]

What was now not in doubt at all was the dismay and the anger in the
specifically Jewish world induced not only by the rebroadcasting of the
legend that Jews consumed Christian blood, but by the ease with which
it had been accepted, *especially* in Paris, as not inherently improbable.
There was horror. There was shame. And there was too a small undercurrent of thought among the acculturated young that here was proof, if
proof was needed, that there was something radically wrong about Jewish responses to defamation and persecution of this or any other kind.
When he read the news of what had transpired in Damascus, a preco-
cious, 15-year-old Ferdinand Lassalle wrote down in his diary:

There is a horrible truth in one sentence of the reporter's: 'The Jews of this town
submit to cruelties that none but these pariahs could endure without being provoked to terrible attempts at reprisals.' That means even the Christians are surprised at our mean spirit, that we do not rise and prefer death on the field of battle
to one in a torture chamber. . . . Cowardly race, you deserve no better fate! Even
a worm will turn: you crawl more abjectly. You do not know how to die, or how
to destroy, you know nothing of just revenge, or how to go down to the same
grave as your enemies, tearing their flesh from their bones in the last death struggle! You were born to be slaves![131]

Heine, a close, and particularly pitiless observer of the scene, believed
that 'a great many Frenchmen [are] not averse to the belief that Oriental
Jews drink human blood at their Passover celebrations' and that it was the
enlightened among them, generally speaking, who were prepared to

[130] Ratti-Menton to Thiers, 27 July 1840, Affaires Etrangéres, no. 33.
[131] Entry for 21 May 1840, cited in David Footman, *The Primrose Path* (London,
1961), 17.

believe any evil thing of religion. He thought, however, that 'no such obtuse opinions . . . could gain ground in Germany', and that this was 'a sign of our [i.e. the Germans'] greater learning. The German people is so steeped in historical knowledge that even the most savage resentment dare not use these ancient bloody fables to achieve its dire purposes.'[132] Heine was wrong. The hold of the charge of ritual murder of Christians by Jews over the imagination of the greater part of Christian Europe, the German *Kulturbereich* (or cultural—as opposed to political—realm) included, remained tenacious. Repeated *ex cathedra* affirmations of its total falsity by Popes, monarchs, and genuinely eminent scholars— Grotius for one—had consistently failed to kill it. No textual demonstration of its inherent absurdity, namely that it ran entirely counter to so much that traditional Judaism had always rigorously insisted upon—the shedding of blood as the most heinous of crimes, human sacrifice (Moloch) as the supreme abomination, the detestation of blood in ordinary food as the foundation of the entire system of *kashrut*—had ever dissolved its tenacious hold on the European imagination. No reference to the judicial record, namely, that there had never been a single properly verified instance of ritual murder as opposed to attempts (some successful, as now in Damascus) to suborn witness and extract evidence of one by torture, had ever sufficed. This was notably the case when, as now, the charge, once advanced, could not be withdrawn without prestige being lost in the interests of nothing weightier than even-handed justice.

But it was certainly the shock administered to French Jewry by what now transpired in Paris itself—in the parliament, in the higher reaches of the government, in the press, and in public opinion generally—that was sharpest. What particularly stirred the thinking, the imagination, and in many cases the hearts of French Jews, as it did, to no small extent, of Jews throughout the rest of Europe, was the fact it was in France, leader of the civilized nations of the world—as French Jews certainly wished to believe and as modernist Jews in all parts tended to believe with them— that the affair came to a head.

Adolphe Crémieux seems to have had no doubt on this score when he took a leading role in the effort to come to the aid of the Damascus Jews. It was, to be sure, no less than what many people in the community expected of him.[133] But Crémieux had first to press the Consistoire Central hard to venture to approach both the king and the government. Successful in that endeavour, he had then to swallow the fact that, while the king had consented to be spoken to on a chance ceremonial occasion, he had displayed no more than polite interest in what was said to him; and

[132] Prawer, *Heine's Jewish Comedy*, 306–7.

[133] A.-A. Créhenge, a prominent French Jewish journalist, to Crémieux. Cited by S. Posener, *Adolphe Crémieux* (Paris, 1933) i. 207.

that the newly appointed Prime Minister and Foreign Minister, Adolphe Thiers, had refused altogether to grant an interview to the Jewish delegation that asked to be received. The bland reporting of the case in ostensibly decently minded newspapers, the lawyers' own *Gazette des Tribunaux* among them, was equally infuriating. It was a 'wretched slander,' said Crémieux, 'born of the infamous prejudices of Christianity in the Middle Ages', to present it in terms which implied that it was by no means improbable that a ritual murder had indeed been committed in Damascus.[134] When, in his capacity as representative of the Consistoire Central in Paris, he travelled to London in mid-June of that year to consult with Montefiore and his colleagues as to what finally should be done, he told the English Jews plainly that 'France is against us!'[135] He was not entirely alone, however. Heine said to him: 'You, my dear Crémieux, are among the few people whom I love and who deserve to be loved.'[136] And Heine, for once, had a good word for Baron James de Rothschild too for having tried his hand at persuading the French government to consider the plight of the Damascus Jews in humanitarian terms, rather than in those it believed to be dictated by high policy in the Near East and the long-term need to maintain the credibility of the French consular service. And it was the other Jewish banker of special renown in Paris, Benoît Fould— the other Parisian *Finanzrabbiner* ('finance-rabbi') as Heine called him— who finally compelled Thiers to say *something* on the subject by declaring in the Chamber of Deputies on 2 June 1840, that

The disappearance of the cleric became an occasion for deliberate religious persecution. The consul of France incites to torture: at a time when the French nation offers an example not only of equality before the law, but of religious equality, it is a Frenchman who instigates exceptional [police] measures, who has recourse to torture, who upholds the arbitrary measures [and] the executioners of the Pasha. The other agents of the European powers were so revolted by this conduct that a kind of council of consuls of the other nations was organized in Damascus.[137]

Nothing would move the government, however. Its response to representations and protests by Jewish notables in Paris, as well as to their effort

---

[134] Posener, *Adolphe Crémieux*, 208.
[135] Poliakov, *History of Anti-Semitism*, iii. 349.
[136] 24 May 1842. Cited by Prawer, *Heine's Jewish Comedy*, 498.
[137] *Le Moniteur Universel*, ci, 155, 3 June 1840, p. 1257, col. 3. Heine, unaware, had attacked Fould bitterly, but memorably, for doing nothing: 'We must, in justice, admit that the great rabbi of the *rive droite*, Baron Rothschild, showed a nobler sympathy for the house of Israel than his scripturally learned antagonist, the great rabbi of the *rive gauche*, M. Benoît Fould, who—while his co-religionists were being tortured and strangled in Syria at the instigation of the French consul—made, with the calmness of soul so characteristic of Hillel, some beautiful speeches in the French Chamber of Deputies about the conversion of annuities and the discount rate of the Bank.' (Cited in Prawer, *Heine's Jewish Comedy*, 302.) When Heine discovered that he had been wrong he apologized.

to rally support for the Jewish position in the press, was to instruct its own organ, *Le Messager*, to affirm the thesis that the superstitions of oriental Jews did indeed prescribe ritual murder and to tell the orientals' western co-religionists that they would be wiser to keep their peace on the subject.[138] Thiers's unwilling, but sharp reply to Fould in parliament was that until what he considered to be fully credible evidence had been produced against Ratti-Menton, he would support him—France's representative—as a matter of principle. 'The more they are attacked by foreign agents, the firmer will be my support for them, above all when they are attacked by the interested parties,' he declared to loud applause.[139] When François Isambert, an eminent Parisian lawyer, pressed the matter of torture, denied by the French consul but by no one else, not even, as the Chamber was told, by a senior Roman Catholic churchman serving in Damascus itself, Thiers's retort, once again to loud applause, was that 'You protest on behalf of the Jews, while I protest on behalf of a Frenchman who until now has fulfilled his duties with honour and devotion.'[140]

Successive governments of France would continue to stick to their guns. No countervailing evidence adduced then or later on the substance of the charges against the Jews of Damascus was ever deemed acceptable. The consular service closed ranks and held together in the face of repeated accusations of misconduct levelled against their colleague in Damascus. When, very reluctantly, a French official was finally sent out to Syria to make further inquiries, he reported back that there could be no doubt at all that 'The circumstances of the murder of Father Thomas and his servant, in so far as may be learned from the Egyptian procedure, seem only too real and, taken together, tend to demonstrate that this double murder, which cannot be explained in terms of hatred or vengeance, was an act of fanaticism.' Meanwhile, he added, 'the condemned of Damascus, they and their coreligionists, boast [*se targuent*] of the impunity they enjoy'.[141] In Paris, in sum, questions of political obligation, loyalty, national identity, and the high policy requirement that France's protégé Mohamed Ali be supported, remained consistently to the fore, unchanged. If an effective initiative on behalf of the Damascus Jews was to be taken, it would have to be from London, if at all.

---

[138] Poliakov, *History of Anti-Semitism*, iii. 360.

[139] *Moniteur*, p. 1258, col. 2.

[140] Ibid. 1258, col. 3.

[141] De Méloizes to Foreign Minister, 27 May 1841. Cited by Zosa Szajkowski, 'Goral ha-tikim be-ministerion ha-ḥuẓ ha-ẓarfati ha-nog'im le-'alilat damesek', *Ẓion*, 19, 3–4 (1954), 169 n. 12. On the long-standing refusal of the Foreign Ministry in Paris to declassify the relevant files (at least two of them baldly entitled 'Affaire du Père Thomas assassiné par les Israélites indigènes') and permit examination by reputable historians on the grounds that it would be 'inappropriate', see Szajkowski, 'Goral', and Parfitt, 'Pride of Israel'.

What followed was a rare demonstration of collective will to act, but also of an unprecedented ability by western European Jews to do so: signal proof of the distance they had travelled in the course of the century that had passed since the great men of Viennese Jewry knelt in the dust at the foot of Maria Theresa's carriage for permission to present her with a petition in favour of their brethren in Bohemia. After discussions held by Jewish notables, Crémieux among them, on 21 April and 15 June in London it was resolved that a deputation consisting of Sir Moses Montefiore and Adolphe Crémieux should set out for the Near East to tackle Mohamed Ali directly. Assurances of British government backing were obtained with little difficulty and were immediately demonstrated for all to see by Montefiore being given passage to France on the first leg of his journey on a vessel of the Royal Navy and then re-emphasized by the British consul in Egypt taking the deputation under his wing upon its arrival in Cairo and presenting Montefiore to the Pasha in person. Initially, Mohamed Ali proved to be unco-operative, however, and the negotiations, in which the Austrian consul joined his British colleague and played a small part as well, were protracted. Even after pressure had been extended through Constantinople and the principle of a full and unconditional release had been agreed to, a fairly acrimonious argument on the verbal formula to be adopted ensued. Louis Loewe, the distinguished orientalist whom Montefiore had taken with him, discovered that it could be inferred from the terminology employed in the draft of the Pasha's order of release that the Damascus Jews had been *pardoned*, the implication being that they had committed an offence after all. Loewe, well versed in both Turkish and Arabic, insisted on the text being altered and Montefiore backed him. Crémieux's own language specialist, Salomon Munk, had Arabic but no Turkish (the language employed) and, possibly for that reason was less intransigent. Crémieux too was willing to compromise on the text, perhaps because it was his inclination as a lawyer not to push things too far against the Pasha and indirectly against the French as well. But Montefiore and Loewe refused to yield and ended by having their way.[142]

There had, in fact, been some friction all along between the two leaders, even in the course of the long, hot, exceedingly uncomfortable sea-voyage to Alexandria. Crémieux was a self-made man and firmly secular, Montefiore immensely rich and scrupulously observant in a style that can only be described as a Jewish form of Victorian piety. And to differences of outlook and temperament there were added the awkward facts that Crémieux's passage had been paid for by Montefiore and that Mohamed Ali, possibly because he had learned of this, had attempted to dismiss Crémieux from the scene altogether on the grounds that he was no more

---

[142] Louis Loewe, *The Damascus Affair* (Ramsgate, 1940), 25–6.

than Montefiore's lawyer. When Montefiore very properly stood his ground, the Pasha dropped his objection, however, and on all other essentials the two men were careful not to allow their need to co-operate to be impaired. The prisoners were released at last on 6 September 1840. On 6 November 1840 the final, formal act in the long-drawn-out affair was concluded by the Ottoman Sultan issuing a *firman* dismissing the charge that the Jews had ever engaged in human sacrifice to obtain blood for Passover rites as a calumny against them and enjoining all concerned to guard them from further molestation in the future. This last was a considerable achievement in itself: in Rome the incumbent Pope Gregory XVI had refused to allow so much as a technical reconfirmation of the two Papal Bulls in which the otherwise similarly hostile Pope Innocent IV had laid down six centuries earlier that whatever else might be held against the Jews the 'blood libel' itself was without foundation. Montefiore and Crémieux and their associates had good reason therefore to be satisfied. It was only in the aftermath that the hard questions arose. Had not proof of the actuality of the 'power of the Jews' been offered? Did it not in some way speak against them? It was remarkable that a Jewish deputy had been able and willing to tackle an unfriendly French Prime Minister and compel him to reply to his parliamentary questions. But what precisely was to be made of Thiers's ironic compliments to the Jews on the great zeal they had demonstrated in their own defence and his own self-congratulation on having stood up to them?

And then permit me to say: something that reflects great honour on the Jews has taken place. They were agitated throughout Europe when the facts were known and brought a degree of zeal and ardour to bear on this affair that, in my eyes, honours them profoundly. And may I say, that they are more powerful worldwide than they claim to be; and that at the present time they are engaged in lodging complaints with all the foreign chancelleries, in which activity they invest extraordinary zeal, an unimaginable ardour. It takes courage for a minister to defend an official subject to such attack. I believe I have shown firmness in this affair, as was indeed my due.

You must know, gentlemen, and I repeat, that the Jews are proceeding with their action [*sont en instance*] in this matter in all the chancelleries and there is no support for our consul except at the Ministry for Foreign Affairs of France.[143]

---

[143] *Moniteur*, p. 1258, col. 3. Later in the year, when Thiers fell from power, the Rothschilds were accused of having had a hand in the intrigue. This was inherently unlikely, nor is there any real evidence to that effect. It was the case, however, that the Rothschild brothers did what they could to reduce tension between the British and the French which they judged to be largely Thiers's doing and that they thought very little of Thiers personally. 'We are condemned to witness, impassively, as this man, of all the upstarts the most arrogant, encircles this country ever more tightly and drags us all into the abyss which his thoughtlessness and pseudo-liberalism has opened up before us.' James Rothschild to his brothers, 22 Sept. 1840. Cited in Bertrand Gille, *Histoire de la Maison Rothschild*, i (Geneva, 1965), 303–4.

When it was all over, the editor of the *Archives Israélites* offered up his journal's thanks to God. But even he could not refrain from adding, 'But you, France, cover your face for your representative in Damascus has compromised your reputation for wisdom and for compassion.'[144] There had been no doubt in Jewish minds that to affirm the innocence of the Jews of Damascus was to uphold the honour of Jewry in its entirety. Awkwardly for French Jews, it had been equally clear that to do so was to cast doubt on the honesty and credibility of the French foreign service. Was it the case, therefore, that the honour of the Jews was irreconcilable with the honour of the French? And if it was, who precisely were the irreconcilable parties to the conflict? Was it indeed a conflict between peoples? Or could it be conceived more narrowly as one between the Jewish people and the French *state*? But was a distinction between the French and their state conceptually and politically permissible in such a case? To most members of the French political class it was plain beyond doubt that to defend an official of the kingdom was to do no more than to rally to the cause of the honour of his service, but also, by extension, to the honour of France itself. And what, for present purposes, was the significance of the twin facts that while the question whether Jews constituted a nation analogous to that of the French was debatable, it could not be more evident that there was no Jewish analogue to the French state? Whatever the answers to these questions, their implications for those who had pinned their hopes on a continual, relatively untroubled unrolling of the process of integration, and of the Jews of France attaining a status within the French nation that was essentially like that of the Protestant minority, were dire.

IX

Two years later, in the course of the French general election of 1842, three well-identified Jewish notables were returned to parliament. Two of the three, Fould and Crémieux, were the men who had done the most in France to explode the calumny against the Jews of Damascus and so, however unwillingly, embarrass and thwart the French establishment. The *Archives Israélites*, for its part, took the result of the election as an augury and its conclusion was triumphant. 'Disagreements' between Jews and non-Jews 'are no longer possible in France after a result like this; there are no longer religious differences among us, no longer hereditary hatreds, no longer beliefs that kill!' Henceforth 'the literary marshals commanding the great army of the press' need to discard the adjective *Jewish* forever. It was not, the editors explained,

---

[144] Philippe, 'Archives Israélites', 104.

that we blush for our beliefs . . .—God forbid!—but because in France, in 1842, the adjective *Jewish* is devoid of meaning; because the Jew, as the dictionary of the Academy knows him, becomes rarer every day; because the Jew whose soul is in Jerusalem and his body in France, scarcely exists any longer in our day; it is because the *Jewish* nation no longer exists on French soil.[145]

It followed that the original challenge of 1789 to French Jewry had been met after all. The Jews—the Jews of France, at all events—had, as required, abandoned all claims to separate nationhood. The corresponding revolutionary promise to admit them as an integral, licit, socially accepted segment of French society had been honoured too.

A thread of genuine conviction did certainly run through this, as did a second thread, intertwined with the first, and spun of the belief that in the struggle to beat back the forces hostile to Jewry it was politic to assert and reassert that this was how the matter stood. And there was a third thread of hope, often passionate, in some cases wistful, hope against hope in fact, that at the end of the day all would indeed be well and that *this* community of Jews, if no other, had reached a safe and permanent haven after all. It was because it was only with very great difficulty that so sanguine a view could be squared with the facts of the case, at any rate as the Damascus Affair had revealed them, that its happy conclusion, no less than its sour origins, posed the eternal question of the authoritative leadership of Jewry all over again and in a new and instructive light.

When Montefiore and Crémieux returned in triumph from Constantinople to be admired and fêted and remembered throughout Jewry to their respective dying days and beyond for what they had done, it could be said of both men that, without much thought for anything but the immediate purpose of rescue, they had propelled themselves into positions of immense personal prestige and unparalleled political potential. Neither, however, was to make much of the position and the implicit challenge. Neither was to seek, nor so far as is known so much as to consider seeking, a position in Jewry that would in any way be analogous to that of those other men, their contemporaries, who sought in some way to lead *their* peoples into the sun. It would remain the case that, among the peoples of mid-nineteenth-century Europe, the Jews were noteworthy for the total absence among them not only of a figure who might reasonably be considered their leader, but of any one at all who had advanced a serious claim to leadership: no Daniel O'Connell, therefore, or Mazzini, or István Széchenyi or Kossuth, or Francis Palacký, or Franz Smolka, or Ludwik Mieroslawski, or, looking somewhat further ahead, Charles Parnell. It is true that the intrinsic obstacles and objections to the

---

[145] 'Les députés israélites MM. Cerfberr, Crémieux et Fould', *Archives Israélites*, iii (1842), 362; 'Les complices d'un adjectif', ibid. 147–55. Cited in Poliakov, *History of Anti-Semitism*, iii. 349–50.

rise of such a figure were very great. It is true too that as a class or social category, certainly as a nation, the Jews of Europe were ill placed for any considered and co-ordinated outlook on their condition to be arrived at and that the cards were very heavily stacked against any individual or group who might presume to take it upon himself, or themselves, to propose measures of improving it. This had long been the case. It was now doubly so. To the ancient habits of political quietism, docility, and self-effacement there had been added, with ever more marked consequences for the ability of publicly minded Jews to act coherently in their own interests both locally *and* across political frontiers, deepening divisions of internal structure, purposes, and mind, and widely differing host societies and regimes. The broad effect was further to reduce the possibility of central leadership, if not to close it entirely. It was only the modernists in Jewry who could be expected to go so far as to consider such an idea. But it was precisely for them, in their overwhelming majority, that it had become more important than ever to deny the reality of the basis on which any readily conceivable *secular* supra-communal leadership would have to operate: the national.

To be sure, the two heroes of the Damascus Affair, Montefiore and Crémieux, were not themselves by temperament or breeding or experience of the class to which the leaders of the oppressed or 'submerged' peoples of the age, their contemporaries, commonly belonged. They were men of prominence in their own right who, somewhat like the intercessors, the *shtadlanim*, of the old school, had set about mobilizing and then successfully employing whatever levers of influence there were to hand in the interests of succouring brethren in distress. Their purpose in the case of the Damascus Affair had been specific, much as the purposes of intercessors had always been and would continue to be: the alleviation of the distress of particular people in particular circumstances. There was no question in their minds of setting themselves to work out a global reordering of the lives of the Jews. They were meliorists and gradualists. They wished to maintain, strengthen, and extend the process of emancipation and integration as practised in England and France especially and as they themselves understood it, no more.

Yet there was a respect in which Crémieux at any rate represented something new. Sir Moses Montefiore was indeed the old-fashioned, government-supported, and generally well thought of philanthropist and social worthy. He was a magnate in his own right. He was recognizably a decent person who would in the course of time proceed to other places, always at great personal inconvenience and at his own expense, to Russia, to Morocco, and to Palestine, performing the public, philanthropic duties he had voluntarily assumed. But whereas his capacity to serve less fortunate Jewish communities than his own was ultimately a function of the favour in which he was held in Whitehall and at Windsor Castle,

Adolphe Crémieux owed nothing to the regime under which he lived. He was not a magnate. He was not in the ordinary sense of the term a philanthropist. He was a public and political figure, an authentic leader of others in a sense in which Montefiore, for all his merits, neither presumed to be nor could have reasonably wanted to be. In a word, Crémieux was that entirely new phenomenon in Jewry, a tribune: the tribune of French Jewry, as it happened, its spokesman and defender—initially in the courts, ultimately in the wider public arena and in parliament, and, when the opportunity presented itself and the case seemed to him to warrant it, even as a minister in the French cabinet. It was this that made him the one man in European Jewry in his time who was possessed of the ability and the status and the personal prestige to play the role of a tribune for all Jewry, at any rate for its modernist, western wing, had he only wished to do so—or had he gone so far as to define a cause which would in some way encompass all or most of the Jewish people and which he would take it upon himself to promote.

Why Crémieux failed to rise to the challenge presented to him can only be a matter for speculation. All that is certain is that had he done so he would have been confronted by at least one, possibly insurmountable, obstacle. The essential origins and basis of his prestige within Jewry lay in his achievements in the world without: as a lawyer of great causes, as an advocate entitled to plead before the nation's supreme court, as a political, and, in the course of time, parliamentary and ministerial figure. For men of his class—there would be others in the course of time—it would always be necessary to maintain their position in the larger world if they were to enjoy one of consequence in the smaller. To go over to the Jewish world soul *and* body was to risk loss of status and power of manœuvre in both—such, at any rate, was the fear, and not without good reason.[146] But even were this not the case, it would still have been necessary to confront an intolerable contradiction. For finally, it was *against* the non-Jewish world—at all events against very substantial parts of it—that the Jews needed to be led. It was thus on the issue of emancipation and civil and

[146] The special case of monied philanthropists apart (on whom more below), there never were more than a handful of candidates for positions of real leadership in Jewry whose influence might have extended, or could have been brought to bear, beyond the confines of a single major community. One who did belong to this select category, however, and who, despite the half-century or so and the Atlantic Ocean that separated them, had much in common with Crémieux was Louis D. Brandeis. In the immediate aftermath of the First World War the leadership of the newly invigorated Zionist movement and, quite arguably, something like the leadership of modernist Jewry in all parts was his for the asking. However, Brandeis preferred to retain his seat on the United States Supreme Court, as was, perhaps, to be expected. Max Nordau was not in the same league as Brandeis and Crémieux, being a literary, not a legal-political figure. But he was a man of not inconsiderable renown in his day (the tail end of the nineteenth century); and such as it was, by joining Herzl in 1897 and devoting himself thereafter heart and soul to a Jewish cause, he killed it.

civic rights. It was thus where the question was defence against the direct ideological attacks upon them. And it was thus, if only by implication, in respect of the largest question of all, namely how—if at all—they were to find a place for themselves within European society.

X

However hostile public and private thinking about the Jews might be in important social, political, and intellectual circles in central and western Europe, nowhere was the state as such the *declared* enemy of the Jews. West of (partitioned) Poland no government and no ruling class either, for that matter, perceived the Jews as a distinct and coherent force that was seriously subversive of state or society. And if no western or central European state was necessarily friendly to Jews, nowhere had the Jews reason to distrust, let alone fear the state and its instruments—as the Jews of imperial Russia learned to do with their mothers' milk. But then while the various policies devised by the men of the Enlightenment to deal with their Jewish subjects had varied over time and from place to place, they had this in common, that they were conceived, as we have seen, with what purported to be the interests of the *state* in mind. The greatest of all problems for Jewry lay, therefore, in the fact that as Europe moved into the second half of the nineteenth century the sum of the change was the ideological and moral reduction of the state in favour of the nation—and the consequent merging of one with the other. The question Jews had therefore increasingly to face was less whether they would be allowed to become citizens of the state than whether they would be granted membership of the nation. And nowhere was the issue posed in so acute and, from the Jewish point of view, so desperate a form as in Germany. This had a good deal to do with the spirit in which the process of German unification was proceeding and the ideological basis on which the greater German state would be established when the unifiers had finally had their way. On the one hand theirs would be a structure in which no space was left for other peoples: fundamentally unlike that of its neighbour, the Habsburg Empire. On the other hand, the people who were to inherit it were conceived increasingly in exclusionary and all but impenetrable terms. The common emphasis was ever less on the cultural and the intellectual, ever more on the ethnic and the racial: on 'seed' therefore and on 'blood' *whence* the ethical was to be derived. The Germans were an excellent people of exceptional qualities, wrote Friedrich Ludwig Jahn (1778–1852), an early advocate of a full-scale return to the supposed original, folkloric virtues and patterns of behaviour of the German people and among the promoters of the all-German association of student organizations, the *Burschenschaften*, an especially notable effort to celebrate triumphant German nationhood. 'Strength, honesty, uprightness, hatred of circumlocution, equity, and good and serious thinking have for several thousand years been the ornaments of our nationality.' But these were precisely the qualities that would be lost if ever the Germans were penetrated and mixed with people of another and inferior kind.

Nationality [Jahn explained] is the true measure of the grandeur of peoples, the scales on which their merits are best weighed. While its existence implies a state, the existence of a state does not imply that of nationality. . . . Just as there are hollow nuts, so there are empty states and peoples devoid of nationality. . . . Hybrid animals are incapable of reproducing themselves; bastard peoples, similarly, lack the life force of proper nations. . . . He who strives to assemble the principal peoples of the earth in a single herd soon risks reigning over the most contemptible scum of the earth. Constantine tried that great experiment; Rome and Greece showed the result. . . . The Spanish proverb 'Trust neither the mule nor the mulatto' is very sound. . . . The most homogeneous people is the best, the most mixed is the least solidly united.[147]

None of this was *necessarily* applicable to the Jews of Germany or any other country. But that these should be the terms in which the matter of the Jews would be ever more commonly perceived, even by some of the leading intellectual lights of the day, was probably inevitable. 'The Jewish race is and remains in Europe an Asiatic people alien to our region,' wrote Herder. Whether it 'belongs' or not to our state was no longer a religious issue and a matter of belief, but of whether and to what degree 'this alien race . . . may be dispensed with, how many are useful or detrimental to *this* and not to any other state—that is the problem'.[148] From this viewpoint to the particular thesis that Jewry and Germany, or 'Judaism' and 'Germandom', were pitted one against the other in inexorable conflict was a short and easy step. 'I do not speak to you in praise of talk of eternal peace or love of the enemy, but rather of talk of war, of valiant resistance, and hatred of the enemy' were the slyly anti-Kantian and anti-Christian terms of a patriotic-mystical appeal to the communal spirit of the Men of Germany in 1814 by Jakob Friedrich Fries, professor of philosophy at Jena, another patron of the *Burschenschaften*. 'What is it, then, that we call a nation [*Volk*]? A spiritual society of people. What is it that gives a band of common citizens its unity? Not the soil, not the edge of the sea-coasts, the river banks, the mountain range—but union of spirit [*Geistesvereinigung*]. How can that come about among men?

[147] Fr.-L. Jahn, *Recherches sur la nationalité: l'esprit des peuples allemands*, trans. P. Lortet (Paris, 1825), 22, 34–7.

[148] 'Bekehrung der Juden' (Conversion of the Jews), published in his journal *Adrastea*, 4 (1802) [the year before his death], reprinted in *Sämtliche Werke*, ed. V. Suphan (reprinted Hildesheim, 1967), xxiv. 61–75. Cited by Rose, *Revolutionary Antisemitism*, 103.

Solely through like habits and modes of life [*gleiche Lebensgewöhnung und deren Formen*].[149] Of the Jews specifically Fries wrote two years later, 'This caste must be exterminated root and branch' and that 'to improve the civic situation of the Jews *means* exterminating Jewry'.[150] And while such ferocity of language was still exceptional, the underlying tendency to reduce complex social and political issues to hugely simplistic national-conflictual terms was rapidly gaining ground—if only because neither was separable from the linked developments of which they were both symptoms and part-causes. These were the disintegration of the old dynastic constitutional and political order of government and the progress being made towards its replacement by one in which national identity and national purposes were the bases and conditions of political legitimacy. In sum, the 'invasion' of the politics of central and east-central Europe by the *Volksgeist*, by nationality as 'the passionate creed of the intellectuals', that was to be, in Lewis Namier's language, the start of 'the Great European War of every nation against its neighbours' had begun.[151] It is true that the revolutionary year of 1848 served to reconfirm—some would say, sanctify—that of 1789. This was certainly the case in France, but it was the extension eastwards of the reforms of the original Great Revolution that was the more dramatic. The irreversibility in the west of much that had been set in train earlier was already established. It was the abolition of residual feudal rights and obligations proclaimed in Vienna on 7 September 1848 that was quite rightly celebrated as the true final nail in the coffin of the old nobiliar-agrarian order. Even the abolition of peasant servitude in Romanov Russia could now be regarded with some confidence as being on its way to realization.

There were, to be sure, other less immediately obvious, but in important ways deeper, and to the minds of some acute observers distinctly troubling, respects in which '1848' signalled change. What remained of the old reliance on, and respect for, law and precedent was further diminished. The disposition to reorganize society and to formulate and justify policy on the basis of first principles was greatly strengthened, but as the rights of *nations* moved to the fore, the rights of *man* as understood and proclaimed in 1789 lost their primacy. It was true that in the very short term the Year of Revolution ironed out some of the discrepancies and inconsistencies that had characterized the general libertarian trend in Europe. Thus for all or almost all Europeans, thus for some of the Jews. In the kingdom of Sardinia-Piedmont the Jews (after some delay) were

---

[149] J. F. Fries, 'Bekehrt Euch! (1814)', in *Zwei Politische Flugschriften 1814 und 1817* (Munich, 1910), 10–12.

[150] *Über die Gefährdung des Wohlstandes und Charakters der Deutschen durch die Juden* (Heidelberg, 1816), 18, 10. Cited in Pulzer, *Jews and the German State*, 17. Emphasis added.

[151] L. B. Namier, *1848: The Revolution of the Intellectuals* (London, 1946; repr. 1992 with an introduction by James Joll), 33, 73.

granted full civic and political rights along with access to the civil service. Most of the smaller Italian states followed suit. When the Pope fled from Rome, the walls of the Roman ghetto were pulled down. And something of the sort transpired in the Germanies and in Austria too. At the new National Assembly at Frankfurt, where it was laid down as one of the Basic Rights of the German People that 'the enjoyment of civic and citizens' rights is neither conditional upon, nor restricted by religious belief',[152] a handful of Jews took seats as elected members. One of their number, Gabriel Riesser, served briefly as its Second Vice-President. Eduard Simson, a baptized Jew, was elected its President. But a proposal to decree total emancipation evoked protest and opposition, a counter-proposal to limit the rights of Jews in the new Germany-to-be was put forward in the plenum in rebuttal, and the entire subject had then to be thrashed out privately in committee, those who opposed emancipation taking the line that while the emancipation measure might be right in principle, it would be unpopular in the country.[153] Still, the *mood* at Frankfurt was such that there really was no answer to the ringing words Riesser addressed to the Assembly in support of the measure. Speaking as a Jew, a German, a liberal, and a proponent of a unified German state, he told his colleagues that he was prepared to admit that the Jews, an oppressed people, had not as yet

reached the Sublime, the patriotic spirit. But nor had Germany. Under just laws, the Jews will become the ever more enthusiastic and patriotic followers of Germany. With and under the Germans they will become Germans [themselves]. Put your trust in the power of justice, in the power of the equal laws, and in the great destiny of Germany! Do not believe that it is possible to make special laws [*Ausnahmegesetze*] without the whole system of freedom sustaining a fatal fissure, without the seed of ruin [*der Keim des Verderbens*] being placed within it. It has been suggested to you that part of the German people should be sacrificed to intolerance and hatred. But this, Gentlemen, you would never do![154]

Modernist German Jews had some reason therefore to be encouraged by the developments at Frankfurt and to point with satisfaction to the fact that substantial numbers of young Jewish men had participated in the rebellions that had brought the Assembly into being in the first place. It was true that, upon the return of the established rulers of the states of central Europe to power in the following year, the Frankfurt Assembly was

[152] Part VI, Article V, paragraph 146.
[153] Reinhard Rürup, 'The European Revolution of 1848 and Jewish Emancipation', in Werner E. Mosse, Arnold Paucker, and Reinhard Rürup (eds.), *Revolution and Evolution: 1848 in German-Jewish History* (Tübingen, 1981), 21 n. 52.
[154] 'Rede gegen Moritz Mohl's Antrag zur Beschränkung der Rechte der Juden, 29 August 1848.' Gabriel Riesser's *Gesammelte Schriften*, iv (Frankfurt and Leipzig, 1868), 409–10.

wound up and its decisions largely annulled or ignored.[155] Analogous provisions of the Austrian constitution of March 1849 met the same fate. Legal disabilities were reimposed on Jews in all the Italian states—with the important exception of Sardinia-Piedmont. The walls of the Roman ghetto were rebuilt. Still, when the excitement of 1848 and its immediate aftermath had died down it was hard to deny that a mark had been left and precedents of a moral kind had been established. Some small steps towards unreserved, formal, and final emancipation had been taken after all. Within a decade or two, three at most, legal equality would indeed be the rule virtually everywhere in western and central Europe, even in a shadowy way in Switzerland where in 1848 it had been hotly and explicitly refused. As for the more fundamental trends and developments that the Frankfurt Assembly had symbolized and which '1848' as a whole had served to articulate, these would be revealed in the longer term.

At the heart of the problem that the 'Springtime of the Nations' set the Jews—in central Europe especially, but ultimately in all of Europe—was that what had underlain and moved it was the conviction that social policy needed to be formulated a priori and that the first principle from which policy was to be derived was that the rights (in truth: the self-interest) of the nation—any nation in its proper domain—overrode all others. Inexorably, Jewry as a distinct and historic ethno-religious category stood condemned. It could be argued, very theoretically and without regard to real circumstances, that had the Jews been willing to establish themselves as one European nation among others their situation would have been different. But no such argument was put forward at the time; and no serious grounds can be discerned in retrospect for thinking that the Jews might have succeeded in reconstituting themselves politically in Europe had there in fact been a reasonable number among them who were prepared to undertake such a venture and press the appropriate claim. It was a notion or vision that would arise many years later, as we shall see, but in totally altered political and territorial circumstances. And even then, as events would demonstrate, it would enjoy only very moderate support within Jewry itself and no serious prospect of fulfilment in any readily foreseeable future. In any event, it was very far from being the case in mid-nineteenth-century Europe that claims and aspirations to politically expressed national status were admitted by all concerned on behalf of all who pressed them as a matter of course. Least of all were such claims likely to be admitted by those who already enjoyed that status when their own interests and ambitions seemed likely to be affected. Few Hungarians, Poles, Germans, Englishmen, or Russians saw any reason

---

[155] The Act of 27 Dec. 1848 in which the Declaration of the 'Basic Rights of the German People' was incorporated was formally repealed by the Diet of the German Confederation on 23 Aug. 1851.

either in practice or in principle to accord to Slovaks, Ruthenes, Czechs, Irishmen, and 'Little' Russians respectively the status and future they had long since assumed for themselves and had every intention of maintaining. In the minds of those who regarded themselves as members of great, 'historic' nations (or, in the central European terminology of the times, *Nationen*), their destinies were sharply and rightly to be distinguished from those of lesser, puny, 'nationalities' (or *Nationalitätchen*). References to the latter in the all-German Frankfurt Assembly were typically hostile and contemptuous. 'Mere existence does not entitle a people to political independence: only the force to assert itself as a State among others' and 'Freedom for all, but the power of the Fatherland and its weal above all!'[156] were the slogans in force. It is true that the complex, unwieldy, multinational empires remained in being—notably the most genuinely (if still incompletely) multinational of all, the Austro-Hungarian. None of the concessions made to the new forces in 1848 or soon after turned out to be fatal to them, or really decisive. Some concessions were shamelessly withdrawn at the first possible moment. On the whole, the insurrectionary, revolutionary opposition to the post-Napoleonic regimes was successfully seen off—in some cases with great brutality, in others without any really serious trouble. In the short and perhaps the middle term too, Germans, Poles, and Hungarians, and in their rather different circumstances the Italians as well, remained some way off from achieving full and satisfactory political expression for their respective purposes. In this respect, therefore, matters were otherwise than they had been in the wake of 1789 when the central changes made were to prove irreversible, at any rate in France. And yet, the overall drive towards polities of a sharply different kind, because founded on different principles and promising or threatening a wholly different future for the peoples of which they were constituted, continued to gather force. The dominant socio-political characteristic to which the men of 1848, the central European 'Liberals' of the day, would strive, and in the course of time almost all political forces with them, would be the very opposite of imperial, ethnic, linguistic, and cultural complexity. It would be to the terrible simplicities that come from uniformity of ethos, behaviour, and purposes that they would strive. And in so doing, they would end by sealing themselves off one from the other and by entering into, and virtually sanctifying, endemic conflict.

The Enlightenment had left little room for eccentricities and exceptions to whatever was held to be the general rule. Now the space left for the anomalous would be further diminished. And this applied *a fortiori* to the Jews irrespective of whether they chose to regard themselves as a submerged and subject *nation* or not. Habsburg Austria, unlike Romanov

---

[156] Cited by Namier, *1848* (1992), 88.

Russia, never formally recognized them as a nation, not even as a second-class *Nationalität*. Neither the Hebrew language nor the Yiddish that was still the vernacular of most of the empire's Jews were among the eight national tongues recognized under the terms of the Liberal constitution of 1859. The onus, as never before, was now upon the Jews themselves to choose their course. In principle, they could accept extrusion from the body politic, although what this might now come to mean in practice no one could tell, except that it would be to fall into a sort of socio-political limbo of some kind. For the modernists among them the logic of the situation seemed therefore to point exclusively to firm and unconditional identification with whatever rising nation they happened to be embedded in, to which they were, in consequence, drawn by the ties and skills of language, education, and general culture that they had come to acquire by accident of birth or domicile or education. When the young Dr Adolf Fischhof, leader of the Vienna students in the rising against Habsburg government in March 1848 and a prominent member of the new, revolutionary Reichstag, preached co-operation to the nations of Austria it was the Germans, the Slavs, the Magyars, and the Italians he had in mind. The Jews as such had no role to play in his vision of inter-national fraternity. Fischhof's father was a Moravian Jew, his mother a Hungarian Jew, his own birthplace was Budapest. He himself identified with the Germans, his quality as a 'German' hinging on his having lived for a little over a decade in Vienna, first as a student, then as a practising physician.[157] Such identification with one of the ruling nations was not a personal betrayal, least of all a conscious one. What was at issue in 1848 was the political role, rights, and life of the nations. But the idea of the Jewish people as one of their number, namely as a *political* nation, or indeed a nation of any kind at all, was, to repeat the point, utterly remote from the thinking of modernist, cultivated people, and fated to be easily dismissed as preposterous when raised. A political nation understood in conspiratorial, underhand, illegitimate terms—perhaps. But openly and as one nation among others—not at all. Even in Greater Poland where the Jews were, as all could and did see, numerically and proportionately one of the constituent peoples of the country along with the Poles themselves, the Lithuanians, the White and the 'Little' Russians (or Ukrainians)—even there none regarded them as candidates for what was now increasingly thought of as normal political existence.

In sum, there was nothing in the rise of nationality as epitomized in 1848 to ease the undoubted problem and the consequent dilemmas which the Jewish people's ancient ethos and internal structure presented both to themselves and to others in the modern age. On the contrary, they served powerfully to drive Jewry somewhat further along the path of

[157] Namier, *1848*, 27.

anachronism, uncertainty, and social and political incompatibility with its environment and its neighbours. The closer and faster the other nations of Europe—the ruling or 'historic' nations before all others—moved towards *their* political apotheosis the more clearly the Question of the Jews unfailingly came into focus and the firmer the refusal all round— here silent, there vociferous—to fit them into any of the versions of the new scheme of things that were, so it was imagined, in the making. By the same token, the faster the other nations of Europe were consolidated, the faster the Jewish people (taken collectively rather than as a con- geries of individuals) was bound to crumble and its position rendered precarious.

The immensely complex ethnic map of central and eastern Europe ensured, moreover, that no neat state/nation solution acceptable to all parties could be worked out anywhere, even where there was the will to do so. Once the claims of one nation—or what purported to be a nation—were proclaimed paramount, conflict with others was inevitable. That one of the differences between the Jews and any of their neighbours in any part of Europe lay in the fact that the Jews were neither actual nor potential competitors for state power should, therefore, have eased their position. And it did so to some extent. On the other hand, the fact that none of the Jews' own neighbours, great or small, needed ser- iously to consider them rivals in the ordinary politico-territorial sense, served to render them more anomalous as ever. It was Lewis Namier's view that, while 'the growth of urban agglomerations and of an urban civilization stimulates the rise of a non-territorial ideology . . . unless there be a complete return to the conditions of the horde, the basic elem- ent of territory cannot be eliminated: there is no escape from the inter- play between groups of men and tracts of land, which forms the essence of history.'[158] And there is much to be said for his dictum, the more so as it is intuitively, but very well understood in all modern societies. Its effect, in any event, has been to pose the question of the Jews' *national* existence and structure in more insistent terms than ever. If they were an anom- alous category in multinational empires, they were fated to be rendered entirely unacceptable and incomprehensible in nation-states.

Yet in the short and middle term it was 1848 as the crisis of the old rul- ing classes that counted for most. Theirs were the structures upon which the Jews had traditionally relied; they were the people who, none doubted, had sought invariably to exploit, use, and manipulate the Jews for their personal or étatist purposes; it was they who had determined the administrative topography through which the Jews had had to make their way; and it was with them that Jews had either achieved a *modus vivendi,* even if a painful and undignified one, or had gone under. But if these were the classes, and theirs were the forms of government, administration, and regulation, to which the Jews had grown accustomed, the question with whom a *modus vivendi* should now be sought had become an open one. So too the question of its terms: what would be the consequences? what would be its price? Gravest of all, if not immediately apparent, was the question whether a *modus vivendi* on anything like the old model, or on any acceptable basis at all, was possible. In a world of competing peoples, was there any space left over for one which, traditionally, as much by force of habit and circumstances as by ingrained and explicit doctrine had abstained from competition hitherto? Even the making of alliances, should it be attempted, had been rendered more difficult by the fact that the image of Jewry projected by new-model Judaeophobia was protean and contradictory: Jews were subversive of the social order, Jews were pillars of the social order; Jews were ignorant, Jews might be learned but in undesirable or absurd branches of knowledge; Jews were dangerously talented, Jews were unteachable; Jews were about to take over the citadels of European culture, Jews were incapable of comprehending and internalizing European culture; Jews sought to penetrate society, Jews kept themselves apart; Jews exploited their customers by selling dear, Jews undermined the market by selling cheap; the nastiness and meanness of the Jews was manifest *inter alia* in their insistence on the letter of the law, their wickedness was evident in their talent for circumventing it; Jews were rich, Jews were poor; and so on and so forth.

The catalogue of charges was endless and infinitely elastic. It was so of epistemological necessity, as it were, since systematic evidence supporting any of the central propositions put forward was in no case ever offered and only very rarely asked for, and whatever it was that might be said on any of these scores drew at least part of its strength from the teachings of the Churches and the folklore of Europe. Besides, in practice, the particular charges selected for emphasis in particular cases varied with the circumstances: with the speaker or publicist articulating them, with the audience, with the *Zeitgeist*, and in a general way with whatever the market and the traffic were thought likely to bear. Tone, content, and intensity varied widely from one case to another. What could be said openly and without fear of contradiction in a Prussian officers' mess was unlikely to be heard, except perhaps *sotto voce*, in the corridors of the French Chamber of Deputies. If the general view of Jewry in the higher reaches of the Roman Catholic hierarchy was no less hostile than that held by certain leading members of the English intellectual and literary establishment, the origins and the concerns underlying it in each case were very different. Yet all varieties and subclasses of modern anti-Semitism, as it was to be called and as it took shape and gathered political and emotive force through the breadth and length of Europe, had this in common: that taken all in all, the Jews were incurably alien and that in one way or another, whether as individuals or collectively, they were sources of social evil and disturbance. They were therefore deeply and incorrigibly undesirable. Most striking and in the long run most telling was the rise of single-issue, very specifically anti-Semitic movements in the final decades of the nineteenth century and their successful entry into the political world. It is true that their fortunes rose and fell and that they were never considered to be entirely respectable even by those political conservatives who had some sympathy for them, let alone by such—Bismarck among them—who, while they had nothing but contempt for them, were prepared to use them for their own purposes. On the other hand, the presence not merely in the general political arena, but in parliament itself, of a coherent and identifiable group propagating a notably ferocious anti-Semitic creed, as a permanent fixture of German political life from 1879 onwards marked an important step towards the eventual reversal of the role of the state in the lives of the Jews from protector to principal enemy. Germany was not alone in this respect. There were parallel developments in Austria and in Hungary. But it was in the new, united imperial Germany that the trend was initially most pronounced and, to the Jewish community in question, most disturbing. And there, party-political developments aside, it is necessary, once again, to distinguish the social from the official and constitutional.

At the highest and most influential levels of German society there was no question of accepting Jews as equals. They might be tolerated (and used) for their wealth or special knowledge or connections or, more rarely, their native wit and ability. But they remained interlopers. The banker Gerson von Bleichröder, as great a man in crude terms of wealth, influence, and connections—and native talent too—as any in his day was tormented throughout his life by a never fully requited thirst for social acceptance. Some of the externals for which he hungered and supplicated—a patent of nobility, decorations, the right kind of guests at his dinner table—he obtained. Some he did not. True social acceptance was never granted him. Bismarck, whom he served for years as regular and intimate financial adviser and as jack-of-all-confidential-trades, kept him carefully compartmentalized and out of view and never so much as mentioned the tremendous services Bleichröder had performed for him in his memoirs. But it is the language in which a Prussian policeman felt free to report to his superiors on Bleichröder's comportment *after* his elevation to the nobility that is most telling:

[The man] almost bursts with pride . . . no longer entertains his former friends and associates, and keeps himself apart from them even in his walks: on his promenades in the Sieges-Allee he walks on the western side instead of on the eastern with the great majority of promenaders, who are almost all Jews. Asked why . . .

is supposed to have answered that the eastern side smelled too much of garlic.[159]

Walther Rathenau, unlike the vulgar Bleichröder, was elegant, sensitive, and intellectually and artistically gifted. Unlike Bleichröder again, his wealth was inherited: his father, Emil, an engineer by training, had been the founder of what would be the largest electro-technical firm in Germany, the Allgemeine Elektrizitäts-Gesellschaft (AEG). Upon Emil's death Walther, very thoroughly groomed for the post, became the head of AEG himself. He was unlike the banker too in his being cursed by a drive to submit himself to continual self-examination and self-criticism and by an equally intense, although certainly meritorious regard for personal dignity. He exceeded Bleichröder in his unconquerable sensitivity to the matter of his Jewish identity too. Of the 'Jewish tribe' itself—of which, while he withdrew formally from the Jewish community, he was careful to announce himself a member—he thought little and said as much. He saw them as deeply unsatisfactory, a *Furchtvolk*, a frightened people, much of what could be said in their favour, notably their intellectual ability, being, he thought, a product of the fear that was endemic in them. 'Look at yourselves in the mirror!' he wrote when a very young man in his initially pseudonymous, subsequently famous appeal 'Höre, Israel!' ('Hear, O Israel'), published in Maximilian Harden's *Zukunft* in 1897. 'Nothing, unfortunately, can be done about the fact that you all look frighteningly alike, that your individual vices, therefore, are attributed to all of you', and that they were of 'east Mediterranean appearance'. They needed to recognize that their build was 'unathletic', their shoulders 'narrow', their shape 'round', and that this determined the miserable view taken of them by 'northern tribes' brought up in 'a strictly military fashion'. The lamentable result was that

In the midst of German life [there is] an alien and isolated race of men. Loud and self-conscious in their dress, hot-blooded and restless in their manner. An Asiatic horde on the sandy plains of Prussia. . . . Yet I know, that there are some among you who are pained and shamed by being strangers and half-citizens in the land, and who long to escape from the stifling ghetto into the pure air of the German woods and hills.[160]

Years later, in 1911, by which time Rathenau had established himself as one of the great men of early twentieth-century Germany and was very nearly at the height of his career, prestige, fame, and powers as an industrial magnate, a regular and trusted consultant to the mighty, and an

---

[159] Cited in Fritz Stern, *Gold and Iron: Bismarck, Bleichröder, and the Building of the German Empire* (New York, 1979), 476.

[160] English trans. in Harry Kessler, *Walther Rathenau: His Life and Work* (London, 1929), 35–9; and P. R. Mendes-Flohr, and Jehuda Reinharz (eds.), *The Jew in the Modern World: A Documentary History* (New York and Oxford, 1980), 234.

authentic, proven intellectual in his own right, he wrote: 'In the days of every German Jew's youth there is a painful moment which he remembers for the whole of his life: when he becomes fully conscious for the first time that he has entered the world as a second-class citizen and that no skill or merit can ever free him from this situation.'[161] It is scarcely conceivable that a figure of analogous prominence in England or France—any of the Rothschilds, for example—would have expressed himself in such (justifiably much quoted) language, or even, so one supposes, have thought such exceedingly dour thoughts. Rathenau was to go on to greater things yet during the war and, especially, in its aftermath when he was appointed Weimar Germany's foreign minister. That last appointment cost him his life, however, at the hands of people who were outraged (as he knew they were) by the spectacle of a Jew holding such an office, doubly so when the policy he pursued on the government's behalf was one that implied at least temporary and partial acceptance of the Versailles treaty. But even apart from the tragedy of his murder, it is an occasion for shock, and perhaps for pity, to discover that a man of such attainments and deep and utterly genuine German-patriotic feeling[162] should be as wracked by insecurity and desperate for acceptance as an equal by the 'blond, steel-blue eyed men' around him as any Bleichröder. It remains only to admire him for the precision of his judgement. For, unlike Bleichröder, Rathenau saw the barriers to achievement of genuine insider's status that both men craved, and with them many tens of thousands of other upper middle-class German Jews, for what they were: impenetrable. He had grasped, as not all were inclined to do, that if you do not wish to be regarded as an interloper and are determined to stand on your dignity you need to take very great care.

Theodor Herzl (of whom more later) was not a German Jew at all, strictly speaking, but he was as close an observer of the scene in Germany as he was of his not entirely different native Austria-Hungary, and as desperately aware as Rathenau of the snares into which Jews might fall in this respect. It is not too much to say, that before all else it was his recognition of the hopelessness and the attendant, humiliating intricacies of the Jewish social condition that were at the root of his conviction that a radical transformation of the status of the Jews was needed if they were ever to be swept away. A single instance will serve as an illustration. On

---

[161] 'Staat und Judentum', *Gesammelte Werke*, i. 189, cited in Pulzer, *Jews and the German State*, 191.

[162] The almost unbearably passionate patriotism (Prussian, perhaps, rather than German) that Rathenau wore on his sleeve, but quite evidently was deeply meant, is well illustrated by a poem he wrote shortly before the First World War: 'Blond und stahlblau Korn und Lüfte | Himmelsaugen heiliger Seen | Dunkler Kiefern Waldesgrüfte | Blasser Dünen Schaumeswehn. . . . Mußte sich der Mensch verschließen | Daß das Herz umpanzert bliebe, | Endlich darf es überfließen | Land, mein Land, du meine Liebe.'

7 October 1898 Herzl held a meeting which he had reason to regard as of extreme importance with the German ambassador at Vienna. This was Count Philipp Eulenburg, the key figure in both men's effort to induce the German government to press the Turks to be more accommodating to the Zionists. Eulenburg himself was a very considerable Prussian grandee. When, at Eulenburg's request, it was agreed that the meeting should take place at the count's Liebenberg estate, near Löwenberg, some fifty kilometres from Berlin, Herzl prepared himself with extreme care and his diary account of what transpired is scrupulously accurate and typically self-observing.

the Count's dogcart was waiting for me [at the station]. The coachman surveyed me haughtily when I asked whether he was waiting for Dr Herzl. He had been told only: a tall gentleman with a black beard. I am probably the first Jew he has ever driven. . . . In a brief half-hour we were at Liebenberg. . . . Two footmen were waiting outside the gate. One of them announced me to the Count. In the hall, hunting weapons and trophies. The whole, grand style. The Count came out at once. He was in hunting costume, and it seemed to me the first thing he did was to take stock of my clothes. I had carefully considered what I should wear, and had taken my grey frock-coat and trousers, although under different circumstances the light-coloured lounge-suit would have been more appropriate. The light-coloured suit would have been informal. However, I certainly did not want to give the impression that I considered myself a guest. I was coming on business, a shade less *habillé* than if it had been in the city—that is, grey rather than black.

I believe he found me suitably dressed.

A long conversation on the political matter in hand was then held in the course of a stroll through the grounds of the estate. As it came to an end

A game-keeper with two dogs straining at the leash came into view. The Count had been showing signs of impatience for some time now. I declined his invitation to eat a second breakfast, which had been set out especially for me, on the pretext that I was anxious to get back to Berlin. . . . A waving of hats, and then Liebenberg lay behind me.

[The same coachman] drove the horses. But this time, I think, with greater respect, for he had seen the Count stand in the gateway until my departure.[163]

Not all German and German-speaking Jews were Bleichröders, Rathenaus, and Herzls. Not all men who were placed—or had chosen to place themselves—in unusually prominent and exposed positions evinced such extreme, if not obsessive behaviour. Hermann Steinthal, a philologist of very high repute, was a member of the teaching staff of the University of Berlin for fifty years until his death in 1899. Because he was a Jew and a devoted one at that, the status of *ordinarius*, or full professor,

---

[163] *The Complete Diaries of Theodor Herzl*, ed. R. Patai, English trans. Harry Zohn, ii (New York, 1960), 687–92.

was denied him to the end. But Steinthal's outlook was stoic. A Jew could not be an officer in the army? 'Well, then, he cannot.' Nobody can stop him from being an effective human being, so let him try *that*. Berthold Auerbach, Steinthal is recorded as pointing out,

> was proud of being acknowledged as a German poet by Jacob Grimm [and] suffers greatly [because] he is looked upon by the antisemites not as a German poet but as a Semite. I do not care. . . . It is absolutely my own affair to which nation I belong.[164]

But Bleichröder, Rathenau, and Herzl do all point, as extreme cases so often do, to what some German Jews continually, and all western and central European Jews at some point in their lives, had to cope with. There was the matter of how one dressed and appeared in public. There were the language and the turns of phrase one employed. There was the exceedingly touchy matter of the posture to adopt in relation to those things that had already been half- or wholly abandoned. Gershom Scholem recalled his family as

> a typical liberal middle-class [one] in which assimilation to things German, as people put it at the time, had progressed quite far. In our home there were only a few perceptible relics of Judaism, such as the use of Jewish idiomatic expressions, which my father avoided and forbade us to use, but which my mother gladly employed, especially when she wanted to make a point. . . . The *Kiddush*, the Hebrew blessing for the Sabbath, was still chanted [on Friday nights] but only half understood. That did not keep people from using the Sabbath candles to light a cigarette or cigar afterwards. Since the prohibition on smoking on the Sabbath was one of the most widely known Jewish regulations, there was deliberate mockery in this act. . . . On the other hand, once or twice a year my father used to make a speech at the dinner table praising the mission of the Jews. According to him, that mission was to proclaim to the world pure monotheism and a purely rational morality. Baptism, he said, was an unprincipled and servile act.[165]

It was not entirely impossible to maintain a foot in both worlds or in the limbo of the interstices between them. Not all found the constant slithering in and out of things Jewish and *per contra* German even in the intimacy of home and hearth as intolerable as Scholem did: Christmas, he remembered, being celebrated 'with roast goose or hare, a decorated

---

[164] Adolph Asch and Johanna Philippson, 'Self-defence at the Turn of the Century: The Emergence of the K.C.', *LBIYB* 3 (London, 1958), 130. Berthold Auerbach, a German-Jewish writer of very considerable fame in his time, was both a noted collector and fancier of German folklore and a man devoted to the fusing of what he judged to be the essentials of Jewish and German cultures. On his exceedingly painful and emotional response to the anti-Semitic campaign as it began in earnest at the end of the 1870s, see Rose, *Revolutionary Antisemitism*, 224–47.

[165] Gershom Scholem, *From Berlin to Jerusalem: Memories of my Youth*, trans. Harry Zohn (New York, 1988), 9–11.

Christmas tree . . . and the big distribution of presents for servants, relatives, and friends', on the stated grounds, that it was, after all 'a German national festival, in the celebration of which we joined not as Jews but as Germans'.[166] At the communal level the scrambling for a stable and honourable social posture was manifest in the multiplication of forms in which traditional beliefs and practices could, it was felt, be legitimately accommodated to the exigencies of life as citizens of Germany and a claim to membership in the German nation. It would be much encouraged and facilitated by the passing of the Law of Withdrawal (Austrittsgesetz) of 1876 which allowed groups holding different religious views on observance and ritual or doctrine to establish separate, legally recognized communities of their own. This ended once and for all what remained of the supremacy within Jewry of traditional orthodoxy and allowed religious reform and ingenuity and imagination in ritual to flourish as never before. At the private level again, something may be gleaned too from the most acute of all modern indicators of social and cultural breakdown in Jewry, the rate of intermarriage. Already on an upward curve, as has been noted, it continued, inexorably it would seem, to rise. In 1910 10.2 per cent of all German-Jewish women marrying contracted a mixed marriage; 10.6 in 1911; 11.2 per cent in 1912; 11.7 per cent in 1913; 17.3 per cent in 1914. The comparable figures for men were consistently higher: 12.7 per cent in 1910; 12.3 per cent in 1911; 12.5 per cent in 1912; 15.1 per cent in 1913; and 23.2 per cent in the obviously exceptional year of 1914. To put these figures in sharper perspective, it needs to be noted that the absolute number of endogamous Jewish marriages in Germany in these years was falling: 3,880 in 1910; 3,814 in 1911; 3,833 in 1912; 3,626 in 1913; and 2,617 in 1914. On the other hand, unlike the trend in the earlier decades of the century, the number of German Jews apostatizing remained virtually constant, the trend, if anything, being downwards. In all 639 Jews joined the Evangelical Church in 1901, 687 in 1902, 663 in 1903, 656 in 1904, 598 in 1905, 567 in 1906, 643 in 1907, 657 in 1908, 557 in 1909, 625 in 1910, 630 in 1911, 542 in 1912, 608 in 1913, 582 in 1914. One possible explanation for the stability of this figure lies in the fact that there was less insistence over time on baptism as a condition of intermarriage, notably when the bride was Jewish. A second lies in the slow, but steady spread of secularist views in all segments of the population, especially among the urban educated—the class German Jews were most likely to encounter socially.[167]

However these figures are read, they cannot be advanced as evidence

[166] Scholem, *From Berlin to Jerusalem*, 28.

[167] Source: J. Kreppel, *Juden und Judentum* (Vienna, 1925), 382, 388, 393. On the grimmest of all responses to the pain of accommodation and alienation, suicide, see below, p. 316.

of a community that was in any real sense at peace with itself and its surroundings. It is evident, too, that this restlessness had much to do with what can plausibly be offered as the central fact of socio-political life for German Jews, namely that in practice, and to some extent in theory as well, matters social and matters constitutional were interconnected and mutually reinforcing. Jews, that is to say, were regularly, disagreeably, and in a variety of ways reminded of what Rathenau had termed their status as 'second-class citizen[s from which] no skill or merit can ever free [them]'. They would hear this, of course, from fully established and identified anti-Semitic demagogues whom they had, perhaps, some reason to ignore. They might hear it *sotto voce* from their neighbours and colleagues. But they would hear it too from men of impeccable academic status and probity, who could not be ignored so easily. It needed an especially thick skin or a very high degree of general obtuseness not to take what was articulated at the University of Berlin, for example, as the settled view of the German social, political, and academic establishment at its most powerful and influential. Whence the importance—and for some the shock—of the direct, at times brutal, and thenceforward notorious pronouncements on the subject by Heinrich von Treitschke.

Treitschke was an academic historian of considerable renown, the author of what had become the standard, immensely influential history of modern Germany. His five volumes achieved a status that was not unlike that of Macaulay's *History of England* and his consequent prestige was at least analogous to that of Lord Macaulay the man. Both historians were engaged in accounting for, and celebrating, the rise of their respective countries to greatness. Both, that is to say, had written 'Whiggish' history. Both dabbled in politics; both had seats in their respective national parliaments; both had party-ideological affiliations. In their actual social and political outlook, on the other hand, Treitschke's narrow, self-congratulatory nationalism was a world away from Macaulay's genuine, open liberalism. And, unsurprisingly, their respective views on the specific matter of the Jews were entirely different.[168] Where, however, they were alike once more, was in their having extended into the contemporary arena and in relation to contemporary issues, each in his way, what had long been embedded in their historical writing. When, at the end of the 1870s, Treitschke, a long-time member of the Reichstag, decided to give public support to the views articulated in the Anti-Semitic Petition of 1880,[169] devoting special attention to the *contemporary* Jewish Question, much that he had to say could be traced to notions adumbrated in his historical works: his view that the entry of Jews into German public life was in the nature of an 'intrusion' (*Einbruch*), for

---

[168] An ardent supporter of Jewish emancipation, Macaulay had devoted his maiden speech in Parliament to the subject.
[169] See below, p. 267.

example.[170] Hence the weight attached to his pronouncements, over and above the plain circumstance that a man of high repute had gone out of his way to declare the organized waging of an anti-Semitic campaign no more and no less than a natural reaction of the authentic Germans to the active presence of 'a foreign element'. When he explicitly congratulated the German people on their instinctive perception of the 'grave danger' confronting it, the impact on respectable, educated, middle-class German Jewry could not have been, and indeed was not, other than deep dismay. It is true that Treitschke's uninhibited use of his professorial platform in Berlin to expound his views, along with the underlying nastiness of a good deal of what he had to say, would impel a body of his colleagues led by Theodor Mommsen, a greater historian than himself, to protest. It remains, that Treitschke's entry into the arena on the side of the anti-Semitic party, the occasional brilliance of some of his coinages ('The Jews are our misfortune') and the vulgarity of others, among them his notorious remark about multitudes of young trouser salesmen from Poland invading Germany, all left an indelible impression. It is also the case that his careful re-emphasis of the thesis that the Jews' complete integration and acceptance had always been and would long continue to be conditional upon their total abandonment of whatever elements of their original identity, particularity, and customs they had retained was neither original nor especially new. The same may be said of his stated view, that the Jews, with rare exceptions—Julius Stahl, for example[171]—had failed to meet the conditions set them; and that furthermore they were most probably incapable—probably inherently incapable—of doing so. What was new was the powerful thrust these theses were now given by virtue of their being affirmed *ex cathedra* by an academic of the first rank in a land and at a time that accorded such men extraordinary respect. And it was in the same unusually peremptory language that he informed his public of his major conclusion: it followed, he argued, that the Jews had forfeited their right to a voice in the national affairs of the country.

Among established academics who took it upon themselves to pronounce on these matters Treitschke was an especially fierce example, but he was not alone. Werner Sombart, an economic historian of somewhat lesser, but by no means negligible, renown, advanced the (ostensibly learned, if, in fact, implausible) argument, that the Jewish contribution to the economic growth and development of Europe through capitalism was fundamental. Where the Jews had come, there the sun shone and life sprouted, Sombart wrote. When they departed all thereupon decayed. The Jews' great talent was their ability to see the world rationally. Its

---

[170] Hans Liebeschütz, 'Treitschke and Mommsen on Jewry and Judaism', *LBIYB* 7 (London, 1962), 153–82.
[171] On Stahl, see above, p. 128f.

source was their religion.[172] In its way, this was intended as a compliment. But Sombart was also of the view that, while the legal equality of the Jews should not be impaired, it would be wisest for the Jews and very much better for all concerned if they refrained from asserting their participatory rights in German public life.

Most telling of all, however—certainly in retrospect, but also because it took the form of a public *attack* on Treitschke and because the intention *vis-à-vis* the Jews was not unfriendly—was the advice Theodor Mommsen thought it his duty to tender *all* varieties of German citizens in his celebrated article 'Auch ein Wort über unser Judenthum' ('Yet another word about our Jewry').[173] Mommsen's principal criticism of Treitschke was that he had demanded of the Jews that they *become* Germans. But 'they already are, as much as he [Treitschke] is or I myself,' Mommsen retorted. ('Sie sind es ja, so gut wie er und ich'.) Of course, there were differences between the Jewish Germans and other Germans. And the Jews did undoubtedly have their defects (*Fehler*). What the other Germans had no right to do—however justly they attributed these defects to the Jewish Germans—was to attempt to remove them from the ranks of the German people as a whole. The 'inequality . . . between the German Occidentals and Semitic blood [*der Ungleichheit . . . zwischen deutschen Occidentalen und semitischen Blut*]' must be considered and dealt with in very different terms and with 'greater clarity'. There would have to be 'some mutual accommodation between the tribes leading to the formation of a German nationality in which no single ethnic group will dominate' and it would have to be a process in which the great cities, Berlin before all, took the lead. It was true that 'the Jews have been active in this direction', but that, wrote Mommsen, 'does not appear to me to be a misfortune [as Treitschke believed], and in my view, Providence has understood better than Herr Stöcker[174] why it would be well if a few percentages of Israel were added to the German metal'.[175]

But Mommsen had a good deal to say *to* the Jews as well. It was only right and honourable that the principle of equality before the law should be maintained. We, the Germans, owed this to ourselves, he said, and to this duty the actual behaviour of the Jews was irrelevant. What could not be done, however, was to protect them from the feeling of alienation and

---

[172] Werner Sombart, *Die Juden und das Wirtschaftleben* (Leipzig, 1911), 24, 15. Cited in Pulzer, *Jews and the German State*, 9.

[173] Published in 1880. Text in Walter Boehlich (ed.), *Der Berliner Antisemitismusstreit* (Frankfurt-on-Main, 1965), 210–55.

[174] Adolf Stöcker, a pastor in the Evangelical Church, Court Preacher, orator, social worker, but passionate enemy of the Social Democrats, had sought to form a Christian workers' party. In 1879, his office of court chaplain notwithstanding, he added to his themes what would be a long-drawn-out attack on the intrusion of the Jews into German life in a form that was very similar to Treitschke's.

[175] Boehlich, *Berliner*, 218.

inequality that stemmed from the social attitudes of German Christians. It was true that there was an evident danger of a 'civil war' (*Bürgerkrieg*) being waged at some time in the future by the majority against the minority. It was also true, that 'Christianity' no longer meant what it once did. On the other hand it was the only term that comprehended modern international civilization. True, the Jews were under no obligation to make the break and accept it for themselves without reservation. They were fully entitled to retain their particularities if that was their choice. But they must know that if they did so, if, more particularly—for reasons of conscience, for example—they refused to renounce Judaism and accept Christianity in its place, why then they would have to bear the consequences. Mommsen left none in doubt about his own view of what constituted the correct choice. The Jews' continued separatism was an anachronistic remnant from the days of the 'protected Jews' (*eine Nachwirkung der Schutzjudenzeit*). 'If these secondary effects are to disappear on one side, they must disappear on the other side as well. There is indeed much to be done on either side. But admission into a great nation has its price [*der Eintritt in eine große Nation kostet seinen Preis*].'[176]

Some Jews were well satisfied by Mommsen's riposte to Treitschke. Berthold Auerbach believed that 'One can again be joyful to see that the cause of the Jews is not just theirs alone, but also the cause of freedom and humanity'.[177] And he was not totally mistaken. An Association for Defence Against anti-Semitism (Verein zur Abwehr des Antisemitismus) was founded in 1890 under prominent and predominantly gentile auspices. Mommsen was among the figures who subscribed to the Abwehr-Verein and, broadly, its approach was the one he had adumbrated in his response to Treitschke ten years earlier. But if many Jewish spirits had been warmed by the spectacle of one distinguished professor waging battle with another on their behalf, the fact that such a debate should have taken place at all in 1880 and would be kept up in various forms for many years thereafter served only to show that the old demand for an act of total cultural and historical self-abnegation by the Jews, far from fading in the course of time, was being asserted more vigorously than ever. Moreover, while the two professors had disagreed about the legitimacy or otherwise of anti-Semitism, Mommsen no less than Treitschke—each in his own way, of course—had made it his business to take the Jews themselves to task. And what was crucial and more than evident was that, major variations of style and minor variations of content apart, both had expressed what to all intents and purposes was the rationale underlying the Jewish policy of imperial Germany itself—that policy which the Reich's masters, most notably its Prussian masters, would have articulated themselves

---

[176] Boehlich, *Berliner*, 225.
[177] Rose, *Revolutionary Autisemitism*, 242.

had they ever felt the need to justify it publicly. To the fundamental question, whether it was conceivable that the Jews be reduced to something like their old status of frank, legal inferiority, both men had given an answer that was no better than a qualified no: Treitschke's qualifications being rather firmer than Mommsen's. What neither had denied, any more than any one else of major consequence or repute in modern Germany, was that the *status quo ante* was indeed at issue. As for authority itself, when the question was put to it directly, *its* answer turned out to be no better than muted. The Anti-Semitic Petition of 1880 (for which over a quarter of a million signatures had been collected) purported to turn on much the same point that Treitschke and, in his milder way, Mommsen too had made: the Jews' failure to keep their side of the bargain on which the emancipation, it was argued, had originally been based. The Jews had been given the opportunity to become Germans and they had not responded. In the case of the authors of the Anti-Semitic Petition this, to be sure, was mere demagogy. Their real claim—and here they differed somewhat from Treitschke and entirely from Mommsen and most of the other, as it were, respectable critics of Jewry—was that the Jews were *incapable* of doing so: incapable of honouring bargains, incapable of becoming decent Germans. It was for the government, therefore, to proceed to the abrogation of the legal equality that had mistakenly been granted the Jews, restrict or stop the immigration of Jews into Germany, and generally restore at least something like the *status quo ante*. Submitted to the Chancellor and Minister-President of Prussia (Bismarck), it elicited no response at all. When the Petition was debated in the Prussian parliament and the government asked to state its position, Bismarck chose to be absent and have the Vice-President of the Prussian Ministry of State respond. Count Otto zu Stolberg-Wernigerode then informed the deputies that the Ministry of State 'does not intend to advocate a change in the legal conditions or the existing legislation which declares equality of status among the religious denominations in civil matters'.[178] He was cheered. But the equivocal spirit in which the government approached the matter of the status of the Jews could hardly have been more effectively conveyed. Those who, in the face of the general *public* anti-Semitic offensive, had sought a counterbalance and solace of some sort from the *state* were implicitly informed that they were entitled only to marginal relief, if to any at all.

None doubted that, subject to these limits, the Jews of Germany had been granted freedoms of which their ancestors would not have dreamed and which all knew their brethren across the border within the Russian

---

[178] Stenographische Berichte über die Verhandlungen des preussischen Abgeordneten-hauses, 22 Nov. 1880, l, 227 ff. cited in Richard S. Levy, *The Downfall of the Anti-Semitic Political Parties in Imperial Germany* (New Haven and London, 1975), 131 f.

Empire, to say nothing of the Islamic lands, continued systematically to be denied. They had freedom of movement, freedom to enter the schools and universities, freedom to practice the liberal professions, freedom to engage in journalism and the arts, freedom to enter the world of politics, and, most famously—and some would say, most decisively of all—untrammelled economic freedom as well. By and large they had made the most of these opportunities: opportunities which those who were still embedded in the eastern, especially Polish regions of Greater Germany and Austria-Hungary (Posen, Silesia, and Galicia) were increasingly alert to and ever more anxious to enjoy. In sum, the pedlars had gone, as had the toll-gates; systematic police harassment was a thing of the past, at all events in Germany proper; and German Jewry, as we have already seen, had emerged as an increasingly urban, well-educated, quite solidly acculturated, and generally prosperous middle-class segment of the total population in ways that answered very well to the original late-eighteenth-century demand that their freedom be conditional on their being useful and respectable citizens. Objections to this process were voiced almost from the onset, as has been noted. As it progressed, so the objections became more strident, implicitly supported by the central circumstance that both the machinery of state and the upper reaches of the hierarchical social system remained closed to them, surrounded by a moat that no Jew, no matter how effectively acculturated, politically loyal, and in all the senses of the old Enlightenment term 'useful' was allowed to cross.

The technical-constitutional position was clear. The principle of full religious equality for all remained as laid down under the terms of the 1869 Law of the North German Confederation, adopted by and for the entire empire in 1871. It was the law's application by the state that continued, as before, to be highly unequal and restrictive both at the imperial or Reich level and at that of the component states: Prussia, first and foremost because it was of course much the largest and most powerful, followed by Bavaria, Hesse, Baden, the Free City of Hamburg, and so on down what was still a long list. There were slight variations from state to state, but overall the limits on the degree to which Jews might participate in the government and administration of the country were narrow everywhere, well defined, and zealously maintained. In Prussia they were enforced with much the same rigidity that characterized the Prussian aristocracy's and gentry's effort to preserve their mastery of the machinery of German government in all its ramifications. The prosecution service was closed to Jews from top to bottom. The highest ranks of the judiciary were closed too. At the lower ranks of the judiciary there had been some small relaxation in the course of time, but grudgingly, and regarded by some as fundamentally unsound and unwarranted. Catholic Bavaria, as it happens, was somewhat more even-handed: by the turn of the century three Jews had been admitted to the bench of high court judges and ten to the prosecution service. Baden was more liberal still.

Tenured Jewish university professors were exceedingly rare throughout Germany, but not for lack of candidate scholars. In 1909 Jews formed no less than 10 per cent of all *Privatdozenten*, the lowest rank, but only 7 per cent of the assistant professors and 2 per cent of the full professors. By 1917 the latter figure had been cut by half; and, notoriously, there were fields from which they were excluded entirely: German language and literature and classical philology. Many scholars of the utmost distinction remained junior professors to the end of their careers. Paul Ehrlich was not elected to a full professorship until six years after being awarded the Nobel prize, at the very end of his life, and that was at Frankfurt, unusually a non-state, substantially non-discriminating private university— unlike the University of Berlin where he had worked for the greater part of his life. Primary and secondary school teachers were rarer still: twelve Jewish secondary school teachers in the whole of Prussia in the final years of the empire, but then the idea of entrusting the education of Germany's children to Jews was unacceptable virtually everywhere, the relatively liberal city of Berlin being one of the few partial exceptions. No more than a handful of Jews could be found at the senior administrative level of government. There was a single case of a Jew holding ministerial rank in one of the lesser German states. There were no Jews at all in the Prussian and Reich administrations at their higher reaches; but the lower reaches— policemen, customs officers, and the like—were effectively closed to them as well. Of the diplomatic service there could be no question at all: a rule to which, however, there had been two exceptions in the course of time. Wilhelm Cahn, having served in the Bavarian legation in Paris before 1870 was admitted into the imperial Foreign Ministry after the establishment of the Reich. He served for a decade. He was not replaced. The exceedingly well-connected Albert von Goldschmidt-Rothschild, having been refused admission to the officer corps despite intense pressure exerted on his behalf by Reich Chancellor Bülow himself, was appointed an attaché at the German embassy in London.[179] The question facing all German Jews in one way or another—at all events in principle—remained. What was to be done? More pragmatically. What could be done? Should anything at all be attempted?

Of course, most German Jews, most of the time, went about their daily business without much more than an occasional thought, sour or otherwise, about the status allotted them by their masters. Virtually all accepted that they had a duty to themselves, to their families, and to other Jews too, to be on their best behaviour. The standard German model of civic propriety—authentic or otherwise, but certainly much trumpeted—namely that of the hard-working, law-abiding citizen who was all loyalty and modesty was one which Jews in Germany had no difficulty adopting for themselves. And for all their disappointments, it was not until the 1930s, as we shall see, that substantial numbers abandoned *all* hope that the process of equalization would be restarted at some time in the future and that one way or another matters would continue, if only erratically, to improve—if not in their own lifetime, then in that of their children. Even those in whom irritation or frustration at the indestructible combination of semi-officially tolerated anti-Semitism and officially and publicly established second-class status for themselves had bitten unusually deeply tended not to allow themselves to lose total confidence in the German state or nation. But unhappiness was rife. And here and there it took organizational shape.

Consider the grounds on which the first Jewish duelling fraternity was established at the University of Breslau in 1886. A little band of a dozen or so Jewish students had been infuriated by what confronted them upon admission to the university. Their complaint was that they were considered unfit to meet other, non-Jewish undergraduates on an equal social footing. The immediate, burning issue, grotesque in retrospect, but keenly felt at the time, was *Satisfactionsfähigkeit*. This had to do with honour, in practice whether the other, *non*-Jewish German students were prepared to fight any one of their Jewish fellows according to the elaborate rules and rituals that had been evolved in the duelling fraternities that had been formed in virtually all German universities in the course of the century. Increasingly, but most especially after the formation of the country-wide, explicitly anti-Semitic student association (Verein Deutscher Studenten) in 1881, the rule was that Jews were not *satisfactionsfähig* and were not to be admitted to the fraternities. Jewish students in Breslau, as elsewhere, were therefore apt to discover upon entry into what, on other grounds, were halls of genuine learning, that their upright Christian German fellows felt free to insult them publicly, that they frequently made it their business to do so, and that they then systematically refused to grant 'satisfaction' (i.e. a duel) to the offended Jew because he was inherently a degraded being.

The Jewish students in question drew up a manifesto. They declared that those who claimed that anti-Semitism was dying were mistaken. On the contrary, the anti-Semites had sown their seed and it has duly taken root throughout the German nation. 'No further cultivation is needed.' The result was manifest: 'We Jews are hated, despised, or at least looked upon as foreigners and not as equals by vast sections of the population.' Most painful of all to the student-authors was to see these same sentiments adopted by the educated classes. They noted too that when, as was the case from time to time, a Jew was accepted for membership in a fraternity it was either because he had hidden his origins or because there had been a conscious and deliberate decision to make an exception in his case. He had then to shun other Jews. The upshot for all was that they were required to accept the idea that to be of Jewish descent was to suffer an irreparable misfortune that needed to be 'endured with patience'. It was shameful and intolerable. It was not to be acquiesced in. On the contrary, the proper course was to 'raise the badge of independent Jewry'—in their particular case to set up a frankly Jewish fraternity that would meet the other students on equal ground.

They proceeded to do so. When 'satisfaction' was nevertheless continually denied, their counter-tactic was to pick quarrels with the other side, punch them, and when the Christian Germans involved still refused to ask for 'satisfaction' to march off the scene in manly triumph. But what this sad exercise in belligerence actually hinged on was an appeal to the better nature of the Germans. There was no question in the Breslau students' minds of a return to, or resurgence of, Jewish separatism. What they hoped for was that

By openly and courageously confessing their descent, the members of such an association [as they proposed to form] will teach their opponents a better opinion of the Jews. . . . The position which the Jewish minority holds within the Christian majority is the touchstone of a nation's nobility of character and civilization. It seems to be the mission of the Jews to teach the nation to which they belong respect for the convictions of others.[180]

It was a forlorn enterprise. The most common response among non-Jewish students was indignation or, at best, indifference. There was no question of a compromise. There would be no lowering of the banner of German exclusivity and inherent superiority. The university authorities, to whom the established fraternities protested, tended cautiously to come down on their side, not on that of the Jews. And while the campaign begun at Breslau 'openly and courageously [to] confess . . . descent' and follow it through with all deliberate pugnacity was taken up by some Jewish students elsewhere the number of those involved was tiny. In any given year in the last three or so decades before the First World War the total number of Jewish students in German universities who were prepared freely to identify themselves as Jewish has been estimated at c.2,000. Of these substantially less than 10 per cent went so far as to join one of the constituent fraternities of the two main country-wide associations of Jewish student societies that were established in due course.[181] And the

[180] Asch and Philippson, 'Self-Defence', 122–5.
[181] M. Zimmermann, 'Hashpaʿat ha-leʾumiyut ha-germanit ʿal ha-leʾumiyut ha-yehudit—irgunei ha-studentim ha-yehudiim be-germania be-reishit ha-meʾah ha-ʿesrim', *Zion*, 45, 4 (1980), 306–8.

most that can be said for their initiative was that it left a trace in the form of a small band of educated German Jews who continued to assert what they considered to be their *double* heritage and identity with some force and no apology—a trace, but no more.

For very many years the established and vastly more popular position had indeed been that there should be no pugnacity and no all-embracing, country-wide Jewish organizations, either of students or, indeed, of any other kind, no 'front' or lobby or party therefore to act on behalf of German Jewry as a whole, no systematic and organized promotion of its special interests and of its defence against attack. Any such body, it was reckoned, would run counter to the integrationist project and do no more than provide the anti-Semites with ready ammunition. It would in any case have proved exceedingly difficult to establish an all-embracing, representative organization of any kind in a post-emancipatory, ever more fragmented community of which the very term 'community' was rapidly losing such substance as it had ever had. Still, the noisy entry of declared anti-Semites into the major political arenas, their far from negligible success in getting their men elected to state parliaments and to the Reichstag itself, and their unremitting performance as highly vocal and energetic speakers for a single-issue political movement which all the relevant German governments were prepared at certain junctures to deal with could not fail to alarm. The result, early in the reign of the new Kaiser Wilhelm II, was a departure from the old rule, unwelcome to many Jews and to some minds dangerous: the establishment in 1893 of the carefully named Central Association of German Citizens of Jewish Faith (Centralverein deutscher Staatsbürger jüdischen Glaubens).[182] Its founders, all upper middle-class German Jews of impeccable professional and business standing, were far from being natural, public leaders of their people. Nor did they claim to be. The Centralverein (or CV) was not intended to be a formally representative body in the way the Board of Deputies of British Jews, for example, purported to be representative of Anglo-Jewry. It was closer in nature to what in our own times would be termed a lobby. It sought to counter the defamation of the Jews by sober and reliable presentation of the facts and to work for the defeat of anti-Semitic candidates for political office. But it was reluctant to take up a clear position of its own on social questions and for long was indecisive when it found itself in the invidious position of having to choose between an anti-Semite and a socialist: having to contemplate the election of the former in the event of failure to contribute what they could to the election of the latter. It took a full decade for the Centralverein to muster up the courage to lay down the rule that its members should in

---

[182] As the title of their association indicates, they did not consider themselves 'German Jews', but rather Germans of 'Jewish faith'.

all cases vote against an anti-Semite regardless of the likely upshot in the case of his defeat.

How successful the CV ever proved to be in the political arena is hard to judge. It has been estimated that it could, with reason, be said to have represented a membership of about one hundred thousand or, roughly, a fifth of all German Jewry, a substantial segment as such things went. But as members of the electorate their direct influence as electors could count for something only in a few of the major cities, the more so as they were not especially well supplied with funds. Where they did make a distinctive mark was in the effort to pin down and discredit anti-Semitic canards and, where anti-Semitic activists could be shown to have been guilty of defamation and other offences against the law, to appeal to the police, to the courts and, when possible, to the state governments directly to intervene. Their careful collection and publication of unsavoury data on the past careers of notable anti-Semitic candidates for office did put numbers of the latter out of public business for a while. Attempts to lobby the various government administrations directly in the matter of official discriminatory practices—refusal to accept qualified Jewish candidates for posts in government, for example—were necessarily more cautious. But if the results were meagre, they were not negligible. Set against the fall in appointments to senior university posts in the last decade or so before the First World War, there was an improvement in the matter of the judiciary that has been credited at least partly to the Centralverein.[183] Closest of all to the bone of the matter of collective action was the question whether the CV should go beyond support for anti-anti-Semites running for political office and support *Jewish* candidates as such. In the 1898 elections to the Prussian *Landtag* they did so; and again in 1903. Their support may not have been crucial, but that it should have been offered at all did indicate a small retreat from past positions and a notable access of daring. It did not go so far, however, as a determination to form a Jewish political party.

The idea of forming a distinctively Jewish party of some kind—one modelled, for example, on the Catholic Centre Party—was raised in the years leading up to the First World War, but never taken up very seriously, least of all by people who were of sufficient standing and influence in Jewry and in the country at large to be capable of doing so to some purpose. It was probably closest to maturation in 1906 when, under Chancellor Bülow, there loomed the danger of a broad political coalition directed against the Social Democrats and the Catholic Centre in which all other parties would participate. By this time German Jews were overwhelmingly middle class and anxiously, but genuinely patriotic. The parliamentary parties to which they tended to be most sympathetic and

[183] Levy, *Downfall*, 157–65; Pulzer, *Jews and the German State, passim.*

were most inclined to trust were the left-liberals of the Deutsche Freisin-
nige Partei (German Free Thought Party). But in the event of such a
coalition being formed, the left-liberals would have been in alliance with
parties hostile to the Jews; and Jewish voters would then have had to
choose between the allegedly unpatriotic 'reds' and 'blacks' on the one
hand and those parties in which anti-Semites of various orders of intensity and dedication were liable to make the running on the other. The
prospect was unpalatable. The question whether, as a way out, the Jews
should field candidates of their own was almost inevitable. There were
talks—held in great secrecy. Potential candidates were considered.
Unusually, the possibility of co-operation between the Zionists (who
were mostly favourable to the idea) and the leaders of the Centralverein
and other passionately anti-Zionist organizations was raised. But nothing
came of the idea, certainly not a plan. To go so far as to set up what a
German-Jewish periodical that had got wind of what was in the offing
quite correctly called the 'emerging political organization of German
Jews' would have been altogether too bold a step for people of consequence
to swallow, let alone to mount themselves of their own volition and on
their own responsibility. The notables who were indispensable to the plan
dropped out. The project was aborted.[184] It is only its hypothetical implications that remain of interest.

There were two main obstacles to such a project. Nothing could have
been more strikingly contrary to the fundamental principle on which
virtually all German Jews had now been brought up, even the ultra-
orthodox among them. This was that, however 'Jewishness' was conceived, it belonged to the private domain, a matter of home and
synagogue. In the public domain they were *Germans*. To promote the
entry of a distinctively Jewish party into the political arena was to erase
that distinction. It was true that taken all in all this was not a distinction
that the public at large or the governing authorities of the country
accepted, not as the CV in particular was accustomed to conceive it, at all
events. The German state cleaved implacably to rules of its own devising
in which the status of Jews as citizens of the second class could not have
been set and articulated more firmly and the public, by and large, followed when it did not actually applaud. Yet there was no escaping what
everyone knew, namely that emancipation had from the first been a
process promoted from above. It needed to be ordained, if it was to be
ordained at all, by government. In France the process had been relatively
swift and was now complete, at least on the face of things. So too, by a
somewhat meandering route, in Great Britain. In Russia there had never
been much prospect of such a process being mounted; it was shortly to be

---

[184] Jacob Toury, 'Organizational Problems of German Jewry', *LBIYB* 13 (London,
1968), 72–7.

clear that there was no prospect of such a development at all. In Germany, in contrast, it had had a beginning and had gone far. It had then stopped short. The Jewish view, instinctively but correctly, was that only state policy and authority could restart it. And only state authority, moreover, was likely to induce a corresponding change in public opinion, although that, at best, would only be over the long haul and very probably with limited results. The centrality of state action in the matter of the Jews was, of course, a universal phenomenon in all of modern Europe. But as an issue it was posed most strongly in Germany where strong anti-Jewish prejudice was of immensely long standing and the state of extraordinary authority and prestige.

It seemed to follow, therefore, that to improve their position and keep up the momentum of liberation it was necessary to fight the all-determining state. But this was precisely what German Jewry, taken as a whole, could under no circumstances afford to do. Were they seriously to attempt to do so, they would only discover what they knew intuitively to be the case, namely how slender and inadequate were such political weapons as they had to hand and how fragile was their position. They knew too, and their enemies knew, some intuitively, some by simple observation, that they were devoid of reliable allies in this or any other matter. The frankly radical opponents of the government were either the anti-Semites themselves or the socialists. The anti-Semites were their declared enemies. The socialists, as to some extent we have seen and we shall see again in further detail, might not in all cases be expressly hostile to Jewry, but were adamant in their refusal to accept the legitimacy of a distinctively Jewish social interest, much less a political one. All had to be subsumed under the general scheme of socio-economic class. The solution to such problems as the Jews might have would come with solutions to the general and fundamental problems of society as a whole. There would therefore be no aid for them on the left any more than on the nationalist right. But in any case, while rebellion against the total state system made sense of a rough sort in Russia, as we shall see, in Germany, for all but a tiny minority, it was unthinkable. The overwhelming majority of German Jews continued to see themselves as beneficiaries of the national political system as it had evolved since the Napoleonic wars. They wanted nothing better than to be part of *Germania* as they knew it, not to alter it or to flee it. In their eyes, the fundamental basis of the emancipatory process, even at its most imperfect, remained what it had always been. The state—however distantly and disappointingly—was friend, not foe. To lose the state was to lose everything—as time, of course, would show.

The second obstacle to collective political action lay in the continuing, crucial role played in all German Jewry's supra-communal affairs by their 'notables', which is to say, by those among them who were exceptionally wealthy or professionally and economically successful and who, none the less, continued actively to associate themselves with communal business. There was no consistory as in France, no equivalent to the Board of Deputies of British Jews, no Chief Rabbi (or *ḥakham bashi*) as in the Ottoman Empire, no uniquely privileged figure like Baron Horace Guenzburg in Russia whom lesser folk were content to accept as their commonly recognized lay leader, and, as it is almost needless to say, no Hasidic *rebbes* as in Poland or supreme scholarly rabbinic authorities as in Lithuania. The establishment of an elected *Judentag* or Jewish Diet was discussed from time to time, but the *Austrittsgesetz* of 1876, it was discovered, by removing the last formal boundary identifying and enclosing German Jews in a potentially structured world of their own had effectively put paid to any such scheme. After that date all individuals who wished to leave the legally established and recognized communities were free to do so without undergoing baptism; and all coherent groups who wished to form distinctive communities of their own apart from the established, legally recognized ones were free to do so too. Fragmentation was the positive order of the day, not structured cohesion. Over and beyond the matter of there being ever more sharply differing views on public affairs, there neither was, nor, it seems, could there easily have been organized, a systematic, reasonably democratic manner of ordering German Jewry's affairs.

Whenever an important Jewish matter of whatsoever kind is concerned [observed the *Israelitisches Gemeindeblatt* of Cologne in 1900], some members of the notability convene and arrive at a decision without much ado. An appeal to the public, a Jewish mass-meeting, are of the utmost rarity. Hence, all our Jewish organizations lack a broad and really democratic base. They consist of lawyers, physicians, bankers, industrialists, etc. The Jewish middle class, the big majority of the Jewish community, the small people, are kept entirely in the background.[185]

What remained for the disgruntled? They could go their own way: contributing further to the process of fragmentation. They could seek solace in those political activities or trends or parties that aimed at the total reform of the state after all, notably the socialists. But the difficulties were substantial. The socialists had been very successfully branded with the stigma of disloyalty to the German nation and state. Marxist socialism itself, as we shall see in greater detail below, implied that same abandonment of historic identity that even relatively friendly critics of the Jews had always demanded of them. The mechanism would differ. It would be dissolution by (and into) class rather than by and into church or nation. And impatience with the Jewish reluctance to evaporate was likely to be

---

[185] Cited in Toury, 'Organizational Problems', 67.

greater and the tone harsher than elsewhere. Why come to me with your special Jewish sorrows? was Rosa Luxemburg's response when asked to take a public stand on the persecution of Jews in eastern Europe. 'I feel just as sorry for the wretched Indian victims in Putamayo, the negroes in Africa. . . . I cannot find a special corner in my heart for the ghetto. I feel at home in the entire world wherever there are clouds and birds and human tears.'[186] The position was consistent with her pre-war attempt on behalf of the German Social Democratic Party (SPD) to draw the Polish working class in German-ruled Silesia away from the distinctively *Polish* Socialist Party (PPS) and persuade them to vote for the SPD in elections to the Reichstag on the grounds *inter alia* that the vision of Polish national-political revival was illusory. It was consistent too with her rigorous internationalism and her belief, as she told her German judges at her trial towards the end of the First World War, that her true fatherland was the working class.

But the real and, for great numbers of thoughtful German Jews, the starker alternative to acceptance of things as they were was of another kind. It was to draw the conclusion that, with all its benefits, the 'price' of emancipation (as Mommsen had put it) might be too high after all. If their integrity and dignity and much that they valued and believed in was to be preserved, it might be necessary to move in a totally different direction and to look a great deal more searchingly inwards than they had done in the recent past. Some did so; and the result, as we shall see, was that unexpectedly and to no small degree paradoxically it would be out of the German *Kulturbereich*, which is to say, not out of Germany alone, but out of that central European sphere in which Germany and Germandom were political and cultural leaders, that there would emerge the catalysts that would precipitate at least two of the more important of the movements that were to set modern Jewry politically, and to a marked extent culturally, in its definitive form. The intensely modernist and secular Zionist movement and the ultra-orthodox Agudat Yisrael were in virtually every respect at cross-purposes. But each in its singular way, as we shall see, sought to take the measure of an unhappy, imperfectly emancipated, imperfectly modernized, and severely disoriented segment of Jewry and to define and resolve the central dilemmas confronting it.

[186] Cited in J. P. Nettl, *Rosa Luxemburg*, ii (London, 1966), 860.

PART II

Aspirations and Equivocations

WITH hindsight, three dates may be invested with capital importance in the history of European Jewry in modern times: 1789, 1881, and 1933. The fall of the Bastille marks the point at which the long, final chapter of the history of the Jews of Europe begins in earnest. The seizure of power in Germany by the National Socialist party marks that at which the chapter draws to its end. The Great French Revolution and the Nazi *Machtergreifung* (or seizure of power) had this in common, however, that in each case the matter of the Jews was part of a vastly larger whole. For the men of 1789 and their immediate successors the impact upon the Jews of what they were about was incidental to their central purposes. It was an afterthought, initially unintended. For Hitler and his men and for the great majority of the vast numbers who followed them in Germany and elsewhere in Europe the matter of Jewry was, of course, much more closely bound up in their minds with their ambitions for Germany and its cognates and for themselves. It formed an essential part of the material out of which they had fashioned their springboard to power. It was integral to their philosophy, beliefs, and political outlook. Still, it was one item among others on the list of abominations that marks the history of Germany and its people between 1933 and 1945, even if the most horrible and, perhaps, the most revealing of the nature of the society the National Socialists had so successfully pulled together. In a shadowy and tragic way, 1789 and 1933 are therefore tied together—ostensibly against all logic and contrary to what each date would otherwise be taken to represent. One marks the beginning of the socio-historical process with which this study is concerned. The other marks its reversal and collapse.

The significance of 1881 is of a different order—as much in real terms as symbolically. The redirection of the general course of Russian history consequent on Alexander II's assassination and his son's accession on 1 March 1881 (OS) did not form a landmark of such supreme importance in the general historical evolution of Europe as a whole as did, each in their way, the events of 1789 in France and those of 1933 in Germany. And it is as a reversion to the political norm in Russia, not as a deviation from it, that the freshly invigorated spirit of harsh and heavy government under the new reign of Alexander III invites closest attention. For the Jews matters were otherwise, however. So far as they were (and are) concerned, the year 1881 marked a turning-point as significant in retrospect as 1789 and as sharp and dramatic and as fraught with initially incalculable but profound consequences as 1933—duly impressed upon their consciousness by a great wave of violence mounted against them at the time, but no less profoundly by what amounted to the first great internal social and political crisis in the modern era. If 1933 and the years immediately subsequent to it mark European Jewry's culminating agony, 1881 marks the first great milestone on the road towards it.

4

Movement

I

OGROMS were attacks by mobs composed preponderantly of peasants and urban workers (who were themselves mostly of recent peasant origin), unskilled as a rule, often unemployed, but laced, as often as not, with elements of the petty criminal class all of whom together were bound on pillage as much as on punishment of the Jews for whatever were supposed to be their historic, economic, or recent political misdeeds. The first of the series in Elizavetgrad in the Kherson *guberniya* (governorate) broke out on 15 April 1881 (OS). By the end of the year at least 200, but very likely 250 or more other Jewish communities in southern and south-western Russia had suffered some form of violent attack. The results were severe. Before the wave in its entirety had petered out tens of thousands of Jews, their houses and workshops sacked, found themselves homeless or without means of livelihood or both. The total value of property destroyed ran into several hundreds of millions of roubles. But worst of all were the human casualties: the dead, the wounded, the women raped, the traumatized. The incidence of violence against persons varied greatly from place to place. The number of the victims might add up to no more than a handful. In many cases there were none at all, only damage to property. In other cases the number of dead ran to several dozen. In the well-documented case of Balta in the Podolia governorate, when the Jewish community was attacked in a second wave of pogroms in the following year and the rioters had a free run of the Jewish quarter for three days between 10 and 12 April 1882, nine men and women were killed and over two hundred injured, some very severely. Damage to property was corres-pondingly immense. Close to a thousand homes and several hundred Jewish-owned shops, workshops, and taverns were destroyed. Above all there was the scene. 'What I saw [in Balta] defies description,' a journalist for the prestigious, once notably anti-Semitic Russian newspaper *Golos* reported. Of one great building on Bulvarnaya Street housing shops and residential apartments nothing remained but

heaps of debris of furniture, household utensils, and merchandise. I move on to a second building, then a third—the picture is the same everywhere! I go to other streets and find the same picture of devastation. It took me seven hours by the clock, walking and riding in my carriage, to traverse the most important parts of a town—in which, in one word, everything that had belonged to Jews had been demolished, destroyed, sacked. . . . Nothing remained standing other than the carcasses [of buildings], the walls and the roofs. . . . The entire Jewish population of Balta at this moment lacks clothing, furniture, beds, household utensils, crockery. The sacked homes are without windows, doors, and often without stoves. Most of the unfortunates were without food for two days until several casks of baked bread sent them from Odessa [had arrived].[1]

To all of which there needs to be added the terror and the humiliation suffered by those who had had to cower in cellars even when able, after a while, to emerge unscathed. Of the mood in Odessa—his own and that of his neighbours—M. L. Lilienblum[2] wrote in his diary on 5 May 1881:

It is as if we were besieged. The courtyard is bolted shut. . . . We sleep in our clothes . . . for fear that robbers will fall upon us and so that we can then quickly take the little children . . . and flee wherever the wind will carry us. But will they let us escape? . . . And will they pity the infants who do not yet know they are Jews, that they are unfortunate. . . . Till when, O God of Israel?[3]

In sum, the pogroms in southern Russia in the early 1880s were the Hep! Hep! riots of Germany in 1819 writ very large; and it is before all else because the wave was so large and because it extended over several years that there is much to account for and explain. Part of the explanation, but also part of the puzzle, lies in the fact that the civil and military authorities failed to maintain order and were exceedingly slack and in many cases positively reluctant to restore order once violence had erupted. Two full days and nights passed before troops were brought to Balta to put the rioters down and disperse them; and this was the pattern even in great cities like Kiev and Odessa, to say nothing of the lesser centres and the villages and Jewish townlets to which the violence spread as by infection. There were documented reports (but also many undocumented and plainly doubtful reports too) of the mobs having been egged on by 'outsiders', of handbills calling for an offensive against the Jews having been distributed, of early warnings of trouble ahead and rumours of hostile crowds gathering for an onslaught having been registered, and of worried communal representatives appealing to the authorities for protection well before any violence had actually taken place. There were cases of efforts by Jews to defend themselves in an organized fashion being systematically broken up by the troops or by the police and of punishment being meted out to them for their impudence. There were very numerous cases of perpetrators of violence—pogromshchiki—who had

---

[1] Cited in AIU, *Bulletin mensuel*, 4 (Apr. 1882), 69. For a Jewish eyewitness report of the pogrom season of the early 1880s, see, for example, P. Sonin, 'Vospominaniya o yuzhnorusskikh pogromakh 1881 goda', *Evreiskaya Starina*, 2 (1909).

[2] On Lilienblum see Chapter 5.

[3] Moshe Leib Lilienblum, *Ketavim otobiografiim*, ed. S. Breiman, ii (Jerusalem, 1970), 188.

been caught in the act, stopped, and arrested, being set free or dismissed after very summary justice and minimal sentences or none at all. In short, the one central, more than merely adequately documented feature of virtually all the pogroms in all the provinces of southern Russia and the Ukraine was the extreme weakness of the official response, the well-nigh universal refusal of the authorities to take steps to inhibit mob violence when it was impending, and, in very great numbers of cases, to stop it when it had already begun. Even when forces were finally sent to the scene they tended initially to be inadequate and to be concerned primarily to ensure that the violence did not spill over into non-Jewish quarters or, worse, degenerate into a generalized assault on property and property-holders of all kinds and on established authority as a whole and as such. And the entire, wretched pattern was capped in very many instances by the ultimate disgrace of the soldiers themselves—sent in, as often as not, when it had become evident both that something had to be done and that the police were too few and too infirm of purpose (or too embarrassed by the need to defend the Jews against their own countrymen) to do it—joining the mob and participating in the general merriment themselves.

What was it that had moved these crowds of mostly artless, illiterate, essentially leaderless men, normally quite peaceful and tractable in their daily conduct, to such behaviour? Was it no more than what had been embedded in them by their priests? Was it the well-nigh universal belief at all levels of Russian society that the Jews exploited the indigenous people of the country economically beyond all measure wherever they had been allowed to settle and had been given the slightest chance to do so? Was it the vaguer, brand-new, still more dangerous notion that the Jews were to be held responsible in some way not only for the current depressed state of economic affairs but for the political disarray and nervousness of the times and perhaps for the assassination of the Tsar as well? To none of these questions was any clear answer ever forthcoming or, indeed, possible. There did seem to be a proximate answer to the related question, how far in any particular case it was the immediate prospect of drink and plunder and the sudden, hugely inviting freedom to go after loot and generally run amok in a normally alien, daunting, chiefly urban environment that determined behaviour rather than any sort of deep-rooted, pent-up urge to wreak vengeance on the Jews for their supposed sins. Anecdotal evidence tends generally to suggest that it was the former rather than the latter that counted for most. The first outbreak in Elizavetgrad was therefore characteristic of those that followed not only by reason of its brutality and the initial indifference and weakness of the local police, but in the immediate precipitant having been a tavern brawl—the tavern, typically enough, being Jewish, the customer a Russian or a Ukrainian, and the time Easter. But something more urgent than loosely held religious and political opinions was needed to gather and energize a mob to such a point of ferocity and sustain it in its nastiness for two or even three days at a stretch—until sheer weariness had overtaken it and the police, or more often than not the army, had intervened in overwhelming force. That factor, evidently, was the prospect of loot and the joys of casting off all restraint. But even that could not be the whole of the answer.

One striking feature of the scene was the incidence of pogroms in the years 1881–4 being confined to the seven provinces of southern Russia and the Ukraine.[4] The Jews of Warsaw were attacked in December 1881, but otherwise the ten *gubernii* of Russian-ruled Poland were quiet, so too were Bessarabia and the six provinces of Belorussia and Lithuania,[5] all heavily populated by Jews. Was this by design? Were these regularities—a manifest breakdown of public order in one part of the Pale of Settlement, firm maintenance of order in the other—indicative of a guiding, hidden hand? Was there a conspiracy? If so, at what level of government had it been set in train? And most important of all, at what level of government had it been sanctioned? These questions and suspicions exercised observers and historians from the start. They have continued to do so to some extent ever since. The initial, unquestioned, slack response to violence in the streets, the seeming indifference to a hugely visible, not far short of generalized breakdown of public order seemed to require a better explanation than that of the (undoubted) inadequacy of the local police in virtually every case and the endemic inefficiency of the Russian administrative machine at all levels, but especially in the provinces. No regime, least of all one of the quality and habits of mind of the Russian Autocracy, can afford to stomach a collapse of order in the streets without fear of dire consequences for itself. Its failure to respond to what on any objective reading of the situation was a challenge to its own authority was tardy and pitiful. Could this be accounted for *except* by the assumption that it regarded the mobs as serving a purpose of its own devising? Certainly, the speed and confidence with which rioters were dispersed once a decision to do so had been taken and local ringleaders were arrested, charged, and in certain cases flogged or sent as convicts to Siberia when it had been decided that things were truly getting dangerously out of hand, served to confirm those who suspected design and intention to be at the root of the entire affair in their convictions. Such, famously, was the view of the doyen of early twentieth-century Jewish historians, S. M. Dubnov, and of many of his followers. Piecing the scattered evidence together, firm in their hatred of the regime and their intimate knowledge of Russian officialdom's set

---

[4] Kiev, Kherson, Ekaterinoslav, Poltava, Chernigov, Volhynia, and Podolia.
[5] Kovno, Vilna, Vitebsk, Grodno, Minsk, and Mogilev.

approach to the matter of the Jews, never doubting the immense power at the disposal of the Autocracy and its determination to maintain social control before all else when it chose to do so, they could hardly have come to any other conclusion. The plan or purpose or logic of the operation that they tended strongly to discern centred paradoxically on a growing fear at senior levels of the governmental machine lest a *loss* of social control, notably in southern Russia, be in prospect. The official establishment sensed the danger of some sort of rising or jacquerie of landless peasants accompanied by the new urban lumpenproletariat that was emerging in consequence of the hugely mismanaged emancipation of the serfs, the rise in both agrarian and urban unemployment, and in parts of the country actual famine. The assassination of the Tsar had revealed serious weaknesses in the state's security system. And if the danger of outright political collapse as a result of revolutionary action was not a very serious one at this stage, it was the case none the less that the revolutionaries had struck successfully at the very heart of the Autocracy. Finally, there was the consideration that many peasant minds may have been struck by the possibility that the death of the Tsar Emancipator could lead in some way to their own emancipation being reversed. Taken together, therefore, these were circumstances in which men who operated at a high level of government and who had been duly shocked and frightened by the assassination were sure to be casting about for an appropriate response. They had good reason to conclude that there was far too much explosive energy in the air about them, that it endangered them, and that it needed to be deflected into safer and, from their point of view, harmless channels. Why not channel it, they must have thought, towards the Jews?

But if none of this was inherently implausible, for none of it was there any direct evidence. And with much of the supporting, circumstantial evidence for the case against the Autocracy *as such* being (and remaining) rather weak, historians of a later generation have tended to discount the possibility of a conspiracy. That there was much sloth, confusion, numerous cases of civil and military authorities failing to co-operate effectively, and repeated misjudgement of the seriousness of the threat to public order and of the danger of it spreading by a process of infection from town to town—of all this there has never been any doubt at all. Nor is there any serious question of failure at the police level being compounded, and to some extent encouraged, by a section of the Russian press having turned violently against the Jews in the wake of the Tsar's assassination or, where the Jewish population was concerned, of the bureaucracy's set posture being one of ill will and disdain. But the notion that there had been a coherent plan of some sort; that the populace had been deliberately let loose upon the Jews; and that, in consequence, the pogroms of 1881 (let alone those that followed until this particular wave petered out some three years later) were met in St Petersburg and the major provincial capitals with winks of approval in high places —this has generally been discounted.[6] Much direct evidence points in the opposite direction. The new Tsar Alexander III was certainly not a man marked by the remotest sympathy for his Jewish subjects. His views were entirely conventional, reinforced under the influence of the arch-, deeply anti-Jewish ideologue of his regime, K. P. Pobedonostev, the *Ober-Prokuror* of the Holy Synod of the Russian Orthodox Church. But Alexander did display genuine dismay and dissatisfaction when reports of the weak and ineffective conduct of the security forces were brought to him; and fury when he learned of cases of military officers and men having actually joined the mob. *His* instructions were to deal firmly with rioters; to see to it that their leaders were severely flogged; and to make clear to the civil and military authorities alike that their business was to restore and maintain order before all else.[7] It is of some interest too that the Tsar himself and his new (more positively and aggressively anti-Semitic) minister of the interior N. P. Ignatiev as well, had themselves begun by looking for a hidden hand before being drawn, as we shall see, to more conventional conclusions about the sources of the violence. For them as for other 'believers in the basic goodness of the common folk, in the spread of enlightenment, and the artificiality of Judaeophobia, it was almost a necessity to accuse some outside agency' of responsibility for this 'outbreak of long-dormant "medieval" passions and hatreds among the Russian masses "who are, religiously speaking, a tolerant people and whose relations to the Jews have, on the whole, been marked with friendliness" '.[8] They suspected revolutionary agitators of responsibility for the outbreak—and not entirely without reason, as we shall see[9]—before coming round to the view that, as Tsar Alexander put it, it was all 'very sad, but I see no end to this: these Yids [*zhidy*] make themselves too

---

[6] The argument against conspiracy is admirably summed up by Hans Rogger, especially in 'Conclusion and Overview' in J. D. Klier, and S. Lambroza (eds.), *Pogroms: Anti-Jewish Violence in Modern Russian History* (Cambridge, 1992), 317 n. 2. But the evidence accompanying the earlier view that pointed to the regime's broad, culpable responsibility deserves attention. See, for example, S. M. Dubnov, 'Materialy, dokumenty i soobshcheniya: Anti-evreiskoe dvizhenie v Rossii v 1881 i 1882 g.', *Evreiskaya Starina*, 1, (1909), 88–109, 265–76; and E. Tcherikower, 'Homer hadash le-toldot ha-pera'ot berusiya be-reishit shenot ha-shemonim' in id., *Yehudim be-'itot mahapekha* (Tel-Aviv, 1957), 341–65. In orthodox circles there was barely any doubt at all regarding the government's culpability. See, for example, Ya'akov ha-Levi Lifschitz, *Zikhron Ya'akov*, 3 vols. (Kaunas, 1923–30, repr. Benei-Berak, 1968), iii. 18.

[7] I. M. Aronson, 'The Prospects for the Emancipation of Russian Jewry during the 1880s', *Slavonic and East European Review*, 55, 3 (1977), 351–2.

[8] Rogger, 'Conclusion and Overview', 317, quoting R. M. Kantor, 'Aleksandr III o evreiskikh pogromakh 1881–83 gg.', in *Evreiskaya Letopis'*, i (Petrograd-Moscow, 1923), 151.

[9] See Chapter 5.

loathsome [*slishkom oprotivli*] to Russians; and so long as they continue to exploit Christians this hatred will not diminish'.[10] All in all then, while much was murky in official Russia at this time, the grounds for positing a momentarily disoriented, intrinsically inefficacious government not so much stimulating as failing to cope with simmering, popular, general-ized discontent seem solid enough. In contrast, the case for positing a conspiracy is a deal weaker—except, no doubt, in Balzac's sense, that all power is in the nature of a permanent conspiracy.[11] In sum and alas for all concerned, the explosion was symptomatic of a permanent condition of social and political instability and would recur under the Romanovs and after them as well for roughly similar reasons and at ever higher levels of mindless and triumphant violence by some and suffering, danger, and fear for others.

What is not so simply accounted for is the depth and magnitude of the response to these events of the Jews themselves. This first great wave of pogroms in modern Russia was not, after all, entirely without precedent. There had been a serious pogrom in Odessa ten years earlier—localized and chiefly perpetrated by Greeks rather than by Russians or Ukrainians, but not materially different in form. It had lasted for four days, six persons had been killed, twenty-one wounded, some fifteen hundred homes, shops, workshops, and other places of business had been sacked. There had been one in Bessarabia in 1865. The pogroms of 1881–4 in southern Russia were themselves contemporary with anti-Jewish riots in West Prussia and Pomerania. The post-Napoleonic era had been ushered in, as we have seen, by riots in eastern France and in Germany. And the way in which riots had been dealt with in the Germanies in 1819 and, most especially, the way in which they had spread through central Europe by report and example and, as it were, contagion, anticipated the pattern of events of some sixty years later in Russia very remarkably. There would be a succession of especially violent anti-Jewish riots in Algeria (perpetrated by Europeans, not Arabs) through the last two decades of the century. And the nineteenth century would end in the early winter of 1899 with a full fortnight of what the London *Jewish Chronicle* primly described as 'excesses' in Bohemia and Moravia, per-fectly harmless and worthy Jewish subjects of the Habsburgs fleeing to the safety of famously anti-Semitic Vienna.[12] In sum, anti-Jewish riots consisting of violence against persons and the pillage and looting of their property—commonly termed *pogroms* in Russia, on some occasions *besporyadki* or *razgromi*, and elsewhere in some such term as 'disturbances' or 'disorder' or 'excesses' in whatever happened to be the relevant

---

[10] Kantor, 'Aleksandr III', 149–58, cited by Aronson, 'Prospects', 352.
[11] 'Tout pouvoir est une conspiration permanente' (*Sur Catherine de Médicis*).
[12] *Jewish Chronicle*, 1 Dec. 1899.

official language—had never ceased to be a feature of the lives of the Jews anywhere. The 1881–4 wave of pogroms in Russia was certainly the most severe and sustained that Europe had known for a very long time. But it cannot be said of it that it represented anything that was truly *foreign* to Jewish experience. Why then should it not have been slotted into place as one more, if greatly extended and intensified, instance of generalized nastiness?

The questions relating to responsibility for the outbreak and the inadequacy of the official response to it at the police level of affairs certainly counted for something. When anti-Jewish 'excesses' broke out in Bohemia and Moravia in 1899 Austrian troops and gendarmes were promptly despatched to the areas in question, arrests were made, justice was speedily meted out, and when it was discovered that Jewish children were being harassed at school the Habsburg Ministry of Education took steps to protect them. On the other hand, if, at ground level, in Russia itself, it cannot be said of the conduct of the authorities that it was other than disgraceful and disappointing, it was by no means out of known character. Again, the onslaught of 1881–4 could not fail to be seen as one of uncommon violence, extent, and duration. By the relatively civilized standards that still obtained in nineteenth-century Europe, even in Russia, it was therefore an altogether shocking affair. And it is, indeed, essential to an understanding of the trauma that minds—non-Jewish no less than Jewish—had grown unused to violence of such a nature and on such a scale and that some years would pass before observers—Jewish no less than non-Jewish—would tend to take such occurrences in their stride. On the other hand, while the memories of Jews were often long, they had been taught—and were accustomed—to accept afflictions of this kind quietistically on the whole, as events that needed so far as possible to be swept under the carpet of consciousness if life was to continue. Besides, where questions were posed, the only authoritative answer to be heard was one that had been cast in terms of a divinely ordained system of reward and punishment that led ultimately, but only ultimately, to final Redemption. The End of history was for God alone to define. Better therefore not to press the inquiry at all. Nevertheless if such had been the norm, it was soon evident on this occasion that the old, broad fatalism had lost something of its hold over the people who had been held in its thrall for so long. For remarkably, the pogroms were followed with very great rapidity by an entirely unprecedented movement both of ideas *and* of people, a movement in which independent, personal, secular volition replaced self-abnegation as the supreme determinant of conduct. There had been no precedent for such a transformation in the recorded history of the Jews in their Exile. Its effect would be to alter both the demographic structure and the general quality and direction of Jewish public life out of all recognition.

II

Broadly speaking, the special impact of the events of 1881–4 on the Jews
of Russia lay somewhat less with the blows delivered by the *pogromshchiki*
and the failure of the police and the army to offer a minimally decent gesture of protection than with what followed in the aftermath. Principally,
that is to say, it lay with the fact that the shock of the pogroms was almost
immediately compounded by an aftershock of new anti-Jewish administrative measures accompanied in turn by an official version of the events
cast in exceptionally hostile terms. Initially, the imperial government was
in two minds about what had occurred—and to some extent divided into
two parties. On the one hand it set itself to lay bare the roots of the problem that had given rise to the violence. On the other hand it wished to
take a stand of some kind, perhaps any kind, with minimal delay and
devise a policy for immediate implementation. Inspectors were sent out,
a Committee on the Jews was established at the Ministry of the Interior,
and committees of inquiry (*gubernskiye kommissii*) were appointed in
each of the governorates of which the Pale was composed under instruction
to report most particularly on those aspects of Jewish economic activity
that were to be considered 'especially dangerous' to the welfare of the
'indigenous population', on the measures needed to be taken to 'prevent
Jews from violating the law', and how an end was to be put to their evil
influence on those branches of the economy in which they were
engaged. In contrast, a body of a very different kind with very much
more serious purposes was established at the All-Russian level. This was
the State Commission for the Revision of the Current Laws Concerning
the Jews, known too as the Pahlen Commission after the longest-serving
and most influential of its chairmen, Count Konstantin Ivanovich
Pahlen, an official of great seniority and long service in the Ministry of
the Interior and as minister of justice. But the times were very different
from those in which the Committee on the Improvement of the Jews was
established under Alexander I.[13]

The provincial committees were so composed and their inquiries (when
these were taken at all seriously) conducted in such a way that their conclusions, besides being superficial and all but oblivious to the realities of
Jewish life in Tsarist Russia, could not fail to be other than profoundly hostile to the Jews.[14] Count Pahlen's Commission seems to have been
intended to be of genuine importance. It took its duty of inquiry very seriously, with little show of initial prejudice, and with as open a mind on the
subject of its investigations as could reasonably be expected of a group of
senior members of the official hierarchy in the early 1880s. But, inexorably, it found itself engaged on yet another exercise in the perennial

---

[13] See Chapter 1.   [14] See Dubnov, 'Materialy', 99 ff.

attempt to square the fact of a large Jewish presence in Russia with what the Autocracy conceived to be the only proper quality and composition of the society which it sought to rule: a hopeless task and one which soon turned out to be irrelevant to the events that had prompted its establishment. It was only set up, moreover, after a delay of just under two years after the initial outbreak at Easter 1881. The best that could be said of its labours was that it sought an approach that was founded on some regard for natural justice as well as being workable in practice. When it submitted its report five years later, Pahlen and the rather more liberal majority of Commission members were frank enough to recognize the truth to which so many of their predecessors (most notably those of the Committee on the Improvement of the Jews of 1804) had unfailingly been drawn, namely that

Without granting [the Jew] equal rights, we cannot, properly speaking, demand of him civic obligations. . . . It is therefore not surprising that the Jews, trained in the spirit of a century-long repressive legislation, have remained in the category of those subjects who are less exact in the discharge of their civic duty, who shirk their obligations towards the State, and do not join fully in Russian life. No less than six hundred and fifty restrictive laws directed against the Jews may be enumerated in the Russian Code, and the discriminations and disabilities implied in these laws are such that they have naturally resulted until now in making the life of an enormous majority of the Jews in Russia exceedingly onerous.[15]

However, official minds had been made up on all the essential issues long before the Pahlen Commission could possibly have produced its report. Firmly, and irreversibly, the government was already set in a direction that was diametrically opposed to what its own most serious and prestigious commission of inquiry would eventually tend—however apologetically and laboriously—to recommend. Its position, taken with great rapidity, was founded on the basis of a three-part combination of outright hostility to Jews, absolute refusal to accept that, individual malefactors apart, either Russian society or the Russian government bore even so much as an indirect and unintentional responsibility for what had happened, and the conviction that it would be highly impolitic and eccentric to appear in any way to favour the Jews. At an informal and to some extent grass-roots level its approach was epitomized in the conduct and, still more, the language of the governor of Odessa. Having first been marginally more energetic in defence of local Jews than some of his colleagues, notably his colleague in Kiev, he instructed his minions to make certain that along with the actual rioters arrested and tried in the course of the effort to restore order substantial numbers of Jews were flogged and otherwise punished as well. When representatives of the community remonstrated, the governor explained, that

---

[15] Cited in S. M. Dubnov, *History of the Jews in Russia and Poland* (Philadelphia, 1916–20), ii. 364 (slightly amended).

I caused the Jews to be flogged in order to quiet the people; and ordered the Jews to be shipped to sea in the company of 800 of the prisoners implicated in the riots in order to show that I do not favour the Jews. . . . It would be madness on my part to show any sympathy for the Jews since they drain the blood of the Christians. I do not blame the Christians in the least for having attacked you: you fully deserve it. I am convinced the Emperor holds the same opinion.[16]

And indeed this did not differ materially from the view of the emperor. When a delegation of Jewish notables, after long delay, was finally accorded an audience of the Tsar to ask for protection for their people and generally plead the cause of the Jews he turned them down flatly. Their request that he scotch the rumours that Jews had been closely involved in the assassination of his predecessor and that he himself had ordered their punishment was refused. Instead he lectured them on their people's iniquities for much of the twenty minutes he had granted them and then had them dismissed. The imperial logic was clear. The Tsar had been greatly disturbed by the pogroms on general law and order grounds, as well he might have been, but he was no more prepared than were any of his officials to appear as a 'protector' of the Jews. And, after consideration, the early tendency to ascribe the pogroms to 'anarchists' and to revolutionaries and explain the attack on the Jews as part of an effort to undermine the regime generally was allowed to fade lest it be implied that there was a deal of tinder available to the revolutionaries to ignite, that the true roots of disorders lay in widespread, if generally inarticulate, discontent with the social and political order as a whole, and therefore ultimately with the Autocracy itself. This was not a line of reasoning that the Tsar and his principal minions were prepared to countenance. Much the simpler line to take, and to cleave to, was that blame lay with the Jews themselves, hated for their excessive economic power and for their habitual and unjust exploitation of the country's other inhabitants. In sum, the turn taken by events demonstrated beyond all possible doubt that the relatively liberal period inaugurated by Alexander II for all of Russia, and for the Jews among his other subjects as well, had ended. The reversal was not total. The horrors of extended military service under the cantonist regime, abolished under Alexander II, were not reinstituted. Jews continued to be allowed to attend Russian state schools and universities, although, that said, a rigorous quota system (unknown even under Nicholas I) limiting their entry was introduced some years later. The moderate easing of the residence restrictions that had occurred under the Tsar Emancipator was not wholly or suddenly reversed in all its particulars. But the Pale of Settlement as the foundation of Jewish life in the Russian Empire, the basis and symbol of their unequal status, was maintained and an entirely fresh series of laws, rules, and regulations, the

---

[16] *Jewish Chronicle*, 17 Nov. 1882.

common purpose of which was further to constrain and confine the Jews within stated territorial and professional spaces, was now inaugurated.

Some regulations were petty; some were exceptionally offensive. On 30 January 1882 it was decreed that Jewish artisans who had previously been allowed to live and work outside the Pale would no longer enjoy that privilege where they operated *machinery*—on the grounds that the term 'handicraft' had to be understood literally as implying manual labour exclusively. On 15 March of that year it was decreed that no Jew might be elected from that time on to the board of an orphan asylum. On 10 April the proportion of Jewish military surgeons was reduced and set at a maximum of 5 per cent. Ten days later Jews were formally forbidden to manufacture or sell icons, crosses, and other objects of Christian piety. Later church candles were added to the list of items Jews were to be prevented, presumably, from defiling. But it was the set of 'Temporary' Regulations (commonly known as the 'May Laws'), proposed by the minister of the interior, Count N. P. Ignatiev, and whittled down somewhat by the Council of Ministers, but promulgated in due form on 3 May 1882 that, taken together, constituted much the most striking item of the series. Nominally, these were no more than a set of temporary measures enacted in anticipation of a general revision of the status and rights of the Jews in the empire. In practice, no such revision was ever undertaken and the 'May Laws' remained in force, subject to minor amendment from time to time, to the end. The central clause of the Temporary Regulations provided that 'Until further orders, the execution of deeds of sale and mortgages in the names of Jews is forbidden, as is the registration of Jews as lessees of real estate outside towns and townlets and the grant to Jews of powers of stewardship or attorney to manage and dispose of such real property.' The obvious intention underlying this convoluted language was to make it increasingly difficult, ultimately all but impossible, for Jews to live and work in the *rural* areas of the Pale—which is to say, of course, in much the greater part of it. Its practical effect would be to crowd them into the towns without regard to real possibilities for employment and housing and to separate them to a very great extent from those with whom they had traditionally traded and for whom they had long provided various commercial services. Moreover, as would soon be apparent, under cover of this regulation Jews would not only be prevented from settling in the countryside, but every possible excuse would be employed to eject even those who had long been settled there: a return from an extended journey could, if the police so wished, be regarded as taking up residence afresh and therefore placed under the ban. For the rest, a giant step had been taken towards the further impoverishment of the greater part of the Jewish population.

The May Laws reflected with the utmost clarity the long-standing desire of those who had served the Autocracy as its ideologues in these

matters from time to time—Derzhavin among them, of course—to separate the Jews from the peasantry and so protect the latter from the harm
supposedly done them by the former. But they proved to be the corner-
stone of an entire system. They were followed regularly, year after year, by
other items of anti-Jewish legislation. Some were promulgated to clear-
up ambiguities in the central provision of the May Laws: the ruling, for
example, that a Jew who had retained the legal right to inhabit a particular village did *not* for that reason have the right to move to another village
(29 December 1887). Some were designed to reduce what had long been
the accepted classes of privileged Jews: where the right of domicile in all
parts of Russia had once been the privilege of all discharged soldiers,
henceforth it would be limited to those who had served only under the
old and terrible conscription system associated with the reign of Nicholas I.
Those who had served under the reformed system inaugurated under
Alexander II in 1874 would, on completion of their service, no matter
how meritoriously performed, be obliged to return to the Pale (11 November 1885). It was an ever-expanding list. The rights, duties, professional functions, residence, and terms of employment of midwives and
lawyers, distillers and tavern-keepers, apothecaries and stockbrokers,
domestic servants and political exiles, military conscripts and jurymen,
schoolboys and university students, holders of foreign university degrees
and merchants of the first (privileged) guild—were from this time on
subject to ever more restrictive regulation. The legislation would be
accompanied irregularly, but far from infrequently, by measures of
enforcement, namely by inspections, razzias, expulsions, and whatever
else the regime at any particular time considered condign punishment in
the event of infraction. And the entire enterprise was informed and
inflamed not only by ancient, Christian religious objection to—not to
say horror of—Jewry, but the belief, at all events the repeated assertion,
that the presence of the Jews in the land was not only an offence to its
indigenous population, but a part—indeed, a very great part—of the
explanation of Russia's misery.

There was also in all of this an extreme, patently dishonest (even if in
many cases unthinking) application of the thesis that commerce verges
on—if it does not actually blend with—the criminal. It was dishonest
because there was no question of the thesis being applied to non-Jews. It
was absurd in that it was not applied with special force, if at all, to the privileged and affluent among the Jews, but extended vigorously to the meanest Jewish craftsmen and shop- and tavern-keepers. Nor was any valid
evidence to the effect that the Russian peasantry and urban proletariat had
benefited, or were ever likely to benefit, from the extrusion and impoverishment of their Jewish neighbours ever adduced. What is chiefly evident—and plain enough to observers of all origins and rank at the
time—was that, taken together, the effect of the various measures

designed to tighten the regime to which they were subject contributed vastly to their further impoverishment and to the shattering of the optimism that had seized many of the modernists in Russian Jewry once the terrible years under Nicholas I had passed. The Autocracy's policy had been rendered sharper, harsher, more punishing, less ambiguous, altogether nastier, and certainly more explicit than ever before. It would be given public expression unashamedly, without embarrassment, if anything rather proudly and complacently—the more so as in what for these purposes may be termed Konstantin Pobedonostev's Russia the last traces of Enlightenment influence and thinking were rapidly evaporating. It would be very much more difficult from this time on for any Jew in or out of Russia to write, let alone think of the empire as it now stood in the terms the Hebrew poet Yehuda Leib Gordon had chosen to write of it a generation earlier, namely as a 'land of Eden', 'open' to its Jews, a land whose 'sons now call [the Jews] "brothers" ' and from whom the Jews themselves should no longer stand apart.[17] The clearest of all messages conveyed to those who were disposed to listen was that the Autocracy no longer regarded itself as having any serious responsibility for the lives and well-being of its Jewish subjects. No concern for the ordinary Jew's ability to earn a minimally decent living for himself and his family would trouble its collective mind or deflect it from its course. From top to bottom, with the rarest of individual, local exceptions, it would proceed to demonstrate as never before its long-established and for the Jews themselves dangerous ambivalence in all that concerned them: unforgiving hostility mitigated, in the final analysis, only by its concern to safeguard ultimate social control and as much as might prove possible of the essential structure of a *Rechtsstaat*. The attempt that had begun under Nicholas I to transform and generally interfere with the lives of its Jewish subjects had been given up. What faced them from this point on was an ever more determined and deliberate consolidation of a system of deliberate oppression, the qualities and infamies of which had something in common with those Edmund Burke had ascribed to the penal laws to which the Irish had been subjected a century and more earlier: 'A machine of wise and elaborate contrivance, and as well fitted for the oppression, impoverishment, and degradation of a people, and the debasement, in them, of human nature itself, as ever proceeded from the perverted ingenuity of man.'[18] But it was in another respect that the affairs of the Irish and the Jews chanced to run most closely parallel to each other. Both were nations

---

[17] 'Hakiẓa ʿami' ('Awake my people'), 1863.

[18] There are other curious and instructive analogies to be discovered when the Irish and Jewish experiences are compared, but only Conor Cruise O'Brien (from whose book *The Great Melody: A Thematic Biography and Commented Anthology of Edmund Burke* (London, 1992), 480, this quotation has been taken) has seemed to be fully aware of them. It is surely an Irishman's intuitive understanding of the Jewish-Israeli predicament that makes

whose response to harsh conditions led to spontaneous emigration on an extraordinarily large scale. In each case, in consequence of this migration, respective national demographic and cultural maps would change out of all recognition. In neither case can the subsequent social and political evolution of either people be fully accounted for without careful attention being paid to the vast movement of population each had undergone.

III

Who were the migrants? A mass of statistical material is available to form the basis for an answer to the question.[19] Not all of it is of adequate accuracy and such sets of figures as appear to be of tolerable reliability are not always strictly and precisely compatible. The best figures for the Jewish population within the Russian Empire towards the end of the nineteenth century are those provided by the Imperial Russian census of 1897. Precise figures on emigration out of Russia are unobtainable, however. The Russian authorities kept no tally. Nor did all the relevant authorities in the countries through which and to which migrants travelled. Where a tally was kept it was not always done for the entire period in question at this stage, namely 1881–1914. The best, most revealing, and historically most important figures are those for immigration, more exactly actual admission into the United States (along with figures for the rejection of potential migrants at American ports of entry). But again, precise figures for *Jewish* immigration into the United States are not available for the years prior to 1899—when a formal distinction between Jews (termed 'Hebrews') and non-Jews from Russia, Romania, Austria, and so forth

his earlier work *The Siege: the Story of Israel and Zionism* (1986) much the best book on the subject to be written by one fortunate enough (in this case) to be an outsider.

[19] The statistical data that follow in this section and in Section IV have been abstracted, collated, and extrapolated principally from the following sources: S. Adler-Rudel, *Ostjuden in Deutschland 1880–1940* (Tübingen, 1959); *Encyclopaedia Judaica*, xvi (Jerusalem, 1971), cols. 1518–29; A. Ginzburg, 'Emigratsia evreev iz Rossii', in *Evreiskaya Entsiklopediya*, xvi, cols. 264–8; Hebrew Sheltering and Immigrant Aid Society, *Third Annual Report* (New York, 1911); L. Hersch, *Le Juif errant d'aujourd'hui: étude sur l'émigration des Israélites de l'Europe orientale aux Etats-Unis de l'Amérique du Nord* (Paris, 1913); *Jewish Immigrants: Report of a Special Committee of the National Jewish Immigration Council appointed to examine . . . illiteracy among Jewish immigrants and its causes*, US Senate Document No. 611, 63rd Congress (Washington, 1914); S. Katzenelenbogen, *L'Émigration juive* (Brussels, 1918); I. M. Rubinow, *Economic Condition of the Jews in Russia* (Washington, 1907; repr. New York, 1975) (useful for its provision of essential extracts from the imperial Russian census of 1897); the Imperial Russian Census of 1897: *Pervaya Vseobshchaya Perepis' Naseleniia Rossiiskoi Imperii 1897 g., Obshchii Svod. i–ii* (St Petersburg, 1905); the Annual Reports of the US Commissioner-General of Immigration; Zentralwohlfahrtsstelle der deutschen Juden, *Jüdische Bevölkerungspolitik* (Berlin, 1929); Felix A. Theilhaber, *Der Untergang der deutschen Juden* (Munich, 1911); Jack Wertheimer, *Unwelcome Strangers: East European Jews in Imperial Germany* (New York, 1987).

was first drawn. Figures from Jewish sources tend to be still less comprehensive: it needs to be borne in mind that the migration from Russia was
for all practical purposes unorganized (leaving aside the moderate assistance provided emigrants by Jewish philanthropic societies in Germany,
Great Britain, and elsewhere *en route*). It was a matter of a vast host of
individuals taking individual decisions on a basis, in most cases, of *sauve
qui peut*. The same may be said of the less dramatic, but parallel, contemporary, in some ways analogous and in any event very substantial streams
of emigrants out of Austrian-ruled Poland (Galicia) and Romania. But if
the detail is often lacking, the outlines and main features of the migration
of the Jews westwards are clear. In one sense, it was part of the very much
greater, general migratory stream from east to west that was in progress
from land to land within Europe itself to some extent, but more especially
and much more massively out of eastern *and* western Europe altogether
that was so striking a feature of the nineteenth century and the early years
of the twentieth. In another sense, its special features and its sheer intensity distinguish it from almost all the rest, as we shall see.

   Two aspects of the whole are paramount: the sharp rise in the absolute
numbers of Jews leaving Europe, especially eastern Europe, after 1881;
and the fact that while there were substantial variations from year to year,
a very high rate of emigration—so high that it cannot be fairly described
as anything but mass flight—was maintained without interruption until
the outbreak of the First World War. In the four decades 1840–80 some
200,000 European Jews migrated overseas. Between 1881 and 1914 well
over ten times that number—the estimates vary between 2.4 and 2.7
million—moved out of Europe to North and South America, South
Africa, Palestine, and the Antipodes. When to this enormous figure are
added the great numbers of eastern European Jews going no further than
western Europe (at least 100,000 settling in Great Britain alone in this
period) it is apparent that despite the moral and physical hardships that
migration inexorably imposes on those who undertake it even in the best
of times, and for all that the emigrants were under no specific external
compulsion to leave, a quarter of the entire Jewish people chose to evacuate
their homes in the course of a little under three and a half decades.[20]

   The common estimate for the total world Jewish population at the
turn of the century—by which time the migration from Europe was well
in train and had taken on a certain regularity—is *c*.11,000,000. Of these,
c.9,000,000 were still in Europe, 1,100,000 were already in the Americas

---

[20] No precise figures for the overall distribution of migrants by countries of ultimate
residence are available, but a fair idea of the trend is provided by figures compiled by one of
the Jewish philanthropic organizations of the time, the ICA, for 1910 in respect of emigrants
from Russia. Their destinations in percentages of the total were: Argentina: 9.7; Canada:
2.8; other European countries, but Great Britain especially: 2.5; Palestine: 1.9; South Africa:
0.8; other countries: 0.5. All the rest, 81.8 per cent, travelled to the United States.

(the majority being recent arrivals from Europe), 700–800,000 were in Asia, Africa, and Australia (the latter of European origin). The migrants were overwhelmingly from eastern Europe. So were the Jews of Europe as a whole: the Jewish populations of Russia, Austria–Hungary, and Romania comprised over five-sixths of all European Jewry between them. The Jewish population of the Russian Empire alone numbered 5.2 million. It accounted for 5 per cent of the total population of European Russia, 4.2 per cent of the total population of the entire empire, and no less than 11.5 per cent (4.9 million) of the provinces comprising the Pale of Jewish Settlement specifically.[21] It followed that the Jewish population confined within the Pale of Settlement constituted over half of the total Jewish population of Europe and approximately 45 per cent of the Jewish people worldwide.

The Jewish population of Austria–Hungary at this time (c.1900), the second great concentration, amounted to 1.2 million in the Austrian lands, 0.85 million in Greater Hungary: accordingly some 2,000,000 altogether or 4.6 per cent of the total population of the Habsburg Empire. The 811,000 souls, three-quarters of Austrian-ruled Jews, to be found in Galicia alone (11 per cent of the total population of the province) may be seen as 'Polish', close kin in almost every significant socio-economic respect to their brethren in 'Congress' (i.e. Russian-ruled) Poland rather than to the substantially Germanized, rapidly modernizing Jews of Bohemia and what would now be termed Austria proper. In the single and famously multinational, multicultural province of Bukovina, 13 per cent of the population (95,000) was Jewish. The number of Jews in Romania has been much debated. Officially it stood at c.250,000, but it may have been substantially larger.

It is against these absolute figures, but still more these proportions and this distribution that the scale and rapidity of the migration is best seen. In the course of the twelve years 1899–1910 no less than three-quarters of a million Jews migrated to the United States from Russia alone: one-seventh of the total Jewish population of the empire at an average rate of some 65,000 per annum. In absolute and relative terms, the migration from Hungary was smaller: a total of 180,000 for the same period, or just under one-tenth of the total Jewish population in question, at an average of 15,000 per annum. It is of interest and great importance too, that, despite the losses due to the huge and regular migration, the Jewish

---

[21] Strictly speaking, a distinction needs to be drawn between the ten provinces of the kingdom of Poland (in which Jews accounted for 1.3 million souls or 14.1 per cent of the population) and the fifteen provinces of the Pale of Settlement proper (in which Jews accounted for 3.6 million souls or 10.9 per cent of the population). However, the differences, so far as the Jews were concerned, between Congress Poland and the western provinces of Russia were minimal by the end of the century and it is convenient and not significantly inaccurate to refer to all twenty-five provinces as the 'Pale'.

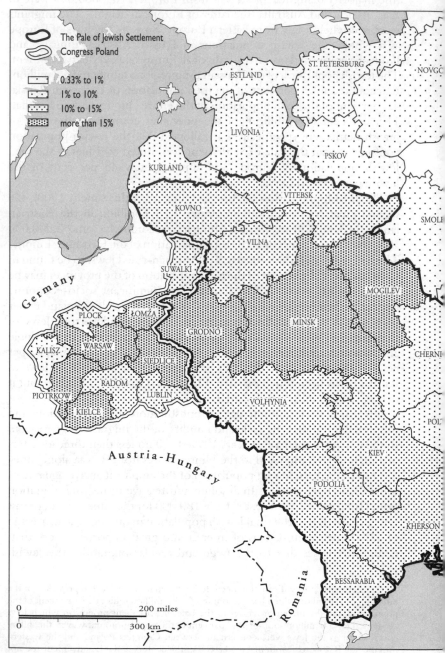

MAP 1. The Jewish population of the Russian Empire in 1897

Jewish population in absolute
numbers and as a proportion of
the general population

*a. The fifteen provinces of the Pale of Jewish
Settlement*

		%
Bessarabia	225,637	11.65
Chernigov	114,630	4.99
Grodno	276,874	17.28
Kherson	337,282	12.32
Kiev	427,863	12.03
Kovno	212,230	13.71
Minsk	338,657	15.77
Mogilev	201,301	11.92
Podolia	366,597	12.15
Poltava	111,417	4.02
Taurida	66,125	4.57
Vilna	205,261	12.90
Vitebsk	175,678	11.80
Volhynia	397,772	13.31
Yekaterinoslav	100,736	4.77

*b. The ten provinces of Russian-ruled
Congress Poland*

		%
Kalisz	72,339	8.59
Kielce	82,427	10.82
Łomźa	90,912	15.69
Lublin	153,728	13.26
Piotrkow	222,229	15.83
Plock	50,473	9.13
Radom	113,277	13.89
Siedlice	122,370	15.84
Suwałki	58,808	10.09
Warsaw	349,943	18.12

*c. Ten provinces beyond the Pale with a
Jewish population of 0.33% or more
of the total*

		%
Don Mil. Dist.	15,440	0.60
Estland	1,396	0.33
Kharkov	13,725	0.55
Kurland	49,313	7.33
Livonia	28,654	2.24
Moscow	8,749	0.36
Novgorod	4,740	0.35
Pskov	6,454	0.58
St Petersburg	21,270	1.01
Smolensk	10,496	0.69

*Total Jewish population of the European
provinces of the Russian Empire:*
          5,082,342   5.44%

population in eastern Europe continued to rise. In the 15 *gubernii* of the Russian Pale (i.e. not counting Congress Poland) it rose from an estimated 1.0 million in 1847 to 2.9 million in 1881 to 3.6 in 1897—an increase of 260 per cent in the course of fifty years and of 24 per cent in a period of 16 years of heavy emigration. The Jewish population of Austrian-ruled Galicia (whence emigration was substantial, but never at the Russian rate) stood at 700,000 in 1880 and 870,000 in 1910—an increase of 25 per cent in thirty years. At no time, therefore did the rate of emigration exceed the rate of natural increase.

In rough socio-economic terms the migrants were of a piece with the broadest, most impoverished strata of east European Jewry: they tended overwhelmingly, although never exclusively, to be the less skilled, the less well educated, and altogether the less well established. It was certainly the less acculturated or Russified, who tended most strongly to leave Russian territory, the less Polonized to leave Poland, the less Germanized or Polonized to leave Galicia, and so on. But then the professional class in Russo-Polish Jewry, even on a very wide interpretation of the term (so as to include rabbis and schoolmasters, for example), was an exceedingly small one. It was slightly larger, proportionately, than that of the population of the Russian Empire as a whole which, as might be expected considering that a good 60 per cent of the non-Jewish population was engaged in agriculture alone, was smaller still, but small all the same: some 5 per cent of all Jews who were gainfully employed, according to the imperial census-takers of 1897. However, when the occupational structure of those who had gone so far as to pull up such stakes as they had in Russia and Poland and emigrate overseas is compared with the overall occupational structure of Russian Jewry itself, it is evident that the emigrants stemmed disproportionately from its poorest and less skilled sectors. Contrariwise, as can be seen in Table 4.1, Russian Jews of whom it is reasonable to surmise that they were in relatively comfortable circumstances tended strongly to stay put—among them those the census-takers classed as 'clergy', which is to say rabbis and others who performed religious (or synagogue) functions of one kind or another.

However, because the truly salient feature of eastern European Jewry (its steady increase in absolute numbers apart) was of a people plagued by endemic and ever deepening poverty, the emigrants presented a telling picture of what they were leaving behind. A substantial fraction of the Jewish population of imperial Russia was to all intents and purposes outside the working population altogether. In some communities the pauperized—meaning those devoid of skills, resources, and specific occupations and largely or even wholly dependent on charity—might form as much as 40–50 per cent of the population. It has been said of the endemic poverty of the Jews of eastern Europe with great truth, that it

TABLE 4.1. *Jews in selected occupations as a proportion of all Jews in 'gainful' occupations*

	Within the Russian Empire (according to the census of 1897) %	Among arrivals in the United States (preponderantly from eastern Europe), 1901–6 %
All professions	5.0	1.3
Clergy	0.4	0.0006
Teachers and educators	2.3	0.18
All manufacturing and mechanical pursuits	37.9	63.0
Manufacture of clothing /tailoring and dressmaking	16.6	29.8
Domestic and personal service	19.4	25.2

Note: Arrivals 1901–6 in gainful occupations (the right-hand column) have been calculated on the basis of the grand total figure for all Jewish immigrants in the period (581,883) less those (251,310) listed as of 'no occupation', yielding 330,573 who had (or claimed to have) an occupation. For example: 78,502 who were listed as 'tailors' and 20,502 as 'seamstresses and dressmakers' entered the US in these six years. Together (99,004) they constituted 29.9 per cent of 330,573. It needs to be stressed, however, that while Russian and American definitions of occupational categories were analogous they were not identical. 'Professions' included lawyers and physicians, as might be expected. But these were a negligible category statistically among Jewish migrants. 'Clergy', employed both by the Russians and the Americans, is problematical because it is not an entirely appropriate term in the Jewish context. It is likely that the Russians and the Americans conceived it similarly when applying it to men holding formal rabbinical appointments. But not all genuine and functioning rabbis held formal appointments. Moreover, the full class of those whom the Russians termed 'persons serving churches, etc.' would have to include cantors, *melamdim* (traditional school teachers), ritual slaughterers, *mohalim*, and the like—all of whom might well have been, and probably were, entered under the appropriate, but separate Russian rubric, but not noted separately (and perhaps not always listed as 'gainfully' employed at all) by the Americans and therefore not included in the figures given here. But they were very numerous in Russia. The Russian census-takers counted over 14,000 of them, as opposed to some 6,000 'clergymen, non-Christian', i.e. officiating rabbis. Oddly, they counted an additional 173 male and 21 female 'clergymen, orthodox' and 82 male and 2 female 'clergymen, other Christian' among the *Jews* of the empire: apostates, presumably. Whatever the social significance of these latter figures might be, the manner in which the census-takers presented them offers indirect, but firm evidence of the distinction Russian officialdom drew as a matter of course between religion on the one hand and nationality on the other.

is not the poverty of the great European cities, nor is it the poverty of the Russian peasant. . . . Jewish poverty has no idea what a factory looks like, for it exists in the *shtetl* where it has its origins in fathers and grandfathers who have been wretchedly poor since time immemorial. The Russian peasant, poor as he may be, is the proprietor of a small piece of land. And his condition is not hopeless—one feels that sooner or later it will improve. But Jewish poverty is utterly without a cure; the Jew has no available means for improving his condition, which will remain abject as long as he lives among alien peoples. In villages where life should have brought him closer to the earth, he lives as though he were in the city.[22]

For it needs to be understood too that the non-pauperized half of the population, comprising those who formed the effective Jewish working force of the empire, were crowded overwhelmingly into occupations, crafts, and trades (domestic service, tailoring, carting, shopkeeping, and the like) that were very poorly remunerated. It was a rule—rough to be sure—that applied even to crafts, cabinet-making, for example, that required a high degree of skill. Moreover, the crafts and trades Jews exercised tended strongly to be ones in which they themselves were very prominent or which they actually dominated. This was a source of economic weakness and social vulnerability, not strength, however, apart from strengthening the grounds for regarding the Jews in question as having the features—as Max Weber pointed out—of a 'caste'.[23] Be that as it may, the rewards for Jewish labour, skilled or unskilled, were commonly abysmal. A cobbler was unlikely to earn more than 200 roubles per annum, a competent tailor perhaps half as much again, a carpenter anything between 100 and 300 roubles—and all this when it took at least 300 roubles per annum (about £30 or $150 at the rate of exchange current at the time) to maintain a family. As for the conditions under which the great majority of working men, women, and children laboured and in which a high proportion had no choice but to live out their lives, these were horrendous regardless of whether work was performed within the home, as was often the case, or in employers' workshops: in either case small, damp, ill-lit, overcrowded rooms and very long hours (a work day of twelve, fourteen, or even sixteen hours being common). A passage in a report on living conditions in the city of Vilna—the intellectual and cultural capital of east European Jewry, 'the Jerusalem of Lithuania'— submitted to the British Royal Commission on Alien Immigration early in 1903 epitomizes the shock registered by virtually all visitors, Jewish and non-Jewish, from the relatively comfortable west when confronted with the greatest of the blights on eastern European Jewish life: its poverty. Visiting

the miserable dens and cellars in which the people live [Major Evans-Gordon found] . . . the walls of the houses were blistered and rotting, as if poisoned by the pestilent atmosphere within. Two or three families would be found in one miserable room or cellar rented at 45 roubles [£4. 10s.] a year. They were mixed up

---

[22] 'Ba'al Maḥshoves', a Yiddish literary critic, cited in I. Howe, *The Immigrant Jews of New York* (London, 1976), 14.

[23] Defined in the *Shorter Oxford English Dictionary* as a 'hereditary class of socially equal persons, united in religion and usually following similar occupations'.

together, regardless of age and sex and health. In one room I found a lunatic as a lodger among a family of young children. . . . I was surrounded by a crowd of gaunt, curious, anxious faces—sad, careworn, hungry-looking people. Some openly begged alms. . . . Others seemed to spend most of their time in the synagogues reading and rocking themselves into oblivion.

Major W. E. Evans-Gordon MP, a member of the Commission, was intent on restricting the immigration of such people into Great Britain and not a man who on any count might be charged with special sympathy for the Jews in Britain itself or elsewhere. Unlike any of his colleagues on the Commission, however, he had taken the trouble to travel to Russia, Poland, and Romania to see for himself what it was that lay at the root of what he (and others of like mind) termed the 'alien invasion' of Great Britain. He proved to be an observant and reliable witness. His written report to the Commission remains a remarkable document,[24] a notably vivid one too. Visiting Lodz, the 'Manchester of Eastern Europe', as he described it, he compared the relatively modern textile factories in which Jews were *not* employed (although there were many who had the requisite skills) with the home-based hand-loom weaving with which they generally had to make do and where 'the very best men working 15 to 18 hours a day can only earn at the outside seven roubles [14s.] a week'.

The conditions under which the work is done are appalling. I shall never forget the terrible places and rooms in which I saw this trade carried on. It would need the pen of a Zola to do justice to them. Three or four looms are crammed into one room with as many families. I have never seen human beings living under more awful conditions even in Vilna or the East of London. Those who have seen Hauptman's grim masterpiece, 'Die Weber,' can form an idea of the reality. The people had the appearance of half-starved consumptives.

The streets are narrow, and the houses mostly of wood. Some of them are four or five storeys high, and are packed solid with humanity. The number of children is incredible. The roofs of these houses slope very steeply, and I found people living in the apex of the angle between the topmost floor and the wooden tiles. Into these receptacles one could hardly creep on one's hands and knees.[25]

But although poverty was a root and continuing cause of the heavy migration of Jews from eastern Europe (as it was for members of other nationalities who moved westwards in great numbers in this period), it does not explain why the pattern of Jewish migration differed in important and characteristic ways from that of virtually all other European peoples. The Jews of Europe were a notably, although far from exclusively, urban people. A well-founded contemporary estimate by a Jewish philanthropic

[24] Royal Commission on Alien Immigration, *Minutes of Evidence* (London, 1903), 451–66.
[25] Ibid. 459.

organization puts the urban Jewish population of the Pale as high as 78 per cent. Where and when they were rural they were to be found over-whelmingly in non-agricultural occupations and trades: serving the peasants and landowners, very rarely landowners and peasants them-selves. In many of the towns and even in some of the cities of eastern Europe (Minsk, for example) they constituted the absolute majority of the population. In all cases they formed a highly distinctive segment of the population socially, culturally, and linguistically, and for all these reasons taken together, economically as well. And Jews tended to live among other Jews, to work with and for Jews, and typically, as has been said, in well-defined occupations. All these features contributed to the main-tenance and reinforcement of their identity both as a national collectivity and as private individuals. The Russian census-takers of 1897 reported 5 million or 97 per cent of the total Jewish population of the empire as giving Yiddish as their mother tongue. Within the Pale of Settlement alone the proportion was slightly higher: 98 per cent. They were distinctive too in that eastern European Jews demonstrated a higher rate of literacy in their languages (Hebrew and Yiddish) and often, if to a lesser degree, in the languages of the country (Russian, Polish, German, and so forth) than did their neighbours in their respective languages. True, the precise rate of literacy among Jews is a matter of debate. It was not as high as legend often claimed it to be, but it was certainly higher in every case than that of those whom Russian officialdom was accustomed to term the 'indigenous' peoples. The official Russian (1897) census rate of 49.9 per cent for illiteracy among Jews of both sexes was almost certainly too high. United States immigration service figures were lower, although it needs to be said that Russian and American figures were not precisely comparable: the Russians examined the literacy of persons of 10 years of age or over, the Americans did so for persons of 14 years of age or over. In any event, American figures for illiteracy among Jewish immigrants in the years 1899 to 1913 average out at *c.*25 per cent and where they can be broken down by sex reveal, as might be expected, a substantial discrepancy: in 1912 16.5 per cent of males were judged illiterate (on the basis of their ability or otherwise to read a Jewish prayer book) as compared with 33 per cent of females (on the same basis). When Jewish philanthropic organizations that had been both surprised and dismayed by these figures ran their own surveys, they produced slightly lower, but still generally similar results. Since total illiteracy was in principle an obstacle, if not an absolute bar, to admission into the United States, and since it can be assumed that, all other things being equal, it is the marginally (but no more than marginally) better educated who would attempt emigration, there is some reason to accept that illiteracy, however it might be assessed, would be higher among those who stayed behind than among those who departed. Even so, the official Russian figures, as published, seem inordinately high despite the fact that official figures for non-Jews were, as might be expected, higher still: 72 per cent of the population over 10 years of age in Russia proper were judged illiterate; 60 per cent of the population in Congress Poland. Austrian figures (as provided by the 1900 census) for Galicia were much the same: illiteracy at 59 per cent of the Polish population of 6 years of age or older; 72 per cent of Romanians; 76 per cent of Ruthenes (Ukrainians). The degree to which eastern European Jews tended, or were obliged, to crowd into certain occupations and avoided or were excluded from others is equally well illustrated in American statistics for all immigrants in the years 1899–1910. In no less than twenty-five listed crafts or trades ranging from hatters and book-binders to bakers, carpenters, and printers—Jews classed as 'skilled' formed the largest single group. In no less than eight crafts[26] out of the twenty-five, Jews formed the absolute majority in the years in question. After the Scots, they were far and away the most skilled of all the various and numerous ethnic groups of immigrants, the Spaniards, the Germans, and the English following upon them in that order.

However, where Jewish migration westwards differed most sharply from that of (almost all) other European peoples was that, by and large, the Jews left their original homes never to return. Unlike the Greeks and the Italians, but in this respect like the Irish, they migrated for the most part as entire families. Accordingly, women and children accounted for a very large proportion, female immigration being no more than very slightly under half of the total. Jewish female immigrants into the United States formed 43.4 per cent of all Jewish immigrants between 1899 and 1910, where female immigrants of all nationalities and denominations in the same period taken together formed 30.5 per cent of the grand total, the Jews themselves, constituting a very large fraction of the total, skewing the fraction representing the full female contingent upward. Taking adults alone, Jewish women immigrated into the United States at the rate of 768 per 1,000 men, as compared with a rate for German women of 685/1,000, for Polish women 440/1,000, for Italian women 259/1,000, and for Greek women a rate of 52 per 1,000 Greek men. In the same period, on average, children under 14 years of age accounted for one-quarter of the total Jewish migration into the United States (267,656 out of 1,074,442), a sixth of the German migration, between an eighth and a ninth of the Italian migration, and one-eleventh of the Polish. Many factors entered into play here for all migrants: personal and family responsibilities, economic conditions in the lands of origin, economic conditions, actual and prospective, in the west, the idea of scouting out the land before making a definite, perhaps irreversible move, and so forth.

[26] Hatters, furriers, bookbinders, tailors, watchmakers, tinsmiths, cabinet-makers, and dressmakers.

What is evident is that in Jewish cases *strictly* economic considerations were rarely preponderant.

Consider the rate of *return* from the United States to the original home country. In the years in question here (1899–1910) the rate of foreign emigration from the United States was, as it happened, relatively high: no less than an estimated 50 per cent of the figure for immigration in the economic crisis year of 1908, falling to about 30 per cent the year after, and falling further to a somewhat more normal 19 per cent in 1910. Taking these three years together, it may be seen that in general the rate of immigrants returning to their homes was high: 61 per cent for northern Italians and 56 for southern Italians, 30 per cent for Poles, 25 per cent for Greeks, and 20 for Germans, all the way down to a relatively low 12 per cent for the English and the Welsh. The rates for the Irish and the Jews were lowest of all (7 and 8 per cent respectively). Plainly, economic conditions in the United States itself had little or no effect on their decision to stay or to leave.

Finally, the Jewish migrants from Russia specifically —much the greatest contingent in quantitative terms, but, in the years leading up to the First World War, much the most significant historically too—may be compared with those who were closest to them socio-economically, but subjects of the substantially different regime in force in the Austrian province of Galicia. Migration figures for both directions, i.e. to and from the United States, by Jews and Poles in both empires, demonstrate both the very much stronger tendency of ethnic Poles as compared with Jews to return to their original homes, but also the no less significant difference between the Russian and Austrian (specifically Galician) Jews in this respect. As Table 4.2 shows, Jewish subjects of Austria were significantly more disposed to turn around in certain circumstances and return to their original homes in (Austrian) Poland than were Jewish subjects of Russia to (Russian) Poland and to Russia proper—and that by a factor of about 1.7.

TABLE 4.2. *Migration of Jews and Poles to the United States from both the Russian and the Austro-Hungarian Empires and back, 1908–1910*

	Arrivals in USA	Departures from USA	Departures as percentages of arrivals %
Jews			
From/to Russia	170,952	12,723	7.4
From/to Austria-Hungary	36,866	4,565	12.4
Poles			
From/to Russia	139,352	33,313	23.9
From/to Austria-Hungary	123,581	47,949	38.8

As for the Jewish exodus from Russia itself as a proportion of all Russo-Polish Jewry, figures for the relatively typical year of 1910 suggest that Jews proceeded abroad at a rate of 8.4 per 1,000. Ethnic Germans left Russia at a rate of 4.1 per 1,000, Poles at 3.5 per 1000, and Latvians and Lithuanians at 3.3 per 1,000. It follows that Jews emigrated at roughly twice the rate of ethnic Germans and two-and-a-half times the rate of Poles, Latvians, and Lithuanians. Ethnic *Russians*, it may be noted, emigrated at a rate (relative to total population) of barely more than one two-hundredth of the Jewish rate, which is to say hardly at all.

In sum, while poverty and the beguiling prospect of socio-economic improvement were undoubtedly twin, fundamental, and continuous sources of the great drive to the west—thus in most cases, thus in the case of the Jews as well—in the case of the Jews specifically, other factors were clearly at work. Personal security was now in question as it had not been for many decades. Despite its obvious failings and inadequacies, the Russian *Rechtsstaat* had been relied upon in the past for at least a measure of fair dealing and had of late even begun to be thought of, as we have seen, as being on the road to genuine liberalization. After 1881 the general sense was that it could no longer be relied on, that so far as the Jews were concerned—but in many other respects as well—all was going rapidly downhill. But that is not all. Beyond the vital considerations of livelihood and security, exceedingly radical and—for Jews—novel doubts and ideas had begun to infiltrate into their society. There will be a good deal more to say about some of the ideas later, but there was one of great simplicity and of special importance not only because it underlay the rest but because it was crucial to the precipitation and the maintenance of the great human flow from east to west.

A change of steadily rising intensity and force had taken place in the approach of the Jewish man in the street to his own affairs. Where previously he was tended strongly to take guidance from authority, he was now inclined as never before to act on no authority but his own and to seek out or define purposes and models of conduct of his own choosing. A hitherto unknown independence of spirit had begun to inform the conduct of ever greater numbers of Russo-Polish Jews, the effect being rapidly—if rarely completely—to undermine positions and opinions that had been set and established long before in all social spheres, but most especially that of obedience to traditional leaders. These, as we shall see, were now concerned, almost to a man, to ensure that the population stayed put. This, precisely, was what in overwhelming numbers it was no longer prepared to do; and in so far as bald statistics can serve to illustrate the workings of a sea-change of this kind and magnitude in a hitherto compact society given to quite uniform and predictable conduct when under threat it is the ever greater determination of the Jewish population to set Russia and Poland behind them that the emigration figures demonstrate. In 1880 an estimated eight thousand Jewish immigrants were registered at American ports of entry. Between 1881 and 1890 their numbers rose fairly steadily: from between fifteen and twenty thousand to slightly over forty thousand per annum. In 1891/2, a year in which a massive and savage expulsion of Jews from Moscow and certain classes of villages took place, the number rose again to 76,000. Subsequently it fell back, remaining, however, at a fairly steady 25–45,000 per annum. In 1903, the year of the great pogrom in Kishinev,[27] it rose to 78,000, then to over 90,000 in the year following. In 1905/6, the year of the first Russian revolution, but also, as we shall see, of the greatest and bloodiest wave of pogroms thus far, it rose to 125,000. And while Jewish emigration from Russia later fell back again somewhat, it remained at almost as high a level until it was brought to an abrupt end by the outbreak of war in 1914.

IV

While vast numbers of eastern European Jews were bent on escape from a condition of poverty compounded and intensified by official persecution, those among whom they now appeared—either to re-establish themselves or, as was more likely, *en route* to another destination—were, as we have seen, very differently placed. By the last decades of the nineteenth century the settled German, Austrian, Hungarian, French, Dutch, Italian, and British Jews had all achieved legal emancipation. The economic progress they had made was impressive, in many cases spectacular. East of Poland and the less developed, non-Magyar territories of Greater Hungary, pedlars, tavern-keepers, petty shopkeepers, semi-skilled self-employed artisans, and the like, to say nothing of the out-and-out pauperized, were all now exceptional. Crucial too to the situation of the Jews of western and central Europe in so far as it may be compared with that of their brethren to the east was the fact that if they were still to some extent victims of discrimination, the forms it took bore no real practical (as opposed, perhaps, to philosophical) resemblance to those practised in Russia or Romania. Even where it had remained institutionalized, as it still was, notoriously, in the German army, school system, corps of judges, civil servants, and to an extent in the German universities too it was rarely as oppressive, nor practised so defiantly and sanctimoniously as in Russia. Finally, western Jews were now rarely under threat of violence at the hands of their immediate neighbours and in those rare instances where trouble had arisen and 'excesses' so-called had occurred the origins were invariably local and the dimensions limited.

---

[27] See Chapter 6.

Serious suspicion of a hidden hand at work was unknown and would have been beside the point. The state and its police could be relied upon to provide protection—not, to be sure, out of specific regard for those identified as Jewish citizens of the state, rather as a matter of straightforward duty and routine. In sum, the times were such that the formally emancipated Jews of western and central Europe were able to live out their lives in conditions of relative comfort and security. And the difference between their condition and that of their cousins to the east was further demonstrated by the fact that their own tendency to migrate overseas, or even within Europe itself, had virtually come to a stop. If the western and central European communities were beset by population loss almost as severe in quantitative terms as that which the eastern communities had begun to suffer, it was of a wholly different nature qualitatively and in some respects more ominous.

Consider the principal demographic trends in pre-First World War German Jewry, much the largest, in some ways the most advanced of the western communities, in many eyes the most important. Three trends are especially noteworthy: the rise of the foreign-born segment of the Jewish population; the continuing shift from country to town; and the continuing decline of the native Jewish population itself.

The steady rise of the foreign (eastern European) component of the Jewish population in the Second Reich was part the product of the contiguity of Germany to the eastern European Jewish heartland and part the fact that the greater part of the migratory stream out of Russia and Poland passed across it, a fraction, as we shall see, going no further than Germany itself.

As a proportion of the total, the rise in the foreign element in the provinces and cities lying closest to Poland is especially noteworthy. In Leipzig, where the Jewish population was always small (3,300 in 1880; 9,400 in 1910), the foreign element within it shot up from 10 per cent to 68 per cent between 1880 and 1910. In distant Munich the rise was less dramatic, although even there it was by no means negligible: the alien segment accounted for 9 per cent of the city's total Jewish population of 4,100 in 1880; by 1910 aliens accounted for 27 per cent of the total Jewish population of 11,000. Apart from the migrants there was a continuous flow of eastern European Jews into Germany to study, a class of travellers that was small in absolute terms, but socially and politically of the highest importance. While the absolute number of native-born German-Jewish students in Prussian universities remained virtually unchanged between the mid-1880s and the mid-1900s and actually fell in relative terms (8.6 per cent of the total student body in 1886/7, 6.8 per cent in 1908/9), the number of foreign Jewish students (the overwhelming majority of whom were from eastern Europe) increased in these same twenty years by a factor of three and doubled in numbers as a proportion of the total body of Jewish students. As a proportion of the entire body of foreign students in Prussian universities, Jewish students accounted for 17 per cent in 1886/7, 32 per cent in 1905/6, and a still very substantial 26 per cent in 1908/9.

A second noteworthy, long-term trend in German Jewry—apparent throughout the nineteenth century—was the move from country to city. It followed directly upon the improvement in the legal status of German Jews and the opening up of inviting economic and cultural possibilities that many reckoned were theirs to seize provided they left the small towns and villages in which most German Jews were chiefly to be found at the beginning of the century. The native Jewish population of all major German cities rose from c.4,000 in 1880 to c.9,000 in 1910 in Munich for example; from 2,000 in 1880 to 3,500 in 1910 in Dresden. But the trend is best epitomized by the remarkable figures for Berlin where the native German Jewish population alone doubled in the course of as little as thirty years: from c.50,000 in 1880 to c.120,000 in 1910.

But it is the third demographic trend that is most instructive of the general direction in which German Jewry was evolving. In total absolute numbers the secure and relatively comfortable native Jewish population of the Second Reich had levelled off in the course of the nineteenth century and had then begun to fall. As a proportion of the entire population of the empire it had fallen drastically. There were important regional differences, to be sure. In Bavaria the Jewish population followed the overall trend: virtually static at 55–60,000 from the middle of the nineteenth century to the beginning of the twentieth, dropping sharply from 1.4 per cent in 1840 to 1 per cent in 1880 and to 0.8 per cent in 1910 as a proportion of the entire (rising) Bavarian population. The Jewish population of the great city of Hamburg rose, much like that of Berlin, from 14,000 in 1871 to 20,000 in 1905. As a proportion of the city's entire population it fell from 4.1 per cent in 1871 to 2.2 per cent in 1905. The Jewish population of Prussia increased steadily throughout this period (see Table 4.3), an increase that owed a great deal to the unique attractions of Berlin, naturally enough, but was necessarily at the expense of other parts of the country. But from the 1880s on the rise was due mostly to the influx of foreign Jews. Even so, while the Jews constituted 13.6 per cent of the total population of Prussia in 1861, by 1905 their fraction of the whole had fallen to 11 per cent. The most telling figure of all, however, is that of the *rate* of increase of the native-born Jewish population of Germany. Between 1861 and 1871 it stood at 22.5 per cent and was therefore comparable to the rate of increase of the Jewish population of eastern Europe. In the course of the 1880s it fell to 2.4 per cent, which is to say by a factor of 10. It rose very slightly again in the 1900s to 4.1 per cent, but never really recovered thereafter. The difference in this particular respect between native German Jewry and the eastern European Jewish communities in

TABLE 4.3. *Foreign Jews as a proportion of all Jews in Second Reich Germany*[28]

	Second German Reich				Prussia			Saxony			Berlin		
	(a) Total Jewish population	(b) Foreign Jews	German Jews	(b) as % of (a)	(a) Total Jewish population	(b) Foreign Jews	(b) as % of (a)	(a) Total Jewish population	(b) Foreign Jews	(b) as % of (a)	(a) Total Jewish population	(b) Foreign Jews	(b) as % of (a)
1880	561,612	15,000	546,612	2.7	363,790	10,000	2.7	6,516	1,000	15.3	53,916	1,954	5.5
1890	567,884	22,000	545,884	3.9	372,059	11,390	3.1	9,368	2,800	29.9	79,287	5,077	6.4
1900	586,833	41,113	545,720	7.0	392,322	21,800	5.6	12,416	5,637	45.5	92,206	11,651	12.6
1910	615,021	78,746	536,275	12.8	415,926	48,166	11.6	17,578	10,378	59.0	143,965	21,683	15.1

[28] Principal source: Adler-Rudel, *ostjuden*, 164.

the last decades of the nineteenth century and the early decades of the twentieth is therefore striking. The latter, despite heavy, continuous losses through migration, kept pace with the general population and in global, absolute numbers continued to rise. Native German Jewry consistently lagged behind, as Table 4.4 makes clear.

TABLE 4.4. *Jewish citizens and non-citizens of Second Reich Germany, compared*

	(a) Total population	(b) Native German- Jewish population	(b) as % of (a)	(c) Foreign Jewish population	(d) Total Jewish population	(d) as % of (a)
1880	45,600,000	547,000	1.2	15,000	562,000	1.23
1890	49,428,000	546,000	1.15	24,000	570,000	1.15
1900	55,780,000	546,000	0.98	41,000	587,000	1.05
1910	64,311,000	536,000	0.83	79,000	615,000	0.96

In 1911 Dr Felix A. Theilhaber published a justly famous, because unusually frank and clear-sighted examination of the vital statistics—and, by extension, the general demographic health of what in his day and age was still the leading Jewish community *west* of Poland. *Der Untergang der deutschen Juden* (*The Decline of the German Jews*) was an untidy and somewhat amateurish work of compilation.[29] But the data were drawn from what must have been virtually every official source available to Theilhaber, his material was reliable, by and large, and however untidily laid out, it supported the essential validity of his diagnosis. This, in a nutshell, was that native *German* Jewry was set firmly and very probably irreversibly on a course of long-term demographic decline. Jewish mortality was falling in consequence of better hygiene and medicine, improved standards of housing, and so forth, as was to be expected. Jewish fertility was falling a good deal faster, however. The overall Jewish population of Prussia had grown by about a fifth between 1875 and 1907, but the more telling datum was the fall of the excess of births over deaths. In 1880–5 Jewish births exceeded deaths by 22,000. Twenty years later the excess stood at half that figure, an inexorable consequence of the dramatic fall in the Jewish annual birth rate in the kingdom from 32 per thousand in 1875 to 17.1 per thousand in 1907, and an exceptionally low rate for any population group in contemporary western and central Europe. The comparable figure for the entire population of Germany in 1907 stood at 33 per thousand; that for Austria at 35.4; that for Great Britain at 27. Even the

[29] *Der Untergang der deutschen Juden: Eine volkswirtschaftliche Studie* (Munich, 1911).

rate for France, where the fall was commonly thought to be precipitous, stood at 20.5. In Bavaria, where the Christian population had been increasing steadily all the while, the Jewish population had grown hardly at all in the last decades of the nineteenth century and the first decade of the twentieth. The influx of eastern European Jews into the kingdom being minimal, the fall in the excess of births over deaths among Jews was dramatic: from 800 in 1876 to 32 (*sic*) in 1909.[30]

Theilhaber's figures further revealed that profound and irreversible changes in the structure, quality, and ethos of family life were at work in German Jewry. Jews of both sexes were contracting marriages later in their lives. The proportion that remained unmarried was extraordinarily high and rising—whereas celibacy had always been comparatively rare in Jewry. And since the proportion of unmarried women was rising faster, and was in absolute terms consistently greater than that of men, there was cause to anticipate not only a further drop in the fertility rate, but a perpetuation of that fall. It would fall further and faster still, moreover, in consequence of the rising rate of intermarriage between Jews and non-Jews (especially between Jewish men and non-Jewish women) that has been noted. The rise from 240 marriages between Jews and Christians contracted in Prussia in the years 1875–9 to 3,300 such marriages contracted in the years 1904–8 was wildly disproportionate to the rise in the kingdom's overall Jewish population.

There was much here that was in no way peculiar to Germany. Intermarriage was not of equal intensity in all parts of western and central Europe, or in all parts of Germany itself. But it was fast becoming a characteristic phenomenon of the age. In Denmark it was exceptionally high: by the early 1900s the rate of exogenous marriages had approached equality with that of endogenous marriages. In Budapest the rate (8 exogenous marriages for every 100 endogenous marriages) was very much lower than in Copenhagen, but still thought of as far from negligible. It is hard to detect a norm for western and central Europe, but the rate in Prussia may be said to be representative at 12 exogenous to 100 endogenous marriages—comparable therefore to the rates in contemporary Amsterdam and in Vienna, for example. In some parts of Germany (in Baden, Bavaria, and Hesse, for example) the rate of intermarriage was somewhat lower than in Prussia. In others it was higher. In Hamburg it was substantially higher: the ratio of Jewish men who had contracted exogenous marriages to Jewish men who had not done so having risen from 6.7:100 in 1885 to 34.8:100 in 1905/6. That was higher than the ratio in Budapest (13:100 in 1896–1900; 17:100 in 1903/4), but not as high as in Denmark (55:100 in 1880–90; 96:100 in 1901–5.[31] Similar

---

[30] Ibid. 25, 54–7.   [31] Ibid. 98–109.

figures may be adduced for France and Great Britain. In sum, the common trend was upwards;[32] and closely interwoven both with the fall in the overall marriage rate and with the striking rise in exogenous marriages was the fact that in all cases, those of endogenous no less than of exogenous marriages, the *family* itself was getting smaller all the while. In all-Christian families in Germany in the early years of the twentieth century the average number of children stood at *c*.4.1 and was rising slightly (4.07 in 1900, 4.13 in 1904). The comparable figure for all-Jewish families was a third smaller than the Christian and falling (2.83 in 1900, 2.65 in 1904). The average number of children in a family of mixed (Jewish-gentile) parentage was smaller still and falling faster: *c*.1.5 (1.42 in 1900, 1.31 in 1904, 1.13 in 1907).[33] Finally, it is worth noting too that while cases of Jewish children born out of wedlock still accounted for a smaller proportion of any given cohort than Christian children, their number was rising both absolutely and relatively.

These were grim figures. Grimmest of all, admittedly of negligible importance quantitatively, but arguably the most closely indicative of all of the presence of a creeping socio-psychological *malaise* of some kind in German Jewry, was the rise in the incidence of suicide—doubly significant because in the past it had generally been rarer among Jews than among their neighbours. It needs to be said, of course, that outright social causes can rarely be disentangled from the distinctly personal. Still, that the ambiguity of their social status was a source of extreme pain to some of the more sensitive minds in German Jewry and contributed massively to their anguish seems more than merely likely. And suicide as the extreme response to the pains of social accommodation and alienation is anything but unknown. Here, at any rate, there was no decline. Assuming the figures compiled by Theilhaber are to be relied upon, it appears that while the Jewish population of Prussia had doubled between the 1840s and the 1900s, the absolute number of suicides among Jews increased in the course of these sixty years by a factor of 6; and while the absolute figure for Jewish suicides in the years 1845–55 had been slightly smaller than that of the (more numerous) Prussian Roman Catholics and between a third and a quarter of the number of cases in the kingdom's vastly greater population of Protestants, by 1900–7 the Jewish figure was three times as large absolutely as the Catholic and a sixth larger, again in *absolute* terms, than the Protestant.[34]

---

[32] Reaching 50 per cent in the residual communities later in the century.

[33] Ibid. 113.

[34] Ibid. 145. Theilhaber's figures may be compared with those offered in J. Kreppel: 32, 35, and 41 suicides per 100,000 Jews in Prussia in the years 1912, 1913, and 1914 respectively, figures which exceeded the comparable rates for the general population of 22, 23, and 21 per 100,000 by between 50 and 100 per cent (*Juden und Judentum* (Vienna, 1925), 382, 388, 393). For the post-1933 years, see below, p. 826.

The sum of this condition was a steadily shrinking community subject to no evident countervailing social forces operating from within. The influx of eastern European Jews, for all its importance, was too small to halt, much less reverse, the overall trend. Besides, despite the immense differences between the two groups homogenization, given time, was sure to take place. To be sure, it would be preceded relentlessly by friction, embarrassment, and misunderstanding, by good will and ill will, by charity and by resentment, and by a good deal of condescension on either side. The most likely prospect none the less, all other things being equal, was that the newcomers in their turn, not immediately but at any rate unfailingly, would before very long assume and internalize the habits of mind, the patterns of behaviour, and to a very large extent the social, economic, and political ambitions of the natives. The underlying pattern of decline, indeed of entropy, would remain. There was no reason to think of it as other than inexorable and, in the circumstances, irreversible.

V

None of this suffices in itself to explain the dismay with which, by and large, the settled and emancipated communities of western and central Europe confronted the sudden appearance on their doorsteps of a huge, untidy, endlessly marching army of distant cousins from the east: there were other causes, external as well as internal. As evidence accumulated that some among the migrants out of the east sought to remain in Europe the settled communities had to cope with unnervingly hostile clamour against themselves. The Rothschilds, complained the Parisian *L'Estafette* (of 10 October 1882), in their 'beneficent and humanitarian spirit', had brought about 'a Semitic invasion' of France by 'hybrid Jews from the Orient'. There was fear, genuine in most instances, especially in Paris and London, that foreign Jews would undermine the position of French and British workmen by accepting lower wages. In Great Britain this led to public protests against the 'alien invasion' as it came to be called. As it happened, British forms of xenophobia and anti-Semitism were of a weaker sort, on the whole, than those that were characteristic of Third Republic France: thus in society as a whole, thus in the socialist and trade union movements. But the actual numbers of eastern European Jews migrating to Great Britain, especially to London, being substantially larger than those entering France, the problem was a real one, and the outcry against them in the event was better organized. It may be said too to have notched up more substantial achievements. The formal remit of the Royal Commission on Alien Immigration (already referred to) set up in 1902 was squarely to inquire into 'the character and extent of the evils [sic] which are attributed to the unrestricted immigration of aliens, especially in the Metropolis. . . . and to advise what remedial or precautionary measures it is desirable to adopt in this country, having regard . . . to the absence of any statutory power to exclude or expel any individual Alien or class of Aliens from its borders'. For the fact was, as the Commission soon discovered, that Great Britain was the only significant state in Europe to be without the simplest of police powers to limit the entry of aliens or even to expel those among them whom the authorities regarded as for one reason or another undesirable. One result of its labours was a Report, issued with remarkable speed in the following year, which, with the Minutes of Evidence appended to it, remains the most serious attempts by any governmental authority in Europe, Russia apart, to examine the contemporary condition of the Jews in detail. A second was to make it possible for the government of the day, after much debate and several false starts, to persuade Parliament in 1905 to enact a measure designed specifically to regulate and restrict 'alien', but in intent and practice Jewish, immigration into England. This had its oddities. The inroads of political and systematic anti-Semitism in Great Britain remained as before less marked than in France or Austria or Germany where no such acts were passed. The British political class remained reluctant totally or even substantially to abandon the tradition of free admission to the country of people persecuted for political or religious reasons. The Conservative government that pushed the act through was therefore (for a while) quite defensive about what it had done; and the Prime Minister of the day, Arthur Balfour, seems to have remained defensive, if not apologetic, about it to the end of his days. On the other hand, the new Liberal government that took office in 1906 after a triumphant landslide election refrained from sticking to the guns it had fired during the 1905 parliamentary debates on the bill and made no attempt to repeal or even seriously to amend it. The final oddity was the fact that while the trade union objections to the entry of impoverished aliens were attentively listened to and any number of private investigations of the immigrant Jews' subjection to—and readiness to accept—conditions of sweated labour were made, there was agreement all round that the economic problem they seemed to pose was unlikely to be more than minimal. The Jews could be relied upon to take care of their own, was the common refrain. 'It is well known,' *The Times* put it in 1888, 'that English Jews only exceptionally suffer the poorer members of their community to become chargeable upon the rates, and that the duty of administering to their wants is committed to a voluntary body called the Jewish Board of Guardians which has ever since [1859] set a conspicuous example of effectual charity in combination with sound discretion.'[35]

---

[35] Cited in I. Finestein, 'Jewish Immigration in British Party Politics in the 1890s', Jewish Historical Society of England, *Migration and Settlement* (London, 1971), 128–30.

This was true. The long-serving, non-Jewish chairman of the local charity board in Whitechapel testified that the 'Jewish Board of Guardians almost entirely relieve us of any burden with regard to the alien population'.[36] But the Board of Guardians was not extravagantly generous. Its actual policy was to discourage immigrants from settling in the country, especially in London, and for some years to that end it extended no assistance at all to immigrants who had been in the country for less than six months. This did certainly ease matters for the settled Jews somewhat as well as for the London rate-payers. But as a philanthropic system it carried a sting. Charles Booth, the great investigator of the condition of the London poor, conceded in 1887 that

The numbers now arriving are less than they have been, but certain districts are overrun, and the effect has been to flood many established trades with unhealthy cheap labour. Miserably destitute themselves, they also increase the destitution of their own people, and of our own people. The Jewish Board of Guardians are fully cognisant of this deplorable state of things, and have made great exertions to check the influx and to send back or send further those who have come.[37]

In brief, the view was that the influx had to be checked: on that there was agreement all round. But could it be checked? Could the migrants be sent back? Was it right and proper to attempt to send them back? And if so, how? And if not, what then? These were questions that now began to preoccupy not only Jewish notables in London, but all of those who passed for leaders of western and central European Jewry anywhere. All found them difficult to grapple with, all found themselves impelled into awkward situations and reversals of position. The one well-established Jewish institution that had long since assumed an explicit duty to extend what care it could to distressed Jews in all parts was the Alliance Israélite Universelle in Paris. Their response to the migration when it first began to flow was equally frantically to do what could be done to stop it and persuade those refugees who had left Russia to return—in which effort, initially at any rate, they were at one with leading communal figures and institutions in the United States as well as with their institutional analogues in Vienna and London, and, not least (as we shall see), with many of those who counted as the leading personalities in Russian Jewry itself. Remarkably, none of these generally well-meaning people seemed to have doubted that it was legitimate for them to seek to control the migratory movement, indeed reverse it, or that it was within their power to do so, or, more curiously still, that the set-upon and impoverished Jews of

---

[36] Royal Commission on Alien Immigration, *Minutes of Evidence*, 366; and see Eugene C. Black, *The Social Politics of Anglo-Jewry 1880–1920* (Oxford, 1988), especially 71–103.

[37] *Condition and Occupations of the People of the Tower Hamlets 1886–7*, Paper read to the Royal Statistical Society, May 1887, 47. Cited in Finestein, 'Jewish Immigration in British Party Politics', 128 n. 1.

eastern Europe who had taken the hard decision to leave their homes would end, reluctantly to be sure, by accepting their authority. It is, of course, this firm, but manifestly ill-thought-out approach to the problem that explains such extraordinary exercises as the effort made, albeit as a final resort, to persuade the *governments* concerned to co-operate with them in this general endeavour: the Austrian governor of Galicia, for example, being asked by the representative of the Alliance on the spot (i.e. on the Austrian–Russian border) to request the Russian Ministry of the Interior to permit the refugees' return and so clear the way to their expulsion from Austrian territory and their return to Russia!

It was only when it became evident to them that they would fail in endeavours of this kind that they set themselves to tackle the obvious alternative: doing whatever could be done to hurry the migrants on their way overseas, going so far, initially, as to try to get the men to leave their womenfolk and children behind them in the interests of their speedier economic integration in America. For failure and disappointment in the Americas and other distant territories would, they feared, bring the migrants all the way back to Europe and, more than likely, to western Europe in particular. The Alliance was especially desperate to divert immigrants away from France; and within France away from Paris. But in this too, they were to be far less successful than they had hoped to be. The provincial Jewish communities in France on whose good will the dispersal of immigrants within the whole of metropolitan France (the 'hexagon') necessarily depended commonly refused to take more than very small numbers under their care and in many cases refused to care for any refugees at all. And then, of course, the easterners had minds and purposes of their own.

The migrants were under no compulsion to accept the dictates of the Alliance or any other Jewish institution. The migratory move was fuelled by more powerful urges than any that the philanthropists of Paris, London, Vienna, or Berlin could muster in the interests of damping it down. And the peremptory language they tended to employ in this connection, while it reflected their thinking with great accuracy, could not have been more ill-suited to the situation with which they proposed to deal. Refugees 'who have no serious professions' and were therefore unlikely to establish themselves in America, 'must be sent back to Russia', was the instruction handed down to one of their representatives in the Galician town of Brody, an important staging-post for the early waves of emigrants headed west.[38] When it was realized that nothing of the kind could be done, that the effort to keep the great mass of east European Jewry intent

---

[38] Zosa Szajkowski, 'How the Mass Migration to America Began', *JSS* 4, 4 (Oct. 1942), 303 n. 60 and *passim*; Michael R. Marrus, *The Politics of Assimilation* (Oxford, 1971), 159–60.

on emigration locked in place was doomed to failure, and that there were no conceivable circumstances in which these people would be amenable to manipulation from afar, the Alliance resolved to drop out of the picture almost entirely. Only their unconquerable fear of an army of migrants marching across Europe and their anxiety about the likely consequences remained vigourous. It was a fear that rose somewhat from time to time with the ups and downs of pressure on the Jews of Russia within the empire itself. But the tone changed, turning a good deal soberer in the course of time, indicating a lesson well learned and a desire to avoid responsibility for what might, after all, transpire.

What we have feared up to now, were we to intervene, was a migratory movement which, if it were to be on too great a scale, would lead to difficulties of such gravity that all the resources of Jewry taken together would be insufficient to surmount them. We are ready to assist and support our co-religionists in Russia, but we must avoid anything that might lead them to rush headlong *en masse* towards the frontier without thought of what would become of them and before others knew what to do with them.[39]

The many other questions raised by the so-called 'alien invasion' remained. Given public objections to the entry of the easterners, should the settled, relatively well-integrated western Jews take a clear-cut public position of their own on the matter? Should they accept that they had a social responsibility for the newcomers that went beyond the strictly charitable; and if so, in what terms was its nature to be defined? Some communal worthies wondered whether they were not under an obligation to play their role as members of the host nation to the full, making common cause with their non-Jewish neighbours and opposing the foreign influx without too many reservations, if any at all. Several Jewish candidates running for election to Parliament from London constituencies under the Conservative standard, believed that that was no less than what was required of them and argued that if the migrants were not hurried along on their way overseas there would be grounds for banning their entry into Great Britain altogether. In Vienna, where the migration was still in its early stages and its eventual, immense dimensions were as yet unimaginable, the question, 'Was it worth-while to endanger the position of one and a half million Jews in Austria-Hungary for the sake of a few hundred refugee families in Brody' was posed still more clearly.[40] The American-based Hebrew Aid Society's representative in Europe,

[39] Confidential circular, 1 June 1891. Cited in Szajkowski, 'Mass Migration', 309 n. 93.
[40] By Joseph von Wertheimer, a noted philanthropist and educationist, and leading figure in the Austrian branch of the Alliance Israélite Universelle, writing to Baron Edmond de Rothschild in Paris, 14 July 1882. Cited in Adler-Rudel, *Ostjuden in Deutschland*, 8. Wertheimer's considered view was clear: 'the emigration to America should be stopped'.

knowing in which direction the local wind was blowing, demanded of European Jewish philanthropic organizations that they be more helpful to their American opposite numbers on whom the greatest burden of dealing with the migrants was falling and would continue to fall. For if they did not lend a substantial financial hand, why then, he warned them, 'the continued shipments from Europe of Emigrants will end badly . . . [and] they must expect many of these Emigrants [to be] reshipped [back] to Europe'.[41]

Beyond all questions pertaining to the mechanics and the costs (social and financial) of philanthropy or even of the very possibility of extending organized and purposeful philanthropic aid and guidance to the easterners, there was a notion abroad, therefore, that the newcomers embodied a threat to the position, so recently improved, of the long-settled Jewish population of western and central Europe. Not all accepted it with equal conviction or in its entirety and without reservation. But it was common enough and it had to do with what for many people was a genuinely hard and frightening question: whether the arrival of easterners in great and ever increasing numbers would not end, however unintentionally, by drawing the westerners back into the ranks of the unemancipated and unintegrated all over again. Might they not revive the image of the Jews as a people deeply and ineradicably alien to western society in something like its ancient vigour and cause the entire post-1789 trend towards equality and civil dignity to falter and the existing, if still sustainable pressure to restore the *status quo ante* gather lasting and decisive force? In sum, for all who, despite the pain and the anxiety intrinsic to their condition, continued to pine for the full social acceptance that still eluded them the influx of the easterners was a source of mounting concern, if not horror. Were they, the settled Jews of Germany, France, the Low Countries, and Great Britain, now to be linked in various awkward, perhaps downright dangerous ways to these fearfully unwelcome people—yoked to them in the minds of their rulers and neighbours, and later too, Heaven forfend, in their social purposes and their outworn notions on the role and true nature of the Jewish people? As objections to the easterners' appearance multiplied, so fears of this nature tended to be articulated with diminishing restraint. That they 'bring Poland with them . . . is more than a misfortune, it is a calamity', was the view of the *Jewish Chronicle* (12 August 1881), then under the direction of Asher Myers. 'Our fair fame is bound up with theirs; the outside world is not capable of making minute discriminations between Jew and Jew and forms its opinion of Jews in general as much, if not more, from them than from the Anglicized portion of the community.'[42] Ten years later this was still the newspaper's view:

[41] Adler-Rudel, *Ostjuden.*
[42] Cited in David Cesarani, *The Jewish Chronicle and Anglo-Jewry 1841–1991* (Cambridge,

'English Jews have the greatest material interest in diminishing the stream of Jewish immigration to these shores.' The settled western Jews would not go so far as to 'invoke state interference' to that end. But it was right to dissuade the prospective immigrants themselves from coming to Great Britain. 'As long as there is a section of Jews in England who proclaim themselves aliens by their mode of life, or by their very looks, by every word they utter, so long will the whole community be an object of distrust to Englishmen, however unmerited that distrust may be' (7 August 1891).

Still, this was not the whole of the picture. Some among the very few men in western Jewry who were of sufficient prominence to set the public tone in these matters one way or the other preferred to keep silence. Thus Bleichröder, immensely active, as we shall see, in the matter of the Romanian Jewry only a few years earlier, was unwilling to take the lead in his own German community on a subject that had landed on his own doorstep. But there may be set against Bleichröder and Rathenau and some others too the example of Sir Samuel Montagu (later Lord Swaythling), a near equivalent to Bleichröder as a Jewish banker of very great prominence in the City of London in his day. Montagu cleaved to the Tradition freely and openly in two cardinal respects. He remained an observant orthodox Jew to the end of his life, wholly unprepared to countenance deviations from the prescriptions of the Law (the rule of endogenous marriage among others), notably in his immediate family. And he was prepared to stand up for the easterners, in Parliament itself if necessary, because they were, in matters of the Tradition, his natural allies, and because his native sense of loyalty and obligation to the wider community of Jewry so dictated. 'I know these people intimately', he told the House of Commons in the course of the debate on the Aliens Bill which he opposed both as a Jew and as a Liberal. 'I have been in and out among them all of my life. I am proud not just to be their friend, but prouder still that there are many amongst them whom I reckon to be my best friends.'[43] And Leopold Greenberg, then editor and publisher of the London *Jewish Year Book*, later editor of the *Jewish Chronicle*, gave full vent to his well-known opposition to restrictions on immigration as well as demonstrating his contempt for what he called 'flunkey Judaism' when he was called to give evidence before the Royal Commission on Alien Immigration. What was most profoundly at issue, he told the Commission, was the political and legal status of the Jews. They for their part were struggling to raise it, and rightly so. They needed to be able to rely upon themselves and to be equipped to fight whatever was threatened

1994), 76; and see Bernard Gainer, *The Alien Invasion: The Origins of the Aliens Act of 1905* (London, 1972), 55–9 and *passim*.

[43] *Jewish Chronicle*, 20 Jan. 1911. Cited in Black, *Social Politics*, 64.

to reduce their political and legal status—which, unfailingly, is what restrictive legislation would do. It was for this reason, as well as for what he considered to be the interests of Great Britain itself, that he opposed it. Major Evans-Gordon, the man who had done most to impel the government to set up the Commission (of which, in the customary manner, he had been appointed a member equal and opposite to the Jewish member, Lord Rothschild) taxed Greenberg on his loyalties.

EVANS-GORDON. I understand you regard this question almost solely from a Jewish point of view?
GREENBERG. Not solely, but largely.
EVANS-GORDON. Mainly?
GREENBERG. Largely.
EVANS-GORDON. The question of the faith of the Jews being involved is the principal concern, in your eyes?
GREENBERG. No, not principally in my eyes.
EVANS-GORDON. That is the tendency of your evidence. You place that first?
GREENBERG. No, I do not place it first.
EVANS-GORDON. The fact of their being, most of them, your coreligionists, is the fact that weighs most with you?
CHAIRMAN [Lord James of Hereford]. I think you may say, prominently?
GREENBERG. Prominently, I agree.[44]

This sort of language and the self-confidence with which it was employed was a world away from that of Bleichröder or Rathenau. But then they were in any case members of a dying breed: two instances of the unsuitability of the old-style plutocratic leadership to the unprecedented dimensions and intensity of the problems afflicting contemporary Jewry. Torn between such traditional communal responsibilities as he was still prepared to assume and his necessarily countervailing private needs, estate, and ambitions, the *gevir* as leader was virtually defunct—in the west, at all events. No single social type in modern Jewry was as receptive to the pull of non-Jewish society at its brightest, highest, but often most hostile too. No single social type—the orthodox rabbinate always excepted—was as resistant to prospects of *radical* change in Jewry. And none, not even in the higher reaches of the rabbinate, was likely to be so discomposed by the failure of other, lesser members of the Jewish people to pay him due attention and respect. Where Moses Montefiore had been one of the last and most successful of the old breed, Crémieux had pointed the way to an alternative: bolder in thought, less afraid, at one and the same time both secularized and loyal to the Jewish interest as he perceived it, free of the encumbrance and peculiar personal responsibilities of great wealth, but in every essential respect his own man. In the

[44] Royal Commission on Alien Immigration, *Minutes of Evidence* (London, 1903), 626.

very small class of those who approximated to such a model Leopold Greenberg was a prominent member. Paul Nathan (1857–1927) was another and the organization which he (with James Simon) helped to found and direct, the Hilfsverein der deutschen Juden, was intended to fill the void that was one of the outcomes of the situation just described.

How much substance there was to the issues, more precisely the anxieties, to which the great migration had given rise in central and western Europe was debatable. But if they were more acutely felt in Germany than elsewhere the reasons went well beyond the unfortunate, but undeniable fact that the migration from Russia happened to coincide with the rise of organized, partly political anti-Semitism in its German form. Some migrants did seek to pass through Dutch and Belgian ports; and others through British ports on their way to North America. The majority, however, to the initial horror of the German government and to the intense discomfort of most settled German Jews, preferred the shorter, cheaper route through Hamburg and Bremen. This in itself did not mean settling in Germany. Even so, the authorities found themselves torn between their instinctive desire to prevent these undesirable people from entering the country and their countervailing obligation to take the commercial interests of the German merchant marine into account. This was not an age—the age of German *Weltpolitik*—in which it was politic to stop the Hamburg–Amerika Line and the Norddeutscher Lloyd shipping companies from making the most of the lucrative business of providing passage for travellers whose individual inability to pay more than the lowest fares possible was handsomely offset by their numbers.[45] The German government gritted its teeth, contented itself with the establishment of special border mechanisms to control the traffic, hurry the migrants on their way, and reduce to an absolute minimum the danger of some of them falling by the wayside and remaining in German territory, possibly for good. Entry was conditional on possession of travel documents, tickets for the entire journey, and a set sum of ready cash (so much for adults, less for children). When it was discovered that temporary lodging, food, and medical care had in many cases to be made available along with reliable advice on travel arrangements and some protection from those who were set to prey upon them, the institutions of German Jewry itself were called in to lend a hand as well. They did so somewhat sporadically at first and on a local basis, but found, in the course of time, that aid to the migrants had to take an organized form and proceed under central direction. They found too that the scale being immense, the burden on the various German-Jewish communities would be substantial. By 1901, when the full country-wide organization, the Hilfsverein der deutschen

---

[45] The traffic built up steadily after 1881. It has been estimated that at its peak, between 1905 and 1914, at least 700,000 Jewish migrants passed through German ports.

Juden, was founded to provide these services systematically, between 40,000 and 50,000 souls were being catered for in a typical year at an annual cost to the community of several million marks.

Paul Nathan, the central founding figure in the Hilfsverein, was in no sense a man of the old plutocratic class of communal leader or, indeed, of the new. He was not a traditionalist himself. In some respects he was in the Crémieux mould: wholly modern, secularized, and acculturated, a man who knew little or no Hebrew and who was devoid of any other substantial component of Jewish learning and intellectual influence. While he was a man of some scholarly attainment, his doctoral dissertation at Heidelberg could not have been more remote from the concerns of Jewish learning either of the traditional kind or of the *Wissenschaft des Judentums* variety: a study of Rabelais's 'Gargantua and Pantagruel'. In contrast, Walther Rathenau, curiously enough, an entirely competent engineer by profession, a man who for all his obsession with the status of the Jews was reluctant to stir a finger on behalf of eastern Jews or any other special class, did take some trouble to acquaint himself with the elements of Hebrew and Jewish law and lore. And Rathenau differed from Nathan in the further respect that he believed that Jews should avoid public prominence of any kind—political involvement before all else. It was very reluctantly, in the end catastrophically, that he become so involved after the First World War. Nathan's inclinations, however, like Crémieux's, were unmistakably political from the first. He did not attain to Crémieux's distinction, nor could he have done so in late nineteenth-century Germany. And he did not have Crémieux's rhetorical skills and charisma. He was, it would seem, cut out for the second rank, where Crémieux had been cut out for the first. But Nathan did become a close and valued associate of Eduard Lasker and Ludwig Bamberger, leaders of the German Liberal Party (and Jews themselves). And he served for many years as co-editor of the Liberal review, *Die Nation*.[46] It was only upon the general shift to the political right that occurred towards the end of the century in Germany, and what seemed to Nathan to be the all-but-permanent relegation of moderate liberalism of the kind to which he was attached to the sidelines, that he withdrew from politics, a respected figure, hardly an eminent one. What he had always been and remained, however, was a man who inspired trust and whose intentions were unmistakably, and in the literal sense of the term, philanthropic. (That too must have counted against his going far as a politico.) And then, secular Jew that he was, Nathan had been somewhat shaken and disheartened by the surge in organized, party-political anti-Semitism in Germany at the end of 1870s. What stung him particularly (again like

[46] Ernst Feder, *Politik und Humanität; Paul Nathan: Ein Lebensbild* (Berlin, 1929), 71–84.

Crémieux) was the revival of the ritual murder charge against Jews, the so-called Blood Libel, in the early 1880s in the form of criminal charges brought before regular courts of law with all due solemnity according to the supposedly proper judicial procedures practised in the heart of Europe itself, as opposed, say, to distant, despotic and 'oriental' Damascus. Appalled by the *probability* of ritual murder committed by Jews being taken up as a subject fit for serious debate, he undertook the preparation of a careful study of the then most notorious of contemporary cases in central Europe, the ritual murder trial held at Tisza-Eszlár in Hungary in 1883. But to the depressing matter of the case itself and the outrageous manner in which it had been handled by the Hungarian authorities,[47] there was then added, to his dismay, the response in the Jewish circles he frequented. This was to urge him *not* to publish his findings on the grounds that the Tisza-Eszlár trial would surely be the last of its kind, that its impact would fade in due course, and that it was wrong and from the point of view of Jewish interests and the collective reputation of the Jews counter-productive to make too much of it. But cases continued to crop up from time to time, one of them in Germany itself when a charge of ritual murder was brought against a Jewish butcher in Xanten in the Rhineland. Nathan subjected it to detailed investigation in turn. And in 1892 he published three substantial studies: the hitherto unpublished examination of the Tisza-Eszlár trial, his account of the Xanten case,[48] and a larger, critical study directed principally at those who were evidently intent on keeping the charge of ritual murder alive.[49]

It is evident that, as in the case of the Damascus Blood Libel half a century earlier, the hurt induced in so modern, thoroughly acculturated, essentially hopeful, and forward-looking a western Jew as Paul Nathan by events on the ground, namely at the mundane public and police level, was compounded by the insistence of people whom he had evidently expected to know and behave better (members of the Prussian state parliament in formal session, for example) on treating the charge of ritual murder by Jews as intrinsically serious and very possibly valid. The best he could do to diminish the affront was to cross historical perspective with irony:

The Crusaders [once] slaughtered the Jews in Xanten: that occurred on June 27, 1096. On June 29, 1891, exactly 795 years and two days later, a poor child with his throat cut was found in that same Xanten, and fanaticism raged again. But they demolished only one house and they dragged a single innocent, suspected

[47] See Chapter 6.
[48] On the Xanten case, see Chapter 6.
[49] *Der Prozess von Tisza-Eszlár. Ein antisemitisches Kulturbild* (Berlin, 1892); *Xanten-Cleve. Betrachtungen zum Prozess Buschhoff* (Berlin, 1892). *Der jüdische Blutmord und der Freiherr von Wackerbarth-Linderode, Mitglied des Preussischen Abgeordnetenhauses. Ein antisemitischen-parlamentarischer Kulturbild* (Berlin, 1892).

Jew no further than the vicinity of the scaffold. That certainly amounts to a difference, and who would deny that in the course of 795 years we have made
progress.[50]

In any event, it was at this point that Paul Nathan began to turn whole-
heartedly and, before long, on a full-time basis, to the Jewish charitable
causes in which he had begun to be increasingly interested—while
remaining careful to subsume them so far as possible under a concern for
universal human rights and values. He participated in one of the earliest
attempts to fight anti-Semitic defamation with facts and reason, serving
as vice-president—indeed, as the moving spirit—of the Comité zur
Abwehr antisemitischer Angriffe formed in 1893. In 1901 he took on
what would be his major role in Jewish public life in the Hilfsverein.

The Hilfsverein der deutschen Juden became at one and the same time
the German analogue of the Parisian Alliance Israélite Universelle and a
notable product of the failure of the Alliance to establish itself as a genuinely worldwide Jewish organization dedicated to the supra-communal
problems that could not be properly dealt with on any other basis.
Whatever chance there may originally have been of such an institution
being set up and made to work, and it was always small, was wiped out by
the Franco-Prussian war and the multiplication of political traps into
which all efforts at Jewish supra-communal co-operation were liable to
fall towards the end of the century and in the early decades of the one following. As its title indicates, the Hilfsverein was more modest in its stated
original intentions than the Alliance. On the other hand, but again unlike
the Alliance, it was not afraid to seek to deal with the problems of large-
scale migration. It saw them as one of its primary concerns both in the
sense of catering for the needs of the migrants and, much like the Jewish
establishment in Great Britain, doing what it could for the Jews of Russia by taking the Russian government to task whenever there was a
chance to do so. It says something for the energy the Hilfsverein devoted
to this latter cause and the rapidity with which it had gained access—if,
to be sure, not much more than access—to high places, that in the revolutionary month of October 1905, and again in 1906, Nathan set out for
Russia to press for protection and equality for the Jews. On the first occasion he was received politely enough by the prime minister (Witte) and
by the minister of the interior (Obolensky). On the second occasion, he
was received rather more coolly by the new prime minister (Stolypin)
and very resentfully by the minister of finance (Kokovtsev). None of his
interlocutors denied either the injustice of the system or the need *in principle* to reform it. But the terms in which all spoke of the political impos-
sibility of moving faster amounted to denying the possibility of any

---

[50] Cited in I. Schorsch, *Jewish Reactions to German anti-Semitism 1870–1914* (New
York and Philadelphia, 1972), p. 106, slightly amended.

movement at all. Accordingly, nothing concrete was achieved except for the grim lesson that nothing could be achieved—other than a fresh contribution to the clarification of the central issue in Jewish public life in all parts in the years leading up to the First World War, namely that the Jewish people was locked in unequal conflict with imperial Russia.[51] For the rest, much like the Alliance, and to some extent in competition with it, the Hilfsverein took it upon itself to work for the socio-economic improvement of Balkan and Near Eastern Jewry by fostering modern, especially technical education among them. Again, like the Alliance, it recognized that its efforts in that direction would be most likely to prosper if it had the backing of its own government; and this, on the whole, it did achieve and at a somewhat lower cost in subservience to Germany's political needs and interests in the Balkans and the Near East than was regularly (albeit willingly) paid by the Alliance Universelle Israélite to the French.

It needs to be added, however, that it would be a mistake to dismiss philanthropy of the kind dispensed by the Hilfsverein or any of the other institutions as little more than the product of panic fear and calculation. In all cases, it accorded with, and owed much to, the duties and responsibilities—pious in some cases, well meaning in all—that had always been expected of decent, communally minded Jews in comfortable and secure circumstances at any level of society. That some form of assistance would be rendered them by their German, French, British, Dutch, Austrian, and other cousins was no more than what many of the migrants expected; and despite the irritation and objections occasioned by their arrival a good deal of aid was always forthcoming sooner or later. The same held true for those who came to the western cities to stay. In these respects, however, there was a line of sorts to be drawn between traditionalists and modernists even if not one that was always entirely clear-cut. The general rule seems to have been that the more closely the settled Jews of western and central Europe remained attached to the religious tradition, to their organized community, and to close involvement in its affairs, the more likely they were to agree that whatever could be done to ease the progress of harassed, impoverished, and travel-wearied Jews and render their journey a little more secure and a trifle less painful should be done. It was true that it was apparent to all classes of settled Jews that they had little real choice in the matter. Substantial numbers of migrants were bound to fall by the wayside in the various countries of transit if efforts were not made to smooth their progress. The greater the numbers the greater the irritation of the authorities, the greater the public clamour, and the greater the embarrassment therefore for all settled Jews—an embarrassment

---

[51] On the renewed hammering of the Jews in 1905 and the response to it within Russian Jewry itself, see Chapter 6.

compounded by the fact that, as suggested, the settled communities were expected to assume a large measure of responsibility for their eastern brethren. Moreover, what held for those in transit held *a fortiori* for those who went no further. The Jewish notables in Great Britain, represented in the Board of Guardians, the Board of Deputies, and the several synagogue federations, had begun by being as appalled as any by the growing number of actual or potential 'indigent aliens' who had decided for one reason or another to remain in the country. Once it was apparent to them that the mounting and ever more vociferous objections to the presence of resoundingly alien and alienated Jews in well-identified sections of the major cities of the realm could not be fought off without their concerning themselves directly and actively with the immigrants' welfare and seeking to ease their way into the economy and, in the course of time, into British society as well, they set out to help. And with the recognition of the need to act came an extensive, increasingly systematized and institutionalized exercise in social welfare and education. It was not long before this took on a momentum and rationale of its own.

Mutatis mutandis this was the pattern everywhere. What was paramount in each instance was the question of the pattern and quality of the relations between the members of the settled communities in each western country and the newly arrived immigrants. The cultural differences were often immense. How then were those relations to be defined, determined, and understood? Who was to determine them? Did the initial responsibility assumed by the settled Jews for the welfare of the newcomers imply anything more than temporary material dependence of the latter on the former? Was it for the immigrants to accept and internalize as best they could the established social norms of the settled communities, defer to their leadership, accept their guidance, keep a low profile, and generally know their proper place until such time as they had earned a better one? Most acutely of all, as the initial shyness and disorientation of immigrants evaporated, as they found their feet, learned the language of the country, and began to articulate their needs and purposes for themselves, were they to invade and ultimately participate in the management of the communal institutions? As the immigrants' numbers rose the matter of control and authority within and over the communities became a source of unending disquiet and tension.

Estimates of the total Jewish population of Great Britain at the end of the century vary, but it was unlikely to have been much greater than 60,000 in 1880. By 1914, however, it had grown by a factor of 4 to about 250,000. In London alone, the Jewish population grew from 40–45,000 in 1880 to perhaps as many as 145,000 by 1905 of whom, according to an analysis of sufficient rigour to be presented to the Royal Statistical Society in 1905, as many as 120,000 lived in the single borough of Stepney in the East End of London. It is probable that by 1914 the total Jewish population of the metropolis had risen to 180,000, the majority being foreign born.[52] This was sufficient in itself, in the course of time, to seal the fate of the old, mostly Sephardi leadership of British Jewry.

In France the process whereby the immigrants assumed a role in communal affairs was slower. Their numbers were smaller both absolutely and relatively than in Great Britain; and at least until the turn of the century they were not in fact the most important category of newcomers in the capital. The Jewish population of Paris had indeed grown from 30,000 in 1869 to 40,000 in 1880 (by which time it constituted two-thirds of the entire Jewish population of France). By 1914 it reached 65–70,000. But this very steep rise is to be accounted for chiefly (over and above natural increase) by the movement of French Jews from the eastern provinces of France. It had been continuous since the Revolution. It was greatly accelerated by the decision of very many thousands to remain citizens of France, leaving Alsace and Lorraine for good when those provinces were annexed by Germany in 1871. It was this, not immigration from eastern Europe, that did most to increase the Jewish population of the capital from the minute proportion of 0.01 per cent of the total population of the city in 1789 to 2 per cent a century or so later and to establish the Jewish population of Paris as the greater part of French Jewry country wide. It was only after the further, still sharper deterioration of conditions in Russia in the early decades of the twentieth century that the immigrant population begin to grow as rapidly and conspicuously as in Great Britain.[53] However, while the influx was substantially smaller both relatively and absolutely than in London, the social tensions between the established native Jews and the newcomers were if anything more acute.

Both in Great Britain and in France these were quarrels and rivalries that were kept within the family for the most part. Few who were entirely outside Jewry took much interest in them. The communities being formally defined as of a religious nature, membership in them was in any case a private and voluntary matter and communal institutions were without compelling statutory authority over Jewish individuals. The struggle for leadership, such as it was, was fated to be resolved either by an orderly retreat of the veterans in the face of the newcomers' invasion, once it had become clear that their own influence over the direction of communal government was waning; or by the newcomers setting up autonomous communities of their own. In Germany, however, while the tensions were of an analogous kind, matters in this particular, institutional respect were otherwise.

[52] Sources: Geoffrey Alderman, *Modern British Jewry* (Oxford, 1992); Lloyd P. Gartner, *The Jewish Immigrant in England, 1870–1914* (London, 1960); V. D. Lipman, *A History of the Jews in Britain since 1858* (New York, 1990); V. D. Lipman, *Social History of the Jews in England 1850–1950* (London, 1954).

[53] Michel Roblin, *Les Juifs de Paris: démographie-économie-culture* (Paris, 1952), 51–67.

Throughout Germany membership in a church, and, where Jews were concerned, membership in a religious community of their own, was compulsory. The only relatively new exception to the rule was the one provided for under the terms of the *Austrittsgesetz* (Law of Exception or Departure) of 1876 which laid down a procedure for formal withdrawal from one's original community and personal registration with the authorities as a person who was explicitly *konfessionslos* (undenominated). It was possible, therefore, even if rare, for the individual to escape the hold of the community despite the fact that much of the quite substantial power, prestige, and monopolistic authority of the German-Jewish *Kultusgemeinde* over their members derived from the state itself and was therefore of a kind unknown in non-étatist, common law Britain or étatist but firmly *laïc* France. On the other hand, much of the trouble that would ensue in Germany between old-timers and newcomers was greatly aggravated by the circumstance that Jews were normally bound into a legal framework that required them to be members of a formally established community and, at the same time, required of each community that it accept all Jews within its purview. What of alien Jews, however? The most common interpretation of the law in the various German states was that, like it or not, regardless of their *civic* status, aliens were equal members of the community with all others. They were entitled to full voting rights and had the important privilege of sending their children to *Gemeinde*-run schools if they so wished. On the other hand, they were not compelled to join an established *Gemeinde*, not in Prussia at all events, if they did not wish to do so. Those among them who found the local *Gemeinde* synagogue services and school curricula too liberal for their taste were free, under the *Austrittsgesetz*, to secede if they insisted on doing so and form a community of their own, a so-called *Austrittsgemeinde*. How strong the inner tendency to do so may have been is hard to judge. Like the formal withdrawal of an individual from his community the establishment of such *Austrittsgemeinde* seems to have been much inhibited by the requirement that it be preceded by a public declaration of intent in the form of a petition submitted to a court of law. On balance, immigrant Jews preferred to keep a low profile and adhere to the established communities—with the partly paradoxical result that their involvement in communal affairs tended to be greater in Germany than it was in other western states. On the other hand, once it had been recognized by the established communal leaders that no exception could be made in the case of alien, notably eastern European Jews—namely that the immigrants were entitled to full membership untrammelled in any way by their origins or their civil status—the question how far their presence, views, manners, and needs would actually be allowed to influence the running and governance of the *Gemeinde* arose in all its inevitable ferocity. In itself, that is to say, common membership in the *Gemeinde* did little to smooth away the inevitable social and, in the course of time, political differences subsisting between native Jews and *Ostjuden* (eastern European Jews). The fear of the former that the latter tended to discredit Jews of all qualities in the eyes of other Germans was exceptionally long lived—not least because the arrival of the *Ostjuden* was employed as a primary stick in the hands of the anti-Semites with which to beat the settled Jews of the country. But there was a more narrowly political dimension to the dismay with which many good German Jews greeted their eastern brethren's arrival. It is true that nowhere in Germany was there a serious prospect of foreigners actually outnumbering the natives: nowhere did foreigners account for more than a fifth of any community; nor was there serious evidence anywhere indicating that easterners as a class were in fact determined to take the communities over, make public statements on behalf of all or even on their own behalf, adopt positions, or even so much as band together to maintain their rights. What the easterners did tend to do, at any rate in the short term, was to strengthen the orthodox-traditionalist, as opposed to the liberal-reformist, tendency in German-Jewish religious life much to the dismay, of course, of the now normally preponderant modernists. In the search for appropriate candidates for rabbinical office, for example, they were apt to tip the balance in favour of one of conservative inclinations.[54] Disputes of this kind impelled liberals in German Jewry to work to deprive the easterners of their rights within the *Gemeinde* while paradoxically maintaining pressure on the government to ease its policies towards them in the social and political spheres. Hence there were repeated appeals to government authorities to disqualify easterners from participation in *Gemeinde* affairs, attempts to frighten immigrants into passivity by reminders that they were in permanent danger of expulsion from the country, and even efforts to rig the results of communal elections by establishing a sort of curia system based on private income—all with mixed results. In 1897 the Prussian governor of Upper Silesia rejected a plea by the community in Neustadt to order participation in *Gemeinde* business to be limited to the native born. But similar attempts in Bochum in 1912, in Cologne and Dortmund in the same year, in Danzig and Chemnitz in 1913, and in Münster in 1914 were successful. The issue was bedevilled, however, by it being state, rather than imperial law that was in question, and by the government of the largest and most influential German state, Prussia, taking the line that since the *Gemeinde* were 'confessional', i.e. religious rather than national or political institutions, foreign Jews were not to be debarred from participation in them. Much later, in May 1914, it would be laid down

---

[54] Mordechai Breuer, *Modernity within Tradition: The Social History of Orthodox Jewry in Imperial Germany* [*Jüdische Orthodoxie im deutschen Reich 1871–1918*, trans. Elizabeth Petuchowski] (New York, 1992), 307–8.

formally that while temporary residents had no rights of participation, foreign Jews who were long resident in the community had. The demand advanced by Jewish opponents (there were none others) to deny aliens the right of full and active participation in Jewish community affairs, so drawing a formal and absolute distinction between German and non-German Jews, was one that was never to be officially accepted, at any rate in full.[55]

All these matters touched in one way or another on some of the most sensitive strains in the modern history of Jews: the famous problem of identity and its twin, the precipitous fall in moral self-confidence that was now a pervasive feature of the lives of the modernizing, acculturating, secularizing Jews of the west; the fact that remarkable progress in many departments of their lives had failed to assure them of a fixed status as full and worthy members of the national societies to which they belonged; the fact that it could be said of very few that they had arrived at their destination and that while some were moving faster in the requisite direction than others, some had failed to move at all; the fact that while a negligible minority had resolved from the first not to embark on the journey into the alien culture, virtually all had gone some distance, and some had gone very far, towards an internalization of the values, loyalties, and opinions of the society in which they now mingled so much more freely than in the past and in which most did actively seek acceptance. The result was that the heartache, torment, humiliation, and laceration of self that in varying degrees had been the lot of Rahel Varnhagen, Heine, Börne, Disraeli, Lassalle, and the many others who had set out to pioneer the road to assimilation and acculturation were now common elements of the social experience of many hundreds of thousands of otherwise unexceptional men and women. In brief, to all of this the appearance of the eastern Jews on western doorsteps—those Jews for whom these particular, quintessentially western aspects of the contemporary Jewish predicament were at least initially totally foreign, imperfectly comprehensible, and, when grasped in whole or in part, often contemptible as well—could not fail to contribute mightily.

VI

There was one aspect of the disarray into which events in Russia had thrown western Jewry that ran deeper than the immediate and discomfiting problems raised by the great migration. It was evident that the greater problem was that of Russo-Polish Jewry itself *in situ*: a community in deep distress whose affairs could not be approached, nor any

---

[55] The entire subject is admirably reviewed in Wertheimer, *Unwelcome Strangers*.

alleviation of its difficulties attempted, in terms that were in any way analogous to those in which the Damascus Affair had been dealt with forty years earlier or even those that had seemed appropriate in the case of the admittedly larger and more complex struggle for the civil rights and status of Romanian Jews (to be discussed in detail below[56]). The Jews of Damascus and of newly independent Romania had been (indeed, still were) in need of protection from their rulers. In each case, for different reasons, international political and diplomatic circumstances happened to provide an opening for intervention by foreign powers on their behalf following intercession by a small number of well-placed, well-meaning Jewish notables who had understood what needed to be done and had gone on to make the most of their personal access to the relevant European statesmen and chancelleries. Strictly speaking, these had been variants on the ancient model of intercession. The novelty, such as it was, in the operation Crémieux and Montefiore had mounted in 1840 lay partly in their having grasped that it had become possible to appeal to general principles of justice and decent conduct with reasonable expectation of a response of some kind in some quarters. Provided there were no serious countervailing considerations even men of great power and international standing preferred to be seen as honouring, rather than flouting them. It lay too, as we have seen, in the freer, less inhibited, in certain cases quite courageous, behaviour of some of the Jewish notables concerned. Finally, there had been established the precedent of Jewish co-operation across frontiers (across the English Channel in the first instance), much additional weight and tactical advantage being gained thereby. But while all these were changes of consequence, they spared none of the individuals or institutions who sought to play a role in Jewish public affairs from a loss of nerve and direction as the true dimensions of the crisis precipitated in 1881 for all European Jewry, if of course for Russian Jewry in the first instance, became apparent even to the least instructed of eyes. None of the new institutions of Jewry, those established in France and Great Britain among them, ventured to take a line that might reasonably be termed forceful. All would grasp very soon that the (seemingly) triumphant precedents of Damascus in 1840 and Romania in 1878 could not be built upon and that, most particularly, no common, supra-communal approach to the matter of Russian Jewry could be so much as formulated, let alone put into operation. Nor would any way be found to prevent a dangerous re-exposure of the Jews' endemic vulnerability for all to see.

The efficacy of high-level, confidential intercession in combination with open public pressure (as practised in the Damascus and Romanian cases) had always been contingent on the object being narrowly defined.

[56] Chapter 6.

In the Syrian case it had been a straightforward one of rescue. In the Romanian case it could be reduced to the need to gain for the Jews recognition as citizens of the country in which they were domiciled and a high proportion born, but which flatly denied them civil rights. The matter of Russian Jewry was a deal more complex. Its roots lay deep in the inner nature and structure of Russian society, the Russian polity, and Russia's particular version of Christendom's ancient inability to endure the continuity and, worse, the presence of the Jews. And, of course, Russia was a very great European power, potentially if not actually the greatest of all. These were aspects of the case that no Jewish institution and no single group of Jewish notables, no matter how eminent, well meaning, and suitably equipped with letters of recommendation from the great men of other European states, could conceivably tackle in the Crémieux-Montefiore manner or, as we shall see, in the way perfected by Bleichröder in the case of Romania—certainly not in a direct way. But nor could any other institution external to Russia, nor any foreign state no matter how prestigious or diplomatically and militarily powerful. On the contrary, the better the matter of Russian Jewry was understood in all its ramifications, the greater the reluctance to raise it. Carefully enfeebled gestures on behalf of the Jews might be made from time to time when either domestic considerations or, as was not entirely unknown, the dictates of decency and a liberal conscience required it. But the great and powerful Russian state was not, and could not be expected to be, amenable to the kind of pressure that the Pasha of Egypt had encountered in his day and the Romanian delegates to the Congress of Berlin and their leaders in Bucharest had been met with in 1878.[57]

The pattern and quality of power-political relationships between the major states of contemporary Europe at the tail-end of the nineteenth century and the early years of the twentieth was thought to require that access to the Autocrat and his minions was kept open and on as even a keel as possible. Knowing that official Russia was unwilling to countenance any attempt from without, no matter how discreet, to induce it to soften its Jewish policy there could be no question of anything remotely resembling forceful intercession on this matter. The afflictions of the Jews under the Autocracy were simply not a subject that any senior European diplomat worth his salt regarded as justifying the slightest risk of souring relations with St Petersburg. And this being very well understood by those Jewish notables of western and central Europe who had nevertheless taken it upon themselves to be concerned about their brethren in Russia their own attempts to rally support were deeply inhibited from the start. It was all very well to *hope* to wean the Autocracy away from the

---

[57] Quite apart from the circumstance, soon apparent to all, that the Romanians were now bent on reneging on their formal undertakings.

exceedingly hard line it had adopted after 1881. To attempt to do so in practice was to beat helplessly against the wall of persistence and encounter repeated and predictable rebuffs. But for private individuals to be so rebuffed was to suffer a measure of public humiliation. To suffer such humiliation was to have the personal status and prestige on which all such well-meaning activity depended called into question. And neither the passage of time nor the steady deterioration of the condition of the Jewish subjects of the Tsar, and the vastly more ferocious violence to which they would be subject in the early years of the new century,[58] were to alter the terms of this pathetic equation—before all was altered in the middle of the second decade of the new century by war and revolution. Besides, the ever more widely accepted notion that the political loyalty of western Jews to their respective countries had repeatedly to be demonstrated put paid to any thought of taking up a position that could be judged disturbing, let alone damaging, of whatever was officially conceived of as the national interest in each case.

When the first great wave of pogroms erupted in 1881 the urge to act was evident almost everywhere. But it tended in certain cases to be decidedly muted. In France two committees of (mostly non-Jewish) notables, all of the first order of personal prestige, were formed: one was presided over by Victor Hugo with Waldeck-Rousseau and Gambetta among its members, the other led by Alphonse de Rothschild. The Alliance Israélite, for its part, as we have seen, proceeded to devote very considerable attention, men, and material resources to the plight of the refugees who had gathered—dangerously, as the people of the Alliance thought—at Brody in Austria-ruled Galicia, just west of the Russian border, unable or unwilling either to proceed further or to return. But there was no question of holding a great public meeting on the lines of the one held in London at the Mansion House on 1 February 1882 under the auspices of the Lord Mayor of the City 'to express public opinion upon the outrages inflicted upon the Jews in various parts of Russia and Russian Poland'. The Earl of Shaftesbury, the Bishop of London, and Cardinal Manning all attended the Mansion House in person and spoke at length and messages of support from the Archbishop of Canterbury, the Duke of Westminster, the Master of Balliol, the Poet Laureate (Tennyson), and a dozen other notables of the nation flowed in and were read aloud to the assembly. In Paris the general sense, not least in the Jewish circle most directly concerned, namely that of the Alliance Israélite itself, was that it was neither possible nor desirable to attempt anything of *that* kind. And of public political pressure being mediated through the French government there was no question at all. When the Jewish deputy Jules Steeg approached Charles de Freycinet, the prime minister of the day, in February

---

[58] See Chapters 6 and 8.

1882, going no further than to ask him privately and politely about French intentions in regard to the persecution of Jews in Russia,

His answer [Steeg recorded] was the one I foresaw: that it was a question to no purpose because it was not one the government could respond to, it being the case that on no account could it meddle in the internal affairs of a foreign country.

He called my attention too to the fact that in England there had been some popular agitation, public meetings, items in the press; whereas in France nothing or almost nothing is known of these sad matters and that the country would not understand why the government should take any interest in it.[59]

Later, as France moved towards a military alliance with Russia, even so very cautious an inquiry as this would be ruled out as a matter of course and only the very gentlest of eleemosynary approaches to the matter of the Tsar's Jews remained permissible. To go to the aid of 'our brothers in Russia' was indeed to do no more than obey 'one of the most legitimate of sentiments'. But it 'should not lend itself to any misinterpretation,' declared the Grand Rabbi of France, Zadoc Kahn, in a pastoral letter to the Jewish communities of France in 1891.

As French Jews we are pleased with the recent events which have so brilliantly raised the prestige of our country and have crowned twenty years of efforts, of moderation, of wise and fruitful negotiation. But misfortune [does have] its claims upon us, our pity must go out to those who suffer, and we know that an immense population, bound to us by the most sacred ties, is undergoing terrible trials.[60]

And once the alliance had been concluded, such simple caution was apt to give way to the grotesque. As Tsar Alexander III, the Autocrat under whom and with whose approval the entire system of administrative oppression had been revivified and intensified, lay dying in 1894, prayers were offered up on his behalf in all the synagogues of Paris. Alexander III, it was authoritatively explained, had indeed 'greatly persecuted Jews'. None the less, he was an honest man and a believer. What he had done he had done according to the dictates of his conscience. And then, 'above all, we must remember that he was a friend of France and that in the interest of our fatherland his life is precious'.[61] Upon his successor's enthronement two years later special prayer services were held again. On this occasion the Russian-Jewish colony in Paris was assured by the chief rabbi that French Jews, in their attachment to France, understood the sentiments of their Russian co-religionists very well: 'living amongst us,

    [59] Cited in Szajkowski, 'How the Mass Migration to America Began', 293 (slightly amended).
    [60] 'Lettre pastorale du Grand Rabbin de France', L'Univers israélite, 1 Dec. 1991. Cited in slightly different form in Marrus, The Politics of Assimilation, 158.
    [61] Ibid. 157.

they faithfully retain the memory of their country of origin, much like the exiles from Judaea who, on the river-banks of Babylon, thought so feelingly and tenderly of Jerusalem.'[62]

Unquestionably, Crémieux was dead in spirit no less than in body. The Alliance Israélite which he had done much to found and had then led for many years remained the one lay institution of French Jewry that was explicitly committed to the welfare of Jews who lived beyond the borders of continental France. But his nominal successors had neither his political prominence nor his pugnacity and were in most other ways lesser men. It was true, that to defy Thiers in 1840 on matters that were arguably on the margin of France's national interests and when there was evidently more than one answer to the question of where national honour might lie was one thing. To cross or even so much as disturb the government of a bloodied, humiliated, insecure, and fundamentally revanchist post-1870 Third Republic desperate for major military allies was another. If matters were easier in Great Britain it was at least in part because Britain's place in the world of international politics was easier too.

Montefiore, Crémieux's partner in the original effort to explode and resolve the Damascus Affair, had subsequently taken a great interest in the affairs of the Russian Jews. In 1846 he had travelled to Russia where, on the strength of his status as a British notable and protégé of the British government, he was received politely enough by the foreign minister, the minister of education, and finally by Tsar Nicholas I himself. Those were easier times all round, or so they appeared to Montefiore who declared himself favourably impressed both by the emperor and by what he termed the 'spiritual and social condition' of the Jews themselves. Their condition had improved, he informed the representative body of British Jews, the Board of Deputies and would continue to improve. Russian Jews had 'abundant reason to cherish grateful feelings towards the Emperor, to whom their prosperity is in so great a measure attributable'.[63] Whether Montefiore, like others in and out of Russia, had been truly blinded by surface changes in the regime to which the Jews had been subjected, or had given way to no more than his own native, somewhat incorrigible optimism, or had suffered a mild clouding of judgement consequent on an inevitably imperfect grasp of the realities of Russia remains an open question. Certainly his best years were behind him. When the great crisis broke in 1881 he was a very old man indeed,[64] and incapable of any action at all. Still, the informal tradition that he had done much to consolidate continued to be respected. The government in

[62] *Archives Israélites*, 11 June 1896.
[63] Lucien Wolf, *Sir Moses Montefiore* (New York, 1885), 218.
[64] Montefiore died in 1885 at the age of 101.

London continued to lend a polite, at times even a genuinely sympathetic, ear to what the recognized, lay representatives of Jewry wished to tell it about the condition and persecution of Jews in foreign lands. And the principle that HM Government was prepared to consider what, if anything, it could do in such cases was maintained, much as expressions of public outrage by some of the great and the good of the kingdom continued to be forthcoming when news of violence against Russian Jews emerged, as would be the case from time to time. Actual robust backing for a Jewish cause was another matter, however. Overt intervention and public support for a Jewish cause in the Palmerstonian mode and for Palmerstonian reasons was a thing of the past. As Great Britain moved towards a political understanding with Russia early in the twentieth century that would be solidified in the course of time under the terms of the entente of 1907 even the discreet transmission to the Russians of remarks on the undesirable impact the hammering of the Jews was having on public opinion in England became very rare and the participation of active politicians—the now substantial contingent of Jewish ministers and Members of Parliament among them—in public protests rarer still. The Anglo-Russian entente had been concluded by a Liberal government; but it had been supported with little hesitation by the Conservative opposition. In these circumstances, it was not surprising that none of the 16 Jews elected to Parliament in 1906 (12 Liberals, 4 Conservatives), or the 14 elected in January 1910, or the 15 elected in the second election held in that year in December, was prepared to take an independent line and break free from his party whip on this issue. It was with unusual bitterness that the *Jewish Chronicle*[65] complained in the spring of 1910, when reports of razzias and other forms of harassment of Jews in Kiev reached London, along with warnings that a massive expulsion of Jews was imminent, that

This monstrous cruelty is being done in the teeth of protests and appeals from Russian citizens. The [Kiev] Merchants' Guild, the Stock Exchange Committee, and a number of Christian householders have petitioned for its abandonment. . . . Even now, however, at the eleventh hour, we hope to hear some voice raised in some civilized State against the atrocious proceedings that are imminent. There are a large number of Jewish members of the House of Commons, to say nothing of the three Jewish members of the Government. Do the private members not feel even a single twinge of pity for their hunted coreligionists— pity enough to persuade one of them, at all events, even say, to put a question in Parliament upon this governmental iniquity?[66]

The Jewish members of the government the *Chronicle* referred to were Herbert Samuel, Rufus Isaacs, and Edwin Montagu. Samuel was a fairly

---

[65] Since 1907 under the much more robust editorial direction of Leopold J. Greenberg.
[66] *Jewish Chronicle*, 22 Apr. 1910.

senior member of the Liberal party: he had entered the cabinet as Chancellor of the Duchy of Lancaster in 1909, the first professing Jew to be a member of cabinet. A year later he was appointed Postmaster-General. Later still he would serve in other offices, the most prestigious being that of Home Secretary. Isaacs had recently been appointed Solicitor-General, an office of state of no more than middling importance and one that has never carried a cabinet seat. But he was a man to mark: later in the year, upon promotion to the post of Attorney-General he would be given a seat in the cabinet—the first Law Officer to have one. Later still he would serve successively as Lord Chief Justice of England, ambassador to the United States, and Viceroy of India—a remarkable succession of offices of state crowned eventually by the title of Marquess of Reading. Montagu was the most junior of the three. Early in 1910 he held the post of Parliamentary Secretary to the Prime Minister. In the course of the autumn reshuffle of offices he would be appointed Parliamentary Secretary to the Secretary of State for India. He had been, as for some years he would remain, unusually close to the Prime Minister, Herbert Asquith, and would hold higher office in the course of time. Taken together, the three men served to demonstrate how far Jews could now go in British politics: quite as far as could be gone in France, far beyond what was even conceivable in Germany or Austria, let alone Russia. But on what might or what should be done as and when matters that were specifically Jewish arose each of the three took a line that was distinctly his own, as we shall see in some detail later. In general, however, Isaacs and Montagu kept in the shadows on such occasions.[67] Samuel, a cautious man and no less ambitious politically than the other two, was less afraid to plead a Jewish cause. He had denounced the Alien Immigration Bill when it came before the Commons in 1905. But the Alien Immigration Bill was the work of the Conservative government of the day. As a member of the Liberal opposition Samuel was relatively free to say what he thought of it as it was being pushed through Parliament. In the following year, as a junior member in the new Liberal government with an appointment in the Home Office and some responsibility for the administration of the new restrictions on immigration, he behaved rather more circumspectly. He appears to have done what he could to ensure a more generous approach to Jewish refugees arriving in England than they might otherwise, perhaps, have had to confront; and the established leaders of Britain Jewry did not consider that they had serious cause for complaint in his regard.[68] Matters of foreign policy were in a class of their own, however. To touch on the major question of the entente with Russia even indirectly was to be very daring and exceptionally careless indeed of one's

[67] See Chapter 7.
[68] Bernard Wasserstein, *Herbert Samuel: A Political Life* (Oxford, 1992), 88–91.

political prospects. In the event, on the substance of the *Jewish Chronicle*'s charge against Samuel and his two colleagues, it may be said that there is no evidence that it ever occurred to Samuel, let alone to his two Jewish colleagues, to rally publicly or otherwise to the cause of Russian Jewry in the precise, political sense the newspaper's editor had in mind. And given the rules of the political game as all understood it, it would have been surprising if any of them had done so. It was for those Jewish notables who had assumed an explicit public responsibility for Jewish welfare and had been accepted both by the Jewish public and by British officialdom as the legitimate representative leaders of British Jewry to act if and when they thought it necessary and useful to do so. In such cases other informal, but equally binding and well-understood, rules applied.

When David Alexander of the Board of Deputies and Claude Montefiore[69] of the Anglo-Jewish Association,[70] went to the Foreign Office on 25 April 1910 to ask for British intervention on behalf of the Jews of Kiev they were told firmly, in well-rehearsed language, that 'of course . . . no official representation which would amount to interference in the internal affairs of a friendly Gov[ernmen]t,' could be made. The official receiving them then softened his response somewhat by adding that 'The most we could do,' he recorded himself as saying, '(and I was not sure that we could do that) was to telegraph St Petersburg instructing Sir A[rthur] Nicolson [the ambassador] to say privately that the rumour had reached us and had alarmed the Jews here and to ask whether such an intention existed.' It turned out that he was mistaken, however. This was much more than his superiors were prepared to sanction. All the Foreign Office authorized in the event was a laconic telegram to St Petersburg requesting the ambassador to seek to discover whether the reported expulsion from Kiev had indeed been fixed to take place on the date mentioned, 28 April. No explanation was given. No mention of Alexander and Montefiore was made. No action was requested.[71] Nicolson did London's bidding to the extent of making inquiries at the Foreign Ministry in St Petersburg where, as might have been expected, nothing was known about the affairs of the Jews in Kiev—a city that, like Moscow and St Petersburg itself, was normally closed to Jews other than those explicitly privileged to live there. But the ambassador made it very clear to London that that was as far as he himself would wish to go. 'It is difficult for me to make enquiries [on such a matter] in official quarters without

---

[69] Sir Moses Montefiore's great-nephew.

[70] The Board was the elected and representative body that spoke for British Jewry. The Anglo-Jewish Association was, in spirit and to some extent in intent and activity, the analogue of the Alliance Israélite in Paris and the Hilfsverein in Germany.

[71] Foreign Office minute, 25 Apr. 1910; and Grey to Nicolson, 25 Apr. 1910, PRO, FO 271/979/14378.

causing offence,' he told them.[72] Alexander and Montefiore persisted. Could 'you . . . not see your way,' they wrote to the Foreign Secretary, 'to suggest to Sir A. Nicolson that he should take a suitable opportunity of intimating in an unofficial manner to the Russian Government that any large expulsion of Jews from Kiev would certainly create a very painful and unfavourable opinion in this country[?]' And why, they asked, had the question of illegal residence of Jews in Kiev arisen in the first place? The city was *within* the Pale of Settlement. Even if the Russian system of restricted residence was accepted, surely there was an additional injustice here? But on this second occasion the Foreign Office was not to be moved. Alexander and Montefiore were informed in terms that had long been familiar to them and would long continue to be employed, that the Secretary of State

cannot see his way to instruct [the embassy] in the sense which you desire. Such an intimation would be calculated to cause irritation at any time as an unwarrantable act of interference on the part of a foreign Govt. in the internal affairs of Russia and at the present moment, when public opinion in that country is unusually sensitive as the result of the intervention of various individuals and public bodies in the question of Finland, the effect produced could not fail to be the exact opposite of what is desired.

Moreover the fact that, so far as can be judged from the information hitherto received, the Russian Govt. appear to be acting in accordance with the law, makes any intervention the more inadvisable.[73]

And yet, the machinery of the Foreign Office and the Diplomatic service, having been engaged, continued to turn over.[74] What was the truth of the matter of the expulsion from Kiev, they wanted to know. On 5 May the Foreign Office informed the embassy in St Petersburg what the British consul in Kiev, who happened to be on a visit in London, knew of the subject: 1,000 Jewish families were indeed to be expelled, although, it was to be noted, 'They were of the poorer classes and not members of the First Merchants Guild.' At the embassy itself, the technical legalities or otherwise of the planned expulsion to which Alexander and Montefiore had called attention were then gone into. It was discovered (what no one at the embassy had previously realized), that while Kiev was 'geographically' within the Pale, in legal terms it had always been treated (like Yalta and Sevastopol) 'as being without it', forbidden to Jews, that is to say, certain specific and narrow categories excepted. Some days later it was learned that the planned expulsion had been postponed;

[72] Nicolson to Grey, 27 Apr. 1910, PRO, FO 271/979/14494.

[73] Foreign Office to Alexander and Montefiore, 31 May 1910, PRO, FO 271/979/18279.

[74] For a useful review of such instances in the 1880s and, especially, the 1890s, see V. V. Timofeev, 'Evreiskaya emigratsiya iz Rossii v kontekste rossiisko-britanskikh otnoshenii kontsa xix veka', University of Kharkov thesis, 1993.

later still, that while there would indeed be expulsions, they would not be massive; and finally that the relevant regulations being of great intricacy, a special commission had been set up to investigate the precise 'titles of individual Jews' to reside in Kiev on a case-to-case basis. In mid-June it was reported that the number of persons slated for expulsion had dropped to 446. In July the embassy was informed by the British consul in Kiev that as of the first of the month the number of Jews actually expelled was 'only' 101 and that the 'Authorities have been most lenient in their deal-ings with this question and no extreme measures have been resorted to'.[75] In the end, stage by stage, by inevitable progression, the affair of the expulsions from Kiev receded from London's view altogether. Certain people in the Foreign Office had been rendered a mite more familiar with the matter of Russian Jewry and its afflictions than they had been before. Nothing of consequence had been done to ease the Jews' actual condition: but then, to the relief of those of whom action had been requested, nothing, seemingly, needed to be done, not urgently at any rate and not in connection with the specific matter which had brought Alexander and Montefiore to the Foreign Office on this particular occa-sion. As for Alexander and Montefiore themselves and for their col-leagues and associates in the Board of Deputies of British Jews and the Anglo-Jewish Association, the general sense of the exceedingly narrow limits within which they might hope to operate to any useful purpose so long as they, no less than the government, kept to the accepted rules, had been further reinforced.

But the heart of the problem that confronted the new specialists in Jewish public affairs and continuously sapped their will to act with a fair degree of confidence and vigour lay in the fact that the turn taken by the affairs of the Jews of Russia (and of Romania too) in the last two decades or so of the century cut across the grain of the central assumption on which the Jews of western and central Europe had now come over-whelmingly to found their lives. This, as we have seen, was that the con-temporary state could, in the final analysis, be relied upon—if not, perhaps, as a friend, then at least as an ally of sorts, but certainly as a protector. His-torically, the state (or the ruler) had always been looked to for protection. In modern times, while the alliance between the state and its Jewish sub-jects might be lacking in mutual regard and respect, it had ceased to rest on the ephemeral private, personal, and therefore contingent interests and inclinations of the ruler. It had come to be founded on the ostensibly more solid basis of the logic on which the modern, generally enlightened state was expected by most of its own citizens to conduct its business. This was the assumption; and since the balance of the evidence in much of

Europe supported it, it was one Jews of all classes were strongly inclined to cherish. In any case, no acceptable alternative thesis was seriously on offer. In most Jewish quarters, therefore, to recognize that hostility to Jewry and Judaism was still alive—even in what all agreed were the distinctly civilized parts of Europe—was not to reject this assumption, it was to cleave to it.

But what if there was continually mounting evidence to show that it was fundamentally inapplicable to Russia? Was it then the case that the common western view, that the *general* drift in society and government did broadly favour the Jews, was not, after all, of universal, but only of local, contingent, and limited application? If so, were ideas such as these, the origins and applicability of which were specifically, perhaps exclusively western, to be subjected to fresh, closer, and much more sceptical examination? Alternatively, if the view that the broader trends in the contemporary world did favour a beneficial readjustment of the terms of Jewish life turned out to be well founded, what was to be made of the Russian exception? Did it mean that Russia was in some important respect beyond the pale of the fully civilized nations and states? Or was it Russian Jewry itself that was in some way the distorting factor? And if that was the case to what extent were western Jews entitled—let alone wise—to press for intervention on behalf of their unfortunate but wayward brethren in the east and in this and other ways set themselves at cross purposes with their own governments?

Finally, there was the largest question of all. If Russia and Romania remained exceptional in Europe because their governments were adamant in their refusal to treat their respective Jewish populations with minimal equity and justice, what was to become of those great communities? What could be done for them? What could not be done? What would be the further implications of so gigantic a movement of population if it continued? If they were to remain in Russia, did that mean that to all intents and purposes they were—at all events for the foreseeable future—condemned? Was that acceptable? But to speculate along such lines as these was necessarily to begin to think the hitherto unthinkable. To refuse to speculate, on the other hand—could that be other than to put the great westward migration, as well as the circumstances that had precipitated it and kept it in being, out of one's mind and so to acquiesce once again in the awful endemic vulnerability and helplessness of the Jewish people?

It is with those who found that they were unable to banish such questions from their minds and who persisted in concerning themselves with a problem for which it was sufficiently evident there was no ready solution that the next chapter is principally concerned.

5
Auto-emancipation?

I

EUROPEAN JEWRY was now divided. It was divided *de facto* and more than ever before in conscience. It was one thing to observe events in Russia from without and at the immense distance in space and mind separating the barbarities inflicted on the Pale of Jewish Settlement from the comparative order and civilization of central and western Europe. It was another to suffer, or even merely to observe, them at first hand from within the empire itself. Sympathy and benign concern for the easterners when contemplating their disasters were not uncommon sentiments in Berlin, Vienna, Budapest, London, and Paris, as we have seen. For the Jews of Russia and Poland themselves matters were of course vastly more immediate, depressing, and, above all, urgent. For the great majority within the Pale, but also for the very small minority allowed to live outside it, for the rich, for the poor, for the high and for the low, for firmly orthodox believers no less than for those who had been touched (or more) by secularism and by indigenous Russian culture, for those who had escaped molestation almost as much as for those who had suffered it at the hands of the mob or those of the authorities—for all these, for all classes, some sort of reckoning had now to be made. The central, haunting question for the Jews, as for most subjects of the Tsar, each class or group or tendency for its own reasons, was *what was to be done?*

In August 1881 and again in April 1882 Baron Horace Guenzburg gathered two dozen carefully selected notables and rabbis in the privacy of his St Petersburg home to discuss how it might be best to proceed in the wake of the recent events. It was accepted by all, within the higher reaches of the Russian bureaucracy itself as well as in the vast Jewish community itself, that Guenzburg was the one figure in Russian Jewry with a claim to the kind of pre-eminence that was commonly ascribed to the Rothschilds in Britain and France and, if rather more surreptitiously, but still as a matter of course, to Gerson Bleichröder in Germany. He had the attributes of wealth and political and economic connections that had long been understood and accepted as supremely relevant to high status of that nature. Uniquely for Russia he had the advantage of a formal title of nobility as well—even if, strictly speaking, it was a non-Russian one. There was certainly no question at all, but that Guenzburg and his near equivalents (S. S. Poliakov, the railway magnate, and the Brodski family who held a dominant position in the sugar industry among them) were in every sense pillars of the established order and recognized and accepted as such by the Autocracy at all levels. And indeed, their public posture and political philosophy were founded, as was appropriate, on their set belief that the Autocracy's good will was essential to the prosperity of Jewry and that, ultimately, the claim to legal equality would be granted. It was their view, therefore, that under no circumstances was the government to be crossed or slighted, let alone actively quarrelled with. The care with which they trod the narrow path of legal freedom allowed them was exemplified in Guenzburg not only being required to ask prior permission from the Ministry of the Interior to hold his little, private meeting, but in his requesting it.

The oligarchs had been appalled by the phenomenon of massive flight from the empire of continually rising numbers of their brethren. They read it, and they thought that that was how it would be read by the authorities, as an immense vote of no confidence in the regime, one that fell just short, if short at all, of a silent declaration of enmity. It was likely, they thought, to undo their own patient work of decades. It would foreclose all good prospects for the future. But more than anything they were struck, by no means unreasonably, by fear lest the *idea* that it was possible to rid the country of the Jews—by provocation, by violence, conceivably by fiat—would gain fresh ground among those, especially in very high places, who had always been uncompromising in their objection to the presence of the Jewish people on the holy soil of Russia. They were horrified when the new minister of the interior, Ignatiev, stated in the course of an interview granted a representative of the liberal Russian-language Jewish weekly *Razsvet* on 16 January 1882 that 'the western frontier [of Russia] is open', that many Jews had already taken ample advantage of the opportunity to leave, and that the emigration of Jews from the empire would no longer be hampered by the state. And they were furious with the editor of *Razsvet* for publishing it. What Ignatiev, had had to say was not at all what they, or for that matter all those lesser folk who since the advent of the late liberal Tsar had cleaved to some form of optimistic modernism and Russification, had ever wanted to hear. They themselves had been given to understand that the government opposed the flight of the Jews. They had been told too that they were expected to put a stop to it. And they had in fact done what they could to oblige. They did not now dare criticize Ignatiev; but Isaac Orshansky who had interviewed him was denounced for what was seen as gratuitously providing an opportunity for the minister to speak his mind, to frighten and depress the Jews, and, worst of all, to contribute massively to the crystallization and articulation of a policy that was deeply unwelcome to them.

To be sure, the position in which the traditional leaders of Russian Jewry now found themselves was untenable. At the local level, the formally installed leaders of the communities continued to perform the tasks laid upon them by the state. The notables, lay and clerical, remained shorn of anything better than an informal, indeterminate status as much within their own society as in society at large a *vis-à-vis* the state machine. Membership of the inner circle fluctuated. No formally established, authoritative, country-wide, and in any useful sense *representative* institution was allowed them. In the Russian Empire, as we have seen, nothing remotely comparable to the Board of Deputies of British Jews or the Consistoire Central in Paris or the Centralverein deutscher Staatsbürger jüdischen Glaubens was permitted, the Autocracy's objection to country-wide organization being consistent and all but total. A modest request for permission to systematize and expand the funding and work of trade schools for young Jewish people submitted to the all-powerful Ministry of the Interior in the final years of Alexander II's reign by a number of well-meaning Jewish philanthropists was met with nothing firmer than provisional and conditional approval. Twenty-six years would pass before final approval of its perfectly innocent operations was granted.[1] The refusal of the authorities to permit Jews of any category, lay or clerical, to form a social organization of their own for any collective purpose whatsoever even blocked attempts to render simple charitable assistance to those who had suffered injury during the pogroms. The rule in Russia was that only people of officially recognized status, loosely defined so as to include directors of hospitals, *zemstvo* men, priests of the Orthodox and Catholic Churches, and the like, were entitled to conduct social welfare operations on a basis that extended beyond the strictly local. But while priests were officially recognized for such purposes most functioning rabbis were not; and Jews of any other class, being debarred from official positions of almost any kind, were effectively ruled out for such purposes too. Large-scale public assistance to the victims of the pogroms, if it was to be rendered at all, had to be channelled through committees that were staffed and operated by non-Jews, bodies that, in the nature of things, were apt to be hostile to the Jews as such and ignorant and dismissive of their special needs. The ordinary, purely local communal Jewish leadership would do what it could, but it was inherently ill-equipped for major tasks of the kind that needed to be performed. The experience was lacking. So were the country-wide connections. Communal worthies tended—at least in the short term—to be ill-informed about events transpiring beyond their immediate horizon. A great deal of what would eventually, but slowly, become common knowledge was unknown to them—or very imperfectly known—in real time. It is true that the Jewish press in Russia did much to maintain what in the circumstances was,

---

[1] This was to be the organization known as the ORT, prodigiously active in many parts of the world in the same field of technical training to this day.

in fact, a fairly high degree of intellectual and cultural coherence in this vast and scattered community. But it was profoundly handicapped by heavy censorship, the operating logic of which required that the more grievous the event the greater the obstacles raised to its being promptly reported, or in many cases reported at all. Much of what was of keenest interest to Jewish readers could be published only after long delay, often one of weeks on end, and then only in watered-down or veiled 'Aesopian' terms. The pogroms were never frankly spoken of in the Jewish press, only alluded to in a phrase such as 'storms in the south'. On the work of the official committees that had been set up in the various provinces of the Pale to examine the Jewish Question,[2] no reporting was allowed at all. This could not and did not totally obstruct the eventual, widespread circulation of essential information. Much passed from mouth to mouth. Russian Jews, like literate Russians of all classes, were skilled interpreters of 'Aesopian' texts. Among the fully literate, both traditionalists and members of the new, Russifying intelligentsia, extensive private correspondence was habitual. Events were reported, opinions expressed, action debated—always cautiously for fear of postal censorship, but ever more systematically. And it was not long before the semi-private reporting of events in Russia was extended to Jewish institutions and notables abroad, rabbinical and lay. Initially, it was to plead for help. But a larger, more specific, and therefore, given the nature of the Russian police state, more daring purpose was assumed in the course of time: that of encouraging Jews in the free countries of western Europe to marshal public, more especially political, opinion in the lands of their settlement.

The hope, at its most modest, was that pressure brought to bear on the Russian authorities would induce them to recognize their responsibility for the safety and welfare of their Jewish subjects. To that end, namely to provide a basis for public, private, eventually even diplomatic intercession with the Autocracy on behalf of the Jews, the relevant facts and figures needed to be collected and transmitted abroad. This had never been done systematically and would not be done now. No country-wide network dedicated to the collection, collation, and transmission of information was established. The initiative remained local in all cases, typically that of a single individual with access to friends or associates abroad—of which the most notable example, perhaps, was the activity in Kovno, the driving force provided by the headmaster of the local religious school, the higher auspices and moral authority by the eminent rabbinical figure, Rabbi Yiẓḥak Elḥanan Spektor. Strictly speaking, the Kovno centre for the collection and distribution abroad of information on the vicissitudes of Russian Jewry was in the nature of an underground operation. So it would certainly have been regarded had it been discovered by the police.

[2] See above, Chapter 4.

The initial line of communication out of Kovno ran by letter post to an official of the Great Synagogue in London. The real addressee, the man relied upon to bring knowledge of the treatment meted out to Russian Jewry to the attention of the London press and through it to the political world in Great Britain, was the accepted lay leader of British Jewry, Nathaniel (the future Lord) Rothschild. From time to time other prominent Jews, lay and clerical, in other European capitals were added to the list of correspondents to be informed of events by the people in Kovno and elsewhere and first results were promising. Detailed reports on the persecution of the Jews were published in *The Times* in mid-January 1882. The great public protest meeting at the Mansion House attended by British notables of the first rank,[3] was held in February. But in its larger purpose the campaign ran, as it was fated to do, into a dead end. Public protest meetings and a bad press in western capitals were embarrassing to the Autocracy, but not gravely so. They were not—nor could they be expected to be—frequent. And there was some plausibility, besides, to the contemporary belief that within the Russian bureaucracy itself there were those who thought that a demonstration of the Autocracy's readiness to deal harshly with its own subjects was positively advantageous to it diplomatically.[4] Still, the more decisive limits to what Rabbi Spektor and his associates and analogues could hope to achieve were internal. There was the police to contend with: what might be regarded as legitimate activity in the west was impermissible criminal conspiracy in Russia and a reason in itself for Rothschild's approximate opposite number in Russia, Baron Guenzburg, to be kept out of the loop and for operations of this kind to remain local and sporadic. It was obvious that the small plutocratic class in Russian Jewry to which he belonged was especially fearful of compromising itself in the eyes of the authorities. Worse, some of its members could be relied upon to do what they could to stop what Rabbi Spektor and his friends were doing if ever they were in a position to do so.[5] But it was the reed on which such operations really depended that proved to be broken. The logic by which Rabbi Spektor and his friends were guided was straightforward. They were firm in their belief that responsibility for the pogroms lay with the government. They recognized that this was odd: governments were assumed to be interested before all else in the maintenance of law and order, not riots and pillage

---

[3] See above, Chapter 4.

[4] Leo Motzkin (ed.), *Die Judenpogrome in Russland*, i (Cologne and Leipzig, 1910), 230.

[5] Ya'akov ha-Levi Lifshitz, *Zikhron Ya'akov*, 3 vols. (Kaunas, 1923–30; repr. Benei-Berak, 1968), iii. 20–63 and *passim*. See also I. Oppenheim, 'The Kovno Circle of Rabbi Yitzhak Elhanan Spektor: Organizing Western Public Opinion over Pogroms in the 1880s', in S. I. Troen and B. Pinkus (eds.), *Organizing Rescue: National Jewish Solidarity in the Modern Period* (London, 1992).

in the streets. But they reasoned that in Germany something of an analogous nature had been the case when Bismarck employed anti-Semitism for political purposes on the grounds, as Ya'akov Lifshitz, the memoirist of the group in Kovno, put it, that it was 'better that they (the Germans) should concern themselves with the Jews instead of worrying about how they might improve their own condition'. If this was true of the Germans, why not of the Russians as well? There was the difference, of course, that 'In an enlightened and civilized country like Germany hatred of Jews only took the form of slander and mild oppression ['*alilot ve-eizeh redifot*], while in Russia the form was one of simple and terrible pogroms.'[6] Here, precisely, were the grounds for their belief that support from the west, Jewish and non-Jewish, would lead eventually to effective pressure being applied on St Petersburg. Their hopes were especially high when, after extensive correspondence, Samuel Montagu (later Lord Swaythling) and Dr Ascher, the driving spirits behind the western protest movement in favour of the Jews of Russia, came out to Poland and Russia in April 1882 to see things for themselves. Alas, it became obvious that what had moved Montagu and Ascher to travel so far from home was the matter of Jewish emigration to England, and that what the English Jews wanted of Rabbi Spektor and his colleagues was a serious effort to reduce it, 'lest', as they put it to the Russians, 'the wrath of the [gentile] inhabitants of England be provoked'.[7] One way or another, therefore, in their larger purposes, that of deflecting the Autocracy from its steadily hardening approach to all matters relating to the Jews, and, on the other hand, that of contributing something of substance to the safety and welfare of Russian Jewry generally, the people in Kovno (and others who had come together in like spirit in other cities from time to time) were driven before long to the conclusion that there was small cause to rely on western help after all.

Nor, taken as a whole, was there cause to rely on the Russian rabbinate itself. For among the class to which he belonged, that which comprised the senior figures in the orthodox Russo-Polish rabbinate of the day, Rabbi Spektor of Kovno was an unusual figure. He was vigorous. He was more than willing to resist petty, but unacceptable governmental attempts to obstruct observance of the norms of Jewish life. His approach to such hard cases as were brought to him in his rabbinical-judgemental capacity was generally lenient. He was prepared to co-operate in the Jewish public interest not only with lay notables of the established type, of which Guenzburg in St Petersburg, once again, was the leading exemplar, but when necessary, and more controversially, even with *maskilim*. On all counts, therefore, he proved to be a man of strong character and an independent turn of mind, as concerned with his people's immediate

---

[6] *Zikhron Ya'akov*, iii. 18–19.
[7] Ibid. 94–5.

material needs as with their continuing observance of the letter of Talmudic law. That he sought positively to keep these largely incompatible concerns reasonably balanced and did to some extent succeed in doing so, and that he was able to go as far as he did without serious damage to his eminence in his own, otherwise closed world of uncompromising, hugely conformist orthodoxy, marks him out as an especially interesting figure—but something of a puzzle as well.

For by and large, the leaders of religious orthodoxy in Russia and Poland cleaved to their quietism. They did so on what they continued to regard as pragmatic grounds, i.e. fear of incalculable consequences for themselves and for other Jews if they did not. They did so out of habit. And they did so, in many cases, on explicitly philosophical-religious grounds of the kind that had long since been formulated, for example, by the original, immensely influential master of the ḤaBaD hasidim, Rabbi Shne'ur Zalman of Lyady.[8] Shne'ur Zalman had laid it down towards the end of the previous century that it was objectionable in principle to seek to improve one's temporal circumstances, that suffering should not be resisted but accepted with love, and that to do otherwise was to reject the will of God. The proper course for the God-fearing was to make of suffering a means of purging sin (meiruk 'avonot) and grounds for self-improvement through worship. That and that alone would bring about the changes in this world that good men desired.[9] It was, of course, change itself that the orthodox of all tendencies (leaving aside the relatively few, generally uninfluential, modernist, state-trained and state-authorized 'crown Rabbis')[10] feared more than anything. Their hostility to modernism, their sour view of emancipation where it had been granted, their disinclination to press for it where it had been blocked, all these were founded on much the same argument that the Ḥatam Sofer of Pressburg had formulated a good three generations earlier.[11] Change in the established mode of public responses to events, even dire events, change in comportment, change of place and occupation when it was likely to lead to cultural and socio-economic transformation—these were to be feared and inhibited wherever possible. Jews were to avoid quarrels with the authorities; they were not to join those seeking (vainly) to pull the whole structure of oppression and injustice down; they were not to seek to go any real distance towards meeting the indigenous Russians

---

[8] On R. Shne'ur Zalman, see above, Chapter 2.

[9] E. Etkes, 'Darko shel R. Shne'ur Zalman mi-Lyady ke-manhig shel hasidim', Ẓion, l (Jubilee vol.), (1985), 330 and passim.

[10] On the all-but-heretical views of, for example, R. Solomon (Zalkind) Minor, Crown Rabbi of Moscow from 1870 to 1892, see 'Azriel Shoḥat, 'Hashkafotav ha-asimilatoriot shel Zalkind Minor, ha-rav mi-ta'am shel kehilat Moskva', Ẓion, 44 (1979), 303–20.

[11] See above, Chapter 2.

on common cultural ground as Russifiers on both sides of the Jew–gentile divide demanded that they do. But nor were they to pull up stakes and venture into the unknown, away from such influence as their traditional leaders believed, at all events hoped, that they would long be in a position to exercise over them. Migration was as profoundly undesirable, therefore, as any other radical social or political move.

By the tail-end of the nineteenth century, however, the influence and authority of the rabbinate had begun to wane even in eastern Europe. The decline was slower than in the west. The world of orthodoxy was only fraying at the edges not undergoing the disintegration at the centre that had taken place in central Europe. Much the greater part of the Jewish population of Poland, Russia, Romania, and the eastern provinces of the Habsburg Empire remained essentially untouched by modern influences. It was besides with modernism pure and simple that eastern European orthodoxy had to contend, not with systematic religious reform on, for example, the German model. Apostasy was too insignificant statistically to worry about unduly, the more so as baptism, while not unknown on opportunistic grounds, was chiefly bound up with cases of coercion— in the army, for example. Exogenous marriage was effectively debarred by law. And, crucially, the question of identity and national or communal loyalty simply did not arise in Russia in the manner that had become familiar in western and central Europe. There was no question at all of a Jew becoming, or seriously believing himself to be, a *Russian* in the sense that German and French and even English Jews were manifestly tempted, and in a certain sense entitled, to think of themselves as Germans, Frenchmen, and Englishmen. Russification was an option, but it was a cultural, linguistic, and intellectual one, not a national, least of all a political one. Russian-speaking Jews remained Jewish nationals of Russia, never Russians, never ever members of the *korennoe naselenie* (or indigenous population). Thus socially, thus legally. The orthodox rabbinical establishment[12] had no objection to this state of affairs. On the contrary, it corresponded very reasonably to its own conception of both the religion of the Jews and their national-ethnic identity—which was one reason why the rabbinate had never been entirely hostile to the regime, any more than the regime itself had been entirely hostile to the rabbinate. In its curious, half-hearted way, and for its own particular reasons, the Autocracy had always been willing to co-operate—if only indirectly— with the traditionalist party in Jewry. It was reluctant to dispense with a system which enabled it to harness the many minor local leaders of the Jews to its service as tax-farmers and recruiting sergeants. It was now

---

[12] With two very minor exceptions—the Karaites, who kept their distance from other Jews, and a tiny, dissident, semi-Christian Jewish sect—Judaism in its religious aspect was present only in its orthodox form in eastern Europe.

prepared to do what it could, as it had not been in Uvarov's day, to strengthen the traditionalists in their effort to reduce the flow of Jews into the society of the empire as a whole—a phenomenon which it, much like the rabbinate, regarded with mixed, chiefly negative feelings. In principle, this was incompatible with the Autocracy's long-standing, well-articulated judgement on Jewish orthodoxy as hopelessly obscurantist and fanatical. The basis for co-operation was therefore inherently restricted and fragile, the more so as, from the strictly Jewish point of view, co-operation with the oppressor was always of doubtful legitimacy. Now, in the wake of the pogroms, the questions posed the orthodox leadership cut still closer to the bone. What were *they* to make of these events? What, as a body, were they prepared to do? Rare and isolated exceptions (such as Rabbi Spektor of Kovno) apart, to neither question was there ever a clear answer or, in fact, any answer at all. Special prayer services were held after the pogroms. Days of fasting were decreed. Petitions were submitted to the authorities. But, for the rest, the leaders of Russian and Polish orthodoxy had little to say to their flock except to call on them to hold to the Tradition itself in its firmest, most unbending, ritualized form. When pressed, they put their faith in the old forms of intercession (*shtadlanut*). It would be argued that harassment and even large-scale persecution could only be met, if indeed they could be met at all, by seeking out the immediately relevant minister, official, policeman, and such like with a view to warding off or at least softening the blow. Private argument, appeals to reason, and if all else failed bribery—these were the only weapons the Jews in their Exile had ever been capable of wielding. Thus in the past, thus in the present. There was something in this, to be sure. As Richard Pipes has put it, 'For the overwhelming majority of officials, self-seeking and bribery were a way of life to which they could conceive of no alternative. The conservative historian Nicholas Karamzin had them in mind when he used to say that if one were to answer with one word the question: "what goes on in Russia?", one would have to reply "thieving".'[13]

The traditionalists claimed that the modernists' position was flawed on other counts as well. *Their* argument had been—had it not?—that once the Jews were allowed to move into the mainstream of Russian life equality of rights with all other Russian subjects would follow to the mutual benefit of all, Jews and Russians alike. This had always been wildly speculative. It had now been totally vitiated by the fact, evident to all, that the thesis was not one to which the Autocracy itself was prepared to pay the slightest attention. The grandest of the modernists, the notables in St Petersburg and Moscow among them, had achieved nothing. The notion that further modernization of the Jews—indistinguishable in orthodox eyes in any case

[13] *Russia under the Old Regime* (New York, 1974), 287.

from secularization—would lead to change either in the higher policy of
the Autocracy towards the Jews or in the severity and efficiency with
which that policy was implemented was patently untenable. The frontal
approach to the Tsar and his ministers had failed. The organized attempt
to consider what should be done at Guenzburg's home had amounted to
nothing more than a decision to press the government yet again to accord
civil rights to the Jews. But to hold that the root *cause* of the afflictions suffered by the Jews lay in the unequal and unjust status forced upon them was
mistaken. The claim that once their equality with all other subjects of the
Tsar had been openly and authoritatively proclaimed the bullying of the
Jews and worse would come to an end was illusory. It was futile to argue
that to keep the Jews in a state of penury, legal inferiority, and vulnerability to the mob was to serve the Russian economy and the Russian people
itself ill. It was certainly commendable to invest time and resources in the
modernizing of the Jews, in training or retraining the vast host of semi-
skilled or totally unskilled among them in useful crafts and professions,
especially the 'mechanical arts', in the improvement of their command of
the Russian language, and generally in converting a nation of pedlars,
shop- and innkeepers, cobblers, tailors, wagoners, and so-called *luftmenshn*
(people devoid of any security or any real role in the economy at all) into
productive members of society. But none of this, no matter how successfully accomplished, was likely to make the slightest impression on the
Autocracy. The modernists and Russifiers in Jewry failed utterly to see the
wood for the trees. They attached more importance to the admission of a
single Jew to a university than to the expulsion of great numbers of impoverished families from their land and their homes. They consistently
demonstrated how little they knew of the conditions in which their
brethren within the Pale lived, how negligible was their knowledge and
understanding of the Tradition, and how baseless was their notion that the
salvation of Israel lay in secular education.[14] They failed—or refused—to
see that the ultimate consequences for the integrity of Jewry and for the
continuity and strength of Judaism of what they were about would be catastrophic. They were appalled by the charges the very harshest of orthodox
critics brought against them: that these catastrophic consequences were
precisely those which the modernists intended; that it was in the decline or
destruction of Judaism in its traditional form that their real, if hidden
purposes lay—in which respect the *maskilim*, whose criticism of the established lay leadership was not dissimilar, were as guilty; that the fact that they
aimed to revive the use of the Hebrew language for profane purposes
revealed their true hand; that in their effort to reform Judaism from within,
they were to all intents and purposes at one with the out-and-out Russifiers, their nominal opponents.

---

[14] Lifshitz, *Zikhron Ya'akov*, iii. 13–16, 106, and *passim*.

It is only to blind us [to the truth] that they claim to speak for the honour of Hebrew, as we [for so they say] do not, or that they want the Jews to be accorded equal rights and that the means whereby this is to be brought about is education: that once the Jews are 'educated' they will have the privilege of full citizenship in Russia.

The truth was otherwise.

What the *maskilim*, in their heart of hearts, really intend is to bring a spirit of free-dom and wantonness [*hofesh ve-hefkerut*] to bear upon the young and to poison the souls of the children of Israel with the drug of absolute heresy.[15]

Ferocity of language and indiscriminate ascription of evil purposes apart, there was, to be sure, much in this critique of the modernist position in its several variations that was acute and valid. But valid or not, it availed those who habitually articulated it very little. The decisive circumstance was that the shock of 1881 failed to rouse religious orthodoxy from such set responses and positions and propose a course of action that was other than old, worn-out, and to ever more minds in ever widening sectors of Jewry irrelevant to the new circumstances. It had become clear in the aftermath of the pogroms, as it had not been before, that the Jews' condi-tion would now be governed by the fact that a great European state had declared itself against them. Minute, wholly marginal concessions might be wrung from it from time to time. In the essentials of the case it had shown itself to be implacable.

But if Jewish orthodoxy could still take what had occurred in its con-ceptual stride, the modernist Jewish intelligentsia, some totally, some partly Russified, some tending towards the *haskalah*, some not, was in shock. It was not only the treatment accorded the Jewish population at the hands of the government that appalled it, it was the almost total silence of those whom they looked upon, as did most educated Russians, as the leaders of Russian literary and intellectual life, Tolstoy and Tur-genev among them. The modernists were now mostly people who had already made great, on the whole successful efforts to adapt to the cultural norms of educated Russians. They had attended Russian schools. They had adopted the Russian language as their own. They had sought most earnestly to devise a method whereby they might become an accepted constituent of Russian society, albeit without abandonment of their own origins, identity, and religious and intellectual heritage. They were pre-cisely those in Russian Jewry who were most anxious to see the Jews emerge from the morass in which they were placed, those who had been most deeply persuaded of the validity and significance of the reforms pro-mulgated under Alexander II: the elimination of the cantonist regime, the easing of military service generally, reduced taxation, freer entry into the universities, and the rest. They believed that they, for their own part, had responded well to what they had taken to be a clear and friendly invitation. Now they had to consider whether they had been betrayed. The shock reached even beyond the margins of Jewry proper. Semyon Yakovlevich Nadson (1862–87) was among the most popular of late nineteenth-century Russian poets, his popularity extending posthumously into the following century, especially among the educated young. Nadson had probably been aware of having a distant genealogical connection with Jewry, of which nothing at all, however, seems to have been known to his admiring public, but that was all. His father had been of Jewish descent, quite possibly of mixed descent himself, but certainly baptized. Nadson's mother was Russian. Like his parents, he had been brought up in the Russian Orthodox faith. As a proper upper-class Russian he had been educated at a cadet school. It is certain that in no way had he ever associated himself, or been associated by others, with things Jewish, or been inclined or even in a position to do so. None the less, the pogroms and the policy pursued by the government shook him to the core of his being. In the aftermath he turned to the Jews, 'my own people, of bitter destiny!' He had, he wrote, been raised an alien to them. The traditions and sorrows of this 'outcast people' had been foreign to him. Now, however, as 'your enemies, like a pack of savage hounds, | Blood-stained, roaming, tear you to pieces,' he would stand with and fight with those who were prepared to defend them. The full sense and ring of Nadson's short poem is difficult to convey. Its quality as poesy and the poet's own strongly and effectively expressed feelings aside, what is remarkable is that it should have been written at all. The tone which Russian literati, major and minor, were accustomed to adopt on those rare occasions when the affairs of the Jewish people swam into their ken was most commonly hostile, condescending at best. Very rarely was there a trace of what dominates Nadson's poem, his grasp of the desperate degree to which the Jews were exposed and isolated.

But, of course, the defining feature of the Russian Jewish diaspora in the early 1880s was not the response of the intelligentsia, Jewish or non-Jewish, but the steady departure from the empire of massive numbers of independently motivated, uninvited, determined emigrants who, overwhelmingly, were of another social order. It was migration, more powerfully than any other factor, that set the Jewish public agenda for all. It was migration with which all those who were disposed to take it upon themselves to give the Jewish public a lead had willy-nilly to deal. And it was because it had not been intended, was not governed by any central authority, but at the same time was far too massive to be ignored that the questions it raised were so insistent. Was it, finally, to be welcomed and encouraged? Was there any plausible alternative to what it seemed to augur, namely total and irreversible departure from the empire—

that is if the Jews were ever finally to extricate themselves from Tsarist rule?

The notion of a full-scale, perhaps total evacuation of the Jewish component of the empire being in train could not fail to evoke powerful mythic and historic precedents: the Exodus from Egypt, the Return to the Holy Land from the Babylonian Exile, the expulsion from Spain in 1492, and others. At the practical, contemporary level, however, nothing was easier to dismiss as fantasy than the idea of deliberate and planned migration. An evacuation of Russia would be no mere matter of thousands, even tens of thousands of souls, but of millions, literally so. It was true that to mount so great an enterprise in the age of steam navigation, the railway, and communication by telegraph was to encounter formidable, but hardly insurmountable, problems of organization. Still, even on the most optimistic of calculations it would take years to execute. It would require the establishment of a Jewish public body equipped more than merely adequately with gifts of will, ability, and material means—none of which were on view. It would constitute an endless race against time. We now know,[16] but it seems to have been sensed at the time, that the Jewish fertility rate and general population growth were high enough to keep the Jewish minority within the Russian Empire, measured in absolute figures, virtually unchanged—short of emigration being pushed to astronomic and panic proportions and, in all likelihood, being imposed from above as well. Besides, as was becoming apparent, there would be the reluctance of the countries of transit and settlement to admit Jewish migrants in what they judged to be excessive numbers to contend with as well: an incalculable factor, not crucial as yet, but not one to be overlooked. Still, all this said, it was not in fact the technical feasibility of mass migration that was principally at issue. Even assuming that Russian Jewry could be evacuated *in toto* (as the leader of the Decembrists had proposed they be),[17] was it right to try to do so? And would it truly benefit the Jews themselves? The refusal of any of the Jewish public bodies in the west to take up the matter of mass emigration except in an attempt to reduce its scale was matched by the still more passionate refusal of virtually the entire body of Russian Jewry's own traditional leaders—lay notables and rabbis of all major tendencies—to grasp the nettle of emigration other than to crush it as rapidly and thoroughly underfoot as they were able.

On the other hand, as the affair of the interview in *Razsvet* indicated, not all were as put out as Baron Guenzburg and his friends had been by what the minister of the interior had had to say. With the scenes in southern Russian streets ever present in their minds, Dr Orshansky and other members of what was rapidly becoming a distinctly radical tendency

[16] See Chapter 4.
[17] See above, pp. 207–9.

were increasingly inclined to regard the grandees and those who allowed themselves to be guided by them with contempt. Orshansky, so Mordekhai Ben Hillel ha-Kohen wrote from St Petersburg, was to be praised, not condemned, for tearing the mask off liars and hypocrites. Baron Guenzburg 'sets himself up as King and Saviour of Israel' and orders the Russian-language *Russky Evrei* and the Hebrew-language *Ha-Meliz*[18] to lie to the people to reassure them of their future because what he and his minions fear most is being charged with disloyalty to the empire. But to the real import of what Ignatiev's deputy Gotovtsev[19] had said quite openly they were blind: that the Jews were foreigners; that they would so remain; and that nothing short of conversion to the Orthodox faith could possibly redeem them from their alien status. Ha-Kohen went on to argue (somewhat less reasonably) that what the notables of Russian Jewry failed to understand was that the one thing that might cause the government to reconsider its policy was precisely the prospect of its Jewish subjects emigrating *en masse*. That apart, anyone with eyes in his head should be able to see that the real reason for the magnates to be so strongly opposed to *organized* migration and to the setting up of an office to manage it systematically—which was no more than what Ignatiev himself had proposed[20]—was fear lest they be called upon to do more than fast and pray for their people. They would most certainly have to do better than to contribute the paltry sums (1,500 roubles in Guenzburg's case) offered the victims of the pogroms thus far.[21]

These were private, not public attacks. If the notables were aware of the criticism directed against them, they were unmoved by it. In the very first of the resolutions passed and published at the end of the April 1882 conference held at Guenzburg's home they announced their absolute rejection of 'all thought of organizing emigration as being subversive of the dignity of the Russian body politic and the historic rights of the Jews in their present fatherland'. They went on to restate their set view that the sole way to 'regulate' relations between the Jews of Russia and the

---

[18] The Russian-language Jewish weekly *Russky Evrei* was strongly opposed to emigration from Russia. The Hebrew-language weekly *Ha-Meliz* was undecided in its editorial policy at this stage. Later it was to side with the proto-Zionist Hibbat Zion movement (on which more below).

[19] Dmitrii Gotovtsev, deputy minister of the interior, had been appointed chairman of the committee set up within the ministry to look into the causes of the pogroms and to co-ordinate the local committees set up in each of the relevant *gubernii* to the same end.

[20] Strictly speaking, Ignatiev had done no more than speak of the institutionalization of emigration as a possibility.

[21] Mordekhai Ben Hillel ha-Kohen to Yehuda Leib Levin ('Yehallel'), 30 Jan. / 11 Feb. 1882. *Ketavim le-toldot Hibbat-Zion ve-yishuv Erez-Yisrael* (henceforward *Toldot*), ed. Alter Druyanov, 3 vols. (Odessa, 1919; Tel-Aviv, 1925–32); *Toldot* rev. edn., ed. Shulamit Laskov, 7 vols. (Tel-Aviv, 1982–93), i, no. 30, 154–6; and in the same spirit, M. M. Dulitsky, Bialystok, to M. Padova, Brest-Litovsk, 21 Mar. / 2 Apr. 1882, ibid., no. 45, 206 f.

country's indigenous inhabitants was by abolition of the existing, discriminatory legislation—namely by emancipation. They expressed cautious criticism of the passivity displayed by provincial authorities in the
course of the disorders. And they asked for ways to be found to compensate the victims of the pogroms for the consequences of inadequate police
protection. Theirs was a statement, therefore, that could be read as
limited and indirect criticism of the conduct of the authorities. But it was
remote from the blunter terms in which, for example, the distinguished
Kiev ophthalmologist Emmanuel Mandelstamm—like Orshansky an
independent spirit—had put the dilemma facing the entire community.
'We have been sold and betrayed in this wretched country,' he said in June
1881. The Jews were like sufferers from a malignant disease that only radical means would cure: equality of rights or emigration. But in practice,
Mandelstamm went on, there was no hope at all of equal rights being
granted them. On the contrary, there was good reason to anticipate further restrictions on such limited freedom as they now possessed. It followed that there was no alternative to emigration.[22] To remain in Russia
was to be condemned to permanent inferiority of status and very probably to much worse. In sum, the Jewish cause *in* Russia was hopeless.

   That the magnates' judgement was inseparable from their moral and
material stake in the existing order by virtue of their economic role and
resources and their privileges was manifest. It is worth noting, however,
that men of Mandelstamm's type were beneficiaries of the system too.
Many of them had acquired higher education and professional qualifications. Much more thoroughly modernized and Russified than the common run of Russian and Polish Jews, or even the notables themselves by
and large, they had to some degree internalized the contemporary currents of political and social opinion fashionable in Russian society too.
Possibly, but not necessarily for that reason, they were apt to be bolder
and fresher in spirit, less patient with precedent, more rebellious, therefore actual or potential dissidents both in respect of the internal norms
and institutions of Jewry and in respect of the Autocratic state itself. Differences in outlook between magnates in St Petersburg and professionals
in Kiev and Odessa can be partly accounted for too by the paradox, that,
although linguistic, social, and professional attributes rendered the latter
substantially more *Russian* than the common run of Jews, they were in
general less protected in their persons from the depredations of the mob
and from harassment at the hands of junior officials and policemen than
the former. But whatever the reason, what counted was that the new
Jewish intelligentsia regarded itself as closer in mind to the common,
Yiddish-speaking Jewish people and were in fact more sensitive generally
to the realities of its wretched condition than the bankers, factory owners,

---

[22] Israel Klausner, *Be-hit'orer 'am* (Jerusalem, 1962), 94.

railway entrepreneurs, and the like who still presumed to seek to lay down the law for all. Hostility was likely to be especially intense where a relatively radical social outlook was combined with a solid grounding of Jewish learning and culture acquired in the critical spirit promoted by the *haskalah*.[23] This was a class—of which Mordekhai Ben Hillel ha-Kohen and Yehuda Leib Levin ('Yehallel') were precisely representative—that was far from sure that it knew what needed to be done. Yet painfully aware of being remote in distance and experience from the centres of political and social power in the Empire, it saw itself, like the people around it, as desperately in need of support, allies, above all leaders who would have the will and the talent to translate ideas that were all still exceedingly loose into sharper terms and into forceful, collective action. It was therefore not altogether inconsistent for four especially accom-plished men of this class, along with one other, to swallow their pride and, as the notables gathered at Baron Guenzburg's for their second con-ference in April 1882, to address one last plea to the great man to recon-sider his views and bring what they had to say before his colleagues.

It was true, they wrote to the banker, that they themselves were men of little consequence and standing, no more than writers. He, in contrast, was a very great man indeed, a veritable 'captain' (*aluf*) of the Jewish people. But they had seen and heard much that he and many of his friends had not: the beatings, the weeping, the destruction of all the earthly possessions of whole families, the utter helplessness of victims of assault, arson, and rape, the turning upside down of an entire world, Sodom and Gomorrah. They, not he, had had to bear with the spectacle of charity raining down upon them, the origins of which extended all the way from the Baltic Sea to the Mississippi River while *here*, in this vast and rich country, the notables of Russian Jewry, flesh of the victims' flesh, had moved hardly a finger or emptied more than a few coins from their purses in aid of the survivors. Nor (with some honourable exceptions, Guenzburg among them) had they so much as been willing to deprive themselves this past summer of their customary journey to Switzerland and to the watering places of southern Germany. But so be it. The question was,

Are you prepared to do something for the good of the nation and its survival, or are you not? . . . What we for our part have to say, is this, that even if times were to change for the better, there is no assurance that the wheel will not turn again; and that therefore what is needed [now] is a great effort to reduce the number of Jews here [in Russia] . . . for the benefit and safety of those who leave the Empire, but even more for those who remain.

What Guenzburg and his associates must understand was that if it were widely known that the notables of Russian Jewry were sympathetic,

[23] See Chapter 2.

effective, and full participants in their own people's affairs the impact on the public mood would be dramatic. Nothing would raise the stock of the grandees so high and for generations to come. Conversely,

If the notables fail to listen to the voice[s] calling to them and continue to stand apart from the public, why then they will have as good as admitted that they have no part in it, that they are not saddened by its afflictions and that they do not share in its joys—upon which the people will see plainly what it is that confronts it, namely that salvation will have to come to the Jews from some other quarter.[24]

Not all the signatories were out-and-out modernists. One of their number, Ya'akov ha-Levi Lifshitz, being a man of impeccable orthodox roots and views, might otherwise have been expected to be a natural opponent of socially radical positions of any kind. But his dismay at the insensitivity of the magnates of Russian Jewry was much like that of his modernist colleagues. When there was famine in the Pale, he recalled in his memoirs, 'our dear brethren in Germany and France', formed committees, collected money, and took in children who had been orphaned to educate them in their homes. Whereas all that while

not a sound [was heard] from our people's aristocracy [*azilim*] in Petersburg and Moscow and not a penny in charity [was granted] in aid of the hungry unfortunates within the Pale. Why so? Because the same oppressive state legislation [*gzeirat ha-malkhut*] that forbade an ordinary Jew to cross the Pale of Settlement set the residents of St Petersburg and Moscow apart from their brethren within the Pale more decisively than the ocean to America distinguishes and cuts off [one branch of Jewry from another].[25]

But it was idle to expect so much of Guenzburg and those he had gathered round him. The circumstances might cry out for a strong will and a fresh imagination leading to a new departure. But to do otherwise than cleave to the *status quo* and refuse to modify their old set theses on the gradual integration of the Jews into Russian life as they knew it, would have been to cut across the grain of the terms in which they were accustomed to regard both their own internal social function and their relations with the government. How far they realized that, having nothing to offer, nothing to propose, and nothing of substance to say to those whom they still presumed to lead and speak for, they were condemning themselves to irrelevancy is unclear. As in the case of the rabbis, so in that of the St Petersburg grandees, the failure to grasp not only the significance of what had happened but to consider what now might seriously be done was before all else a failure of imagination and spirit. The *haute bourgeoisie's* fear that Jewish emigration would be taken (and exploited) as

[24] S. P. Rabinowitz ('Shefer'), Warsaw; M. L. Lilienblum, Odessa; Y. L. Levin, Kiev; Y. Lifshitz, Kovno; and S. Friedenberg, Grodno, to Baron Horace Guenzburg, St Petersburg, 29 Mar. 1882, in *Toldot* rev. edn., i, no. 43, 196–203.

[25] Lifshitz, *Zikhron Ya'akov*, iii. 6–7.

proof positive of the Jews' shallow roots in the country and confirmation of their essentially alien character was founded on error. The government had no real objection to the Jews' departure and it had never been seriously supposed in the relevant Russian political and social quarters that the Jews were other than aliens, irreparably distinguishable from the indigenous Russian population. It was true that the government continued to speak in several voices and to gesture in several contrary directions even on the immediate but central issue of emigration. Ignatiev's statement of January 1882 had helped to set the scene for mass departure and had certainly encouraged it. On the other hand, it had been informal in nature, just conceivably off the cuff, and it had been a Jewish weekly, not an official or semi-official organ of any kind, that had ventilated it. No explicit licence to leave the empire had been granted Russia's Jews. Young, healthy men, precisely those whom everyone knew to be best fitted for departure and rapid settlement elsewhere, the natural forerunners of any major exodus, would continue to be refused permission to leave on the grounds that they were liable for military service.

Russian public opinion—in so far as the preponderantly anti-Jewish and censored Russian press may be taken as reflecting it—was similarly ambiguous. No objection to the departure of the Jews *on principle* was expressed. Commonly, as a solution to the problems of which they were thought to be the cause, it was welcomed. So too were what were seen as the practical possibilities it opened up. The notion that in general there was much to be said for giving the Jews a rough time had been voiced with special stridency at the onset of the pogroms.[26] And often, given the evidence that the more uncomfortable life became for them the more likely they were to leave, the grounds for causing them still greater discomfort were held to have been reinforced. There was, it is true, a parallel, ostensibly countervailing tendency to dwell on what were supposed to be the impracticalities of large-scale Jewish emigration, although not because their departure was judged undesirable in itself, rather because it was reckoned to be doomed to failure. Hard work in rough country was what settlers in a new land needed to undertake. But did not all good Russians know that hard work was not the Jewish style? (Besides, if the Jews were prepared to labour, why should they not stay in Russia?) The danger, it was pointed out, was that once prospective host countries saw whom they had to deal with their response was likely to be cast in the same justly critical spirit in which decent Russians had long regarded their Jewish neighbours. And what then? Would the Jews return? Would they *be* returned? That would be doubly calamitous. Still, the common

---

[26] The notorious article entitled 'To beat or not to beat' in which the pros and cons of pogroms were discussed without the least embarrassment was published in *Novoe Vremya*, 1 May 1881.

thread running through all these themes was that which Ivan Sergeyevich Aksakov (1823–86), a celebrated Slavophil writer and a man of implacably anti-Semitic views, articulated. On reflection, Aksakov decided, there was little to be said against the Children of Israel, as he put it, selecting emigration (once again) as the cure for their ills and much to be said for it. He himself rejoiced at the prospect and invited his readers to do so too.[27] Nor did anyone of any consequence at all suggest otherwise—on the basis, as it would have to be, that a *modus vivendi* for the Jews in Russia could be worked out after all. Even a man as critical of the treatment and continual, wholesale defamation of the Jews by both government and society as Vladimir Solov'ev could see no reason to posit common ground of that kind. It was the hopeless differences between the Jews and the Russians that struck him hardest.

The Jews, in all places and all times regarded Christians, and dealt with them in practice according to the dictates of their *religion*, their *faith*, and their *laws*. The Jews invariably treated us in a Jewish manner [*po-iudeiski*]; we the Christians, on the other hand, to this day, have never learned to treat Jewry in a Christian manner [*po-khristianski*]. On no occasion in our connection did they ever violate their religious laws, whereas we constantly violated and continue to violate in their connection the precepts of the Christian religion.[28]

The Jews themselves, in their numbers, were caught therefore between two hopelessly destructive forces. One was active: a front, fuelled by an especially vulgar form of anti-Semitism in which most sectors of Russia's officialdom and society had at least a share—even the revolutionaries, as we shall see in a moment—was bearing down upon them from without. The other was reactive: the established leadership of Russian Jewry itself, lay and clerical, that with rare exceptions was determined to preserve what it imagined to be the *status quo* and to damp down the individual and collective attempts of lesser folk to escape. So far as it was concerned, there was to be no question of radical social or political change in the light of the new circumstances. Its refusal to lead in any direction at all commensurate with what corresponded to a reasonable reading of the Jews' real condition was total. There were two results. There was the flight from Russia of enormous numbers of Russian Jews who had resolved, on their own, to close the Russian option altogether by voting with their feet. It was unquestionably this great migration that was the

---

[27] *Rus'*, 10 Apr. 1882. I am indebted to Dr John Klier for an opportunity to read his chapter on the contemporary Russian press in an early draft of his book *Prejudice into Policy*. For Aksakov's major articles on the Jewish Question, see the volume of his collected works entitled *Pol'skii vopros I zapadno-russkoe delo; Evreiskii vopros—1860–1886* (Moscow, 1886).

[28] Vladimir Sergeevich Solov'ev, 'Evreistvo i khristiansky vopros' ('Judaism and the Christian Question'), Dec. 1885. Repr. in V. F. Boikova (ed.), *Taina Izrailya* (St Petersburg, 1993), 31. Emphases in the original.

most immediately revealing aspect of the mood of the Russian Jewish public as a whole. It spoke of a pot of fear and resentment boiling over, of immense impatience, and of a rising spirit of rebellion. It offered spectacular evidence of steadily deepening loss of regard for the old norms and habits of Jewish life as well as for those who continued to uphold and teach them. It indicated a rare level of excitement and a readiness—a dangerous readiness, in the old guard's view, needless to say—to listen to fresh and untried voices. Inexorably, it raised questions of a programmatic and ideological nature to entirely unusual prominence. The second result, simply put, was the entry into the public life of the Jews of Europe of the idea of political action: initially in Russia and Poland, in the course of time elsewhere. At first, it would be barely perceptible. Ten to fifteen more years would pass before it could be regarded—even then with difficulty—as having borne palpable fruit. On the whole it ran counter to what would still be, and would remain well into the following century, the most profound and most widespread of all tendencies, almost as deep in its way and almost as widepread as the urge of huge numbers of private individuals to leave their homes and abandon their social and ideological customs altogether. What both trends had in common was that they had been precipitated by the positive and negative forces pounding Russo-Polish Jewry, by the failure of the established leaders to propound a viable course of action for it, and by the general thirst for action of almost any kind at all provided it offered change in a new and promising direction. But the difference between the two trends was at least as important as the ground they shared. The migrants, by and large, looked abroad, as Jews had done so often in the past, in search of a land in which they had better reason to expect if not generous treatment at least minimal justice. These were not people who were inclined, therefore, to dwell on larger matters, on an alternative destiny for the Jewish people as a whole or on the likelihood of political change in Russia itself. Still less did it occur to them to think of themselves as participants in efforts devoted to effect either the one or the other. To emigrate was to undertake an individual and private act. It was one's own and one's family's interests that one had set before one: a narrowly circumscribed horizon, to be sure, but one—or so it seemed—that might actually be attained.

The progenitors of national political action and those who followed their lead belonged to a different mental world. At the foundation of what they were about were the barely spoken convictions that nothing could be understood and nothing would be accomplished without prior and systematic thought. They wished to examine the situation of the Jews afresh. They were unwilling to be incessantly inhibited by ancient precedents, habits, fears, and pressures. Having rethought the Jews' condition, they wished to alter it. Their approach was therefore ideological: first analysis, then programme. And it was purposeful. They sought—

awkwardly, often ineffectively, but almost always passionately and urgently—to act, to organize, to influence, to lead, and to produce tangible results. The sum of this was that they were resolved to convert the social unrest and dissatisfaction that was all around them, and which they themselves shared to a very high degree, into a thoroughgoing revolution. And revolution being their purpose, they formed, taken together, the embryo of a political class such as the Jewish people had neither benefited nor suffered from since the onset of the Exile.

On the nature of the revolution they had in view, they were very sharply divided, however. One school believed in common with the migrants that much—perhaps all—hinged on the transplantation of the Jews out of eastern Europe, indeed out of Europe altogether. It was a school that would evolve, as will be seen, on very broad lines. It would contain—often with some difficulty—an entire range of contending subsets, coteries, tendencies, and parties. Few would be easily compatible one with the other; some would be wholly at cross purposes. The other school was founded on assumptions that ran entirely counter to the call to migrate. This was partly on what were held to be pragmatic grounds, but partly on principle. It sought to deal with the afflictions of eastern European Jewry by political and social change within Europe—especially eastern Europe—itself. Accordingly, it would lead its adepts very far from the established and familiar social norms of Jewry—just as the other school was being led by the logic of its position in an entirely different and in some ways more radical direction. But both schools would be nourished by the same rebellious impatience that now began to sweep through all of eastern European Jewry. Both had concluded that the Jews' sovereign, alien rulers were hopelessly hostile. Both wished to bring the Jews' submission to them to an end. One sought to do so by removing the Jews from the purview of alien power altogether. The other sought to alter the specific identity, quality, and purposes of those who governed them and to help to have them replaced by others. The first preached self-reliance before all. The second, ostensibly more modest, preached common cause with other subject peoples.

II

It is necessary, at this point, to introduce a factor to which barely any reference has been made thus far. The place occupied by the ancestral Land of Israel in the minds and sentiments of the Jewish people in its Exile cannot be precisely calculated. It formed a central part of their cosmology and theology, their Law, their religious ritual, their history, and their world-view. It was a component of the supremely important realm reserved in Jewish belief, culture, literature, and conduct for elegy and lament, for nostalgia and yearning, but also for hope and for release. The second great rebellion mounted against Rome in CE 132, put down three years later after horrific fighting and massive, punitive slaughter, spelled the end of dense Jewish population of the country. Most of what was left of the traumatized people scattered. The city of Jerusalem, in the dramatic, but tolerably accurate word of the authors of the Mishna, was 'ploughed up'[29] and its very name decreed defunct and altered to 'Aeolia Capitolina'. And the basis of a normal national existence having thus been swept away, all reasonable prospect of political autonomy within the Roman system (or any other) was lost. The implications of this defeat were immensely far-reaching. An all but irreversible adjustment to a life of political self-abnegation was ordained for the Jews by their spiritual and philosophical masters: a matter of expediency to begin with, but very rapidly established as one of theological and cosmological principle to which all among them who were righteous and God-fearing were expected to adhere. And adhere they did. They might, as instructed, continually bewail the interminable Exile and mourn the loss of the Land of Israel (Erez Yisrael) specifically. But as the possession of the Land receded in time and the reality of Exile took hold, it was the positive, theological teaching of the causes and nature of the Exile that became preponderant in their thinking. Doctrine held that the Exile had been divinely and punitively ordained. Only in God's good time and in consequence of his judgement might the Jews expect to return to their ancestral Land and reassume a form of direct responsibility for their own destinies. An attempt to defy the dictate of Heaven and to seek to wind up the Exile autonomously could not be other than wicked and would, in any event, be doomed to failure. Only obedience to the will of God and continual dedication to the study of his Law held promise of an eventual reopening of the gates of the ancient kingdom. In the interim the Jews were neither to press nor even to pray excessively for a Return. They were not to indulge in—and endanger themselves by—futile attempts to 'hasten the end'. Return was contingent upon Redemption.

Nevertheless, both in doctrine and as a component of folk memory, Erez Yisrael remained *the* Land and *their* Land. Each nation had been granted a particular land by the Almighty, ran one famous and characteristic line of argument. *This* was the land he had granted the Jews. It was the land *from* which they had been exiled. It was the land *to* which they would return. It stood in permanent contrast, therefore, to each and every one of the many lands in which Jews happened, in their exile, to settle. It was the one land in which resettlement would finally free them of all that was painful, unnatural, anomalous, and unhappy in their condition. These were firm, indelible, and deeply internalized ideas,

---

[29] The Mishna, Ta'anit, 4: 6.

moreover. No man, woman, or child was allowed to forget them; and, indeed, there was little in their ritual and their lore that did not remind them and speak to them of their once, but also future commonwealth in one way or another, over and over again, directly and indirectly. Thus in their regular daily prayers; thus in seasonal prayers such as those they were required to offer up as a matter of course in rainy, snowy Europe for the blessings of Providential rain in semi-arid Palestine; thus in the celebration of the harvest festival of Shavu'ot (Pentecost) for all that they were a people that had long since been forced out of agriculture; and thus in the prescribed, diligent study of the Talmud, not excluding close attention to tractates regulating the administration of civil and criminal law in what had become a phantom polity.

The question whether the various historical, mythic, utopian, and romantic threads with which the matter of the Land had come to be shot through might usefully be disentangled did not arise. In any case, the weight of learned, rabbinic opinion was opposed to any such examination. The closely interconnected myths of the Covenant concluded between the Jewish people and the Almighty and the Promise of the Land made to them were much too close to the central nerve of Judaism to be permissible subjects of inquiry. Besides, the survival of the idea of an ancestral Land to which the Jews would eventually return owed something too to the natural propensity of a people in distress to find solace in myth and memory and to seek to resolve the paradox of a benevolent deity presiding over a people who despite submission to his will were eternally and so drastically reduced to misery and humiliation. But if, so long as the Tradition reigned supreme, none dared, and few greatly desired, to subject the matter of the Return to the Promised Land to pragmatic—or even philosophic—examination, it was the case too that for very many centuries there was nothing in the actual condition of the Jews that especially impelled or encouraged any of them to do so.

Such was the rule. It was a rough rule, however, and it admitted some exceptions. A good deal depended on the internal condition of the Land itself, which is to say, on the tolerance or otherwise of those who actually governed it to its remaining Jewish inhabitants and occasional Jewish travellers. Under Christian sovereignty—Byzantine or Latin—systematic, principled persecution rendered a Jewish presence all but impossible. Under Muslim sovereignty the principles differed and while conditions were generally hard they were not so hard as to rule Jewish settlement out entirely. Accordingly, over time, the Jewish presence in the Land rose and fell; and, broadly, the Land was rarely—some scholars would say, never—without one. In the Middle Ages particularly intrepid individuals travelled to it as pilgrims. In early modern times, as part of the fanning out of the Jews of Spain on their expulsion from Iberia, a small community began to build up all over again, its most famous component being that of the Cabalistic mystics who congregated in the Galilean town of Safed in the sixteenth century. By the beginning of the seventeenth century Safed could boast almost a score of Talmudic colleges and a like number of synagogues. But then this was a stage, at which it was indeed the mystic and magic attributes of the Land that drew Jews to it. The Hasidic saint Rabbi Naḥman of Bratzlav, having set out on the long and difficult journey from eastern Europe at the turn of the eighteenth century, found, as he later told his disciples, that it was enough for him to have set foot on the Land for all that he had known and understood before to be reduced to insignificance. Whereas prior to his journey all had been confusion in his mind, thereafter he could hold the Law whole. 'As soon as he had walked four ells in Ereẓ Yisrael', so ran the authorized account of his journey, the rabbi 'had accomplished what he had wished to achieve'.[30] After the briefest of visits to Tiberias, Rabbi Naḥman returned to Poland. He had seen no reason to linger, not even long enough to visit Jerusalem. The greatest Talmudic scholar of the age, Rabbi Eliahu, the Ga'on of Vilna, never stirred from Lithuania at all. Nor was he in the ordinary sense a mystic. But he did encourage his disciples to make their way to Palestine. A group settled happily there early in the nineteenth century. In their reports back to Vilna they extolled the Land for its air, water, and climate in contrast to what they recalled of north-eastern Europe. They extolled it too, more particularly, for the spiritual qualities that were its special gift to all who were so fortunate as to live within its (ill-defined) borders. Other folk began to percolate into the country. Some were scholars, some were mystics, some were quite ordinary, but elderly people who wished to assure themselves of burial in holy soil. Some, like Rabbi 'Akiva Schlesinger of Pressburg (1832–1922) and his followers, came because they believed that the processes of social integration and political emancipation they had observed in Europe spelled the ruin of the Jewish people. Only in Ereẓ Yisrael, they believed, in the cradle of both the nation and its religion, might corruption be avoided and decadence fought off with confidence. All told, the Jewish population of Jerusalem—despite Rabbi Naḥman, it was Jerusalem consistently that held the greatest attraction for observant and pious Jews—grew rapidly in the course of the nineteenth century: at over three times the rate at which the Muslim population was increasing. By 1880 Jews accounted for well over half the city's total population (17,000 out of 30,000).[31]

---

[30] A. Ya'ari (ed.), 'Mas'ot Ereẓ Yisrael (Tel-Aviv, 1946), 480, 487; Martin Buber, The Tales of Rabbi Nachman, trans. Maurice Freedman (Bloomington, Ind., 1962).

[31] These are still the best figures available. See Y. Ben-Arye, 'Hitpatḥuta shel Yerushalayim', Keshet, 12, 4 (1970), 37. There are no truly reliable figures for the years prior to that (1922) in which a proper census was taken by the British administration, by which time the population had doubled. The proportions, however, remained the same: total population: 62,600; Jews: 34,000; Christians, 14,700; Muslims: 13,500.

All this was devoid of political implications. For very few of the members of the old *yishuv* (settlement), as it came to be called, were the larger, mundane destinies of the Jewish people—its safety, or its ordinary material well-being—matters of great moment. Their concerns, their own simple survival apart, were of the spirit—their own in the first place, that of others only in the abstract or very marginally if at all. They did not see the Land as the focus or the instrument of national, or even religious revival except, it needs to be said, in chiliastic terms, namely as it might pertain to the unfolding of the Latter Day. They were in no sense, therefore, the forerunners of those who would now seek to enter the Land in greater numbers and with very different purposes. And were it not for their extraordinary, eventual impact on the history of the Jewish people in its entirety—and, to some degree, on that of other peoples as well—the migrants who began to trickle into the Ottoman-ruled provinces of Palestine from eastern Europe in the 1880s would justify little more than a flicker of special interest either. These were people who were impelled by the same collapse of trust in established authority and the same spreading mood of disquiet and rebellion that was at the root of the decisions taken by other migrants. They too were moved by the same rising propensity to think for themselves and to conclude that the narrowing of life and spirit in the lands of their birth was no longer tolerable. They may be seen, therefore, before all else—which is not to say exclusively—as part and parcel of the great migratory movement of escape from Russia, Poland, and Romania to central and western Europe and on to North and South America, South Africa, and the Antipodes that would change the geographical distribution of all Jewry between the 1880s and the outbreak of the First World War. Yet that said, there were three cardinal respects in which they did differ after all from the great majority. Firstly, they formed a minority within the migratory mass so small as to appear eccentric: rarely more than 2 or 3 per cent of all migrants out of eastern Europe in any given year. Secondly, their destination—Palestine—could not fail to differ sharply from all others not merely in compass terms, but in inner significance. Thirdly, their *purposes* differed: in some cases very radically indeed.

All courses of action adopted by migrants out of eastern Europe to all destinations were necessarily shot through with risks and uncertainty. In all cases it was therefore the young, the healthy, the unattached, and, most especially, the bold and the enterprising who were most likely to be drawn to assume those risks. But that said, the difference between North America and the other destinations to which migrants were most commonly bound on the one hand and the Jews' own ancestral land on the other was dramatic—and very widely understood to be so. To set out on the hugely uncomfortable voyage to New York or Cape Town or the less demanding, but still strenuous, journey to Paris or Liverpool was daunting enough. In all cases, what awaited one on arrival was never likely to be better than an extended effort to find one's feet in an unfamiliar, possibly hostile environment. The process was bound to be painful. It might be very prolonged. It might never be completed. It might fail totally. Still, the risks could almost always be roughly assessed. And there was much to encourage people of the right age and native ability to assume them. The major destination, the United States, was not only vast, but, as a country that was explicitly open to immigrants, inviting. Finally, there was the circumstance that a Russian, Polish, or Romanian Jew setting out for New York or Baltimore knew that he or she would be in the company of many thousands, and, before too long, many hundreds of thousands of people who were much like him- or herself—and embarked on the same purpose.

To set out for a tiny, impoverished, sparsely populated, in part malaria-ridden, provincial backwater of the Ottoman Empire was another matter altogether. Palestine was unwelcoming, ill-policed, and—to put the matter at its most favourable—negligently governed. To immigrate was not so much to assume incalculable risks as to plunge into an adventure—but not by any means a private adventure for private profit. There was no private advantage to be extracted from the Palestine of the day. Nor was there any to hope for. The pattern of migration to Palestine was fuelled from the first by ideology—which largely accounts in turn for the distinguishing fact that in most (but not all) cases it took the form of coherent groups moving in accordance with some prearranged collective plan. The group might continue to cohere on arrival. It might break apart very quickly or do so by stages over an extended period. The plan agreed upon might turn out to be well or ill conceived. The original ideological and social purpose underlying the enterprise might be defined with greater or lesser rigour and might be further elaborated upon on arrival or set aside totally in the course of time. But in all cases, whether it was one of a coherent group acting in concert or of individuals braving the unknown on their own, action would be coloured to an exceptionally high degree by conscious social purposes and convictions.

The history of one tiny group formed chiefly of students at Kharkov University will illustrate the qualities and purposes found—generally in milder and looser form—in all. It begins with a discussion circle formed after the events of 1881 and in response to them that then set itself the task of working out a set of well-defined and exalted social purposes and (more hazily) political ambitions for a regenerated Jewish People in their repossessed Land. They would call a new, autonomous society into being. It would be one that was imbued with the highest principles of duty and comportment. They themselves—the Kharkov students and some others who were joining them—would form its guiding elite: socially conscious, utterly dedicated men and women who, by their personal example, would serve best of all to illustrate the intended ethos for all to see. The seriousness and intellectual energy invested by these very young people in the formulation of all seventy-eight clauses of the book of rules by which they proposed to govern both their own tightly knit association and the larger society of which it would take the leading part stood in ironic and fatal contrast, as might be expected, to their own small numbers (under three score) and the paucity of their resources.

We hardly had any money for the journey [one of them related after arrival]. The future did not frighten us and we were ready for anything. However, we were too confident of the sympathy of our brethren. The newspapers were full of false information about fantastic donations for the colonization of Palestine and we believed everything. The moment we reached Jaffa we had to look for work; and as we wished to get acquainted with agricultural labour in order to be able to work our own land we started looking around. We applied to many [of the independent Jewish farmers, new arrivals themselves]. We were rejected everywhere. And truly, how could people have any faith in youngsters who all their lives had to do with books and had no idea whatsoever about agricultural work.[32]

Both the facility with which the Biluim, as they termed themselves,[33] invented intricate structures for an entire, but non-existent and inherently unlikely, society and their undying belief in the value and the duty of personal example betrayed the influence upon them of patterns of social thought that had become exceedingly common among members of the Russian intelligentsia as a whole. So too did their initial and in individual cases fatal failure to take the true measure of the obstacles they faced. The co-operative village of Gedera some 25 kilometres south of Jaffa was the sum of their concrete achievement. But the Biluim set a precedent for movement and settlement on a collective basis; and their example—or what was advanced as an elaboration upon their example—would be followed by members of a later generation with much the same kind of initial enthusiasm, but with greater stamina and in more substantial numbers. For the time being, namely the last two decades of the century, the more important and to some extent defining model was set, as it happened, not by politically minded students and other candidate-members of the new Jewish intelligentsia, but by ideologically staider parties of mostly middle-class and lower middle-class Jews from Romania.

Unlike Russia, there had been no sudden, unanticipated explosion of violence in Romania. But the plight of Romanian Jewry was, if

---

[32] Hayim Hissin to Warsaw subcommittee of Ḥibbat Ẓion, 21 July / 2 Aug. 1885. *Toldot*, rev. edn., iii, no. 648, 423–4.

[33] From BILU, an acronym derived from the name they devised for their society: Beit Ya'akov lekhu ve-nelkha (i.e. 'O house of Jacob, come ye and let us walk [in the light of the Lord]', Isaiah 2: 5). On BILU generally, see D. Vital, *The Origins of Zionism* (Oxford, 1975), 74–88.

anything, more evil than that of their Russian counterparts. At the formal, constitutional level, their affairs were governed and indeed epitomized by the sweeping, judicially proclaimed principle that Jews, having no country of their own, belong to no state whatsoever. They were not only technically, but inherently alien. Arbitrary expulsion from places of settlement, confiscation of property, and physical persecution and humiliation by the mob and the police were endemic. Entry into the professions and the civil service at any level was barred to them as a matter of course. So long, however, as the new Romanian state was held in a form of international tutelage, the worst was to some extent mitigated by the intercessionary and supervisory role which the European powers were formally entitled—and were from time to time actually disposed—to play. But tutelage ended in 1878 under terms laid down at the Congress of Berlin and on the basis of explicit undertakings required of Romania and agreed to.[34] The most important of these was that independent Romania should formally and freely award its Jewish subjects citizenship and civil rights. It became evident almost immediately, however, that the Romanian authorities had no intention of abiding by their undertakings; and when matters on the ground deteriorated still further a very substantial exodus from Romania to much the same destinations to which Russian and Polish Jews had been moving began in earnest. A fifth of the country's entire Jewish population, 67,000 souls, left for the United States alone within three decades. A very much smaller fraction resolved to make its way to Erez Yisrael. Quite unlike the Kharkov students, they proceeded to mount a carefully planned operation. Public meetings to debate the ways and means of settlement in Palestine were held. Cooperative associations of those who had made up their minds to move were formed. Delegates—with journalists and local worthies in attendance—gathered in Focşani in Moldavia at the end of 1881 to establish a central, country-wide organization to oversee the entire enterprise. Funds were collected. A small committee was dispatched to Palestine to find and purchase the tract of land on which the migrants were to establish their village and, in the language and spirit that was characteristic of the entire enterprise, work for their livelihood in 'field and vineyard' and for the greater honour of their people. Building materials and tools were bought and packed. Shipping was booked. In May 1882 an initial party of some two hundred Romanian Jews left for Haifa where temporary housing was found for the women and children and from which the menfolk could set out for their final destination in the southern foothills of Mount Carmel. The land was cleared. Housing was constructed. Within a year or so the village of Samarin (later renamed Zikhron Ya'akov) was a going concern: faltering in some ways, but a reality.

---

[34] See Chapter 6 for a fuller discussion.

Others followed from Romania, more, of the same kind and in the same spirit, from Russia itself in the course of time.

Common to all these people was the intention to settle not only in, but *on* the Land of Israel. They were alert, as Jews had always been, to the historic and emotive virtues of the Land, but it was central to their outlook that these were indissoluble from the moral and social virtues of agriculture. Life in the one and labour at the other were, they thought, the twin keys to the regeneration and restoration of the Jewish people. But what would have been worthy of respect, but not especially surprising, in Swedish or German peasants setting out to establish themselves as independent farmers in the American Middle West was the sharpest possible deviation from all that had been known and could reasonably be expected of European Jews, mostly petty traders, clerks, urban artisans, and such like from Wallachia, Moldavia, and the Pale of Jewish Settlement, only a bare handful of whom had skills that were directly relevant to the undertaking. There were besides other obstacles to overcome.

The Ottoman authorities had been quick to note that these Jews were unlike any they had been accustomed to see in Jerusalem and the other towns (Tiberias, Safed, and of course Hebron) that Jews regarded as especially holy. The old-style inhabitants tended to be not only pious, but meek. They were devoid of national-political ideas, let alone ambitions. Few were economically independent. Fewer still were troubled by the fact that they were heavily dependent on charity. They were most obviously the very last people in the world to constitute a source of concern, let alone actual or even potential trouble, to the authorities. The Turkish authorities knew this. And they could see too, by the same token, that the new arrivals were of a different breed. They had, as the Turks immediately discerned, something in common with activists among the Bulgarians and the Armenians and some of the other restless subject populations of the empire. And the Turks knew too, by a flash of undeniably percipient intuition, that they did not want these people. It was therefore laid down in very short order as a matter of Ottoman policy, but in the spirit of the Laws of the Medes and the Persians, that it was necessary to make it as difficult as possible for their kind to enter the country or to remain in it if they had managed to gain admittance and had none the less bought land and in other ways established themselves within Palestine. No secret was made of this being the Ottoman view or these being their intentions, nor of the reasoning that lay behind them. Jews, it was announced from time to time, were welcome to settle within the empire; but not in Palestine[35] or in Syria, only in Anatolia or Mesopotamia, and then in relatively

---

[35] In administrative and political terms 'Palestine' has to be understood as an anachronism. What in modern times was a stretch of the Mediterranean littoral carved out of the Ottoman Empire after the First World War and delineated by the British and the French

small groups. Happily for would-be settlers, the efficacy with which policy formulated in Constantinople tended to be implemented in practice left much to be desired. The regulations themselves were poorly drafted. Circumvention was not excessively difficult. Blanket rules of any kind on the movements and the rights of foreigners ran counter to Ottoman obligations under the capitulations to various European powers. As a result Jews who were nationals of the relevant powers could appeal to them for support and that support might well be forthcoming. Venality was not unknown among the members of the official hierarchy of the empire or in the ranks of the Ottoman police. Nevertheless, however weakly and irregularly implemented, the resulting impediment to further Jewish settlement was substantial and continual. Entry was obstructed, petty bureaucratic harassment was a real and constant threat, police protection from marauders and common criminals was anything but assured, land prices rose unceasingly, and expulsion was always a possibility.

But the greatest obstacle of all to large-scale migration to Palestine—the country's own poverty of resources apart—was presented by the fact that, by and large, people of property, means, and influence throughout European Jewry not only refused to participate in the venture in their own persons, as was to be expected, but were firmly, often ferociously opposed to settlement in Palestine as a matter of principle.[36] Their opposition was at least as great as their opposition to emigration to the west. Very commonly it was stronger. It would have had to be a very dull person not to sense—correctly, of course—that more was involved here than in the case of emigration to other destinations. There was the specific fear that there was no knowing what these *enthusiasts* (a term used with pejorative intent) might eventually be up to other than that they would certainly fail and that the resulting damage—for example, to the quiet philanthropic and educational work in which the Alliance Israélite Universelle and its analogues were engaged in the same part of the world—would be considerable. Actually to assist them 'against our own

as Palestine did not exist under Turkish sovereignty as more than, at best, a geographical expression. The northern half of what would be the territory allotted to Great Britain under the terms of the League of Nations Mandate was a minor district of the Vilayet of Beirut. The land lying east of the Jordan River belonged administratively to the Vilayet of Damascus. The land lying south of a line extending roughly from a point just north of Jaffa to one on the Jordan some 25 kilometres north of the Dead Sea up to the border with (British-ruled) Egypt was termed the *muta-sarriflik* (governorate) of Jerusalem, its special status epitomized by the governor, unlike the chief officer of any other region of comparable size, reporting directly to Constantinople.

[36] Such was the rule. Among the exceptions were the then Grand Rabbi of France, Zadoc Kahn, who was cautiously sympathetic to the idea of resettling Palestine, a handful of relatively affluent Romanian Jews without whose help the settlers in Zikhron Ya'akov might never have left Romania, and an analogous (but lonely) figure in Russia who made the settlement of Rishon le-Zion possible.

judgement' would, as F. D. Mocatta of the Anglo-Jewish Association put it, render 'ourselves responsible for the ruin which, most of us think, must inevitably follow'.[37] The best qualified western observer on the spot, E. F. Veneziani of the Alliance Israélite Universelle, warned his principals in Paris in 1883 that the cost to the western Jewish institutions if, as was likely, they were eventually called upon to rescue these people would be enormous. Great numbers of those who arrived in Palestine had been prevented from landing, he reported, and had nowhere to go. Most of those who had managed to land were without means of support. Those who had initially done somewhat better than that were soon reduced to beggary for lack of farming experience or any other useful skills. 'Every impulse to emigrate to Palestine and every attempt at colonization, however timid it might be,' Veneziani wrote, 'must be absolutely and expressly checked for the time being by all means within our power. . . . It is time this tragedy ended.'[38]

Veneziani was responding to what he had observed in Jaffa and elsewhere in Palestine much as he and his colleagues had responded to the spectacle of refugees from southern Russia crowding into the Galician border town of Brody—and, more generally, to the vastly greater exodus to the major lands of immigration in the west. But the disquiet was deeper. To the basic view that it would be better for all if everyone stayed put, there was added a particular lack of sympathy in the relevant Jewish circles in Paris, London, St Petersburg, Berlin, and Vienna for this unexpected, but surely absurdly anachronistic enthusiasm for a Return to Zion. On the substance, Veneziani was correct. The outlook for the half-dozen farming villages established in 1882 and for the some 500 souls inhabiting them could not be described as other than shaky, for some among them no less than grim. It was perfectly reasonable to hold that the venture was bound to end in ignominious collapse and retreat back to Europe, or transfer to the Americas. But while the failure to produce a demonstrable success was evident, there was no collapse. The toehold the settlers gained for themselves in Palestine in the early 1880s was maintained. Two factors militated in their favour.

As the representative of the Alliance could see for himself, a distinction needed to be drawn between two classes of immigrants. There were those who arrived in Palestine much as immigrants arrived in America: as members, that is to say, of an essentially incoherent crowd, virtually or utterly penniless, trusting to their ability to muddle through until a paid job and a roof for themselves had been found. But there were also, as we have seen, a few relatively well-organized groups, insufficiently financed to be sure, but not totally impoverished, such as those that had set out

---

[37] *Jewish Chronicle*, 19 May 1882.
[38] Alliance Israélite Universelle, *Bulletin mensuel*, July 1883, 98.

from Romania and a similar group led by the eminently practical and determined Z. D. Levontin that had set out from Kremenchug and Kharkov and had found, bought, and settled a tract of land south of Jaffa to form the farming village of Rishon le-Zion. The case for doubting whether the future held any promise for the former class, in what was beyond all question a small, poorly endowed, and generally unfriendly land, beyond failure and misery was strong. Matters were less clear-cut in the case of the latter. There was no question of their determination and stamina, they inspired a measure of admiration even in the generally hard-boiled, congenitally sceptical Veneziani. He had found the Romanian Jews at Samarin, he reported, to be hard-working and sober. They knew what they wanted and what they were about. The majority were literate. Some spoke two or even three languages. A few were 'well-educated'. It was evident that to ensure the overall success of their venture they were prepared to deny themselves a good deal in the way of daily comfort. Perhaps, therefore, success was not to be ruled out after all. A few even had some knowledge of farming. 'And the rest,' wrote Veneziani, carried away for once by pleasure at what he had seen at Samarin, 'could, in time, become good and sturdy farmers if they persist with the good will and enthusiasm that animates them.' In brief, something might eventually be made of these people *provided* they had proper technical guidance and that their resources proved adequate over the long haul.[39] The great question was whether such resources would ever be forthcoming. In the event, it would be the great good fortune of the settlers in Samarin and several other villages that they were forthcoming—albeit from an inherently unlikely and unexpected quarter, from a charter member of the very class that was apt to be most suspicious and dismissive of all of Jewish social initiatives and eccentricities of this or any other kind.

Baron Edmond de Rothschild (1845–1934) was himself a maverick of sorts. He was not a banker or railway entrepreneur. Responsibility for management of the Parisian branch of the family firm was left to his elder brother Alphonse. But Edmond's somewhat dandified appearance aside, he was more than merely another member of Parisian high society whose great wealth permitted him to indulge his social and aesthetic tastes. Remarkably, he was a genuine philanthropist and especially devoted to Jewish affairs and concerns, a man who took his philanthropy very seriously, moreover, mixing generosity with caution and with an insistence on proper reporting and accounting as well. Like the rest of his class he was firm in his opposition to mass migration from the east. Nor could he see any advantage in migration to Palestine in particular. But he knew a thing or two about actual conditions in the Land and had more than a

[39] Ibid., Apr. 1883, 47–8.

passing interest in the welfare of the *yishuv*, the condition and welfare of the old Jewish *yishuv* in particular. His family had assumed a measure of responsibility for it, built a hospital, and established a modern school in Jerusalem. Whatever one thought of the purposes of the new settlers, the fact that they were in Palestine counted for something in his eyes, as did the fact that most of them were in distress. So while Edmond de Rothschild was less than welcoming when approached on their behalf with a request for aid, he did not turn the application down entirely and out of hand. He agreed to make a small grant, laying down conditions that severely limited its use. When approached a second time, he was somewhat more forthcoming, laying down further conditions, one of them being preservation of his own anonymity, another being regular inspection of the results by his representative. At that point a pattern had been set, one that would be maintained over a very substantial period with great regularity, the consequences of which were unseen. The more generous Rothschild became, the more precise the stipulations as to what might and what might not be done by settlers fortunate enough to be in receipt of his largesse. But, of course, the more binding his instructions, the more dependent upon him they became; and the more dependent the settlers whom the Baron was prepared to subsidize became, the greater was his evolving obligation to support them. By the end of the century his grants to selected villages in the new *yishuv* had reached a total of well over a million and half pounds sterling. It is commonly estimated that in the course of his lifetime Edmond de Rothschild contributed between 5 and 6 million pounds—a vast sum for the times.

The settlements—some, not all—were saved for the time being. But the irony of the tie to the millionaire in Paris was profound and to many minds sad. Intentions on all sides, not excluding those of the Baron himself, were beyond reproach. The result, however, was to reproduce in a particularly sharp and unanticipated form something of the ancient dependence of the plain man in Jewry on the seemingly all-powerful, distant, often overbearing *gevir*. Rothschild's determination to keep a tight rein on his protégés and to see to it that they prospered was reasonable in itself. The cumulative effect was to stultify, irritate, at times humiliate the settlers, and slowly and subtly—in some cases not subtly at all—to corrupt them. Besides, while Rothschild's munificence was crucial to the survival of the settlements which he undertook to assist, not all were recipients. And while it was the case that his material contribution to the new *yishuv* was far and away the greatest it ever derived from a single source, it was never the sole source from which aid of some kind was expected or was actually forthcoming. Finally, there was the matter of the all-important moral and ideological purposes driving the entire enterprise. Rothschild's contribution to the morale (and the morals) of the new *yishuv* varied between the inconsequential and the obstructive. The

motor forces promoting and fuelling the new *yishuv* emanated from eastern Europe. They did not and could not come from the eighth *arrondisse-
ment* of Paris. He and his delegates on the spot did a great deal to keep the
fragile enterprise going. His agents performed yeoman service as instructors in the relevant agricultural skills—the art of wine-making, for example. But neither he nor they had anything of social or political value to
teach, nothing, that is, that impinged on the *raison d'être* of the new
yishuv, not positively and helpfully, at any rate. Nor, of course, did the
yishuv and its affairs impinge in any noteworthy way as yet on the affairs
and the thinking of Jews in Paris or in any other important western centre
of the Jewish Diaspora. What the settlers had accomplished, however, by
the fact of their existence was to establish themselves as an object of
public attention, a target to which very many pairs of eyes, some friendly,
some hostile, were regularly directed, a topic to which the Jewish press,
for example, devoted ever more space and which was therefore a subject
for frequent, lively, at times ferocious private and public discussion. This
was true throughout the world of Jewry. It was especially the case in eastern
Europe. And indeed the *locus* of such public debate as was likely to be of
most consequence for the *yishuv's* future lay firmly there, in eastern
Europe—not in Paris or London or Berlin, or indeed even in Erez Yisrael itself. The *yishuv* itself was as yet no more than an outpost of eastern
European Jewry: peripheral to the Jewish people's true centre of gravity
not only geographically and demographically, but functionally as well. It
was not itself the arena in which debates on the affairs of Jewry which
were in any real sense pivotal were likely to be held and preferred outcomes decided upon.

Along the vast chain of communities in the Jewish heartland that
extended from the Baltic to the Black Sea, there would now begin to
cohere a distinctive subcategory of circles of the like-minded for whom
the *yishuv* was the material embodiment of their cause. By the Jewish
calendar year of 1882/3 at least a dozen such pro-settlement,
'Palestinophil' societies had sprung up in Russia alone. Three years later
their number had risen tenfold. Given the Russian administrative principle governing associations of any kind, namely that what had not been
officially sanctioned was *ipso facto* illicit, such societies were obliged to
proceed in semi-secrecy. No *non*-Russian organization of nationalist tendency however mild could be approved of and that counted against them.
On the other hand, a movement that set out to encourage Jewish emigration was not one that senior members of the Russian bureaucracy
would want to obstruct. A measure of light surveillance over them was
exercised. But they were not interfered with as a rule so long as they kept
an appropriately low profile. With the bureaucracy's not wholly
unfriendly attitude in mind, anxious to demonstrate, if necessary, that all
was above board, elaborate rule-books were drawn up, minutes were

recorded, regular consultation by correspondence between local societies, but especially with the central leadership in Odessa, was conducted. But there was no real hierarchy and no uniformity of structure or size or prestige. Some local societies were very small, numbering no more than a hundred or so signed-up, dues-paying members in all. Some were larger: a membership roll of 500 or 1,000 was common. Largest and most important of all local societies was the one in Odessa with several thousand members. Next in importance was the society in Warsaw. There were societies in the capital cities of St Petersburg and Moscow as well. But as access to them was difficult for Jews resident in the Pale and it was, in any case, in the Pale that feelings on all relevant counts were strongest and potential membership greatest,[40] the *de facto* centre of operations was in Odessa. Odessa had the advantage of presenting no problems of access other than that of distance. It was the natural port of embarkation for Palestine through which all emigrants to Palestine passed and needed to be cared for to some extent while they awaited shipping. But before all else it was the home city of the man who had done most to push what had begun as a spontaneous and poorly focused rebellion of spirit towards conversion into something that was a little more like a revolution.

Yehuda Leib Pinsker (1821–91) was an unlikely candidate for a revolutionary role, even a very muted one. He had none of the personal characteristics and inclinations that made for political activism of real quality and vigour. He was totally lacking in the traits of brutality and single-mindedness that are the necessary marks of the 'professional revolutionary'. He was not a man of violence or ambition. He was not particularly a man of action. He was devoid—entirely and unmistakably—of such qualities of leadership as are suggested by the famously loose term 'charisma'. And if his virtues were many and very real, they were of a private, not a public nature. The respect accorded him by most of those who knew him was inspired by his solidity of character and his personal integrity. Pinsker's social and political outlook was a moderate one, moreover. Seen in the context of general (i.e. Russian) politics his views can be classed as typically liberal and 'western'. Had he been born a generation later and survived into the second decade of the twentieth century he would have fitted easily into the Russian Constitutional-Democratic party, the Kadets. In sum, on the eve of this good man's

---

[40] Societies of a cognate character, loosely connected to those in Russia and Poland, appeared in the west as well, notably in university cities where students from eastern Europe were present in substantial numbers: in Zurich, Heidelberg, Berlin, Vienna, Paris, Montpelier, and as far away as Leeds and Manchester. But these were discussion circles, essentially. Their importance over time had to do with their function as incubators of future members, in some cases leaders, of the movement rather than with anything they might themselves be doing, or expected to do, to sustain the settlements either materially or with their own persons.

world being turned upside down in 1881, the face he presented was that of an elderly, somewhat retiring bachelor, a practising physician of repute, a citizen with a strong sense of public responsibility and, at the same time, a man whose stock with the authorities was fairly high as well. There needs only to be added the salient fact that, as was perhaps to be expected of a member of the first generation of Jews to have been admitted to Russian universities, he was an active participant in the work of the St Petersburg school of believers in, and promoters of, the social and economic and, above all, the linguistic integration of Russian Jewry into Russian society as a whole. Pinsker was among those who reasoned that the Russian language had not only to be acquired by the Jews, but needed to become a (if not quite *the*) principal vehicle for the articulation and display of their learning and literature. This would benefit those Jews who would be acquiring it in ever greater numbers in any case; and it would be of benefit and indirect instruction for cultivated ethnic Russians as well. The Russian language would then play a role analogous to that which Arabic had once played for the Jews of the Islamic world and the German language now played for the Jews of the contemporary German *Kulturbereich* (or German cultural sphere). The underlying assumption was integrationist: it was necessary, but it was also possible for the Jews to reconstruct their role and place in the great multinational empire in which they lived and to bridge the vast social and cultural gap between ethnic Russians and themselves.

Jews of Pinsker's view (and that of Baron Guenzburg and his associates) did not go so far as to urge total assimilation, or apostasy, or any other form of self-abnegation that was likely to entail loss of heritage, identity, or dignity. They did not want any such attempt to be made; and they did not believe that such an attempt would succeed, the more so as it was manifest that the Jews of Russia, overwhelmingly, would want none of it. Nor, they contended, would anything be accomplished by the Jews continuing their stubborn refusal to make a move of their own towards the middle ground. It was true that neither the Russian state nor Russian society had gone as far as they might have done, and should have done, towards that middle ground themselves. Still, the state had shifted its position somewhat in recent years (i.e. under Alexander II) and in the right direction, notably in the sphere of education and culture, but also in the formal, more difficult realm of legislation as well. It followed that the assumption that Russian society and the Autocracy were intrinsically wicked or hopelessly and irrevocably ill-disposed towards the Jews was unwarranted.

Pinsker, not entirely coincidentally, was a long-established citizen of Odessa, a city that was notorious for its Russian-Jewish community being the least encumbered of all by the minutiae of the Tradition. He knew very little Hebrew, but had excellent Russian and German. In essence, if not in name, he was a free-thinker in matters of religion.

Above all, perhaps, he was a living exemplar of the still small, but steadily growing class of those who had had the benefit of the easing of the framework in which the Jewish subjects of the Autocracy were required to live out their lives. If he did not say so, he certainly hoped that others would emulate him—not, however, as renegades intent on turning their backs on the mass of Jewry, but as members of a class of Jews who were in the process of becoming—in ways and to a degree barely known until the latter years of Alexander II's reign—*Russians.*

The events of 1881 shattered Dr Pinsker. His innocence was lost. His optimism went up in smoke. His belief in gradualism and bridge-building and in language, education, and culture as the primal instruments of change evaporated. Moshe Leib Lilienblum, his colleague in the movement they were jointly to lead, described the scene in which, with uncharacteristic ferocity of language, Pinsker announced his change of mind at a meeting of the St Petersburg-based, Guenzburg-backed Society for the Propagation of Culture among Jews and proclaimed the futility of its labours. They—and he with them—had been doing no more than 'amusing' themselves. Tens of thousands of terrorized and impoverished people were in flight to the borders of the empire. The Jews in their numbers had never before been in such dire straits. It was not the education of individuals that was now at issue, but the fate of the entire nation.[41] Yet what, he asked himself in the aftermath, were the cause and nature and, physician that he was, the aetiology of the double curse laid upon the Jews: the circle of active and dangerous hostility in which they were enclosed and what he identified as the disease of Judaeophobia with which the gentiles were evidently afflicted. He proceeded to formulate a diagnosis and prescribe a cure. The conclusions to which he was drawn on both counts can be summed up under five heads.

(*a*) At the root of the Jewish predicament lay the fact that it was not so much a matter of the probability or otherwise of the Jews of Russia ever being granted emancipation, as of the improbability of their emancipation ever sparing them from the afflictions to which they were prey. The emancipation of western Jews had been a great event so far as it went, but it was only of a legal, not a social nature. It was the product of reason, not natural, unencumbered sentiment. Millennia would pass before brotherly love all round became a common human attribute. And until such time the Jews, for their part, were fated to remain what they were at present, a foreign element in each society in which they happened to be embedded. To believe otherwise, namely that emancipation would come to them as a function of such general human and social progress as was in train, was to delude oneself.

(*b*) Pinsker's second thesis was that the afflictions of Russian Jewry and

[41] *Kol Kitvei M. L. Lilienblum,* iv (Warsaw, 1913), 182.

the dangers to which they were exposed were peculiar neither to them as
Russian Jews nor to Russia as such. They were functions of the intrinsic
condition of all Jews at all times and in all places.

(c) His third was that if the Jews were ever to emerge out of the mire in
which their history had placed—and abandoned—them they would have
to dig themselves out of it themselves.

(d) His fourth was that while the Jews of Russia had many virtues, they
lacked the experience, the leaders, the institutions, and the necessary,
minimal conditions of freedom usefully to set about the organization of
their own salvation. The Jews, as a people, would have to resolve, collectively, how they were to proceed to their own rescue. But it would be for
the relatively free, influential, practised, and independently minded Jews
of the west to take the lead.

(e) His fifth and most important thesis was that the only viable basis for a
solution, and therefore the only target at which the Jews should aim, was
a territorial-political one. Their one sure course was to establish themselves on a territory that was all their own, equipped and empowered,
once again, as masters of their own destiny.

Some of this bore the mark of the thinking and writing of Pinsker's
younger contemporary, Moshe Leib Lilienblum (1843–1910)—as,
indeed, he was ready enough to acknowledge. Lilienblum was a figure of
a very different cut, background, temperament, and personal status. In
origin and by training he was a classic product of the world of the Talmudic academies of Lithuania at their most austere and demanding. But
as one of the first and greatest of its inhabitants to turn against it and pil-
lory it for the pitilessly stultifying mental and social strait-jacket in which
it enclosed its adepts and—through them—the Jewish people as a whole,
he was, at the time, a very rare phenomenon. Life and Law needed to be
rejoined, he wrote in a celebrated article published in 1868, 'Orḥot ha-
Talmud'. It was the function of the rabbis to attempt to do so, to institute
changes in the rules of religious observance that would permit Jews who
were still loyal to their people to be faithful to the essentials of their heritage as encapsulated in what was truly central to Judaism, the prophetic
texts of the Bible. If they did not, catastrophe was inevitable. The fabric
binding the Jews one to another would crumble and the centrifugal
forces acting upon them would then destroy them as a coherent people
altogether. Proponents of the Jewish enlightenment, the *haskalah*, welcomed Lilienblum to their camp. Lilienblum's peers and superiors were
outraged. In orthodox eyes, his demand for change was heretical and all
the more scandalous for it having been made by a man who was eminently one of their own. Isolated, vilified, and cast out, Lilienblum left
Lithuania for the freer air of Odessa. He set himself to acquire the elements of the secular education that he had never had, supporting himself on

the edge of pauperdom as a *melamed* and, later, as an equally meanly paid secretary of a local burial society. But he continued to write and his reputation, among the *maskilim* at any rate, grew steadily.

The corner-stone of Lilienblum's thinking remained, as before, his immovable conviction that there was much in the life of the Jews that was no longer tolerable and that there must be fundamental, internal change—change of values, change of structures, change in conduct—if ever they were to be rescued. But the shock of 1881 (of which he wrote memorably in his diary[42]) led him to re-examine his position, not so much to alter as to radicalize and extend it out of the relatively familiar country in which internal social change was contemplated and on to the unfamiliar one of reflection on the totality of the Jewish condition. It was evident, he concluded, that the salient characteristic of the Jews was their eternally alien status. As such, as strangers, they were invariably at risk, invariably vulnerable to criticism, to bullying, to defamation, and worse. It was therefore to this alien condition itself that an end had to be put if they were ever to be free of threat to their persons and their dignity and released from the absurdity and humiliation of being expected to imitate their persecutors and to be grateful for each and every act of mercy and simple decency accorded them. 'For more than six hundred years we have been repeatedly proving to Europe that we neither eat human flesh nor drink Christian blood—but in vain. . . . We think ourselves fortunate when some learned Christian attests that, truly, we do not cook Passover dishes with human blood. What disgrace, what shame!' His operative conclusion was simple. It was time to abandon Europe. But, it was not to America that they should turn. For there they would be strangers once again. Their central need was to return to the one country in which and to which they had historic rights and would not, in consequence, be aliens. These were ancient rights, to be sure, but they had not, for that reason, been forgone. The Jews had no more lost their right to their country upon the loss of their sovereignty over it than had the Balkan peoples lost their rights to their lands when they lost power over them. It might take a very long time, perhaps an entire century, to evacuate Europe and resettle the people in Erez Yisrael. But a beginning could be made. And in the meanwhile there must at least be an end to continued self-deception and suppression of dignity. The Jews had witnessed and enjoyed a relatively liberal period, in Russia as elsewhere. But it had been no more than a respite, as recent events in Russia had demonstrated. 'How many more pages inscribed in blood the present chapter

---

[42] 'I am glad I have suffered torment,' he wrote on 7 May 1881 after the pogrom in Odessa. 'For once in my life I have felt what my forefathers felt all through their lives. They lived continually in fear and terror; why should I not feel something of the dread which they felt throughout their days?' (*Ketavim otobiografiim* (Jerusalem, 1970), ii. 187–9). And see above, p. 284.

may be holding, nor what chapters will follow the present one, nobody knows.'[43]

But it was the less naturally eloquent, less learned, less historically minded, and altogether less subtle Pinsker who, in a pamphlet of his own, was to catch the general imagination. The doctor had gone abroad in 1882, his immediate purpose rest and a 'cure'. But he sought out those leaders of central and western European Jewry to whom he had access and who, he thought, might be persuaded to take the matter of contemporary Jewry in hand. He pressed his ideas upon them at every opportunity. He wanted deeds and leadership. He believed a great world conference of the notables of Jewry should be convened to work out and then proclaim a programme of general rehabilitation and realignment. It would select and authorize a smaller group to set such a programme in train and equip the Jews as they had never been equipped before with a body that was both prepared to see the problems of the nation whole and to do something lasting and decisive about them. But he found no one of much consequence who agreed with him on the substance of his case and none who shared his sense of urgency. Adolf Jellinek, an old acquaintance, now the most influential rabbi in Vienna, received him kindly enough, finding the doctor much changed, even shockingly so, as he reported later. But he made no bones about his disagreement. Was this Jewish *nationalist* the man who had once studied at Leipzig, Heidelberg, and Berlin and filled his mind with the latest advances in the sciences? Was Pinsker proposing to convert him too to Jewish nationalism? Rabbi Jellinek advised his much troubled visitor from Russia to travel to Italy without delay, as originally planned, for a period of rest and recuperation after the shock he had experienced and charged him to remember that as the Jews had once survived Vespasian and Titus, so they would now survive Ignatiev. 'Do you seriously imagine,' Jellinek put it him, 'that I could agree to all your assumptions and conclusions and actually join you in raising the blue and white banner of a Jewish state and a Jewish political nation? Why, I should have to deny my entire past and all I had ever preached and published in the course of over thirty years!' Did Pinsker want all that had been invested in the fight for emancipation since Moses Mendelssohn and the Great French Revolution down to this very day to be cast away? Were western Jews expected to agree with their enemies, namely to accept that they were nomads, that it was indeed the case that they had neither home nor motherland of their own, and that they were incapable of having feelings of patriotic loyalty to the countries of Europe in which they lived as their fathers had before them?

We are at home in Europe [the rabbi told him]. We feel that we are sons of the country in which we were born and educated, whose language we speak, whose

---

[43] 'Obshcheevreisky vopros i Palestina', *Razsvet*, 49, 9 Oct. 1881, 1597 ff.

culture forms the basis of our spirit. . . . We are Germans, Frenchmen, English-men, Magyars, Italians, and so on, down to the marrow of our bones. . . . We have lost the sense of Hebrew nationality.

Pinsker should be in no doubt: if it were possible to ask the Jewish people what it thought of his programme, all European Jews—those of his own country (Russia) excepted, perhaps—would be found to reject it.[44] The doctor heard more in this vein. Some of those he talked to were more hostile still. Almost all were in one way or another dismissive of his case for fresh thought and urgent action. Among the scattered exceptions to the rule was the President of the Board of Deputies of British Jews, Arthur Cohen. But he refrained from committing himself to more than an expression of sympathy and to advising Pinsker, sensibly enough, that he would do well to set out his argument in publishable form. The advice was taken. Breaking his return journey to Russia in Berlin, writing in the German language for the *western* audience to which he believed it was vital that he address himself,[45] he produced a pamphlet which he entitled *Autoemancipation! Mahnruf an seine Stammesgenossen von einem russischen Juden* (*Auto-emancipation! A Russian Jew's urgent warning to his kinsfolk*).

The pamphlet was a manifesto, the first of its kind in the public affairs of modern Jewry, the most effective ever written. It was straightforward in structure, markedly devoid of the qualifications and circumlocutions that were the common characteristics of statements on Jewish affairs des-tined for the public domain, and pitiless.

Though you prove yourselves patriots a thousand times . . . some fine morning you will find yourselves crossing the border and reminded by the mob that you are, after all, nothing but vagrants and parasites, without the protection of the law.

But its power lay too in the fury and the anguish which it conveyed.

When we are ill-used, robbed, plundered, and dishonoured, we dare not defend ourselves, and, worse still, we take it almost as a matter of course.

The nub of its argument, much like Lilienblum's, was that the illness of the Jews lay in the fact that their afflictions had little or nothing to do with their being the friends or the foes of any other people. It had everything to do with their being aliens and strangers everywhere and at all times. Unlike all other peoples, they had no country of their own in which others who entered it were required to accept the alien condition. By surviving, astonishingly and in defiance of all common experience, they had done no more than to render themselves doubly anomalous: 'A people without a territory is like a man without a shadow, a thing unnatural,

---

[44] A. Druyanov, 'Pinsker u-zemano', *Ha-Tekufa*, 16 (1923), 318–25.

[45] There was in any case no certainty, for the time being, that the Russian censors would pass it.

spectral.' It was this anomalous and unnatural condition that gave rise to superstitious fear of them, to hatred, and then to a Judaeophobia that passed from generation to generation like a disease, a pathological condition so profound, so regular in its manifestation, so plainly 'an inherited aberration of the human mind' that no rational argument or pragmatic consideration was proof against it.

But Pinsker's central business was with the Jews themselves. They needed to *see* the 'tragicomic figure' they presented to others. They needed to reconcile themselves once and for all to the idea that other nations would forever reject them. It was essential that they take the elemental forces at work here into account. And they should not complain. On the contrary, they were 'duty-bound to take courage, rise, and see to it that we do not remain forever the foundling of the nations and their butt'. They must aspire to equality, urgently, but they must understand that equality would only be attained when they had returned to the ranks of the nations as an independent people living in its own homeland. And they needed desperately to understand that others would not achieve that for them, that it would be achieved, if at all, only by an effort of their own. In sum, escape and release from their morally and materially degraded and insufferable condition depended on two fundamental conditions being fulfilled. Firstly, they must have a territory of their own, although it need not (*pace* Lilienblum and others) be Palestine necessarily. It was territory as such and the concentration of the greater part of Jewry within it that would be crucial, not this or that particular geographical location. Secondly, their re-entry into the ranks of the nations as equals had to be their own achievement. They must cease to look to others to emancipate them. They must understand once and for all that they needed to emancipate themselves. It was *auto*-emancipation that they should strive for.[46]

Autoemancipation! did not go unnoticed in the central European Jewish press, but such attention as it received was mostly very unfriendly. Where it was not dismissed out of hand, it was denounced as narrow in outlook, or as anachronistic, or as insufficiently appreciative of what had been achieved in consequence of emancipation in the west, or as excessively impatient when it was evident that progress in the east was bound to be slow, or as absurd in its insistence on likening the case of the Jews to that of the Serbs, the Bulgars, and other submerged and unhappy peoples. Back in Russia itself, however, matters were otherwise. The religiously orthodox paid no attention to Pinsker. They knew little or nothing of him or of his pamphlet. Theirs was a largely hermetic world. Few among them had—or desired to have—access to such Jewish periodical

---

[46] Y. L. Pinsker, *Autoemancipation! Mahnruf an seine Stammesgenossen von einem russischen Juden* (Berlin, 1882). English trans. (used here in amended form) by D. S. Blondheim in B. Netanyahu (ed.), *Road to Freedom* (New York, 1944).

publications as had reported the manifesto's publication in the west and passed on its content, in some cases in full, in Yiddish, Hebrew, and Russian.[47] Nor were they likely to have any interest in what a man of his unabashedly modernist and secularist stamp had to say. Among those who had veered away to some extent from orthodoxy and were inclined to modernism, but belonged to the older, moderate school that followed the lead of the magnates of Russian Jewry, much as Pinsker himself had done in the past, the response was similar to that which his pamphlet had met in the west. They were, in any case, likely to perceive the essay as, among other things, an attack upon themselves. But within the Russian Jewish intelligentsia proper—among those who had been shaken for all time by the pogroms, had been embittered by the government's response, had come to despair of the established leaders of Jewry, and had begun to doubt the relevance of universalist social and political prescriptions to the very specific matter of Jewry as well—among such men and women the response was in many cases electric. It was, indeed, a measure of the degree to which this small, but rapidly growing fraction of Russo-Polish Jewry hungered for new ideas, for a new direction, and, above all, for leadership in one form or another, that the pamphlet's author was almost instantly recognized and accepted as the man of the hour, as a tribune. The Hebrew poet Y. L. Gordon, the champion of a Jewish cultural renovation founded on a revival of Hebrew as a literary and spoken language in combination with uncompromising opposition to rabbinical orthodoxy, gave quintessential expression to the mood with a bitter poem entitled ' 'Eder Adonai' ('The Herd of God')[48] in which the Jews were excoriated for their limitless weakness and resignation. Gordon dedicated it to the still anonymous author of *Autoemancipation!* Others of like standing, among them Lilienblum himself, Mandelstamm, and Lev Osipovich Levanda, *uchĕnyi evrei* ('learned Jew', i.e. official expert on Jewish affairs) to the governor-general of Vilna, but also a novelist and journalist of repute and an important figure in the east European wing of the *haskalah* movement, hurried to express their admiration to the author when they discovered his identity. More, they pressed him to take the lead—not, it needs to be said, in the realm of ideas in which each one of them had a

---

[47]   The first Hebrew version was printed in Vilna in 1883. The classic Hebrew translation is by Aḥad Ha-'Am, published in Y. Klausner (ed.), *Sefer Pinsker* (Jerusalem, 1921). The liberal Jewish newspaper in St Petersburg *Razsvet* issued a Russian translation in the latter half of 1882. A Yiddish translation by the celebrated author Sh. Y. Abramowitsch, known best by his pen-name 'Mendele mokher seforim', was printed in Odessa in 1884.

[48]   A few lines will give the flavour of Gordon's poem: 'The herd of God, the holy cattle are we, | The earth is an altar set before us . . . | To be a sacrifice we were created.' The poet had been among those *maskilim* who had displayed abiding confidence in the good intentions of the Autocracy prior to 1881. His dismay at the turn events had taken was correspondingly and typically intense.

certain status of his own, but in the one practical enterprise that seemed to them at least to point a way out of the morass.

The local Palestinophil societies that had sprung up in Russia, Poland, and Romania were all very well, they felt. They attested to good will. They encouraged migration to Palestine and mobilized moral support for the settlers. But if material help was to be adequate and if, as was hoped, their status was ever to be regularized so as to allow them to emerge from the awkward, unfamiliar, and possibly dangerous twilight of illegality in which they were operating, something better had to be devised. There had to be central organization and direction, if possible an adaptation to the admittedly very different circumstances of Russia of that now pre-eminent model of institutionalized Jewish public activity, the Alliance Israélite Universelle. It would, to be sure, be focused exclusively on the needs of the new settlements. It would be imbued with the spirit and viewpoint encapsulated in the name by which the Palestinophil settle-ment movement had begun to be known: Ḥibbat Ẓion (Love of Zion). And if there was to be a central organization, there had necessarily to be a central figure to lead and represent it. The natural candidate for the role was Pinsker himself.

The urgency with which Pinsker was pressed to take this on is not immediately explicable. His notoriety as the author of *Autoemancipation!* counted for a very great deal. But that he was very far from being a nat-ural leader of men and that, as it turned out, he was exceedingly reluctant to assume the responsibilities demanded of him, was never in doubt. Cer-tainly, he was a 'distinguished and honoured' man, as Lilienblum was to put it later. But his distinction was regional. The sources of such honour as was commonly meted out to him were limited to Odessa. In the realm of strict ideology his views were not, and were known by all concerned not to be, those of Lilienblum and the great majority of his other col-leagues. None doubted that on the necessity of migration out of Europe and some form of territorial resettlement of the Jews on the basis of an autonomous regime of their own all were agreed. In contrast, on what for most people was the equally central matter of Palestine—of Ereẓ Yisrael itself—as the specific *locus* of such resettlement, disagreement was pro-found. For the Palestinophils there could be no question of a territorial solution to the Problem of the Jews on any territory other than the ances-tral one. Pinsker, for his part, had no objection to the effort to return to Ereẓ Yisrael. But he thought it unlikely to succeed; and he did not think it essential to try. In this respect, as in others, he was a man who saw things with a colder, more sceptical, wearier eye than most of those who now gathered round him. His social outlook was simpler than theirs. Unlike Lilienblum and Levanda and many of the rest he had never been sub-jected to the old forms of Jewish intellectual training. He carried less of a burden than they and was in no need at all of working out a middle way

between a deeply internalized, closely studied, thoroughly familiar Tradition on the one hand and an incomplete, in many ways still somewhat
alien modernity on the other. His Palestinophil colleagues had gone very
far towards modifying their original, inherited views of both the condition and the Tradition of the Jews.

But they had not gone as far as Pinsker or the colleague who was probably closest to him in outlook, Emmanuel Mandelstamm. These two
men, both physicians, were products of a form of schooling and training
that was exclusively and explicitly secular. They had lived and performed
professionally for a great many years in a world—the world of science as
opposed to that of letters—in which history, religion, culture, and even
ethnic identity played very small roles, if any at all. Had they been natives
and residents of France or Germany they would, most probably, have
been out-and-out assimilationists of one kind or another, proponents not
only of the emancipation of the Jews as the process was understood in the
west, but of substantial, if not complete, social and cultural integration as
well. In Russia, where any such possibility was effectively ruled out, they
had begun by seeking a middle way of their own. It had only been when
the prospect of some such middle way was demolished that they moved
on to a fresh position somewhat nearer to the mainstream of Jewish life.
It had, as perhaps some on the fringes of Ḥibbat Ẓion hoped it would,
brought them closer to the Tradition too, at least in the modified form
espoused by the *maskilim*. In practice, it was rather to a secularized form
of Jewish nationalism that they were drawn, one which, in its essentials,
as some of Pinsker's critics in the west had correctly pointed out to him,
had a good deal in common with other contemporary varieties of political nationalism. What was uniquely Jewish being in many ways reduced
or absent, the gap between Pinsker, Mandelstamm, and some others and
the much more numerous members of the Palestinophil school was correspondingly wide. Could a bridge be thrown over it? If so, could such a
bridge be better than temporary, fated to be swept away by the first flood
of strong ideological feeling that arose? Why then have the good Dr
Pinsker as leader?

The short answer was that Dr Pinsker was a man who had shown his
colours. Whatever his failings he was a man of courage and conviction.
And then, there was no one else in view. It had become plain to all, as it
had rapidly been made plain to Pinsker himself, that it was futile to wait
for the westerners to come to their rescue. It was equally evident that
there was little to hope for from the well established and affluent in Russian Jewry itself. Some reckoned that that might change. Perhaps with
Pinsker at the head of the new movement, given the respect in
which he was held locally, the higher levels of the Jewish bourgeoisie
in Odessa could at least be counted on not to be obstructive. Later
their example might be followed by their analogues in other Russian

cities.[49] These were not strong arguments; and there are hints all along that their weakness was recognized. In the course of time, especially after Pinsker's formal election as chairman of the entire movement at Ḥibbat Ẓion's first general conference in 1884 (of which more later), even Lilienblum, Pinsker's great champion, came, on reflection, to regret the choice. The good man was not really one of their kind, he noted in his recollections, not a Ḥovev Ẓion (lover of Zion), not a dedicated one, at all events. He was most certainly a person of the highest integrity. It was not to be doubted that they could console themselves with the thought that their chosen leader was devoted to their cause. 'But I knew very well,' Lilienblum wrote, 'that he was ill and weak, that he had a bad heart, and that despite the best of intentions he was incapable of doing anything that required much energy and was of real substance.' That those who had attended the conference had chosen the one amongst them who was best qualified for the task was not to be denied. But if that was the case, what, Lilienblum asked himself gloomily, could 'we hope to accomplish if the best of the Lovers of Zion . . . is a man devoid of strength, whose weakness of body and spirit renders him incapable of coping with a task which is of such evident immensity?'[50]

Pinsker too, once he had succumbed to the pressure and agreed to preside, had to make the best of things. He held to his belief that what was needed was a great national assembly meeting in one of the capital cities of Europe at which fundamental decisions on policy for all Jewry would be taken. He knew it to be unattainable. He accepted that the best that could be managed was a minor gathering of some thirty delegates, all with a genuine interest in the affairs of the movement, all more or less self-selected, all but three from eastern Europe, none (with the partial exception of Pinsker himself) of much more than regional prominence at best. The delegates assembled early in November 1884 in the Silesian town of Kattowitz on the German side of the border with Russian-ruled Poland. Kattowitz had been chosen partly because access to it from Russia was relatively easy, partly because on German territory they would be free from Russian surveillance,[51] and partly too because it was the one town in all of what was technically Germany in which a local society of Ḥovevei Ẓion had been formed. But much as the form and scale of the Kattowitz conference was a very far cry from what Pinsker had originally had in mind, so too was its outcome. The major political and ideological issues raised directly and indirectly in his *Autoemancipation!* pamphlet were not discussed, only vaguely referred to. There was no serious

---

[49] M. L. Lilienblum, *Derekh la'avor golim* (Warsaw, 1899), 11.

[50] Ibid. 21–2.

[51] One delegate at least is known to have been interrogated by the Russian police on his return.

discussion of ways and means whereby the movement might be made to go beyond its present size and structure and expand its numbers and influence, although none doubted that it needed to do so if it was to move purposefully towards its targets. It was accepted that it was essential to set up some sort of office in Berlin to provide a freer base of operations than the main existing ones in Odessa and Warsaw, one that could at least attempt to mobilize support in the west. But no decision to do so was taken. It was resolved that an effort would be made to try to persuade the Ottoman government to relax the multiple obstacles to entry and settlement in Palestine. How this was to be accomplished and by whom was left undiscussed and undecided. Pinsker's leadership was confirmed, however. It was resolved without debate that as best as it was able the movement would continue to support those settlements in Palestine which Edmond de Rothschild was for one reason or another unwilling to subsidize. But it was resolved, too, that no new responsibilities were to be assumed and no new settlement of the country was to be encouraged—not, at any rate, until such time as the existing settlements were judged to have been consolidated and the movement's leadership had made an intelligent assessment of conditions as a whole.

For what purported to be the foundation conference of a national movement this was a weak, not far short of defeatist outcome. Some comfort could be taken in the thought that Kattowitz was a step in the right direction. But even those participants who thought so were hard pressed to agree that the enthusiastic language adopted by the Warsaw Hebrew daily newspaper *Ha-Ẓefira*, when it spoke of it as a great parliament of Jewry,[52] was really warranted. There had been some in Pinsker's circle who had hoped that a counterweight to the Alliance Israélite Universelle in the shape of a 'World-wide Palestinian Union' would emerge. Activities in Palestine would then be re-energized and reorganized; and, of even greater significance, 'our people would be emancipated' and it would be made possible for them 'to go their own way without being influenced by the rich and the plutocrats who are much more interested in the stock exchange . . . than in the fate of our people and their country'. Accordingly, it would not be a mere 'philanthropic but rather a [political] institution'.[53] But there was no cause whatsoever to believe that an organization, formidable enough to rival the Parisian Alliance Israélite Universelle, had in fact been in the making.

---

[52] 11 Nov. 1884. The article in question was published after the conference, but it is plain enough that it had been written before the delegates to Kattowitz had convened.

[53] Mikhael Shlyaposhnikov to Pinsker, 18/30 Sept. 1884. *Toldot*, rev. edn., ii, no. 396, 523–4. The term employed in the original Russian was 'state . . . institution [*ne filantropicheskago, a gosudarstvennago uchrezhdeniya*]'. But the intention, given the context, was clearly to 'political' or, perhaps, 'national' (*Toldot*, i, no. 129, col. 252).

Still, there was novelty enough in the Kattowitz conference to infuri-
ate those who were opposed to what it was taken to represent. The Warsaw Jewish weekly *Izraelita*, speaking for 'Poles of Mosaic persuasion',
conceded that there might be something to be said for Ḥibbat Zion as a
philanthropic enterprise—were it no more than a provider of employment in agriculture for the poor. Indeed, if nothing could be done for
them within the empire, there was no reason why something should not
be attempted in Palestine. But that was not its true purpose. It was evident
that what Ḥibbat Zion really aimed at was the revival of the Hebrew
nation. Its people wished to lay a corner-stone for an independent Jewish kingdom in the country of their forefathers—a purpose which all sensible Jews were obliged to proscribe as a fantasy injurious to the masses
and incapable of realization. The Russian-language Jewish newspaper
Voskhod in St Petersburg reaffirmed its opposition to emigration: as such,
to any destination whatever, and regardless of underlying private or public purpose. Migration from Europe to America was bad enough.
Because of its *national* colouring and the likelihood that it would divert
people's attention from the really essential task of educational and
professional improvement, migration to Palestine was worst of all. The
most important of all German-language Jewish periodicals, Ludwig
Philippson's *Allgemeine Zeitung des Judentums* in Berlin, declared itself
hostile for much the same reasons. So too did Rabbi Jellinek's *Neuzeit* in
Vienna:

We must firmly oppose whoever wishes to establish the settlement of Ereẓ
Yisrael on national foundations [and] on Messianic hopes of national rejuvena-
tion. . . . We do want to come to the help of our persecuted brethren in Russia.
But we do also strongly require of them that they not embarrass the Jews of
Europe and abstain from offering fresh grist to the anti-Semites' mill, such that
the latter be able to argue that the Jews of Europe were foreign nationals after
all.[54]

Back in Russia, Pinsker and his associates were at one in their refusal to
pay attention to such pleas for discretion. And all, not excluding those
whom he had distressed by his indifference to what they held to be indispensable, were united in their desire to avoid an ideological rift on matters of high principle. Compromise had been formally established as a
guiding principle well before the meeting at Kattowitz, when the new
Odessa Committee's first public statement of purposes was drawn up.
Remarkably, even the possibility that there might well be more than one
legitimate viewpoint was explicitly conceded: 'The prime aim of the
committee will be the establishment of a settlement centre, in Ereẓ Yisrael *if possible*, for those of our impoverished brethren in all countries of

[54] Cited in S. L. Zitron, *Toldot Ḥibbat Zion* (Odessa, 1914), 259–63. Cf. *Toldot*, iii, no.
1241, col. 711 n. 3.

origin who are capable of such labour and can not find employment in their countries of origin.'[55]

In practice, however, the movement continued to devote itself to the promotion of settlement in Palestine exclusively. Pinsker accepted his new colleagues' absolute dedication to the ancestral land with understanding and, so far as is known, good grace. As Lilienblum was the first to affirm, he performed his duties as their leader without complaint and with all the energy he could muster. He made no attempt to impose his own point of view. Only when he was asked to revise the written text of his own *Autoemancipation!* to accommodate their Palestinophil sentiments did he stick to his sceptical guns and refuse outright. The compromise was therefore somewhat lopsided, more a matter of language than of deeds—the first of many, as will be seen—and for that very reason a greater source of weakness than was realized at the time. The general, root dissatisfaction with the current condition of Russo-Polish and Romanian Jewry and the determination to initiate change that had brought them together continued to unite them. But the purposes and rationale of the still embryonic movement were left substantially less well defined than they might have been. Much that in analogous national movements would have been rigorously debated and articulated was allowed to remain unstated, at best implicit. That little was really clear-cut and unambiguous in the relevant circles of the nominally one-minded goes some way to explain, however, why Pinsker's pamphlet had made so great an initial impact on actual and potential Ḥovevei Ẓion. *Autoemancipation!* was nothing if not muscular and unambiguous. On the other hand, that same robust quality that had distinguished it helps to explain in turn why the pamphlet's subsequent reputation would be somewhat shadowy: a statement members of the movement were inclined to refer to on occasion, but which many understood incompletely and many more left partly or even wholly unread. Despite its original galvanizing role it never attained the status of an official, canonized statement of Ḥibbat Ẓion's—and later Zionism's—aims and purposes, *the* manifesto of the movement it had done so much to bring into being.

There was one further respect in which the inveterate tendency to refrain from bold and clear-cut programmatic purposes and definitions determined the course of events. As deep, if not deeper than the largely silent quarrel between Pinsker and his school and Lilienblum and his friends was the incipient, ultimately inexorable conflict between those who were still loyal to religious orthodoxy and those who had substantially abandoned it. The leaders of east European orthodoxy, in so far as they deigned to take any notice of Ḥibbat Ẓion, had initially been uncertain how to deal with it. Not all were anxious to admit what the Turks,

---

[55] Lilienblum, *Derekh la'avor golim*, 15 f. Emphasis added.

for their part, had noted immediately, namely that the new settlers in Erez Yisrael were fundamentally different from those who constituted the old *yishuv*. Some sought to keep their distance from Ḥibbat Ẓion without opposing it openly. Some hoped that much would be clarified in the course of time. Very few were willing to lend it an active hand or offer a word of positive encouragement. Only one rabbi of recognized standing and impeccably orthodox credentials agreed to take part openly and with a good will in its activities. This was Rabbi Shemu'el Mohilever of Bialystok. Rabbi Mohilever had long shown great interest in the affairs of the new *yishuv* from its beginnings. He had been one of the two men who helped to talk Edmond de Rothschild into making his initial grant-in-aid to the settlers in the autumn of 1882.[56] His attendance at the Kattowitz conference, as well as at the general conferences held subsequently (at Druskieniki near Grodno in June 1887 and at Vilna in August 1889) followed naturally and if, in Odessa, it was seen as a considerable achievement to have induced him to turn up so, up to a point, it was. It was undeniable that Mohilever's participation served what almost all agreed to be the tactical need to found the Ḥibbat Ẓion movement on the broadest possible social basis and to play down, so far as that might be possible, issues that touched on religious observance and belief. None doubted that to do otherwise was to risk an open quarrel with the rabbinate, even with Mohilever and the very few like him who were prepared to help: to quarrel with them was to break with them and to break with them was, most probably, to cut themselves off from a large and potentially friendly public. It became evident, however, that it would be difficult, and perhaps impossible, to play the differences down entirely. Debate on fundamental principle could, perhaps, be avoided. Seemingly technical-legal issues on which the Law was precise could not be. The cultivation of land in Erez Yisrael itself by Jews raised the question, for example, of the applicability or otherwise of the antique biblical injunction to leave all land fallow during the Sabbatical Year. Were the new settlers to observe it? To the orthodox mind a clear biblical injunction was beyond dispute and it was the duty of the movement to insist on all its people honouring it. For decent, observant Jews, *a fortiori* for respectable members of the rabbinate, to participate in a movement that failed to do so was unthinkable and impermissible. To the modernists, on the other hand, the idea of calling upon the exceedingly hard-pressed novice farmers in Palestine to

---

[56] The respect Rothschild accorded Mohilever on this occasion (as opposed to the much more dismissive treatment accorded Yosef Feinberg who had been delegated by the settlers of Rishon le-Zion to approach the Baron for the same purpose) recalls the oddity of semi- or totally secularized western magnates habitually regarding implacably orthodox rabbinical leaders as the authentic representatives of eastern European Jewry and therefore the only people they were obliged to talk to if they wished to achieve anything of value in those communities' regard.

abstain for an entire year from any attempt at all to squeeze whatever they could out of their land was absurd on every possible practical ground and potentially destructive of the entire enterprise.

Then there was the matter of the Ḥibbat Ẓion's own leadership. To the orthodox-rabbinical mind there could be no question of a man of Rabbi Mohilever's class and quality accepting the legitimacy of secular leadership in a specifically Jewish organization or institution—short, at any rate, of some form of clerical surveillance and control over it. The primacy of the immensely respectable Dr Pinsker was, perhaps, at a pinch, acceptable. That Moshe Lilienblum, the renegade, should serve as the Odessa Committee's secretary was not. When the matter of office-holders came to a head at the second general conference at Druskieniki in 1887 some points of specific disagreement were papered over by common consent, but some could not be. Grumbling *sotto voce* about 'Jesuitry', Pinsker refused to budge. Mohilever, very possibly with an eye on Pinsker's failing health, retreated by choosing to regard all arrangements agreed upon as temporary and making do with a refusal to add his signature to the conference minutes. But the retreat was tactical. Nothing had been resolved. And if the desire of all parties to abstain from conflict and avoid a rupture was evident, how well it served the movement in the long term remains a puzzle. Shying away from confrontation suggests a lack of toughness and determination. It betokens a certain modesty too and a recognition that there are alternative and contradictory views on the course to be taken that are not to be dismissed, not out of hand at any rate. From caution of this sort it was only a step to the explicit view that consensus was an end in itself to be striven for even at the cost of basic ideological clarity and consistency. This had governed the odd choice of Pinsker himself as leader. All this was prudent; but it was remarkable too. Moderation on issues of principle and a tendency to draw back from final and irreversible confrontations and disagreements were qualities for which the radical movements that were taking form in Russian society as a whole at this time were anything but notable. And unfortunately for Ḥibbat Ẓion, if these other movements were beginning to prove especially attractive to the young, modernistically, and secularly inclined members of Russian Jewry who formed the reservoir from which Ḥibbat Ẓion itself would have to draw its membership if it was not merely to survive on the margins of Jewry but to gain a position of strength within it, it was to no small extent because a great part of their attraction lay in their positions being very sharply defined and deliberately confrontational.

There would therefore be a price to pay for leaving so much unsaid, unthrashed out, unfought over. In a world in which the bonds of traditional social principles and attitudes were loosening at great speed, Ḥibbat Ẓion needed to compete with many rivals for the attention of the modernist Jewish intelligentsia, but also, increasingly, for that of the man

and woman in the street, members of the artisan class, of the urban proletariat, and the great, grey lumpenproletariat itself. All these were in a
state of incipient mental and social rebellion against the *gevir* and the rabbi
and, indeed, against the Tsar and all that *he* represented as well. In the
competition for their hearts and minds it was the strong, ostensibly rational argument, not always the sentimental one, and certainly not one
that was ambiguously and less than confidently formulated, that was most
likely to carry conviction. Ambiguity and subtlety of purpose were not
much admired by the increasingly politicized urban classes of late
nineteenth-century and early twentieth-century Russia, Jewish and
non-Jewish. Least of all was lack of clarity in regard to the Autocracy
likely to be understood and accepted. In this respect, Hibbat Zion, a
movement anxious to remain on the right side of the law in Russia, was
especially badly placed. None could doubt that its members' loathing of
the government was intense. But there were two respects in which its
members, certainly the most prominent among them, were imbued with
traditional Jewish caution. You did not attempt to fight the *rashut*, the ruling
power in the land, least of all openly and directly. You did not lightly
abandon such legal and political advantages as you held no matter how
limited and fragile they might be. Pinsker and his colleagues had not only
no wish to fight the authorities, they had been anxious from the first to
gain official sanction for their activities. They were, after all, very much
men of the middle class. Pinsker, Mandelstamm, Levanda, Shlyaposhnikov,
and many others were as fully respectable members of Russia's small professional and learned bourgeoisie as any Jew could hope to be. If, in the
sense used here, they were revolutionaries, the revolution they wished to
mount pertained exclusively to the internal Jewish arena. In the general
Russian context, and by its standards, they were nothing of the kind.
They were far from being political radicals in the ordinary sense. They
were not participants in any of the dissident, let alone revolutionary
movements. They had a quarrel with the Autocracy, but they did not
wish to fight it if they could avoid doing so. To do so was to risk being
crushed—but to no great purpose if it was on the removal of the Jews
from the authority of the Russian state that they were intent. It was characteristic of their approach, therefore, that their first considered statement of principles of September 1883 was rounded off with the sentence,
'It goes without saying, that those who wish to leave their country to join
[the] settlements [in Palestine] must first fulfil their obligations to the
governments of the countries which they will be leaving'[57]—the 'obligations' they had in mind being the military ones to which Jews, like others,
were subject under the terms of the conscription laws. They wished so far
as possible to forestall official objections to what they were about. They

---

[57] Lilienblum, *Derekh la'avor golim*, 15–16.

were persuaded that the legal status they craved would be granted them sooner or later if they were cautious.

If we outline openly and straightforwardly our true aim, which, as it seems to me, is not in conflict with any Russian interest, governmental or general, we shall deprive the government of any grounds for seeing some hidden purpose in our aim (which it truly lacks). . . . If we choose to hide our true aim under all sorts of 'cleverly' interwoven purposes, we shall tie our own hands and feet, shall be paralysed in our activities, and shall have to run in circles round our real aim, in all probability never reaching it. . . . I think it essential that it be clearly stated in the Application [for legal status] or even in the [movement's] rules and principles themselves, that we plan to help and encourage immigration to Palestine of such Jewish elements as, having found no way of making a living in Russia, are a burden to themselves, to society, and to the Government.[58]

Thus Levanda, the governor-general of Vilna's *uchënyi evrei*, a man with some knowledge of the internal workings of the bureaucracy, to Dr Pinsker. Whether it was necessary for them to be so very cautious and to try quite so hard not to give offence is uncertain. Emigration to Palestine (mostly through Odessa) was no more impeded by Russian officialdom and police than emigration to the west. The movement itself was never at any time without the benefit of very nearly as great a measure of *de facto* toleration as it could reasonably wish to have granted it *de jure*. And that too would be granted to it before very long. Renamed The Society for the Support of Jewish Farmers and Artisans in Syria and Palestine to suit the Russian authorities, the Odessa Committee was officially registered and approved in the spring of 1890 to the great satisfaction of its members. But if some thought that a milestone of some sort had been passed, nothing of substance changed. When Pinsker died in the following year Hibbat Zion was still bravely inching forward, but no more. It had not declined in numbers, but nor had it grown more than moderately. The Ottoman government continued to demonstrate from time to time that the rules it had established for itself as a guide to the way in which the new Jewish settlers in Palestine were to be treated were immovable. On the contrary, fresh efforts were made periodically to strengthen the machinery by which the relevant regulations—especially those dealing with entry into the country—were to be enforced. Discreet intercession in the Turkish capital, even at the ministerial level, by a variety of well-meaning Jewish notables (among them the American Minister in Constantinople, Oscar Straus, who tried as hard as his official duties permitted him to be helpful) rarely yielded more than a polite restatement of established policy. A lighter hand was promised from time to time, but that was all. When, after repeated applications, Edmond de Rothschild was authorized in 1887 to proceed with the construction of additional houses to

[58] Levanda to Pinsker, 19 Feb. 1885, *Toldot*, i, no. 230, col. 443.

accommodate settlers in villages for which he had assumed a general responsibility it was thought a considerable achievement. But at no time was there any doubt of the Ottoman regime's desire to show that it drew a line between its hostility to the new settlers and what it assumed they were about and its determination to continue to treat its own long-established Jewish subjects correctly and with reasonably good will. A request by the Alliance Israélite Universelle in the very same year to look to the safety of a group of Jews who had been attacked and pillaged in the vicinity of Damascus was acted on without delay.[59]

But if Ottoman policy loomed as the greatest obstacle to progress, it offered only one illustration among others of the disparity between what all thought needed to be done and the little that all knew they were able to do. Here lay the greatest and most decisive of the movement's weaknesses. The resources available for the expansion and consolidation of the settlements were wretchedly inadequate. Ḥibbat Ẓion was at all times a movement that relied on contributions in kopeks as well as in roubles. Only very rarely did it manage to muster a sum in excess of £5,000 in any given year—barely enough, by the strictest calculation, to equip a score of families at most with the land and the implements they needed if ever they were to strike root. A shift from the spirit of high enthusiasm in which it had been born to one of scepticism and depression was therefore inevitable. The tendency to accept a lowering of original expectations and to seek short-term satisfaction in petty administrative routine became in some cases all but ungovernable. Some among the leading figures of Ḥibbat Ẓion began to argue for a full recasting of the movement's purposes and methods both in Palestine itself and in the Diaspora. Most notable among them and to greatest effect in his strictures was Asher Ẓevi Ginsberg (1856–1927), a brilliant essayist, something of a philosopher, one of the few undoubted intellectuals to occupy a position of influence in the movement, best known both in his lifetime and posthumously by his somewhat falsely self-deprecating pen-name Aḥad Ha-'Am (One of the People). At no time, however, did he, like some, drift away, for all that the movement's true relevance to the needs and prospects of a public that was being continually buffeted by rising social and political tensions and measures of deliberate persecution was open to question once again. What, it began to be asked among those who might otherwise have been its adepts and activists, could be the use, finally, of this small, weak, middle-class, anxiously respectable, law-abiding, loosely structured movement other, perhaps, than serving as so much further evidence of the unrest and dissatisfaction to which eastern European Jewry was now increasingly prey? The danger of marginalization well before anything of real substance had been accomplished was

[59] Kalmanovich to Pinsker, 7 Dec. 1887, *Toldot*, rev. edn., v, no. 1128, 485–7.

manifest—the darkening mood within Ḥibbat Ẓion itself contributing to it mightily.

The sum of this was that the undeniable, near-fatal weakness from which it suffered was not, after all, of a methodological, still less of a doctrinal order. It was that nothing it might reasonably hope to do to relieve the *material* distress of the Jews of eastern Europe could conceivably be better than marginal and that the two central questions it had put before the public—whence indeed the source of its attraction to some at least among the modernists of contemporary Jewry—remained unanswered. *Auto*-emancipation . . . but did the Jews wish to emancipate themselves? And could they do so if that was what they wished? Dr Pinsker had lit a long, thin fuse under the structures of Jewish life. That it was sputtering was an achievement in itself. But if it were as suddenly to peter out neither the upholders of the ancient structures of Jewry nor those who were trying to mount a rebellion against them would have had reason to be surprised.

III

By the end of the nineteenth century the process by which the public life of the Jews of Europe was being riven by deep, endemic, and to some extent overlapping quarrels of a kind for which there had been no precedent in their historic past was well in train. Traditionalists denounced modernists, nationalists confronted assimilationists, the orthodox fought religious reformists on the one hand and secularist *maskilim* on the other, opponents of migration condemned its proponents, Palestinophils (shortly to be transmogrified into Zionists, as we shall see) drew apart from Americanophils, and—pragmatically rather than programmatically—westerners took their distance from easterners. The overall pattern was fluid. The contending schools were protean, each subject at one time or another to sharp variations in internal self-confidence and intensity of conviction, gains by one commonly entailing losses by others. All would continue well into the following century to trouble men's spirits and to influence their conduct. Of all the symptoms of the changes wrought in the lives of the Jews in the course of the long run-up in *all* parts of Europe to the crisis precipitated by the events in Russia in the early 1880s it is this multiplication of schools that is perhaps the most telling. In it were reflected the multiple contradictions between the application of the principles of the Enlightenment to the particular matter of the Jews and the resistance to it encountered for different reasons in both the Jewish and the non-Jewish worlds, the interplay between the forces marshalled along the several lines of division of opinion and interest within Jewry itself leaving marks that were in certain ways very nearly as profound as those left by the external conflict visited upon the Jews by hostile forces without. Deepest of all was the ideological—and, by extension, social—fissure precipitated and continually nourished by the effort to recombine the elements of socio-political rebelliousness that appeared among the Jews in Russia in the aftermath of the pogroms of the 1880s into revolutionary activity proper. None was so precisely reflective of the contradictions between Enlightenment principles and the realities of the public and private lives of the Jews as this. None—largely for that reason— would be so conspicuously destructive of what had been European Jewry's once justly celebrated social and political cohesion.

The participation of individual Jews in radical and even revolutionary movements in central Europe has been noted. That Jews should take an active and open role in the general political life of their respective countries was a striking departure from past practice. But it was no more than a natural, perhaps inevitable consequence of the multiple and mutually reinforcing processes of cultural assimilation and the absorption of the social (not excluding political) values of the relevant sectors of society at large. It was equally natural that by and large Jews should tend to prominence in the socially radical, left-wing side of the political divide in each case, the moderate left in some cases, the extreme left in others.[60] But it was very rare indeed for Jews entering the western and central European political arenas to announce themselves, or even to see themselves, as representing a distinct Jewish constituency. Here and there, as in the case of Samuel Montagu who represented a preponderantly Jewish constituency in London's East End, the Jewish vote and the local interests of the Jewish community came to be of some immediate, marginal political relevance. In no case before the end of the century did the participation of Jews in the political life of their country owe anything of importance to a declared or conscious or even unconscious *primary* concern for the condition and status of the Jewish community in question. Even where a Jew's political prominence and acceptance went unquestioned and some

---

[60] I have not ventured a definition of 'left', but I have found no better term to indicate an approach to social and political matters that presupposes a pressing need to pass control of the existing socio-politico-economic order into new and nominally (which is not always to say, actually) more numerous hands; a belief that the social order as a whole is in fact amenable to rational and purposeful control; and a conviction that, once the dust has settled, the new order will prove to be better than the old for *all* concerned and the cost, if any, justified. That people who have themselves reaped immediate and visible benefits from processes of formally legislated and imposed social reform should tend to think that there was much to be said for its extension to other areas and to other sectors of society was probably inevitable. It may have been naïf. It was not for that reason discreditable. Placed well outside the established fortresses of privilege and power, the sympathies and understanding and possible alliances of newly emancipated Jews who were in any way disposed to political action would very naturally be with members of other social classes who, like themselves, were bent on breaking into the political arena, rather than with those who were already inside it and were concerned chiefly to avoid being joined by others.

of the glory attained by the individual was thought to reflect on the community, the tendency for both sides, of the community itself no less than its politician-member, was to make the disengagement of the one from the other as clear and public as possible. And the more radical the politics in question, the greater the effort to do so. However, where the community itself was not, or did not believe itself to be, under threat and where the political tendency to which the individual Jew who had entered the political world subscribed could be contained within whatever had been set as the outer limits of constitutional respectability, there the root phenomenon of Jewish participation in general politics had ceased to be a source of positive anxiety, at any rate among the Jews themselves. It might irritate their opponents and critics. It might worry those Jews who were particularly prone to social and political quietism and timidity. But generally speaking, the evidence encouraged a more relaxed view: figures as prominent, flamboyant, and disregarding in their contempt for many of the niceties of public life as Ferdinand Lassalle and the young Disraeli had plainly failed to disrupt the pattern by which the German and English Jewries were evolving. However, where the politics subscribed to were not merely radical-reformist, but conceived and practised as a deliberate threat to the structure and quality of the state and to the social order that supported it, there matters were otherwise.

They were doubly so, naturally enough, where the masters of the state and the social order in question had shown themselves to be explicitly and actively hostile to Jewry, rather than merely indifferent or at worst unfriendly to it. No Jewish community could then keep a comfortable distance from the political arena. It would be vastly more difficult to shy away from the question where the community's own, collective political interests ultimately lay. It would be altogether impossible to avoid the community in question being regarded as a reservoir of potential recruits from which movements seeking to overthrow the existing political order were likely to seek and find their men—and women. In a word, the probability of Jews *in the mass* being seen by their enemies not only as the 'objective' allies of politically subversive movements, but to some extent being in the process of becoming actively involved, would be enormously enhanced. All this took on an exceptionally heightened form in Russia for there, indeed, the fundamental, general, and urgent political question was that of the nature and future of the regime itself. The question posed to all politically minded persons, Jews among them, was whether to accommodate oneself to it or to oppose it? And if to oppose it, was one to do so in thought or in deed? And if in deed, by moderate or extreme methods? In brief, did one or did one not both think and promote revolution?

Until the 1870s, Russians of revolutionary sentiment and purpose were still preponderantly members of the nobility, much as the

Decembrists had been, bound together to a certain extent by common social origins and upbringing. By the same token, there were very few Jews among them. As Jews began to percolate into the Russian school system and, especially, the universities, and as revolutionary fever rose throughout the intelligentsia, this changed. Their entry into the ranks of the extremist Narodnaya Volya was the first to be marked—encouraged, and made possible in all likelihood by that movement's particular belief in what an exceedingly small, compact group could do if it had adequate resources of energy and courage and knew how to identify the right targets for attack. Attacked and attackers being in all cases individuals, the role any young person might play provided only his or her dedication and readiness for sacrifice were absolute, was therefore of indisputable (and glorious) value regardless of origin. By the middle of the 1870s—which is to say, well before the dramatically steep rise in their numbers in the aftermath of 1881—Jewish recruits to the revolutionary movement in its early populist form had at any rate ceased to be exceptional. A breakdown based on official records of the calling, social status, and origin of 1,054 revolutionaries arrested, tried, condemned, and sent into punitive exile or placed under police surveillance in the course of the round-up of dissidents in 1873–7 showed that 68—6.5 per cent—were Jews. Of 79 condemned to exile 12 were Jews: 15.2 per cent.[61] These were not immensely large figures, but they do illustrate the fact that the Jewish contingent was already strikingly in excess of the Jewish proportion of the total population of the empire.

Many of these young people were of the same type and class as other populists, that is young, middle-class *intelligenty*. Typically (but not exclusively) they would be students, sons and daughters of 'privileged' Jews (merchants of the First Guild, for example), who, being legally resident in Moscow and Kiev and other cities and areas outside the Pale of Settlement, were not only products of the Russian system of secondary and higher education, and therefore Russified in great measure, but well on their way to total cultural integration and much affected by the climate of ideas in the more advanced and literate sectors of contemporary society. Gregorii Davidovich Goldenberg is remembered for having shot the governor of Kharkov, Kropotkin, in February 1879, an assignment from which he managed to escape undetected, but equally for having subsequently been caught in possession of explosives destined for an attack on the Tsar and for having been entrapped by his interrogators, but more especially by his own self-importance, into revealing fatal information on other conspirators. On realizing the absurdity of his attempt to negotiate with his captors on behalf of the movement and the damage he had done,

---

[61] 'Statisticheskiye svedeniya o propagandistakh 70-kh godov v obrabotke III otde-leniya', *Katorga i ssylka. Istoriko-revoliutsionny vestnik* (Moscow, 1928), xxxviii. 47.

he committed suicide. Gesya Gelfman was one of the group caught and tried in connection with the actual assassination of Alexander II in 1881. She was of sterner character than Goldenberg, unco-operative with her captors, and unrepentant when sentenced to hang. The sentence was not carried out, however, when it became known that she was pregnant, but imprisonment in the Peter-Paul fortress destroyed her anyway and she died the following year. Unlike Goldenberg and Gelfman, Osip Vasil'e-vich Aptekman (b. 1849), a student at Kharkov University in the early 1870s, was a member of the non-violent *Chorny peredel* wing of Narod-naya Volya that pinned its hopes on what it supposed to be the spon-taneously rising revolutionary spirit in the peasantry and the role the *narodniki* would be privileged to play once the peasants accepted them. Aptekman went so far as to convert to Russian Orthodoxy as a necessary preliminary to his 'going to the people', saying of his apostasy later, that it was only upon his baptism he had felt himself 'literally renewed' and truly drawn to the peasants among whom he intended to live. Franco Venturi's observation, that political factors in this Rousseauist movement were 'inextricably mixed with the desire to express long-repressed feelings' [and that] 'the political content cannot be separated from the [populists'] desire to break with the civilization of their fathers', is peculiarly apt. The sense of a wish to break free from the burden of Jewish ancestry is unmistakable, being part, no doubt, of a general craving for a form of freedom that, paradoxically, turned out to be conditional on the accept-ance of even simpler absolutes. To go to the people was not only to lend them one's strength, share the joys of a people's revolution with them along with its pains, but to put aside all one's own habits and culture. It was necessary, 'once and for all, to shed one's own cultivated skin [*sbrosit' s sebya kul'turnuyu shkuru*] and appear before the people in the coarse, labourers' skin that was theirs'. Thus Aptekman in retrospect, long after he had been arrested (in 1880), tried, exiled to Yakutsk, and had returned.[62] Another early Jewish recruit to Russian revolutionary populism was Lev Grigorevich Deich (Deutsch), described by Venturi as 'one of the most active revolutionaries of the last thirty years of the nineteenth century and the beginning of the twentieth, and one of the founders of the Russian social-democratic party'.[63] Deich is probably best remem-bered as one of the authors, with Plekhanov and Vera Zasulich, of the 'Open Letter to the Petrograd Workers' of 28 October 1917 in which the Leninist 'October Revolution' of that year was condemned as an 'historic disaster' that would provoke a civil war that would end with a retreat from the achievements of the 'February Revolution' of that year. But it may be

---

[62] O. V. Aptekman, *Obshchestvo 'Zemlya i Volya' 70kh godov* (Petrograd, 1924), 128.
[63] Franco Venturi, *Roots of Revolution* (New York, 1966), 570; and see Nora Levin, *Jewish Socialist Movements, 1871–1917: While Messiah Tarried* (London, 1978), ch. 4.

Lazar (Eli'ezer) Tsukerman's career that best epitomizes the role his kind and generation played in Russian populism. He was responsible for setting up Narodnaya Volya's printing press. He was captured and arrested in 1880, tried and sentenced to fifteen years *katorga*, penal servitude in Siberia. Five years later, at the age of 35, he committed suicide.

These were early days, however. A great deal turned—ever more in the course of time—on two intertwined questions. On what terms might individual Jews expect to be admitted to radical, but especially revolutionary movements of any description? And, more fundamentally, on what terms—if any at all—were the reforming, radical, but especially the out-and-out revolutionary-conspiratorial movements prepared to concern themselves with, and cater for the specific, collective needs and disadvantages of the Jews of the empire as one legitimate item among others in the catalogue of social ills they had taken it upon themselves to remedy?

The crux of the matter lay in the fact that the answer to the second question was apt in the most important of cases to be flatly in the negative. That this would bear heavily on the role Jews might play in the revolutionary movements and on the ability of the movements to recruit Jews to their ranks was inevitable. But the subject would be repeatedly bedevilled, as we shall see, by the extreme reluctance of almost all concerned first to recognize the issue and then to confront it. That there was an issue to be confronted became abundantly apparent when the common outlook in Narodnaya Volya on Jewish affairs generally and on the pogroms of the early 1880s specifically followed a logic that differed very little from that which informed the regime itself. The principal revolutionary movement of the day, that is to say, adopted a position of publicly proclaimed hostility to Jewry and then, after surveying the scene in the spring of 1881, went further than the government itself by offering direct and open encouragement to the *pogromshchiki* by word of mouth and in print as well. On 1 September 1881, the first wave of the pogroms of that year not quite over and many more cases of pillage and violence against Jews in the southern provinces of Russia and elsewhere still to follow, the executive committee (*ispolnitel'ny komitet*) of the Ukrainian branch of the movement distributed a printed manifesto addressed to the 'good people, the honest Ukrainian nation'. The Tsar (for whose assassination it took explicit responsibility), the police, and the gentry were all denounced for their crimes against the people. So were the Jews, Jewry in its undifferentiated entirety, that is to say, but more precisely, in the carefully abusive language of the manifesto, '*the* Yids' (*zhidy*). The people—in practice, the Ukrainian peasantry—were now called upon to recollect the time when their forefathers were still free, the land was theirs, and the Poles had not yet come to seize their land and enslave them or the Jews to exploit and cheat them. All their enemies were conspiratorially linked, they were informed. When the peasants very properly sought to expel the Jews from Elizavetgrad and Kiev had not the Tsar immediately and typically set out to save them? Had not Russians (*Moskaly*) been brought in for that very purpose and honest Christian-peasant blood been spilled? Was not this collusion between Tsar and Jews the best possible evidence of the Autocrat's essentially evil nature? Narodnaya Volya had already judged one Tsar, the Ukrainian people were told, sentenced him to death, and duly executed him. It had then warned his successor of what would betide him if he did not bring the oppression to which the 'people of the Orthodox Church' were subject to an end. The young Tsar had shown indifference to their demand, but he was gravely in error. For,

Good people, we shall achieve nothing except by force and by mutiny. Blood alone will wash human sorrow away. You have already begun to rise against the Yids. You have done well. Soon the entire land of Russia will rise in mutiny against the Tsar, the [Polish] gentry [*Pany*], and the Yids. It is as well that you be with us.[64]

It needs to be seen that there was rather more in this than a simple, cynical tactical position. It reflected the revolutionary populists' long-standing view that it was essential not only to 'go to the people' in the self-assumed role of political mentors, recruiting sergeants, and manipulators, but to accommodate in every way possible the peasants' way of life and established opinions. One needed to live among them, work with them, and learn and practice their agricultural and artisan crafts, in so far as young, educated souls from middle- and upper-class families—separated, therefore, from the peasants by an almost unimaginable mental gulf—might be able to do so. One needed to refrain from questioning firmly held peasant beliefs in the tricky realm of religion, for example. One needed to recognize that it would be illegitimate to oppose, or even so much as criticize, the 'toiling masses' when these were embarked on what could only be construed as a form of class warfare. From this to a positive adoption and enthusiastic propagation of certain peasant beliefs was therefore a very short step, notably so when such adoption and propagation offered an opportunity to display one's own (revolutionary) sympathy with them *and* the general revolutionary purpose of disruption and disorientation was served. The logic behind the view that it was opportune to encourage violence even in the form of pogroms and to play on the peasants' deep strain of anti-Jewish sentiment seemed a firm one. So did the parallel attempt to employ the authorities' effort, such as it was, to restore order as a stick with which to beat it for its supposed collusion

[64] *Ispolnitel'ny komitet Ukrains'komu narodu: Ob'yavlenie.* Text and accompanying annotations in Y. Ma'or, 'Ha-keruz ha-antishemi shel "narodnaya volya" ', *Zion*, 15 (1950), 150–5.

with 'the Jews'. But there is no reason to suppose that such simple political opportunism did not in fact fit in very well with what many of these
young people had been brought up to think and readily accepted as the
truth of the matter of the Jews in Russia well before the events of 1881
brought the question to a head. An easy, blanket vilification of the Jews
that differed in no important respect from what was thought and said in
the highest official and social circles of St Petersburg, and was well established in Russian literature that was otherwise of the highest quality, had
long been sufficiently common among *narodniki* for it to have been a
source of disquiet, even mild embarrassment, for some at least of the
more reflective spirits in the revolutionary movement. Five years before
the outbreak of the pogroms 'this crude lack of understanding and this
unconscionable attitude' was complained of in an article offered to
Vperëd!, much the most important oppositional periodical of the day. The
author (unknown, but, on internal evidence almost certainly not a Jew
himself) warned that it 'will bring, that it already has brought, no small
damage not only to the Jews, but to the socialist–revolutionary [cause]
itself. . . . Do you really and truly believe, that Jewry comprises exploiters
and deceivers exclusively, that there are no exploited people among them
too . . . that the Jewish people has no working class of its own?' He then
went so far as to speak at some length of the shame that all in the movement should feel at what he judged to be the stupidity of those whose
attack on Jews in general was unsparing even in the case of devoted members of the populist movement itself. Peter Lavrov, the editor of *Vperëd!*,
had some sympathy for this position and little patience, for example, with
Bakunin's habitual and particularly gross anti-Semitism. But even the
gentlemanly Lavrov seems to have found this particular variety of internal criticism too unpalatable to publish, filing it away, after reflection,
without further comment or reference.[65]

The considered view, even of many of the Jewish members of
the movement—Lev Grigorevich Deich, for example—was that the
dilemma facing the revolutionary populists was a very real one and that
no simple course of escape from it presented itself. One might regard the
pogroms with distaste, but they did seem to provide powerful evidence of
a mutinous spirit abroad among both the peasants and the urban lumpenproletariat. Surely this was to be encouraged. Surely it was wrong to try
to inhibit it. Whether the violence presaged actual revolution was, of
course, a matter for separate debate. In general, initially at any rate, the
revolutionaries did think so and were, if only for that reason, strongly
inclined to cheer the *pogromshchiki* on. Hence the Ukrainian manifesto
referred to above and others like it. It was only on further, somewhat

---

[65] M. Mishkinsky, ' 'Al "ha-de'ot ha-kedumot shel ha-soẓialistim ha-mahapakhniim
shelanu neged ha-yehudim" ', *He-'Avar*, 21 (1975), 20–34.

more mature reflection that some tended to consider that the *pogromshchiki* may have been mistaken in concentrating their attention, their bitterness, and of course their violence on the Jews after all. If some Jews were, indeed, exploiters and class enemies, it was undeniable that most Jews were nothing of the kind, that very great numbers of them were as hellishly impoverished and as ill done by as the Russian and Ukrainian peasantry, if not more so. Still, when due regard had been paid to the awkwardly plain and observable socio-economic facts, it remained that mutinous, popular violence of any kind was a phenomenon to be welcomed, not decried. The sum of the populist position was that harmless individuals might suffer injury, but resort to violence by the common people was bound to inculcate a stronger sense of their rights as men and citizens in the Russian populace than they would otherwise have and do wonders to stoke up the energy and the will to defend those rights to the utmost with whatever weapons were to hand against those who would deny them.[66] But, most important of all, it seemed to the *narodniki* there was really no alternative. To denounce the pogroms was to side with the Jews. To side with the Jews was unthinkable.[67]

In sum, those who were the Autocracy's most active and dedicated enemies at this time were at one with it in their sentimental, semi-mystical view of the peasants as the uniquely good, innocent, and in the catch-phrase *fundamental* people of Russia, badly in need of guidance, to be sure—such as it was their peculiar duty and function to provide. And both, by the same token, regarded the Jews primarily in terms of what was imagined to be their insidious commercial role among the peasants. Both subscribed to the same conventional wisdom, namely that the pogroms needed to be understood—and to be presented publicly—as so many linked cases of justly aggrieved, morally worthy people rising against an alien caste that had long abused them and against whom they were themselves hopelessly ill-equipped to defend themselves. The differences between the servants of the Autocracy and their most dedicated enemies were not, for any of these reasons, insubstantial. The government knew that, however it might choose to account for the 'disturbances', it owed it to itself to damp them down. The revolutionaries, in contrast, thought that they had reason to rejoice at the spectacle of disorders that were to some extent undermining the authority of the state. Again, sober, senior members of the government bureaucracy understood, and made no secret of their understanding, that there were grounds for distinguishing between the various classes, types, ideological

---

[66] Editorial in *Chernyi Peredel*, 4, p. 298, 1 Mar. 1881, cited by M. Mishkinsky, ' "Black Repartition" and the Pogroms of 1881–1882' in J. D. Klier, and S. Lambroza (eds.), *Pogroms: Anti-Jewish Violence in Modern Russian History* (Cambridge, 1992), 79.

[67] Mishkinsky, ' 'Al "ha-de'ot" ', 20–34.

and religious tendencies, occupational categories, and so forth into which Russian Jewry was actually divided—if only as a latter-day variation on the old distinction between 'useful' and 'useless' Jews. The activists of Narodnaya Volya, by and large, displayed no interest in such niceties and were happy to denounce Jewry in its entirety.

Still, the varieties of social class and economic condition to be found among the Jews, blindingly apparent to observers of even the narrowest vision, could not be ignored indefinitely. Nor could the presence—and significance—of a growing number of Jewish recruits within the revolutionary movement itself. Aron Isakovich Zundelevich (1854–1923) was the very model of a revolutionary activist of the early period: a born conspirator, 'the tireless technician' of Zemlya i Volya, later Narodnaya Volya,[68] exceptionally courageous and enterprising, and highly regarded by all for his exploits, but most notably for the organization of regular— and therefore especially dangerous—traffic in smuggled publications, printing equipment, explosives, and people across Russia's borders. Zundelevich had been a student at the state rabbinical seminary in Vilna.[69] He was therefore a man with a firm foot in both worlds, a native of the Pale who had acquired, apart from an admittedly something less than fully orthodox training in rabbinics, a standard Russian secondary education and access to Russian literature and to contemporary thinking and writing in Russian radical circles. In 1872, with A. S. Liberman, he led a circle of politically minded fellow students at the seminary. A spell abroad in Germany brought him in touch with central European socialists, systematic social democracy, and an acquaintance with assimilated and largely emancipated central European Jewry. It was an experience that appears to have contributed strongly to his early, very firm, hugely superficial misreading of the Jewish condition in his own part of the world. It led him to write at the time of his most intense conspiratorial activity in the 1870s, that 'to none of us Jewish revolutionaries did Jewry seem to be a [genuine] national organism, a phenomenon worthy of support'. Jewish nationalism, Zundelevich went on to assert, very much in the terms central European socialists, Jewish and non-Jewish, had already made their own, was inherently illegitimate. 'The only element binding the Jews together as a single, discrete entity—religion—is one which in our settled view is utterly regressive.'[70] He was arrested in 1879, three years after entering Narodnaya Volya in which he had become what would later be called a 'professional revolutionary', tried in the first great trial of its members, that of the 'sixteen', in 1880 and sentenced to hard

[68] Venturi, *Roots of Revolution*, 684.

[69] On the foundation of the two state rabbinical seminaries at Vilna and Zhitomir under Nicholas I in the 1840s, see Chapter 2.

[70] Cited in Yehuda Erez, 'Aharon Zundelevich—yehudi 'amami be-ẓameret ha-narodnikim', in E. Shaltiel (ed.), *Yehudim bi-tenu'ot mahapkhaniyot* (Jerusalem, 1982), 57.

labour for life. Fifteen years later the sentence was reduced to one of twenty years. In 1905 he was allowed to leave Siberia. He then left Russia, first for a brief period, then for good, settling eventually in London. He had written to friends, shortly after his trial: 'If I were free, I would not stay in Russia one day longer'; adding: 'As you know, I have never been fond of Russia and if I remained here it was because I felt an obligation to suffering comrades. Now I too am suffering.'[71]

In essence, Zundelevich was more of a straightforward, western-style revolutionary libertarian than a characteristically Russian, peasant-intoxicated populist. There is some evidence, too, that whatever he may have affirmed on the theoretical level he never quite threw overboard such Jewish concerns as he had acquired with his mother's milk. It has been plausibly argued that the Jewish revolutionary 'David Stern', a character in S. M. Stepnyak-Kravchinsky's once celebrated novel *Andrei Kozhukhov*, is a plain portrait of the man. Kravchinsky knew Zundelevich well and is said to have held him in high regard. There is a passage in the book in which a Russian charges Stern/Zundelevich (and by implication all other Jews in the populist-revolutionary movement) with failing in loyal attachment to Russia. 'We are strongly attached to our people. You are not,' he tells him. Stern/Zundelevich does not answer for a while. 'No, I am not attached to your people,' he says at last. 'Why should I be?'

We Jews love our own race, all that is left to us on this earth. At all events, I love it with all my heart. Why should I love your peasants who murder my people and treat them barbarically? Tomorrow they may rob my father—an honest labourer—just as they have already robbed thousands of other Jews who have worked all their days by the sweat of their brows. I can pity your peasants for their suffering, just as I might pity the Arabs, the Ethiopians or the Malays, or any other suffering beings, but they are not close to my heart. What I cannot do is dream your dreams and bow down before your people. As to what is called high society, the upper classes—what should I feel for them, cowardly rabbits, other than contempt? No, in your Russia there is nothing to revere. But I hold the revolutionaries in esteem and I do love them, even more than my own people. I have kept faith with them and I love them like brothers and it is they who form the sole tie binding me to your country.[72]

Less striking than Zundelevich the brilliant operator, but intellectually and ideologically more acute, was his fellow student and fellow conspirator at the Vilna seminary, Aharon Shemu'el Liberman (1845?–80). Liberman was older than Zundelevich, less daring, more thoughtful, and never able or willing to shake off his Jewish concerns at all. He found it especially difficult to operate in an ideological environment that left little

---

[71] Cited in Erez, 'Aharon Zundelevich', 63.
[72] Cited ibid. 64. Cf. the English language tran. published as *The Career of a Nihilist*, 2nd edn. (London, 1890).

or no room for *non*-Russian national sentiment and attendant loyalties even in the somewhat milk-and-water version of Jewish nationalism which he was inclined to promote. However, when he made his way to London in 1875 after having to flee Russia, he was welcomed into the Lavrov-Smirnov circle there as, at all events, one who had manifestly tried to follow Lavrov's well-known dictum of the need to live one's life 'according to nature and truth'.[73]

London, it may be noted, was on the point of becoming the locus of a specifically and unmistakably *Jewish* urban proletariat not too easily distinguishable from the one Liberman would have known in Vilna. Being overwhelmingly immigrants from the Pale of Settlement they were much the same kind of people. In so far as the pressures of daily life left them time and energy for consideration of social and political doctrine of a general kind they were open to much the same influences as those that had worked upon them in Lithuania, Poland, and the Ukraine. Indeed, for all immediate political purposes they are best seen at this stage as exiles rather than immigrants—one foreign colony among others in a country which had traditionally allowed exiles a very large measure of freedom to pursue their purposes. To be sure, none of the exiles from Russia, least of all the Jews among them, deluded themselves about their role and potential: it was what occurred and what was done within Russia itself that counted, not what they could accomplish from afar. And if that was so where major figures of Herzen's and Lavrov's class were concerned, it was doubly the case for the obscure Liberman in his lonely attempt to find in socialism a little room for the Jews so that the specifics of the Jewish condition were recognized, at least in part, rather than ruled totally out of court a priori. The Jews, he thought, were after all very well fitted to a revolutionary role in the socialist movement. Socialism was in no way naturally alien to them. It was to be found embedded, even if easily overlooked, in the norms of Jewish communal life and to a great extent in traditional Jewish Law. Jewish property and land law, for example, could be said to comprise moderate, but distinctly restrictive, anti-capitalistic elements in such provisions as the law of the Jubilee Year and the law of the Sabbatical Year. And there was much in the prophetic tradition itself and in the hardening of communal discipline and purposes that the effort to withstand repeated acts of persecution over many centuries had induced in the Jews that was directly conducive to their being of a potentially rebellious disposition not only individually, but collectively. The revolutionary camp was the natural place for them. And it would be much to the benefit of the revolutionary camp if it accepted

---

[73] Jonathan Frankel, *Prophecy and Politics: Socialism, Nationalism, and the Russian Jews, 1862–1917* (Cambridge, 1981), 29; Boris Sapir, 'Liberman et le socialisme russe', in *The International Review for Social History*, 3 (1938), 25–88.

them—accepted them as they really were, that is to say, rather than as some thought they should be.

But these were not terms in which anyone hitherto had ever seriously proposed to consider the Jews. For most socialists and revolutionaries in or out of Russia, the idea that the Jews in some sort formed a proletarian nation, let alone a revolutionary one, was preposterous. The common approach, not least among socialists of Jewish origin themselves—revolutionary or moderate-constitutional—was to circumvent the specifics of the Jewish predicament by universalizing them. Thus, famously in the west, as in the notable cases of Marx and Lassalle, as we have seen, and in many others, some of whom will be referred to below. But thus in the east too where socialism necessarily took a much more radical and daring form because there it could only mean working directly against the regime. In the east it was a matter of revolution rather than mere rebellion (in Schumpeter's or, for that matter, Camus's sense of the distinction between the two): in no conceivable situation was there room for so moderate and circumspect a *constitutional* position as that of the Social-Democratic Party in Germany, for example. There was the further difference between east and west, however, that the specifics of Jewry and Judaism itself could not be so easily circumvented in the east as they could be in the west. Precisely for that reason they had to be heavily discounted. 'The Jews of Russia are not a nation,' a Ukrainian revolutionary comrade wrote to Smirnov in London in protest against Liberman,

but an entire class which lives exclusively at the expense of the petty-bourgeois population. The weight of their exploitation is great and their harmfulness unlimited. . . . If we find it possible to preach revolution, and only revolution, against the nobles, how can we defend the Jews? . . . We, cannot have any faith in the laughable 'Yiddish International' nor in the sympathies of the Yids for the revolution.[74]

But the fact was that the Jews of eastern Europe did manifestly constitute a discrete, readily identifiable social group that for all practical and theoretical purposes did constitute a nation. Thus legally under Russian imperial law and official practice. Thus effectively in social and economic and of course political relations. Thus in the minds of all who had dealings with them. And thus, of course, most decisively of all, in their own minds as well. What had become problematic, certainly questionable, in the west was hardly so in the east. It was precisely because the distinct and substantial Jewish proletariat inhabiting the Russian Empire was possessed of visible and palpable national characteristics that its affairs and the climate of opinion within it were of such high relevance. In the west, recruitment of Jews to the socialist parties, certainly to what functioned

---

[74] Cited in Frankel, *Prophecy and Politics*, 34.

there as the revolutionary camp, was invariably on an individual basis. They came, to employ a Shakespearian trope, as 'single spies'. In the east, in contrast, but quite as plainly, there was at any rate immense potential for their joining it in 'battalions'. No informed and unjaundiced view of Jewish society in Russia could fail to recognize that, uniquely, there was the possibility, perhaps the probability, of a large and fully Jewish urban proletarian component taking up an exceedingly important place within the revolutionary armies—in a country, as all knew, in which the general population consisted overwhelmingly of peasants still firmly anchored to the land. Lavrov too had his doubts about the compatibility of Liberman's views with socialist orthodoxy as he understood it. But wiser and more tolerant than others, he allowed Liberman to publish in *Vperëd!*, supported Liberman's attempts to organize Jewish working men in London, and went so far as to speak approvingly of 'our Jewish comrades'.[75]

At the theoretical and ideological level—the level at which policy was chiefly hammered out by nineteenth- and early twentieth-century socialists in all parts of Europe—the difficulty of incorporating the matter of the Jews into any of the acceptable schemata and scenarios remained a source of permanent discomfort. And it was permanent because it was ever harder to deny those socio-economic features of the Jewish population of Russia, Poland, and the Baltic lands that in the specifically social-ist and revolutionary context were evidently salient. The proletarian character of the great majority of the Jewish inhabitants of Vilna, Warsaw, Minsk, Lodz, and the other rapidly industrializing centres in eastern Europe—along, it may be said, with pockets of Jewish inhabitants in some of the great cities of the west, London, Paris, Amsterdam among them—could not seriously be in question regardless of what political activists were minded for one reason or another to ascribe to them. Nor could it be denied that they offered the prospect of immense political, syndicalist, and ultimately revolutionary potential. What was really at issue, therefore, was the question of the *auspices* under which this poten-tial would be brought into play and the precise nature of the cause for which it was reasonable to expect it to be mobilized.

What transpired in practice was a rise in the salience of the Question of the Jews in all sectors and varieties of eastern European, but especially Russian, radicalism, extending all the way from those who still pinned some faith on constitutional reform to those who were determined to pursue outright, revolutionary conspiracy. But it was the tendency, founded on a combination of tactical and ideological considerations (peppered in some, but not all cases with substantial elements of com-mon, Judaeophobic sentiment and prejudice), to refuse particular con-sideration of the Jews as a distinct social category (or even subcategory)

[75] Ibid. 38.

that gained most rapidly in vigour and coherence. A distinction would have to be drawn eventually between the populist and distinctively Russian branch of the overall socialist movement and the non-nationalist, Marxist, social democratic branch. Jews would be found in both camps, although it was in the latter, as might be expected, that they were generally more at ease. At the same time, countervailing, centripetal forces tended to pull some of the actual and potential revolutionaries in Jewry back to what they knew, and most—not all—were prepared to recognize as the genuine peculiarities and special needs of their own people and to insist on what they had no doubt were the most appropriate terms in which agitation for the revolutionary cause should be conducted within the Jewish population if it was to succeed.

The history of the Jewish 'left' in eastern Europe—and to some extent in central and western Europe as well—is to a large extent that of the degree to which men and women would be pulled in one or other of these directions. It would hinge, therefore, in each case on the degree to which activists of undoubted Jewish origin were prepared or intellectually able or, indeed, anxious to subsume the case of the Jews and its attendant anomalies under the general, commonly accepted class categories to which socialists in all parts of the continent now subscribed. Those who agreed to do so needed to hold that the observable particularities of the Jews were historically transitory, so many pieces of ostensibly odd, but none the less genuine epiphenomenal evidence of the truly fundamental socio-economic processes with which alone it was their business as revolutionaries to concern themselves. What was specific to the Jews could then be safely disregarded. Or if not totally disregarded, then condemned for the psychological and political mischief it embodied by endlessly diverting innocent elements in the Jewish public from their true concerns, obligations, and responsibilities. Those who found such theses difficult to swallow either because they cut across the grain of deeply inculcated and equally deeply felt loyalties or because they were far too sharply at variance with the observable realities of the condition of eastern European Jewry had to go elsewhere. The former tendency was one composed of people who were inclined to conceive society first and foremost in the abstract—either for lack of first-hand knowledge of the relevant cases or out of conviction that social thought needed in any case to be pursued a priori and that certain overwhelmingly powerful principles of analysis were conveniently to hand. The latter tendency was inclined to allow its opinions to be governed a good deal more decisively by direct observation and intimate knowledge of the case. More often than not it was therefore those whose roots and formative years had been in the heartland of contemporary Jewry, in the Pale of Settlement itself, who evinced greatest disquiet at the ease with which the matter of the Jews was refused serious attention by the Russian revolutionary movement in its various manifestations as well as by the socialist movement in all its varieties in Europe generally. Yet there was no simple and invariable line of distinction to be drawn here. Individuals passed fairly freely, in some cases back *and* forth and more than once, both between loose schools of thought and, in the course of time, as political trends and the terms in which doctrines came to be articulated and solidified, even between one formally instituted party and another.

IV

The most remarkable of all attempts to resolve the multiple contradictions to which each one of the efforts to cope with the crisis of eastern European Jewry necessarily gave rise was the General Jewish Workers' Party of Lithuania, Poland, and Russia (Algemeyner yidisher arbeter Bund in Lite, Poyln, un Rusland) commonly known as the Bund. It was at once national, secularist, class oriented in the Marxist mode, syndicalist, and, unlike any other specifically Jewish movement, revolutionary-conspiratorial. Fundamentally demotic in ethos, it was at the same time genuinely concerned to encourage art, science, and literature at every level, not excluding the highest. It took form, therefore, not simply as a party in the strict political and organizational sense of the term, but as an entire society, the lines separating political and syndicalist activities from the cultural and social tending to dissolve somewhat on close inspection. In the sense that it was founded on the absolutes of Jewish identity and loyalty it was unlike all other revolutionary parties. But it was as deliberate and explicit in waging uncompromising war against *all* things that it judged demeaning and oppressive of the Jewish people, those which emanated from within as well as those which emanated from without: religious orthodoxy, therefore, and the established Hasidic and anti-Hasidic rabbinate, the Jewish bourgeoisie, but also the modern Hebraists and *maskilim* whom the Bundists insisted on associating with all that was clerical, middle class, and narrowly or 'chauvinistically' national. There was therefore much in its outlook that relied on circular argument: the Bund identified enemies which it then regarded itself as bound to fight. And there was much that assumed a greater coherence of outlook among its various opponents and rivals than could realistically be detected in practice. But then central to the ethos of the Bund was *class*; and its particular trademark was an insistence on the employment of the common language of the Jews of eastern Europe, Yiddish, for every conceivable purpose not excluding the austerely academic. For the Bundists' defining merit was their abiding attention to the here and now of the condition of Jewry as it presented itself in eastern Europe in practice and *in situ*. No other organized group, movement, or party in modern Jewry was so closely and authentically reflective of the impoverished, perpetually set-upon, labouring people who formed what was manifestly the great majority of the Jews of the Pale of Settlement and its outlying areas. Nor was any so uncompromising in its rejection of plans and remedies that turned on distant and future redemption.

Appropriately, the Bund emerged where those features of Jewish life with which it would always be most closely associated were most in evidence, namely in the north-western provinces of the Russian Empire. These (with Poland) were the most heavily populated by Jews at the end of the nineteenth century (14.1 per cent of the total population as opposed to 11.5 per cent for the entire Pale and 4.2 per cent for the empire as a whole).[76] The Jewish population itself was the most highly urbanized in the empire, forming the absolute majority (52.6 per cent) of the region's entire urban population. Jews whom the Russian census-takers had defined as 'workingmen'—chiefly factory workers, as opposed to those engaged in commerce, innkeeping, and the like—formed no less than an estimated two-thirds of the total number in the region: a remarkable figure in itself, besides being above the average for the entire Pale of Settlement (an estimated 30 per cent). Parallel figures for independent or semi-independent Jewish artisans further confirm the picture of a Jewish population that was now well advanced on the road to proletarianization:[77] 12.6 per cent of the Jewish population (where the average for the entire Pale was 10.2); a lead in absolute numbers in every category of industry and craft with the sole exception of textiles (in which the Jews of Poland were slightly more numerous). But since artisan and factory skills were not enough to ensure a decent livelihood, occupation was not the whole of the story.[78] In a confidential report submitted in October 1903,[79] the Russian governor of Vilna informed higher authority of his finding that Jewish foundrymen, turners, and fitters employed in the production of agricultural machinery—all quite highly skilled—as well as weavers, glaziers, and workers in the leather and tobacco trades were unlikely to attain an annual income of more than three or four hundred roubles (£30–40 at the current rate of exchange). In very many cases they had to be satisfied with less than two hundred. Women and girls earned substantially less. A very large segment of the Jewish population was

---

[76] For the chief sources for these figures and those that follow see above, p. 297 n. 19, to which there need to be added figures collected by the Jewish Colonization Committee reproduced in I. M. Rubinow, *Economic Condition of the Jews in Russia* (Washington, 1907), especially 491, 493, 502, 522, 542–4; and those cited in the learned and invaluable article on Vilna in *Evreiskaya Entsiklopediya*, v, cols. 572–97.

[77] Levin, *Jewish Socialist Movements*, 225.

[78] Other than in such exceptional cases as those of very senior typesetters in the printing trade.

[79] Of which the Bund obtained a copy and arranged to have published in Geneva in Mar. 1904.

therefore partly or wholly dependent on charity; and, as the governor observed, the magnitude of the problem of penury among Jews in the city of Vilna—two-fifths of its population[80]—could be measured by the fact that half the Jewish working population was without permanent employment and that in the single year of 1903 the local synagogue authorities distributed funds and unleavened bread for the celebration of the Passover to no fewer than five thousand families (perhaps a third of the entire community). It was this endemic poverty, the governor argued, in combination with the new, disloyal, 'educated proletariat' that had been left high and dry by the narrowing of educational, professional, and economic opportunities for Jews decreed in the 1880s, that had opened the way to the dangerous and exceedingly undesirable politicization of the Jewish population. To this politicization, he noted, the Bund was making a massive contribution.[81]

The industrial proletarianization of Russo-Polish Jewry would have advanced faster and more pervasively were it not, however, for the factors which gave the Jewish population much of its special character and cohesion: the refusal of most Jews to accept employment that required work on the Sabbath and Jewish holy days and the difficulties—regular mistreatment and abuse in many cases—that they were likely to encounter when working with or under non-Jews. Jewish factory workers tended overwhelmingly, therefore, to seek employment in factories owned and managed by other Jews and in which people of their own kind formed at least the greater part of the workforce. There were two consequences. One was that industrial relations—and, of course, industrial unrest—tended most commonly to be a matter of Jewish employees confronting, and being confronted by, industrialists who were themselves Jews. This contributed heavily to the general process whereby Jewry as a whole was losing its once celebrated social and mental cohesion and gave a very particular spin to class consciousness among the Jewish working men. The second consequence was an enhancement of the spontaneous movement of Jewish workers, notably the independent and semi-independent artisans among them, towards a mild, embryonic, but because illegal, somewhat dangerous form of syndicalism. Initially, this took the form of welfare and self-help societies. By the 1890s these had become fairly common in over a score of trades in some of the major cities of the northwest, notably Vilna and Minsk. The numbers were small and the rate of growth modest—1,500 working men all told in Vilna by 1897, 1,000 in Minsk, out of a total strength of what could just begin to be seen as

---

[80] 64,000 out of a total population of 155,000—or 41.3 per cent according to the Russian census of 1897.

[81] Text of the governor's report in Y. Klausner (ed.), 'Tazkir 'al ba'ayat ha-yehudim be-rusiya me'et sar ha-pelekh ha-vilna' i Pahlen', *He-'Avar*, 7 (1950), 95–122.

organized labour of about 3,000 in all parts. But it was a more rapid development with more far-reaching short-term consequences than anything taking place at this stage among the Russians and the Poles.[82] As confidence grew, and experience of elementary forms of collective action was acquired, a more precise and determined form of syndicalism took shape. By the middle of the decade, to the horror of the authorities no less than that of the employers, there were occasions on which Jewish workers struck—and struck successfully—for higher wages. Well over fifty strikes were recorded in Vilna in the years 1895 and 1896 and about the same number in Minsk between 1894 and 1897. These were mostly for straightforward industrial, *not* political purposes: higher wages, healthier conditions, shorter hours (no more than the twelve hours long since laid down as the maximum by Russian law but not observed, rather than the much more usual fourteen or even sixteen).[83] G. V. Plekhanov, the veteran Russian Marxist, no friend at all of the Bund, reported to the 1896 Congress of the Socialist International with 'special satisfaction' on what he counted as the progress of social democratic agitation among the Jews of Russia:

These pariahs . . . who do not even have the paltry rights that the Christian inhabitants possess, have shown so much staunchness in the struggle with their exploiters and such keenness in understanding the socio-political task of the contemporary workers' movement, that in some respects they may be considered the avant-garde of the workers' army of Russia.[84]

By the end of the decade, with the Bund in place, but only just beginning to establish itself, strikes by Jewish workers had become sufficiently numerous for the Bundists to count and analyse them and determine how many had ended in a victory for the workers and how many in defeat or compromise.

But if a firm foundation for a coherent, bold, and self-conscious Jewish proletariat had been laid well before the Bund came into being, it was the proto-Bundists who struck the sharper notes, sounded the broader arguments, and, above all, introduced and propagated the fundamental notion of class struggle. When Jewish workers at a tobacco factory in Vilna went on strike in 1895 the police called in a compliant rabbi to try to ensure a peaceful conclusion to the conflict. To the astonishment of all the rabbi took it upon himself to berate the workers for endangering the Jewish population by encouraging the authorities to view the Jews as a seditious and rebellious people, rather than the peaceful disciplined folk they were in truth. This was bitterly resented, the rabbi was shouted

---

[82] Henry J. Tobias, *The Jewish Bund in Russia: From its Origins to 1905* (Stanford, Calif., 1972), 37–8.
[83] Ibid. 38
[84] Cited ibid. 61.

down in his own synagogue, and the Marxist group that was shortly to set about the formal foundation of the Bund added to the general fury by denouncing him in semi-biblical language for pleading the cause of the employers in the 'temple' itself. The significance of the affair, they stated in a pamphlet they entitled *The Town Preacher (Der shtot mogid)* lay deeper still: 'There is no longer any single Jewish people . . . The great Jewish people are now divided into two classes whose enmity is so great that it does not stop for the holiness of the temple . . . not even for the strength and cruelty of the all-powerful Russian police.'[85]

Vilna, it needs to be recalled, besides providing exceptionally fertile ground for assembling a radical Jewish working-men's party was, famously, the long-established, universally recognized intellectual capital of eastern European Jewish orthodoxy, the so-called 'Jerusalem of Lithuania' and the combination of great socio-economic and inter-ethnic ferment on the one hand and a concentration of bearers of the highest intellectual tradition in orthodox Jewry on the other proved explosive. It was in Vilna, as we have seen, that Zundelevich and Liberman began their careers as socialists and revolutionaries. It was in Vilna that it was most natural—if not inevitable—for the two classes of actual and potential dissidents, newly free-thinking intellectuals and syndicalistically minded working men, to join forces twenty years later in a common resolve, as they hoped, to work out the means whereby they might press together towards their respective social and political goals. But while the groundwork for such an alliance was being laid locally in the course of the early 1890s,[86] it was a relative outsider to the place and to the society in question who, as not for the first time in the annals of modern national movements, would do most to pull the threads of the argument together and formulate the essential case for a formally constituted General Jewish Workers' Party of Lithuania, Poland, and Russia.

Iulii Osipovich Tsederbaum (1873–1923), also known and better known as Martov, sometime ally of Lenin, later his arch opponent within the Russian Social Democratic Workers' Party as leader of the *Mensheviki*, had a distant connection to the modern Jewish cultural revival through his grandfather, Alexander, an eminent Hebraist. He needs to be

---

[85] *Der shtot magid (The Town Preacher)*, cited ibid. 41. The pamphlet has been ascribed by some to Iulii Martov, future leader of the Menshevik faction of the Russian Social Democratic Party. Others, Tobias among them, believe it to have been written by Shemu'el Gozhansky (ibid.). Gozhansky played an important role in the moves taken towards the foundation of the Bund, but joined the Communist Party after the Revolution of 1917. He was arrested and sentenced in the purges of 1936–7 and did not survive.

[86] Related in meticulous detail in M. Mishkinsky, 'Mekoroteiha ha-ra'ayoniim shel tenu'at ha-po'alim ha-yehudit be-rusiya be-reishita', *Zion*, 31, 1–2 (1966), 87–115; and in still greater detail in the same author's *Reishit tenu'at ha-po'alim ha-yehudit be-rusiya: megamot yesod* (Tel-Aviv, 1981). For the standard English-language account, see Frankel, *Prophecy and Politics*, ch. 4.

seen, however, before all else, and for all practical purposes, as a member of that small, substantially Russified and acculturated body of Jews who, by reason of their wholly Russian education and/or their economic standing, were privileged to live in inner Russia and, most significantly, in either of the capital cities of St Petersburg or Moscow. These cultivated men and women, mostly of solid character and reputation, tended to be drawn very powerfully into the more liberal of the literary and political currents of the day. As one generation succeeded another and ties to Jewry and Judaism became ever more tenuous, the only limits on the process were those set by the laws of the empire and the common (but not absolutely universal) refusal to go so far as formal apostasy. It was characteristic of Martov's class and milieu that, while he had neither been baptized nor properly introduced even to the essentials of Judaism and Jewish history, there was never any question in his mind or anyone else's of his national identity as defined by law and as prescribed by the norms of Russian society as a whole. It was equally characteristic that like many others of his class and type he should have been drawn to revolutionary politics quite early in his life, the first of many rounds of activism terminating in 1893 when, at the age of 20, he was arrested, tried, and sentenced to two years' exile in Vilna. Forced residence in the Pale of Settlement for a Jew accustomed to life in inner Russia was a mild punishment, but punishment all the same. There was little the successfully Russified Jew was apt to dislike so much as being dumped in the teeming mass of his less enlightened brethren.

Still, Martov was as fair a representative as any of one of the important strains in what would be the leadership of the Bund: that which consisted of sons and daughters of middle-class, either *haskalah*-minded or substantially Russified people who did not necessarily know Yiddish properly, but who did soon learn that if they were to 'go to the Jewish people' they would have to speak to them in their own language. Some of these were or had been students; many had already been in Russian jails as political offenders, others would suffer imprisonment and exile in due course. Plainly, these young men and women had much in common with the *narodniki* of the previous generation. Where they differed from their predecessors was in their adoption of Marxist socialism as it began, in the 1890s, to be understood and applied in Russia. Principally, this meant acceptance of the thesis that it would be the mobilization of the urban proletariat, not the peasantry, that would serve as the key to revolution and general progress. It meant that terrorism as practised by the Narodnaya Volya was to be eschewed on the grounds that it was founded on a romantic delusion about the role of individuals and the individual act in history. And it meant, not least, that along with class it was cosmopolitanism, not nationalism, that needed to be the operative principle. Some of the burdens that had been laid upon otherwise willing Jewish recruits

to the revolutionary movements were eased thereby. A populism oriented towards the peasantry was not one in which Jewish militants, by
and large, could find a place for themselves without very great difficulty,
the more so as it was one in which the Jewish population as a whole could
not be expected to play a part. In contrast, where all was supposed to
hinge on the urban proletariat, the place of the Jewish population of
Russia was necessarily at or near the centre of the enterprise and those
who spoke to—and for it—were bound to have a substantial role to play
if only they were bold enough to take it up.

Plainly, these were people who were light years away from the older
generation of gentleman-revolutionaries in Russia, so many of whom
had been well educated, well provided for, and, generally speaking, politics aside, entirely natural members of the class that by service to the Tsar,
or at least silent acquiescence in the Tsarist system, had managed to serve
its own interests at least as well as it had served the Autocrat himself. Least
of all had they anything in common with the famously effete of Russia,
the 'superfluous men', the otherwise perfectly decent, well-intentioned
members of the service nobility who, pining for an end to the monstrous
structure of government under which they lived, were rendered miserable by knowledge of their own political impotence and loss of social
direction. But the middle-class founders of the Bund differed from other
social democrats, most notably, although not exclusively, from the Bolsheviks among them of whom, as we shall see, some were gentiles, some
Jews like themselves, in that there was a respect in which theirs was a case
in which experience finally outweighed principle and doctrine. What set
them apart was that they were unable to succumb to a corseting of their
understanding of their environment by theory. They *knew* that the determinants of the condition of the Jews were otherwise than those laid down
by the received ideology to which their social democratic colleagues subscribed. They could detect no grounds for believing that matters would
be otherwise for as long and as far as the prophetic, but more especially
the sober eye could see. It would be too much to say that they were in any
serious sense even distant disciples of Herzen. They were given to thinking in the abstract and to devising theoretical schemata from which rigid
operative rules might be derived much as were other Marxists. But they
were unable to sublimate what they knew in their bones to be the rough
reality of the life and true prospects of the Jews in Russia or anywhere else
in eastern Europe into any kind of finer, doctrinally more palatable metal.

What Martov found in Vilna on his arrival there was a unique opportunity to work out his ideas on the social democrats' besetting problem in
Russia: how a revolutionary socialist movement conceived in Marxist,
which is to say western and distinctly non-Russian, terms was to proceed
in a country that was famously devoid of an urban proletariat of anything
like the quality and numbers needed for performance of the role Marxist

theory allotted it. For there was a labouring class in Vilna that did conform, roughly and imperfectly to be sure, to theoretical requirements
after all. Moreover, as was particularly promising and encouraging, it
conformed quite closely too to what might be termed subjective expectations: symptoms of revolutionary—at any rate syndicalist—ferment
were present and observable; so was a notable desire for political education. So far, then, so good. On the other hand there was no doubting that
one of the defining characteristics of the population in question was that
its members were Jewish and Yiddish-speaking; and that deeply ingrained
cultural and socio-economic features separated its members from those
who might otherwise have been their fellow proletarians. Plainly, therefore, if the Jewish working class of Vilna and the surrounding provinces
was to be drawn into the wider social democratic movement-to-be by
'agitation', and its undoubted potential for revolutionary action
exploited to the full, both those aspects which conformed to theory and
those which did not do so needed to be addressed.[87] In a lecture to an
audience of worker-activists—or 'agitators'—on 1 May 1895, by which
time, two years after his arrival, he was reasonably familiar with local conditions, Martov delivered what would remain the clearest of all statements of the grounds for the foundation of an independent, mass Jewish
working men's organization.

Martov's primary argument was that it was not simply to the workman
who stood above the ruck by reason of his intellectual qualities, but to the
'ordinary Jewish workman of average qualities who laboured under the
usual burdens' that the still embryonic movement needed to address itself;
and that if this was to be done to any good purpose it would have to be
done in the light of that ordinary workman's real needs and in his own
language. This was not only the right and proper course to take, but one
that was exceedingly worth while. The working-class movement had put
the mobilization of the masses at the very centre of its programme. It was
to the masses, therefore, that its propaganda and education needed to be
adapted. Since, syndicalist and proto-revolutionary progress among Jews
was evidently greater than among Russians, special attention should be
paid to them—meaning, in practice, ensuring that propaganda and
education among them had a distinctively Jewish character and was
conducted in the Yiddish language. To that end, 'we must repeatedly and
openly declare our purpose, namely that the purpose of the Jewish social
democrats is to establish a distinctively Jewish workers' organization that
takes it upon itself to lead and educate the Jewish proletariat in its

---

[87] The proto-Bundists' switch from mere discussion and study to mass agitation among
members of the Jewish working class seems to have occurred in the course of 1894. The
argument for doing so was laid out by Aleksandr Kremer (with Martov's stylistic help,
according to Tobias, *Jewish Bund*, 27) in his Russian-language (not Yiddish) essay *Ob agi-
tatsii* (Geneva, 1896).

struggle for economic, civic, and political freedom'. The case of the Jews was decidedly one, moreover, in which the proletariat would lead. Among the Poles matters were more difficult. There there was a revolutionary, *non*-socialist national movement. Where the Jewish proletariat was concerned there was no reason to fear a source of danger and confusion of that nature. The Russo-Jewish bourgeoisie, unlike the Russian-Jewish working class, was not only passive in social terms, but passive in political and national terms as well, content to await the mercy (*hesed*) of the regime. Nor was anything to be feared or expected of the Jewish (bourgeois) intelligentsia. Its 'national passivity and indifference [had only been] a source of weakness to our movement in its initial period'. But now, expecting nothing of the Tsar nor anything as a result of 'independent action by the Jewish people itself', the Jewish proletariat, once organized, was ready to take its rightful place in the international workers' movement along with the Russians and the others in the general advance towards freedom for all. Lastly, briefly, almost in passing, Martov reminded his listeners of another, darker reason for a specifically Jewish workers' organization to be founded.

As in the past, we cannot rely on the Russian proletariat. . . . We must remember that the Russian working class will encounter obstacles as it evolves, each tiny achievement requiring an enormous effort. It follows, of course, that the Russian proletariat, when obliged to withdraw certain demands to make some progress, will assuredly want to withdraw those demands that concern the Jews alone—religious freedom or civil equality, for example.[88]

However, Martov parted company from his colleagues in Vilna after his return to St Petersburg shortly afterwards. They duly set about the establishment of the 'separate Jewish labour organization' which he and they had favoured. Such interest as he had ever had in Jewish separatism as a cause to be pursued for other than purely tactical reasons lapsed. He could see very well that Jews were more likely to form part of the great proletarian army he believed to be massing if they were spoken to in their own language and allowed to form a distinctive division of their own. He recognized that they were entitled to justice and equality no less than others and were more likely to achieve both the one and the other—even at the hands of their fellow proletarians—if they held together at least until the final, all-proletarian victory had been won. But he had no interest

---

[88] Published by the Bund in due course in Yiddish under the title 'Di naye epokhe in der idisher arbayter-bavegung' ('The new epoch in the Jewish workers' movement') (Geneva, n.d., but probably very early in the century) and in Russian under the slightly amended title 'Povorotnyi punkt v istorii evreiskogo rabochego dvizheniya' ('A Turning-point in the History of the Jewish Labour Movement') (St Petersburg, 1906). In neither case is the author referred to, Martov having long since moved on to a position of open hostility to the Bund, to the creation of which his contribution, while it may not have been crucial, was certainly substantial. The citations are based on the Yiddish version.

in, and seems to have attached no intrinsic value to, that very attachment to language and identity—and by extension, to culture in the broadest sense—that made it so necessary to address the Jewish working man in his own terms and language in the first place if he was to be addressed at all. These were people who needed to be humoured, he seems to have thought. No progress would be made or, if at all, then not as rapidly as might otherwise be possible, if they were not so addressed. But on what they actually held to and, indeed, on the independent value of their national existence he had nothing to say that implied value. Those aspects of the ethos of the Bund that were not reducible to strategic or tactical, but in any case opportunistic considerations were foreign to him. It would be on these, however, because they were at the root of the irreducible nature of the Bund's claim to autonomy as the one authentic and effective representative of the Jewish proletariat within the Russian Empire, that the long argument, shortly to begin, about its place and ranking within the Russian social democratic movement would turn. No issue was to trouble the Bundists in the years between the foundation of their movement in October 1897 and the First Russian Revolution of 1905 more than that of their status within the larger Russian social democratic movement of which, at the outset, they formed an integral, if distinct part, but in which a force that was as hostile to them as it was to Martov and what he would come to represent was contending for supremacy.

In practice, the actual, formal founding of the Bund in early October 1897 had most to do with semi-tactical, defensive considerations. Moves towards the establishment of a full-scale, all-inclusive social democratic party in Russia were in progress and near conclusion. Martov's former associates in Vilna welcomed the prospect and participated in it from the first. But, they reasoned, unless they set up their own shop first and staked a firm claim of their own to responsibility for the Jewish sector, Jewish interests and needs would end by being swamped. Their fear that specifically Jewish ground would be pre-empted by others was heavily reinforced by the consistent hostility to the very idea of separate Jewish activity displayed by their neighbours the Polish socialists who were also on the point of forming their own party, the Polska Partja Socjalistyczna, and whose great ill will was reaffirmed at the PPS's foundation Congress in Warsaw in November 1897 by a ferocious denunciation of the Bundists for their alleged 'denial of solidarity with the Polish and Lithuanian proletariat in their struggle for liberation from the Tsarist invader'.[89] The Polish position was that the Jewish proletariat was under a primary obligation to accommodate the majoritarian proletariat in the country it inhabited. The Bundists' position was that both Poles and Jews were subjects of the Tsar and that the Polish position was one that

---

[89] Tobias, *Jewish Bund*, 72.

effectively denied the Jews that same right to national unity that the Poles claimed for themselves. Equally objectionable to the Bund was the unmistakably anti-Semitic touch the Polish socialists gave to their charge: the attention paid to the Bundists abroad was so excessive, they complained, that one was liable to think that all socialists had turned Jewish; the Russian revolutionary movement was of Jewish inspiration; the Bund was in any case the child of the Jewish bourgeoisie; the Jews were partners in the Russian occupation of Poland; the course the Bund had chosen to follow would lead to heightened anti-Semitism all round, and so forth. The upshot, naturally enough, was to confirm the Bundists in their belief that their course was the correct one: however one looked at the Polish position, its necessary implication was that the Jews needed to remember that they were outsiders in Poland, that they had to be put in their place, and that they should not be allowed to forget that their fate was dependent on Polish good will, not proletarian solidarity or anything of that sort.[90] But the Bundists' confidence in the propriety of their position was reinforced above all, and repeatedly, by the circumstance that in its early years it was much the most active and best organized of all the segments of the new Russian Social Democratic Workers' Party, and as daring as any as well.

Like other segments of Marxist social democracy, the Bund was opposed to political terrorism and hostile to the army, the ultimate instrument of government and repression. It seemed to follow, therefore, that it was no less than a positive virtue and a social duty to avoid military service. What possible justification could there be for serving the emperor as a slave and a cog in a vast and oppressive machine that might at any moment be called upon to crush men like oneself? Besides, military service was doubly awful for Jews. In the language of one of the Bund's early manifestos (1901) to recruits, 'The Jewish soldier is treated with far greater brutality than any other. Mockery and degradation are our lot even when we meet our duty to emperor and country.' On the other hand the army was composed overwhelmingly of members of the general population, kin, therefore, to those whom social democrats of all origins regarded themselves as representing. The remedy for the 'military affliction' was as for all other ills: socialism and agitation. Bundists 'who have now been torn out of our ranks and thrown into barracks' should be employed to spread the ideas of social democracy 'which, like sparkling stars, will light the oppressed soldiers' painful path, call them to our red flag . . . [and] bring them over to our side along with all others [who struggle] to put an end to slavery and exploitation'.[91] The Russian armed

---

[90] See esp. ibid. 64–9.

[91] Cited in P. Schwartz, 'Revolutsionere arbet fun "Bund" in der tsarishe armei', *YIVO Bletter*, 42 (1962), 127–8.

forces needed to be attacked. The way to attack them was by the propagation of radical ideas among the troops, teaching them to be critical of the orders and advice given them by their superiors, seeking to induce them to refuse to be employed against striking workers—and to reject attempts by their officers to set Christian against Jew. In sum, it was a positive duty to infiltrate one's own enlightened, class-conscious, politically minded, and indoctrinated men into the army's ranks.

There is indeed some evidence of small-scale agitation among the troops by Jewish revolutionaries as early as the late 1880s. It became more intense at the turn of the century when the Bundists took the assignment in hand. Demonstrations protesting recruitment to the army were organized (in an early case, in Dvinsk in 1901, 300 people took part). Manifestos directed at recruits, at serving soldiers, and even at officers were prepared and distributed in their thousands, in some cases in tens of thousands, in Yiddish, Russian, and when necessary in Lithuanian. There were occasions on which actual strikes—of Jewish military artisans, for example—were successfully organized. The results were not remarkable: so many flea-bites on marginal segments of the vast body of the Russian military machine. But they did not go unnoticed. Agitators, when discovered, were pounced upon and severely punished. And the campaign, such as it was, confirmed a notion, long since lodged in many military minds but still inaccurate for the most part, that Jewish soldiers were inherently disloyal and untrustworthy. In general, the Russian high command was well aware that political agitation among the military was in progress and that the instigators were of many varieties and origins. It concluded, however, as A. N. Kuropatkin, the minister of war, put it in a secret circular issued in 1902, that where Jewish soldiers were concerned there was cause for special vigilance to be exercised. It had been shown, he claimed, that when in touch with the local Jewish population they were particularly likely to be engaged in the dissemination of revolutionary propaganda.[92]

Where the Bundists were not at one with their Marxist brethren was on the matter of the *nation* and on that of the Jewish nation in particular. It was a respect in which they found the position that members of other tendencies in the RSDWP adopted towards them not only unsatisfactory and even offensive, but manifestly superficial, marked by continual refusal to attend to perfectly well-known social facts. The position they encountered was roughly that which Karl Marx himself had outlined half a century earlier, namely that Jewish society was unamenable to change, that it was shot through with essentials or 'essences' formed in antiquity, and that these remained inseparable from capitalism and the pursuit of gain.

---

[92] Circular No. 54, *Poslednie Izvestiia*, 103 (1902–3). Cited by Schwartz, 'Revolutionere', 140.

These were notions that were endlessly repeated along with the still more encompassing idea that it was proper and necessary for alien minorities in the empire to merge with, and assimilate into, the majority population. In that way alone would unnecessary—therefore doubly regrettable—conflicts between nations be avoided. The proper, primary concern of all Marxists was social revolution. Nationalism, where it obtained, was an irrelevance at best, at worst a positive obstacle to progress—one that was promoted and sustained, moreover, by the bourgeoisie in its own characteristically selfish interest. Stated in so strong and uncompromising form, the implication, where accepted, was devastating for the Bund, cutting the ground entirely from under its ethos as a distinct and largely self-contained organization. But what of the principle of the matter and distant eventualities? What of the likelihood and desirability of the eventual withering away of the nations altogether, the Jewish nation among the rest? And what, so far as the Jews were concerned most specifically, of assimilation? The most influential proponent of a rigorously articulated position for the Bund on this, the most delicate of all subjects for a Jewish movement of any kind that was less than explicitly traditionalist, was Vladimir Medem (1879–1923).

In his origins, Medem was in some ways even more remote from things Jewish than Martov. He had been baptized in infancy into the Russian Orthodox Church, both his parents having converted to Lutheranism early in their adult lives on much the same cynical-opportunistic-desperate grounds that Heine had made famous. The family was totally acculturated: firmly Russian-speaking, all things Jewish, the Yiddish language among them, firmly absent. They knew themselves to be Jews, however, not least Vladimir Medem himself who seems, for example, to have associated mostly with other Jewish boys when at school. And the fact that he had passed most of his boyhood in Minsk, a largely Jewish city, and therefore legally and socially quite unlike the cities of inner Russia, must have counted for something too. As a student at the University of Kiev he turned to politics in what was probably a fairly minor way. But he was caught, expelled, and returned to Minsk under police surveillance (pod nadzor). From that point on his shift to systematic political action occurred at an accelerated rate. Medem's approach to political dissidence and revolution was in some ways original. His was a romantic view of the worker and the suffering, fighting working class. It was a 'Prometheus in chains' and asleep, but soon to be fully awake, that partook at least as much of the older Russian peasant-oriented populism (narodnichestvo)—of which it was in some sort an urban version—as of the sterner, classic Marxist view of the proletariat's role. There was certainly none of the thinly disguised contempt for the worker in Medem's outlook that was common among stricter Marxists, and in Russia among the Leninists especially: a view of the proletarian (to say nothing of the peasant) as a being that was far too passive, ignorant, and deferent to his social superiors ever to take the lead himself and therefore crucially in need of being led and organized from above. What Medem could see all around him in Minsk was what Martov had seen in Vilna. What he concluded was that Jewish workers fitted his semi-populist bill far better than any of the other urban ethnic groups—to which recognition there needs certainly to be added Medem's growing nostalgia for other things Jewish, even to things Jewish *per se*. At Kiev he had envied the Jewish students their organized society and collective dining arrangements. To a direct question put to him on one occasion, his response was that 'I felt a longing to return home.' In his autobiography he recalled that

Were I to be asked—indeed I have been asked—how I became a Jew once again, I would be compelled, unfortunately, to reply: 'I simply do not know.' For it was no sudden transition, no leap, no conscious decision. It came of itself, gradually by degrees so that I myself scarcely noticed it. I can only identify the two terminal points: my childhood years, when I considered myself a Russian; and the later period, the time of adulthood, when I considered myself a Jew.[93]

Medem had no doubt at all that it was the matter of assimilation that separated the Bund from its sister parties in the Social Democratic movement. His own, firm position was that it had to do with culture essentially, not politics, and that it was legitimate and needed to be free and unobstructed. Jews were entitled to absorb, and adapt to, other cultures if they so wished. They were entitled no less, however, both collectively and as individuals, to promote and develop a culture of their own. How the various processes of acculturation on the one hand and of change and development in existing, ancient national cultures at the hands of their respective modern heirs on the other would evolve ultimately was not, he thought, a matter on which it was wise or possible or useful to pronounce. The proper position for the Bund itself was therefore *neutrality*. 'Free from external pressure, the folk organism itself, in the course of its development, determines its own fate.'[94] In contrast, on the political aspects of the national question, the Bund had to take a clear stand of its own; and only two answers seemed to him and to his colleagues to be acceptable. One was an entitlement to political independence and to civil and political rights for all nations as such and without exception in line with what would later come to be called the principle of national self-determination. The other was an entitlement to national rights, on a basis of equality to be sure, but within a single, multinational state. What the precise content of those rights would be in the latter case

[93] S. A. Portnoy (trans. and ed.), *Vladimir Medem: The Life and Soul of a Legendary Jewish Socialist* [English trans of V. D. Medem, *Fun mayn leben*] (New York, 1979), 129.

[94] 'Sotsialdemokratiya . . .', *Vestnik Bunda*, 4 (July 1904), 8, cited in Tobias, *Jewish Bund*, 275 n. 92.

had still to be worked out. They need not be and could not be, so the Bundists thought, *full* political rights. But they had certainly to provide for cultural autonomy at the very least. They could and should cater, for example, for state schooling of a kind that would permit and encourage, rather than obstruct, the free development and articulation of the distinct culture and cultural life to which all nations were entitled—that of the Jews among them.

Alas for the Bundists, and to their dismay, all this was dismissed out of hand by their colleagues in the newly established Russian Social Democratic Workers' Party, notably by the Iskraite faction led by Lenin, but including Martov and his friends too at this stage. They argued that the Bund's position signified nothing less than political and social fragmentation, recognition and legitimation of national separatism, and—in the sad event of the Social Democrats going so far as to subscribe to such absurdities—a federal structure for their party. That Martov, while opposing Lenin on the broader matter of the internal structure of the movement, should have become an especially fierce opponent of the Bund's claim to autonomy, was especially distressing to the Bundists, but should not really have surprised them. At its foundation congress in 1898 the RSDWP had indeed accepted the Bund as a constituent, but autonomous organization. It had been agreed by all concerned that it would retain the right to handle its affairs within the Jewish sector in the light of its own understanding of the needs of that particular and manifestly idiosyncratic constituency. Whatever their reservations, none of the leaders of the RSDWP doubted that the Bund's contribution in numbers and organization would be a very considerable one, at any rate in the short term. Initially, in fact, it was the largest single component of the full RSDWP. Even several years into the new century, by which time much had been done by the all-Russian party to extend its membership both in numbers and throughout the imperial territory, the Bund remained a valued partner. None of this was contested. But there were distinct counts on which the incorporation of the Bund into the RSDWP, while it might be thought both just and opportune in short-term Russian terms, might in the broader perspective of the social democratic movement be fairly judged anomalous.

European social democracy had long been predicated on non-recognition, if not outright dismissal, of the intrinsic validity and reality of national-cultural, as opposed to class differences. If, with various tactical, organizational, and distinctly temporary considerations in mind, the various great national segments of the existing world proletariat did have to be confronted and accommodated, the notion that such considerations were applicable to a specifically *Jewish* proletariat was an exceedingly— for some social democrats an impossibly—difficult one to swallow. There was, once again, the conviction, deeply rooted in virtually all segments and varieties of the European left, that the Jews were a fundamentally bourgeois people—if they were not, indeed, the very embodiment of bourgeois values. They were therefore by their very nature enemies of the proletariat and enemies of the revolution, as well as being deeply and inherently pernicious on many other social counts as well. That had been the teaching of Fourier, Proudhon, and Bakunin, as we have seen,[95] no less than of Marx. Then there was the objection, one to which socialists of Jewish origin themselves were especially (and not unnaturally) sensitive, that any recognition of Jewish nationality, for whatever reason and however limited, would be destructive of the one great promise that socialism purported to hold out to (deserving) Jews, namely the final reduction to a nullity of the anachronistic religio-ethnic category to which they belonged. Lastly, there was the straightforward, tactical consideration, that to support or defend or in any way at all to appear to favour a Jewish cause was to embark on a course that could not be other than deeply and damagingly unpopular.

All this had been played out with unusual clarity, some drama, and in prototypical form for all to note several years earlier at the Second Congress of the Socialist International in Brussels in 1891. No specifically Jewish socialist party having yet been formed, the especially contentious question of formal Jewish *national* representation in the International had still to arise. It was only the ostensibly more limited, to some minds non-contentious matter of the persecution and mistreatment of Jewish working men, most specifically those among them who had ventured to form trade unions of their own, that was raised, as it happened by the representative of newly formed Jewish trade unions in the United States. Abraham Cahan (1860–1951) was yet another radical native of Vilna who, on fleeing arrest by the Russian police for revolutionary activity in Vitebsk in 1882, had left Europe for New York. It was there, rather than in Russia, that his career and eminence as a socialist and trade unionist, but also as a journalist and novelist and eventually as one of the best-known Jewish newspaper editors of his time, began in earnest. But he is best seen in the present context as a very remarkable member of what was becoming the great extension across Europe, and across the Atlantic, as well, of Yiddish-speaking, Russo-Polish, and Romanian Jewry: for the time being something of a Diaspora of the Diaspora, still very much a product of its original environment despite residence and employment in London, Paris, and, especially, New York, Chicago, Philadelphia, and several other great North American cities. Events in Russia and developments in Europe were therefore very naturally on his mind—hardly less so than concerns that were narrowly specific to trade union activity in New York City itself. They were equally on the minds of those to whom he now

[95] See Chapter 3.

addressed himself, although that failed to gain him a sympathetic hearing. What Cahan asked for was not action, only a formal, verbal condemnation of the persecution of Jews and a declaration of sympathy and support for the victims—and for the hard-pressed Jewish working class generally. What he discovered was that the overwhelming majority of those attending the Socialist Congress were unwilling to take up any position that might be read as support for Jews—not, at any rate, unless it was couched in the most ambiguous and, as events would prove, most obfuscatory terms ingenuity could devise. For Cahan, in his innocence, had put the 'Jewish Question' before the Congress. That was the language in which his motion was recorded in the official summing-up of the Congress's proceedings.[96] That was how the delegates, the press, and, most especially, two of the most prominent of the delegates attending, Victor Adler of Austria and Paul Singer of Germany, understood it. Adler and Singer were Jews themselves (with the caveat, in Adler's case, that he was at one and the same time a convert to Roman Catholicism, a man who had never ceased to regard himself as a Jew, and one who throughout his life was so regarded by others). They were horrified by Cahan's 'tactlessness'—which would do no more, they told him, than provide grounds for anti-Semitic defamation of the socialists as champions of the Jews. And they proceeded to bring all the pressure they could muster on him to persuade him to withdraw his motion. When Cahan stood his ground, Adler and Singer did what they could—which was commonly believed to have been a very great deal—to sabotage his effort before it had properly begun, in which pitiful enterprise their success was virtually complete.

Cahan was not denied the floor. And when it was granted to him, he made it clear that he had not come to relate the 'grievances of the Jewish race'. What he did want, he said, was equality for the Jews, in all respects, but in the manner too in which the socialist movement itself approached them. Others could rightly be charged with responsibility for the continual warfare between Jews and Christians. It was for the socialists, none the less, to take a position.

In America there are trade unions that refuse to admit Negroes to membership. If there were trade unions in Russia they would refuse to admit Jews. All Russian newspapers attack the Jews and say that the socialist workers [too] detest the Jews. What you are asked to declare is that that is not true, that you are the enemies of all exploiters whether they be Jews or Christians, and that you have as much sympathy for Jewish workers as you do for Christian workers.[97]

[96] Namely, as 'De l'attitude que les travailleurs organisés de tous les pays doivent prendre concernant la question juive', *Congrès international ouvrier socialiste tenu à Bruxelles du 16 au 23 août 1891*, *Rapport* (Brussels, 1893), 41–4.
[97] Ibid. 42.

Cahan was politely applauded, but it was the Belgian socialist Jean Volders who, by arrangement, rose to reply who was cheered. Volders dismissed the idea of issuing a statement of sympathy for Jews as 'unnecessary' and 'superfluous'. Socialists knew that they were nothing if not supporters of the oppressed of all origins. They were supporters of the Jews as well, he seems to have wanted to imply, being careful at the same time not actually to say so. But the anti-Semitic campaign was, after all, 'the invention of high capitalism and derives from the hatred the Christian capitalist bears for the Jewish capitalist who is more cunning than he'. There was therefore nothing in this matter that the socialists needed especially to concern themselves about. Cahan's motion was denied. But as the subject could not be entirely swept away, an alternative resolution was put to the Congress and approved. It recalled that socialists had always affirmed that there could be no genuine, non-artificial 'antagonisms' between races and nations, only between classes. The only authentic struggle was between proletarians and capitalists and that pertained to all races. But it was the key clause of the resolution that was uniquely disingenuous:

The Congress . . . while it condemns anti-Semitic and philo-Semitic provocations as manœuvres by which the capitalist class and governmental reaction seek to divert the socialist movement and divide the workers;

Resolves, that there is no cause to deal with the subject put forward by the delegation of American socialist groups of Jewish language and proceeds to the business of the day.[98]

In eastern Europe itself there was no escaping the issue by such sophistry. For one thing, the facts were far too plain to be denied. For another, there would shortly be within the socialist movement itself a party dedicated, amongst things, to a refusal to its being dismissed. What was possible in Brussels, at any rate for the time being—and, of course, in Vienna and Berlin—was untenable in Vilna, Minsk, and Warsaw. But just how 'the National Question' was to be defined remained exceedingly difficult for the Bundists to decide. Several years would pass before it was taken up in earnest, debated at length at the local level for very many months, and finally discussed as the principal item of business at the party congress (the fourth in 1901). The result was uncompromising and, all things considered, the stand taken pugnacious. It was resolved that it was not only the oppression of one class by another and of citizens by their government that were 'incompatible' (nedopustimo) with the spirit of social democracy, but that of one nation by another and the 'ascendancy' (gospodstvo) of one language over another. Russia, it was stated, being a country that comprised a great many nationalities, should therefore become a federation in which each nationality enjoyed autonomy

---

[98] Rapport, 43–4; E. Silberner, 'Austrian Social Democracy and the Jewish Problem', Historia Judaica, 13 (1951), 125–9.

'regardless of the territory it [actually] inhabits [*nezavisimo ot obitaemoi eyu territorii*]'. And lest there be any doubt or confusion about its intention the congress went on to declare firmly that the concept of nationality did emphatically apply to the Jewish people. The sole concession to opposing voices heard outside—and, perhaps, to arguments for caution heard within—was a clause laying down the view that for the time being no explicit demand for national autonomy for the Jews would be made on the ground that all energy should be devoted to the common fight against immediate oppression.[99]

However, the countervailing voices heard outside the Bund were growing louder all the while. In April 1903, with the Second Congress of the RSDWP to be convened in Brussels at the end of July in view, Martov set out his own draft constitution for the party. Famously, it differed very sharply from Lenin's proposals. Where Lenin insisted on the membership consisting effectively of 'professional revolutionaries' and the party being ruled for all practical purposes by its Central Committee, Martov wanted a broader membership, a looser organization, and much left to local initiative and authority. Martov's draft, it has been argued,[100] would have allowed national-regional unions—the Polish social democrats (the PPS) and the Bund, among them—a semi-autonomous status. It would have granted them a large measure of freedom to work among their own nationals too. But it held to the proviso, none the less, that general policy was to remain firmly in the hands of the party's central committee in the interests of ensuring that the autonomy of such national unions was limited both functionally and as a matter of constitutional principle. Martov and the other dozen or so non-Bundist Jewish social democrats at the Congress who opposed real autonomy for the Bund did not deny, and were, for the most part, happy to concede, that the oppressed Jews of Russia had created a distinctly admirable movement in their own small corner of the Empire. But its locus, they argued, was too remote from the real centre of Russia and from those strategic points within the empire that were most likely to be of direct relevance when the time came for the central effort facing the movement to be made, the attempt to overthrow the regime. Ultimately, therefore, it would be a false expenditure of time and energy to recruit Jews in the Pale of Settlement into a special organization of their own. The correct approach and the proper obligation was for all available forces to unite. The Autocracy would be overthrown only by an integrated proletariat. It was true that as things stood the Russian social democratic party was hardly strong

[99] 'Chetvertyi s'ezd vseobshchago evreiskago rabochago soyuza v litve, polshe i rossii ("Bunda")', *Materialy k istorii evreiskago rabochago dvizheniya* (St Petersburg, 1906), 119–20. The fifth congress of the Bund, meeting two years later in Geneva, i.e. just before the second congress of the RSDWP, confirmed the position taken at the earlier congress.

[100] I. Getzler, *Martov* (Cambridge and Melbourne, 1967), 70.

enough to do all that was necessary. It needed such reinforcement as the Jews could bring to it both within the Pale and outside it. But that was insufficient reason for narrow, 'tribal' Jewish interests to be allowed to get in the way of the general effort and the central purposes of the party to which they should, on the contrary, be firmly subordinated. To admit the validity of the Bund's project for an independent *national* workers' party by which Jewish proletarians would be separated off from Poles and Russians was to 'create an artificial antagonism between those who ought to be united in the common struggle for common tasks'.[101]

It was Martov, again, not Lenin (but serving Lenin's purpose no less than his own), who then led the attack at the Second Congress that was to drive the Bund out of the party which he had helped to form no more than five years earlier. The autonomy that had been granted the Bund at the First Congress in 1898 did not imply 'exclusivity' (*isklyuchenie*), Martov argued. Other 'committees' had been granted as much. In any event,

At the basis of the project lies the proposition that the Jewish proletariat is in need of an independent political organization to represent its national interests in the ranks of Russian Social Democracy. Irrespective of the question of party organization being on federative or autonomous principles, we cannot allow this or that segment of the party to represent the group or professional or national interests of a particular stratum of the proletariat.[102]

The only possible justification for an extension of the Bund's autonomy was 'revolutionary convenience'.[103] Martov was prepared, in the language of the resolution he offered to the Congress for approval, to countenance 'independence for a Jewish workers' movement in matters relating to the particularities of agitation in the Jewish population consequent upon peculiarities of language and mode of life'.[104] But no more. The Bund's pretension to go beyond these limits were unacceptable and misguided. The Congress should therefore determine the issue on the basis that

the closest unity between the Jewish proletariat and the proletariat of those races amongst which it dwells was absolutely necessary in the interests of its own struggle for political and economic emancipation; [and that] only such close unity would guarantee success for social democracy in the struggle with all varieties of chauvinism and anti-Semitism.[105]

---

[101] Iu. Martov, 'Edinaya russkaya sotsialdemokratiya i interesy evreiskogo proletariata', *Iskra*, 36 (15 Mar. 1903). Cited in Getzler, *Martov*, 57–8.
[102] Rossiiskaya Sotsial-demokraticheskaya Rabochaya Partiya, *Vtoroi s'ezd, iul'-avgust 1903 goda: Protokoly* (Moscow, 1959), 55.
[103] Ibid. 57.
[104] Ibid. 57 n.
[105] Ibid.

But to the ears of the Bundists themselves this high sentiment was almost as falsely reflective of the real state of relations between 'the races', and therefore of the true needs of the Jewish working class, as the resolution passed in Brussels a decade earlier—to which, indeed, Martov had gone so far as to refer approvingly in his remarks.[106] It was, indeed, as disingenuous and as patronizing in tone into the bargain as well. The yoking together of 'chauvinism'—plainly, a half-hearted reference to *Jewish* nationalism—and anti-Semitism may have been no more than thoughtless. Even so, it could hardly have encouraged the Bundists to relax their position, 'to come to their senses', as some think Martov had greatly hoped they would, and to refrain from pressing their case to the bitter end.[107] But the five Bundist delegates present at the Congress (Vladimir Kossovsky, Arkady Kremer, Mark Liber, Vladimir Medem, and Noah Portnoy) stuck to their guns.

The immediate beneficiary was Lenin. On the matter of the general structure of the RSDWP the Bundists had been Martov's natural allies. They too favoured a relatively loose, open, and democratic structure. The Bund itself was—and long remained—a party of precisely this kind. With the Bund Martov commanded a majority for his cause. Without them, it was the Leninists, dedicated to a strictly hierarchical, highly centralized and professionalized party who became the majoritarians (*Bolsheviki*), so determining both issue and relevant party nomenclature for several generations to come. How far Lenin may have anticipated this result it is impossible to say. That he assessed the strength of Bundists' feeling and conviction and understood the logic of their position better than others—better, notably, than the many non-Bundist Jews who attended as delegates—is likely. What is plain is that he recognized that the principles of internal organization on which the Bund was insisting were incompatible with those which he, for his part, was determined to establish. There was no longer any room, now that he was in his stride, for what he and others had originally been prepared to concede to the Bund upon the formation of the RSDWP, namely 'complete autonomy in matters concerning the Jewish proletariat'. Lenin does not seem to have wished to force the Bund out, still less to humiliate it, to give it, as he put it, a 'kick in the teeth'. But he did foresee that they might very well have no alternative but to leave the party and he appears to have decided in advance that he would have no regrets on that score if they did. In practice, he left the confrontation in Brussels to the Jews among his supporters—almost all of whom were as adamant as he in rejecting the Bundist position either on what purported to be high party principle and strategy, or out of private concern to maintain the logic on which their own position in an *all*-Russian party was founded, or both.

[106] Ibid.   [107] Getzler, *Martov*, 60–1.

The argument for the existence of the Bund had been predicated from the start on the thesis that the special condition, interests, and vulnerabilities of Jewish working men required a dedicated, autonomous organization of their own. Lenin's Iskraites, like other social democrats in and out of Russia, met this by refusing to budge from the established socialist thesis, namely that anti-Semitism was an exclusively bourgeois phenomenon and that the charge of working-class hostility and brutality to Jews of the same class was either a monstrous imputation on proletarian honour or an unwarranted conclusion from scattered and trivial incidents. It was to the union of all proletarians that all good socialists should aim. It was also what all should be required to submit to. The Bundists were, of course, fully in favour of unity on the general socialist-proletarian front. They were not so foolish as to doubt their incapacity to fight the government and the 'bourgeois system' as a whole single-handed, let alone bring either one or the other down on their own. But nor could they free themselves of the fear that the Jewish proletariat would end by being crushed by the steamroller of proletarian revolution once it had begun to move in earnest. At the heart of their quarrel with Lenin and the tension between the Bund and the greater part of the socialist movement there was, that is to say, a condition of ineradicable foreboding and largely unspoken distrust. Trotsky, who served as Lenin's and Martov's principal ally in the concerted effort to diminish the status of the Bund within the party, perceived this. Like others, he argued that to grant the Bund its claim to autonomy would be to open the way to other demands and, finally, to the reconstruction of the party on a federative rather than integrative basis. But he objected quite as profoundly, he said, to the Bund's fundamental claim that it alone was entitled to teach socialism to Jewish workers. The rules for party organization that the Bund proposed amounted, he said, to nothing less than 'formulated distrust [*formulirovannoe nedoverie*]'. The demand for a monopoly over activities within the Jewish sector was no less than an expression of disbelief in the integrity of the non-Jewish members of the party. The Bund, Trotsky said, was free not to trust the party, but it could not expect the party to accept that and to limit its own freedom of action now and in the future accordingly. To do so would be to perform an act of 'moral and political suicide'.[108] These were very shrewd thrusts; and the Bundists could do no less than reply with an affirmation of the warmth of their feelings for their colleagues. Otherwise, however, this deeply rooted, always imperfectly articulated issue was left in the air, none of those present, so it seems, being disposed to thrash it out in earnest. Conceivably, it was in the nature of such things that it could not be.

---

[108] *Vtoroi s'ezd*, 71.

As a formal issue, the Bund's status continued to exercise the Congress either in the plenum or in committee until its twenty-seventh session on 18 August (by which time, at the urging of the Belgian police, it had moved from Brussels to London). But there was no possibility of agreement without a fundamental concession being made by one or other side to the dispute, a dispute so fundamental that in retrospect, at any rate, it can be seen that there was never any likelihood of an appropriate concession being made. Even the *scope* of the Bund's activity proved unamenable to agreed definition. There was some further debate, then a final protest by the Bund's principal spokesman at the Congress, Mark Liber, then a vote: 41 to 5 (the 5 Bundists) with 5 abstentions.[109] Lenin, with Martov's and Trotsky's important help, had had his way—to Martov's subsequent great cost. The Bundists withdrew from the Congress and from the party itself, determined, for the time being, to march to a drum of their own.

V

In the great swirl of radical thinking on social questions that was now one, but only one, of the hallmarks of European Jewry no single movement of ideas would be quite as far-reaching and strike quite so penetrating a note as that which would soon be known as Zionism. Put simply, it amounted to the reconstruction of Pinsker's and Lilienblum's loosely conceived and still more loosely led Ḥibbat Ẓion as a movement that was recognizably the child of its parent, but was forever tending towards a very different and scandalously unprecedented form. It would be tighter and more coherent in structure than Ḥibbat Ẓion had ever been. It would be surer of its ground and its methods and clearer as to how they should be articulated. It sought from the first to place itself at the head of the Jewish people by defining what it believed to be their ultimate collective interest and offering itself as the one sure instrument whereby that interest was most likely to be achieved. In practice, therefore, what had not been much more than a church would be transformed into a political movement that, for its time, was of great originality, an early version of what many decades later would become familiar to all as a movement for national liberation. It needs to be said, however, that the originality that was intrinsic to the phenomenon of Zionism owed a very great deal—some would say, everything—to its being to an extraordinary extent the invention of a single individual whom colleagues, followers, rivals, journalists, biographers, and

---

[109] A grand total of 43 delegates holding 51 mandates and 12 non-voting observers attended the Second Congress. The full Bund delegation was of 5 voting members and 1 observer.

historians, all without number, have been at pains to exalt, denigrate, explain, explain away, but at any rate to account for ever since.

There was a great deal in Theodor Herzl (1860–1904) that was typical to the point of banality of the large and steadily increasing class of well-educated writers, artists (musicians especially), academics, lawyers, doctors, journalists, and other such members of the high central European Jewish intelligentsia to which he belonged if not precisely by birth, then certainly by upbringing. Born in Budapest of wealthy parents, of a father who was barely one generation away from Jewish orthodoxy, but of a mother who was rather more remote from it, he himself became primarily attached to the German language and to German culture. He trained as a lawyer in Vienna and took up permanent residence there as a matter of course, but not to practise law, rather to pursue the goal that was initially closest to his heart: a place of consequence in the world of (German) letters. He gained a name for himself as a playwright of recognized if (as we may now judge) no more than moderate talent, as an excellent journalist, and, especially, as a clever, often brilliant essayist to whom the light and somewhat sardonic manner popular in Vienna in his day came naturally. However, neither in his successful achievement of a name for himself in his chosen field nor in the parallel, seemingly contrary circumstance that he was haunted all along by the inconsistencies, circumlocutions, confusions, and humiliations with which the lives of the Jews—*all* Jews, as he initially thought—seemed fatally and intolerably shot through was there anything strikingly unusual for his time and place and social class. What was unusual in this otherwise excellent and elegant man of popular Viennese letters was the explosion of an unquenchable urge to act on and for the Jewish people. At some point in 1895, in his thirty-fifth year, he decided that he would attempt to alter its destiny.

Just how and why this self-induced conversion to the Jewish national interest occurred has never been adequately explained. It has often been said—with great conviction, but scant evidence—that it was precipitated, if not caused, by his having witnessed Captain Dreyfus's public military degradation to the accompaniment of a Parisian crowd baying for the death of all Jews in 1895. Were this the case, it would, of course, have been well before the full Affair as such erupted, which is to say well before the possibility of Dreyfus having been framed by his officer-colleagues had so much as occurred to anyone of real consequence. In fact, there has never been any hard evidence to justify the fancy, nor has repetition rendered it intrinsically plausible, except as an instance of *se non é vero é ben trovato*. Of what there can be no question, however, is that Herzl's time in Paris between 1891 and 1895 as resident correspondent for the leading Viennese newspaper, the *Neue Freie Presse*, afforded him an opportunity to observe (and report) on modern European anti-Semitism at a moment and in a country in which it had taken on a notoriously vicious form and to do so with the optical advantages of an outsider.[110] That his four years in Paris added mightily to his sense that the Jewish condition was fundamentally and finally intolerable is beyond question.[111] That his time there served to tip the long-standing, intrinsically, and permanently unstable balance between his craving for glory in letters and his hitherto repressed, but powerful drive to act publicly and politically is equally certain. In the end, however, his own simple statement before the Royal Commission on Alien Immigration in London in 1902, says almost all that really matters.

Seven years ago, when I was living in Paris, I was so impressed with the state of Jewry throughout Europe that I turned my attention to the Jewish question and published a pamphlet which I called 'A Jewish State'. I may say that it was not my original intention to publish the pamphlet or to take part in a political movement. But, after placing before a number of influential Jews my views upon the Jewish question, and finding that they were utterly oblivious of the danger which I then foresaw—that they could not see the large black cloud gathering in the East—I published the pamphlet which resulted in the establishment of the Zionist movement.[112]

This astringent account of a journey into the internal and external politics of Jewry corresponded, it may be supposed, to what Herzl judged appropriate to the occasion of testimony before the Commission. It stands in striking contrast, however, to what we know of his fundamentally romantic outlook on life in general and on what his own role in society might be. Still, as an account of his genesis as a national leader it needs to be only moderately broken down and expanded upon, not least because it reflects best of all his almost overpowering tendency to simplification: simplification of problems and issues, simplification of solutions. For what Herzl had set himself to do in 1895, grand *simplificateur* that he most certainly was—in his great innocence and ignorance, as some would say, in his arrogant presumption, as other would have it—was to devise a plan for the solution, once and for all, of the Problem of the Jews.

---

[110] What Herzl's editors at the *Neue Freie Presse* (Eduard Bacher and Moritz Benedikt, both Jews themselves) would *not* allow in their newspaper was any reference to his own political activities or, indeed, to Zionism generally. They were happy to keep Herzl himself on their staff. They permitted him to go off on his political travels from time to time. But, being, as a great Vienna correspondent of *The Times* was later to note, 'fanatically devoted to the propagation of Jewish-German "Liberal" assimilationist doctrine' (Henry Wickham Steed, *The Hapsburg Monarchy* (London, 1914), 188), they remained unalterably opposed to everything he was about, his light literary contributions to their paper excepted.

[111] It is worth noting that while Herzl was tireless in his attempts to tap every possible political opening in every one of the major states of Europe, he rarely returned to France and seems not to have tempted to take advantage of any of the contacts he had developed in Paris in the course of his years there as a senior journalist.

[112] Royal Commission on Alien Immigration, *Minutes of Evidence*, 7 July 1902, 211.

And if the peculiarity of what follows is to be fully appreciated, it must be remembered that Herzl had made no attempt to study the afflictions of his subject before collecting his thoughts on how these ills might finally and forever be cured; that he had never been to eastern Europe and was not to attempt a visit to the heartland of Jewry to see his flock *in situ* until the very tail-end of his short career eight years later; that he knew nothing as yet of Pinsker and had certainly never read *Autoemancipation!*;[113] that he was only very distantly aware of the existence and accomplishments, such as they were, of Ḥibbat Ẓion; and that all in all his thinking on the matter of the Jews was shot through with, and very seriously vitiated by, the most common and stereotypical, not to say vulgar, notions about the people to whose rescue he was to devote himself. To the end of his short life, Herzl was never to be more than superficially, and then often inaccurately, instructed on the life, mores, strengths, and weaknesses of his people. Therein lay one of his own great weaknesses; but also a great—if not greater—strength.

For Herzl needs to be placed in that minute class of men who, in Winston Churchill's memorable phrase, have at some period in their lives made the weather. He was a member too of that other (not infrequently overlapping) class of popular leaders who stem from the margins of the nation they presume to lead, or from outside it altogether, but in any event are atypical in important and entirely obvious respects of the ordinary run of the people at whose head they have placed themselves. They turn out to be of all kinds and qualities: decent, evil, reasonable, fanatical, even saintly in very rare cases. Some leave the people in question a horrendous legacy, others one that, on the whole, turns out to be worth while: Hitler the Austrian, Lenin the quarter-Russian (or less), Stalin the Georgian, and Hafez al-Assad the Alaouite will be found in one subclass; Napoleon the Corsican will be found in another; in yet another, one that bears an especially instructive resemblance to the Jewish case, will be some of the most notable proponents of Irish nationalism: Wolfe Tone, leader of the United Irishmen at the tail-end of the eighteenth century, Charles Parnell, the most prominent leader of the Irish nationalists a century later (both born into the Protestant Ascendancy), and Eamon de Valera, the sternest and most unrelenting of Irish national leaders in the twentieth century (foreign born and of mixed parentage). Other examples are not difficult to find. And so, perhaps, *mutatis mutandis*, Herzl's remoteness in background, experience, but above all *mind* from the eastern European Jews for whom Ḥibbat Ẓion had sought to speak and to act,

---

[113] Or, for that matter, a still earlier analysis of the condition of modern Jewry by Moses Hess, sometime early communist and associate of Marx, whose *Rome and Jerusalem* (1862) tended in a similar direction. Hess would be rediscovered as the Zionist movement grew, many taking the view that his account of the matter remains the most penetrating of all.

but for whom he set out to care and proceeded to do so with uncommon results, should not puzzle us unduly. The gulf between him and the Jewish man in the street is attested to by any number of telling indicators from the root fact that it was to German culture and, in a distinctly mawkish way, the German people to whom he was most deeply drawn,[114] to an indifference to the common currency of Judaism so great as to extend his tardiness in arranging for his own son's circumcision to *years*. None the less, at no stage did he ever doubt or question his membership of the Jewish people. Nor did his feeling for things German affect his conviction that it was Germany rather than France that had long been and still remained the true *Hauptsitz* (or natural centre) of European anti-Semitism.[115]

Herzl's short programme for the rescue and general moral salvation of the Jews was worked out between the spring of 1895 and the winter of 1895/6 in the course of a series of solitary cogitations punctuated by attempts—but more especially failures—to bring his ideas to the attention of various members of the class of Jewish notables whose residual ascendancy in western Jewry he would later set himself to overthrow. Among these were the Grand Rabbi of France, the Chief Rabbi of Vienna, the greatest of contemporary Jewish plutocrat-philanthropists, the railroad magnate Baron de Hirsch, the most prominent of Jewish Members of the British Parliament, Sir Samuel Montagu, and, inevitably, the Rothschilds—whom Herzl, like so many others, conceived of as a coherent clan and whom he imagined himself addressing in formal 'family council' especially convened to listen to him. Some refused to see him. Some of those who did receive him rejected all or most of what he had to say out of hand. Some, while patient and friendly were openly sceptical. He fared best of all with two men of his own kind, Max Nordau and Israel Zangwill, two of the best-known Jewish men of letters of the day. It was only with them that he met with real sympathy and succeeded in occasioning that leap of the listeners' imagination that engenders understanding. But sympathy and understanding were all either of them could offer for the time being. The interview with Hirsch and the correspondence that followed it led nowhere. As for the Rothschilds, it was the head of the Viennese branch of the family to whom Herzl chose to address himself, a natural choice, perhaps, given Herzl's own prominence in the world of Viennese letters and journalism, but an unfortunate one. Baron Albert Rothschild was notorious for having as little to do with Jews

---

[114] At the very crisis of his life, as his ideas and plans for the Jews (and for himself) were taking shape, he noted in his diary, in that extraordinarily direct and honest way that distinguished both him and it, that 'If there is one thing I should like to be, it is a member of the old Prussian nobility', *Complete Diaries of Theodor Herzl*, ed. Raphael Patai, English trans. Harry Zohn, 5 vols. (New York, 1960), 5 July 1895, i. 196.

[115] Ibid. 28 June 1895, i. 190.

socially as might be possible. For that reason or out of some more general notion of his own importance, he failed to accord the journalist so much as the courtesy of a reply. It was a little nastiness that helped to confirm Herzl in his lasting detestation of Jewish bankers—the *Finanzjuden*—a sentiment he shared with Nordau; and it did much to prompt him to take his next step. Herzl was aware that the grandees of contemporary Jewry were at one in their aversion to the airing of the internal affairs of Jewry before the general public, that few things were so likely to upset them as the publication of radical ideas on Jewish questions, and that, most hateful of all, were assertions of the *national* quality of the Jewish people. To publish his views was therefore both a tactical circumvention of the notables by bringing what he had to say before the public directly and a delicious act of deliberate and public defiance of their social authority.

There is much in this that was reminiscent of Pinsker. Like the good doctor fourteen years earlier, Herzl laid out and published his analysis of the Jewish condition and his programme for its cure in pamphlet form for maximum distribution. Like Pinsker, again, and following a very similar line of argument, he was adamant in his fundamental claim that there was no future for the Jews in Europe. Each and every one of the nations among which they had lived had proved to be either overtly or covertly anti-Semitic. Assimilation, where it had been attempted, had failed. The unending effort made 'to merge ourselves in the social life of the surrounding communities' had availed the assimilationists nothing. 'Everything tends to one and the same conclusion, clearly enunciated in that classic Berlin phrase: *Juden raus!* (Jews out!).' And, indeed, the Jews must depart, except that they must do so not in scattered groups in ways and directions that would serve only to restart the process of objection, rejection, and subjection elsewhere. Their departure must be massive, orderly, and planned. It needed to be—and it could be—conducted in such a manner as to 'involve no economic disturbances, no crises, no persecutions'. And, the really essential point, it must be intended from the first to ensure that the migrants take up residence, citizenship, political identity, and independence in a *Judenstaat*—a state of Jews—a state of their own.

Thus far, the similarity to Pinsker, style and terminology apart, is striking. But where Pinsker conceived his manifesto as a warning (*Mahnruf*), a call for help and attention to which others, so he hoped, would respond, Herzl's was conceived as a political act in itself, a preliminary to a campaign in which he proposed to play the central role himself. Unlike Pinsker again, Herzl laid his emphasis less on diagnosis than on prescription, and less on mental states (either among the Jews or among the non-Jews) than on the method and the machinery whereby the former were to be extricated from their condition among the latter. Most characteristically, where the title of the Odessa physician's manifesto was formulated as a challenge in the abstract—*Autoemancipation!*—that of the Viennese journalist was specific and concrete: *Der Judenstaat*,[116] and the subtitle equally bold and unambiguous: *Versuch einer modernen Lösung der Juden-frage (An Attempt at a Modern Solution to the Jewish Question)*. Pinsker's was altogether weaker and not devoid of pathos: *Mahnruf an seine Stammesgenossen von einem russischen Juden (A Russian Jew's urgent warning to his kinsfolk)*.

Where he thought it useful and necessary Herzl was happy to employ bold and provocative language. In general, however, he was at pains to insist that his plan entailed nothing really new or revolutionary, least of all anything wild or impractical. He wished his readers to find, on proper examination of his tract, that all was sensible, sober, practical. 'The idea that I have developed in this pamphlet,' reads the first sentence of *Der Judenstaat*, 'is a very old one: it is the *restoration* of the Jewish State.'[117] While the evacuation of most (never all) of the Jews from Europe obviously implied a massive piece of social surgery, it was his continuing claim that it could be managed peaceably, rationally, efficiently, and in such a way as to ensure that all would benefit from it, Jews and non-Jews alike. The Jews would be restored to social health, but so would the nations they left behind. In fact, the latter would positively prosper from the Jews' departure. 'An inner migration of Christian citizens into the positions the Jews had evacuated' would occur. A very great source of internal tension, irritation, and dispute would be removed.

Herzl made no serious attempt to examine the twin questions that had tormented Pinsker: *Why* did the Jews constitute a source of perpetual tension and conflict? *What*, when all was said and done, were the true roots of anti-Semitism and its explanation? But that hardly mattered. He himself, without his knowing it, was very like an answer to Pinsker's original prayer: a westerner of some prominence, a man who was both free and prepared to act in the public domain as none in the east was able, and none in the west, thus far, had been willing to do. He was a man, as Pinsker's legatees would soon see for themselves, who had identified the great questions facing the Jewish people in much the same light as Pinsker and Lilienblum and others in the east, one who proposed very much the same solution, and one who was very plainly calling, as had Pinsker in his time, for a firm 'national decision' to be taken by those who were free and competent to promote that solution. Indeed, Herzl had gone a good deal further. For one thing, he had thought things out. He had gone beyond the proclamation of need and principle. And he was specific. He proposed the establishment of two linked, but distinct organizations. A

[116] *Not*, as commonly, perhaps unavoidably, rendered: 'The Jewish State'. The distinction between a state preponderantly inhabited and in some important formal sense possessed by Jews and a state that, in some other, perhaps deeper, necessarily cultural and philosophical and no doubt religious sense would be *Jewish* has been from Herzl's time to our own both important and profoundly vexed.

[117] Emphasis added.

'Society of Jews' would take up the political tasks, treat with governments, assume responsibility on behalf of the Jewish people for the 'neutral piece of land' to which they would remove themselves and in which they would reconstitute and rehabilitate themselves, and administer the territory pending the establishment of regular, liberal, and enlightened parliamentary government. It would undertake scientific study of the needs, resources, and wishes of the Jews. It would determine the forms of government and administration best suited to them. It would investigate the territory or territories to which Jews might be able, and would actually wish, to migrate. It would resolve the question how a decision on this great matter might be taken and, most probably, what that decision would be. It would, in sum, be 'the organ of the national movement'.

The second organization, the 'Jewish Company', would deal with grittier matters. Herzl imagined it as a semi-commercial chartered company on the model Britain had developed for some of its outlying territories. It would be established in London itself very likely, under English law. It would deal with the liquidation of the emigrants' assets in Europe, the handling of their actual migration 'to better ground', and the provision of housing, land, employment, schooling, and other social needs upon their arrival. It is characteristic of Herzl's approach and his repeated insistence on the *feasibility* of his plan that it should be to the Jewish Company and to its mundane duties that the longest chapter in his pamphlet is devoted.

In sum, while, like Pinsker and Lilienblum and those who had followed their lead, Herzl saw no future for the Jews in Europe, his emphases and, on close inspection, his essential point of departure, were different. What drove him to the common conclusion that all the nations among which the Jews lived were either overtly or covertly anti-Semitic, hopelessly so, was his own specifically central and western European experience, his judgement that assimilation, while honestly attempted, had failed. No such massive attempt to assimilate had—or could have—taken place in eastern Europe anyway, as we have seen. No Russian or Polish or Romanian Jew would or could have written, as Herzl did, of the Jews' unending efforts 'to merge ourselves in the social life of the surrounding communities' and go on to complain that these efforts had availed them nothing. Where Herzl also differed—somewhat more subtly, yet vitally—from the easterners was in his passionate insistence on honour: his own in the first instance, no doubt, but, with an intensity that rapidly overwhelmed his private concerns, his people's. The Diaspora, he had concluded, dishonoured the Jews. That, finally, was why he wished its destruction. He had grasped, intuitively but reasonably enough, that however the Jewish collectivity might be defined—whether as nation, people, social class, or any other category—their honour as a group was in some way the precondition of honourable status for individual members. Such concern with honour—namely with status, respect, dignity, and, more generally still, with the terms in which one was perceived by others—was pre-eminently and prototypically a concern of western, most especially central European Jews. It was exceedingly rare for eastern European Jews (some Polonizers excepted) to regard themselves, let alone Jewry as a whole, as in any sense dishonoured by their condition and by what *others* made and thought of it and of them. They would all agree that they were oppressed. Some, not all, accepted that they were in need of deep internal reform. But none thought that they were in some intrinsic moral or social sense *inferior* to others—least of all to any of the broader eastern European nations and societies (Russians, Ukrainians, Poles, Lithuanians, Romanians, and so forth) in which they chanced to be materially, but not socially enveloped. Only very rarely—on the extreme political populist left, as we have seen, and among minute pockets of Polonized Jewry—were there to be found exceptions to the general rule which was, indeed, that eastern European Jews were disinclined to view themselves individually or collectively through what could only seem to them to be irrelevant, inappropriate, and, in effect, vulgar gentile spectacles. But then, of course, if something of this sort—namely, this tendency to view Jewry through non-Jewish spectacles—was by no means uncommon in the west, it was because it was part and parcel of the general processes of social and cultural integration and assimilation which were now central to the western experience, but which touched eastern European Jewry only at its very margins. The springs from which Herzl's nationalism flowed were therefore substantially different in kind from those that had moved the people who had rallied to Pinsker and, more especially Lilienblum, who formed the bulk of the membership of Ḥibbat Ẓion, and who were, as he himself soon discovered, the most likely recruits to his own movement. Here lay some of the barriers to mutual understanding between Herzl and many of those who, while they would end by agreeing to follow him, would do so reluctantly and with foreboding. That such differences were capable of being overlooked and even to some extent overcome or circumvented—initially, at any rate— and that Herzl should indeed have found any colleagues and followers at all not only in the ranks of Ḥibbat Ẓion, but among its leading figures as well, is therefore puzzling.

Part of the explanation seems to lie in the fact that, if Herzl's diagnosis of the Jewish condition failed overly to impress even those who were disposed to take it seriously, what he proposed to *do*, and the genuinely original mode in which, explicitly to some extent, but certainly implicitly, he proposed that Jewish public life be conducted, did tend to be taken very seriously indeed. It aroused controversy, but it aroused fears as well. It was evident that what this new man had to say bore directly on the purposes and operations of Ḥibbat Ẓion. It followed that the members could not fail to attend to what he was about and to consider with some care, not so much how they might assist him, but rather how he might get in their way. For all the novelty and controversial character of their own purposes and their own enterprise, the Ḥovevei Ẓion tended, as we have seen, to be firmly embedded in the cautious and in so many ways fearful and self-abnegatory mental world of Jewry—too firmly not to be at least as wary of the new man as some among them were fascinated and encouraged by him. The dilemma Herzl presented them was therefore acute. The view taken of him by the local leaders of Ḥibbat Ẓion in the Austrian-ruled Polish province of Galicia was characteristic in its ambivalence.

It is just as undesirable for Ḥibbat Ẓion to lend a hand to [Dr Herzl] and to co-operate with him in his enterprise as it would be to oppose him totally and to rubbish what he has to say [to us]. If [following Herzl's lead] the [Odessa] Committee-men were to turn to politics, all their labour would be in vain and they would find that they had accomplished nothing at all for our people. Heartfelt honour is due Dr Herzl and his ideas on the matter of the Jews, but we have to warn Ḥibbat Ẓion not to think that their affairs will now move rapidly in the direction to which he wishes to lead us. Dr Herzl has been very precipitate in publishing his book and in his activities generally. For that reason he will fail.[118]

Reinforcing inbred wariness was the worrying knowledge that Ḥibbat Ẓion's one great benefactor in the free west, Edmond de Rothschild, was violently opposed to everything that Herzl represented. This was on general principles, but equally because of what this journalist and playwright sought to do specifically. When in the late spring of 1896 Herzl reluctantly resolved on a second approach to the Rothschilds, and Max Nordau went to rue Lafitte on his behalf to put his case to Baron Edmond directly, the millionaire made no secret of the severity of his view. He expressed himself with very great force, at very great length, and in a manner that was openly domineering. It was only very briefly and 'with trouble and some lack of courtesy [mit Mühe und einiger Unhöflichkeit]' that Nordau, as he later reported to Herzl, managed to get some words in. The Russians, the Baron told him, would never allow Palestine to fall under Jewish influence. No Turkish promise—if one were ever made—would be of value in any case. The entire enterprise was 'dangerous and harmful': dangerous because the patriotism of the Jews would be shown to be cant; harmful because it would be the ruin of what Rothschild, with great difficulty, was himself trying to do in Palestine.[119]

Nevertheless, in Odessa, Kiev, Moscow, St Petersburg, Vilna, Warsaw, Cracow, and other eastern European centres of Ḥibbat Ẓion, while the fears were of much the same order the response was different. After

---

[118] 'Ha-zeman kazar ve-hamelakha meruba', Ha-Magid, 15 Oct. 1896, 316.
[119] Nordau to Herzl, 15 May 1896, CZA, H VIII 614.

months of hesitation, almost at the last moment, it was decided that Herzl's invitation to attend the Congress of Zionists he wished to hold in Basel at the end of August 1897 had to be accepted after all. The clamour that had arisen *against* such a congress being held, notably among moderately reformist rabbis in Germany, had caused hearts in Ḥibbat Ẓion to warm to Herzl somewhat. The sense that he might be offering an opportunity for a new departure and that Ḥibbat Ẓion might end by being strengthened in numbers and morale by the new people who had begun to gather round Herzl in the east itself no less than in the west began to take on an almost palpable dimension.[120] But it was the underlying anxiety about the necessarily incalculable consequences of his being left to his own devices that was uppermost in the minds of those who were most active and prominent in Ḥibbat Ẓion, the Odessa Committee people especially. And it seemed to most of them that the shortest way to a resolution of the dilemma with which he had presented them was to attend his Congress in Basel after all—with the intention, in some cases half-spoken, in others explicit, of reining him in when necessary.

Herzl's explicit talk of a 'state' had horrified the Ḥovevei Ẓion almost as much as it had those assimilationists who were prepared to pay attention to him. All who were in any way concerned with the new *yishuv* in Palestine were aware of Ottoman objections to what was still an exceedingly painful and limited effort to establish a modern Jewish foothold in the country and knew that the chief Turkish objection was to a Jewish population that might turn out to have distinct, national political ambitions of their own. The people in Odessa and Warsaw were therefore mollified somewhat when Herzl rapidly removed the term 'state' from his lexicon. Their minds would be further set at rest at the Congress itself, at Basel in the summer of 1897, by his approval of the awkward circumlocution devised by Nordau for the wording of the new Zionist movement's formal goal. 'Zionism aims at the creation of a home [*Heimstätte*] for the Jewish people in Palestine to be secured by public law' was the wording of the governing sentence of what came to be known as the Basel Programme. The phrase 'public law', all but meaningless jurisprudentially, was intended to imply a special, in some way internationally approved status for the 'home' in spite of everything; and with that all were expected to be satisfied. Later still, the concrete end to which all efforts were being directed would be transmuted into the marginally more precise term and concept of a 'charter'. In any event, the term 'state' was dropped and would not be heard of again—authoritatively, at any rate—for some decades. But most encouraging of all, as things were seen in Odessa, was that there was now evidence that Herzl could be

---

[120] On the long-drawn-out preliminaries to the convening of the First Congress, see Vital, *Origins*, 321–53.

moved from his original position, that he had learned something in the course of his initial attempt to treat with the Turks, and that he was prepared to accommodate Hibbat Zion. The evidence was not conclusive. The dour view, that there would never be any knowing precisely what this irresponsible fantasist might be up to, was not without foundation. Men who had long since set their minds on a careful, incremental building up of the new *yishuv* had reason to remain anxious.

One of the great difficulties about Herzl for those who felt they could not afford to ignore him, but could not overcome their reservations about him either, was that his purposes, standards, and *modus operandi* were all deeply influenced, if not substantially dictated, by his perception of the world of states and what he took to be the rules and practices that governed it. It needs to be recalled, of course, this was still a world that was wholly external to Jewry and from which Jews as individuals had long been excluded. Herzl believed that while in the management of their affairs the leaders of the great, 'civilized' (in practice, European) nations of the contemporary world might or might not be personally of a liberal and generous disposition, they could be relied upon to tend, ultimately, to a fairly dispassionate calculation of their own interests. Such interests—again, ultimately—would, he thought, be more or less identical with those of the *collectivity* for which the ruler or other leader held himself and was held by others to be responsible. Whatever they were and however they were defined, it would necessarily be the leader's responsibility to protect and where possible enhance them. The operative rules were clear. On the one hand, nothing of value was likely to be conceded to an alien entity without good and sufficient cause. On the other hand, sensible, sober, and rational men were open, so it could be assumed, to sensible, sober, and rational argument concerning those interests or assets. It followed that negotiation was always possible, provided it was conducted on the basis of *do ut des*, of give and take. It followed, too, that the essential prerequisites for progress in any serious matter that entailed change in the configuration and quality of the world of states were three: access to the true and effective leaders of the nations in question; the ability of one party to offer an asset of its own in exchange for whatever benefit it was it wished to derive from the other; and confidence on both sides in each other's integrity and essential good will. In sum, political calculation turned, invariably but reasonably, on considerations of advantage and need, *not* on sentiment or moral or philanthropic principles. And this last being a universal rule, it applied to the Jews no less than to any other social entity that had, or wished to have, a place in the general political arena. Nothing of substance would be or could be achieved for them, therefore, except on the basis of give and take and recognition and understanding by all parties of what their respective interlocutor's interests, no less than their own, might be. The most urgent business of negotiators was to identify their own assets and to consider how these might be turned not merely and exclusively to their own advantage, but in some way or other to the advantage of the other party as well.

Such thinking was foreign to the Jewish experience—at all events to their experience as it had traditionally been interpreted. The Jews' exclusion from the world of autonomous politics in the course of two millennia had led them to rely little and rarely on rational calculation of national or state interest, very much more on what great men might conceive to be to their own private advantage. This was not necessarily because the notion of rational calculation of state or national interest was unfamiliar *per se*, rather because experience suggested that, likely as not, it would turn out to have been pursued in the service of bigotry and rancour, rather than as genuine, objectively generated *raison d'état* might properly dictate. Herzl's view of the manner in which the Jews should now proceed was therefore diametrically, and to some extent consciously, opposed to the spirit and the logic that had most commonly underlain the forms in which the affairs of Jewish communities had traditionally been handled: the intercessionary. The logic of his approach required that the relevant men of power be actively sought out rather than so far as possible avoided, that the matter of the Jews be brought to a head rather than tucked out of sight, that the purposes of the Jewish people be very clearly and publicly defined and then publicly articulated and acted upon—in that order. It was strikingly in defiance of the ancient, deeply ingrained precepts that enjoined a low profile and avoidance, so far as might be possible, of the 'ruling power'. And there could hardly have been a greater challenge not only to the standing but to the rationale that underlay the authority of the traditional leaders of Jewry in almost all parts, that of the rabbis as well, of course, as that of the *gevirim*. Even for the men in Odessa and other centres of Ḥibbat Ẓion the thought of what such boldness might imply for their own modest enterprise was troubling, even when privately and in spite of themselves they warmed to the unfamiliar, but open, large, and confident spirit that informed it. Not the least of the many puzzles to which the appearance on the public scene of this unusual man gave rise, therefore, was the fact that the institutions he invented for his movement and fashioned to facilitate his *modus operandi* survived long after his demise, in very much the form he had set them, and serving much the purposes he had had in mind for them too. And the puzzle is the greater for his having had no true heirs of his own, his most important successors tending to be largely at odds with him in his lifetime and, in the most notable of cases, critical and dismissive of him after his death as well. And yet they drew much of *their* strength from what they and others judged to be their ability to step into shoes which Herzl had cobbled out of what, in his own time, could not but have seemed thin air.

All that is evident beyond doubt is that Herzl's ability to create a

Jewish national movement explicitly dedicated *before all else* to a territorial-political solution to the Jewish Problem as this was understood at the turn of the century owed a very great deal to his ability to tie all the strands of his activity indissolubly, and as it were organically, together. There is no way in which his ideas and his method, his proven ability to be received (however improbably) as a legitimate representative of the Jewish people by emperors, kings, ministers, and other great men can be separated in practice (as opposed to merely analytically) from his success-ful establishment of the Congress of Zionists as a self-proclaimed parlia-ment of Jewry. Nor can his insistence on running all the Zionist movement's affairs and institutions under a very tight rein be disentangled from his entirely genuine, fair-minded encouragement of successive Congresses to evolve as genuine parliaments in which the fundamental (as opposed to tactical) issues facing the movement would be ironed out and an entire range of contending schools of thought would emerge and cohabit under the single roof he, and none other, had constructed for them. What certainly lay at the heart of Herzl's persona and conduct was confidence: his own immense, virtually unthinking self-confidence in the first place, but the backing provided him by the confidence of a suf-ficiency of other men as well. These were never as many as he had hoped for, nor were they, by and large, of the kind and quality on which he had hoped to rely. But many more were drawn to his side than to any other contemporary secular figure in Jewry, arguably to any figure of any qual-ity at all. The source of the confidence others placed in Herzl remains, as is in the nature of such things, somewhat mysterious, difficult if not ultimately impossible to account for persuasively, difficult too not to put down to that indefinable, doubtful factor, charisma. 'I knew at once that he would be our leader,' one of his early and most loyal followers noted on meeting him for the first time.

His appearance filled me with joy and pride. A splendid man. It was thus, roughly, that as a pupil of the top class in the *gymnasium* I had imagined Hector, the hero of Troy. More than anything it was his eyes and his mouth that captured my heart. Spirit and courage and kindness, strictness, softness and humility, were all combined in him.[121]

Thus in Herzl's own time; thus, to some extent, long after his death. There were many even within the movement who thought the near-worship of Herzl ill-founded, unjustified, and perhaps, in all the various senses of the term, absurd. Nothing is easier than to point to the absence of really massive popular backing for anything he did, or to the dearth of the resources on which he sought to base his 'negotiations' with the Turks, or his desperate ignorance of, for example, the true nature and

---

[121] Max Bodenheimer, *Darki le-ẓion* (Jerusalem, 1952), 71.

structure of the Ottoman Empire and the considerations by which it tended to be ruled. Yet it could be seen that nothing, not even his absolute, admitted failure in Constantinople, would deter him from pursuit of his goal of political-territorial settlement. Failure in one capital moved him to try another, failure of one tactic led him to devise a second and a third. Failure to gain a formally recognized, politically negotiated status for the Jews in Palestine moved him to attempt something of the same sort, if only on a temporary basis, in what he liked to think of as the neighbourhood of the ancestral land—in the Sinai or in Cyprus. Repeatedly defeated—by the Germans, for example, who promised him powerful political support in Constantinople, but, as we will see in a moment, quite as easily resolved to shake him off once they had tested the waters in the real Near East—he was never crushed. Nor—until the end—could he be deflected by objections from within. His leadership was therefore of the most infuriating and, to some minds, dangerous kind. But it had its magnificence. To accept it was in some sort to surrender to it. To object to what he was about in any single instance or connection appeared to be, and was to some extent, to object to him in, as it were, his entirety. Some within the Zionist camp itself did so, yet always in moderation, or semi-privately, never to the end, never so far as to break with him. None, even among his most severe critics, failed to realize that without him there would have been no Congress, no Central Office, no Greater Actions Committee serving as a sort of interim Congress, no German, Hebrew, and Yiddish printed and regularly published organs of Zionist opinion, no slowly growing salaried officialdom, in a word no Zionist *organization*, very probably no real Zionist movement of any kind at all. There would be Hibbat Zion—worthy, decent, cautious, modest, but unmistakably and hopelessly devoid of the élan and electricity and sense of great things emerging from admittedly small beginnings that were all part of Herzl's undoubted contribution to the general effort and atmosphere. All this came to be seen with some clarity when the very real differences between Herzl and a large segment of his colleagues and followers erupted to the point of real crisis; and when Herzl himself could see that the opposition to what he was doing threatened the coherence and integrity of the movement he himself had created virtually *ex nihilo*. On the one hand, his opponents were unwilling to go to the point of rupture. On the other hand, he himself was prepared to make a limited, but not insubstantial retreat.

But there are four more particular reasons why the crisis precipitated by what came to be known (inaccurately) as 'the Uganda Scheme' has merited the close, alas often tendentious, examination it has generally received. It encapsulated both the uses and the failings of Herzl's method. It demonstrated the kind of circumstances in which serious, international-political interest in the Zionist movement (and, just possibly, assistance for it) might be available, and on what terms, and within what limits. It illustrated the profundity, if not virtual insolubility, of the dilemma in which the attempt to confront the complexities of Jewish life and history head-on placed even so radical and dedicated a movement for social and political change in Jewry as Zionism. And it very largely determined, at any rate in broad outline, the path the movement would tread from that time on.

In its immediate origins, the quarrel between Herzl and a substantial number of the most prominent Zionists that erupted in the spring of 1903—so deep and so genuine that it all but tore the movement apart— was an odd, very marginal, and fortuitous outcome of the British determination to reset the pattern by which eastern and southern Africa were to be ruled. It occurred in the wake of a strong desire in London to integrate the non-British European inhabitants of southern Africa into the British imperial system at the end of the long and costly (and at first woefully unsuccessful) war waged against them on as generous a basis as could be managed. But it also had to do with the particular personality and political—more especially, imperial—intentions and imagination of the man who took this matter in hand and was, besides, as it happened, much the most important and independently minded British politician of the day. Joseph Chamberlain had set out for Africa towards the end of 1902 on a mission of inspection and reconciliation, reconciliation with the defeated Afrikaners in South Africa in the first instance, but inspection of the other British domains that he would encounter on his way as well. Among them was Kenya; and among the projects to which he was to pay special attention was the newly completed Uganda railway which ran from Mombasa on the coast up to Nairobi in the hills and on to the lands of the Kikuyu and the Mau escarpment. The railway was very naturally seen by all concerned, not least by Chamberlain himself, as precisely the sort of great public enterprise that was needed in Africa if British imperial rule was to prove effective, constructive, and profitable. Another—and interconnected—concern of the British imperialists of the day was settlement, where possible, by hardy, independent, and enterprising Europeans.

Chamberlain was a close, diligent, and intelligent observer. Reaching the highlands of what would eventually be called Kenya, perched on a seat specially constructed for him on the engine buffer of his train, he was much impressed by the country revealed to him as he rode through it. He thought it as attractive as southern England and eminently suitable for settlement and cultivation by Europeans. And it occurred to him in passing, as he duly wrote down among the notes he drew up before leaving Africa, that 'If Dr Herzl were at all inclined to transfer his efforts to East Africa, there would be no difficulty in finding land suitable for Jewish settlers.' To which observation he added, thus reflecting greater attention to what he had learned from and about the Zionists than he might otherwise have been given credit for, that 'I assume that this country is too far removed from Palestine to have any attraction for him.'[122]

Herzl had had a brief series of meetings with Joseph Chamberlain in the course of 1902 and 1903. It seems fair to say that the rapport established between the two men marked the high—as it happened the final— point in the Zionist leader's long, unrelenting pursuit of that political alliance which, he never doubted, was the necessary, although far from sufficient, condition of the Jews' entry into the world of independent nations. It had begun with his setting out for Constantinople in June 1896, more than a year before the convening of the Congress, indeed many months before it had so much as occurred to him to convene one. Herzl knew, as did all reasonably informed Europeans, that the Ottoman regime was hard pressed politically and financially, that it was heavily in debt to European banks, and that it was bound to a humiliating system whereby foreign officials not only substantially controlled its finances, but foreigners enjoyed a large measure of extraterritorial judicial and police power of their own within the empire. Here, Herzl imagined, was an opening for a combination that would be fruitful to both Turks and Jews and, conceivably, to worried European creditors as well. The Sultan would be offered the financial means to get the foreigners off his back, the great *Finanzjuden* of Frankfurt, Paris, London, and Vienna who could provide those means would be shown how they might, with proper discretion and elegance, get the problem of oppressed, impoverished, and above all migrant Jewry off *their* backs. The Sultan would then reward the Jews by allowing massive Jewish immigration and settlement into Palestine and the country's reconstitution as an autonomous, but distinctly Jewish entity within the Ottoman Empire. The Jews of Palestine would return the compliment by pledging political loyalty to the Ottomans. The European Powers, seeing the great majority of their Jewish subjects depart, would applaud in their turn—the more loudly for recognizing that a strong Jewish presence in the Holy Land was preferable to the present chaos. And finally, *pari passu* with the decline of anti-Semitic ferment that would follow the departure of most Jews and the virtual winding up of the European Diaspora, those who were determined to forgo the great adventure and remain put would be set free at long last to attend uninterruptedly and uninhibitedly to their private affairs.

It was a neat and, despite its simplicity, ingenious scheme. With rare exceptions, the monarchs, ministers, and other great (necessarily non-Jewish) men before whom Herzl unfolded his plan, were attracted to it and inclined to help. Some (the Grand Duke of Baden, for example)

---

[122] 'Notes on Mombasa and East Africa Protectorate by the Right honourable J. Chamberlain', Ladysmith, 2 Jan. 1903, PRO, FO 2/722, p. 7.

because they sympathized with the plight of the Jews; some (like the German Kaiser) because it struck him as offering an additional way in which he might manage to cut a very fine figure internationally; some (like the Tsar's ministers Witte and Plehve) because it suggested, if not a way of expediting the Jews' departure, at any rate a purpose that might encourage them to turn away from revolutionary activity within Russia itself as well as improving Russia's image somewhat where the Jews were concerned without requiring any change in its system of legalized oppression. But details aside, almost all found something else that was new and promising in what Herzl had to say to them. He spoke to them as no Jew had ever done before and of things which no Jew had ever raised before. Therein, of course, lay one of the two great flaws in his scheme. The men within Jewry on whom it depended, the *Finanzjuden*, the plutocrats of Jewry, those who actually possessed the one resource the Jews—more precisely some Jews—could be said to have had and on which Herzl had begun by thinking he could rely, were the people least disposed to have any sympathy with it or with him.

The other, still greater flaw was the absolute refusal of the Ottomans themselves to contemplate a special, openly proclaimed, and recognized *political* status for the Jews, one, that is to say, that went beyond their continuing to constitute a *millet*. They wished the Jews to continue as a legally established, obligatory ethno-religious community analogous to that of the Greeks or the Armenians, subject to their rabbis when that suited the sovereign ruler, directly to the Ottoman authorities when it did not. And if that was the operative principle throughout the empire, it was doubly to be insisted upon in the case of Palestine. Turkey stuck inflexibly to the policy for Palestine formulated in 1882: immigration of Jews into Anatolia or Mesopotamia in small, scattered groups was permissible; immigration of non-Ottoman Jews into Syria and Palestine and purchase of land for their settlement there was not.

Friends[123] of Herzl who knew a great deal more than he did about the Ottoman style and system of government, of the relevance of Islam to that system, and of the obligations incumbent upon the Sultan as Caliph in connection with Palestine and Jerusalem in particular had warned Herzl that he would get nowhere in Constantinople with his grand scheme for the rescue of the empire on the one hand and the Jews on the other. And, indeed, repeatedly, on each one of his journeys there, he found that on the central issue of a special Jewish regime for the country he would be put off with a dusty answer or with a reformulation of set

---

[123] Two in particular: Richard Gottheil, professor of semitics at Columbia University, and Arminius Vámbéry (né Hermann Wamberger), professor of oriental languages at the University of Budapest and sometime tailor's apprentice, tutor in European languages at the Ottoman court, explorer for the Hungarian Academy, and highly valued (and well-paid) secret agent for the British government.

policy on Jewish immigration as laid down in 1882.[124] However, six years would pass before this otherwise normally perceptive and experienced professional journalist finally concluded that the Turks were 'like sea foam', that 'only their expressions are serious, not their intentions',[125] and that there was nothing further to be done in or about Constantinople other than to wait for some vast change of mind or, perhaps, regime. To the question why it took him so long to draw what cannot fail to seem a straightforward conclusion, several answers suggest themselves.

There was the matter of Turkish tactics. These appear to have been decided upon immediately, which is to say, upon Herzl's first attempt to penetrate the slippery halls of Ottoman power and to cope as best he could with a succession of regular ministers and government officials, palace courtiers and secretaries, contact men, agents of influence, and agents *tout court* of every conceivable kind. It was a crowd through which he had somehow to find his way, at times aware, at other times unaware, that the Turkish authorities took more than routine interest in him, that he was followed, that spies were attached to him. It is certainly the case that he was regularly reported on, that the proceedings of the Congresses over which he presided were noted (very imperfectly, it needs to be said), and that generally speaking the Turks were sufficiently intrigued to wish to know what this Viennese journalist was up to and who, if anybody, was behind him. It is equally the case, however, that the Turks received him and in a sense recognized him for what he claimed to be and as one entitled to treat with them. At no stage did they question, let alone deny his authority to speak on behalf of the Jewish people. Ministers at the Porte, the Sultan's powerful secretaries, the Sultan himself—all, in effect, were prepared to deal with him on the basis that they took Herzl at his word whatever they may have thought of him and his pretensions privately. He was treated with great formal courtesy. He was awarded a decoration.[126] Several of his numerous visits to Constantinople were in response to a Turkish summons to come for talks. This seemingly inexplicable behaviour is most plausibly explained by positing that they concluded very early on that the simplest way of keeping him under observation was to receive him at something like his own estimation of his role, namely on terms that bordered on, while never being strictly identical with, formal honour. There is evidence that at one stage in these protracted and

---

[124] Its final version, dictated to Herzl in French on 2 Aug. 1902, read as follows: 'The Jews can be admitted and established in the Ottoman Empire on condition that they be settled ununited [*non réunis*], that is to say dispersed, in such places as are judged suitable by the Government. They will be accorded Ottoman citizenship [*la sujétion ottomane*] and charged with all civic duties, including military service, and as Ottomans be subject to all the laws of the land' (*Theodor Herzls Tagebücher*, 3 vols. (Berlin, 1922–3), iii. 274).

[125] 31 July 1902, *Diaries*, iv. 1334.

[126] Commander of the Mejidiye Order.

tiresome proceedings the Ottomans desired to show a French financial group with which they were negotiating a consolidation of their public debt that they had others irons in the fire, a Jewish iron as well. But chiefly, overall, behind what cannot fail to seem in retrospect to have been a futile game of cat and mouse, there seems to have been something that was not unlike that wariness of the Jews that had so long bedevilled and would long continue to confuse relations between Jews and non-Jews in the Christian world. It is true that the masters of Islam had rarely been as attentive to matters Jewish as great men in Christendom have often been, not least the doctors of the Church. Nor had Muslim rulers, until quite recently, ever considered that they had need to be wary of their own Jewish subjects, let alone foreign Jews. But it remains that while the reception accorded Herzl in Constantinople could be read as evidence of the validity of his method, it pointed repeatedly and more strongly to the futility of what he was about.

Long before Herzl drew the desperate conclusion that he must abandon hope for an established presence for the Jews in Palestine in any conceivable future it became clear to him, therefore, that he needed to try a new tack if any concrete progress was to be made. The Turks refused to budge. The plutocrats of Jewry were consistently unhelpful. Perhaps something could be made of foreign political influence in Constantinople. If one of the great European powers subscribed to his argument for the re-establishment of a Jewish territorial and political entity of some kind in the Near East, might it not be prepared to press the much weakened and in part dependent Ottoman state to be more flexible? And if it did so, would not elements within the Jewish world itself be inclined to rethink their position? Germany held a strong position in Constantinople. It was led by a young emperor anxious to cut an exceptional and inventive figure on the world stage (besides being sufficiently anti-Semitic to relish the idea of promoting a Jewish evacuation of Europe). The way to him might be opened through his helpful and friendly uncle, the Grand Duke of Baden, the first figure of any consequence at all on the European stage to have received Herzl and retain a strong and favourable impression of him. It seemed a promising route to follow; so it proved to be. With the Grand Duke's help and after knocking on a series of doors of steadily ascending importance, Herzl had his request that German pressure be exerted on the Sultan put to Kaiser Wilhelm and in the summer of 1898 the German ambassador in Vienna, Count Philipp zu Eulenburg, an intimate of the Kaiser, was instructed by his master to look into the matter of Zionism systematically.

There ensued a rapid flowering, followed by a still more rapid wilting, of Herzlian diplomacy. The Zionist's ideas and programme caught Eulenburg's imagination. Herzl himself impressed the German aristocrat and courtier in what one may suppose were the very terms he would have

wanted to be regarded by such a man. 'Undeniably one of the most interesting personalities I have ever met . . . extraordinarily gifted . . . a militant [*streitbaren*] Jewish leader from the age of the Jewish kings without a
particle of what we call "trading Jews" [*Handelsjuden*]. My association
with this high-minded, *selfless* [*selbstlosen*] distinguished man will remain
in my memory forever.'[127] Eulenburg reported to the Kaiser on both man
and plan very favourably; and Wilhelm, momentarily intoxicated by a
vision of 'undreamt-of prosperity' being brought to the Holy Land and
of the Sick Man of Europe being cured by vast sums of Jewish money
pouring into 'Turkish money-bags'—intermingled, to be sure, with his
intention of playing a statesmanlike role in the Near East on the occasion
of his coming visit there—agreed to take up the Zionists' cause. It was a
fine and immensely promising idea, he decided. 'The tribe of Shem'
would be 'directed to worthier goals than the exploitation of Christians'.
The advantage to Germany if, in view of 'the tremendous power represented by international Jewish capital in all its dangerousness . . . the
Hebrew world looked up to our country with gratitude', was certainly
not to be underrated.[128] He would therefore readily undertake, in the
course of his journey to Constantinople and Jerusalem in the following
month, to 'intercede [on their behalf] with the Sultan very exhaustively
and as urgently as possible'. Thus Eulenburg, writing to Herzl on 27 September under seal of secrecy, but on the highest authority. The Kaiser
believed, moreover, that it would be exceedingly appropriate if a delegation of Zionists were to await him in Jerusalem for their wishes to be put
to him in person and formally. And Wilhelm's enthusiasm for the Zionist cause was further underlined by the ambassador writing to Herzl once
more, two days later, plainly at the Kaiser's urging, to reaffirm both the
undertaking to intercede with the Sultan and the invitation/command to
meet the emperor in Constantinople and Jerusalem in even more unambiguous and emphatic language.[129]

The German emperor's promise turned out to be as easily broken as it
had been given. It was made clear to him on his arrival in Turkey, that this
was not a subject on which the Sultan would tolerate his intervention,
nor was it one that those of his own officials whose work bore on
German–Ottoman relations thought there could be any serious reason to

[127] Cited in A. Bein, 'Zikhronot u-te'udot 'al pegishato shel Herzl 'im Vilhelm ha-
sheini', in *Sefer ha-yovel li-khvod Dr. N. M. Gelber* (Tel Aviv, 1963), appendix 2, 16.
Emphasis in original. Eulenburg made almost as powerful an impression on Herzl—for his
toughness of character and 'iron' self-possession, however, rather than for his moral qualities. On the extreme care with which Herzl planned one of his important meetings with
Eulenburg, see above, pp. 259–60.

[128] Wilhelm II to his uncle, the Grand Duke of Baden, 29 Sept. 1898. Text in Bein,
'Zikhronot', appendix 8, 22–4.

[129] Eulenburg to Herzl, 27 and 28 Sept. 1898, CZA, HS 2; and Bein, 'Zikhronot',
appendices 6 and 7, 19–21.

take up. Accordingly, without further ceremony, Zionism was dropped; and Herzl, when he turned up to meet the Kaiser in Palestine as requested, was hastily brushed off with just that combination of thought-lessness and crudity for which the emperor and his entourage were rapidly making a name for themselves elsewhere. For Herzl himself, needless to say, the German promise having been made, and he himself having dropped incautious hints of unspecified great things to come, the immediate disappointment was, if anything, greater than any rendered him by the Turks or by the Rothschilds or, had he but known what would follow, by his own supporters too in due course. The Germans had betrayed him. But it was his own judgement that was now in question.

Herzl's original decision to champion the Jewish national cause and his absolute conviction that he knew, as others did not, how the Jews might be rescued materially, socially, and morally—but speedily and irreversibly too—had been bound up from the first with what had turned out to be a long, painful, and ultimately futile effort to strike a deal with the Turks. In his own lifetime, the ins and outs of his Turkish venture lent themselves handily to the charge of a certain absurdity in all that he was about. In retrospect, while the man's single-mindedness and obstinacy command admiration his reputation is clouded by the persistent question when and how far the sober political calculation by which he himself held such store was in fact deflected and distorted by flights of imagination and sheer fantasy. All that is plain is that at some point in 1901 or 1902 he awoke from his Turkish dream and that he did so without abandoning his cause and his movement—as he might well have done on seeing his ori-ginal, grandiose plan collapse. It is equally evident that from this point on his management of the matter of Zionism was dictated by a cooler, if more melancholy realism than had been in evidence before.

It is undeniable, too, and inevitable in the circumstances, that by this time, namely by the turn of the century, the internal pressure on Herzl—here unspoken, there beginning to be vociferous—to show results for his efforts had begun to weigh with him. His own efforts to persuade his crit-ics within the movement that his path to national salvation was one that they would do well to follow because it would, eventually, deliver them at the gates of Palestine became unrelenting. He had to persuade them to grant him more time to prove himself. They needed to be asked, repeat-edly, to continue to comprehend and tolerate his refusal to share the burden of tactical calculation with any but a tiny handful of colleagues—among whom only Max Nordau was in a position of close enough trust to offer advice that would be seriously attended to even if not always taken. And Herzl had the still more difficult task of demonstrating the worth of Zionism *per se* to the great mass of Jewry that remained outside the movement altogether, in part unconvinced by the arguments advanced in its favour, in greater part either indifferent to it and its works, poorly informed about them, or ferociously opposed to what it took the movement and leader to stand for.

By 1901, therefore, it had become evident that a new tack was needed if there was not to be a radical departure from the old course or, worse, a total collapse. The Zionist movement was voluntary. Members moved in and out of it at will. Public relations, public image, spirit, hope, faith, but in the final analysis concrete achievement were therefore all. But was there any prospect of concrete achievement? Or if the whole loaf was unobtainable, as seemed to be the case, was there perhaps something to be said for making do with half? But what could *that* be? What could be less than a self-governing autonomous home for the Jews in Palestine? It needed at the very least to be in something like the same class as the ultimate goal and related to it in some visible way as well. What was certainly indispensable was the political element, namely that upon whatever else the movement resolved to compromise, it needed to be able to demonstrate that a political-territorial arrangement for the Jews was indeed viable, that it was not an absurdity, and that it could contribute very substantially to the rescue and rehabilitation of the Jews of eastern Europe. If that was ensured it should prove easier to compromise on the identity and location of the territory than on the status Jews would have within it. Might it not be acceptable, for example, for the territory in question *not*, for the time being, to be identical with the Land of the Jewish people itself, provided it was at least on that Land's periphery geographically and associated with it and with the history of the Jews in some way? It was plain that there would be ferocious ideological and sentimental objections to such a venture. Great arts of presentation, not to say sleight of hand, would be required to make it acceptable. But something of the central aim of Zionism would have been achieved. The indispensable precedent of properly negotiated, duly recognized territorial autonomy would have been established. Jews and non-Jews would begin to accustom themselves both to the principle and to the real merits of a territorial and political solution to the Jewish Question.

In practice, to think along such lines was, necessarily, to think of Great Britain. Germany had a measure of influence in the (Ottoman) Near East. France had old, but still lively ambitions there. Britain alone had a solid territorial presence: in Cyprus since 1878 and in Egypt since 1882. Moreover, to evident geo-political facts there needs to be added the warmth of the regard in which all European Jews—notably, but certainly not exclusively, the Jews of Russia and Poland—tended to hold 'England the mighty, England the free' (the words are Herzl's, but he was speaking to a Jewish audience that knew exactly what he had in mind). All knew it as the greatest of the world powers of the day, mistress of the seas, diplomatically prestigious, renowned for a capital city that was not only the most populous of all contemporary urban conurbations and the unquestioned centre of world finance, but the seat of the most wide-spread empire the world had ever known. It was besides—and in Jewish eyes before all else—a politically free and open society known for its hospitality to foreign exiles.

But it was distant knowledge. Herzl did not know England at first hand, only superficially and at one or more removes, in a manner that bore comparison with his knowledge of Turkey as opposed to his close and detailed grasp of people and politics in France, Germany, and, of course, Austria-Hungary itself. He was not ignorant. He knew enough to be aware that one of the men who counted for most in British politics at the turn of the century was Joseph Chamberlain. But he did not know enough to understand that Alfred Austin, the Poet laureate, counted for nothing at all either as laureate or as poet. He believed with others that the British Empire was not only immense, but flourishing. There is no reason to suspect that he had read Kipling's 'Recessional' (1897) or been taught by any one else to ponder the empire's most likely future. But even had he done so he would have been wrong to draw an operative conclusion from, for example, Kipling's famous warning against selfish complacency. Herzl's outlook in his quest for an ally was short-term, relatively speaking. Given his purposes, it was correct.

The immediate question, as always, was how to make contact with those people in London who mattered, an exercise that he found to be much more difficult to accomplish than in the Germanies. In 1900 he had decided to hold the Fourth Congress of Zionists in London rather than in Basel, as was usual, in the hope of making a splash there. It was an unpopular decision in the movement itself. London was a great deal further from Russia than Basel, more difficult of access therefore for delegates who had to travel all the way from eastern Europe at their own expense. It earned him a good press in Britain, but it availed him nothing otherwise, any more than had the establishment in London of the Zionist Organization's financial arm, the Jewish Colonial Trust, or an attempt to put up a Zionist candidate for Parliament in the East End of London that had duly come to nothing. Almost to a man, the grandees of English Jewry refused to have anything to do with him. The impact in the larger, political world was nil. Not until Leopold Greenberg engineered his being called to testify before the Royal Commission on Alien Immigration two years later did matters change.

In an instant, Zionism was converted from an unknown, or at best exceedingly remote and improbable, Jewish fantasy into a movement that touched—or was thought capable of touching—on a domestic British concern. This, of course, was the matter of coping with, if necessary limiting, Jewish immigration into Great Britain. It had been this particular, somewhat embarrassed concern that had prompted Arthur Balfour's Unionist government to set up the Royal Commission in the first place.[130] Any plan to make it possible—amicably and on a voluntary basis—to divert the torrent of eastern European Jewish migrants away from Great Britain was likely to excite some hopeful interest. The further notion that a place might be found for them within the empire itself was trickier, but, for men who were masters of, or even—as in Joseph Chamberlain's case—confident believers in a multinational, multiracial, and necessarily multi-religious empire, the notion of a small segment of it being set apart for the Jews was not especially difficult to swallow. Some might be sceptical of the Jews' capacity to succeed in any such—in the accepted sense of the term at the time—colonial enterprise. Others, Chamberlain for one, might dislike Jews *en bloc*, but never doubt their energy, commercial enterprise, and iron determination to succeed in whatever they undertook. It was, besides, an article of faith among the more articulate imperialists of the day that if the great resources of the empire were ever to be put to good use much would have to depend on its lands being settled by Europeans. Minds set firmly on a hierarchy of races—Europeans being superior to Asians and Asians to Africans, and so on—subscribed to equally fixed notions about Europeans. Of course, Jews were not the best sort of Europeans. They were plainly inferior as colonists, and indeed for most other purposes as well, to the English themselves or to the Dutch or the Germans. But they had their merits; and in any case Asians and Blacks, none doubted, were, in their turn, inferior to the Jews. In a word, Britain could do very well without (an excess of) Jews in Whitechapel and Houndsditch. But it might be able to make good use of them overseas. The question was, where?

Herzl was introduced to Chamberlain after testifying before the Royal Commission. (And treated a good deal more courteously by its Jewish member, Lord Rothschild, thereafter as well.) Cyprus was mentioned, but Chamberlain dismissed the possibility out of hand on the grounds that the Greeks who formed the greater part of the population would object—vehemently in all probability—to any such project as Herzl had in mind and he, Chamberlain, as the minister responsible for the colony, would have to support them. A more promising possibility was Sinai, more precisely the El Arish region in the north-east corner of the peninsula. Virtually uninhabited, El Arish suggested none of the problems Cyprus would have offered both the British and the Jews had Jewish settlement on the island been attempted. From the Zionist point of view Sinai had the added advantage of being both literally and historically on the doorstep of the Promised Land. On the other hand, it was not British territory, strictly speaking, not sovereign territory that is, not a colony, but rather, if somewhat vaguely, a dependency of Egypt. Nominally, Egypt itself was Ottoman territory governed by a Khedive or viceroy in

---

[130] See above, Chapter 4.

the name of the Sultan. In fact, for all major purposes, it was controlled by Britain. Its real ruler was a British official sent out from London to perform the double duty placed on all British colonial and imperial satraps of looking after the interests of the local population as best they understood them and caring for the higher interests of the empire whenever these appeared to be relevant. Ottoman sovereignty was therefore a fiction. The reality was a British protectorate. In the interests of maintaining the fiction, however, the philosophical significance of which was that British rule was temporary, the British governor of the country bore the deliberately modest title of agent and consul-general rather than, say, governor-general; and he reported to the Foreign Office in London, rather than to the Colonial Office. And all this being the case, once the matter of El Arish began to be discussed as a serious possibility, Chamberlain had to pass Herzl on to the Foreign Secretary, Lord Lansdowne, and Lansdowne, in his turn, had to pass Herzl and his project on to the consul-general in Cairo, *de facto* ruler of the country, for closer examination.

Egypt's ruler at this time was the very experienced, and exceedingly strong-minded Evelyn Baring, Lord Cromer, now twenty years in his post. Lansdowne and Baring, each in his turn, took a cooler view of Zionism, and indeed of Herzl personally, than Chamberlain. Moreover, unlike Chamberlain, neither had their eyes on the British domestic scene. And if both, in the strict sense, were men who saw it as their duty to promote, uphold, and if possible expand the British Empire, neither was inclined to place much emphasis on economic development. They were old-fashioned servants of the state, reluctant to rock existing boats and upset what they regarded, rightly or wrongly, as delicate local balances of current power, influence, and social structure. Zionism in its concrete form, namely as a movement intent on promoting the migration of a great mass of alien Jews from one part of the world into another, could not but seem to them to entail disturbance of such a balance were the migrants ever to intrude into the realm for which they held themselves responsible. Still, Chamberlain having recommended Herzl to Lansdowne's good offices, the Foreign Secretary could not, without discourtesy, avoid passing him on to Cromer with his own (very moderately worded) request to see what he could do for him. Cromer, on meeting Herzl, promptly rated him 'a wild enthusiast',[131] and thought very little of his project. But again, given the position Lansdowne had adopted in deference to Chamberlain, he too seems to have decided that a gesture had to be made and he agreed, grudgingly, to El Arish being looked at by a committee of technical experts as a possible site for Jewish settlement.

---

[131] Cromer to Sanderson, 28 Mar. 1903. Cited in R. Patai, 'Herzl's Sinai Project', *Herzl Year Book*, 1 (New York, 1958), 116. Herzl, for his part, noted in his diary that Cromer was 'the most disagreeable Englishman I have ever faced', 25 Mar. 1903, *Diaries*, iv. 1446.

When it turned out that all would depend in the first instance on water being piped to Sinai from Egypt proper,[132] he wasted no time, however, in dismissing the Zionists and their projects from his mind and from his official agenda as well. So far as he was concerned, there had been more than enough there to kill the idea—quite apart from objections raised by the indigenous Egyptian authorities once they were informed of what was in the offing and were asked for their views. Cromer's own firm view from beginning to end had been that no British or Egyptian interest would be served by such an enterprise from which, in all probability, only various kinds of still incalculable political unpleasantness would result. Accordingly, when Herzl pressed the Foreign Office, in effect, to over-rule Cromer, he was politely, but firmly informed, that 'Lord Cromer has evidently been much impressed by [the] objections to the scheme, and [that] they appear to Lord Lansdowne [too] to be of so cogent a nature that he is constrained to tell you that in his opinion no favourable result can be expected from the further reference which is now being made to Cairo'.[133]

However, East Africa as a region for Jewish settlement was still in play and Chamberlain now pressed his idea on Greenberg, who had begun to stand in for Herzl in London on a regular basis. Greenberg reported the Colonial Secretary as telling him that the territory in question,

was on very high ground with fine climate and every possibility for a great colony which could support at least a million souls. . . . If [the El Arish plan] comes to nothing, [Greenberg reported Chamberlain as saying] I do hope Dr H[erzl] will consider very seriously the suggestion. . . . I asked him if it w[oul]d be possible, providing you considered the scheme[,] for us to have local self gov-ernment and he replied 'Certainly'. He said it would be necessary to send out a Governor—'Who would be a Jew?' I asked. 'Who could be a Jew,' he replied. Anyway, he said, let Dr H[erzl] consider this and I shall be glad to hear further upon it.[134]

The attractions of the proposal were plain. An offer of a place of refuge made in the aftermath of the great pogrom in Kishinev at Eastertime 1903[135]—which, apart from its actual horrors, seemed to announce a return to semi-tolerance of murderous mob violence against Jews after twenty years of relative peace in Russia—could not but be welcomed. As a response to Zionist insistence on internal autonomy and an open, for-mal recognition of the national Jewish character of the territory they were to inhabit it was all they could desire, certainly for the moment.

---

[132] Wrongly, as we now know, there being ample underground supplies of water for purposes of cultivation in Sinai itself and in the El Arish area in particular.

[133] Sanderson to Herzl, 19 June 1903. Cited in A. Bein, 'Ha-masa u-matan bein Herzl le-vein britania ha-gedola be-'inyan el-'arish', *Shivat Zion*, 1 (Jerusalem, 1950), 219.

[134] Greenberg to Herzl, 20 May 1903, CZA, H VIII/292.

[135] On which, see below, Chapter 6.

There were the questions of the precise location, the extent, and the actual suitability for settlement of the territory Chamberlain had in mind, all of which would have to be gone into, although it was more than likely that the answers would prove to be promising. But, above all, the long, immensely tiring, continually criticized political-diplomatic campaign Herzl had initiated did seem, at long last, to have borne fruit. A great power, for reasons of its own, had offered the Jewish people almost precisely what the Zionist movement, its self-appointed, but now manifestly recognized representative, had called for. Here, at long last, was a concrete, political achievement. Here, it would seem, was proof of the validity of the Herzlian method and outlook. And here, for Zionism, was a moral victory of the first order.

The one great snag to the offer was more than apparent: to Herzl himself, to Greenberg, and to Max Nordau (the only other of his friends whom he was prepared to consult on the subject) as well as to Chamberlain himself, as we have seen. The Kenyan highlands were not Palestine. They could not conceivably be regarded as lying on the doorstep, or in the general neighbourhood of Palestine. It could not be said of them that they bore a relation of any kind whatsoever to the Jews' ancestral land. Contrariwise, it could be said of them, and would be said of them—with some justice—that to settle upon them was to enter yet another land of exile, one that was devoid, moreover, even of such bitter-sweet, but at any rate authentic historical, cultural, and religious associations as Babylon (Mesopotamia), the Rhineland, and the Iberian peninsula, for example, were capable of evoking in the minds and hearts of some segments of the Jewish people.

The dilemma was acute, but it was not equally acute for all, nor did all admit that it was a genuine dilemma. The argument that the Zionist Organization had no choice but to accept the proposal was not implausible. It was the great imperial power Great Britain, through one of its most influential politicians, that had made the offer. *Mirabile dictu* a powerful, friendly hand had been held out to the Zionists in precisely the spirit and with the kind of intention—namely co-operation and enlightened self-interest rather than charity—that not only augured best, but had been what they had sought for from the first. There were therefore exceptionally strong grounds for taking care in these unique circumstances not to appear churlish or unreasonable, not to offend, and, above all, not to terminate the one political dialogue which had proved to be productive before it had really properly begun and its possibilities had been fully explored. But none of this proved decisive and the rest is soon told.

The British offer, of which nothing had previously been known in the movement at large, was brought before the Sixth Congress of Zionists in Basel (23–8 August 1903) with great caution.

The new territory [Herzl told the delegates] does not have the historic, poetical-religious, and Zionist value that even the Sinai Peninsula would have had, but I do not doubt that the Congress, acting as the representative of the entire Jewish people, will receive the new offer with the warmest gratitude. . . . Considering the plight of Jewry and the immediate necessity of finding some way to ameliorate this plight as much as possible, I did not feel justified, when this proposal was made, in doing other than obtaining permission to submit it to the Congress. . . .

Although it is evident that the Jewish people can have no ultimate goal other than Palestine . . . the Congress will recognize the extraordinary progress that our movement has made through the negotiations with the British government. . . . I believe the Congress can find a way to make use of this offer. The way in which this offer was made to us is bound to help, improve, and alleviate the situation of the Jewish people without our abandoning any of the great principles on which our movement was founded.[136]

The first response of the assembled delegates was to cheer Herzl to the rafters. But once the first burst of enthusiasm had passed and the full import of what had been offered and what Herzl was proposing—namely that the Congress take up the offer provisionally and agree to its being examined to see what, if anything, could be made of it—the mood changed. A substantial minority rapidly backtracked: theirs had been no more than an emotive and thoughtless response, they tended later to claim. Bitter debate both in open session and in the lobbies ensued, culminating, at the penultimate point, in a mass walk-out of malcontents. Herzl himself was denounced personally, if still cautiously—which is to say, privately rather than openly—for betrayal of the movement, for having proposed the sale of the Jewish birthright to the Land of Israel for a mess of East African pottage. And for the first time the elected head of the movement found himself faced with organized opposition. The old undercurrents of doubt and misunderstanding, in some cases outright suspicion and alienation, to which Herzl had given rise from the first, notably among the easterners, came together and to a head, strictly ideological and tactical objections being fatally reinforced by the private and the emotive.

Opposition to the East Africa scheme was heightened further by lingering objections to Herzl's having treated with the notoriously reactionary Russian minister of the interior, V. K. Plehve, in the course of his recent (first and only) visit to the heartland of Jewry.[137] Plehve, before all other servants of the Autocracy, was now the most hated and despised of all the Tsar's principal servants, regarded by all decent Russian liberals as the man who embodied most perfectly all that rendered the regime itself

---

[136] *Stenographisches Protokoll der Verhandlungen des VI. Zionisten-Kongresses* (Vienna, 1903), 8.

[137] The sole small fraction of which he was allowed to see was Vilna. Otherwise his visit to Russia was limited to a stay in St Petersburg.

vicious and intolerable. The Jews in Russia held him in special loathing for his systematic promotion of anti-Semitic policies and for what was commonly (but probably incorrectly) believed to be his personal responsibility for the great pogrom perpetrated in Kishinev several months earlier.[138] It was indeed the case that Herzl had tried very hard to obtain an invitation to Russia to meet Plehve. But it was at the behest of the Russian Zionists themselves, in the first instance, that he had wanted to make direct contact with the Russian government and, in accordance with his very reasonable principle that it was to the men who wielded real power in any given state that one needed to talk, no matter what one thought of them in private, he had particularly wanted to meet Plehve.

The Russian police paid closer attention to the Zionists after the formal foundation of the movement in 1897 than they had ever paid to Hibbat Zion, the weaknesses of which they seem to have recognized from the first. They disliked the Russian Zionists' international connections. They noted, and of course objected to, the semi-secrecy with which the movement conducted its affairs within Russia, for all that it turned out to be an organization that was quite easily penetrated by the government's agents. They wondered whether its stated purposes were in fact its ultimate purposes, which is to say whether these might not be more sinister. They noted the sharp increase in interest in the Zionist idea among Russian Jews. The commander of gendarmerie in Livonia reported with alarm, not long after the movement's foundation, that 'the number of Zionists in Riga had reached 4,000. [And that] if account was taken of the fact that more than 24,000 Jews live in Riga and that of these 10,000 are men, it can be seen that the movement has drawn in [okhvatilo] almost half the [the city's Jewish] adult population and was steadily expanding [ono vse bolee rasprostranyaetsya]'.[139] This was a wild exaggeration, not uncharacteristic of Russian police reporting on Jewish matters,[140] but was bound to strike a nerve in St Petersburg. The authorities' deepest and most lasting objection was to what one senior policeman defined as the 'intensification of Jewish separatism [usilenie obosoblennosti evreev]'.

Still, there were countervailing considerations. Zionism did at any rate

---

[138] See Chapter 6.

[139] A. Lokshin, 'Formirovanie politiki (Tsarskaya administratsiya i sionizm v Rossii v kontse XIX—nachale XX v.)', Vestnik evreiskogo universiteta v Moskve, 1 (1992), 44 and passim.

[140] No absolutely firm and reliable figures for membership in the Zionist movement have survived. Such internal data as are available suggest at the turn of the century no single local association of Zionists ever accounted for more than about a fifth of local heads of families and that the common proportion in the Pale of Settlement and in Poland was one-twentieth or smaller. In the provinces of Kurland, Livonia, and Estonia there were at most 350 'shekel-holders'—i.e. paid-up members—constituting an estimated 10 per cent of 'bread-winning heads of families'. See J. Goldstein, 'Some Sociological Aspects of the Russian Zionist Movement at its Inception', JSS 47, 2 (Spring 1985), 168.

divert Jewish attention from much more dangerous internal revolutionary purposes. In most respects its members were law-abiding and respectable. And, the crowning feature in its favour, the movement was intent on promoting emigration. For some years, for all these reasons, the question what finally should be done about the Zionists, if anything at all, was left unresolved. Provincial governors who asked for instructions were given little more than a promise that a policy decision would be handed down, eventually. No attempt was made to destroy the movement or even seriously to restrain it. From time to time more rope than would normally have been expected was allowed it. In 1902 the police went so far as to permit a large, public conference of delegates representing the entire Russian branch of the Zionist movement to be held in Minsk (with representatives of the police present to watch the proceedings). Still, there was uncertainty. As Mandelstamm once put it, the fear lest Zionism in Russia be suddenly 'immobilized for years with a single stroke of a pen at the whim [*die Laune*] of some drunken bureaucrat in the Ministry of Finance or the Ministry of Interior'[141] was unending. And the wind did change after the Minsk conference and with it a first serious effort in St Petersburg to formulate a policy.

Doubts about the uses of Zionism from the regime's own point of view had arisen. As an organization encouraging emigration it did not, after all, seem to be as effective as might have been hoped. A special study of the movement prepared for internal consumption in the ministry concluded in the following year that if the conference at Minsk had achieved 'nothing of substance [*nichego sushchestvennogo dostignuta ne bylo*]' it had, none the less, been of 'tremendous propaganda significance for the Zionists as a demonstration before Russian Jews of the Government's toleration of the movement'.[142] But was such toleration wise? The authors of the report were unsure. Increasingly, it seemed to the police, Zionism, concerned in one way or another to encourage straightforward national sentiment, was performing a function that no Russian government could fail to regard as unwelcome. A nationalist Jewry was necessarily a politicized Jewry. That was certainly not a trend to be encouraged. The upshot was that a general crackdown on the movement was in the offing: heavier censorship, prohibition on the importation of Zionist literature, restrictions on the transfer of membership dues to the central office in Vienna, and a much heavier hand in the event of discovery of illicit meetings—in practice, therefore, virtually *all* meetings great and small, since all, in default of specific permission to hold them, were illicit. Leaked to the Zionists, these were measures that registered, as Mandelstamm for

---

[141] Mandelstamm to Herzl, Kiev, 13 June 1899, CZA, H VIII 541.
[142] Russia: Ministry of Interior, *Sionizm: istoricheskii ocherk ego razvitiya. Zapiska, sostavlennaya v departamente politsii* (St Petersburg, 1903), 143, CZA, K14a/13.

one feared, as quite possibly 'the beginning of the end'.[143] And such doubts as there were that hard times were in store for the Zionist movement, and for the Jews generally, were removed by further news that on 7 July 1903 the long-awaited general instruction on the matter of Zionism and the Jewish national movement had finally been circulated to all provincial governors and senior police commanders by the minister of the interior. The Zionists, it read in part, had evidently 'postponed to the distant future' their plan to promote Jewish emigration to Palestine and found an independent Jewish state. They were directing their efforts instead at

the development and strengthening of the Jewish national idea, advocating the uniting of the Jews in closed organizations in the places of their present habitation. This direction, given that it is inimical to the assimilation of the Jews into the other nationalities and that it aggravates ethnic dissension, runs counter to the bases of the Russian state idea and thus, for that reason, cannot be tolerated.[144]

The propagation of Zionist ideas, notably among the lower orders of the Jewish population, was therefore to be stopped, meetings and conferences were no longer to be allowed, local associations that showed signs of public activity were to be closed down, Zionist activists were not to be allowed to travel abroad on the movement's business, and the collection of funds was to be prohibited. Jewish institutions known to be connected in any way with the movement were to be put under surveillance. Candidates for rabbinical and lay office in the communities were to be vetted.

That it had been to persuade Plehve to rescind this order that Herzl left for Russia on 5 August 1903 was sufficiently widely known at the time in the movement as well as elsewhere for it to be reported in the London Jewish Chronicle almost immediately.[145] But, on arrival, as his second item of business, Herzl went on to ask for Russian political influence to be exerted in Constantinople on the movement's behalf as well. Remarkably, both requests were granted him, subject to the condition that his movement continue to want to 'create an independent state in Palestine' and to 'organize the emigration from Russia of a certain number of her subjects' so reducing the Jewish population of the country. To these aims, Plehve declared in a written memorandum handed to Herzl after authority to do so had been obtained from the Tsar, the Russian government itself was 'entirely favourable'. So long as the Zionists stuck to their original purposes they could count therefore on Russia's moral and material support. Russia was prepared to back the Zionist representatives in Constantinople ('protéger les mandataires sionistes près du gouvernement

---

[143] Letter to Herzl, 27 Oct. 1902, CZA, H VIII 541.
[144] Ministry of Interior, Police Department, Circular 6142, 24 June 1903 (OS). Text in Evreiskaya Starina, 7, 3–4 (1915), 412–14. Emphases in the original.
[145] 14 Aug. 1903.

ottoman'). And it would 'facilitate the work of the emigration societies' as well.[146]

That the Russian Autocracy should have issued an undertaking of this or of any other kind to a Jewish organization was without precedent, of course, and except in one respect out of character: all that was typical was the forthright brutality of mind which it reflected. But that was of small moment. Plehve's intentions were evidently serious. Herzl had reason to consider that to have obtained these undertakings from him was a triumph. The heat on the Russian branch of the movement had been lifted. Firm evidence of his continued loyalty to Zionism's central purposes in Palestine had been provided. However, by the time of his return from Russia and arrival in Basel for the Sixth Congress on 28 August tempers were running so high that the substance of the agreement between the two men was thought of little account, at any rate by the most vocal members of the rising opposition to him, almost all of whom were themselves from Russia. That he had travelled to Russia at the urging of the Russian branch of the movement and in response to their fear of heavier police persecution was ignored. What counted in their eyes was that he had treated with Plehve at all: an incomprehensible and morally flawed act and, in the context of internal Russian affairs, embarrassing to them as members, marginal or otherwise, of the class of Russia's enlightened. In the summer of 1903 none could know that nothing would come of Plehve's promise, partly because Russian diplomats in Constantinople disliked the idea of backing the Zionists, but chiefly because both he and Herzl would be dead before twelve months were out. Herzl died of heart disease on 3 July 1904. Plehve was assassinated by the Socialist Revolutionaries' 'fighting organization' a few weeks later on 28 July. New men with other ideas would take their place. In the meantime, it was less Plehve or the sins of the Autocracy or how the Zionists—and perhaps the Jews generally—were likely to fare in Russia if no state-approved *modus vivendi* was devised for them that engaged the Congress than Chamberlain's East Africa scheme. It had now been formally offered to the Zionists for their consideration. It was on this that all attention was now concentrated.

The questions to which the Congress had to form its answers boiled down to two. One was ostensibly practical: would acceptance of the British offer divert attention, energy, and people from the repeatedly reaffirmed, long-term goal of the Jews' return to their ancestral land? The other was conceptual and in a very loose sense philosophical: was it conceivable that a movement for Jewish national revival be associated with

---

[146] CZA, H VI/D4. Plehve's memorandum was published in the original French with a German translation in the movement's chief organ, *Die Welt* on 25 Aug. 1903, almost immediately upon Herzl's return from Russia, on the eve of the Zionists' Sixth Congress.

any territory other than that to which the Jews had repeatedly turned, and returned, and on which in various but clearly fundamental senses their destinies had always hinged?

The deeper origins and nature of the matter of the Jews and the ultimate place and role of the Jewish people in the world of nations had never been matters of great concern to Herzl and his school. It was *equality* with other nations that they wanted, not continued particularity. It was the current manifestations of the Jewish predicament that struck them hardest and had brought them to where they now stood. The pathos of the Jews' long and difficult history was to be regretted, not dwelt over. As for the future, the governing assumption of the Herzlians was that the Jews' independent state, once established, would correspond as a matter of course to that model of open, decent, secular, generous, and to some extent participatory parliamentary democracy to which, in a characteristic mixture of innocence and wishful thinking, they fancied that most major western European states subscribed or at least aspired. That a Jewish society and polity so conceived might in many ways be strange, alien, and because alien incomprehensible and disappointing to those who were most likely to wish, or need to enter it, had not seriously occurred to them. Herzl himself had outlined his views on the new Judaea in a shallow utopian novel about the 'Old-New Land' in which the Jewish state and its accompanying society were to rise. He seems never to have doubted, as his fiercest critics were happy to point out, that the Jewish society-to-be would be one in which the very language of the country was likely to be German or French or English, not, as others might think, obviously and necessarily Hebrew or Yiddish. And there were many other ways in which it did not seem to be in any seriously detectable sense Jewish. What Herzl did believe with all his heart was that the Jews should not only recognize the need for general improvement and *aggiornamento* in their mental and material condition, but have the confidence to strike out purposefully and coherently to achieve it. But in what direction? And with what likely results? His opponents wanted these questions answered, authoritatively. They themselves had no doubt what the correct answers should be, but, most fundamentally, whatever was done with an eye to the future had to be done with an eye—if, to be sure, a critical eye—on the past. There could be no question of tossing two, perhaps three thousand years of law, literature, customs, social norms, and the rest of the Jews' vast cultural baggage overboard. Else what of continuity? For if continuity were lost, what would be left of the purpose and sense of the entire exercise? On this formidable issue, of the degree to which the Jews' historic past in all its aspects could, but also should, eventually be brought to bear on the shaping of the autonomous society-to-be towards which all were striving, most Zionists had always tended to part company from Herzl. Not all admitted as much, even to themselves. For many years only a few had been so bold as to say so openly. But, finally, it was on these intermingled issues of the ways and means of moving towards the immense undertaking of auto-emancipation in daily practice, of what they should strive for, and of what they were likely to find were their goal ever attained, that the origins of the East Africa crisis and much else that would bedevil the Zionists from this time on (and the Bundists too in different ways) lay.

When the smoke had cleared, Herzl could be seen to have had his way, but only after a fashion. At his insistence, the Congress resolved that the uses of the African territory in question for Jewish settlement would be looked into and an expedition would be dispatched to Africa to that end. But there were two limiting provisos. Funds for the expedition would have to be found from other than the Organization's own regular resources; and only when the expedition's findings had been reported back to the Congress would a final decision on the matter be made. It was further laid down that whatever those findings might be and whatever was decided about the East Africa scheme itself, the Zionist movement's devotion to the Land of Israel as a matter of absolute and undeviating principle remained fundamental and unimpaired.

In the rows and wrangling that had led up to this resolution as well as in the internal debate that followed long after, the play of personal ambition was unmistakable. The presence and rising confidence of men who aimed at attaining power within and over the Organization for themselves began to be marked. This was not a negative development. Herzl himself could see in it, were he so minded (and there is some reason to think that he was indeed so minded), encouraging evidence of the growing solidity of the Zionist Organization as an effective and established political movement. But the reality was that much in the movement had changed, irreversibly. It had become evident that Herzl, Nordau, Zangwill, Mandelstamm, and others of his school would fail to carry the movement with them if, when the subject came up again at the next Congress, they insisted on the British offer being taken up. None of the arguments for acceptance made any real impression on the majority: neither that it was necessary to maintain the relationship with Great Britain that had so surprisingly developed, nor that a self-governing Jewish territory anywhere at all in the world should be valued for the precedents it would shatter and for the precedent it would establish. Even the most serious argument of all, that there would be a territory which Jews could enter freely *and* within which they could maintain their society intact, was not one that many in the ranks of the opposition were prepared to listen to. There had been a compromise. Herzl had not been defeated. But something of his prestige had been lost; and he had now to face at least the beginning of an organized, if still *ad hoc* opposition. To be sure, it was not one that was so inflexible in its purposes, so coherent in its membership,

or so confident of its strength as to decide that the movement could dispense with its leader. No one went so far as to claim Herzl's seat. His
sternest critics, Yeḥiel Tchlenov and Menaḥem Ussishkin, late of Ḥibbat
Ẕion, now leaders of the Russian wing of Zionism, were unwilling to
contemplate an effort to defeat him openly. Whether this was because
they recognized that there would be insufficient support for so drastic a
move or because they feared the damage such a shock would cause the
movement as a whole we shall never know. What they did seek actively
was to alter the direction he had taken. Herzl himself, for his part, had
learned both at the Congress itself and at the equally stormy meeting of
the Greater Actions Committee held in April of the following year that
even if he was assured of a parliamentary majority at the Congress his
opponents were people who had to be listened to and reckoned with if
the movement was to hold together. He could not have failed to note
that, while the majority of delegates at the Congress and, very likely, the
great majority of rank-and-file members of the movement as a whole
continued to support him and trusted him not only personally but with
particular reference to the East Africa scheme specifically, man for man
the social and political weight of those who opposed him was greater. In
their majority, the young, the educated, and the members of the higher
ranks in the movement opposed the scheme. When the roll-call vote was
held at the Congress they either opposed it openly or abstained.[147] So
while Herzl's leadership of Zionism was reconfirmed, cracks in its structure had appeared for all to see.

At his death the matter of East Africa was still technically unresolved.
In practice, as a scheme to which the World Zionist Organization was
prepared to pay serious attention (as opposed to marking time and saving
faces all round) it died with him. Joseph Chamberlain who had dreamed
it up retired from politics, desperately ill, in September 1903. The Foreign Office had never much liked the idea. The English settlers in East
Africa wanted the place for themselves and wished to see no Jews beside
them. At the Seventh Congress in 1905 the final, formal decision to
shelve what had come inaccurately and peculiarly to be called the
'Uganda' project was taken, but by then the British had lost all interest
anyway. The moment had come and gone. Greenberg, who had served
as the chief link with the British government, and Israel Zangwill and
Emmanuel Mandelstamm and others who had favoured it were furious.
They promptly led a segment of the membership out of the movement
and into a wholly distinct one that would be known as the Jewish Territorial Organization (ITO). Nordau remained in the WZO, relieved on

---

[147] For a detailed breakdown of the vote by age, occupation, standing in the movement,
and country of residence, see D. Vital, *Zionism: The Formative Years* (Oxford, 1982),
479–94.

the whole. He had supported Herzl in the latter's lifetime as best he could, but had always regarded the scheme sceptically. Tchlenov, Ussishkin, and many others of what might have been called—but never was—the Lilienblum wing of Zionism were triumphant.

Still, the Zionist movement emerged from its first great crisis in better health than might have been expected. Its new leaders would be of smaller calibre than its founder. When Max Nordau refused to follow Herzl as president, the Congress elected David Wolffsohn, originally from eastern Europe, but long established as a timber merchant in Cologne, a self-taught, self-made man of little imagination or political flair. But he was transparently honest and well intentioned, not without a certain earthy good sense, and, having been very close to Herzl and supportive of him from the beginning, trusted by the Herzlian school not to deviate too far from the late leader's policies. All told, a man for the interim, a man to mark time, to keep the ship afloat as the 'Territorialists' who had insisted on following the East Africa scheme through fell away and the membership dropped.[148] He did so. His one achievement, by no means negligible, was to put administrative order into the organization's machinery, moving its central office to his own home city of Cologne for convenience. However, for a movement of this nature to mark time was to decline. And under Otto Warburg (1859–1938), who succeeded Wolffsohn in 1911, the signals pointed frankly to retrogression. Warburg was a figure of a very different sort, anything but a self-made man, rather a member of a very proper and prominent German-Jewish family of bankers, a scientist of distinction and established academic status, uninterested and distrustful of political action, contemptuous of all that smacked of utopianism and irrational thought. It was to the affairs of the movement as they were before Herzl appeared on the scene to brush

---

[148] Precise figures for total membership of the movement have been available for most years of the movement's life because membership carried with it the all-important right to participate in the contested elections to the biannual Congresses and was contingent on a small fee being paid. The sum of all fees constituted the basic revenue of the movement and rigorous financial records were kept from the first. Total membership stood at 114,370 worldwide in 1899, it dropped slightly in 1901, more than doubled (232,645) in 1903 at the peak of Herzl's career, then fell again after Herzl's death to 137,071 in 1905. Thereafter, it climbed slowly back towards its 1903 peak, 217,231 members participating in the elections to the last Congress to be held before the war (the Eleventh Congress of Zionists held in Vienna in Sept. 1913). The majority of these 100,000–200,000 people were Russian subjects. Just how many can no longer be known. Records were not always kept for fear of the police, or if kept for a while were soon destroyed, or if not destroyed lost in the course of revolution and civil war. What the meticulous financial records kept at the central offices of the organization in Vienna, Cologne, and Berlin successively suggest, however, is that some 70 per cent of the Organization's total income from the *shekel* (the membership fee) originated in Russia. It is likely therefore that the average paid-up membership of the Russian branch of Zionism in the years 1903–7 stood at about 125,000 or at about 4 per cent of the empire's adult Jewish population. Cf. more detailed calculations in Vital, *Formative Years*, 412 n.

them aside that he, Warburg, was drawn: to the slow and careful implantation of Jewish agricultural settlements in Palestine, that is to say, to anything but activity that was at or near the central stage of international politics. Warburg too moved the movement's central office to a more convenient location, to Berlin in his case, so giving it, quite unintentionally, a German cachet that, while unwarranted in practice, was to be a source of some political difficulty to the Zionists in the years leading up to the outbreak of war in 1914 and beyond. But in any event, as intended by his supporters, Warburg's elevation to the presidency confirmed the supremacy of those who had distrusted Herzl and who, towards the end of his life, had begun to oppose him openly.

Caution, retrenchment, consolidation, and the preservation of what had already been achieved, especially on the ground in Palestine, now determined the order of the day, not flights of imagination and great daring and risky, but deliberately (or hopefully) spectacular political initiatives in the Herzlian style. The lower profile adopted owed much to the fact that there was now no one of decisive influence who insisted on a higher profile, no leader (as yet) who, in the course of his efforts to advance matters, was prepared, and to some extent able, to rely on his personal qualities and personal touch. Still, Herzl's disappearance from the scene and his replacement by lesser men does not entirely explain the flattening of the curve. A desire to know and understand where the movement was going had overtaken most members. Sobriety—both of thought and of action—was rated once again as a value, virtually a determining value. And it would be, above all, towards Palestine that thinking would now be directed. It would be to the *yishuv's* evolution, expansion, and development that the movement would devote its attention, directly, almost exclusively, as far as possible systematically, and with all such resources in manpower and money as it was able to mobilize. Herzl's contempt for 'infiltration', for the unending, surreptitious—and to his mind impermissibly undignified—effort to enter and settle Palestine in twos and threes in defiance, and more especially in circumvention, of the Turkish authorities on which Ḥibbat Ẓion had necessarily to depend, was forgotten.

What was lost in élan and for lack of a major personality at the helm of the movement in these years cannot easily be calculated. What was gained was the final consolidation of the democratic-parliamentary and bureaucratic order that Herzl himself had stood for, of which he was the progenitor, but with which, at the same time, he was temperamentally at odds. The affairs of the movement would be handled henceforth in a less autocratic and high-handed manner. Formal institutional proprieties would be more carefully respected than in Herzl's day. The Greater Actions Committee would come into its own as the movement's effective decision-making body. The business of the organization would be much more efficiently handled from Cologne and Berlin than ever it had been from Odessa or Warsaw or even Herzl's Vienna. The Zionists would be clearer in their minds as to what they were and were not about. The practical and technical (and, most notably, agricultural) sphere of activity in Palestine would be dealt with a good deal more systematically. But while, on the face of things, nothing in either the proclaimed purposes and programmes or the institutional structure of the Zionist Organization was changed so far as inner quality and spirit and final purposes were concerned, the World Zionist Organization from this point on until the outbreak of war in 1914 is best seen as Ḥibbat Zion revivified. Substantially, the central ethos would now be that which had obtained before the advent of the extraordinary man who had created it.

6
Crystallization

I

ONE cardinal respect in which something of the old world of unemancipated, unacculturated Jewry survived the great social changes undergone in the nineteenth century was the rule of mutual assistance: the fundamental operative principle on which the unity and integrity of Jewry in its entirety relied. It may never have been absolutely and in all circumstances operative. But it spoke, and it continued into the modern era to speak, to all Jews of certain common, rock-bottom interests, responsibilities, and obligations. It lay at the heart of the greater part of Jewish public business. It was the Archimedean point on which all calls for aid and co-operation and all efforts to respond to them turned: thus within particular communities, thus across communal and state boundaries as well. For actual force and effectiveness it depended partly on the sympathy—but perhaps more especially the empathy— which supplicants for assistance normally evoked. It depended equally on it being recognized as the incontestable moral obligation of all collectivities, institutions, and individuals in Jewry—notably, of course, but not exclusively, those perceived as well placed and fortunate—to render whatever aid and protection they could muster to the less fortunate, above all to those in immediate, evident distress.

In principle, the obligation to respond was a matter of private conscience. So far as the law of the land had it, it was, of course, distinctly voluntary—thus in normal circumstances, at any rate. In the real social context of Jewry, however, it was less a matter of choice and personal discretion than a firm duty: an obligation in no case to be shirked—perhaps to be finessed by some, but never totally avoided by anyone. It provided the salient, *public* measure of the virtue, decency, loyalty, and, of course, generosity—or otherwise—by which those to whom justifiable appeals had been made would be judged. In the rapidly changing circumstances of the modern age it came to be one of the most telling of the many indicators distinguishing those who were about to depart from Jewry, or had already departed from it, from those who still considered themselves, and wished others to consider them, members of their people in good and honourable standing.

However, where the fortunes of the Jews had altered most dramatically for the better and where, in consequence, charitable assistance was most likely to be available, there the forms in which it tended to be granted had undergone a change of structure. There was a growing preference in western and central Europe for channelling philanthropic assistance of all kinds through specialist institutions that operated on fixed budgets and according to established rules—more systematically, therefore, more rigorously in financial terms, and on a more depersonalized basis. None of this excluded individual initiative or more traditional methods. But the characteristic form in the new age was institutional. It was thus for local purposes, namely within particular communities, but also, with historically more important consequences, at the supra-communal and international level where it was the pioneering Alliance Israélite Universelle, founded in Paris in 1860, that set the form. The AIU model was adopted with some modifications by the analogous Anglo-Jewish Association in Great Britain, later by the Hilfsverein der Deutschen Juden in Germany, and by the Israelitische Allianz zu Wien in Austria. 'You are aware what considerations gave rise to the formation of our Association,' an officer of the Anglo-Jewish Association explained to a correspondent in the United States,

it was the conviction that we English Jews as a body did not sufficiently identify ourselves with the mass of our oppressed brethren in imperfectly civilized countries, that the feeling of oneness was not sufficiently intense among us and that we consequently lagged behind in the discharge of the sacred duties which brother owes to brother, although it must be admitted that this reproach could not be made against individual members of the Anglo-Jewish Community.[1]

Despite its title and despite the fact that the great majority of its members (some four-fifths of the worldwide total of about 13,000 in the early 1870s) were not nationals of France, the Alliance Israélite Universelle was never in any useful, operative sense *universal*. It was French. It did seek to enlist individual members in all of Europe (and in the United States as well). It was more than happy to agree to the establishment of local branches wherever it was feasible and politic to do so. But throughout its history it was French in spirit, in outlook, and in day-to-day management. Its president and senior officers were always French nationals. French Jews held the majority of seats on its central committee. The secretariat and office staff of the headquarters in Paris were local people. And while there was no abandoning of the original pretension to 'universality' it was the consistent effort of all concerned over many decades to maintain the French character and French orientation of the organization as a matter of the first order of importance. The collective mind of the AIU was therefore often divided. Its claim to a sort of primacy in

[1] Cited in Zosa Szajkowski, 'Conflicts in the Alliance Israélite Universelle and the Founding of the Anglo-Jewish Association, the Vienna Allianz and the Hilfsverein', *JSS* 19 (1957), 31 n. 4.

Jewish life in all matters that were conceived of as worldwide, more particularly all-European, led it, as a general rule, to refuse invitations to join other Jewish organizations in *joint* projects, protests, and initiatives. It opposed, for example, the convening of a conference on Romanian Jewry in Vienna in December 1902. It refused to take a full part in a conference in Berlin called in the wake of the pogrom in Kishinev in 1903. It rejected an invitation (tendered by the Zionists in this case) to attend a conference in Brussels early in 1906 to discuss the calamitous condition of Russian Jewry after the revolution the previous year.[2] It beat down attempts by its own local branches in other countries to assert a measure of genuine, even if not absolute, independence so far as it was able. And where the cause of hegemonic rule had evidently been lost, there the people of the Alliance were apt to prefer formal disengagement to co-operation between equals. The process of separation could be swift, simple, and relatively amicable. The claim of British Jews to independence was barely contested; and the deed done, the AIU and the new Anglo-Jewish Association, the AJA (founded in 1871) had no difficulty in co-operating thereafter either in the strictly philanthropic and charitable sphere or in respect of the more complex and delicate political matters that would arise and multiply, as we shall see, in the course of time.[3]

In contrast, relations between the German branch of the AIU and the Paris headquarters were soon marked by acrimony. The readily comprehensible desire of members of a substantially larger and on the whole less secularist, more religiously observant network of communities to play an equal, although perhaps not necessarily greater role than that played by French Jews led to argument, debate, and the exertion of pressures and counter-pressures over a considerable period. Personal vanity and ambition seem to have played a role and there can be no question but that relations between French and German Jews, here as in other connections, were further bedevilled by the intensity of the Franco-German political and military rivalry as it took shape after the humiliating defeat of the French in 1870. It was an early instance of an essentially strategic and diplomatic conflict at the supreme level of high international politics extending into the full range of economic, social and cultural, and even philanthropic activities wherever these were thought to touch, however marginally, however unnecessarily and absurdly, on the interests and prestige of the countries concerned. In such a climate of opinion citizens of either country—Jewish citizens among all others, naturally enough—

---

[2] Zosa Szajkowski, 'Jewish Diplomacy', *JSS* 22 (1960), 145–6; Paul A. Alsberg, 'Documents on the Brussels Conference of 1906', *Michael*, 2 (Tel Aviv, 1973), 145–53. On the Brussels conference specifically, see below, pp. 596–9.

[3] The Central Committee of the AIU eased the swallowing of the pill by resolving that the new Anglo-Jewish Association could be *deemed* to be the 'new central branch of the Alliance Israélite Universelle in England' (Szajkowski, 'Conflicts', 30).

assumed an obligation, almost as a matter of course, to do their mite to promote respective national purposes in any way possible and to resist whatever they perceived as an encroachment on their own national sphere by the recognized national rival. Proposals to move the AIU's headquarters from France to another country after the débâcle of 1870 were made and duly noted with great indignation in Paris, as were reports that Romanian Jews were being advised to look to Berlin as the new centre of Jewish influence.

But there were positive as well as negative reasons for all these institutions to seek to align themselves politically with their home countries. It accorded with their essentially conservative and peaceable character. It accorded equally well with their central purposes, namely the protection of weaker, less fortunate communities in Jewry and the enhancement—through education and technical training—of the capacity of the people concerned, notably the young among them, to cope with the stresses and disadvantages that were their lot. Protection was, of course, protection from the severe, often barbaric pressures exerted by the governments and societies under whose boot the Jews of eastern Europe and the Balkans were placed. In this sense, especially where Russia and Romania were concerned, the enterprise in which these otherwise apolitical institutions were engaged in was in fact socially reformist and improving; and therefore, not surprisingly, one which the Russian and Romanian governments regarded as impertinent, if not subversive, and in any event incompatible—as indeed it was—with the purposes and policies they themselves were intent on pursuing towards their Jewish subjects. But if the AIU and its analogues were socially reformist and on occasion militant in their activities, they were only so abroad: in no case was their reformism and militancy directed towards their own home state, society, and country. There it was their innate conservatism and social quietism that ruled.

The logic underlying this strict distinction was simple enough. Where Jews had been emancipated and (stated exceptions apart) enjoyed equitable treatment under law, and where government itself was rule bound rather than arbitrary, there there was no call, generally speaking, to press for change *on their own behalf*. And in the rare event of an intervention of one kind or another being judged necessary, its natural form would be that of a demand for common justice, not, as in the rapidly receding past, mercy or special privileges. By extension, where the effort was on behalf of a *foreign* community of Jews, there the goal was to induce the foreign government concerned to accept such rules, laws, and procedures as the home government had long since agreed to abide by and could be relied upon to continue doing so. Either way, therefore, it was on the western *status quo* that everything hinged. And that being the case, no move that might appear in any way to put the treatment of emancipated Jews in their home countries at risk could be contemplated. But while the spheres of activity the philanthropic institutions had particularly assigned to themselves were in the relatively distant regions where no transformation of the Jews' status on the western model had yet occurred—in eastern and south-eastern Europe, in the Near East, and in North Africa—none was inert politically. All were in one way or another subject to the close political and strategic attention of the western and central European powers themselves.

In the Balkans, the Near East, and in North Africa the continuing efforts by France and Germany to penetrate and extend their influence appeared to the leaders of both the Alliance and the Hilfsverein to work in their favour. The Alliance's particular pride and joy was the extensive school system it had built up with great care and assiduity in the major towns and cities of Algeria, Bulgaria, Egypt, Turkey-in-Europe, Mesopotamia, Morocco, Palestine, Persia, Syria, Tripolitania, Tunisia, and Turkey-in-Asia: 34 schools in 1880, 134 schools for a total of 40,000 pupils by 1907. There is no evidence that a positive interconnection between the good works they pursued on behalf of indigenous Jewish communities and the power politics pursued by the Second Napoleonic Empire and subsequently by the French Republic had been anticipated. But a coincidence of interests and purposes between France as an enlightened state and Jewry itself, in what the men of the Alliance did not doubt was *its* most enlightened and advanced state, was soon apparent to both sides. It was a source of particular satisfaction to the leaders of the AIU to feel that they were contributing to the consolidation of French positions and interests overseas and to know that their services were duly recognized by the relevant branches of French government and by a wider, but well-informed circle of men of influence as well. It was with high approval that the distinguished historian Anatole Leroy-Beaulieu pointed out in the *Revue des Deux Mondes* that the Alliance's schools were to be seen as the work of an eminently French institution, founded in France, 'née chez nous', whose headquarters were and had always been in Paris. Their schools, he wrote, were 'French schools where French was the language of instruction' and, he pointed out correctly,

That, indeed, was one of the reasons for the Alliance, in its rehabilitative work among the Jews of the Orient, not always encountering, as it seems, the foreign co-operation to which one would think it was entitled. The Jews of Germany and Austria-Hungary, those of the United States too, hold it against [the Alliance] that it gives pride of place to our language and so promotes our influence.[4]

That central European Jews would object to French as the common language of instruction in such schools was therefore inevitable. It was

----

[4] Anatole Leroy-Beaulieu, 'La Langue française et les révolutions de l'orient', *Revue des Deux Mondes*, 79 (15 Apr. 1909), 866–7.

equally inevitable that the Zionists, notably, would tend very strongly to object to the employment of both French and German—rather than Hebrew—in schools and higher educational institutions sponsored by the Alliance and the Hilfsverein in Palestine: for much of the language logic operated in the case of the Hilfsverein as well. One of the arguments the founders of the Hilfsverein had offered the Alliance by way of explaining, but also justifying, the final act of separation from the original parent body was that they wished 'as German Jews [to bring] the German language and German culture' to the Jews of the Near East.[5] They believed, and thought it would redound to their credit, that by encouraging the use of the German language among the Jews of eastern Europe and Asia they would be doing their part to promote German influence and commerce.[6] And they had the word of the German Foreign Ministry that it, for its part, approved heartily of what they were about and could assure the Hilfsverein of its backing.[7]

But it was not only the language of instruction in which these externally sponsored Jewish schools were run in the Balkans, the Near East, and North Africa that flagged them nationally for all to see—and, as the case might be, to object to. There was the somewhat trickier question of the actual curriculum and what can only be described as the general spirit in which the schools were run. These tended to provide even stronger and better-founded grounds for approval or criticism. Leroy-Beaulieu had no doubt that he was paying the Alliance a compliment when he observed of their schools, that 'Instruction is imbued with a truly modern spirit and great tolerance, so much so that the old rabbis and the old orthodox Jews are often inclined to view it with suspicion.'[8] But even quite moderate traditionalists in Germany, to say nothing of the largely secular Zionists in all parts, judged the curricula in the Alliance schools to be seriously lacking in authentic Jewish content and objected heatedly to what they did not doubt was the essentially non-Jewish spirit in which they were run. Protests were especially loud when Salomon Reinach, a particularly influential member of the AIU directorate, was elected vice-president. Reinach, well known for his *dreyfusard* credentials, was a member of the Institut and an eminent philologist, archaeologist, and student of ancient religions. Where Judaism was concerned he was known, however, to have made no bones in his scholarly writings about the mythological character of significant portions of the Bible and the small regard, if not contempt, in which he held the Talmud. For Jewish ritual he appears to have had no use at all. His public position on the question of

    [5] Szajkowski, 'Conflicts', 40.
    [6] Ibid. 47 n. 76.
    [7] Simon Dubnow, *Die neueste Geschichte des jüdischen Volkes*, x (Berlin, 1929), 488 n. 1.
    [8] Leroy-Beaulieu, 'La Langue française'.

education was that he wanted to see the Jews emancipated spiritually no less than legally and on a basis—there could be no other, in his view— that was essentially secular. He had no sympathy for any of the various attempts, that of the Zionists among others, to maintain the *national* identity and character of the Jewish people. The knowledge that within the inner circle of the Alliance Reinach was not alone in his views added further fuel to the endemic rivalry between the Alliance and mainstream German-Jewish opinion.[9] In contrast, no such happy—some were inclined to think dangerous—coincidence of state interests and Jewish charitable concerns may be discerned in the case of the Anglo-Jewish Association. There was little or no British effort at this time, at all events at the governmental level, to encourage the teaching and use of the English language in areas that were not directly under British political control or political influence. There was indeed nothing quite comparable to the heavy French insistence on French-style formal education even where the British did rule.

But, in any event, the really hard questions lay in the more decisive context of attempts to enlist the powers in the effort to extend western-style liberal government and the general rule of law eastwards and southwards. There were two questions. How strong was the intrinsic disposition of the major western or central European government in question—if, indeed, there was any such disposition at all—to attend to such charitable Jewish needs as had been brought to their attention either by the relevant philanthropic organization or, as might equally be the case, by especially influential Jewish individuals? And to what extent was the government in question likely to judge what was about to be asked of it as politically convenient? In neither respect, in the case of none of the relevant governments, is it easy to discern a consistent pattern. Broadly, the British tended to be somewhat readier than France, Germany, or Austria-Hungary at any rate to listen and consider—and, now and again, when especially pressed, actually to pursue—a purely humanitarian purpose. They did not always do so with energy, nor was it likely to be the case, where some action had been taken, that the governing motive was particular interest in matters Jewish. But then, apart from those aspects of the matter of the Jews that were prompted by their migration from east to west, no official in any of the chancelleries of Europe was likely to think of their affairs, when he thought of them at all, as meriting special attention anyway. What did incline the British government and more particularly the Foreign Office, as we have seen,[10] to pay some limited and

   [9] See for example A. S. Yahuda's strictures on the Alliance and on Reinach in particular, 30 May 1911, as reported by the Zionist Press Bureau, Cologne, 5 June 1911, CZA, Z 2/551.
   [10] See Chapter 3.

selective attention to requests by Jews who were British nationals that British influence in foreign capitals be applied to the mitigation of oppression of foreign Jews was the long-established, semi-philosophical principle that Britain was under a very general moral obligation to do what it could to promote justice and reduce blatant abuses of power whenever and wherever it was in a position to do so. In alternative terms, British statesmen, almost uniquely, were apt, all other things being equal, to be susceptible to the argument that foreign, no less than domestic, policy was not to be entirely disentangled from ethical considerations. Something of this sort had informed Gladstone's famous 1876 denunciation of Britain's then pro-Turkish political orientation. It had not been without precedent in modern British diplomatic history and something of the Gladstonian approach lingered on long after the great man had left the stage. To those who subscribed to such a view, intervention on behalf of persecuted Jews might be thought of as in a class with refusal to support Turkey against Russia because of the atrocities Turkish forces had committed in Bulgaria or, more likely, the long-standing British effort to put down the slave trade. When Lord Rothschild took it upon himself to ask the Foreign Office to do what it could to protect the Jews of Hamadan from an especially nasty bout of persecution in 1893, the British minister in Teheran was instructed to take up the matter with the Shah himself; and Rothschild was informed in due course, that

At an audience with the Shah . . . Sir F. Lascelles had taken the opportunity of expressing to His Majesty the regret with which he had heard that the persecution had not ceased and he added that he feared that a very bad impression would be created in England if it were allowed to continue.

The Shah said that the new Governor of Hamadan had not yet reached his post and had not therefore been able to execute the strict orders which His Majesty had given him on the subject, but His Majesty had no doubt that all complaints would cease as soon as the Governor arrived.

In a subsequent interview with the Sadr-Azam [Prime Minister], Sir Frank Lascelles pointed out to His Highness how unwise and short-sighted a policy it was of the Persian Government to outrage the feelings of the Jewish community throughout the world by action of this kind under the present circumstances of that Kingdom.

The Sadr-Azam replied that he entirely agreed in this view and he expressed the hope that in a short time the Jews of Hamadan would have no cause for complaint.[11]

But the obstacles facing appellants for London's favour in respect of Russia's Jews, as opposed to Persia's, were of a very different order of difficulty. For Russia was conceived, correctly, of course, as part of Christian Europe. It was culturally, if not, strictly speaking, geographically, a

---

[11] Foreign Office to Rothschild, 26 May 1893, BoD, C11/2/1.

good deal closer to home and generally more familiar territory than Persia. Besides, a Jewish cause in the Islamic world was one thing. A Jewish cause anywhere in Europe was another, and not one to be seen by anyone in England as quite so straightforward as, say, that of the Bulgarians of whom virtually nothing was known *except* that great numbers of them had been massacred and that they were Christians. Nor was a Jewish cause likely to be perceived in the strong, simple terms in which African slavery, for example, was regarded, namely as raising matters of absolute and overriding principle. And then, it was one thing to set the Royal Navy to harry Arab slavers in the Persian Gulf and along the east coast of Africa where it had a very free hand. It was quite another to try to induce the Tsar's ministers, let alone the Tsar himself, to alter long-established Russian policy in a sphere in which, manifestly, no ostensibly fraternal foreign government had any *locus standi*, let alone power, at all. The most that could be expected of an always reluctant British ambassador in St Petersburg was that he bring to the attention of his Russian colleagues the unfortunate impact measures taken against the Jews, pogroms among them, were having on *British* public opinion. The Russians could not be spoken to in the terms and tone easily adopted in the case of the Persians, nor could they be expected to respond in such mild language as the Shah and his minister would employ in conversation with the British envoy in Teheran. And what was true of the British in these respects applied with still greater force to the Germans, the Austrians, and the French, all of whom were even warier of undertaking humanitarian missions of this nature. Each of the continental states had its counter-vailing strategic and diplomatic considerations to bear in mind. None shared the peculiarly British disposition to intercalate, rather than compartmentalize, morality and foreign policy. Always and in all connections, they were more hard headed in defining the national interest and less apologetic about pursuing it once it had been satisfactorily defined.

For all these reasons, applications by Jewish philanthropists, both individual and institutional, to exert leverage on behalf of distressed Jews in any part of the world needed to be drawn up with great care and submitted apologetically and defensively. No suspicion of conflict of interest—the Jewish with the national—could be allowed. Always it would be assumed that the merest hint of incompatibility with the foreign purposes and policies of the home government sufficed to rule the venture out of court however authentically and transparently charitable the purposes of the appellants might be. The Jewish appellants' loyalty to the nation-state had repeatedly to be demonstrated. The best and safest general policy to pursue was therefore to limit one's own activities to such as could be shown to be likely to *reinforce* state policies, if only marginally; and, for the rest, to accept that where diplomatic considerations proper were especially complex and were likely to be perceived, reasonably or otherwise, as touching on national interests and the security of the state (as in the case of France's alliance with Russia), there distinctively Jewish concerns were best abandoned altogether. The practice of taking preliminary soundings in the relevant official quarters prior to embarking on a fresh initiative was therefore a common one. Preferred habits of work were private. Open, public action was very rarely contemplated and then only with reluctance, after much heart-searching, and where the benefits were judged substantial and the risks negligible. By the same token, attempts by outsiders to gain more or less regular access to government in London, Paris, or elsewhere independently of—and therefore necessarily in competition with—the established representatives of local Jewry were regarded with extreme displeasure and anxiety everywhere and so far as possible resisted. This helps to account for the instant hostility of the leaders of both the AIU and the AJA to almost everything Herzl, his followers, and his eventual successors were about. But it is worth noting that the roots of this somewhat eunuchoid approach to the contemporary problems and afflictions of Jewry ran deeper than a mere preference for making policy on one's own behind conveniently closed doors.

It followed that appeals by Jews to their own government, or indeed to any government or any non-Jewish body at all, on behalf of other, foreign Jews could be said to be founded on a contradiction. The principles relied upon were universal. The actual driving, underlying motive in all such cases was nothing if not particularist: a product—or manifestation—of just such historically ingrained common sentiments, concerns, and obligations as were widely known to typify Jews and did tend (among many other factors to be sure) to set them apart. Such sentiments and concerns could not be denied; nor was there any evident moral reason to do so. There was nothing politically or philosophically illegitimate about a plea for intervention on behalf of distant kinsmen. But the stronger the claim to undifferentiated membership in the national society to which one belonged by law and, increasingly, by culture, the greater the ambiguities of one's relationship with the kinsmen on whose behalf and for whose benefit one wishes to act. The founders of the Alliance Israélite Universelle sought to tackle the issue head-on in their opening manifesto (1860). Why, they asked, should such entirely humane and worthwhile social purposes as the organization intended to promote not be pursued on a truly *universal*, rather than an exclusively Jewish, basis? They went on to offer the following answer:

universal union is among our aspirations without any doubt; and we consider all men our brothers; but just as the family comes before strangers in the order of affection, so religion inspires and memory of common oppression fortifies a family sentiment that in the ordinary course of life surpasses others. . . . Finally, there is the decisive consideration for not going beyond the religious confraternity: all other important faiths are represented in the world by nations—embodied, that is to say, in governments that have a special interest and an official duty to represent and speak for them. Ours alone is without this important advantage; it corresponds neither to a state nor to a society nor again to a specific territory: it is no more than a rallying-cry for scattered individuals—the very people whom it is therefore essential to bring together.[12]

These matters were less acute in Britain and Germany. There was no real equivalent in either country to the formal, as it were philosophical insistence of the French on all citizens of France being Frenchmen—a proposition denied by many Frenchmen in practice, to be sure, but always available as a rebuff to the Jews when judged appropriate and, in any case, one that the Jews of France themselves held to be of supreme importance. In any event, as the will to identify with the host nation and the true social and cultural basis for doing so both grew, so too did an enduring ambivalence of approach to these matters of assistance and calls for intervention and a need to manœuvre between what were indeed two imperfectly compatible orders of public behaviour. In hard cases the effect was to sap the confidence of the appellants or to cause them to refrain altogether from appealing for support. In all cases, it led to the rule that appeals, if they were to be made, needed to be very carefully managed by especially skilled and experienced representatives. The eventual result, as we shall see, notably in the course of the First World War, would be to accelerate the entry into the diplomatic arena of spokesmen for Jewry who could speak for distinct Jewish interests without restraint and unencumbered by other, countervailing considerations and loyalties. In the shorter term there was a role left for intercession on the very much older, pre-emancipatory basis in which private and public concerns and capabilities were intermingled and the efficacy of the spokesmen for Jewry was a function of personal status and private connections. However, there were likely to be people who were only very distantly associated with one or other of the new philanthropic institutions, if at all, and who would in any case be unwilling to take guidance, people who were free to press the cause in question or abandon it at will, people who enjoyed the advantage of being answerable to no one, who risked none of the strains and perils of public responsibility, and who, above all, had no need to justify their position in public.

There would indeed be one last great, seemingly immensely promising occasion on which private and semi-private initiatives did indeed come into play in something like the old style of intercession (or *shtadlanut*). This was the culminating stage of the extended western effort finally to ensure the safety of the Jewish minority in Romania when all appeared to hinge on the ability of a handful of central and western European Jewish

---

[12] 'Manifeste de juillet 1860'. Text in André Chouraqui, *L'Alliance Israélite Universelle et la renaissance juive contemporaine* (Paris, 1965), Annexe no. 3, 411.

grandees to persuade the masters of the major European states to act upon the issue.

II

As Turkish suzerainty over Moldavia and Wallachia was reduced, so effective government in the Danubian Principalities fell into the hands of shifting combinations of Romanian landowners and members of the country's small urban professional and merchant class—to which, in 1866, there was added a royal house and court headed by a German prince drawn from the cadet branch of the Hohenzollern dynasty. Whatever other qualities this new governing elite may have had, it sought to distinguish itself by a particularly raw, mean-minded, and nervous nationalism: thus in their handling of most of their public affairs; thus, with added force and special venom, where those Jews who now had the misfortune to find themselves under their political control were concerned. The leaders of the newly united and autonomous Romanian principalities conducted themselves, it may be said, in a spirit and from an angle of vision that would be very common in Europe after the First World War, but which were still rare—and insufficiently understood—in the comparatively relaxed climate of the middle decades of the nineteenth century. The gist of the matter was that the Jews of Romania were now at their mercy and that it was soon evident that in fact little or no mercy would be shown them. They would, on the contrary, be the object of an unrelenting campaign of physical, legal, and economic pressure and incessant, uninhibited verbal vilification the like of which had no parallel anywhere else in Europe at that time. Pogroms, expulsions, and legal restrictions on residence, occupation, access to schooling, property rights, and other similar basic human needs all multiplied. In a narrow sense the condition of Romanian Jews in the 1860s and 1870s was analogous to that of their cousins in Russia and Poland twenty, thirty, and forty years later. There were important ways, however, in which it was worse and showed signs of likely further deterioration in the future.

All population figures for nineteenth-century Romania are questionable and often tendentious. Those for the Jews of the country are probably less reliable than others. It is likely, however, that the Jewish population in the 1870s was of the order of 250,000, some 7 per cent of the total; also that it was rising, partly through natural increase, partly due to immigration into Romania from Russia and Poland. In social structure the community was not unlike the Jewish population of Greater Poland: engaged preponderantly in small trade, innkeeping, and the minor crafts, a generally urban population, forming a substantial segment of the population of major towns and cities. Later (c.1900) figures show 40,000 Jews out of a total city population of 282,000 in Bucharest; 17,000 out of 32,000 in Botoşani; 12,000 out of 63,000 in Galatz (Galaţi); 40,000 out of 78,000 in Jassy (Iasi). Romanian Jewry was weaker than that of Russia and Poland in the higher professions as well as in the proportion of settled, modernist middle- and upper middle-class people among them; and it was notably lacking in influential centres of traditional rabbinical leadership.

But the crucial difference lay not so much in the size or quality of the communities as between the regimes to which they were subject. The Jews of Russia, as we have seen, were indeed second-class citizens of the empire. But they were citizens. Theirs were diminished rights—as were, for different reasons and in different respects, those of the peasants of Russia as well. But they were not without rights; and both in theory and in administrative practice their legal situation and their freedoms were superior to those of the peasants. The individual Russian Jew had many good reasons to distrust the authorities. But he did not have to assume that recourse to them or, for example, to the courts was necessarily and invariably useless or that the (undoubted) general hostility with which he was regarded meant that he was always and totally at the mercy of the meanest jack-in-office, drunken peasant, or politically excited student. The innumerable complexities of his condition hinged precisely, as we have seen, on there having been left to Russo-Polish Jews a certain small political and administrative space within which, despite the difficulties and the pain visited upon them in minor packets day by day and in major blows at increasingly frequent intervals, they were able, generally speaking, both as individuals and as a collectivity, to keep their societal ship afloat. In the 1860s, in the reign of Alexander II, that space had been—or at any rate was commonly reckoned to have been—in the process of enlargement. From the 1880s on, under Alexander III and Nicholas II, it would manifestly be in the process of being reduced. But no attempt (as yet) had been made to eliminate it altogether. The imperfections of the Russian Empire as a *Rechtsstaat* were plain enough and a source of embarrassment to most educated Russians both within the circle of government and outside it. What cannot be said of nineteenth-century Russia—particular and particularly nasty instances apart—was that it was lawless or that the procedures of its government were wholly arbitrary. Thus in general. Thus even in respect of its Jews. Romania was otherwise.

Contrary to Russian practice, let alone that of the central and western European states, the new rulers of Romania set out not only to deny Jews ordinary civic rights, but to place them outside the law of the country altogether and to subject them to a system of arbitrary and punitive rule. This in itself amounted to behaviour of a kind and to a degree that had been rare in any age, but which in modern times, in those parts of Europe that had been touched however slightly by the Enlightenment, were as yet unknown. But there was a more specific question than that of humane government and natural justice at issue. The publicly proclaimed policy of the newly autonomous rulers of Romania was in violation of the terms on which, by successive stages, the major, controlling powers of Europe had agreed to release them from Turkish rule and grant them political autonomy. The conference of representatives of the powers, which had gathered in Constantinople in 1856 to prepare the definitive Convention of Paris (1858) that was intended, among things, to impose a new order throughout the Balkans, had very solemnly laid down the principles on which the population of the Principalities would be governed: 'All the religions and those who profess them shall enjoy equal liberty and equal protection' (Article XIII); 'All Moldavians and Wallachians without exception shall be admissible to public employment' (Article XVI); 'All classes of the population, without any distinction of birth or religion, shall enjoy equality of civil rights and particularly of the right of property in every shape' (Article XVIII). Later, at the Paris Congress itself, at the urgent request of the Romanians, these rules were watered down somewhat, the Prince of Moldavia having pleaded the need to take account of the many unassimilated Jews in the Principalities. The principle of equality was 'excellent in itself', he assured the Congress. All he asked for was gradualism. The result was the definitive Article XLVI of the Convention of Paris (19 August 1858) which, in deference to this plea and on the strength of a promise of good intentions, laid down that

All Moldavians and Wallachians shall be equal in the eye of the law and with regard to taxation, and shall be equally admissible to public employments in both Principalities. Their individual liberty shall be guaranteed. No one can be detained, arrested, or prosecuted, but in conformity with the law. No one can be deprived of his property, unless legally, for causes of public interest, and on payment of indemnification.

The Convention then went on to distinguish between the civil (or civic) rights that were guaranteed to all absolutely on the one hand and political rights on the other. Moldavians and Wallachians of all Christian confessions would enjoy political rights. 'The enjoyment of these rights may be extended to other religions by legislative arrangements.'

This was a defeat for the Jews, although not, as things appeared at the time, a major one. The Romanians' obligation to grant *civic* rights was now absolute and beyond question; and they were *understood* to have undertaken to grant Jews political rights in the course of time as well. On neither of these two points was there any doubt in the relevant political circles abroad, namely in the major capitals of Europe. What was very soon apparent in Romania itself, however, was that besides having no intention of keeping their half-promise to grant Jews political rights, gradually and in the course of time, the reinvigorated Romanian authorities had no intention of granting the Jews civic rights either. The plain meaning of the Treaty of Paris and the undertakings accepted under its terms would from this point on be systematically circumvented by the absurdly simple expedient of declaring the Jews not to be 'Moldavians and Wallachians' (i.e. Romanians) at all. Previously, they had been classed as an alien but none the less indigenous people entitled, in principle, to apply for naturalization on an individual basis. In practice the process was designed to be long and difficult, so long and so difficult as to amount to a virtually insurmountable obstacle. In June 1866 even this dubious privilege was withdrawn. To the accompaniment of popular demonstrations and a pogrom in which Jews in Bucharest were molested, homes and businesses plundered, and the city's central synagogue put to the sack, the national parliament enacted Article VII of the country's new constitution. This laid down, now wholly unambiguously, that 'only foreigners of the Christian religion may obtain the status of a Romanian'.

The passing of Article VII signalled further re-energizing of the campaign of legal persecution and diminishment against the Jews. 'Gentlemen,' Ion Bratianu, minister of finance at the time and leader of the campaign, had declared in parliament after the passing of Article VII, 'the government has no intention of handing the country over to the Jews, nor of granting them rights which encroach upon or injure, however slightly, the interests of the Romanians;'[13] and Bratianu and his fellows were as good as their word. In September 1866 the government revived an older regulation under the terms of which *all* Jews, regardless of origin or condition, were formally defined as members of a vagabond race, rendering them legally subject to expulsion.[14] The right of fixed residence in the countryside was denied them. Local authorities were instructed to enforce the law against 'vagabondage' with all possible rigour. And when Bratianu, now minister of the interior, travelled up to Jassy some time later to supervise their work, he chose to mark his arrival by ordering the police to institute a razzia against the Jews. The police, Jewish communal leaders telegraphed to London, had already been engaged for some days

in taking up numbers of Jews in the streets, without any judicial proceedings, without distinction of age or condition . . . put[ting] them in irons, and with unheard-of brutality transport[ing] them in troops across the Danube. This sad spectacle, accompanied on the one hand by the derisive shouts of the population,

[13] Cited in Carol Iancu, 'Adolphe Crémieux, l'Alliance Israélite Universelle et les Juifs de Roumanie', *Revue d'Études Juives*, 133, 3–4 (1974), 487 n. 18.

[14] In 1877, in a notorious case concerning an Austrian Jew who had been denied the right to acquire a building in Jassy on the grounds that his status was in no way different from that of any other Jew, a Romanian court declared flatly that since 'Jews have no fatherland it follows that they do not properly belong to any State'.

and on the other by the cries of distress raised by the wives and children of our unhappy co-religionists, is repeated every instant in the streets of Jassy; and every day the state of things becomes more threatening.[15]

As the British consul in Jassy put it in a report to his superiors, the effect of Romanian public policy was 'neither more nor less' than to show 'bad characters among the Christian population' that Jews had been

excluded from the privileges of the Constitution and the laws which guarantee the safety of individuals in Roumania, and that they, as it were, may be treated as outlaws; and many such persons here have in consequence had meetings where they talk of pillaging, and even of massacring the Jews as just and allowable acts.[16]

There were other brutalities. In a series of nasty incidents in northern Moldavia in the summer of 1867 several hundred Jews were expelled from their villages. Some managed to bribe their way back. Others were successfully forced across the Danube at bayonet point. All were subject to great suffering. Some died. But again, what was clear to all, participants and observers alike, was that the true energizing source of the campaign was the ruling power in the state. The initiative in such cases came from above: 'The junior officials in charge [of these operations] do not in any way hide the fact', the French consul in Galatz reported to his superior in Bucharest 'that they are under orders to treat these wretched people without the slightest pity, as outlaws.'[17] And brutalities were backed up by a long series of discriminatory enactments. The legal profession was restricted to Romanians by birth or naturalization under the decree of 4 December 1864. By the decree of 25 October 1869 that of pharmacists was similarly restricted. By the law of 3 February 1868 tenders for public works were to be accepted only from persons possessing full civil rights. By the law of 3 February 1872 the manufacture and sale of tobacco was similarly restricted as was, by the law of 13 February 1873, with especially severe consequences for the country's many Jewish tavern-keepers, the retail sale of spirits.

No one doubted that the Principalities would be granted full independence before very long. It was plain therefore that if nothing were done for them the situation of the Jews would deteriorate further. However, as the actual accession of Romania to full sovereignty was in the gift of the powers some thought it might be possible to make it conditional on Jewish emancipation. When one of the grandees of English Jewry,

[15] Jewish community in Jassy to Sir Moses Montefiore, Sir F[rancis] Goldsmid, and Baron Rothschild, 23 May 1867, 'Correspondence respecting the Persecution of Jews in Moldavia', Parliamentary Papers (London, 1867), No. 1, 1.

[16] A. B. St Clair to J. Green (Bucharest), 29 May 1867, ibid., No. 9. encl. 1, 7.

[17] Archives du ministère des Affaires étrangères, Correspondance politique, Turquie, Galatz, 30 juillet 1867. Cited in Iancu, 'Adolphe Crémieux', 491 n. 31.

Sir Francis Goldsmid,[18] raised the matter of the persecution of Romanian Jewry in the House of Commons in 1868, the Foreign Secretary, Lord Stanley, was more than sympathetic.

I can assure the hon. Baronet that he cannot feel upon the subject more strongly than I do. I really think it is a question that concerns Christians even more than Jews, because if the suffering falls upon the Jew the disgrace falls upon the Christian. I know of no instance in our times of a series of oppressive acts committed so completely—I will not say merely without provocation, but so far as I can see, without any reasonable and intelligible motive whatsoever. In so far as these acts were connived at, or encouraged by the local officials, or, as I fear must have been the case, in some instances by the Roumanian Government itself, I can only explain that connivance or encouragement by the tendency of a weak, and not very scrupulous, Government, to trade upon the worst popular passions.[19]

The auguries were good, therefore, and the internal force driving western notables to pursue the issue was a powerful one. European Jewry was now quite sharply divided between those who lived under relatively liberal regimes in the west and those who lived under notoriously oppressive ones in the east. The prospect of the eastern system being extended westwards in a particularly evil form, under joint Russian *and* western auspices—as would necessarily be the case if the powers granted Romanian independence—was therefore doubly intolerable. And side by side with the standing moral argument for action, there was yet another practical one to be evoked as well. Severe persecution as practised in Romania and the denial of civil rights as a matter of national legal principle on the odious grounds that the Jews were an inherently 'vagabond' race could, in the long run, mean one of two things. They would be hammered totally into the ground or forced to emigrate. Emigration would indeed soon become a marked feature of Romanian Jewry, gathering force steadily in the last quarter of the nineteenth century and the first decade of the twentieth. But the first signs of a migratory stream forming had already appeared in the 1860s and the question how likely it was to grow along with the more painful and awkward one whether it should and could be forestalled or, on the contrary, encouraged were already much in the minds of all concerned. In general, those who presumed to speak either for western or Romanian Jewries opposed it. The only proponent of emigration of any note was an American Jew, Benjamin Franklin Peixotto, who, unusually for his place and times, had an absorbing interest in worldwide Jewish affairs. Through the intermediary

[18] The first Jew to be admitted to the English bar, subsequently the first to be appointed Queen's Counsel (1858). His father, Isaac Lyon Goldsmid, a financier and philanthropist who played a prominent part in the founding of University College, London, was the first Jew to be made a baronet (in 1841, five years before Moses Montefiore).

[19] Quoted by Goldsmid in the House of Commons, 19 Apr. 1872, Hansard, 3rd series, ccx (1872), col. 1588.

of the California banker Abraham Seligman and the latter's East Coast contacts, Peixotto had managed to persuade President Grant to appoint him unpaid consul of the United States in Bucharest. And on the agreed and declared purpose that he was to hold a watching brief for the Romanian Jews and to do whatever was possible on the ground to protect and succour them in practice, several fellow American Jews had agreed to support him financially while he held that office and pursued that end. Peixotto served in Bucharest for all of five years (1871–6) and in at least one respect was highly successful. His semi-diplomatic status in still less-than-sovereign Romania allowed him both to investigate specific events fairly freely and, through the consular corps of which he was of course a member, to call attention both abroad and in Romania itself at the heart of the government in Bucharest to specific acts of persecution and miscarriage of justice. A notable instance was his diligent investigation and exposure (with the help of most of the rest of the Bucharest consular corps) of events in Ismail, a town close to the Russian border, on 24 January 1872, in which an especially ferocious pogrom had been followed by police brutalities, false imprisonment of Jews, and further pogroms in neighbouring localities.

The Romanian Jews themselves were divided, however, in their attitude to Peixotto, his purposes, and the way he went about trying to realize them. The lower orders were grateful to him, as were, of course, local worthies whom, by badgering the authorities, he had freed from prison and from the prospect of worse to follow. But those in the community who were relatively well placed—a very small segment of the whole, to be sure—were frightened by his bull-in-a-china-shop tactics; and the more he irritated the Romanian authorities by digging into their affairs and diligently making them public, the more agitated the Jewish notables of Romania itself became. The solution to the problem of Romanian Jewry that he had rapidly arrived at and did not hesitate to make public, namely that much the best thing for them would be to leave the country altogether, infuriated them. And the fact that Peixotto, for his part, made little secret of his contempt for them added further fuel to the quarrel. Assured that there were charitable organizations in the United States that were prepared to facilitate their evacuation, Peixotto addressed his views on the indispensability of mass emigration to the public in general, to the leaders of the Alliance, and on at least one occasion to the Romanian authorities directly. This was entirely intolerable: those among them who still hoped for the best in Romania knew that while the Romanian nationalists would be happy to see the last of them, it was the nationalists' practice to proclaim that in the possibility that some or all of the Jews had it in mind to leave lay more than sufficient justification for mistreating them. 'If the Jews emigrate, [it was argued in the national press] why that is because they are not patriotic and therefore do not merit equality of

rights; if they do not emigrate, that is the best proof that they are not persecuted and that all the accusations in the international press are therefore
false and mendacious.'[20] But Peixotto's views for a solution to the problem of Romania's Jewry, as opposed to treatment of it *in situ* was no more
acceptable to the notables of western Jewry, those of Germany in particular. His proposals were taken up when leading figures from Austria, Belgium, France, Germany, Great Britain, and the Netherlands, as well as
Romania itself and, unusually, the United States as well in the person of
an American-Jewish banker resident in London and Peixotto himself,
gathered in Brussels at the end of October 1872 to concert Jewish forces
on the matter of Romanian Jewry. But all those present, other than
Peixotto himself and one of the Romanian delegates, gave them short
shrift—on grounds, it may be said, that were not materially different from
those on which Romanian nationalists themselves liked to rely:

The conference unanimously rejects all thought of emigration from the soil of
Romania. Such thinking is in any event regarded as criminal [*sic*] by the Jews of
Romania whose devotion to their country was splendidly in evidence in the
course of the conference deliberations; the conference affirms that any such decision would amount to the casting of an aspersion on the justice of the Romanian
Christians to whom their brothers, the Romanian Jews, owe their support in the
effort to secure and consolidate the destiny of their common fatherland.[21]

The operative decisions actually taken at Brussels were of a less contentious nature. A permanent executive committee briefed to promote
the social welfare of Romanian Jews would be established at Vienna.
Representatives of the Romanian Jews would submit a petition to their
own parliament in which the demand for equal civil and political rights
would be clearly stated, phrased however in the local and humble terms
that were thought to have a better chance of acceptance than foreign and
peremptory language. In the event, style proved irrelevant. A form of
petition to the Romanian parliament was indeed drawn up later in the
year and, after some time, published. But on a Jewish delegation to the
prime minister being told plainly that they could be sure that no notice
would be taken of it, the petitioners refrained from submitting it and the
westerners, for their part, reverted to attempts to apply pressure from
without.

Meanwhile, anti-Jewish legislation piled up. Every effort to seal apparent loopholes in existing laws and regulations was made. In 1874, for
example, it was discovered that while Jews were clearly barred from

---

[20] *Românul* (organ of the Liberal party), 7/8 Aug. 1878. Cited in Carol Iancu, 'Benjamin Franklin Peixotto, l'Alliance Israélite Universelle et les Juifs de Roumanie. Correspondance inédite (1871–1876)', *Revue d'Études Juives*, 137, 1–2 (1978), 92.

[21] Bulletin AIU, 2ème semestre, 1872, p. 56. Cited in Iancu, 'Benjamin Franklin
Peixotto, etc.', 95.

national elections it appeared, anomalously, that the law as it stood did
not entirely exclude them from municipal elections. The electoral law
was then revised. It was laid down that Jews might not take part unless and
until they had satisfied a number of specific (effectively insurmountable)
conditions, among them service in the army in at least non-commissioned
rank, 'regular' studies at a lycée or university, and, quaintly, to have shown
evidence of 'Romanian morals and feelings'.[22] On the other hand, the
prospects of an eventual rescue by intervention from without continued
to appear to be uncommonly favourable. Romania, as yet, was in no formal
sense an independent state. It remained a supplicant for acceptance and
recognition—a difficult, proud, and irritable one, no doubt, but a supplicant
none the less, its affairs and ultimate destiny still firmly in the hands of
'Europe', which is to say, Europe's principal powers. The temptation to
consider its leaders to be vulnerable to external pressure was therefore a
natural one. When a greatly agitated Adolphe Crémieux, now the grand
old man of western European Jewry, turned to Napoleon III in 1867 to
protest against their conduct he was assured that 'this oppression can
neither be tolerated nor understood. I intend to show that to the Prince
[Charles].' As good as his word, the emperor telegraphed a reprimand to
Bucharest, marginally softened by the ironic conclusion that 'I cannot
believe that Your Highness's government authorises measures so incompatible with humanity and civilization'.[23] The Hohenzollern prince,
only recently installed as ruler of the country, still sufficiently uncertain
of his status and throne not to be embarrassed by the image Romania and
he himself might be presenting to 'Europe', took action. Bratianu was
made to resign. Émile Picot, one of the prince's private secretaries, was
sent to Paris to meet the directors of the AIU in person (on 22 July 1867)
and give them as good an account of the government's position as he
was able. Crémieux presiding, the meeting passed off civilly enough
although, as Picot's assurances of the good intentions of the Romanian
government failed to correspond to what the AIU knew of the true conditions on the ground in Romania itself, the effort to mollify the Parisian
notables failed. Crémieux then addressed himself directly to Prince
Charles. Hardly less than imperious, his language speaks volumes both
for the mounting indignation with which the condition of Romanian
Jewry had come to be regarded by leading members of the western
European Jewish communities and for the historically unprecedented
self-assurance with which many of them now approached their public
duty. 'The moment has come, Prince,' Crémieux wrote, 'to employ
[your] legitimate authority and break off this odious course of events.'

[22] Isidore Loeb, *La Situation des Israélites en Turquie, en Serbie et en Roumanie* (Paris, 1877), 203.
[23] Cited in Iancu, 'Adolphe Crémieux', 488–9.

Bratianu should be dismissed 'absolutely'. The savage measures taken against the Jews should be annulled. The unfortunates who had been torn violently from their homes must be allowed to return. For the rest,

Inform [the country] that nothing will be neglected to erase the traces of this evil, pursue without respite the newspapers that have for the past year continually engaged in incitement to hatred, contempt, assassination, and expulsion of the Jews, dismiss all the cowardly officials who have lent a violent hand to this dreadful persecution and deal energetically with all violence directed at the Jews from this time on.[24]

One may assume that this made unpleasant reading for Prince Charles, but it remained without real effect. Bratianu was not dismissed 'absolutely'. He was, on the contrary, given a new post. The press was not restrained. Officials engaged in active persecution of Jews were not removed from office. And after 1870 and the plummeting of French prestige, Émile Picot, a Frenchman, was out of favour in Bucharest anyway and the channel he had opened to western Jewry collapsed—as, of course, did the political weight ascribed in Bucharest to the AIU itself.

The two real questions facing the western notables were therefore how firmly would the Romanians seek to resist such pressure as might be applied to them; and how insistently and for how long were the powers, for their part, likely to uphold Jewish claims to equitable treatment. The answer to the first question was unknown; the likely bearing of the answer to the second question upon it was largely disregarded. In the event, the determination of the Romanians to have their own way in the matter of the Jews turned out to be very much greater than outsiders, Jews and others, had commonly assumed. As for the answer to the second question, while, on the evidence initially available, it appeared to be that the powers would be uncompromising, it too turned out to be mistaken.

In the circumstances, these were venial errors. The crisis of Romanian Jewry peaked at a moment in the history of European Jewry when the governments of the major states of western and central Europe had proclaimed themselves to be sympathetic at any rate to the Jews' formal claim to equality. It was a moment, moreover, when these same governments appeared to be in a unique position to have their way with the Romanians were that their wish. As the affair moved to its climax at the Congress of Berlin in the summer of 1878 where, among other things, full recognition of Romania as an independent state was finally to be decided upon, the response of the great men of Europe to the protests addressed to them and to the pleas that they insist on the Romanians acting in good faith were almost invariably encouraging. The main contentions of the

---

[24] Iancu, 'Adolphe Crémieux', 490 n. 30.

Alliance and the other Jewish bodies were accepted without demur: the broken promises, the steady deterioration in the Jews' condition since the conclusion of the Treaty of Paris, the conversion of the Jews from unenfranchised Moldavians and Wallachians into total aliens and outcasts, and their subjection to endless and innumerable acts of malicious and barbaric persecution, and the rest. No one regarded the central demand that equal political and civil rights for the Jews be explicitly provided for in the Romanian constitution as in any way egregious or unreasonable. Gerson von Bleichröder who, by virtue of his close relationship with Bismarck, had now moved to the centre of the Jewish stage in this connection, did not doubt at all that 'if Romania and Serbia ask for independence they will find that they have to accept the conditions that Europe is in a position to impose upon them'.[25] The unusually unequivocal (but characteristically heightened) language of the memorial which the AIU submitted to the Congress on the eve of its opening is equally suggestive of confidence that, at long last, something would be done:

> In the name of the Jews of all countries, we respectfully address ourselves to Europe on behalf of our wretched co-religionists. It is [Europe] that we expect to bring their suffering to an end. . . . Let Europe make its powerful voice heard, let it proclaim the equality of men independently of all religious belief, let it demand the inclusion of this principle in the Constitution; and finally let it become the vigilant watchman [of that Constitution].[26]

But the sheer staying power and general bloody-mindedness of a national movement on the eve of achievement and in its immediate aftermath were still imperfectly understood and woefully underrated.

Of course, Jewish representatives were in no sense participants or accredited observers at the Congress. There was no question of their being invited to outline their case before the Congress in person. They had to be content with such opportunities as were available to them to publish their views and to lobby the participants either directly or through such intermediaries as Jewish members of the Austro-Hungarian and German parliaments, for example. This had chiefly to be done before the Congress actually assembled in Berlin on 13 June 1878, only to a limited extent while it was in progress. But this was the tail-end of a long-drawn-out and to some extent steadily maturing campaign that had begun in earnest a year and a half earlier when some sixty-five delegates from the principal Jewish organizations assembled in Paris to consider their strategy and tactics.

Initially, it had gone well. Austria-Hungary, France, Germany, and

---

[25] Bleichröder to the Central Committee of the AIU, 21 Feb. 1878. Cited in Carol Iancu, *Les Juifs en Roumanie (1866–1919): de l'exclusion à l'émancipation* (Aix-en-Provence, 1978), 155.

[26] 9 June 1878. Text in AIU, *Bulletin mensuel*, 6, v, 2878, pp. 84–9.

Great Britain all committed themselves—admittedly, in varying degrees of firmness of language—to look kindly at the Jewish claim. Germany, the leading power at this juncture, had done so repeatedly and, as long before the Congress actually assembled or been seriously planned as January 1877, the State Secretary (Bülow) at the German Foreign Ministry assured a German-Jewish delegation of the fact in writing.[27] For his part, the French ambassador in Berlin, Count de St Vallier, had assured Crémieux that 'so far as I am concerned, if the Congress assembles and I am called upon to take part, I shall consider it my duty in justice and humanity to search for means of improving the lot of the Jews of the Orient according to the old and generous traditions of French policy'.[28] Andrássy, the Austro-Hungarian Foreign Minister and Hungarian Prime Minister, Disraeli (now Lord Beaconsfield), Lord Odo Russell, the British ambassador in Berlin, and Count de Launay, the Italian ambassador, had all expressed themselves in roughly similar terms as well.

At the Congress itself, presiding, and much the most influential of the assembled statesmen, was Bismarck. Publicly, he tended to keep his distance from the issue of Romanian Jewry. In private, however, he made no secret of his interest which derived partly—but probably no more than marginally—from his general, on the whole not unenlightened outlook on the question of civil and political rights; and partly from an acquired, positive dislike of the Romanians. It owed something too to the heavy pressure exerted upon him by his banker and close adviser Bleichröder to whom he had long been under an obligation to act. It owed most, as Professor Fritz Stern has shown with great clarity,[29] to Bismarck having found it a useful weapon with which to bring the Romanians to heel on quite other counts, notably that of the heavy and financially disastrous involvement of some of his own social and political peers and allies in a long-standing, exceedingly sordid Romanian railway-construction venture. But it was Bleichröder again, at Bismarck's particular insistence, who had undertaken, at much trouble and great expense to himself, to try to save something from the wreckage, who rounded out the circle of interconnected German-Romanian-Jewish interests. Bismarck's lofty view of the affair in *all* its aspects was probably best reflected in what he

---

[27] Bülow to Kristeller and Goldschmidt, 7 Jan. 1977. Cited in N. M. Gelber, 'The Intervention of German Jews at the Berlin Congress 1878', *LBIYB* 5 (London, 1960), 227. A year later Bülow repeated these assurances, informing representatives of the Berlin Jewish Community that Germany would support any effort to obtain 'for the members of any religious persuasion in the countries concerned the same liberties as those to which they were constitutionally entitled in Germany' (ibid. 229).

[28] St Vallier to Crémieux, 27 Mar. 1878. Cited in Iancu, *Les Juifs en Roumanie*, 157.

[29] See the superb analysis of Bismarck's and Bleichröder's intertwined, but by no means common purposes in respect of Romania in general and the Jews of Romania in particular in Fritz Stern, *Gold and Iron: Bismarck, Bleichröder, and the Building of the German Empire* (New York, 1979), especially 351–93.

told St Vallier when it was all over. The Romanians were 'crooks and savages', but 'one fine day, two [German] dukes, one general who is aide-de-camp [to the Emperor], a half-dozen ladies in waiting, twice that many chamberlains, a hundred coffee-house owners and all the cabmen of Berlin found themselves totally ruined'. Clearly, something had to be done for them. For the rest, it was a convenient opportunity to help the Jews 'whom I need to coddle, win over, and who can be very useful to me in Germany and whom I like to pay in Rumanian money; don't you call that funny money?'[30]

The sum of this was that, on the face of things, the Romanians had cause to be concerned. In July 1877 their foreign minister, Mihail Kogalniceanu, sought to deflect Jewish pressure by assuring representatives of the Vienna Allianz that equal rights would be granted to all Jews who agreed to be naturalized and had acquired the Romanian language. In practice, no actual steps facilitating naturalization were taken, and the promise of more equitable treatment was simply repeated from time to time in one watered-down or plainly deceptive form or another, laced increasingly with warnings to the Jews that, by seeking to involve the Berlin Congress in what was a purely internal matter, they were committing a dangerous error. Late in June 1878, as the Congress was sitting, Kogalniceanu told a Jewish deputation in Budapest that 'We are aware that you are agitating abroad, in fact through Herr Bleichröder. You are gravely mistaken, however, if you believe that foreign intervention can force us to give you equal rights. We are independent and masters in our own house.'[31] This was understood as a threat, as it was so intended, and an attempt by the leaders of Romanian Jewry to dissociate themselves from the westerners' effort to intercede on their behalf followed. The westerners themselves, smelling victory, saw no reason to change their tactics although a closer look at the actual record of the conduct of the European Powers would have shown that the signs of a favourable outcome were not as conclusive as they judged them. For all their growing sophistication, the leaders of western and central European Jewry failed to pay due attention to the universal urge of diplomats, high and low and of all nations, to tidy up their desks, simplify their agendas, and, whenever possible, reset such items as still remained to be dealt with in a fresh and more convenient order of compelling political priority. It had been a major talking-point of Jewish spokesmen, for example, that whatever might be thought or said of Romanian treatment of *indigenous* Jews, there ought to be no question at all of the major states of Europe agreeing to their own nationals being so treated. France and Great Britain proved firm on this score; others less so. A commercial agreement concluded between Austria-Hungary and Romania in June 1875 had recognized

---

[30] Cited ibid. 383 and n.   [31] Gelber, 'Intervention', 228, 240, 243.

the Romanians' right to apply their anti-Jewish laws and regulations to resident Austrian and Hungarian Jews (despite the fact that Austria-Hungary itself was one of the guarantors of the Treaty of Paris). In March 1878 the Italian government approved a trade agreement with Romania in which the rights of Italian Jews were simply ignored.[32]

Still, at the Congress itself things went well. Conveniently, questions relating to Bulgaria, Serbia, and Romania were taken up in that order. A French proposal that equality of creeds should prevail in the new state of Bulgaria was accepted without excessive argument. Serbia was a more difficult case, however. When, on 28 June, it was proposed that the condition laid on Bulgaria be laid on Serbia as well, the Russians objected. The Russian Foreign Minister, Prince A. M. Gorchakov, conceded that no one would consider denying political and civil rights to the Jews of Berlin, Paris, London, or Vienna. But western Jews, he argued, should not be confused with the Jews of Serbia, Romania, and some of the Russian provinces. In those lands they were 'a real scourge to the native populations'. Bismarck responded with a dig at the Russians by observing that 'it might be [more] to the purpose to attribute the lamentable condition of the Jews to the restrictions placed upon their civil and political rights'. Rather more solemnly, the French Foreign Minister, Waddington, said that he considered it important to seize the opportunity

to procure an affirmation by the Representatives of Europe of the principles of religious liberty. . . . Servia, which demands to enter into the European family upon the same footing as the other States, should in the first place acknowledge the principles which form the basis of social organisation in all the States of Europe, and accept them as a necessary condition of the favour she solicits.[33]

When, despite outraged Russian's objections, the western and central Europeans had their way and Serbia's admission to diplomatic parity as a sovereign state was made conditional on equal rights for its Jewish population, the way to dealing with Romania on a similar basis seemed clear. Doubts did arise when the Romanian delegates, Bratianu and Kogalniceanu, were allowed, again despite strenuous Russian objections, to present their case before the plenum—a case which, among other things, comprised a claim to Bessarabia—doubts arose. But these dissipated when it became clear that this had been intended as no more than a diplomatic kindness to the Romanians: the greater part of the province having been annexed by Russia there was no question whatever of the Congress considering its incorporation into the new Romania. Still, the Russian hand had been weakened somewhat and when the matter of the Jews of

[32] Gelber, 'Intervention', 232 n. 33.
[33] Congress of Berlin, Protocol No. 8, Sitting of 28 June 1878, House of Commons Parliamentary Papers, 1878, vol. lxxxiii, p. 120.

Romania came up, it was the French foreign minister once again who struck the decisive note. Romania should be granted independence on the same basis as Serbia, Waddington said. There were, to be sure, 'local difficulties', but it was

better not to depart from the grand rule of the equality of rights and freedom of worship. It would be difficult, moreover, for the Roumanian Government to reject within its territory, the principle admitted by Turkey for its subjects. [He, Waddington] thinks that there can be no possible doubt that Roumania, in demanding an entrance into the great European family, ought to accept the obligations and even the drawbacks of the position, the benefit of which she claims. . . . As for the local difficulties . . . they will be more easily surmounted when those principles shall have been recognized by Roumania, and when the Jewish race shall have learnt that it has nothing to hope for but from its own efforts and from the union of its interests with those of the indigenous populations.[34]

Bismarck supported the French, as did Disraeli who added that he 'could not suppose for a moment that the Congress would recognise the independence of Roumania apart from this condition'.[35] The Austrian and Italian plenipotentiaries agreed. Outnumbered, the Russians withdrew their objections and it was laid down that the independence of Romania would indeed be recognized on the same terms as that of Bulgaria and Serbia, namely equality of treatment for members of all religious creeds. All that remained was to formulate what would be Article XLIV of the Treaty, as follows:

In Roumania the difference of religious creeds and confessions shall not be alleged against any person as a ground for exclusion or incapacity in matters relating to the enjoyment of civil and political rights, admission to public employments, functions and honours, or the exercise of various professions and industries in any locality whatsoever.

The freedom and outward exercise of all forms of worship shall be assured to all persons belonging to the Roumanian State, as well as to foreigners, and no hindrance shall be offered either to the hierarchical organisation of the different communions, or to their relations with their spiritual chiefs.

The subjects and citizens of all the Powers, traders or others, shall be treated in Roumania, without distinction of creed, on a footing of perfect equality.

This was acceptable to most participants, but not to all. When it was pointed out by a member of the drafting committee that the text still left the question of the *nationality* of the Jews dangerously open, an Italian delegate, Count de Launay, proposed that the Article be strengthened by the insertion of an additional clause that laid down an explicit rule that the Jews of Romania who had no other nationality would acquire

Romanian nationality as a matter of right (*de plein droit*). But, with Bismarck now in the van, the Congress turned the Italian proposal down, arguing, not wholly unreasonably, that Article XLIV as it was drafted established the principle of equality of civil and political rights with adequate rigour and answered to the purpose the Congress had in mind. The delegates moved equally by the knowledge that the Romanians objected violently to the obligations already laid upon them and that it might be unwise to push them too far and make their humiliation complete. And then, in general, those among the participants who may fairly be described as men of good will judged the wording of Article XLIV in the form incorporated into the Treaty as more than sufficient. 'Defending . . . the Jewish cause at the Congress we have defended the cause of justice, humanity, and civilisation' the French ambassador wrote to the Secretary of State at the Vatican.[36] As for those in Jewry who had worked so long and hard to achieve this very end, the temptation to see it as marking the final coming together of modern, liberal, and not ungenerous Europe on the one hand and Europe's various Jewries on the other was irresistible. Bleichröder, on whom all had come increasingly to rely and who was justly considered to have done more than anyone to pull it off, was in all eyes, not least his own, the hero of the day. In Romania itself, whatever reservations there may have been previously, joy, initially, was boundless. 'Hallelujah!' a group of Jewish notables telegraphed Crémieux from Bucharest. 'We are free. God be praised! Glory to you, noble and illustrious champions of our cause, glory to the Alliance!'[37]

Indeed, it was hard not to regard this by-product of the Congress of Berlin as a famous victory. Nor, in the circumstances, could the Bleichröders, the Crémieuxs, the Goldschmidts, the Montefiores, the Netters, the Peixottos, the Kristellers, and the rest of what had become a small army of Jewish men of independent standing labouring to protect and succour their Romanian cousins be expected not to relish it as a victory over what all without exception regarded as an infamous regime. 'In this lovely Rumania, this excrescence rather than protectorate [*Schmutz- nicht Schutzstaat*] of the Great Powers,' Moritz von Goldschmidt, the Viennese banker, had written to Bleichröder the year before to urge him on, 'the poor Jews suffer, nothing is exaggerated, everything is true, and if so far it has not been brought to light, the terrorism of the rulers and the weakness of the consuls are to blame.'[38] But if it was a victory, it was no more than a temporary and tactical one. As in the aftermath of the signing of the Treaty of Paris twenty years earlier, so now on the ground, namely in Romania itself, little or nothing changed. The Romanians would show, once again, that they were not to be moved, not even by the

[36] *Le XIXᵉ siècle*, 6 July 1878. Cited in Iancu, *Les Juifs en Roumanie*, 162.
[37] Ibid. 162.   [38] Cited in Stern, *Gold and Iron*, 374–5 n.

solemn provisions of the Treaty of Berlin, and that it was possible, by systematic stonewalling on the essentials, retreat on the trivial, and barefaced
mendacity whenever pressed into a corner, for a second-rate power to
have its own way after all. Romanian representations to the signatories of
the Treaty remained unchanged. If the Jews were not aliens in law, they
were manifestly aliens in fact: foreign in religion, language, customs,
morals, and aspirations too. They were uncivilized. They were fanatical.
And, anyway, there were too many of them. Were they to be enfranchised
a fatal blow would be struck at the homogeneity of the Romanian society and its national character. If Article XLIV of the Treaty of Berlin were
fully implemented the effect would be to endanger rather than promote
the cause of religious liberty. In Bucharest itself, in debates upon the subject in parliament, arguments were of a different class, the tone in certain
instances strident to the point of hysteria.

And I [one deputy cried in the course of debate], so far as I am concerned, why
I have the courage to say from this rostrum, that I shall never agree to the Jews
of Romania, *en masse*, enjoying political rights. (Applause) . . . If it turns out
that injustice goes as far as Europe demanding any such a thing, the Powers
will have first to pass over my body rather than get me to join in the murder of
my country.[39]

What counted equally was that once the Congress of Berlin had dispersed
the signatories of the Treaty turned out to be somewhat less than deaf to
these contentions. They did not think them wholly without merit. Nor
were they oblivious of the absolute refusal of the Romanian political
class, almost to a man, to countenance even a marginally more generous
policy towards the Jews however strongly they were pressed to soften
their position even by their own Prince Charles. When after eighteen
months of further argument the Romanians offered the signatories a
slightly improved version of the selfsame promise they had made at Paris
over two decades earlier (and which, as we have seen, there had never
been any attempt to keep), Austria and Italy agreed to accept it and
France, Germany, and Great Britain, after some additional exchanges and
a slight tightening of the new Romanian undertaking, followed on. The
new Romanian undertaking was to rewrite Article VII of their constitution. In its revised form it would provide for the division of the Jews into
three categories: outright foreigners, Romanian subjects, and Romanian
citizens. Foreign Jews would be entitled to the treatment accorded all
other foreigners. Jewish subjects of Romania would enjoy a number of
rights hitherto denied them, among them that of serving in the Romanian army, but also, it was promised, the right to acquire real estate, to
practise law and other liberal professions, and to serve on juries. On the

---

[39] *Monitorul Oficial*, 24 Feb. 1879. Cited in Iancu, *Les Juifs en Roumanie*, 165.

issue of citizenship in the strict sense the Romanians were even less forth-coming. It would no longer be denied to Jews absolutely and as a matter of national and legal principle. It would be granted as a matter of right to all Jews who had served in the Romanian forces in the course of the War of Liberation and, indeed, the 883 ex-servicemen in question were duly naturalized in relatively short order. But otherwise, and in the future, it would be conferred, if at all, only individually and by special legislation in each individual case. The upshot was that Jews would not be granted full citizenship *en bloc* and as of right, but only in minute numbers and in exceptional cases. The three powers that had held out for full and true obedience to the Treaty requirements informed the Romanian foreign minister, Vasile Boerescu, on 20 February 1880, that it was still their view, that they 'cannot consider the new Constitutional provisions . . . as being a complete fulfilment of [their] views'. But, they gave him to understand, that they would not insist. Instead, they would put their trust, they informed Boerescu, in

the determination of the Prince's Government to approximate more and more . . . to the liberal intentions entertained by the Powers, and taking note of the pos-itive assurances to that effect which have been conveyed to them, . . . [and] being desirous of giving the Roumanian nation a proof of their friendly sentiments, have decided to recognise the Principality of Roumania as an independent State.[40]

The campaign mounted on behalf of Romanian Jewry had been remarkably well organized and well supported. No case of this kind had ever evoked so high a degree of unity of opinion in the most influential quarters in Jewry since the effort to rescue the Jews of Damascus several decades earlier.[41] But the differences were striking and exceedingly sig-nificant. The matter of Romanian Jewry was writ very much larger than that of the Jews of Damascus. It was played out over years, not months, and on a very much more public and diplomatically central international stage. The goals sought by those who militated in favour of the Jews of Romania were much more far-reaching than any Moses Montefiore and Adolphe Crémieux had had in mind a generation earlier and the obs-tacles to their achievement were of a very different political and ideo-logical order. It was not the release of a small number of Jews from the dungeons and torture chambers of an oriental satrap that was asked for, rather the permanent inclusion of an entire community within a nation-state's system of justice and legal equality. Supporters were not facing a somewhat isolated, if powerful local despot and a handful of his minions, but the entire political establishment of a highly self-conscious, emerging nation adamant in its contemptuous refusal to accord equitable treatment to Jews *qua* Jews, insistent on keeping them down as a distinct and hugely vulnerable social, economic, and political underclass. And then, of course, the campaign to assure Romanian Jews of their civil and political rights differed from the rescue in Damascus in that while the latter succeeded, the outcome of the former was failure. The exertions of the notables and philanthropic organizations of western and central European Jewry on behalf of the Romanian Jews added more than a mite to the mythology of the 'international power' of the Jews. In fact, there could have been no clearer demonstration of the exceedingly limited capacity of Jews in one part of Europe to come to the aid of Jews to any good and lasting purpose, that is, in another. On the ground, in Romania itself, in the aftermath of the Congress of Berlin and after the amendment of Article VII of the Romanian constitution, most of the laws restricting the Jews in their private and communal lives, in their occupations, their places of residence, and their access to public education and the public service remained in force or even intensified. Brutality of treatment at the hands of the police was no less common after Berlin and after the amendment to the Romanian constitution than before. The atmosphere, as travellers to Romania were apt to discover, was as poisonous. When Bernard Lazare travelled to Austrian-ruled Galicia and to independent Romania a full quarter of a century later to see things in eastern Europe and in the Balkans for himself no one stopped or molested him in Galicia or, initially, on his reaching Romania, at Jassy. But on his arrival in Bucharest itself all changed. He was met by demonstrations and an organized attempt to force him to discontinue his investigations—not, as he wrote in protest to the French Foreign Minister, merely by

irresponsible agitators who came in groups to demonstrate under the windows of my hotel shouting death cries against the Jews and against me. The printed handbills calling for these demonstrations, a sample of which I have the honour to attach, were distributed in the streets of Bucharest on Monday the 19 May [NS] by uniformed policemen. The meeting held on Tuesday 20 May [NS], following which the commotion [*le tumulte*] took place, was presided over by an official of the Ministry of Public Instruction and Religions (what irony!), M. Nae Dimitrescu. [42]

After Berlin, the Jewish organizations in the west would continue to try to do their duty as best they saw it, but their hour had passed. This was partly, of course, because the pass had been sold: Romania was now a fully recognized sovereign state. It was partly too because even where an opportunity for the powers to press the Romanians to abide by their undertaking was glimpsed the disposition to seize it had lapsed. The

---

[42] Open letter to Théophile Delcassé, 23 May 1902, *L'Aurore*, 28 May 1902. On Bernard Lazare, see below, pp. 554 ff.

representatives of the major European Powers and the spokesmen for the grandees of Jewry went through certain motions from time to time, but never with anything like the old conviction. When, twenty years on, the Conjoint Jewish Committee[43] in London brought up the subject of what the Foreign Office primly called 'recent legislation in Roumania likely to affect the position of the Jews in that country', they were told that the British minister at Bucharest had indeed 'repeatedly called the attention of the Roumanian Government to the matter and will continue to do what he properly can [d]o to further the interests of the Jews'. But they were also told that while the Foreign Secretary, Lord Lansdowne, was ready to 'consider any further communication on this subject which you may desire to address to him', he did not think that 'any advantage would be gained by his receiving a deputation from the . . . two bodies which you represent'.[44] When yet another occasion for the major European Powers to play an active, leading, and collective role in the Balkans arose in 1913—Romania hoping at this point to gain something for itself from the detritus of the Balkan wars—the Conjoint Committee tried again. It asked the British government to

refuse their sanction to this or any similar proposal. We do so on the grounds (1) that Romania, being in default in regard to the conditions imposed upon her by the Treaty of Berlin for the recognition of her independence, is not entitled to any such consideration at the hands of the Great Powers [;] and (2) that any territorial aggrandisement of that country would have the undesirable effect of enlarging pro tanto the area within which its Government practises a policy of Religious discrimination and intolerance in defiance of the Treaty of Berlin and in violation of the solemn pledges given to the signatories of that instrument in 1880.

Adding valiantly, if somewhat desperately, that

We feel confident that His Majesty's Government, who have not been slow in the past to express their sense of the bad faith and inhumanity of Roumania and their sympathy with the oppressed Jews of that country, will refuse to countenance any such scheme, unless and until they receive satisfactory guarantees from the Cabinet in Bucharest for the fulfilment of their obligations under Article XLIV of the Treaty of Berlin.[45]

---

[43] It was to strengthen their collective hand somewhat by avoiding damaging internal disputes and presenting a united front, that the London Committee of Deputies of British Jews, after first refusing to co-operate with the newly founded Anglo-Jewish Association, changed its mind. By the terms of the Heads of Arrangement finalized in May 1878 it was agreed that 'no communication shall be made on behalf of either party to the British Government seeking the interference of the Government in reference to the affairs of Jews in foreign parts' before consultation in a joint committee composed of equal numbers of representatives of the two organizations; and that should no agreement 'on the course to be adopted' be possible 'the subject should be referred to the Parent Bodies and each Parent Body shall then be at liberty to act separately and independently as it may think fit', BoD, C11/1/2.

[44] Sanderson to Montefiore, 2 June 1902, ibid., C11/2/2.

[45] Alexander and Montefiore to Grey, 11 Jan. 1913, ibid., C11/2/4.

The Foreign Office did not dispute the facts as presented to them. It was well aware, it replied, that the amendment to the now notorious Article VII of the Romanian constitution passed in October 1879 had been no more than 'technical' and that 'the intentions of the Powers in formulating the Treaty of Berlin have remained in a great measure unfulfilled'.[46] But as regards the Committee's proposal that advantage be taken of the coming repartition of the Balkans, the position was that

It is uncertain whether any question connected with Roumania will come before the Great Powers for sanction, and that though the grievances of the Jews will be borne in mind, the present moment, when the Great Powers are so fully occupied with the war and its complications, is hardly one when the question can be raised by His Majesty's Government with any prospect of success.[47]

But by this time in any event, in Romania as elsewhere in Europe, the salient and most palpable indicator of the Jewish condition had become the flow of population out—or into—particular countries. It had become clear by the end of the century that in Romania the Jewish population was falling. The 68,000 Romanian Jewish immigrants who travelled to the United States alone between 1881 and 1910 constituted no less than a quarter of the country's entire Jewish population. In the single peak year of 1903, the 8,562 Jews leaving for the United States (Jews accounted for 90 per cent of *all* emigrants from Romania to the United States) constituted 3.3 per cent of the total Jewish population at that time.[48] Nineteenth- and early twentieth-century Romanian population figures were notoriously unreliable. But it has been estimated, extrapolating on the basis of the known rate of natural increase, that the Jewish population of Romania should have reached 310,000 by 1912. In fact, emigration out of Romania, especially but not exclusively to the United States, reduced it from an estimated 250,000–270,000 in the 1870s and 1880s to 240,000[49]—which, if accurate, represents an *absolute* decline in numbers that was unique.

[46] Campbell to Emanuel, 20 Apr. 1907, ibid.

[47] Mallet to the Committee, 17 Jan. 1913, ibid. Later the Romanians were induced to promise that *all* the inhabitants of the newly annexed territories, 'whether of Jewish or of other nationalities . . . would of course enjoy the full political and civil rights which they had under Bulgarian rule' (Mallet to the Committee, citing the Romanian minister in London, 9 June 1913, ibid.). Of political and civil rights in Romania proper nothing was said.

[48] Joseph Kissman, 'The Immigration of Rumanian Jews up to 1914', *YIVO Annual of Jewish Social Science*, 2–3 (New York, 1947/8), 176–9.

[49] H. S. Halevi, *Hashpa'at milhemet ha-'olam ha-sheniya 'al ha-tekhunot ha-demografiyot shel 'am yisrael* (Jerusalem, 1963), 94. Both the numbers and the social features of Romanian Jewry would change dramatically after the First World War with the incorporation of Transylvania into the kingdom. But it is worth noting too that there would be a drastic fall in the birth rate and in the rate of natural increase: 46.5 per thousand in 1871–82 falling to 14.8 per thousand in 1934 and 20.8 per thousand in the nineteenth century falling to 1.04 per thousand in 1935 respectively (Halevi, *Hashpa'at*).

III

What the unusually intense and long-drawn campaign to ensure decent treatment for the Jews of Romania served to demonstrate most effectively was therefore less the latent power of the Jewish people to care for their own than their absolute vulnerability to persecution and spoliation at the hands of any government determined to punish them. What it demonstrated with equal clarity was that the social transformation undergone by the Jews of Europe in the course of the nineteenth century had in no way diminished the one consistently determining factor in their lives which was the power held over them by the territorial state. The identity and purposes of their political masters, the spirit in which they operated, the social ends the masters of the state held in view, the means employed to further those ends, and the efficacy with which this was done—these, to be sure, had always been sources of anxiety. But where the essential lore of Exile had been that it was in the nature of things that the question of state policy towards Jews was one which would never be finally and definitively settled one way or the other, the lesson of the new age had appeared to be that it did lend itself to final and, what is more, favourable settlement after all. Wherever and whenever an opportunity to move the matter of the Jews' civil and political status still further along in the appropriate direction appeared to arise, those who had taken it upon themselves to lead the Jews in these new fresh directions were thus greatly tempted—besides being under some public pressure—to seek to play an active, if possible determining role of their own.

Inexorably, the question arises whether such confidence in the autonomous ability of Jews of any quality and position to play such a role to good purpose was not inherently idle. While it admits of no certain answer it is clear, at any rate in retrospect, that the obstacles to Jewish entry into the political arena in an explicitly Jewish interest were more considerable than many had begun to imagine them to be. What was no less imperfectly grasped was that these obstacles had in all cases as much to do with the changing structure and quality of the European state itself. For this was now, increasingly, a nation-state. If it was not yet entirely so in substance it was likely to be so in principle. If it was not so in daily political and social practice, such at any rate was the ideal to which many of its masters and ever greater numbers of their subjects were likely to have in mind. And, crucially, it was the nation-state that had begun to be conceived of as a proper—and to some minds even indispensable—building-block of the European political system. The obstacles both to domestic and international *autonomous* political action by Jews in state and polity were therefore three. The question of the simple and, as would be claimed, anomalous presence of Jews could be and would be raised with still greater force than before. The legal, practical, and ideological objections to Jews playing a social, certainly a political role on their own behalf would be claimed by some and seem to very many more to be if not unanswerable at any rate reasonable. And as a criterion for admission to working membership in the international system the congruence of state and majoritarian nation had come closer to eventual establishment as that which must be allowed to override all others.

The implications of this climate of sharpening national-political values for all of Europe's Jews were detectable everywhere to some degree towards the end of the nineteenth century. It had been a matter of chance that it was in the relatively remote and seemingly eccentric case of Romania that they were so very clearly apparent initially. It was equally fortuitous that it would be there that the ability of nominally well-placed Jews in one part of Europe to act on behalf of a Jewish community in great distress in another part would be most severely tested. It remained that the great significance of the Romanian case lay in its pointing to the future, in the precision with which it indicated what lay ahead for the Jews in all parts of the continent in the century to follow.

Meanwhile, it was still in Russia—more properly, in the Russian Empire—that it seemed most likely that the destinies of the bulk of the Jews of Europe would eventually be played out and the prospects for the Jewish people as a whole decided. As the century drew to an end it was, at any rate, on the great Russo-Polish segment of the whole that most thinking minds in Jewry were concentrated—whether out of straight-forwardly sympathetic and humane concern, or as a consequence of rational analysis of its condition, or for fear of the impact upon themselves were the dam to burst and a still greater migratory flood engulf everyone and everything.

IV

No single incident in the implacably deteriorating condition of Russian and Polish Jewry came so rapidly to take on an emblematic character as the pogrom that began in Kishinev, the capital of Bessarabia, on 19 April 1903, continued the following day, and was not entirely over until the day after that. Why this should have been so—and not only at the time, but for very many decades after—is unclear. It was certainly the case that the pogrom was an exceedingly violent one: more so, as many remarked, than any single one of the pogroms visited upon the Jews of southern Russia a generation earlier. Fifty-one Jews were killed outright. Eight more died of their wounds subsequently. Close to 500 were injured, some very severely . Crowbars and axes had been the weapons of choice. There were numerous (but, as was common, mostly unreported) cases of rape. Blood and gore apart, huge damage was inflicted on property as well. It was reliably estimated that a fifth of the Jewish population of the city found itself homeless and destitute when the streets had at last been cleared and the business of picking up the pieces began. It was, no doubt, because the casualties at Kishinev were so numerous and the damage to property so great and calls for help from the local community to Jewish communities in Russia and abroad therefore immediate and especially desperate, that news of the pogrom spread unusually widely and rapidly and prompted exceptionally detailed coverage in both the domestic and foreign press. On the other hand, by the standards that were to be set and made familiar two or three years on (of which more later), the assault on the Jewish population of Kishinev at Easter time, 1903, was a relatively limited affair; and the much higher incidence of violent death and plunder inflicted upon Jews in the final years of the Tsarist Empire generally would itself be overshadowed by what they would be forced to undergo in the aftermath of its collapse. But it is Kishinev as a single epitomizing incident that would be longest remembered; and one is left with the conclusion that this was chiefly so because, in a characteristic mixture of crushed optimism and grim foreboding, it seemed to most Jewish observers at the time that, nothing on this scale having occurred in the past twenty or so years, a sharp change for the worse in the social and political weather was in the offing

As is common in such cases, there is no knowing with certainty how far the action of the mob was spontaneous in the admittedly limited sense that it had been steamed up by, say, some minor instances of dispute between Jews and gentiles, and how far, as many suspected at the time and would argue long after the event, it was the deliberate creation of *provocateurs*. But there was not then, nor is there today, any question but that the pogrom was preceded—and in that sense prepared—by continuous and poisonous anti-Semitic agitation in the local press and in the street: better prepared and better fed by more poisonous and more effective material than any of the pogroms that had taken place in the earlier wave in the 1880s. Nor is there any doubt that the principal agitators enjoyed the protection, or at the very least the carefully studied and therefore encouraging indifference, of the local authorities. The most notorious among them, one Pavolachi Krushevan, was a Moldavian who had taken to promoting the full cultural, social, and political integration of Moldova/Bessarabia into Russia and had been rewarded with a helpful, intimate connection with the authorities. In 1897 he had been granted the considerable privilege of publishing and editing the only newspaper licensed to appear in Kishinev, the *Bessarabets*. In 1902 he was granted the additional, equally valuable right to publish a newspaper of his own (*Znamya*) in St Petersburg itself. That the otherwise omnipresent and always vigilant censorship left him free to pursue a sedulously and virulently anti-Semitic editorial policy announced another form of official favour and approval. It was virtually inevitable and entirely in character, therefore, that in the very early spring of 1903 Krushevan's Kishinev newspaper should seek to make as much as it could of rumours that Jews had been responsible for the ritual murder of a teenage boy whose body had been found in the nearby town of Dubossary, every piece of gossip and speculation being seized upon and where possible embellished. Despite the local authorities in Dubossary itself having immediately looked into the matter and dismissed the allegation on the basis of professional medical advice and Krushevan's intention being very deliberately inflammatory, there was no attempt by higher authority in Kishinev, let alone St Petersburg, to interfere with his campaign.

The recrudescence of the blood libel, the nastiest of all medieval inventions about the Jews, in the nineteenth century and early twentieth century was by no means limited to Russia, as we have seen and shall see again. But like virtually all other charges of general and endemic wickedness in the Jews, the consequences of a focused attempt to recirculate it were likely to be more serious in Russia than anywhere else. No one either in the Jewish communities concerned, or among those with official responsibility for the policing of the population as a whole, could be in any doubt about the consequences for public order if a story of this kind were not immediately investigated. But whereas the authorities in Dubossary itself had indeed acted promptly, the more senior officials in the provincial capital Kishinev itself were a good deal more relaxed. The Orthodox metropolitan (or bishop) of the city—whose word on this particular subject was of course especially important in such a context— proved to be hostile when a Jewish delegation approached him with the request that he formally discredit the charge of ritual murder. Far from doing so, he gave them to understand that he tended to subscribe to it himself. As further signs of coming trouble multiplied and as tension (and the Jews' fears) mounted, the city's Jewish notables applied to the civil and police authorities for specific preventive measures to be taken and, if all else failed, for protection. They received an equally dusty answer. No one troubled to deny that trouble of some kind was possible and even likely. But only marginal, hopelessly inadequate precautionary measures were taken. From that point on events followed the common pattern: scuffles in the market-place degenerating into drunken attacks on Jews, followed in turn by rioters setting out in more or less organized groups of a dozen or so to vandalize and pillage Jewish homes, shops, and workplaces, the provincial civil and military authorities refusing all the while to intervene. On the second day mob violence escalated sharply. Two, and by some estimates three thousand men armed with axes, clubs, crowbars, and in some cases revolvers roamed the city, many drunk, all fired up by hatred, pious self-satisfaction, and greed, clearly on the loose and out of control. The governor and army commander, still sitting on their hands, confined their activity to exchanging messages with each other, at greater pains to determine what measures might or might not be acceptable at this or that level of authority above them in St Petersburg than to deal with the violence on display before their eyes. All the police were prepared to do, and that with all possible speed, was to put down the limited and, in the circumstances, brave attempts by small, scattered parties of Jews to organize their own defence. Not until the city had finally and formally been turned over to the military and the garrison commander had been as good as ordered by his superiors in St Petersburg to intervene was the rioting stopped—stopped in a matter of hours and without serious resistance as had always been possible. Then came the questions. Had the local authorities been deliberately and criminally negligent in their response to early warnings of trouble or only slothful and ineffective? To what extent had their conduct been determined by private loathing of the Jews and covert or even overt sympathy for the rioters as opposed to the absence of adequate force at their immediate disposal and poor co-ordination between the civil authorities and the military? No firm answers being available, only uncertainty and learned debate on what might have been the truth of the matter remained. Thus at the time; and so to some extent ever since. So far, then, much as always.

Yet not all was exactly as before. For once the respectable wing of Russian conservatism, though hostile to Jewry and Judaism as a matter of course and unforgiving of what it did not doubt were the Jews' multiple sins and offences against Russian society, was as disturbed by mob violence against them as were the liberals. The semi-official *St Peterburskiye Vedomosti* went so far as to report to its readers on what it did not doubt was the unpardonably disgraceful behaviour of 'the better class of the Christian public' in Kishinev. That it did so at all, and with some freedom and precision, may have had something to do with the fact that Bessarabia was not Russia strictly speaking, not 'Inner Russia' at all events. Still, to complain that Christians of one class had done nothing to stop Christians of another class from attacking Jews was unusual. Members of this 'better class of the Christian public', the newspaper reported, had 'walked calmly along and gazed at these horrible spectacles with the utmost indifference. Many of them even rode through the streets in their carriages in holiday attire in order to witness the cruelties that were being perpetrated.'[50]

Leo Tolstoy who had had nothing to say about the pogroms of the early 1880s was now quick to denounce the government for the 'horrible

---

[50] Quoted in the *Jewish Chronicle*, 8 May 1903. Among those who went out to observe the scene with such equanimity was Yakov, the Orthodox metropolitan who had refused to say anything in refutation of the blood libel. The bishop went so far, it was later reported, as to bless the rioters as he travelled past them in his carriage (Edward H. Judge, *Easter in Kishinev: Anatomy of a Pogrom* (New York, 1992), 52).

events in Kishinev'. What he felt most deeply, he wrote, was 'horror of the criminals who were responsible for all that had occurred, horror of the Government that with its clergy and its bandit horde of officials, keeps the people in a state of ignorance and fanaticism'.

The attitude of our Government towards these events is fresh proof of their brutal egoism which does not flinch from any measure, however cruel, when it is a question of suppressing a movement which they deem dangerous, and of their complete indifference—much like the indifference of the Turkish Government to atrocities conducted against the Armenians—to outrages that do not affect their interests.

As for the Jews themselves, the best advice Tolstoy could offer them was not 'to fight the Government with violence—a weapon to be left to the Government itself—but by virtuous living [*borot'sya s pravitel'stvom nye nasiliem . . . a dobroyu zhizn'yu*]'.[51]

Of greater consequence than the undeniably distasteful images evoked by reports of the events in Kishinev in the Russian press was the interest taken in the affair, notably in its deeper origins, by the foreign press in central and western Europe and in the United States. This owed a good deal to the inability of the central government to shake off the widespread, exceedingly stubborn conviction in most Jewish quarters, and to some extent in influential, non-Jewish circles abroad too, that whatever doubts there may have been about the conduct of the regime twenty or so years earlier, on this occasion it had indeed been closely, directly, and maliciously involved. The inspiration for the pogrom, so ran the most common thesis, had not been local on this occasion. It was the strong man of the day, Minister of the Interior Plehve himself, who had either deliberately precipitated it or, at the very least, had made it possible by ensuring that when the time came the Jews of Kishinev would be without police protection. The charge against Plehve was never proven. A message which purported to have provided proof of his culpability turned out to be a forgery. And, strictly construed, the charge against him

---

[51] Letter dated 27 Apr. [OS] 1903 to editors of *Kishinev* 1 (Aug. 1903). Russian text in H. Shurer, *et al.* (eds.), *Ha-pogrom be-kishinov* (Tel Aviv, 1963), 178–81. One wonders what Alexander Herzen would have said of Kishinev had he been alive. When Jules Michelet wrote of the Russians, in response to their treatment of the Poles, that they were brutal savages not to be included among the civilized nations of Europe, and that they lacked 'the essential attribute of man, the moral faculty, the sense of good and evil', Herzen replied with great force that it was to the regime that attention should be paid, 'to see if this strange empire has indeed no other reason for its existence except that hideous vocation which has been given to it by the Government of Petersburg—to be a stone blocking up the high-road to humanity. . . . There is no longer existence, but a mere waiting, an anxiety. Everything is overturned. No more legality, no more justice, not even the phantom of liberty; an irreligious lay Inquisition reigns absolutely; the laws are replaced by martial law as of a place in a state of siege. One sole moral force presides, dictates, ordains,—Fear' (*The Russian People and Socialism: A Letter to M. Jules Michelet* (Coniston, Windermere, 1855)).

was almost certainly without foundation. On the other hand, his ministry had been devoting substantial resources to the concoction and propagation of anti-Semitic ideas and material; and it was not in doubt that Plehve himself was exceedingly hostile to the Jews on general principles of one kind or another and that, like Ignatiev, his predecessor of a little over twenty years earlier, he was inclined to punish them for what he supposed to be their sins. In any event, the relatively tough and unbending Alexander III was gone, the new Autocrat was his weak and incompetent son, and the empire itself was a structure beset by both real and imaginary enemies and increasingly unsure of itself. There would be no question at all of inflicting condign punishment on the guilty in Kishinev.

The idea that the time might finally have come to soften the iron framework of punitive regulations under which Russia's Jewish subjects were obliged to live out their lives never seriously arose. Only the old argument that, however nasty they might be, the pogroms were no more than the Jews' comeuppance for continually and systematically exploiting the common folk among whom they lived was trotted out—along with the somewhat newer charge that it was for the Jews themselves to put their own house in order before all else: let them stamp out the revolutionaries in their ranks and recognize their own responsibility for what had befallen them before claiming the support and protection of the government. Once more, then, much as always. And yet, again, not entirely so.

As questions multiplied and foreign exercises in what in our own times would be called investigative journalism dug deeper it came to be understood in St Petersburg that if imperial Russia's reputation was not to suffer greater damage than its master and his minions could absorb in comfort, the Autocracy would have to try a good deal harder. And try it did, seeking briefly to demonstrate to the world at large that despite appearances its intentions were decent and honourable after all. Wholesale personnel changes at the highest level of Russian civil, military, and police officialdom in Bessarabia were instituted—capped, not undramatically, by the installation of a new, manifestly untainted official as governor of the province. This was Prince Sergei Dmitrovich Urusov, until then deputy governor of Tambov, now suddenly promoted and transferred to Bessarabia at the end of May 1903—very rapidly indeed, therefore, by Russia's usual administrative standards. Urusov had no record of dealing with Jewish matters: his service had been confined to 'inner Russia' where Jews were not ordinarily allowed to settle. But he was considered to be relatively free of the usual prejudices and to be a decent and fair-minded man all round; and so he proved to be. Unusually for a Russian official, Urusov was unafraid of being accused of 'philo-Semitism'—always an awkward, unpleasant, and for a senior Russian bureaucrat probably damaging allegation, but one which those who treated the

Jewish population on an even-handed basis were apt to incur.[52] Some other gestures of limited good will towards the Jews were decided upon as well, the most imaginative being to reverse a long-standing position on the Zionists, grant Herzl permission to visit Russia (very briefly, it needs to be said), and treat him with a degree of courtesy and a display of apparent plain dealing such as no Jew had been accorded since Sir Moses Montefiore travelled to the empire fifty-seven years before.[53]

It was not long, of course, before the public protests aroused by the pogrom died down and whatever hope there may ever have been of a change of substance or intensity in the Autocracy's approach to matters Jewish was put to rest. Urusov's appointment, it became clear, was no more than a sop to public—and to some extent Jewish—opinion. Herzl came and went; and nothing else of any consequence occurred to soften the initial, in the event enduring impression left on Russia's Jews or to encourage those who had half-forgotten the earlier wave of violence to wrench it out of the recesses of their minds. Nor had anything arisen to resolve the paradox of a government that was demonstrably intent on maintaining itself as, at one and the same time, an oriental despotism, a bureaucratic police state, and a forward-looking *Rechtsstaat*, while remaining morally incapable of bringing itself to keep order in the streets of its cities when the likely victims of the mob were Jews. The social impact of the Kishinev pogrom was not as fundamental as that of the first great wave in the early 1880s. It was not the occasion for another great change of direction in mind and conduct in eastern European Jewry. But it served an entire generation as the readiest of all illustrations of what was intolerable in the behaviour of *all* concerned: the Russian government, the Russian public, but also, as we shall see, in exceedingly important respects, the Jewish public as well.

V

The one question still open in the long aftermath of the pogrom in Kishinev was how the Jews themselves, within Russia and outside it, would respond. Within Russian-ruled Jewry itself the shock had been electric. Recovery was easiest for the inveterate sceptics, of course. Strict and devoted traditionalists could take some comfort from recital of the supplicatory prayer to the Merciful Father (*Av ha-raḥamim*) customarily offered up on such occasions on behalf of the innocent and the pious

[52] Urusov's recollections (*Memoiren eines russischen Gouverneurs: Kischinew 1903–1904* (Stuttgart and Leipzig, 1907)) are still worth reading, if only for a hint of a Russia that might have been.
[53] On the immediate purpose of Herzl's visit to Russia and the conflicting views of it within his own movement, see Chapter 5.

whose blood has been shed and from reiteration of the vengeance on their killers foretold in the Book of Psalms.[54] For the rest, they tended to keep their heads down and together. Matters were much more difficult for those whom Kishinev had struck as before all else anachronistic: a horrible reversion to forms of public and official behaviour that the Russians, like other Europeans, were thought to have put behind them, that their government would no longer tolerate, and that the Jews of the empire would therefore no longer have to contend with. It would be some time before this massive error of judgement was grasped and internalized. Not all well-meaning people accepted that this was indeed the case and attempts by those who continued to believe and rely on the eventual transformation of Russia into a liberal state to tackle the masters of the imperial machine of government followed. They sought to point out that the case for some attention to be paid to the grievances of the Jews was now stronger and more evident than ever. To demand fair treatment, physical protection, and a through investigation of the events in Kishinev itself was, they claimed, no more than reasonable, neither disloyal nor provocative. Bolder spirits thought they even glimpsed a genuine opportunity to press for a fundamental change of attitude, although except for the appointment and vigorous behaviour of the new, eminently decent governor of Bessarabia there was in fact nothing to support them in their optimism. When the powerful national police director in the Ministry of the Interior, A. A. Lopukhin, finally took the trouble to travel down to Kishinev to see things for himself, local Jewish communal leaders prepared a carefully, somewhat obsequiously drafted memorandum for him on the immediate causes of the events.[55] But the great man received their memorandum without comment and, in the best tradition of the higher Russian bureaucracy, treated the delegation itself with studied coolness. A stronger delegation of Jewish notables that waited upon the minister of the interior himself in St Petersburg (on 23 May) was dealt with somewhat more courteously,[56] but got very little further. Their criticism of the local authorities in Bessarabia and their carefully phrased, but unmistakably critical remarks on the relevant arms of the central government itself were dismissed as impudent and unacceptable. Their request for an official *ex post facto* public statement condemning the attack on the Jews of Kishinev was rejected out of hand. Their demand—inevitable once the discussion with the minister moved (at Plehve's own initiative, as it happened) from the particular to the general—for a serious

---

[54] 'Wherefore should the heathen say, where is their God?—let him be known among the heathen in our sight by the revenging of the shed blood of thy servants.' And the Lord 'shall judge among the heathen, he shall fill the places with the bodies of the dead' (Psalms 79: 10; 110: 6).

[55] Cited in Shurer, *Ha-pogrom*, 106–10.

[56] But carefully, if surreptitiously, searched for concealed weapons beforehand.

revision of the entire corpus of anti-Jewish legislation was turned down as unfeasible. They had to make do with a vague ministerial promise to rein in the more poisonously anti-Semitic publications, an affirmation that they were entitled to see the dismissal of the governor of the province as an earnest of St Petersburg's ultimately good intentions, and an invitation to return for a second round of talks. However, this being less than even the pessimists in the group had hoped for, the delegation resolved to refrain from taking up the minister's invitation. Still, if the flame of their belief in the need and in the possibility of the Jews of the empire—a reformed empire, to be sure—eventually finding a decent place for themselves within it was sputtering, it cannot be said to have blown out.

Among the more assertively secular nationalists—Yiddishists as well as Hebraists, Bundists as well as Zionists—the response was of two kinds. The Yiddishist-populists, the Bundists in particular, found that their familiar dilemma confronted them once again. While it could be argued in the abstract that the case for lining up with all those in Russia who were intent on the total demolition of the entire, evil structure of Tsardom had been strengthened, in practice their long-standing conviction that it was necessary for the Jews to fight their corner on their own in the first instance had been confirmed. The language and tone in which the Bund chose to pronounce publicly on the event was, in the style of the times, unequivocal and pugnacious. The Jewish proletariat was praised for, 'alone in all the Jewish people, having thrown down the gauntlet before the chief culprit—the government itself—and being engaged in a courageous struggle against it'. The Jewish bourgeoisie was denounced for 'crawling at the feet of the Russian government', protesting its loyalty, and going so far as to ask for protection of a government that was known not to have hesitated to launch the pogrom in the first place and which, with its army and its police, bore unmitigated responsibility for what had occurred. It was the minister of the interior himself who had threatened 'to drown the Bund in Jewish blood'.[57] So far then, so simple, except that, in fact, the pogrom had shone a harder light than ever on the obstacles to the Bund's playing anything like the role it had conceived for itself in the general political arena as one of the participants in the general, *militantly* revolutionary struggle against the Autocracy. The Bundists continued to insist that 'the anti-Semitism that expresses itself from time to time in pogroms was only a particular case of the kind of hatred that was common between different peoples' and that while it might flourish in certain social conditions it was bound, by the same token, to disappear in others. 'Here in Russia,' the argument went, 'it was Tsarism that played the principal role in the setting of one nation against another. . . . Being unsure of

---

[57] Statement by the Central Committee of the Bund, 3 May 1903. Cited in Y. S. Hertz *et al.*, *Di Geshikhte fun Bund*, ii (New York, 1962), 58–60.

itself, beside the hangings, the floggings, the whips and Siberia [to which the Autocracy has recourse, it] misses no opportunity to set Russians against Poles and the two together against the Jews . . . so as to weaken the revolutionary spirit of the people and cloud its political understanding.'[58]

But while there was some truth in this it was not the whole truth. Whatever the Bundists or anyone else might have to say about the causes of anti-Jewish pogroms and about the identity of those to whom immediate responsibility for provoking them in each case could confidently be ascribed, it was manifest that the pogrom in Kishinev had been an exceedingly *popular* event. It had earned the open and enthusiastic support—and to a marked extent the active participation—of the non-Jewish, urban working class. At no point had there ever been any question of the working class as such, or of any significant fraction of it, standing shoulder to shoulder with the Jews as natural partners in the central revolutionary struggle against the regime and its bourgeois allies. Instances of moral support for the Jews had been rare enough. Cases of active opposition to the mob by non-Jews of any social class at all were rarer still. The rules of behaviour being otherwise, there was no substance or relevance—not in Kishinev, at any rate—to the distinction the Bund sought to draw between the 'ignorant and the provoked' and the 'wise and class-conscious' who had, actually, 'fought with us under the single banner of international socialism'.[59] And what was true of the simple, the ignorant, the unwashed, and therefore, perhaps, the pardonable was almost equally true of the educated and the politically sophisticated and—accordingly—the unpardonable. It was the case, and could be noted with due satisfaction, that those closest to the Bund in general political outlook had been quick to report and denounce the pogrom in Kishinev and to excoriate the government for its wickedness and the craven middle classes for their weakness and malevolence. However, what neither of the two newly separated wings of the RSDWP, Bolsheviks and Mensheviks, were moved to reconsider was the hostility (somewhat mitigated by respect) with which they approached the Bund itself. Their determination to insist on the institutional integration of the Bund within the larger movement as a stage leading to its eventual dissolution remained implacable. That the pogrom in Kishinev occurred only weeks after the Bund's angry withdrawal from the RSDWP[60] on just this issue may have contributed something to the isolation in which the Bund found itself. But it is worth recalling that, on the occasion of the less well-known because less bloody pogrom in Czestochowa the year before, their then nominal political allies had behaved in much the same way.[61]

[58] *Di kishinever hariga* (London, 1903), 8–11. Cited in I. Halpern (ed.), *Sefer ha-gevura: antologiya historit-sifrutit*, iii (Tel Aviv, 1950), 21.

[59] Ibid.   [60] See Chapter 5.

[61] Henry J. Tobias, *The Jewish Bund in Russia* (Stanford, Calif., 1972), 192, 221 f., 287.

At all events, with the leading segment of the Russian Social Democratic Workers' Party now fairly firmly under Lenin's (newly christened) Bolshevik thumb, the pogrom in Kishinev was less likely than ever to prompt even so much as a marginal reversal of its position on the matter of the Jews—which was, as we have seen, that all in all anti-Semitism was a bourgeois phenomenon, that it would diminish as the class struggle hardened, and that it would evaporate entirely once the governance of the proletariat had been established. Nothing could have been more alien and distasteful to a man as firmly bound in by his a priori vision of the world around him and the way it worked as Lenin than to modify it in the wake of a pogrom, or of any other mere *event*, and so to accept, if only implicitly, that the Bund's case for continued autonomy within the larger movement might be a reasonable one after all. Nothing of this nature was likely to move the Mensheviks either. Neither Martov who, after all, knew all about the Bund that he himself had done so much to found, or Trotsky who had taken such fierce umbrage at what he had (not unreasonably) called the Bund's 'formulated distrust' of the RSDWP, could have been firmer in their views on the proper role for Jews in the revolutionary struggle.[62] *Iskra*, now in Menshevik editorial hands, did offer its readers regular and fairly detailed reports on pogroms as they occurred. But it took care to play down the role performed by Bundists, and *a fortiori* by the Zionists, in the continuing and mounting efforts to mount organized self-defence by and for Jews (of which more later) and to celebrate, grossly exaggerating its dimensions, the contribution of undefined, but by clear implication *non*-Jewish, as it were generic 'Russians' and 'workers'.[63] In sum, far from serving as the effective link between the Jews of the empire and the most consistent, least romantic, and (so far as Jews themselves were concerned) least hostile and ideologically most accommodating of the various parties on the revolutionary left, the Bundists found themselves isolated within the revolutionary 'camp' along lines that were very similar to those in which Russo-Polish Jewry as a whole was enclosed. That the case for reliance on overall working-class solidarity had been damaged was hardly in doubt. Whether it had crumbled entirely remained to be seen. And if the question was not one the leaders of the Bund relished examining, they all knew perfectly well that it touched on just those matters that were of greatest and most urgent concern to the ordinary working-class Jew—the man to whom their appeal was principally addressed—moving him more strongly than ever to emigrate rather than, as the Bund wished, remaining in Russia to fight it out. Prospects of revolution in the long term—or even, for the truest

---

[62] See Chapter 5.
[63] Y. Erez, 'Ha-hagana ha-ʿazmit ha-yehudit be-rusiya bi-shenot 1903–1905', He-ʿAvar, 3 (1956), 82–94.

believers, the short term—and estimates of the configuration of conditions and forces most likely to bring it about were one thing; the urgent
and immediate need of the man in the street for basic physical and
economic security for himself and his family was another. The Bund's
position on emigration—that it was tantamount to flight—set it at cross-
purposes with a large and steadily growing segment of its natural constituency. Its continued rejection of the calls for Jewish unity on the
ground that the fundamental aspect of the Jewish people, like all other
nations, was that it was riven by fatal and endemic class struggle further
entrenched it in its isolation. But then few things were so feared by the
leaders of the Bund as being driven into a straightforward nationalist position unmitigated and uncorrected by Marxism and therefore all but
indistinguishable in substance from Zionism.

However, matters were hardly easier for the other great wing of what
may loosely be called the modernist national party in eastern European
Jewry, that of the *maskilim* and the not quite congruent Zionists. These,
for lack of so all-embracing and seemingly compelling an ideological
scheme as Marxism to guide them, had never at any time been entirely in
agreement among themselves on the question of what was to be done
here and now, in Europe itself, but especially in Russia. And they were to
be further divided when Herzl's long-awaited and much wished for visit
to Russia in the immediate aftermath of the Kishinev pogrom unintentionally but neatly encapsulated the dilemma facing them and greatly
intensified the discomfort which the standing issue of Zionist *non*-
participation in internal Russian politics had always aroused. To plunge
into the domestic arena would reduce the distance between Zionism and
other approaches and ideologies to the problems and afflictions of the
Jewish people. But it would necessarily shift attention, energy, and such
resources as were available away from the essential Zionist purpose of settlement in Palestine. And, as surely, it would invite more severe and dedicated police repression than anything they had known up to this point
when the principal reason for pressing Herzl to seek to visit Russia in the
first place had been the hope that he would find a way to avert a serious
effort to crush them. Would their essentially respectable and, as the
Bundists never tired of arguing, preponderantly bourgeois party survive
a police campaign if one were ever launched against them? They could
only wonder. Might it not be wiser to stick to respectable 'political' (or
'diplomatic') Zionism as Herzl understood and practised it after all, setting sentiment (and perhaps honour too) aside in this instance on the
grounds that in any case the sole true and viable solution to the problem
of the Jews was the territorial one outside Russia altogether? Yet if the
political road to national salvation was going to be a very long one indeed
and there was effectively nothing to be done in any of the social or political spheres that were of immediate concern to the Jews at least until

Herzl's (or his eventual successors') effort to find allies among the European Powers had borne some small fruit, was there not a danger in the interim of the Zionist movement dying of sheer irrelevance?

I said to myself [wrote Herzl's arch-critic], that surely we would for once see the truth, namely that what life demands of us before all else is to be *men*, to rid ourselves in our *inner beings* of our meanness and our servility and cease to be sheep to the slaughter;[64] to show the masters of this country that five million souls have to be reckoned with, that they are self-respecting men and women, not animals capable only of looking pleadingly at their slaughterers. But—all in vain! Our old leaders have reverted, contemptibly, to intercession. Our new leaders have thought it an appropriate occasion to make propaganda for *their* kind of Zionism—as if really and truly it was in the power of Zionism to put an end to the likes of Kishinev.[65]

Where most modernists were at one—Bundists and Zionists too for once, but also such essentially independent figures as the distinguished historian S. M. Dubnov—was in their outrage. Dubnov was no Zionist. He believed firmly, almost to the end of his life, in the need and propriety, but in the actual possibility too, of creating terms for a decent, self-respecting structure of social and cultural autonomy for the Jews within the existing ethno-political structure of eastern Europe. It would have to await the foundation of a reformed, democratic, multinational Russian state to be sure. When, after the First World War, matters turned out to be otherwise, he pressed for autonomy of a limited nature in the succession states. Dubnov was already at this time the pre-eminent historian of the Jewish people: the very worthy, yet very different, successor to Heinrich Graetz: different because he was more social historian than historian of ideas, but also, very much more than Graetz, a man who sought an active role for himself in the contemporary arena, although in the role in which he rightly thought he could best make a contribution, as a contemporary historian. His personal account of the shock induced by first reports of the Kishinev pogrom was much like that of others in the Russian-Jewish intelligentsia:[66] anger, heartbreak, restlessness, an inability to resume the daily routine, reflection on the difference between the pogroms of the 1880s and the one that had just erupted, and a craving for

[64] The phrase 'like sheep to the slaughter [ka-zon la-tevah]' appears in the prayer service for regular recitation on Mondays and Thursdays as one of the supplicatory prayers (*tefilot tahnunim*) in which Jews address the Lord and plead with him to look down upon them from his seat in Heaven to see them as they are, reduced to ridicule and derision and led like sheep to the slaughter ('Habet mishamayim u-re'eh ki hayinu la'ag ve-keles ka-zon la-tevah yuval').

[65] Ahad Ha-'Am to Y. Eisenstadt in Jaffa, 24 May 1903. Cited in *Igrot Ahad Ha-'Am*, iii (Tel-Aviv, 1957), 250. Emphases in original.

[66] See for example Ahad Ha-'Am, writing to Klausner on 29 Apr. 1903: 'The massacre in Kishinev is all I can think of; I cannot bring myself to take up any other matter . . .', *Igrot Ahad Ha-'Am*, iii (Tel-Aviv, 1957), 240.

action of some kind.[67] Somewhat like R. Elḥanan Spektor and his friends twenty years earlier, Dubnov, Aḥad Ha-'Am, H. N. Bialik, and several other members of his circle (largely at Dubnov's urging) began the urgent collection of all available hard data on the events in Kishinev for transmission to the west for wider distribution and publication.

But they went further. They knew that here and there, notably in Odessa itself, plans for organized Jewish self-defence against the mob were already in hand. They knew too that it was the declared policy of the Ministry of the Interior to stamp out all attempts by Jews to defend themselves on the grounds that these were of an intrinsically 'revolutionary' character. But it seemed to them right and necessary to encourage communal self-defence by issuing a general call for it to be circulated on a semi-conspiratorial basis to a limited number (no more than a hundred or so) of communal leaders in the empire. It would be drawn up in Hebrew as a minor precaution but also, most probably, because that would make it more effective. Its language would be at once clear and emphatic, critical of the government to be sure, but at the same time, on the assumption that the text would fall into the hands of the police sooner or later, not violently so. The difficult task of steering between straight talking and abuse was given to the recognized master of pellucid modern Hebrew, Aḥad Ha-'Am. The result was as penetrating and well written an analysis of the predicament of Russian Jewry as had ever been composed, offering, by implication and extension, an anticipatory view of the quandary into which all the Jews of all Europe would finally be placed. The full dark truth of what awaited them was, of course, beyond the imagining of the great essayist who drafted the manifesto or of any of the other members of his committee in the summer of 1903. On the contrary, running through it all there can be discerned a thread of hope that not all was lost, that the government of Russia would end by recognizing its responsibilities, that something would be saved from the impending wreckage after all, and, that, generally, the Jews would be spared the catastrophe of total and implacable confrontation with the Russian state. There was much in it, therefore, that reflected, in however shadowy a way, the principal moral and political uncertainties in which the modernist, generally liberal, essentially middle-class Jewish intelligentsia— Zionists among them, but not the Zionists alone—found itself.

The prescriptive passages of the Dubnov–Aḥad Ha-'Am manifesto were unambiguous. 'It was a disgrace for five million souls to depend on others, to bare their necks to the slaughterer, to cry for others to succour them without attempting to defend their property, their honour, and their lives themselves.' In that disgrace alone lay one of the root causes of the contempt in which Jews were held by the other peoples of the empire

---

[67] *Ha-Tekufah*, xxiv, 2nd edn. (1934), 416.

and, at the same time, the answer to the question how it could be that a few hundred drunks, armed with nothing better than clubs and axes, had dared to fall on a great, 40,000-strong Jewish community[68] to kill, mutilate, and pillage at will. The least the Jews could do now was to learn their lesson and act upon it, the lesson, quite simply, being that the Jews must take responsibility for their own, organized self-defence. They must make such dispositions as would give them early warning of an enemy's approach. They must ensure that the able-bodied in their number did all rally immediately to the point of danger. They should be in no doubt at all about the need or the right to defend themselves. Nor could the government properly deny the justice of their cause nor their specific, elementary right to self-defence. But whether it did or not, the leaders of the relevant Jewish communities must know that they were under a moral and social obligation to act both separately, each in their domain, and collectively, in conference, to consider the condition into which the Jews of the empire had now been propelled and what needed to be done on their behalf.[69]

But the government, for its part, never deviated from its absolute, repeatedly proclaimed opposition to any and all attempts by Jews to defend themselves against the mob or any other hostile body. And no such gathering of principal communal leaders as Dubnov, Aḥad Ha-'Am, and the others had called for was ever convened. Whether the latter had seriously expected one to assemble is unclear. It is not improbable that their hopes had never been high. While their manifesto had the form of a prescription for public action as well as an analysis of the Jewish condition it is best read as a *cri de cœur*, an important indicator of the mood that had begun to overtake the modernists in Russo-Polish Jewry, one marked by unusual pugnacity and a mounting determination to break out of the old quietistic-submissive shell in which Jewry was habitually encased. These were now common sentiments, although none would voice them with more precision and to greater public effect than the same Odessa literary circle's special delegate to Kishinev himself.

Ḥayyim Naḥman Bialik was 30 years of age in 1903, not yet the supreme representative of the contemporary national cultural revival that

---

[68] The 1897 imperial census listed the Jewish population of Kishinev as 50,237 out of a total of 108,483 (46.3 per cent). Moldavians and Russians together accounted for almost exactly the same proportion of the population as Jews. How many of these were in fact ethnic Russians is less clear: official figures gave 29,000, but the Russians may, in fact, have accounted for fewer than 10,000. Moldavians were officially 19,000, but may have been more numerous. There was a small community of Ukrainians.

[69] Text in *Ha-Tekufah*, xxiv. 417–20. In the event, much to Aḥad Ha-'Am's displeasure, the manifesto, dated 20 Apr. 1903 (OS, i.e. 3 May 1903 NS or two weeks after the pogrom), was not signed openly by Aḥad Ha-'Am himself, S. M. Dubnov, Ben-'Ami, Y. H. Ravnitzky, and H. N. Bialik as had been planned. Instead, it was dispatched to a selected list of about a hundred communities on behalf of the Society of Hebrew Writers in Odessa—an added, if useless precaution against its falling into the hands of the police.

he would soon become, but already widely known, recognized, and appreciated, especially in Zionist and Hebraist circles. He had made a name for himself as a master of the Hebrew language in all its intercalated biblical, Mishnaic, medieval, and now modern layers. He was, moreover, a wholly original literary figure, a poet whose verse derived much of its power from an incomparable and historically almost unprecedented combination of simplicity, clarity, and unmistakable social passion. Of old, exilic Jewry, condemned, as he saw it, to squalor and to immobilism, he had long despaired. In one of his very early poems, written on a return from the relative light and sparkle of Odessa to the gloom of the grandpaternal home in Zhitomir in the very heart of the Pale of Jewish Settlement, the picture is typically uncompromising: shrivelled age, stagnation, rot.[70] And it was from Odessa once again, now well established there in his own right, that Bialik set out for Kishinev, charged formally by the Jewish Historical Committee in that city to discover and document what had really happened and why. Dubnov, characteristically, had armed him with very precise tasks and careful procedural instructions, leaving, as he supposed, relatively little to the poet's imagination. Bialik was to interview and photograph all available witnesses, to attend and follow up the trials of such *pogromshchiki* as had been brought to justice, to visit cemeteries and hospitals and examine their registers, to collect or copy all relevant documents he could lay his hands on, to ascertain the true facts in suspected cases of rape, and to establish what had and what had not been done by the authorities and by non-Jews generally, but also by the Jews themselves.[71]

Bialik went about his task with exemplary thoroughness, in just such a determinedly investigative spirit as Dubnov had hoped for. He did so, however, in what the local people who assisted him in his duties later described as a state of mounting internal tension[72]—the more, perhaps, as he had already had something to say about the pogrom. ' 'Al ha-shehita' ('On the slaughter'), written in the immediate aftermath of the atrocity, is a short poem (four verses of seven lines each in all), exceedingly intense, almost unbearably bitter. What marks it most strongly, however, is that it is fuelled by sentiments that are firmly and consciously antithetical to those which Jews had traditionally been wont to express in the midst or in the aftermath of persecution and are precisely articulated, as we have seen, in the traditional prayer to the Merciful God (*Av ha-rahamim*). *If*, Bialik writes, *if* there is a God in heaven, and *if* a pathway to him—one which the speaker-victim-poet, for his part, has yet to discover—*can* be found, then let Heaven itself pray for him, for his heart is dead. He can no longer pray. His strength is gone. He has abandoned hope. 'Behead me

[70] 'Biteshuvati' (1891).
[71] P. Lahover, *Bialik: hayyav vi-yzirotav*, ii (Tel-Aviv, 1944), 424–6.
[72] Y. Berman, ' 'Im H. N. Bialik be-kishinov', in Shurer, *Ha-pogrom*, 75–80.

like a dog,' the speaker tells the executioner; 'the entire earth is my scaffold. . . . Strike me, and the blood of babes and greybeards will spurt on
to your shirt never to be wiped away.' The poet speaks of revenge as well:
but only to say that it would be beyond the power of Satan himself to
devise condign retribution for the spilling of a child's blood. Thus Bialik
the poet on first hearing and reading of what had happened in Kishinev.
On his return from Kishinev, the greater part of his duties for Dubnov
and his other colleagues accomplished, his mind now crowded with what
he had seen and heard on the spot, he set about the composition of the
greater work by which he is best remembered to this day.

'Be-'ir ha-hareiga' ('In the city of the slaughter') is a long poem composed chiefly, but irregularly, of loosely rhymed couplets. It is set in a
steady, rhythmic iambic heptameter to which it must owe something of
its power, the regular beat of its near-biblical Hebrew carrying other
associations to which his readers could not fail to respond. The consistently prophetic, even apocalyptic thrust Bialik gives to what he had to say
is further strengthened by its being set in its entirety in the imperative
mood. But the tone and the exceedingly precise choice of language
being almost infinitely bitter and pitiless, the biblical comparison is only
partly valid. In Jeremiah there are great and extended moments of pure
sorrow and empathy. In Bialik there are none. The four opening lines
announce the 268 lines that follow in all their implacable harshness:[73]

Rise and go to the city of the slaughter, enter the courtyards | and with your own
eyes see and with your own hands touch—on the fences | and on the trees and
on the stones and on the wall plaster— | the dried blood and the hardened brain-
matter of the dead.[74]

Bialik repeats, in somewhat more veiled terms on this second occasion,
the theme of the earlier poem, ' 'Al ha-sheḥita': the abandonment of man
by God and the abandonment of God by man. His real concern is now
with men alone, however, more specifically the Jews themselves: with the
victims in the first instance, but more especially with the survivors. In so
far as the theme of abandonment is repeated, it is therefore in terms of the

---

[73] I have made no attempt to translate the poem into equivalent English and do proper
justice to the ferocity of Bialik's verse precisely because it is a poem of great and (in Yeats's
celebrated coinage) terrible beauty and stands to this day, even in the long aftermath of the
Second World War, as the supreme expression of all that was most horrible in the condition of the Jews in Christian Europe. What follows is no more than a literal, unavoidably
lame prose rendering of such lines as have seemed to me to convey most succinctly what
Bialik had to say and are known to have struck great numbers of his readers most unfor-
gettably. However, bolder spirits have tried their hand at rendering it into English verse,
among them Abraham M. Klein, in *Selected Poems by H. N. Bialik*, ed. Israel Efros (revised
edn., New York, 1965).

[74] 'Kum lekh el 'ir ha-harega u-ba'ta el-haḥazeirot, | U-ve'einekha tir'eh u-
veyadkha te-mashesh 'al-hagdeirot | Ve-'al ha-'ezim ve-'al ha-avanim ve-'al gabei tiakh
ha-ketalim | Et-ha-dam ha-karush ve-et-ha-mo'akh ha-nikshe shel-ha-ḥalalim.'

abandonment of man by man and, very powerfully, of woman by man. The mindless cruelty of the mob is alluded to. The poet flinches from none of the revolting details that form the material essence of the matter of a pogrom: bellies ripped apart and stuffed with feathers, skulls crushed with nailed clubs and hammers, bones smashed with crowbars. But this is only preliminary to his taking up the conduct of those—the Jews themselves, not the Moldavians or the Russians—who *lived* through the pogrom, who 'fled like mice and hid like beetles and died like dogs wherever they were found', 'the sons of the sons of the Maccabees'. These were men who, when it was all over and they could emerge into the light of day from 'the latrines and pigsties and other filthy, excremental places' into which they had retreated, could do no more than bring themselves to weep and pray and repeat *Av ha-raḥamim* 'with not so much as a resolute curse upon their lips'.

How many proud and passionate souls had thought such thoughts about their own kind in the course of the long dark past of the Jews of Europe one does not know. Few had ever given voice to them. None had ever done so in such ferocious terms as these. But harder still was the passage that no reader of Bialik's poem has ever forgotten: even more intensely expressive of the rage, pity, heart-break, and barely governable revulsion that had overwhelmed him at Kishinev—although to some minds, the least warranted of all that the poem contained.

And you went down and came into the dark cellars, | There among the stores where the decent daughters of your people were defiled, | One by one, under the uncircumcised [who came at them] seven by seven, | The daughter before her mother's eyes, the mother before her daughter's, | Before the slaughter, during the slaughter, after the slaughter; . . . | And see too: there in the dark corner, | Under this mortar, behind that house, | There lay the husbands, the sons-in-law, the brothers, peeping through holes | At the holy bodies writhing under the flesh of asses, | Choking in their defilement, swallowing their blood | . . . There they lay, in their shame and watched—neither moving nor flinching, | Neither tearing out their eyes nor going mad— | And perhaps only praying, each man in the privacy of his soul: | O God Almighty, perform a miracle—let *me* be spared the evil.

'The pain of it all', Bialik wrote in what is, perhaps, the most succinct and telling and in its way conclusive of all his lines, 'was very great; so too was the disgrace. Which then was the *greater*?'[75] The poet offered no answer to his terrible question. He may have thought it enough to have posed it.

'Be-'ir ha-hareiga' was completed early in the autumn. It was December 1903, however, before it could be published in the bi-weekly Hebrew language *Ha-Zeman* in St Petersburg. *Ha-Zeman* was a less prestigious vehicle than, for example, *Ha-Shilo'aḥ*, published in Odessa itself at that

---

[75] 'Ve-gadol ha-ke'ev me'od u-gedola ha-klima—u-ma mi-sheneihem gadol?'

time, founded by Zionism's own philosopher-king, Aḥad ha-'Am him-self, with which Bialik had a close and continuing connection. The deci-sion to offer it to *Ha-Zeman* was deliberate and calculated, however, for the problem facing Bialik and his friends in the matter of publication was to ensure that it came before a reasonably well-disposed censor. The chief censor of Hebrew books in the capital, was a former Lubavitcher *ḥasid* turned Russian Orthodox Christian. It was thought that he was much more likely to fit the bill than his less independently minded, more junior colleague in Odessa. The chief censor was known to be friendly; and, conveniently enough, mildly corrupt.[76] Even so, certain cuts had to be made. Famously, the title of the poem was altered to 'Massa Nemirov' ('The Vision of Nemirov'). This was an allusion to a vast and well-remembered massacre of Jews in the Ukrainian town of that name by Cossacks in the course of the Chmielnicki rising of 1648: a great pogrom to be sure, but one that had taken place in an age when Poles, not Rus-sians, were the rulers. Nevertheless, lines that could be interpreted as crit-ical of the authorities or simply blasphemous had to be excised. But the bulk of the poem got through and could be published as written; and no Jewish reader was ever in any doubt that the true subject was Kishinev. As the text of 'Be-'ir ha-hareiga' began to be known and when, in fairly short order, to the original Hebrew there were added first a Yiddish translation[77] and then one in Russian,[78] the impression on the literate, socially minded public was often shattering. Ya'akov Mazeh, crown (or state-appointed) Rabbi (*kazyonny ravvin*) of Moscow—but, exception-ally among the holders of that doubtful office, a man who commanded almost universal respect—promptly declared, all a-tremble, that the prayers of lamentation traditionally said on the anniversary of the ori-ginal 1648 massacre should now be replaced by 'Bialik's vision'. The irre-pressible Vladimir Jabotinsky, on the very verge of entering into his role as Zionism's perpetual *enfant terrible*, observed that a poem of such qual-ity offered all the reason anyone needed to learn the Hebrew language; and went on to provide a preface to his Russian translation of 'Be-'ir ha-hareiga' in the form of a poem of his own. Joseph Klausner, perhaps the most important scholarly authority on Hebrew language and literature at the time, and Bialik's contemporary and friend, wrote to Bialik that the poem had almost driven him mad. 'For three consecutive days after read-ing it I neither slept at night nor worked in the daytime. This is no exag-geration; it is the absolute truth. . . . The Devil knows what one is to make of it: it is not really a poem, it is not a lyric, it is more of a prophecy by Jeremiah or by Ezekiel. You have attained the uppermost peak of Hebrew poetry,' he told Bialik, 'and perhaps of poetry in general.'[79]

---

[76] Lahover, *Bialik*, 435–6.　　[77] By Y. L. Peretz.
[78] By Vladimir Jabotinsky.　　[79] Lahover, *Bialik*, 437–8.

But it is, perhaps, the recollections of the young men who had been deputed by the Kishinev community to help Bialik in his investigations for the Historical Committee that best convey the immensely charged contemporary reaction to his poem, notably the reaction of those who, in the long term, would count for most.

Each and every word [one of them was to write] was like a skewer of white hot iron, each and every line a consuming fire: it was all bitter derision, contempt, and rage pouring into the depths of one's soul like so much boiling lead. But not on the heads of those who had done the driving, the persecution, and the beating, rather those who had been driven, persecuted, and beaten—those who only a few weeks earlier had [in roughly Bialik's own words] touched the dried blood and the hardened brainmatter of their fallen brethren on the plaster of their walls . . . We read the poem a second and a third time; we studied it over and over again—and then, wonderfully, the longer we read and reread it, the better we understood it: the rebuke was not a rebuke . . . the wounds were the wounds of one who loved and wished to cure [us]. . . . The chisel of his language had broken open the Jew's closed, sorrowing heart, injecting it with an ancient spirit of heroism and energy.[80]

It was not Bialik, of course, certainly not Bialik single-handed, who precipitated the change of mood among the radical, modernist young in Russian Jewry following Kishinev. But he did contribute to the change mightily; and he expressed it with immense and unequalled power. Thereafter, there was no contesting his status as the national poet; and the fact that he became so very widely recognized as such speaks volumes in itself for the state of Jewish public opinion in the eastern European heartland at this time and after. Great segments of that public would now see itself and its predicament in terms that, if they were not identical, were certainly analogous to those in which the other 'submerged' nations of Europe had come to perceive themselves in the course of the nineteenth century and, still more urgently, the early decades of the twentieth century. They were a people that would have to learn to strike out if they were not to be repeatedly and perhaps totally struck down. This was not an entirely new sentiment. But from this point on it was sharper and more explicit than it had ever been before.

VI

In Gomel, Mogilev governorate, the scene of the next major pogrom five months later,[81] events pursued a course for which, up to that point, there had been no real precedent. The early stages were the usual ones. Rumours of trouble brewing had begun to circulate in workshops,

---

[80] Berman, 'Bialik', 76.   [81] 29 Aug. and 1 Sept. 1903 (OS).

taverns, and stores frequented by non-Jews some two weeks earlier. Telegrams to the governor of the province warning of riots in the offing and asking for protection were ignored. A dispute of the utmost banality between a Jewish woman stallkeeper in the market-place and her non-Jewish customer turned rapidly, possibly by design, into generalized street violence which gave rise, in turn, to a false tale of a sober Christian having been killed by angry Jews. On the familiar general signal 'Beat the Yids!' ('*Bei zhidov!*') being sounded, gangs of hooligans who had been gathering meanwhile in the market set upon individual Jews, their homes, and their places of business. There were some casualties on both sides, the police refusing to intervene at this stage and displaying every intention of cleaving, so far as the Jews were concerned, to customary hostile neutrality. A short break ensued. Then, three days later, a large number of Russian workmen bent on violence, plunder, and general mayhem, among them several hundred railroad employees, entered the town and the pogrom proper began. Once again, then, so much as usual, except that on this occasion a Jewish response had been prepared. As the mob in the market-place set out to carry the attack to parts of the town known to be populated by Jews they were regularly met by lightly armed and centrally (if loosely) directed groups of young members of the Jewish community, Bundists and Zionists, and among the latter the Zionist-socialists of the Po'alei Zion wing of the movement especially. Initially, they were successful, able on each occasion to beat the mob back. Later, however, they had to cope not only with rioters, but with the police itself, and later still, in some cases, with troops who had been moved in to shield the rioters and punish the Jews for their impudence. This was a great deal more difficult, in the final analysis well beyond their power. Still, the results were not unsatisfactory. The pogrom as such had not lasted as long as the one in Kishinev, the casualties were not as numerous, and there was substantially less arson and general damage to private and commercial property. This reduction of the horror owed something to the decision evidently taken by the authorities in the course of the lull between the first round and the more serious second round of the affair not to allow things to get entirely out of hand. But there can be little question that the resistance offered by Jewish youth groups played as great if not a greater role in keeping the scale of bodily injury and material damage down: directly, by meeting and discomposing the mob; indirectly, by encouraging the governor and his people to do their duty lest the confrontation between Jews and Christians end with a palpable victory for the former.

That it was a victory of some sort was hardly in doubt. Jewish casualties, for once, turned out to be substantially, if not entirely, offset by those incurred by their attackers. The sources are not unanimous about the precise numbers, but it is likely that the number of dead counted when it was all over on 14 September 1903 (NS), four days after it began was twenty or under. Of these a dozen or fewer were Jews, some killed by rioters, others, significantly enough, shot or bayonetted by the troops. The remaining eight were Christians, more precisely rioters.[82] How much damage had been done to Jewish property before the police and troops finally closed in remains uncertain. The governor's report on the causes and course of the pogrom speaks of 200 Jewish homes being heavily damaged. The total may have been greater: in general, as we shall see in a moment, his report was wildly mendacious. It remained that 'Gomel' was not 'Kishinev' and the boost to Jewish morale—at all events among those who were radically inclined—was therefore beneficial and long lasting. 'What had occurred . . . was a fight rather than a pogrom,' were the terms in which the only Yiddish language newspaper to be published legally in Russia summed it up.[83] Indeed, a corner had been turned, a precedent set, and a lesson both taught and learned. To activists of all kinds it was immensely encouraging. To the Bundists it was doubly so. What had transpired in Gomel, the RSDWP committee in Kharkov proclaimed in a congratulatory message, had 'taught the Russian workman, as dozens of good books would never have taught him, to respect his Jewish comrade as a fighter. The Jewish proletariat is now to be seen in its new role . . . as the defender of the impoverished Jewish masses whom the government, promising plunder, had incited an ignorant throng to attack.'[84]

The police, through postal intercepts and agents' reports,[85] were well aware of the change of mood in certain segments of the Jewish population and greatly disliked it. The idea that it might now be evident to the Jews that they were capable of scattering the mob when necessary and had the will to do so—certainly in cities like Gomel in which they constituted half or even slightly more than half of the total population[86]—was one that the Russian authorities were not prepared to countenance. Such independence and, as they saw it, such impudent and ideologically intolerable behaviour, needed to be stamped out. This was the meaning of the regularity with which the police, followed by the troops, had more or less

---

[82] A contemporary Bundist source announced a total of eight dead on the Jewish side: six Jews and two Christians who had joined the Jewish self-defence forces.

[83] *Der Fraind* (St Petersburg), 20/7 Sept. 1903. Cited in Tobias, *The Jewish Bund in Russia*, 227.

[84] Cited in Hertz et al., *Di Geshikhte fun Bund*, ii. 70–1.

[85] An intercepted letter, written immediately after the Gomel pogrom and thought of sufficient interest to be sent to St Petersburg, speaks of 'such occurrences encouraging us to maintain the struggle' and of the 'hope that next year we shall be able to join the ranks of the fighters for liberty and freedom from slavery' (18 Sept. 1903, RSA, DM00, 1903, D555, MA 1129).

[86] In all 20,385 (or 56.4 per cent of the total population) according to the imperial census of 1897.

spontaneously turned upon the Jews rather than on the actual rioters in the course of the pogrom itself. It would be made clearer still and entirely explicit in the aftermath when, in anticipation of a fresh wave of criticism from abroad, the government-controlled press took the line that it was the Jews of Gomel who had criminally and provocatively attacked the police and the troops, all of whom had been sent in exclusively to quell disorder and with the best of intentions.

The tone of the government's response had been set very early, however. When the governor of the province, having chosen initially to ignore all early warnings of trouble ahead, turned up in Gomel (no more than three hours' train journey from his seat in Mogilev) at the concluding stage of the pogrom to see things for himself, he chose to begin by haranguing the Jewish delegation that had come to see him on what he claimed was *its* responsibility for the affair. Once again, he told them, the Jews had displayed their well-known impertinence and stubbornness, the disastrous impression they had made on the government being greatly exacerbated on this occasion by their having illicitly armed themselves. He pointed triumphantly to the fact (that none denied) that the Bund was relatively strong in Gomel and charged the Jews of Gomel with harbouring social democrats in their midst. There had been a time, the governor wished to remind them, when Jews took no part in politics and when, in consequence, there were no pogroms. He then contradicted himself by telling his audience that the pogroms of the 1880s had had to do with the 'attitude of the Jews to the Russian population', not politics. In any event, now matters were otherwise: 'Jews have become the instigators [*sdelalis' podstrekatelyami*] who incite and lead all [*sic*] anti-government movements.' The Bund in its entirety and all these other social democrats too were Jews. True, there were cases of Christians joining these movements, but only after Jews had incited them to do so. You have lost all respect for the authorities, the delegation was told. You are contemptuous of Christians. You conduct anti-state propaganda. You fire on troops who come to protect you. It is we, not you, who have to act in our own defence.[87] And in his formal report to the emperor, a minor masterpiece of distortion and mendacity, the governor summed up the affair along similar lines, namely that the true cause of the trouble at every stage was to be sought in the Jews' aggressive and insubordinate behaviour.

On 29 August in the city of Gomel [the Tsar was informed] in the market square, a peasant who had quarrelled with a Jewess about the quality of her goods struck

---

[87] From notes taken down by one of the Jewish participants and distributed (in Yiddish) to interested communal leaders elsewhere, intercepted and translated into Russian by the police in Warsaw, and dispatched to St Petersburg, 4 Sept. 1903, RSA, DP00, 1903, D555 MA Ya/dd/1/ob 100. See also Memorandum submitted to the Ministry of Interior by representatives of the Jewish communities in Gomel, 18 Sept. 1903 (OS), RSA, DP00, 1903, D2719 m7–9 kob.

her in the face. A crowd (or multitude: *tolpa*) of Jews immediately fell on the peasant and a fight broke out in the course of which a Christian was wounded and later died. When the fight was over the Jewish crowd began throwing rocks and shooting at the police; whereupon a police officer responded by firing in the air, accidentally [*sluchaino*] hitting one of the Jews. The day ended with the Jews considering themselves the victors and openly boasting as much.

On 1 September a group of workmen[88] entered the city intent upon a pogrom. They were dissuaded from carrying through by the police and the whole affair would indeed have ended peacefully had there not appeared at that very moment a multitude of armed Jews, some 800 men all told. Their intention being to attack the workmen, the workmen began to pillage Jewish homes. The task [set] the police was to prevent these masses of people from reaching the city centre. Some hours later the army took over and calm was restored to the population . . .

While these disturbances are widely considered to have had the character of an anti-Jewish pogrom, I for my part find it necessary to point out, that it is the Jews themselves who should be held responsible [for what occurred] inasmuch as they conduct anti-government propaganda, incite workmen to disturb the peace, and strike a disdainful attitude [*prenebrezhitel'noe otnoshenie*] towards Christians.[89]

The upshot was that, along with those among the actual rioters whom it had been decided to arrest and prosecute, thirty-six Jews were brought to trial as well and that in very short order the official view of the affair was that the behaviour of the Jews had been at least as violent as that of the *pogromshchiki* proper, in important respects more so. Still more seriously, it had been—as that of the *pogromshchiki* evidently had not—rebellious. Upon this having been established and duly articulated all concerned at all levels of the administration knew how they were to deal with the Jewish population in analogous situations and how to speak to them too when it was thought imperative or merely convenient to do so.

Where the Jews themselves were concerned, it would be a great deal too much to say that the passivity and self-abnegation that had so shocked Bialik was to be a thing of the past after Gomel. But there had for once been a response to danger and attack that was nothing if not robust and it was in no more danger of being forgotten—in modernist, nationalist circles of all relevant tendencies, at any rate—than the horror, and as many thought the shame, of Kishinev. The lasting effect of the two pogroms was therefore to move Jewish opinion a step forward in radicalization of mind and action, to a further reinforcement of its alienation from the Russian state, and so to preparation of a further twist in Russian Jewry's long-maturing crisis of social orientation and purpose. To which it needs

---

[88] It was characteristic that whereas the governor spoke of a 'crowd of Jews', he described the rioters as a 'group of workmen'.

[89] 4 Sept. 1903 (OS), RSA, GA RFF 102 DP00 1903 D555 LA 153–57.

to be added that the crisis could not be that of Russian Jewry alone. The condition, fortunes, and internal evolution of the greater part of European Jewry could not fail to impinge in some degree on the destinies, qualities, social coherence, and broad course of development of all—so long, at all events, as movement out of Russia was free and the Russian Empire formed part, awkwardly or otherwise, of the European cultural and political system.

But for the time being it was the hardening of Russian attitudes and purposes that was felt most strongly. There was, of course, nothing new in it being the preponderant view at all politically influential levels of Russian society that whatever else one might think of the Jews they were, and deserved to be treated as, an alien people immiscible with the rest. What was to be marked was that much of the ambiguity that had long dogged Russian policy where its Jewish population was concerned dropped away in the course of 1903. The Autocracy found it easier than in the previous century to permit its enmity to be revealed as beyond mitigation even by sober calculation of its own immediate short- or long-term interests or, as before, by frank but divided mind on the matter. It followed that what the Jews themselves, as a body, had now to cope with was not a party, or circle, or particular group of bureaucrats or politicians or intellectuals, not even the court, but more than ever the state itself *in toto*, driven virtually without reservation or compunction by an engine of government that was remarkable before all else for its will, if indeed not always its ability, to control the society over which it ruled. Russia was a case, that is to say, of a country so organized bureaucratically, so policed, and so served by its officials that Jews who were unfortunate enough to inhabit it were for all practical purposes held supine in a condition so dire in every material and psychological respect that the only conceivable treatment for it was shock. A shock had been delivered. Further shocks were to come.

At some point in the years leading up to Kishinev official Russia had implicitly abandoned what had always been the basic operative principle by which the political men of the Enlightenment, in Russia no less than elsewhere, had sought to square their negative judgement upon Jewry and Judaism with their views on what the proper management of the state and the economy required in actual and fruitful practice. Most commonly, as we have seen repeatedly, this was reducible to the old distinction between 'useful' and 'useless' Jews that had been formulated at its clearest under the Habsburg Emperor Joseph II, but which was then followed by virtually all the European states, the only important exceptions to the rule (in the nineteenth century) being France, Great Britain, and the Netherlands. The 'useless' were conceived of as forming the great majority, the 'useful' as a small, even negligible minority. The channel by which individuals might pass from the large class to the small was expected to be a narrow one. But however strictly defined, it was there to be negotiated—by the very talented, by the rich, and, as often as not, by the unscrupulous. Thus even in Russia, until in 1881 a process whereby the passage was to be almost totally blocked off was begun and the old useful/useless distinction discarded. This was not done explicitly. Nor was it done with efficiency or (by standards that would become familiar several decades later) with especial ferocity. It can even be said of Tsar Alexander III and his closest and most influential advisers that they were less than clear in their minds about what it was precisely that they were embarked upon. Something of the old ambiguity about the way to proceed in the matter of (in practice: against) the Jews was evident to the end of Alexander III's reign and for some time after. But now, in these early years of the twentieth century, the last of the awkwardness and the uncertainties that had dogged the Autocracy in these respects since the time of Catherine II[90] were being swept away: in practice and, increasingly, in principle as well. What could not as yet be stated officially with full freedom nor, as we shall see, acted upon wholly without inhibition, could be said at home and even abroad at any rate by unofficial spokesmen for what was known, politely, as Russian conservative opinion. M. O. Menchikov, editor of the semi-official, uncompromisingly anti-Jewish St Petersburg newspaper *Novoe Vremya*, writing in the London *Monthly Review* in February 1904 and setting out the relevant credo, deserves to be quoted at some length.

The danger for Russia of the Jewish settlements may be summarized in the following points. The Jews within our Empire form a closely organised political community of some 8,000,000 [*sic*] souls, a community not merely foreign in creed and language, but decidedly hostile to the country. A vagrant tribe amid established nations, they are totally unfit for husbandry, and almost invariably season their petty trades and other transactions with various tricks and usurious practices. They are mostly keepers of bars or brothels, pimps, smugglers, receivers of stolen goods, moneylenders or pawnbrokers, counterfeiters of coin, etc.; in other words, 'go-betweens' of every branch of preposterous business. Some are small farmers and contractors; as workmen they live from hand to mouth. Settled between two seas within the fifteen Russian provinces nearest to Western Europe, and residing chiefly amid two great Powers—Russia and Austria—the Jews could no more raise the culture of the country than develop a rich industry or big trade. Far from being well-off, they are part and parcel of the miserable proletariat and quite incapable of sound work. The progressive incursions of this hungry yet well-organised alien colony is, therefore, justly regarded as a source of great danger for our Empire. The much talked of 'demarcation line' [marking the Pale of Jewish Settlement] is nothing but a crumbling dam, not proof against the infiltration of the turbid waves of Judaism. Together with merchants of the first-class guild, mechanics, and other workers of higher education,

---

[90] See Chapter 1 above.

who also possess the legal right to reside in Russia, innumerable Jews stole in who could boast no definite trade or business. As a result, hardly a century had elapsed before the whole of the trade in South Russia was practically in the hands of the Jews. In 'White Russia' they are landowners, whilst in the several capitals they have found access to the liberal professions. The Russian press, for instance, is largely Jewish property.

Generally speaking, Russia is distinctly hospitable to foreigners. Our Government entertains not the slightest objection to a foreign people bringing into the country their own specific talents, knowledge, and capital. But the Jews do nothing of the kind, nor do they mix easily with the native population; it is a fact that five hundred years residence in Poland and [Lithuania] has failed to make them into either Poles or White Russians. Besides, Jews, taken as a whole, are ignorant and anything but naturally gifted. With two or three exceptions, they have given no remarkable men to Russia. Hostile both to Christianity and to Russian independence, they are as a dissolvent in the national culture and organism.

Finally:

The Jews are the victims of their own history. They are the only race in Europe which has not been assimilated by Christianity. They should either found a kingdom of their own—outside Europe!—as the Zionists propose, or else renounce their nationality. The real Ghetto of the Jews is Judaism itself, an old creed which congeals its followers in a serfdom heavier than that of ancient Egypt. To me it seems that the only possible Canaan for all, including the Jews themselves, would be Christianity, and the assimilation of the Jews with those nations among whom they are now living.[91]

VII

In western, even in central Europe, nothing remotely like Kishinev had occurred in living memory. The view that such an incident as this was not merely bestial, but 'medieval' and anachronistic, and *ipso facto* foreign to the advanced societies of the west was not without grounds. On the face of things, Jewish and non-Jewish observers alike had reason to say, even to believe, that nothing of so brutal a nature could now occur in the general area lying west of Poland. It was true that western and central European Jews had no more been spared a recrudescence of the ancient—indeed, medieval—charge of ritual murder than their cousins in the east. And in the west, as in the east, particular cases were apt to be accompanied by mob violence—although admittedly, always on a smaller and less murderous scale. In central Europe a certain ambivalence on the part of the authorities was detectable as well. In 1882, upon the disappearance of a young Christian girl in the north-eastern Hungarian

[91] *Monthly Review*, Feb. 1904.

town of Tisza Eszlar, the local police, the examining magistrate, and the Catholic parish priest were all resolved on bringing a large group of local Jews to trial on a charge of murder to obtain her blood. At the higher levels of the state prosecution service there were none who doubted that the accused were innocent. All knew that no body had been found. And it was well known too, and would be shown in court to be the case, that the sole testimony against the wretched people brought to trial was perjured, having been extracted by heavy-handed police pressure on the young son of one of the accused. But with numerous parliamentary deputies in Budapest pressing for a trial to be held and the Jews' supposed iniquities exposed, it was inconvenient politically to have the charges quashed.

The affair caused a sensation. It was followed closely by the public, the local and foreign press, even by the diplomatic corps. The atmosphere in the trial court was heated, the more so for the President of the Court, as foreigners were quick to observe, being unashamedly partisan. He conducted himself, the British ambassador in Vienna reported, 'more like an unscrupulous advocate for the prosecution than a judge . . . almost encouraging the intimidation of the witnesses for the defence by the fanatical audience in the Court'.[92] But it was evident that there was no case to answer and in the closing stages of the trial the public prosecutor himself decided that he had no choice but to propose that all the accused be acquitted, as indeed they were. The verdict was appealed, but upheld—in the courts, however, not in the streets. The acquittal of the accused was followed by attacks on Jews in Budapest and elsewhere in Hungary, some serious enough for a local state of emergency to be declared. Later, it was discovered that the girl whom the Jews of Tisza Eszlar were supposed to have killed and bled had committed suicide by drowning.

A similar charge of ritual murder was raised in the case (already alluded to[93]) of Adolf Buschoff, a Jewish butcher in Xanten in the Roman Catholic German Rhineland. The accusation was first sounded in the local press. Later it was taken up by the police. Buschoff was arrested, but discharged fairly promptly for lack of evidence. However, when the noted anti-Semitic court preacher Adolf Stöcker,[94] outraged by what he considered to be the authorities' failure to deal with the matter with all due severity, brought the case before the Prussian Diet, the wretched Buschoff was re-arrested and brought to trial after all. Once again the charge was found to be without foundation—on this second occasion by a jury. Buschoff was acquitted. There was a similar pattern of events in the East Prussian town of Konitz in 1900 where the central circumstance was

[92] Elliott to Granville, 14 July 1883, PRO, F0 7/1050. Cited in N. Katzburg, *Anti-shemiyut be-hungariya, 1867–1914* (Tel Aviv, 1969), 239.
[93] See Chapter 4.   [94] See Chapter 3.

the readiness of the local police to credit a charge of ritual murder by Jews, leaving it to the courts to rule in due course what they themselves could easily have discovered—or, as is likely, had in fact known all along—namely, that the evidence had been fabricated. An acquittal was mandatory. But the charge, having been brought, sufficed to precipitate riots against the local Jewish population.

Set against what had occurred in eastern Europe in the early 1880s and would recur repeatedly and in rising degrees of horror in the years leading up to the First World War, and then, with yet greater severity in its aftermath (as will be seen), such incidents in central and western Europe were very small beer. At no time was there cause to fear a serious breakdown of security in Germany, France, Italy, Austria-Hungary, or Great Britain. In no case did suspicion of deliberate provocation and manipulation by the central authorities of the countries concerned arise, nor any cause to doubt their devotion, if not to their formal, constitutional responsibilities *vis-à-vis* their Jewish subjects, at any rate to the need to preserve general law and order in the streets of their cities as a matter of fundamental political principle. The sum total of injury to Jewish life and limb, and damage to property and other worldly goods—even in the cases of the earlier anti-Jewish riots in Alsace in the revolutionary years 1830 and 1848 or those that spread through France as the Dreyfus Affair approached its climax—was never more than negligible, however nasty the consequences for those under attack in each case. That charges of ritual murder should have arisen, however, and been taken up at some level of officialdom, even if only a junior one, in the ostensibly more enlightened western half of the continent was shocking and especially wounding to Jewish opinion. It faced the more alert and better informed sons and daughters of those who had been similarly outraged by the Damascus Affair half a century earlier with the thought, perhaps the actual possibility, that they could be no more certain than their parents had been that the response to such dangerous nonsense in the west might really be no different materially from that which was common enough in the more obviously backward and obscurantist east. Whether a meaningful distinction could be drawn between the conduct of the French Prime Minister in 1840[95] and the Hungarian minister of justice forty-two years later (neither of whom was able to bring himself to dismiss the blood libel out of hand) and that of some of the less enlightened men at the top of the Russian bureaucratic hierarchy might be considered an open question. In this respect even the undoubted differences between the Orthodox Church (as instanced by its leading representative in Kishinev in 1903) and the most important of all western churches, the Roman Catholic, were negligible. It was true that the Church of Rome *as such* had long since dismissed the charge of ritual murder as a nasty fiction.[96] But the verbal portrayal of Jewry as the embodiment of evil, not least because its members habitually indulged in ritual murder, was a staple item in no less an organ of the Church than the Jesuits' *Civiltà Cattolica*. And what emerged from the smoothly and carefully written pages of *Civiltà Cattolica* differed in no real sense from the systematic, verbal, *and* visual portrayal of 'the Jew' in the flagship of French anti-Semitism, Édouard Drumont's *Libre Parole* newspaper, as a member of a knife-wielding, sub-human species, his disproportionately long, clawed fingers dripping blood.[97]

But, in any case, the resurrection from time to time of the blood libel was only one particularly disturbing contribution to the unremitting flow of provocative incidents, practices, insinuations, and supposed tales out of school, some important, some merely nagging, with which the more alert, sensitive, and insecure among central and western European Jews were obliged to cope. Those whose place was on the lower rungs of the socio-economic ladder were apt to be more immediately and materially vulnerable. The Jewish populations of Xanten and Konitz declined rapidly after the traumas visited upon them. But no Jew, however well and securely placed, could entirely ignore the battering. And, commonly, it was those who had travelled farthest socially and economically, who had been transformed most thoroughly by the great integrationist and assimilatory thrust, and who identified most closely with the society around them who were touched most painfully—if only in the deeper recesses of their minds and souls. It is true that in Germany the state, as we have seen, while less than friendly by and large and openly discriminatory in certain well-defined respects, showed no inclination to reverse the emancipatory process, or even pay serious attention to those who, whether from within the magic circle of government and influence or from outside it, called upon it to do so. It did not seem to members of the German political class that it was within the power of mere parliamentary politicians, preachers, publicists, historians, or journalists, let alone private individuals, however socially or politically prominent they might be, or for Churches, political parties, and related ginger groups, or for editorial committees, associations of students, or for any other type or class of organization or institution, parliamentary or extra-parliamentary, legal or illegal, to provoke a really powerful movement for change. No doubt

---

[96] See Chapter 3.

[97] In the autumn of 1881, not long therefore before the Tisza Eszlar affair, the editors of *Civiltà Cattolica* ran a series of articles (datelined Florence, 6 and 27 Oct., 10 and 24 Nov., and 7 Dec. 1881) in which, on the alleged basis of hitherto secret documents, they offered their readers, as already promised, 'authentic proof of the existence of a religious Talmudic-rabbinic law that obliged Jews to celebrate their Passover with Christian blood' (*Civiltà Cattolica*, 8, series 11, 225–31, 344–52, 476–83, 598–606, 730–8).

all contributions of whatever nature to the general mood and climate of opinion impinged on the thinking of those who, being in political authority, were in a position from time to time to consider and decide some aspect of the matter of the Jews in its determining, *political* mode, the more so as the tendency to seek refuge behind the argument that state policy needed *ultimately* to be a function of public sentiment was a growing one. In practice, however, in this connection as in so many others, what might ultimately be the case was hardly relevant; and of an impending change in state policy in the short or middle term in respect of the Jews there was no sign. The rule throughout the Hohenzollern and Habsburg empires and the liberal west of Europe was that much as emancipation had in each case been the gift—or, as some of the very orthodox among the Jews held it to be, the curse—of whoever held power in the state to grant, so it remained within the power of the state exclusively to modify or withdraw it. In this sense, the political terms on which the condition of the Jews hinged at the end of the nineteenth century were still consistent with those on which the history of the Jews throughout their Exile in Europe (and, indeed, elsewhere) had been contingent, namely on the interplay between approaches to their affairs that derived from religious teaching, folk memory, simple xenophobia, and whatever else happened to be socio-politically fashionable at the time on the one hand and what was perceived to be dictated by *raison d'état* on the other.

So far as the Jews themselves were concerned, the traditional view had been that where considerations of *raison d'état* governed the thinking of their rulers, there they were tolerably safe. It still obtained, generally speaking. So did its corollary that it was where cold, calculable, and, in a word, pragmatic considerations of state (or of the ruler, personally) were overridden, or even significantly coloured, by private views and interests, by religious dogmas and over-arching social theories, that danger loomed. By the same token, it was where the machinery of the state had come to be harnessed openly and unmistakably to such notions that danger was manifest. It was precisely this that had occurred in Russia. But there was no fear in Germany, Austria-Hungary, the Netherlands, Italy, Great Britain, or France of any of the visible arms of government—the police, the military, the tax authorities—turning against law-abiding Jewish subjects in the Russian or Romanian manner as a matter of daily practice. The questions that German Jews whose full civil emancipation could be said to have been longest delayed had reason to ask themselves were of another order. When were the last of the restrictions and limitations on appointments to judgeships, to senior university and secondary school positions, to admission to the officer corps, to positions in the higher ranks of the bureaucracy and the like, and, more distantly and less hopefully, to a ministerial or other political position of real power in government likely to be done away with? And when, if at all, and then on

what terms, would the social and cultural integration of the Jews in German society be completed—*at least* in the sense that the debate upon it
and the tensions and objections it continued to arouse among non-Jewish
Germans would come to an end? The decisive circumstance was that
while the condition of the Jews in Germany was not wholly satisfactory
for all, for most it was unsatisfactory only at the margin of their lives. The
especially ambitious, their purposes being thwarted, and the especially
sensitive, their dignity being continually hurt, had been rendered restless
and in some cases, as we have seen, incurably unhappy by the tension
between what they had hoped for and what they knew they were likely to
be granted. Some sought to keep a stiff, but bitter upper lip. Some sought
solace in a self-generated vision of an eventual Jewish-German cultural
symbiosis. Some, soberly and even happily, thought such a symbiosis was
actually in train. One way or another the sum of the German Jewish experience in the final decades of the Second Reich suggests that a substantial
measure of social and political estrangement, even hostility, could be
borne by emancipated Jewry everywhere provided only that such
estrangement remained unmatched and unarticulated in the day-to-day
treatment accorded them by the state and its major instruments. It was
because the Dreyfus Affair gave cause to consider whether in this very
particular respect matters might in fact be closer to a breakdown in republican France than in imperial Germany that the initial shock to the morale
of western, but especially French Jewry itself needless to say, was so great
and its moral repercussions, even if only in a smaller and less lasting way,
were not wholly unlike those of Kishinev in the east. In France, as in Germany, as we have seen, there had long been calls from a variety of quarters
to reverse the process of emancipation and exclude Jews from society—if
not from the country entirely. What was revealed, as the Affair moved
towards its technical denouement, was that calls for the reduction of the
Jews had gained far more in power and resonance since the Revolution
than had generally been suspected and that the balance of considerations
governing the terms on which the state and the major components of its
machinery dealt with its Jewish citizens had either shifted substantially or
was likely to do so in a quite readily foreseeable future.

VIII

It is necessary, for present purposes, to distinguish between the Dreyfus
Affair as a crisis in the history of France and the Affair as a crisis in the his-
tory of the Jews, at all events in the history of the Jews of France. Charles
Péguy, one of the most devoted, intransigent, and enduring of *dreyfusards*
was of this view—although it needs to be added that he believed that the
Affair marked a crisis in the history of Christianity as well. Certainly, it is

necessary to separate the *case* of the wretched Captain Alfred Dreyfus from the *Affair*—the Affair writ large, that is to say—to which he so unwillingly gave his name. The fate and the sorrows of the competent, but by no means distinguished or especially promising, junior staff officer who was arrested on a monstrously false, deliberately concocted charge of treason, secretly tried and convicted, but publicly degraded, shunted off to Devil's Island for life, and only released, pardoned (for a crime he never committed), and ultimately rehabilitated in the wake of an unprecedentedly huge and intensely bitter and divisive public and political row—all that was one thing. The conflict between the defenders of the spirit and principles of the Revolution of 1789 and the Third Republic that was thought to embody them and those who either looked back to the *ancien régime* and the primacy of the Catholic Church or forward to something as yet undefined, but in every way better than the intolerably mediocre, corrupt, bourgeois, and in certain ways alien polity that had emerged out of the shambles of the 1870 débâcle—all that was something else again. The case of Captain Dreyfus may be regarded as having caused the deeper, wider conflict over the past and future of France to explode. It certainly provided—fortuitously—an occasion for the principal lines of stress and conflict in modern France to be laid bare as never before. But except in one cardinal respect, the two aspects of the whole are best kept apart—not least because, in general, those who were impelled for one reason or another to play a role in one were apt to have little interest in the other. When the Affair as a daily wrangle had at last died down, Péguy complained that whereas he and other *dreyfusards* had been prepared to suffer ruin and even die for Dreyfus—or, more precisely, for what he and others were to call *Dreyfusisme*—Captain Dreyfus was not prepared for equivalent sacrifice himself. It was this absolute devotion of *others* to the matter of Dreyfus that, to Péguy's mind, lay at the heart of the Affair and gave it its uniquely passionate and moral character, whereas all that Alfred Dreyfus wanted, and his devoted brother Mathieu with him, was to have his name cleared.

He did not die; but there were several who died for him—making, sanctifying, and sanctioning a mystique. Others died for him. He was not ruined in his own cause. He is not the man to ruin himself for another. Yet many were ruined for him. Many sacrificed their career, their bread, their life itself, their wives' and their children's bread. Many threw themselves into inexpiable misery for him, resulting, sanctifying, and sanctioning a mystique.[98]

Neither Alfred nor his brother wanted to fight the army that had betrayed him, let alone a Republic that was prepared to back the army. Once he had been fully rehabilitated, the case, so far as he and his family were concerned, was at an end.

[98] *Notre Jeunesse*, in Charles Péguy, *Oeuvres en Prose 1909–1914* (Paris, 1961), 545.

Where, none the less, the case of Captain Dreyfus and the Affair when writ large may be seen not merely to touch, but to have been organically connected from the first and throughout, was in the cardinal respect of Alfred Dreyfus being a Jew. It is safe to say that had he not been a Jew, he would not immediately have been held suspect, let alone falsely and maliciously accused. Nor is it likely that a non-Jewish officer *justly* convicted of treason would have been so bitterly and publicly denounced and degraded. It is equally unlikely that a non-Jewish officer so placed would have found such ardent defenders. It is because what would otherwise have been regarded by all concerned as neither the first nor the last squalid instance of betrayal, best left in decent obscurity and forgotten as rapidly as possible,[99] turned, as the truth began to seep out, into a blatant instance of prejudice and injustice run wild that it became an issue of recognizably high moral importance for great numbers of Frenchmen of other categories. The socialists, most notably, were disposed at first to dismiss the conflict between *dreyfusards* and anti-*dreyfusards* as no more than a quarrel between one segment of the bourgeoisie and another. In the end the majority admitted, although many held out, that the unjust pillorying and punishment of any individual—even one who, being wealthy, a career officer, and a Jew, combined in his person almost everything they had long been taught to detest—was in some serious way incompatible with the principles with which any decent society needed to keep faith. And this would include the society that they would make were they ever to gain power.

The Jewish population of late nineteenth-century France was among the smallest in the major continental states of Europe both in absolute terms and as a proportion of the total population of the country. In finite numbers it was only a quarter of German Jewry, for example, and as against approximately 1.3 per cent of the total population of Germany the Jews of France constituted no more than 0.4 per cent of the total population of France. French Jewry would have been smaller still but for the change in its internal distribution following the annexation of Alsace and Lorraine by Germany under the terms of the 1871 peace settlement when the impact of the loss of the two eastern provinces was mitigated somewhat by the decision of a full third of Alsatian Jews (slightly over half the total Jewish population of France) to opt for French citizenship and resettlement in France. Knowledge that the status of Jews was less

---

[99] In Oct. 1890, a Lieutenant Jean Bonnet who had been shown conclusively to have been in receipt of regular monthly payments 'from abroad', was arrested at Nancy, tried for treason, and condemned to five years' imprisonment. But as Bernard Lazare was to point out, for a brief report on the affair of Lieutenant Bonnet you would have to look in the inside pages of the Parisian newspapers under 'news from the provinces' and even then verdict and sentence would hardly be mentioned (Bernard Lazare, *L'Affaire Dreyfus: une erreur judiciaire* (Paris, 1897), 10).

favourable in Germany than in France was not irrelevant to this remarkable decision. Those who had prospered under French rule as state officials and school teachers, for example, had good reason to be concerned about their future. But, in the last resort, everything hinged on French Jewry's now immovable conviction that France, even after defeat, would remain true to the principles of the Great Revolution.[100] Once the most inward looking and traditionalist of French-Jewish communities, Alsatian Jewry had in the course of a continuing process of acculturation been transformed into one composed not merely of loyal, but in many cases fervent citizens of the Republic. And there could have been no more tangible and massive expression of their devotion to France as they had come to know it and of their undeviating confidence in France as the original, consistent, and most faithful of the emancipating European states than their migration out of what would be German territory. It was therefore among the many ironies of the Affair that the Dreyfus family had been prominent among these Jewish loyalists migrating to Paris and that Alfred Dreyfus's entry into the French officer corps and his posting to the general staff in due course were taken as splendid confirmation of the validity of their belief and confidence in their country.

It is true, of course, that the ancient undercurrent of objection to the presence of Jews in France had never dried up. On the contrary, as we have seen, the original revolutionary decision to emancipate them had revived it; and it had been subsequently nourished from two fixed sources that had in common their wish to demolish the republic as it stood and rebuild state and nation according to radically different socio-political principles. On the political right the Church and its allies were active promoters of primitive Judaeophobia, traditional Christian demonization of the deicide race having been reinvigorated by Rome's massive contemporary effort to push back the rising tide of secularism and liberalism for which it held the Jews, along with the Masons, as at once responsible and emblematic. On the left it was fed by the now well-established socialist convention that the Jews were at one and the same time representatives, manipulators, proponents, *and* beneficiaries of the bourgeois money economy. Each of these two great wings of French political and social opinion repeatedly and assiduously made it its business to point in outrage to the fact that the Jews of France had been allowed to prosper not only in finance, commerce, and the professions as, so it was implied, was to be expected, but—uniquely in Europe—in the hierarchies of most (if not, in fact, all[101]) of the *grands corps de l'État*, namely the principal arms of the state itself: in the all-important corps of teachers in secondary and

---

[100] Vicki Caron and Paula Hyman, 'The Failed Alliance: Jewish Catholic Relations in Alsace-Lorraine 1871–1914', *LBIYB* 26 (1981), 5.

[101] The French diplomatic service was effectively closed to Jews.

higher education, in the civil service (not excluding the corps of departmental prefects and subprefects who administered the country), and even
in that holy of holies, the armed forces. Very slowly—and, in the event,
incompletely—a wing of the socialist movement came round to the view
that there was no real reason either in theory or practice to distinguish
Jewish from Christian capitalists, the more so as most Jews could be safely
categorized as proletarians.[102] But on the whole, at least until the Affair
was at its peak, reactionary right and socialist left were very nearly at one
on the matter of the Jews, suggesting, in the mental and political turmoil
that followed in the wake of the great débâcle of 1870, the possibility of
a future, particularly frightening marshalling of forces against them. A
complete and effective synthesis of leading contemporary Christian and
socialist ideas on the matter of the Jews did not emerge, however, until
the publication in 1886 by Édouard Drumont of his triumphantly best-
selling catalogue of Jewish iniquities, *La France juive*.[103]

Drumont's book was a much padded, hugely untidy, but briskly and
here and there even brilliantly written rehash of Alphonse Toussenel's
forty-year-old *Les juifs, rois de l'époque*.[104] But it was not so much the
explicit argument that struck home. It was rather the author's monstrously assiduous piling up of every allegation, insinuation, and legend—
true, partly true, or totally and demonstrably false—that he could lay his
hands on so long as it served his purpose of distinguishing 'the Jew' as a
being set apart from the rest of mankind by his intrinsic nature ('peculiar,
so very long-lived, so completely different from all other beings'), that it
contributed to 'the Jew's' absolute discredit, and that it helped to tear the
scales off the eyes of the normally peaceful, well-meaning, but lament-
ably innocent citizens of France. The burden of the book was simple: as
the Jew rose, so France fell; as the Jew fell, so France rose. ('Quand le Juif
monte, la France baisse; quand le Juif baisse, la France monte.') There had
been 800,000 Jews in France in the fourteenth century, Drumont told his

[102] Even after Jean Jaurès, unlike Jules Guesde and some of the other leaders of the
socialist movement, had determined that while Dreyfus was indeed a Jew and a wealthy
one to boot, the issues raised by the Affair were of the highest *republican* principle, the view
that capitalism was in some intimate way associated with Jews and Judaism remained a
staple of his thinking. 'The Jewish race, single-minded, passionate and subtle, constantly
consumed by a kind of fever, . . . is especially gifted at handling the capitalist system,' Jaurès declared in June 1898. 'But,' he went on to ask, '. . . If the whole of capitalism is
detestable and iniquitous, why point particularly to Jewish capitalism?' Cited in Nancy L.
Green, 'Socialist Anti-Semitism, Defense of a Bourgeois Jew and Discovery of the Jewish
Proletariat', *International Review of Social History*, 30, 3 (1985), 398.

[103] One hundred thousand copies were sold in its first year of publication. By 1912
there had been 200 printings of the original French edition alone. See Stephen Wilson,
Ideology and Experience: Antisemitism in France at the time of the Dreyfus Affair (Rutherford and
London, 1982), 171.

[104] See above, pp. 203–4.

readers (with characteristic contempt for the facts[105]) before their failure
to render any useful service, their intrigues, and their usury 'obliged' the
landowners to chase them away. Thereafter, all went well. From that
point on France enjoyed magnificent prosperity. Alas, later they were
allowed to return. 'They came back behind the Free Masons in 1790 and
became the absolute masters of a country that they detached bit by bit,
with prodigious cunning, from all the traditions that had given it its
grandeur and its power.'[106]

What is really important about Drumont, however, is that he had
caught and articulated existing undercurrents of feeling and thinking on
the subject with a precision unequalled by any publicist before him. That
apart, the sheer internal energy fuelling the book made it the masterpiece
of tendentious, dishonest, and therefore singularly effective political
propaganda that it was. 'Anyone who has read Drumont's books will have
easily discovered in them a certain number of powerful images around
which the facts seem to group themselves as in a sort of magnetic field',
wrote Georges Bernanos who had first read Drumont at the age of 13 and
remained in his thrall throughout his life.[107] La France juive injected into
the ancient but ever lively issue of the nature, social role, and appropriate
final disposition of the Jews of France hitherto unknown levels of passion,
invective, and violent public debate. It raised anti-Semitism to the level of
a central political idea in its own right. It left the Question of the Jews
lodged in the public consciousness more firmly, and couched in harsher
terms, than it had ever been before. It contributed enormously to the
final and irreversible establishment of that Question as a matter of critical
national importance of which all were invited to take account. In sum,
La France juive, in conjunction with the newspaper La Libre Parole in
which Drumont proceeded to keep his ideas (and himself) before the
public eyes, did as much as, if not more than anything else, to till and fertilize
the ground on which the seed sown by Dreyfus's accusers some years later
would grow into the Affair. It is therefore not too much to say that it is
1886, the year of the publication of his book, rather than 1894, the year
of Dreyfus's disgrace, that marks the watershed between what, all told,
had been an age given to little more than periodic rumbles of anti-
Semitic sentiment and the very different, vastly more explosive age that
would follow.

In this atmosphere it was impossible for Jews in France not to find the
matter of Dreyfus's alleged treason intensely embarrassing and to consider
not only how they would do best to respond to it, but whether they

---

[105] The best estimates suggest a figure of no more than 100,000 in all of France before
the expulsion of 1306; and some 350,000 in the rest of Europe.

[106] La France juive: essai d'histoire contemporaine, i (Paris, 37th edn., 1886), 515–16.

[107] Cited in Jacques Petit, Bernanos, Bloy, Claudel, Péguy: quatre écrivains catholiques face à
Israël (Paris, 1972), 17.

should make any attempt to do so. Some individuals, seeing themselves directly or indirectly insulted, had recourse to duelling. (Unlike their German cousins, French Jews were not normally denied 'satisfaction'.) The poet André Spire, at the time an *auditeur* (or junior official) at the Conseil d'État, was one such proud young man, although, curiously, he was later to describe himself as a person who had not yet come to feel himself a Jew 'as mounting anti-Judaism compelled me to little by little', but rather as 'an *israélite*, a Jew with a small "j", one of the kind the great scholar Sylvain Lévi, professor at the Collège de France . . . wanted to have called Jewish Frenchmen [*Français-juifs*]'.[108] A Jewish captain in the dragoons challenged Drumont and fought a duel with him. So did the anarchist man-of-letters Bernard Lazare. So did the newspaper editor Arthur Meyer. The most famous case of such private defence of public reputation was that of a Captain Armand Mayer, an officer in the army who challenged the marquis de Morès, a man as notorious for his anti-Semitism as for his skill with the sabre. Mayer paid for his sense of honour with his life. But, these were all exceptions. The most common response was to close the shutters and wait for the storm to pass. And indeed, initially, there was little else anyone could do as the news of the arrest filtered through, as reports of the secret trial itself began to be published followed rapidly by official confirmation of Dreyfus's conviction and, finally, the public degradation in the courtyard of the École Militaire, the baying of the mob, and the huge, country-wide display of anti-Semitic *schadenfreude* and general nastiness all took place. Knowing little or nothing of Dreyfus himself, still less of the material facts of the case, it occurred to very few upright French Jews to doubt that the man, however improbably, was guilty and that justice—very rough, but still condign justice—had been done. But there was a particular sense in which the position of the few who had begun to doubt the validity of the actual judicial proceedings and were determined to fight for his release and acquittal was itself not materially different from that of those who were disinclined to make their views known one way or the other. Even the first great *public* denunciation of the trial, Bernard Lazare's devastating book-length rubbishing of what had been presented as the primary evidence of Dreyfus's guilt—the supposed identity of his handwriting with that of the author of the famous *bordereau*—was carefully subtitled *A judicial error (une erreur judiciaire)*, which could be taken to mean that it was an error that Dreyfus's judges had committed, not a crime. And it is not insignificant that Dreyfus's greatest personal defender, his brother Mathieu, tireless in his effort to save him, the man who had recruited Lazare to serve this legitimate, but still private cause, insisted on the book's publication being postponed for somewhat over a year while he continued

---

[108] André Spire, *Souvenirs à bâtons rompus* (Paris, 1962), 36.

efforts to have Alfred Dreyfus's case dealt with through quieter and more regular channels than outright public protest. So long as the army remained adamant in its refusal to reconsider the case those who considered mounting a public campaign to induce it to do so had to reckon with the fact that to save Dreyfus would be to disgrace the army. To disgrace the army, it was widely argued and felt, would be to disgrace the Republic. To disgrace the Republic was in some sense to disgrace France itself. Mathieu's fight for his brother was thus to fight the tide of opinion even within the limited circle of the notables of French Jewry for whom there could be no question at all of quarrelling with the republican state to which the Jews of France did not doubt that they were all beholden and to which they were indeed devoted as a matter of primal civic faith. It *had* to be assumed that the republic would end by doing justice to Dreyfus. To believe otherwise was to accept that the state was incorrigibly, even if only selectively, hostile to its Jewish citizens; and that was intolerable. It was, besides, to encounter the massive defence mounted by the army itself, supported by the greater part of the French press, and, as the Affair approached its climax, by a frightening rise in sympathetic background noise.

In the early months of 1898, largely in response to the opening of the main *dreyfusard* campaign for revision of the original conviction, anti-Jewish riots spread through much of France. Some of these were deliberately precipitated by organized agitators, some were more or less spontaneous. All were directed against Jews specifically—not, for example, at government offices, or at private non-Jewish homes, businesses, and people. There was a good deal of noisy marching through the streets accompanied by arson, pillage, stoning of individuals, and, needless to say, verbal insults as well. Some riots were perpetrated by quite small groups, some involved crowds of many thousands. Two well-known instances were the demonstrations held in the north-western department of Ille-et-Vilaine (Dreyfus's second trial was held in its *chef-lieu*, Rennes) and in Nantes where, by some estimates, the anti-*dreyfusard* crowd numbered 15,000. But arenas for violent protest were provided by most of the major cities of the country, Paris, Marseilles, Lyons, Bordeaux, and Dijon among them, and very many minor centres as well. In some cases the rioting lasted for several days in succession. Here and there troops had to be brought in to reinforce the police and gendarmerie. But there was little bloodshed, at all events in metropolitan France.[109] Cries for a general campaign of violence were not unknown. The term 'massacre' was to be heard: advanced as a useful possibility by some, denied as a serious

---

[109] In French Algeria matters were otherwise. In the city of Algiers itself there were pogroms in the authentic east European sense of the term between 18 and 25 Jan. 1898: murderous violence against Jews, sacking, looting, and firing of Jewish property, local authorities openly sympathetic to the rioters, inadequate police protection, indifferent military (Wilson, *Ideology and Experience*, 106–24 and 655–70).

intention by others. But in the main the onslaught on people was verbal. Calls at public meetings and in the press for the wickedness of the Jews, and of the Jewish 'syndicate' in particular, to be exposed were endlessly repeated as were demands that the freedom accorded Jews be reduced by denying them entry into political life and the state service. The more extreme demand that the decrees emancipating them be totally repealed was to be heard too, but more rarely.[110] The desire to see France shot of the Jews entirely could be heard too. The popular novelist 'Gyp' (Sybille-Gabrielle Marie-Antoinette de Riquetti de Mirabeau), who doubled at this point as a correspondent for Drumont's *Libre Parole*, is recorded as explaining that what she wanted was '*To see them leave France*, and hence to really scare them! I don't personally ask them to be killed. I am not so ferocious as that. But let's drive them out, let's not do like the Russians who keep them and herd them in special areas.'[111] A salient feature of the barrage was that it was continually accompanied by deliberately demeaning and dehumanizing physical portrayal. The leading organ of what Péguy called 'l'Église tartufiée',[112] the Assumptionist Order's *La Croix*, reported the opening of the trial of Emile Zola in characteristic terms. Zola himself was labelled a 'pornographer', the presence of 'Jewish noses' in the courtroom was offered as a sinister reminder of who, supposedly, was behind him, and the trial itself was presented to the reader as a further instance of the struggle to the death between 'Catholic France and Jewish, Protestant, and free-thinking France'.[113] That much of this was undeniably mindless and automatic—and of a semi-ritual character—in no way lessened its lasting impact on the social climate in which Jews had now to learn to live, the more so as the view from Rome was much the same. Thanks to the 'error' of emancipation, the editors of *Civiltà Cattolica* contended, there was now in France

this fistful of Jews pullulating within and stealing in from without that had risen to a level of power that a hundred years earlier would have seemed totally imaginary. Under the shield of civic equality it had laid its hands on everything: the judiciary, the press, commerce, the banks, the railways, the universities, literature, science, public administration, and a large portion of the legislative authority and even of the army. . . . [Paris] a metropolis that takes the place of the lost Jerusalem, with its institutions and universal leagues and opulent Croesuses . . . is now the stronghold of world Judaism where all the [necessary] strings by which the unity and solidarity of its scattered offspring is maintained throughout the world are held and tightened.[114]

---

[110] This was the main demand formulated at the Antisemitic Congress convened in Lyons in 1896.

[111] Cited in Wilson, *Ideology and Experience*, 677. Emphasis in original.

[112] 'Le Ravage et Réparation', *La Revue Blanche*, 20 (1899), 427.

[113] *La Croix*, 8 Feb. 1898.

[114] 'Il caso di Alfredo Dreyfus', *Civiltà Cattolica*, series xvii, i, 1143 (5 Feb. 1898), 275–6.

If in practice, therefore, efforts to disentangle the specific, narrowly defined fight to save and rehabilitate Captain Dreyfus from the larger fight for what was soon believed to be the reputation, dignity, and very soul of France were bound to fail there was no way either of disentangling the case, status, and future of Dreyfus the man from the case, status, and future of French Jewry in its entirety. This enormous widening of the stakes and of the field of conflict, signalled most particularly by Emile Zola's celebrated intervention in January 1898 and the rallying of some of the socialists (led by Jaurès), a steadily multiplying host of other political figures (Clemenceau among them), and, most famously, the *intellectuals* of France, was at once therefore a source of encouragement to the Jews of the country and a source of embarrassment as well. For some it was anxiety, for some fear: fear of being tarred with the same brush as Captain Dreyfus himself, fear of provoking—perhaps of having already provoked—stronger and more widespread attacks than could be coped with, fear of a sea-change in French opinion that would prove to be irreversible, fear of the unknowable paths the crisis might take, fear of what the absurd and imaginary, but wholesale charges against Jewry—famously and most critically, that they were in one way or another secretly and conspiratorially linked and inherently disloyal and alien—might eventually lead to. This latter charge, in comparatively civilized mode, is reflected in the passage in *À la recherche du temps perdu* in which Proust deals with Swann's having revealed himself to be a *dreyfusard*. The duc de Guermantes is outraged:

'It is true that Swann is a Jew. But, until today . . . I have always been foolish enough to believe that a Jew can be a Frenchman, that is to say an honourable Jew, a man of the world. Now, Swann was that in every sense of the word. Ah, well! He forces me to admit that I have been mistaken, since he has taken the side of Dreyfus (who, guilty or not, never moved in his world; he cannot ever have met him)[115] against a society that had adopted him, had treated him as one of ourselves. It goes without saying, we were all of us prepared to vouch for Swann, I would have answered for his patriotism as for my own. Ah! He is rewarding us very badly.' . . .

'Don't you see,' M. de Guermantes went on, 'even from the point of view of his beloved Jews, since he is absolutely determined to stand by them, Swann has made a blunder of incalculable magnitude. He has shewn that they are to some extent forced to give their support to anyone of their own race, even if they do not know him personally. It is a public danger. . . . People will say: *Ab uno disce omnes.*'[116]

The anti-*dreyfusards* had indeed been quick to claim that the great campaign mounted to save Dreyfus and against themselves was in itself proof

---

[115] '. . . puisqu'il prend parti pour ce Dreyfus (qui, coupable ou non, ne fait nullement partie de son milieu, qu'il n'aurait jamais rencontré) . . . '

[116] *Sodome et Gomorrhe*, part 2, ch. 1, pp. 678–80 in vol. ii of the Pléïade edn. English trans. by C. K. Scott Moncrieff, *Cities of the Plain*, i (London, 1967), 108–11.

positive of the power of the Jews to manipulate the leaders of opinion: a monstrous, but typical illustration of their ancient practice of extending unconditional protection to their own. In fact, nothing could have been further from the truth. Perhaps only so unusually perceptive and, in his way, so demanding an observer of things Jewish as Charles Péguy could see that in France, at all events, matters were very distinctly otherwise.

The politicians, rabbis, and communities of Israel, in the course of century upon century of persecution and ordeals accustomed themselves politically to the sacrifice of some of their people in the interests of peace: the peace of political management, the peace of kings and grandees, the peace of their debtors, the peace of populations and of princes, the peace of anti-Semites. They asked only to recommence, to continue, to sacrifice Dreyfus, to avert [*conjurer*] the storm. The great majority of Jews are like the great majority of [other] members of the electorate. They fear war. They fear confusion. They fear disquiet. More than anything they fear, indeed they dread simple disturbance. What they want more than anything is silence and tranquillity. . . . Their greatness has been forced upon them. They go to their great and sad destiny only because a handful of troublemakers, a busy minority (*une minorité agissante*), a band of energumens and fanatics, and of madmen, all grouped around a few leaders who are none other than the prophets of Israel themselves force them to do so. Israel has supplied innumerable prophets; and heroes, martyrs, and warriors without number. But when all is said and done, in ordinary times the people of Israel are like all other peoples, they ask only not to be embarking on extraordinary times. . . . Israel has supplied innumerable prophets; more, it is itself a prophet, it is itself a prophetic race; take it as a whole, as a single body, it is a prophet. But all it asks for, finally, is this: that it be unnecessary for prophets to exercise their calling, for it knows what the costs might be. . . . The policy of Israel in its entirety, then, is to make no noise . . . (there has been more than enough), and to buy peace by a prudent silence.[117]

Péguy's language was harsh and unforgiving, but what he had to say was the truth. By and large, the grandees of French Jewry sat on their hands. The Consistoire Central, presided over by Alphonse de Rothschild, avoided all involvement. The Alliance Israélite Universelle kept equally aloof, intent on concerning itself exclusively with its philanthropic activities abroad (for which it continued to have the blessing of the authorities), and if it ventured to touch on anti-Semitism then only on its manifestations abroad. Of the awkward matter of anti-Semitism in France itself it was determined to steer clear.[118] The rabbinate too, with rarest of exceptions, shut itself up in its synagogues. Only the Grand Rabbi himself, Zadoc Kahn, and a few like-minded men went so far as at any rate to consider action in the face of what they recognized as an intense and exceedingly dangerous anti-Jewish campaign, their chosen instrument a Comité de Défense Contre l'Antisémitisme formed at the

[117] *Notre Jeunesse*, 547–9.
[118] Michael R. Marrus, *The Politics of Assimilation* (Oxford, 1971), 236–9.

end of 1894. Yet nothing could be more revealing of the view they took of the very real quandary in which the steadily mounting waves of hostility beating against French Jews had placed them, than the extremely narrow terms in which the half-dozen or so members of the Grand Rabbi's committee defined their self-appointed task. Their first, very preliminary, highly confidential discussions had revealed that while the participants in the circle Rabbi Zadoc Kahn had gathered round him were united in their concerns, they were sharply divided on what could and should be done. Some, led by the Grand Rabbi himself, wanted to proceed to the establishment of a broadly based, fully public body that would operate on lines similar to those of the Verein zur Abwehr des Antisemitismus founded four years earlier in Germany.[119] Others were opposed to any form of organized, collective, and public action. A third group was prepared to act, but only provided the existence of the directing body remained secret. There being insufficient support among the notables of the community for public action even in the milk-and-water mode the Abwehr-Verein had made its own, it was plain that it would be in a secretive and exceedingly limited form that the Comité had to take shape if it was to function at all.

In composition the Comité de Défense Contre l'Antisémitisme was notably respectable. Narcisse Leven, president-director of the Alliance Israélite Universelle, Salomon Reinach, an eminent archaeologist and historian and a Member of the Institut, and I. Levaillant, a retired departmental *préfet* and senior official in the Ministry of the Interior, were among its members. None of the great Jewish plutocrats of France participated, however. The Grand Rabbi, his post being in some respects an official one, does not seem to have taken part either, although it is probable that he maintained a position for himself in the very near background. And precisely what the committee sought to accomplish other than very moderate purposes in the general realm of public relations remains unclear. It had limited funds to disburse. It left little or no mark on events in the Dreyfus years. It survived, so far as is known, until 1902, at which point, it set out—unsuccessfully it seems—to widen its circle and reinvigorate its operations. When it breathed its last is unknown.[120] But in retrospect, in any event, the committee remains of interest less for the little that it did than for the extraordinarily great pains to which it went to define its purposes and outlook and these, at least, are known from a document made public in 1902—the fact of the committee's existence having indeed been successfully kept secret until then.

[119] Although the Abwehr-Verein was founded under predominantly gentile auspices. See Chapter 3.

[120] Michael R. Marrus, 'Le Comité de Défence Contre l'Antisémitisme', *Michael*, 4 (Tel Aviv, 1976), 163–8; Julien Weill, *Zadoc Kahn 1839–1905* (Paris, 1912), 168–71.

Events, so founders of the committee argued, had shown that it had been imprudent of the Jews of France to imagine that 'wars of religion and race' were no longer possible at the end of the nineteenth century and that the general public could be relied upon to show good sense and take the true measure of the odious and absurd attacks made upon their Jewish fellow citizens. It was indeed because no resistance to anti-Semitic propaganda had been offered that the injury sustained by French Jewry had been serious. The committee's purpose—its sole purpose, it was emphasized—had been (and continued to be) to put an end to this intolerably weak and indecisive state of affairs. They had sought to fight anti-Semitism 'in all its forms and in all its incarnations, whether it presents itself with an open face or behind the borrowed mask of nationalism'. But, they went on to emphasize, they did not by any means consider their cause to be a narrowly Jewish one: the cause to which they had devoted themselves was that of equality before the law for all Frenchmen. The sole distinction they were prepared to draw was between those who were partisans of the principles of the Revolution and those who were its adversaries. It had been for these reasons that the committee had been careful to resolve on what it would not concern itself with and in what it would not engage and had specifically been determined *not* to take up the case of Alfred Dreyfus directly.

Born in the course of the terrible crisis that the Dreyfus Affair had unleashed, its settled purpose was not to intervene in the judicial proceedings . . . but to respond to the very dangerous situation in which our co-religionists were placed as revealed by the affair.

Nor had the committee been prepared to enter into 'confessional' matters. It held anti-Semitism to be directed against Jews as persons, not against their religion. All Jews—reformists, orthodox, and free-thinkers, as well as those who had detached themselves entirely from the community—were under attack equally. On the other hand, its concern had been and would continue to be with French Jews, and French Jews alone.

We are certainly not insensible to the suffering of our co-religionists in other countries and some among us have been associated with the work of the 'Alliance Israélite Universelle'. But in regard to the particular purpose which we set ourselves we have acted not as Jews established in France but as French citizens of Jewish origin, the rights of whom were breached (*battu en brèche*) and who were determined to safeguard them.

In retrospect, from the vantage point of 1902, the members of the Comité de Défense Contre l'Antisémitisme affirmed their conviction that in the interim matters had greatly improved. The condition of the Jews was less critical. The authorities had shown that they were prepared to treat them more equitably than before. Most reassuring of all, the central lesson of the Affair had been widely absorbed. The authors of the document believed, therefore, that

In the light of these events, the parties that stand for the ideas of 1789 in our country have finally understood that anti-Semitism does not only threaten a religious minority but puts in question all the achievements of modern France. The present struggle is not between anti-Semitism and the Jews, but between anti-Semitism and the principles of the Revolution. We are therefore neither isolated nor deserted.[121]

In sum, while there was no denying that the Jews of France had been hugely involved in the Affair both in their minds and their persons and that their situation had been revealed to be a deal more precarious than they themselves had previously been inclined to think, the determination to join the fight—if at all—only as undifferentiated citizens of the republic, *never* as Jews, had, the committee implied, proved to be correct. Despite the claims and insinuations of the anti-Semites, no clash—not even a notional one—between the Jews of France *as such* and the republic, let alone the army, had occurred. The storm had been weathered, the winds were now dying down.

That the position adopted by the (short-lived) Comité de Défense Contre l'Antisémitisme was not an especially bold one was one thing. That it did not accord with established Jewish practice was another. *Pace* Péguy, their refusal to consider that they had a duty to see to the rescue of one of their number when in dire straits ran wholly counter to the ancient Jewish rule—and instinct too (as the conduct of the leaders of French Jewry itself had demonstrated in the course of the Damascus Affair). As a judgement on the relevant aspects of French society in general, their views, in so far as these may be said to have been held seriously, were certainly quite remarkably sanguine and superficial. But it may not be irrelevant that this, their credo, had been put together in the course of an appeal for open and wider support. Its authors could be relied upon to know what would and what would not be acceptable to the majority of French Jews. And it needs to be said, too, that it is far from clear what other position they could have adopted so long as their view of the revolutionary and republican dispensation towards the Jews remained unchanged and they retained their absolute and not unreasonable conviction that they were among the Revolution's most fortunate beneficiaries. To think, still more to behave otherwise—to take up a position, even as self-proclaimed *dreyfusards*, on grounds that were specifically Jewish rather than universal—seemed to the overwhelming majority of Jews in France, the Dreyfus family itself among others, to be perverse or

---

[121] Circular letter from the Comité's steering group, addressed, so it appears, to a circle of 'co-religionists' thought likely to be willing to serve as participants in, or as supporters of, its work, 14 Nov. 1902. Cited in Marrus, 'Le Comité', 169–75.

anachronistic. It was perverse because to think and act otherwise was to set oneself apart from society-in-general, of one's own volition, and to re-establish oneself as an oddity and an eccentric. Proust was to say of his character Swann—terminally ill, but in the wake of the Affair newly and unexpectedly insistent on his identity with other Jews—that he was turn-ing into a prophet.[122] Péguy wrote of the real Bernard Lazare, whose central thesis was that the case of Dreyfus was indissolubly tied to the general Question of the Jews, that he *was* a prophet.

The prophet, in that great crisis of Israel and the world, was Bernard-Lazare. Let us salute one of the greatest names of modern times . . . one of the greatest of the prophets of Israel. As for me, if I live long enough, I should consider it one of the great rewards of old age to be able to restore and establish the portrait of that extraordinary man.[123]

And stripped of heightened and theistic language, Péguy's characterization of Lazare was not without substance. His crucial role in the Affair in its early stages has already been alluded to. In retrospect, however, it was the change that occurred in his view of the Affair and of its interconnection with the matter of the Jews in general and with that of the Jews of France in particular, that is of enduring interest.

It is probablay crucial to Bernard Lazare's personal history (b. Marcus Bernard Lazare, 1865; d. possibly of cancer, 1903) that he was a native of Nîmes and inclined, perhaps not wholly without cause, to regard himself and his kind as lineal descendants of the ancient community of Jews who had inhabited France since Roman times, longer therefore than the Franks. These were people who, having been subjects of the Pope rather than the king, had been spared the great fourteenth-century expulsion. And there were sundry other ways in which they deserved, they thought, to be distinguished from the much larger, mostly Ashkenazi segments of French Jewry. Lazare's actual grasp and knowledge of Jewish Law and trad-ition were very slight; and everything about him suggests that to the end of his short life he remained unencumbered by religious belief. His real education was secular. He was a product—by no means a brilliant one—of the school system of the republic at all its levels, the last being in the form of a period at the École Pratique de Hautes Études in Paris. But what Lazare lacked in aptitude for formal scholarship he made up for, on his arrival in Paris as an aspiring young man of letters, in assiduous attention to social questions and uncompromisingly radical politics. He is commonly classified as an anarchist; and, indeed, if an intensely unfor-giving hostility to all forms of government amounts to anarchism, the cap fits. On the other hand, violence, not excluding anarchist violence, was

---

[122] 'Swann était arrivé à l'âge du prophète' (*Sodome et Gomorrhe*, part 2, ch. 1, Pléiade edn., ii. 690.
[123] *Notre Jeunesse*, 551.

foreign to his nature and his outlook. He was to the end a man of ideas. Only in the wake of the Affair, and as his concern with the Jewish Question in France *and* abroad became the very axis on which his life would finally turn, did action—even then principally in a literary mode— follow.

Lazare's early views on Jewry in the *mass* were harsh, very much less than well founded historically and sociologically, and, taken together, quite evidently functions of his own initially strong view of himself as an authentic and undifferentiated Frenchman. He subscribed to the view that French Jews, respectable citizens of the republic, were to be distinguished sharply from the eastern Europeans who had begun to enter the country in the 1880s. The former were honest, hard-working, eminently satisfactory 'Israélites', the latter, as often as not, worthless, money-minded, money-grubbing, unsociable 'Juifs'.

To welcome these contemptible people to our country [he wrote in 1890], to help them, to patronize them, to implant them in a soil which is not their own and which does not nourish them in order to facilitate their conquest? For whose benefit is this? For the benefit of the cosmopolitan *juif* who has no ties with any nation, no affection for any nation, who is [like] the Bedouin moving his tent about with complete indifference.[124]

This of course was little more than yet another version of the old, but still popular distinction between 'useful' and 'useless' Jews intermixed with elements of the socialist outlook on the matter as propounded by Fourier, Marx, Proudhon, and Toussenel among others. In his first serious attempt to tackle the problem of anti-Semitism, Lazare dwelt, like the others, on the fact that

The wealth [*l'or*] of the Jew is said to have been won [*conquis*] from the Christian ... by fraud, by deceit, depredation, by all possible means, but principally by reprehensible means. It is this, that I shall call the moral grounds [*grief*] for anti-Semitism, and it can be summed up as follows: the Jew is more dishonest than the Christian; he is totally without scruples, a stranger to loyalty and to candour.

Is this charge well founded? It was so and still is so in all those countries in which the Jew is kept outside society; where he receives a Talmudic education exclusively, where he is subject to persecution, to insult, and to outrage, where the dignity and autonomy of a human being are denied him. The moral condition of the Jew is of his own making as well as of external circumstances; his soul has been moulded by a self-imposed law as well as that which has been imposed upon him.[125]

Language of this kind brought him within an ace of Drumont and even earned him Drumont's approbation for his 'impartiality' and his

---

[124] 'Juifs et israélites', *Entretiens politiques et littéraires*, 1 (Sept. 1890), 178–9. Cited in Marrus, 'Le Comite', 170.

[125] *L'antisémitisme: son histoire et ses causes* (Paris, 1894; repr. 1982), 179.

determination 'not to yield to the impulses of his race'.[126] But it was not his final position. Good socialist that he was, Lazare's study of the history and causes of anti-Semitism (1894) ended on a positive note. Judaism was weakening much as Catholicism and Protestantism were. Generally, 'positive, determined, limited religious sentiment is fading day by day'. The notion that the Jews were racially distinct from their neighbours was unfounded. It was human solidarity and the brotherhood of nations that would soon be the order of the day. Anti-Semitism was therefore destined to fade—although, ironically, not before serving a vital social purpose. In its origins, to be sure, it was a reactionary movement. Its proponents were the property-owning classes who employed it to incite the middle classes, the *petit bourgeois*, and at times the peasants too, against the capitalists of Jewry. But in so doing, they did no more than help prepare their own destruction. For the effect of infusing the lesser orders with such ideas was to lead them to socialism, to clear the ground for anarchy, to induce a hatred for all capitalists and, above all, for capital as such. It was only those Jews who persisted in maintaining their national identity who would encounter hostility and have to put up with it.[127] Lazare's book on anti-Semitism was finished in April 1894. Then came the Affair in which he would very rapidly assume the role of central, if not prime mover in the campaign to beat back the army and those who stood with it and rehabilitate the victim of its injustice.

The impact of his plunge into the Affair upon Lazare himself was profound. An entirely new vision of the matter of the Jews was borne in upon him. He was not alone in this, but he was unique among Jewish *dreyfusards* in his boldness, in the freedom with which he called a spade a spade, in his willingness to pin the conspiracy against Dreyfus squarely on the man being a Jew, and in his pointing to what he did not doubt were the lessons of the Affair for all other Jews. Captain Dreyfus, he wrote (in the book in which he set out to demolish the case for the prosecution) had been arrested, charged, judged, and condemned without anyone knowing on what grounds any of these judicial steps had been based. And yet, 'Despite all that, public opinion unhesitatingly accepted that he was guilty and heaped its anger and abhorrence upon him. Even the instinct of self-defence moved none of his fellow citizens to stand up and cry: "If that is how one arrests, judges, and condemns, so much for anyone's liberty." ' It would be said, that Captain Dreyfus had been tried by his peers. How was it then that even as an accused, let alone as a man on trial, there were none among his peers to defend him? True, there had been enormous excitement all round at the time of his trial. There was no denying

[126] *La Libre Parole*, 10 Jan. 1895. Cited by Robert S. Wistrich, introduction to English edn. of Lazare's essay, *Antisemitism: Its History and Causes* (Lincoln, Nebr., 1995), p. xv.
[127] Lazare, *L'Antisémitisme*, 196–8.

'the siege mentality fever that burns in all nations living in a condition of armed peace'. But it was not enough to explain the relentless and incredible animosity (*l'incroyable acharnement*) displayed towards him. The explanation lay elsewhere. 'Have I not said, that Captain Dreyfus belonged to a class of pariahs?'

He was soldier, but he was a Jew and it was as a Jew before all else that he was persecuted. It was because he was a Jew that he was arrested, it was because he was a Jew that he was judged, it was because he was a Jew that he was condemned, it was because he was a Jew that the voice of justice and truth cannot be made to be heard in his favour, and the responsibility for the conviction of this innocent man falls entirely on those who provoked it by their despicable incitements, their lies and their calumnies. They needed a Jewish traitor to take the place of the classic Judas, a Jewish traitor whom they could refer to continually, every day, to ensure that his disgrace fell upon an entire race; a Jewish traitor who could be made use of to sanction a long campaign of which the Dreyfus Affair was the last act.[128]

There was in this line of thought, over and above the uncompromising terms in which it was expressed, more than sufficient cause for Mathieu Dreyfus to hesitate before allowing the man he seems to have begun by thinking of as a hired hack to proceed to the publication of his findings and analysis. And while *L'Affaire Dreyfus: une erreur judiciaire*, when published, did serve its purpose admirably as the first serious attack on the military conspirators who had landed Dreyfus on Devil's Island and were determined to keep him there, it served equally to set Lazare apart from most of those who would otherwise have been his natural allies. The socialists jeered at him for acting, as they claimed, as a hired spokesman for high society, a man who was evidently at one and the same time anarchist and loyal admirer of his majesty King Rothschild, and whose book represented the latest tactic of the financial and Jewish press for sowing doubt in the public mind about a convicted traitor's guilt.[129] When it was all over Lazare referred with evident pride to 'the days, bitter and sweet, when I knew the keen delight of fighting all alone under mud and abuse'.[130] Earlier there had been no escape from pain and seeming contradictions in his position.

If, as Péguy thought, it was Lazare who emerged as the most admirable and most memorable of all in the great gallery of *dreyfusards* it was because, in truth, he was that very great rarity, a man of absolute and uncompromising intellectual integrity, but also one with a consistently and diligently kept open mind. Restless, inquiring, insistent on all positions being examined, watchful for deviations from fundamental moral and

---

[128] *L'Affaire Dreyfus: une erreur judiciaire*, 8–9.
[129] 'Une apologie de Dreyfus', *La Petite République*, Nov. 1896. Cited in Edmund Silberner, 'Bernard Lazare ve-ha-ẓionut', *Shivat Ẓion*, 2–3 (1951–2), 331–2.
[130] 'Lettre ouverte à M. Trarieux', *L'Aurore*, 7 June 1899.

social principles, he could not fail to be not only an exceptional figure, but a solitary one. At journey's end, certainly, his views, his arguments, and his essential purposes could not be other than totally at variance with those on which French Jewry as a whole had for some time been firmly united, and which had been expressed with such clarity in the 1902 statement drawn up by the Comité de Défense Contre l'Antisémitisme.

Lazare had seen that what had occurred in France was the first great demonstration of the intrinsic fragility of the emancipatory contract under the terms of which the Jews had been admitted to both citizenry and society in exchange for abandoning their own social structures and accepting the culture and values of the host nation. This was what Stanislaw de Clermont-Tonnerre and his fellows had famously demanded of them in December 1789. This, with the rarest of exceptions, was what they had done. As a leading Jewish scholar of the day put it: 'In exchange for liberty and the common law, Israel has given up its dreams of political restoration and has ceased to wish to become a nation once again, [content] to be no more than a religious grouping: a painful transformation, but an inevitable one that has precedents in antiquity in Alexandria and in the middle ages in Spain.'[131] This had been the basis and logic of the emancipatory process and the measuring rod by which it was commonly judged wherever it had been set in motion. But, of course, as a basis on which Jews would finally be free to live and prosper without harassment or worse, it was contingent on government being in fact a government of law. It was because Russia's credentials as a state governed by law had worn so thin and Romania's pretence at being one was clearly so hollow that Jews had been fleeing both the one and the other. It was because, when all was said and done, both Germany and the major components of Austria-Hungary seemed reasonably reliable and consistent in this respect that the never-ending internal contradictions and nastinesses which their Jewish populations knew they had to face in certain well-understood and well-remarked contexts were regarded by most of those concerned as tolerable after all.

What Lazare had concluded, and was prepared to say, was that the lesson of the Dreyfus Affair was that France was not to be relied upon, not blindly at all events. For the question on which everything ultimately hinged was not that of the origins and formal structure of the republican state, admirable though they were, but rather the general outlook and political intentions of those who happened at any particular time to be its masters. The thought to which his argument led was not merely the common one that the Affair writ large was a struggle between two great, opposing coalitions. It was that while the *dreyfusards* could, with some

---

[131] Théodore Reinach, *Histoire des Israélites depuis la ruine de leur indépendance nationale jusqu'à nos jours* (Paris, 1901), p. xiii.

justice, end by considering themselves the victors, it remained that the fight might have gone the other way—from which it was a short step to the unspoken corollary, that on some future, unfortunate occasion it might do so. And indeed, regardless of where one placed one's emphasis—whether on the grim fact that the Affair should have erupted at all or, in contrast, on what many, Captain Dreyfus among them, considered the satisfactory if much delayed conclusion—the lasting impact of the Affair on some Jewish minds was the shadow of doubt it cast on France in the very role in which the Jews of Europe had long been accustomed to see it: leader of the Enlightenment in so many ways; the one major state that had emancipated them as a matter of principle rather than political and/or economic expediency or friendliness or mere failure to find a way out of what seemed to be the obligations laid upon all those who wished to be considered civilized. In the Germanies, in the Habsburg domains, and of course in Russia, matters had been otherwise from the beginning; and so they had remained through the greater part of the nineteenth century. England, in this respect, as in so many others, was the odd man out, as we have seen: never going down the straight, Gallic, poplar-lined road of absolute and undeviating principle; but rather, on the other hand, moving step by step, now easily, now reluctantly, until, in practice, it had arrived at a position similar to that of France in all but name. Together, the two western powers stood in contrast, therefore, with the major continental states. But it was still France, not England, that had first set the standard by which the matter of the Jews as a constitutional issue had come to be measured in western and central Europe. Measured there in the first place, but ultimately in all parts of the world where the status of the Jews and the liberties and opportunities accorded them were in any way at issue. The case of France was crucial therefore to a general reconsideration of the true condition and the likely future prospects of emancipated Jewry were one to take place. To be sure, once Dreyfus had been rehabilitated and the Affair at its bitterest was over, the overwhelming tendency in French Jewry was to put it behind them and to take as cool and philosophical a view of the matter as possible: to try to see it as an unfortunate, essentially fortuitous, therefore passing social phase, a typically unpredictable turn of the wheel of history and fashion, not one to dwell over excessively, not as a danger signal, rather as a famous victory.[132] But then there was always more to the relief felt by French Jews as the Affair began to wind down than mere desire to get on with their lives much as there was more to their patriotism than mere sober calculation of the benefits that had accrued to them as a consequence of emancipation.

[132] Proust's comments on the relevant social mechanism are apposite: 'Like a kaleidoscope which is every now and then given a turn, society successively arranges elements which one would have supposed to be immovable in different orders, and composes a fresh pattern. Before I had made my first Communion, right-thinking ladies had been

Captain Dreyfus was not alone in his absolute devotion to, and confidence in, France. There was in all sectors of French Jewry an intensity of gratitude and of personal and cultural attachment to what none doubted was their country that had no real parallel anywhere else, not even in Germany.

In our own times it is somewhat more difficult than it was a century ago to credit this sentiment. It may be appropriate, therefore, to cite as scrupulous a statement by a French Jew of his love for his country as has ever been written. The great medievalist Marc Bloch begins his celebrated account of the débâcle of 1940 with the following words:

By birth I am a Jew, though not by religion, for I have never professed any creed, whether Hebrew or Christian. I feel neither pride nor shame in my origins. I am, I hope, a sufficiently good historian to know that racial qualities are a myth, and that the whole notion of Race is an absurdity. . . . I am at pains never to stress my heredity save when I find myself in the presence of an anti-Semite. But it may be that certain persons will challenge the evidence which I propose to put on record [i.e. in the account that follows] on the grounds that I am an 'alien', I need say no more in rebuttal of such a charge than that my great-grandfather was a serving soldier in 1793; that my father was one of the defenders of Strasbourg in 1870; that both my uncles chose to leave their native Alsace after its annexation by the Second Reich; that I was brought up in the traditions of patriotism which found no more fervent champions than the Jews of the Alsatian exodus; and that France, from which many would expel me today (and may, for all I know, succeed in doing so), will remain, whatever happens, the one country with which my deepest emotions are inextricably bound up. I was born in France. I have drunk of the waters of her culture. I have made her past my own. I breathe freely in her climate, and I have done my best, with others, to defend her interests. [133]

Men and women of this outlook—members of Marc Bloch's generation,

---

stupefied, while paying calls, to meet a smart Jewess. . . . The Dreyfus case brought about another pattern, at a period rather later than that in which I began to go to Mme Swann's. . . . Everything Jewish, even the smart lady herself, fell out of the pattern, and obscure nationalists took her place. The most brilliant drawing-room in Paris was that of a Prince who was an Austrian and an ultra-Catholic. If instead of the Dreyfus case there had been a war with Germany, the base of the kaleidoscope would have turned in the other direction, and its pattern reversed. The Jews, having shown to general astonishment that they were patriots, would have kept their position, and no one would have cared any more to go, or even to admit that he had ever gone, to the Austrian Prince's. . . . The one thing that does not change is that it seems each time that "something in France has changed."' ('La seule chose qui ne change pas est qu'il semble chaque fois qu'il y ait "quelque chose   de changé en France" ', À l'ombre des jeunes filles en fleurs, part 1, Pléïade edn., 517).

[133] L'Étrange Défaite, trans. as Strange Defeat by G. Hopkins (New York, 1968), 3. Marc Bloch (1886–1944), a serving officer in both world wars, joined the Resistance after the French collapse in 1940 and his discharge from military service. He was caught, tortured, and executed by the Germans. The shabby treatment accorded him by his 'aryan' academic colleagues, Lucien Febvre among them, once Franco-German persecution of French Jews began in earnest, cast a final, melancholy light on the life of this brave man, one of the most distinguished historians of the age.

a fortiori their seniors—judged their loyalty to France and the foundations of their status as Frenchmen *à part entière* to have been confirmed and vindicated, not rubbished, by the Affair. There was among them little or no interest therefore in going back and reviewing what had happened with *critical* intent. There was no patience at all with the very few (Lazare among them along with outsiders like Herzl and Max Nordau) who thought it right and necessary to do so, nor can the sensitivity of the nerve touched by those who insisted on doing so be exaggerated.

It had always been plain to Herzl, and it would be equally plain to his successors, that their theses on the condition of Jewry would never be acceptable to more than a statistically insignificant minority in any of the countries of central and western Europe. Least of all, as Herzl had learned very rapidly for himself, would they be acceptable to Jews in France—with the partial, but telling exception of those among them who were themselves recent arrivals from the east. Such was the case even while the thunder of the Affair beset all Jewish ears in France—those of Herzl himself among so many others—but so it was later 'Obviously, there is no helping the French Jews,' he noted in his diary after a visit to Paris at the very height of the Affair in 1898. 'They heat themselves by setting fire to their beds. They seek protection from the Socialists and the destroyers of the present civil order. Zadoc [Kahn, the Grand Rabbi] was of good cheer because [the Affair] no longer involves Dreyfus, but [rather] Zola, and Picquart.' A day later, he wrote down: 'The French Jews are absolutely unavailable to us. Truly, they are not Jews any more. To be sure, they are not Frenchmen either.'[134] And indeed, the only French Jew of some or any public standing who thought, as Herzl did, that it was vital to return to the ancient concept of the Jews as a discrete nation and that Zionism was relevant to the French case after all was Bernard Lazare. But then what other secular Jew in Paris at the turn of the century can be imagined setting down the thought that rather than assimilation bringing the wretchedness of the Jews to an end it was likely, on the contrary, to be a source of new miseries? Or daring openly to compare Christianity to Judaism to the advantage of the latter:

'It is the soul that sinneth that shall die,' says Ezekiel. 'The son shall not die for the crime committed by his father.'

What moral progress there! Punishment is individual. How far we are from the crime for which seven generations may have to bear punishment. What daring of the prophet, mindful as he must have been of the so-called Mosaic precepts, and how retrograde is Christianity [*comme le christianisme est une régression*) with its original sin and eternal expiation and the substitution of the innocent for the guilty.[135]

---

[134] Entries (slightly modified) for 29, 30 Sept. 1898, *The Complete Diaries of Theodor Herzl* (New York, 1960), ii. 672–3.
[135] *Le Fumier de Job* (Paris, 1928), 111–12.

Lazare and Herzl had much in common: age, high literary ambitions and undoubted (if, perhaps, not really first-rate) literary talent, and a moderate name for themselves as journalists and men of letters. Neither had more than the most tenuous ties of the traditional sort to the established Jewish communities. Neither had more than a scrappy, superficial grasp of the elements of the Tradition. Both loathed the moneyed Jews before all other species of humanity. Both found the servility with which the grandees of Jewry tended to be surrounded within their communities intolerably offensive. The common folk of Jewry moved them to pity on account of their condition and to shame on account of their passivity and fatalism in the face of persecution, but they thought they needed to be led, not relied upon. And it was the instinct of both men that the crucial factor in life, but also in politics, was that of dignity.

As long as Christianity exists, [Lazare told a group of Russian Jewish students in 1897] the Jews, scattered among the peoples, will arouse hatred and wrath, and the position created for them will be either materially or morally inferior; whether they are unable to enjoy their rights as citizens or men, or whether they are exposed to some variety of scorn, the result is the same. What solution is there for this? I am well aware that for the Christian peoples an Armenian solution [i.e. massacre] is available, but their sensibilities cannot allow them to envisage that. On the other hand, it is impossible for us Jews to accept conditions of life incompatible with our dignity as men. We have the right to develop ourselves in every fashion, this right must be guaranteed to us in an effective way, and (since I pass by the great majority of emancipated Jews, who are probably quite contented— for which I do not give them any praise) we must discover what remedy we may apply to millions of non-emancipated Jews.[136]

That Lazare was an early recruit to Zionism is not to be wondered at therefore—any more than that he would be Herzl's only significant French recruit.[137] He had responded instantly to Herzl's pamphlet *Der Judenstaat* when it appeared in Vienna in February 1896.[138] And when the two men met in Paris five months later they warmed to each other immediately. 'Talked to Bernard Lazare,' Herzl noted in his diary. 'Superior type of a good, intelligent French Jew.'[139] Lazare, for his part, set himself to help Herzl in every way possible. He tried to arrange for a French edition of *Der Judenstaat* to be prepared and published (with limited success).

---

[136] 'Jewish Nationalism', Mar. 1897, published as *Publications du Kadimah* (1898), No. 1. English trans. in Bernard Lazare, *Job's Dungheap* (New York, 1948), 68.

[137] The greatest of all Herzl's recruits to his movement, Max Nordau, a celebrated, if highly controversial man of letters in his day, was a long-time resident of Paris, but, like Herzl himself, a native of Hungary. Upon the outbreak of war in 1914, in the evening of his life, he was forced to leave France as an enemy alien.

[138] Nelly Wilson, *Bernard Lazare: Antisemitism and the Problem of Jewish Identity in Late Nineteenth-Century France* (Cambridge, 1978), 224.

[139] 'Vorzüglicher Typus eines guten, gescheiten französischen Juden', *Theodor Herzls Tagebücher*, i (Berlin, 1922), 488.

He smoothed the path to people whom Herzl wanted to meet. He presided over meetings at which Herzl spoke. Herzl was grateful and, wishing to draw Lazare into the Zionist Organization once it had been formally established, had Lazare elected to its executive. But while each man retained a high opinion of the other to the end of their short lives (Lazare died in 1903; Herzl, it will be recalled, the year following) the political association between the two was of short duration. Lazare took no part in the actual running of the Organization and attended none of the Congresses held in his lifetime. Visits to Vienna were planned, but repeatedly put off. Ill health, his own heavy, concurrent involvement in the Affair, and finally sharp disagreement with Herzl on matters which he, Lazare, believed were of fundamental principle came between them. By 1899 he had decided that he could no longer stomach either the manner in which Herzl ran the movement or the strategy and tactics he was prepared to pursue. Herzl was too high-handed, he thought, insufficiently respectful of democratic procedures, too forgiving of things and persons of doubtful integrity, too secretive, too manipulative. 'You are bourgeois in your thinking,' he wrote to him in his typically frank and pugnacious style. 'You therefore wish to guide our impoverished, miserable, proletarian people . . . to lead them from without and from above in a direction of your choosing, as a herd.' The idea of a *bank* as a major instrument for the Organization was typically misconceived: 'What irony to make of a bank the foundation[stone] of the Jewish nation! Ezra and Nehemiah carried arms as well as the Law—the word and the sword— and they were poor men because they had left the rich behind them in Babylon.' Besides, Herzl was too intent on putting a good face on things when, plainly, they were ugly. He had established a government before creating a people. And

like all governments you wish to conceal [*farder*] the truth, to be the government of a respectable people, the acme of your duty being never to display the nation's shame. I, on the other hand, have no objection to it being displayed, to poor Job being seen on his dung-heap scraping his sores with a shard. . . . Our people are set in the most vile of mires: it is for us to roll up our sleeves and set off to look for them there where they moan, there where they wail, there where they suffer. Our nation needs to be recreated—that is the really solid job of work, the strong job, above all the first job of work [to be taken up]. The nation needs to be re-educated, shown what it is, made to grow before its own eyes—when it will grow in the eyes of others—and have its heart and its spirit raised. When that has been done it will be fit to win its place.[140]

Some of this was fair, some of it less so. Herzl tried gently, and at some length, to point out what to his mind was not.[141] But in any case it was not

---

[140] Lazare to Herzl, 4 Feb. 1899, CZA, H VIII 479/11.
[141] Herzl to Lazare, 16 Feb. 1899, *Igrot Herzl*, iii (Jerusalem, 1957), no. 743, 269–72.

in their respective views on the rules by which delegates were elected to the Congress or on the obscure matter of a certain Seidener who had been accused, almost certainly unfairly, of misconduct in his handling of land purchases in Palestine, or, again, on the admittedly more central question of the bank that their decisive differences lay. Least of all did they differ on ultimate purposes. There were differences of character and temperament. Lazare bridled at Herzl's too casual reference to him as a man of letters and informed him severely and humourlessly, that 'I cease to be a man of letters when it is Zionism and the interests of the Jewish people that concern me.' 'Am I really so bourgeois?' Herzl had protested in his turn. 'I really do think that that, and the matter of my personal character generally, are questions of secondary importance.'[142] Where they differed fundamentally was in their understanding of the nature and purposes of political action. They disagreed too on what was required in practice of those who undertook such action and to what constraints they ought properly to be subject.

What Herzl had grasped—and what to a large extent marks him out amongst contemporary Jewry—was that the indispensable conditions of political action were pragmatism and a certain single-mindedness—egoism, in fact. One judged what needed to be done from the standpoint of the interest of the collectivity one had chosen to represent. The weaker and more exposed one's position, the greater, for example, the need for allies. But effective allies were hard to come by, notably so for the weak and the exposed. They needed to be sought wherever they might be found. And where actual or prospective allies were left unrewarded for their aid, there there would be no holding them. It was true that high principles were what distinguished the legitimate from the illegitimate political enterprise. But high principles were poor determinants of method and still poorer guides to policy. It was one thing to be scrupulous in one's personal affairs.[143] It was quite another to be over-scrupulous and fastidious in the management of the political affairs of an entire people.

None of this, if it was understood at all, could be to the liking of Bernard Lazare. There was, besides, an irony to the difference between the two men, which neither is known to have noticed, in that it touched on the very issue on which the Dreyfus Affair had ultimately hinged. For Péguy this was whether or not France would be 'faithful to her

---

[142] Herzl to Lazare, 16 Feb. 1899, *Igrot Herzl*, iii. 269–72.

[143] None could have been more scrupulous than Herzl who allowed his small, inherited fortune to be swallowed up in the interests of keeping the movement going, who refused to accept a penny from it when it was suggested that he accept a salary, and who, despite a punishing, never-ending round of travel, conferences, and negotiations with great men and small, worked as a wage-earning journalist to the end of his life to keep his family in some comfort.

revolutionary past'.[144] Maurice Paléologue, the Quai d'Orsay official who had been instructed to follow and document the Affair for his ministry, was somewhat closer to the nub of the matter, however, when he remarked that the greatness of the struggle convulsing the country arose from the fact that it was one in which two 'sacred sentiments' were pitted against each other: 'love of justice and the religion of patriotism.'[145] And indeed, what was the argument of the more thoughtful and less vulgar of the anti-*dreyfusards* if not that the interest of France and of the army had to come before that of a private individual? And was it not the ultimate argument of the *dreyfusards* that, on the contrary, it was in the interest of the country and the nation as a whole that justice be done, though the heavens might fall, for nothing less would ensure that France were 'true to herself'. It was precisely in these respects, namely in the matter of the ancient but ageless problem of political morality, that Herzl thought that Lazare was indeed always more *littérateur* than statesman, more moralist than political tactician, always a man who could be relied upon in fair weather and foul to put principle before praxis. These were great virtues. With his personal physical and civic courage they formed the sources of his justly acquired reputation for integrity. But they were private virtues. Their value for action in the public arena could not be other than limited. And there was this to say too: here was a respect in which Lazare was not alone after all. There were many more in Jewry who for very similar reasons were unwilling to set out along the dusty and disagreeable road Herzl had chosen to travel, taking an entire people along with him if he could. There would be very many more who, for much the same kind of reason, would refuse to accompany either him or, in the course of time, his successors. In his own stiff way, Lazare ended his short stint as a Zionist by wishing Herzl well:

Whatever the opinions, principles, and ideas that divide us may be, nothing will alter the fact that I retain the greatest friendship and the most affectionate admiration for you. You have known how to stir the depths of Israel, you have brought it your love and your life, you have awakened it; no Jew deserving of the name must ever forget that, nor forget to bear witness before you of his gratitude.[146]

But on the nub of his complaint he was adamant: 'You are establishing a government before creating a people.' It was a shrewd remark. In a people devoid of a general structure of authority of any kind—no exilarch, no supra-communal council of elders, no aristocracy, nor, for that matter, any easily identifiable and agreed common interests—there was indeed no way, as we have seen repeatedly, in which even the greatest and

[144] 'L'Affaire Dreyfus et la crise du parti socialiste', *La Revue Blanche*, 20 (1899), 127.
[145] Cited in Jean-Denis Bredin, *The Affair: The Case of Alfred Dreyfus* (New York, 1986), 257.
[146] Lazare to Herzl, 4 Feb. 1899, in Silberner, 'Bernard Lazare', 359.

most pressing of public issues could be so much as brought up for systematic public discussion. Nor, of course, was there any way in which an
encompassing decision might be taken, let alone implemented.

If Herzl was a driven man it was because of his impatient understanding that the affairs of the Jewish people had been rendered desperate by
drift and inertia; that it was the invertebrate structure of Jewry that made
their predicament so extraordinarily intractable. It was evident, he wrote
in *Der Judenstaat*, that the Jewish people in their exile were incapable of
conducting their political affairs for themselves. That being the case,
others had to do so for them—at all events, initially. It had never been the
least of Herzl's purposes to provide the Jews with a mechanism for general discussion, debate, and decision and in this vital sense, as Lazare had
perceived, create for them at least an approximation to government. To
Lazare he wrote in his parting letter: 'You know what Bismarck said: put
Germany in the saddle and it will ride off on its own. I limit myself too
to wanting to put the Jewish people in the saddle, after which it will ride
along whatever path it chooses to follow.'[147] And then the Jewish people
in their great majority were far to the east.

IX

It was the First Russian Revolution of 1905 that finally brought the long
maturing crisis of Russo-Polish Jewry to a head. It greatly exacerbated—
and illustrated for all to see—the dangers to which its Jewish population
was exposed. At the same time, in apparent contrast, it seemed to hold
out a promise of improvement in their condition in ways and to a degree
that had previously been all but inconceivable. And thirdly, it posed more
acutely than ever the question with which all thinking people in the
empire had long been wrestling, namely what, in the circumstances, was
to be *done*. For while the Revolution, as we shall see, brought about a partial, generally welcome breakdown of the Jews' political isolation in
Russia, the question whether the change was likely to be other than transitory would continually hover; as would the question of the fate that
awaited the Jews once stability and public order had been restored *whatever* form post-revolutionary regular government took. Even among the
most optimistic in Russo-Polish Jewry, those, that is to say, who did not
doubt that the Revolution had much to offer them, there were many
who worried whether on balance it was wise for Jews to seek positively
and autonomously to make the most of what appeared to be the new
opportunities opened to them.

In its essentials, the Revolution was, of course, devoid of any intrinsic

Jewish aspect or content. It was a further stage in the long-drawn-out evolutionary process by which Russia was emerging from Muscovite despotism to government of some other, still indefinable kind—a remarkable stage, to be sure, but manifestly neither the last nor the most decisive. The rumble of endemic rebellion had been audible in Russia since at least the abortive Decembrist revolt eighty years earlier at a time when the Jews were still totally quiescent politically. The deeper causes of the unrest that had done most to pave the way to the actual upheaval of 1905 were equally matters in which the Jews of Russia as an identifiable social category neither played nor, arguably, could play a part: chief among these were the mismanaged emancipation of the serfs and the pitiless processes by which vast numbers of peasants had been swept up from the countryside and redeployed for industrial employment and a semi-pauperized existence in the cities. Nor did Jews, individually or collectively, play a part of any consequence in the setting of the fuses that actually detonated the Revolution: the military and naval setbacks suffered by Russia in its incompetently waged war with Japan, the great wave of industrial unrest that struck St Petersburg in the autumn and winter of 1905, the stupidity and brutality of the authorities that produced the scandal of the Bloody Sunday massacre (9 January 1905) of hugely disgruntled, peaceful workmen whose *political* loyalty, up to that point at least, had never been in doubt.

Matters were somewhat different as regards the massive movement of organized protest and general strikes that broke out in many of Russia's major cities. But even so, the involvement of Jews at this point had less to do with their peculiarities than with those of their social characteristics that brought them into the general social and economic orbit. Their high rate of literacy, urbanism, craft, and business skills put a relatively high proportion of the Jewish working class squarely among the more active, disgruntled, and easily inflamed urban industrial workers. Jewish high school and university students were to be found with other students in demonstrations held against the regime. Jewish professionals were apt to join other professionals in the various liberal and libertarian movements of protest that were to combine in the all-Russian, but still politically moderate 'Union of Unions' which, although intensely critical of the regime, was not out to subvert it. In much the same spirit, namely that of joining in what was clearly a generalized struggle for political and social change, Jews who had already placed themselves on the extreme revolutionary left, the Bundists most notably, aligned themselves with the other revolutionaries. As the crisis intensified, the central committee of the Bund distributed one hundred thousand copies of an 'order of the day' for the 'liquidation of the Autocracy'[148] and Jewish radicals harangued

---

[148] Cited in Jonathan Frankel, *Prophecy and Politics: Socialism, Nationalism, and the Russian Jews, 1862–1917* (Cambridge, 1981), 158.

Jewish audiences in the streets and in the synagogues in the same ferocious manner that dedicated radicals of similar views, but other ethnic
origins, performed what they considered to be their socio-political duty.

But this was no more than to be expected of a people who tended disproportionately to belong to the literate, urban, more politically alert
sectors of the population of the empire and who were bound therefore
to be swept up equally disproportionately in the fever of social and political eruption with which so many other subjects of the Tsar had been
smitten. Besides, at the two really crucial points in the long chain of
events that led up to the true denouement of the Revolution, those that
particularly shook the Tsar and his intimates and forced them into temporary political retreat, the Jews of Russia as a distinct category were
totally irrelevant. These were the paralysing shutting down of the entire
Russian railroad system in the course of the summer of 1905 and the
mounting evidence of widespread disaffection, not excluding cases of
actual mutiny (famously, but not solely, in the Black Sea fleet), in the
Russian armed forces. It was these last features of the new landscape that
were immediately and indeed correctly seen in St Petersburg as altering
it out of recognition and therefore requiring a swift and decisive response
of some kind—in practice, so the Tsar's chief advisers at that moment
believed, one that would have to go beyond mere fixing of bayonets and
loading of rifles. Faced with the intolerable prospect of having to rely on
troops whose loyalty would be doubtful in the event of any attempt to reimpose authority by force, and the almost equally grim likelihood that
much blood would be shed however things went if he chose to try to
do so, the Tsar drew back. He did so in a form, moreover, that was close
enough to capitulation for very many clever people to think that that was
what had occurred. In practice, however, while the imperial Manifesto of
17 October did promise constitutional government, it left the main outlines of the system that was to replace old-fashioned, straightforward, and
uncompromising Autocracy to be determined later. The result was that
while a genuine revolution seemed to many to have taken place, a great
deal about it remained very uncertain. It was at this point, namely in the
course of the subsequent effort to spell out the implications of the Manifesto in sober constitutional terms and the mustering of the forces dedicated to the nullification of any change whatsoever in the Autocratic,
despotic, Russian-nationalist, and Orthodox Christian bases on which
the empire had so long been governed, that the Jews as a more or less
coherent collectivity may be said to have entered—more precisely, to
have been propelled—into the arena in their own name, for their own
purposes, and to their great cost.

Signs that the Jews might be drawn into the maelstrom *as such*, as a distinctive social category, willy-nilly and with dire consequences for themselves, had not been absent during the preliminary ferment, which is to

say before the October 1905 climax. But it was as the high point of the Revolution was reached and more especially in its immediate aftermath that a threat of unprecedented magnitude to their lives, limbs, property, and livelihood took definitive shape. In its origins it had less to do with the vicissitudes of the Revolution itself, however, than with the struggle that the Tsar's apparent capitulation had precipitated between the two great, still imperfectly coherent parties in which political Russia now came to be divided: between those who wished to entrench and extend the new, fragile system of quasi-constitutional government or do away with the monarchy altogether and those who wished—with equal determination but, if anything, greater passion—to reduce, or better still nullify the Revolution and erase its meagre results altogether. Both sides held the struggle to be as much for the soul of Russia as for its control. There was therefore much about it that was symmetrical. But whereas the opponents of the Autocracy in its traditional form were all of one mind at least in their desire for change and in their agreement on the identity of their major opponent—the Tsar, his entourage, and the existing machinery of government—those who sought to set the affairs of Russia in reverse were faced with an insoluble and, for some among them, embarrassing dilemma. Fervent, not to say mindless devotees of the principle that the Tsar was the sole legitimate source of law and authority in Russia found themselves bitterly opposed to his decision to allow a system of government that implied, even if it did not explicitly affirm, the negation of the Autocracy as all had hitherto understood it. The Tsar could not be criticized directly for having so decided. His weakness could only be regretted. But he could be fortified in his resistance to the forces seeking to undermine him and ruin much else that the adepts of the Tsarist system held to be of value. It was a time therefore for his enemies to be identified, hunted down, put to flight, and, if all else failed, destroyed. The launching of the heaviest and thus far most extensive of the several waves of violence to which the Jews had been prey since their original subjection to Russian rule at the end of the eighteenth century followed this logic. It was at this point that it became virtually impossible for socially and politically minded Jews of any class or tendency to avoid the question whether they should not now enter the general political mêlée as a clearly defined people, as a coherent force, and bent upon purposes that were unambiguously their own. The answers would vary. The question would not go away.

Sporadic attacks on Jews, some of them very severe and evolving into full-scale, murderous pogroms, broke out in several towns in Russia in the course of 1904 and 1905. The immediate causes varied. Cases of reservist soldiers who had refused orders to serve in the war in the Far East and who proceeded to riot ignited what were still essentially local fires. Of a different character, however, and very much more devastating was the chain of explosions that occurred on the very morrow of, and as an explicit articulation of objection to, the Tsar's October Manifesto: 660 Jewish communities in towns and townlets of varying sizes and importance in the southern sector of the Pale of Jewish Settlement alone were attacked between 18 and 29 October 1905. Each one of the eight governorates in question (Bessarabia, Chernigov, Ekaterinoslav, Kherson, Kiev, Podolia, Poltava, and Taurida) were heavily populated by Jews—the Jewish segment in each case ranging between 4–12 per cent of the total. But unlike 1881–4, hardly any part of Russia was entirely untouched by the fever, not even relatively remote places in the governorates of 'inner Russia'—those of Kazan and Yaroslavl, for example—where Jews were very few on the ground, always 'privileged', Russified for the most part, and therefore comparatively inconspicuous socially. For intensity, simultaneity, sheer numbers of victims, and material damage there had certainly been nothing comparable since the middle of the seventeenth century (under Polish rule). Of the pogrom in Odessa, the bloodiest of all on this occasion, Leo Motzkin, a firm Zionist, but one, as we shall see, who differed from most of his colleagues in his careful and persistent attention to the *details* of the condition of eastern European Jewry, wrote:

For almost four days and nights blood flowed in Odessa as on a battlefield, but without the generally valid laws of war prevailing. There rushed through over one hundred streets tens of thousands. Soldiers, policemen in and out of uniform, government officials of various categories, the blind civilian troops of Reaction [*die blinden Ziviltruppen der Reaktion*] in their various shapes from householders from distant quarters of the city to aimless companies of workmen and peasants—and all these elements robbed stole, raped, and murdered until Jewish Odessa was like a field of rubble strewn with corpses.[149]

And compiling what remains to this day the most painstaking account of the events of October 1905, Motzkin found that 302 Jews had been killed in the city of Odessa alone, leaving 140 widows and 593 orphans. A further 5,000 suffered serious physical injury.[150] He estimated material damage at 3.75 million roubles, noting that because, as was almost always the case, it was chiefly the poorer sections of the Jewish population that had suffered it was doubly painful. Thousands emerged from the horrors of those four days in Odessa to discover that they were ruined: simple artisans, for example, who, having lost their tools and workshops, were reduced instantly to pauperdom. In the full governorate of Kherson of

[149] 'A. Linden' [Leo Motzkin], *Die Judenpogrome in Russland* (Cologne and Leipzig, 1910), i. 195.
[150] Other, substantially higher, but by no means improbable figures have been advanced. On any reading, Motzkin's remain the most conservative. Cf. Sh. Lambroza, 'The Pogroms of 1903–1906', and R. Weinberg, 'The Pogrom of 1905 in Odessa: A Case Study', both in J. D. Klier and S. Lambroza (eds.), *Pogroms: Anti-Jewish Violence in Modern Russian History* (Cambridge, 1992).

which Odessa was the major city the total number of dead reached 371. And if in other governorates in southern Russia the reckoning were not on so horrific a scale, it was bad enough: 110 dead in Bessarabia, 23 in Chernigov, 131 in Ekaterinoslav, 31 in Kiev, 31 in Podolia, 18 in Poltava, 53 in Taurida. Taking the governorates of Minsk, Mogilev, Vitebsk, and Don into account as well, the grand total for the October pogroms was of at least 880 killed.[151] The corresponding total estimate of damage to property—homes, workshops, tools, commercial enterprises, and so forth—was proportionate: in the thirteen governorates where pogroms were fiercest and most numerous just under 200,000 Jews (roughly 4 per cent of the entire Jewish population of the Pale) were hurt directly and severely in one way or another, if not bodily then materially. Motzkin's estimate of the total economic damage done to Russo-Polish Jewry in the course of October 1905 alone was 60 million roubles (or £6 million at the rate of exchange prevailing at the time) at least—at the time an immense sum for a generally impoverished segment of the population.[152]

Still, in one respect, the pattern was much like that which had obtained in the pogroms of the early 1880s and at Kishinev two years earlier. Contrary to common belief, there was no evidence of central planning and direction although encouragement, or *per contra* discouragement, of *pogromshchiki* by people in local authority was another matter. Where the local governor, police chief, or military commandant was willing to perform his manifest duty, and with dispatch, pogroms, if they occurred at all, were quickly snuffed out. Where, as was notoriously the case in Odessa, the provincial governor was especiallly hostile to Jews and openly helpful to elements of the rapidly strengthening and multiplying philo-Tsarist, Russian nationalist, dedicatedly anti-Semitic movements operating in his domain (to the extent of providing them with firearms), matters were otherwise. Where the restoration of order meant dispersing a mob bent on wreaking vengeance on the Jewish population, police and troops would be unavailable or very late in arriving. Where Jewish self-defence groups appeared and it was a case of putting them down, there police and troops were likely to be readily available and encouraged to employ the force at their disposal unreservedly.[153] Were not the Jews inveterate agitators and troublemakers? Had they not wanted freedom? Well, now, they would get a taste of it, so the governor of Odessa, Dmitrii Neidhart, made a point of telling a delegation of Jewish notables who had waited upon him to ask for protection.[154]

It was indeed a salient feature of the entire episode, namely of the succession of pogroms that began in 1904, reached its peak in October 1905,

[151] Motzkin, *Die Judenpogrome*, 213.   [152] Ibid. 218.
[153] For the testimony of participants see Halpern, *Sefer ha-gevura*, 100–53 and *passim*.
[154] Weinberg, 'Pogrom of 1905', 271.

and only tailed off the year after, that among ever more numerous young Jewish people the gut feeling was that they had little to lose by putting up a fight—even against police and troops, if necessary—and much to gain in self-respect and national pride. The mark left by what many regarded as the shame of Kishinev was still palpable. But locally and independently organized self-defence was not only in the nature of a moral response to physical attack and pillage. It was—or so the braver, younger spirits tended strongly to argue—an absolute necessity in a country teetering on the brink of chaos. It was certainly these freer elements in Jewish society—students, social democrats, socialist revolutionaries, trade unionists, typically—as opposed to the older and established ones, who undertook to mount some form of organized defence against the mob. Very little was owed to the regular communal authorities. Almost everything was the work of the politically organized and the ideologically oriented—in alliance in some places with sympathetically minded non-Jews of more or less the same politically dissident outlook and quality. Lawlessness on the one hand and politicization on the other, both in degrees that were well beyond what any man or woman alive could recall, were thus mutually reinforcing, the Bund being prominent in this connection almost as a matter of course. Alone in the Jewish world the Bund had the necessary organizational experience and framework, the numbers, and the discipline. And here and there, for the moment at least, it had allies among the other social democrats to call upon as well. However, it was where the Bund was weakest, in southern Russia, that pogroms were most numerous and most ferocious. There the main burden tended therefore to fall on other Jewish groups. In Elizavetgrad, for example, a city in southern Russia with a long local history of anti-Jewish violence, the Zionists and the so-called 'non-party' men associated with them, together with a handful of socialist-revolutionaries and some (non-Jewish) Russian supporters, formed the largest of several groups of organized defenders: 380 in all. Jewish social democrats formed a second group numbering somewhat over 160. The Bundists came last in this instance with 25. In Orsha, on the other hand, in the northern Vitebsk *guberniya* where the Bund was relatively strong, it did duly play the leading role in effective self-defence, as may be gauged indirectly by the casualties it suffered: 16 of the 21 members of the local Jewish self-defence force killed in the fighting at Orsha were theirs.[155]

The total number of participants in Jewish self-defence is unknown, but clearly it ran into many thousands: some 2,000 in Odessa alone. Nor is it known what the total death toll throughout all the ranks of the pitifully armed,[156] hastily mounted, and, of course, easily outnumbered

---

[155] Motzkin, *Die Judempogrome*, 130, 395 n., 397–8.
[156] Pistols, at best, and rarely enough of them; for the rest clubs and 'cold' weapons.

Jewish defence forces came to. What is known, thanks to Motzkin, is that in the course of October 1905 alone 132 young men were killed, 55 in Odessa alone—in itself an indicator of the intensity of the violence and the danger the defenders encountered, notably at the hands of the police and the troops. For what the Jewish self-defence forces soon discovered was that mere rioters, many of them drunk, could generally be scattered. A crowd armed with chains, pistols, scythes, and the like, plainly bent on huge mischief, and proceeding down a Jewish street with portraits of the Tsar and icons and other religious symbols held high, could commonly be seen off too, except that much would depend, none the less, on whether the pogrom makers had been joined by policemen and soldiers, in or out of uniform. However, where properly organized and officered troops had been brought into play and it was plainly the rioters they had come out to protect and the political dissidents, Jewish or others, they were pleased to punish, there the attackers could not be met head-on at all.

The real difficulty about the phenomenon of Jews resisting the Autocracy's self-proclaimed loyalists in an organized fashion and so, as officials and policemen were quick to conclude, indirectly defying the Autocracy itself was that it greatly magnified the desire to inflict punishment upon them. Among the Jewish militants themselves it raised the question, therefore, whether the effort at self-defence was justified even in the short term as an immediate measure of protection for the Jewish population. The cautious answer is that it probably did, but only at the very margin. What it chiefly signified—whence its legacy for the future—was further reinforcement of the change in spirit alluded to earlier in this chapter, namely the assumption among the young and the politically minded of a much more self-confident, activist, independent, above all pugnacious posture than had been evident in Jews of any given class previously. This was accompanied by a recognition among all classes and age-groups of a general need for new and tighter forms of internal organization if anything of social value was to be accomplished in any sphere. That some 2,000 or more young people could be involved in one way or another in the effort to protect the Jewish population of Odessa in October 1905 owed a very great deal to the fact that plans for organized self-defence had been drawn up months earlier. This had occurred fortuitously on the (classic) occasion of the Passover of that year when it was already feared that a pogrom might ensue. By October a skeleton organization was in place and there had already been some serious thinking about how to proceed in the event of a fresh threat materializing. Something of the very practical frame of mind in which the young leaders of the new self-defence groups approached the duties they had assumed for themselves unbidden is conveyed in the language of one of the printed handbills prepared for distribution to the population.

Armed parties will be ready to defend the Jewish inhabitants, but remember that
such defence will be insufficient. . . . Band together with your neighbours to help
one another and set watchmen at street corners. Put the women and children on
the upper storeys; but the men must not remain in their homes to defend themselves each man for and by himself. Do not [attempt to] fight singly, they will
slaughter you all. As soon as a riot is in the offing, go outside, all of you, and defend
your street together. There will then be a great many of you and your numbers
will make it easy for you to withstand attack. Be prepared and fear nothing. Fight
hard and bravely, one for the other. Give as good as you get; and do not repeat the
shame of Kishinev. Defend your children and the honour of your nation![157]

But what the October 1905 pogroms—as well as those that had preceded
them and those that were to follow in the course of 1906—most especially imprinted on Jewish minds, over above the *scale* of the hammering
to which Russian and Polish Jews were subject on this occasion and the
now established practice of at least an attempt at self-defence, was the
incidence of distinctly *murderous* violence. As before, as in the 1880s,
there was much pillage and common, brutal, and so to speak feral
molestation. But it was evident too that minds were set much more deliberately and specifically than earlier on murder, rape, and mutilating
injury—in a word, on punishment. Something of this had always been
integral to the Russian pogrom,[158] but as part of the whole, not necessarily as the essence of the matter. No longer. From this point on a pogrom
would rightly be taken to spell death and crippling injury before all else
and, increasingly, to the exclusion of all else.

The shock the pogroms of 1903 had administered to the more hopeful and economically and professionally more successful in Russian Jewry
was now repeated. It had taken an especially sanguine and trusting mind
to believe that the killings in Kishinev and Gomel[159] two years earlier had

---

[157] Cited in Halpern, *Sefer ha-gevura*, 140 n.

[158] As opposed to the devastating massacres conducted by the Ukrainian peasant rebels
against Polish rule in 1648.

[159] The son of a highly regarded Jewish attorney (who had been exiled from Moscow
to Gomel in the heart of the Jewish Pale of Settlement as punishment for overly energetic
insistence on justice for a (non-Jewish) victim of police ill-treatment) recalled what he had
witnessed as a boy:

'Rumours began to spread of an impending pogrom. I did not think much about it
because somehow it seemed too far-fetched that an anti-Jewish outbreak should in any
way affect our family. Then one morning I heard a commotion in the street and ran out to
see what was happening. There I saw an orderly procession of peasants marching several abreast with sticks, stones, hammers and other simple weapons. At the head of the procession a number of men carried holy images, flags, portraits of the Czar. Throughout the
line were numerous crosses. It was that day that instilled in me a fear of the cross.

Although I was thirteen, I still could not account as a reality what I saw. As the men
passed our gate, I asked one of them where they were going. He turned on me his open,
simple, good-natured face and said in an uncertain tone, "Well, my boy, the police told us
that we might come to town and trim the Jews and there would be no interference."

I followed the crowd for several blocks. Suddenly someone threw a rock at the window

been essentially isolated incidents to be explained primarily, let alone exclusively, in local terms. Now the evidence pointed overwhelmingly to the likelihood of Russian Jews being set to endure more numerous, more frequent, and, in all probability, steeper waves of officially sanctioned administrative persecution on the one hand and extreme, more or less officially tolerated, private. and public violence on the other. There was a distinct sense, therefore, that as the significance of the crisis of the Revolution bit into the consciousness of Russian society in general, so in regard to the Jews the wind had shifted even further against them. The regime, it seemed, in so far as it could be said to have made up its collect-ive mind about anything, was determined to bar all roads, mental as well as official, such as might lead, at least in the course of time, to a decent *modus vivendi* between it and its Jewish subjects. And there was an equally disagreeable feeling too of being enmeshed not only in an incurable and dangerous conflict with the state but, if to a less measurable but still unquestionably massive extent, with the Russian, Ukrainian, and Polish peoples of the empire.

There were some—notably in the upper, more Russified strata of Jew-ish society—who had always hoped against hope that this might not be the case, that it might be possible, with patience, to reduce the tension and dissolve the evident confrontation, and that, at a minimum, it might be possible to make common cause with the other subject or 'submerged' peoples of the empire. But the dominant mood in this regard was now an exceedingly sour one. And to darker thoughts and observations about the future of the Jews among what the bureaucracy now tended to call the 'territorial' peoples of the empire, there was soon added the evidence that the Autocracy itself was proving more resilient than the majority of its critics and enemies had originally imagined it capable of being. The replacement of Witte by Peter Stolypin as chairman of the Council of Ministers in July 1906 was followed in short order by an almost complete reassertion of pre-revolutionary social control, the unexpected dissolu-tion of the First, relatively liberal and independently minded Duma, and the fixing of elections for a new parliament on a more restrictive basis— all clear indicators of what was likely to follow. It was evident that at its

---

of a Jewish store, the crowd became a mob, rushed the stores and attacked men and women assembled on the sidewalks. I watched in bewilderment until, out of the mêlée, one of my father's cronies emerged—Rimbalovitch (I shall never forget *this* name), secre-tary of the District Court—directing the incipient robbers and murderers. When he saw me, he halted for a second, then screamed, "Hey, you little Sheeny, get the hell out of here before one of the boys cracks yours skull!" I turned and walked home, too overwhelmed to run.

Later, Father left the house and was gone some time. When he returned, his face was bloodless. All he could say was, "They are beating . . .".' (Joseph V. DePorte, 'Boyhood and Revolution: The Story of my Early Years', *Per/Se*, 2, 1 (n.d.), 40–1.)

highest and determinant level the government was adamant in its intention to restore the *status quo ante*, that it proposed to do no less than nullify such constitutional reforms as had been extracted from it when the country was in turmoil, and that the Tsar was now the first to regret what he regarded as a moment of disorienting weakness. As for its Jewish subjects specifically, the regime now set itself to demonstrate, both by its half-overt, half-covert sponsorship of such profoundly—and, as Motzkin would have put it, 'candidly'—anti-Semitic organizations as the Union of the Russian People and its hooligan satellites, the Black Hundreds, and by a fresh series of anti-Jewish enactments, deliberate perversions of justice, and other public acts, that it had turned against them once and for all and that under no circumstances would it consider them candidates for equal treatment with any of the other peoples subject to its rule. Finally, there was the evidence that in both respects, namely the general constitutional one and that which pertained specifically to the Autocracy's deeply ingrained anti-Semitism, that the Tsar and his ministers were not alone in their attitudes. On the contrary, there was everything to show that they had a substantial part of the general population marshalled behind them where the Jews were concerned. The state, that is to say, and large segments of the organized public subject to its rule were of similar mind and held positions that were mutually reinforcing.

One needs to be clear at this point about what was commonly paraded by all who supported the regime as well as by its actual masters as the nature of the endemic conflict between the Jews and the state. Jews had indeed, by this time, come to form a substantial and—having regard to their total numbers—disproportionate part of what was never to be more than a very small army of political radicals of various degrees of determination and ambition in Russia, the so-called 'professional revolutionaries' among them.[160] There were, of course, very good reasons for Jews to be hostile—disproportionately so—to the regime; and for the young and politically minded among them to be drawn—again, disproportionately—into the revolutionary stream. The Bund apart, the roster of Jews known to be active as dedicated 'professional revolutionaries' in both the Menshevik and Bolshevik wings of the RSDWP and, still more dramatically and deviantly (given ancient Jewish practice), in the Socialist Revolutionaries' 'fighting organization' had in the course of a very few years become a long and notorious one. Plehve, Witte, and the many others among the masters and servants of the state who chose repeatedly, however disingenuously, to make what they could of this when charged with

---

[160] A report by the commander of the Siberian military region in 1905 gives the number of persons detained under political surveillance there as 5,426. Of these 1,676 (or 31 per cent) were Jews—7.5 times their proportion of the total population of the empire according to the 1897 census figures (Richard Charques, *The Twilight of Imperial Russia* (London, 1965), 82).

responsibility for oppression of the Jews, did at least have the plain and narrow facts of the matter on their side. What was not true was that those whom the authorities recognized, informally of course, as being in some sense or other the established leaders of the community had anything like their own former, let alone their forefathers', powers of social control. All could see that the radicals emerging from Russo-Polish Jewry at a steadily mounting rate in the course of the previous quarter-century or so were engaged in a double rebellion: against the established, part-rabbinical, part-notable management of the Jews' public affairs quite as much as against the state. Nor was it true that the radicals, when heads were counted, formed more than a small fraction of Russo-Polish Jewry in its entirety. Even the Bund, at this time much the most numerous and best organized of any of the dedicatedly revolutionary parties or movements in the empire, numbered no more than 20,000–25,000 members, most of whom were to be found on the western and north-western periphery of the empire, far from 'inner Russia'.[161] The greater part of Russo-Polish Jewry, impoverished, unskilled, politically uninformed, instinctively traditionalist, and therefore quietistic in general socio-political outlook, was still far too deeply mired in its Sisyphean struggle for sheer existence to spare more than an occasional thought for the advantages of semi-constitutional government, let alone such benefits as might, but again might not, follow in the wake of outright revolution. To be sure, Jews, by and large, were more inclined than the common run of Russian or Ukrainian peasants, or even members of the non-Jewish urban working class, to listen to the voices calling for the overthrow of Tsarism. There was no question, moreover, but that they were disaffected in ways and to a degree unknown in the general population. Regardless of station and condition, Jews were entirely incapable of regarding the Tsar as their distant, but benevolent Little Father, the *Tsar' batyushka*. They were equally deaf, needless to say, to the political teachings of the Orthodox

---

[161] Later the numbers would rise. The total Jewish membership of the principal social-ist parties of both strict and moderate Marxist tendencies in all of Russia and Poland in 1905–7—years of revolution, but also years in which parties were able to achieve a partial legal status—has been estimated at about 170,000. Of these the two wings of the social democratic party proper (the Bolsheviks and the Mensheviks, in both of which the Jewish membership was substantial) accounted for 46,000 and 38,000 respectively, or, taken together, slightly under half the total. The other half was accounted for by the four specif-ically Jewish socialist parties. The Bund led with 33,000 or one-fifth of the total. The two Zionist-socialist parties followed with 16,000 for Po'alei-Zion ('Workers of Zion') and 26,000 for the Zionist Socialist Workers' Party (which inclined towards Zangwill's and Mandelstamm's 'territorialist' outlook), a quarter of the total altogether. The non-Zionist Jewish Socialist Workers' Party brought up the rear with 13,000 members, or a little less than one-tenth of the total. None of these figures is certain. Nor do they necessarily reflect the actual intensity and efficacy of political and syndicalist activity. In any event, at about 5 per cent of the total adult Jewish population of the empire, membership of the Jewish socialist parties were clearly far from dominant. Nor, of course, were the Zionists.

Church. If, on the whole, they tended none the less to be obedient to Tsar and state, the grounds for submission to both the one and the other were pragmatic rather than moral—all of which was perfectly well understood by those in authority who had troubled to look beneath the surface of events and ask themselves why a people noted throughout the ages for their quietism were rapidly sloughing it off. There were, that is to say, within the administration itself, officials—policemen among others—who were sufficiently clear-headed to see that the Jews would not cease to constitute a threat, however small, to the regime until some other, milder way of dealing with them had been devised.

It had indeed been decided in 1901 to apply to the Jewish sector of the industrial proletariat in Lithuania and Belorussia something like the tactic that had begun to be employed, with some success, in the Autocracy's campaign against the revolutionary parties generally. This was 'police socialism' conceived and employed by the innovative and imaginative chief of the political, or 'defence' (*okhrana*) department of the police in Moscow, Colonel S. V. Zubatov, who held a special brief for waging war against revolutionary organizations. It amounted to recognition of the dire economic and social straits in which the working population of Russia had fallen, the well-founded fear that unattended socio-economic distress fertilized revolution, and the notion that a *successful* workers' movement devoted purely and strictly to the satisfaction of the workers' legitimate demands would wean the men and women concerned away from the dangers of true politics. Zubatov proposed the establishment of a licit trade union movement which, while genuinely catering to the needs of the workers under discreet police supervision, would steer the lower urban orders away from all that smacked of political subversion. The plan succeeded beyond all expectations until it crashed on Bloody Sunday at the opening stages of the First Russian Revolution of 1905.

Zubatov had no great liking or respect for the Jewish population, but as a good policeman he had studied them and he believed that if the principles underlying 'police socialism' were applied to them *mutatis mutandis* similarly useful results could be obtained. He knew that the revolutionaries were far from being in the majority in the Jewish population which was politically divided on very many other counts as well. He believed that much illegal activity would cease if certain quite simple demands were satisfied: if the government allowed a Yiddish-language newspaper to appear, for example, much of the very extensive illegal Jewish press would sink. More generally, if a show was made of listening to the Jews and of having some sympathy for their genuine socio-economic needs, the bulk of the Jewish population could be won over to the regime. And, once that were done, there was good reason to suppose that the dangerous elements in Russian Jewry—the Bundists, notably—would be isolated. Still, to remove them entirely from the centre of the radical stage it was necessary to create a rival, syndicalist in nature too, but not strictly speaking socialist, and in any event harmless *politically*. Having a handful of Bundists of a somewhat less than usually doctrinaire cast of mind conveniently to hand in his prisons Zubatov set out to establish such a movement. Handling them with great care, subjecting them to meticulous penitential interrogations in which the sorrows and difficulties of the Jewish working class were fully and sympathetically discussed, he proved that not insubstantial numbers could be induced to believe in the ultimately benevolent intentions of the state even where the Jewish population was concerned.[162] An Independent Jewish Workers' Party was duly established—under licence, so to speak and with the primary function (so far as Zubatov was concerned) of entering into competition with the Bund. In the event, it was not an especially successful enterprise. No officially (even if secretly) sponsored programme of this kind could be expected to survive the blow delivered the remnants of Jewish confidence in the good intentions of the regime by the massive recrudescence of pogroms that was shortly to follow. But there was some benefit—to the community if not to the police. It was this fresh attention paid to the pervading mood and aspirations of Jews by a handful of perceptive and independently minded policemen that led to a lighter hand at the beginning of the century where the Zionists were concerned.[163] One notable instance was when the commander of the gendarmerie in Minsk allowed the Russian branch of the movement to hold a convention on the grounds that their activities helped to draw the working population away from the social democrats and the revolutionary organizations and set them on a peaceful way to achieving an improvement in their economic circumstances.[164]

The phenomenon of national separatism was an entirely familiar one to official Russia. The only question it raised was how it was to be met. Were the Jews, for instance, to be put down, crushed, and dissolved into the larger Russian mass by force? Were they to be extruded? Might it perhaps be more expedient to appease and placate them in some way in the interests of reducing their trouble-making capacity and establishing at least a temporary *modus vivendi* with them while minor, but more dangerously dissident, subgroups were dealt with first? In any event, Jewish separatism puzzled no one in the higher and middle reaches of the administrative hierarchy, least of all in the one branch of government that

[162] M. Mishkinsky, 'Ha-"Soẓializm ha-mishtarti" u-megamot bi-mediniyut ha-shilton ha-ẓari le-gabei ha-yehudim (1900–1903)', *Ẓion*, 25, 3–4 (1960); Jeremiah Schneiderman, *Sergei Zubatov and Revolutionary Marxism* (Ithaca, NY, 1976); Y. Goldstein, *Manya Vilbusheviẓ-Shoḥat: perek ha-manhigut ha-mahapkhanit* (Haifa, 1991).

[163] See Chapter 5.

[164] Russia, Ministry of Interior, *Sionizm: istoricheskii ocherk ego razvitiya. Zapiska, sostavlennaya v departament politsii* (St Petersburg, 1903), 130.

was supposed to look directly and clear-mindedly at the real questions posed by the condition of Russian Jewry and actually did so from time to time, the police. But Zubatov's experiment was not allowed to last very long. The colonel had overstated his case somewhat when he assured the Ministry of the Interior that 'it was necessary to encourage the Jews' because 'after that one can twist them around one's finger. Thanks to their solidarity,' he had gone on to claim, 'the slightest attention to them is instantly transmitted to all corners, and everyone learns about it. Bring the crowd to heat by your attention and the masses will follow you, and thanks to their unity, they themselves will betray the revolutionaries.'[165] Zubatov was probably right in thinking that if he were allowed to maintain and expand the systematic manipulation of radical elements by going some distance towards recognizing the validity of their purposes and the real needs of the common folk in Jewry for whom they sought to act, he could go far to draw the Jews' revolutionary sting. But there was the difficulty (among others) that a central feature of the Russian state system was its abhorrence of autonomous sources of power and authority intermediate between subject and Autocrat. In principle and in law all in Russia, high and low, were in some sense the Tsar's slaves and the kingdom his property. The Tsar himself was, as has often been said, *dominus*. In practice, and after 1905 to some extent in theory too, the autocratic principle was less in evidence than it had been earlier. But the theory of the autocratic state was never wholly abandoned and Nicholas II, encouraged by his entourage, thought of his function and duties in these terms to the end. It followed that for any coherent national group to be allowed to aspire to a measure of autonomy was to run against the constitutional grain of the empire itself. The *Zubatovshchina* as an expression of the always very thin, but never entirely negligible strain of ambivalence that had marked Russian state policy towards its Jewish population since the time of Catherine II was therefore bound to fail. What put an end to it, however, was less cold-blooded calculation of the underlying danger of a more coherent and purposeful and independently minded Jewish population than considerations of another order altogether.

The various, rapidly mobilizing, angry, frustrated, but in some cases immensely dedicated armies of the Russian right both within and without the state machine needed desperately to slake their thirst for action on the master's behalf. Their leaders were not, on the whole, politically imaginative people, nor were they of high intellectual calibre. Dmitrii Khomyakov, an important spokesman for one of the earliest right-wing formations, the Union of Russian Men (Soyuz Russkikh Lyudei) was exceptional both as regards personal quality and in being prepared, for example, to distinguish between the undesirability of non-Orthodox

---

[165] Cited in Schneiderman, *Sergei Zubatov*, 236.

persons, the Jews of course among them, participating in the country's social and political life on the one hand and their constituting *ipso facto* a class bent on the subversion of the state on the other.[166] But, in general, the best that can be said of the Russian right was that it was not composed of people who were inclined to examine the events that had precipitated the crisis, let alone the broader circumstances that promoted political disaffection in large segments of the population, in anything like the cold light of day. Witte was a reliable witness for once when he judged the rank and file 'dark-minded and ignorant' and rated their leaders 'unscrupulous political adventurers' devoid of honest and constructive ideas, bent only on goading and exploiting the mob, cowardly, savage, and uncreative—'unhanged villains', therefore, a negligible minority of the Russian nobility who fed 'on the crumbs, rich crumbs indeed, which fall from the Czar's table'.[167] Plainly, for such as these, the temptation to follow old and, so to speak, tried and true precedents by punishing all who could be conveniently identified as actual or presumed enemies and were, as it happened, equally conveniently to hand, was irresistible. Pogroms required little planning. All concerned knew almost instinctively how to go about preparing them. Nothing was easier than to make out whether the provincial governor in the case or the army or police commanders or all three together would allow the *pogromshchiki* a free hand or go further still and actually co-operate. The probability that pogrom-makers would indeed be allowed a free hand was now higher than it had been before. The gendarmerie officer who had said squarely that a pogrom could be easily tailored to order—ten people participating if that is what was wanted, or ten thousand if that was what was preferred[168]— had indeed uttered a 'historic phrase', as Urusov had put it, when he quoted him in the Duma in the course of the debate on similarly bloody events in Bialystok (14–16 June 1906).[169] In brief, there was now a climate not only of extreme, but of active hostility. Its roots might be ancient; but they had been newly fortified in the shallower minds that operated at the pinnacle of Russian power by the conviction that the role of the Jews in the recent troubles was truly enormous.[170] And it was shot

---

[166] Don C. Rawson, *Russian Rightists and the Revolution of 1905* (Cambridge, 1995). Dmitrii Khomyakov was the son of A. S. Khomyakov, a leading figure in the Slavophil movement in the middle of the previous century and therefore, so to speak, of first-class lineage.

[167] S. Yu. Witte, *The Memoirs of Count Witte* (New York, 1967), 191–2.

[168] 'Pogrom ustroit' mozhno kakoi ugodno; khotite na 10 chelovek, a khotite i na 10 tysyach'.

[169] Gosudartsvennaya Duma, *Stenograficheskie Otchety, 1906 g., sessiya pervaya*, ii (St Petersburg, 1906), 8 June 1906, 1131.

[170] 'Because nine-tenths of the trouble-makers are Jews, the people's anger turned against them. That's how the pogroms happened,' Nicholas wrote to his mother on 27 Oct. 1905. Count Lamsdorff, the foreign minister, advised the Tsar early in the following

through with a nastiness epitomized in the Tsar's invariable, vulgar practice of referring to Jews as *zhidy* (i.e. 'Yids', rather than using the proper,
neutral *evreii*). 'In his attitude toward the Jews,' Witte wrote in his memoirs, 'as in all other respects, the Emperor's ideas are at bottom those of the
Black Hundreds. The strength of that party lies precisely in the fact that
their Majesties have conceived the notion that those anarchists of the
right are their salvation.'[171] In sum, the post-1905 climate was not one in
which reform was seriously conceivable. No minister who valued his
office could allow himself to press the Tsar to permit it.

In practice, therefore, while the *Zubatovshchina* was in progress the
recruitment of Jews to the revolutionary forces in Russia never did fall off
and when it was over the Autocracy's anti-Jewish posture was revealed to
be as implacably hostile as ever. The one result of the failure of the curious attempt at Jewish police socialism was further, if only marginally, to
reinforce the regime's hostility to its Jewish subjects, its approach now
irredeemably poisoned by the conviction that they were not only deeply
undesirable on socio-economic and theological grounds, but were in the
nature of an inherent and permanent threat to the state itself. This had
rarely been entirely absent from the thinking of the Tsar's policemen in
the past, as we have seen; but it had been one strain of thought among
others. From this time on it was in the nature of established and in most
official eyes incontrovertible doctrine. Few, even at the highest reaches of
the Autocracy, would refuse to admit, privately at all events, that the phenomenon of Jews adhering to the revolutionary forces was functionally
related to the oppressive system to which they continued to be subject.
But since every proposal, no matter how mild, to soften or blunt that system—and such proposals were rare—were fated to be rejected out of
hand by the very small-minded man who sat on the imperial throne the
impasse was total.

It was true that, side by side with the establishment of the Union of the
Russian People, the Black Hundreds, and similar organizations and
movements as permanent features of Russian society and politics, there
was a countervailing body of opinion in the political centre and on the

---

year that 'our revolutionary movement is being actively supported and partly directed by
the forces of universal Jewry'. The idea that western Jewish money was behind eastern
Jewish revolutionaries was sufficiently popular in official circles in St Petersburg for it to
be taken up by foreign diplomats, the British among others, and reported back as, at least,
a distinct possibility. The Foreign Secretary in London (Lansdowne) thought it not impossible that 'the strike movement has been largely supported by Jewish money'. On efforts
by Jewish notables to press for British diplomatic intervention on behalf of Russian Jewry
in 1905, see E. Feldman, 'Pera'ot 1905 be-russiya ba-pe'ilut ha-diplomatit ha-britit',
He-'Avar, 22 (1977), 59–83.

[171] Witte, *Memoirs*, 189–91. While Nicholas was not devoid of certain personal virtues,
fastidiousness of language was not one of them. The Japanese were habitually referred to
as 'monkeys'.

moderate right, indeed even here and there in the higher reaches of the Tsar's government itself, that took the view that the treatment and consequent condition of the Jews was a scandal and a national disgrace. But it was a view that was most commonly expressed privately, if at all, and then with reservations and apologies. Even the Constitutional Democrats, much the most important and promising of the new parliamentary parties, proved reluctant to take up the issue of the legal restraints under which Jews lived and to press for urgent and *specific* attention being paid to it in the Duma. In any case, as the regime reasserted its powers and made plain its refusal in all but name to permit the Duma to perform genuine parliamentary duties, the external determinants of the condition of the Jews were effectively reduced once again to two: the state itself and the street. And as the state reasserted its power over the populace and its ability to delineate the limits set on the freedom of the mob to invade the streets of the cities of Russia, so, once again, it was the binary relationship between state and the Jews that counted for almost everything. It was an ever grimmer relationship, however, utterly hopeless, fatally dialectical. And on what general lessons needed to be drawn from the entire bitter and protracted episode of the Revolution the Jews themselves were, once again, divided.

There was little disagreement on the broadest of all possible conclusions, namely that instability in Russia led inexorably to the ravaging of the Jews: that pogroms, in other words, needed to be understood as integral to, and characteristic of, Russia's fundamental political and social make-up. Such, upon completion of his massive study of the October pogroms, was the view of Leo Motzkin, one of the closest and most systematic of contemporary observers of the lives of the Jews of Russia, and there do not seem to have been many who thought otherwise. Anti-Semitism, Motzkin wrote, had grown more audacious and candid (*kühner und offenherziger*) in Russia than ever. And 'Pogroms, alas, in one form or another, were a constituent of Russian Jewish destiny.'[172] It was for the Russian Jews themselves, no doubt, not for others, to choose their response, he went on. But it would be well, especially in times of relative—although, in fact, no more than surface—calm, if they bore in mind that there was therefore a choice that they would have to make sooner or later.

Loosely, but for the most part tacitly, this was indeed the conclusion drawn by the politically *un*instructed commonalty of Russo-Polish Jewry as well; and it was duly reflected, as before, in the vicissitudes of the migratory flow. After 1903 (Kishinev) the surge had been dramatic. Now it would reach its peak. Assuming, as is customary, that between 70 and 80 per cent of all Jewish immigrants into the United States in the first

[172] Motzkin, *Die Judenpogrome*, 404.

decade of the twentieth century emanated from the Russian Empire,[173] estimations of Jewish emigration from Russia alone to the United States alone in the years in question may be seen in Table 6.1.

TABLE 6.1. *Jewish emigrants from the Russian Empire to the United States*[174]

1901	40,000
1902	40,000
1903	53,000
1904	74,000
1905	91,000
1906	111,000
1907	115,000
1908	72,000
1909	40,000
1910	60,000
1911	65,000

But even so remarkable an *annual* rate of emigration, namely one that never fell below *c.*1.0 per cent and reached 1.5–2.0 per cent of the total Jewish population of the empire at its peak, left a vast and ever more troubled and turbulent community in place. Once again, as in the early 1880s, the impulsion among those who remained behind—some hopeful, some bitter, some comfortable, some pauperized, some politically instructed, some not—was to mull over recent events, all of which were now widely reported, and to consider what it was in the structure of Russian society and politics that was so singularly conducive to violence against them. As always, the answers varied. What varied hardly at all was the immediate, operative conclusion which was that when all was said and done, but notably when times were hardest for all, the Jews stood alone. That their established enemies were glad to pounce upon them was evident and to be expected. That in the main those who had been thought of as civilized and moderate neighbours placed somewhere to the left of the political centre, or even squarely within the political left, had by and large proved to be content to avert their eyes and leave them to their fate came to some as a surprise: but not to all, nor did all draw the same conclusion.

The dominant tendency among Jews who had located themselves on the political left was to keep their eyes on the matter of the larger Revolution towards which they were striving. Having refused to recognize

[173] In 1907 Russian Jews are believed to have accounted for as much as 77 per cent of the total Jewish immigration into the United States in that year.

[174] Sources: I. M. Rubinow, *Economic Condition of the Jews in Russia* (Washington, 1907; repr. New York, 1975), 503–4; *Evreiskaya Entsiklopediya*, xvi (St Petersburg, 1913), cols. 264–5.

particularities in the afflictions of the Jews, they chose either to remain undismayed by actual Jewish circumstances or to avert their gaze from them altogether. When circumstances were such that this had become impossible to do without abandoning all pretence of objectivity and decency, the common approach was less to insist on the Jews being undeserving of special attention than to argue that, in any event, *chem khuzhe chem luchshe*: the worse things were the more rapidly and surely the grand and decisive Revolution with its many benefits would be upon them all, Jews as well as gentiles. This, as may be recalled, was a view that had long retained its resonance. The Sages themselves had held that the agonies that would afflict the world prior to the coming of the Messiah would at the same time announce his imminent arrival. But it was not a view that all were now prepared to subscribe to. Dubnov, among contemporary sages, was infuriated by what he judged to be the irrelevant and deeply misguided application of class-war concepts and theories to the travails of their own people by Bundists and by others who had placed themselves on the revolutionary left. It was, he thought, the duty of members of a nation subject to such stresses as those that afflicted the Jews to close their ranks and deal with harsh, contemporary reality directly rather than dangle fanciful notions before their fellows about the impending conversion of Russia into a social republic in which the causes of internal, ethnic conflict were certain to be speedily resolved.

Those thousands and tens of thousands of workers, peasants, *meshchane* [petty bourgeois], and *raznochintsy* [educated commoners] who across the length and breadth of Russia, from Odessa to Tomsk, broke Jewish heads, tore out children's eyes, raped women and cut them to pieces . . . were doing what their fathers and brothers did in years past and will do again given favourable circumstances. . . . The leading paper of the organized Russian proletariat—*Novaya Zhizn*—passed by the pogroms almost in silence as if they were some minor episode in the revolutionary struggle. . . . Those dozens of . . . students and other Russians who took part in Jewish self-defence and fell victim . . . were no more than wonderful exceptions to the miserable rule. . . . You [on the left] will doubtless answer us with references to 'counter-revolution', to 'mass psychosis', and to 'the line of least resistance'. . . . But what will you do with the people, those Jewish masses who—in the space of one week—have just lived through all the horrors of the Middle Ages taken together . . . making 1905 analogous to 1648 (read 1648, not 1848).[175]

But, in any case, the strength of the revolutionary left, where the Jewish population of Russia was concerned, lay much less in the theories and theses its spokesmen chose to propagate from time to time than in its real, compelling circumstances. And these, of course, were such that nothing

---

[175] Sh. Dubnov, 'Uroki strashnykh dnei' ('Lessons of Terrible Days'), *Voskhod*, 47–8 (1 Dec. 1905). Cited in Jonathan Frankel, *Jewish Politics and the Russian Revolution of 1905* (Tel Aviv, 1982), 12.

was now less natural for the Jews in Russia than to stand entirely aside from the wider struggle to reduce, if not destroy the Autocracy. The central questions posed by and for those who now constituted the Russian-Jewish political class were the terms on which Jews should seek to participate actively in the political life of the country and what their own particular and final purposes in that regard should be.

In the early stages of the revolutionary crisis there had been only sporadic calls from Jewish quarters to place their own specific grievances and proposals before the Tsar, his ministers, and the public and argue with any force at all that the Jewish Question was a subject worthy of renewed examination and fundamental reform. Two of these were of more than nominal importance. Ignored by the government, to be sure, they remain of interest none the less because they indicate an accession of boldness, confidence, and hope where extreme prudence, not to say timidity, had hitherto been the rule. On 27 February 1905, responding with alacrity to the Tsar's rescript of 18 February 1905 in which private persons and institutions were explicitly and, against all precedent, invited to propose ways of achieving 'the perfection of the well-being of the state', the very respectable Society for the Diffusion of Enlightenment among Jews in Russia (Obshchestvo dlya rasprostraneniya prosveshcheniya mezhdu evreiami v Rossii) set out its views. Founded under the auspices of the very wealthiest and best connected of Russian Jews as long ago as 1863, it had always been carefully non-political and non-confrontational where the authorities were concerned. The Society now chose to depart from previous, exclusively philanthropic and educational, chiefly Russifying practice. An adequate and properly organized system of education for the Jews of Russia was only possible, it asserted, when the Jews of the empire had themselves been granted full equality of civic rights with the rest of the population

As a firm guarantee of the untrammelled cultural development and the complete equality of all nationalities, it is necessary that the legislative power and the administrative control of the country shall have the co-operation of popular representatives, to be elected upon the basis of the universal, direct and secret vote of all citizens of the country, without any distinction of nationality, denomination or calling.[176]

Of greater importance, and of a more ambitious and encompassing character, was the foundation, a short while after, of a specific League (or Union) for the Attainment of Full Rights for the Jewish People in Russia (Soyuz dlya dostizheniya polnoraviya evreiskago naroda v Rossii). Its founders were men who were not unlike those who had been active in the Society for the Diffusion of Enlightenment: modernist in outlook,

---

[176] Cited in S. M. Dubno[v], *History of the Jews in Russia and Poland*, 3 vols. (Philadelphia, 1916–20), iii. 111.

Russian speaking, university educated, and in many cases professionally qualified—lawyers, typically. They were privileged Jews for the most part, people who were entitled to reside in inner Russia, notably in the capital cities, and who, commonly, had been admitted (not unconditionally, to be sure) to a normally restricted profession. It was not unnatural, therefore, that while the foundation meeting of the League was held in the heart of the Pale of Jewish Settlement, in Vilna (on 25–6 March 1905), sixty-seven communal leaders from thirty-two towns or cities in Russia and Poland in attendance, the centre of its activity thereafter would be in St Petersburg and the tone and style of much that it did would be determined by a small group of St Petersburg lawyers who were as intent on joining in the general fight for the liberalization of the regime as for pressing as actively and energetically as they thought feasible for equal rights for the Jews specifically. To establish the League's executive committee in the political capital of the empire, rather than in provincial and comparatively remote Vilna, was not unreasonable, the more so as the founders had, quite characteristically, set up what they termed a *Byuro zashchity evreev*—namely an office for the protection of Jews that was to operate along juridical lines that evidently dictated a strong presence in St Petersburg itself. But the decisive factor was the determination of these lawyers to run in double harness politically: as Jews but also as Russian liberals.

The major figures, among them most notably Maxim Vinaver himself, the unquestioned leader of the group, would soon be playing a considerable role in the leadership of the moderate, liberal all-Russian Constitutional Democratic (Kadet) Party. It was indeed Vinaver's view that it was possible to be active on both fronts, that they were not incompatible but reciprocal, and that all groups in Russian Jewry could and should now unite in a common effort to achieve full suffrage for all and full civic and political rights for Jews as individuals in particular. Vinaver had not despaired of the future of the Jews in Russia, even in a Russia that remained in important respects an outgrowth of the Russia he had always known. He believed that the Jews were not, after all, without allies and that a constitutional regime, once installed, would end by releasing them from their bondage. His prominence in the Kadet Party and his election in due course to the Duma by a distinctly non-Jewish St Petersburg constituency served, not unnaturally, to confirm him in the confidence with which he held to his views.

Vinaver was greatly admired and respected as a lawyer, but also for his courage as a public figure and as a man of the utmost probity. It was not uncharacteristic of the spirit in which he and his fellows in the League chose to operate that they laid great stress on the openness of their proceedings and the candour with which they pressed their case. Great care was taken, for example, to deflect the charges of conspiracy and unconscionable intrigue that were customarily and well-nigh automatically levelled at Jewish organizations whatever their nature and purposes. Resolutions passed at the League's meetings were in most cases promptly published. When the first serious pogroms erupted (in Zhitomir, Melitopol, and elsewhere in the spring of 1905) the League protested promptly and very publicly and took steps to provide legal—and therefore, once again, public—protection for victims. When the decision to call and convene the State Duma had been made and suffrage laws were enacted (in a form, after some debate at the highest level of government, that did not, in the event, totally exclude the participation of Jews), the League sought to make the most of the new possibilities, acting scrupulously, however, within what was now the law. Young lawyers were sent out to the Pale of Jewish Settlement to explain the complex system of indirect elections by curiae which, while it militated heavily against Jewish representation in parliament, did not entirely exclude it. Handbills and cheap editions of books dealing with the social problems and political issues of the day were prepared, printed, and distributed. In sum, the League's activities were not only of a kind unknown in the community until then, but were all eminently and unusually worthy, energetic, forward looking, above all earnest and high-minded. The very respectable, professionally reputable, well-connected people who were its most prominent members were not unlike those in the west who, in vastly less troubled and dangerous circumstances, made up the active membership of the Alliance Israélite Universelle, the Anglo-Jewish Association, and the Hilfsverein. It was not that they were of a kind hitherto entirely unknown in Russian Jewry. It was rather that never before had such people attempted to launch themselves into the public arena, least of all in a body.

But there had, after all, been a revolution. Might it not be the case that, despite the horrors of Odessa, Kiev, Bialystok, and so many other cities, towns, and villages in Russia and Poland, and despite the open, imperial sponsorship bestowed on those, the notorious Union of the Russian People (Soyuz Russkago Naroda) before all others, who held that the salvation of Russia *depended* on the crushing of the Jews (among other proclaimed actual or supposed enemies of the regime), that a corner had been turned? Even when, in the course of 1906 and 1907, the concessions of October 1905 had been whittled down, was not the larger lesson that in any event the ice had finally been cracked, that a process of liberalization had been set in train, and that while there had been and would be setbacks, in the final analysis the shift to constitutional rule could not now be other than irreversible? In sum, was not the Autocracy in retreat? Was it so very absurd to read the concessions made, limited though they might be, as Portents—terribly belated, to be sure—of further, more fundamental, and necessarily beneficial changes to come *even* in respect of the Jews? It was true that matters had been so arranged that the Jews would be consistently and miserably underrepresented in the new State Duma.[177] But that Jewish deputies should be present there at all, that they would be taking part in the regular proceedings of a major state institution on a basis of formal equality with all other deputies—surely this was a dramatic departure from anything known or conceivable in imperial Russia previously?

Indeed, in the event, it did prove to be in the power of the Jewish deputies to the First Duma to raise matters of Jewish concern in the course of general debate on government policy, to do so again in the wake of the exceptionally severe pogrom mounted in Bialystok in June 1906,[178] and to go so far as to call the minister of the interior himself, to his great embarrassment, to account. On these occasions Maxim Vinaver and M. Ya. Ostrogorsky took the lead in calling for civil equality, Vinaver warning the government, in carefully measured terms, that there would be no peace in Russia until equality had been granted to all, the Jews included. Shmaryahu Levin, a Zionist, was less restrained. When the conservative spokesmen, Count Geiden and Prince Volkonsky, argued for 'realism' and caution on the grounds that emancipation for all, peasants, Jews, and women included, was necessarily a complicated business; that all knew that the Jewish problem had been solved nowhere; and that it was therefore best not to be hasty about dealing with it in Russia, Levin retorted that to speak of the complexity of the issue as an argument for postponing the effort to deal with it was intolerably misguided. As for Prince Volkonsky's plea that the special condition of Russia be taken into account to this end, was it not odd that a Russian patriot should want to place Russia on a level with Romania rather than with Germany, England, and France? The complaint that the Jews were excessively agitated was equally odd. Of course the Jews were agitated; but that should occasion no surprise. 'Gentlemen, you must understand us. If we are agitated when the matter is one of the liberation from slavery [*osvobozhdeniye ot rabstva*] of the six million-strong Jewish people, nothing could be more intelligible and natural. We are entitled to such agitation; and no one in this sphere should try to limit our giving expression to it.'[179]

---

[177] In principle, suffrage was universal. As was to be expected, the government found it difficult to make up its mind about the Jews, but did finally decide to permit them (and the peasants too) to vote and to stand as candidates, although on the basis that elections to the Duma would be indirect and carefully weighted to facilitate the admission of deputies representing segments of the population likely to be supportive of the regime. In the peasants' case, the results were unsatisfactory: the peasant deputies proved much more troublesome than had been expected. In the case of the Jews the manipulators were more successful.

[178] The Jewish community in Bialystok had already been very badly scarred the year before and the complicity of both the local police and police headquarters in the capital was not in doubt. The parliamentary commission investigating this last, still bloodier eruption reported that 82 Jews and 6 Christians had been killed (Gosudartsvennaya Duma, *Stenografichestie Otchety*, 22 June 1906, 1584).

[179] Ibid. 8 June 1906, 1104.

The Duma set up a committee to draft a law on civic equality. When evidence of dereliction of duty by the police in the course of the Bialystok pogrom was offered the Jewish deputies were handsomely supported by some of the Kadet deputies and by a former assistant minister of the interior, Prince S. D. Urusov.[180] But it was all to no final purpose. An impatient and irritated government dissolved this First Duma well before any of these matters had reached their climactic stage; and subsequent Dumas were less liberal in political make-up and a great deal less tolerant of Jewish demands for justice in particular. After the dissolution many of the liberal deputies, Vinaver among them, went on to sign the defiant Vyborg Declaration in which all Russians were called to defy the regime by refusing to pay taxes or heed the call-up to the armed forces. Their proclamation had little effect, however, other than to make it easier for the government to send some of them to prison for brief periods and to bar all the signatories to the manifesto from further participation in Russia's parliamentary life. The opportunity for vigorous parliamentary action on the Jews' behalf, if that is what it was, passed.

At the second convention of the League for the Attainment of Full Rights for the Jewish People in Russia (on 22–5 November 1905, in St Petersburg, not Vilna, on this occasion and well before the First Duma was convened), representatives from thirty cities in the empire discussed the October pogroms as the first order of business, as was to be expected. They demanded an examination of the circumstances in which violence had been allowed to occur and of the case, if case there was, for judicial proceedings against those who had been derelict in their duty. A demand that the victims be compensated by the government was voiced as well. Few of the some seventy participants present could have imagined that the imperial government would respond favourably to such demands or even respond at all. But it was a proper and, all in all, a fairly brave step to have taken. Of greater moment, however, was the decision taken to convene a country-wide ('all-Russian') conference of the representatives of Russian Jewry in its entirety to consider 'the forms and principles of Jewish national self-determination and the basis of its internal organization [*ustanovleniya form i printsipov ego natsional'nogo samoopredleniya i osnov vnutrennei ego organizatsii*]'. This was a very new note to be struck in a forum in which St Petersburg notables were prominent, even if these were no longer in the strict majority; and indeed, in the event, while a printed text of the relevant resolution was prepared, care was taken, presumably at the last moment, *not* to distribute it publicly. The leading members of the League still saw it as their chief task in the short term to encourage the Jewish population to vote in the elections to the Duma.

But the essential issue that underlay the technical proposal to convene

---

[180] Governor of Bessarabia after the Kishinev massacre. See above, pp. 514–15.

an all-Russian national Jewish congress arose in another form and was not of a nature to be so easily postponed. At the third conference of representatives of the League on 10–13 February 1906, once again in St Petersburg rather than in Vilna (or some other centre in the Pale of Jewish Settlement itself), the most urgent question regarded the manner in which Jewish deputies were to conduct themselves in the Duma itself. Several of the future deputies were prominent members of the League. And if the League itself, as a body, took a proprietary interest in the subject this was partly because it ascribed the fact that any Jewish deputies at all had been elected to its own efforts very largely; and partly because Jewish representation seemed to it so very clearly to constitute the first great step towards emancipation all round that its people hoped for. None doubted that the Jewish deputies would press for full civil rights for the Jews as a matter of course. What proved to be unacceptable to some in the League—among them Vinaver himself—was the further, more politically pregnant proposal that there be established a regular Jewish faction or caucus or bloc (or, as the term went at the time, a 'Jewish national group') in the Duma, such as the Poles, for example, had been quick to organize. Vinaver and his friends were insistent on it being entirely sufficient if, on matters that concerned Jewish civil rights directly, Jewish deputies worked in unison. They could do this without difficulty regardless of the differences in general political outlook and consequent party affiliation that separated them. On the other hand, to go beyond such *ad hoc* co-operation and form what would to all intents and purposes be a Jewish *party* would be to render their membership as individuals in the existing parties—notably that of the Kadets in which Vinaver himself was exceptionally prominent and influential—nugatory. More precisely, it would mean the abandonment of positions of influence which could otherwise be brought to bear in the service of the central Jewish cause and all to much greater effect than a Jewish bloc could hope to engineer unaided. But the question was not only one of tactics. It touched heavily, as everyone understood, on the entire—and to some painful—matter of Jewish nationhood, assimilation, and separatism. Vinaver had his way for the moment,[181] but not for long. The matter of a Jewish parliamentary bloc soon came up again, the Zionists being particularly insistent on some form of group organization and discipline being established.

Meanwhile, the Duma had assembled. Of the twelve Jewish deputies who had been elected, all associated with the League, nine were members of the Kadet Party, three joined the Trudovik or Labour (chiefly peasant) Party. Five of the twelve were Zionists. One defined himself as a

---

[181] At this point, in Mar. 1906, to ensure that it fell in with the requirements of a new law of association, the League changed its name. Henceforth it would be the Society for Full Rights for the Jewish People in Russia (Obshchestvo polnopraviya evreiskago naroda v Rossii).

non-Zionist Jewish nationalist. Most were members of the liberal professions, all had had a Jewish education as well as a secular one. All wanted full civil and civic rights for the Jews. Otherwise, notably on the question of the form Jewish participation in the public life of Russia should take, they were divided. None was socialist, it should be noted: the socialist factions and parties, the Bundists among them, firm in their belief that revolutionary forces should confine themselves to the business of achieving the total overthrow of the regime, had boycotted the elections to the First Duma and were intent, moreover, on persuading the public not to participate.[182]

A very great deal was expected of the Jewish deputies—principally, it seems, because initially much was expected at this early stage of the Duma itself. The question how they were to conduct themselves was therefore rated one of special importance both as an issue of principle and as a practical matter; and when the League activists met once more early in May, the question of the basis on which they would act in concert was debated more heatedly than ever. It had become plain, meanwhile, that what the Zionists, now a majority in the League, were moving for was not simply an agreed working relationship among Jewish members of the Duma and acceptance of the principle that Jewish deputies should give priority to Jewish issues and to the fight for civic rights for Jews—to which no one in the League was opposed. It was the Zionists' insistence that the fight be for *national* rights for the Jewish people within the empire that aroused disagreement. A formally structured Jewish faction within the Russian parliament would, of course, do a great deal to establish this as the direction in which Russian Jewry, broadly speaking, wished to move. It was precisely on this question, however—namely, whether the Jews should aim for civic equality as individuals or for a recognized, equitable, and permanent status as one of the constituent nations of the empire—that a crucial, ultimately unbridgeable division within Russo-Polish Jewry as a whole now opened. Liberals of the Vinaver school were on one side, along with Jewish social democrats and socialist revolutionaries. Zionists and, in their way, the Orthodox too as well as, if somewhat less firmly, the Bundists were ranged on the other. When within the League the Zionists pressed the issue to a vote they were able to win the argument by a fair, if slim majority of 57 to 44.

However, when to the dismay of all, Vinaver, five other deputies who supported him, and all those among the other participants who were of his mind found this unacceptable and announced their withdrawal from the League altogether, the matter was dropped for the time being by general consent. All knew that Vinaver had done more than anyone else to

---

[182] The socialists were not alone in boycotting the elections, however. The liberal Union of Unions (of which the League for the Attainment of Full Rights for the Jewish People was a constituent, but went its own way in this connection) had also resolved on a boycott.

found the League, that it was he who had presided over it all along, and that in an entirely informal way he had come to be recognized by all as the pre-eminent public figure in Russian Jewry. It was impossible for the Zionist faction or for any other to be seen as forcing him out into the cold. Yet the issue on which they were divided was too urgent and too precisely encapsulated what all perceived to be of fundamental, perhaps transcendent significance to be put aside for long. That it should have been brought up again in the course of the elections to the Second Duma (in which Vinaver himself, as a signatory of the Vyborg Declaration had been forbidden by the authorities to participate) was therefore inevitable. Once again the League found itself hopelessly divided, the more so because the difference was extended to the question whether to run a distinctly Jewish party in the elections. The Russian Zionists stuck to their guns and entered the new electoral campaign independently, although in the event it availed them little. The new electoral law, designed to bolster conservative representation in the Duma had the incidental (but from the regime's point of view desirable) effect of sharply reducing that of the Jews. Even the First Duma's twelve Jewish deputies (out of a total of 486, i.e. 2.5 per cent) had been strikingly disproportionate to the Jewish population of the country (5.2 million out of 125.6 million or 4.1 per cent, according to the 1897 census, the figures for which were now substantially out of date).[183] In the Second Duma there would be only four Jewish deputies, in the Third Duma two, and in the Fourth and last three.

By 1907, the League itself had collapsed. It had no longer been able to contain the ever more coherent, ever more strongly held, but fatefully divergent approaches to the matter of the Jews in Russia that had developed in consequence of the limited access to the all-Russian political arena that the Jews of the empire had so belatedly and grudgingly been granted. The plan to convene an empire-wide Jewish congress evaporated by default. Only the issue of the essential basis on which Jews should participate in the political life of the country, if at all, remained unresolved and fully alive.

X

The death of Herzl in the summer of 1904 left the Zionists without an effective and self-confident leader. Many had been at odds with him, but

[183] It is worth noting, too, that fierce Polish opposition to the election of any Jewish candidates at all—and, by and large, even to the participation of Jews in the elections at any level—had left the Jewish population of that country (in which they constituted 1.3 million out of 9.4 million or 14 per cent of the population) totally unrepresented. On elections to the first three Dumas in Poland, see especially Yiẓḥak Gruenbaum's accounts, initially published in the Yiddish and Polish-language Jewish periodical press, reprinted in his *Milḥamot yehudei Polin (1906–1912)* (Warsaw, 1922), 132–52. In Russia itself matters were otherwise

it was he who had been uniquely capable of sounding a trumpet call to which all paid attention. He was alone, moreover, in having gained access and a certain informal recognition in what were still conveniently known as the chancelleries of Europe. It was, in short, the central fact about Theodor Herzl, and, perhaps, his largest claim to fame, that he had become a *national* leader: in his own eyes, to be sure, but also in the eyes of his colleagues and followers; in the eyes of his opponents and enemies, however slowly and grudgingly; and thus too, ever less doubtfully, in the eyes of many of the most influential people in turn-of-the-century Europe—kings and prime ministers, ministers and lesser minions, and here and there men of letters of distinction as well. There was no precedent for such status in modern times. It may be said that there was no precedent for any such figure in Jewry for the past fifteen centuries at least. What was no less significant was that Herzl had taken it upon himself to be—and had indeed become—a national leader in the further, double sense that he posited a *nation* in the contemporary European way, namely as one nation among others, and that he sought to lead it in a specific direction, towards the attainment of reasonably well-defined goals in the interests of radical social change.

Seen in terms of the general, contemporary drive towards sharper national self-definition all round and some form of political autonomy for the 'submerged' peoples of Europe in particular, Herzl falls easily therefore, as has already been suggested, into the class epitomized by, say, Mazzini and Parnell. Seen in terms of the full sweep of the history of his own people, on the other hand, he was before all else a rebel. For Jewry, as he found it, was, as has been repeatedly noted, wedded before all else to the preservation of its heritage and, so far as possible, to the inhibition of change. Those, still in the majority, who remained loyal to the Tradition *knew* what they had been taught, namely that one of its central implications was that the Jewish people were not, could not be, and should not try to be one people among others. Those, on the other hand, who wished to circumvent or escape the Tradition altogether desired change with all their hearts but for the most part rejected the notion that the Jews were or could be a nation. What neither school, for its own particular reasons, could countenance was public action grounded on open political institutions in the interests of national political autonomy and, perhaps, ultimately, full independence on the accepted international model. It followed that everything Herzl stood for as a political man of action drove a coach and horses through the mind-set of most of his own Jewish contemporaries high and low: he was a threat to the norms and structure of Jewish communal life and, by extension, to the immediate interests of most of Jewry's existing leaders and notables, both religious and lay.

initially. Vinaver and one other Jewish deputy had been elected to the First Duma by a St Petersburg constituency in which Jews formed a negligible fraction of the electorate.

That in salient respects Herzl should have been a man who was initially very much on the margin of Jewish life and was never to have more than a very superficial knowledge and understanding of what that life entailed socially and intellectually (even in his own times, let alone much earlier), is therefore much less paradoxical than might at first appear. It was most certainly one of the great sources of his strength. As easily resoluble is the seeming paradox in his greatest popular strength being in those parts of Europe where the Tradition itself was strongest. On the one hand, it was, of course, precisely there that the desire to escape its heavy hand was most passionate—and, it may be said, necessary. On the other hand, it was there that both heritage and actual circumstances had combined to imbue virtually all Jews with an ineradicable consciousness of belonging to a distinct and independent nationality—the denial of which entailed arguments which few even among the most hopeful of Russifiers and Polonizers could bring themselves to consider as anything but bogus. Whatever reservations his followers and, more particularly, his senior colleagues in eastern Europe may have had about his management of the affairs of the movement, to say nothing of the role within it that he had assumed for himself as a matter of course, they were at one with him on the *national* principle underlying Jewish life and history. And none of this was in any way affected either by his death or by the revolutionary turmoil in Russia that, as chance would have it, followed soon after.

What the Revolution had brought about among the Russian Zionists, however, was a certain drawing back into the storms of Russia itself. Short- and middle-term social and political developments of a general order were having a greater impact upon their thinking than had been the case earlier. A somewhat more localized, locally determined, and in some ways more parochial view of things was in vogue. No doubt, the ground for this refocusing of attention had already been prepared somewhat by the dissatisfaction with Herzl's leadership that had been evident in the movement before his death, by the frustration induced by the knowledge that the Russian Zionists themselves were incapable, if only for police reasons, of taking over the movement with all the force that their numbers, quality, and energy entitled them to do. But now, after his death, what even Herzl's fiercest critics had been prepared to leave in his hands because they knew how much they owed to him, few were content to concede to David Wolffsohn and to the staff this loyal, well-meaning, but uninspired and uninspiring man had gathered round him in Cologne.

The fact was, however, that there was very little the World Zionist Organization—under Wolffsohn or any one else for that matter—could do for or about the Jews in Russia in their distress. The limited funds available to the movement allowed it to offer only very small measures of relief. The meticulous inquiry into the origins, unfolding, and consequences of the pogroms that was ordered and for which Motzkin had been engaged[184] could not be of other than historical importance. That the feeling in Cologne was that something more hopeful and, if possible, dramatic was needed was natural in these circumstances; and it was essentially for lack of anything more substantial to do that Wolffsohn decided to call a general Jewish conference to review the plight of Russian Jewry and consider what might, after all, be done by Jewry *collectively*, all forces joined together on its behalf. The conference was therefore conceived of as being as broad as possible in composition. All major philanthropic and charitable and communal organizations in Europe and North America were invited to participate, the only condition, an implicit one at that, being that nothing be said or done that might harm or further complicate the condition of the Jews of Russia themselves. Otherwise, as Wolffsohn sought repeatedly to emphasize, no topics, possibilities, or nostrums were to be ruled out of order either a priori or in the course of discussion. It was not to be in any sense a *Zionist* conference, therefore; only an instance of Zionist *initiative*. It was to be founded on the recognition all round that a huge community was in dire straits and that it was intolerable that the more comfortable half of European Jewry should sit by as onlookers. But it did certainly reflect the Zionists' underlying belief in the value and necessity of a national, supra-communal approach to the matter of the Jews. And it was, among other things, a step taken by men who knew they were playing from weakness and wished to strengthen their hand and heighten their prestige.

Wolffsohn's plan met with a very cool response even within the movement over which he presided. Primarily, this was because, having just rubbished the East Africa scheme, the now triumphant Practical Zionists, as the anti-Herzlians had come to be called, thought it excessively 'political' in character and derivative of a dangerously 'Territorialist' view of things. They recognized that the evacuation of Europe, of eastern Europe in particular, was fundamental to the Zionist scheme of things, but they feared that too great an emphasis on the need for urgent action, desperate measures, and a swift solution to the particular problems of Russian Jewry would drive the movement back in a Herzlian—or worse, 'Territorialist'—direction. And it would revive interest in East Africa itself or in an analogue of some kind. It would divert thought and resources away from the solid and imperturbable concentration on the movement's set purposes in Palestine which they favoured above all. In sum, the reluctance to support Wolffsohn had less to do in the first instance with what he actually had in mind than with the steadily sharpening division between the dwindling circle of men who thirsted for action and wished to *rescue* the Jews in their distress and the worldly wise Practicals and the Culturals whose eyes were on Palestine, to be sure, but equally and in the

---

[184] See above, p. 570.

final analysis preponderantly, on the Jews' internal, socio-cultural evolution. All these were people, therefore, who wished to pursue more limited, as they thought more attainable, but also ultimately more fundamental purposes; and it was they, by and large, who were now making the running in the movement as a whole. Wolffsohn's simple, contrary view was that failure to try to deal with what was plainly an unprecedented emergency would drive the ordinary folk in Jewry massively into the arms of the Territorialists or other, still less desirable varieties of migrationists, but in any case away from Zionism proper.

But there was genuine scepticism about his plan as well. Few within the movement believed that anything would actually be accomplished by the sort of gathering Wolffsohn had in mind. Aḥad Ha-'Am, as so often in the past, was foremost in articulating his doubts. Maintaining the unique role he had created for himself within proto-Zionist Ḥibbat Ẓion, he had soon become Herzl's most ferocious, but also most penetrating, critic within the Zionist movement as well. He was now well on his way to becoming not only the (almost) universally acclaimed moral teacher of the Zionists but of the men and women of the Jewish Enlightenment of the last decade or so of the nineteenth century and of the early decades of the twentieth. Aḥad Ha-'Am did not think that a period of evident crisis was in fact one in which long-term plans could usefully be drawn up. He did not believe that anyone really knew what could be done for Russian Jewry. He did not expect very many Jewish organizations to agree to attend a conference convened by the Zionists. And, he asked, who could blame them when the division between nationalists and all others in Jewry was so deep and evident. It was true that Wolffsohn and his associates had made it as clear as they could that it would not be a *Zionist* conference. What they had not realized was that, in so doing, 'they had [implicitly] denied any possibility of considering the Jewish Question in all its aspects and of offering *fundamental* proposals for the not-so-immediate future. For such proposals [if ever they were made] would unfailingly touch on the matter of Zionism somehow or other, positively or negatively.' On the other hand, to do no more than discuss the organization of aid to the victims, support for the refugees, and other philanthropic measures was to concern oneself with what was being done anyway 'before and without the conference'.[185]

Nordau too had his misgivings although no one had been more loyal to Herzl in his lifetime and to his legacy after the leader's death, and no one was further removed from Aḥad Ha-'Am in his outlook on the affairs of the Jews in general and on those of the Zionist movement in particular. The truth, Nordau thought, was that there was little or nothing the

---

[185] Letter to Sh. Barabash, 23 Jan. 1906, *Igrot Aḥad Ha-'Am*, iv. 6–7. Emphasis in original.

Jews could do. Pressure from abroad would leave the Russian government unmoved. Action within Russia could only be undertaken by the Jews of Russia themselves. There would be no harm and perhaps some good in encouraging and if possible helping them to improve their own internal arrangements for confronting current dangers: facilitating the circulation of such information as was relevant to their safety and welfare, for example. It would be proper too to try to make the system for rendering material assistance to the emigrants more efficacious. The fight for equal civic rights should certainly be kept up—in co-operation, however, as was necessary, with the Russian liberals. None of this partook of Zionism, strictly speaking. But what else was there for the Zionists to do 'outside Zionism'? He had every sympathy for those who wished to *act*, he told Wolffsohn. But to act, and then end by achieving nothing was always a mistake. In some circumstances it was a greater mistake than doing nothing at all. He himself would not attend the conference.[186]

Outside the Zionist movement the response to Wolffsohn's plan was entirely unfriendly. Scepticism about the benefits eastern European Jews were likely to derive even from a really massive effort by the westerners on their behalf was virtually universal. But it was opposition among the leading Jewish communal and philanthropic organizations in western and central Europe to so much as a hint of an attempt by the Zionists to assume a leading role in the general Jewish arena that was most intense. The determination to fight the Zionists and wherever possible diminish them was now of long standing. As always, it stemmed partly from opposition to what the Zionists stood for specifically, but equally from a more general determination on the part of the established leadership of the western and central European Jewish communities to abstain from anything that might be judged 'political'. It was composed preponderantly of people who were adamant in their insistence on sticking—prudently, as they saw it—to tried and true relief work, to assistance to needy migrants, and to other worthy, charitable, but politically innocent, activities. Wolffsohn and his friends might not have something of a specifically Zionist character in mind. But a 'general Jewish conference' of any kind, one at which accredited representatives of the Jewish people would try to work out the ways and means of initiating improvements in the Jewish condition—and so, quite possibly, in the ability of the Jews to beat off their oppressors—spoke necessarily of Jewish nationalism in some form or other and of a move forward to some kind of large-scale, conceivably permanent supra-communal organization as well. None of this was acceptable to the men of the Alliance in Paris or the Anglo-Jewish Association

---

[186] Nordau to Wolffsohn, 29 Nov. 1905, M. Eliav, *David Wolffsohn: ha-ish u-zemano* (Jerusalem, 1977), 71, 338–9; and 26 Jan. 1906, Sh. Schwartz, *Nordau be-igrotav* (Jerusalem, 1944), 130–1.

or their analogues elsewhere. Yet what doomed Wolffsohn's General Jewish Conference to failure absolutely was, once again, the view the great majority of the independent notables of European Jewry in all parts of the continent, in eastern Europe, therefore, no less than in the west, took of the matter of *migration*. Long before it had convened in Brussels on 29 January 1906 and over and above the refusal of most of those who had been invited to take part, this was the issue on which all was made ultimately to turn. Nothing could have been plainer to all concerned than that no discussion of the affairs and condition of eastern European Jewry was separable from the matter of migration—*massive* migration— either as a social phenomenon or in terms of its desirability. And the position of virtually all those whom Wolffsohn had invited to Brussels was, broadly but very firmly, that migration from Russia, from all parts of Poland, from Lithuania, and from Romania was not to be encouraged and that it would be well if it could be greatly reduced.

It was a note that had been sounded often enough in the past. It was sounded again, and the tone for all that was to follow was set, at a meeting in London in mid-November 1905—within weeks, therefore, of the October pogroms in Russia—of as influential and well connected a body of men in Jewry as could then be imagined. It had been called by Paul Nathan of the Hilfsverein and the New York banker Jacob Schiff, was chaired by Lord [Nathaniel Mayer] Rothschild, and attended by representatives of all the major philanthropic organizations. The participants resolved on the immediate dispatch of a mission to Russia to assess what aid should be provided in order to set the communities that had been most seriously hit by violence and arson back on their economic feet. They discussed in detail how the necessary funds were to be collected, transmitted, and distributed. They reasserted their view that emigration offered no solution to the problems of Russian Jewry. They expressed their hope and belief that the aid they would be providing would help to make emigration from east to west unnecessary: 'The overall points of view that have guided us in our relief work remain unchanged, [and are] as follows: the prevention of migration [*Verhinderung der Auswanderung*] so far as that may be feasible; no charity, but rather the grant of prompt assistance to those who are in a position to take up their original economic activity, even if only on a modest scale.'[187]

When the mission of inquiry returned from Russia a larger, more widely attended meeting of representatives of the philanthropic organizations was convened in Frankfurt on 4 January—no more (conceivably by intention) than a few weeks before Wolffsohn's conference in Brussels was due to meet. The Zionist Organization itself was not invited to send representatives to Frankfurt: that would have implied a form of

---

[187] Cited in Alsberg, 'Documents on the Brussels Conference of 1906', 150 n. 16.

recognition the convenors were unwilling to grant. It could be argued, too, that being neither a charity nor having any funds of its own to disburse, the Zionist Organization was in no position to contribute anything more substantial than ideas, when, of course, it was the Zionists' ideas that the convenors abominated most particularly. There was the further, and from the convenors' point of view typical difficulty about the Zionists, that they were known to be involved in the promotion and organization and, where possible, the equipping of Jewish self-defence groups within Russia, an activity of which the strict philanthropists strongly disapproved and which they had no intention of supporting, or of being involved with in any way at all. But the decisive reasons for keeping the Zionists out of the Frankfurt conference were identical with those that had moved them to refuse to join Wolffsohn in Brussels: Zionist leadership in a sphere which the philanthropists regarded their own—or indeed in any sphere at all—was unacceptable; and the philosophical differences between their respective, contending schools were manifestly too great for any attempt to bridge them being made or, if made, likely to succeed. What Wolffsohn, like Herzl before him, was taken as representing before all else, was a *catastrophic* view of the condition of eastern Jewry, if not, indeed, ultimately of that of all of Europe. If the condition was indeed catastrophic, the only recourse, if recourse there was, was indeed to that massive emigration to which they were all opposed—the Russians among them (the most prominent of whom was Baron David Guenzburg) no less than the Germans, the French, the English, and the others. Since those attending the Frankfurt conference took care to keep their deliberations confidential, it may be taken as a measure of the extreme importance they ascribed to the continuing need to oppose emigration from Russia that it was the one substantive item referred to explicitly in the brief communiqué issued on its conclusion.

There were other ways in which the proceedings at Frankfurt went far to epitomize fundamental differences in outlook between the principal contending schools of thought and action in Jewish public affairs: between privately and plutocratically led philanthropy and benevolent, always intensely discreet intercession on the one hand and the new, popularly mandated forms (represented by the Bundists no less than by the Zionists) founded on belief in the value and necessity of vigorous descent into the public political arena on the other. Neither the great plutocratic notables nor the new men who were at once their functionaries and their intellectual allies wished to deny that the homes of the Jews in Russia were burning or that the Jews in all of eastern Europe were under intolerable material and moral stress. What they were unwilling to accept was that the present emergency called for measures that were radical and untried, rather than palliative and familiar. The possibility of an appeal to the Grand Duke of Hesse, the Tsar's brother-in-law, to intervene on behalf of Russian Jewry was discussed at great length, until finally dropped as an entirely hopeless undertaking. Much time too was devoted to a report by Baron David Guenzburg of St Petersburg on his conversations with two Russian ministers, Count Ivan Tolstoy and Prince Alexei Obolensky, who had advised him in seemingly friendly fashion not to press too hard for emancipation for the time being, and to the more general question whether anti-Semitism was or was not really and truly rooted in the Russian people, Guenzburg insisting that it was not: 'It is true that anti-Semitism exists; but it also true that anti-Semitism is not a product of the Russian nation.'[188]

All this was remote from anything the Zionists had in mind and was to some minds predictable. Leopold Greenberg, Herzl's old ally in London, having been the most energetic of all those who favoured a great conference under Zionist auspices 'to concert measures for dealing with the Emigration from Russia', expected nothing better. The Frankfurt conference, he wrote Wolffsohn, would be 'like one called together to see how best to deal with a number of victims of some plague that has broken up in a town—what hospitals they shall be sent to and what sanatoria are available. [Our] Brussels Conference is to see whether something might not be done to the drains and waterworks of the town, so that further plague ravages should be prevented or at least guarded against.'[189] But right or wrong, none of this was helpful to Wolffsohn. All that the people in Frankfurt were prepared to recognize in the Zionists was that they retained a certain nuisance value. And it was to reduce that nuisance to a minimum that they ended by grudgingly agreeing that the Hilfsverein— but the Hilfsverein alone[190]—would be represented at the Brussels conference after all. Paul Nathan would attend, holding a watching brief. It would be his duty to do whatever was needed to prevent an outcome which he and other philanthropists of the older school might find undesirable or embarrassing. And indeed, in the event, Nathan and his friends duly had their way at Brussels. The Zionist sponsors of the conference kept their promise to maintain it on neutral lines. Leopold Greenberg's by no means 'Zionist' proposal that the conference should resolve to press for equal civic rights for the Jews of Russia and for the 'regularizing' of Jewish emigration was defeated. The Hilfsverein's own proposal that the conference declare its opposition to all efforts to promote the emigration of destitute Jews from Russia was successfully rammed through. And the result, as the people in Frankfurt had hoped, was that even as a forum in which concrete, uncontroversial measures of relief might be planned

---

[188] Cited in Y. Heilperin, 'Nisayon shel intervenziya politit le-ma'an yehudei russiya aharei pera'ot oktober', *Zion*, 20, 3–4 (1955), 171.

[189] Greenberg to Wolffsohn, 30 Dec. 1905, CZA, W. 78.

[190] Even the Chief Rabbi of Brussels refused to turn up.

Wolffsohn's conference led nowhere. The prestige of the Zionist movement was in no way enhanced. The waters of Zionist belief and doctrine,
darkening all the while and unquiet in any case, were further agitated.
And the steady shift of the movement's centre of gravity that had been in
train since the death of Herzl away from central Europe and back to the
heartland of Jewry in Russia and Poland—where, so it might be said, it
had always belonged—accelerated. This in turn helped to bring the question of the attitude the Zionists should adopt towards the Russian state
and to internal Russian politics further to the forefront.

This was a question that had always been a source of immense trouble,
indeed anguish to the Russian Zionists. After the death of Herzl it bid fair
to tear them apart. There was, to begin with, a question of strict doctrine:
surely they had written off the possibility of there being devised and
established a decent *modus vivendi* for the Jews in any part of Europe, but
in Russia itself before all other lands? There was a practical consideration:
would not their work in Russia be enormously facilitated by their being
accepted and legalized by the Russian authorities rather than repressed?
There was the matter of moral and social principle: could they stand aside
from the contemporary struggle against the hated Tsarist tyranny? And
were they to do so, would they not lose the best, most energetic, and most
passionately political of their young people to the revolutionaries? But
what would then be left of the respectable, law-abiding approach which
Herzl in the west had dictated to the movement in all parts, which he
himself epitomized in all his affairs, and which many of his older followers found natural and sensible and were quite as ready to adopt, much as
the proto-Zionists under Pinsker and Lilienblum had done as a matter of
course a generation earlier? Was prudentialism not, as Herzl had argued,
a necessary condition of dialogue with the powers that be—without
whose sanction nothing at all in Palestine itself or anywhere else was ever
likely to be achieved?

But not all who subscribed to the basic tenets of Zionism were themselves attracted to respectability, least of all in Russia. Great, indeed
increasing numbers were now consumed by hatred for the Tsarist system,
deeply and instinctively sympathetic to one or other of the many combinations of socialist ideology and conspiratorial-revolutionary practice
that furnished the contemporary Russian political arena so amply, and
therefore hugely drawn to the prospect of marching towards liberation in
the company of other parties and movements, and other nations too. One
of the salient effects of the Revolution of 1905 was, in many people's
minds, to boil these various, mostly conflicting considerations down to
one: was it possible for Zionists, any more than for other Jews (the dedicated quietists of the rabbinically guided traditionalist world excepted) to
stand aside from the contemporary struggle—which, if it was not, so far
as all participants were concerned, directed at the outright overthrow of

the regime, was aimed at the very least at the establishment of constitu-tional government on something like the western European model? In its essentials the question was far from new. But the form it had come to take upon the outbreak of the Revolution was sharper, more specific, and more peremptory than it had been earlier; and in its ramifications wider. If indeed it was improper, even impossible for the Zionists to resolve on abnegation, on what basis were they to align themselves with resistance to the regime? Should they enter into an alliance with one or other of the all-Russian parties to the struggle? Should they operate on a wholly autonomous basis, namely as Jews fighting, to be sure for reform in gen-eral, but before all else for reform of their own condition and in the name of their own people? If they were to be engaged in the general struggle for reform, should it be along the new constitutional lines or should it be in the older, now parallel, revolutionary form? In sum, should the Zion-ist position be that the Jews, as one of many peoples subject to the Auto-cracy's rule, should seek an acceptable accommodation with it, or ought they to reject that possibility altogether and apply such forces as they were able to muster to its overthrow? And either way, with what precise pur-pose in view: should the Zionists aim for equal civic rights for Jews as individuals or fight for collective Jewish *national* rights? The initial success of the Revolution had opened up the unfamiliar prospect—distant, but perhaps no longer unreal—of an eventual easing of the condition of the Jews of Russia, Lithuania, and Poland and of a humane and equitable resolution of the most pressing of their problems. The rapidity and brutality with which that prospect was destroyed had brought the entire complex of their intolerable circumstances to a head all over again—directly as Jews, but indirectly too as one category of subjects of the Tsar among many others. There was no escaping these issues in some form or other for any tendency in Russian Jewry. But the dilemma for the Zionists in particular was acute. To resolve on participation in Russian politics would be to imply that the Jews could find their way to social salvation within the Diaspora after all, so negating what Zionism stood for most fundamentally.

Of course, the stronger the centripetal pull into the vortex of Russian politics, the greater the propensity to set such troubling thoughts aside. Nervousness, fluidity of opinion, an urgent need to act to some purpose, or to any purpose at all; or, alternatively, a sense of being overwhelmed by the forces of oppression and stagnation, of the forces confronting Jewry being too great, too hostile, and too bloody-minded for the Jews to repel; and the final desperate conclusion that migration alone, not 'internal migration' but actual migration overseas, promised release—all these in one combination or another were more powerfully the sentiments of the Tsar's 5 to 6 million Jewish subjects, the Zionists among them, than they had ever been before. The social and political attitudes that had been tending ever since the trauma of 1881—against all previous historical precedent in Jewry—towards the taking of extreme positions were now subject to further intensification. The entire stretch of time extending from the beginning of the new century to the outbreak of the First World War was marked, much more than in any earlier period, by a particular sense of all things moving rapidly towards a climax of an as yet indeterminate nature, to be sure, except that, quite possibly, it bore within it the seeds of greater upheaval yet. Thoughts, paths of action, recruitment to existing political organizations and movements, the formation of new political societies, tendencies, and parties—all these would be subject to repeated and often very radical change, to multiplication and to perpetual internal reformation and reconstruction. It was fully characteristic of the times that no less than three new parties made their appearance on the political left alone in Russian Jewry: the Jewish Social-Democratic Workers' Party-Po'alei Zion (Evreiskaya Sotsialdemokraticheskaya Rabochaya Partiya-Po'alei Zion); the Zionist-Socialist Workers' Party (Sionistsko-sotsialisticheskaya Rabochaya Partiya); and the Jewish Socialist Workers' Party (Evreiskaya Sotsialisticheskaya Rabochaya Partiya). Each, somewhat like the now veteran Bund, defined itself as both Jewish (in the secular national sense) and socialist, the differences between them hinging on the degree to which strict Marxism happened to be diluted either by specifically Jewish national concerns or by such looser forms of socialism as were represented in Russia by the largely peasant-oriented Socialist-Revolutionary Party. Each had its affinities with mainstream Zionism and sought to place itself at a distinctive point of its own between the Bund on the one hand and Zionism proper on the other. But like the Bund, all appealed to Jews to participate with all their hearts in the general effort to overthrow the Autocracy—with the consequence, that while the Russian police was less willing than before to wish to understand the phenomenon, it unfailingly noticed it, objected to it, and sought to stamp it out.

It was a time, in short, in which the stupendous fact of revolution in modern Russia, even an aborted one, could not fail to suggest to all who were socially and politically minded that the outlook for an equitable and humane alleviation of the afflictions visited upon the Jews of Russia had improved at least in the sense that the tunnel through which the Jews were passing had finally widened somewhat and that it was within their power, as it had not been before, to embark on independently generated action. Even on what might (somewhat invidiously) be termed the right in Jewry, namely in the world of unbending religious orthodoxy, there too, against all precedent, an entirely new socio-political structure was about to take shape. Even Max Nordau, more than ever after Herzl's death the Grand Old Man of the Zionist movement and far and away the most articulate and prestigious of spokesmen for the strict Herzlian 'political' or 'diplomatic' school that had begun by forswearing participation in domestic politics, found the events in Russia to be compelling.

The profound changes towards which Russia is moving [he told the Seventh Congress in the summer of 1905] will have enormous influence on the fate of six million Jews. Zionism, the meaning of which is freedom, self-determination, renaissance, and resurgence, would be denying its own principles were it not to support popular sovereignty and enlightenment against absolutism, repression, and the force of darkness with conviction and determination.

It is true that the Zionists do not believe for one moment that upon the attainment of freedom and equal rights by the Jews of Russia the Jewish Question in general or the Jewish Question in Russia alone will finally be solved. The ideal of Zionist Jews in Russia as in other lands remains the renaissance of the nation in the Land of the Fathers. But nothing will prevent the Jews of Russia from fighting with the best elements of the Russian people for a progressive constitution that will assure them full equality of rights. For only free Jews will be able to train themselves without hindrance to be fit citizens of the future Jewish land.[191]

There was another view, however. In Russia itself it was held most commonly and most tenaciously by those who had been present at the foundation of the movement in its pre-Herzlian form and who continued to accept as fundamental the original article of faith formulated by Pinsker and Lilienblum when they asserted their thesis that there was nothing to be hoped for from European liberalism west or east. It had been all-round agreement on this thesis that had made the joining of the proto-Zionists of Ḥibbat Ẓion to Herzl and his followers possible. Still wedded to the principle of exclusive attention to the ancestral land of the Jews and to the rule of 'practical' work on that land in the liberating form of agriculture, the lineal legatees of Ḥibbat Ẓion refused to be diverted from the purpose to which all their energies had been devoted since Pinsker's time, namely that of agricultural settlement in Palestine however painful the process and limited the immediately visible results. And, tellingly, it was the man who, thanks to the quarrel over the East Africa plan, had emerged as their principal spokesman and leader, Menaḥem Ussishkin, who was now (1906) inaugurated as chairman-in-charge of the old bastion of Ḥibbat Ẓion in Odessa.

Never short of confidence in his own judgement, Ussishkin had been among the least inhibited of the critics of Herzlian diplomacy and of Herzl's leadership of the movement generally. He had argued, plausibly enough, that because very few men—perhaps no more than one—were needed for diplomatic and political work, the question of what there remained for the others to do was left open and unresolved. Were they destined, he wondered, to be no more than silent, uninformed spectators

---

[191] *Stenographisches Protokoll der Verhandlungen des VII. Zionisten-Kongresses*, 27 July–2 Aug. 1905 (Berlin, 1905), 23–4.

of the diplomatist's progress from capital to capital? Was close observation of the leader and blind loyalty to him enough to sustain an entire movement? Contrariness and ambition apart, Ussishkin (an engineer by training), had an unquenchable thirst for action, especially such as could be pursued at the practical, ground level of affairs as opposed to that of high politics. And by the position he had gained for himself at Odessa, the original centre of Zionism in Russia, and still in important respects at its heart, he was in a position to do what he wished to do above all, namely to 'concentrate all the Zionist work and all the practical work for Erez-Yisrael in one place',[192] as he wrote a friend—the 'place' being Odessa, the hands, unstated, his own.

There was nothing new in the programme Ussishkin devised for the Zionist movement as it stood. It amounted to a continual effort to purchase and settle land in Palestine, bit by bit, man by man, and to expand Hebrew education both there and in the Diaspora. Only the energy which he was prepared to infuse into the enterprise was fresh. And there was the further difficulty that while this was necessarily of a lesser order of drama and brilliance than Herzl's and this could be judged a virtue, it suffered only slightly less than had Herzl's diplomacy from what Ussishkin himself had correctly perceived as the latter's great weakness: it left unanswered the question of the function of the vast majority of rank-and-file Zionists in the meanwhile. But then what could Zionism, as conceived by Ussishkin or anyone else, offer Russian and Polish Jewry when the tide of contemporary, internal Russian politics was flowing so strongly against them, entry into Palestine itself was all but barred by the Turks, and the funds needed to settle those who could get in and stay were only available in penny packets? Ussishkin and his friends could choose to abstain from engaging directly in the contemporary constitutional and revolutionary struggle. They had no choice but to condone, however half-heartedly, the legitimacy of what other Zionists were doing, hoping the movement as a whole could avoid being explicitly and dangerously committed.

Not unnaturally, the stalwarts of Ḥibbat Ẓion in their Odessa fastness were imperfectly reflective of the dominant mood and trends among the leading activists of Russian and (a distinction that was now beginning to make political sense) Polish Zionism. Odessa, both for historical reasons as the original centre of Ḥibbat Ẓion and because it was the port of exit from Russia for migrants to Palestine, remained the natural centre for all that pertained concretely to Practical Zionism. But it had been decided at the Seventh Congress that now that the Russian Zionists were likely to be somewhat freer to manage their affairs without interference from the

---

[192] Letter to Yehoshuʻa Barzilai, July 1906. Cited in Sh. Schwartz, *Ussishkin be-igrotav* (Jerusalem, 1949), 121.

police, they would do well to place their new Central Office for the Russian branch of the movement in Vilna—a city that, as the 'Jerusalem of Lithuania', was commonly, if of course only informally, recognized as the capital of eastern European Jewry, certainly as the pre-eminent centre of its cultural and intellectual life. Vilna had the further virtues that unlike Odessa it was well within the region of greatest Jewish concentration and, on the other hand, was less tumultuous and dangerous a place than Odessa had repeatedly proved to be. Finally, it was the centre of Bundist activities: it had not escaped the Zionists that by planting their flag in Vilna they would be reasserting their intention to compete with the strongest of their rivals for the attention of the Jewish public. The result, in any event, was to provide the movement with an alternative arena that, by virtue both of its location within the empire and the structure of its population, was exceptionally open and sensitive to the new winds blowing through the Tsar's domains. There the purposes of Zionism could not fail to be looked at afresh in the light of the new circumstances.

It will be recalled that barely a year after the proclamation of the October Manifesto it had become evident, sound and fury aside and a few cosmetic changes apart, that not one element of real substance in the elaborately restrictive system under which the Jews had to pursue their lives had been modified, let alone annulled.[193] It might be constitutional government of a sort—a very special and limited sort—but it promised the Jews of the empire nothing. The Zionists might be confident that they had a better understanding than the revolutionaries on the one hand and the liberals on the other why this was so; they might believe they knew the true nature of the afflictions of the Jews generally, namely that these were a function of competing, incompatible, and endemic national-cultural-historical rivalries, ambitions, and prejudices and that they ran too deep and were much too violent to be resolved either by new constitutional arrangements or by a class struggle fought to the finish. But so far as the actual, day-to-day safety and welfare of eastern European Jewry in the mass and on the ground were concerned, they had accomplished no more, nor were in a position to promise more, than anyone else. As in Herzl's time, so in that of his successors, and for the same reasons, efforts to induce the Ottoman government to agree to a lifting, or even a softening, of the legal and bureaucratic obstacles it had put in place specifically to obstruct them had repeatedly failed. There could be no doubt that the larger hope of persuading the Turks to countenance a politically based, autonomous status for the Jews in Palestine had to be set aside for the foreseeable future. And if these disappointments had not

---

[193] One of a handful of very minor exceptions to the rule was the permission granted veterans of the Russo-Japanese war to reside outside the Pale of Jewish Settlement.

brought the enterprise to an absolute halt, they had greatly dimmed the movement's members' original, shining, and heartening view of their actual prospects and of the Zionist *idea* itself. Hope explained the sharp rise in membership in the early years of the movement. Disappointment accounts for the failure to sustain that steady, rapid growth in numbers that would at least have helped to confirm the Zionists' claim to be the pre-eminent representatives of the Jewish people and its interests and their Congress to be as close an approximation to a national parliament as might be achieved in Jewry's present circumstances.[194]

The failure to hold the movement together after the final, formal rejection of the East Africa scheme by the Seventh Zionist Congress in the summer of 1905 was a particularly hard blow—even if only the exceptionally perceptive or those exceptionally loyal to Herzl's memory perceived it as such. There was the brute fact of a group led by Israel Zangwill and a number of other stalwarts of the movement, Emmanuel Mandelstamm among them, breaking away from the main body with the intention of reviving and pursuing the East Africa scheme on their own in defiance of the now formal decision by the Congress to reject it. It was compounded—although, again, imperfectly understood—by the discovery made by Zangwill and his friends that the British had lost interest in what had originally been their own idea: a development in which the Zionists proper were inclined, understandably, to rejoice, was in fact an omen they would have done better to take to heart. Desperate to find a substitute for the ancestral land forbidden them, the new Jewish Territorial Organization (ITO) discovered that it was impossible to induce any government, anywhere at all, so much as to consider the establishment of anything remotely like the East Africa project in the terms Joseph Chamberlain, as British Colonial Secretary, had conceived it, however vast the empty tracts of land at its disposition and however well established the dearth of useful immigrants to settle those lands. The governments of Australia and Canada were applied to, as were the Canadian province of Ontario and the Australian state governments of South Australia and Western Australia. The possibility of settlement in Cyrenaica, Mesopotamia, and Angola were also looked into. How far the objections in Canada and Australia especially were to large-scale Jewish immigration *per se* is hard to assess. On the evidence they were unlikely to have been negligible. What is certain is that none of the governments applied to was prepared to countenance a Jewish *corpus separatum* of any kind, much less self-government within a defined territory. Back, therefore, to Russia and to Zionism proper.

The occasion—and opportunity—for a much needed redefinition of purposes was the convening of an all-Russian conference of Zionists in

---

[194] On membership figures, see above Chapter 5, p. 473 n. 148.

the relatively free atmosphere of Helsingfors (Helsinki) on 4 December 1906. Although formally an affair of the Russian branch of the movement alone, the decline of the central leadership under Herzl's successor greatly enhanced both the freedom with which the participants cast about for a fresh approach and the importance of their eventual decisions for a redefinition of purposes for the movement as a whole. The radicals' argument, now familiar in outline, was that the Jews had no hope of achieving either the social conditions to which they were entitled or the civil and political rights that were their due unaided and alone. It was questionable whether anyone would trouble to fight to attain those rights for them if they did not fight for them themselves. And when the Jews did fight for their rights they were, in practice, whether they knew it or not, advancing the cause of rights for all. Their integration into the larger struggle for radical political and social improvement in all Russia for all peoples and on behalf of the working classes in particular was therefore both right and indispensable. There remained the question of the form their participation would take and the precise nature of their assignment. These were difficult, but unavoidable questions, more obvious and still more acute in the case of the Bund, as it happened.

Where the Bundists were concerned the emphasis had shifted from the training of cadres and the education and indoctrination of the more gifted and malleable working men to mass action and agitation, and the question of the form an alliance with other dissident forces should take had risen once more to the top of the movement's agenda. In 1903 it had led, as we have seen, to the Bund being effectively expelled from Lenin's Russian Social Democratic Workers' Party. It was accepted in the aftermath of the Revolution that the terms of the Bund's relations with the RSDWP needed to be reformulated. Somewhat sheepishly and with a good deal of casuistry, its leaders agreed to rejoin the party—to the fury, it may be said, of an intransigent segment of their movement. The uncertainty about which way it should finally turn, and in which way it *had* actually turned, was never fully and satisfactorily resolved, however. Its role and presence in the Russian Social Democrat Workers' Party remained ill-defined and its relations with the roughly parallel Polish parties were positively painful, the Polish Socialist Party being exceedingly reluctant and the Polish Social Democratic Party entirely unwilling to concede the right of separate organization and ethos to Jewish social democrats under any terms whatsoever. Tension between the Bund and the socialist parties in Poland was further compounded by the Bundists finding the world of the Russian social democratic movement at any rate more congenial intellectually and culturally than that of the Poles. It was one, moreover, in which they thought they had at least a chance of finding an honourable place for themselves in due course, the Russians being opposed at this stage to national divisions and particularisms of any kind, not excluding 'Great Russian chauvinism' itself. In contrast, the Polish social democrats, were unfailingly and jealously nationalist, doubtful of the possibility of any genuine internal revolution occurring in Russia, deeply (which is not to say unreasonably) suspicious of the Russians as such and intensely critical therefore of non-Russians who subscribed to the all-Russian (i.e. empire-wide) revolutionary cause.

The Bundists were opposed neither in principle nor in practice to independence for Poland. But they reckoned that post-revolutionary Russia would be constituted a multinational or a-national state, whereas post-revolutionary Poland, whatever its borders and status, was unlikely to be. The sum of the Bundist view, therefore, was that satisfaction of the needs of the Jewish masses lay with a full, united, revolutionary effort by all the socialist forces. To this, namely to the 'all-Russian' effort, the Jewish national role would have to be subordinated; and so would the national role of the Poles, which was totally unacceptable to the Poles themselves. These differences between distinctively Jewish socialists and Polish socialists being irreconcilable, they were fated to colour the Bund's affairs indelibly once Poland had achieved independence and politics were practised under somewhat easier conditions than under imperial Russian rule. At heart, however, they were no more than a contributory element to the larger issue, namely whether any accommodation at all between the Jews of Poland and their needs and aspirations and the needs and aspirations of the Poles themselves as represented—or propelled—by any of the major Polish political formations was possible. The basis for this potentially damaging, but still mostly latent conflict had been laid well before the full take-over of the kingdom by the Russians at the end of the eighteenth century, as we have seen. What was now in evidence during these twilight years of semi-constitutional Russian imperial rule, was the early shaping of the form it was going to take under modern, twentieth-century conditions. By the end of the decade, Polish public opinion, as the commanding general of the Russian police in Warsaw reported to the Police Department in St Petersburg,

was preoccupied with relations between Jews and Poles which had altered greatly . . . as a result of radical change in the outlook of the Jews since 1904. New revolutionary movements had drawn young Jewish people to the socialist camp, where they supported the Polish revolutionaries, but were concerned less to realize socialist ideals than to achieve equal rights for the Jews themselves. Members of the older generation of Jews did not participate personally in the revolutionary movements, but assisted them financially because they were seen as offering a way to the achievement of equality. When the revolutionary movement failed [some] Jews hastily moved over to our [i.e. the Russian] side, while among others there developed a new aspiration: towards nationalism. This aspiration has been encouraged by Zionist propaganda on the one hand and by Polish nationalist intolerance on the other. This intolerance required of the Jews absolute obedience to Polish orders and, at the same time, by the establishment of agricultural co-operatives, reduced the turnover in Jewish commerce and harmed the Jews' standard of living, especially in the villages. . . . The Law on Autonomous Municipal Administration in the provinces of the Kingdom of Poland further embittered the relations between Poles and Jews in consequence of the fact that the largest of the Polish parties, the National-Democratic, was firmly in favour of those clauses of the Law that restricted the rights of the Jews. It also turned out to be the case, that the National-Democrats were hostile not only to 'Lithuanians' (i.e. Russian Jews) and to [traditionalist] Hasidim, but to 'Polish [i.e. Polonized or assimilated] Jews' as well, demanding of the latter that they resolve on being [*sdelalis'*] either Poles or Jews.[195]

If the Zionists had the prospect of emerging from a consideration of these and similar dilemmas in somewhat better shape than the Bund, it was because, in the main, they were under no analogous impulsion to hold distinct and in important ways incompatible sets of considerations— national and Marxist—in a working balance of some sort. But they were very far from being altogether free from internal doctrinal contradictions.

The conference of the Russian branch of Zionism held in Helsingfors at the end of 1906 was the third of its kind, somewhat grander than the first all-Russian Zionist conference held privately and semi-secretly in Warsaw in 1898, more modest than the second at Minsk in 1902. Of the one hundred delegates elected eighty turned up. But diminished numbers counted for less than imperfect representation of differing currents of opinion. That the Territorialists were absent altogether was probably inevitable: they had abandoned the Zionist movement as such. More serious was the absence of both the socialist and the orthodox wings of Zionism. Most serious of all and most clearly indicative of the Russian branch's loss of coherence and of the prevailing uncertainty as to how it would be wisest to proceed in the new circumstances was the decision taken by most of the Russian members of the full movement's ruling body, the Greater Actions Committee (GAC) that served as the parliamentary authority in the movement in the interim between the Congresses, to stay away as well. Ussishkin remained in Odessa. Aḥad Ha-'Am, not a member of the GAC, but Zionism's leading man of ideas, failed to turn up. Among the recognized leaders of Russian Zionism, only Yeḥiel Tchlenov, an old and well-liked Ḥovev Zion and Ussishkin's sole rival for personal pre-eminence in Russian Zionism, attended. The result was that other men, all of the second rank at the time, who had taken the trouble, however, to prepare the ground for what was to transpire at Helsingfors well ahead of time were free to set the tone. These were a group of journalists, all well known in the movement for their contributions to Zionist periodicals in major cities of the empire, of a

---

[195] 14 Jan. 1911, RSA, GA RF ADP.00. D. 20. Ch. 9 MA.

lesser order of eminence in the movement than Ussishkin or Tchlenov, let alone Aḥad Ha-'Am, but fresher in their minds and less encumbered by old quarrels. Most were younger too. Meeting privately in Vilna well before the gathering in Helsingfors, they had set themselves to devise an answer to the question how, in the post-revolutionary circumstances in Russia, the movement might best succeed in keeping its head above water. Two were especially prominent in the discussions. Yizḥak Gruenbaum, editor of the Polish-language Jewish periodical *Glos Zydowski*, was a man who, unusually in these circles at this time, was well versed in the particular intricacies of Polish politics (as well as Russian). Against what seemed to be overwhelming evidence, he believed that Jews could find an honourable place for themselves *alongside* Poland's other national groups after all in the event of independence being attained. Vladimir Ze'ev Jabotinsky, was another journalist, but one who, exceptionally, wrote with great success for the Russian (i.e. non-Jewish) press as well. A man of remarkable rhetorical talent, in many ways more of a Russian than a specifically Jewish *intelligent*, he had already, with great rapidity, made a name for himself as the *Wunderkind* of the Zionist movement. An older and more senior figure, Avraham Idelson, editor of the leading Russian-language Zionist weekly *Razsvet* had played an influential role in the course of the group's preliminary discussions at Vilna, but in the interim, having offended the Russian censorship, he was prevented by the police from travelling to Finland and had to leave it to Gruenbaum and Jabotinsky to speak for him.

Tchlenov, presiding, opened the debate by likening the present condition of Zionism to that of the German Social Democrats upon their having lost their belief in the imminence of revolution. Having reluctantly accepted that there was no prospect in the foreseeable future of their attaining Palestine by political means, the Zionists had at any rate had the good sense to turn their energies to 'practical' purposes and 'practical' work. Sooner or later, one way or another, the country would be theirs, he assured his audience. In the interim there were matters which, while they bore no direct relation to the movement's fixed and ultimate purposes, had none the less to be faced and dealt with. The general thrust of the discussions thus set, the delegates got down to cases. Some attention was paid to the weakness of internal organizational arrangements in Russia as revealed in the course of the revolutionary crisis and to means of strengthening them. But the real business of the conference, as everyone knew, was charting a direction for the movement. Zionism, all agreed, needed to be redefined. The formula most were ready to approve was encapsulated in the term 'synthesis' (probably Idelson's invention), offered to the conference as a judicious blend of the major strains into which the movement was evidently in danger of fragmenting. The idea was that Ḥibbat Ẓion-like, Palestinocentric concentration on settlement work would be pursued with all possible vigour on the one hand, but Herzlian high politics and diplomacy would not be neglected. They were not the incompatible strategies on which so much ink had been spilled and argument wasted. On the contrary, properly understood and carefully applied, they were mutually and beneficially reinforcing. How precisely they were to be pursued in tandem and in what proportions was less easily settled. What shape the movement was likely to take in the event of 'synthetic Zionism' being the order of the day was equally unclear. All were agreed that a very different approach to Constantinople had to be devised if the Zionists were to stick to their minimal purposes and yet retain some hope of making progress towards them. But the question what that approach should amount to beyond some scaling down of proposals put to the Turks was left unanswered. One proposal was that the hitherto fixed Herzlian demand for a binding public Charter in which the rights, privileges, and obligations of the Jewish entity in Palestine would be duly and irrevocably set out by the Ottoman government should be abandoned. If less was asked, so the argument ran, the greater was the likelihood of the Turks being a little more forthcoming. However, this pertained to the external policy of the movement and was therefore a subject to take up with Wolffsohn in due course and eventually put before the Congress. No formal decision could be or needed to be taken at Helsingfors. In any case, it was on affairs in Russia that the delegates really had their eyes.

The new coin of 'synthetic' Zionism had a reverse side, Gruenbaum pointed out. It implied—indeed it could be said to entail—the abandonment of the 'catastrophic' mode of Zionism: the root notion, the very trade mark of the now nearly defunct Herzlian Zionism, meaning that the Problem of the Jews was of such urgency that only some great, but at the same time simple revolutionary stroke was appropriate to dealing with it. Drop the idea that the nation was on the brink of an immense if still undefined catastrophe and the need to press *urgently* for a Charter fell away too and other, more readily obtainable targets suggested themselves. Diplomacy was not to be abandoned therefore; only maintained in a minor key. The main thing was that 'practical' work could then be pressed forward with greater energy than had previously been devoted to it and less interference from the movement's own leadership.

What then of that great segment of European Jewry that Zionism in its 'catastrophic' mode had sought to rescue? Would 'synthetic' Zionism remove it from its sights? The solution adumbrated at Vilna and then presented to the conference in Helsingfors was that this was a matter to be taken up under the increasingly popular rubric of 'current tasks' (*Gegenwartsarbeit* in the jargon of the movement). 'Current tasks' had originally been understood to cover educational, cultural, and national consciousness-raising activities. Measures designed to promote action in this sphere had been repeatedly discussed and recommended at successive Congresses and only the religiously observant Zionists, absent from this particular conference at Helsingfors, had voiced serious objections of principle to their being taken up. Now, however, it was meant to include the much more controversial 'task' of integrating Zionism into the general movement for political and constitutional reform of the Russian Empire as well. But how was this to be done? Could it be done at all? And what would then be left of Zionism's original and presumably still fundamental content: its rejection of Exile, its belief in the need to relocate a very great part of the Jewish people, its aim to reform their internal ethos and social organization, and the thesis that underlay all else, namely that the Jews must finally form a majority of the population on some defined territory of their own *somewhere* and be their own political masters once again?

Gruenbaum, leading the debate, turned these questions around. He put it to the conference that what was most urgent of all for the movement was to respond to the 'masses' ' demand that they be given answers to the questions 'of the day'. It was true that emancipation would do nothing to relieve the deepest causes of Jewish misery. Only a national territory into which the Jews were free to enter and in which they were able to rebuild their lives would accomplish that. But the immediate circumstance was that it was the pressures of the (Russian) state upon the Jews that prevented the proper flow of energies in the requisite direction. To relieve them of these pressures would be to release those energies. A democratic constitution, civic and civil rights for all, freedom of speech and assembly, and some form of institutional autonomy for minorities were all necessary conditions for progress towards the political organization of the Jewish people and of the Jews' advance towards what Zionism called for most fundamentally: to advance national-political goals of their own devising. It followed that it was not only right and proper, but vital for pragmatic reasons, for the Jews to join the majoritarian people of the Russian Empire in the general demand for a liberal constitution.[196] This prompted the retort that the example of western and central Europe demonstrated the opposite: emancipation had led Jews in a variety of new directions; least of all, however, had it led the Jews to rally to the cause Gruenbaum and all other Zionists had in mind, namely that of a national renaissance centred on the ancestral Land of Israel. And what were the prospects for a fruitful alliance with other national groups in Russia? Thus far the record offered grounds for nothing better than scepticism in this regard.

---

[196] *Die Welt*, 28 Dec. 1906. See also Gruenbaum's account: 'Ha-pegishot shel ha-'itonut ha-ẓionit', in Y. Gruenbaum, *Dor be-mivḥan* (Jerusalem, 1951), 64–70; and 'Ha-ve'ida be-helsingfors', ibid. 71–7; Shelomo Netzer, 'Yiẓḥak Gruenbaum ke-ish ẓa'ir—ẓemiḥato shel manhig ẓioni be-folin', *Kivunim*, 10 (Feb. 1981). For a contrasting views, see Joseph Goldstein, 'Jabotinsky and Jewish Autonomy in the Diaspora', *Studies in Zionism*, 7, 2 (1986), 29–232.

It was Leo Motzkin, however, who offered the most acute analysis of the dilemma the Revolution of 1905 had posed for the Zionists. The specifically Zionist solution to the Problem of the Jews was, after all, no more than a means to a larger national end—the renaissance and rehabilitation of Jewry. On this all were agreed. Alas, it was undeniable that the Jews themselves in their numbers were not markedly drawn towards it; and, further, that their attitude would be all but unaffected by what transpired in Palestine—the more so as the present prospects of the *yishuv* were so poor. The arena in which the fate of the Jewish people would actually be decided was that of the Diaspora itself. The central question facing it, how Jewry was to manage its affairs *there*, had not changed. What had rendered the question more urgent and more complex was that the Jews could not allow themselves the luxury of pursuing interests of their own where those interests appeared to run counter to what humane and ethical principles of a general or universal character prescribed. Strong nations might do so for a while, but even they might not do so for long. Weak nations condemned themselves to destruction if they did so. The Jews must therefore align themselves with the progressive and democratic forces even at a certain cost to themselves, even, that is to say, when it was apparent that such forces were unwilling to concede anything of substance to them and to their particular needs and customs and were generally unwilling to accept them as a distinct and equal nation. Eventually, recognition would come, Motzkin thought. But much would depend on how the Jews conducted themselves in the wider political sphere as well as how they ordered their own internal affairs. In general, it was the Zionists' duty to devote themselves to the organization and coherence of the Jews as a nation and as an autonomous political force— notably, but not exclusively in Russia. But the indispensable key to their future as a distinct and coherent people was language. It was language that was now especially under threat in consequence of the Jews' own powerful tendency to make the most of the opportunities to assimilate other cultures. There was therefore no more important 'current task' for the Zionists to perform than the reinforcement and, where necessary, the systematic inculcation of the Jewish languages.[197]

Motzkin had gone somewhat further than any of his colleagues had been prepared, or were perhaps able, to go. Some years would pass before the full force—but also the weakness—of his thesis (and the role he himself would play in seeking to pursue it) would begin to be apparent. For the time being, by general consent, the conference contented itself with the recognition that in practice the greater part of the Russian branch of the movement was already engaged in the fight for the liberalization of

---

[197] Ibid.; A. Rafa'eli, 'Ve'idot arẓiot shel ẓionei rusiya', Kaẓir [I] (Tel Aviv, 1964), 82–90; A. Bein (ed.), *Sefer Motzkin* (Jerusalem, 1939), 74–5.

the Russian regime. The 'natural entry of the Zionist masses into the liberation movement of the territorial nations of Russia' was approved. 'The union of Russian Jewry for the attainment of recognition of Jewish nationhood and legally established self-government in all matters relating to Jewish national life' was defined as a central goal. Much of what Gruenbaum and Motzkin had had to say was then incorporated into specific political demands formulated in the following terms:

1. The democratization of the Russian regime on a strict parliamentary basis; broad political freedom, autonomy for national territories; and guarantees for national minorities.
2. Complete and absolute equality of rights for the Jewish population.
3. Assured representation of national minorities in state and local elections conducted by universal, equal, direct, and secret ballot irrespective of sex.
4. The recognition of Jewish nationality as an entity entitled to self-rule in all spheres of national life.
5. The convening of an all-Jewish national assembly to lay the bases for national organization.
6. National-language rights in the schools, in the courts, and in public life.
7. The right to substitute the Sabbath for Sunday as a day of rest in all parts of the country.[198]

This was a very long way from the Basel Programme as Herzl and Nordau had formulated it and the First Congress of Zionists, nine years earlier, had established it as the movement's ideological corner-stone. Tchlenov, characteristically flexible, sought to make out that little of real and central substance had changed. Herzl, if he were alive, he assured the delegates, would surely approve of what they had done. Gruenbaum, more robust, had no doubt that this was not the case at all. But 'there is no future without a present', he told the delegates; and it was to the present, he thought, that the Zionists—and, by implication, all Jews—should direct their attention. The Russian police, for their part, promptly drew the very conclusion that Herzl had always wanted to avoid, namely that 'Russian Zionism has abandoned its indifference to [domestic] political problems . . . and has sanctioned the adhesion of the Zionist masses to the liberation movement of the territorial nations of Russia.'[199]

XI

In the conservative environment where the orthodox rabbinate still set the tone of public as well as private life, such large prescriptions for active

[198] Rafa'eli, 'Ve'idot', 98–9; *Die Welt*, 28 Dec. 1906.
[199] Cited in A. Lokshin, 'Formirovanie politiki (Tsarskaya administratsiya i sionizm v Rossii v kontse XIX—nachale XX v.)', *Vestnik evreiskogo universiteta v Moskve*, 1 (1992), 54.

treatment of the Jews' collective ills and afflictions drew little attention and carried no conviction. The rule was quietism. Political impotence[200] remained integral to the mechanism by which Jews were to accommodate themselves to their condition, the abnormal in their lives effectively remade as normal, their existential weakness a source of strength. Those who sought release from the tension of an otherwise intolerable discrepancy were taught to avert their gaze from what lay without and attend chiefly to what was internal and private in Jewry itself, to that which lent itself, after all, to determination by the Jews themselves. The men of greatest moral authority in orthodoxy were blind neither to the recent horrors of the pogroms nor to the accelerated abandonment of eastern Europe by vast numbers from within their flock. But there could be no question of their tackling contemporary issues in terms that were even remotely analogous to those which the modernists in Jewry were very successfully making familiar: to wonder, for example, whether, in the circumstances, the Tradition could—or even should—be preserved in its entirety; or whether what they themselves conceived of as a divinely ordained Exilic condition was ultimately, humanly, tolerable. What the rabbis did see most clearly and what most profoundly dismayed them were the inroads of modernism. It was the accelerating processes of acculturation and alienation of great numbers of Jews from their people and from Judaism itself, namely as a creed and a culture, that were the sources of chief disquiet. All understood that the threat to the Tradition that Ḥatam Sofer[201] and others had identified a century earlier had materialized. Some among them had become very conscious of the inadequacy of the means available to them to stem the tide. But the divisions within the world of orthodoxy itself on matters of doctrine and behaviour, the absence of a hierarchy, the proud independence of mind and status of the most eminent figures among them, and the fact that there was no immediately apparent and effective way in which the Law as they knew it could be made to serve as a practical guide to collective conduct in modern conditions—all these made it just short of impossible for recognized leaders to take stock together, much less devise a plan of positive joint action. Besides, while few in the world of orthodoxy disputed the thesis that the gift of emancipation, where granted, was in one degree or another poisoned, the world of those most loyal to the Tradition was not of one view on what might constitute a doctrinally acceptable and at the same time socially viable approach to the Jews' civil liberation.

---

[200] Expressed quintessentially in the Talmudic dictum that until the coming of the Messiah it is enslavement to alien kingdoms that will continually mark the lives of the Jews: 'Ein bein ha'olam ha-zeh li-imot ha-mashiaḥ ela shi-'ebud malkhuyot bilvad' (Zera'im: Berakhot 34b).

[201] See Chapter 2.

Emancipation, acculturation, and secularism having bitten more deeply into the German-Jewish community, its own wing of orthodoxy had been more directly, not to say dramatically, challenged than its analogues in eastern and southern Europe. The lines distinguishing orthodox practice and strict observance from religious reform and moderate performance had been drawn publicly and institutionally in central Europe in a way that had no parallel further east. This had been done, moreover, at the behest of those who wished to retain, rather than modify, the old forms of worship and social organization and practice, wherein, so far as they were concerned, the point and value of the German *Austrittsgesetz* of 1876.[202] It was this that had made it possible for what had become a minority within Jewry to avoid being swamped by the more liberal majority, to be in a position to set up its own schools, synagogues, burial societies, and such like, and to manage its financial and fiscal affairs on its own, rather than in a form that would have left it permanently subordinate to the established, but now doctrinally more moderate communal institutions. But the ultra-orthodox in Germany differed most of all from their brethren in eastern Europe in their social outlook. They had ceased to envisage maximum divorce from the rest of civil society as a desirable, let alone a feasible end. They knew themselves to be more vulnerable to the inroads of religious reform and assimilationist trends generally than the powerful leaders of the vastly more numerous communities of Hasidic and non-Hasidic Jews in eastern Europe—certainly more vulnerable than the leaders of the eastern communities still believed themselves to be.

Accordingly, German orthodoxy, even in its doctrinally strictest vein as taught by the Frankfurt rabbi Samson Raphael Hirsch (1808–88), had been prepared to move in ways and in a direction that by and large were still anathema further east. It allowed and even encouraged, as eastern European orthodoxy did not, some real involvement in the secular, non-Jewish world. This had to be selective and carefully measured, to be sure. It could only go so far as such involvement was compatible with strict observance of rite and ritual and the maintenance of communal and inner private life in a form that left its essentials virtually unchanged. But they were of a disposition to distinguish the primary from the secondary and the fundamental from the trivial. They ceased to insist on 'Jewish' dress or on an exclusively, or even predominantly, Jewish education. Unlike the great eastern European branch and the smaller, but equally intransigent Hungarian branch of religious orthodoxy, it had dropped objections to more imaginative and cosmopolitan architecture for its synagogues. It permitted its religious functionaries to dress themselves in a mode that was not too distantly removed from that of the Protestant clergy. Many of

---

[202] See above, Chapter 4. A similar law had been passed in Hungary.

the leaders of this school, Hirsch himself and 'Azriel Hildesheimer (1820–99), rabbi of the orthodox congregation Adass Jisroel in Berlin among them, had themselves acquired a command of the German language and had attended German universities: ventures into totally alien cultural territory that had no equivalent in the east except, to some extent, among the Russian state-appointed crown Rabbis whom the strictly orthodox despised as ignoramuses and virtual secularists.

The effect was not only to legitimize the acquisition of the German language by all their followers, but to promote—intentionally or otherwise—an internalization of the manners and to some extent the values of German society. In certain circumstances even formal observance of religious ritual could be regarded as less than a cardinal and absolute duty. When Rabbi Hildesheimer of Berlin discovered why young people were regularly absent from his Sabbath morning synagogue service—because his congregants insisted on their children attending *Gymnasium*, the indispensable road to regular secondary education—he ruled that the ritual reading of the Torah would be held in the afternoon after school hours and that part of the morning service be repeated for their benefit.[203] This was a concession of a kind that would never have been so much as dreamt of in eastern Europe. In sum, German orthodoxy, even at its strictest, had been taken over by devotees of *Bildung* as this was then understood. Secular education, far from being ruled out, was encouraged. Little or no attempt was made to avoid military service. And it was accepted that integration in general society and its multiple hierarchies in *some* form was doctrinally acceptable and could be actively sought. Where a passable track, if one was ever found, between the largely contradictory obligations of Jewish traditional practice on the one hand and German citizenship on the other would lead was less clear. To manœuvre between even limited participation in the life of a country given over to ever more feverishly nationalist agitation on the one hand and the rock-bottom, but still very substantial obligations that were the mark of Jews who remained fully loyal to the Tradition on the other required extraordinary casuistical skill. But the possibility of such a middle way between the two being delineated and adhered to was not forgone.

It remained that this intricate and demanding enterprise of adjustment could not fail to seem exceedingly doubtful, if not incomprehensible and ultimately impermissible, to the strict constructionists in the east, the real and ultimate guardians of the fortress of orthodox legitimacy. And it appears to have been to some extent the need to justify both in their own minds and in the minds of others the evident inconsistencies and contradictions in their position that goes furthest to explain the emergence

[203] David Ellenson, 'German Jewish Orthodoxy: Tradition in the Context of Culture', in Jack Wertheimer, *The Uses of Tradition* (New York, 1992), 11–12.

from within the relatively small community of S. R. Hirsch's strict and separatist followers of a group of articulate and energetic individuals who were intent on bringing the western and eastern worlds of orthodoxy into a congenial, but also institutionalized relationship. Some were officiating rabbis. Some were laymen. Uniquely in the world of strict orthodoxy, they had not only the ability and imagination, but the independence of mind to formulate an ideological basis for a venture into what in all but name was politics and to lay down the ideological and programmatic bases for a common organization that would, despite all the evident difficulties, prove acceptable to the always demanding, sceptical, and hidebound men in the east on whose approval everything, ultimately, depended.

In their organizational skill and intellectual rigour, modified somewhat by a certain practicality and pragmatism, the three most prominent advocates of the effort to bring the orthodox in all parts of Europe under a single roof were well representative of the strengths of German Jewry as a whole. The original impetus is customarily traced to a Isaac Halevy-Rabinowitz (1847–1914), a man of impeccably ultra-orthodox views, but of considerable modern as well as traditional learning. His bias was firmly towards the latter. He was noted for being an especially fierce critic of the methods and purposes of the *haskalah*[204] or Jewish enlightenment, of the Wissenschaft des Judentums movement, and so, perhaps inevitably, although a diligent amateur historian himself, most particularly of Heinrich Graetz, far and away the most eminent Jewish historian in the latter half of the nineteenth century. Having moved from Poland to Germany as a comparatively young man, he emerged, none the less, as one who was willing and capable to some extent of straddling both worlds, the adopted German as well as the eastern European from which he stemmed and to which in very many ways he remained quite faithful. A greater role would be played by Jacob Rosenheim (1870–1965), a man in whom the ostensibly incompatible qualities of German *Bildung* and Jewish religious orthodoxy were very remarkably and much more closely and organically combined. He would be seconded in important ways by a man of a more distinctly intellectual stamp, Isaac Breuer, but it was Rosenheim more than anyone else who would tip the balance between the inertial quietism that was so deeply characteristic of Jewish orthodoxy and something that was more like public action.

Rosenheim regarded himself as a pupil of S. R. Hirsch of whose school of orthodoxy in its most notable social and institutional manifestation in Frankfurt he was indeed a pillar. He was a layman, however. The name he made for himself in Jewish circles in Germany owed most to his activities as the proprietor and combative editor of the *Der Israelit* newspaper, the

---

[204] On the *haskalah*, see Chapter 2.

principal organ of German orthodoxy, and as a notable initiator and organizer of charitable and philanthropic enterprises. Of his deep attachment to the ancient Jewish tradition there can be no question, but he was not an obscurantist. Nor was he insensitive to, much less ignorant of, the world around him—in which, he did not doubt, Jewry in all parts had to make its way, like it or not. At the core of Rosenheim's position was the view that this could indeed be done without anything of really genuine importance being abandoned. Dress, for example, to which many in the east attached great symbolic weight, was of no significance in his eyes. His opposition to secularism was total. But he was as firmly—if more cautiously (given his continuing effort to obtain the indispensable sanction of the rabbinate at its most eminent for all that he was about)—opposed to anti-modernism in its extreme and uncompromising forms as well. When Nathan Birnbaum, briefly a Zionist himself, not only turned against Zionism and all he believed it to represent, but went on to argue that the Jews had become 'addicted' to a culture of science and godlessness and revolutionary modernism generally whence it followed that no potential ally whatsoever deserved to be overlooked in the vital struggle against these evils, not even the anti-Semites provided only that they were godfearing, Rosenheim was quick to draw a line. However severely one judged those who had left the fold and however right and proper it was for the orthodox to fight them, under no circumstances might orthodoxy go so far as to ally itself to the anti-Semites against other Jews. That would be unconscionable, dishonourable, and contrary to everything that was worthiest in the Jewish tradition.[205]

Ideas apart, he was a man with a useful gift for plain, but effective language, one which he was to put to good purpose in the course of his long effort to pull the world of orthodoxy together and into something like the modern age. The straightforward terms in which Rosenheim set out his views publicly at the end of 1908 appear to have done much, perhaps more than anything, to set the tone and content of a meeting of rabbinic notables at Homburg the following year in which the plan for a worldwide orthodox *movement* was first seriously adumbrated by people of considerable standing and influence. Characteristically, Rosenheim sought to convey confidence and strength laced with pragmatism. It was true, he wrote, that in western Europe the orthodox ('the loyal sons of traditional Judaism') were now a minority. They knew as well as any that the spirit of the times was anti-religious and therefore against them. But they had kept going and they had kept together and they could and would continue to do so because it was their rightful conviction that it was they and they alone who maintained that continuity by which Jewry and

---

[205] Yosef Fund, 'Agudat yisrael mul ha-ẓionut u-medinat yisrael—idiologiya u-mediniyut', Ph.D. thesis, Bar-Ilan University, 1989, 35–6.

Judaism had always laid enormous store. Their numbers were now small, but numbers were not decisive. 'We represent historic Judaism; and wherever ten of our orthodox brothers gather for God's purpose,[206] they and none other represent eternal Israel, for within them dwells the soul of this people, within them lies God's Law and Teaching.' Besides, the orthodox were only in the minority when 'the hundreds of thousands and even millions of our brethren in eastern Europe and even in the west beyond the seas' had not been taken into account.[207]

Isaac Breuer (1883–1946) was of a different stamp: a man of ideas rather than of action. In a movement founded on exceedingly strong views, but loath to engage in fundamental doctrinal debate, he was at once, so it may be argued, its most distinguished philosopher-theologian and to a certain extent its odd man out. As a grandson of Samson Raphael Hirsch himself he was by lineal descent a member of the inner circle of German orthodoxy in Frankfurt,[208] of which, being learned in the traditional mode, a graduate of German universities, and a lawyer by profession, he was almost perfectly representative. He wrote prolifically on the dilemmas of orthodoxy and the terms on which they might be resolved offering formal argument for what he considered a doctrinally and intellectually viable middle way between strictest orthodoxy and moderate modernism. Unusually for a member of his class, he made at least two attempts to articulate his case in popular, fictional terms as well.

Breuer's central thesis was a daring one for a German Jew of any tendency. He minced no words about the essential character and quality of Jewry: 'The Jewish people are not merely a religious community with a divine mission; they are also a *nation* comparable to the German nation, the French nation, and others.' On the other hand, there was a cardinal respect in which the Jewish nation was exceptional. Other nations shaped their laws. In the case of the Jews it was the Law that had shaped them. They were less a nation by virtue of their history—for all that their history had been a factor of huge importance in their evolution—than by virtue of Torah. It was Torah, God-given Law, that defined them and to which the content and primacy of human wisdom, experience, and will were all fundamentally irrelevant. It was Torah that had made them what they were. It was Torah, and Torah alone, that had served them in the past as their national constitution. And it would necessarily be Torah that

---

[206] An allusion to the *minyan*, the ten male adults who constitute the minimal number for conduct of a public prayer service. Cf. the original German: '. . . daβ der Judentum der Geschichte, wie wir es vertreten, jedes *Minjan* gesetztreuer Juden im tiefsten Sinne zu einer Vertretung des unsterblichen jüdischen Volkes, die Thora, wohnt.'

[207] Jacob Rosenheim, *Agudistische Schriften* (Frankfurt-on-Main, n.d.), 110–11. See also Jacob Rosenheim, *Ausgewählte Aufsätze und Ansprachen*, 2 vols. (Frankfurt-on-Main, 1930); and Jacob Rosenheim, *Zikhronot* (2nd edn., Benei Berak, 1979).

[208] He was born in Hungary, as it happened, but at the age of 7 he was taken to Germany where he remained until 1936.

would serve them as their constitution in the future. It was therefore 'impossible to be a national Jew without being loyal to the national law. Only we who observe Torah and its precepts are truly national Jews—[as opposed] to the Zionists who, it is true, look upon themselves as nationalists, but have a distorted view of the Jewish nation [seeing it merely as one] among [others].'[209]

Zionism, Breuer maintained, encapsulated a very great presumption. This was not to say that in its purposes it was necessarily and entirely wrong. He could agree with the Zionists that a people separated from its homeland was necessarily a crippled people, culturally and spiritually. What he rejected was their view—which they held in common with the other national movements and programmes that had emerged in Europe in recent times—that the Jews were free to rely on autonomously generated human ideas and independent human action. The ultimate purpose and final end of Jewish history was *not* political independence. It was Redemption. Independence would be restored to the Jews in due course, but by divine will and intervention, not human agency. The commonwealth-to-come would not be and need not be a sovereign state of the usual kind at all. All that was required was that Jews have free access to their ancestral land and that the community be re-established according to the rules and principles of *halakha*. Zionism had done much to awaken national consciousness. That was all to the good. But it aimed at a secular, not a *halakhic* state and for that reason remained inherently inimical to the people it sought to sustain and at cross purposes with their true and higher destiny. On all this Breuer was uncompromising. The Zionist movement, he was to write some years later, was 'the most terrible enemy that has ever risen against the Jewish nation'.[210]

If it is curious, it is at the same time intelligible that the immediate precipitant of the final stage in the process by which much of the orthodox world agreed to come together in something like the organized fashion Rosenheim had in mind in the movement that would be known as Agudat Yisrael was a row in the opposing camp, among their arch-rivals the Zionists. In the first instance it was a quarrel that concerned Zionism's own small orthodox faction, the Mizrahi, but it had larger and deeper-lying implications as well sparked by the resumption, at the Tenth Zionist Congress in 1911, of a debate on 'culture' begun a full decade earlier. At its more or less concrete level the principal issue was the duty—or otherwise—of the Zionists to venture into the field of education: most specifically, but by no means exclusively, the promotion of the Hebrew language as the national vernacular and as the vehicle for literature and other secular endeavours. A second, not unrelated issue was the effort to

[209] Cited in Jacob S. Levinger, 'Introduction', in Isaac Breuer, *Concepts of Judaism* (Jerusalem, 1974), 4 (slightly amended).

[210] *Judenproblem* (Halle, 1918?), 89. Cited in Levinger, 'Introduction, 6.

enforce—or *per contra* to resist—such limitations on public and private life
in the new Jewish settlements in Palestine as traditional rules of behaviour
did unquestionably dictate: strict observance of the Sabbath being the
most notable example along with the (economically ruinous) biblical
precept of a Sabbatical year which laid down that all agricultural land be
left to lie fallow every seventh year. Herzl's view on all these and similar
matters had been that the Organization should so far as possible steer clear
of them and that as little as possible be done to offend the orthodox or
make their presence in the movement more difficult than it was in any
case. But there was no way in which the underlying differences of view
could be diminished or papered over for very long. Feelings on either
side—tempers too, often enough—ran far too high for the issues at stake
not to re-emerge with depressing and damaging regularity—on the
whole, with added force on each occasion—for the ideological and
philosophical chasm within the body of the Zionist movement not to be
revealed for all to see.

A display of ill feeling and bad tempers of this kind was precisely what
had scarred the Tenth Congress held at Basel in 1911, the more so as it
was anything but unexpected. The Mizraḥi, in its forebodings and ill
temper, had gone so far as to gather privately in Frankfurt before the
Congress actually met, the better to establish its position and prepare its
strictures on the way in which, for example, settlers on land purchased by
the relevant agency of the Zionist movement, the Jewish National Fund,
had been allowed to breach the Sabbath. When at the Congress itself the
spokesmen for Mizraḥi duly voiced their complaints and demands from
the platform, they were promptly and unsurprisingly met by the preponderant secularists' charges of 'clericalism' and renewed insistence on the
movement remaining wedded to freedom of thought and personal conduct. Care was taken not to trespass on the basic principle established in
Herzl's time that the Tradition was always to be accorded formal respect.
None of the resolutions passed could be fairly described as explicitly anti-
religious. But it did emerge, not for the first time, that the balance of
opinion within the movement remained overwhelmingly secular and
that while nothing would be done deliberately to offend the orthodox
they were not about to have their way in matters which the others, in line
with the now established attachment to 'current tasks', deemed essential.
Some among the Zionist orthodox found this intolerable and withdrew
entirely from the movement soon after. Others, among them R. Reines
their leader, remained in the not altogether vain hope of bringing the
movement round to something more like their own viewpoint in the
course of time. In the short term, what counted most was the residual
feeling both within and without the movement that the lines had been
drawn a good deal more sharply than in the past and that an exceedingly
divisive issue had been allowed to get out of hand.

While few developments in modern Jewry had disturbed the leaders of orthodoxy in all parts of the continent so much as the establishment of the Zionist movement, not all among them dismissed it out of hand. What moved almost all of them to resolve eventually on total opposition was the failure of those who had had some initial sympathy for it to gain a role within it for themselves as governing moral and spiritual guides. This, they made plain, was the condition on which they were prepared to play any sort of part in it at all. But negotiations between the few (on either side) who had been reluctant to forgo the possibility of union or at least mutual tolerance foundered very soon in a climate of mutual recrimination: denunciation of disloyalty to the Jewish heritage and refusal to obey the people's rightful guides on the one hand; cries of 'No, no, we shan't go to Canossa' and such like on the other.[211] Herzl's repeated appeals to the orthodox rabbinate to support the movement fell on deaf ears. Zionism, and Herzl himself, were anathema to the most illustrious and influential of eastern European rabbis almost as a matter of course. Where the orthodox were concerned, there were the doctrinal issues already alluded to. There was also the judgement that a national movement that partook so blatantly of the spirit of contemporary European nationalism instead of being informed by the Jews' own Holy Law and Teaching could not be other than intrinsically ill founded and misconceived. There was too the exceedingly serious, although never explicitly mentioned, threat the Zionists had mounted, partly by intention, partly not, to the supremacy and authority of the rabbinate itself. Finally, there was fear of rebellion within orthodoxy.

Among the developments that had particularly irritated, offended, and, beyond all doubt, worried its established leaders was the formation within the Zionist movement itself in 1902 (with Herzl's warm encouragement) of an orthodox faction, the Mizraḥi. Like Po'alei Zion—the original generic name for what would be a full set of factions professing socialism in varying degrees of severity and confidence within the larger Zionist movement—Mizraḥi was syncretist in nature. It stood for strict religious orthodoxy. It sought to stand equally for Zionism—at any rate for Zionism in its Herzlian, political form, which is to say, non-socialist, neutral on cultural matters, seeing the political-diplomatic task of gaining a formal, legal, internationally recognized foothold for the Jews in Palestine as primary and the question of the structure and quality of the society to be established there in due course as one that was best left to one side while Herzl and his chosen few got on with making the evacuation of the most vulnerable and needy of Europe's Jews and their resettlement elsewhere possible. The leaders of Mizraḥi knew perfectly well that Zionism, both in its early form under Pinsker and Lilienblum and in its more mature form under Herzl and his successors, was incompatible with religious orthodoxy in several, fundamental ways, one of which was especially difficult for them to swallow. There was no denying that the Zionists were no less dedicated to the continuation and coherence of the Jewish people than the masters of traditional religious orthodoxy. But it was equally plain that they were in no need of Judaism in its traditional religious form for any of their purposes; and, what was worse, that they were busily engaged in creating powerful and popular secular substitutes for it in the now familiar and (to the orthodox) hateful spirit of the *haskalah*.

Accordingly, while favouring the major goals of Zionism, the people in Mizraḥi were at one with the non- and more especially the anti-Zionist leaders of Jewish orthodoxy in rejecting and condemning those Zionist activities that had come to be grouped under the generic designation 'culture', namely the promotion of the Hebrew language and its literature and of formal, secular education at all levels conducted *in* Hebrew. They could now see, as their more prestigious analogues in the very much larger anti-Zionist orthodox camp had seen almost from the first, that Zionism in all its forms, but most particularly in the hands of the devotees of 'culture', offered not a variant on religion in the manner of the religious reformists, but something far more dangerous: a complete substitute for it. They continued to differ from orthodox anti-Zionism in their somewhat greater sensitivity to the material condition of the Jews, the selfsame Jews who constituted the greater part of the orthodox flock. They refused to view the material afflictions of the Jews with that fatalism that was so dangerously, and to some minds infuriatingly, close to equanimity. They had always been at one with Herzl in seeing the political task of making the rescue and rehabilitation of the Jews possible as Zionism's overriding purpose. And they had drawn comfort from his opposition to the common secularist plea for the promotion of 'culture' as a matter of high priority, untroubled by the fact that it derived from tactical considerations, rather than from reasons of principle. To Nahum Sokolov's plea for humanism and pluralism in Jewry and for the 'modern development' of the Jewish people at the Fourth Zionist Congress in London in 1900, Mizraḥi's leader, Rabbi Y. Y. Reines (1839–1915) retorted that it was not culture the people needed most urgently, but food. Those gentlemen who insisted on bringing up the question of culture, the rabbi went on, either did not understand Zionism, or if they did they were undermining it. The object—the sole object—of the movement was to accelerate the ultimately inevitable Return to Ereẓ-Yisrael.[212] Reines was therefore in no real way inconsistent, when he

---

[212] *Stenographisches Protokoll der Verhandlungen des IV. Zionisten-Kongresses*, 196–210, 212, 221, 281.

resolved, after much searching of his soul, to support Herzl on the issue of East Africa in 1903. If the Jewish people went under, he argued, there would be none to return to the earthly Zion in Erez-Yisrael anyway when the time for restoration, divinely determined or otherwise, finally arrived.

So while they had to fight the devotees of 'culture' on their own, there was a sense in which the essentially symbolic victory of the secularists registered as a defeat not only for them, but for what was left of the Herzlian school of exclusively political Zionism as well—and for the dead Herzl's immediate, admittedly dull and mediocre, but always loyal successor David Wolffsohn personally. It may be that this was bound to happen. The anti-Herzlians had long since been released from the inhibitions generated in them by the combination of awe, appreciation, and puzzlement in which all but the Founder's fiercest opponents within the movement regarded him in his lifetime. There had always been those who believed the movement would do better if it set its collective mind on other things than high politics and a diplomacy geared to face-to-face confrontation with kings, presidents, prime ministers, and the like, not forgetting the Sultan of Turkey and the Pope in Rome. On the evidence, they claimed, nothing would be achieved that way, Herzl's way; not for the time being, at any rate. The movement should attend to the so-called 'practical' work instead, to settling Palestine itself, bit by bit, village by village, man by man, much in the spirit of, although more efficiently than, its predecessor Hibbat Zion.[213] And then, if it were truly realistic, if it took the full measure of what could and what could not be accomplished in the foreseeable future, it should consider the *moral* state of the Jewish people in its Exile as well and what the Jews were actually in a condition to make of political independence if ever they achieved it. 'It cannot be,' wrote Ahad Ha-'Am in his capacity as arch-priest of this, the 'moral' or 'spiritual' variety of Zionism, after the First Congress in 1897,

that after thousands of years of untold evil and affliction the people of Israel will rejoice upon attaining, at long last, to the rank of a small and mean nation, its state a plaything in the hands of great neighbours and incapable of survival except by the machinations of diplomacy and perpetual abasement before whomever fortune happens to have smiled upon; an ancient people which was a light unto the gentiles cannot be satisfied with no more than this as a reward for its hardships— when many other nations, of unknown origins and without culture, have achieved it in short order without first suffering a fraction of what it had undergone.[214]

The fact was, he wrote on another occasion, that the political conditions on which Herzl set such great store were far from being such as

[213] On Hibbat Zion, see Chapter 5.
[214] 'Ha-kongres ha-zioni ha-rishon', *Ha-Shilo'ah*, 2, 6 (1897).

would allow the Jews to proceed as directly and as smoothly to independence in their ancestral homeland, or indeed anywhere else, as he and his
colleagues hoped; and for that reason, if no other, it was questionable
whether *political* independence was properly the first priority. The Jews
did certainly need to return to their historic centre. It was there alone that
they would be able to

live a life of natural development, to apply [their] powers to all components of
human culture, to develop and complete [their] natural heritage, and so once
more to contribute a great national culture to the storehouse of humanity, the
fruit of the free labour of a nation that lives according to its own spirit, as in the
past.[215]

But if Jewry in its present sorry state was ill equipped morally and spiritually—and by the same token culturally—for such a task and the Zionist movement itself was manifestly too small, too weak, and too poor in
material and political resources to handle the immense task of massive
physical relocation that the Herzlians in their naïvety had assumed on its
behalf, there was much it could do in more modest, less dramatic, but
ultimately more fundamental spheres. Aḥad Ha-'Am did not employ the
term *Bildung*, but it is the term that corresponds most closely to what he
had in mind—at which point the theses of the Aḥad Ha-'Amian so-called
'cultural' (or sometimes 'spiritual') Zionists tended to merge with those
of the 'practical' Zionists. For in the last years of peace in Europe all, even
the remaining Herzlian loyalists, had concluded not merely that 'diplomacy' had failed to yield tangible results, but that the movement must at
all costs avoid being left in the doldrums if it was not to decline. Pending
great changes in the strategic and diplomatic structure of the Near East
that might, perhaps, soften Ottoman objections to what the Zionists
were about, it was vitally necessary, therefore, to provide it with fields of
activity in which useful results could be shown to have been achieved.
The movement had in fact no choice but to set itself 'current tasks'. In
Europe itself it had already proved to be excessively difficult, if not impossible, totally to avert the Zionists' collective eye from the internal politics
of Russia in favour of absolute concentration on the movement's admittedly essential, stated aims in Palestine. As for Palestine itself, whatever
one's view of the uses of further moves to gain a politically recognized
foothold there, all could agree on the promotion, improvement, and so
far as possible multiplication of the tangible agricultural settlements of
the new *yishuv*. Such meagre resources as could be mobilized to that end
were already being channelled rather more systematically in that direction, subject to the obstacles raised from time to time by the Ottoman
authorities and to some extent by the Arab population of the country.

---

[215] 'Medinat ha-yehudim ve-ẓarat ha-yehudim', *Ha-Shilo'ah*, 3, 1 (1898).

And upon Wolffsohn's resignation at the 1911 Congress and his replacement by Otto Warburg, the whole thrust of the movement towards the 'current' and the 'practical' would, it was hoped, be confirmed and so to speak sanctified more or less in the spirit of the resolutions passed by the now firmly dominant Russian branch of the movement five years earlier.

But 'practical' work too was far from being without its difficulties. It was inherently slow and often tiresome. It was unrewarding in the short term. For those immediately concerned it was generally ungrateful, dangerous to health (notably because of endemic malaria in Palestine), and to some extent dangerous to life and limb as well. When the Tenth Congress was over Aḥad Ha-'Am might declare with evident satisfaction that the old 'official' Zionism, as he called it, was dead or dying and that it had come to be accepted that the true aim of the movement was not the achievement of 'a secure refuge for the *people* of Israel' after all, but of 'a fixed centre for the *spirit* of Israel'[216]—although if this was the case it was a negation in substance as well as in name of the movement's original purposes. What was certain and more critical was that there had been a lapse into a mode of thought that brought the movement appreciably nearer the minimalism and quietism that had for so long been the decisive characteristics of Jewish conduct in the public sphere everywhere and at all times in the Exile: precisely that approach to the miseries of the Jews that Pinsker and Herzl and the tougher minds among their followers had sought to do away with. But while, for these reasons, whether they knew it or not, the Tenth Congress had brought the Zionists somewhat nearer their opponents than they had been earlier, there was still very little in it to cheer the religiously orthodox either within the movement or outside it.

The Aḥad Ha-'Amian distinction between the 'spiritual' and the 'material', its implicit renunciation of responsibility for the life and welfare of living men and women as opposed to the Jewish people and Judaism conceived generally and in the abstract, and the abiding dismissal of the Herzlian vision of a state that in all essential respects was to be a state like any other—all these strictures were much like those that had been habitually voiced by the harshest critics of Zionism as it was originally (and correctly) understood. On the other hand, there was no mistaking in them an emphasis on—and an attempt to invest new energy in—forms of Judaism which, in so far as they drew sustenance from the traditional literary and historical sources did so selectively, in a critical rather than pious spirit, and with a markedly secular conception of both the national heritage and the national future in mind. For the Mizraḥi, therefore, as already noted, the Aḥad Ha-'Amian turn taken by the Tenth Congress

---

[216] Aḥad Ha-'Am to Ladizhinsky, 22 Aug. 1911, *Igrot Aḥad Ha-'Am*, vi. 223; and 'Sakh ha-kol', *Ha-Shilo'ah*, 16, 3 (1912). Emphases in the original.

added to the pain it had caused them on other counts. They knew themselves to be to some extent Herzl's creation. They had found in his exclusively political line a solution to the problem with which Zionism, by its advocacy of a *non*-Messianic Return, confronted them as orthodox believers. They had duly supported Herzl on the East Africa project. They had been willing to swallow the election of Nordau as Herzl's successor when that was proposed despite Nordau's being married to a non-Jewish woman; and when Nordau refused the crown, they had (somewhat grumpily) accepted David Wolffsohn as the new leader for all that, unlike Herzl, or Nordau for that matter, the man was clearly second rate. But in the interim they had seen that even under Wolffsohn the movement was moving slowly and steadily in the opposite direction: a characteristic and, for Mizraḥi, peculiarly infuriating project had been the establishment in 1909, under explicitly Zionist auspices and to Zionist applause, of the distinctly secular Herzlia Hebrew *Gymnasium* in the new Jaffa suburb of Tel Aviv. The sum of it all was that by the eve of the Tenth Congress little of the approach thought to have been enshrined in the original Basel (political and economic) Programme of 1897 was left, the Mizraḥi itself was in disarray, and its most influential figures had no choice but to consider—some of them to reconsider—their position. In other words, the issue of orthodoxy as a whole versus Zionism had been brought to a head.

In the wider world of orthodoxy as a whole the matter of Zionism had continued to fester too and objections to it, as formulated notably in Germany (rather than in eastern Europe), had become increasingly coherent. Zionism was clearly *secular*. That its chosen means and fields of endeavour were now distinctly cultural served to emphasize the fact. There was no doubting its contempt for the traditional, authoritatively fixed view of the destiny and cosmological role of the Jewish people and of the consequent propriety of the Jews' 'yearning for redemption' (*kisufei ge'ula*) and anticipation of Messianic deliverance. Far from arising out of religious motives or in the interests of furthering religious purposes, it was part and parcel of the general awakening of nationalism in Europe and of modernist Jews' reaction to anti-Semitism in particular. It was entirely *irreligious*: 'Zionism is a wholly national-racial movement that has nothing at all to do with religion.' The Zionists might pride themselves on their tolerance, but that only counted against them: 'By offering an equal welcome to orthodox and reformists [they merely] demonstrated [their] intention to rehabilitate the Jewish people without any regard whatsoever for the Jewish religion.'[217] And besides, their much proclaimed tolerance of orthodoxy was deeply suspect too: what had been divinely

---

[217] Cited in Ya'akov Ẓur, 'Ha-ortodoksiya ha-yehudit be-germaniya ve-yaḥasa lahit'argenut ha-yehudit ve-la-ẓionut', Ph.D. thesis, Tel Aviv University, 1982, 374–5.

ordained, firmly anchored in the Torah, and fundamental to true Judaism was known to be regarded by many of them as little better than the prattle of rabbis and literati (*Rabbiner und Literaten Geschwätz*). The orthodox refusal to make common cause with them was not to be understood by any means therefore as a failure to pay due attention to the travails and afflictions of eastern European Jewry. Orthodox Jews were as concerned as any other body or group in Germany or elsewhere. What they did insist upon, however, was that philanthropy be extended in a manner free of philosophical content that ran counter to the established norms of Jewish orthodoxy. It was because so much that the Zionists were engaged in did directly and indirectly do so that the adherence of strictly observant and God-fearing Jews to the Zionist movement in the manner of the Mizraḥi was scandalous, an impermissible breaking of orthodox ranks, a further muddying of Jewish waters. But for action to be taken, for the inertia of the leading figures in European orthodoxy to be overcome by the likes of Halevy and Rosenheim, and for the truly illustrious and therefore indispensable figures in orthodoxy to be induced to leave their strongholds and join in a common effort of some kind, developments in Jewish public life that would illustrate the merits and urgency of their argument beyond all doubt had to occur.

It was this that was provided by the debate on culture and religion at the Tenth Zionist Congress—savage at times—and the bitter response to it of the Mizraḥi[218]—although, that said, it would probably not have sufficed to provoke a departure from normal practice had it not been for the impact of the terrible events in Russia some years earlier. What seems finally to have induced the great men of eastern European orthodoxy to lend their authority to a venture of the kind Rosenheim and his colleagues had in mind were developments in Russia in their own world in the wake of the Revolution of 1905. 'The recent great revolution and the devastation visited upon our people, have moved all the best in Jewry to consider the condition of the people and how it might be improved.' Thus Rabbi Ḥayyim 'Ozer Grodzienski of Vilna, second only (if at all) to Rabbi Ḥayyim Soloveitchik of Brest-Litovsk in eminence among the non-Hasidic (and by the same token more scholarly, less mystically inclined) rabbinic leaders. The Jews, he pointed out, were now divided into distinct 'companies' (i.e. parties or factions), each organized according to its particular outlook. Sadly and paradoxically 'the largest of all companies in our nation and it alone—that of the faithful [i.e. orthodox] in Israel—has failed to take a similar step'. The orthodox were of one mind, but they were scattered and divided. It followed that they were

---

[218] It was certainly Rosenheim's view that it had been the resolutions passed by the Tenth Congress that served him and his colleagues as the final and necessary precipitant. See Rosenheim, *Zikhronot*, 116.

now drastically in need of organization, of a general, permanent institution of some kind, one that would tackle 'the questions facing the nation in an orderly fashion and in a spirit appropriate to those who keep the faith'.[219] What Grodzienski and some of his colleagues had had in mind initially was an organization encompassing the orthodox within the Russian Empire alone. They wished to do no more than keep the existing orthodox communities in being, guard the ancient dikes that surrounded them, and plug the holes in them as they appeared. None of their purposes was therefore in any sense socially radical. They were confident that the prominent, socially conservative laymen who would rally to their side could be relied upon to be submissive to their authority and ensure that all would proceed in a firmly moderate direction. They therefore expected to have the approval of the authorities for what they were about and initially, if somewhat grudgingly, they were indeed allowed to hold a series of consultations in which some of the grandest names both in the Russo-Polish rabbinate and among the lay notables of Russian Jewry participated (on one occasion at least with representatives of the Ministry of the Interior present) between 1907 and 1910. All plans collapsed, however, upon the Russian government's refusal, in the event, to permit such a movement being established. Never explicitly articulated, its grounds were never in doubt. The Autocracy's well-established objection to a mass movement that, while plainly and satisfactorily traditionalist and politically neutral, even politically innocent, would none the less be devoted to the raising of religious and national consciousness among the Tsar's Jewish subjects still stood. At this point, his plan having collapsed, Grodzienski became a readier listener to Halevy's ideas for a Europe-wide, perhaps even worldwide union of the orthodox; and he agreed to participate actively in the drawing up of plans for an alternative.

To move from remonstrance and censure of the enemies of orthodoxy to the establishment of a supra-communal, potentially worldwide orthodox *organization* was a very considerable step, however. That it had become possible to contemplate it owed something to the successful establishment of a modest east–west functional relationship between the two wings of orthodoxy for philanthropic purposes. It owed more to the idea itself having taken hold, slowly and incrementally, in the course of a series of attempts to bring the leaders of orthodoxy in all parts of the continent together to consider their position and chart a common direction. It had already been adumbrated at a rabbinical conference held in Cracow in 1903, although nothing was resolved, followed in turn by a more important, although still not decisive meeting of rabbis from Russia (Rabbi Grodzienski among them), Poland, Germany, and Hungary at

---

[219] Circular letter, 5 Feb. 1908, Ḥayyim ʿOzer Grodzienski, *Aḥiʿezer: kovez igrot*, ed. Aharon Suraski, i (Benei Berak, 1970), 257–60.

Homburg in August 1909 under Halevy's chairmanship.[220] But it was all extremely slow moving. Serious preparations for what would be the founding conference of Agudat Yisrael were not begun before the end of October 1911 (shortly after, and directly in the wake of the Tenth Zionist Congress); and were not concluded until the spring of the following year on the eve of the conference itself. Only on the 27–8 of May 1912, after further prolonged and difficult negotiations with the leaders of European orthodoxy, did 228 mostly rabbinical figures from Austria, Belgium, Belorussia, Congress Poland, England, France, (Austrian-ruled) Galicia, Germany itself, Hungary (a disappointingly small delegation), Latvia, Lithuania, Moravia, Palestine, Russia, Switzerland, and the Ukraine gather in the Prussian border town of Kattowitz to consider and resolve on an explicit course of action.[221]

There were two salient classes of participants at the Kattowitz assembly. There were the black-coated, heavily bearded men, many of them elderly, bent, and scraggy, all well aware of their standing within their own closed world, mostly indifferent, when not contemptuous, of virtually all that lay outside it, but moved on this one occasion to venture somewhat beyond it by a newly heightened sense of the national responsibility they believed to be theirs and by the recognition that Jewry as they knew it was visibly beset by decomposition. Among them were some who by general consent were the most eminent figures of the day in the world of traditional Judaism in eastern Europe: Rabbi Ḥayyim Soloveitchik of Brest-Litovsk, Rabbi Eli'ezer Rabbinowitz of Minsk, Rabbi Eli'ezer Gordon of Telschi, Lithuania, Rabbi Ḥayyim 'Ozer Grodzienski of Vilna, and the President of the Council of orthodox communities in Hungary, Adolf Frankl. The two most influential of all Hasidic leaders, the 'Gerer *rebbe*' Rabbi Mordekhai Alter and, the 'Lubavicher *rebbe*' Rabbi Shalom Dov Baer Schneersohn, did not appear in person, but sent their representatives. On the other hand, at once leading, and deferring to the rabbis, were a number of younger, more vigorous, more worldly men who were in some respects of their own kind, yet of a very different appearance and comportment, whose beards were trimmed, whose dress was 'European', who not only knew the German language thoroughly, but spoke it from choice, and whose outlook on the world in general was freer, more open, and to a marked extent less a priori. Among the latter were some of the Mizraḥi people who had participated in the preliminary talks held in Frankfurt in October 1911 in the wake of the Tenth Zionist Congress and who had now begun to look for a new direction—although it needs to be said that the tendency on all sides at

Kattowitz was, so far as possible, to play down the role of the Zionist Congress as the immediate precipitant of their own assembly.

The working out of the definitive, public articulation of a common outlook and purpose by all these people, the eminent among them being in general the proudest and the most difficult to handle, fell to Rosenheim. His was the moving spirit and his too the conviction that if dignity was to be maintained the new Agudat Yisrael must not appear as the Zionists' rival, let alone analogue. He saw too, and no one seems to have contested his view, that it was best to argue that it had been the general dilemmas with which orthodox Jewry was, indeed, so obviously confronted that had brought the people at Kattowitz together: nothing less, that is to say, than the entire trend of events in Jewry since the onset of emancipation and of the accompanying, destructive processes of acculturation and secularization. Accordingly, no formal resolution on the matter of Zionism itself was passed. Nor was there to be any explicit reference to the theologically tangled question of the resettlement of the Holy Land. The question whether the condition of Exile was or was not intrinsically anomalous, on which the modernists in Jewry were so sharply divided, was not referred to either. Most tellingly of all, the material distress of the Jewish people itself was passed over in silence as well. The new movement was simply declared to be a religious and philanthropic organization dedicated to 'resolving the various questions arising from day to day in the lives of the Jewish people [*kelal Yisrael*][222] in the spirit of the Law and the Precepts [*Torah u-mizvot*]'. It was a careful formulation, to some minds a deal too careful. Breuer, for example, found it deeply unsatisfactory: by seeming to say everything it said nothing.[223] As a contribution to the resolution of the many questions that would, as most of the participants appear to have realized at the time, face Agudat Yisrael in the future both within the camp of Jewish orthodoxy itself and in its hostile confrontations with Zionists and others—the exceedingly difficult question of the attitude to take towards the resettlement of the Holy Land, for example—it failed totally. But then the immediate concerns of the organizers at this early stage lay elsewhere.

Two issues raised well before Kattowitz by the easterners and by the Hungarian ultra-orthodox (who, while invited, had resolved in the event not to attend) could under no circumstances be avoided. One had to do with the continued independence and particularity of the various orthodox communities themselves. Would any of them be in any way obliged, in consequence of their adhesion to a supra-communal organization of the kind proposed, to accommodate themselves to some general, preconceived model? Besides their own, there was the German model

---

[222] Literally: the entirety or generality of Israel, namely the Jewish people, or the Jewish public, as a whole.
[223] Fund, 'Agudat Yisrael', 51–2.

admirably represented by Rosenheim himself. It was natural that the easterners would have it very much in mind. All knew that German orthodoxy was explicitly predicated on the pragmatic principle of *Torah 'im
derekh-erez* ('Torah and the way of the land') which was intended to
mean, roughly, that while the inner life of orthodox Jews should (and by
implication could) remain unchanged, in externals and especially in their
relations with the general population, speech, dress, conduct, and so
forth they would so far as possible conform to the common norms. Of
this, however, the easterners and the ultra-orthodox in Hungary would
have none. They held it to be essential that Jews remain distinct and separate in every possible way, not least in externals.[224] They needed to know
that there would be no attempt to induce them to order things otherwise
in their own parishes.

The other, not unconnected matter was that of the formal status of the
specifically orthodox public (in some cases ultra-orthodox) within the
Jewish community as a whole in each country. Once again, there was a
German model. The *Austrittsgesetz* had sanctioned the peeling off of separate, regular, officially recognized orthodox communities—separate,
that is to say, from the rest of the Jewry in each German state and city. It
was of crucial importance to the Hungarian and German orthodox to
assert and maintain such separation if they were not to be swamped by the
moderately observant and the outright reformists. But in Poland and the
Pale there had been no such fission of the observant community into discrete, doctrinally distinct segments. The eastern European rabbis were
confident that on their own home ground they had the great majority of
the local Jewish population behind them and that they were not alone in
their instinctive abhorrence of such multiplication of Judaisms in circumstances that implied that the more moderate forms of orthodoxy—
perhaps even the hugely despised, but also greatly feared Reform Judaism
as well—needed to be recognized as in some degree or other legitimate.
The approval of the easterners, led by Rabbi Soloveitchik, to the plans of
Rosenheim, Halevy, *et al.*, was flatly conditional on their demands and
interests in these respects being met to the full.[225]

---

[224] The flavour of unrelenting orthodoxy is conveyed by an exchange at an assembly of
rabbis in November 1868 at Budapest in the course of which an extreme conservative, one
Rabbi Zevi Hirsch, denounced a proposal that lay teachers be appointed to teach secular subjects at advanced *yeshivot* (rabbinical seminaries), saying 'A rabbi in Israel should have nothing
to do with *Bildung*, secular subjects, or the sciences! It is enough if he knows how to sign his
name in German or Hungarian, and no more.' Cited in Michael K. Silber, 'The Emergence
of Ultra-Orthodoxy: The Invention of a Tradition', in Wertheimer, *The Uses of Tradition*, 44.

[225] Rabbi Hayyim Soloveitchik (1853–1918) is commonly considered to have been the
foremost Talmudic scholar and authority of his time, noted for his development of an
especially austere and abstract mode of study and analysis. It is more than probable that had
he decided to oppose it Agudat Yisrael would never have been established. It is certainly
evident that he took his duty in regard to it very seriously, formulating eighteen specific

But if there was to be no approved and binding model for the country components of the movement-to-be, how was it to be structured and what would be the nature of its central authority—if, that is, there was to be one? Was it to be no more than a talking-shop? Ought Agudat Yisrael strive to be as large and encompassing a movement as possible, one in which even orthodox Zionists might eventually find a place for themselves? Should it, on the contrary, be driven by an especially tough, demanding, and therefore restrictive view of what constituted its proper clientele? What emerged from the conference at Kattowitz was less than clear-cut one way or the other. It had become evident that the movement would have to cater for at least four fairly distinct tendencies: eastern European orthodoxy proper in its relatively austere 'Lithuanian' form; the Hasidim of eastern Europe; the ultra-orthodox of Hungary; and the orthodox of Germany and their analogues in other western countries. It was agreed that each was legitimately distinctive and that none would be under an obligation to accommodate itself to anything to which it was unaccustomed or of which it disapproved. That, however, was as far as pluralism would be allowed to go. In most other respects a strict and exclusive, rather than inclusive approach to membership would be the rule, founded on what the founders took to be the role they hoped to play in the future evolution of the Jewish people. The actual formulation, once again, was Rosenheim's. The structure and continuity of Jewry had been ruptured by emancipation, he told the Kattowitz conference in his keynote address to it. The task of organized orthodoxy was to reconstruct it—*not*, however, by remaking the Jewish people into a nation in the usual, modern form, nor by merely founding one more association among other associations. 'Our supreme goal is the revival within the civilized world of an ancient Jewish possession [*Besitz*], the traditional idea/notion of *kelal Yisrael*—the entirety of Israel, faithful in all solemnity to the Torah that is its very soul.'[226]

demands to be met as the condition of his approval. Curiously, the paper in which his demands were itemized—much the most important document to be considered at and by the Kattowitz conference—was never published and the original is said to have been lost. Rosenheim was later to confirm the loss, while asserting, still more curiously, that in practice Soloveitchik's conditions had not been especially important after all. The upshot, in any case, was that the terms on which Agudat Yisrael was born and set on its way obviated any attempt by westerners to intervene or interfere in local matters in Russian Jewry, while, on the other hand, as Rosenheim noted with concern (Rosenheim, *Zikhronot*, 169) underlying distrust of the religiosity of the German orthodox to which Soloveitchik's document had given voice was never quite dissipated. Rosenheim was in constant fear of some sort of coalition of opponents of his plans drawn from the Lithuanian and Hungarian rabbinate being formed. While the conference lasted he suffered, he was to recall, sleepless nights and 'hell on earth'.

[226] 'Was will "Agudas Jisroel"?' in Rosenheim, *Ausgewählte Aufsätze*, ii. 164–73. Emphases in original; 'kelal yisrael' and 'Torah' in Hebrew characters in the original); and see Fund, 'Agudat Yisrael', 29–30, 98; Zur, 'Ha-ortodoksiya', 399.

It followed that in its founders' view Agudat Yisrael was not to be regarded as a new creation, let alone a simple organization, party or faction *within* Jewry. Their claim was that it was no less than authentic Jewry itself—*kelal Yisrael*. But the circle they proposed to draw around themselves to define their movement and to distinguish those who subscribed to it and followed its teachings from those who did not did none the less leave the latter in doctrinal limbo and the question how they were to be dealt with undecided. In the eyes of those who carried most doctrinal weight at Kattowitz the proper position was the strict and unyielding one, namely that co-operation with those who failed to accept the Torah as the basis for public, no less than private, activity was impermissible. The more moderate position was that in certain dire circumstances co-operation might be necessary and because necessary possible—*provided* strict guarantees against the irreligious majority drawing Torah-loyalists into impropriety of any kind obtained. In the event, the actual, infinite complexities of the lives of the Jews in Europe would ensure that there would be no really effective rule in this respect, only uncertainty, disagreement, and much awkward manœuvring between the dictates of principle and the demands of practice.

Where Agudat Yisrael would find itself on still more unstable ground was within its own nominal domain. In western terms, the Hirsch school of German orthodoxy counted as very strict, if not quite ultra-orthodox. In eastern eyes it remained intrinsically doubtful. The notion that it might be possible to combine forms of modernism and external adaptation to the norms of society at large with traditional Jewish orthodoxy brought it far too near—some would say right up to—the borders of the hated, much feared, and totally rejected *haskalah*. For the German orthodox to have dared to mount the Kattowitz conference was therefore, among other things, to have risked division in the world they themselves wished most dearly to unify. And telling differences of viewpoint and customary behaviour were on display even in the plenum of the conference itself, its proceedings being conducted in German, for example, a language not all those present understood and for which quite lame apologies had to be made. If the gamble succeeded, it was not only because all accepted the notion that if they stood together they would do substantially better than if they stood alone, but because the more difficult proposition that they could only do so if all, without exception, swallowed the idea that each community was, morally and practically entitled to go its own way was accepted too—or, as the learned Aramaic phrase evoked at Kattowitz went, each river in Jewry would continue to flow in its own set path (*nahara nahara u-feshateiha*). None, except, perhaps, for the original enthusiasts among the founders of the movement, could bring themselves to regard this essentially pragmatic, operative approach as really satisfactory. The need to reiterate and reinforce and, especially, reconfirm its validity would therefore arise repeatedly once the movement got into its real stride after the First World War. But none seriously contested the carefully worded thesis Rosenheim laid before the conference in his main address, the sum of which was that eastern and western European Jewries had diverged and that if friction and instability were to be avoided respectful attention had to be paid to local particularities. Country associations would do well, therefore, to refrain from seeking to impose such particularities as they had developed in the course of time on the movement as a whole.[227]

It followed that the Aguda, conceived as a coherent movement, rested on a contradiction. Demanding conformity, the dominant, majoritarian traditionalists in eastern Europe knew they must never waver in their insistence on social control. The Germans who had originated everything and with whom the ultra-traditionalists were prepared to go along to some extent, by maintaining their claim to have found a middle way through the thickets of modernity after all (*Torah 'im derekh erez*) had effectively relinquished social control. How then was the movement to proceed? Rosenheim's solution to the dilemma, adumbrated in his opening, programmatic address to the assembly, was simple. On the one hand, overall coherence of the movement would be ensured by the institution of a supreme rabbinical council—to be known as Mo'ezet Gedolei Yisrael[228]—which would possess absolute authority to lay down general lines of action, to pronounce on what was and what was not permissible when 'measured by the yardstick of Torah', and, generally, to stand for the ultimate sovereignty of Torah. On the other hand, as a matter of cardinal 'organizational principle', Agudat Yisrael would be decentralized.

While the general character of the necessary solution to the questions agitating the totality of Jewry today is clear, it is equally clear that there will be many local distinctions to be taken into account. Things have taken such different forms in East and West in the course of centuries of development that it is only with the most scrupulous regard for the peculiarity of Jewish circumstances in particular countries that friction and convulsions can be avoided. To the planned country organizations, so far as the general structure of their constitutions is concerned, there must therefore be accorded far-reaching autonomy, while, on the other hand, a distinct measure of restraint will be required of them where the carrying over of particular rules to the full organization is in question.[229]

The upshot, curiously, was that for all the evident organizational and, of course, ideological differences between them, the position the Aguda adopted for itself was analogous to that of the Bund—by no means analogous to that of the Zionists, least of all those who remained devotees of

---

[227] Rosenheim, *Zikhronot*, 151.
[228] Later known as Mo'ezet Gedolei ha-Torah.
[229] Rosenheim, *Ausgewählte Aufsätze*, ii. 171.

Zionism in its original, Herzlian mode. Where the Bund predicated its legitimacy and purposes on socio-economic *class* as the fundamental, politically, and socio-economically crucial criterion by which proletarian sheep were to be distinguished from bourgeois goats, Agudat Yisrael predicated its case on *piety* as the cardinal quality by which the elect were to be distinguished from the fallen and were to be guided through the dangerous complexities of social action. The Zionists, in contrast, had at any rate begun by claiming to speak for the Jewish people in its entirety: the actual, vocal members of the movement, of course, but for all others as well, and most especially the terribly needy, virtually voiceless Jewish rank and file. Specific programmes and purposes aside, it was this huge— many would say overweening and impossible ambition—that more than anything else had set them apart from other contemporary Jewish movements and tendencies. Others—religious reformists, assimilationists of all varieties (Germans and Poles of Jewish or 'Mosaic' faith, and the like), socialists, and of course the ultra-orthodox and the Bundists—had this in common, that while they were generous with their advice, rarely, if at all, did they wish to speak, let alone act, on behalf of the Jewish people *in its entirety*. Even when the claim in each case was that they constituted what was now Jewry's leading and decisive segment, the silent assumption was that those who failed to rally to their own particular flag would, in the fullness of time, drop away altogether. What the Kattowitz conference had made plain was that even the concerns of mainstream orthodoxy were from this point on no longer with all of Jewry, but with the faithful alone—Jewry, it might be said, as they felt it ought to be, by no means as it really was and as it was likely to remain or evolve in the future. The unintended effect of their having come together and raised their ideological flag for all to see in the manner chosen, was therefore to place themselves, despite their claim to unique national validity and authenticity, much more narrowly in place as one of the several constituent factions in modern Jewry than they were prepared initially to recognize.[230] There was certainly no question of their seeing themselves, however remotely, as one among equals or even near-equals. There was no more disposition than there had been before to examine, if only to seek to understand, what the modernists were about even where such examination might

---

[230] Which is not to say that this was how they, or even those among the orthodox who remained loyal to the Zionist movement, saw the matter. Rabbi Meir Berlin, editor of the religious Zionist weekly *Ha-'Ivri* (leader of the Mizraḥi after the First World War), wrote after Kattowitz that while the World Zionist Organization, not being founded on Torah, was indeed to be regarded as one party among others in Jewry, Agudat Yisrael, in contrast, was the embodiment of the true, historical *kelal Yisrael*. It alone was entitled, on the solid basis of Torah, to represent Jewry in its entirety. ('Sie wird die Vertretung der jüdischen Gesamtheit auf der festen Basis der Thora bleiben.') In his memoirs Rosenheim quotes Berlin with evident satisfaction (*Zikhronot*, 170; *Erinnerungen*, 125).

yield fuel with which to stoke the continual effort to attack and ridicule them, impugn their motives, and generally dismiss them for their wickedness or foolishness or both. The customary style remained one of tedious rant and denunciation, very little in the nature of genuine evidence or serious argument ever being advanced. The Jewish enlightenment, wrote Rabbi Ya'akov ha-Levi Lifschitz of Kovno, was nothing less than a deliberate, satanic plot generated in Vienna and Berlin designed to alienate the Jew from his Judaism and to teach him 'heresy and absolute permissiveness . . . and, in the manner of the gentiles, denial of the truths of Torah and of the Prophets'. It was typical of the methods of the *maskilim* that they 'sought to introduce the Jews to tales of lust and sensuality . . . in the guise of "literature" '. Neither compromise with the *maskilim* nor tolerance of any of their offerings were possible for that way only led, as the *maskilim* dearly wished it to lead, to the ruin of religion. No deviation, no matter how small, from the path of righteousness and faith in search of freedom—even limited freedom—could result in anything but a plunge into total freedom and unremitting impiety.[231]

But then it was in the nature of what was at issue that the orthodox had little choice but to denounce the other streams in Jewry if they were not to find that they had, after all, entered into dialogue with them when dialogue was inherently impossible. There was no response they could conceivably make to those whose 'bitterness [was] against the past and against all those who had bequeathed us their opinions and their thoughts'.[232] Nor was there anything useful the orthodox could say to those who shared even in weakened form M. Y. Berdyczewski's judgement that 'The greatest public tragedy of all is the tragedy of the Jews: a people of ten millions dispersed to all four corners of the earth whose life is without purpose and without hope' and who went on to ask, 'What purpose did this centuries-long suffering serve? To what actual purpose does the people of Israel exist?'[233]

---

[231] Ya'akov ha-Levi Lifschitz, *Sefer Maḥazikei ha-dat* (Piotrków, 1903), 79–95.
[232] 'Le she'elat he-'avar' (1902). Cited in Micha Yosef Berdyczewski, *Yalkut* (Tel Aviv, 1983), 280.
[233] *Pirkei yoman 'amal yom ve-haguto* (Tel Aviv, 1974), 46.

PART III

New Dispensations

THE nineteenth century—the 'long nineteenth century'—was Jewry's last age of innocence. There were moments of anxiety and foreboding in every one of the schools of thought contending for the moral and social leadership of the Jewish people; and for good cause. But in no instance did the public or private treatment meted out to the Jews in practice, however disappointing or plainly evil, go so far as to shatter the morale of any one of these schools or undermine its leading members' confidence in their having identified and taken possession of the key to their people's material or spiritual salvation. Each school or category, each in its way—traditionalist or modernist, Lithuanian ultra-orthodox or Polish Hasidic, freethinking secularist, assimilationist or nationalist, Bundist or Zionist, respectably bourgeois or anarchically Bohemian, law-abiding liberal or revolutionary universalist, Hebraist, Russifier, east European Autonomist, German of Jewish Faith, Jewish Englishman, Francophone Israélite, Magyarized Neolog, any one of the several varieties of schools of more radical religious reform—each and all of these continued to be moved by its members' virtually unshakeable combination of confidence in the precision, validity, and relevance of their own particular diagnosis of the Jewish condition and their own distinctive prescription for its cure. All had this in common too that each presumed to know not only what was right and proper for themselves, but, by and large, what was right and proper and salutary for most of the rest of Jewry as well. All assumed—for the most part silently, some unconsciously, but some openly and explicitly—that choice of school, direction, and way of life generally was open and free: thus for the private individual; thus too, by and large, for the community in its entirety.

Whether there had ever been a firm basis for making such an assumption and whether it had been reasonable to think and act upon it in the course of the century and a quarter separating the Great French Revolution from the Great European War of 1914–18 must remain a matter for debate. What is not in doubt is that *thereafter*, namely in the aftermath of the First World War, such grounds as there may have been for an essentially sanguine approach to what lay at the heart of the Jewish condition were fast eroding. The catastrophe that very few had been prepared to contemplate before the war would now be upon them: in eastern Europe immediately, in the centre of the continent within a decade to a decade and a half, in the west half a decade or so later. The ancient balance between Christian Europe's social (and of course theological) repulsion of the Jewish people and its contrary disposition in certain saving instances to grant them—at a price—conditional asylum had always been a delicate one. But it had made the survival of Jewry considered as a caste or class and of the Jews themselves as private individuals possible. In the aftermath of the Great War the balance crumbled. Upon the collapse of the multinational European empires the long-standing, often grudging process by which legal emancipation and technical equality had been in the process of being granted to them, stage by stage and bit by bit, came to an end. On the other hand, too, the contradictory and to some minds regressive principle of Jewish nationhood and nationality was accorded an unprecedented degree of formal recognition. And there were other ways in which, as we shall see, the ambivalences that had long formed the basis of the Jewish presence among peoples hostile to them in one degree or another—that of the rulers towards their Jewish subjects and that of the Jewish subjects towards their rulers—were deprived of their internal logic and ceased to be socially and politically sustainable. It only remained for the foul winds started up in 1914, and which were to blow thereafter ever more powerfully for the three to four decades to follow, to strip those saving ambivalences totally away, leaving the overwhelming majority of the Jews of Europe naked and desolate before the blast. Small wonder that the capacity of those who had assumed—or allowed to have attributed to them—the leadership of Jewry would be tested for wisdom, moral courage, and imagination beyond anything ever demanded of their predecessors not merely in living memory but since the onset of the Great Exile itself.

The crisis of European Jewry was therefore finally to be played out between the end of the Great (or First) World War and the outbreak of the Second. If, in the course of the First World War, there had been intimations of a catastrophe looming for the Jews of eastern Europe, it was hardly over before disaster was indeed upon them. It took two forms. The first was the consequence of the breakdown of state power throughout the enormous territory in which the Russian Autocracy had previously held sway. The other followed upon the nature and guiding purposes of government in the several states that then took shape as successors to imperial Russia, in other states that were contiguous to them, and then, by stages, yet others that were contiguous to *them*. The sum of it all was a radical change in the general political climate, one aspect of which was the abandonment of what had become in the course of the nineteenth century the more or less established view of the most efficacious way to deal with the Jews—that which had evolved under the influence of the Enlightenment.

It was true that the resulting system had been an uneasy one. From time to time and in particular locations it had proved to be temporarily untenable. It had been shot through, as we have seen repeatedly, with innumerable ambivalences, reservations, resentments, and anxieties on *both* sides, the Jewish as well as the non-Jewish. The differences between the practice in western Europe and the rules, written and unwritten, in central Europe revealed themselves on inspection to be fundamental in principle and substantial in content. And western European and central European customary practice taken together were, in turn, a world away from the system (or systems) enforced in eastern Europe. And then, almost everywhere, there was backsliding of one kind or another. As the Great French Revolution receded from memory, opposition not only to the participation of Jews in civil society, but to their presence within it as well, took on new life and its proponents new force. On the other side of the divide, the flight from Jewry turned from a trickle to a river; and the flight of Jews of all sorts, classes, and opinions from Europe itself became a flood.

It was, however, of the essence of the total regime to which Jews were subject in the course of the 'long nineteenth century' that in no case did any of the *states* (with the exception of Romania) go so far as unambiguously to reverse themselves. None retreated in form or in fact to the old, pre-Enlightenment regime. None *totally* shook off the new norms of conduct that the overwhelming majority of the political masters of Europe great and small had internalized in spite of everything since the Great French Revolution. Some listened more intently than before to other voices. Some bent with the newly reinforced anti-Jewish winds. In some cases the political masters of the day sought to exploit them in their own private political interest. It remained that none of them succumbed definitively and unambiguously to the arguments and pressures of the steadily gathering, radicalized, and radicalizing forces that proclaimed themselves enemies of the Jewish people and preached some combination or other of reinvigorated, theologically inspired, and justified anti-Semitism with more fashionable racial and class-oriented theses. Nor was there any case in which a European government had withdrawn decisively from the relevant public arenas, leaving the power to set the determining logic by which Jews were expected to live out their lives to others—in practice, to extra-legal, extra-constitutional authority, or, more plainly still, to the mob.

In the final analysis, therefore, however loose, irregular, and, in a word, defective it may have been, the regime to which Jewry throughout the continent had come to be subordinated, and to which by the beginning of the twentieth century it had become accustomed both for good and for ill, held. And it was because it did hold by and large that the crisis of European Jewry was so very slow to mature and it took the cataclysm of the First World War to bring it to a head—although, to be precise, it was not so much the war itself as what occurred in its aftermath as a function of the immense social, political, and ideological dislocation it had brought about. For there followed in its aftermath the making up of several Procrustean beds in which the Jews, along with a great many other European peoples, were forced to lie and to which they, taking all in all, were inherently incapable of accommodating themselves—not, at all events, without suffering immense and irreparable social injury.

At the basis of what many hoped, and some seriously intended, would be the new postwar Europe lay three leading principles-cum-slogans: the principle of nationality; the principle of popular sovereignty; and (somewhat less generally held and in some quarters very hotly contested) the principle of class as *the* (or at least *a*) fundamental social determinant. Each either contained an element of undeniable social truth or could be shown to follow from those rules of customary morality to which service is paid in most societies as a matter of course. Each, when converted into purposeful and operational terms, appeared to promise genuine social and material benefits to very great numbers, but especially to those inhabitants of Europe who had reason to consider themselves deprived. Their political uses were so great, so evident, and so easily applicable (with suitable variations) to all societies, that it was not long before they were to be heard from the mouths and read on the banners of virtually all the most determined political activists of the day. And since each of these principles lent itself easily to reformulation in all-embracing and incontestable terms and could be taken to imply (and justify) exceedingly bitter, implacable, hugely destructive, and unending socio-political conflict, the consequences for all the populations of Europe could not be otherwise than dire.

If the consequences for the Jews among them would be doubly and trebly catastrophic it was in large measure because, exceptionally, that was indeed in many cases the intention. But even when conceived and applied in a moderate and genuinely benevolent spirit—a paradoxical and in any case rare occurrence in itself—these principles required of the Jews a huge, ultimately impossible degree of adjustment and accommodation *if* anything that was authentically and historically characteristic of the Jewish people or customarily valued by them was to be preserved. Taken to their extremes, as was more commonly and, as may be thought, always most likely to be the case, they left hardly any room at all for a social existence of the kind to which even the comparative modernists among the Jews of Europe had more or less accustomed themselves; and no place at all for the great majority that was still faithful to the Tradition and could not as yet conceive of an acceptable alternative to it. In some cases the driving forces fuelling the attempt to apply these leading principles to the raw society in question were local and in some degree spontaneous. In others there could be discerned a great and deliberate effort to re-engineer society in its entirety. In all cases, the final effect was to bring the nineteenth-century regime—always ambiguous in character, but for that reason not wholly and consistently intolerable—to an end.

7

War

THE Jews of Europe passed through the valley of the shadow of death during the years 1914–18 with the rest of the continent's population—which is to say, as best they could. That they were no more spared the crippling horrors of the war than any one else was at once the result and the supreme expression of the radical change in their circumstances. The days when, insignificant exceptions apart, it was natural, but also possible, for Jews to keep out of the way when the gentiles foolishly and incomprehensibly fought each other were over. Where their participation in continental warfare, if any, had been on an essentially individual basis—as bankers and provisioners, but only very rarely as soldiers—it was now first and foremost as ordinary fighting men in the ranks of each of the armies of the belligerents. Countless numbers of perfectly ordinary, non-political Jewish people marched off to war and to personal, often fatal involvement in the great and terrifying events that proceeded to unfold from August 1914 onwards along with all the other ordinary, non-political people who were marching off to war. They did so, moreover, for all the world as if it were a natural and (in central and western Europe) a worthy and desirable thing to do. Their political masters had still to determine whether, and if so in what way and to what degree, further advantage was to be taken of their services. And in this respect there were differences. In Russia there was no question at all of access to positions of influence and authority of any kind. In Germany too the contradiction between what wartime state interest appeared to dictate and the political and military classes' refusal to acquiesce in a really serious relaxation of the rules by which society had been governed in the past remained incapable of resolution to the end. It would be worn down somewhat by undeniable necessity—as in the case of the sullen (and temporary) appointment of Walther Rathenau to a post as a principal organizer of the German war economy—but, no lasting change occurred. In the west Jews were taken on freely enough wherever they seemed likely to bring advantage and, unlike in Germany, regret at the prospect of irreversible change in the social order tended to be wistful rather than bitter. The unspoken rule remained, however, that while, when it was really necessary to do so, Jews might be admitted to the inner sanctums where high policy was decided, they would only be given places below the political salt, those reserved for specialists and experts, not those that would entitle them to wield real power.

Admission into the ranks of the armies themselves was free and unrestricted everywhere. In the dire circumstances of the times and the universal, unslakable thirst for men to man the trenches, the old assumption that the Jew was useless as a fighting man was forgotten. In an environment that had generally been alien and hostile to him, the Jewish soldier was apt to be treated rather more decently than he had been in the past. If he distinguished himself in battle he was more likely than before to be awarded the honours that were his due. In some armies distinction in battle opened the way to promotion as well. But not in all. The imperial Russian army stood its ground in this respect to the end: its high command, with the full approval of the Tsar, refusing to sanction the granting of officer rank even to the most able, willing, and battle-proven of Jewish soldiers whatever the occasional fair-minded regimental commander might say on his behalf. But even here matters were not absolutely cut and dried. Officer rank as military surgeons was conceded to Jewish doctors. Here and there, where the dearth of literate, willing, and responsible *echt*-Russian candidates had reduced a battalion or brigade commander to desperation, the official eye might briefly overlook an individual Jewish soldier's being given *de facto* authority to perform an officer's role.[1] (Of the flatly infamous treatment to which the Russian army's high command subjected the *civilian* Jewish population in the areas through which its forces moved on their way to the west and, more especially, on their retreat back towards the east, more will be said in a moment.)

The German army, previously at one with the Russians in this respect, now rescinded its once unwavering refusal to promote suitable Jews to officer rank. By the end of the war some two thousand Jews had been commissioned. Still, no Jew was allowed to reach senior rank in the German army, unlike the Austro-Hungarian army in which, interestingly, some Jews had held rank as general officers even before the war. And the true spirit in which the German high command viewed the matter of their Jewish citizens, and that of Jews in uniform in particular, is conveyed by its notoriously bloody-minded decision in October 1916 to launch a formal investigation into the contribution of the German Jews to the national war effort and of Jewish soldiers to service in the trenches by initiating a systematic counting of heads. This so-called *Judenzählung* (or Jew-count) was not only nastily hostile, but unwarranted. Actual Jewish *Frontsoldaten* (front-line soldiers) were outraged. It was, someone said, 'as if the yellow patch had been sewn back on'.[2] A tiny handful of pacifists

---

[1] See Yoḥanan Rattner's autobiography, for example: *Hayyai ve-ani* (Tel Aviv, 1978).
[2] Cited in Peter Pulzer, *Jews and the German State* (Oxford, 1992), 205.

and extraordinarily courageous and determined social democrats had indeed opposed the war and been jailed or otherwise hounded out of society and home. But rare exceptions apart, German Jewry's support for the war had been immensely (in retrospect almost embarrassingly) wholehearted at every level: from men of the greatest academic distinction (Hermann Cohen, the Kantian philosopher, and Fritz Haber, the chemist, for example) down to the simplest and least politically imaginative *petit bourgeois*. When the war was over, the society of Jewish *Frontsoldaten*, the stain on their honour still burning, conducted a meticulous survey of its own. It found that at least 100,000 Jews had served in the German armed forces or 18 per cent of the total Jewish population of imperial Germany of 550,000. Of these 12,000 had been killed in action or died of wounds: namely 2.2 per cent of German Jewry. Their study further demonstrated that these figures were virtually identical with those for the population of the city of Munich (a fair comparison, the Jews being a largely skilled and educated, urban population, much like the citizens of Munich): 645,000 citizens in all; 13,700 war dead.[3] The German general staff's own figures were never published. But perhaps the most ominous aspect of the *Judenzählung* was that when it was proposed and brought up in the Reichstag it was supported not only by the right wing, as was to be expected, but by the Catholic Centre Party and the National Liberals under Gustav Stresemann as well.

No such inquiries were instituted in other countries; nor were any warranted.[4] The general record of Jewish participation in the fighting forces of the various belligerents was in each case at least as high as that of the general population and in some cases higher. No figures as precise as those collated in Germany are available, but it has been fairly reliably estimated that some 450,000 Jews served in the immense Russian army—where it appears, moreover, that in consequence of the severely restrictive rules governing the military functions Jews might or might not perform, they tended to serve somewhat more commonly than others as front-line infantry soldiers and to suffer higher than average casualty rates in consequence. Some 275,000 Jews served in the Austro-Hungarian

---

[3] The Reichsverband Jüdischer Frontsoldaten's compilation was published in 1932 as the 423-page *Die jüdischen Gefallenen des deutschen Heeres, der deutschen Marine und der deutschen Schutztruppen 1914–1918; ein Gedenkbuch*. It consisted chiefly of the names, regimental affiliations, and dates of death of the war dead (where known). The great warlord himself, Hindenburg, now president of the republic, contributed a friendly preface.

[4] One partial exception was the case of Jews of Russian nationality who had settled in Great Britain, who for the greater part of the war were neither obliged nor permitted to serve in the British army, and who regarded consequent pressure to return to Russia to serve the Tsar as absurd, if not monstrous. They were therefore a source of unending embarrassment to the established segments of English Jewry, but of opportunity to the Zionists who saw them as natural recruits to the 'Jewish Legion' that they founded to fight alongside the Allies (on which more below).

army: *c*.11 per cent of the total Jewish population of the empire; 41,000 served in the British armed forces or a little under 14 per cent of British Jewry;[5] 35,000 in the French army: or *c*.20 per cent of the total Jewish population of France. The overall figure for Jews serving in all belligerent armies (including the American army, in due course, in which the proportion of Jews was exceptionally high) was of the order of 1,500,000 or about 2 per cent of all mobilized manpower. It was therefore roughly double that of the Jewish proportion of the entire population of the countries concerned.[6]

There was thus a sense—an ironic one, one may think—in which the Great War, in practice, was the supreme occasion on which the Jews of Europe were called upon to be 'useful' to each of the several states of which they were nationals in very much the sense that those men of the Enlightenment who had troubled themselves either to think about or to legislate for the Jews or both had had in mind. The Jews' skills, knowledge, experience, and native energy—coupled, in the central and western states, but not totally absent even in the east under the Russians, to their habitual loyalty to the sovereign power in the land and their manifest desire to please it—proved as easily available for harnessing to the machinery of war as Joseph II of Austria or his advisers had ever wished. And the total effect, again very much as the men of the Enlightenment would have wished, was further to promote and hasten their acculturation. The war initiated none of the essential processes of social and cultural change to which European Jewry was subject. But by dint of scattering and dissolving great numbers of young Jewish men into the larger mass of mobilized society on a basis that was unprecedentedly random it did greatly accelerate them and intensify their impact. It loosened the ties binding the individual to his community. It provided Jewish soldiers—much as it provided great numbers of other disoriented people—with new, alternative, if of course no more than temporary focuses of loyalty. And while it lasted there would be much else in its impact to support those who felt that the now century-old, imperfectly kept promise of fair dealing and equitable integration had not, after all, been false. None the less, perversely, the lasting impact of the war so far as the Jews were concerned was to reassert and re-emphasize the ascription to the Jewish people of their ancient status as a distinct—and for certain purposes justifiably autonomous—national entity. The major powers of Europe were moved, each in its way, in varying degrees, and, to be sure, with unequal consequences, to consider

---

[5] The proportion of the general population serving the British armed forces was 11.5 per cent (Geoffrey Alderman, *Modern British Jewry* (Oxford, 1992), 235).

[6] A. G. Duker, 'Jews in the World War', *Contemporary Jewish Record*, 2, 5 (Sept.–Oct. 1939); Y. Slutsky, and M. Kaplan, *Hayyalim yehudiim be-ziv'ot eiropa* (Tel Aviv, 1967); *Encyclopaedia Judaica*, xi, col. 1550; Felix A. Theilhaber, *Die Juden im Weltkriege* (Berlin, 1916); Michael Adler, *The Jews of the Empire and the Great War* (London, 1919).

whether and how their own urgent national-political needs and interests might be squared with what were reckoned to be the collective needs, interests, and aspirations of the Jewish people. This was a most dramatic alteration of perspective, as remote from the ordinary hostility that fuelled policy towards them in some cases as from the somewhat more considerate, but always unsystematic and severely limited, philanthropic basis on which their affairs were viewed (when they were viewed at all). Nothing, certainly, could have been more remote from the legacy and purposes of the Enlightenment itself.

II

A salient strategic feature of the First World War—at least until the winter of 1917/18—was the fine balance in which the forces were arrayed against each other. One result was that each increment of manpower, economic resources, political influence, and even mere sympathy to one side tended to have ascribed to it by the other a value that was often out of all proportion to its intrinsic weight. The fight had become so hard, so costly, and so dangerously uncertain that there could, besides, be no question any more—assuming that such had ever entirely been the case—of state policy being managed wholly within, and directed exclusively at, the magic circle of the 'chancelleries of Europe'. It became an axiom of political and diplomatic warfare almost everywhere that public opinion in general needed to be attended to with some care. Anything and anybody capable of helping to tip the balance of military power in one's favour or, contrariwise, of serving the enemy's countervailing effort to tip the balance against oneself became an object of observation. And where an advantage was perceived as attainable, there the disposition to pay a price, to make a promise, and, if necessary, to grant immediate political, institutional, military, or financial support was, if not boundless, at any rate well in excess of anything that would have been thought reasonable previously. In this sense, the supply of gold to Arab rebels against their Ottoman suzerains by the British and the financing and dispatch of Lenin and his companions back to Russia to foment revolution by the Germans were of a piece. In all cases, the determining consideration was the need to prosecute the war to a successful conclusion.

Long-term consequences and responsibilities were secondary—although that is not to say that they were taken to be of no account at all. But while each of the major belligerents would pay closer attention than in the past to society and opinion in the now neutral countries, it would be the western Allies, France and Great Britain, that would pay closest and most consistent attention to the submerged and subject peoples in Europe and the Near East. They would do so in a form, moreover, that, even before the adhesion of the United States to the Entente as an 'Associated Power' in April 1917 and the elevation of the entire subject of 'national self-determination' to the status of political dogma, was intended to persist beyond the war. For once British, French, and, in due course, American sights had been set so very high in this respect, the race was one in which the major central powers, multinational, continental states with territorial ambitions of a much more conventional kind for themselves, and burdened with the submerged nations most anxious (and most likely) to wish to work themselves free, were exceedingly ill placed to compete. Nor was this a political game in which the western powers' great eastern ally was equipped to participate. Russia might seek, not too seriously, and wholly irresponsibly (considering the likely consequences), to draw the Armenian subjects of the Ottomans to its side. But it itself, some soft words apart, manifestly proposed to remain the 'prison house of nations' as before, presenting Russia's own allies with an insuperable political and ideological difficulty: the Poles and the Baltic peoples and, arguably, the Ukrainians too, were notoriously among the subject nations now brooding on—and in some cases already fighting for—their freedom. And then there were the Jews.

The case of the Jews was plainly of a very different order from that of the Poles or even the Ukrainians. The political significance of the Jewish population of Russia so far as the actual military prosecution of the war was concerned was less obvious—initially at all events. Upon its entry into Russian-ruled Poland the German and Austrian army went to the trouble of informing its Jewish inhabitants in specially printed wall-posters in the Yiddish language that they came as liberators. And so they did to some extent, initially, although what the Germans and the Austrians expected of the local Jewish population is unclear. By and large, Russo-Polish Jews proved to be too wary to support the German side whatever they might think privately of the apparent advantages to them of an eventual transfer of the territories in question from Russian to German, or better still Austrian hands. One shrewd observer was to remark that even in the early stage of the occupation he could see no reason to rejoice. 'We have not been let out to freedom, but passed from one slavery to another; and who can tell if the later will not prove harder than the earlier?'[7] Besides, subsequent German behaviour towards them positively discouraged them from doing so. Rough treatment, forced and inequitable loans, sporadic (probably only half-serious) threats of mass expulsion to Palestine and Syria, and oppressive restrictions on movement and labour followed before long. By the end of the war, as French military intelligence reported, the German occupation authorities in Poland were treating Jewish inhabitants

[7] Yizḥak Nissenboim, 'Alei ḥeldi (Warsaw, 1929), 323.

with a severity that is equal at least to that which was once displayed by the Tsar's administration. A strong anti-Semitic current prevails everywhere in the occupation authority and every measure of harassment, notably against the 300 or 350,000 Jews of Warsaw, is permissible, the most usual being refusal to issue passports and laissez-passer. It is even said that they have been completely forbidden access to the Saxon Gardens, the largest park in the city.[8]

But it was *Russian* treatment of its own Jewish population, as well as of the Jewish population in foreign territories which came under Russian occupation from time to time, that was to merit closest international attention and have palpable political consequences. It is not inconceivable that had treatment of the Jews continued on the basis, more or less, that had been established since the 1880s, namely hostile in spirit, harsh in execution, blatantly discriminatory, and steadily impoverishing, but only sporadically violent and not totally and invariably devoid of the occasional flash of decency and fair-dealing, the now established matter of Russian Jewry would have been tucked away for the duration even in the minds of the Jews themselves. It was to be expected that the mobilization of close to half a million Jewish men (almost a tenth of the total Jewish population of the empire) would accelerate the process of pauperization. That the condition of the Jews in large parts of western Russia and in those areas that were adjacent to Russia (Austrian-ruled Galicia, for example) which came under Russian military occupation would deteriorate further as the war continued was equally to be expected: an immense war of movement was being fought precisely where the Jewish population of Europe was thickest. In sum, none could imagine that the Jews of what, roughly, had once been Greater Poland, would not suffer brutal dislocation and hardship of all kinds. What transformed the familiar miseries of a civilian population caught between great armies into a disaster and an outrage were the vast unanticipated dimensions attained by inevitable suffering *coupled* to the manifest responsibility of the Russian military authorities for its extension. And it needs to be stressed that this was not the result of genuine and perhaps unavoidable 'military necessity', but the consequence of a deceitful and cowardly attempt to deflect attention from the army's own incompetence and failure in the field.

The year 1915 was decisive in this respect, marked by a continuous series of massive, arbitrary, wholly unnecessary expulsions of the civilian Jewish population—now preponderantly composed of women, children, the elderly, and the infirm, a high proportion of able-bodied men having been mobilized for military service—from the Baltic lands and the western regions of Russia. Hundreds of thousands were summarily

---

[8] SHAT, Aff. Milit. (Pologne 1914–19), Box 7N 1449.

ordered to leave their homes and employment, often at no more than twelve hours notice, in some cases with no prior warning at all, crammed into trains when these were available, forced to move on foot when transport was lacking, and dumped without ceremony or resources or shelter to fend for themselves in towns and cities in the eastern parts of Poland and the Pale of Settlement or even beyond the Pale of Settlement altogether. The declared justification for this outrage was national security, namely the need to remove a disloyal and dangerous population from the area of combat. And to the large-scale misery inflicted on the Jews of great parts of the western territories of the empire there were added the more precise and often more terrible cases of specific charges, all invariably trumped up (as in due course would be plain), of espionage, sabotage, and co-operation with the enemy of every other conceivable kind, these being dealt with by collective punishment, the taking of hostages, and summary trial by drumhead court martial followed by execution.

At the time, censorship of the press and postal traffic made it difficult to ascertain the precise dimensions of the horror and to discover what truth, if any at all, lay behind the allegations. But it was evident even to passive observers that something very terrible was going on. In some rural areas where Jews had formed 80 per cent of the population none was now left. The greater part of the Jewish population of the provinces of Courland, Kovno, and Grodno—some 200,000 people in all—had been forced to leave their homes at forty-eight hours notice or less. In May 1915 the Jewish community of Warsaw alone was attempting to cope with over 100,000 refugees. In the early summer of 1915 the committee established by Jewish notables in Petrograd and elsewhere to organize relief estimated that as many as 600,000 people had been forcibly displaced all told. It was not long before the picture, at all events in broad outline, percolated out of Russia and began to be broadcast to the west, but most especially to Jewish institutions in the United States, often in the desperate form of which the following passages from a long telegram sent through an intermediary in Copenhagen to New York in the summer of 1915 provide an example:

Continual evacuations expelled Jews causes Russian Jewry indescribable panic . . . expelled from Kovno Kurland . . . thousands families lost children wives infirm relatives special inquiry offices established Wilna Minsk Riga Utjany seek lost persons local authorities often refuse reception arriving mass trains stop twenty-two freight waggons expelled forbidden enter Lubny respectively other destination-places compelled return Wilna therefrom sent back province Poltawa unfortunates thus [s]hunt forward backwards five weeks dreadful freightwaggons stop . . . official placards announce throughout Russia Joseph and Schlioma Salzmann and Freidenberg hanged because accomplices Mjassojedows but in reality innocent persons stop please publish Jewish and general press without name undersigned.[9]

---

[9] Simonsen to the American Jewish Committee, 9 July 1915, CZA, A126/41/5. Myasoyedov was an ethnic Russian officer of gendarmerie serving in the department of

In Petrograd itself the Russian Council of Ministers was fully aware of what was transpiring in the western war zone. And it did not doubt for a moment that the motive force driving the army was the attempt, initially by local commanders, then under the more august authority of the Russian high command itself under the Grand Duke Nikolai Nikolayevich and his chief of staff General N. N. Yanushkevich, to help provide an exculpatory account for the humiliating reversals it had suffered. As the Russian minister of the interior (Prince N. B. Shcherbatov) put it to his colleagues ('one does not like to say this, but we are among ourselves . . .'), the army wished, by imputing to the local Jews imaginary actions of sabotage against the Russian forces, to represent them as being 'responsible for its own failure and defeat at the front'. 'In the flood of refugees [of all kinds],' noted another participant at the Council, one can especially discern

the Jews, who are being chased out of the frontal zone with whips and accused— all without discrimination—of espionage, signalling, and other methods of helping the enemy. . . . Of course, this whole Jewish mass is extremely irritated and arrives in the new regions it will inhabit in a revolutionary mood; and the situation is complicated by the fact that the local inhabitants, suffering more and more heavily the burden of military disasters, receive the hungry and homeless Jews in by-no-means a friendly manner.

This 'revolutionary mood . . . growing irrepressibly in the Jewish masses' was bad enough, the ministers felt. It could be contained, however. What could not be, and was therefore a deal more serious to their minds, very notably so in the view of the minister of finance (P. L. Bark), was the firing of anti-Russian sentiment among Jews *abroad* and, to a lesser extent, foreign public opinion in general. Foreign financial markets were being closed to Russia, the ministers were told. It had proved impossible to place the last great loan the government had wished to float. And the minister of finance himself had been made to understand, so he informed his colleagues, that there would be no solution to Russia's

police in the Ministry of the Interior. He had been charged, tried, and executed for espionage. Several Jews were charged, falsely, with complicity and hanged with him. Ostensibly, this was a characteristic effort to minimize the disgrace by implying ultimate Jewish responsibility. So it was seen, naturally enough, by the Jewish organizations and political parties in Russia who did what they could to bring the mistreatment of Russian Jewry at the hands of the army to the attention of the public abroad. (See for example W. Kossowsky, *Les Persécutions des Juifs en Russie* (Berne, 1915), published by the foreign committee of the Bund.) In fact, it was an even nastier case of judicial murder, if that were possible. Myasoyedov, while certainly of unsavoury reputation, is thought not to have been guilty of espionage, but of unpardonable zeal in the service of one of the factions in which the overall command of the Russian army was composed. Grand Duke Nikolai Nikolayevich's field command, the *stavka*, wished to get rid of him in a way that would discredit his master Sukhomlinov, the minister for war. In June 1915 Sukhomlinov was dismissed, arrested, and incarcerated in the Peter and Paul Fortress. (See Norman Stone, *The Eastern Front 1914–1917* (London, 1975), 26, 197–8.)

evident financial difficulties until a clear move in the proper, i.e. liberal, direction on the Jewish question had been made. The minister of agriculture (A. V. Krivoshein) agreed. So did the foreign minister (S. D. Sazonov): Russia, he said, could not 'conduct a war both against Germany and against the Jews'. The minister of the interior, reluctantly, was of the same view. 'What can we do when the knife is at our throat? If the evil influence of the Jews is undebatable, the necessity for money with which to conduct the war is equally undebatable, and the money is in Jewish hands,'[10] But the Council of Ministers had no authority over the army and such pleas for change as some ministers were prepared to make went unheeded. And in fact, no great effort in that direction seems to have been made. Even within the Council of Ministers itself the opposition to real and dramatic concessions to the Jews was substantial although in this respect, as in others, the government was now to some extent behind informed political opinion. The pre-eminent leader of the extreme, anti-Semitic faction in the Russian political arena, V. M. Purishkevich, had moderated his position somewhat. He still hated the Jews, he told the Duma in February 1916. But he saw no reason to blame them for things with which they were in no way concerned.[11]

Russia being their wartime ally, French and British diplomatic and military representatives were inclined to accept that the empire was immovable on the subject of the Jews,[12] and so far as possible play down the scandal of the treatment meted out to them by the army. In February 1915, for example, the French ambassador informed Paris that the main body of Russian Jewry had, up to that point, 'suffered no collective violence whatsoever'. Matters were otherwise in 'the zone of operations', he conceded, but even there, he pointed out, nothing very serious had occurred: 'A few hundred Jews had been hanged for espionage: that is all'.[13] The ambassador's easy remark about executions bears comparison with that of a senior British officer on attachment to the Russian army,

---

[10] *Arkhiv Russkoi Revolutsii* (Berlin, 1926), xviii. 43–4. Trans. Michael Cherniavsky (ed.), *Prologue to Revolution* (Englewood Cliffs, NJ, 1967), 39–43, 56–72, 85–7, 121–3, 194–5.

[11] Where the Poles were concerned, the war had caused Purishkevich to change his mind entirely. He had hated them too, he said. Now he thought they should be given their rights without further ado.

[12] In Aug. 1916 Jews were granted temporary right of residence in all Russian *towns* with the exception of Petrograd and Moscow and such towns as were under special (e.g. military) administration. But it needs to be noted that numerous 'villages' were larger than 'towns' and apt to offer greater possibilities of employment; and that given the flow of expellees and refugees from the western provinces there was a sense in which the measure was before all else a recognition of a *fait accompli*. If it had been intended to be of dramatic effect it failed, the more so as the right to acquire real property while promised was not accorded and all other restrictions were kept in force.

[13] Paléologue to the Ministry for Foreign Affairs, 4 Feb. 1915, AE, Guerre 1914–1918, Sionisme, vol. 1197, 22.

duly passed on to London, to the effect that 'the whole German spy system in Poland is said to have been carried out by Jews, and . . . [that therefore] in the circumstances . . . no Russian general in command of an army in Poland would be justified, in view of the pro-German attitude of the Jewish population, in not evacuating the Jews out of the occupied area.'[14] Less apt to rely on official Russian sources, more concerned with what he could see for himself, and much less concerned about keeping the alliance on an even keel, the British vice-consul in Moscow reported (9 August 1915) widespread Jewish 'discontent' and called his superiors' attention to the fact that Jewish fear of pogroms was 'not altogether unjustifiable'. He affirmed that 'the Russian Government has been assiduously fostering anti-Semitic sentiments among the people' and went on to offer his own assessment of the probable outcome. 'The Jews, as Jews,' he thought, were unlikely to be able to cause 'serious trouble at the present moment'.

The feeling of the country is against them, and a Jewish pogrom is far more probable than a revolutionary movement financed and fomented by Jews. The Jews can, however, and do act against the Russian Government in other ways. Needless repressive measures against the Jews at the present moment seem ill-timed, and the effect of a Jewish pogrom on public opinion in England and America might have far-reaching consequences.

As customary, Vice-Consul R. H. Bruce Lockhart's report was submitted to the ambassador in Petrograd for approval prior to transmission to London. Sir George Buchanan took the opportunity to append his own remark.

As regards the question of the treatment of the Jews . . . the subject, as you are aware, is one of the greatest difficulty. Public opinion in Russia is as a whole so hostile to the Jews that I am inclined to think that the Government are, if anything, in advance of it in their view of the question.[15]

But whatever allied ambassadors and other foreign representatives in Petrograd might try to make of it, they were unable to prevent the matter of Russian Jewry becoming a subject of quite serious concern and embarrassment in London and Paris. This was partly because the Germans and the Austrians had thereby been presented with a small, free, and— given their initially fairly decent conduct in the 'zone of operations'—by no means undeserved propaganda gift. But much closer to the bone was the Allied discovery early in the war that so long as it lasted they would be crucially dependent on American industry for vital military supplies and quite as critically dependent on the American financial markets for the money with which to purchase those supplies. Their own resources were

[14] Cited by De Bunsen, a senior British diplomat, in a letter to Lucien Wolf of the Conjoint Committee, 3 Mar. 1916, Mocatta Library, AJ/204/2.
[15] Buchanan to Grey, 12 Aug. 1915, circulated to the cabinet, PRO, CAB 37/133.

dwindling rapidly. There was no question of the United States, still a neutral power, granting them direct financial or material aid. Huge loans
would therefore have to be floated in Wall Street in the ordinary way: a
costly and somewhat uncertain endeavour at the best of times and now
dependent as well on the silent approval of the federal authorities in
Washington. American sympathies were by no means entirely with the
democratic Allies. Opinion was strongly divided on the steadily growing
role of the United States as military supplier. The view that nothing
should be done in or by the United States that was liable to impair
its much trumpeted posture as a neutral power was very strongly
entrenched. So indeed were powerful countervailing forces: the initially
surreptitious, soon unmistakably pro-Allied policy of the administration
itself and, rather more decisively, the enormous benefit the American
munitions industry and the American economy were sure to derive from
massive British and French purchases. But the principle of rigorous neutrality was a popular one that would not be entirely overcome until the
United States itself had entered the war as an 'associated' power in the
spring of 1917. It went hand in hand with minority ethnic sentiment in
certain cases. German-Americans tended, naturally enough, to be moderately pro-German, although the effect of this could be offset to some
degree by suitable emphasis on the free and democratic nature of society
and government in Great Britain and France. Irish-American sentiment
was firmly, not to say congenitally anti-British and was the more serious
politically for there being no conceivable way in which sympathy for the
Irish nationalist cause could be seriously appeased; this was undoubtedly
so before the Easter Rising in Dublin in 1916 and doubly so thereafter.

Prevailing views in the growing Jewish community in the United
States were marginally like those of the German-Americans, but were
not without affinities with the Irish. As Allied representatives in Washington correctly and repeatedly pointed out, it tended to be pro-
German, but out of 'dislike and fear of Russia'[16] rather than because of
any intrinsic sympathy for Germany itself. The French ambassador
(Jusserand) noted with foreboding the damage done to the Allies 'in a
country where the Jews are powerful and numerous' by reports of mistreatment of Jews by the Russian forces. His British colleague (Spring
Rice) observed that while 'the principal Jewish journalists in New York,
the editors of the "Sun" and the "Times", are strongly in favour of the
Allies and . . . have done us a very great deal of good', there was no question of Jewish bankers, some of them of the first rank, being other than

---

[16] Spring Rice to Chirol, 13 Nov. 1914. Cited in Stephen Gwynn (ed.), *The Letters and Friendships of Sir Cecil Spring Rice*, ii (London, 1929), 242. Spring Rice to Primrose, 1 Apr. 1915, PRO, FO 371/2559. Jusserand to Delcassé, 26 Jan. 1915, AE, Guerre 1914–1918, Sionisme, vol. 1197, 22.

unfriendly. The ambassador did overstate his case when he wrote to the Foreign Office that 'German Jewish bankers are toiling in a solid phalanx to compass our destruction'. But it was true that among those bankers, there were some—notably Jacob Schiff, head of one of the two or three leading investment houses in New York and commonly regarded as the most prominent and influential single figure in the American Jewish community as a whole at the time—who preferred, to the great discomfit of the Allies, to stick immovably to what the French termed 'correct neutrality'. 'As a Jew,' Jusserand wrote of him after the war, Schiff 'had ardently represented and supported in the United States the material and moral interests of his co-religionists. . . . German by origin and taste, he had retained very close ties with his first country, but he was before and above all else a Jew; his conduct when the Anglo-French [loan] was being floated showed this clearly.' And indeed, when his firm, Kuhn, Loeb and Company, was approached by the firm of J. P. Morgan with an invitation to co-operate in the handling of the especially large ($500 million) loan the Allies wished to launch in the late summer of 1915, Schiff laid it down as an explicit condition that he would co-operate only if he was assured that the Russians derived no benefit from the venture. He 'judged the [Russian government's] attitude to the Jews contrary to the principles of humanity and justice,' Jusserand wrote. And, 'it being impossible to give [him] an assurance on this matter, the House of Kuhn, Loeb refrained from joining the syndicate'.[17] The ambassador's assessment was a fair one. 'I am perfectly frank to say, my sympathies in this lamentable and terrible conflict are on the side of Germany,' Schiff wrote to Lucien Wolf on 14 June 1915, 'because I have not only been born and educated there, but because also my forebears have lived in Germany for many centuries. . . . Nevertheless, I have in reality no anti-English feeling, and am perfectly willing to concede that liberty—especially as far as the Jews is concerned—has in the past gained vastly more from England than from Germany[.] . . . Whether this will be so in the future, with the venom and poison which the Russian Alliance appears to have already instilled into English feeling for the Jew, seems to be at least doubtful.'[18]

Schiff's venture—some might think it an intrusion—into the world of high politics was of the old-fashioned kind to be sure.[19] On the face of

[17] 'Note sur la maison Kuhn, Loeb et Co.', 17 June 1921, AE, Jusserand papers, box, 33, Otto Kahn file, fos. 8–12.

[18] CZA, A77/3a.

[19] It was also of a kind in which Jacob Schiff himself had already engaged and had gained some experience. He had participated in the long-standing effort to induce the Russians to abandon their restrictions on the temporary entry of foreign (specifically American) Jews and at the time of the Russo-Japanese war of 1904 had played an important role in the effort to deny financial aid to the Russians and grant it instead to the Japanese. In all these cases he made no secret of his primary aim which was the shaming of Russia for its treatment of its own Jewish subjects.

things it was once again a case of the needs and interests of a large, but distant community being defined, articulated, and pursued by a well-meaning, but self-appointed, socially and institutionally unrepresentative, fortuitously well-placed private individual. He was tougher in his pursuit of what he considered to be the Jewish interest than Bleichröder[20] had been some four decades earlier, more direct and more demanding too, not to say peremptory. Early twentieth-century America was, of course, a world away from Bismarckian Germany. And Schiff was much better placed than Bleichröder had ever been in his time: more secure socially and in need of no great man as private client and secret political patron. But if Jacob Schiff was for some time the leading figure in the long-standing effort to bring pressure on Russia, he was not alone. The terms in which the president of the American Jewish Committee, the most important country-wide Jewish institution in the United States at the time, summed up the issues for the benefit of a Russian intermediary testify amply to the confident unity prevailing in the leading circles in American Jewry on all the relevant questions.

The leading Jews in the United States, including Mr Schiff, have no hesitation in giving the assurance that arrangements can be made to secure for Russia a loan of one, or even two, hundred million dollars, if the money be expended for such purchases as shall hereafter be made by Russia in the United States, but solely on the following conditions, which are to be complied with before any money is forthcoming:

First: The Duma, with the approval of the Council of the Empire and the sanction of the Czar, shall enact and put into operation by appropriate proclamation, permanent laws, which shall for all time abolish the Pale of Settlement and confer upon all Jews the same freedom of habitation and sojourn in any part of the Russian Empire as shall be possessed by any other of its subjects, and which shall repeal all laws and regulations restricting them in respect to education, business pursuits, occupations and professions, or hampering them in their civil and religious liberties.

Second: A new treaty of commerce and navigation shall be entered into with the United States, in which is to be mutually recognized the right of expatriation and the equality of all Russian and American citizens, respectively, in the enjoyment of all rights, privileges and advantages conferred by such treaty, regardless of race, religion or previous allegiance.

I am convinced that a glorious day will dawn for Russia were such a program to be effectuated. She would thereby gain the undying friendship, as well as the admiration, of every true American, and the grateful prayers of every Jew.[21]

[20] On Gerson Bleichröder's efforts on behalf of Romanian Jewry, see Chapter 6.
[21] Louis Marshall to M. A. Guinzburg, 23 Oct. 1915, BoD, C11/3/1/1. Marshall was president of the most prestigious of American Jewish institutions, the American Jewish Committee. The Guinzburg (or Guenzburg) in question was not a member of the well-known Guenzburg family led until shortly before the First World War by Baron Horace Guenzburg but, most probably, Moisei Akimovich Guinzburg, a Baku oil magnate.

But while all this could—and it did—give the governments of Great Britain and France (as well as that of Russia, of course) food for thought, Schiff and his friends could no more succeed in their purpose than, in the end, could Bleichröder in his. The problem presented by Jewish hostility to Russia—and thus indirectly although rarely by intention, to the Allied cause generally—had therefore more than ethnic origins and certain tactical features in common with that presented by prevalent Irish-American opinion. Both were characterized by there being no way in which the true and evident cause of distress—Irish in one case, Jewish in the other—could actually be tackled to some good purpose. None but the British could alter the state of affairs in Ireland; and this, for the time being, they were neither willing nor, given the current structure of politics in the United Kingdom, able to do. Only the Russians could alter Russian policy; and while, as we have seen, there were voices within the Russian government at a level that fell just short of that of the Tsar himself that favoured going well beyond the one grudging gesture that had been made to the Jews—a promise that their affairs would be looked at once the war was over—the response to all such proposals was firmly negative. Gentle probing in St Petersburg by the French and the British neither could nor did, nor was ever expected to, lead anywhere. No one in Paris or in London was prepared seriously to consider exerting really heavy diplomatic pressure on their wartime ally in any internal cause, least of all a Jewish one. Nor had anyone the wit to suggest what form such pressure might take were a decision to exert it ever taken.

The British ambassador in Washington thought that influential British and French Jews should be encouraged to call their co-religionists in New York to order and warned that it would go ill with them in due course in France and Great Britain if no results followed.[22] But if there were people in Whitehall/Downing Street and the Quai d'Orsay who were tempted to go this far and who imagined that the almost inevitable scandal[23] could somehow be sloughed off, there were many more who understood that representations of such a kind from such a quarter would cut very little ice with a man like Jacob Schiff or with any one else of

---

[22] Spring Rice to Cecil, 29 Jan. 1916, PRO, FO 371/2835. On a later occasion the ambassador wrote semi-privately to Hardinge, the new Permanent Under-Secretary at the Foreign Office: 'I think it would be a very good thing to warn English Jews of the very great danger Jews will incur in the allied countries if in this neutral country the Jews as a whole use their organisations and political power against the Allies . . . The Jews here [i.e. in the United States] are living in a neutral country. If they take part as an organisation against the allies it must be for some reason. If the reason is that the victory of Germany is to the advantage of Jewry the Jews are rather dangerous citizens to have in our midst [i.e. in the United Kingdom]', 14 July 1916, PRO, FO 800/242.

[23] On the prompt and unusually fierce response of the regular spokesman for British Jewry when offered polite advice of the kind the ambassador had in mind, see below, pp. 669f.

appropriate standing in the United States. It was not that the problem of
Jewish opinion in the United States was rated one of catastrophic proportions. The support of the more powerful firm of J. P. Morgan had
been assured the Allies from the start. But it was an irritant. It would not
go away. It and its analogues seemed likely to crop up elsewhere in other
contexts and in different forms. It induced the Allied powers to take serious note of Jewish hostility to Russia and Jewish reservations about the
Allied cause in the United States. And people in high political places
acquired the habit of thinking of Jews as not only being in possession of
significant levers of influence and even power, but as a substantially more
coherent body of people than it had once been usual to assume. From this
to thinking of them as a people who not only needed to be dealt with
because of the impediments they were placing before the Allied cause
but as one that it might be useful to harness in its favour was only a short
step. Lord Robert Cecil, Parliamentary Under-Secretary at the Foreign
Office, but a political figure of greater influence than the title of his office
might imply, noted on one occasion: 'I do not think it is easy to exaggerate the international power of the Jews'.[24] Cecil's dictum was neither
especially friendly nor unfriendly in spirit or intention. In due course it
would be revealed, moreover, as anything but well founded. But it encapsulated this new attitude with great precision.

   Yet 'the international power of the Jews' was an odd notion. Neither it
nor the actual decision to deal with 'the Jews' head on (to which it may be
said to have done much to lead) were the outcome of anything that could
reasonably be thought of as a systematic inquiry and analysis of the Jewish factor in international affairs and of the weight it would be proper to
attach to it. The Jews, as the professionals of British diplomacy ought to
have known (and those of France, as it happened, rarely doubted) had no
'international power' whatever that curious term might be held to mean.
They had, that is to say, no means—and (the Zionists apart) little desire—
to come together to wield autonomous power in their own collective
interest. Nor, as we have seen repeatedly, did they have the means of
ascertaining in just what their collective interest might consist. The
steady flow to Paris, London, and Petrograd of reports on Jacob Schiff,
the Rothschilds, and other Jewish notables, their view and their loyalties,
real or alleged, left their cumulative impact on all three governments. But
it was the predisposition to read more into them than the evidence could
actually bear that was decisive and remains, in retrospect, question-
begging.

[24] Cecil was commenting on a dispatch from McMahon, the British High Commissioner in Cairo, reporting a conversation with the head of the Jewish community in
Alexandria who had argued that a British declaration in favour of Zionism would do
much to swing Jewish opinion in Britain's favour. McMahon to Grey, 11 Feb. 1916,
PRO, FO 371/2671.

It both reflected and fed the underlying assumptions governing the Allied governments' approach (that of Great Britain especially) to matters Jewish as it evolved during the war. It goes far to explain the Allied powers' critical, but logically and empirically unwarranted, leap from the observable to the speculative and from the speculative to the operative in this connection. Yet it was one thing to recognize that the affairs and interests of the Allies intersected with those of the Jews at a variety of by no means negligible points. It was another to assume that the scattered, normally disconnected, in some respects contentious Jewish communities could, despite appearances, be effectively dealt with as if they truly pertained to some sort of ultimately integrated or at any rate interconnected, supra-communal whole. It may be surmised, no doubt, that the deeper source of the belief in 'the international power of the Jews' lay with those pieces of conventional and malicious wisdom about the Jews that men and women in high European society had long been happy to dispense—mostly without much thought, or fear of rebuttal, or need to examine the observable facts. In essence, that is to say, it was a feature of the commonest of attitudes to Jews among members of the privileged classes, especially to those Jews who approximated to them socio-economically: part resentful, part admiring, and a trifle fearful.

In sum, the dramatic conclusions otherwise quite sensible men were now inclined to draw in regard to the Jews cannot be fully accounted for without allowance being made for their sharing the common, but in fact ancient propensity among non-Jews of all classes and all levels of social and political sophistication to ascribe to Jewry features that bore little or no relation to the observable evidence. For where organic unity was posited, there merely cursory inspection would have revealed that Jewry was an aggregate of groups, parties, communities, institutions, societies, and particular individuals of widely differing types and purposes, bound—if that is the word—only by quite tenuous and uncertain ties. And where defined, recognized, and compelling *interests* were so easily presumed to operate, there the ties, such as they were, that bound the various communities to each other pertained only to things of the mind and the heart. It was precisely for lack of a strong, evident, common interest in the hard, political sense of the term and for lack of strong, generally accepted leadership capable of articulating and pursuing a common interest that the Jews were in fact devoid, and mostly chose to continue to be devoid, of 'international power'. All Jews knew this: some as a plain and evident feature of their lives, some simply in their bones, by instinct. It was among the observers of Jewry from *without* that the myth of an organic Jewry and of consequent Jewish international power held a fascination, was believed or half-believed in, and tended from time to time to influence the interpretation of data and serve as a basis for political action. This was such a time. There were some, it is true, who saw through the clouds of lore and excited prejudgement in which the matter of the Jews began, for a while, to be enveloped. It would not be very long—less than a generation would pass—before the notion of the Jews' 'international power' would be revealed throughout Europe, and in the United States as well, as empty of all significant political content. But—a crucial 'but'—it was to have its (wartime) moment; and while that moment lasted it set off a chain of events that in ordinary circumstances would have been judged not only remarkable but improbable.

III

In December 1915 a committee for propaganda among Jews in neutral countries[25] was formed by the French government. It was to operate under the combined auspices of the Foreign Affairs Committee of the Chamber of Deputies and the Government itself and was to be composed of men of suitable distinction, Jews and non-Jews, deputies, scholars, men of letters, one of whom, Victor Basch, a professor at the Sorbonne, had already been to the United States at the behest of the Quai d'Orsay to scout out the territory. Basch had been gratified to find much sympathy for France 'whose tenacity and calm valour is admired' even in 'German-Jewish circles'; and he reported too (somewhat smugly) on a strong current of antipathy towards Great Britain. As for Russia, he found that hatred of it and contempt were almost universal.

The great point of departure is now religious persecution and it is the two million Jews of America, a million and a half of whom are to be found in New York, and a million and a half of whom are Russian and Polish Jews who have escaped the pogroms, who lead the campaign against Russia. The organs of anti-Russian propaganda are the Yiddish-language newspapers, some of which, like the *Vorwärts*, have a circulation of 200,000 copies and buildings as sumptuous as the *New York Times* and the *World*; the popular speakers; the rabbis; and finally the great bankers of Wall Street headed by the greatest financial force of all in America, Jacob H. Schiff. They act by mounting appeals for victims of the war, appeals which, thus far, have yielded 1,300,000 dollars and which provide an opportunity to hold great meetings at which inflammatory speeches against Russian barbarism are delivered; and there are publications like the Black Book in which all instances of persecution suffered by the Jews of Russia since the beginning of the war are recounted.

Basch thought it would be very difficult to fight this anti-Russian movement, but not impossible.

It is necessary at one and the same time to touch the popular masses, the newspapers, the rabbis, and the great bankers. One finds staunch allies among the

[25] Formally entitled Le Comité français d'information et d'action auprès des Juifs des pays neutres.

Zionists, the socialists, among some of the Yiddish writers, and among some of
the bankers. The [right] tactic is to try to demonstrate that the fatherland of anti-
Semitism is not Russia at all but Germany; that the real Russians, the Russian
people, are in no sense religious fanatics; that Russian anti-Semitism is the work
of the bureaucracy and the German [*sic*] police for the most part; that the Russian political parties, with the sole exception of the men of the Black Hundreds
and the [pro-German] party, are agreed on the need for Jewish emancipation;
that after the war emancipation will certainly be realised and that if the Russian
ghetto will be opened one day soon, it will never be like the German ghetto
which is a moral ghetto that rests on the ineradicable conviction shared by German scholars as well as by the people that the Semitic race is an inferior race,
admixture with which threatens to contaminate the German.[26]

Professor Basch's analysis of affairs in the United States, while highly
coloured, was not seriously inaccurate—unlike his view of the (relative)
absence of anti-Semitism among ordinary Russians.[27] But it led to no
dramatic consequences. It was the propaganda committee's approach
(through Jacques Bigart, secretary of the Alliance Israélite Universelle) to
Lucien Wolf, secretary of the Conjoint Committee of the principal representative institutions of British Jewry, with an invitation to join them
in the appointed task of swinging the Jews of the United States to the side
of the Allies that was to bear real fruit—although fruit that would be
altogether too ripe, as things turned out, for the French themselves to
stomach.

Wolf responded with alacrity. Approaching the Foreign Office in the
first instance for their approval, he told them that a similar committee
should be set up under British auspices, not least because it was likely to
be more effective than anything the French could mount. And he took
the opportunity to offer his own views on the way Jewish opinion in the
United States was best tackled if it was to be tackled at all seriously. There
was no actual harm in re-arguing the well-established grounds for supporting the democracies rather than the militarist and anti-Semitic Central Powers *despite* Russia—as the French intended. But it would advance
matters very little. To cause the Jews to overlook the Russian factor and
support the Allied cause positively, there needed to be an appeal to their
own inner sentiment and loyalties. And here, alas, the facts were plain. 'In
any bid for Jewish sympathies to-day,' he told Lord Robert Cecil, 'very
serious account must be taken of the Zionist movement. In America the
Zionist organizations have lately captured Jewish opinion, and very
shortly a great American Jewish Congress will be held virtually under

---

[26] 'Résumé de lettres de Victor Basch' [n.d.], CZA, A77/3a.

[27] Which it is curious to compare with the contrary, equally false view on the *relative*
weakness of anti-Semitism in government circles when compared with that which prevailed among the common people to which, for example, the British ambassador subscribed and on which he reported. See above, p. 657.

Zionist auspices.' He wished to make clear that he himself 'deplore[d] the
Jewish National Movement. To my mind the Jews are not a nationality. I
doubt whether they have ever been one in the true sense of the term.' But
he did not doubt that this was 'the moment for the Allies to declare their
policy in regard to Palestine' and to do so in a spirit that was acceptable to
Zionist ears. The Zionists probably recognized that the Allies could not
'make a Jewish State of a land in which only a comparatively small minority of the inhabitants are Jews'. But Britain and France could say to them
'that they thoroughly understand and sympathise with Jewish aspirations
in regard to Palestine, and that when the destiny of the country came to
be considered, those aspirations will be taken into account'. He thought
too that assurances of 'reasonable facilities for immigration and colonisa-
tion', for the establishment of a Jewish University, and for the recognition
of Hebrew 'as one of the vernaculars of the land' could be given. Were
all that done, the Allies, Wolf did not doubt, 'would sweep the whole of
American Jewry into enthusiastic allegiance to their cause'. It was true
that this still left the question of the *political* disposition of the country
itself open. The Zionists, he had reason to believe, would look forward to
Great Britain becoming the 'mistress of Palestine'. No doubt, as he himself recognized, it might be difficult for the British themselves to touch
on the subject in view of the well-established French claims to Syria and
the equally well-established French view that Palestine itself was part of
'Syria'. But again, if the assurances about Britain's sympathy for Zionism
and its willingness to guarantee rights of immigration and settlement in
Palestine to Jews that he proposed were proclaimed, the purpose immediately in view, namely the attachment of American Jewry to the Allied
cause, would be achieved. Wolf did not go so far as to say that the Zionists would end by being reconciled to French rule. He probably thought
it unwise to venture into what he knew was sensitive political territory.
Besides, it was not for him to speak for the Zionists. He limited himself
to pointing out that, so far as he knew, 'what the Zionists fear above all is
an increase of Russian influence, or an Italian annexation which would
fill the country with Sicilian peasants, or an International Commission
which would be soulless if it were not a hot-bed of demoralising
intrigue'.[28]

In fact, whatever Wolf may have thought of the Zionists, which was
not a great deal, and of their outlook and purposes, of which he disapproved, he was well informed about them. He knew that their movement
was in disarray in direct consequence of the war and that it was no longer
as clear as it had once been who precisely was entitled to speak for it,
let alone take decisions on its behalf. When Harry Sacher, a figure of

[28] Wolf to Cecil, 'Suggestions for pro-Allies propaganda among Jews in the United
States', 16 Dec. 1915, PRO, FO 371/2579.

moderate standing in the small English branch of the movement, representing Chaim Weizmann,[29] who was of firmer status (in that he was a member of the Greater Actions Committee) but still only of middle rank, sought 'a means of co-operation' with the Conjoint Committee towards the end of 1914, Wolf's response was testy. 'I find at the outset,' he wrote to Sacher, 'that I am confronted by the enquiry: who are the persons and organisations representing your views and in what measure do they represent the great body of Zionists?'[30] Well-entrenched disapproval apart, Wolf and his principals, D. L. Alexander of the Board of Deputies and Claude Montefiore of the Anglo-Jewish Association, had been infuriated, the latter especially, by Weizmann's wholly independent efforts to tackle senior figures in the British political establishment directly on what purported to be his movement's behalf. They saw these episodes as characteristic of the conduct—disorderly, unwise, and irresponsible more often than not—which they had always attributed to the Zionists. Sacher was therefore informed that if Weizmann were really anxious to co-operate with the Conjoint Committee he would be 'very ill-advised' to continue to 'pursue his negotiations with politicians'. 'The Conjoint Committee,' Wolf pointed out in the especially stiff language he employed when dealing with, or reporting to, others on the Zionists, 'was the appointed body elected for that purpose by the Anglo-Jewish Community, and it would only make trouble if the Zionists were to trespass on their functions.'[31] But a meeting was arranged and an extended exchange of views, some of it in writing, followed—although not with Sacher or Weizmann, in the event, but with Naḥum Sokolov and Yeḥiel Tchlenov. Sokolov's and Tchlenov's seniority and prestige in the movement were substantially greater than Weizmann's. They had been formally accredited to act in London for the movement's Executive (the Actions Committee). And so if Alexander, Montefiore, and Wolf were not disposed to offer them an especially warm reception when they arrived in London (which, as Russian citizens they had been free to do, unlike Warburg and several other leading members of the movement who were German nationals), to refuse to see and listen to them altogether would have been unthinkable.[32]

But nothing of substance was agreed upon. The validity of Zionist insistence on the need to begin to think hard about the peace conference that would eventually follow the war was not disputed. Their view that the Jewish people's claims on the attention of what would surely be a major international forum needed to be defined, agreed upon, and then

[29] On whom more below.
[30] Wolf to Sacher, 26 Nov. 1914, BoD, E3/204/1.
[31] Wolf reporting to Alexander, 16 Dec. 1914, ibid.
[32] Wolf thought it proper, however, to report the proceedings in full to the Foreign Office, PRO, FO 371/2488.

pressed forward at war's end by a single and coherent body—and that it would be tragic if the opportunity to do this were missed—was accepted as well founded. So too was their position that such a delegation would be duty-bound to concern itself with the standing and the rights of the Jews in Palestine no less than with the civil rights and liberties of the Jews in Europe. But on details or priorities, still less on the underlying purposes to which it was proper to aim—which is to say, on how these otherwise very proper intentions should be spelled out in practice—there was no meeting of minds at all. When the central ideological issues that had always divided the two camps were, as was inevitable, so much as touched upon the gulf between them could be seen by all to be unbridgeable. There could be no joint approach to the powers on the condition of eastern European Jewry, for example, without prior agreement on the matter of emancipation. The Zionist thesis on emancipation—namely that while it was right and proper for Jews to demand it, it was nevertheless doomed to failure: in eastern Europe certainly, possibly elsewhere as well—was not remotely acceptable to the Londoners. The Conjoint Committee, Wolf informed Sokolov by way of bringing what had been nothing better than a passage of arms to an end, remained

unshaken in their belief that the 'Nationalist postulate' of the Zionists and the projected special rights for Jews in Palestine would stimulate anti-Semitism and would hopelessly compromise the whole movement for the emancipation of the Jews in lands where they are still suffering civil and political disabilities. The fact cited by the Zionists that anti-Semitism existed before Zionism does not affect this belief, seeing that anti-Semitism bases itself on a theory of the perpetual alienage of Jews which, in the view of the Conjoint Committee, the 'Nationalist postulate' is calculated to justify.[33]

On the face of things it was odd, therefore, that Wolf and his colleagues should resolve on making proposals to the Foreign Office on, in effect, the Zionists' behalf—although entirely, as needs to be stressed, without the latter's knowledge.[34] It was, of course, proof—if proof were needed— of their patriotism and their undeviating intellectual honesty. The notables of British Jewry were nothing if not anxious to do what they could to further the war effort, and anxious too to demonstrate beyond all possible doubt that this was in fact their intention. Moreover, the twin mat-

[33] Wolf to Sokolov, 11 June 1915, Mocatta Library, AJ/204/4.

[34] There was as yet no contact either official or unofficial between the Zionists and the Foreign Office. Weizmann had been received on one occasion (Apr. 1915) by Cecil, but there was no follow-up, possibly because Cecil seems to have taken a dislike to him, more likely because little or no interest was taken in the Zionist movement before Wolf and his colleagues drew attention to an important, if indirect connection between Zionism and anti-Russian feeling among Jews in the United States. On the other hand, there were no illusions about the differences between the people Wolf represented and the Zionists.

ters of the Jews of Russia and Jewish sentiment in America belonged,
they thought, to a sphere in which they possessed a firm standing and particular authority and, therefore, by extension, some responsibility as well.
This was the view, as they chanced to be reminded at about this time, in
Whitehall as well. But there it had rather different implications. They
were more than a little put off when Lord Robert Cecil, prompted, possibly, by what the ambassador in Washington had had to say on the uses of
cautioning British Jews about the eventual consequences for *them* if their
American co-religionists continued to be obstructive, went so far as to
warn the Conjoint Committee that their 'co-religionists' should bear in
mind

that the triumph of Germany in this war must be disastrous to Jewish interests in
Russia, and if it were thought that that triumph had been assisted in any way by
Jewish efforts on neutral or Allied countries, they would necessarily lose a great
part of the sympathy which at present exists for them in France and England.[35]

Wolf, as the accredited representative of the Board of Deputies of
British Jews and the Anglo-Jewish Association, responded with unusual
acerbity: 'While we shall always do our best to induce our coreligionists
in other countries to support the policy of His Majesty's Government, we
cannot be held responsible', he pointed out, 'for anything they may judge
proper to do in the very different circumstances in which they are placed.'
Whereupon Cecil retreated somewhat. Wolf's views, he was told, were
'appreciated' and would be borne in mind.[36] But if they were, it was not
for long. Some weeks later, after a conversation with a rather less senior
official at the Foreign Office, Wolf felt obliged to protest in still stiffer
language.

I have been thinking over our conversation of last Monday, and it seems to me I
ought to repeat in writing what I then told you, namely, that while we British
Jews are most anxious to do everything possible to bring the case for the Allies
before our American coreligionists, and to impress upon them our conviction
that the cause of Jewish emancipation, social, civic, and religious, must gain by
the triumph of the Allies, and can only be prejudiced by a German triumph, or
by an inconclusive peace, we cannot take any responsibility for any line of action
the American Jews may choose to follow. I thought I detected, both in the
dispatch of Sir Cecil Spring Rice and in your own observations, a tacit assumption of a solidarity, apart from their confessional identity, marking the Jew off
from the nations among whom they live. This assumption finds perhaps some
little justification in the mischievous and ill-considered doctrine of the extreme
Zionists, but it is none the less a fallacy. The Jews are a religious community like
any other, but unlike some others, they have absolutely no international organization, either for religious or political purposes. Politically, they belong to the

---

[35] Cecil to Wolf, 24 Feb. 1916, Mocatta Library, AJ/204/2.
[36] Wolf to Cecil, 29 Feb. 1916; Cecil to Wolf, 1 Mar. 1916, ibid.

countries in which they dwell, and in the politics of those countries they never form a separate party, but share or reflect the views of their non–Jewish fellow–citizens in like proportions. Hence we cannot answer for the American Jews and their views on the war, though, of course, we will do our best to persuade them.[37]

In the event, two of the Conjoint Committee's proposals were dismissed out of hand: the one that Britain and France should promote an understanding between Russia and the United States on the matter of discrimination against Jewish citizens of the United States travelling to Russia—an ancient subject of contention; the other that the Entente powers 'urge' Russia to abolish *some* restrictions on Jewish residence and employment in the empire 'pending the complete revision of the laws relating to Jews already promised by the Imperial Government' after the war. Wolf was told very firmly that 'Any attempt at the present moment to induce the British and French Governments to intervene directly or indirectly in Russia's internal questions would be a great mistake.'[38] 'Nor do I think it would be even in the interests of your co–religionists,' Cecil had added. The idea that a British committee be formed for propaganda work in the United States along the lines of the one the French had set up was approved, but perhaps with something less than enthusiasm. Lord Reading (Rufus Isaacs), Lord Chief Justice, was spoken of as its leading member. When Reading refused to participate the plan fell apart, however. But the Foreign Office did adopt and persisted in for some time with mounting enthusiasm in what lay at the operative heart of Wolf's memorandum, that which came to be called the 'Palestine Idea'. 'It would appeal powerfully to a large and influential section of Jews throughout the world,' ran the key Foreign Office minute in which the 'Idea' was restated for internal digestion and sent up for approval by the Foreign Secretary, Grey, and his deputy, Crewe (Lord President of the Council). 'It is clear that the Palestine scheme has in it the most far–reaching political possibilities and we should, if I may be allowed to say so,

---

[37] Wolf to Montgomery, 5 Apr. 1916, PRO, FO 371/2835. The ambassador in Washington had written to London: 'It seems to me that the real remedy for this state of things is representations from the Jewish community in England. If the attitude of the Jews here becomes generally known in England and France the result cannot fail to be very unfortunate for the Jewish residents in those countries, who are regarded in every sense of the word as our countrymen. It is evidently their interest that the Jewish community here [in the US] should not take an active part in the pro–German movement. It seems to me to be more the business of the Jewish community in England and France than that of the British Government to explain to their Jewish brethren here what would be the effects of their taking sides with us.' Spring Rice to Cecil, 29 Jan. 1916, PRO, FO 371/2835. And see above, p. 661 n. 22.

[38] 'Memorandum' [18 Feb. 1916], PRO, FO 371/2835; Cecil to Wolf, 24 Feb. 1916, ibid.

be losing a great opportunity if we did not do our utmost to overcome any difficulties that may be raised by France and Russia.'[39]

Approval was speedily gained and the Russians and the French were then invited to join Britain in considering 'an arrangement in regard to Palestine completely satisfactory to Jewish aspirations'. The definition of 'Jewish aspirations' Wolf had offered to the Foreign Office was forwarded to the Allied governments for examination as it stood along with the terms on which the Foreign Office itself proposed that an offer to the Jews be made. Wolf's terms were modest:

In the event of Palestine coming within the sphere of influence of Great Britain or France at the close of the war, the Governments of those Powers will not fail to take account of the historic interest that country possesses for the Jewish community. The Jewish population will be secured in the enjoyment of civil and religious liberty, equal political rights with the rest of the population, reasonable facilities for immigration and colonization, and such municipal privileges in towns and colonies inhabited by them as may be shown to be necessary.

The Foreign Office, however, wished the French and the Russians to know that they themselves favoured a substantially stronger formulation:

We consider . . . that the scheme might be made far more attractive to the majority of Jews if it held out to them the prospect that when in the course of time Jewish colonists in Palestine grow strong enough to cope with the Arab population they may be allowed to take the management of the internal affairs of Palestine (with the exception of Jerusalem and the Holy Places) into their own hands.[40]

The Russian response turned out to be friendly. Sazonov, the foreign minister, told the British ambassador (Buchanan) that Russia welcomed the migration of Jews out of Russia to Palestine or anywhere else. Their only proviso was that the (Christian) Holy Places be placed under an international regime.[41] In contrast, the French response was ferociously negative, first and foremost because it seemed to them that the 'Palestine Idea' touched impermissibly, even if only obliquely (but perhaps not unintentionally), on their own strategic and colonial ambitions in the area. It had only been after much difficult argument that the details of the Anglo-French (Sykes–Picot) Agreement on the postwar partition and control of the Near East had recently been settled (long before either British or French armies had made any military headway against the Turks in any of the territories concerned, it may be added). Beyond a brief and essentially technical reference to the 'conscientious desires' of

[39] Minute by O'Beirne, the official principally concerned with Jewish affairs at this time, 8 Mar. 1916, PRO, FO 371/2817.
[40] Telegram to Bertie in Paris and Buchanan in Petrograd, 11 Mar. 1916, PRO, FO 371/2817.
[41] Buchanan to the Foreign Office, 14 and 15 Mar. 1916, PRO, FO 371/2817; and Sazonov to Paléologue, 26 Apr. 1916, AE, Série A, Paix, vol. 174, fo. 101.

Judaism 'in regard to the status of Jerusalem and the neighbouring shrines' there was no allusion in the Agreement either to historical or contemporary Jewish interest in Palestine. Only the very politically minded director of British naval intelligence, Captain W. R. Hall, commented, when he saw the draft of the Agreement, that 'the Jews have a strong *material*, and a very strong *political*, interest in the future of [Palestine]' and recommended that 'the question of Zionism . . . be considered'.[42] But no attention seems to have been paid to his views on this matter at the time and now it was too late: the Agreement awaited final signature. As the well-informed and level-headed British ambassador in Paris (Bertie) had warned London as soon as he received his instructions on the subject, the French proceeded to make clear to the British beyond a shadow of doubt that they were not prepared to countenance anything of the kind.[43] It was their position that the British proposal to enter into negotiations on the future of the Near East constituted 'official and formal recognition of our rights on the eastern coasts of the Mediterranean'. As for Palestine, Picot, on being delegated to conduct the negotiations, had it laid down for him in his written instructions, that

The term 'Syria' has always been understood in France in a large sense, the treaty of 1840, in which Palestine was called southern Syria, only reflected general opinion. It follows that our abandonment of any part of the Syrian coast would not be understood, and you are therefore to insist on our possession stopping only at the Egyptian frontier.[44]

For the rest, France's view of Jewry was at once more hostile and more sceptical than that of its British analogue. Zionism did not commend itself to the Quai d'Orsay or any other arm of French government in any way at all. French diplomats judged it (wrongly) to be an essentially pro-German movement and (correctly) to be in hopeless conflict with the

---

[42] Hall to Nicolson (Permanent Under-Secretary at the Foreign Office), 12 Jan. 1916, IOLR, MSS Eur. F112/265. Emphases in original.

[43] Like any good ambassador, Lord Bertie had thoroughly internalized the preponderant view of things taken by those among whom he represented his country and could be relied upon to convey it to his principals at home. He had, as it happened, already heard something of Zionism. He thought it 'absurd', observing in his diary: 'What would the Pope, and Italy, and Catholic France with her hatred of Jews, say of this scheme?' (*The Diary of Lord Bertie of Thame* (London, 1924), i. 105–6). And he thought little of the Jews: they were not, he wrote to Grey, 'a combative race. How would they fare against the warlike Arabs unless physically supported by England and France?' (Bertie to Grey, 13 Mar. 1916, PRO, FO 800/176). He followed his instructions, needless to say, doing what he could to make what the Foreign Office had in mind a trifle more palatable to the French. Grey's resolute 'Our sole object is to find an arrangement which would be so attractive to the majority of Jews as to enable us to strike a bargain for Jewish support' underwent cosmetic treatment. 'Attractive' became 'appealing'; 'us' became 'the Allies'; 'bargain' became 'arrangement' (Grey to Bertie, 11 Mar. 1916; and Bertie to the Ministry for Foreign Affairs, 12 Mar. 1916, PRO, FO 800/176).

[44] Briand to Picot, 2 Nov. 1915, AE, Guerre 1914–1918, vol. 871, fos. 32–6.

zealously patriotic, not to say subservient, Alliance Israélite Universelle. They believed (again, correctly) that there was less support in Jewry for the aspirations of Zionism than the British seemed to be ascribing to it. And they judged those aspirations as in any case to be pitifully unrealistic. They were a good deal less impressed than the British by what Cecil had termed the Jews' 'international power' and were convinced that no declaration in favour of the movement would suffice to counter or deflect Jewry's ineradicable hostility to Russia and draw it effectively to the Allied cause.

There is reason to ask [Briand, the French foreign minister, observed] if the project outlined by M. Lucien Wolf will really influence Jewish opinion as anticipated, it being the case that the attitude of those members of this community who are hostile to the Allies derives from concerns which have nothing in common with Zionist aspirations and which the realisation of those aspirations will not cause to disappear.[45]

A French declaration in favour of a Jewish state would, therefore, as the director of Asian affairs at the French Foreign Ministry was to put it a little later,

be laughable and to no purpose. We have Israélites in France and anti-Semites, but in reality we have very few 'Jews'. In contrast, we have Christians who believe fervently that Jerusalem is the Holy City and that it is our duty to deliver it and rule over it. The less talk therefore the better. I was among those who wished to include Palestine in our share [lot] not because of the Holy City, but because of the port of Jaffa and the fertile valley of Esdraelon. The decision has been otherwise. To draw the attention of the French public to this region would, it seems to me, be quite unwise.[46]

But the decisive consideration in their eyes had less to do with the Jews than with their own aspirations. The 'Palestine Idea' as it had come to be conceived and developed in London was entirely incompatible with what, as the French (not unreasonably) saw it, they and the British (with Russian assent) had just been in the course of settling as the details of the postwar division of spoils in the Near East. It had been difficult enough for them to agree to 'Palestine' (as the country would be defined after the war) being divided into four parts,[47] the greater part of which would be placed under international governance of some sort rather than under undivided French control. They had wanted it for themselves. Picot, the French negotiator, was furious when he learned from Sykes, his British

[45] Briand to Bertie, 21 Mar. 1916, PRO, FO 371/2817.
[46] Jean Gout, n.d. probably Aug. 1916, AE, Guerre 1914–1918, Sionisme, II, vol. 1198, fo. 45.
[47] The north of the country (Galilee) would come under direct French control; an enclave around Haifa would be British; the southern desert area (the Negev) would be British 'protected'; and the rest, including Jerusalem, would be internationally regulated.

counterpart, of the new, totally unexpected 'Palestine Idea' that the Foreign Office was in the process of floating. There was no question in his mind that a special status for the Jews in the country was to add insult to injury and was therefore totally out of the question. 'M. Picot on hearing the sense of [Grey's] telegram made loud exclamations and spoke of pogroms in Paris,' Sir Mark Sykes reported. 'He grew calmer but maintained [that] France would grow excited.' Sykes, who was accepted in official London as an authority on the Near East, then went on to list the difficulties the 'Palestine Idea' would encounter. Arabs would be outraged: 'The Shereef [of Mecca] will be in a position to say to us, "You propose to introduce idolatrous Indians into Mesopotamia to oust Moslem Arabs; impose French rule on Syria to Frenchify Arab Christians; and now decide to flood Palestine with Jews to drive out Arabs whether Moslems or Christians. Turks and Germans are preferable." ' However, as for the Jews, 'I urged on M. Picot [the] inestimable advantages to [the] allied cause of active friendship of Jews[,] of the World force of which he reluctantly admitted. However[,] Zionists should, I submit, give some demonstration of their power; accentuation of German financial straits and glow of pro-Allied sentiment in certain hitherto anti-ally neutral papers would be [a] sufficient indication.'[48]

When it had thus been made plain to London through all the many channels available that the French saw nothing in the 'Palestine Idea' to recommend it and many reasons to oppose it the British drew back. No one in London seems to have been moved to question the actual logic on which the 'Palestine Idea' had originally been founded other than conceding that there was much about it that was indeed speculative. What was decisive was that there could be no question of a fresh quarrel with Britain's principal ally on what, after all, was a relatively minor matter. Anglo-French rivalry in the Near East was an old and familiar subject. A new flair-up in that quarter was unthinkable while the war was on, the more so as Britain's own interests in the area (and in Palestine itself) as the government of the day had defined them had been completely satisfied by Sykes–Picot. All Asquith and Grey had ever wanted was a protected line of communication eastwards towards Mesopotamia and on to what counted for most, if not everything, in the British imperial scheme of things: India. The allocation to Britain of the Haifa enclave would provide that very adequately. It was not until Lloyd George replaced Asquith as Prime Minister in December 1916 that the 'Palestine Idea' would be taken out of the files in which it was now to lie buried for a while, refurbished somewhat, and restored to life as an item of active public policy. In sum, by the early summer of 1916 the 'Idea' had been dropped—quite as quickly, that is to say, as it had originally been picked up. It only remained

[48] Buchanan to Grey, 14 Mar. 1916, PRO, FO 371/2767.

for the Foreign Office to give some sort of explanation to Wolf. He would be told, it was decided, that there had been opposition in Paris, but he would not be told why, the Anglo-French (Sykes–Picot) Agreement on the carving up of the Near East being a dark diplomatic secret for the time being. Wolf, in the event, drew the wholly mistaken conclusion that it was the Zionists who had somehow or other interfered. 'It appears,' he noted bitterly, '. . . that the Zionists have used their efforts to get our formula, which was intended as a concession to them, rejected. That is to say, that they would rather have no privileges at all in Palestine than have the equal rights and the colonising privileges we ask for.'[49]

IV

The First World War presented the Zionist Organization with a problem it was peculiarly ill-fitted to solve. The phenomenon of the inner world of Jewry being riven through and through by lines of political and military battle to which the Jews themselves, as such, were immaterial was in itself far from new. It was the scale, the duration, and the intensity of emotional, ideological, and political impact on the Jews of Europe as citizens and subjects of the countries they inhabited that were all without precedent. Most Jewish organizations, being of an essentially communal nature, continued to look almost exclusively inward and to attune their purposes and subordinate their activities to the war effort of the country and nation in the midst of which they operated and with which they were formally, but of course also socially and culturally, identified as a matter of course. Movements whose ethos and structure were supra-communal, whose general method of operation required regular communication across borders in writing and the perpetual crossing and recrossing of frontiers by their activists in person, were in another case altogether—doubly so when their purposes, explicitly or otherwise, were political. Agudat Yisrael, hardly formed, went to ground for the duration. The well-established Bund tried to keep going. So did the Zionists.

The Bund had been hard hit by the repression that all revolutionary movements suffered after the Revolution of 1905. It had moderated its revolutionary stand somewhat by associating itself finally with the Menshevik (rather than Bolshevik) faction in the Russian Social Democratic Workers' Party,[50] and by going so far as to participate in the elections to the Fourth Duma in 1913. But on the outbreak of war it had remained faithful (as the French and German socialist parties had not) to the principle of

---

[49] Memorandum, 5 July 1916, BoD, C11/3/2/1.

[50] The Mensheviks had effectively dropped their opposition to Jewish national and cultural autonomy—to which the Bolsheviks continued to be adamantly opposed.

working-class internationalism. It had subscribed to the Zimmerwald Manifesto of September 1915 against the war; and it made no secret of its continuing dedication to the overthrow of the Autocracy. There was no question therefore of the Bund (or, of course, of any of the other Russian social democrats) participating in some sort of Russian equivalent of the German *Burgfrieden* or the French *Union sacrée*—had such a political truce been proclaimed. The Zimmerwald Manifesto expressed general hopes and principles in the form of a call to workers to put aside chauvinism and end the killing. It did not call for an immediate revolutionary campaign, for civil war all round, especially in Russia, to bring the world war to an end and the RSDWP to power as Lenin had wanted. It may be said of the Bund, therefore, that it had effectively opted for sitting out the war in expectation of more promising times and better opportunities to come when it was over. In the course of time it even agreed to co-operate with the major (pronouncedly bourgeois) philanthropic organizations of Russian Jewry in the organization and distribution of relief.

The case of the Zionists was different. Their movement had reached a plateau of sorts some years before the war—at a modest and unexciting altitude, however. The Organization functioned, Congresses were convened, the Actions Committee met, the wheels turned over—better than ever before in fact. A little band of efficient (now salaried) administrative appointees—civil servants in all but name—had gathered round the Central Office in Berlin: solid, reliable, well-educated, dedicated German, or at any rate German-speaking Jews. They saw to it that business was transacted in exemplary fashion, that proceedings and decisions were recorded, regular correspondence with the various branches of the movement maintained, bulletins issued to the press, periodical publications and useful books sponsored, and the movement's financial affairs handled openly and scrupulously. All this was as Herzl had always wanted it to be and it rested on the foundations he himself had laid. In his time, he had handled a great deal of the business of the movement himself, the rest, perforce, being left to volunteers. When funds were lacking, as was very often the case, he supplied the lack out of the small fortune his father had left him—until, some time before his death, it had been exhausted. Under Wolffsohn and now under Warburg the unpaid, somewhat personal, voluntary character of the movement at its institutional centre was much reduced. The World Zionist *Organization* was bureaucratized. There was something to show for the new efficiency. Some additional moderate (now, characteristically, more orderly and systematic) progress in the resettlement of Palestine by Jews in more or less self-sufficient agricultural 'colonies'[51] had been achieved—to which the contribution of

---

[51] A term which, as it may be superfluous to point out, carried none of the damning negative overtones that began to accompany it in the second half of the twentieth century.

the movement's Palestine Office established in Jaffa in 1908 was not negligible. But more was owed to the influx of several thousand radically minded young people from Russia in the wake of the events of 1904 and 1905: a quantitatively small, but qualitatively vital leap in the total character of the new *yishuv*, lending it a touch of the socially innovative and the personally heroic such as it had not had before. For all major practical purposes, all of which hinged on the re-entry of the Jews into Palestine on a very large scale, matters were precisely where Herzl had left them in despair in 1901 and had begun to think, reluctantly or otherwise, of alternative lands to which the Jews might be channelled and allowed to set up a polity of their own.

   In such circumstances it was hard for the more energetic and unquiet members of the movement—people of moderate standing in the first instance, but rank-and-file Zionists too—not to think that the movement might finally have run into the sand. Certainly there was little emanating from Berlin to cause them to think otherwise. Otto Warburg was a thoroughly decent and well-meaning man. But as a leader of a movement dedicated to the restructuring and rehabilitation of the Jewish people he was not merely mediocre, he was socially and psychologically incongruous. Increasingly, the active, passionate, and imaginative spirits began therefore to be found not in the formally defined inner circle of the Organization, but rather, for good or for ill, in its outer reaches; and not among the honourable, but inevitably somewhat staid, culturally German, functionaries at the Central Office, but rather among the self-employed, mostly Russian-, Yiddish-, and now increasingly Hebrew-speaking *and* writing journalists, professionals, and actual settlers in Palestine itself who were, almost to a man (or woman) from eastern Europe. Of the beginning of the failure of the centre of Zionism to hold as Herzl had managed to hold it, although even then with difficulty, while he lived, the Helsingfors conference had been the first considerable augury. It had gone far to revise the climate of ideas in which the Zionists operated. Yet neither Wolffsohn, the movement's leader at the time, nor any of the people in his entourage had been involved or been consulted. It had been an entirely Russian affair.

   Upon the outbreak of the war Zionism's institutional centre in Germany was cut off in fresh and still sharper ways from its largest and most important branch in Russia. Indeed, founded on a system of country branches, the representatives of which were expected to come together at stated intervals for consultation and decision-making, the Zionist Organization as Herzl had structured it was virtually debarred from functioning at all. For a worldwide movement desperately seeking entry into the world of international relations and a measure of real, if cautious, involvement of the Jews in the affairs of the 'Nations', the division of Europe into two warring blocs could not, it seemed, be less than paralysing. All the original Herzlian assumptions underlying *political* Zionism were in question. There was plainly no way now in which striving for the patronage of any of the major states of Europe and the Near East could fail to be other than dangerous—for the movement itself, but very possibly for Jews of all kinds in all places. Totally to align the Zionist movement—or any other Jewish movement with claims to a national-representative role, for that matter—with one or other of the belligerents would be madness itself. As individuals and as members of discrete communities Jews were now under an almost universal impulsion, some very willingly, some resignedly, to serve whatever country chance had led them to inhabit. Even committed Zionists tended to align themselves with the country of which they were citizens, although few went quite so far as those in Germany who raised loyalty to the Kaiser's empire to the level of ideological principle. In his first considered message to his members after the outbreak of war, the elected leader of the German branch assured his people that the preservation of 'our Palestinian undertakings' was certainly the movement's first concern, but he was especially proud to report to them that 'our friends in the movement have all without exception fulfilled their duty by the German Fatherland. The members of the Zionist Federation of Germany have demonstrated practical patriotism [*Patriotismus der Tat*] in exemplary manner.'[52]

Still, once the fever of the early months of the war had passed, it seemed to the more sober people in and around the Central Office in Berlin that a reversion to the old Jewish rule of keeping Jewry *per se* as far out of the way of the 'Nations' as might be possible was the better part of wisdom. And this despite the fact that, as has been said, German troops, upon their entry into Russian territory, appeared to eastern European Jews in the role of liberators. It was soon apparent too, at a time when the Turks were turning ever more harshly against the new *yishuv*, most of whose members were Russian subjects and therefore enemy aliens, that there were advantages in the official headquarters of the movement being in Berlin and the principal representative of the movement in Palestine itself (Arthur Ruppin) being a German subject. The relative warmth with which some Jews welcomed German troops cooled before long. The Zionists' German connections, such as they were, failed to save the *yishuv* from the massive expulsion of mostly Russian citizens ordered in 1915. Ruppin himself was expelled by explicit order of the local Ottoman satrap Djemal Pasha in the autumn of 1916. And it could be argued plausibly that Zionist prospects in Palestine, in the event of victory by the central powers in Europe and the Near East, were likely to be darker rather than brighter. A strengthened Ottoman Empire would be less, rather than more, likely to give ground and its German ally was the

---

[52] Arthur Hantke to the branches, 26 Aug. 1914, CZA, A126/41/4.

least likely of the great powers to press it to do so. Finally there was the overriding consideration that a close political association with Germany might end by impinging on the movement in Russia and on Russian Jewry generally. To most of the leading figures in the movement both in Germany and in Russia itself it seemed best therefore if the Zionists lay low until the war was over. Inaction could be prettyfied somewhat by entitling it 'neutrality'. But it too presented difficulties.

If a policy of 'neutrality' was to mean more than mere prudence and was to redound positively to the credit of Zionism after the war it had at the very least to be formally determined and proclaimed by the central institutions of the movement as a binding decision. There was then the question how precisely such a policy of 'neutrality' was to be conducted if the movement was not to go totally to ground for the duration and risk being beyond awakening when the war was over. And there were issues that required immediate settlement: seemingly formal or symbolic in nature, but in fact shot through and through with genuine political content. Should the seat of the movement remain in Berlin, for example? If it did, how precisely was business of any kind at all to be transacted? There could be no question of a full Congress being convened while the war lasted; that much was clear. But could the central executive organ of the movement, the Actions Committee, be allowed to fall into desuetude as well? If it was to meet from time to time, where and how and with what attendance? In the event, it was not until December 1914, with the war in its fifth month, that it proved possible to bring the two, now seriously reduced components of the Actions Committee together in neutral Denmark: with four of the six members of the Smaller Actions Committee, the movement's standing executive body present, but only five of the twenty-four members of the larger, more representative and ultimately more authoritative Greater Actions Committee (GAC). All present did duly agree on 'neutrality', defined as non-involvement in the affairs of the belligerents; and the decision was rammed home by a case in point being energetically dealt with. Leading members of the German branch of the movement had alarmed and infuriated the Russians by joining a committee of German-Jewish notables that had been set up to deal with problems arising in territories occupied by the German armed forces. In so doing, it was now argued, they had implicitly approved the occupation. The Actions Committee resolved formally to condemn 'the participation of leading Zionists in endeavours likely to endanger the security of Jews in any of the countries at war' and the relevant resignations were offered and accepted.

The Committee then went on to consider what it could and should do to relieve immediate distress in eastern Europe—as opposed to devoting all its energies and meagre resources to the preservation of the *yishuv* which were now thought likely (and would indeed soon prove) to be in some danger. This was evidently a much more difficult issue to resolve, being no more than a new variation on the now familiar question, where Zionism's true and compelling priorities lay—in Europe itself or in Palestine? The wording of the Actions Committee's eventual resolution illustrated the quandary in which it found itself, while amounting in practice to little more than a reformulation of the issue it had been trying to confront. Zionism, the Committee declared, aimed 'at the fulfilment of the Jewish people's national demands on the basis of concurrent work for our Palestine programme and for the attainment of equal rights in those countries where these are not yet possessed'. And the Actions Committee was no better at making up its mind about the seemingly more technical question, whether the Smaller Actions Committee (the EAC) and the Central Office of the Zionist Organization should be left in Germany or transferred to the United States or some other neutral country for the duration. Warburg opposed a move from Berlin on the not unreasonable grounds that it would be seen as anti-German at a time when relations with the Wilhelmstrasse and the rest of the German bureaucracy were good and were no less than vital when and where intercession with the Turks on behalf of the *yishuv* was called for. On the other hand, it was equally clear that there could be no question of Berlin continuing to be the locus of the centre of Zionist activity, however limited that might be in wartime. Torn between equally impossible alternative courses, the Actions Committee decided to skirt the issue by setting up a liaison office in neutral Copenhagen to be run by Leo Motzkin. It would have no special authority of its own, but it would, it was hoped, make more or less regular exchange of views and central distribution of information on the movement's affairs possible. And it would serve from time to time as a base for meetings of leading members of the movement at which matters that could not otherwise be dealt with would be thrashed out. Meanwhile, as a further sign of life, senior people in the movement would visit those capital cities to which Warburg and his collaborators, as German citizens, had no access. (This was the assignment that had brought Tchlenov and Sokolov to London in the early summer of 1915.[53])

The establishment of the Copenhagen liaison office was both sensible and, at the same time, a characteristic fudge. It fulfilled its technical functions successfully throughout the war. It did not and could not compensate for a leadership that had reduced itself to a state of semi-abdication by its refusal to move from Germany and a parallel, but contradictory insistence on 'neutrality'. The first attempt to reconvene the full Actions Committee early in 1915 failed: only two of the twenty-four members of the GAC turned up. A third meeting in mid-June of that year was more promising. No Austrians were present. Nor were any delegates from

---

[53] See above, pp. 667–8.

Great Britain—a detail which would not have mattered much in the past, yet now, with the English Zionist Federation beginning to have an importance that was out of all proportion to its membership, could be considered unfortunate. Nordau, the grand old man of Zionism, could not attend: he remained in Spain, to which the French authorities, despite his many years of residence in Paris, had expelled him as an enemy alien. But Warburg and Hantke arrived in Denmark from Germany as did the principal Russian figures in the all-important Russian branch of the movement: Ussishkin, Tchlenov, Jacobson, Goldberg, Motzkin, Rosov. Otherwise, there was no movement, least of all of ideas. With the EAC locked into the German orbit no serious attempt to pull the Organization out of the condition of suspended animation into which it had been allowed to fall seemed possible to those present; and none was proposed. The policy of neutrality was reconfirmed. The question where Zionism's fundamental priorities lay was touched upon once more: refugees from the war zone had been flooding into Austria and it seemed right that the Zionist movement should undertake relief work among them. On the other hand, Turkish pressure on the *yishuv* was now very severe. To the assistance of whom should the Zionist Organization now apply its resources when it was plain to all that in absolute terms these were far too limited for it to be other than absurd to try to spread them evenly? Ussishkin, ever the stalwart of uncompromising 'Palestinophilism' as it was called, ever the man to speak his mind plainly, had no doubt. There was a 'Jewish duty', certainly, to go to the assistance of people still in Europe. But there was a 'national duty' to stand by the *yishuv*.[54] Everyone else thought the dilemma insoluble. What had turned out to be equally insoluble in the meanwhile—and which for practical, not theoretical or ideological reasons left the established leadership of the Zionist movement even more agitated—was the rise of independent and dissident spirits who, from within the movement, spoke openly and critically of their leaders and with increasing vigour offered alternative views on how the movement should conduct itself while the war lasted. They professed continued basic loyalty, but they left no one in doubt that they were prepared to disregard set policy and defy—if necessary ignore—those who had been responsible for its formulation.

The dissidents were few in number, hardly more than a handful, all relatively young men, between ten and twenty years younger than the elected leaders. All were Russian, but less inward-looking and more worldly than was usual among Jews from Russia and Poland. All had made a mark of some kind in the non-Jewish world—as journalists, or members of the professions, or, in one case, as a revolutionary, and in

---

[54] Copenhagen to Central Office, Berlin, 4 Nov. 1915, CZA, L6/88; and circular letter from Copenhagen, 15 Feb. 1916, CZA, L7/18/1.

another as a soldier. They had a more confident (which is not to say a necessarily more accurate) grasp of affairs in the greater world that lay outside Jewry, and were certainly a good deal less wary of it, than were their
seniors. But what had most specifically brought them together and served
to distinguish them from those who had been leading the movement thus
far was that they had come to believe strongly, even passionately, that the
world they knew was manifestly in violent, probably irreversible, flux and
that it might be fatal to the Zionist interest to wait patiently on the sidelines for the war to end and for the political business of Europe and the
Near East to be restored to some sort of pre-war normality. It was precisely because the world was undergoing radical change that it was necessary for the Jews in general and for the Zionists in particular to seize the
moment and make what they could of whatever opportunities came their
way. Rather than sit out the war, the Zionists needed to plunge into it—
very much as groups of Poles, Finns, Czechs, Armenians, Arabs, and *tutti
quanti* were in the process of doing, each in its own way, each for its own
particular purposes. Moreover, they thought it evident, increasingly so as
the war progressed, more plainly than ever when the Ottoman Empire
formally aligned itself with the central powers, that the future of the Jews,
and the future of the Zionists in particular, lay with the western democracies. This was partly because France and Britain were indeed liberal and
democratic. It was partly because the Entente now stood quite firmly for
national self-determination. And it was partly, but crucially, because they
proposed—admittedly in ways that were still unknown—to reconstruct
the Near East. No such prospect of reconstruction was likely to present
itself in the event of a victory of the central powers. It followed that at
long last, remarkably, a window of opportunity had opened; and that this
being the case the die had to be cast. There were risks in doing so. It
meant a gamble, possibly a dangerous one. But then all one could be
entirely sure of in the present circumstances was that extreme prudence
of the kind mandated by the Actions Committee would lead nowhere
at all.

The dissidents adhered to one of two schools. The first school saw the
war primarily in its military aspect. It believed that eventual political
advantages, if any, would hinge, and properly so, on Jews *qua* Jews participating in distinct, uniformed, fighting formations. Their chief and
immediate purpose was therefore to promote the raising of a 'Jewish
Legion' on something like the model of Pilsudski's Polish Legions
(although, of course, on the Allied, not the Austrian side). They saw this
as a matter of practical politics. But they saw it too as a matter of principle. If there was to be a military struggle to wrest Palestine (and much
of the rest of the Near East) from the Turks, as seemed increasingly likely,
if the Jews continued to lay a claim to their ancestral country, and if, especially, they hoped, when the war had ended, to gain that position of

power or influence within the country or over it that had until now been
denied them, why then they were no less than honour bound to participate in the fighting. Political calculation was not foreign to their thinking. But it was shot through with—and therefore, in the nature of things,
was at once reinforced and diluted by—a romanticism of very much the
kind that the horrors of the war itself were in the process of eliminating
from most men's minds: honour counted for a great deal in their eyes; so
did the linked principles of personal participation and equality of sacrifice; and they were animated by an especially strong desire to bring to an
end the long estrangement of the Jewish people from military life and
military values.

Seen in the strictly Jewish context this made them firm, even supreme
modernists. Seen in a broader social context there was much about
them—especially about the leading (and politically longest-lasting) figure among them, the sometime *Wunderkind* of the Zionist movement
Vladimir Ze'ev Jabotinsky—that, as the war progressed and Europe in its
entirety was thrust irreversibly into the twentieth century, would soon be
old-fashioned, *passé*, and therefore, even to many minds in the Zionist
movement itself, misconceived. Still, for the time being these qualities
were a source of strength, the very substance of their call to other young
Jewish men to enlist in the units that the British military authorities were
eventually, with great difficulty, persuaded to form. The first was the
'Zion Mule Corps', a supply and transport battalion for service in the
Gallipoli campaign composed of locally enlisted men, most of whom
were members of the new *yishuv* whom the Turks had expelled from
Palestine. Later there were the three infantry battalions of the Royal
Fusiliers—comprising in fact, if not fully in name, the Jewish Legion that
Jabotinsky and his friends[55] had begun by asking to be allowed to form
and fight under British command.

None of this was to the liking of the old guard. And had they known
about the NILI espionage ring set up in Palestine itself by Aaron Aaron-
sohn as another form of service to the British forces camped in Egypt
prior to their push to the north they would have liked it still less.[56] They
saw the 'activists', as Jabotinsky and his colleagues had begun to call
themselves, as rebels and adventurers who were guilty of breaking ranks
and ignoring set policy in especially dangerous times. They sought to
warn the movement at large against them and to ridicule their arguments
for abandoning neutrality. It was absurd to suppose, they claimed in a

[55] On the others who were especially prominent members of this school, Yosef
Trumpeldor, Pinḥas Rutenberg, and Meir Grossman, see D. Vital, *Zionism: The Crucial
Phase* (Oxford, 1987), 136–56 and *passim*.

[56] On NILI see, for example, Eli'ezer Livneh, *NILI: toldoteiha shel he'aza medinit*
(Jerusalem, 1961).

confidential memorandum circulated from Copenhagen, that putting a Jewish Legion of several thousand men at the disposal of one of the powers was likely to contribute seriously either to the actual conquest of Palestine or to that power's eventual decision to back the establishment there of a Jewish state.[57] But the men who gathered in Copenhagen (or the Hague) from time to time avoided a full and open confrontation with the dissidents. The great and damaging controversy over the British East Africa scheme which had divided and somewhat reduced the movement between 1903 and 1905 had not been forgotten. The 'activists', for their part, were unabashed. They were in no doubt about the differences between themselves and the old guard, but they believed there was a very strong case for exposing them in full.

It may be that our leaders have grown old; it may be that Zionism itself has been struck with a sickness of age. Whichever is the case, an operation is called for. . . . Why, we speak almost different languages. You [the established leaders] argue: what will the gentiles say? We for our part want the truth itself. . . . You speak to us of harmony within the family. We reply: Zionism itself and the freedom of our people matter a great deal more than the Organization. . . . You speak to us of discipline, obedience, and silence. Are we to hide? . . . We want to illuminate both Zionism and the Organization, to see that the Idea matches the gravity of the hour.[58]

The leader of the other school of dissidents was a more formidable, if in some ways a more conventional, figure than any of those who belonged to what might be termed the 'military' school. When Chaim Weizmann (1874–1952), first appeared on the Zionist political scene in 1903 as one of Herzl's opponents, there was no immediate reason to think of him as in the running to become the founder's first true successor—no mere *primus inter pares* in the manner of Wolffsohn, Warburg, and later Sokolov but, for the fifteen to twenty years that followed the First World War, Zionism's barely disputed and to very many minds indispensable *leader*. There were other crucial aspects of his career that were unexpected, and indeed fortuitous and paradoxical. He had attained no more than a second-rank position in the Zionist movement before the war as one of the Russian members of the GAC and had compounded his failure to go further by removing himself from the centre of affairs and taking up residence on the periphery of the Jewish world in England. Once there, moreover, he sought hardest of all to establish himself socially and professionally as an academic and industrial chemist—again, crucially for what followed, with mixed results. He was appointed to a teaching and research post at Manchester University. But he was denied a professorship

[57] Copenhagen Liaison Office, confidential circular, 26 Oct. 1915, CZA, L6/18/1.

[58] Meir Grossman, 'Shelom bayit' [domestic harmony], *Di Tribune* (Copenhagen), 8 (5 Feb. 1916).

and he failed to leap the key hurdle to distinction in British science, election to the Royal Society. On the other hand, Weizmann in his prime was a very good chemist, sufficiently expert in his chosen field to be taken on for wartime work by the Ministry of Munitions and the Admiralty where, in the course of time, he made his mark as the inventor of a new, desperately needed method for the production of one of the ingredients of cordite. This led in turn to his deferment from military service (to which he had been called when conscription was introduced) and to substantial monetary reward when the war was over along with the concomitant boon of financial independence. These were not mean achievements for a recent Jewish immigrant who had been granted naturalization only in 1910; and they were to be of enormous help to him once he had decided to cut a path of his own to the great men who ran the country during the war and after in what he had privately determined were Zionism's best interests.

The interesting, wholly speculative question whether Weizmann would have dropped away from an active role in the movement had he done better academically remains. It is not improbable that he would have done so, but unlikely. His loyalty to the Zionist movement was undeviating. He was always drawn powerfully to the public arena where, as he correctly felt, his greatest talents lay. Even in retreat in Manchester he made good use of his time, developing such political contacts as could be reached, chief of whom was C. P. Scott, the celebrated and influential Liberal editor of the *Manchester Guardian*. It was Scott who (repeatedly) brought Weizmann to Lloyd George's attention during the war and who was assiduous in smoothing Weizmann's path to the political centre of Britain in every other way open to him. Still, it was the war itself that altered his priorities most sharply and irreversibly and confirmed him as a political man rather than one of any other variety. Like Jabotinsky and his friends he had grasped very rapidly that, however the war ended, when it was over the world would be transformed. Like them he was prepared to disregard established Zionist policy. He too was temperamentally disposed to striking out on his own—although at first at any rate more discreetly, not to say surreptitiously.

There were two main differences. Weizmann saw nothing objectionable in the establishment of a Jewish Legion to fight alongside the Allied forces in Palestine or anywhere else. But at bottom, like the members of the Actions Committee against which he was to mount his own quieter, deeper, and in the end more thoroughgoing and decisive rebellion, he did not think that the addition of a few thousand Jewish troops to the Allied armies would ever count for a great deal in itself. The other difference lay in the role he was intent on shaping for himself. Much like Herzl a generation earlier, he was a man who contained within himself the indispensable ingredients of political leadership at its most powerful. For the central fact about Weizmann is that from the very first and before all else a combination of huge ambition, almost unshakeable self-confidence, and very great reserves of cunning marked him down for all but the blind to see as one who was likely to go very far in whatever public course he chose finally to pursue. If his rise to very great prominence, when it came, was swift, it should not, that is to say, have been unexpected. And the speed with which his authority was accepted virtually throughout the movement after November 1917 suggests, over and above the political achievement attributed to him (of which more in a moment), that in some sense a great deal had, after all, always been expected of him. It needs to be said too that Weizmann was well served by the quite extraordinary resources of energy on which he was able to draw when he felt called upon to do so—compensated, it is true, perhaps wisely, by periods of puzzling lassitude and withdrawal. He had a great advantage too in his view of the world being practical and empirical: where Herzl had been painfully principled and Motzkin, for example, perpetually insistent on total devotion of person, and often of family too, to the common cause, Weizmann was apt to be easygoing. On the other hand, very unusually for a member of the Russian-Jewish intelligentsia, there was a streak of impenetrable arrogance about him, at all events where other Jews were concerned. That too was to serve him well in his race to the very top, once he had embarked upon it. Of impressive bearing, flexible and persuasive in argument, he had in sum the gifts needed to create and foster the role he was to fashion for himself as, in his time, the uniquely authoritative voice in, but more especially *of* Jewry.

It was a remarkable achievement, the more remarkable for his never having the benefit of *organized* popular support (as David Ben Gurion would have) nor ever seriously seeking to create it. Like Herzl before him, he was to be a leader around whom not a party, but a court was to form. Again, like Herzl and others in the small class of effective national and (for want of a better word) charismatic leaders, Weizmann never doubted that he did really know what was best for the people in whose interests he laboured and that it was therefore a chore to consult them and unnecessary to attend closely to their wishes. And like Herzl, like all supreme national leaders, he would remain to the end of his life a somewhat solitary figure: head and shoulders above the ruck, always somewhat distant from, and independent of, those with whom he chose to labour, although (unlike Herzl, on the whole) not without something like the common touch.

Where Weizmann differed from most leaders of analogous quality was in his ability to alter course, at all events in his early years. The modest name he had made for himself in the movement before the war was as an opponent, rather than as a supporter of Herzl whom he charged, in company with other 'synthetic', 'practical', and 'cultural' Zionists, with being too much wedded to 'diplomacy' and too uninterested in, and unfamiliar with, Jewry in its allegedly true and authentic, namely eastern European form. A sharp critic of Herzl in his lifetime, Weizmann became openly derisive of him once the great man was in his grave. None the less, without ever turning a hair, in the role he would create for himself in Jewish public life when the war came he would follow Herzl's example and teaching with precision. Like Herzl, but with still greater passion and confidence, he looked to 'England the mighty, England the free, the England that looks out over the seas'.[59] And as in Herzl's case, the central basis on which Weizmann believed it was indispensable to proceed comprised three components: personal and confidential political relations, a great and friendly ally under whose auspices the indispensable formal, legally defined, internationally acceptable foothold in Palestine might eventually be gained, and untiring reliance on the root argument that Zionism offered advantages to Jews and gentiles alike. In times of uncertainty overweening self-confidence is, of course, apt to be a source of strength and influence rather than weakness and flexibility, a positive virtue rather than a sin. And, in the event, the speed and thoroughness with which Weizmann's turn-about was accomplished was matched only by the speed with which those who noticed it forgot it. This leaves the interesting question why he succeeded where Herzl had failed—to which the probable answer lies in the unique and unanticipated combination of stress, circumstances, and desperate calculation induced by the war that allowed the Zionists finally to float to the surface. What may be noted, however, was that this would never have happened had the Zionist movement not managed to keep itself alive despite its deeply disappointing failure to make decisive and visible progress. And there lies the indirect evidence, if evidence is needed, of its having come at any rate to *stand* for a real need and to represent a substantial segment of opinion in Jewry after all.

V

There has long been debate on the true origins of the Balfour Declaration of 2 November 1917 in which, with reservations (on which more below), the British government promised to 'use its best endeavours to facilitate' the 'establishment in Palestine of a national home for the Jewish people'.[60] So too on its meaning and intention. For the British

---

[59] *Stenographisches Protokoll der Verhandlungen des IV. Zionisten-Kongresses*, 13–16 Aug. 1900, 5.

[60] The literature on the subject is now immense: one product among many others of the continuing and bitter conflict between Jews and Arabs which it helped to fuel, a function of the attention paid to Weizmann himself, and of the long hiatus between the event

themselves it was an episode among innumerable others in their wartime
diplomacy: at the time reckoned likely to be useful, even necessary; in the
long aftermath bitterly regretted. In its essential content it was a reformulation of the 'Palestine Idea' which the British government under
Asquith and the Foreign Office in particular under Grey had wished to
issue well over a year earlier and which the French government had
insisted that they put aside. Its resurrection under Lloyd George as
Prime Minister (after December 1916) and Balfour as Foreign Secretary
stemmed from fresh considerations, however.

One new set of considerations had little to do with Jewish opinion in
the United States and the hostility of American Jewry to Russia. It had
more to do with Jewish opinion in Russia itself. The question that now
exercised the Allies was how the ever more vociferous calls in Russia to
conclude a separate peace with Germany, even at great territorial cost,
might be countered. The western Allies had no doubt that every conceivable effort to deflect the new, democratic Russia from such a course
should be made. The February 1917 Revolution had finally freed the
Jews from the web of official restrictions and semi-punitive legislation
under which they had lived for so long. The resulting influx of newly
emancipated, now possibly influential Jews into the Russian political
arena suggested to those who had accepted the argument advanced in
favour of the 'Palestine Idea' the year before that it might now be dusted
off and applied to the present issue. 'One of the best methods of counter-
acting Jewish pacifist and socialist propaganda in Russia,' it was thought
in London, 'would be to offer definite encouragement to Jewish nation-

(or events) in question and the release of what appear to be (but then again may not be) the
crucial relevant British and French documents. The classic statement of the view, long
accepted by the Zionists themselves, that the Declaration was very largely Weizmann's
own doing is Sir C. K. Webster's eloquent, often penetrating, but hopelessly dated 'The
Founder of the National Home' in his *The Art and Practice of Diplomacy* (New York, 1962),
113–32. This was punctured for all time by the Mayir Vereté's path-breaking article, 'The
Balfour Declaration and its Makers', *Middle Eastern Studies*, 6, 1 (1970), in which its place
in the weave and woof of British wartime policy and its essential character as an item in
British policy for the purposes of which the Zionists would have had to be invented had
they not been readily to hand was amply demonstrated. Leonard Stein's meticulous, full-
length *The Balfour Declaration* (New York, 1961) continues to command respect for all that
it had undertaken before the full release of documents occurred and that, sadly, it is weaker
than it might have been by reason of Stein's disinclination to impose a clear judgement of
his own at any major point. Isaiah Friedman's *The Question of Palestine* (New York, 1973)
is not as broadly conceived, but is well documented and by no means lacking in a point of
view, as is the second volume of Jehuda Reinharz's indubitably important biography of
Weizmann (*Chaim Weizmann: The Making of a Statesman* (New York, 1992)) despite or
because it seems to have been conceived in something like the respectful spirit in which
Victorian biographers handled Great Men. My own detailed account, based on my own
reading and, in important respects, quite different interpretation of both the wartime
scene as a whole and the relevant documents themselves, will be found in Vital, *Zionism:
The Crucial Phase*.

alist aspirations in Palestine.'[61] This was a very different sort of argument from the one originally advanced in favour of the 'Idea': it concerned Russian Jewry directly, not the view taken of their situation in America. That did not mean that it was entirely without merit. Membership was greater and general pro-Zionist sentiment was stronger in Russia and Poland than anywhere else.[62] On the other hand, the misery and turmoil of the war itself, the prospects opened up by the Provisional government's prompt, blanket annulment of anti-Jewish legislation, and the general domestic political ferment which had seized the country were all of more immediate concern to most Jews, certainly to the modernists among them, than statements, whatever their source, about the eventual fate of distant Palestine.[63] That there was a substantial number of Jews among the Bolsheviks who were loudest and most consistent in their call to leave the war was not in question. But nor was the fact that they, of all people, were deaf to blandishments from London of this or any other kind.[64]

Approval of Zionism accorded neatly, however, with what was now the accepted western view of the matter of nationalities. By this stage of the war there was no question at all in either of the major Allied capitals that when the time came for a general political settlement it would be necessary, as Balfour put it to the cabinet on one occasion, to set about the 'rearranging of the map of Europe in closer agreement with what we rather vaguely call "the principle of nationality" '.[65] Unlike the French, members of the English political class had never been reluctant to think of the Jews of Europe (when they thought of them at all) in terms analogous to those in which they thought of the other submerged nations of the continent, and also increasingly, by natural extension, of the peoples of the Near East as well. They tended very readily, that is to say, to accept that it would be best for all concerned if the Jews too were granted some form of national political and territorial expression. But this, like the application of the 'Palestine Idea' to Russia, served as no more than a contributory factor in the taking of the decision to issue the Declaration,

---

[61] Cecil to Buchanan, 24 Apr. 1917, PRO, FO 371/3053.

[62] The Russian branch of the movement reckoned that after the February Revolution, when it became fully legal, its paid-up membership rose to 140,000 organized in 640 branches. EAC *Protokoll* 29–31 July 1917 at Copenhagen, CZA, L6/64i; and EAC *Bericht* for March to October 1917, CZA, L6/18iii.

[63] The ambassador in Petrograd, to his credit, had little time for the idea. He did not believe there was as much enthusiasm for Zionism as all that among Russian Jews; and, more generally, but also characteristically, he thought that 'the less said about the Jews the better'. Buchanan to Foreign Office, 27 Apr. 1917, ibid.

[64] In any event, the Bolshevik 'October' Revolution which, as chance would have it, fell five days after the Declaration had been published, soon put paid to the notion that support for a Jewish cause might have a bearing, however indirectly, on Russian national policy.

[65] 'The Peace Settlement in Europe', 4 Oct. 1916, PRO, CAB 37/157/7.

the climate of political opinion serving to ease the way somewhat towards what might otherwise have been rejected as quite an excessively bizarre policy decision. The decisive consideration emerges as a function of British imperial policy, newly defined and applied to Palestine itself.

Where Palestine was concerned, foremost in the British government's mind, but most urgently and consistently in that of the new Prime Minister himself—David Lloyd George being very much more aggressively inclined in imperial matters than his predecessor Asquith—was the desire to revise the terms under which Britain and France had planned to divide the Near East between them. In the course of the spring of 1917, with the Ottomans on the point of being expelled from Palestine by an overwhelmingly British force (to which the French had been able to attach no more than token units), there crystallized in official London the view that a way had to be found to 'secure such a modification of the [Sykes–Picot] agreement with France . . . as would give Britain definite and exclusive control over Palestine'.[66] The enclave around Haifa which the British were to receive under the original agreement was now judged too small; and it failed, moreover, to solve the problem of non-British forces being too close to the Suez Canal for comfort. The 'Palestine' which the French and British had agreed in May 1916 to internationalize had therefore to be increased in size (from the Egyptian border all the way up to the Litani river, if possible) and placed under British rule in its entirety. None doubted that this could be achieved only over the strenuous objections of Britain's principal ally; and that the problem of what in London were thought of as French 'pretensions' and 'sentimental' claims to the country—France in the role of Christian Protector of the Levant, for example—was a serious one. It had been with great difficulty that the French had been persuaded to agree to 'international' control of Palestine, comforting themselves with the thought that whatever the structure it would be they themselves who would play the leading role in it. It would now be doubly hard to talk them into abandoning the function of protecting (later 'mandatory') power to the British altogether, British 'pretensions' to the country having more to do with right of conquest and the presence of its troops on the spot in very large numbers than anything else.

Something more was needed therefore if there was not to be an ugly quarrel and it was to this end that the Zionists were thought capable of making a vital, if unconscious contribution. They had their own 'pretensions' to the country. They could be trusted to prefer Britain to France as the protecting power. They could be asked to say as much to the French or to anyone else who might be interested and listening (the Vatican, for example). Zionism, in brief, might serve as that largish fig leaf under

---

[66] Imperial War Cabinet, Report of [Lord Curzon's] Committee on the Terms of Peace, 28 Apr. 1917, PRO, CAB 21/77.

which a gentle, but firm effort to dislodge the French from any part at all in the future management of Palestine could proceed, Weizmann personally functioning as one of the elements of the equation.

Weizmann had rapidly emerged (in British eyes), after trial and close observation, as one who was safe: a 'shrewd observer' in whom the establishment could allow itself to have as much confidence as it could bring itself to place in anyone who was not strictly speaking one of their own.[67] He had especially pleased the government by helping to foil a somewhat inept attempt by Henry Morgenthau, formerly United States ambassador at Constantinople, to negotiate terms on which Turkey would detach itself from the central powers and leave the war—a move that would have upset both British and French plans for the Near East, queered relations with the Arabs if they were to suspect the Allies of negotiating with the Turks, and, as a British summary of the episode was to put it, caused 'anxiety' among the Armenians and the Zionists as well.[68] When news of the Morgenthau mission broke Weizmann was rushed to Gibraltar to head off Morgenthau and talk him out of proceeding with his plan before any real damage was done—a task which he accomplished to everyone's satisfaction, especially that of Sykes.[69] Not long afterwards it was finally concluded in official London not only that he was evidently the coming man in the Zionist movement itself but that he could probably be relied upon when the time came to steer it into appropriate channels—autonomously determined, to be sure, but useful or at any rate harmless from the point of view of the British themselves. The relationship with Weizmann would not be that of patron and client, but symbiotic. But that would suffice.

Very little of what the British had principally in mind was grasped by the Zionists themselves: not at the time, nor indeed for many years to come. Not a word was said to any of those with whom Sykes, Graham, and in due course Balfour himself were in touch, not even to Weizmann. The Jews were to know nothing at this stage of the existence, let alone the ramifications, of the Sykes–Picot Agreement. They were allowed to think that it had been their own powers of persuasion and the evident justice of their cause—forming a convenient combination, it may be said, with what all parties expected to be the equally evident imperial uses of a solidly loyal Jewish settlement to rely upon in a region that was otherwise notorious for its political vagaries—that had brought the British round. No attempt was made to disabuse them of this, the *soft* interpretation of the origins of the Anglo-Zionist link as it were. There were even

---

[67] Minutes by Graham and Balfour, 13 July; and Graham to Hardinge, 23 July 1917, PRO, FO 371/3057.

[68] 'Memorandum on Turkish Peace Overtures', 20 Nov. 1917, PRO, FO 371/3057.

[69] Sykes to Clayton, 22 July 1917, Hull University Library, Sykes Papers, 11/61.

some on the British side, Sir Mark Sykes himself, Leo Amery, and W. G. Ormsby-Gore, for example, who were inclined to think of it in roughly similar terms themselves. Much in the later history of Zionism would hinge, however, on the question of the terms on which the link had actually been established and to what purpose, and on the degree to which they continued to be valid—or, alternatively, were amenable to revalidation. Much in the internal evolution of the movement would hinge on the belief that the central motor force all along had been that of the Zionists. Among the participants who were closest to the scene Aḥad Ha-'Am alone, with his usual preference for sober truth over agreeable illusion, kept a level head after the event. 'In the months preceding the publication of the "Balfour Declaration"', he wrote some years later, 'we were busy in London with formulations of its text for submission to the English government for signature. Several drafts were prepared. . . . But in the end the government issued *its own* formulation and paid little attention to our proposals.'[70]

Within Jewry itself, however, the effect of the Declaration was instantly to pluck the Zionists out of what their critics had long and not all that unreasonably judged to be the never-never land of earnest fantasy in which they had been lodged for the past thirty-five years. It set Zionism down in the real political world once and for all: to fight its corner, to be sure, but now on what approximated to its own terms and equipped at long last with virtually all that up to that point its protagonists had ever seriously asked for. The Zionists, therefore, despite the drift their movement had suffered before the war, had finally gained a march on their rivals among the traditional leaders of Jewry, rabbinic as well as plutocratic. It is important to see how this had occurred and what it chiefly signified.

VI

The people in Whitehall and Downing Street who were concerned with the making of policy were aware that Jewry was deeply divided on many of the relevant issues. Early in 1915 Asquith had circulated confidential memorandums for and (vehemently) against the restoration of the Jews to Palestine as a politically independent (or at least autonomous) nation by Herbert Samuel and Edwin Montagu respectively.[71] Wolf, as we have seen, had repeatedly made clear where the established leaders of the Jewish

---

[70] Emphasis in original. Aḥad Ha-'Am's own editorial footnote (no. 1) to a letter to Sokolov (11 July 1917), printed in *Igrot Aḥad Ha-'Am*, 2nd edn. vi (Tel Aviv, 1960), 74.

[71] Samuel's 'The Future of Palestine', Jan. 1915, PRO, CAB 37/123; and 'Palestine', Mar. 1915, ISA/100/1; and Edwin Montagu's memorandum of 16 Mar. 1915, HLRO, LlGP, C/25/14/1.

community in Great Britain and, of course, he himself stood. And
Weizmann, once he got the ministerial and official ear had done the same
at every opportunity too. There were innumerable references in Whitehall—some bemused, some irritable, all wary—to the internal divisions
in Jewry. 'Mr. L. Wolf cannot be taken as the spokesman of the whole of
Jewry,' Crewe (deputizing for the ailing Grey) minuted on 8 March 1916.
'If and when we are allowed by our allies to say anything worth saying to
the Jews it should not be left to Mr. Lucien Wolf to say it.'[72] 'When Jews
fall out it is none too easy for Christians to decide whether Zionists or
anti-Zionists are in the wrong.'[73] And the Zionist question 'is a matter
upon which the most representative Jews are utterly divided and it seems
to me that H. M. G. may be laying [in] stores of trouble, if they encourage a scheme which commits them to Zionism', another Foreign Office
official minuted on 30 March 1917.[74] Both the Permanent Under-
Secretary (Hardinge) and Balfour himself agreed with him at this point
and it was not long before they had more than prudent reason to do so.

In April Wolf and his people finally caught wind of what was afoot and
hurriedly asked the Foreign Office for clarification. Was it true? Was the
government going to proceed without troubling to ask the Anglo-Jewish
community what it thought of the scheme? That would be 'a great injustice' and 'a very serious mischief would result, . . . more especially as the
gentlemen with whom His Majesty's Government have so far been in
negotiation are all foreign Jews, having no quality to speak for the native
Jews of the United Kingdom with whom, for the most part, they do not
co-operate in the affairs of the community'.[75] There was no way of avoiding a row, and the Conjoint Committee, in its desperation, decided on 17
May to precipitate one by issuing a formal statement of its position for
publication in *The Times*. This was answered, as was inevitable, by com-
munications to *The Times* from the Zionist side, then by further statements from supporters of the position taken by the Conjoint Foreign
Committee, and, by way of capping it all, a leading article by the editors
of *The Times* themselves in which they came down on the Zionist side.
The round ended with a bitter and unusually well-attended debate in the
Board of Deputies of British Jews on the content, but equally on the
propriety, of the CFC having published its views without consulting its
parent bodies in the first place, followed in turn by the collapse of the
CFC itself. All this had proceeded before the public gaze, contrary to
precedent and traditional instinct. A second, parallel debate, almost as

---

[72] PRO, FO 371/2817.
[73] Lancelot Oliphant, the Foreign Office's chief specialist on Jewish questions, on 10
Dec. 1916, PRO, FO 371/2817, fo. 163.
[74] PRO, FO 371/3101/65760.
[75] Wolf to Oliphant, 21 Apr. 1917, PRO, FO 371/3092.

heated in character as the one conducted in public, but one which the official establishment could under no circumstances ignore because it had been initiated by a member of the cabinet itself, Edwin Montagu, the Secretary of State for India, was being conducted meanwhile within the inner recesses of government itself.

None of the issues was new nor, in their essentials, were the arguments offered. For the CFC there were two that counted: that Judaism was 'a religious' system to which it was anachronistic to ascribe national, let alone political significance; and that Zionism was likely to turn the settled and established Jews in Britain, as well as all those who enjoyed a similar status in other countries, into 'strangers in their native lands'. The Zionists denied both propositions. As regards the first, they claimed that most Jews and most non-Jews had always thought, and continued to think to this day, that the Jews did constitute a nationality. As regards the second, they argued that it was totally without foundation: those who had identified themselves with the countries in which they lived would continue to be loyal to them as before. It was not so much the content as the fury and—in the case of the anti-Zionists the pathos too—which the protagonists invested in them that was remarkable about these exchanges, especially when they were conducted in private. Claude Montefiore of the Anglo-Jewish Association 'begged' Lord Milner, a member of the War Cabinet, not to 'commit ourselves to Sokoloff or Weizmann'[76] and followed up his talk with Milner with a written plea 'to trust your own fellow citizens, who, at all events, are Englishmen through and through, and whose sons are serving in England's armies, rather than foreigners who have no love for England, and who, if the fortunes of war went wrong, would throw her over in a trice and hurry over to Berlin to join the majority of the Colleagues'.[77] Edwin Montagu was more agitated and vehement still. And it was he, a minister, privy to a good deal of what had transpired and present at the War Cabinet by special invitation when the 'Palestine Idea' in its latest form was discussed, who compelled the government—of which he was now the only Jew of ministerial rank—to consider the matter as he saw it in some depth. Montefiore, Wolf, and other opponents of the scheme could be put off. Montagu could not be, either constitutionally or, more simply, as a colleague—the more so as he was at very great pains to fight it out. He submitted two formal cabinet papers, one of them entitled 'The Anti-Semitism of the Present Government', the other a demi-official letter to Lord Robert Cecil which he had printed and circulated to his colleagues as well. He arranged for each member of the cabinet to be supplied with a great

[76] Milner to Cecil, 17 May 1917, PRO, FO 800/198.
[77] Montefiore to Milner, 17 May 1917, CZA, A77/3B.

quantity of polemical anti-Zionist material.[78] He sought to show in some detail that Jewish opinion was not pro-Zionist, that the rabbis were divided on the subject, that there were conclusive local political grounds for a Jewish Palestine to be rated wholly impracticable, that the Declaration contemplated by the government would result in the citizens of 'every country' being driven out to Palestine, and why it was the case anyway that 'there is no Jewish nation'. He wrote to the Prime Minister that he believed 'firmly, that if you make a statement about Palestine as the national home for Jews, every anti-Semitic organisation and news-paper will ask what right a Jewish Englishman, with the status at best of a naturalized foreigner, has to take a foremost part in the Government of the British Empire' and he hinted at his resignation in the event of the Declaration being issued.[79] He could not possibly be ignored. Ministers were provided with a Foreign Office paper that sought to refute his argu-ments one by one.[80] And Balfour, in cabinet, painted the larger picture as he claimed to see it. There was

nothing inconsistent between the establishment of a Jewish national focus in Palestine and the complete assimilation and absorption of Jews into the nation-ality of other countries. Just as English emigrants to the United States became, either in the first or subsequent generations, American nationals, so, in the future, should a Jewish citizenship be established in Palestine, would Jews become either Englishmen, Americans, Germans, or Palestinians.

In any event,

What was at the back of the Zionist Movement was the intense national con-sciousness held by certain members of the Jewish race. They regarded themselves as one of the great historic races of the world, whose original home was Pales-tine, and those Jews had a passionate longing to regain once more this ancient national home.[81]

This was consistent, implicitly, with the terms in which Balfour, then Prime Minister, had justified the presentation before Parliament of the Aliens Bill (1905) that broke the long-standing tradition of virtually free entry of refugees, now Jewish in the main, into Great Britain: 'The medieval treatment of the Jews was a permanent stain on European annals; and he [Balfour] agreed that if they could do anything to wipe it

---

[78] Lord Swaythling (Edwin Montagu's brother) to Major L. Storr of the Cabinet Office, 10 Oct. 1917, PRO, CAB 21/58.

[79] 'The Anti-Semitism of the Present Government', 23 Aug., PRO, CAB 24/24; Montagu to Cecil, 14 Sept., PRO, CAB 24/27; 'Zionism', 9 Oct., PRO CAB 24/28; Montagu to Lloyd George, 4 Oct. 1917, HLRO, LlGP F/39/3/30. Montagu did not resign.

[80] 'Note on the Secretary of State for India's Paper on the Anti-Semitism of the Gov-ernment', n.d. [end of Aug.? 1917], PRO, FO 371/3083.

[81] War Cabinet 245, 4 Oct. 1917, PRO, CAB 21/58.

out, if they could do anything to diminish its effects in the present time, it would be their bounden duty to do it.' Balfour agreed, he had told the House of Commons, that the anti-Semitic spirit 'disgraced a great deal of modern politics in other countries of Europe and that the Jews of England were a valuable element in the community'. But he thought too that it was possible to imagine conditions in which 'it would not be to the advantage of the civilisation of the country that there should be an immense body of persons who, however patriotic, able, and industrious, however much they threw themselves into the national life, still, by their own action, remained a people apart', not merely holding a religion that differed from that of the vast majority of their fellow countrymen, 'but only intermarried among themselves'.[82]

There was greater concern in the cabinet, however, about the likely response to the proposed Declaration in France and the United States, but on that score the cabinet was assured that all was well, the Zionists themselves having been helpful in this regard, Sokolov in Paris,[83] Louis Brandeis in Washington.[84] A great deal of attention was paid to the precise wording of the Declaration itself and the text was repeatedly revised. 'Jewish people' was substituted for 'Jewish race'. The original 'His Majesty's Government accepts the principle that Palestine should be *reconstituted* as *the* National Home of the Jewish people' became the substantially weaker 'His Majesty's Government views with favour the establishment *in* Palestine of *a* national home for the Jewish people'. The matter of the true seriousness and popularity of Zionism, the known poverty of Palestine itself (as Curzon stated: 'A less propitious seat for the future Jewish race could not be imagined'), and the question of the country's other inhabitants (Curzon asking: What was to happen to them? Were they to be got rid of?) were all brought up as the cabinet moved towards a decision. Balfour, Sykes providing the arguments,

---

[82] 10 July 1905. Hansard, *Parliamentary Debates*, 4th series, vol. 149, cols. 154–5.

[83] The terms of French acquiescence as delivered to Sokolov deserve to be quoted in full: 'You have been good enough to outline the project to which you are devoting your efforts, the object of which is to develop Jewish colonization in Palestine. You believe that if circumstances permit and the independence of the Holy Places is assured, it would be in the interests of justice and reparation to render assistance to the re-birth, under the protection of the Allied Powers, of Jewish nationality on this land from which the people of Israel were expelled so many centuries ago. | The Government of France which entered the present war to defend a people that had been unjustly attacked, and which pursues the struggle to assure the triumph of right over force, cannot but feel sympathy for your cause, the triumph of which is linked to that of the Allies.' Jules Cambon to Sokolov, 4 June 1917, PRO, FO 371/3058, fo. 153.

[84] On 19 Oct. 1917, after much uncertainty, the Foreign Office was informed that 'Colonel House put [the] formula before [the] President, who approves it, but asks that no mention of his approval shall be made before His Majesty's Government make [the] formula public, as he has arranged that American Jews shall then ask for his approval, which he will publicly give.' Cabinet memorandum on 'Palestine' by the Secretary of State for the Colonies, 13 Mar. 1923.

assured his colleagues that the Jews would be able to work out their own salvation there and were anxious to do so. And such anxiety as there was about the fate of the existing Arab population was met by the insertion of a clause affirming that 'nothing shall be done which may prejudice the civil and religious rights of the existing non-Jewish communities'. No one suggested that the *political* rights of the 'existing non-Jewish communities' deserved discussion, let alone assurance. It may be presumed that Arab political rights were considered to have been adequately dealt by the terms of the rest of the Sykes–Picot Agreement under which most of the huge territory from which the Turks were to be expelled would be allotted to a semi-independent Arab state (or states) under a combination of French and British protection. It was rather to the question of the political rights and status of the Jews—not Jews in Palestine, but Jews elsewhere—that the attention of the cabinet had been particularly drawn. And what had become clear as the process moved towards a conclusion was that Lloyd George's cabinet had no choice but to adjudicate what many of the notables of contemporary Jewry regarded as the gravest internal issue to have arisen within Jewry since the onset of the emancipation. To that end the cabinet decided to ascertain the views of 'representative persons in Anglo-Jewry', both Zionists and those opposed to Zionism.

This last was a curious exercise. It was conducted by the Cabinet Office in great secrecy and with dispatch. A list of ten major figures was drawn up, Montagu being asked to offer names of opponents of Zionism, Weizmann to suggest supporters. Each was supplied with the draft text of the Declaration (still in its penultimate form) and, 'in view of the apparent divergence of opinion expressed on the subject by the Jews themselves', to comment upon it. The replies were soon in. Six opinions were favourable.[85] Four were hostile.[86] Of course, it was therefore anything but a systematic sounding of opinion. As a preliminary to a (still secret) cabinet decision, perhaps it could not be. It is probable that it was intended principally as a way of appeasing Montagu or, at the very least, taking some of the wind out of his sails. And indeed, thereafter, there was not much he could do or say, the more so as one of those he had named as a probable opponent of the Zionists (Stuart Samuel) had replied in unexpectedly favourable (if hardly enthusiastic) terms. Nor was there much that was especially new in any of the replies which, together with some additional material on the state of the Zionist movement in Russia and the United States, were submitted to the cabinet on 17 October. After

[85] Herbert Samuel, the Chief Rabbi (Joseph Hertz), Lord (Lionel Walter) Rothschild, the new president of the Board of Deputies (Sir Stuart Samuel, who was rather more reserved than the others), Weizmann, and Sokolov.

[86] Sir Philip Magnus (of the League of British Jews), Claude Montefiore, L. L. Cohen (chairman of the Jewish Board of Guardians), and Montagu himself.

further minor, technical delays the matter was brought before the cabinet for a final decision on 31 October.

Balfour rehearsed that part of the case for the Declaration (in its amended form) that pertained to the Jews. There was no doubt, he informed his colleagues, that 'the vast majority of Jews in Russia and America, as, indeed, all over the world, now appeared to be favourable to Zionism'. Accordingly, 'if we could make a declaration favourable to such an idea, we should be able to carry on extremely useful propaganda both in Russia and America'. As for 'the difficulty felt with regard to the future position of Jews in Western countries', why rather than hindering the process of assimilation the evidence was that the establishment of a Jewish National Home would go far to hasten the process. There was no argument. Montagu, on his way to India, was not present. Balfour sailed over the precise and careful written arguments that Montagu, Monte-fiore, Magnus, and L. L. Cohen had submitted with his inimitable facil-ity for turning a fine and confident phrase. Anglo-French rivalry in the Near East and the British strategic interest in Palestine went unmen-tioned. The Foreign Secretary had his way and the publication of the notoriously unwieldy and ambiguous statement of official intent on the Jews and on Palestine was authorized.[87]

The more I study it, the more disastrous it seems to me [was Lucien Wolf's bit-ter reaction]. The saving clause about our political status almost suggests that it is a mere technicality. It sounds hollow by the side of the declaration that our national home is in Palestine. Henceforth we are only temporary sojourners here enjoying a political status which we obtained by some oversight and which will not be disturbed, but which is none the less artificial. What a triumph for the anti-Semites. What are we to say in the future, when Dmo[w]ski and Bratianu propose to treat the Jews as foreigners and deny them political rights? I suppose we shall have to call on the British Government to give them protection as nationals of Palestine.[88]

Zionism, of course, was a cause. But it was not a British cause. The view taken of it in British political and official circles—along with the view taken of the Jews and their affairs generally—varied from minister to minister and from official to official: approval of a vague kind here, a good deal of scepticism there, some lightly veiled hostility elsewhere. What none doubted, however, was that the only proper issue before the

---

[87] War Cabinet 261, 31 Oct. 1917, PRO, CAB 21/58. The 'Balfour Declaration' in its final, famous form read: 'His Majesty's Government views with favour the establish-ment in Palestine of a national home for the Jewish people, and will use its best endeav-ours to facilitate the achievement of this object, it being clearly understood that nothing shall be done which may prejudice the civil and religious rights of existing non-Jewish communities in Palestine, or the rights and political status enjoyed by Jews in any other country.'

[88] Wolf to C. G. Montefiore, 12 Nov. 1917, CZA, A77/3b.

government was whether Zionism would serve Britain's purposes. And it is to the British ministers' belief that it would—however extraordinary this may appear in retrospect—that everything that preceded and much that for a while at least followed 2 November 1917 was due. But there were features of the way in which the cabinet arrived at its decision, especially the fact that it inquired into, and then—to its own satisfaction, at all events—adjudicated an intense confrontation between major schools of social thought within Jewry itself, that deserve special attention.

The immediate and lasting effect of the Declaration was to tip the balance between the various contending schools in Jewry in the Zionists' favour. In itself, this was no more than an additional, but striking illustration of the rule that the standing of any major group within Exilic Jewry is ultimately a function of its standing *vis-à-vis* the relevant ruling power—and, through the latter's mediation, *vis-à-vis* the world of real political power in general. So far as the Zionists were concerned, if the Balfour Declaration meant anything at all, it meant that they stood to obtain virtually everything that Herzl had asked for and considerably more than any of his immediate successors had hoped to receive: a 'charter' formally establishing rights of entry and settlement in Palestine; international recognition of the Zionist Organization as licit representatives of the Jewish people—the latter, it is true, being left undefined and the question of the status of other, possibly equally licit contestants for that role left unresolved. It was therefore unquestionably a huge step forward towards at least *de facto* primacy among all such organizations and institutions as sought to play a role of more than local significance. They could now function in their people's interests in fact, and in name too, on the world stage. Thus in the abstract and in symbolic terms. Thus in practice too.

From this point on the Zionists would have two inestimable advantages. One lay in the fact that for some years to come they would enjoy the open backing of one of the leading world powers and, to a certain extent, the backing of other governments as well, notably those that had been Great Britain's wartime allies. Faced with what had become official policy in the countries which they inhabited and to which they owed primary political loyalty, this tended to cool the ardour of those in France, the United States, and Great Britain itself who continued to oppose Zionism in all circumstances.[89] The other feature of the Zionist Organization's new situation was that Britain's backing (while it lasted) led first

---

[89] Even in the United States where Louis Marshall of the anti-Zionist American Jewish Committee warned David Philippson, one of the leading lights of the equally anti-Zionist religious Reform movement, that 'To combat Zionism at this time is to combat the Government of England, France and Italy, and to some extent our Government in so far as its political interests are united with those of the nations with which it has joined in fighting the curse of autocracy' (CZA, 264/26–8).

to the grant of a poorly defined, but still unquestioned *locus standi* in
Palestine while the country was still under military occupation. Later,
under the terms of the League of Nations Mandate for Palestine, its status
and authority would be reconfirmed and very greatly strengthened by
the creation of the 'Jewish Agency for Palestine' which would be virtually
indistinguishable in practice from its own Executive (the pre-war Smaller
Actions Committee). This Jewish Agency/Zionist Executive would
then be entitled in turn to a degree of social and economic, but above all
political, autonomy of a degree and significance—and also promise—
such as Jews had not known since Roman times in Palestine. Less than
two decades later, when a British Royal Commission (formed to 'ascertain
the underlying causes of the disturbances which broke out in Palestine in
the middle of April [1936]')[90] examined its function, it found that,

Speaking generally, it may be said that the Jewish Agency has used to the fullest
extent the position conferred on it by the Mandate. In the course of time it has
created a complete administrative apparatus. This powerful and effective organization amounts, in fact, to a Government existing side by side with the Mandatory Government.[91]

No other organization or institution in Jewry was remotely of this
class, nor sought to be. No Jewish community other than the one in
Palestine had, or was likely to have, what distinguished the *yishuv*, namely
a *government* of its own in the strict sense which the authors of the Royal
Commission's *Report* had in mind. In the Zionists' offer of a complete
and internally consistent alternative to every one of the other forms of
Jewish life that had evolved in the course of the Exile there had always
been implicit a threat of lasting structural differentiation (and therefore
disunity in Jewry). The Balfour Declaration went far to convert this
threat into probable reality. It opened the way to the great bifurcation in
Jewry which has been one of its dominant features ever since the First
World War.

What, contrary to appearances, the Declaration failed to do was to
move the most fundamental of all questions in the public life of the Jews
closer to the centre of debate and, therefore, to resolution. The great
unresolved issue in Jewry remained as before that of the ultimate and
decisive operative principle on which questions of public interest turned.
Ought it to be essentially abstract and collective in character? Ought the
highest of all priorities be ascribed to the continuity and collective identity of the Jewish people as such and as a whole and the preservation of its
national, cultural, and religious tradition? Or ought the resolution of all
serious questions be geared before all else to the private needs, interests,

[90] i.e. the Arab Rebellion that was to last until 1939 and be transmuted in the course
of the following decade into a full-scale Arab–Jewish war.
[91] Palestine Royal Commission, *Report*, Cmd. 5479 (London, 1937), 174.

and desires of the Jews themselves as individual men, women, and children
to whose personal safety, welfare, and dignity all other considerations
were ultimately to be held subordinate? Neither alternative entirely
excluded the other, but it was the latter that, in the last resort, had ruled
the minds of Herzl and Nordau, as it had ruled Pinsker's before them,
and, in his odd way, Zangwill's too. Their successors did not go so far as
to deny that the wants and fate of the individual were rightly considerations of high priority. But they had not accepted that these were of a
class to which all other considerations had finally to be subordinated. And
it was this deeply traditional outlook on the affairs of their people that
implicitly, but fundamentally, cut them off from other modernists. If, in
general, modernism in Jewry seemed to promise a shift of emphasis
towards the pragmatic end of the stick and to an overriding concern for
the Jews as living individuals rather than as, in the final analysis, dutiful
bearers of an inherited culture, so far as the new leaders of the Zionists
were concerned the most that can be said is that the issue awaited clarification and resolution. On this central question the new men in the Zionist movement, undoubted modernists and, as triumphant beneficiaries of
the British policy decision encapsulated in the Balfour Declaration,
undoubted victors in a decades-long argument with their opponents,
were almost hopelessly in two minds. 'We must not be told as the Poles
are trying to do,' Weizmann wrote to the foreign editor of *The Times* only
a year later, ' "You have your Palestine, clear out of here!" [For] if so, we
shall have all the miserable refugees who will be driven out of Poland,
Galicia, Rumania, etc., at the doors of Palestine. We shall be swamped in
Palestine and shall never be able to set up a community worth having
there.'[92] And on the other hand there were the voices that called the
movement's attention, and equally the attention of all Jews, to the real
condition in eastern Europe in different terms, a different style, and,
implicitly, very different implications. There were repeated warnings
throughout the war of horrors to come. Writing to the Zionist Central
Committee in May 1916 on the strength of the reports coming to him
out of Russia, Motzkin described the picture as he saw it: four and a half
million defenceless and desperate persons, subject to the mercy of every
lowly jack-in-office, liable to be put before courts martial on the slightest suspicion and dispatched to Siberia or worse at the merest whim of
those set over them, a people drained of hope for an improvement in
their condition, terrified of what was in store for them.

The general feeling is that after the war, however it may end, the catastrophe that
will occur will be without parallel in history. There is a search for a scapegoat on
whom all the mistakes, the blunders and the failures can be laid and it is obvious

---

[92] Letter to H. Wickham Steed, 30 Nov. 1918. *The Letters and Papers of Chaim Weizmann*, no. 45, ix. 50.

that the Jews will be chosen to play that role. There is no interest now in the possessions of the Jews, rather in their lives; and if the pogrom-campaign now being diligently and methodically prepared does take place it is possible that to the bloodstained pages of the history of the Jews there will be appended the bloodiest.[93]

---

[93] Motzkin to Berlin, no. 1142, 12 May 1916, CZA, L6/88.

8
Peace

I

THE formal and unambiguous grant of civil rights to all citizens decreed by the Russian Provisional government on 20 March 1917,[1] was confirmed in the aftermath of the subsequent October Revolution. As a constitutional principle it remained unquestioned under subsequent Bolshevik rule; and the consequences for the lives of those Jews who now found themselves in what would be the Soviet Union were dramatic. Overt and unashamed (as opposed to allusive and deliberately subliminal) dissemination of anti-Semitic ideas and programmes was forbidden. Pogroms (on which more below), once the civil war was over, became a thing of the past. The massive entry of Jews into civil and military state service[2] from which they had been totally excluded from office of virtually any kind in the past was both revolutionary in spirit and revolutionary in its social consequences. So, of course, was the notorious and still more remarkable presence of Jews in the true centres of power in the USSR, the party and the secret police. Their numbers were never as great as was commonly thought either within or without Russia to be the case, but they were not negligible, at all events at the outset. In 1917 five of the twenty-one members of the Communist Party's Central Committee were Jews,[3] and it has been estimated that at the early post-1917 party congresses between 15 and 20 per cent of the delegates were Jewish.[4] Later, these numbers would fall absolutely and proportionately. Once Stalin's hold over party and state had been consolidated they would be diminished drastically. But they would never be totally eliminated. Admission of Jews to lesser, but still

---

[1] 'All restrictions established by existing legislation on the rights of citizens of Russia by reason of their adherence to a particular religious denomination or sect or by reason of nationality are abolished.' There was no specific reference to Jews.

[2] G. K. (Sergo) Ordzhonikidze, People's Commissar for Workers' and Peasants' Inspection, reported to the Fifteenth Congress of the Communist Party in 1927 that Jews filled 10.3 per cent of all administrative posts in Moscow, 22.6 per cent of civil service posts in the Ukrainian SSR, and 30.6 per cent in Byelorussian SSR. William Korey, 'The Legal Position of Soviet Jewry: A Historical Enquiry', in Lionel Kochan (ed.), *The Jews in Soviet Russia since 1917* (Oxford, 1978), 92.

[3] Sokolnikov, Sverdlov, Trotsky, Uritskii, and Zinoviev. Kamenev, with one Jewish parent, is commonly added to their number.

[4] Zvi Y. Gitelman, *Jewish Nationality and Soviet Politics* (Princeton, 1972), 106.

important governmental, industrial, and academic, scientific, and literary and cultural institutions, an equally prominent feature of the early years, would be cut down too in the course of time. But it would never be entirely stopped; and it would never be held—as it had been under the Tsars—to be intrinsically unthinkable that Jews be civil or military servants of the state. Nor was the freedom Jews had been granted in the spring of 1917 to settle virtually anywhere in the country, but most notably in Moscow and Leningrad,[5] and to engage in any profession of their choosing formally rescinded. In sum, the abolition of the Pale of Settlement along with the many hundreds of laws and ordinances which had in one way or another constricted and humiliated the Jews in virtually all their affairs since the time of Catherine the Great remained a continuing, and for those who remembered the bloody-minded rigidity of the old regime, a valued fact of their lives.[6]

Still, one cannot properly speak of the *emancipation* of the Jews—or indeed of anyone else—in the slave state Lenin and his colleagues and their immediate successors proceeded to erect upon the bodies of the peasants, workers, and miscellaneous city-dwellers (some 'proletarians', some 'bourgeois') of all the various races, classes, denominations, and nationalities contained within the reconstructed Russian empire. For one thing, what actually transpired was a change in the internal structure and quality of Russian Jewry and in their attributes as a component of the Russian body politic as a whole that bore a striking similarity to those to which the old regime in Russia itself—in its more clear-minded moments, at all events—had always aimed. Nicholas I would have understood and probably approved both of what the Bolsheviks intended and, in the event, of what they accomplished.

Driving the Russian state, as before, was the totalitarian imperative: the imposition of near-absolute social control through equalization and standardization of all social and *a fortiori* political institutions. In this respect the purpose and spirit moving Bolshevik Russia had marked affinities with what in Nazi Germany would be termed *Gleichschaltung*, the principal difference being that the Bolshevik version of *Gleichschaltung* was pushed through with greater efficacy and (the matter of the Jews excepted) vastly more far-reaching and deadly results. Unlike the Nazi rulers of Germany, the new Bolshevik rulers of Russia neither sought alliances with any of their potential rivals nor made any except very briefly and as a preliminary to crushing and disposing of them as soon as that might be possible. Again unlike the Nazis, the original sources of

---

[5] The Jewish population of Leningrad, 17,000 in 1897, had reached 52,000 in 1923 and 84,000 in 1926; that of Moscow was 8,000 in 1897, 86,000 in 1923, and 131,000 in 1926.

[6] Except in the very last stages of Stalin's life and career.

their onslaught on Jewish society in particular were not specific to the Jews themselves, but lay with the terms which Bolsheviks—much like contemporary social democrats of all categories—conceived of as being applicable to society as a whole. In principle and to a considerable extent in practice too, the attack mounted soon after the seizure of power on the religious functionaries and institutions of Russian Jewry—and therefore, as was plainly the intention, on the religious practices of the Jewish man or woman in the street as well—derived from the same ideological sources and was designed to achieve the same political ends as the simultaneous and more formidable attack launched against the Russian Orthodox Church and on the religious practices of the Russian faithful generally. The denigration and dispossession of the Jewish propertied class was part and parcel of the offensive mounted against the Russian propertied class as a whole. Once the Bolsheviks had seized power, Jewish political parties were bound to go under along with all other political parties. The Bund and the socialist Zionists were fated to be crushed along with all other distinctively national (especially Ukrainian) offshoots of the major socialist parties. And what was left of the Jewish centrist groups would be flushed away with the Socialist Revolutionaries, the Mensheviks, and the surviving remnants of the Kadet Party for essentially the same reasons. The mainstream Zionists had to go too: damned in Bolshevik eyes by the strong support they had gained for themselves within the Jewish community, damned again as 'bourgeois' and 'chauvinist', and damned once more by their having important foreign connections and by the fact that the locus of their purposes and interests lay, unpardonably, outside Russia altogether.

That all this was bound to be perceived by the Bolsheviks as a small but necessary part of the general clearing of the decks that had to precede the installation of a full totalitarian system followed from the strength and distribution of the Jewish parties revealed in the course of the elections to the Constituent Assembly held in late November 1917. Even when no allowance was made for the fact that the Bund, the mainstream Zionists, and the several varieties of socialist Zionists had refrained from presenting candidates in *every* constituency where the Jewish vote was likely to be significant, and for it being obvious that Jews had not given their votes exclusively to specifically Jewish parties, the achievement was too substantial to be ignored. It could be seen, for example, that in what was left of the heart of the former Pale of Settlement (Poland and a good part of the other fifteen provinces being still under German and Austrian occupation at the time) the political sympathies and loyalties of the Jewish population were quite massively behind *Jewish* parties. Half a million votes went to the Jewish parties: a little under 2.5 per cent of all votes cast. But, as Table 8.1 shows, in some provinces the vote for Jewish parties was greater in absolute terms than *total* popular support for the Bolsheviks.

For all these reasons, there could be no doubt in the Bolshevik mind that organized and distinctively Jewish political opinion would have to be confronted and neutralized: thus on the general grounds of the need, as they saw it, to make a clean sweep throughout their new dominions, but also for the more particular reason that the Jewish parties had all along been among those most vigorously opposed to Bolshevik rule. But clearing away organized political parties and political activists by proscription, arrest, imprisonment, exile, and summary execution did not dispose of the people itself.

TABLE 8.1. *Elections to the Russian Constituent Assembly*[7]

	Socialist-Revolutionaries	Bolsheviks	Ukrainian parties	Jewish parties	Total vote	Jewish parties as a percentage of total vote
Kiev	19,201	59,413	1,256,271	122,386	1,627,727	7.5
Minsk	181,673	579,087	—	76,110	917,246	8.3
Podolia	10,170	27,540	656,116	76,407	830,260	9.2
Poltava	198,437	64,460	760,022	40,624	1,149,256	3.5
Volhynia	27,575	35,612	569,044	55,967	804,208	7.0

Lenin had laid down long before the Revolution that the idea of a separate Jewish people was untenable scientifically and reactionary politically. He accepted that there was indeed a Jewish Problem. But he saw the solution to it, if the Jews were not to remain in total social isolation, as one that turned on assimilation into the general population. It was to this that the Party should therefore bend its efforts. This accorded with the wider social democratic claim, that all nationalities were destined ultimately to be dissolved; and that all their members would end by being integrated into a single, *class*-defined people—a Soviet people as it would later be called. It might be necessary to make interim concessions to the so-called 'territorial' nations—the Ukrainians, the Byelorussians, Georgians, and the Muslim peoples of the Caucasus and Central Asia—and a form of national-territorial existence allowed them. But the *principle* of dissolution all round as both the necessary and the desirable end was not affected thereby. Least of all was this the case where the Jews were concerned. They were not a true nation anyway. Certainly, they were not a 'territorial'

---

[7] Source: O. H. Radkey, *The Election to the Russian Constituent Assembly of 1917* (Cambridge, Mass., 1950). The Assembly, the first and last democratically elected body in Russian history before the collapse of the Soviet Union in 1989, was closed down by the Bolsheviks after a single sitting.

nation.[8] They were, Lenin wrote on another occasion, 'a caste'.[9] He conceded that, caste or nation, they were not a negligible quantity, not in absolute numbers, least of all when their massive presence in the urban, labouring population of the western provinces was taken into account.[10] There was no question, therefore, of their being allowed to drift, unharnessed and untouched by the plans the Leninists had in store for the population as a whole. And then, beyond the general grounds for dealing with them there were pressing and immediate reasons for action in the Jewish sector. There needed to be a means of operating politically in those territories that were still under German occupation, which the new regime was far from abandoning, and in which the Jewish population was both substantial and of an especially urban–proletarian character. It was necessary, therefore, to organize them. On the other hand, there could be no question of defying the Germans so blatantly as to assign the task to an organ of the new Soviet government. Objections, if any, to operations by the *Party* would, it was reckoned, be easier to counter. In any event, one way or another, both within the borders agreed upon with the Germans at Brest-Litovsk or beyond them, the Jews had to be dealt with and brought into the fold.

The difficulties were evident. While there was no doubting that, as a group, they were likely to be quite docile politically, it was not to be doubted either that they would, as was their wont, be enormously resistant to outright pressures to conform to the new social model. Secondly, as was now borne in upon the magnates of the Party, the politically minded Yiddish-speaking Jews of the western provinces of Russia had until now been left effectively to the Zionists and the Bund; and the Communist Party itself lacked cadres that were equipped to deal with them even had they desired to do so. If the affairs of these people were now to be handled by the Party itself, the handlers had to be people who knew them and were capable, at the very least, of speaking to them in their own language both figuratively and literally. Such people were rare among the Bolsheviks. The operative conclusion, not to be stated in so many words, but undeniable none the less, was that the argument on which the Bund had always founded its claim to a free hand in the Jewish

[8] Stalin's famous definition of a nation (which would be much relied upon by communists in all parts in the course of time) accorded very well with Lenin's view: 'A nation is a historically constituted, stable community of people, formed on the basis of a common language, territory, economic life, and psychological make-up manifested in a community of culture' ('Marxism and the National Question', Jan. 1913).

[9] 'Critical remarks on the National Question', 1913.

[10] It is probable that Jewish components of the populations of the Ukraine and Byelorussia at this time were 1.5 million (or 7 per cent) and c.0.5 million (or 10 per cent) respectively. But the Jews accounted for between 25 and 40 per cent of the urban population of the major cities of the Ukraine and somewhat under half the urban population of Byelorussia.

sector within the social democratic movement, namely that it alone was equipped to propagate the faith among the Jewish urban proletariat and organize them, had been a valid one all along. It followed that a new, necessarily more pragmatic approach to the matter of the Jewish population had to be resolved upon if anything useful was to be done and it was characteristic of the speed and efficacy with which Lenin and his colleagues were capable of functioning that little time was lost doing so. In February 1918 a Commissariat for Jewish Affairs was established within the new People's Commissariat for the Affairs of Nationalities (under Stalin as People's Commissar) and Semyon Dimanshtein (1886–1937) was appointed to head it. Dimanshtein himself was an Old Bolshevik. He had joined the Party in 1904 and been a staunch Leninist (and an opponent of the Bund and all it stood for) ever since. But he was a rare bird among the Jewish veterans of the Party. Quite unlike such totally Russified Jews as Trotsky and Sverdlov, he had undergone formal training as a rabbinical student at a distinguished *yeshiva* and was well versed in Jewish Law and in the Hebrew and Yiddish languages—for which, it seems, despite his firm Marxist-Leninist outlook, he was not without some residual sympathy.[11] Shortly afterwards, in parallel with the Commissariat as an organ of government, it was agreed to establish Jewish sections of the Party too, known in Soviet newspeak from this point on by the generic term *Evsektsia* (in the singular).

The primary assignment of all these new institutions was to bring Russian Jewry under effective social control. They had, Dimanshtein informed them on the first grand occasion on which the future activists and agitators had been gathered for instructions, 'the technical task' of disseminating propaganda among Jewish workers in an appropriate form, namely in the workers' own language, and the political task of 'establishing the dictatorship of the proletariat in the Jewish street'. But they needed to understand the limited terms on which their campaign was to be conducted:

The new Jewish sections will be composed of the new comrades who are now joining the Party. Old Bolsheviks, in contrast, will undoubtedly remain in the ranks of the general [i.e. all-Russian] Party. We shall therefore have to see to it that those who join the [Jewish] sections are not drawn to nationalist tendencies of any kind. . . . We are not a special or independent party. We are no more than a part of the Communist Party that comprises Jewish workers. And being internationalists, we do not set ourselves national tasks of any kind, only proletarian-class tasks, exclusively. While we ourselves speak a different language [i.e. Russian], we are under an obligation to meet the intellectual and cultural needs

---

[11] Y. Berger-Barzilai, *Ha-tragediya shel ha-mahapekha ha-sovyetit* (Tel Aviv, 1968), 31–3. After the dissolution of the *Evsektsia* in 1930 Dimanshtein was relegated to official obscurity for a while. Later, in 1937, along with so many other Old Bolsheviks, he was shot.

of the Jewish masses in their own language. But we are not devotees of Yiddish: it will not, so far as we are concerned, be 'holy-Yiddish'[12] as it is in the eyes of Jewish nationalists. Not at all; the language itself means nothing to us.[13]

Stripped of Party jargon, the purposes set both the Commissariat and the *Evsektsia* were therefore kin to those that had been at the root of pre-revolutionary state policy in Russia at least until 1881: the precipitation, acceleration, and intensification of all such processes as promised to lead to the *de facto* disintegration of Jewish society. As under the Autocracy, so now, in the early years of Soviet rule, there was to be a concerted attempt to reform the Jews socio-economically and to make them a more 'useful' people by, for example, encouraging their settlement on the land, by extending secular schooling for their children—Yiddish-language schools where necessary to begin with, but channelling them into Russian-language state schools wherever and whenever possible—and so preparing them for tasks in the economy that heretofore most Jews had been ill-equipped to undertake. But the spirit in which the Soviet state would now pursue its aims was less inhibited and more single-minded than that of its predecessor. The pace would be faster and the means more brutal. There was the interesting difference, too, that while both before and after the Revolution there was never any question of inquiring seriously into the wishes of the population concerned, matters being determined from above as a matter of course, the rulers of Soviet Russia were initially content to leave much of the actual labour of denaturing Russian Jewry and the crushing of all that preserved it as a recognizable and coherent social entity to elements in Jewry itself. For while the Leninist-Stalinist complex of state and party, and its undeviating policy on the nationality or otherwise of the Jews, provided the necessary conditions for bringing what would prove to be the greatest and most systematic of all the many efforts made in the course of nineteenth and twentieth centuries to dissolve a culturally coherent and distinctive Jewish social presence into the larger society around it, these were not sufficient conditions. It was indispensable that there should evolve, and be available for the execution of this purpose, a class of men, of whom Dimanshtein was by no means the sole exemplar, who were able and willing—some of them much more than merely willing—to take on the assignment. It was necessary too that the opposition from within Russian Jewry to what they were about should not, after all, be adamant.

That both these latter conditions were amply fulfilled owed much to the fact that for a time at least (notably from 1918 to 1921), the ranks of

---

[12] A play on Yiddish-speakers' common reference to Hebrew as *loshen-kodesh*—i.e. 'holy language'.

[13] Cited in Hayyim Sloves, *Mamlakhtiyut yehudit bivrit ha-moʿezot* (Tel Aviv, 1981), 16–17.

the Jewish sections of the Communist Party steadily thickened. In due course both the Commissariat and the *Evsektsia* would be stuffed with former Bundists and the more determinedly Marxist among the socialist-Zionists—people who had decided *faute de mieux* to throw in their lot with the Bolsheviks while the Bolsheviks would still have them. Therein, with that irony that is so common in the history of the Communist Party, lay at least part of the basis for the *Evsektsia*'s relative success in fulfilling its assignment but also the principal seeds of its own eventual destruction. The more successfully the Jewish sections drew the people to whom they addressed themselves into the Communist fold, the weaker—from Moscow's point of view—became the grounds for keeping such distinctly Jewish structures in the Party in being. At the same time, it seemed both promising and useful, in what would now be Stalin's Russia, to charge specifically Jewish party institutions (along with all other groups suspected of purposes that Stalin had no reason to regard as his own) with 'right-wing deviationism' or 'petty-bourgeois tendencies' or 'nationalist', 'chauvinist', or 'clericalist' tendencies, and other imaginary offences as part of the ritual preliminary to destroying them. There was a sense, of course, in which all this was foredoomed. It had, after all, been laid down from the very first that there was to be no question of a distinctively Jewish communist party being set up. Jews who joined the Party were to be enlisted in the Party proper, the 'Communist Party of the Soviet Union (Bolsheviks)'. The Jewish sections were organs of the Party administration, not genuine, let alone autonomous subsidiaries. The last thing that anyone in real authority in Moscow wanted either in the early years of Soviet rule or later was the formation, even in modified form, of what would unfailingly be in some sort a successor to, or a substitute for, the Bund. And yet, it was first and foremost to the survival of that very particular combination of Jewish national sentiment in its secular and Yiddishist form on the one hand and a yearning for some degree of social and cultural autonomy on the other that had always been the motor force driving the Bund that the Jewish sections of the Party owed their ability to find willing recruits, to mobilize some popular support, and to get the process of communizing the Jews of the old empire started. It is true that as hope of the old empire being replaced by a democratic state was abandoned, so the desire of many who had been active in the Menshevik, Socialist-Revolutionary, and Bundist parties, and in the more left-leaning of the socialist Zionists as well, to find a place for themselves in the new political hierarchies grew—for safety's sake, if for no other reason, and as a function of the political animal's natural and universal aversion to being left out totally in the political cold.

But it was not all trimming, time-serving, and hypocrisy. At their most honest and constructive, the Jewish sections of the Party did what they could to offer professionally ambitious and politically minded Jews a corner of their own in the new totalitarian state: a half way (if in the event temporary) house between full-blooded national self-abnegation in the form prescribed by Bolshevik (and, for that matter, Menshevik) doctrine on the nature of Jewish peoplehood on the one hand and continued insistence on Jewish continuity in one at least of the now familiar modernist forms—traditional, Bundist, Autonomist, or Zionist. Many former Bundists seem to have hoped that the *Evsektsia* would form a sort of Bolshevik Bund; and for a while this was indeed the case. In this sense, both the moves to de-legitimize and disband the Jewish sections (that began as early as 1923 and lasted until 1930) *and* the countervailing, but exceedingly cautious, yet unmistakably brave attempts by some of their *apparatchiki* to forestall liquidation when it began to stare them in the face fall into place. The Jewish sections, that is to say, both represented and did to some extent actually provide for a real social and cultural need. Alas for those concerned, it was a need which Jews alone were liable to feel—and by no means all of them. It was not a need that the regime had any perceived interest of its own to recognize, let alone satisfy, except briefly and reluctantly and then hedged around with very firm restrictions on its natural growth and development. By the same token, the final, formal liquidation of the Jewish sections in 1930 marked the burial of any hope at all of the new Autocracy agreeing to a *modus vivendi* such as would have allowed the Jews of the Soviet Union a place within the whole complex and gigantic enterprise that would in some sense or other be their own.

The other necessary condition on which the ability of the Commissariat for Jewish Affairs and the Jewish sections of the Party to function successfully hinged was that there be, at least initially, some general and so to speak unfocused public support for the new regime within Russian Jewry at large. And the fact was that while they lasted, for all that they aroused more suspicion than support within the Jewish commonalty, they were able to earn some moderate approval. In their role of shadowy successors to the Bund and several other varieties of Jewish modernism in pre-revolutionary Russia, the Jewish sections of the Party were able to draw upon long-standing popular antipathies to social and religious orthodoxy, to Jewish traditionalism in general, and to the rabbinical and plutocratic establishments in particular. There was, that is to say, a ready audience for a good deal of what the propagandists had to say about Jewish 'clericalism' and 'reaction' even when the terms were harsher than anything previously articulated in public in the eastern European 'Jewish street'. Still, it was a limited audience. The objections to what the *Evsektsia* and the Commissariat were chiefly about remained profound. They were, after all, while they lasted, the very symbols and spearheads of the attack launched against the forms, the structures, and the content of the collective life of the Jews on which so much in their private lives as well had always necessarily hinged. Synagogues, rabbinical academies, and

Talmudic libraries; all genuine and authentic and, above all, internally
generated and sustained communal, philanthropic, educational, and, of
course, political institutions; all national Russian-language or mother-
tongue (Hebrew and Yiddish) journals, publishing houses, newspapers,
scholarly societies, and theatre companies; and, generally, all formal and
informal structures in which the breath of authentically Jewish cultural or
social freedom and autonomy might be detected within them or so much
as held to subsist were either proscribed outright and liquidated in very
short order or taken over by placemen and systematically drained of
whatever native content and spirit they might have had as a preliminary
to their eventual dissolution.

It was a devastating attack on the social and cultural structures of
Russian, now Soviet Jewry. It succeeded because it was conducted on the
authority of the state and the Party and with their resources and power to
call on when necessary. Even so, it was a long process. Active, open resistance was relatively rare, always non-violent, and local in character. There
was no central direction or guidance either from within the Soviet Union
or from abroad: that, as was quickly recognized, would have been too
dangerous to mount. And by way of compensation and deflection of
opposition a constant show of ambivalence on certain matters allowed
the diehards in Jewry to retain some hope that, appearances notwithstanding, not all was lost. Secular Jewish culture—schooling, literature,
theatre, and its associated art forms—all continued to be tolerated in
principle (provided operations were under state or Party auspices and the
language vehicle was Yiddish rather than Hebrew), while at the same
time being steadily reduced. Religious practice was in some ways both an
easier target for the Bolsheviks and a harder nut to crack. While communal institutions, religious institutions among them, could be closed by
fiat—on the grounds, for example, that they were performing a social and
educational function that belonged properly to the state,[14] religious
observance itself was more difficult to tackle directly. In principle, all citizens of the Soviet state were free to practise their religion if they were
determined to do so and were prepared to face the continuous officially
sponsored, greatly inhibiting campaign mounted against all such alleged
absurdities and superstitions. But whereas the Russian Orthodox
Church, while oppressed, was allowed a twilight existence, the organized
community that was the foundation of all Jewish religious practice was out-
lawed. Rabbis were forbidden to adjudicate, collective worship and study
were heavily obstructed, the Sabbath became ever more difficult to keep,
as were the dietary laws, and circumcision became a rite that was best

---

[14] N. Romanovna, 'Dokumenty evreiskogo otdela Petrogradskogo komissariata po
delam natsional'nostei', in D. A. El'yashevich (ed.), *Istoriya evreev v Rossii* (St Petersburg,
1993), 154.

practised privately if not secretly. Only very firm minds were likely to persist in going their own way for any length of time. Only very brave souls were capable of standing up to a hostile, barracking mob, knowing that the consequence of resisting the pressure brought to bear upon them by the Party was almost certain punishment.

It was a hopeless, fruitless, and personally very costly road to travel. Some did. But not many. By the time the Jewish sections of the Party were disbanded in 1930 the social and the institutional fabric of Russian Jewry, having been first publicly denigrated, then institutionally and socially undermined, was in tatters. Saddest of all for those who had been most hopeful was the refusal, upon the consolidation of the USSR, to grant them even minimal formal, *constitutional* recognition as one of the nations of the Union. Stalin himself had laid down at the Twelfth Party Congress in 1923 that delegations representing such Soviet republics in the Soviet of Nationalities (the upper house of the new parliament) as were themselves manifestly multinational were under an obligation to see to the representation of the minorities contained within their borders.[15] It was not much to be grateful for. But it would have accorded the Jewish people at least a modicum of recognition and (in Soviet terms) respectability had Jews been appointed or elected as such, as of right, and as a matter of course to membership of the Ukrainian and Byelorussian SSRs, in both of which they formed substantial proportions of the total population. The promise was never fulfilled. With the dissolution of the all-Soviet People's Commissariat for the Affairs of Nationalities (and the Commissariat for Jewish Affairs with it) in the same year it had begun to be apparent to all that the brief chapter of open, formal, and nominally non-contentious acceptance of Jewish nationhood—hedged around with reservations though it had always been—was about to be closed. By the 1930s it was over. The Jewish citizens of the Soviet Union continued to be defined, officially, as of Jewish nationality. The Jewish nation itself was reduced to the status of a ghost.

In the long aftermath of the October Revolution, in the course of which the Bolshevik totalitarian system was consolidated and its direction set, it was the fact that the vehicle spearheading the attack on the social institutions of Jewry had been manned by Jews that would be most frequently and bitterly recalled by all but the most unquestioning devotees of the Communist Party itself. It was, that is to say, with their role as agents of the regime in the execution of the Party's essentially negative and destructive purposes that the *Evsektsia* people came principally to be associated in many Jewish minds both at home and abroad. And indeed,

---

[15] 'As there are a number of distinct nationalities in certain republics . . . the delegations [to the Soviet of Nationalities] should be so constituted as to provide for every one of those nations to be represented.' Cited in M. Altshuler, *Ha-yevsektia bivrit ha-mo'ezot (1918–1930): bein le'umiyut le-komunizm* (Tel Aviv, 1980), 130–3.

by the same token, it is possible to see in much of what was accomplished for the Soviet regime through the agency of the *Evsektsia* the playing out—in an unexpectedly extreme and often brutal form, to be sure—of what in Russia (but not elsewhere) would turn out to be the final round in the long-standing conflict between the plutocratic and traditionalist leadership of eastern European Jewry on the one hand and its radical and modernist wing on the other. For some among the modernists this tended to soften the blow somewhat. It needs to be recalled, that is to say, that, at least in the early years of Soviet government, the standing of the *Evsektsia* people as the agents of the Party and the regime was not invariably held against them. All Jews were aware that, uniquely among the peoples of Russia, they had had no stake at all in the old regime and a very limited one in Russian society at large as it had been constituted before the revolution. They were neither peasants nor landowners. They had been totally excluded from the bureaucracy, the judiciary, and the officer corps. They had no reason to regard the Autocracy as a system, and the Tsar as a ruler, as other than alien, untrustworthy, and incurably hostile to them in particular. Other than their material possessions, they had, in short, nothing to lose by a change of regime—and their material possessions, in the overwhelming majority of cases, were exceedingly meagre, as we have seen.

These were positive reasons for welcoming the February Revolution and negative, but by no means negligible, reasons for acquiescence in, and resignation to, the October Revolution that followed—to which there needs to be added the cumulative impact of confrontation with the Bolsheviks' ready employment of force, their brutality, and their absolute refusal—indeed, inability—to take under serious consideration views that differed from their own. But before all else it was the shattering experience of being subjected to the most intense and widespread campaign of violence known in modern times (thus far) that dissolved the will and reduced the ability of the very great majority of Russian Jews to resist the imposition of comprehensive and virtually irreversible cultural and social mutation. Whatever doubts or fears Jews might have about the Bolsheviks *per se* and the eventual consequences of the October Revolution, they were in no doubt at all about the murderous and hysterical Judaeophobia of the forces against which the Red Army—for reasons which, of course, had nothing intrinsically to do with the Jews at all—were arrayed. The Communist Party, the new Soviet government, and, *by and large*, the Red Army too,[16] did at least offer those Jews who found themselves under their rule a degree—in the course of time a high degree—of safety and protection. It is true that in the immediate aftermath of the Revolution a very great part of Russia was sucked into the chaos and brutality of

---

[16] But see below, p. 722 n. 29.

a long civil war. For the Jews among them, however, notably where Jews were most numerous, the common evils of civil war were compounded by the very disaster which Motzkin had anticipated two years earlier. Now it was less the possessions of the Jews that their enemies were interested in than their lives.[17] In these circumstances Bolshevik supremacy seemed at all events to promise life rather than continual fear, humiliation, and a high probability of death or mutilation. It was a datum that in most minds could not fail to outweigh—if not cancel out—all other possible considerations.

II

The defining feature of the south-western provinces of what had been the Russian Empire during the four years that elapsed between the political separation of the Ukraine from Russia in July 1917 and the establishment of effective and lasting Soviet rule in 1921 was the absence of government in any of the commonly accepted senses of the term. The country was given over to mutually competing, perpetually advancing and retreating armed forces of various kinds and sharply varying military significance: regular and irregular Ukrainian nationalist troops; Bolshevik forces that tended in the course of time to be absorbed into, or be replaced by, the Red Army proper; and 'White' forces of anti-Bolshevik counter-revolution, chiefly represented in this part of the old empire by the 'Volunteer Army' led by General Denikin. Minor, politically motivated forces, among them Nestor Makhno's anarchists, and the innumerable, unambiguously criminal bands with which the whole vast area was infested, some of which painted themselves from time to time in what they deemed to be appropriate political colours, others not troubling with such nonsense, completed the grim picture. Except in the cases of the Red and Volunteer Armies discipline was exceedingly poor. Brutality was extreme and universal. All, while they controlled some segment of it, held the ordinary inhabitants in each locality totally at their mercy. None—other than the Bolsheviks towards the end of the period—were capable of holding any part of this immense territory for long. For those who were not themselves actually engaged in charging up and down the land in a ferocious effort to possess it for themselves, the sum of things in the southern and western provinces of Russia was therefore first and foremost a long and terrible eclipse of the *state*. And the outcome for all concerned, the armed and the unarmed, the victims and the victimizers, was much the same stunting and brutalization of their humanity and society as central Europe had had to endure during the Thirty Years' War.

---

[17] See above, p. 702.

And yet, for the Jews among them, some 10 per cent of the total population, the results were incomparably worse. 'In the district town of
Proskurov, province of Podolia,' the Danish Red Cross Delegation in
Moscow informed its Copenhagen office in May 1919, citing reports
from the scene,

there occurred on February 15 to 18 a Jewish pogrom. The town at that time was
in the power of the 'Directory of the Ukrainian People's Republic'. In the
morning of February 13 a revolt took place in the town against the Directory for
the restoration of Soviet power. The attempt, utterly weak and unorganized,
was immediately suppressed without any difficulty. On the same day, under the
pretext of fighting the Bolsheviks, pillaging, robbing and ill-treating of the Jews
began. As was subsequently learnt, some sixty peasants' carts had been brought
up to the town from the surrounding villages during the preceding night by
order of the military commander of the town, one Kivertchuk, a former non-
commissioned officer of the Russian army, and these peasants had begun to dig
common graves near the station. . . .

The pogrom was carried out very systematically. Detachments of ten to
twenty Haidamaks [Ukrainian Cossacks] surrounded the houses and killed all the
Jews in them, without distinction of age or sex, sparing neither infants in arms
nor aged people. The massacre was carried out in the houses, in the streets and
also at the station, which is two-thirds of a mile distant from the town, and where
any Jewish passengers who happened to arrive were taken out of the train. The
streets were full of corpses and wounded. Relations were not allowed to bury
their dead, nor were the corpses handed over to them. It was forbidden to give
help to the wounded. . . .

By the evening [of February 16] the aspect of the town was horrible. On all
sides were looted shops, broken window panes, doors forced open, streets
streaming with blood, household effects and chattels in fragments and scattered
on the pavement. The statements of eye-witnesses are harrowing. They tell of a
two-months' infant with six wounds, of mounted Haidamaks chasing old men
and women who could scarcely walk without assistance, of pregnant women
ripped open, of murders of children in their sleep, of eyes put out, of hundreds
of violated girls.

It is difficult to establish the total number of killed and wounded. After the
arrival of the Soviet troops, that is after April 7, an approximate 'dead census' was
taken of the regularly domiciled Proskurov inhabitants, when it was found that
the number of those killed or wounded exceeded 1,500; but that total does not
include travellers from other places, or recent arrivals, or persons passing through
the station for various reasons connected with the war. It was known that over
100 dead were buried in one common grave only by Klave's Brewery near the
station. Local inhabitants estimate the total number of victims at no less than
3,000 to 4,000. . . .

The slaughter came to an end in the evening of February 18, after some negotiation which resulted in the commander of the Zaporog Cossack Brigade of the
Ukraine Republican army, Hetman Semosenko, acting on behalf of the Com-
mander-in-Chief Petl[y]ura, consenting to accept from the Jewish inhabitants
of Proskurov 'as grant in aid to the Detachment' a sum of 300,000 roubles. The

money was taken by Semosenko's aide-de-camp, a captain, who counted it at the Town Hall.[18]

The slaughter in Proskurov is thought to have been among the worst of the massacres of unarmed, non-combatant Jewish villagers and townspeople that occurred in the Ukraine in this period.[19] Perhaps for that reason, it is one of the better documented. But in its essentials it can be taken as standing for all. Something of the sort, commonly on a lesser scale, but often enough on one that was only marginally smaller, took place in very many hundreds of towns and villages up and down the Ukraine and in the areas to its immediate west and north. The numbers mounted rapidly. By the summer of 1919, long, therefore, before the full killing season was over, thirty thousand Jewish civilians had been killed by Ukrainian forces of all kinds—regular and irregular troops and simple bandits. The most cautious estimates for the entire period, taking into account the later, equally massive killings perpetrated by the Cossacks of General Denikin's counter-revolutionary Volunteer Army and those dispatched by the Red Army as well, speak of at least fifty to sixty thousand dead. And it has been soberly suggested, and is indeed far from improbable, that the true sum total of the dead was twice as high. When to those done to death on the spot or so badly wounded that death followed soon after, there are added the many tens of thousands of heavily wounded and mutilated men, women, children, and infants who survived and the untold thousands of women and girls of all ages, grandmothers and grandchildren, who had been raped and, when not shot or bayoneted on the spot after use, left mentally shattered and infected with venereal disease,—it can be seen that the Jewish population in the Ukraine (of some 1.6 million at the time) had been literally decimated.[20]

All this said, it is important to see that this massive flailing of the Jewish population of the southern and western provinces of what had been the Russian Empire was not a new wave of 'pogroms' on something like the familiar pattern—although, to be sure, that was how it came most

---

[18] Committee of the Jewish Delegations [compiled by J. B. Schechtman], *The Pogroms in the Ukraine under the Ukrainian Governments (1917–1920)* (London, 1927), Annex No. 28, 189–91.

[19] The worst of all single incidents, so far as is known, was in the townlet of Tetiev two years later in which some 4,000 Jews were slaughtered.

[20] Vladimir N. Brovkin, *Behind the Front Lines of the Civil War: Political Parties and Social Movements in Russia, 1918–1922* (Princeton, 1994), *passim*; Committee of the Jewish Delegations [Schechtman], *The Pogroms in the Ukraine*; *Encyclopaedia Judaica*, xiii, cols. 698–701; N. Gergel, 'The Pogroms in the Ukraine in 1918–21', *YIVO Annual of Jewish Social Science*, 6 (1951); Elias Heifetz, *The Slaughter of the Jews in the Ukraine in 1919* (New York, 1921), 175–82; Peter Kenez, 'Pogroms and White ideology in the Russian Civil War', in J. D. Klier and S. Lambroza (eds.), *Pogroms: Anti-Jewish Violence in Modern Russian History* (Cambridge, 1992), 293–313; Richard Pipes, *Russia under the Bolshevik Regime* (New York, 1993), especially 99–114; N. I. Shtif, *Pogromy na ukraine (period dobrovol'cheskoi armii)* (Berlin, 1922).

commonly to be thought of, especially abroad. None doubted, as even the most cautious figures testified, that it was vastly greater in scale and more horrific in quality than any of the waves of violence and destruction that had preceded it since the 1880s. It is the comparison with the so-called Khmelnitsky massacres of 1648 that observers with any knowledge of the past were (and remain) inclined to make, and with good reason. What was less well understood was that it was not only the scale that was vastly greater than, say, the sufficiently devastating pogroms of 1905, but that it was radically different in kind as well.

One of the sad, but undeniable paradoxes of imperial Russian rule had been, as we have seen, that, while the Autocracy was indeed ineradicably hostile to its Jewish subjects, it did offer them, reluctantly and very imperfectly to be sure, a good deal of necessary protection from the Jews' various sworn and declared religious, class, and political enemies. More remarkably, it did this against its own deepest instincts and against those of its own masters. The regime's hostility was evident, manifest, and often very hard to bear. But it was never allowed fully to be played out in practice. For the most part, the slender bonds of Enlightenment thinking held the Russian political and military class back, along with, as needs to be said, its reluctance to cut too nasty a figure in what most educated Russians tended instinctively to think of as the more civilized parts of Europe. Now, however, the Autocracy gone, the Jews of Russia, in the very place where they were most numerous, most alien culturally, and most easily identifiable, were left with only such protection as they themselves were able and willing to muster. And this, in the new circumstances, was more limited than ever. In practice, therefore, those who wished to attack and punish them were now uniquely free to do so.

It is more difficult to explain why there should have been so strong an inclination to attack them, and why the attacks were carried out with such extreme violence and to such murderous purpose. Part of the answer must lie in a feature of social and political breakdown that is common enough to be considered universal. Civil war, notably when it is prolonged, is inherently conducive to latent political and social hatreds and suspicions rising rapidly to the surface, to private and public accounts being settled with great alacrity and ferocity, to savage searches being made for whomever may be conveniently held guilty of having precipitated the general misery, and to society, generally, being reduced to its most violent and bestial. The death-dealing gangs of Ukrainians and Cossacks seem plainly to have been seized, as people are apt to be seized in such dire circumstances, by the sudden, terrible emptiness of the political space in which they found themselves once they had lost the compass and direction that had been provided them by the old regime. Horrors perpetrated on the bodies of so enormous a number of people, all demonstrably harmless militarily and innocent politically, ostensibly on the basis that they were Bolsheviks one and all, or, if not Bolsheviks themselves, then at any rate in secret league with the Bolsheviks, or if not that then in some other way responsible for the ills of Russia and the disgrace into which the empire and society itself had fallen, point inexorably to mass psychosis. But not to psychosis alone. The slaughters were not isolated, marginal, unusual incidents. They were repeated over and over again throughout an exceedingly wide area over several years in succession, and consistently in a manner that suggests prior intent. They speak of a climate of political opinion in which friends and enemies were clearly identified and the latter demonized. They speak too of a climate of moral opinion peculiarly conducive to the eager shedding of blood in circumstances of maximum bestiality. Rare and trivial instances apart, the executioners proved to be deaf not only to pleas for mercy, but to argument of any kind at all: uninterested, that is to say, in the political truths of the matter (namely, that the Jewish population was in fact overwhelmingly anti-Bolshevik), unwilling even to be bought off by ransom money in the old style. No doubt, the almost absolute freedom to operate without fear of punishment served as an invitation and an encouragement. Instances of Jewish self-defence forces operating in sufficient strength of men and arms to repel minor Ukrainian gangs were not unknown, but no central organization ever came into being and it is probable that none was possible.[21]

For the greater part of the period the Ukraine was cut off from the political centres of Russia, Moscow and Petrograd, where the most self-confident and experienced Jewish activists were to be found. In Kiev itself men of adequate stature were too few in number even to fill such posts in the national government as were open to them.[22] Information in what we would now call real time was totally lacking. The nationalist Ukrainian press and the press operating under White auspices were irredeemably and violently hostile. The Soviet press, while full of venomously critical reports on the Volunteer Army, paid scarcely any attention to the atrocities committed by Denikin's people against the Jews (unlike the Menshevik press which, alas, functioned only abroad at this time and was therefore of little practical relevance). The villages and townlets in which most Jews were still to be found were therefore uninformed or ill-informed about what was taking place all around them and were that much more easily picked off by the troops one at a time. On the other hand, those located near the railway lines were more liable to be attacked than those who were remote from them if only because much of the fighting was for control of the lines and the presence of troops was

[21] [Dov-] B[e]r Slutsky, 'Ha-hagana ha-'aẓma'it be-ukraina', 1923, publ. in *He-'Avar*, 17 (1970).
[22] M. Hindes to the Zionist Central Office, 8 May 1918, CZA, Z3/893.

therefore heavier where the lines ran. Safety lay in total isolation, but total isolation was rare.

In sum, the central and defining feature of the whole ghastly episode was that the Jews of the Ukraine had been catapulted into a condition—not unfamiliar in earlier times, but rare until now in modern times—in which they were effectively without the means, direct or indirect, to withstand or deflect the killers, disembowellers, torturers, and rapists who had set upon them. They had been marked down as targets for immediate destruction and deprived, in a manner rare even in the long and bitter history of the Exile, of any of the means by which they had attempted in the past, often enough with success, to fend off or diminish the sentence laid upon them. None, therefore, in what would soon become the Soviet Union, craved more ardently than they the restitution of elementary law and order: law and order of any kind at anyone's hands—even, if all else failed, at the hands of the counter-revolutionary forces of whom they knew very well that the best they could expect was the re-establishment of the old regime in all its original rigour and nastiness.[23] And it is precisely characteristic of their condition that where, in their innocence, Jewish representatives did set out to welcome Denikin's forces, they found that they were either deliberately ignored, or laughed at for not grasping what everyone else knew was about to be done to them, or told to their faces that bread and salt and words of welcome would most certainly fail to save them from the coming slaughter.

The behaviour of the leaders of the newly independent Ukraine was less brutally simple, but in the final analysis not much better. Initially, at the highest level of the infant Ukrainian state there was a genuine ambivalence towards the Jews, as there was with regard to other national minorities (Poles and Russians). The Ukrainian nationalists had begun, sensibly enough from their point of view and their own calculation of interests, by offering the Jewish minority generously defined national minority rights. Between July 1917 and January 1918 the status and rights of the Jews as a national minority were formally recognized, a Jewish notable was appointed vice-minister for Jewish Affairs, the candidates of Jewish national parties were admitted to seats in the Central Rada (or parliament),[24] and the Rada itself went on to pass laws regulating elections to Jewish community councils and establishing 'Jewish National-Personal Autonomy' for the Jewish population as a whole. For their part, the principal Jewish parties in the Ukraine gave their support to the movement for Ukrainian independence (the Bund, it is true, by reason of its affiliation with the RSDWP, with somewhat less enthusiasm than the others).

---

[23] On this see especially Shtif, *Pogromy*, *passim*.

[24] The Rada comprised 809 deputies: among them 624 Ukrainians, 94 Russians, 50 Jews, 20 Poles, 5 Romanians, 3 Germans, and 3 Tatars.

All seemed to be set fair, therefore, for co-operation and a long period of good feeling. 'It is our purpose to demonstrate,' the president of the Rada, V. K. Vinnichenko, told a French diplomat in Kiev in August 1917,

how the future League of Nations should be constituted. That is why we have agreed to all the ethnic minorities being represented in the Central Rada. We shall probably be the first country in the world to put *personal autonomy* into effect, a question of particular interest to the Jews who have no territory, but who in Russia form the precisely defined Jewish nationality.[25]

But the original Ukrainian state fell apart in the course of the war of all against all that ensued after the October Revolution. Ukrainians fought Ukrainians, Whites fought Reds, and each in turn fought the Ukrainians. Government by the Rada was replaced by a German puppet regime under Hetman Skoropadski, which was replaced in turn by a five-man Directory upon the Germans' withdrawal at the end of the war in the west. No one's writ ran throughout the entire province, or anywhere at all for long, until the final and definitive take-over was achieved by Lenin's army. As one kaleidoscopic change followed another, the founder-members of the first government gave way to new, harder, and always more desperate men. Military units disintegrated. Troops formed a multitude of armed, criminal bands. Initially, as attacks on Jews multiplied and mounted steadily in mindless ferocity, the protests of Jewish members of the Rada were answered with promises of an improvement in the general discipline of the army that no one seriously proposed to try to keep (or imagined it possible to do so). Later, such protests met only counter-charges: that the Jews themselves, by being excessively critical of the republic, were displaying their disloyalty; that they were indifferent if not hostile to the idea of an independent Ukraine itself; that it was more than likely, as the common people tended to think, that they were in league with the Bolsheviks anyway. By the time Skoropadski had been catapulted into power by the Germans at the end of April 1918, good feelings and, to a large extent, good intentions too had evaporated on both sides. The Germans restored a semblance of order. On the other hand, the Rada was dissolved, the Ministry of Jewish Affairs and the Jewish National Council were abolished, the Law of Jewish National-Personal Autonomy was repealed, and the tone in which Skoropadski and his minions proceeded to govern the country so far as the Jews were concerned is adequately indicated by the language in which the semi-official press chose to formulate its outlook. 'The Jew of the Ukraine and

---

[25] Cited in M. Mintz, 'The Secretariat of Internationality Affairs (*Sekretariiat mizhnatsional'nykh sprav*) of the Ukrainian General Secretariat (1917–1918)', *Harvard Ukrainian Studies*, 6, 1 (Mar. 1982), 41 n. 65. Emphasis in the original.

White Russia,' declared a leader writer in a newspaper published under the auspices of the 'Ministry of War of the Ukrainian State',

having cut himself off from the local language and the local culture, is an outsider, a pathological excrescence on the body of the two nations. The Jews were on the side of Poland when we waged war against her, and for that they have paid heavily. Now Ukraine is fighting Moscow, and once more the Jews are on the side of our enemies. They will pay the penalty for that also.[26]

By the time the third and last independent Ukrainian regime—the Directory headed by Semyon Petlyura—had replaced Skoropadski upon the withdrawal of his German sponsors, only a semblance of the original, multinational Ukraine remained. The country was given over to warlords. What remained of the Ukrainian army was reduced to a multitude of competing, increasingly wild armed parties of various sizes, all free to operate with that special liberty of action that accrues to the totally unscrupulous. The Directory itself proved to be more led by those over whom it held nominal authority than leading and was powerless to control them. Thus it was in most respects, but especially so in respect of the country's Jews. Gestures were made from time to time. Condign punishment of the worst offenders was promised. Notice (as opposed to evidence) of the execution of several of the more notorious killer-commanders having been carried out was published. The Jewish population waited for Denikin. Then, when he and his people had shown their true faces, they waited for the Bolsheviks.

Initially, the Bolsheviks were little better than the others. Like Petlyura and his men and like the White generals, the Bolshevik leadership (its Jewish members among them) refused to be exercised by reports of atrocities, even atrocities committed by units of the Red Army that had joined in what Cossack commanders in all three armies were apt to call the 'fun'.[27] 'Same old story,' Isaac Babel noted in the diary he kept when he was riding with the Red Army's Cossack cavalry; 'the Jews . . . expected the Soviet regime to liberate them, and suddenly there were shrieks, whips cracking, shouts of "dirty Yid" '.[28] But the Reds were relatively minor participants in the horrors,[29] and as their army consolidated discipline was insisted upon, and the system of rigorous political control from the centre having been perfected persecution by the Bolshevik

---

[26] Committee of the Jewish Delegations, *The Pogroms in the Ukraine*, 19.

[27] Orlando Figes, 'The Red Army and Mass Mobilization during the Russian Civil War 1918–1920', *Past and Present*, 129 (Nov. 1990), 195–6.

[28] *1920 Diary*, trans. H. T. Willetts; ed. C. J. Avins (New Haven, 1995), entry for 11 July 1920, 12.

[29] It has been calculated that Soviet forces were responsible for 8.6 per cent of all major and minor incidents and 2.3 per cent of those killed, the comparable figures for Petlyura's forces being 40 and 53.7 per cent and for the Volunteer Army 17.2 and 17 per cent (Gergel, 'Pogroms', table vi, 248).

forces ceased. This was soon known by all to be the case. Optimists in Russian and Ukrainian Jewry were therefore tempted to place their hopes on Lenin's triumph. Might it not spell a new world after all, nothing worse, at any rate, than a return to something akin to the Tsar's Russia in its better days? Pessimists took comfort in the thought that Bolshevik rule was preferable to further chaos or rule by the likes of the men around Denikin or Petlyura if that was the alternative. As for the measures of restrictive control which the Bolsheviks were known to impose on the population in its entirety whenever they were in a position to do so— the clamping down on free movement within, but especially out of the country; the reinstitution of censorship; the re-establishment of the police as the primary instrument of government; direction of labour by the state; exile as the commonest of acts of administrative punishment; and the courts themselves as engines of state repression—these, after all, were of a familiar nature to people who had so recently been subjects of the Tsar. And in any event, in the murderous chaos of the times few had either the necessary clarity of mind or the will to speculate usefully about the immense social cost that would soon be borne by all in consequence of the severity with which these and other similar measures were in the process of being imposed. Nor, of course, would it have greatly aided the Jews of Russia taken all in all had they actually stopped to consider what was likely to become of them and seek at so late a stage to set about determining their private and collective destinies for themselves.

What had not been envisaged at all, on the other hand, was that the new rulers of Russia should decide, after some initial hesitation, to bring the hitherto (relatively) free emigration of the Jews from their dominions to an end. No doubt, the closing of the gates and the enclosure of the entire population of the USSR behind a barrier so heavily policed as to be all but impenetrable to ordinary people was no more than a reversion to times and conditions for which there were well-established precedents in the history of the Russians themselves. For the Jews of the country, however, the blow was shattering. No such barrier to their movement either as individuals or as whole communities and to free—or even secret—communication between their communities on so great a scale, of such long duration, and with such dire results for their cohesion as a people had ever been known, not in Europe, at all events. The consequences were immediate and severe. There was a freer hand than ever there had been before for all who were intent on pursuing the campaign finally and irreversibly to denature Russian Jewry. Forbidden participation in the general complex of worldwide Jewish life on pain of dire punishment, the Jews of Russia were from this point on effectively removed from sight and, in the course of time, very largely from mind as well. Calls for help to the outside world died down after a while: they were becoming too dangerous to make; no clear lines of communication were available; and in the end there were none left who was in a position of sufficient moral authority to make an appeal of the strength required. The hermetic enclosure within the borders of the USSR and the elimination of all organized internal communal life were mutually reinforcing. And if the effect on Russian Jewry itself and on the structure of world Jewry as a whole was less immediately palpable than the campaign against their institutions and certainly less horrific than the slaughters, in the long term, in important, moral ways, it was to prove as devastating. The great Russian segment of European Jewry would be left culturally, no less than politically, crippled—barely a people at all except in the narrowest of formal legal senses: their being individually labelled as Jews in their official papers. As a branch of the Jewish people capable of playing the leading role—indeed any role at all—within the larger context of the public affairs of Jewry, they had been demolished. Contrary to all reasonable expectation, the Russian Revolutions of 1917 were the ruin of Russian Jewry.[30]

Still, in the short and middle term, it is the physical violence done them—and where not done at any rate constantly threatened—that deserves closest attention. It can be no part of the purpose of this book to inquire into the psychopathology, if that is what it is, of those substantial segments of Russian, Ukrainian, and Cossack society that were intent on disposing of the Jews not merely politically and socially (like the Bolsheviks) but, so far as possible, physically. That task needs to be left to specialist historians of the societies in question, if not to students of human behaviour in general. But there is one distinction that needs to be drawn quite clearly: that between the locally raised Ukrainian forces and Denikin's Volunteer Army. The latter's behaviour was not only as grim as that of the former, it was of a more far-reaching, ominous, and ecumenical significance. It was no rabble, but in every sense a real army: well armed, on the whole well disciplined, initially very powerful, commanded throughout by professional officers. It was, if anything, over-officered: so encumbered by officers and officer cadets of the old Russian army that entire units up to battalion level had necessarily to be composed of them, generals serving as battalion commanders, colonels in the role of subalterns. It was unlike the Ukrainian nationalists too in that it enjoyed the advantage of serious political connections with, and the backing of, foreign, notably western powers. It is true that Denikin's Cossack troops were allowed to loot and cart away whatever property they thought of value to them. But in essentials it was none the less a true and effective military force and that not least because all ranks within it

---

[30] I am aware, as I write this, that in the final years of the twentieth century there has been a distinct effort to breathe life into Russian Jewry—more properly into what is left of it after close to three generations of Soviet rule and massive emigration in its final stages and immediately thereafter.

were politically united in their dedication to the re-establishment of the
Autocracy and genuinely imbued with the connected, driving conviction that at the root of Russia's tragedy and their own political discomfi-
ture as a military class lay the Jews. If their Russia was ever to rise again
from the ashes in which it now languished, the Jews, so ran their common
and exceedingly tenacious belief, needed to be punished, indeed
destroyed. Given the spirit moving them and the armed power at their
command, it was inevitable that the consequences should go well beyond
the Cossacks being allowed a few days' amusement—as Denikin's subor-
dinates were apt to put it—in the Jewish quarters of the towns and villages
through which they swept when advancing towards the centre of the
country and again, in darker mood, early in 1920, as they retreated. In the
view of the thinking members of the Volunteer Army, there lay upon
them a positive duty to rid Russia, and by extension Christian Europe
generally, of 'the Jew'—'the Jew' in general, that is to say, conceived
generically and without regard to his or her actual sex, or age, or station
in life, or political affiliation (if any at all). No explicit obligation to kill
was laid upon Denikin's officers in the field. So far as is known, no central, binding order to do away with the Jewish population was ever issued.
But the climate of opinion in which they were engulfed encouraged it.
And on those rare occasions when they were questioned about it *critically*—for example, when hostages had been taken, a brief delay had
ensued, and there was a sufficiency of non-Jews (town councillors and
the like) bold and decent enough to protest against the imminent proceedings—the grounds would be articulated without reserve. The Jews,
it would be said, were all Bolsheviks; the troops were therefore free to
slice them up and kill them: '*Vse zhidy bol'sheviki, ikh mozhno rezat' i
ubivat'*.'[31]

It needs to be recalled that the destruction of entire communities by
disciplined, uniformed, military or para-military troops acting on the
authority of their regular commanders or, at the very least, with their
tacit permission and approval, was not as common in Europe in the early
decades of the twentieth century as it would later become. The officers
and men of the *Wehrmacht* and its ancillary forces upon their entry into
the same lands twenty-two years later wasted little of their time and
energy mutilating or torturing those it proposed to put to death. Nor did
German troops occupy themselves with the rape of Jewish women on the
immense scale practised by Denikin's Cossacks. Mid-twentieth century
German military and police commanders were too intent on the central
business of extermination (besides fighting their war) to be inclined to
permit their troops 'to stroll' (*pogulyat'*) through the Jewish quarters of
the towns they occupied for the 'lawful three days' (*zakonnye tri dnya*)

---

[31] Cited in Shtif, *Pogromy*, 14.

allowed Denikin's Cossacks[32] before final and more systematic punishment of the inhabitants was inflicted. What the two armies did have in
common were mind-set and bestiality. The term 'genocide' had yet to be
coined, but no sane contemporary observer of the scene in the Ukraine
at the time of the Russian civil war could doubt that *that*—crudely and
imperfectly, to be sure—was what was being attempted. 'This wave [of
violence] has for its objective the entire annihilation of Ukrainian Jewry
and in several instances whole communities, men, women, and children,
have been put to death,' the Kiev committee of the Russian Red Cross
reported on 2 October 1919.[33]

But the cardinal matter was that of political outlook—if that is not too
grand a term to apply to the crudities of Russian counter-revolutionary
thinking. The counter-revolutionaries believed that at the root of the
Russian Revolution lay a Jewish-Bolshevik conspiracy, that 'the Jews'
were ultimately responsible for Russia's disasters—for how else were
those disasters to be explained?—and that, more generally, the Jews had
engineered themselves into a position of great political power. It was a
view that they held with great tenacity, and which they proceeded, with
some success, to spread round the world. Others who sought an explanation for these and the other terrible events of the time would pick it up
with still more terrible consequences. The notion that the Jews constituted an 'international power'—not in the sense that Lord Robert Cecil
and his colleagues in London had had in mind a few years' earlier,[34] but
in a much more direct and very much more malevolent sense—would fall
on ready ground. This ascription of power and of secretly planned and
deeply destructive purposes to a construct labelled 'the Jews' would
haunt the real Jewish people in all its affairs hereafter. Was it an oddity of
their history that this should be so when there could have been no more
vivid illustration of the crippling impotence of Jewry than what had
transpired in eastern Europe in the course of the war years and more
especially in its aftermath? Or was it an oddity of the history of Christian
Europe? It was, of course, the case that individual Jews were prominent
in the Bolshevik wing of the Russian Social Democratic Workers' Party,
much as they were in the other revolutionary movements, as we have
seen. But they neither dominated the Communist Party nor any other
party (apart from the exclusively Jewish Bund and the left-leaning Zionist socialists, of course). Nor, as has been noted, did they form more than
a minority, although a substantial one, within the Communist Party in
particular at any of its levels. And in any event, as we have seen, and as was

---

[32] Shtif, *Progomy*, 20.
[33] Cited in the English translation of a report passed to the west through Zionist channels, untitled and undated, but evidently drawn up towards the end of 1919, CZA,
A18/50/1. The original Russian text has not been found.
[34] See above, p. 662.

abundantly evident at the time, the one true common denominator of the Jewish members of each of the three major revolutionary parties, the Bolsheviks, the Mensheviks, and the Socialist-Revolutionaries, was their fixed, quite passionate determination to *disengage* themselves from specifically Jewish interests and from the Jewish collectivity itself in any of its forms. As for the Jews of Russia as such, they, in their great majority, had always been opposed to the Bolsheviks as all who took the trouble to inquire, not least the Bolsheviks themselves, knew very well.

But the greater, underlying question raised by this allegation of a Jewish–Bolshevik nexus, the latest of the various sets of charges that had been preferred against Jewry in the course of its history, had little to do with the facts of the matter. It had to do with the participation of Jews in the political life of the states in which they formed a minority—therefore *all* states at this point—in any form and to any purpose at all. Their entry into politics, chiefly as individuals, but here and there in distinctively Jewish parties as well, had, as we have seen, been one of the more striking consequences of their emancipation. Such was manifestly the case where emancipation had been granted them. Such, for equal and opposite reasons, was the case too where, as in Russia, it had been denied. Were the Jews of Europe now about to pay the price of their presumption? The murder of Walther Rathenau, now foreign minister of republican Germany, in January 1922 could be seen as suggesting as much. In the minds of his enemies, certainly in those of his assassins, his well-known Jewish origins were heavily intermingled with the political grounds on which they opposed the policy he had been trying to pursue since the end of the war. The vicious verbal and physical abuse to which Léon Blum's enemies subjected him a decade and a half later was another small sign testifying to the continuing vitality of the old objection to the free and equal membership of Jews in civil society. The response in postwar Hungary to the brief reign of a Communist Party in which Jews were especially prominent had very bitter consequences for the entire Jewish population of what remained of the country after the peacemakers of Paris had had their way with it.

In sum, there would now spread throughout Europe, in degrees of intensity which accorded more or less with the nature and seriousness of the difficulties and tensions with which particular societies were afflicted, an entire range of variations on the original basic stab-in-the-back argument with which the Russian generals sought to explain their defeats in the course of the war and the Denikinists and their analogues chose to account for the collapse of the Autocracy itself. It is not surprising that this should have happened. The thesis of direct and fundamental Jewish responsibility for the ills of state and society—all states and all societies—had always offered those who propagated it extraordinary polemical advantages. It was not without superficial plausibility. What were Trotsky,

Zinoviev, Sverdlov, Bela Kun, and the rest—possibly Lenin himself, as some falsely argued[35]—if not Jews? It was very simple. It was susceptible neither to verification nor to falsification. It drew on ancient, nourishing theological, social, and folkloric roots. It served admirably to shift the enduring question of public and political responsibility for national events well away from those who had actually wielded political power at whatever was held to be the critical moment. In sum, as never before, anti-Semitism would now take on the features, and deliver the corresponding impact, of serviceable, secular, political myth. And the Jews themselves, regardless of actual quality, rich and poor, 'useful' and 'useless', politically involved and politically innocent, would be ground increasingly between state and people and vilified, here to their faces, there behind their backs, for being so presumptuous as to seek to serve their own interests in precisely those connections and contexts where it was manifest that in fact they were doing nothing of the kind.

'We are ancient people, exhausted,' Babel noted in his diary on 21 July 1920. He then consoled himself with the thought that 'we still have some strength left' after all.[36] Two days later, however, he wrote:

Dubno synagogues. Everything destroyed. . . . Ancient buildings, squat, green and blue . . . nondescript architecture. I go into the Hasidic synagogue. It's Friday. Such misshapen little figures, such worn faces. . . . Religion? There are no adornments in the building, everything is white and plain to the point of asceticism, everything is fleshless, bloodless, to a grotesque degree, you have to have the soul of a Jew to sense what it means. But what does the soul consist of? Can it be that ours is the century in which they perish?[37]

III

The cutting off of Russia shifted the active centre of Jewish public life to the west almost immediately. In the short term, that would have been the case even if the civil war had ended differently and the Russian Empire, or a liberalized version thereof, were still intact. It was the Paris Peace Conference, the greatest diplomatic gathering since the Congress of Vienna a century earlier, and much more ambitious in intent, that drew the eyes of all politically minded Jews much as it did those of their analogues among the other 'submerged' peoples of Europe and the Near East. There, in mid-January 1919, the great men who were to function on this one brief occasion as the world's veritable masters assembled to

---

[35] Lenin was of mixed Russian, Kalmyk, German, Swedish, and Jewish origin. His maternal grandfather was a baptized Jew, Alexander Dmitrievich Blank. See Dmitri Volkogonov, *Lenin: Life and Legacy* (London, 1994), 4–9.

[36] Ibid. 28.   [37] Ibid. 33.

revise the European political order and much else besides. But later too, throughout the quarter-century that followed, the axis of Jewish concerns and political strivings would continue to lie alongside the line that stretched from London, through Berlin, and on to Warsaw, coming to an end for all practical purposes at the Russian border. This owed a very great deal to the fact that the public life of the greater part of what had loosely been termed *Russian* Jewry was over, leaving only ever weaker and more futile efforts to save something from the wreckage. But it had much to do too with the fact that the Paris Peace was not only committed to the final abolition of the collapsed continental empires that had been situated west and south-west of the Soviet Union, but that its plans for replacement were such as would alter the terms of Jewish life quite as thoroughly as those of the other peoples, rulers and ruled, that inhabited the vast area in question. All that lay between the Rhine and the (still imperfectly determined) western frontier of the new, Soviet Russian Empire was now set to be reordered according to the 'principle of nationality'.

Of this principle much had been said and promised while the war was still being fought. Understood as *self-determination*, it was conceived, certainly in President Woodrow Wilson's mind, but (with minor reservations) in those of his major colleagues as well, in very positive, operative terms. It was not 'a mere phrase'. It was, on the contrary, the President told the United States Congress, 'an imperative principle of action which statesmen will henceforth ignore at their peril'.[38] Wilson had recognized, however, as had—more readily still—his British, French, and Italian colleagues, that in practice self-determination would have to be compounded with, and therefore mitigated by, other equally 'imperative' considerations: by such wartime promises as had been made to the Italians, for example; by the ethnographic map of Europe being far too untidy for the continent to be divided into neat and even roughly homogeneous and coherent political societies; by Europe's physical geography and the concomitant economic and strategic considerations to which it gave rise; and by the not unnatural, if strictly speaking improper, tendency to deal a good deal less than equitably with the quondam master peoples of central and eastern Europe, the Germans and the Magyars, as opposed to those they had once ruled—the Poles, the Slovaks, the Czechs, the Romanians, and the South Slavs. The consequence of ensuring that few or no Romanians remained in Hungary was the incorporation of the substantial Magyar-speaking population of Transylvania into a grossly enlarged Romania. If the historic and strategic boundaries of Bohemia were to be preserved, the new state of Czechoslovakia would

[38] 'The Four Principles', 11 Feb. 1918. See H. W. V. Temperley (ed.), *A History of the Peace Conference of Paris*, i (London, 1920), 437.

necessarily contain a high population of Germans; and other contingents of Germans would find themselves enclosed in a resurrected Polish state and in an enlarged and much strengthened Italy. Similarly, there would be Turks in Greece, Greeks in Turkey, Ukrainians (Ruthenians) in Poland, and so on down a long and, for the peacemakers, tedious list—at the bottom of which, in an irritatingly different category, were the Jews. In sum, the supreme difficulty raised by the establishment of the principle of nationality as the guiding principle for the drawing of new maps was that no state—no state at all, anywhere, but certainly no state in east-central, eastern, and south-eastern Europe in particular—no matter how conceived and whatever geographic configuration was devised for it, would be devoid of national (or, as some preferred, ethnic) minorities. It followed, that if nationality was the key consideration, the resulting proliferation of national *minorities* had in some form or another to be taken into consideration as well.

All this touched in some way on the 5.5 million Jews inhabiting the states that would now take form in the area (over and above the great number trapped in what would be the Soviet Union). But in what way? And with what likely consequences? The governing rule in each case, subject to minor variations, was that the Jews constituted a distinctive and more or less coherent social minority in the very particular sense that had now acquired major, if not decisive significance. On the other hand, however they might be defined and regarded—and their precise and appropriate status was invariably a matter of dispute—they were *not* held to be members of what would be the planned and recognized preponderant nation of the nation-state in question. This was consistent with the common tendency among all those who would now come into what they considered to be their full and rightful inheritance—the Poles, the Romanians, the Lithuanians, the Greeks, and so on—to play down, reduce, and if possible dismiss the claims of members of other nationalities, of native speakers of other languages than their own, of bearers of other historic traditions, and, of course, of members of other religious denominations to equality of status and, by extension, a share in government. Few things were so obviously fraught with danger for those social groups whose equality of status was held to be open to question, or was simply denied. But such was the spirit of the times and nothing was considered to be more natural than that this should be the case, not least because, strictly speaking, there was nothing especially new in it. These were the terms on which the German and Russian Empires and each one of the two halves of Austria–Hungary had been ruled. The difference lay in the consequent dangers to the non-preponderant—now 'minority'—peoples. Despite their imperfections and the great injustices to which they had given rise, the continental empires had been recognizably multinational states and there had always been some minimal understanding of the advantages of preserving some sort of inter-nation peace even when resented and displaced in practice by contrary considerations. But the polities that were about to replace the old empires were founded on concepts, the sum of which was a flat denial of multinationalism not only *de facto* but *de jure* too and as a matter of highest political principle. Rational, efficacious, and so far as possible peaceful administration ceased to be accepted as a central criterion of good government. The romantic principle of nationality replaced it as the one by which all acts of state were to be judged and justified. And this being the case, the implications for the Jews could not be other than dire.

Much had happened since the Congress of Berlin four decades earlier, not least the fact that there floated before all eyes, among the political and diplomatic experts at the Conference in the first instance, but to some extent among the principals whom they were there to serve as well, the lesson the Romanians had subsequently done so much to inculcate: namely that this was a sphere in which no one was to be wholly trusted, that safeguards and guarantees were of the essence, that written treaty undertakings were unlikely to suffice—least of all when they were couched in general terms. There was little or no disagreement among the Big Three and their minions that whatever framework was imposed on eastern and south-eastern Europe, the Jews of those parts did constitute a distinct social (i.e. not solely religious) category, that whatever the results of the Conference's labours might be they would bear heavily upon them, and—a crucial consideration—that the Jews were seriously in need of protection. If there were doubts on any of these scores at the beginning of the process of discussion they were largely put to rest by the reports flowing in from the Ukraine and neighbouring Polish-controlled territories on the actual fate of the Jewish inhabitants there and by the hostile, in some cases ferocious response of the master-nations of the new and enlarged states that were in the process of being established to proposals that Jewish needs and fears be explicitly catered for.

But in other respects those present in Paris to determine how central and eastern Europe was actually to be refashioned piece by piece were not all of one mind. The British and the Americans were generally prepared to consider the relevant questions in terms of what they themselves reckoned to be the viability and even the rough justice of such proposals as were under examination. The French were less inclined to adopt a detached and objective approach: their minds were on other things for the most part; and in so far as they attended to the affairs of eastern Europe and the Balkans, notably where the larger states, Poland and Romania, were concerned, it was their strategic potentialities as military allies of France that interested them most. It was widely recognized that there was a new mood among the Jews of eastern Europe. It was noted at the time in an official French publication that 'Little by little, the Jews of these countries have awakened to their ethnic individuality, an awakening promoted by Zionist propaganda and by the movement of nationalities precipitated by the war. Today, the great majority of Jews claim not only the rights of citizens, but also, and most especially, collective national rights.[39] But to the question whether this meant that the Jews were therefore to be considered one of the constituent *nationalities* of eastern Europe there was no agreed answer. There was only a great reluctance to deal directly with the issue and an absolute refusal all round to accept that Jewish national sentiment might ultimately be allowed to have real political consequences—consequences *in Europe*, that is to say. There was less difficulty, it needs to be said, and for the British no difficulty at all, about Jews *from* Europe—or from any other part of the world for that matter—having a recognized national status and appropriate national political institutions and national political aspirations in Palestine. This was consistent with the approach embodied in the final, carefully worded formulation of the Balfour Declaration. It followed that where Palestine was concerned those in Jewry who can be described, roughly, as Jewish nationalists—the Zionists, of course, among them—were very well placed.

Great Britain's allies had accepted the principles embodied in the Declaration and went along, in due course, with its textual embodiment in the League of Nations Mandate under which Great Britain was to administer the country—the central prescriptive obligation of which was that this be done in the interests of the Jewish National Home.[40] The French, it is true, did drag their feet somewhat in this respect. When Weizmann, Sokolov, and Ussishkin came before the Council of Ten to put the Zionist case, the Quai d'Orsay put up Sylvain Lévi, its man in the Alliance Israélite Universelle, to explain with great sincerity, but at somewhat self-defeating length, why it was a poor idea after all and why, therefore, many Jews of considerable standing opposed it. When the French chairman of the Committee on New States wanted his committee to hear Joseph Reinach, a firm opponent of Zionism, speak on the subject, there were objections on the grounds *inter alia* that 'what Zionism has in mind is the creation of a state, a political question of the highest degree, and not the protection of ethnic minorities'. And while sufficient pressure was exerted to ensure that Reinach be heard, the effect was diminished by all concerned informing the chairman that they were attending

---

[39] Ministères des Affaires Etrangères et de la Guerre, *Recueil de Documents Etrangers. Supplément périodique aux Bulletins de presse étrangère* (Paris, 31 July 1919), no. 46, 254. Cited in Nathan Feinberg, *La Question des minorités à la conférence de la paix de 1919–1920 et l'action juive en faveur de la protection internationale des minorités* (Paris, 1929), 38.

[40] The Preamble to the League of Nations Mandate repeated the text of the Balfour Declaration and laid down that Britain was responsible for putting it into effect, repeating the injunction in Article 2, on which see below, p. 868 n. 54.

his meeting exclusively in a private capacity.[41] The British duly had their way in the end. The Zionist programme (somewhat whittled down) sailed through the relevant committees and conferences. In an initial, admittedly still very fragile form the renewed Jewish national foothold in the ancestral land was assured—and not before time, one might add: it would not be long before most of the British statesmen and officials concerned had concluded that they had taken on a great deal more than they had ever bargained for. Where there was no such relatively plain sailing for the Zionists, however, and for those who were prepared to go along with them was in respect of the views and programmes concerning the Jews in Europe itself which they, the Zionists, had been quick to formulate and were equally keen to press upon the principal governments represented at the Peace Conference.

One of their difficulties was that they were far from having the stage to themselves. The Zionists' old opponents and rivals for the ears of western statesmen and diplomats, the Alliance Israélite Universelle and the newly reconstructed Joint Foreign Committee representing the Board of Deputies of British Jews and the Anglo-Jewish Association, were present in Paris in force and had very clear ideas of their own. They regarded the welfare of Diaspora Jewry as their own firm, long-standing, supremely legitimate and well-nigh exclusive responsibility. They felt themselves to be, and there was none to deny it, the heirs of Adolphe Crémieux and Moses Montefiore. The Alliance's seniority among Jewish public, quasi-political institutions, along with the twin facts that it was at home in Paris and that it maintained an exceedingly close relationship with the French government sufficed to assure it of a respectful hearing among officials of other governments and among the representatives of the other Jewish bodies present on the margins of the Conference as well. The JFC too commanded general respect, grudging in some quarters, but real enough—a tribute before all else to the formidable talents, experience, drive, expert knowledge of eastern Europe, and first-rate contacts within the British establishment of its executive secretary, Lucien Wolf. Neither body could be dismissed or ignored. And the result was all-round competition for the attention not only of the almost unapproachable great men who had assembled in Paris to make the final decisions, but more particularly and more intensively for the attention of the nominally lesser, but recognizably influential, figures soldiering in the great army of diplomats and specialist advisers who made up the bulk of the assemblage.

Fortunately, there was no difficulty of any consequence about persuading the experts themselves to listen to what Jewish representatives

---

[41] 26 Sept. 1919, AE, Palestine 1918–1929, 14 (E 3124] Sionisme, fo. 22. Reinach summed up his hostile, but forceful view of Zionism at this time in a leaflet entitled *Sur le Sionisme* (Paris, 1919), BNat. A 18364.

had to say and to read their written submissions with care—one obvious
difference between this Paris Peace Conference of 1919 and other great
international gatherings that had preceded it. An equally remarkable difference was the absence from the scene of any of the magnates of Jewry.
A few polite pilgrimages were made to Baron Edmond de Rothschild.
And the Baron seems to have been in sporadic contact with the Quai
d'Orsay. Messages from important addresses in London were transmitted
from time to time and taken note of in both diplomatic and Jewish quarters. Effectively, however, the public business of the Jewish people was
now in the hands of men who could begin to be seen as professional
politicians, of specialists, and of such as may fairly be described as public
servants. This made for greater efficiency in communication and in the
transaction of business, but heightened the problem presented by the
presence of a considerable range of Jewish bodies of a great variety of
incompatible characters and notions of what needed to be done on eastern European Jewry's behalf—at least a score before the Conference was
over. Rivalry was intense. Each watched the others jealously, at times
with dismay, at other times with anticipatory *schadenfreude*.

I hear that the Zionists are very busy organising their new Bureau for the treatment of the questions which the *Alliance* and the Joint Committee have hitherto
been dealing with [Lucien Wolf noted in his diary on 19 March 1919]. I do not
think they will find their task an easy one. They propose to support the extreme
exponents of Jewish National Rights in Eastern Europe. This will bring them in
conflict with the Allied Delegations which, as things stand at present, are strongly
disposed to favour our moderate formula of cultural autonomy. They are also no
less likely to find themselves repudiated by the Roumanian Jews, whose cause
must be hopelessly compromised by any demand for National Rights and
who are consequently overwhelmingly against the Zionists. Personally I have no
reason to regret the attitude of the Zionists on this point, as their extremism can
only make our moderation the more acceptable both to the Allied Governments
and the Poles. Still it is a pity that at the moment there should be dis-union on
this important question in the Jewish community. Happily the responsibility is
not ours, for I have neglected nothing to come to an agreement with the Zionists,
and I am still without an answer to my last letter to Sokolo[v] in which I
expressed my readiness to discuss with him his very dubious scheme of united
action.[42]

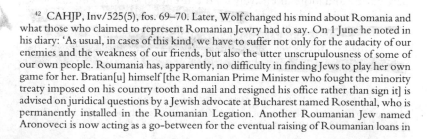

[42] CAHJP, Inv/525(5), fos. 69–70. Later, Wolf changed his mind about Romania and
what those who claimed to represent Romanian Jewry had to say. On 1 June he noted in
his diary: 'As usual, in cases of this kind, we have to suffer not only for the audacity of our
enemies and the weakness of our friends, but also the utter unscrupulousness of some of
our own people. Roumania has, apparently, no difficulty in finding Jews to play her own
game for her. Bratian[u] himself [the Roumanian Prime Minister who fought the minority
treaty imposed on his country tooth and nail and resigned his office rather than sign it] is
advised on juridical questions by a Jewish advocate at Bucharest named Rosenthal, who is
permanently installed in the Roumanian Legation. Another Roumanian Jew named
Aronoveci is now acting as a go-between for the eventual raising of Roumanian loans in

None doubted that this general and incoherent scramble for attention was unfortunate and possibly dangerous. There was an evident risk that much of the force of what needed to be said to the makers of policy and their minions would be lost. No one denied that it would be wiser and better if the spokesmen for Jewish causes worked as a united delegation. Several attempts to form such a delegation were made, each collapsing in acrimony, charges and counter-charges of bad faith and presumptuous arrogance being the common reward of all concerned, both those who were genuinely prepared to modify or moderate their positions and those who were immovable. The final and grandest attempt to achieve at least temporary unity was an immensely long debate held at the offices of the Consistoire and extending over two days, 5–6 April 1919. Virtually everyone of some personal and institutional standing and with something to say on the matter attended, just under four dozen people in all. Nothing new was said. Well-known positions were rehearsed. Fundamental incompatibilities of outlook corresponding, roughly, to the old east–west divide were rendered clearer than ever. And tempers were frayed as perhaps never before. Sokolov insisted on a demand for 'national' rights in Poland being made. Elsewhere, if it proved absolutely necessary, he would agree to the term 'ethnic' being substituted for 'national', pointing out quite correctly that in eastern Europe, unlike the west, 'nationality' did not necessarily have political connotations, but such as were essentially ethnic and cultural. Still, if the Jews were to be capable of playing their due and proper *proportionate* role in the new states unhampered, constitutional matters could not be ignored. In Poland and in other countries with a large and coherent Jewish population there needed therefore to be a curia electoral system such as would allow Jews to be represented in parliament in due proportion to their numbers in the population.

Claude Montefiore for the JFC and Eugène Sée for the Alliance would have none of this. Montefiore stuck to the principle he and his colleagues had formally agreed upon in London in December of the previous year in anticipation of the Conference, namely that the idea that 'Jews constitute a separate political nationality all over the world' was itself

England. . . . Yesterday by a singular coincidence the well known Jewish economist who is also a member of the Jewish Consistoire, Georges Raphael Levi, delivered a lecture to a fashionable audience on the economic [re]sources of Roumania, the object being to puff the country for the benefit of the money market. Nor are these the only instances I could mention of Jews serving the anti-Semitic Government of Roumania and even worse Roumanian rascals than the Anti-Semites. No wonder Bratian[u] assumes a pose of injured innocence when he is called upon to give guarantees to the fair treatment of the Jews' (ibid., fos. 155–6). Prime Minister Ion C. Bratianu was the son of Ion Bratianu, minister of the interior in the 1860s and Romanian delegate to the Congress of Berlin, referred to in Chapter 6 above.

inadmissible.[43] He repudiated charges made by some of the nationalists present that the western Jews, having their own interests in mind, had betrayed the easterners in the past and were about to do so again. The westerners had no selfish interests to serve. And in any case, the present dangers were not to this or that community, but to 'the higher interests of Judaism'. He himself was proud to be an Englishman; he was prouder still to be a member of the 'universal Jewish community'—and it was this which was endangered by the attempt to transform the Jews into one or many political nationalities. What he was prepared to support was a claim to a measure of autonomy in the religious and cultural spheres. Sée, for the Alliance, was unwilling to go even that far, upon which Ussishkin in rebuttal, fresh from the Ukraine and accepted willy-nilly as the most prominent and authentic spokesman-leader of Russian Jewry present in Paris at the time, lectured the assembly on the example of the Jews of the Ukraine. They were now in the process of being organized as a national community. This was the example to be followed elsewhere. He spoke too of the formation of a world Jewish parliament and of the admission of the Jews as a distinct people, some fifteen million strong, into the League of Nations. To the horrified objections of Sée and the other anti-nationalists, Ussishkin retorted by pointing to a painting of the Napoleonic Sanhedrin that hung on the wall of the room in the Consistoire in which the meeting had been convened and warning them that the time would come when it would be replaced by one of the First Congress of Zionists at Basel. An indignant Sée replied that had it not been for the Sanhedrin the Jews of France would still be in the ghetto and unable to help others, but that was not an argument likely to impress Ussishkin, or Sokolov either, for that matter.[44] No meeting of minds being possible, the Zionists and the Americans (not all of whom were themselves Zionists) formed themselves into one camp, the Alliance and the JFC into another.

The 'Palestine Idea' having been approved by the major powers dominating the scene in Paris, the Zionists had gained for themselves a tactical and psychological advantage over the others. They were now locked as no Jewish group had ever been before into the western diplomatic system by virtue of their involvement in high Near Eastern politics (as the representatives of eastern European orthodoxy, for example, could never be, needless to say). At the same time, being for the most part eastern European Jews themselves, they were commonly perceived as far and away the most effective and authentic spokesmen for their countrymen (as neither Sylvain Lévi or Lucien Wolf, regardless of their good intentions, could claim to be). And while in the contemporary chaos of

[43] JFC Minutes, 11 Dec. 1918, CZA, A77/3/c.
[44] Wolf, diary, fos. 86–9; Oscar I. Janowsky, *The Jews and Minority Rights 1898–1919* (New York, 1933; repr. New York, 1966), 299–302.

eastern Europe no accurate counting of heads was possible, the evidence really did point to the Zionists being the current leaders of Jewish public opinion—by their assumption of a dominant role in the majority of the communities in the new Poland, for example.[45] Finally, their salience at Paris owed something to theirs being the clearest and most uncompromising statement of Jewish requirements, one, moreover, that had manifestly been written with the new Wilsonian Europe in mind and that was closely geared to what no one seriously doubted were the contemporary realities of Jewish life.

It is now virtually impossible to disentangle the many lines of contact, debate, and influence exerted by the many various and conflicting representations made on behalf of the Jews of eastern Europe and to assess the precise weight of their influence on the peacemakers collectively and separately. What deserves special note, however, is that it can be assumed that had there been no pressure from Jewish organizations of all kinds, nationalist and anti-nationalist, for *some* system of protection for the Jewish minorities to be devised, it is unlikely in the extreme that their interests would ever have been attended to. James Headlam Morley, later to serve as Historical Adviser at the British Foreign Office, but at the time of the Peace Conference the man most intimately involved on the British side with Jewish affairs, observed in a confidential memorandum some ten years later, that

No specific reference to the protection of minorities was included in any of the reports presented by the territorial commissions to the Council of Four, and when the recommendations of these reports were accepted by the Council and included in the text of the treaty, they were not accompanied by any clauses dealing with this matter. It appeared, indeed, as if the importance of it had escaped the attention of the Council and would go by default. That this did not happen seems entirely the result of the action of the Jews.[46]

There was, however, one other factor, as Headlam Morley went on to observe. Jewish concern about the future had been especially and justifiably fuelled by what was rapidly becoming known about the catastrophic condition of the Jews not only in the Ukraine and other areas in which the Russian civil war was raging, but in the territories that had been taken over by the new and the enlarged lesser states of eastern Europe and the Balkans, most especially Poland. 'Reports . . . showed that the situation was gravely unsatisfactory, and there was just ground for apprehension that unless provision were made for their protection, the Jews might be subjected not only to discriminatory legislation, but also to open violence and ill-treatment.'[47] The Historical Adviser's carefully chosen,

[45] A dominance they would lose when things calmed down somewhat.
[46] 'Memorandum respecting the Minorities Treaties', 17 May 1929, PRO, FO 371/14125.
[47] Ibid.

exceedingly prim language referred to a state of affairs in Poland that, as he well knew, differed in scale somewhat from that obtaining in the Ukraine, but not at all in kind: a wave of executions, mutilation, systematic humiliation, heavy looting, floggings, collective fines, such displays of military superiority as forcing women to march barefoot in the winter cold and then neck-deep into the icy waters of the nearest river, the systematic disarming and prohibition of Jewish self-defence forces—in brief, much the same range of varieties of viciousness that were on display across the border in the Ukraine together with such additions as imaginative Polish mob leaders, army officers among them, had happened to think up. Cracow, Kielce, Lida, Lwow, Lublin, Pinsk, and Vilna were the scenes of major eruptions of violence, but the communities in very many dozens of other towns and villages, in Galicia especially, were attacked.[48] All this was evident by the time the Peace Conference had assembled: 110 pogroms of varying degrees of gravity had been perpetrated in the month of November 1918 alone. It was equally evident that the Polish army, police, and gendarmerie were active, and in the most serious cases were principal participants in the violence, notably so where unprovoked and organized slaughter by firing squad was recorded—as in Pinsk on 5 April 1919. The excuses offered on the rare occasions when the authorities had been asked to account for themselves were equally of a kind with those that were being voiced in the Ukraine: that the Jews had aided the enemies of resurgent Poland—either the Bolsheviks or the Ukrainians—or had displayed disloyalty to the republic in some other way.[49] In fact, no evidence corresponding in any way at all to the magnitude and horrific nature of the punishment inflicted on the republic's new subjects was ever adduced. And the sum of it by the late spring of 1919 was that even Lucien Wolf, contrary to his every wish and instinct, had given up the

---

[48] Telegram, 10 Feb. 1919, Zionist Bureau, London, to Zionist Organization, New York, CZA, A264/9; L. Chasanowitch (ed.), *Les Pogromes anti-juifs en Pologne et en Galicie en novembre et décembre 1918* (Stockholm, 1919); Pawel Korzec, *Juifs en Pologne: la question juive pendant l'entre-deux-guerres* (Paris, 1980), 75–81.

[49] A statement issued by the Polish military commander at Lemberg (Lwow) on 25 Nov. 1918 incorporates a typical mixture of false charges, threats, and sanctimonious protestations of honest intentions: 'During three weeks of the fighting for Lemberg the greater part of the Jewish population not only failed to maintain neutrality *vis-à-vis* the Polish troops, *but on several occasions offered them armed resistance and sought treacherously to prevent our troops' victorious advance.* There are established cases of firing on our soldiers from behind cover, of boiling water being poured [on them], and of our patrols being attacked with axes. The Polish command, none the less, wishes to resist the *natural movement* of the Polish population and soldiery. All citizens without religious distinction have been placed under the protection of the law. Martial law has been declared to this end. Still, it is the imperative duty of the Jewish population to warn *that party among its co-religionists* that continues to act in this manner that *it may in consequence provoke the most terrible catastrophe* for the Jewish population in its entirety.' See Chasanowitch, *Les Pogromes anti-juifs*, 61–2. Emphases in the original.

attempt to establish a meeting of minds with the Poles by fighting what he regarded as the Jewish nationalists' egregious demands for autonomy. He now drew the grimmest of conclusions.

Both Marshall [President of the American Jewish Committee] and I received further batches of horrors from Poland to-day, and we are bombarding our respective Delegations with them. I am afraid it is no good resisting any longer the proposed campaigns against Poland. We are in the presence of what certainly looks like a deliberate attempt to thin out the Jewish population by massacre.[50]

IV

The sharpest articulation of Jewish demands for national autonomy in eastern Europe had been issued by the Zionist liaison office in Copenhagen on 25 October 1918, well before the Peace Conference assembled, but when it was already clear that the war was finally drawing to a close. The Copenhagen Manifesto, as it came to be known, called upon the Peace Conference that all expected to be convened to assure the Jewish people of four things: of Palestine, 'within the limits fixed by historical tradition and political and economic necessities', being recognized as their National Home; of 'full and actual equality of rights for the Jews of all countries'; of 'national autonomy, cultural, social and political' for the Jews in countries where they formed a mass population, but in other countries too, provided the local Jewish population demanded it; and of admission of the Jewish people to the 'League of Free Nations as an equal of its fellow-members'.[51]

The truly burning concerns of the principal Zionist leadership and of the movement's main bureaucracy as they now began to regroup around Weizmann in London were, not unnaturally, with the National Home, while 'Current tasks' in the Diaspora itself were relegated to a second tier within the movement and the only major figure to play an active role in both arenas was Naḥum Sokolov. This was not fortuitous: Sokolov was the only figure of primary standing in the pre-war movement to survive politically into the new age. Where Palestine affairs were concerned he

---

[50] Wolf, diary, fo. 136. 'I don't know what you people are doing in Paris, but I know what you ought to be doing. There are more than a million Jews in the New Poland being starved and persecuted to death. There are more than six hundred thousand in Eastern Galicia, now partly battle ground between the Poles and the Ukrainians, partly what is almost as bad, Ukrainian territory subject to all kinds of lawlessness. These six hundred thousand are slowly also rotting to death.' Thus Henry G. Alsberg, a former member of the American Foreign Service who had been attached to the American Zionist delegation to Europe, beginning a detailed report from Warsaw on the Jews' condition to Felix Frankfurter from Warsaw, 12 May 1919, CZA, A264/7.

[51] CZA, A18/20.

had been locked into subordination to his sometime junior, Weizmann, in the course of 1917. In the arena specific to the Diaspora he had a freer hand, the more so as his activity there left Weizmann himself to deal unhindered with what was undoubtedly closest to *his* heart and mind. This implied a clear ordering of priorities for the movement generally, of course, and was a source of dissatisfaction therefore to those whose lives (and hearts) were still in eastern Europe. Semyon (Shimshon) Rosenbaum, a former member of the Duma, now deputy foreign minister in the new Lithuanian government and a staunch believer in both the right and the need for the Jews in eastern Europe to establish an autonomous political framework for themselves *in situ*, complained bitterly, after a visit to Paris, of what he judged to be the Zionist leadership's neglect of the matter of Jewish requirements in the Diaspora. It was Rosenbaum's view that the reason Weizmann refused to be involved in such matters was because he was before all else a pragmatist, a man who was only interested in what would work, and convinced that what was being asked for— national rights for the Jews along with other minority peoples—was in practice unattainable and unworkable. The result, as he saw it, was that the single most influential voice in Jewry at that juncture spoke almost exclusively of other things. Rosenbaum took some comfort in Sokolov having resolved to take up the burden, but not much.[52] In fact, however, the line between the two arenas—and between the two men—was never drawn with anything like the precision Rosenbaum and some others ascribed to it. Weizmann could be found seeking to impress upon the British government the need to induce the Poles to desist from violent persecution of Jews in the territories now under their control.[53] Sokolov's initial position in 1919 had been, as he explained to a senior foreign official, that 'the Zionist organization as such was not an organization concerned with these European problems though individual Zionists may have their views upon them. The Zionist organization existed for Palestine only and the Zionist question was geographically limited to Palestine.'[54] But the issue Rosenbaum had in mind was a real one.

While Zionism itself was nothing if not a movement born of the actual material and mental afflictions of the Jews of Europe, so long as Herzl governed it the rule was to go no further than to affirm this as a truth. In practice, all eyes and efforts were to be directed towards Palestine. Rigorous abstention from participation in the domestic affairs of the states and societies in which the Zionist Organization had established a presence was adduced as one of several good reasons for governments to view it with favour. When it had begun to seem to the great majority of Zionists that the Palestine goal, as a practical proposition, was receding into an intolerably remote future while the problems assailing the Jews in Europe were steadily changing for the worse, this, as we have seen, became a position that could no longer be sustained. Now the wheel had turned again. Diplomacy, secrecy, personal contacts in very high, alien places, and the rest of what Herzl had come to stand for in the eyes of those who disparaged him had been revived—and were judged to have proved themselves after all. One of his greatest critics had turned out to be the most distinguished champion and practitioner of his method. And it had become quite as natural for Weizmann and his school to doubt whether it was wise or even possible to do other than concentrate exclusively, or almost so, on matters Palestinian as ever it had been for the Master whom they had long since confined, not very reverently, to shadowland.

The difficulty about this was that in the actual heartland of Jewry, far from London, Paris, and Jerusalem, the shattering deterioration of conditions seemed, if anything, to call for a very much heightened and expanded, rather than diminished, version of the pre-war 'Helsingfors doctrine'.[55] There where the condition of the Jews was most dire the sudden improvement in Zionism's prospects tended to reimpose a double—and therefore somewhat equivocal—vision of things on the movement's activists. In the appalling turmoil and horrors of Russia and the Ukraine there was, indeed, no choice but to take a firm and public stand on what was here and now and all around one as well as on what lay in the future. It was both natural *and* necessary for Zionists to press for recognized national-political status for the Jews in the Ukraine and the rest of eastern and east-central Europe not only because it accorded with their fundamental outlook, but because it was that which the commonalty was most likely to support and because it did in practice reflect better than any perceivable alternative their true situation and immediate needs. The Zionists were therefore drawn quite as powerfully as were other secular nationalists to active participation, for example, in Ukrainian parliamentary affairs. And as reports on the slaughter in the Ukraine and on the widespread physical persecution of Jews in newly independent Poland flooded into Zionist centres in the west activists in Copenhagen, Paris, London, and New York found themselves serving as key conduits for their further dissemination and as spokesmen for their brethren in the east. They were themselves, it needs to be recalled, preponderantly from eastern Europe. They now had at their disposal the best-organized, most widespread, and most coherent supra-communal Jewish organization of all—which was, besides, the only one of its kind to straddle the east–west

---

[55] See above, pp. 612–16.

divide. They had recently achieved a triumph that could fairly be termed revolutionary. The task could not possibly be shirked. On the other hand, the question at what targets, and in what proportions, they should direct their efforts had still to be faced—if faced it could be.

In the event, no great debate or grand redefinition of purposes occurred. The issue was never allowed to be brought to a head and fully thrashed out. Nor could it be, one supposes, without the structure of Zionism as ideology and as movement being torn to pieces there and then. In practice, the upshot was only a rough and ready division of labour. The Zionist movement would proceed along twin, yet separable tracks: one Near Eastern, the other European. There would be those whose eyes and concerns remained fastened firmly and exclusively on the movement's eponymous task of establishing and consolidating the Jewish National Home. It had now been promised them by the British government. It was in the process of being confirmed internationally. The British undertaking would shortly be incorporated formally into the League of Nations Mandate for Palestine that would in some sort serve as the country's constitution. And since it had almost immediately become plain that this would be an exceedingly difficult and an increasingly perilous undertaking in itself, one that would be beset with obstacles and formidable enemies, the grounds for mobilizing all available forces in its pursuit were, as it would be argued for many years to come, indisputable. Weizmann himself was the natural, not to say inevitable exponent of this, the more stringent, in some ways pitiless, school. At the same time, there were those whose belief in, and commitment to, the classic Zionist territorial path out of the morass of the Diaspora was in no way diminished, but who none the less refused to avert their eyes from the immediate condition of those whom the entire enterprise was intended ultimately to liberate. Leo Motzkin, Weizmann's old antagonist, began at this point to take his place as the effective leader and driving force of this, the second school.

Motzkin's initial, exceedingly simple, in due course celebrated argument, set out at the first postwar general conference of Zionists (held in London February–March 1919) was that the most one could assume of emigration to Palestine was that it would proceed at an annual rate of 50,000. But since the natural increase of the Jewish population in Europe and elsewhere was likely to continue at an approximate annual rate of 200,000, it was plain that if the Zionists aspired to leadership in Jewry they had no choice but to accept a great measure of responsibility for Jewish conditions and rights in the Diaspora as well as in Palestine. The issue this raised was an old one: in its bare essentials it was much the same as that which had all but torn the movement apart at the time of the great debate over the East Africa scheme in 1903: Palestinophilism versus immediate relief. It had a great deal in common too with that which served to distinguish the *purs et durs* of Zionism from the several varieties of Diaspora nationalists: the Bundists, the Autonomists, and the rest. Having regard to the real condition of the Jews, however, the terms of the dilemma were harsher than they had been before the war and it would not be long before they would become harsher still. For the time being, however, at the Peace Conference, it was the Copenhagen Manifesto that did duty as a basis for discussion among those delegations, chiefly the Zionists and the Americans, who came together to form what would in due course be termed the Committee of Jewish Delegations to the Peace Conference (Comité des Délégations Juives auprès de la Conférence de la Paix).[56]

But it had first to be refashioned into a document that could be presented in due form to the Peace Conference and whittled down somewhat too if it was to have any chance of being considered. The demand for Jewish membership in the League of Nations was abandoned, as was the demand for compensation for material damage suffered in the course of pogroms and for a proportionate share of war indemnities.[57] The main demands put to the Council by the Zionist-American coalition were cast in very general terms, moreover. No more was asked for the Jews than, so it was argued, was rightly due all 'national, religious, racial and linguistic minorities' in central and eastern Europe. All these were entitled to be recognized as 'distinct and autonomous organisms' by the states in question, as was their consequent right to manage and control their own educational and social institutions, and the Jews with all others. The original, all-encompassing demand for 'national autonomy, cultural, social and political' for the Jews specifically was softened: the term 'political' did not appear in the final document. But it was strengthened somewhat by being spelled out: all national minorities, the Jews among them, to be sure, should be entitled to elect representatives to all state, departmental, municipal, and other public elective bodies in proportion to their respective numbers in the total population. And three other precise demands were submitted: the right to a measure of independence in education coupled to an obligation by the state to support the minority's school system financially; measures to protect the Jews from attempts to turn their observance of the Sabbath against them economically and politically; and a system whereby, under certain circumstances, it would be open to the League of Nations to adjudicate complaints levelled against any of the states in question for having violated its undertakings under the relevant treaty.[58]

---

[56] See Léo Motzkin, 'Les Revendications nationales des Juifs', in *Les Droits nationaux des Juifs en Europe Orientale: receuil d'études* (Paris, 1919), 7–27.

[57] Motzkin's point had been that the imposition of an obligation to compensate the victims of persecution would have a deterrent effect on governments—no pogrom ever having taken place without some degree of official connivance (ibid. 24–5).

[58] Comité des Délégations Juives auprès de la Conférence de la Paix to the President and the Members of the Peace Conference, 10 May 1919, CZA, L6/80.

When the Peace Conference first assembled the French proposed that a specialist committee on Jewish affairs be established. The plan was soon dropped, however. Matters concerning the Jews, it was resolved, were to be discussed under the general rubric of 'the rights of [all] ethnic and religious minorities'.[59] Foremost in the minds of the peacemakers was the view that however deserving of sympathy the Jews and certain other subject peoples might be (the Ukrainians who were fated to be included in the new Poland, for example), in straightforward political terms the most difficult and much the most urgent aspect of the new European map-in-the-making was the fact that the minorities most in need of consideration and protection were those who belonged to nations which had hitherto been in a position of supremacy: the Germans and the Hungarians. The peacemakers were clear in their minds that there could be no such ready acceptance of Jewish claims to collective rights and to a collective national status as there was to their claim to individual civil rights and equality, an issue about which there was no dispute at all in any quarter, not openly at all events. It was accepted by all and without question that the Jews *as individuals* were entitled to full civil and political rights in all countries, notably where they had not as yet enjoyed them. And of this the Zionists, the JFC, and the Alliance had all been carefully and unambiguously assured well before the war was over. In June 1918 the British government had affirmed its sympathy with the demand for emancipation and declared itself to be 'most anxious to do everything in their power to secure a just and permanent settlement of the Jewish question eastern and south-eastern Europe'.[60] A month later, the French foreign minister, Pichon, in characteristically different style, but to the same end and in terms carrying the same weight, informed the AIU that

true to the generous traditions of France, not forgetting that the French Republic was the first in Europe to accord Jews the rights of citizenship, the Government of the Republic desires the emancipation of the Jews in eastern Europe and is prepared to do all that is within its power to bring about a just settlement of the Jewish question in those countries.[61]

Inherently more complex, however, but also violently resented by the new states, was the question of the means by which minorities were to be

---

[59] Later, when the Jewish clauses of the minorities treaties had finally to be decided upon, the Council of Four set up a Franco-Anglo-American committee on New States to be presided over by Philippe Berthelot, the French representative. The American member was David Hunter Miller. The most influential and knowledgeable of the three was the British member, James Headlam Morley. They were joined after a while by Italian and Japanese representatives.

[60] A conflation of letters sent on Balfour's behalf, Langley to Sokolov, 15 June 1918, CZA, A18/23; and Graham to Wolf, 28 June 1918, BD, C11/3/1/3.

[61] 24 July 1918. See Alliance Israélite Universelle, *La question juive devant la conférence de la paix* (Paris, 1919), 8–9.

protected from those who would now be their lawful rulers. This was difficult enough in all cases. It was soon apparent that the case of the Jews presented special difficulties, not least for the Jews themselves. Should they press for a non-specific solution of general application? This was the preference of the anti-nationalists, firmly wedded to the principle of at least eventual integration into society as a whole and always reluctant to see the Jews specified and categorized, especially if they were to be categorized at all, as analogues of the Ukrainians or the Germans. The difficulty, as Wolf of the JFC was rather more inclined to recognize than were the representatives of the Alliance, was that there were obvious ways in which ostensibly non-specific legislation and administrative ordinances of a seemingly banal character could be employed to disenfranchise the Jews and discriminate against them—and against them alone. National and local elections could be held on the Jewish Sabbath, for example. Regulations prohibiting work and trade on Sundays would reduce the Jews' working week to five days in all. It was already evident in Poland that their representation in parliament was being cut to the bone by the gerrymandering of electoral constituencies, towns in which Jews were preponderant or even formed the absolute majority of the population being swallowed up in vast countryside districts in which they were necessarily a small minority.

The lesson taught by the Romanians' flagrantly deceitful repudiation of its obligations under the accords of 1878 had long since been learned. Now, as C. A. Macartney was to put it, it 'recoiled upon them' (and upon the Poles and others) by leading to much more stringent terms being inserted into the treaty they would have to sign if they were to be allowed to enlarge their territories. The Romanians sought to persuade the peacemakers that they had mended their ways. They were not believed.[62] When persuasion failed they tried defiance. But that did them little good either, although the preamble to the treaty of St Germain, signed at the very last moment, on 9 December 1919, was sweetened to read less like the *Diktat* that it was; and certain clauses relating very specifically to Jews such as were already contained in the Polish treaty (on which more in a moment) were deleted. Generally speaking, the behaviour of the Romanians and the only marginally less co-operative behaviour of the Poles served to demonstrate how well founded were repeated demands by Jewish representatives and by the representatives of other peoples too for guarantees that went well beyond a new state's mere written promise of good behaviour in the future. The Committee on New States eventually accepted that a procedure by which the members of a national minority,

---

[62] Macartney quotes a Romanian ex-minister who claimed in 1881 that 'We can boast that we have resolved the Jewish question in the national sense, and that we can avow it openly, contrary to the manifest intention and the spirit itself of the Treaty of Berlin.' See C. A. Macartney, *National States and National Minorities* (London, 1934), 169.

or their accredited representatives, might seek an international remedy for ill treatment needed to be devised. But how precise did it need to be and how far should it go? The peacemakers' readiness in principle to grant effective guarantees was heavily offset in practice not only by the heavy opposition of the new states themselves, but by other, more attractive theses on what was needed for the proper management of international affairs—theses which were much more in tune with the general, meliorist climate of opinion and intentions in which the Conference as a whole had allowed itself to be enveloped. It was accepted as virtually axiomatic that hope of an *eventual* recognition by both majoritarian and minoritarian peoples (*a fortiori* gentiles and Jews) of their common interests must under no circumstances be abandoned; that the true goal towards which men of good will should strive was social integration; and that it would be a gross political error to insist on the majoritarian nations conceding more than they could reasonably be expected to stomach: namely that the pride of the greater group deserved as much consideration as the protection of the lesser. The result was that each of the minority treaties would embody two basic, inner contradictions—at all events so far as their application to the Jews was concerned: an implicit refusal to accept that the Jews did indeed constitute a distinct national minority on a par with other national minorities—coupled, however, to a very clear recognition of the likelihood that they would none the less be treated as such by the majoritarian people and by its government; and a recognition of the need to establish some form of international protection for them if they were not sooner or later to be crushed—but again, coupled to, and heavily diminished by, an extreme reluctance to blunt the sacred principle of state sovereignty.

For all this, the primary instance and occasion for the fiercest diplomatic battles was Poland. Poland was the most important and potentially most powerful of the new states. It was the one which possessed the most fervently coherent and patriotic national society. It was not a new state in anything like the same sense that Czechoslovakia and Yugoslavia were. But the circumstances, as was well understood in Paris in 1919, were that, however the new Poland's borders might be drawn, great numbers of non-Polish inhabitants (Germans, Ukrainians, Belorussians, and Jews principally) would be included within them. All told, minorities accounted for a full third of the total, the Jews alone about a tenth.[63]

Everything indicated, and none in Paris seriously doubted, that it was a primary concern of the Polish leaders to ensure unquestioned Polish preponderance in the fragile, not to say porous, nation-state they were in the process of trying to pull together. The Polish republic, having been reconstructed very specifically upon the ruins of Prussia as well as, in a

---

[63] See Table 9.1, Chapter 9, below.

more general sense, out of the debris of three of the four continental empires, was a country under permanent threat. And no one doubted the extraordinary combination of romantic tenacity, political pugnacity, and overweening national pride with which national feeling among the members of the Polish social elite was shot through. Poland provided a paradigmatic illustration, therefore, of the immense, if not insurmountable obstacles to achieving a tolerable balance between the contradictory imperatives of national self-determination, a civil order based on equity and equality for all, and genuinely irenic relations with neighbours that the peacemakers of Paris had identified as their overall purposes. Could there be, on the one hand, a state which the Poles themselves—at all events those who claimed to speak for them—were truly satisfied to regard as significantly and unmistakably their own? On the other hand, could there be a state (the same state) in which all inhabitants without exception were assured of security of person, free private and public practice of religion, equality before the law, fair and equal access to public offices, honours and functions, admission to all professions and occupations, language facilities in the courts and in education for all substantial minorities, and—as the ultimate test of all else—untrammelled individual and collective participation in the country's political life? The idea that, having barely entered into their inheritance, the Polish nationalists should be forced to make what struck them as real cultural and constitutional—and therefore ultimately politico-national—concessions to the aliens in their midst was more than most of them could bring themselves to stomach. That they should agree to external, international protection for the minorities seemed to them to be a still more intolerable attaint on their sovereignty, an imposition of a means of systematic intervention in their internal affairs such as few states, not even defeated Germany, were obliged to put up with. And that these offences were compounded by the insistence at Paris that the Jews—the least wanted, least palatable, and most disliked of all the non-Polish peoples who would now come under their rule—be *explicitly* protected was the final outrage. Both Roman Dmowski, founder-leader of the National Democratic Party (Endecja) and the leading figure in the Polish delegation to the Peace Conference, and Ignacy Paderewski, the titular leader of the country, left no one in any doubt that this was their view, as did all other authorized spokesman and the Polish press as well.

It could be assumed that when the new rulers of the country had found their feet they would be prepared to stop their troops from mounting pogroms in the established Cossack style.[64] It was unlikely that they would fail to restore basic order in the streets and impose something like

---

[64] Even the practice of giving the men a free day or two to pillage and maltreat at will before being called off had been adopted.

the rule of law throughout the territory eventually. But over and above the massive physical violence to which the Jewish population was being subjected even as the treaty was under discussion in Paris, there was abundant evidence of the continuing, generally mindless hostility newly independent Poland's political, Church, and military authorities at virtually every level of the various hierarchies were displaying as a matter of course towards the Jewish inhabitants now under their rule. In content it bore very little relation to the more than evident facts of Jewish life—the extreme poverty of the great majority of Polish Jews, for example. And, to the alarm of western Jews, it was being continually picked up and internalized by western diplomats and soldiers and duly transmitted back to their respective home bases. 'And in the middle of all this,' Captain Charles de Gaulle, then a member of the French military mission in Poland, wrote to his mother, 'innumerable [. . .][65] utterly loathed [*détestés à mort*] by all classes of society, all of them enriched [*sic*] by the war having profited at the expense of the Russians, the Boches and the Poles, and well disposed to a social revolution in which, by sharp practice, they would stand to make a lot of money.'[66]

In sum, there could be no doubt at all that the Jews could expect a hard time in Poland in all circumstances and that the Polish authorities were very likely to circumvent general, *non*-specific treaty rules for the protection of minorities in the particular and—from the nationalist-Polish point of view—especially irritating and objectionable case of the Jews. They needed only to make the most of the always debatable, and indeed objectively equivocal status of the Jews. Were they a religious category? Were they an ethnic or a linguistic one? What business had they anyway in Poland? There was the awkward fact that, unlike the Germans and the Ukrainians, the Jews were scattered throughout the country and rarely if at all present in an absolutely compact mass—awkward for all, Jews and Poles alike, but convenient to the latter if the former were to be disenfranchised *de facto*. Simplest of all for those who meant to exclude the Jews from *l'état légal* as well as, so far as possible, *l'état réel*, was the fact that the Jews were 'Saturday people'. Nothing would be easier for the authorities than to reduce the general protective clauses of the treaty to a virtual nullity whenever they chose to do so by holding national and municipal elections, or setting important professional and academic examinations, on the Saturday. And—this being, of course, the crux of the matter—it was generally expected of them that they would take advantage of the various, all-too-familiar anomalies of Jewish life to drain the treaty of

[65] Thus in the printed text. The reference is obviously to Jews, although as the editors of de Gaulle's papers excised the term used by the future general there is no knowing whether he called them *Juifs* or something a good deal less complimentary.

[66] Letter to Mme Henry de Gaulle, 23 May 1919. See Charles de Gaulle, *Lettres, notes et carnets*, ii (Paris, 1980), 28.

whatever protection it was designed to offer the Jews, sooner or later, if they were not firmly prevented from doing so by appropriately unambiguous language.

Fatally for the Poles, however, but also alas for the Jews of independent Poland themselves, theirs would be the country with the largest free Jewish population in Europe, the locus therefore of the new centre of demographic, political, and cultural gravity of the Jewish people as now constituted. There was really no way, therefore, to paper over or reduce the problem, not so long as the Peace Conference lasted, at all events; and it was, of course, the Peace Conference, through the instrumentality of the peace treaty with Germany, that had it in its power to determine the legal, international status of the new republic and the constraints, if any, within which it would have to operate. 'The Poles have now come to the parting of the roads,' Lewis Namier, much the most penetrating of all observers of the case, wrote to Headlam Morley in Paris from his post in the Political Intelligence Department in the Foreign Office in London.

I had always hoped that Esmé Howard[67] would give them some sensible advice on this question, but as he absolutely failed to do so and merely continues talking about [Jewish] demands for privileges without ever reasonably explaining what he means, there is really need that some one else should do it. It is still in the power of the Poles to effect some kind of reconciliation with the Jews, and the Poles themselves seem hardly to realise how important it is for them to do so. What they seem mainly to wish for is that a few hundred thousand Jews should leave Poland, and that they do not consider how harmful it will be to them if these people leave the country with a feeling of bitterness and exasperation. On the other hand, if they meet the reasonable demands of the Jews and treat them in a sensible manner, the West European and American Jews can reasonably be expected to do all they can for the economic well-being and development of those Jews, and through them for the economic welfare of Poland. Things which were hardly possible under the oppressive Russian *ancien régime* might be done now, and if favourable national and economic conditions were created for the Jews in Poland, all the Jewish influence abroad would come to help and secure the new Poland.

The Jewish demands for educational autonomy are certainly just and reasonable, and it would be to the advantage to the Poles themselves [to satisfy them]. A nation is an organic entity, each part of it can profitably develop in its own proper setting alone, and it can be of no use to either side to cut off an arm from one body and try to graft it artificially as a third limb on the other. Jews can be good Polish citizens in the meaning of citizens of the Polish commonwealth, but they cannot possible partake of the Polish tradition of that *Volkstum* which is bound up with Poland's history, and its villages and fields, and its Church and the graves of their ancestors, and the altars of their saints. Equally undesirable is it that

---

[67] Howard (later Lord Howard of Penrith), a British diplomat dealing with Russian affairs at the Peace Conference, had been the British Commissioner on the Special Interallied Mission to Poland, Feb.–Mar. 1919.

we should drop our own ancient traditions which are second to those of no community in the world, which are strongly and markedly national, and which start from the Prophets and will not end until their prophecies come true. Assimilation such as Esmé Howard glibly talks about but no Pole really desires means crippling both sides. If people want to know the real origin of Bolshevism among the Jews I can tell them that its source is so-called assimilation. I frankly admit that the more I go towards Jewish nationalism—and in this I have advanced even during the last few months—the less respect I have for Bolshevik theories. Nationalism is the opposite to Bolshevism for much deeper reasons than any Socialists imagine. These reasons are: (1) Tradition, which in its very nature must be conservative. (2) The conception, and not merely the conception, but sincerely feeling, that a nation is an entity and not merely a collection of individuals. In a collection of individuals there would be no imaginable reason why one person should be better off than another, whereas in the case of an organic body there are good and obvious reasons why it should walk on its legs and not on its head. If you want to see a striking example of assimilation, look at a man like Rajchman[68] for whom, as you know, I have the greatest admiration. He has lost all trace of Jewish feeling and considers himself a Pole, but there is not in him, and indeed could not be even a trace of Polish national tradition and *Volkstum*. The effect is that extraordinary clear-sighted, almost prophetic objectivism and that extreme logical radicalism. And if you carefully analyse where in that really splendid man the defects come from, you will agree with me that it is from the absence of roots and from the fact that he neither knows nor feels the word of the Prophets which constitutionally ought to be his national inheritance.

Now if the Jews are put into Polish schools their roots will be cut in that manner, and this will not be of an advantage either to the Poles or to the Jews themselves. A fundamental reason why the Poles do not wish to concede to us that educational autonomy (though at bottom they strongly desire that we should be separate so that they should [not come under Jewish influence]) is that to acknowledge us as a national minority would be to some extent equivalent to acknowledging our presence in Poland as fully legitimate. The Poles prefer to give us whatever civil rights they may concede to us, as if by oversight, *qua* individuals, without admitting our right to a gregarious existence. Such a procedure may be right where the Jews form tiny minorities like in England, France and Italy, but nowhere form the majority of the town population. If Poland included nothing but purely Polish territory, it will contain 2 million Jews. Were it to be drawn according to Dmowski's demands, there would be 4 millions. Such masses cannot be treated as 'individuals' and to treat them as such is to deny them some of the most vital rights which a human being possesses. For indeed it is his most vital right to be something more than an individual and to merge his own small personality in the mighty historic personality of the nation which extends over centuries; in our case even over continents.

I have no doubt that in the end the Poles will have to concede these rights to us, especially should they be able to annex any non-Polish territory, because in

---

[68]   One of the representatives of the assimilationist faction in Polish Jewry who came to Paris to plead a case that ran contrary to that of the Zionists and the other Jewish nationalists. He was the son of a baptized Jew.

these annexed territories they will prefer the Jews to register as such (which implies an acknowledgement of the Jewish nationality); the alternative is that the Jews should go to swell the numbers of the non-Polish territories. Undoubtedly, if a Jew in annexed East-Galicia had to choose between registering as a Pole or as an Ukrainian, he would choose the latter.[69]

A French study group under one Professor E. Denis charged to look into the 'Jewish Question in historic Poland' as one of the many questions with which the coming Peace Conference would have to deal, had warned earlier that 'Nations do not like others to be meddling in their affairs, even with the best of intentions, and the Allies would do well to avoid immoderate [*abusive*] intervention.' It had gone on to remark, however, that 'our [wartime] sacrifices do perhaps give us the right to offer advice';[70] and it was in this spirit, in the event, that very heavy pressure had been brought to bear and a long, stern, yet not unsympathetic letter was addressed to them by Clemenceau, recalling in some detail what had been said and agreed upon at the Congress of Berlin.[71] The proposed treaty, Clemenceau argued, was far from constituting a fresh departure in public law; and 'special protection' was necessary for the Jews in Poland in view of the 'historical development of the Jewish question and the great animosity aroused by it'.[72] Further displays of ill will and wounded honour followed, but the Poles were finally induced to sign an agreed text—on the day the Treaty of Versailles itself was signed in the Hall of Mirrors, but separately and in another room. As agreed, the preamble to the Polish minorities treaty stated that 'the Allied and Associated Powers [having] by the success of their arms restored to the Polish nation the independence of which it had been unjustly deprived', were now in due form recognizing Poland 'as a sovereign and independent member of

---

[69] Namier to Headlam Morley, 16 Apr. 1919, Headlam Morley Papers, No. 47. (Some minor corrections have been made to a text obviously written in haste and heat.) Namier's views were, as he said, changing all the while. Three weeks earlier he had written to Headlam Morley: 'So far as I understand it, the Jews ask for two separate things: first of all that they should not be murdered promiscuously and that they should have the full protection of the law; to this they are absolutely entitled. Secondly, they ask that they should have their own schools. . . . Is there anything more which they really want? If not, why use the expression "national autonomy" . . . ?', 24 Mar. 1919. See James Headlam Morley, *A Memoir of the Paris Peace Conference 1919* (London, 1972), 55. Later still he wrote to the Prime Minister's Private Secretary: 'There are thousands of Jews impatiently waiting in Eastern Europe for the day when they could leave the House of Bondage, that torture-chamber which Poland has become for them. Their life in Poland is a daily round of insult and oppression. They are complete outlaws, and there is neither justice nor legal protection for them anywhere, and they are not even allowed to defend themselves. Their economic position is equally hopeless' (Namier to Kerr, 6 Sept. 1919, SRO, Lothian Papers, GD 40/17/216).

[70] Cited in Feinberg, *La Question des minorités*, 40 n. 3.

[71] See above, pp. 497–507.

[72] Clemenceau to Paderewski, 24 June 1919, Temperley, *Peace Conference*, v (London, 1921), Appendix iv, 432–7.

the Family of Nations'. They were 'anxious', however, 'to ensure the execution' of the minority provisions[73] of the Treaty of Peace with Germany. And Poland too, for its part, desired 'her institutions to conform to the principles of liberty and justice, and to give a sure guarantee to the inhabitants of the territory over which she has assumed sovereignty'.

The actual stipulations of the Polish treaty were of three kinds. The *first* was negative in character, in the sense that there were specified the rights and freedoms the new state might *not* deny individuals over whom it would have sovereign authority: life and liberty without regard to birth, nationality, language, race, or religion for all inhabitants, and whether citizens or otherwise, of the new Poland, as well, of course, as the right to practice any faith or religion; equality before the law for all Poles regardless of origin, ethnic and religious identity, and language, along with equality of opportunity, equality of educational facilities, and an equal right to establish charitable, religious and educational institutions on whatever linguistic and religious basis was desired. All this was to be founded on unimpeded access to full Polish citizenship for subjects of Germany, Austria, Hungary, and Russia who now found themselves domiciled in Poland or, alternatively, free departure from Poland for those who so chose, with all their possessions should that be their wish. The *second* class of treaty stipulations was positive. In districts in which there was a substantial proportion of citizens whose language was other than Polish it would be for the state itself to ensure that primary school children were instructed in their own language. Similarly, the state would be under an obligation to afford minorities an equitable and proportionate share of whatever public funds were allocated to educational, religious, and charitable purposes. The *third* class of stipulations defined all such treaty stipulations as 'obligations of international concern', laid down the rule that they were not to be modified without the assent of the majority of the Council of the League of Nations, and set out a limited mechanism for dealing with 'any infraction, or any danger of infraction, of the treaty's provisions through the Council of the League of Nations'. Any member of the Council of the League was entitled to draw the Council's attention to the particular case and the Council, for its part, was entitled to determine the validity of the charge and act upon its finding.

All of this was of general application. The Jews were dealt with specifically in two further articles of the treaty. Article 10 laid down that the 'Jewish communities of Poland' would be entitled to establish 'educational committees' of their own choosing and that these, 'subject to the general control of the State', would receive their due proportionate share

---

[73] Article 93 of the Treaty of Versailles stated that 'Poland accepts and agrees to embody in a Treaty with the Principal Allied and Associated Powers such provisions as may be deemed necessary by the said Powers to protect the interests of inhabitants of Poland who differ from the majority of the population in race, language, or religion.'

of public funds. The sum of Article 11 was that the Jewish Sabbath was to be respected and, in particular, was not to be employed as a weapon against the Jews themselves:

Jews shall not be compelled to perform any act which constitutes a violation of their Sabbath, nor shall they be placed under any disability by reason of their refusal to attend courts of law or perform any legal business on their Sabbath. This provision however shall not exempt Jews from such obligations as shall be imposed upon all other Polish citizens for the necessary purposes of military service, national defence or the preservation of public order.

Poland declares her intention to refrain from ordering or permitting elections, whether general or local, to be held on a Saturday, nor will registration for electoral or other purposes be compelled to be performed on a Saturday.[74]

These stipulations were welcome enough to most of the Jewish delegations. Still, taken together, they were a far cry from what Jewish nationalists of all stripes wanted and had originally hoped for. The treaty's shadowy recognition under Article 10 of 'Jewish communities' as legitimate, perhaps statutory bodies, and of the communities' right to a measure of autonomy in the sphere of education was no more than a single, very modest step in the desired direction. The linchpin of the system, both symbolically and in practical terms, was Article 11. It went further because it did at least *imply* recognition of the separate character of Jewry as being legitimate and inviolable and that in terms that were not altogether remote from those in which the Jews themselves conceived it and wished to maintain it. This in itself, not unnaturally, sufficed to evoke severe opposition not only from the Poles, but from the American and the Italian diplomatic specialists who participated in the negotiations. But it was little enough. And it had been made plain that there should be no misunderstanding about either the true and precise underlying intention or its exceedingly strict limits.[75]

These clauses have been limited to the minimum which seems necessary under the circumstances of the present day, viz. the maintenance of Jewish schools and the protection of the Jews in the religious observance of their Sabbath. It is believed that these stipulations will not create any obstacle to the political unity of Poland. They do not constitute any recognition of the Jews as a separate political community within the Polish State.[76]

Thus Clemenceau in the letter he was induced to write to Paderewski as part of the effort to persuade the Poles to swallow the pill.

It may be asked how an attempt to employ legal-contractual formulae

[74] Temperley *Peace Conference*, v. 441–2.
[75] It was only after submission to the Supreme Allied Council by the British member of the committee that Article 11 was finally approved. Janowsky, *Jews and Minority Rights*, 364.
[76] Temperley, *Peace Conference*, v. 436.

to compel an intensely nationalist and profoundly—indeed, to use Julien Benda's terrible phrase, *sincerely*—anti-Semitic ruling caste to accord its Jewish subjects fair and dispassionate treatment could ever have been expected to succeed. Part of the answer is provided by the special circumstances and the momentarily sanguine spirit and political climate of the time in the immediate aftermath of the First World War, the overwhelming power and prestige of the victorious powers and their historically unprecedented effort to do something for the subject peoples of Europe, even for the Jews. Part can be traced to the general feeling in Paris that the whole complex structure had to be kept together and that no one was really interested in exploding it by excessive political egocentricity. Part is provided by the Jewish delegations' own understandable and ostensibly well-founded conviction that the opportunity presented *them* by the occasion of a grand Peace Conference at Paris had to be seized and made the best of before it slipped their grasp. But chiefly underlying the system of very moderate protection envisaged by the draftsmen of the minorities treaties were the twin assumptions that there would in fact develop a strong and well-respected League of Nations and that liberal democracy would be the rule virtually everywhere in Europe. Neither promise would be fulfilled, of course. And we can only wonder at this remarkable, not to say supreme, instance of the wish being father to the thought.

9

Captivity

I

WHEN the Peace Conference was over and the Jewish delegations took stock they could hardly be in doubt about the outcome. What the minorities treaties marked in practice was less the inauguration of an era of generosity and good will towards the Jews than the point beyond which the European powers, great and small, had refused to go on their behalf. The Alliance Israélite Universelle, always the flag-bearer of the anti-nationalist school in Jewry, did promptly pronounce itself well satisfied with the Polish Treaty. The Alliance had always argued, its spokesmen pointed out, and had affirmed before the Peace Conference itself, that what the Jews needed before all else was full citizenship in each one of the new states: citizenship as individuals, that is to say, citizenship such as all inhabitants were entitled to enjoy without distinction of race, language, or religion—unless, indeed, they explicitly desired otherwise. It was true, their leaders conceded, that in certain circles in Jewry the view was that this failed to accord with the actual aspirations of the Jewish population itself and that

since eastern Europe is composed of ethnic groups of differing tendencies, customs, languages, and religions, the New States should provide for the constitutional recognition of special national minority rights for each one of these groups—Jewish groups among others.

They themselves thought otherwise.

Linked in destiny to their country, participants in its intellectual, spiritual, and political life as well as its economic prosperity, it is important that a new wall of separation should not be established, but that, on the contrary, existing barriers be knocked down once and for all with a view to facilitating the reconciliation of the various elements of the population and bringing about their spiritual unity.[1]

[1] 6 July 1919. *La Question juive*, 37–8. Still, they remained wary. When it was discovered that Article 129 of the peace Treaty of Sèvres with Ottoman Turkey laid down that Jews of non-Ottoman citizenship 'established' in Palestine would become citizens of that country they wished to know whether it would apply to French Jews. The answer from the Quai d'Orsay, much delayed, fell short of what had been hoped for: it was not the intention of the French government to deprive French Jews of their citizenship, but all doubt could be removed by the people concerned if they made an official declaration to the effect that their residence in Palestine was *temporary*. Bigart to the Foreign Minister,

And, indeed, whatever the common feeling in Warsaw or Bucharest or Vilna, let alone Kiev, might be, the salient fact emerging from the entire exercise was that little remained of the idea that the Jewish people could now take its place as one of the fully legitimate, constituent nations of Europe. Those who had been in the vicinity of the peacemakers at the time had come to realize that this would be the case well before the general outline of the treaties had been worked out. If they had begun by entertaining other ideas the general refusal 'to do anything which might in the slightest degree give any countenance to the Jewish National claims' was soon impressed upon them in the somewhat testy, yet not wholly unfriendly spirit in which Headlam Morley put the matter to Namier privately when the Polish Treaty had at last been signed:

I have no opposition to Zionism in the proper sense of the word, viz: the settlement of the Jews in Palestine, if that can be properly carried out, but the other aspect of Zionism by which, while the Jews are to get, if they do, their own state in Palestine, they are also to become an international nationality, influencing every other country, seems to me to be most dangerous.[2]

The sum of it all was that the hostility and danger in which the Jews were enveloped in the greater part of Europe had been recognized. So had the need to make some humane provision for it. But there had never been any serious question of allowing them to take a place that was fully their own in the new Europe—not one of a territorial nature, needless to say, but not one of a notional or symbolic nature either. They were to continue to be what they had always been and as, even in the course of the long, liberating nineteenth century, they had remained: an anomalous and peculiar people for whom no fully acceptable and secure place could be made available either in theory or in practice.

No doubt the settlement imposed by the peacemakers in Paris—'those three all-powerful, all-ignorant men sitting there and partitioning continents with only a child to take notes for them', the ever-perceptive, ever-feline Balfour had complained[3]—was flawed in many ways. Famously, while its severest and most influential critics had promptly pounced on the 'Carthaginian peace' imposed on Germany, there could be more than one view of that matter. The bottom had dropped out of the central political and security aspects of the Versailles system which set out the geopolitical and economic diminution of Germany when the United States Senate refused to honour Wilson's (admittedly contingent)

19 May; Bonnevay to Bigart, 3 Nov. 1921, BoD, E3/187/1. The Treaty of Sèvres itself was aborted by the refusal of the new Kemalist regimen to accept it. It was replaced by the Treaty of Lausanne two years later.

    [2] 30 June 1919, Headlam Morley Papers, No. 66.
    [3] Quoted by Harold Nicolson in a letter to his wife, Vita Sackville-West, 17 May 1919. See Nigel Nicolson, *Portrait of a Marriage* (London, 1974), 151.

promise of American participation in the League of Nations. Thereafter, the central failure of the settlement must be traced back to the Anglo-French Entente's lack of will to enforce the terms they themselves had dictated to Germany while they were still able to do so. But expedient or unworkable, the effort to impose a new political order on Europe was not, *pace* Keynes and his many followers, inherently unworthy. Judged in the light of its authors' intentions, it continues to rate as the first and last genuine effort to refound Europe on an enduringly civilized basis. The sober and on the whole systematic way in which the Conference had applied itself to what its masters considered to be its task continues to represent a political and diplomatic, even a moral peak: a peak of the possible, to be sure, but a peak none the less.

This was true even of the attention accorded to the matter of the Jews. When due allowance has been made for time and place, the effort to meet the interests, needs, and aspirations of the Jews of Europe as these had been articulated at Paris in 1919 was a remarkable one. For sheer seriousness and awareness of the vulnerabilities and peculiarities of the Jews there had never been anything like it. The civil emancipation of the individual conceived as a rule that admitted of no exceptions was confirmed. A measure of legitimacy was accorded Jewish separatism—not, indeed, throughout Europe, but at any rate where the desire for it was greatest and it appeared to reflect social reality most clearly. And a form of territorial national self-determination, limited yet palpable, had been granted the Jews *outside* Europe, chiefly, as all understood, as a consequence of wartime promises and certain postwar calculations, but equally with the needs and wishes of a substantial segment of European Jewry in view. Taken together, these concessions to Jewish needs and sentiments were less than what were asked for by some within Jewry itself, possibly the majority but none could tell. On the other hand, they were substantially more than what was wanted by others. Strictly speaking, no single one of these three concessions to Jewish claims and feelings was compatible with the other two. Nor, in combination, did they add up to anything remotely like a full and honourable solution to the Jewish Question in Europe or anywhere else however that 'question' might be conceived. But that had never been the peacemakers' intention nor, for that matter, had it been the purpose that any of the Jewish delegates who had pressed them to act had had in mind. It was the view in Paris both among those who were there to speak on behalf of the Jews and among the peace-makers themselves that no single, all-embracing solution to that Question was either possible or, in the circumstances of contemporary Europe, and having regard to what it might entail, desirable. That the scene would turn out to be a much rougher one than James Headlam Morley and his colleagues had been capable of imagining should not surprise us, therefore. What emerged from Paris in 1919 was never intended to be more than an exercise in inspired compromise. It fed on an ingrained confidence in the value of incremental progress towards half-understood, carefully ill-defined ends. And the working assumption underlying the system that had been devised was that it would always be possible to rely upon the (European) *state*.

Was not the modern state the very embodiment of modern (understood to mean European) civilization? Was it not safe therefore to assume that the individual state, but also the several states—the 'family of nations'—acting in concert, would be willing to deal with such domestic and external delinquents as might none the less appear among them? Was it unreasonable to suppose that the essential defences against barbarism would remain adequately garrisoned? What cause could there be, therefore, to consider the alternative possibility, namely that the modern state, even when fitted out with genuinely free elections, an authentic parliamentary regime, and other good things, might none the less fall into the hands of barbarians? There was little in the personal histories and experience of the participants in the Peace Conference, major or minor, to equip them to deal with such a hypothesis had it ever been authoritatively raised before them. And despite its antiquity, the antithesis between the civilized and the barbaric in politics, foreign or domestic, had never been clear-cut. While the war was being fought the distinction had lapsed, first reduced to a propagandist's self-serving vulgarism, then buried totally beneath the weight of the unspeakable brutalities the leaders of the belligerent nations had inflicted on their own troops no less than upon those of the enemy. On the other hand, the notion of the civilized state had not been forgotten and by and large it was still fondly remembered. Rather less understandably and more mysteriously, otherwise serious people continued to think of it as of the essence of international relations. Accordingly, when the fighting stopped, the temptation to assume that it would regain its putative validity and, moreover, that it was capable of extension beyond the magic circle of the sometime leading powers proved irresistible. Even violent internal conflict and repression in Hungary and Germany—much closer to Paris and London than the bestialities of civil and revolutionary warfare in Russia, Poland, and the Ukraine—failed to dissipate the general wish to believe that such would, eventually, prove to be the case.

To this sanguine view of the state as the very foundation-stone of civilized society even the most disabused among the Jewish notables of Europe were willing parties. The rulers of states might still be deeply, even automatically suspect in Jewish eyes in ways and for reasons that were the fruit of the Jews' distinctive history and so peculiar to them. On the other hand, reliance upon *the* ruler and upon the machinery at his disposal had, as we have seen repeatedly, been the constant, pivotal assumption on which the pragmatic norms of the long sojourn in Exile had been based. The Sages had taught their people that while, until the coming of the Messiah, their condition, alas, would be one of enslavement to their alien rulers,[4] they had no choice in practice but to rely upon them for such safety as could be hoped for. And the truth embodied in the more general (proto-Hobbesian) injunction that it was no less than the people's duty to 'pray for the safety of the kingdom; for were it not for the fear in which it is held men would devour their neighbours alive'[5] had been inculcated into them no less effectively. To the question what was to be done when reliance on the 'kingdom' turned out to have been misplaced no clear answer had ever been forthcoming. Now, however, there was at least a hint of one in the inner logic of the minorities treaties for the principal argument in their favour was that they seemed to promise a way out of such a dilemma.

This was participation. But there was a double difficulty about participation. The idea of the Jews needing neither to be dissolved into the general population *nor* to be kept apart and constitutionally inferior was barely acceptable even in its negative, minimal form. Translated into positive, maximalist terms, namely in something like those envisaged by Motzkin and his friends and set out in the Copenhagen Manifesto, it was entirely unacceptable: horrifying to the Poles, to the Romanians, and to the others; but unacceptable too to the Headlam Morleys, the Berthelots, and the Millers as well, as we have seen. What then? What form could participation of Jews *as such* in the political and economic life of any country take? The treaty-makers had refused to attempt even so much as a suggestion.

The other difficulty, as was soon apparent, was that the obstacles to the little that had been laid down in Paris as incumbent on the new states to accept and honour were very much greater than had originally been envisaged and were set to grow continually in size and severity. Forces of an intensity and dedication such as had not been seen for centuries were being marshalled against the Jews throughout Europe and in Europe's cultural extensions overseas. In content, the incessant, internally contradictory public denigration and denunciation of the Jews would be much as before: the Jews as revolutionaries, the Jews as reactionaries, the Jews as a people who kept themselves apart from the rest of mankind, the Jews as a people who continually intruded, and, generally and essentially, in an infinity of ways, the Jews as enemies of society and poisoners of its wells. But if, at their most elementary, the themes were of a piece with those which had been widely and often eloquently broadcast in the course of

---

[4] See above, p. 617 n. 200.
[5] 'Hevei mitpalel bi-shloma shel malkhut she-ilmale mora'a—ish et re'ehu hayyim bala'u.' Avot 3: 2.

the previous century, the tone was now less restrained, the force with which these themes were articulated was greater, and there was now a distinct shift in the balance of *intentions*. The order of the day was no longer improvement. Very little was heard at any social or political level of the need to bring the Jews into line with other classes of citizens, or of ridding them of their faults, superstitions, dress, customs, and the like. What was wanted was *extrusion*: in the first instance removal from those societal, economic, academic, and political structures into which Jews had already been admitted; later, in ways still to be worked out, removal from society and, if possible, out of the country in question altogether. The form, the style, and the stated grounds for such calls for expulsion varied; the essential content was one and the same. The older, mitigating distinctions between 'good' Jews and others, between the 'useful' and the 'useless', between the acceptable (or at any rate exploitable) and the unacceptable had lapsed or were in the process of being swept away. The frame of mind in which 'the Jews'—conceived of as both a local and a universal 'problem' or 'question', but as actual men and women as well— would now be altogether more radical, simplistic, and brutal than in the past. In short, the rules of social and political thought and, even more seriously, the norms of political behaviour as these had been set by the Enlightenment had dissolved.

It needs to be said at this point, that it has not been part of the purpose of this book to *account* for the rise and gathering of forces hostile to Jewry either before the First World War or in the years subsequent to it. Their quality and intentions have been sketched from time to time, but only in so far as it has been necessary to place them among the other determinants of the breadth of the political space that was available to the Jews themselves at any particular point. But it is important to see that the prevalence of anti-Semitism and the vehemence with which it would be promoted throughout Europe in the years following the war, especially and most drastically in countries that lay east of the Rhine, had a great deal to do with what had been decided for all those territories and peoples at Paris in 1919. For the Peace Settlement, as those 'three all-powerful men' and their minions had designed it, precipitated two closely intercalated sets of conflict. One was a continent-wide struggle between those who wished to preserve the settlement against those who wished to destroy it. The other was the parallel series of discrete, internal political struggles that developed in virtually every one of the European states that lay to the west of the USSR, conflicts in which extreme nationalists pitted themselves against more moderate opponents. What was in question in each instance was the *status quo*. Extreme nationalists—by which is meant those who had elevated the promotion of the interests of the nation they presumed to represent to the rank of a self-serving moral, and therefore absolute, imperative—were to be found both among the enemies and the supporters of what the Versailles-Trianon-St Germain settlements had prescribed. And there were other variations and variables. The ruling nationalist school in one particular case might be socially and politically conservative, intent on the preservation of as much of the pre-war social order as was possible. But it might, on the other hand, be socially and politically radical—bent, that is to say, on a total reformation of the internal structure of government and society, the old ruling classes and the sources of their power being swept away in the process along with, but for quite separate reasons, all those who were perceived as alien to the nation as well.

For the rest, what marked the European arena overall was that the various domestic struggles for power on the one hand and the conflicts over the 1919 settlement itself on the other fed and inflamed one another. Nor could it have been otherwise. The fundamental building block of both internal and international politics, as the Wilsonian peacemakers had conceived things, was the nation-state and the nation-state, as they understood it, rested necessarily on a one-to-one correspondence between state and nation. Unfailingly, this left very little constitutional and political room—in some cases none at all—to inhabitants who either would not or could not claim membership of the possessor-nation into whose hands the state had effectively been handed as a matter of logic and right. The problem which now confronted the Jews in particular was not, therefore, as their leaders had expected, how and what to build on the slim, but not wholly unpromising foundations established for their protection at the Peace Conference. It was how to prevent those foundations being washed entirely away by forces bent obsessively on dealing with the Jews on an entirely different and explicitly injurious basis.

Here, inexorably, lay the roots of the coming ruin of the Jews of Europe; and it is in the first instance because all these factors were present and active in Poland between the two world wars to a very remarkable degree that the case of Polish Jewry deserves particular attention. In the abstract the prospects for a *modus vivendi* could be read as not wholly unfavourable or unrealistic. Considered in the light of the past history of Poland, but more especially with quite recent events and the climate of Polish opinion generally in mind, it was hard to see how, in fact, they could be other than grim.

II

The migration of Jews in the years leading up to the First World War and its aftermath—massive in the case of the Americas, Africa, and Oceania although in smaller numbers to Palestine—had substantially reduced the

Jewish population of Europe as a proportion of the entire Jewish people. The loss has been estimated to be as great as a quarter: from 83 per cent of all Jewry in 1825 to 62 per cent in 1930. The more telling datum, however, was the seemingly paradoxical, steady rise of Europe's Jewish population in absolute numbers. In the course of the same one hundred years or so, despite migration and the great losses sustained during and immediately after the war, it quadrupled: from about 2.5 million to some 10 million, or slightly under two-thirds of the world's total Jewish population which stood at c.15.8 million in 1930. Of these the Jewish inhabitants of the western and central European states (Great Britain, France, Italy, and the Low Countries in the west; Germany, Austria, Czechoslovakia, and Hungary in the centre) who numbered well under half a million at the beginning of the nineteenth century, numbered c.1.7 million by 1930 or a little over one-tenth of the entire Jewish people. But very nearly three times as many Jews inhabited the eastern European states, while another 3 million were locked away in the Soviet Union.[6] The now greatly expanded Romania accounted for about 1 million. There was a substantial Jewish population in Lithuania as well. And there was the Polish community: far and away the largest, not far short of 3 million on independence (the official figure of 2.7 million was almost certainly too low) and at least 3.1 million in 1931 despite continual emigration at a not insubstantial level,[7] if indeed one that was never comparable to the rates achieved before the First World War.

The Second Polish Republic had been constituted a parliamentary democracy in which its Jewish population had been granted civil rights and liberties previously denied them along with all other inhabitants and had been recognized internationally, as we have seen, as one of a number of Poland's more or less equally placed ethno-cultural minorities. To be sure, the new, post-Versailles Poland had been conceived from the first as a nation-state. Those were most certainly the terms in which all those who spoke for the Polish people at Paris and subsequently saw the reconstructed Polish Republic. Unhappily for everyone, not least for Poland's own leaders, the fact was that in real terms, namely in all relevant, palpable, national-cultural demographic respects, the new Poland (like the old) was nothing of the kind. *De facto*—and, in consequence of the minorities treaty, to a certain extent *de jure* too—it was a multinational state in which Ukrainians, Jews, Byelorussians, Germans, Lithuanians, Russians, and Czechoslovaks (in that order) accounted for a full third of the total population (see Table 9.1).

---

[6] By 1930 the Jewish population of North and South America had risen to a total of a little under 5 million.
[7] It is estimated that all told some 400,000 Jews emigrated from Poland between the end of the First World War and the outbreak of the Second.

TABLE 9.1. *The components of multinational Poland (1931 figures)*

	Absolute numbers	As a percentage of the total population %
Germans	780,000	2.4
Jews	3,114,000	9.8
Ukrainians	5,114,000	16.0
Byelorussians	1,954,000	6.1
Other minorities	310,000	1.0
All minorities	11,272,000	35.3
Poles	20,644,000	64.7
Total population	31,916,000	100.0

But whereas the Ukrainians and the Byelorussians were chiefly peasant peoples and were concentrated in the eastern provinces of the country, the Jews were to be found throughout Poland and formed a high proportion of its urban population everywhere. Three out of four Jews lived in towns and cities (as opposed to one out of five non-Jews), accounting in 1921 for 31 per cent of the total urban population in the country. By 1931 the Jewish segment of the urban population had dropped somewhat (to 27.2 per cent). But as a proportion of the population of Poland's major cities it was still extraordinarily—and to many Polish minds, impermissibly—high: 30.1 per cent in Warsaw, 33.5 per cent in Lodz, 31.9 per cent in Lwow, 25.8 per cent in Cracow, 34.7 per cent in Lublin.[8] Here was much grist to the Polish nationalists' mill: no less than a daily, irritating reminder to them of the Jewish presence. It was equally a reminder to all, Jews and non-Jews alike, that the fundamental political question facing the country was whether it was to be in its essential political character a multinational state in which the Poles, while of course remaining the preponderant group, would share power to some degree at least with others; or *per contra* whether it was to be an explicitly and overwhelmingly Polish nation-state in which all non-Poles were expected (and if necessary compelled) to go to the wall.

Poland was not alone in having to confront the dilemma of a nation-state freighted with minorities. But it did exhibit it in an extreme form. Hungary, previously a great multinational state, had been shorn of a great part of its territorial possessions under the terms of the Treaty of Trianon and reduced in status and population as had no other state in Europe, Austria itself excepted. The Magyars ceased to be the overlords of the Slovaks and the Croats and of a good many Romanians as well. Worse from a Hungarian point of view was the fact that the settlement dictated to them left over 2.5 million ethnic Hungarians, or a quarter of all who

[8] Raphael Mahler, *Yehudei Polin bein shetei milḥamot 'olam* (Tel Aviv, 1968), 18–35.

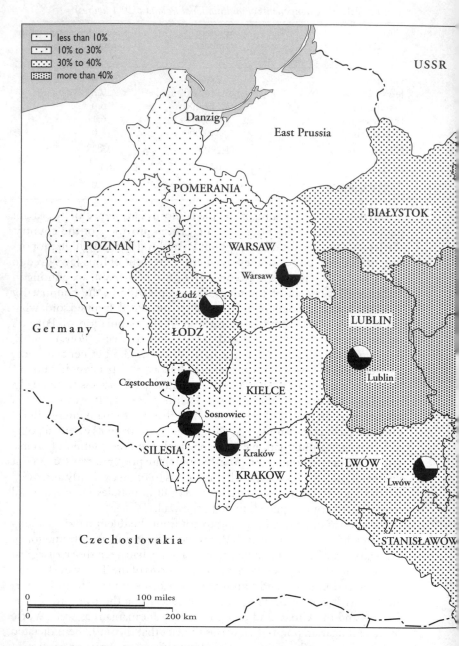

MAP 2. Density of Jewish population in inter-war Poland: provinces and major urban centres (1931 figures)

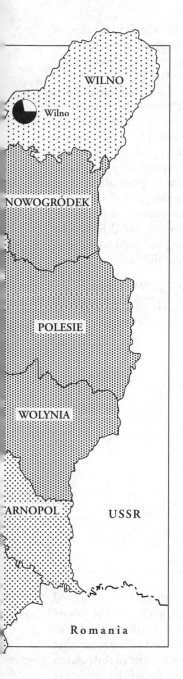

Jewish population as a proportion of total population

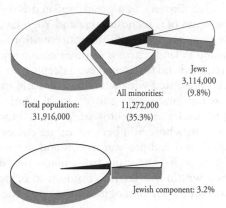

Jews:
3,114,000
(9.8%)

All minorities:
11,272,000
(35.3%)

Total population:
31,916,000

Jewish component: 3.2%

Rural population:
72.6% of total

Jewish component: 27.2%

Urban population:
27.4 % of total

Major centres of Jewish urban population

	total pop.	Jewish pop.	Jews as % of total
Warsaw	1,171,898	352,659	30.1
Łódź	604,829	202,497	33.5
Lwów	312,231	99,595	31.9
Kraków	219,296	56,515	25.8
Wilno	195,071	55,006	28.2
Lublin	112,285	38,537	34.7
Częstochowa	117,179	25,588	21.9
Sosnowiec	108,959	20,805	19.1

counted as members of the Magyar nation, outside the new borders of the country altogether, exchanging place and condition with their former subjects: some 1.4 million Hungarians were now inhabitants, and second-class citizens, of a greatly inflated Romania, the rest citizens of the new states of Czechoslovakia and Yugoslavia. The Poles' great good fortune was that no significant concentrations of ethnic Poles had been left outside Poland, citizens of other countries. On the other hand, the much reduced and (in its own eyes) deeply humiliated Hungarian people had been presented with what the Poles and many others had reason to regard as the inestimable gift of virtual ethnic homogeneity (see Table 9.2). Just under nine-tenths of Trianon Hungary's population were Magyars—to whose numbers the ruling circles in the country, had they so wished, and had pre-war norms and purposes continued to obtain, could have added the some half-million heavily magyarized Jews who remained within the Trianon borders, so bringing the total to a round 8 million (or 92 per cent of the entire population of the country).

TABLE 9.2. *Ethnic minorities in the Hungarian nation-state (1931 figures)*

	Absolute numbers	As a percentage of the total population of Hungary %
Czechoslovaks	104,700	1.2
Germans	478,600	5.5
Jews	444,500	5.1
Romanians	16,200	0.2
Yugoslavs	34,100	0.4
Others	49,200	0.6
All minorities	1,127,500	12.9
Ethnic Hungarians in Trianon Hungary	7,556,500	87.0
Total population of Trianon Hungary	8,684,000	100.0
Expatriate Hungarians	*c.*2,600,000	*c.*26.0 [as a percentage of all Hungarians]

It can be said of virtually all the effective leaders of state, Church, and society in the newly restored Polish republic that while, on the whole correctly, they perceived the Jewish population as distinct and in the main alien—probably irreducibly so—and wished, chiefly for that reason, to rid the country of its presence, not all were alike in the passion they devoted to the subject, nor were all anxious to act, let alone act forcibly. But there were few indeed who did not *wish* the Jews gone. The consequence was that, broadly, in actual political practice, two schools of thought may be discerned. On the one hand there was the school led by Roman Dmowski's National Democrats (the Endeks or Endecja). Their position was well known. It had been formulated and propagated well before the First World War and illustrated by a vast and not unsuccessful boycott campaign mounted explicitly to ruin Jewish traders. They viewed the very ancient Jewish presence in Poland as a permanent outrage, an offence to the eye, soul, and body politic of Catholic Poland, a running sore that needed urgently to be cauterized if the Polish nation was ever to be its own master and entirely in good health. Its people believed—seriously, it seems—that the fate of Poland was bound up with that of the Jews in some fateful way, that pressure upon them had therefore never to be relaxed, and that the need to extrude them from the Fatherland must never be compromised or forgotten. They left no one in doubt that, if they were ever completely to have their way in the country, there would be no room in it at all for the Jews. In all this they enjoyed the advantage of being heavily backed, notably in the early years of the Second Republic, by the Catholic Church both in its *ex cathedra* teaching and by such outward signs of inward approval as members of the hierarchy being seated on Endek benches in the Sejm and the Senate.[9] Spokesmen for the Church did speak a somewhat different language, in the main. It was the duty of the government to seek 'the proper solution to the Jewish question on which *depends* the religious, national, and economic future of the Fatherland'[10] was one formulation although Cardinal Hlond's notorious pastoral letter of February 1936, read from all the pulpits in the country and published in whole or in part in most of the immensely large and influential Catholic press, was cast in rougher terms:

It is a fact that Jews oppose the Catholic Church, are steeped in free-thinking, and represent the avant-garde of the atheist movement, the Bolshevik movement, and subversive action. The Jews have a disastrous effect on morality and their publishing-houses dispense pornography. It is true that Jews commit fraud, usury, and are involved in trade in human beings.[11]

In practice, therefore, the message was the same.

[9] Edward D. Wynot, 'The Catholic Church and the Polish State 1935–1939', *Journal of Church and State*, 15 (1973), 226.

[10] The Rev. Jan Rostworowski for the Union of Catholic Writers, in Warsaw, in 1936. Cited in Wynot, 'Catholic Church', 229 n. 17. Emphasis added.

[11] Cited in Anna Landau-Czajka, 'The Image of the Jew in the Catholic Press during the Second Republic', in Antony Polonsky, *et al.* (eds.), *Jews in Independent Poland 1918–1939, Polin: Studies in Polish Jewry*, viii (London, 1994), 170. These were very common themes. Appealed to by the Union of Rabbis in 1934 to condemn anti-Semitic violence, the archbishop of Warsaw, Cardinal Kakowski, duly affirmed that violence was unchristian and then appalled the rabbis by accusing the Jews themselves of provoking it by their propagation of atheism, communism, and pornography (Pawel Korzec, *Juifs en Pologne* (Paris, 1980), 231). Where the prelates differed from the men of the Endecja was

The other school is best represented by the Polish Socialist Party (Polska Partia Soczjalistyczna or PPS) and to some extent by Marshal Jozef Pilsudski himself and the semi-dictatorial Sanacja or 'cleansing' regime which he put in power by *coup d'état* in 1926 and presided over (from a distance) until his death in 1935. The rightful primacy of the Polish nation in the Second Republic was not in question, so far as the leaders of the Pilsudski-PPS school were concerned. Nevertheless, their view of the matter of the other nationalities, the Jews among them, was somewhat more pragmatic and, without being totally unlike that of their extreme nationalist opponents, somewhat more tolerant and humane as well. Pilsudski's first prime minister, Kazimierz Bartel, told the Sejm on taking office in 1926 that his government would seek to *reduce* friction of a national and religious origin; and that it wished to establish harmonious relations between 'the different nations and cultures of which the population was made up, believing that economic anti-Semitism is harmful to the State'.[12] 'The Government will not allow the just rights of citizens who are not Poles to be endangered. It holds, moreover, that hostility towards any group of citizens because of its language or belief is contrary to the spirit of Poland.'[13] These were new notes in high places and very welcome ones to all the minority peoples. As things turned out, however, they pertained more to ethos than to practical policy; and even as such they proved to be of uncertain quality. Ignacy Daszynski, the leading figure in the PPS in the first fifteen years of independence, was a man with a deserved reputation for fair-mindedness and for what passed in Poland at the time for tolerance of ethnic minorities, the Jews among the others. He had supported Jewish deputies in the Sejm in 1919 when they had demanded a public condemnation of brutalities committed by Polish troops and a parliamentary inquiry. Still, on a more private occasion, comparing the Jews of Cracow with its German inhabitants on one occasion, pointing out that whereas the latter, in the course of several centuries, had become 'excellent Poles', while the Jews remained 'enclosed in their ghetto', he went on to say,

The difficulty lies not only in the number, but also in the occupations of the Jews. They inhabit our cities, centres of science, art, commerce, and industry. Imagine how this compact, foreign mass would be treated in American or English cities. Would they be liked? Would they be given official positions when they differ in their customs and their language? And we too cannot endure them. So long as they say that Poland does not concern them, so long as they inhabit

in their tendency to concede, as Cardinal Hlond put it in 1936, that, yes, 'not all Jews are like this. There are very many Jewish faithful who are honest, just, compassionate and charitable.'

[12] Cited in E. Meltzer, 'Mifleget ha-shilton OZON ve-ha-yehudim be-Polin (1937–1939)', *Gal-'Ed* (Tel Aviv), 4–5 (1978), 400 n. 14.

[13] Cited in Antony Polonsky, *Politics in Independent Poland 1921–1939* (Oxford, 1972), 190.

our cities in such proportions, it must not surprise them that the people of the State [*sic*] are unable to accord them full confidence. . . . Saying that, I do not condone the pogroms. Everyone must denounce them as acts of barbarism that disgrace us in the eyes of the world.[14]

It would be tedious to list more than a few examples of the nastiness, violence, minor, but unpunished pogroms, professional restrictions, economic boycotts, pieces of punitive taxation, and campaigns of denigration launched against the Jews of Poland in the course of the Second Republic's short life, some of which were hugely successful, the heavily discriminatory policy at the universities, for example: a shadowy but effective quota system, systematic mistreatment of such Jewish students as had been admitted, ordinary violence and molestation of individuals and their confinement as a class to so-called 'ghetto-benches' in the lecture halls, an operation begun by the non-Jewish students, by force, then established as a norm by academic authority. The result, as desired, was that the number of Jewish students dropped dramatically both absolutely and relatively: while the non-Jewish student body almost doubled in the two decades of independence, the Jewish student body was halved.[15]

Some measures taken against the Jewish population were ostensibly trivial, in practice profoundly damaging. A 1927 law requiring artisans to pass a formal examination of technical competence laid down that their proficiency in the Polish language be tested as well. Jewish craftsmen formed a high proportion of the total artisan class in Poland and an immense proportion of the Jewish working class, as was very well known, was literate in Yiddish, not Polish. The law confronted them with an obstacle that relatively few among them were in a position to overcome and did nothing in practice to accelerate the spread of the Polish language in the Jewish population—a natural process that needed no formal machinery to promote it. Still more telling of the general trend in these matters were the efforts made in the 1930s to limit the entry of Jews into the liberal professions, that of medicine among them, and to make practice by those who had already entered them as difficult as possible— entirely impossible, for example, where hospital, teaching, and other official appointments were concerned. In 1937 the Union of Polish Physicians resolved, in imitation of laws that had recently been passed in Germany and in concert with the Union of Polish Lawyers, to restrict Union membership to 'Poles of Polish descent'—although, be it said, not without opposition from within the Union and with only partial

---

[14] Statement before a gathering of deputies from Cracow, 21 Jan. 1919, CZA, A126/52/6.

[15] 8,426 Jewish students at Polish universities or 24.6 per cent of a total student body of 34,266 in the academic year 1921/2; 4,113 Jewish students or 8.2 per cent of the total student body of 49,987 in 1938/9, Raphael Mahler, 'Jews in Public Service and the Liberal Professions in Poland, 1918–39', *JSS* 6 (1944), 341.

success when, in the event, the government refused to confirm the resolution until it had been amended to 'Polish citizens of Christian birth'.[16]

Actual government service itself had been closed to Jews to all intents and purposes from the very beginning, very firmly indeed at the central administrative level, but at the less exalted levels of the railway and postal services as well. In Congress Poland this had been easy to do: it needed no more than a decision to maintain in force what had been the practice under Russian rule. In Galicia, where the Austrian authorities had been more liberal in such matters and a fair number of Jews were found to be in office in the relevant services when power was transferred to Polish hands, the solution was to bar the admission of Jews to government employment while allowing those already in service to remain in office until retirement. The result was that in Galicia in 1931 Jews still accounted for 4.5 per cent of the full white-collar strength of the postal, railway, and state and courts services, whereas in the rest of Poland the figures were totally negligible: of the 16,840 postal workers 21 in all were Jews (0.1 per cent); of a total of 28,895 railway officials 44 (0.1 per cent) were Jews; of the 41,905 state administration and court officials 534 (1.3 per cent) were Jews.[17]

A remarkable feature of the untiring effort to make life difficult, if possible unendurable, for the Jews of the country was that the lead was taken not by marginal men, or merely by the educated, but to a quite unusual degree by members of Poland's political, intellectual, academic, and ecclesiastical elite. Where in pre-revolutionary Russia the most cultivated levels of society tended on the whole to be critical or at the very least embarrassed by the constant hammering of the Jews, their Polish analogues, with relatively rare exceptions, were in the grip of a Polish patriotism, admirable in some ways, but intermixed with a form of anti-Semitism which partook equally of modern romantic nationalism and ancient Christian hatred of the Jews as the killers and rejecters of Jesus. It was a potent blend, percolating easily down the social hierarchy, then percolating upwards again, holding prisoner party leaders whose own private views might be milder or more pragmatic than those of the populace, but who were dependent on it for electoral support. To veer from the conventional wisdom on the matter of the Jews, let alone seek to refute it, was at the very least eccentric. Socially it was risky. Politically it could be fatal. To cleave to it could in no way be damaging and was likely to be politically profitable.

The effect, when Pilsudski died and his relatively moderate Sanacja collapsed, was therefore shattering. The Endecja became freer than it had ever been before to promote its message and to harass Jews physically as well as economically whenever it was convenient to do so. And it had the satisfaction of hearing its long-standing insistence on a much firmer

---

[16] Mahler, 'Jews in Public Service', 325–30.   [17] Ibid. 304–5.

anti-Jewish policy being increasingly echoed at the highest reaches of government. Reckoning that it would help to keep them in power, Pilsudski's epigoni altered their language and then, at an accelerating rate, their policy. In June 1936 Prime Minister Slawoj-Skladowski told parliament that economic conflict between Jews and Poles was no less than a struggle for Poland's survival. As the OZON, or Camp of National Unity,[18] established in February 1937 as the Sanacja's successor sought desperately to gather and revitalize what remained of the Pilsudski forces it moved at an accelerated rate towards an accommodation with the ultranationalists, taking up the Endecja themes with increasing confidence and energy on the way. The solution to the problem of the Jews, its leader, General Stanislaw Skwarczynski, announced on 21 February 1938, was contingent on 'a radical decrease' in their number, his only caveat being that 'demagogic and irresponsible terroristic activity' against the Jews would be opposed.[19] Three months later a comprehensive set of thirteen resolutions spelling out how this reduction was to be effected was worked out and formally approved by the movement's Supreme Council.[20]

These, to be sure, were the dying years of the republic when Poland had entered into a wildly misconceived treaty relationship with Nazi Germany. The minorities treaty, some of the stipulations of which had never been honoured,[21] was formally repudiated. Poland was resolved to co-operate with Germany in the dismemberment of Czechoslovakia. Ever widening circles among Poland's ultra-nationalists were beginning to think that Germany's less inhibited treatment of its Jewish population, now manifest for all to see, offered an example they themselves would do well to follow. Here the government held back, however, despite German criticism of what they thought was the OZON's milk-and-water approach to the Jewish Question, notably the refusal to apply blanket racial principles. Clause 11 of the OZON's May 1938 resolutions had indeed laid down that while the overall purpose was not by any means the 'national assimilation' of the Jews, individuals of Jewish origin who, in the course of their lives and by the services they had rendered to the Polish nation had proved that they were Poles, would none the less be recognized as belonging to 'the Polish national partnership'.[22] And at the practical level, the nationalist-clericalist coalition was still capable of overreaching themselves or simply failing through mismanagement or ill timing to achieve their ends. The continuous campaign mounted by Catholic leaders, in concert with the Endecja, to outlaw the ritual

[18] Oboz Zjednoczenia Narodowego.
[19] Edward D. Wynot, '"A Necessary Cruelty": The Emergence of Official Anti-Semitism in Poland, 1936–39', *American Historical Review*, 76 (1971), 1047.
[20] Text (in Polish) in Meltzer, 'Mifleget ha-shilton', 424–6; Hebrew trans. 406–7.
[21] The requirement that Jewish schools be publicly financed, for example.
[22] Meltzer, 'Mifleget ha-shilton', 426.

slaughter of animals (*sheḥitah*) for meat consumption by Jews failed. Appropriate bills were brought before parliament on three separate occasions. But the first was of so uncompromising a nature that the vice-minister of cults and public education, himself a priest, insisted on it being liberalized.[23] It was passed in a limited form in April 1936, *sheḥitah* being restricted to the proportion of Jews, Karaites, and Muslims in any given region. A second attempt at a total ban was made on behalf of OZON itself early in 1938, but parliament was dissolved before it could be acted upon. A third motion was put before the Sejm in 1939, but the debate was cut short by the outbreak of war. In general, the best that can be said of those pressing for the prohibition of *sheḥitah* was that their motives were mixed. Ostensibly, but not convincingly, their argument was humanitarian. In practice, their lesser aim was to strike at an economic sector, that of the cattle and meat trade, in which Jews were prominent. Their greater purpose, as everyone understood, was to strike a moral blow at a very well-known, deeply rooted, and particularistic facet of Jewish life and custom. And the campaign owed something too, it may be thought, to frustration.

It had become very clear to the National Democrats and to their various, ever more numerous allies that while they were in the process of gaining the power to rid the country of its Jewish inhabitants, there was in fact no place to send them. The gates to all other countries were substantially, and in many cases, absolutely closed. One desperate move by the Polish government was to demand of the League of Nations (in August 1936) that Poland be allotted colonies—partly, it is true, as a tribute to what the government considered to be its great power status, but partly to provide a dumping ground into which its Jewish citizens might conveniently be shunted. A committee of inquiry was dispatched a year later to examine Madagascar as a possibility. Nothing came of it. Equally desperate were repeated attempts, especially after the intergovernmental conference on 'political refugees' at Evian in July 1938,[24] to induce the British government to allow more Jews into Palestine or, failing that, into other parts of the empire. In October of that year a senior member of the Polish embassy in London informed the Foreign Office that 'the Jewish question was . . . more than pressing. It was becoming intolerable. It was not a question of any responsible person in Poland wishing to get rid of the Jews merely because they were unpopular, but simply that their number were so great and was increasing so rapidly that it was becoming impossible to find livelihoods for all of them.' Some weeks later, the ambassador, Count Raczynski, tried his hand. The Jewish question in

---

[23] And was hounded out of office for his pains, leaving the minister of agriculture to complain that the measure, if passed in its original form, would be more damaging to the farmers than to the Jews.

[24] See below, pp. 881–6.

Poland should not be confused with the Jewish question in Germany, he stressed. The Germans persecuted the Jews for reasons of doctrine. The Poles, on the other hand, were faced with a real problem. Anti-Semitism was increasing. He himself 'lived in dread of an outbreak of pogroms'. What was needed was a 'large scale scheme . . . in which the Polish Jews could share'. Once that had been mounted, the agitation was sure to die down and the problem could be tackled 'rather more at leisure' and to good purpose too—for, as the ambassador told his English colleague, the Polish Jews, unlike the German Jews,

were labourers and artisans rather than intellectuals. They would make good colonists in such a place as Northern Rhodesia and would be anxious to emigrate at the rate of some 100,000 per year. . . . He feared, however, that if nothing was done for [sic] the Polish Jews the Polish government would inevitably be forced to adopt the same kind of policy as the German Government, and indeed draw closer to that Government in general policy.[25]

But the British were not to be moved; and, just possibly for this reason, a bill designed finally to reduce the Jews to helots was placed before the Scjm a few weeks later by deputies representing the OZON. The constitutional status of the Jews was to be totally and irreversibly revised. Their civil and political rights were to be rescinded. They were to lose the right to vote and the right of admission to government service (the latter being merely formal since in practice it had systematically been denied). They would lose the right to practise law, medicine, or any of the other free professions totally. The right of equal access to, and treatment by, the courts would be denied them. They would lose the right to possess real property. And the government, for its part, was actively to seek their expulsion from the country. It was further proposed, in a characteristic corollary, that the contingent costs of the migration be borne by the Jews themselves, a special burden of taxation being laid upon them to that end. In the event, the government itself hesitated, possibly because, given the sharply deteriorating relations with Germany once the Munich crisis was over and Poland had ceased to be a partner in the destruction of Czechoslovakia, it would have been incongruous to give the project a final blessing.[26] But there could be no further doubt about the end of Poland as the peacemakers of Paris had envisaged it twenty years earlier.

The interesting question is why it took so long for the regime to reach the point towards which the logic of its approach had been carrying it for twenty years. The reasons are necessarily complex and to some extent

---

[25] Jazdzewski to Baggallay, 28 Oct. 1938, PRO, FO 371/21636. Minute by Strang, 9 Dec. 1938, PRO, FO 371/22540. Cited in E. Meltzer, 'Ha-diplomatiya ha-polanit u-ve 'ayat ha-hagira ha-yehudit ba-shanim 1935–1939', Gal-'Ed, 1 (1973), 244–5.

[26] E. Meltzer, 'Li-ve 'ayat ha-giz 'anut ba-ḥevra ha-polanit ba-shanim 1933–1939—le-halakha u-le-ma 'aseh', Gal- 'Ed, 14 (1995), 133.

obscure. Large sectors in the population and important parties active in the political arena were vehemently opposed on general grounds to the ever more authoritarian ways of successive Polish governments since 1926—Pilsudski's original party, the PPS, among them. There was a deep and quite widespread reluctance to tear up any part at all of the Polish constitutions of 1921 and 1935, both of which assured equality to all citizens regardless of nationality or religion and the right of each religious or national (ethnic) group to evolve freely. Sympathy for the effort to deal once and for all with the Jewish Question was all very well; but where would the process end? Who, that is to say, would be next? Except among the Endecja there was too a residuum of moral doubt about the treatment of the Jews tickling the conscience of men in high places at awkward moments, and the dismay of the more worldly members of the Polish social and political elite at the continual, and after 1934, accelerating decline of Poland's reputation abroad. A further brake on firm and clear-cut action was the circumstance that the question of the precise nature of the Jewish community, namely whether the Jews constituted a religious or a national group, had never been resolved either legally or, so far as the Polish nationalists themselves were concerned, ideologically. For the extremists among them there was no question of, and no interest in, Polonizing the Jews either by force or by fiat. But if you could not expel them because there was nowhere to send them, what were you to do? All these aspects of the problem help to explain the rising incidence of brutality towards the Jews not only in choice of language and terms of abuse, but physically in the streets. None was conducive to confident, implacable implementation of a precisely formulated policy of any kind. And there was yet another sense in which successive Polish governments never had a totally free hand in this matter. They had invariably to cope not only with the largest Jewish community in Europe, but with one that was far and away the most turbulent and independently minded.

III

Polish Jewry had come to constitute the Jewish people's natural and primary storehouse of socially and politically but also intellectually and artistically active men and women. It constituted the central, and to very many minds the critical, arena in which all the major social and political *national* tendencies in contemporary Jewry found it necessary to compete for a preponderant role with whatever energy and resources were available to them. It would be in Poland that all parties and organized groups in Jewry sought, some desperately, to draw members and reinforce cadres. And it was the Polish community, as its own leaders well knew, to which the greatest attention worldwide would be paid from this point on. All this owed something to the mixed blessing of perpetual social and intellectual ferment and unbridgeable internal divisions on all the central issues of the day that were among its salient characteristics. It owed at least as much to the combined effects of endemic impoverishment and the continual efforts already alluded to of political and commercial groupings of the highest order of influence in Poland to drive the Jews collectively and individually to the wall. The enduring question for the Jews of Poland was therefore what, if anything at all, should be done to cope with the punishing straits in which they found themselves. To confront them was to recognize a bitter and a depressing instance of the ancient and unending quarrel between the Jews and their neighbours. It was also to respond to a predicament that had arisen out of totally new and on the face of things initially promising conditions.

While the politics of the Jewish condition were necessarily uppermost, the poverty and galloping pauperization of the Jews of Poland can under no circumstances be neglected as a factor determining behaviour and morale. In 1921, for example, which is to say very early on in the history of the Second Republic, only one-third (33.9 per cent) of the Jewish population of the country was effectively self-supporting, the majority (66.1 per cent) being classed as dependants. The rate of dependence was high among non-Jews as well, but the proportions were reversed: 56.7 per cent self-supporting as opposed to 43.3 per cent dependants.[27] And the especially widespread condition of dependency among Jews was further aggravated by Jewish workmen and craftsmen tending preponderantly and disproportionately to be self-employed: 55.5 per cent of the economically active among the Jews or a little over twice the proportion of the self-employed among the non-agricultural gainfully employed nation-wide.[28] Moreover, those who were not self-employed tended, much to their detriment, to be employed in very small enterprises—once again in stark contrast to non-Jews who, for their part, tended overwhelmingly to be employed by large enterprises (see Table 9.3).

TABLE 9.3. *Factory employment of Jews and non-Jews compared*[29]

Number of workmen	Jews %	Non-Jews %
1	17.0	1.0
2–3	29.8	3.2
4–5	13.7	2.9
31–50	3.9	12.2
50+	8.5	59.3

[27] Mahler, 'Jews in Public Service', 46.
[28] In 1931 Jews alone accounted for 21 per cent of all those gainfully employed nation-wide in non-agricultural occupations: 1,123,025 out of a total of 5,335,466 (ibid. 50).
[29] Source: Lucjan Dobroszycki, 'The Fertility of Modern Polish Jewry', in Paul

The cumulative effects of nominal economic independence were social no less than economic. Men and women employed in very small enterprises were devoid of minimal social security and unemployment relief and were effectively without trade union support. Their condition was therefore part cause but also part consequence of the enduring rift of alienation between members of what was nominally the same urban working class. If the self-employed Jewish artisan and trader enjoyed a greater measure of independence than his Polish analogue, his hours were longer, his income less assured, and, for the most part, substantially lower. He was obliged to pay an annual licence fee of about 40 zloty if a shop-keeper and 7–8 zloty (or about $1.50) if an artisan. It was a striking measure of their disastrous condition that the burden of such a licence fee, small though it was, was such that three out of ten such independent traders and craftsmen were unable to sustain it without communal assist-ance—total weekly earnings being unlikely to be higher than a few zloty more in each case. But the two most telling, certainly most conspicuous indicators of the continuing, seemingly ineradicable poverty afflicting the greater part of Polish Jewry, and serving without doubt as the most potent, permanently depressing factor in their lives, were the appalling conditions in which so very many of them were housed and the massive degree to which they relied on general communal charity. A survey conducted among the Jewish working class in Lodz in the early 1930s showed that over 70 per cent of families (comprising 5–8 persons on average) lived in a single room, that a little under a fifth of such rooms were either in attics or in cellars, and that three out of ten such rooms served as daytime workshops as well as night-time living quarters. Lodz may have presented the hardest cases, but conditions in Warsaw, Vilna, and Bialystok were not much better. The other indicator of ineradicable poverty—a classic measurement in Jewish society at all times and in all countries—was the extent to which charity was dispensed at Passover-time. It has been estimated that 25.8 per cent of the entire Jewish popu-lation of the country requested assistance in 1934, that nine out of ten such requests were granted, and that the average grant was 7.83 zloty per family. The proportions were a trifle lower in Warsaw, substantially higher in Lodz and in Vilna. The general tendency over time was for the rate to rise. In a hundred cities and towns surveyed (urban conditions dif-fered somewhat from conditions in the countryside) charitable assistance was granted to 22 per cent of the population in 1935; to 24.6 per cent in 1936; to 26.2 per cent in 1937. It is to be noted too that only a quarter of those in receipt of such charity belonged to the expected marginal or

Ritterband (ed.), *Modern Jewish Fertility* (Leiden, 1981), 71. And see Bina Garncarnska-Kadari, 'Shikhvot ha-'ovdim be-polin bein shetei milḥamot 'olam', in *Gal-'Ed*, 3 (1976), 157–63.

inactive economic categories: widows, orphans, professional beggars, and the like. The great majority belonged to the normally—and willingly—productive members of society: traders, artisans, labourers, clerks, waggoners, and so forth.[30]

Polish Jewry in the period between the world wars may thus be seen as in some way the successor to what had previously been chiefly thought of as 'Russian' Jewry—but which, of course, was always more properly the Jewish population of the Tsar's Russia in which the Jews of Russian-ruled Poland formed a very considerable proportion. Material conditions apart, what the substitution of a Polish for a Russian regime had in no way altered was the fact that in their great majority these were people who were unequivocal in their self-identification as Jews. To the relevant census questions in 1921 slightly under three-quarters of those who declared themselves to be Jews by religion declared themselves to be Jews by nationality as well, ergo not 'Poles'. In Congress Poland, which was much the largest part of the state and contained the greater segment of Poland's Jewish population, four out of five declared themselves to be of Jewish rather than Polish nationality. In Galicia, where the Jewish population was a little over a quarter of that of Congress Poland, roughly three out of five declared themselves to be of Jewish nationality. In the city of Cracow the proportion dropped to 50.2 per cent.[31] There had been notable cases of sympathy and support for Polish national purposes before the war. In the main, however, Polish Jewry's self-view was relatively uncluttered by integrationist aspirations and tended to be indifferent to, or sceptical of, Polish national-revolutionary purposes, besides—in Congress Poland—being reluctant to add to their troubles with the Russians by helping the Poles. This was one of the reasons why Dmowski's National Democrats had been so set on punishing them. The Endecja had not only mounted an economic boycott of Jewish traders while all, Poles and Jews, were still under Russian rule, but had subjected the community to a continuous rumble of threatening noises for having had the impertinence to seek to establish themselves in the Duma in their own names rather than put aside their own, specifically Jewish concerns in the interests of furthering those of the Poles.

In newly independent Poland matters then got off to a very bad start, as we have seen: the Jews being subjected to a continuous hail of verbal

---

[30] Mahler, 'Jews in Public Service', 189–95. For an equally dismal picture of the poverty of Polish Jewry based on an analysis of communal membership fees paid and unpaid, see Jacob Lestschinsky, *La Situation économique des juifs depuis la guerre mondiale (Europe orientale et centrale)* (Paris, 1934), 75–8 and *passim*.

[31] Ezra Mendelsohn, *The Jews of East Central Europe between the World Wars* (Bloomington, Ind., 1987), 29–30. The Jewish population of Congress Poland in 1921 was 2,217,000, that of Galicia 607,000. The Jewish population of the ex-Prussian province was a negligible 20,600 in 1921.

attacks and widespread violence, much of it of an exceedingly cruel and humiliating nature vented for no objectively comprehensible grounds. Nor was it in the pre-revolutionary manner, namely by mobs, but by Polish troops acting in most cases with the support and approval of their commanders. The auguries were therefore clear enough. The Jews of Poland had been taught to perceive their own basic interests as a community and as individuals as being irreconcilable with Polish nationalism in the form in which it had been demonstrated to them most strikingly; and the belief that it was therefore necessary to strike out in a direction of their own choosing naturally and very rapidly gained ground. It was not the view of any of the established Jewish parties, however, that they had cause to be hostile to Polish independence or to the Polish Republic as such. It was rather that there was no escaping the fact that, like it or not, they were at cross purposes with those who, over the greater part of the period in question, were to hold political power. A certain mild hopefulness did obtain at the very beginning, much encouraged by the relatively good results obtained in the elections to the first or constitutional Sejm, and then again when Marshal Pilsudski seized power. But in general, and in the long run, there was no shying away from the fact that so long as it was the National Democrats and their various ideological, ecclesiastical, and political allies, followers, and successors who set the pace, there was much in reconstructed Poland with which it was impossible for Jews of any political stripe to reconcile and identify themselves.

On the other hand, while the international and constitutional rules under which Poland was governed worked against the interests of the country's Jews in some ways, there were others which opened up unprecedented political possibilities before them. These were of much the same kind that had at any rate been hoped for in Russia, had materialized in part for the briefest of moments in 1905, and had then been quickly snuffed out. Elections in the new Poland were expected to be reasonably free. Jews accounted for about a tenth of the population. They were not alone in being a discontented and put-upon segment of the population: there were the other major national minorities: Germans, Ukrainians, Byelorussians; and there were the socialists and the working classes generally whose lot was a hard one in itself. And finally, as we have seen, the Polish nationalists themselves were not all of one piece. Something surely could be made of this, not in the street, to be sure, nor, on the whole, on the shop floor, but at least in parliament. And, indeed, as nowhere else in Europe between the wars—until the Second Republic was extinguished—the Jews of Poland, with the rarest of exceptions, were to be found both free *and* willing to engage in politics on a collective basis, in their own name, that is to say, and in their own interest, directly and unapologetically. Not all approved of the tactics adopted by this or that party. Nor were all prepared to make the very most of the political opportunities that the national constitution and the general social and political configuration of the country appeared to offer them. But Jewish national politics as a component of the total political system did take on a fairly firm structure of its own quite rapidly. And, broadly, three strategies evolved, each being an attempt by one of the three major political formations in Polish Jewry to define a role for the community as a whole and chart a path for it in what no one doubted was at one and the same time a largely open and an intensely hostile social and political environment.

One strategy was associated with the Zionists, more precisely the dominant faction in the movement at the time, the so-called 'General Zionists' (in contradistinction to the several varieties of socialists, the orthodox Mizraḥi faction, and, later, the Revisionist Zionists and its two offshoots the New Zionist Organization and the Jewish State Party). Considered generically, the Zionists had the advantage of having been quick to take the lead at the end of the war in all the principal communities of eastern Europe. The Balfour Declaration and its subsequent incorporation in the League of Nations Mandate for Palestine had raised their stock beyond anything they could have hoped for prior to the war. They had performed to better purpose at the Peace Conference than any of their rivals. The Peace Conference itself had borne what appeared to be substantial and immediate fruit in the form of the Polish minorities treaty. The paramount leaders of the movement, moving and operating on the world stage in a manner that was totally new in Jewish experience, had become a source of pride and encouragement all round. And, to cap it all, the Zionists had the benefit of several exceedingly energetic and effective leaders of their own in Poland itself, the most prominent of whom was Yiẓḥak Gruenbaum (1879–1970), who had taught themselves to speak in what amounted to two voices. They propagated Zionism proper, as ordinarily understood, as the long-term, definitive policy for the Jews to pursue, and the very one that had now, it could be very reasonably argued, come into its own. But they could not and, on the whole, did not avoid the question, posed with mounting anxiety throughout the two decades that separated their triumph at the end of the First World War from the disaster that would engulf them at the beginning of the Second, which was whether they, their movement, and, ultimately, Palestine itself had really very much to offer by way of easing the ever more crushing, short- and middle-term needs of Polish Jewry itself.

The migratory *push* out of Poland in these years was an uneven one: high in the mid-1920s, then low, then high again and rising steadily in the 1930s. The degree to which Palestine could serve as a land of settlement depended on the state of its economy—always a small one, yet one that was demonstrably capable of being enlarged and enriched by the flow into it of immigrants. It depended, secondly, on the resources available to the Zionist movement to allot to the settlement of migrants at any moment. These were always exceedingly slim. It depended thirdly on the immigration policy of the Zionist movement itself. Its consistent preference, especially in the 1920s, was for the young and the fit, the 'pioneers' who were prepared to farm the land, the people whose devotion to socialism in one form or another was beyond all question, and whom the leaders of the movement, partly for objective reasons, partly out of regard for who were most likely to support them politically, thought it would be wisest to supply with such immigration permits—always limited in number—as the British administration was prepared to make available. For finally, and ever more critically as time passed, it was on the number of Jewish immigrants allowed into Palestine by the Mandatory Power itself that Palestine as a land of refuge and as a land in which Jews could rebuild their lives privately, but above all collectively, was contingent.

Emigration from Poland had begun by being quite small: a few thousand a year in the early 1920s. In 1924, however, as the economic and political condition of the Jews deteriorated, it leaped to some 8,000; in 1925 to 18,000. Then it fell once more to the earlier rates of several thousand each year or fewer. In 1928, by which time the gates to the United States had been closed and the pressure to enter Palestine had begun greatly to exceed the number of immigrants the British administration was prepared to admit, only 763 Polish Jews received permission to enter the country.[32] The numbers admittedly picked up again in the early 1930s, reaching 30,000 in the peak year of 1935 (or roughly half of all Jewish immigrants into the country) before falling once more to a few thousand annually in the last years of peace—chiefly because the British administration was becoming immovable on the total number allowed in and the greater pressure for permission to enter was now from Germany, Austria, Italy, and Czechoslovakia. In all, it has been calculated that some 140,000 Jews left Poland for Palestine between 1919 and 1942. This was by far the largest single country group of immigrants, yet they accounted for only 4.5 per cent of the entire Jewish population of Poland and no more than half its natural increase in the course of the years 1931–5 alone: a perfect illustration, therefore, of the validity of Motzkin's thesis[33] that the ability of the Zionists to offer a substantial solution to the problems of European Jewry (Motzkin had only eastern Europe in mind at the time) was exceedingly limited and that their ability to offer Palestine as a refuge would be consistently lower, and over time very much lower, than the demand to enter it. The eventual consequences of this discrepancy between what was needed and what was on offer would be fatal for

---

[32] *Din ve-heshbon shel ha-va'ad ha-merkazi la-histadrut ha-zionit be-polin* (Warsaw, 1932), 132.

[33] See above, p. 742.

immense numbers of European Jews. The immediate consequence for the Zionist movement was a steady sapping of the prestige they had so unexpectedly earned in 1917 and again in 1919.

Gruenbaum was to some extent at one with Motzkin at this time. It will be recalled that he had played a central role at the conference of Russian Zionists assembled in Helsingfors in 1906. He had been one of the authors and promoters of the decision to take up what were termed 'current tasks' (*Gegenwartsarbeit* in the jargon of the movement)—meaning devotion of thought, time, and resources to the improvement of the condition of Jewry in the Diaspora itself as opposed to undiluted emphasis on the settlement of Palestine while Zionism's central and eponymous concerns hung fire. But there was more to his plunge into Polish politics than that of even ordinary personal ambition and thirst for action. Gruenbaum had always seen himself as in every relevant sense a Polish (as opposed to a Russian) Jew. He wrote in Polish. He knew a great deal about Polish politics. It had been his view, and it had long been on the record, that the Jews could indeed find a tolerable place for themselves in the country—not as Poles of an inferior kind, to be sure, but as one of the several national groups that would necessarily inhabit it. It was therefore to be expected that, on independence being achieved, Gruenbaum would seek to lead the Zionists into active participation in Polish national and parliamentary politics. In fact, he went a good deal further. It was true that much could be done, and much was done, by the relevant Polish authorities, to cut down Jewish representation in parliament. Heavy intervention by the state bureaucracy in the conduct of the elections, large-scale gerrymandering in the cities, and systematic overrepresentation of the countryside where the *szlachta* (landowning gentry) was at its strongest and the peasants in the non-Ukrainian and non-Byelorussian areas were assumed to be good Catholic Poles, were all regular practice. And parliamentary life could be made difficult even for those representatives of Jewish parties who had actually managed to leap the many hurdles to election.[34] But the Jews could not be shut out of the parliamentary arena altogether.

As social and economic pressure on the Jews mounted, Gruenbaum set himself to fend it off by devoting his very considerable resources of energy to the creation of a parliamentary bloc in which all the minority nationalities, the Germans, the Ukrainians, and the Byelorussians as well as the Jews, all being discontented and all in one degree or another being at odds with the Polish nationalists, would join in a common effort of resistance and defiance against the dominant national and political forces

---

[34] By, for example, setting the number of deputies needed to support a parliamentary interpellation at a level higher than all the Jewish deputies taken together could muster on their own.

in the country. This, to be sure, was *Gegenwartsarbeit* with a vengeance, as radical a departure from the old Herzlian principle of non-participation in domestic politics as there could be.[35] Not all Zionists liked it. The great majority of Zionism's opponents within Jewry itself disapproved of it. The orthodox Aguda preferred to cleave to the ancient rule of avoiding an open clash with the masters of the kingdom whoever they were. The Bund denounced the minorities bloc as a coalition of bourgeois nation-alists rather than the one towards which they strove, a coalition founded on class. The initial results were promising, however. In 1922 most of the Jewish parties, having under Gruenbaum's leadership entered into an alliance with the parties representing the other minorities, gained thirty-five seats in all or a little under 8 per cent of the total membership of the Sejm. But the success was never repeated. It was apparent after a while that no long-lasting working parliamentary bloc of loyally co-operating deputies representing the interests of the minorities could be formed. The national minorities were themselves in certain respects quite sharply divided. The Germans and the Ukrainians wanted a state of nationalities instead of a firmly Polish nation-state. The Jews, broadly, the Zionists apart, were more receptive to the Polish national view of the Polish nation-state, provided a viable place was left for them. The Ukrainians and Byelorussians were peasant peoples. The Jews were preponderantly urban. The Germans with whom the Jews had most in common demo-graphically and sociologically came under Nazi influence before very long, whereupon such co-operation as there had been with them broke down. And there was the cardinal difference between the Jews and all the others, that all other minorities had a national state, real or nominal, across the border to which they could look for protection and for guid-ance. The Jews, in contrast, were cautious about calling upon foreign Jews to intervene on their behalf and had reason to doubt the efficacy of such intervention anyway.

The formation of the minorities bloc had counted as a famous victory by Gruenbaum and his followers in 1922. By the same token, its failure was spelled out for all to see in the results of the 1928 elections when the Jewish parties found themselves with only thirteen deputies or 2.9 per cent of the total membership of the Sejm. This was about a third of the Jews' proportionate strength in the population and substantially fewer both absolutely and proportionately than the very much smaller German minority which had gained nineteen seats (two more than in the 1922

[35] Very much later, during the Second World War, Gruenbaum's views changed. At a meeting of the Zionist Executive in Feb. 1943 at which he described the miserable con-dition of European Jewry and the indifference of the Allies to their fate, he argued that it had to be 'Zionism above all'. He told his colleagues that he did not believe that there was any possibility at all of stopping the slaughter and he argued lucidly for all resources to be devoted to settlement in Palestine (Roman Frister, *Le-lo peshara* (Tel Aviv, 1987), 286 ff.).

elections), or 4.4 per cent of the total Sejm membership but very nearly twice its relative segment of the population. Gerrymandering and other forms of government manipulation had had something to do with the failure, but were less than the whole of the story. Not all Jews voted for specifically Jewish parties and precisely who supported which party in which election (local, national parliamentary, or communal) was never entirely clear. Many Jews were divided in their own minds about whom to vote for and there was a marked, although not overwhelming tendency by individuals to split their vote, voting for one Jewish party or group in one set of elections—say, the national—and for another party in another set—the municipal or the communal. Where there was no vote-sharing agreement between the parties, there was a further consequent loss to all Jewish parties taken together. All this had been in evidence in the very first round of elections to the Sejm in January 1919 when the ability of the Jewish parties to gain representation in the Sejm was perhaps the highest of all objectively. There were then no less than six major lists. The Zionists did particularly well, especially so in (formerly Austrian) West Galicia where they received 52,661 of a total of 58,034 votes cast for all Jewish lists (which suggests that, very unusually, substantial numbers of orthodox Jews had been among those voting for the Zionists). They had some cause, therefore, to appear at the Peace Conference as the preponderant tendency in all of Poland. They did very well in Congress Poland too, although there Agudat Yisrael received just under a quarter of the votes cast for all the Jewish parties running, or slightly over half the votes cast for the Zionist-dominated Temporary Jewish National Council (Tymczasowa Zydowska Rada Narodowa) list of which Gruenbaum was the leading figure and in which the religious Zionists (the Mizrahi) participated. The Bund, then at its nadir, failed to gain any representation at all.

TABLE 9.4.[36] *Elections to the Sejm, 1919: Jewish parties in Congress Poland compared*

Party lists	Votes cast	%
Jewish National Council	180,234	45.42
Agudat Yisrael	97,293	24.52
Folkspartei	59,229	14.93
Po'alei Zion	27,063	6.82
Bund	16,366	4.12
United Socialist Party	8,883	2.24
Local lists	7,739	1.95
TOTAL IN CONGRESS POLAND	396,807	100.00

[36] No elections at all were held in East Galicia and in the eastern borderlands of the new Poland in 1919. The poor showing of the Bund may have owed something to the dislocations of war and revolution and to the numbers of Jews voting for parties of the

In any case, the full potential force of the Jewish vote in municipal and especially in the more important national elections was consistently weakened by the relatively low participation of Jews generally: twenty percentage points or so less than in the case of non-Jews, male as well as female. This low turn-out, so unlike Jewish political behaviour in western countries, seems to have been partly a function of traditional attitudes to general politics and to what could be taken—and by certain sectors of Jewish orthodoxy were taken—as matters that did not and should not concern Jews; and partly it may be attributed, equally traditionally, to eastern European Jews' ingrained fatalism, namely the conviction that elections would change little or nothing so far as they were concerned. But it owed something as well to the harassment at the hands of Polish nationalists that could be expected at many of the polling stations. All this contributed to, without fully explaining, the underrepresentation of the Jews in the Sejm overall, the case of the 1922 elections excepted.

Gruenbaum was far from having everyone behind him. There was substantial opposition to what he was about among the Zionists themselves on the grounds, correct in themselves, that Polish hostility to the minorities bloc could hardly be other than fixed and in some quarters ferocious. In its original, pristine form, Zionism had tended to be viewed somewhat sympathetically by Polish nationalists for much the same reason that it had been openly favoured in Russia and Germany in Herzl's time and, rather more circumspectly, in Great Britain under Lloyd George and Balfour. Were not the Zionists intent on leading the Jews out of Europe? Was that not sufficient cause to support them? What Gruenbaum and his colleagues were actually about, however, could not fail to appear to Polish nationalists—notably Dmowski's National Democrats, but in one degree or another to those who belonged to the milder and more tolerant schools of thought as well—as precisely that which they were least prepared to stomach: the presence within the Polish body politic of a distinctive and self-directing Jewish presence. Surely this was proof positive of the validity of the extremists' thesis that it was the Jews, given their supposedly monstrous hold over the economy and their overweening political ambitions, who constituted the greatest, because most insidious, threat to the strength and future of the Polish nation? Even those who were less inclined to swallow the bogeyman image of Polish Jewry whole and whose view of the Jews and other minorities was a milder and less excited one, those who followed Pilsudski, for example, drew the line at this point. Here lay the basis for a second Jewish strategy

Polish (i.e. distinctly non-Jewish) left. *Sources*: Ezra Mendelsohn, *Zionism in Poland: The Formative Years, 1915–1926* (New Haven, 1981), 108; G. C. Bacon, 'Agudat Israel in Interwar Poland', in Yisrael Gutman, *et al.* (eds.), *The Jews of Poland between Two World Wars* (Hanover and London, 1989), 23–5.

for keeping afloat in independent Poland: less ambitious, more traditional, and more acceptable too to the moderates in the Polish political establishment, notably after Pilsudski's seizure of power in 1926.

The governmental view of Jewish orthodoxy tended to be a good deal milder than its view of Jewish secularism and Jewish secularists—an important distinction which the more extreme Polish nationalists, by and large, were less inclined to make. The secularist wing of Polish Jewry was resented for its independence of mind and for its efforts to make the most of parliamentary arithmetic. It was held suspect by reason of the large socialist element within it. And it suffered from every Polish government's tendency to blur the very real distinction between rebellious Jews who had totally abandoned the community and its interests and were indeed at war with the regime as well and those who, while exceedingly discontented and highly critical of it, remained politically loyal to the state and wholly and openly devoted to the interests of their community. In practice there was a world of difference between the notionally Jewish members of the much feared, underground Polish Communist Party (Komunistyczna Partia Polska or KPP) and the Bundists, for example, who could not have been further from abandoning all interest or connection with the community in the manner which Rosa Luxemburg had made notorious. For all their criticism of the regime, the Bundists, like the Zionists, remained politically loyal to it and were, on the whole, left free to operate legally and in the open. But they were disliked by the authorities, known to be militant and temperamentally rebellious, and held suspect, along with all other socialists, of being either secretly or at any rate potentially subversive.

In contrast, where the orthodox were concerned, attitudes were more relaxed and followed much the same pattern as had obtained in pre-revolutionary Russia. They were perceived as Jews of a more familiar, more manageable type. Their leaders, it was thought, could be more easily trusted to hold their flocks under a tight rein. Their political ambitions were evidently limited to their desire to preserve their set way of life before all else. Their umbrella organization, Agudat Yisrael, was manifestly more an interest lobby than a political party in the ordinary sense. And, still more fortunately, the orthodox were conveniently riven by divisions of their own: by the old antagonism between the Hasidic and the anti-Hasidic (or in common parlance 'Lithuanian') wings of eastern European orthodoxy; by enduring rivalries between leading Hasidic *rebbes* and their respective courts; and by the idea of venturing into the Polish political arena itself. Some leaders of religious orthodoxy regarded it as intrinsically incompatible with traditional Jewish values and practice. Others believed that those who were loyal to the Tradition had a positive duty to ensure that it not go unrepresented and the arena left to the secularists, the assimilationists, and to those, in some ways the worst of the lot, who formed the small minority within orthodoxy that espoused Zionism and religious orthodoxy in tandem. Finally, the orthodox, being of course, deeply at odds with the secularists, could be relied upon in certain circumstances—once their own special demands were met—to undercut them.

The consultative forum which united the orthodox, Agudat Yisrael, was, it will be recalled,[37] of recent creation, the invention of the rather more worldly and sophisticated German branch of Jewish orthodoxy, to the initiatives of which the eastern European rabbinate had responded hesitantly and somewhat reluctantly. The attempt to consolidate what had been achieved at the Aguda's founding conference at Kattowitz in 1912 had had to hang fire during the war, bar some small progress in the effort to encourage a more sympathetic attitude to it, especially among the followers of the most influential of the Hasidic leaders the *rebbe* of Gur (Góra Kalwaria, not far from Warsaw), by a pair of German orthodox rabbis attached as advisers on Jewish affairs to the German occupation authorities in Poland.[38] But the difference between the German or Frankfurt school of Jewish orthodoxy and the Polish—and the very much greater east European branch generally—had not really been bridged. The Germans' posture *vis-à-vis* the non-Jewish world and, by extension, before the rest of German Jewry, remained defensive. They were inclined to play down the religion–nationality nexus in Judaism. Their Polish colleagues had no such inhibitions. Nothing could be further from *their* thoughts than to resign themselves to a form of separatism within Polish Jewry of the kind the German school of orthodoxy had accepted for itself. Nor did they see any reason to play down the specifically national character of Jewry, however careful they might be to deprive it of clear-cut political implications in their handling of the issue in their relations with the Poles.

What the orthodox establishment in Poland, as it is fair to call it, had in common with the Gruenbaum school of Zionism,[39] was that it was willing, although much more circumspectly than the Zionists, to try to make the most of such constitutional liberties and right of participation in the political life of the country as it thought might be open to it. To that end too the rabbis were prepared to allow their political people to co-operate, if absolutely necessary, with Gruenbaum and his people—notably, as they

[37] See Chapter 5.

[38] Alexander Carlebach, 'A German Rabbi goes East', *LBIYB* 6 (London, 1961), 60–121.

[39] It needs to be recalled that in strict organizational terms Yiẓḥak Gruenbaum was the leader of the middle of the road General Zionists as opposed to the several varieties of socialist Zionists on the left, the orthodox Zionists of the Mizraḥi movement, and the Revisionists on the right—'right' having more to do, however, with intransigence *vis-à-vis* the British government in London and the Mandatory administration in Palestine itself than with principled opposition to socialism in any of its forms.

seemed to have feared might be the case, if they were likely to find themselves without any representation in the Sejm at all if they did not.[40] Once
seated in the Sejm their deputies duly joined the 'Jewish Parliamentary
Club' or caucus—the Kolo Zydowskie—over which Gruenbaum may
be said to have presided, but on their terms, with limited purposes, and
on the implicit understanding all round that if they thought it expedient
to do so they would go their own way after all.[41] And indeed, in practice,
except for short-term parliamentary purposes there was no real political
co-operation between the Aguda and the other Jewish parties. Its people
saw the secularists in Jewry, and Gruenbaum as the most prominent figure among them in particular, as internal enemies to be fought implacably whenever a convenient opportunity arose to do so.

They had always viewed co-operation with the non-Jewish minorities
as undesirable and dangerous on the perfectly solid grounds that since, at
bottom, the Germans and the Ukrainians were opposed to Poland in its
present borders while the Jews as such were not, the latter were unwise to
allow themselves to be dragged into a quarrel that could only envenom
their relations with the Polish government of the day and perhaps all governments thereafter. They objected too to the fairly prevalent notion
among the modernists that the Polish left was an actual or at least potential ally. The Aguda distrusted it politically, feared it socially, and preferred
to rely on such common social ground as it had with the conservative
forces in Poland[42] and the role it could play in the Sejm from time to time
by, for example, casting a swing vote in case of deadlock in committees.
For the rest, it preferred to examine each issue on its specific merit,
namely on the basis of how, if at all, it was likely to affect Jewish interests
(as it itself defined them). In sum, there were few among the staunchly
orthodox who doubted the continuing validity of the wisdom of the
ages, namely that it was not and could never be expedient for the Jews to
quarrel head-on with the masters of the country that they inhabited.
And, finally, they had in view what they did not doubt was a higher interest to protect: their schools. If the reward for co-operating with the government in compassing the defeat of the Gruenbaumites was the
safeguarding of their own traditional educational system, along with
related benefits and additions, why then so be it. And since, by making
the limited concessions that would satisfy Jewish orthodoxy the stipulations of the Polish minorities treaty concerning education could be

---

[40] Ezra Mendelsohn, 'The Politics of Agudas Yisroel in Inter-War Poland', *Soviet Jewish Affairs*, 2, 2 (1972), 47–60.

[41] Gershon C. Bacon, 'The Politics of Tradition: Agudat Israel in Polish Politics, 1916–1939', *Studies in Contemporary Jewry*, 2 (Bloomington, Ind., 1986), *passim*.

[42] The Aguda sided with the conservatives against Gruenbaum when he proposed that clergymen be excluded from the Sejm and it opposed a socialist proposal that state schools be secular. Bacon, 'Politics of Tradition', 155.

largely circumvented, the Jewish political front itself divided and weakened, and the much sterner and more insistent secular Jewish nationalists
in particular severely undercut, there were indeed the makings of a deal
between what in the abstract were firm opposites: Polish conservatives
and nationalists on the one hand, dedicated and prototypical Jewish sep-
aratists on the other.

But while the Aguda had its small successes, on the broader plane of
Jewish needs it was no better placed than anyone else to offer its own constituency of the ultra-orthodox, let alone Polish Jewry as a whole, a
prospect of relief either from endemic poverty or from the mistreatment
and discrimination which afflicted it. Nor did it seek to formulate one, or
to think through the problem of the essential viability of Polish Jewry. Its
leaders relied before all else, as they had always done, on intercession—
now construed, in part at least, in parliamentary terms. They continued
to hope and to pray, as their ancestors had always hoped and prayed, for
better times. They were not blind to the condition of their people. Their
brief moment of co-operation with the Jewish secularists, so contrary to
their strongest instincts, has been interpreted by some historians as stemming from worthier grounds than the merely opportunistic—a one time
only deviation decided upon in protest against the anti-Semitic posture
of the government of the day—from which Pilsudski's coup in 1926 freed
them, however, to revert to their natural position.[43] The return of Pilsudski to power had been generally welcomed by the Jews. He was (at
least in his origins) a man of the left. He was certainly a man of order. He
was not markedly anti-Semitic. And he was a sworn enemy of the
National Democrats. True, he had been brought to power by a *coup d'état*;
but democratic principles in the ordinary sense had never been of great
concern to Agudat Yisrael. Its people had seen no reason, therefore, not
to enter into an alliance with Pilsudski's Sanacja—which did certainly
appear to be a great deal more desirable as the foundation of government
than the ultra-nationalist, openly anti-Semitic Endecja. And if, in the
event, very little of Jewish interest was ever achieved, why that was not a
matter to take too much to heart. Unfortunately for the Aguda, the
alliance collapsed after Pilsudski's death. Sanacja's successor was the
overtly anti-Semitic Camp of National Unity (OZON) and the break
with the Pilsudskian outlook on these matters was cemented by the
OZON government's agreement, as we have seen, to take the campaign
against *sheḥita* (and much else) under its wing. The denunciation of
sheḥita could not have been other than a source of intense objection and
disappointment to the orthodox. Few measures could have been seen
by Polish Jews of any persuasion as being more precisely directed at
Judaism as the orthodox represented it and few could have so seriously

[43] Mendelsohn, 'The Politics of Agudas Yisroel', 52.

undermined the *political* prestige of the Aguda within its own natural constituency.

The great leaders of Polish orthodoxy were retiring men for the most part. They did not descend into the political arena themselves. The labour of fighting the Jewish corner as they understood it was left to the *'askanim* or politicos who came to them for general (and compelling) guidance, but otherwise left them to their studies and to the tending of their flocks. There is no doubt, however, that they did not like what they saw all round them. The accelerating alienation of their flock from the Tradition was far from new. But what some found almost as difficult to stomach were the ever bitterer rifts within the community itself, the violence of language employed, the minor, but unpleasant bodily violence too that tended increasingly to accompany internal political divisions and invariably flared up when elections were held to the Sejm, or to the municipal councils, or to the community's own councils, or, in the case of the Zionists, to the Zionist Congresses held abroad.

I really cannot contain myself on this occasion [the ageing Rabbi Ḥayyim 'Ozer Grodzienski wrote from Vilna as he contemplated the scene in mid-November 1930]. Any one of sense knows that these are times when what is needed is for all the [Jewish] parties to increase their representation [in the Sejm] and to choose the best and most talented people to speak in the houses of parliament for our people, shattered as they are by the economic crisis, as the *'askanim* always did in the past, marching shoulder to shoulder in our people's defence. That is how it was earlier in the course of elections to the [Russian] Duma when the entire people, regardless of party, knew whom to regard as the most competent men to represent them. . . . How different things are in our own times.[44]

The third Jewish strategy was that of the Polish Bund, heirs to the party that had functioned for twenty years with remarkable success under Russian rule—although, as will be recalled, less in Poland itself at the time than in Lithuania and Byelorussia. One of the results of its having to concentrate its activities in Poland, however, was that it was free to shed the features and rhetoric of an illegal, necessarily conspiratorial, revolutionary movement and stage by stage, to some extent unconsciously, but on the whole quite rapidly, transform itself into a party that was prepared, even eager, to operate within the constraints of the Polish constitution. The Bundists remained faithful, as their surviving brethren under Soviet rule could not be, to the syncretistic amalgam of Marxism and Jewish Diaspora nationalism on which the movement had been founded and which had been worked out under the very different conditions of Tsarist Russia. But the balance had shifted. They were now more concerned to defend the Jews against their enemies than to employ them in

---

[44] Ḥayyim 'Ozer Grodzienski, *Ahi'ezer*, ed. Aharon Suraski (Benei Berak, 1970), i. 249–50.

some general campaign to overturn the regime. Marxism had not been abandoned, however: one reason for their somewhat unthinking refusal to join the 'bourgeois' Zionists, their 'class enemy', in the demand for autonomy and minority rights with which the largely Zionist Polish-Jewish delegation to the Peace Conference had armed itself in 1919.

Their devotion to Marxism accounts too for their untiring search for allies on the non-Jewish political left, for remaining hopeful in this respect beyond all reason, and for being prepared in this single connection, as they were in no other, to swallow their otherwise exemplary pride. On the other hand, there would in fact be no common ground between them and the (illegal) Polish Communist Party with whom the original quarrel between them and Lenin's (and, for the moment, Martov's) RSDWP was fated to be replayed over and over again, greatly aggravated by the brutal destruction of the original Bund at the hands of the Bolsheviks, and aggravated again by the Bund's own decision not to join the Moscow-run Third International.[45] The quarrel over the special needs of the Jewish working class and the Bund's own prerogative right to represent it would also be replayed, if in a milder form, with the Polish Socialist Party (PPS)—with whom, in other respects, the Bund had a good deal in common. Both were authentically socialist parties, the Bund being more strictly Marxist than the PPS, however. Neither was willing to accept Moscow's authority. Each was kept apart from the other by national considerations which their common socialism should, in principle, have reduced to a nullity.

The Bundists were determined to think of Poland as their home whatever the ruling Polish view of the matter might be—and not merely in the pragmatic way of Gruenbaum's Zionists or the vaguer, contingent, and at the same time resigned and fatalistic way of the orthodox. Poland, they claimed, was a land in which Jews had full and unquestionable right of settlement and citizenship. The Polish socialists thought of Poland quite differently: as their very own country; and while they were moderate nationalists, they were nationalists all the same, applauding and following Marshal Pilsudski, once one of their own, in his territorial expansionism. The Bundists would not go so far as that and were contemptuous of what they took to be the opportunism of the PPS in this respect—as they were again when the PPS entered into a political alliance with the 'reactionary' (and generally anti-Semitic) Polish Peasant Party (PSL). But the really insuperable obstacle to a lasting and genuinely friendly relationship was

---

[45] But only after great internal stress and dislocation and the loss of its most influential leader, Vladimir Medem, who had gone out of his way to warn against having anything to do with the Leninists and, on being outvoted and it being resolved at an early stage of the extended proceedings to adhere to the Comintern, left the Party and Europe altogether. In 1930 the Bund changed its mind once again and decided to adhere to the Second International.

the adamant refusal of the PPS to recognize the Jews as a distinct nationality. Like the Leninists in this respect, its people regarded the ultimate and proper aim towards which all socialists should strive to be the eventual dissolution of Jewry and the assimilation of its members into the general population. But what had been admissible to the Bundist mind as a worthy, but exceedingly distant prospect in a distinctly multinational state like that of Russia was totally unacceptable in a nation-state, to the essential and exclusive ethos of which the Polish socialists subscribed as firmly, if less brutally, as did their right-wing rivals.

The saving grace of the PPS in this connection, so far as the Bund was concerned, was that, unlike the Communists, it did not oppose special social, cultural, and educational institutions for the national minorities, the Jewish minority among the rest. But this was not enough to pacify an irresolubly conflictual relationship between the PPS and the Bund, punctuated from time to time to be sure by passages of co-operation and/or recognition of common interests, and then marred periodically by the PPS being generally less loyal to its occasional partner than the Bund to it. The PPS was entirely capable of rewarding the Bund for its co-operation at election time by the underhand tactic of putting up Jewish candidates of its own to fight it and reduce, if possible, the very thing the Bund was best at offering its own natural constituency: genuine socialism, as good or better than that offered by any of the other socialist parties, yet socialism with a Jewish face.[46] Still, the relationship between the Bund and the PPS was never as unfriendly as that which obtained between the Bund and the Communists—apart from a brief period in the mid-1930s when the old quarrel was softened somewhat by Communist attempts to woo 'progressive forces' of all varieties and incorporate them in a 'popular front'. On this occasion, while the PPS turned a deaf ear to Moscow's blandishments, the Bund, despite its open criticism of much that had transpired in the USSR since the Revolution, and of the Moscow trials in particular, was initially receptive. 'As in the past, so today, it is our opinion that there is much in common between the socialist and communist workers; they should belong to one organization in which conflicts can be resolved in a democratic manner on the basis of freedom of thought and the discipline of action.'[47]

Later, their suspicions and fears of the Communists mounting, the Bundists moved to a position that was virtually identical with that of the PPS,[48] although as late as 1939 Victor Alter can be found observing that

[46] On this see especially Korzec, *Juifs en Pologne*, 74.

[47] Victor Alter in 'Di moskver ekzekutsyes' ['The Moscow executions'], *Folkstsaytung* (Warsaw), Sept. 1936. Cited in Abraham Brumberg, 'The Bund and the Polish Socialist Party in the late 1930s', in Yisrael Gutman, *et al.* (eds.), *The Jews of Poland between Two World Wars* (Hanover and London, 1989), 80.

[48] A fear well justified. Alter, who had taken refuge first in the Russian zone of

his personal responses to what was transpiring around him were governed by what he conceived of as a hierarchy. He responded to events first and foremost, he explained, as a human being, secondly as a socialist, and only finally as a Jew. As for contemporary anti-Semitism, he was 'unable to regard [it] from a specifically Jewish point of view at all'.[49] There is no doubting that the Bundists, to the end, were prisoners of a deep, almost visceral objection to taking the full measure of the anti-Semitism of the Polish working class and to recognizing it frankly as a phenomenon too firmly seated for genuine 'class solidarity' to be possible where the Jews were concerned. They continued, fatally, to be drawn to the idea that despite everything Communists and socialists were at least potential allies and that the common underpinning of all who were genuinely on the left was an essentially, at any rate ultimately, undifferentiated working class. Where the specifically Jewish parties were concerned their outlook was altogether less inhibited, however.

Total secularists and dedicated critics of the Tradition, the Bundists yielded to none in their denunciation of organized orthodoxy for its obscurantism and the moral subjugation in which it held its people. Their objections were therefore sweeping and fundamental. Their differences with the Zionists—modernists and (in the majority) secularists like themselves—stemmed, to be sure, from their insistence that their rivals were chauvinists and bourgeois reactionaries. But they had more to do with specifics and were therefore more complex. They differed from the Zionists, of course, in that, where for the latter Jewish national autonomy in Poland was a temporary goal to be striven for, a stage to pass through for pragmatic reasons while the struggle to reach the ultimate goal of Jewish political autonomy in Palestine was maintained, for the Bundists it was very nearly the final goal. There was the further difference, one which in the actual circumstances of Polish Jewry between the wars counted for almost as much as a final purpose, that for the Zionists the symbol and, in some ways, the primary engine of the Jewish national secular revival was the revival of Hebrew both as a literary vehicle *and* as a vernacular. For the Bund, on the other hand, it was Yiddish that counted in all relevant respects: as the actual language of the people; because it could, should, and to some extent already did serve as a literary vehicle; as a language of scholarship as well; and because what it breathed was not (to their minds) fustiness, reaction, and the dread Tradition, but modernity and *doikeyt*: staying put.

occupation and then in Russia itself where he had agreed readily and as matter of course to harness himself (and what was left of the Bund) to the Allied war effort, was arrested early in Dec. 1941 along with his principal colleague Henryk Erlich. Erlich died in prison six months later. Alter himself was shot on 17 Feb. 1943.

[49] Cited in Henri Minczeles, *Histoire générale du Bund: un mouvement révolutionnaire juif* (Paris, 1995), 370.

The key to the Bundists' thinking lay in this conception of themselves as staying put. Their autonomous, self-willed, social, and political functions were all predicated on *doikeyt*. They did not deny that there was little enough in the independent Polish state in which they now found themselves to excite their enthusiasm. But they did not propose to fight or subvert it or abandon it—any more than did their ideological near-neighbours, the PPS. In their view, the Zionists' advocacy of large-scale emigration from Poland was tantamount to advocacy of deportation. The motives of the Zionists differed, no doubt, from those of the Endecja and the rest. But the effect was the same: the alienation of the 'Jewish masses' from Poland and their being driven inexorably into conflict with their analogues, the working people of Poland.

Our party has roused, and still rouses, an awareness among the Jewish masses of the inseparability of their fate and the fate of the land in which they live; [the Bund] has developed and is still developing in the Jewish masses the feeling that they are citizens of Poland who are not only entitled to equal rights with others, but are also obligated to equal responsibility with others; [the Bund] has linked, and still links, the Jewish masses ever closer with the life of Poland and with the struggles of the Polish working masses for a better tomorrow and for a fuller liberation in their joint fatherland.[50]

So while in certain cultural and intellectual respects there was much to link the Bundists to the Zionists, even to Gruenbaum's mainstream General Zionists—having the latter's role as promoters of 'current tasks' in mind—the two great parties of modernists were normally at daggers drawn.

On the other hand, they were at one with the Zionists in being willing to set aside their anti-clericalism and contempt for religious ritual and defend traditional Jewish practice where an assault upon it was seen as an attack on Jewry generally. The Bund joined the other Jewish parties readily enough in the effort to beat back the long-drawn-out effort to ban *sheḥita*. It had done the same, inevitably with some reservations, in defence of the Jewish Sabbath too when the issue first arose in the early years of the republic.[51] This added something to its prestige in circles that lay beyond the confines of their natural, urban, semi-secular working-class constituency. But in the eyes of the general Jewish public it was their participation and, increasingly, the lead they took in resisting anti-Semitism in the increasingly violent forms it began to take in the final years of the republic that finally marked the Bund as its most stalwart and vigorous defender.

The defining instance was a pogrom perpetrated in the preponderantly

---

[50] Bernard K. Johnpoll, *The Politics of Futility: The General Jewish Workers Bund of Poland, 1917–1943* (Ithaca, NY, 1967), 218.

[51] Brumberg, 'The Bund', 76–7 n. 2; and Golczewski, 'The Problem of Sunday Rest in Interwar Poland', in Gutman *et al.*, *Jews of Poland*, 158–72.

Jewish village of Przytyk (in the Opoczno district, south-east of Lodz) on 9 March 1936. Several Jews were killed. Several dozen were injured. A good many Jewish homes and workshops were set alight. And despite the fact that the National Democrats were behind the atrocity the Sanacja authorities (still in power) tolerated them on this occasion and the police stood aside. It was an occasion, however, when the first round was followed by a second at which a Jewish self-defence force went into action. In this further fighting a Pole was killed and several dozen of the attackers wounded. When the police finally intervened, arrests made, and trials held it was the Jews who were accused of having fomented the riot, seven of them being found guilty and sentenced to heavy terms of imprisonment (five to eight years). Of the actual *pogromshchiki* forty-two were also tried and found guilty, but sentenced to very much lighter terms (four to twelve months each). Although by the standards set in Poland itself only fifteen years or so earlier, and therefore in living memory, the Przytyk pogrom was a small affair, the outrage was immense, perhaps chiefly because it was one incident among many and was seen, correctly, as speaking volumes about the direction the post-Pilsudski regime was taking.

The Bund, in any event, responded rapidly. On 17 March it issued a call for a general strike which, against all precedent, turned out to be a resounding success. All the Jewish trade unions co-operated, as did the Zionist socialists, the Po'alei Zion. But so did the Polish Socialist Workers' Party (that stood somewhat to the left of the PPS) and the Polish socialist trade unions in all the major cities of the country as well. A brief, temporarily paralysing blow was struck at the economy. An impression—fleeting, to be sure—was made on the general public, a deeper and more lasting one on the Jewish. On the Bundists themselves the impact, naturally enough, was especially heartening. Had they not called for work, bread, and liberty for all the nationalities in Poland; for a protest against clerical reaction as well as against Jewish nationalism; and against reaction, fascism, and capitalism as well as against the boycotting and persecution of the Jews?[52] And had not many thousands of *Poles* duly joined them and marched with them shoulder to shoulder? The pogrom in Przytyk was followed by others, but resistance to violence continued and the Bundists in Poland became as adept in organizing Jewish self-defence—both in the figurative and literal senses of the term—as their predecessors had been in pre-revolutionary Russia.[53] Massive strikes were mounted wherever and whenever possible in protest against

---

[52] Text in Minczeles, *Histoire générale*, 376.

[53] On the 'ordener-grupe' organized by the Bund, see Leonard Rowe, 'Jewish Self-Defense: A Response to Violence', in Joshua A. Fishman (ed.), *Shtudiés vegn yidn in Poiln 1919/Studies on Polish Jewry* (New York, 1974), 105–49.

continued anti-Jewish violence and wrongful dismissal of Jewish employees. Pitched battles between National Democrats and socialist Jewish self-defence forces in the streets of Warsaw, Lodz, Bialystok, Czestochowa, and dozens of other centres of population large and small became a familiar spectacle. The public was provided with some fairly regular protection from hooligans. And if the strikes, while widely followed, altered nothing of a fundamental nature, they served to boost the Jews' public morale and raise a few barriers to absolute despair.

It would not be long before the Bund reaped its first reward when, having suddenly reversed a long-standing decision to abstain from playing a role of any kind in what it had long dismissed as inherently reactionary and useless institutions, it participated in the *kehilla* (community) elections of 30 August and 6 September 1936. The results were stunning. In the country as a whole the Bund gained 11.8 per cent of all *kehilla* council seats: an excellent outcome, considering the number of parties participating, the fact that the communities varied enormously in size and quality, and the fact that the Bund could only expect to do really well in the larger industrial and commercial cities, as opposed to the small towns and villages in which the Aguda was especially well entrenched. They did best of all in Warsaw itself where they left both the Aguda and the Zionists far behind (Table 9.5).

TABLE 9.5. *Warsaw community council elections (major lists only), 6 September 1936*

List	Votes	Percentage %	Seats
Bund	10,767	26.6	15
Zionists	6,982	17.2	9
Agudat Yisrael	5,257	13.0	10
Mizraḥi	2,205	5.4	3
Po'alei Zion (right)	2,046	5.0	2
'Adat Yisrael	1,249	3.1	2
Folkspartei	972	2.4	1
Po'alei Zion (left)	915	2.3	1

The results in the Lodz city council elections held several weeks later were more startling still. The Bund gained 48.1 per cent of all votes cast for Jewish parties, earning them 6 out of the 11 seats allotted to all Jewish parties taken together and 9.2 per cent of the total city poll as opposed to 5.8 per cent for the bloc led by the Aguda and 4.1 per cent for the bloc headed by the General Zionists.[54] And this signal triumph was repeated in the local government elections held at the end of 1938 and in May

[54] Robert M. Shapiro, *The Polish* Kehile *Elections of 1936: A Revolution Re-examined* (New York, 1988).

1939, the last to be held before the war, when they overtook the other Jewish parties again: 17 seats in the Warsaw city council as opposed to 3 for all other Jewish parties; 10 out of 17 Jewish seats in Vilna, 11 out of 17 in Lodz, 10 out of 15 in Bialystok; less well in Galicia and Wolynia, but overall an astonishing 9.5 per cent of the total vote in the larger towns of Poland (where government intervention was least efficacious and elections freest) taken together.[55]

To be sure, the triumph of the Bund was no more than moral. And the ever more oppressive atmosphere in Poland in the late 1930s was only conducive to influential minds in the Jewish population coming together to a limited extent if at all. Bouts of unity of feeling and recognition of common destiny erupted from time to time, but were apt to be rapidly undone by the dissolving power of continuing differences of outlook precisely when positive public action was most urgently indicated. The deepest lying quarrel was about appropriate posture. Ought it to be high or low? Ought Jews to be intent finally on breaking out of the old boundaries or content to remain within them? Were independence of mind and self-assertiveness truly of the essence, as the Bundists and Zionists believed, or was it expediency pushed to the point of self-abnegation if necessary that should rule, as was the orthodox view? Should eyes be on the short and middle term or on the enduring, the ultimate, and the eternal? The philosophical and ideological gulf between the believing orthodox and the atheist and deist secularists was recognizably unbridgeable. Each major tendency and party inhabited a more or less hermetic, morally self-sufficient world of its own. The Aguda had neither the temperament nor the ambition to set its sights as high as the Zionists or the Bundists and was content to enjoy its habitual informal, *de facto* autonomy, asking chiefly, as matters deteriorated, to be left alone. When roused by what it perceived to be a threat to its internal structure or to a Jewish interest that it judged vital to preserve, its procedure was to set about defence on the ancient assumption that some sort of deal could, and therefore most probably would, eventually be cut. A price—political or material—would be paid and the *gzeira* (the anti-Jewish edict or measure or deed) cancelled or withdrawn or at the very least reduced.

But if the sum of all this was that the leaders of the Jewish orthodoxy were therefore in no position to achieve anything that would actually relieve their own people of their multiple miseries, it was equally manifest that the secularists and modernists could do no better. Zionists and Bundists stopped well short of supine submission to their fate: partly because it was a matter of high principle for them, but partly too in virtue

---

[55] E. Meltzer, 'Ma'avak ha-ẓionim 'im ha-"bund" 'al ha-mediniyut ha-yehudit be-polin', in *Ha-ẓionut u-mitnagdeiha ba-'am ha-yehudi* (Jerusalem, 1990), 264; Polonsky, *Politics in Independent Poland*, 442.

of their instinctive recognition that in the new eastern European circumstances of enclosure in a nation-state the old style spelt suicide. They had
attempted, each group in its own way, to stall, circumvent, and neutralize
the Jews' most dangerous opponents by forming alliances with representatives of those sectors of the general population that had reasons of their
own for beating back the rulers of contemporary Poland. The results had
been meagre. Each such coalition relied on a group or groups whose governing sentiment, where the Jews were concerned, was as likely in certain circumstances to prove as ferociously inimical to their quondam allies
as was that of the Polish nationalists themselves. All such coalitions were
therefore flawed, ephemeral, and unreliable, never ever regarded by the
non-Jewish side as coalitions of equals. Nor were they.

There remained the second, but in truth and in fact the major prong of
the Zionists' forked strategy: Zionism proper, the Jewish National
Home, the eventual Jewish state, Palestine. Alas, there, as the Bund continually claimed, but as all could see in any case, the British government
was in the process of rendering these central aims of the Zionists unattainable. When the Palestine Royal Commission sent out to investigate
the Arab–Jewish conflict at the end of 1936[56] recommended that the
country be partitioned and that a small Jewish state of some 2,000 square
miles be established alongside a very much larger Arab one, the British
government itself first wavered, then set the Commission's findings
totally aside. It resolved instead, in the course of 1938 and 1939, on a
series of rapid steps,[57] the substance of which was the repudiation of the
Balfour Declaration and the effective closing of Palestine to Jewish
migration other than in demographically and politically insignificant
numbers. Zionism in its original, 'catastrophic' form seemed therefore,
once again, to have come to what many had long believed was its
appointed end. The principle of *doikeyt* or 'hereness' that had always lain
at the heart of the Bund's own understanding of the Jewish predicament,
the stubborn insistence—admirable in itself—on staying put and fighting
all problems through no matter how mountainous they might appear,
acquired a measure of plausibility that hitherto had been denied it. In a
society in which each political party served its adherents not only as their
guide to the perplexed, but as a home and a refuge and an entire alternative society to the one from which they stemmed and which was evidently failing them, this was powerful stuff: devastating for the Zionists,

[56] Palestine Royal Commission, *Report*, Cmd. 5479 (London, July 1937).
[57] The last of which was the publication of the British government's 'White Paper' of
17 May 1939 (Cmd. 6109) in which it was laid down that Jewish immigration was, after
an interval, to come to a virtual end and a state that would be Arab in all but name and in
which Jews would constitute a permanent minority was to be established subject to 'such
relations between the Arabs and the Jews as would make good government possible'.

invigorating for the Bund, food for thought for everyone. Thoughts and sentiments apart, however, the meaning of the redefinition of British Middle Eastern policy was that the trap in which the Jews of Poland had long been caught was now shut tight.

IV

It is because the Jewish population of Poland was so large and, all things considered, so thoroughly organized, politicized, and culturally coherent; because the Poland of Dmowski, Pilsudski, Cardinal Hlond, and the Colonels was itself far from being a solid and enduring social and political, let alone ethnic, structure; and because on the rock-bottom issues, as opposed to how they were to be handled, there was little disagreement in any quarter, that it is impossible not to wonder whether matters could have been otherwise. There was no mystery about the destructive nature of the pivot on which Polish Jewry's relations with the Polish state and with Polish society had been turning and on which it may be said to have been impaled. *Pace* the Bund, there was no reason to believe that improvement of any kind would come from within the Polish people itself, from any government that might conceivably rule over it or from any of its major institutions: the bureaucracy, the Sejm, the universities, the army, the Church. But could the Jews themselves have done better: by being more difficult to handle and be imposed upon, more rebellious, more violent, and very much more ambitious, or, alternatively, more imaginative, more accommodating, more discreet, and less ambitious? And were they not themselves beset all along by internal weaknesses that helped to drain away whatever lasting and effective power they may have had *potentially* to keep the forces hostile to them at bay? Were the leaders of Polish Jewry ever other than divided about their ultimate purposes and about the tactics they thought it expedient to pursue in furthering them? Was there ever any workable agreement on ways and means of confronting the Polish government and the Polish nationalist and anti-Semitic parliamentary and extra-parliamentary forces? Was there not a still deeper division on the more abstract, but most passionate issue of all because it cut to the very heart of the matter of the Jewish condition: whether a tolerable future for the Jews of Poland was conceivable in any circumstances at all? And all this being the case, what prospect of change in general and of a gathering of all available forces for a fresh and united stand could there be?

But then the reality in Poland, as everywhere else—that with which all in Jewry, modernists and traditionalists alike, had to cope—was the fact that the public and collective life of the Jews was in all cases grounded immutably on an inescapable asymmetry. The monopoly of real and

effective power lay invariably in non-Jewish hands. All battles into which the Jews chose to venture were therefore necessarily unequal. There might be—indeed, there often were—circumstances in which they could hope for an accommodation of one unsatisfactory and impermanent kind or another. Had it been entirely otherwise they would never have survived so long either in Christian or in modern Europe. The style and posture which Jews thought it expedient to adopt in any particular case as they worked their way towards the necessary accommodation could vary greatly. The deep, invariable, often unspoken basis of every accommodation remained none the less the irrefutable prospect that, irrespective of the degree and nature of such punishment as the Jews might succeed in inflicting on their enemies, they themselves would go under if the conflict were pursued to its natural end. For the orthodox this was no less than an obvious truth—a banality. To the Zionist mind this was consistent with their darker view that, ultimately, there was no future of any kind, certainly no decent and honourable future, for the Jews in their Exile. The Polish Bundists, for their part, resisted such pessimism. On the eve of the Second World War, refreshed by their electoral successes, they remained unchanged in their fundamental optimism—as central to their outlook as the tired pragmatism of the orthodox and the over-confident realism of the Zionists were central to theirs. 'The work of Jewish socialists and the decades-long fight waged by the Bund have shown that the Jewish masses have linked their destiny to that of the labouring masses of the entire country,' the Bundist organ *Der Veker* proclaimed in June 1939 with satisfaction. And '. . . the facts show ever more clearly that it is indeed the constant concern of the Jewish working class to form an integral part of the great popular army fighting for liberty and equality'.[58]

Moshe Kleinbaum (later Sneh), who succeeded to the leading position among the Zionists of Poland upon Gruenbaum's departure for Palestine in 1932, thought otherwise. There was no prospect of stability in the relations between Poles and Jews in the present intolerable state of affairs, he wrote in February 1939, because, not least, it was shot through with hypocrisy and insincerity.

From a formal point of view the Jews were citizens enjoying equal rights; in reality they are treated as a 'foreign and harmful element'. It is in the nature of life to destroy all things that are untrue, founded on fiction and on an internal lie. There will therefore have to come a radical change in the attitude of the Polish government to the Jews: for good or for ill, as true citizens or as 'pernicious aliens'. One way or the other![59]

---

[58]   Cited in Minczeles, *Histoire générale*, 385.
[59]   Moshe Sneh (Kleinbaum), 'Ḥoser omeẓ ba-ẓad ha-yehudi', 9 Feb. 1939, in Sneh, *Ketavim: 1928–1939*, i (Tel Aviv, 1995), 274–5.

V

It is conceivable none the less, *pace* Kleinbaum, that were it not for developments beyond Poland's frontiers and well beyond the Polish Republic's control or influence, the condition of the Jews of Poland would have remained fundamentally unchanged. Like that of Jewry under the Russian old regime it would have continued to be a great festering sore of human misery and frustration, isolated from, and only very marginally protected by the more fortunate segments of Jewry, unamenable to change for good or for ill, let alone to cure. The questions of public policy that had dogged the Jews of Europe for the better part of a century would have remained unanswered: that of the terms on which Jews might reasonably expect to live out their lives if and when they embarked on the road to modernity, that of what modernity might actually consist in not merely in their eyes but in the eyes of their rulers and neighbours, and, most fundamentally of all, that of how and to what precise ends they themselves would be free to determine their own private and collective destinies. But the closing of the trap around them in one European country and against them overseas rendered these and other related questions acute beyond anything that Crémieux, Pinsker, Herzl, Nordau, Jacob Schiff, Sylvain Lévi, Israel Zangwill, Lucien Wolf, or any of the many others who had once sought to speak for and to the Jews of Europe might have imagined: acute and, at the same time, nugatory. The internal debate on the ends to which the Jewish people should strive did not abate, but it bore ever less practical significance. As anti-Semitism in its extreme, namely 'racial' form, came to be installed as a fixed and open element of the political, administrative, and, in ever more numerous cases, the constitutional landscape of Europe, and as physical and psychological pressures besetting Jews of all kinds and conditions increased and each one of the gates to *extra*-European lands of refuge were shut against them in succession, ever more tightly, debate ran into the sand. Hopeful interpretations and rationalizations of the Jewish predicament evaporated. Disabused, tougher-minded views of the Jewish condition in its entirety moved to the fore. And it was the desperate idea that there was nothing at all to be done that gained purchase most rapidly. What there was no denying was that three interlocking, mutually reinforcing factors were pushing the Jews of Europe to the wall everywhere.

The first of these was the circumstance that processes analogous and parallel to those that were shunting the Jews of Poland into a dead end were in evidence virtually everywhere else in eastern and central Europe and had begun to percolate, at all events as ideas to be entertained, into the western states of the continent as well. In the Baltic states discriminatory barriers to the admission of Jews to the civil service and the univer-

sities were in the process of refortification. In Latvia, in particular, an entire campaign to reduce the role of Jews in the economy had been embarked upon following a change of government in 1934. In Romania still more punishing anti-Jewish measures were being promulgated and implemented with uncharacteristic zeal. Some had been given formal legislative form; some, in the Polish manner, were the autonomous resolutions of the professional associations concerned. It was decreed that the number of Jews allowed to work in certain industrial or commercial enterprises be restricted. It was made very much more difficult, and in some parts of the country impossible, for a Jew to be admitted to the Romanian bar. Jewish-owned newspapers were suppressed. Non-Jewish-owned newspapers were forbidden to employ Jewish journalists. Jewish households were forbidden to employ non-Jewish women under the age of 40. And, upon the old issue of the right of Jewish inhabitants of the state to Romanian citizenship being resurrected, the civic rights and citizenship of about a third of the community's members were arbitrarily cancelled.

Yet it was in Hungary that the change in the condition of the Jews, considering the distance they had already travelled towards assimilation and the degree to which the major forces in the country had previously eased their way, was most drastic. The change of direction was announced soon after the war: first by the so-called White Terror that followed the fall of the Communist regime in August 1919 being directed with special ferocity against Jews of all political persuasions or none at all; and then confirmed in the year following by the passing of a *numerus clausus* law that heavily restricted the entry of Jewish students into the country's universities to the 6 per cent held to be the Jewish proportion of the population at the time. Incessant protests and pressure abroad, notably at the League of Nations, induced István Bethlen's government, despite furious opposition, to alter its terms somewhat early in 1927, eliminating the racial definition of Jews and so making it marginally less offensive. In practical terms little was altered, however. The access of Jews to academic education continued to be severely limited and, ominously, the principle of exclusion was shown to have commanded the enthusiastic support of the greater part of the Hungarian student body and of the professoriat as well. Other attempts to diminish the country's Jews and undo their previously well-established moral and formal status as Magyars *à part entière* followed, the most considerable of which was an omnibus Law for the More Efficient Protection of the Social and Economic Balance passed in June 1938. Industry and commerce, financial institutions, the medical, legal, engineering, and entertainment professions, and journalism all came under *numerus clausus* rules. Henceforth, no more than 20 per cent of the work-force in any given enterprise was to be of Jewish origin. In the following year, on 4 May 1939, an additional, still more drastic Law

to Restrict Jewish Participation in Public and Economic Life extending
and amplifying the terms of the previous law was passed. 'Jews' were now
very carefully defined, limited exemptions from the category were
meticulously provided for, and a host of penal provisions fell upon those
unlucky enough to fall into the former category. Quotas were further
reduced (12 per cent in commerce and industry, 6 per cent in the professions, 6 per cent of the student body), professions and occupations from
which Jews were to be barred totally were listed, the right to elect and to
be elected to public office restricted, admission to civil and military office
ended.

The second factor steadily, but rapidly pushing the Jews to the wall virtually everywhere, but especially in central and eastern Europe, was the
virtual closing down of the safety valve of free migration that had done
so much in the past to release the Jews of eastern Europe from what
would otherwise have been totally intolerable pressures. Such mass
escape ceased to be possible. This was not, it may be noted, because at this
point in their history either their natural inertia or the Jews' traditional
leaders' ingrained reluctance to see them leave held them back—although
these continued to be quite potent factors, notably among the orthodox.
It was increasingly because the western European states and, more
especially, those extra-European countries to which Jews had migrated in
great numbers before the First World War were now determined to bring
the admission of Jewish immigrants to an end—in some cases (Canada,
for example) absolutely so, in others (the United States notably) as nearly
as might be politically and technically possible.[60]

Thirdly, in 1933, in the mightiest of all European states, absolute but at
the same time popular power was assumed by a political movement that
adopted the Question of the Jews and the need to settle it urgently and
for all time as a quintessential element of its domestic and international
political programme. The change of regime in Germany was, of course,
to have the severest consequences of all. But it needs to be recalled that
here lay not only the most tragic of developments, but much the oddest
and most paradoxical of those to which the matter of the Jews gave rise
after the First World War. That the Jews did constitute a genuine socio-
political problem in Poland seen as a nation-state was beyond question. It
was never as severe as the extreme nationalists of Poland claimed. Nor
would it have been unamenable to treatment and melioration had it been
confronted on either side, but especially on that of the Poles, with more
tolerance and good will than, on the evidence, they were capable of mustering. But in Germany the Jewish Question in any of the forms anyone
in that country ascribed to it, certainly in the terms the National Socialists systematically propagated, was (except for the Jews themselves) a

---

[60] On this central issue of migration as it would develop, see Chapter 10.

minor, not to say artificial and invented matter. And however it might be conceived and whatever importance might be attached to it, the unassailable fact was that the Jewish presence in the country was, as we have seen, in a state of rapid and continuous decline. There were, moreover, two additional differences between Poland and Germany that bore directly on the Jewish Question, at all events in real terms. One had to do with Poland and Germany having different forms of government. They were comparable neither constitutionally nor in respect of the nature and efficacy of the instruments of government available to either state's political masters. Nor were they comparable in respect of the degree to which the two populations were inclined to lend an obedient ear to those who sought to rule them. Polish government before and after Pilsudski's primacy, but even under Pilsudski himself, was always inherently insecure—vastly more so than the German government after 1933. And where Germany had been rapidly and very successfully turned into a totalitarian state, Poland retained its imperfect, yet by no means inauthentic, parliamentary system to the end. The treatment successive Polish governments accorded the Jewish population was, all in all, mendacious, unjust, and in strict terms of expediency unwise. But part of the explanation of the somewhat hysterical and brutal chauvinism that was so much a part of the Polish politico-socio-religious scene where the Jews were concerned was that they did form a distinct, far from negligible, and to some extent ungovernable political factor.

But nothing of *this* kind obtained in Germany. Where Polish Jewry was remarkable for its national cohesion and self-assertiveness, German Jewry had long been marked by social disintegration and self-abnegation. In proven willing service and loyalty to the state, in socio-economic 'usefulness' in the old Enlightenment sense of the term, in demonstrated *in*capacity and lack of will to act together for any political, economic, or cultural purpose of their own other than ever deeper identification with, and enthusiastic accommodation to, German society and the German state, the Jews of Germany, with the very rarest of exceptions, could under no circumstances be faulted. They were a source of no conceivable disturbance, let alone danger, to a German regime of any political complexion. And it was no less than central to the qualitative (as well, of course, to the quantitative) differences between the two communities that there was in Germany nothing remotely comparable to Polish-Jewish political activity: no Jewish parties, no Jewish representation in the Reichstag or in any of the *Landtage* (or provincial parliaments), no participation in local or national politics *as such*, namely as Jews and in the Jewish interest however Jewry or its interests might be conceived.

A second difference between Poland and Germany was the all-important ethnic make-up of the state in each case. Poland, as we have seen, was in every sense except the formal one a multinational state and for that very reason inherently brittle and problematic. Post-Versailles Germany was—like post-Trianon Hungary (leaving the special case of the Jews in either state aside)—as nearly perfect a Wilsonian nation-state as could be asked for. Polish anti-Semitism, inhumane, ill-considered, and morally flawed though it might be, was not, given the struggle of the Poles to establish themselves in a viable state of their own, without a small objective core. German anti-Semitism, in contrast, was depraved. In Poland the compulsive, mindless hatred of the Jews that filled so many minds among the members of the country's political class owed much to the ancient but still lively teachings of the Church. In Germany the models drawn upon were pseudo-scientific in content and very deliberately hysterical in form. It is true, and it was a matter of great moment, that the long-term tendency was for the dominant forms of Judaeophobia in both countries to resemble each other: Polish National Democrats, as has been noted, partook increasingly of the teachings and examples of German National Socialists. As a practical issue of government, social control, and social engineering the Jewish Question ended by being perceived in both countries, at all events by those who held power, in terms that for all *practical* purposes were identical. The differences in each country between the arguments advanced for the extrusion of Jewish inhabitants and the intensity with which these arguments were insisted upon were never wholly negligible. But the actual goals for which each state were striving by the late 1930s and up to the outbreak of the Second World War were substantially one and the same. What had not changed was the fact that whereas in Poland the quality and sheer size of the Jewish community encouraged its leaders to believe that they were not devoid of political resources of their own with which to fight their corner, in Germany no such belief was ever seriously entertained by the Jews nor ever seriously ascribed to them by their National Socialist masters. Yet it was Germany, not Poland, let alone Hungary or Romania, that raised the Question of the Jews to boiling point throughout Europe, confronted the Jewish people in its entirety with dilemmas for which there were neither precedents nor, as it seemed, solutions, and, after some hesitation, set itself with historically unprecedented deliberation to solve the Question once and for all.

VI

There are four aspects of the revolution of 1933 that at one and the same time drove the German state in this direction *and* facilitated the actual execution of such a policy. One was the fact that the Third Reich was a polity in which features of a quite genuinely popular, plebiscitary demo-cracy were closely combined with those of an 'oriental despotism' in the sense in which Karl Wittfogel employed the term, namely one of total power that 'tolerates no relevant forces besides itself'.[61] No less than three-quarters of the electorate voted for the National Socialist Party and its parliamentary allies in the last free elections to be held in Germany before the war (5 March 1933). Positive and, in very many quarters, distinctly enthusiastic support for the regime rose steadily thereafter and was to last at least until the tide of the great European war that the new Reich had inflicted on its own citizens as well as on its neighbours changed against it. It is indisputable that with rare exceptions Germans low *and* high acquiesced in their reduction to the status of minions, not to say slaves of the Leader and his Law; and that they did so rapidly, with little complaint, and with striking and very widespread social consequences for their society all round. This too corresponded closely to Wittfogel's model of an oriental despotism.[62] The acceptance of National Socialist norms not merely as so many facts of life with which all had necessarily to cope, but as a total, binding, and broadly legitimate moral system cannot be wholly disentangled, needless to say, from the rigour with which the population was policed—or at any rate believed itself to be. It had much to do too with the skill with which the propagandists of National Socialism first identified the inner nerves of German society and then proceeded to pluck them—a skill especially evident in the application, as an implacable rule of government, of the precept that all who were not members of the German nation were *ipso facto* outside its Law altogether. Whence the second aspect of the German revolution that is especially relevant to the present topic.

Germany under the short reign of the National Socialists stands to this day as the supreme example of the principle of nationality being applied to all aspects of life without inhibition or reservation whatsoever—ergo *ad absurdum* and with very terrible consequences for all. It was, of course, as we have seen, in the very nature of the principle of national self-determination that it should be as easily applicable to the destruction of a Wilsonian Europe as to its construction. And, indeed, the deliberately punitive terms of peace dictated to Germany at the Paris Peace Conference did face German governments of all political complexions with a temptation to take over the anti-*status quo* pack of states and lead a general, multinational effort to reduce the Versailles system to ruins. But, and this is the third aspect of the rise of the National Socialists to power in Germany that is especially relevant to the present topic, what counted for

---

[61] Karl A. Wittfogel, *Oriental Despotism: A Comparative Study of Total Power* (New Haven, 1957), 137.

[62] 'The fact that the ruler in peace or war may insist on an irrational policy, even when it endangers the very existence of the state, underlines the extent to which power is concentrated in his person. The fact that his minor decisions may profoundly affect the prestige, income, and security of his officials underlines the unique political sensitiveness of the ruling class under the conditions of total power' (Wittfogel, *Oriental Despotism*, 345).

most was the particular spin the National Socialist Party put on the concept of the *nation* itself.

A cardinal element of Nazi doctrine on the principle of nationality was that it was not to be reduced to anything so simple as, say, detectable common ethnic, historical, and cultural origins. It was most certainly not to be identified with citizenship. It had to do with *race*. The National Socialists supposed, and they were very far from being alone in their views on these matters, that humanity was to be seen as a biological species not only in the obvious scientific, but morally neutral sense, but for virtually all social and political purposes as well. Moreover, the decisive datum was that it was a species subdivided into distinct 'races' and that each race, by virtue of its primordial biological and genetic composition, was of certain predetermined and immutable qualities. It followed, they argued, that the principal determinants of men's inner moral nature, no less than of their actual conduct, were inborn, carried down relentlessly from generation to generation; and that since the determinants varied from 'race' to 'race' the salient result was that, taken together, the races formed a hierarchy. The Germans, conveniently, occupied a place at the very top of the hierarchy. The Jews, inconveniently for *them*, but inconveniently too for all those nations into whose bodies politic Jews had been allowed to infiltrate, were at the bottom of the heap. The Jews' place in the hierarchy was therefore not simply beneath that of the Germans and the other 'Aryans'. It was below that of the Slavs, the blacks, and the many other, undoubtedly inferior peoples who, as helots, were predestined to serve the master race. For, unlike most other peoples, the Jews were *sub*human: a hugely and disastrously impaired lot, deeply inadequate in every physical and moral respect, totally beyond improvement and cure.

None of these ideas was original. In many quarters throughout what we have since come to call the western world they were no less than coin of the realm. When T. S. Eliot, neither a German nor a National Socialist of any kind at all, but an eminent poet with an incomparable gift for capturing much that was central to the spirit of these times, wrote that 'The rats are underneath the piles. | The jew is underneath the lot' in 1920,[63] he was expressing in two brief lines what would be the whole of the Nazi charge against the Jews. The National Socialists' contribution to the genre was original and inventive only in the sense that they systematized and popularized such pseudo-Darwinian rubbish on a scale that soared above anything others had attempted and fashioned it into a legitimizing charter under the terms of which they provided an especial punch to their long, but in the end successful, campaign to mobilize

---

[63] 'Burbank with a Baedeker: Bleistein with a Cigar.' For an acute discussion of Eliot's view of the Jewish people see Bryan Cheyette, *Constructions of 'the Jew' in English Literature and Society* (Cambridge, 1995), 248–58 and *passim*.

native German opinion behind them. They made all that could possibly be made of the German–Jew dichotomy; and, once in power, raised it not only to a principle of government, but one of life itself—and then, more purposefully still, of death. The Germans, so National Socialist teaching ran, were innately superior to all other races morally and physically. They were born, therefore, to rule. The Jews, in the pseudo-biological and ecological terminology their propagandists employed to powerful effect among their own people, were vermin. *They* were destined to be exterminated. And, lest these destroyers of culture (*Kulturzerstörer*) corrupt the proper structure of mankind beyond repair, it was the duty of the Germans to see to it that this be done. Adolf Hitler's National Socialist Party made no secret of the essentials of its outlook while it was working its way to popularity and power. And it was crucial to its quality that subsequent to 30 January 1933, the day on which Hitler was appointed head of government and office and power were achieved, no part of this ideological baggage was abandoned. On the contrary, the themes of racial anti-Semitism were propagated with mounting zeal and skill, and to ever greater effect: thus within Germany itself, to be sure, but within the entire German ethno-cultural sphere (or *Kulturbereich*) as well.

Where the National Socialists were less successful was in their parallel effort to tear away the last of the several veils of ambivalence and hypocrisy in which the matter of the Jews had come to be enveloped in the rest of Europe since the collapse of the Enlightenment. This may have had something to do with the fact that the role allotted the non-Germanic nations did not always recommend itself to *them*. It is likely that the German claim to superiority in all things was too evidently self-serving and that the ideological meat of the matter was too obviously absurd for very great numbers outside Germany to swallow whole. But the failure was not total. The vehemence with which racialism in its National Socialist form was propagated and the systematic quality of their effort to impose it worldwide sufficed, in practice, to inhibit many of those who might have spoken with some scientific, if not more civilized validity from coping adequately with the onslaught. Well-informed and intellectually sophisticated non-Germans who dealt with the Nazis professionally and knew what they were about—the statesmen, the diplomats, the journalists who might have been expected to dismiss such rubbish out of hand—tended for many years to avoid open and outright criticism of the Nazi view. In some cases this was out of a secret, partial, even embarrassed sympathy for its general thrust—even if not for all the ways in which Hitler and his party hierarchs went about their business. In other cases the reluctance to contest German racialism arose out of fear of quarrelling with an evidently predatory and dangerous regime and the belief that it was wiser to try to calm and, if possible, befriend it, and, generally, in the vogue language of the time, to *appease* rather than fight it. But it also had a good deal to do with the dual nature of the way in which the new masters of Germany actually pursued their racial policy (at any rate until the autumn of 1938): this being the fourth aspect of the revolution that deserves attention here—not least because it helped cause the Jews of Germany, those most immediately concerned, to mistake both the nature of the regime and its likely intentions towards them.

National Socialist rule was, from the start, one of thugs. Open brutality, concentration camps, the systematic employment of the street as the central national political arena, and murder of both the vulgar and the judicial kind—all these were intrinsic to the party's method of government and to its inner and fundamental nature. Therein, indeed, lay the primary sources of its power both to cow its subjects and to rally them to its ranks as loyal, uniformed servants and supporters. Therein too lay a salient expression of its revolutionary character. But the masters of the New Reich contrived at the same time to present their government as one of law. Short-term tactical necessity dictated this to them in the beginning to some extent. So too did the anxiety common to all revolutionary regimes to make the most of whatever forms of legitimization were to hand. One result was that despite continual murmurs and worse in its own party ranks, notably in the SA—the 'Storm Troopers' who had fought for Hitler and his hierarchs in the street from the beginning—the great socio-economic revolution they had promised was never allowed to materialize. On the contrary, as many as possible of the central institutions of the German state, tamed and converted to be sure to National Socialist use, were kept in being. At least until the six-year European war began in earnest, the face the German government presented to the world, but no less significantly to its own subjects as well, was therefore a double one. The thugs, the torturers, the prisons, the shrieking, threatening, hate-filled party leaders and propagandists reflected one face. The several orderly, well-groomed, well-spoken, long-established, and therefore thoroughly familiar corps of civil servants, diplomats, army officers, university professors, judges, law officers, non-political police, and the like—all winnowed, somewhat, but otherwise much as they had been before, namely pillars of the German *Rechtsstaat* and the established constitutional order—reflected, as they had always reflected, the other. In very many respects, therefore, the Third Reich was continuous in function, style, and to a great extent in personnel as well, with the Second Reich and the Weimar Republic. And the temptation to believe both that the latter represented the true Germany and that the true Germany would end by dissolving and displacing the former was immense. Nor could it be said, on the basis of what was known at the time, that the idea was entirely unfounded or absurd. At all events, great numbers within and outside Germany set their hearts on it. Some, at home and abroad, surrendered to it entirely. Particularly inclined to find the thesis irresistible were the Jews of Germany themselves. In sum, the National Socialists endowed themselves and the very many millions who followed them with sources of immense cohesive strength, self-satisfaction, and self-confidence—as well as, by reason of its sheer vulgarity, with a social and political vision of extraordinary power. The result, fatally and unfailingly, was rule of unspeakable and frightening brutality with which no Jewish community in western or central Europe was equipped to cope, least of all that of Germany itself.

VII

Different in almost every other conceivable way from the Jews of Poland, the Jews of Germany had at least in common with them that they too had finally been accorded full and formal emancipation in 1919, immediately after the war. Under the terms of the new, republican, 'Weimar' constitution all citizens of the Reich were granted equal civil and political rights. Admission to official posts was declared 'independent of religious creed'. Religious practice and membership of a religious body were classed as private matters with which the authorities were neither to concern themselves nor to inquire into except for such neutral, limited, and technical purposes as the collection of statistics and then only when specifically and legally mandated to do so. There was to be no established State Church at all.[64] And, central to the approach adopted in these and cognate matters, the nation was conceived of as being composed of *citizens* rather than of Germans defined in strictly ethnic (or *völkisch*) terms. Opposition to these principles, particularly to the German nation being defined in terms analogous to those in which the French nation had been proclaimed in 1789, was strong and continuing, however. The infant National Socialist German Workers' Party had been quick to declare in its original, never-to-be-altered 1920 programme, that 'only fellow countrymen [*Volksgenossen*] can be citizens'; that 'only persons of German blood can be *Volksgenossen*'; that 'no Jew, therefore, can be a countryman'; and that, finally, for these reasons, no Jew can be a citizen. As non-citizens they would therefore be subject to special legislation. Further immigration of non-Germans would be stopped entirely. And non-Germans who had entered the country after August 1914 were to be expelled 'without delay'.[65] The Nazis' eventual rivals for the right-wing vote, the conservative, socially more respectable Deutschnationale Volkspartei, took the same line:

[64] Articles 135–7 of the Constitution of 11 Aug. 1919.
[65] Programm der Nationalsozialistische Deutsche Arbeiterpartei (NSDAP), Articles 4, 5, and 8.

The Party combats every disintegrating, un–German spirit whether originating in Jewish or other circles. It takes a firm stand against the predominance of Jewry in government and public life which has been ever more fatefully present since the revolution. It urges that the influx of people of foreign origin across our frontiers be stopped.[66]

What is important is that these were not eccentric or unpopular voices. The evidence that the stipulations of the Weimar constitution in respect of equality of treatment for *all* German citizens in *all* spheres were unacceptable to great and important segments of the population is abundant. It was characteristic of the German *pays réel* under Weimar that while the old rules barring the admission of professing Jews into the middle and higher ranks of public administration almost entirely at both Reich and the *Land* levels were relaxed somewhat they were never in any true sense overcome. The difference was that the process by which the barriers to the entry of Jews into bodies from which they had previously been generally excluded tended to be imposed informally and *ad hoc* rather than by more or less open rule. A few Jews did find their way into the foreign service, a few more into other branches of the senior ranks of the civil service and, in larger numbers than before the war, into the judiciary and the professoriat. But the University of Munich, in a famous and characteristic instance, remained unmoved when one of its most distinguished scientists, Richard Willstätter, Nobel prizeman in chemistry, resigned his chair in 1925 upon the university's refusal to appoint the best candidate to a chair in crystallography because he, like Willstätter himself, was a Jew.[67] And it was the case that on the eve of the Nazi take-over there were still only two Jewish professors in all Bavarian universities taken together: one whose academic career had begun under the monarchy, the other being an obvious borderline case in that he was both a convert to Christianity and an authority on the Bavarian constitution. At the very top of the administrative machine under the Weimar constitution only two non-baptized Jews were ever to serve: Walther Rathenau as foreign minister, until his assassination by right-wingers four months after taking office in 1922; Rudolf Hilferding, a Social Democrat, as Reich minister of finance.[68]

The sum of it was that the National Socialists' talent for determining what would and what would not be acceptable to the general public in

---

[66] June 1920. Cited in Ernest Hamburger, 'One Hundred Years of Emancipation', *LBIYB* 14 (London, 1969), 39.

[67] Willstätter, despite many invitations to take up academic posts abroad, chose to remain in Germany after 1933 and—an exceedingly rare case—was left in peace by the German police and allowed to die in his bed. See John V. H. Dippel, *Bound Upon a Wheel of Fire* (New York, 1996), 257–8.

[68] Hilferding fled Germany in 1933, but he too would be disposed of when the French police handed him over to the Germans in 1941.

Germany was never more brilliantly displayed than in their making their own first formal, legal step against the country's Jews the forced retirement of 'non-Aryans' from the civil service under a Law for the Restoration of the Professional Civil Service. Equally inspired by their firm, if instinctive grasp of what was and was not acceptable to the public was the Janus-like way in which they went about the promulgation of this and all the other measures taken to disenfranchise, dispossess, segregate, and generally humble and diminish Germany's Jews, with the aim above all, of encouraging them to leave the country. Bullying, street-fighting, and passionately violent propaganda were made to merge in every instance, sometimes quite subtly, with the regular *modus operandi* of the established, normally apolitical bureaucratic practices of the Reich as everyone, Jews among all others, had always known it. The result was that on the one hand the country's Jews were objects of a continual, deliberately hysterical barrage of state- and party-sponsored vilification designed to frighten them while the general public had dinned into it an undying image of Jewry as a deeply vicious, sexually predatory, politically treasonable social category, at once hydra-headed and monolithic, capitalist and Bolshevik, bloodthirsty and cowardly—in sum, no more and no less than dedicated enemies of the human race in its entirety and of the 'Aryans' in particular.

On the other hand, the Jews of Germany were the subject of an ever more comprehensive structure of meticulously drafted laws, decrees, and regulations setting out the legal framework within which, presumably, they were to live out their lives while they remained in the country. Each such law, decree, or regulation tore a piece out of the always somewhat shaky structure of their emancipation. But it was characteristic of the process that each such measure was accompanied wherever appropriate by precise ancillary provisions laying down, for example, to whom the decree was to be immediately applicable, who, on the contrary, would be exempt from its application on the ground, say, of admission to the relevant status or position prior to 1914 or in recognition of military service at the front in the course of the war, who was entitled to a pension upon dismissal and on what terms, and who was not. The Law for the Restoration of the Professional Civil Service, promulgated on 7 April 1933 within no more than a fortnight of the Enabling Act by which the now tamed Reichstag had passed all effective power to Hitler and his cabinet, was followed in rapid succession by decrees laying down what exactly was to be understood by the term 'non-Aryan' and specifying the fields and functions from which 'non-Aryans' were to be excluded: the Reichsbank, the railway service, the public medical service, the teaching profession, the bar, the peasantry, and so on. A Law against the Overcrowding of German Schools and Universities promulgated on 25 April 1933 set a *numerus clausus* for all educational institutions, private as well as public, with 'non-Aryan' students to be admitted at the rate of 1.5 per cent of the student body. German citizenship acquired by naturalization between the collapse of the Second Reich and the installation of the Third was revoked on 14 July 1933. In September and November 1935 the entire process of categorization, separation, and exclusion and the placing of the Jews of Germany and beyond outside the normal laws of the country was capped by the so-called Nuremberg Laws.

Up to this point there had been a fairly strong tendency among German Jews—other than among those who had identified themselves and were identifiable by others as open political enemies of the regime or who had had their professional lives or the economic basis for their existence totally destroyed—to wait and see, and to hope for a change and for the best. Professionally and economically, socially and psychologically, life had become more difficult for everyone and fairly substantial numbers had in fact decided upon emigration while the going was good. But there had been no massive flight. It did not seem to very many that all doors had been—or were about to be—closed before them. The belief that it might still be possible to reorder their lives in such a way as to earn a ticket of re-entry into German society when, in the fullness of time, the decision to expel them had been rescinded was strong; and the disparate modes in which the state treated them suggested that it itself approached the matter of the Jews in a divided mind. How else was Hans Frank, Reich Commissioner for the Co-ordination of Justice in the States and for the Renewal of Jurisprudence (and future governor-general of occupied Poland) to be understood when he set out to calm Jewish fears early in October 1933 by assuring them that it was

The firm decision of the Reich authorities . . . that there should be a certain pause now in the continued disputation with the Jews. The Reich authorities further desire to state—in particular as far as the world [abroad] is concerned, that Jews living in Germany within the framework of German law may carry out their occupations without hindrance . . . [and that] a certain agreement has now been achieved in the area of disputation with the Jews . . . that the security and life of the Jews is in no danger.[69]

And were there not valid distinctions to be drawn between local and central initiatives, for example, and between short- and long-term purposes? Were there not continual hints that the new masters of Germany themselves were less than sure of what they were about? Were they perhaps having second thoughts? Were their conservative allies not engaged all the while in smoothing the savages' furs? And was the pause that ensued once the burst of violence that had accompanied the *Machtergreifung*, the

---

[69] *Jüdische Rundschau*, 4 Oct. 1933. Cited in Y. Arad, *et al.* (eds.), *Documents on the Holocaust* (Jerusalem, 1987), 44.

seizure of power, was spent really no more than tactical? Visiting Germany shortly after, Arthur Ruppin, now a member of the Executive of the Jewish Agency for Palestine, but a native of Germany and well established too as one of the foremost sociologists and demographers of contemporary Jewry, observed, that

The two weeks in Germany passed without disturbance—for all that I expected all kinds of unpleasantnesses. If I had not known from the newspapers and from private conversations to what extent the economic and political condition of the Jews had worsened as a consequence of the government's penal decrees—I should not have sensed it from what was to be seen in the street, not in Berlin at all events. Customers (Christians among them) still frequent Jewish businesses, cafés on the Kurfürstendamm are still full of Jews, in trains and restaurants Jews are served as before. It is only when you talk to doctors and lawyers, or with village shopkeepers, that the extent of the change becomes clear.[70]

In sum, it was not unreasonable or difficult to believe, certainly while President Hindenburg was alive and Hitler and his companions were still inclined to move with some caution, that a *modus vivendi* of some kind could be worked out. Alfred Wiener, speaking for the most respectable and well established of supra-communal Jewish organizations, the Centralverein deutscher Staatsbürger jüdischen Glaubens, but almost certainly for the greater part of German Jewry at the time, had responded to the Nazi take-over and to the promulgation of the first measures extruding Jews from public office and from the professions by insisting that his people's roots in their German homeland remained firm and lasting. That the new laws classed them as non-Germans devoid of equal rights was undeniable and very sad. However, in their own hearts and minds they, for their part, remained Germans, with full rights, as before. They refused to be categorized as a separate, national minority. And although the result was that they now found themselves 'suspended between heaven and earth,' it remained their firm intention 'to fight with courage and strength to return to earth' both in fact and in the eyes of the state.[71] When a new military conscription law was promulgated in March 1935 the leaders of the newly formed representative body of German Jewry, the Reichsvertretung der deutschen Juden protested the exclusion of the community's sons from the Wehrmacht and called on the government to remember the 12,000 German Jews who had given their lives for their country in the Great War. So, as might have been expected, did the Jewish war veterans association, the Reichsbund jüdischer Frontsoldaten (RjF) which had become a popular substitute home for Jews who had

---

[70] Diary entry, 16 Aug. 1933, Arthur Ruppin, *Pirkei Ḥayyai: be-vinyan ha-areẓ veha'am*, iii (Tel Aviv, 1968), 222.

[71] *CV-Zeitung*, 1 June 1933. Cited in Arad, *et al.* (eds.), *Documents on the Holocaust*, 50–1.

now been entirely banned from membership in German patriotic associations. The RjF was especially incensed by hints that special Jewish units
might be formed. Equal admission to all branches of the armed forces on
the basis of equal citizenship was their demand.

The sharpest invocation of Jewish loyalty to Germany was sounded by
the eccentric, hyper-patriotic, and in quantitative terms wildly unrepresentative Deutsche Vortrupp (German Vanguard). Comprising a handful
of university students led by Hans Joachim Schoeps, founded at the end
of February 1933, within a month, therefore, of the appointment of
Hitler as Chancellor, the Vortrupp's great point was its reaffirmation of
boundless devotion to the state. In somewhat milder form almost all Jewish movements and institutions had done so. But Schoeps and his fellows
differed from most other Jewish tendencies in their general social outlook. The common run of German Jews was liberal or moderately left-
wing. The Vortrupp people thought and spoke insistently in standard
right-wing terms on standard right-wing topics: the 'regeneration' of
German society, for example. They argued that the anti-Semitism of the
nationalist right could be no more than peripheral to its main purposes,
holding that what lay at the heart of National Socialism was indeed the
regeneration of German society, not racialism and race hatred, and that
therefore they were on common ground after all. The Jews, as a group,
needed to be seen as in some sense analogous to the Prussians, Hessians,
Bavarians, and other components of the German nation. Judaism, they
argued, had much in common with Prussianism: moral severity, discipline, and the authoritarian spirit. They did not deny that there was
tension between Jews and non-Jews, but they blamed the *Ostjuden* for it.
Article one of their statement of principles laid down, that 'The
Deutsche Vortrupp's mission is the concentration [*Zusammenfassung*] of
young German Jews in an integrated organization in the interests of fostering national sentiment on an associative [*bündischer*] basis and a deepening of Jewish religious life.'[72]

When Schoeps tried to meet Hitler he was rebuffed. He was rebuffed
again when he tried to meet Hitler's ministers. In his desire to enter into
some sort of dialogue with the new government, however, he was not
alone among those who wished to speak for German Jewry. Nor was he
alone in his declarations of support for German foreign policy. 'At this
historic moment in which the German Reich has reinstituted its unchal-
lenged sovereignty over military service,' the Vortrupp was quick to proclaim when on 16 March 1935 the German government repudiated the
military clauses of the Treaty of Versailles, 'we young German Jews feel
moved to express our satisfaction with this step. Just as our fathers of

[72] Carl J. Rheins, 'Deutscher Vortrupp, Gefolgschaft deutscher Juden 1933–35',
LBIYB 26 (London, 1981), 215 n. 48.

1914–1918 fulfilled their self-evident duty to the Fatherland, so we declare ourselves prepared for military service, true to our motto *Bereit für Deutschland*.'[73] What the members of the Vortrupp and the somewhat similar Verband nationaldeutscher Juden led by Max Naumann or, for that matter, the much more considerable RjF, or, indeed, any of the normally devoutly German-patriotic Jewish organizations and movements, found exceedingly difficult to come to terms with was that the regime had no interest at all in people dedicated to the *maintenance* of a Jewish presence in Germany on any terms whatsoever. In contrast, the government's attitude to the Zionists was mildly favourable (until shortly before the war) on the grounds that they after all favoured the *evacuation* of the Jews.[74]

The Vortrupp and the Verband nationaldeutscher Juden were ordered to dissolve in 1935. Naumann was arrested, Schoeps fled to Scandinavia. But it is important to see that they were not only articulating, however absurdly given the new circumstances, something that had run very deep for many decades in the German-Jewish ethos, but that their expectations were not entirely misconceived. The Army Command went so far as to demand the right, which they were initially granted under a special dispensation, to employ 'non-Aryans' in case of war. In July 1935 it was announced that while young men of 'mixed origins' would be posted to the reserve forces (rather than to immediate active service), non-Aryans were entitled to appeal to a committee that had discretionary authority to admit them to active military service after all. However, some months later this narrow, but for a brief moment not wholly imaginary path to the bliss of *de facto* reincorporation into the German nation, was shut off for good. In September and November of that year the promulgation of the so-called Nuremberg Laws brought all remaining hopes and expectations of this nature to an end.

The Nuremberg Laws comprised a Law for the Protection of German Blood and German Honour (*Gesetz zum Schutze des deutschen Blutes und der deutschen Ehre*) prohibiting marriage and extra-marital relations between Jews and non-Jews, the employment by Jews of female domestic help of 'German or cognate blood' under the age of 45, and the display by Jews of German national colours;[75] a Reich Citizenship Law (*Reichsbürgergesetz*) which finally and formally excluded Jews from German citizenship along with the residual political rights associated with it on the basis that 'members of the state' (*Staatsangehöriger*) must be

[73] 22 Mar. 1935. Cited ibid. 224; ibid. 207–29.

[74] See for example the wording of the instructions issued by the Bavarian political police in the course of 1935 appended to Kurt R. Grossmann, 'Zionists and non-Zionists under Nazi Rule', in R. Patai (ed.), *Herzl Year Book*, iv (New York, 1962), 340–4.

[75] Oddly, but consistent with the internal logic of National Socialist policy at this stage, Jews were explicitly permitted to display 'Jewish colours'.

of 'German or cognate blood'; a decree ordering the summary dismissal of the last remaining Jewish holders of public office (the residual pension rights, if any, of *Frontsoldaten* and certain other narrowly defined categories being maintained, however); and two additional, seemingly routine, but in fact highly significant sets of regulations that provided a formal basis for the general push towards absolute social separation of the Jews of Germany from the rest of the country's inhabitants.

One laid down a final official definition of a Jew. The unsatisfactory category of 'non-Aryan' was replaced by a rendering of the National Socialists' supreme principle of 'blood' into legally usable language for daily application by the police and the bureaucracy. Such nice but to the official mind perpetually baffling questions as how persons of *mixed* descent (*Mischlinge*) were to be classed and treated in practice could now be handled with confidence and efficiency. The other set had to do with the re-ghettoization of the Jews pending their total extrusion from the Fatherland. The establishment of Jewish communal institutions was authorized along with special schools into which Jewish children would be channelled from this point on and other decrees extending and intensifying the application of the letter and spirit of the Nuremberg Laws followed from time to time. The Jews' communal institutions (*Gemeinde*) were to be deprived of their long established legal status, their right to levy taxes on their members, and their exemption, like other religious institutions, from taxes themselves. All Jews, along with their 'non-Jewish consort(s)', were ordered to report and register their entire domestic and foreign property. Henceforth Jews were to be banned totally from the profession and practice of medicine (other than a limited number authorized to treat other Jews exclusively). The state school and university system was to be wholly and absolutely *Judenrein*. And, in rapid, successive stages, Jews were to be eliminated from the economic life of the country at virtually all its levels, in very many cases from their homes as well, and, ordered, for purposes of easy recognition by police and public, to bear given names chosen from an officially determined list, failing which they were to be re-registered as bearing the additional given names of Sarah or Israel.

After 1935, therefore, it was all but impossible for German Jews of any tendency not to see these and other pieces of legislation as amounting to acts of state designed finally and totally to reorder their lives. No longer could there be any doubt either in their minds or in those of the general public as to the direction in which the state was moving: a tidying-up of what until now had been a purposeful but insufficiently systematic process of exclusion and extrusion. The effect was devastating in all sectors of the Jewish public. But perhaps it was most acutely felt in the countryside where Jews had been a fixed segment of the population for centuries in very many cases and so quite solidly integrated, if in certain quarters unloved. It was in the countryside especially that their lives both as private individuals and as members of defined communities had already been most rapidly diminished, their personal security and social status most quickly lost, and the difficulty of keeping head above water economically experienced soonest.

National Socialist policy at both the local and the national level had in fact been directed at removing Jews first and foremost from rural Germany. This had a good deal to do with the romantic strain that was prominent in the party's myth-making: the German peasant being set on a pedestal as a primary symbol of national purity, somewhat in the manner that the Russian *muzhik* had been sentimentalized under the Romanovs and held to be in need of protection from his Jewish neighbour. But it had much to do too with the fact that the structure of rural society rendered a policy of extrusion much easier to implement than in the cities. The Jewish traders, cattle-dealers, shopkeepers, artisans, doctors in general practice, lawyers, pharmacists, schoolmasters, and the like who lived and worked in the villages and market towns of Germany were hugely vulnerable. The short-term protection that urban anonymity and urban numbers afforded their city cousins was denied them, while geography and habits of mind separated them somewhat from the greater, now more representative, in many ways more 'Jewish' segments of German Jewry in the major cities. Their own communities were small. Local community leadership tended to be relatively undistinguished. In the period leading up to the *Machtergreifung* anti-Jewish street brutality and what might be called short-range abuse had been commoner in the country than in the towns. From 1933 onwards harassment in any of the myriad forms it could take, not excluding such ostensibly trivial, but especially offensive acts of hostility as the banning of Jews from places of public entertainment, from swimming pools, from sports and hiking clubs, and so forth, were all common in the countryside well before they became mandatory throughout the country. Personal relations and contact being closer, they soured more quickly. Germans who were bold enough to defend or protect Jews were more easily ostracized by their own kind and, in what were thought to be extreme cases, subjected to exemplary punishment.

Isolated instances of murder and arson peppered the countryside continually in a way that was rare in the cities. By the same token, attempts by the Ministry of the Economy in the early years of Nazi rule to *reduce* attacks on Jewish businesses were more easily ignored: rural enterprises tended to be smaller than those located in the cities and to have no international connections to take into account and Jewish traders and professionals who inhabited rural Germany were therefore under a more urgent impulsion to leave their normal places of residence for larger centres in Germany itself or for abroad than their city analogues. To be

sure, local economic circumstances remained of some account, determining, for example, how rapidly, if at all, National Socialist agitators
succeeded, for example, in persuading the generally depressed farming
community to hold the Jewish cattle-dealers they dealt with responsible
for their plight. Some among the more prosperous cattle traders managed
to keep head above water for a while despite the pressures upon them by
paying higher than market prices to peasants—who, for their part,
having no one else to sell their cattle to in any case, were glad to accept
what they were offered. But less well-established traders and shopkeepers
might have to revert to the ancient Jewish occupation of itinerant trade
for lack of any other way of earning a living.

The religious colouring of a town or village was a further factor. Predominantly Protestant villages in Hessen, for example, tended to be more
anti-Semitic than the Catholic—except in the Fulda region where the
anti-Semitic attitudes of the Catholic population were especially marked.
But much depended too on whether Catholics were in a majority in a
given district, on the position taken by local clergymen, Catholic or
Protestant, and on the support dissidents might expect to be granted by
their bishops. In general, Protestant pastors were relatively prominent
among those clerics who were happy to identify themselves openly with
the Nazis—by taking out party membership, for example, and by participating in its rallies. Roman Catholic priests were apt to be more discreet
politically and somewhat more numerous than Protestants among the
few who made their opposition to Nazi policies plain.[76]

All in all, while in the years prior to the promulgation of the Nuremberg Laws it was still conceivable that in the cities life would continue
on restricted but not wholly impossible terms, matters were otherwise in
rural Germany. Everything that was thought likely to induce rural Jewry
to leave—if not immediately for abroad, then for the cities—was done
and, on the whole, done successfully. False charges of selling spoiled
goods were laid in one place, death threats delivered in another, windows
were smashed, beatings administered, Jews who had been unlucky
enough to draw the attention of local Storm Troopers to themselves
might be forced to run the gauntlet between rows of thugs armed with
iron rods and truncheons, synagogues were broken into, and here and
there people were killed outright or very severely injured. And since in
most, although not all, cases such local campaigns were conducted under

---

[76] Such, at all events, was the view of the Sicherheitsdienst (which had special responsibility for watching the general population) and the Gestapo. See Menahem Kaufman,
'The Daily Life of the Village and Country Jews in Hessen from Hitler's Ascent to Power
to November 1938', *Yad Vashem Studies*, 22 (Jerusalem, 1992), 160, 180; and on public
reactions to anti-Jewish measures generally, as revealed in German police reports, see
O. D. Kulka, ' "Daʻat kahal" be-Germaniya ha-naẓional-soẓialistit ve-ha-beʻaya ha-
yehudit: ha-mekorot u-vaʻayoteihem', *Zion*, 40, 3–4 (1975), 186–291.

the benevolent eye of the local authorities, the courts and the police, almost invariably, were quick to dismiss such complaints or claims for damages as the bolder spirits in the Jewish population had dared to lodge. It was therefore a losing battle. The Olympic Games of 1936 brought about a lull. But thereafter the screws were tightened, implacably. In 1937, a central directive from Berlin finally and formally ordained that all businesses of Jews outside the major cities be liquidated. In 1938 Jewish graveyards in rural Germany were closed, all Jews were forced to sell their homes, even peddling was forbidden. By the middle of 1939 the centuries-old Jewish presence in the German countryside had effectively been liquidated. In 1942 the last (mostly elderly) remnants of the rural Jewish population were deported to eastern Europe to be killed,[77] but by then the distinction between rural and urban Jewry had ceased to count. Long before the outbreak of war the effort to chase the rural Jews out of the countryside and, if not abroad, then into a dark and airless corner into which they could be conveniently crowded while their future was being decided had engulfed the Jewish urban population as well. By the end of 1938 half of all the Jews remaining in Germany were concentrated in Berlin alone.

Summing up what would be his last visit to Germany in the spring of 1938 Arthur Ruppin noted in his diary, that

It seems to me that many Jews in Germany still do not assess with full seriousness what has happened to them. There are still wealthy Jews who live from their investments almost as they did before. So long as they are able to buy the food they need from the grocer near-by—they fail to feel the calamity. They fail to see that their children have no future whatsoever in Germany, not from an economic point of view and not from a cultural point of view, and that it has been resolved that they are to be considered pariahs—at least for several decades, until the government agrees to absorb the few Jews who will be left. There are other Jews who despair, but see no way out. They have become too much a part of the place where they live and their occupation or profession. They are content only here [in Germany] despite the dangers. They lack the flexibility needed to get up and emigrate. People live today—as they say in Germany—from 'substance' (i.e. from capital). Numbers of doctors, lawyers, engineers, journalists, etc., have been left without work and income, have eaten up their savings and are dependent upon charity. The process of impoverishment advances with rapidity. About a quarter or a third of the Jews in moderately sized communities are now dependent on communal assistance. It may be said to the credit of the government that so far as unemployment assistance is concerned it still does not distinguish between Jew and Christian.[78]

But lingering uncertainties about German state policy in their regard were finally dissipated in the course of the organized paroxysm of

---

[77] Kaufman, 'The Daily Life', *passim*.   [78] Ruppin, *Pirkei Ḥayyai*, 298.

violence known as the *Kristallnacht* launched against them on 9/10 November 1938.

What was most notable about what has gone down in the chronicles of Germany under National Socialist rule as the *Reichskristallnacht* was that it brought into focus two of the determining aspects of the European Jewish condition on the eve of the Second World War: the ever more widespread insistence on the exclusion and extrusion of Jews and the consequent mingling of the destinies of western Jews with those in the east; and the impact upon *all* concerned of the tension between the Jews' vulnerability to punishment at the hands of those who chose to persecute them and the penalty they were likely to pay should they be so bold as to attempt to resist.

The course of events leading up to the onslaught was straightforward. At the end of March 1938 the Polish government announced that the passports of Polish citizens resident abroad for more than five years would have to be revalidated. Whether this was linked exclusively to its fear that in consequence of the German annexation of Austria and the immediate instigation of repressive measures there would be a mass flight of Polish Jews back to Poland is uncertain, although there can be no doubt that the authorities in Warsaw had the likely impact of the *Anschluss* upon themselves in mind. On 6 October, at any rate, it was announced that the deadline for such revalidation would be 30 October. The German response was immediate. Already irritated by having found itself, upon its annexation of Austria, with a large *increase* of its Jewish population and now fearful of being left with a large number of stateless and therefore doubly unwanted Jews, the German government decided on 28 October on the immediate deportation of all Polish Jews they could lay their hands on before the deadline expired. An immense *razzia* was set in train. Of the some 18,000 Polish Jews believed to be resident in Germany at the time at least 15,000 were rounded up, mostly overnight, many in the clothes in which they happened to be wearing upon arrest, some therefore in their pyjamas, none allowed to take more than ten marks in cash and a small suitcase of belongings. After a night in police stations and the like they were forced into sealed trains bound for the Polish frontier and, in most cases, unceremoniously pushed across. Some were shoved through established crossing points, others anywhere at all where it might be convenient to do so, in practice, therefore, often illicitly, across the unfenced so-called 'green border' (*über die grüne Grenze*).[79]

Of the Polish response to this horrendous treatment of their citizens the best that can be said was that it was mixed. At some crossing points the refugees were allowed into the country and their passage into the interior

---

[79] *Documents on German Foreign Policy 1918–1945*, Series D, v, nos. 84, 88, 89, 91–2, pp. 111–12, 115–20.

to friends and relations facilitated. At other points admission was refused and thousands of politically harmless and disoriented people, many of them long-time residents of Leipzig, Chemnitz, and other cities and towns in eastern Germany, some from further afield, were left to welter in the autumn mud and drizzle of the open country until, days later, they were shunted into makeshift prison camps in wholly unspeakable conditions. In the most notorious instance of this kind, at least 5,000 and very possibly as many as 8,000 people of all ages and states of health were crowded into a set of unheated, stinking military stables in the small town of Zbaszyn that had been condemned and abandoned as unsuitable for the horses for which it had originally been designed. Help did soon pour in from Jewish philanthropic and communal organizations in Poland and abroad. Certain limited categories of refugees were allowed back into Germany briefly to settle their affairs. But the greater part of those who had been unfortunate enough to be interned in the camps that had been hastily set up to contain them were refused both re-entry into Germany and free entry into Poland itself. There in limbo they were to remain until the war and the Wehrmacht caught up with them on 1 September of the year following.

There had already been several recent precedents for such deportations, all on a smaller scale. Several thousand Jews had been evicted from territories in Czechoslovakia annexed by Germany and Hungary under the terms of the Munich Agreement signed by the four major European powers a month earlier. In one incident, several hundred stateless (*staatenlos*) Jews living in Bratislava had been similarly pushed across the Hungarian border and, when the Hungarian authorities refused to admit them, left to camp out in the open fields between the lines. But scale apart, the October 1938 deportation of Polish Jews from Germany differed because of the two exceedingly significant conditions on which its success depended. The immediate, wholesale deportation of the Polish Jews was ordered by the German Foreign Ministry in the first instance, but had required a high degree of co-ordination between the ordinary police, the Gestapo, the Foreign Ministry itself, and, among other arms of the state, the railways to be set in motion. In the event, not everything went as smoothly as had been hoped and not all the Jews who had been targeted were found. Still, broadly, the aim the government had set itself was achieved. The other condition of success was the grant of at least *ex post facto* co-operation by the Polish government and this, while grudging and imperfect, had been given. Taken together these were important, and for the National Socialist regime encouraging and instructive, precedents for all that they were lost from sight temporarily when the matter of the actual expulsion, brutal and massive though it was, was swallowed up in the public mind, especially in the Jewish public mind, by the explosion of the officially encouraged and orchestrated violence and extortion to which it led.

The precipitating incident was the decision of a young Polish Jew to avenge himself for the wrong done his parents. After learning that his parents had been deported, Herschel Grynszpan, 17 years of age, walked into the German embassy in Paris on 7 November 1938 and shot the first diplomat who agreed to see him, a junior official named Ernst vom Rath. There had been only one such incident before when David Frankfurter shot Wilhelm Gustloff, leader of the German National Socialists in Switzerland in 1936. On that occasion the German government and party leaders did not respond. On this occasion the response was immediate and the Nazi party hierarchs, Goebbels in the lead, decided to teach the Jews a lesson by subjecting all Jews in (the recently much enlarged) Germany to massive public punishment. On the night of 9/10 November the SA, with the police and the fire services in attendance to ensure that Aryans and their property were not inadvertently harmed, were let totally loose for the first time since 1933. Thirty-six Jews were killed more or less outright, a like number seriously injured, at least 20,000, possibly as many as 30,000 were arrested and carted off to concentration camps and prisons (where, within a few months, the death toll reached three figures), hundreds of synagogues, dwelling houses, shops, and warehouses were put to the torch or otherwise destroyed, thousands more had their shopfront glass shattered. On the following day, 11 November, at a meeting at the Air Ministry under Göring's chairmanship, Hitler's order that 'the Jewish Question is to be summed up and co-ordinated once and for all and solved in one way or another'[80] was announced, steps being taken, however, to ensure that no such absurdly wasteful destruction of easily confiscated property be allowed in future. On 12 November it was announced that the Jews of Germany would be subject collectively to a punitive levy of one thousand million marks (£84,000,000), the 'exclusion of Jews from German economic life' as from 1 January 1939 was decreed,[81] they were to repair all damage done to their premises at their own cost, and, in a characteristic touch, they were to forfeit all insurance claims to the state. But it was the violence above all that struck home.

Kristallnacht was an event that was entirely without precedent in Germany in modern times. There had been, as we have seen, instances of local violence and arson. The happy response of a large proportion of the Austrian public, notably in Vienna, to the entry of the German army into Austria earlier in the year had taken the form of widespread arson, looting, some outright murder, and, most especially, much brutal, public, and deliberately humiliating harassment and molestation. But it too had been

---

[80] International Military Tribunal, *The Trial of German Major War Criminals*, Part 9 (London, 1947), 256.

[81] A second decree, tightening the stipulations of the first, was published eleven days later.

of a different order of magnitude. Except for the speed and thoroughness with which it was conducted and, equally tellingly, the rapidity with which it was brought to an end, the onslaught was comparable only with events in Russia in the early 1880s and 1905. And the lesson it taught was essentially of the same kind, if it was not in fact a good deal clearer. After the night of 9/10 October there was no doubt in any quarter that there remained no grounds whatsoever for continuing to ascribe uncertainty or indecision to German purposes in regard to the Jews; nor any reason for the Jews of Germany to retain such hopes as still lingered of there being a way back either for the National Socialists or, more significantly, for themselves. The only possible *argument* for remaining in Germany was now of a moral nature. Such, most notably, was the reason Rabbi Leo Baeck, effectively the moral or spiritual leader of German Jewry, was determined to stick it out. Despite the danger to himself personally he thought it his solemn duty to do so so long as there were those among his people whom age, physical condition, fear of inability to readjust to exile, lack of resources, refusal to be separated from parents or children, or, increasingly and decisively, failure to obtain permission to enter any other country forced to remain.

VIII

Herschel Grynszpan, it is worth noting, was not himself a German national. Nor was David Frankfurter.[82] Among the settled and authentic Jews of Germany there were no such desperate—arguably futile—attempts as theirs actively to resist, or at any rate protest the effort to denigrate, despoil, and extrude them. There were no peaceful, large-scale public protests of the kind mounted by the Bund in Poland after the pogrom in Przytyk two and a half years earlier, nor were any self-defence units on the old Russian model formed to beat back the SA. Certainly nothing of such a kind was attempted before or after the promulgation of the Nuremberg Laws or in the wake of the *Kristallnacht*, and no one at the time (or since) seriously thought or claimed that the eastern European model was other than inappropriate to German circumstances. The Jews of Germany were fewer absolutely and proportionately than those of Poland, less compactly settled, less organized, less isolated socially, altogether less of a single kind and very much less politically minded. The independent and internally fuelled politics and institutions that had made the public life of Jewry in pre-war Russia and contemporary Poland and Lithuania what it was had no German equivalent. The tradition, habit and, as most German Jews saw it, compelling propriety of abiding by the

---

[82] Frankfurter was from Croatia. A student in Germany, he had left the country when persecution began.

law whatever its source and of accommodating oneself to the demands of
state and society with little regard, if any at all, to their nature were very
deeply ingrained in them, as was the awe in which, with rare exceptions,
they tended to hold the massive power of the German state(s).

And then there was the crowning circumstance that, unlike the Jews of
Poland (and of Russia before the October Revolution), they were
entirely devoid of allies. The liberal and social democratic opposition to
the National Socialists had been destroyed. There neither was, nor in the
circumstances of the totalitarian political system that had replaced the
Weimar Republic could there be, a functioning political body analogous
in role and purpose to, say, the Kadets in Russia or the PPS in Poland—
pale allies, to be sure, but *in extremis* likely to be allies all the same. There
was indeed a conservative opposition to Hitler's government and methods,
but this had not yet fully crystallized, nor would it do so to any extent
before the defeat of the Reich began seriously to loom. Besides, there
was no question at any stage of Jews as such, or even Jews at all, being
incorporated into any of the relevant oppositional circles. The affairs of
the Jews were of little interest to the politically and culturally displaced
generals, diplomats, quondam politicians, and aristocrats who formed
the opposition, such as it was, few of whom were as averse to Hitler's purposes as they were to his methods and to the dangers they thought he was
running. But nor were allies to be found at the opposite end of the political spectrum. Within Germany both the Social Democratic Party and
the Communist Party were soon in ruins and what was left of them was
subject to the special attention of the Gestapo. Nothing could be more
dangerous for the Jewish community as such than to allow itself to be
linked with the Marxist left. But nor was there any likelihood of an
alliance of any kind being concluded with the German left anyway, quite
apart from the dangers it would have entailed and its probable intrinsic
futility.

Even in the aftermath of the *Machtergreifung* the position of the Communist Party of Germany (KPD) on the matter of the Jews continued to
be derived from the old refusal to see nationalism, racial or otherwise, as
an independent socio-political phenomenon. It considered it vital to dis-
prove the Nazi claim to genuine 'socialist' content in their programme. It
argued that Nazi anti-Semitism was no more than a tactic employed to
manipulate the masses who were themselves normally free of any such
contamination. It sought to show that the Nazi onslaught against the Jews
was limited in practice to the poorer classes in Jewry and that, as might be
expected, major Jewish capitalists had no more to fear from National
Socialism than their gentile analogues. But it was not above pandering to
popular anti-Semitic sentiment itself. In its clandestine publications, in
the early years of National Socialist rule, the party ridiculed its rival for,
as it argued, manifestly failing to solve 'the Jewish Question' in Germany

despite repeated promises to do so. Later, after the promulgation of the Nuremberg Laws, content and tone changed somewhat. In important instances, in clandestine circulars picked up by the Gestapo in Berlin, for example, and in material published and broadcast abroad, the Nuremberg Laws themselves, and the fresh onslaught on the Jews which they announced, were denounced and the *Kristallnacht* in particular was fully covered too in the party press and dealt with in appropriate language.[83] Still, the subject of the Jews and the attack upon them remained what it had always been to Marxist socialists, both those who took their cue from Moscow and those who did not: a nuisance and a source of ideological and tactical embarrassment. The tendency to play it down when possible and concentrate on other grim aspects of the National Socialist phenomenon was always a strong one. Tellingly, while some individual Jews are known to have operated in the Communist underground, in general they were thought a liability to the cause. Where Jewish party members had not been ordered to withdraw from Germany altogether either for the Party's good or for their own safety, they were most commonly told to stick to such more or less purely Jewish communist groups as had been formed and were still managing, in the ever more dangerous circumstances of the time, to keep afloat—and this despite the fact that Jews who had found their way into Communist formations, or to other left-wing underground organizations, had done so as Marxists of one kind or another, not as Jews, having in most cases left all *that* behind them long before.[84]

As for the general German public, it seems that on the whole the immense and unashamedly *open* display of National Socialist violence on *Kristallnacht* was badly received;[85] and that, as a result, the authorities took care from that point onward to ensure that anti-Jewish procedures, while of mounting severity in themselves, were conducted with greater discretion and to some extent in secret. Such public disquiet as there was failed, however, to be translated into active support for the Jews themselves. The churches, notably, were almost entirely silent, the tranquillity prevailing in their precincts broken only by murmurs of embarrassed concern about the likely fate of 'Christian non-Aryans' and by a very few, distinctly atypical instances of actual, open protest from the pulpit—instantly smothered by ecclesiastical apologies to the authorities for such breaking

---

[83] David Bankier, 'Ha-miflaga ha-komunistit ha-germanit ve-yaḥasa le-antishemiyut ba-raikh ha-shelishi 1933–1938', *Yahadut Zemaneinu*, 2 (1985), *passim*.

[84] Helmut Eschwege, 'Resistance of German Jews against the Nazi Regime', *LBIYB* 15 (London, 1970), 143–80.

[85] See for example Kulka, 'Da'at', 234 ff.; and Paul Sauer, *Die Schicksale der jüdischen Bürger Baden-Württembergs während der nationalsozialistischen Verfolgungszeit 1933–1945* (Stuttgart, 1969), 334 f.

of the ranks and by condign punishment being meted out to the offenders at the hands of the mob or the Gestapo or both.[86]

For all these reasons, there was no cause to expect the Jews of Germany to be bolder in their resistance to the National Socialists as the legal masters of the state than their 'Aryan' contemporaries proved to be. Counter-attack was unthinkable. The chosen strategy, in so far as one may be said to have been *chosen*, was that of orderly withdrawal under fire. The grant of emancipation—always problematic and grudging in Germany, and therefore always the pivot on which both their hopes and their anxieties turned—had been withdrawn. The once much-favoured notion of a German–Jewish 'symbiosis' being in the making had been rubbished. For those who had pinned everything on the one being completed and the other striking root there was now only an especially dark and disorienting night in which to scrabble for a new way to material and spiritual salvation. And it was therefore inevitable in the circumstances that some should give up the struggle entirely. The rate of suicide among German Jews had long been a fairly high one.[87] It was now to rise. No precise and fully reliable figures are available, but it has been fairly estimated, for example, that between 300 and 400 Jews committed suicide in April and May 1933 alone, almost certainly in direct response to the first great public measures taken against them after the Nazi assumption of full powers. In the autumn of 1937 the Berlin Jewish community reported a rate of 70.2 per 100,000 for the years 1932–4 as compared with a non-Jewish rate of 48.8 per 100,000 (itself exceedingly high by the standards of the more stable societies of western Europe). All told, it has been estimated that some 10,000 German Jews and 'persons of Jewish descent' committed suicide, or attempted to do so, when under Nazi rule: or about 2 per cent of the total Jewish population of Germany at its maximum. It needs to be said, however, that the Jewish population of German was one in which the proportion of the elderly was disproportionately high and rising. In 1933 16.3 per cent of all German Jews were over 60 years of age. By 1939, as a proportion of the total Jewish population left in Germany, the elderly so defined formed no less than 32.25 per cent.[88] It is not to be doubted that in very many instances successive injections of

---

[86] On the case of the admirable village pastor Julius von Jahn of Oberlenningen in Württemberg and his punishment, see Richard Gutteridge, *Open thy mouth to the dumb! The German Evangelical Church and the Jews, 1879–1950* (Oxford, 1976), 182–4.

[87] See above, Chapter 4.

[88] The steep rise in the elderly's share of the Jewish population is largely accounted for by the birth rate having fallen with the disintegration of the social regularities that are the necessary foundation of family life and with the relative equanimity with which the young, as opposed to the elderly and the middle-aged, faced the prospect of emigration. In 1933 17.25 per cent of the Jewish population was under 16 years of age. In Sept. 1939 the proportion under the age of 15 was estimated to have fallen by half to 8.1 per cent.

despair, disappointment, and humiliation combined fatefully with the natural and inexorable burdens of age; and, further, that in a community in which the great majority of members had long since taken their distance from the Tradition the ancient Jewish injunction against taking one's own life counted for relatively little.[89]

Still, if self-destruction was commoner than it had been in the past and symptomatic of the great unhappiness to which German Jews were subject, it was never a mass phenomenon, properly speaking. A more usual—although in the circumstances no more than interim—response to the waves beating against them in the twilight years preceding the definitive eruption in November 1938 was to look inward: into the community itself and away from what was visible outside. Mutual assistance was warmer, commoner, and more generous than it had been before, rich and poor tended to come together more easily, families to reunite, private life to be more intense, Sabbath and holiday prayers to be said more regularly, the return of reform-minded Jews to traditional observance a somewhat more frequent occurrence, and the history, culture, and character of the Jewish people generally to be taken up as subjects of deeper and wider interest than they had been for very many decades. Synagogues served once more as centres of Jewish society rather than merely as places for the performance of religious ritual alone. Jewish sports associations multiplied—the efforts of the Zionist Maccabi association and that of the RjF's Schild, the Jewish war veterans' subsidiary, being especially remarkable in this sphere. Artists who remained in Germany fell back on the Kulturbund deutscher Juden that had been formed expressly, with official encouragement it may be added, to provide them (and their audiences) with a substitute for the world from which they had been excluded. In sum, as the social, cultural, professional, and legal ring closed around the Jews there occurred a palpable, if somewhat embarrassed readaptation to something like the old rules and practices of the ghetto: to social and cultural self-sufficiency and self-containment—under the watchful eyes, it needs to be said, of such bodies as the Prussian Ministry of Education (in the case of the Kulturbund) and the Gestapo. None of this was ever to be more than ephemeral and it was all to be steadily pared down after *Kristallnacht* by ever heavier administrative control and by the impact of the decrees effectively eliminating Jews from the economic life of the country. But in truth, while it lasted, it was never more than a set of temporary crutches to which people had recourse while they collected their wits and sought to determine what they might be able to make of the rest

[89] *Sources*: Konrad Kwiet, 'The Ultimate Refuge: Suicide in the Jewish Communities under the Nazis', *LBIYB* 19 (London, 1984), 135–67; Herbert A. Strauss, 'Jewish Emigration from Germany: Nazi Policies and Jewish Responses', *LBIYB* 25 (London, 1980), 318–19.

of their lives. After *Kristallnacht* it was to flight, in any event, that almost all thoughts and efforts were turned.

It has been estimated that between 270,000 and 300,000 German Jews—some three-fifths of the total Jewish population of Germany in 1933—had left Germany by the end of 1939.[90] This accorded well with German purposes although not nearly as well as the government would have liked. Before the outbreak of the war emigration was free and positively encouraged—subject to certain economic penalties to which emigrants were liable in the form of a 'flight tax' (*Reichsfluchtsteuer*)[91] and partial or total loss of property. The actual rate of emigration fluctuated, however. It is believed that 37,000 left in 1933, many of them for political rather than explicitly 'racial' reasons. Later, remarkably, the numbers fell: 23,000 left in 1934, 21,000 in 1935. As the pace and intensity of persecution quickened and the full implications of the Nuremberg Laws were borne in upon the Jewish population the numbers rose once again: to 25,000 in 1936 before falling again to 23,000 in 1937. By mid-1938 about 150,000 had left. After the pogrom of 9/10 November 1938 the rate of departure soared, some 100,000 leaving before the barriers came down altogether upon the outbreak of war. It is evident, therefore, that

[90] The commonly accepted figure for the Jewish population of Germany in January 1933—525,000—is itself a matter of conjecture and a function of definition; and very few of the various sets of figures available quite match. Of these 99,000 (or 18.9 per cent) were of foreign nationality: 56,000 (or 56.6 per cent of all foreign Jews) were Polish, 20,000 (or 20 per cent) were stateless. To the 525,000 some demographers, however, add an estimated 292,000 *Mischlinge* of mixed parentage. By specifically Nazi count the number of so-called *Volljuden* of 'Mosaic faith' was 499,683 (or 0.77 per cent of the total population) in 1933, the number of non-believing or 'separated' *Volljuden* 300,000. By another estimate, the combined total of 'race-Jews' (another Nazi term) and *Mischlinge*, i.e. all those in the country who were liable to persecution of one degree of severity or another on grounds of racial identity, was well over 800,000 in the early years of the regime. The official German census of May 1939 put the number of so-called 'race-Jews' left in Germany at 233,000, noting that of this number 19,700 or 8.5 per cent were not in fact of 'Mosaic' faith. And there is yet another, widely accepted, possibly better figure for the total number of practising and non-practising Jews still in the country at the outbreak of the Second World War: 185,000. In any event, reverting to the 525,000 figure for 1933, it needs to be said that the huge drop of 340,000 (65 per cent) is to be explained not only by the relatively massive migratory movement out of Germany, but by the consistent excess of deaths over births to a total of 47,500 in the course of the years 1933–9. And finally, it is to be noted too that not all those who fled Germany before the war escaped their former masters. Some 30,000 German Jews remained trapped in Europe and, having being caught by, or delivered to, the German authorities by collaborating foreign police authorities, were sent east for destruction. In all, 10,000 German Jews seemed to have survived within Germany itself long enough to see the end of the National Socialist regime: 5,000 in hiding, 5,000 in camps, forming just under 2 per cent of the 1933 total. The principal source for these passages is Strauss, 'Jewish Emigration'.

[91] The 'flight tax', imposed (as from 1934) on persons owning at least 50,000 marks-worth of property or having earned 20,000 marks or more per annum yielded 70 million marks in 1934/6, rising to the immense sum of 342 million marks in 1938/9 (Strauss, 'Jewish Emigration', 343–4).

the speed and determination with which individual decisions to leave the country were made were functions in each instance of the intensity and precise nature of the punishment meted out (or anticipated), the exceedingly deep reluctance to leave the country of birth, language, and culture that marked virtually all German Jews, and, of course, the ever rising, ultimately almost insurmountable difficulty of obtaining permission to enter and settle in any other country (on which more in the next chapter). What can be said in general of German Jewry's response to the campaign launched against it was that it was the sum of several hundred thousand individual decisions, among them the failure or inability in very many cases to decide on any individually determined course of action at all. Still, the Jews of Germany were not totally without a form of central leadership in the crisis that had been foisted upon them and not totally devoid of central institutions capable, within very narrow limits to be sure, of offering a measure of counsel and assistance to their people while at the same time seeking, in something like the age-old manner, to intercede with the authorities on their behalf.

IX

Prior to 1933 the Jews of Germany had been without a central representative institution on either the French model (the Consistoire Central) or British model (the Board of Deputies). Such supra-communal organizations as there were bore the mark of Germany's federal structure, local communities (*Gemeinde*) being grouped in regional organizations (*Landesverbände*), the largest and far and away the most important of which was the Prussian which catered for very nearly three-quarters of those Jews who had not explicitly opted out of any communal attachment whatsoever. Apart from the inherent difficulty of getting hitherto independent and to some extent rival institutions to pull together, there was the fact that the Jewish *Gemeinde* and the *Landesverbände* had always been conceived of as communal institutions in a restrictive sense, their duty being to maintain synagogues, schools, hospitals, orphanages, homes for the aged, and to see to general welfare. There was no experience of authoritative, all-encompassing representation, notably *vis-à-vis* the central government. So if, upon the National Socialist take-over of the state in 1933, it was widely agreed that something more appropriate to the times was needed and that a unified and representative leadership body of some kind had urgently to be set up, it was less certain what its precise nature and mandate should be. Georg Landauer, a prominent Zionist, director for some years of the Zionist movement's Palestine Office in Berlin, appears to have proposed in a working paper dated 18 July 1933 that 'a united organization of the German Jews shall be formed by the

Jewish communities with a supreme leadership, representing all of German Jewry and duly recognized by the state. Every Jew must belong to a Jewish community. All members of the Jewish Community shall enjoy equal rights.'[92] But, effectively, this was a proposal for the voluntary assumption of minority status and minority rights; and few, other than the Zionists (and, indeed, not all Zionists), accepted that the time had come to go so far as to revise established German-Jewish doctrine on the national identity, purposes, and societal quality of the Jews. Landauer's blueprint was rejected. That such ideas might be incompatible not only with long-established German-Jewish purposes, but with the ultimate purposes of the National Socialists as well was still very imperfectly understood, if at all. The new regime wanted to be rid of the Jews. It had little interest in settling a new, formal status upon them other than for temporary manipulative purposes.

The solution chosen by some but not all leading figures in the community was to establish on 17 September 1933 what was originally conceived of as a sort of lobby: the Reichsvertretung der deutschen Juden (or Reich Representation of German Jews). It would speak for most, although not all regional community organizations or *Landesverbände* and major country-wide organizations. The great exception was the Berlin community, the largest and best established in the country and with a hold over the Prussian association of communities in its entirety. A lesser, but instructive exception was the German branch of Agudat Yisrael which refused to accept the leadership of an essentially secular body presided over by a reformist rabbi. A third, emerging in the course of time as a bitter opponent of the Reichsvertretung, was the extreme, dissident wing of German Zionism led by Georg Kareski whose 'State-Zionists' were an essentially ungovernable offshoot of the Zionist Revisionist movement with which it was at loggerheads over the issue of the worldwide Jewish economic boycott of Germany that had been launched in March 1933.[93] Kareski's belief that if the Jews were to be safely and completely evacuated from Germany a way had to be found to co-operate with the Nazis rather than fight them was, perhaps, no more than what was becoming the common view of those with some claim to a leadership position in German Jewry. But in addition to being a hugely controversial, independently minded, and quarrelsome man, he went a great deal further in his efforts to establish a *modus vivendi* with the Nazis than other people could stomach, his easy acceptance of the Nuremberg Laws as more or less compatible with his own views on Jewish national separatism horrifying Jewish opinion both in Germany itself and abroad.[94] But the three major non-communal country associations, the Centralverein deutscher Staatsbürger jüdischen Glaubens (CV), the Zionistische Vereinigung für Deutschland (ZfD), and the Reichsbund jüdischer Frontsoldaten (RjF) did all participate in the work of the Reichsvertretung—with the wholly unprecedented result that somewhat informally, on an unelected, but nevertheless quite widely accepted basis, it was in a position to take the lead.

On the face of things, as an attempt to assume regular, institutionalized leadership over German Jewry, the Reichsvertretung could be seen as a radical departure from past practices. In truth, it was rather more feeble than that. While they had much in common culturally, the Jews of Germany had long been divided by their communal organizations, divided too by political and ideological sympathies, divided in their initial attitudes to the new regime, and deeply and fatefully divided on all matters that pertained specifically to their identity as Jews: religious belief and practice and the linked issues of Jewish nationhood and Zionism. Moreover, being acculturated and assimilated to a very high degree, they were especially ill-adapted to the demands of overall leadership and to collective action and support for the centre of the kind that would now be necessary if their leaders were to be able to function to any useful purpose. The Reichsvertretung was therefore conceded no special authority by and over the communities that it was to represent any more than it was granted formal or official standing by the regime—as opposed to a sort of *de facto* recognition which entailed, among other things, constant surveillance of its activities by the Gestapo. It had no constitution or fixed rules or instruments of its own—no journal in which to articulate and broadcast its position and its advice, for example. For such purposes it needed to rely (successfully in the event) on the existing Jewish press: especially on the two most important periodicals, the Centralverein's *CV-Zeitung* and the Zionists' *Jüdische Rundschau*. Charitable and welfare work remained, as before, within the purview of the *Gemeinde* and other existing institutions. Emigration to Palestine continued to be handled by the Zionists' Palestine Office;[95] repatriation to eastern Europe by the Hauptstelle für jüdische Wanderfürsorge; and emigration to other parts by the Hilfsverein der deutschen Juden.

---

[94] The more so as, perhaps incautiously, he had allowed his views on the subject to be published in Goebbels's newspaper *Der Angriff*. See Herbert S. Levine, 'A Jewish Collaborator in Nazi Germany: The Strange Career of Georg Kareski, 1933–37', *Central European History*, 7 (1975), 268.

[95] The Zionist Organization of Germany was dissolved, along with all other Jewish parties, on 9 Nov. 1938. The Palestine Office, however, was allowed to continue its activities for another six months.

The functions of the Reichsvertretung[96] were therefore essentially those which its founding members defined pragmatically as the occasion demanded: the representation of German Jewry *vis-à-vis* the authorities at both the national level and at the level of the *Länder*, but also the task of doing whatever could be done to deflect and reduce the steadily deepening and demoralizing impact on the Jews themselves of the propaganda, expulsions, expropriations, dismissals, and general bullying to which they were subject. Rules and formal authority aside, however, within the Jewish world itself, the Reichsvertretung did rapidly assume the pre-eminent position among Jewish institutions and organizations in Germany. It provided the focus of attention and authority that had previously been absent and was now considered by almost all to be indispensable. It arbitrated between the many and various Jewish institutions. It treated with major foreign Jewish institutions. There remained only the matter of its relations with the regime—that which counted for most, of course—but in which regard there was very little it could do. The instinct of the very prominent figures in German Jewish life who founded and led the Reichsvertretung had been to try to enter into what they hoped, and seemed to have believed, could be a dignified debate or exchange of views (*Aussprache*) with the new government. They were to be no more successful in this than Schoeps's Deutsche Vortrupp. Hitler refused outright to see them. Göring did consent to receive a Jewish delegation on one occasion late in March 1933, but the exercise was never repeated, there was no follow-up, and from that point on the leaders of German Jewry were restricted in practice to ever more painful contact with officials of steadily diminishing rank. It was a norm to which the Reichsvertretung did its best to accommodate itself, keeping an exceedingly low profile, making it plain repeatedly that what it sought was a *modus vivendi* of a kind that would at least allow the Jews of Germany to hang on:

In the new State the position of individual groups has changed, even groups that are stronger and far more numerous than ours. Legislation and economic policy have taken their own authorized road, including some and excluding others. We must understand this without deceiving ourselves. Only then shall we be able to find honourable opportunities to struggle for all such rights, places, and opportunities and still exist, and German Jews be able to make their way in the new State as a productive, work-accepting and work-providing community.

There is only a single sphere in which we are free to realize our own ideas and purposes, but it is the decisive one: that of our own Jewish life and future.[97]

---

[96] Ordered in 1935 to change its name from Representation of German Jews to Representation of Jews in Germany (Reichsvertretung der Juden in Deutschland).

[97] 'Kundgebung der neuen Reichsvertretung der deutschen Juden', *Jüdische Rundschau*, 29 Sept. 1933.

Thus the constraints laid upon it by the regime and National Socialist purposes on the one hand and the self-denying political ordinances that it had assumed for itself on the other left it virtually no room for manœuvre. When in 1938 the government resolved to reduce it to a Reich Federation of Jews in Germany (Reichsverband der Juden in Deutschland),[98] so converting it in name as well as in fact into an instrument of state through which social control over the Jews was to be maintained, its brief hour was effectively over. It had not been allowed to become the Jews' own, admittedly blunt and soft instrument in their relations with the state. It was on the quality and personal standing of those who had come together to establish it and those, most particularly, who led it to the end, that all, while it lasted, had really depended.

The leading members of the group were notably independent, non-political, men. Rabbi Leo Baeck, *primus inter pares*, had been chairman of the Prussian *Landesverband*. He was the foremost figure in the progressive or liberal wing of German Judaism, a prominent member of the CV. Mildly sympathetic to Zionism and a non-Zionist member of the Jewish Agency for Palestine, he was not in fact a Zionist himself. He made no secret, however, of his view that the history of German Jewry was at an end, while refusing to leave Germany himself and repeatedly turning down offers of appointment to rabbinical and academic positions abroad. So long, he said, as there was a *minyan* to pray with he would remain. Baeck was arrested several times. In 1943 he was deported to Theresienstadt where, almost miraculously, he survived. Only then, when the war was over, did he leave Germany (for the United Kingdom). Baeck's closest and most senior colleague, Otto Hirsch, was a man of somewhat similar outlook, notably on Zionism, but of quite different background and experience. He had been senior government official in Württemberg. His strength was in practical affairs and organization. Where Baeck presided as the moral leader of the Reichsvertretung, Hirsch served as its executive director. Like Baeck he had felt it necessary to stay with the Jews of Germany so long as it was possible to do so and his fate was much like Baeck's except for the end. He was repeatedly arrested. In 1941 he was taken to Mauthausen where he was killed. If Baeck in some sense represented Berlin, Hirsch represented the lesser Jewish centres. Both stood for hanging on, therefore for something like the *doikeyt* of the Bund in Poland—a weaker, more desperate version to be sure and a less practicable one. Still, the principle was there and the Reichsvertretung under Baeck's leadership was its institutional expression.

Some questions were inescapable, however. Had the attempt to hang

---

[98] It was typical of German officialdom's obsessive attention to titles and pseudo-legalisms that a further change was ordered a year later: to Reich *Association* of Jews in Germany (Reichsvereinigung der Juden in Deutschland).

on helped to keep back people who might, in the early stages of the National Socialist regime, have got away? Was there an alternative approach to what was effectively—the case of the Zionists apart—one of every man, woman, and child for him- or herself? The mainstream Zionists were well represented on the Reichsvertretung's board. Their prestige had risen sharply after the *Machtergreifung*, as had their numbers. So had the degree to which people of all tendencies were disposed to listen to what they had to say and follow their advice.[99] The turn of events in Germany had forced even the Centralverein to soften its traditional anti-Zionism. When the Zionists claimed the leadership of organized Jewry for themselves it was denied them. But they were granted a much greater say for their point of view than had been customary before. They, for their part, had been quick to dismiss the hopeful arguments of those who still clung to the belief that it was both necessary *and* possible for the leaders of German Jewry to convince the 'representatives of the State that race is not the prerequisite for creating a uniform national sentiment'; and that 'we as Jews possess those qualities that contribute to the common communal life, those that a National Socialist state demands of its members, namely unconditional fidelity to its principles, acknowledgement of the *Führer*-principle, the subordination of the organization to the movement.'[100] Their view was that where national identity was held to be dependent on 'blood and nature' exclusively, as opposed to 'a mental attitude and its expression', there really was 'no point in advancing arguments that are not directed to the opponent's [real] position; . . . [T]he belief in the power of blood to determine our fate is so deeply rooted in National Socialism that neither reference to patriotic sentiments nor cultural ties, and least of all to cultural achievements, can shake the foundation.'[101]

---

[99] The best measure of public interest was the readership of German Zionism's principal organ, the *Jüdische Rundschau*. No more than between five and seven thousand before 1933, by the end of that year its circulation had reached 38,000 and was to continue at the 35,000 level or thereabouts for four years to come. In contrast, the *CV-Zeitung*, being the organ of the Centralverein deutscher Staatsbürger jüdischen Glaubens and having taken over the century-old *Allgemeine Zeitung des Judentums* when it folded in 1921, had always had a very much larger circulation, commonly assessed at about 60,000 before 1933. Thereafter its circulation dropped to roughly that of the level of the *Jüdische Rundschau* in the same period until both periodicals were forced to cease publication in Nov. 1938. See Jacob Boas, 'The Shrinking World of German Jewry', *LBIYB* 31 (London, 1986), 242–3 n. 12.

[100] Alfred Hirschberg, 'Wege zu Deutschtum und Judentum'. Cited in Uriel Tal, *Structures of German 'Political Theology' in the Nazi Era* (Tel Aviv, 1979), 16. Hirschberg was editor-in-chief of the most important Jewish periodical in Germany, the *CV-Zeitung*. On this occasion he was writing in the Berlin community's house journal, the *Gemeindeblatt der Jüdischen Gemeinde zu Berlin*, 23, 4 (Apr. 1933), 167. On Hirschberg and his insistence on a distinctly and consistently *German*-Jewish way, see Boas, 'Shrinking World of German Jewry', 251–5.

[101] *Jüdische Rundschau*, 7 July 1933. Cited in Tal, *Structures*, 13.

The sum of the Zionists' message to German Jewry at the beginning of Hitler's rule was sounded famously by Robert Weltsch, editor of German Zionism's principal organ the *Jüdische Rundschau* in the form of a positive, defiant appeal to self-respect and dignity. 'Wear it with pride, the yellow badge!'[102] he told his readers. But the fact was that the Zionists had been no less surprised by the rapid turn of events in Germany than the most thoroughly acculturated and complacent members of the community had been. They too, at least initially, were reluctant to accept that all bridges to the Germany they knew had been washed away, or were about to be. A single week after publishing Weltsch's ringing call for self-respect before all else, the *Jüdische Rundschau* affirmed that it was now necessary to 'declare with all clarity that equality of rights for the Jews was at an end', but went on to say that

The German people must know that historic, centuries-old bonds are not all that easily undone. Our profession of Jewish peoplehood has never meant, nor could it mean, the renunciation of what the German spirit has granted us. We were brought up in it and know what we have to thank it for. It has been German letters that taught national Judaism—its own Jewish sources and treasures apart—what character and freedom mean. . . . Today we are once again at a turning point. Thousands of German Jews, products of German education, must leave a country that will no longer allow them to live out their lives within it. The lot of the emigrant is not an easy one to bear, but we know that however many years and decades pass generations will stay true to what they have received in German spirit and culture.[103]

Yet they knew that their long-standing thesis about the intrinsic fragility of the Diaspora condition in the west no less than in the east had in fact been vindicated; that their general analysis of the state of Jewry had been shown to be correct; and that their own purposes and intentions were demonstrably more relevant to the immediate needs of German Jewry than anyone else's. It was in the nature of things, however, that they formed a wasting asset in German Jewry's hour of greatest need. In their inner being the Zionists, the Zionist members of the Reichsvertretung among them, had been long prepared to leave Germany for Palestine. They were now positively anxious to depart; and those who could do so did leave, one after the other. The fearful task of catering for those who would not, or, as was now increasingly likely to be the case, could not join them remained for what was left of the Reichsvertretung to shoulder.

In practice, once hope of Nationalist Socialist policy being modified was abandoned, all that was left for Baeck and his colleagues to do was to try to see to it that emigration and departure were conducted in an orderly way, the only possible tactic left to them being to play for time.

---

[102] 'Tragt ihn mit Stolz, den gelben Fleck!', *Jüdische Rundschau*, 4 Apr. 1933.
[103] *Jüdische Rundschau*, 30/31, 13 Apr. 1933, 147–8.

Attempts by the Gestapo to infiltrate the Reichsvertretung and manipulate it were successfully resisted on the whole. But it was thought necessary to continue to insist on patriotic sentiment, to express open support for German foreign policy, to oppose the economic boycott of Germany that had been launched abroad as a Jewish counter-measure, and to approach the Evian conference on refugees (on all of which more below) with the greatest caution. The Reichsvertretung was a body composed of highly educated, hugely respectable, middle-class, and, when not elderly, middle-aged people, all fatally unused to holding established authority in distrust. The last leaders of German Jewry could not reasonably be expected, therefore, to be less inclined than those who looked to them for guidance to yield to the belief that however bad things might be, worse could be warded off by accommodation: order, obedience, legalism would all help to save them; disorder and rebellion would only loosen the hands of those who wished to destroy them. The sum of their position was therefore that they would not fight the government and that there was to be no question of taking independent political action. They saw themselves, correctly, as captives of the state. The only question that remained to be answered was whether their brethren *abroad* were in a position to do anything for them—unless it was the case that European Jewry in its entirety, when its condition was properly understood, had now to be regarded as a captive people too?

10
Denouement

I

THE curtain was rung down on the history of the Jews of Europe on 1 September 1939. With one moderately sized exception (the British) and three very small ones (the Finnish, the Swedish, and the Swiss) each of the continent's communities would end by being placed either entirely or, as in the case of Russian Jewry, at any rate in great part at the mercy of Germany's army, police, and civil administration. In German-occupied Poland this was immediate. In Hungary this occurred only in the final stages of the war. But the result everywhere was much the same. What transpired throughout the continent was Proskurov,[1] but a Proskurov writ immensely large, not so much another instance of riders descending on a civil population in the tried and true manner of marauding bandits throughout the ages, but the work of a skilled and disciplined official apparatus of government operating under the helpful eye of a fighting army that, regiment for regiment, commanding officer for commanding officer, was probably the finest the continent had known since the Romans at their peak. Having failed to extrude the Jews, it became the purpose of the German state to destroy them. There having been little opposition to their policy towards the Jews in the years leading up to the war, the masters of Germany were left to conclude, correctly as things turned out, that they and their many allies would have an entirely free hand in the business of disposing of the Jews once and for all once the war was in progress. Multitudes of Jews were worked to death as slaves of the German war machine. Very much greater numbers still were rounded up and done to death without any delay at all.

The former task was largely left to private industry. The latter was allocated, initially, to teams detailed off from other, ostensibly more ordinary duties, but was later consigned almost entirely to units especially established to that end. What was remarkable about the doing of the Jews to death, summarily and otherwise, was that the operation relied for its success on the support of an immense array of subsidiary structures manned by many tens of thousands of policemen, railwaymen, office clerks, builders, mechanics, suppliers of poison gas and special apparatus,

---

[1] On the massacres in the Ukraine and in the Podolian town of Proskurov in particular in the aftermath of the October Revolution, see Chapter 8.

distributors of plunder, bankers of all nationalities, paymasters, guards, and, of course, in the crucial supervisory roles, tireless and dedicated staff officers whose function it was to ensure that victims were fed to the actual killers with all possible efficiency and dispatch and that their worldly goods were placed at the disposal of the German state and the German people. German nationals were naturally in the lead throughout, but it needs to be recalled that members of each and every one of the nations that had willingly or otherwise been incorporated into the new, German-dominated continental Europe in the course of the war were to be found alongside them engaged in pursuit of the common purpose in as great numbers as their racial betters and, for the most part, quite as devotedly. That the operation was not *absolutely* successful—in the sense that some Jews did survive, even in the occupied territories, even, a tiny handful, in Germany itself—was due not to any failure of will or conviction on the part of those who had undertaken the task of rooting them out or because insufficient manpower and material resources (rail traffic, for example) had been devoted to so large and intricate an enterprise in time of war. It was that Germany was defeated before the task, by any reasonable calculation, could be completed.

These grim matters pertain chiefly to the period *subsequent* to that with which this book attempts to grapple. Whatever may have been the intentions and ambitions of Hitler and his senior minions, it was the state of total war in Europe that provided optimum conditions for setting what they were pleased to call the Final Solution to the Jewish Problem in train. It is, indeed, exceedingly difficult to imagine it having taken place at all—at any rate in the manner chosen and on so gigantic a scale—except in wartime or in the aftermath of a world war that had ended in a German victory. On the other hand, it is impossible to consider the political affairs of the Jewish people themselves *up* to the actual outbreak of the war except, at least to some extent, in the light—more precisely the shadow—of our retrospective knowledge of what occurred *after* 1 September 1939. The question of the extent to which we are required or indeed entitled to do so is probably unanswerable, at any rate in rigorous terms. So too, ultimately are the larger issues that arise and will, no doubt, continue to torment at least some among those who venture to consider them. Should the effective end of European Jewry in anything like the shape and numbers that characterized it before the Second World War bear on our consideration of the modern period *in its entirety*? Is there a case for seeing the catastrophe as having been in the making very many decades *before* the event itself? What is the validity, if any, of the argument that holds the destruction of the Jews of Europe to be the inexorable consequence of the processes of emancipation and acculturation which had begun to transform them at the end of the eighteenth century and that gathered pace throughout the following century?

These are not questions or arguments that can be dismissed out of hand even if they are not of the kind that can be settled safely and comfortably one way or the other. All that is certain is that if the ground for catastrophe was laid well before its actual onset, so was the ground for other not impossible outcomes: potentiality is one thing, actuality another. Men and women will vary in their power, and certainly in their will, to determine a course for themselves. But they are not all and everywhere and at all times entirely devoid of the quality that makes them, among all other animals, unique and therefore uniquely interesting: all members of the human kind, that is to say, regardless of sort and degree, and except in the most extreme and unusual circumstances, retain some power to choose. It is, at any rate, the assumption that there will always be some people who in some respects and in some degree and for certain purposes are in the nature of free agents that makes the writing of history possible and distinguishes it—both as art and as science—not only from, say, zoology and ethology, but in an important sense from the quantitatively oriented social sciences as well. The limits set by their circumstances on the real ability and freedom of those who otherwise appear powerful and autonomous may be very substantial, often much more substantial than such people tend themselves to imagine. Huge differences in belief in one's capacity for independent action and in one's ability to discern the true features of the surrounding world in which action, if any, is to be taken are among the qualities that distinguish one man from another most sharply. But no problem is commoner for the historian than that of assessing the extent of the discrepancy between what a given individual perceived to be his ability and freedom to act, to do his will, to achieve his purposes, and so on, and the actual, objective limits placed upon his freedom by the true structure of the external world in which he proposed to operate and in which, in the natural course of things, hostile and countervailing forces were sure to be present.

A salient, if not determining characteristic of the National Socialist regime in Germany was, most precisely, that its masters believed that their scope for free, wilful action was, if not absolutely unlimited, at all events extra-ordinary and immense well beyond normal measure. In contrast, an equally salient and determining characteristic of the established leaders of those Jews who found themselves under National Socialist authority was that, much as their forefathers might have done previously, they reckoned *their* scope for free action to be so limited as to be virtually nought. It is because both the Germans in the years of their triumph and the Jews when the trap had closed around them had, indeed, good cause to hold to their respective views of the degree of freedom open to them that it has always been substantially more difficult to open the case of the latter to historical examination than that of the former. But if difficult, not impossible.

For the historian [*wrote Johan Huizinga*] the facts will always be 'a series of events that happened at a given time' [and] it must be added, that could have happened differently. . . . The sociologist . . . searches for the way in which the result was already determined in the facts. The historian, on the other hand, must always maintain towards his subject an indeterminist point of view. He must constantly put himself at a point in the past at which the known factors still seem to permit different outcomes. If he speaks of Salamis, then it must be as if the Persians might still win; if he speaks of the *coup d'état* of Brumaire, then it must remain to be seen as if Bonaparte will be ignominiously repulsed. Only by continuously recognizing that possibilities are unlimited can the historian do justice to the fullness of life.[2]

This has been the spirit in which I have approached the political history of the Jews of Europe during the entire period with which this book seeks to deal. And it has seemed to me that whatever we choose to make of what occurred once the Second World War began, there can be no reason, despite the evident difficulties, to exclude the some six and a half years that elapsed between the National Socialist seizure of power and the outbreak of the war itself. It is true that on the day the Wehrmacht moved into Poland the little that was left of the pre-1914 European world was destroyed for all time. It is hard not to see the fate of the Jews being at that point effectively sealed—sealed in the double sense that they very rapidly lost such limited power as they had had to act freely, autonomously, and collectively and that, contrariwise, their several enemies won greater freedom than ever to do with them whatever it was they wished. Throughout the vast territories that would fall to their control, the German rulers and their allies were in a position not only to say, as many of their predecessors had said, the fourteenth-century Holy Roman Emperor Charles IV among them, that the Jews, their bodies, and their possessions 'belong to us . . . [and that] we may act, make, and do with [them] what we will and please',[3] but to proceed upon that basis in actual practice. Yet up to that point, *prior* to 1 September 1939, all this lay unknown, unknowable, virtually unthinkable, guessable at best, in the future. It was true that emancipation had already been shown repeatedly, and in some cases dramatically, to be reversible. It had become evident in the course of the 1930s that it had been a gift that all—by no means, therefore, Germany alone—were free to withdraw if and when they were of a mind to do so. There had been countless other premonitions of a slide into eventual, if still indefinable catastrophe. It was true that no one at any

---

[2] J. Huizinga, 'De Historische Idee', in *Verzamelde Werken*, vii (Haarlem, 1950). English trans. by Rosalie Colie as 'The Idea of History' in Fritz Stern, *The Varieties of History* (New York, 1973), 292.

[3] Cited by John I. von Döllinger, 'The Jews of Europe', an address delivered at the Academy of Munich, 25 July 1881. English trans. in his *Studies in European History* (London, 1890), 221.

time up to the point at which actual, total continental war broke out had
soberly anticipated or was in any position to anticipate the shape and
dimensions of the eventual, encompassing disaster. This would not happen for nearly two years. All that is certain is that while the lives and freedom of the Jews were being severely reduced virtually everywhere in
Europe prior to September 1939 they were far from having been obliter-
ated. The question how the effective political class in Jewry conducted
itself in these final, desperate years is therefore neither absurd nor one that
it might be proper, in charity or in compassion, to evade.

II

Two simple, overarching questions faced the Jews as individuals, but
more especially and more obviously as a collectivity and therefore most
acutely those who claimed to *represent* them. How was National Socialist
Germany to be confronted; and how were those whose freedoms had
been most severely curtailed and whose lives and safety were under greatest threat to be redeemed? The first question was essentially one to
which, in the nature of things, only the Jews themselves were in a position to determine a response. The answer to the second question, in an
age in which free migration out of Europe and across the oceans had
been brought to an end, depended primarily—although, as we shall see,
by no means exclusively—upon others. What the answers to both questions
were bound to have in common regardless of content was that each was
contingent on the ability of those who *spoke* for Jewry as a whole or for
any of its major constituent segments to pull together. In this respect,
namely the debilitating effect of the long-standing chaos and disunity in
Jewish public life, the rise of the National Socialists to power in Germany
altered nothing. But it did express a need in terms of unprecedented
urgency.

Serious and consistent efforts to reconstruct and rationalize the various, putatively representative institutions of Jewry in the interests of a
grand pooling of their common moral, material, and political resources
had always been rare. Those who made them had invariably been caused
to stumble over a prevailing disinclination in all quarters to re-evaluate set
positions and reconsider well-tried conventions of conduct and thought.
Safety—namely what was thought at any particular time and moment to
be safe—was cardinal. What had been tried in the past without damage
being incurred commonly ended by being relied upon to work in the
future. To go so far as to tackle any of the great, manifestly desperate, continent-wide, very likely insoluble problems of European Jewry head-on,
and to do so moreover with a fresh mind and some readiness to consider
unprecedented action, was precisely the sort of radical venture from

which almost all those to whom the challenge to embark on such a course might reasonably have been addressed automatically drew back. The question whether any common strategy could be devised was perpetually intertwined with the logically but also empirically prior question whether a united Jewish front of any kind could be established for any purpose whatsoever.

The greatest opportunity of all in modern times to construct a common front was that which had been offered by the Paris Peace Conference. But full advantage of it was not taken and there was a continuing failure to build on the little that had nevertheless been achieved. A Committee of Jewish Delegations to the Peace Conference (Comité des Délégations Juives auprès de la Conférence de la Paix) had been set up jointly, it will be recalled,[4] by prominent representatives of American Jewry on the one hand and representatives of the Zionist movement on the other. Those concerned came from outside the class of notables that had dominated the public affairs of the Jews either in Europe itself or in the United States since the middle of the previous century and were in one way or another at odds with it. In general social and political terms they were all of a moderate liberal tendency. In specifically Jewish terms and context they were modernists and if not totally secular at least semi-secularized. In 1919 the auguries were still favourable on the whole. The general international climate of opinion had proved uniquely conducive to the Comité being given a fairly warm hearing. Composed of delegates from an unprecedentedly broad range of public committees, conferences, and councils, some directly, some indirectly elected, some formed on the tried and true basis of co-optation, some well established, some *ad hoc*, most European, but some of the most prominent among them from the United States, the Comité itself was unusually (which is not to say fully) representative. Its people all knew their own minds and had well-defined and well-articulated purposes; minor differences apart, they stood on common ground so far as the Peace Conference was concerned. This owed much, to be sure, to the Zionists and their allies being in the lead in the Comité—the 'allies' being those who, if not ardent Zionists themselves, were at any rate sympathetic to Zionist purposes and to the Zionist outlook on Jewish nationality and what all thought were its implications in and for eastern Europe.

That the leading figures in the coalition of delegations that had formed and run the Comité should wish to keep this coalition in being after the Peace Conference itself had dispersed and provide it with an appropriate institutional form was therefore no more than a natural development. That the leaders of the Zionist Organization proper should approve of this being done was equally to be expected. But ever anxious, under

[4] See Chapter 8.

Weizmann's leadership, to concentrate resources and attention on the complexities and sheer immensity of the task of resettling as many of Europe's Jews as was feasible in what was to be the Jewish National Home in Palestine, they were more than content to divest themselves of what otherwise might have seemed to them to form a part—a large and unwieldy part—of their responsibilities. No really clear dividing line was drawn then or later between those Zionists who continued to devote the greater part of their time and energy to the matters with which the Comité was concerned—close observation of the workings of the minorities treaties, for example, and intervention at governmental or international level where it was urgent to try at any rate to alleviate repression and apparently feasible to do—and those, the majority, who were happier, on the whole, to leave these duties to others. But there was a distinct sense in which the old, pre-First World War argument that Zionists should be engaging in 'current tasks' in the Diaspora[5] as well as in the admittedly absolutely central one of the resettling of Jewry in Palestine had come to an end. Certainly, none suspected that it would reopen a decade and a half later in a fresh and particularly bitter form.

For a while all went fairly smoothly. The Comité, slightly modified in name and structure, became a permanent, formally recognized lobby with a watching brief for Jewish interests at the League of Nations in Geneva. There its primary function was to press for honest and unimpeded implementation of the new rules under which Jews (and of course members of other peoples) were entitled to equal civil and minority rights in the new states. It was then up to the Comité to bring cases of backsliding in this respect to the attention of the Council of the League. However, very much as had been the case at the Peace Conference, so at Geneva, the Comité encountered rivals and opponents from within Jewry itself. Neither the Alliance Israélite Universelle nor the Joint Foreign Committee (JFC) representing the Board of Deputies of British Jews and the Anglo-Jewish Association had agreed to join the Comité when it was originally formed in 1919. Now, joined by revived German–Jewish organizations, they persisted with their objections to the Comité as such and to the Comité's terms of reference in particular, their grounds for doing so being essentially those that had exercised them in 1919. They took the Comité to be an institution of largely Zionist inspiration that had worked its way into arenas in which they felt very strongly, as in the past, that they alone were entitled to operate and to be accepted by all concerned as competent to do so.

On specifics, however, the Alliance and the JFC were not at one in all respects any more than they had been at the Peace Conference. Firm in its conviction that Jews and Jewish communities were to be defined in

---

[5] See above, pp. 613 ff. and 628–30.

religious terms exclusively, the Alliance remained adamant in its refusal to countenance the grant of national rights to Jews anywhere, in any form, and under any circumstances. The JFC, more moderate, more sophisticated, and always better informed about the realities of life in eastern Europe, had long since agreed to a distinction of some sort or other being drawn between what might be appropriate in the east as opposed to what, to their minds, was most definitely appropriate in the west. Somewhat against the grain of their own thinking and aspirations, they had therefore been prepared to press for autonomy for the Jews in the management of their religious, cultural, and charitable institutions and to such statutory protection of national or ethnic minorities as had been granted to Germans and Ruthenians in Poland and to Hungarians in Romania and Czechoslovakia being extended to Jews as well.

None the less, the JFC's general tendency was to close ranks with its old associate wherever possible and it remained undeviating in its determination to keep its distance from the Zionists, whom, opposition on grounds of principle apart, it continued to hold in ineradicable distrust. When in June 1927 the Comité and the American Jewish Congress tried once again to induce the Board of Deputies, the Alliance, and the Hilfsverein in Germany to enter into a form of regular consultation and cooperation the rebuff was immediate. The Comité had argued that

Most of the organizations occupied with the defence of the rights of the Jewish population of central and eastern Europe have long felt the necessity of a central body which shall co-ordinate Jewish activities in relation to the various international bodies concerned with these rights. This necessity has become imperative in the face of the creation of numerous Jewish organizations, large and small, which by their independent and often conflicting activities have sometimes weakened and even compromised in the court of international opinion the very cause they have at heart.

It therefore proposed a general conference to review the full range of issues touching on the protection of Jewish minorities and a special conference in Zurich on 17–19 August to discuss the creation of a 'united Jewish front' to defend their rights.

If, in the judgement of the Zurich Conference, it should not seem feasible to create one central [permanent] organ, we believe that a *modus vivendi* will in any event be arrived at, which, without affecting in any way the autonomy of existing bodies, will serve as a Co-ordinating Council in relation to these organizations. Otherwise all work in defence of the rights of the Jewish minorities remains chaotic.[6]

---

[6] Julian Mack and Stephen Wise for the American Jewish Congress and Naḥum Sokolov and Leo Motzkin on behalf of the Comité itself to the Board of Deputies of British Jews, 30 June 1927, CAHJP, P13/1/22.

So far as the Alliance was concerned, this was entirely unacceptable and the spirit in which the proposal was received may be judged by its leaders' conclusion that this was an appropriate moment for the Alliance and the two western organizations to which it was linked to submit a joint note to the League of Nations in which their contention that the Comité had 'no mandate and does not represent members of the Jewish faith in the several countries of which the undersigned are citizens' was made absolutely clear.[7] The JFC held back, however, thinking the move proposed by its old partner was far too drastic, for all that on the substance of the matter it was at one with the Alliance and the Hilfsverein in Germany besides having its own special objection to co-operation with the Americans and with the Comité. This, as Lucien Wolf put it privately to his principals, was that a deviation from the line set six years earlier when regular contact between the JFC and the Comité had been suspended 'would practically mean handing over the functions of the Joint Foreign Committee to the Comité des Délégations'.[8] In his formal, written reply to Mack and Sokolov and their respective colleagues, Wolf spelled out his objections with more precision. There was no real need to set up a 'co-ordinating council' of any kind, he thought. He was not aware, he said, of the 'evil' they complained of. He did not know of any evidence to the effect that the effort to ensure protection of Jewish minorities had been or was being compromised by 'independent and often contradictory interventions'. And beyond all that, the authors of the invitation must understand that

The Joint Foreign Committee and its parent bodies are composed of British subjects, representing the Jewish communities of the British Empire, and it is impossible for them to contemplate any sacrifice of their independence or any delegation of their functions. In dealing with the rights of Jewish Minorities in Eastern and South-Eastern Europe, the Committee has frequently consulted His Majesty's Government as to the interpretation and application of Treaties of which Great Britain is one of the chief signatories. It cannot share this task with any foreign body which must necessarily be only imperfectly acquainted with British methods and the British outlook in such matters. Moreover, the Joint Foreign Committee, when it approaches the League of Nations in regard to the Minorities Treaties, does so as a representative British body, and this fact has hitherto proved an asset of no small importance in securing the effective operation of the Minorities Treaties.

For these reasons the Joint Foreign Committee can neither merge itself in the

[7] Cited by Wolf writing to Lord Rothschild, 12 July 1927, ibid. The depth of the undeviating hostility evinced by leading members of French Jewry to anything that smacked of Zionism is well illustrated by the attempt in 1933 to persuade the French prime minister (Daladier) to forbid Weizmann to accept invitations to lecture before a distinguished audience at the École de la Paix and at the Sorbonne on the condition of the Jews in Germany. Daladier refused to intervene. See Weizmann to Anthony de Rothschild, 28 Dec. 1933, in Chaim Weizmann, *Letters and Papers*, xvi (London and Jerusalem, 1968–80), no. 180, 195.

[8] Wolf to Rothschild, ibid.

proposed International Central Committee, nor in any other way subordinate its activities to that body. It must remain the sole judge of what events do or do not constitute adequate grounds for its interventions, and of what methods should be employed to secure a successful issue for such interventions. It is of course its duty to consult the Minorities [themselves] on whose behalf it acts and, indeed, only in very exceptional circumstances does it plead the cause of an aggrieved Minority without a direct Mandate to do so. This, however, must remain the limit of its organic obligations in foreign countries.[9]

What Wolf did not refer to were two additional, particular fears to which he and his colleagues were prey. One was that an international Jewish body of any kind, but certainly one that purported to encompass most if not all Jewish communities worldwide, was bound to provide the anti-Semites with just that 'proof' of international Jewish conspiracy that they were continually seeking. The JFC's other fear, long familiar and still very lively, was lest the status of British Jews as Englishmen and as subjects of the British crown be contaminated by links with persons and organizations who, in contradistinction to themselves, stood squarely for the principle of Jewish nationality and were intent, moreover, on promoting the establishment of an independent Jewish state. At the heart of the quarrel, therefore, was the customary disagreement, at once instinctive *and* reasoned, about the nature of the Jewish collectivity itself: a dialogue of the deaf, familiar to all concerned, to which the erection of Woodrow Wilson's new Europe had given a new edge and immediate political implications. The Comité's initiative was therefore bound to abort.[10] And since past experience showed that no gathering under Zionist sponsorship could be other than suspect in the eyes of Zionism's opponents,[11] the question whether further attempts to build a greater structure on the foundation of the Comité were likely ever to succeed seemed to be foreclosed.

Yet who, other than those who took what at least approximated to a national, supra-communal view of Jewry were likely to undertake such a venture? Alone even among those who might reasonably be classed as nationalists of some kind, the outlook of the Zionists was at once political, modernist, and not overly encumbered by sectarian reservations. No other supra-communal organization answered as well as theirs to these specifications. Agudat Yisrael, for example, was political only by indirection. The concessions its rabbinic leaders had made to its central European wing were exceedingly limited. It remained fundamentally

    [9] Wolf to Sokolov, 25 July 1927, in Weizmann, *Letters and Papers*, xvi, no. 180.
    [10] A Conference on the Rights of Jewish Minorities did assemble in Zurich 17–19 Aug. 1927. Once again, the AJC, the JFC, the AIU, and now the Hilfsverein der Deutschen Juden too, declined to participate. And while 65 delegates representing 43 other organizations from 13 countries did turn up, along with a delegation speaking for stateless Jews, taken together they formed little more than a framework for further consultations.
    [11] On reactions to the conference called by the Zionists in 1906, see Chapter 6.

anti-modernist. It wished to preserve the closed world of traditional Jewry, not to open, expand, or in any other way seriously alter it. Its leaders were unwilling, and effectively unable, to overcome deep objections to co-operation with secular Jews on any basis or to any purpose except, perhaps, *in extremis* and even then for exceedingly limited and short-term purposes. The Bund was equally disinclined to co-operate in any such venture and equally unshakeable in its views, bound as ever to the theses that the prerequisite to the solution of the Jewish Problem was socialism, that the Jews were as class-ridden a people as any other, and that there was, in any case, no *common* Jewish destiny to tackle and cater for. There was the additional difficulty that, along with the rest of the Jewish left not excluding the more radical segments of the Zionist left wing, the Bund preferred to play down its undoubted and admitted suspicion of, and hostility to, the regime in the USSR. It was certainly not disposed to attack it, even for the treatment accorded Russia's Jews, not publicly at all events, and above all not in company with those it regarded as representatives of the Jewish bourgeoisie. Besides, its activities and aspirations were now limited to Poland and Lithuania. Small groups of sympathizers could be found in major cities in Great Britain, France, and the United States, even here and there in Latin America. But it could not seriously be rated a worldwide organization.

The men and women of the Comité and their American allies continued their admittedly somewhat desultory efforts to expand the institution, tending steadily, as time went on, towards the creation of a larger, grander, above all more encompassing organization than their own, a World Jewish Congress in name, but also in fact. It was to be a representative parliament of Jewry in its entirety, no less than that comprehensive national assembly (*Nationalversammlung*) that Herzl tried to convene some four decades earlier, although whether they themselves were conscious of the precedent is unclear. Herzl in his time had learned very rapidly that the annual, later biannual, Zionist Congress was not and could not be the fully representative national assembly he had hoped for. Zionism had emerged not as a unifying force in Jewry but, necessarily, as a divisive one. No Zionist assembly, no matter how watered down the thrust of its debates and resolutions, could become a 'national' assembly in the sense Herzl had wanted it to be. He had had, it is true, some cause to congratulate himself on having infused many of the delegates present at Basel in 1897 with the idea that that, in fact, was what they had attended: 'I gradually worked the people into the mood for a State,' he noted in his diary, 'and made them feel that they were its National Assembly.'[12] And it was the case, in the course of time, that the Zionist Congress came closer than

---

[12] Entry for 3 Sept. 1897, *The Complete Diaries of Theodor Herzl*, ed. Raphael Patai, trans. Harry Zohn (New York, 1960), ii. 581. Herzl closed the relevant passage in his diary

any other body formed in the course of the history of the Jews in their Diaspora to functioning as a national assembly or parliament.

By the 1930s it was established for all to see as the only fully elected, representative institution in which the affairs of the Jewish people *as a whole* were consistently the central and invariable matter of open and recorded debate. It had successfully introduced into the Jewish public arena a wholly new, distinctly *political*, and at the same time unquestionably parliamentary-democratic mode of discussion, decision-making, and thinking. It made it possible for its own leaders to go further than men of modest origins and moderate wealth and scholarly attainment had ever done previously towards replacing the class of notables, dominant throughout the previous century, whose hold on all the indispensable keys to social and political action had hitherto been unyielding. The supremacy of prestige within Jewry and the monopoly of access to those who wielded power in the real world were both wrested from them. The Jewish public had begun to grow accustomed to the radical and large-scale political action to which the Zionist movement was devoted and which lay at the very root of its ethos and *raison d'être* and which was, of course, precisely what the notables of Jewry, with the rarest of exceptions, had always refused to undertake. It was the Zionist Congress again that provided the uniquely effective platform from which Herzl and his successors had not only been able to present their radical purposes to all who would listen to them, but to offer themselves as the alternative leaders of Jewry whose special public virtue lay in their being neither self-perpetuating nor self-selected, but elected and responsible. It was therefore to be expected that this was the model the founders of the World Jewish Congress (WJC), mostly Zionists themselves, had in mind, consciously or otherwise, when, after a series of preliminary meetings extending over an entire decade, they managed finally to inaugurate a full and definitive Congress of their own at Geneva on 8–15 August 1936. But the question whether it was possible to replicate it, if only loosely and in outline, in the interests of 'world Jewry' had still to be answered, the more so as the Zionist Congress, while destined in some respects to be the WJC's twin and partner,[13] was at the same time its rival.

with the observation that 'Perhaps the most important episode from the point of view of principle—although it may have gone completely unnoticed—was my introduction of the representative system, that is, the National Assembly. The next Congress will consist only of delegates' (ibid. 585).

[13] The Zionist Actions Committee officially welcomed the WJC preparatory conference in 1932 with support for 'every form of international action by the Jewish people to defend its civic and national rights, as well as its political, economic, and social positions. In these days of unheard-of attacks upon the existence of the Jewish people and of a threat to vital Jewish rights in divers lands, every effort at an international union of Jewish communities and groups of various countries is doubly necessary.'

Unlike the Zionist Organization and *its* Congresses, the World Jewish Congress would be committed to no particular view of what needed to be done on behalf of the Jews, only to the general need to beat back repression by such legitimate means as were available to it and to speak for an otherwise voiceless people in such a way and in such terms as would command closer and friendlier attention to their plight. That a larger measure of unity should now be possible owed much to the closing of the several rings into which the Jews of central and eastern Europe were being compressed. Above all, of course, the dramatic and increasingly frightening march of the German National Socialists and their analogues elsewhere to power softened much of the normal hostility to radical and unfamiliar initiatives. The process was signalled most publicly and dramatically when the old guard leadership in Jewish public life in Great Britain was hurried out of what had long been one of the bastions of Jewish conservatism, a prominent Zionist (Selig Brodetsky) being elected president of the Board of Deputies of British Jews. But this occurred late in the day in 1939.

III

In outline, the written and unwritten rules of membership, debate, type of issue it might be proper to take up or leave to others were all set well before the World Jewish Congress was finally convened in the course of a series of preliminary meetings at which plans for the eventual full Congress were repeatedly adumbrated. Some of these were substantial gatherings in themselves.[14] Fifty-two delegates from eighteen countries attended the conference at Geneva in September 1933, the first to be

---

[14] The long-drawn-out preliminary stages were as follows. A smallish, relatively informal meeting of leaders met to discuss the foundation of such an organization in London on 3–4 Aug. 1926. The Zurich Conference on the Rights of Jewish Minorities referred to above assembled on 17–19 Aug. 1927. Discussions in which Stephen Wise, Motzkin, and Gruenbaum were the principal participants took place in Basel immediately after the 17th Zionist Congress at Basel in 1931 which all three had attended. The first explicitly entitled 'World Jewish [preparatory] Conference' was held at Geneva, 14–17 Aug. 1932. The American Jewish Committee, the B'nai B'rith, the Board of Deputies, and the Centralverein Deutscher Staatsbürger Jüdischen Glaubens refused to attend. But 94 delegates from 17 countries (including Germany) did. No decisions of substantive importance were taken, but it was resolved to pursue the effort to create an adequately ecumenical conference which 'amidst the fragmentation and atomization of Jewish life and the Jewish community' would offer 'real, legitimate, collective representation of Jewry . . . [and] be entitled to speak in the name of the 15 million Jews to the nations and governments of the world, as well as to the Jews themselves'. A second preparatory World Jewish Conference was held, once again at Geneva, on 5–8 Sept. 1933. A third preparatory conference was held at Geneva on 20 Aug. 1934. Two more years passed before the full World Jewish Congress assembled.

held after the National Socialist seizure of power in Germany.[15] The American Jewish Committee, the Board of Deputies of British Jews, the Anglo-Jewish Association, the French Consistoire Central, the Parisian Alliance Israélite Universelle, the Centralverein Deutscher Staatsbürger Jüdischen Glaubens, and the American Jewish Committee all still declined to be represented. But this was expected, and the grounds for their refusal to attend and co-operate might equally have been anticipated. If the Board of Deputies 'became associated with the WJC,' Lionel Cohen, the vice-president of the Board, explained to his colleagues, 'it would . . . lose its influence, for our government would not be satisfied that due regard was being paid to British interests in representations that were made on behalf of the JFC.' And when intense lobbying and some skulduggery at the Board ensured that a Zionist counter-motion recommending partici-pation was defeated, but only by an embarrassingly very small margin (105 to 81), Neville Laski thought it necessary to explain to senior news-paper editors that the vote reflected the views of the 'more responsible elements' and 'what I may now almost term the "indigenous Jew"' as opposed to 'the East European immigrants'.[16]

---

[15] Belgium, Bulgaria, Czechoslovakia, Denmark, Egypt, France, Great Britain, Italy, Lithuania, Morocco, Palestine, Poland, Romania, South Africa, Spain, Switzerland, United States, and Yugoslavia. Communal notables and institutions in Austria, Argentina, Tunisia, and Turkey sent messages of support and approval. There were no representatives or messages from Germany (the conference took place after the Nazi *Machtergreifung*) or from the USSR.

[16] Sharon Gewirtz, 'Anglo-Jewish Responses to Nazi Germany 1933–39: The Anti-nazi Boycott and the Board of Deputies of British Jews', *Journal of Contemporary History*, 26 (1991), 268–70. Laski sought repeatedly to give a structure to this thesis. In 1934 he was at pains to create a 'back-channel' of his own to the Colonial Office by means of which the regular and on the whole not unfriendly contacts between the Colonial Office and the Jewish Agency (of which he was himself one of the non-Zionist members) would be undercut and Whitehall instructed in the true nature of Jewish needs, interests, and loyal-ties, at any rate as his 'section of Anglo-Jewry' understood them. 'You can divide what is known as Anglo-Jewry into two sections,' Cosmo Parkinson, the assistant Under-Secretary of State responsible for Palestine and Middle East Affairs, reported the president of the Board of Deputies of British Jews as telling him: '(1) those Jews who, like himself, put British citizenship first and regard themselves as separated from the Community solely by religion; (2) those who, like Dr. Brodetsky, have a non-British origin and, while friendly to Great Britain as the Mandatory Power for Palestine, are thinking all the time on international lines, and are aiming first and foremost at the establishment of a Jewish state in Palestine. Mr. Laski mentioned Dr. Weizmann in this connection,' Parkinson reported, 'and said that, although Dr. Weizmann had since denied it, he knew positively that Dr. Weizmann had said that a Jew cannot be just a citizen of the country in which he lives, or words to that effect.' Laski did not think it as difficult 'to bridge the gulf between Jewish and Arab interests as the Zionists maintained'. And while his view, and that of his friends, 'was that any individual Jew might, if he so wished, refuse to trade with Germany, . . . it was most improper for British Jews living in this country to attempt to organise a boycott. . . . [As] any other attitude might be extremely embarrassing to His Majesty's Government in its relations with the German Reich.' What Laski wanted, Parkinson con-cluded, were 'secret and informal discussions between the Colonial Office and himself and

But the disappointment, such as it was, did nothing to lower the founders' sights. It was declared at Geneva in 1933 that when the new Congress assembled it would

consider and take action upon all Jewish questions. What the Zionist Congress and the Jewish Agency for Palestine are designed to be and to do in relation to Zionism and the re-establishment of the Jewish Home in Palestine, the World Jewish Congress plans to be and to do in relation to the common Jewish problems in the Diaspora. The World Jewish Congress is to be an assembly not of a handful of Jewish notables, but a group of democratically chosen representatives of Jewish life in all lands, one: for discussion and action by Jews on their common problems, two: for presentation of such problems to that world opinion in which we have not lost confidence.[17]

How democratic representation was to be achieved and whether it was to be attempted at all was not made clear. Some of those present insisted that the WJC be formed of delegates chosen by popular, democratic election exclusively, although it was abundantly obvious that the social make-up of the various segments of Jewry differed far too greatly one from the other for uniform electoral rules to be written, let alone applied. The systems of government to which the various communities were subject differed equally strikingly, as did their own individual social and institutional structures. In the very large communities, in the United States and in Poland, there was no single country-wide *community* to speak of, except perhaps in entirely nominal terms, only congeries of discrete, autonomous, local synagogue communities. Some of these had incorporated themselves into larger networks of communities, but each of these remained defined by some very particular religious or political orthodoxy or was led by its own particular, often singular and charismatic moral and spiritual chief, each therefore tending to be in some degree antipathetic, when not downright hostile, to its neighbours and analogues. It followed that if there was to be a single rule for all it would have to be of such a nature that each constituent country community would remain free to determine for itself, and by itself, how its delegates were chosen. The issue of popular, fully representative government of the

his friends'. The Colonial Office turned him down, however. They thought Laski's strictures on Brodetsky and other Zionists generally unfounded and insisted that the Jewish Agency, in which, in the nature of things, the Zionists were naturally dominant, was 'the accredited body for dealing with the Government in regard to the National Home'. And they had no doubt that if Zionists got wind of secret talks of such a kind as Laski proposed being held behind their backs there would be a most embarrassing scandal. Laski to Cunliffe-Lister, the Colonial Secretary, 31 July 1934; minutes by Parkinson, 15 and 16 Aug.; by J. E. Shuckburgh, deputy Under-Secretary of State, 17 Aug.; by Cunliffe-Lister, 19 Aug. 1934, PRO, CO/733/266/10. On the anti-German boycott see below, pp. 860ff.

[17] Stephen S. Wise at the Comité Exécutif du Congrès juif mondial, 5–8 Sept. 1933, *Protocole de la IIe conférence juive mondiale, Genève, 5–8 septembre 1933* (Geneva, 1933), 22–3.

Congress versus some form or other of indirect election or co-optation was never quite put to rest. On the other hand, after 1933 matters of institutional order and political principle began to count for relatively little. It was how the World Jewish Congress, if and when it was established, and however it was constructed, addressed itself in practice to the burning issues of the day that was to count. Chief of these, of course, was that of the persecution of the Jews in Germany.

The most evident source of weakness in this regard was the political attrition suffered by Jewry as a whole, but the Jews of Europe in particular, once that moment of almost legendary, now clearly fortuitous prestige enjoyed at the tail-end of the First World War had passed. One indicator of the straits to which the Europeans were reduced was the enhanced role of—and reliance upon—America, which is to say the United States and, more especially, American Jewry. It was a small but telling fact that an American, Rabbi Stephen S. Wise, leader of the now well-established American Jewish Congress and a major figure in the Jewish (religious) Reform movement, had taken the rostrum to open the proceedings in 1933. Wise was to continue to play quite as prominent a role in the affairs of the Congress as the real stalwarts of the Comité, Leo Motzkin and his successor Nahum Goldmann, were to assume. While real enough, Wise's importance and influence were essentially contingent. They lay partly in his serving as one of WJC's principal links to the Zionist Organization and *its* Congresses. But in the Zionist movement itself they were contingent first and foremost on his prominence at home, namely in the society, politics, and Jewish community (loosely conceived, to be sure) of the United States. Within the United States his reputation, almost uniquely among men and women who were prominent in Jewish public life, extended well beyond the limits of American Jewry. He was known as a champion of important social causes: women's suffrage and the supervision or abolition of child labour among others. He was known too as one of the leaders of the campaign launched against the new regime in Germany, recognized as such by the National Socialists themselves as headlined reports of his speeches in *Der Angriff* and the *Völkischer Beobachter* attested. Few figures prominent in contemporary Jewry were capable of denouncing National Socialist Germany in such ringing tones as he, nor, in the early years of the regime, were there very many who were willing to try to do so. He had a fairly sharp eye for weakness in Jewry itself. He had nothing but pity, he said, for those German Jews who had assured him and his colleagues in 1932 that Adolf Hitler would 'not dare to be as ruthless and merciless to German Jews as he had threatened to be, and as he has invited his followers to prove themselves'. In fact, said Wise, this was the one respect, 'namely in the matter of delivering the Jews of Germany as prey to be hunted and wronged by the Reich', in which the new regime had immediately been 'equal to its promises'.[18] All told, Wise went further, it seems, than any other single individual towards providing the World Jewish Congress with its indispensable moral guarantee.

In Rabbi Wise's book morality and politics were indeed inseparable. Of his utterly genuine, even passionate, concern for the Jews of Europe in their plight there can be no question.[19] But there was, at the same time, a certain remoteness and lack of specificity about his approach to their affairs, a tendency to see them, and much else too, in universal and therefore somewhat abstract terms. The exception was always where a concrete case of an individual in great and immediate need of assistance was brought before him, but this tendency may have had something to do with the circumstance that the true locus of his life did, after all, lie elsewhere, namely in the United States. The degree to which he had internalized American culture, values, and style (Wise had been taken to live in the United States as a very small child) was more than apparent in the preachy rhetoric of which he was, in fact, an acknowledged master. The Jewish people, he told his colleagues in 1933, had, once again, been

called upon to suffer, for we are the suffering servants of humanity. . . . We do not rebel against the tragic role which we must play if only the nations of the earth may achieve some gain, may profit as a result of our sufferings, may realize in time the enormity of the danger they face in that common enemy of mankind which has no other aim than to conquer and destroy. We are ready if only the precious and beautiful things of life may survive. That is once again the mission of the Jews. We stand on the front line, in the first row of the trenches.[20]

Still, none of this accounts for the lapse of three years between the *Machtergeifung* in Germany and the formal foundation of the World Jewish

---

[18] *Protocole de la IIe conférence*, 21–2. Other delegates recalled the response of the delegates from Germany in sharper terms. W. Wislicki pointed out that at the WJC preliminary conference the year before the German delegates had wanted no discussion of the National Socialist menace at all, that they had claimed that the von Papen government could be trusted to fight Hitler, and that he, Hitler, would not attain power anyway. When Wislicki himself had proposed that a distinction be drawn between Jews who were citizens *à part entière* of a given country and Jews who were members of distinct minority groups, the German delegates 'declared categorically that they would not take up the question of minorities and that before all else they were good Germans and only then Jews'. No delegates from Germany were in attendance at the 1933 meeting, nor subsequently. Ibid. 70f.

[19] Although, as Max Warburg told the American ambassador in Berlin, he and his brother Felix—leading members of the Warburg banking family, Felix in New York and Max in Hamburg, and arch-representatives of the contemporary Jewish plutocratic class—thought otherwise. Wise and Samuel Untermyer were driven by a 'craving for publicity', Max Warburg informed Ambassador Dodd, and the two Warburgs were 'fully in sympathy with Colonel House in his efforts to ease off the Jewish boycott and reduce the number of Jews in high position in the United States' (W. E. Dodd, *Ambassador Dodd's Diary, 1933–1938* (New York, 1941), 147).

[20] Ibid. 62.

Congress as a fully fledged institution, the more so as the promulgation of the Nuremberg Laws was not the only blow delivered to the Jews of Europe in the long interim. The condition of the Jews of Poland had taken the severe turn for the worse after Pilsudski's death that has already been noted. In Romania the exceedingly violent Iron Guard was in the ascendant once more and draconic anti-Jewish legislation was in the process of being implemented. And elsewhere too bits and pieces of legislation understood by all concerned to be harmful to Jews were in the process of being promulgated to a constant background noise of ever nastier, ever more strongly resonating anti-Semitic propaganda. This was either on the new, explicitly racist German model or else the non-specific, but distinctly xenophobic variety of which the French law passed in 1934 laying down that a lawyer of foreign birth would only be allowed to practise his profession ten years *after* naturalization was an eminent example.

As if to confirm that these were auguries of worse to come, James McDonald, the newly appointed high commissioner for refugees at the League of Nations, an American who, for his class and nationality, was unusually sympathetic to the plight of Jews, resigned his post at the end of 1935. His well-meaning effort to engineer massive diplomatic and moral pressure on Germany had come to nothing. The careful disconnection of his functions, along with those of the Commission over which he was expected to preside, from the League of Nations lest Germany be offended had undercut the very limited authority he had hoped to possess. It had become abundantly plain that there was no prospect of the League as such through its Council, or any of the major constituent states either singly or in concert, exerting any pressure on the new German regime. And McDonald's own energetic attempts to encourage the admission of Jewish refugees from Germany and elsewhere into countries in which circumstances seemed objectively favourable to their resettlement had all fallen flat. It was at the members of the League that he addressed his sharpest criticism, his main charge being that he had been given no means of dealing with the root of the problem of the Jews of Germany, namely their persecution, only with the results. But he had already had something to say (privately) about the response of those in Jewry who to his mind were profoundly remiss in their social duty to their brethren.

More and more I am convinced that tragic as is the plight of the refugees and of German Jewry within the Reich, this is merely today's version of a century old problem which will continue to defeat the efforts of those who strive for a solution through temporary and half-hearted expedients. . . . Obviously I, even after my experience of the past two years, am in no position to set myself up as a critic in these matters. Nonetheless, as I come in close personal contact with Jewish leaders and with representatives of the Jewish masses in many parts of the world,

I am again and again struck by the futility of some of the most highly placed and most wealthy Jews. Some of these seem to me, almost in proportion as they have risen in the commercial world, to have lost their moral authority and the will or even the desire to play any worthy rôle in the present crisis. In other words, men who might be expected to do most do least, or at any rate much less than many persons with a tiny fraction of their material resources; and in some situations the utter failure of the natural leaders to lead or to be willing to take the least chance or to make a tiny sacrifice, has made immeasurably more difficult the task of other members of the community.[21]

That the founders of the World Jewish Congress-to-be wanted the full and public backing of the Zionist Organization before they set out to fly their own flag goes part of the way towards explaining the otherwise seemingly inexplicable delay establishing it formally. There was also the loss sustained in the death of Leo Motzkin, long the prime energizer of the effort to create a distinct, supra-communal Diaspora organization of some sort, of almost any sort, at the end of 1933. But his replacement, Nahum Goldmann, while a man of a different stamp, hardly the totally dedicated, somewhat puritanical secular saint that Motzkin had been, but more the relaxed, skilled operator and would-be fashionable man of the world, at any rate had the gift of boundless energy and an insatiable appetite for life. Goldmann would end by being regarded as shrewder and more formidable than was initially assumed, even if, unlike Motzkin, he was always approached somewhat warily and rarely with affection. There was the difficulty, moreover, of his having been appointed the Zionist Organization's own representative at the League of Nations (replacing the veteran Victor Jacobson) in 1935, precisely therefore at the time when the World Jewish Congress was in the process of construction. And this ran right against the grain of what was now, once again, the accepted wisdom in the higher reaches of the Zionist Organization, namely that the related and therefore parallel struggles for the National Home in Palestine on the one hand and for the rights of the Jews as a minority in the Diaspora on the other needed to be kept in separate compartments. This revival of the old Herzlian rule derived partly from the personal preference, already noted, of many of those concerned for a clear division of labour, but there were good technical and tactical reasons for keeping the two operations apart as well. In Poland, as we have seen, the Zionists *as such* had reason to expect support from the authorities. Were their representatives to double as spokesmen for the local Jewish minority, they would find themselves locked in conflict with the Poles like all other Jewish spokesmen. Goldmann, however, was never a man to shy away from the simultaneous assumption of a variety of offices and

---

[21] Letter to Weizmann, 4 June 1935, WA. Weizmann's reply, if there was one, has not been found.

tasks.[22] In the event, by the time the definitive World Jewish Congress convened at last in Geneva on 8–15 August 1936 its umbilical tie to the Zionist Organization was not in doubt. The sister organization conferred its formal blessing on the WJC at its own 19th Congress the year before.[23] Stephen Wise, serving once again as keynote speaker, came to Geneva to reiterate and, as it were, embody the connection. And the question whether anything of importance had been or would be lost by conferring these two sets of responsibilities on Goldmann personally was swallowed up by the larger one of whether the actual strategies and immediate purposes of the two organizations were really compatible.

IV

In general outlook, the leading spirits in both the WJC and the WZO saw eye to eye. 'We live,' said one of the delegates at the founding session of the World Jewish Congress in 1936,

in times when both international law and the internal juridical order of the State are driven by national interest. The organization, legislation, tendencies, and purposes of our society all carry the national label. The very constitution of our world, as provided for by the peace treaties along with the appendices regulating the condition of the minorities, is founded on the national criterion. In these circumstances, inclusion in the juridical order and the ability to follow the general tendency that moves society depends on our own capacity for self-discipline and an organisation established on the same foundations.[24]

No delegate to a Zionist Congress could have put the point more firmly. Still, on the matter of self-definition, the notes struck were somewhat contradictory. The 291[25] delegates from thirty-two countries (eighty from the United States alone) who attended all agreed to declare themselves to be a comprehensive organization representing Jews of all views and conditions, people who had been brought together on 'a new plane', not so much for negotiation as 'for an interchange of views touching every manner of Jewish problems with a view to their solution'. Charity, they wished it to be understood, was no longer enough. It was a time for moral, economic, and political self-defence. 'Unreadiness to act organizedly in defence of, and for the safeguarding of the rights of Jews [was] . . . an invitation, a temptation, and a provocation to the enemies of Israel.'

[22] Nathan Feinberg, *Pirkei ḥayyim ve-zikhronot* (Jerusalem, 1985), 137–8.
[23] *Stenographisches Protokoll der Verhandlungen des XIX Zionistenkongresses, Luzern, 20. August bis 6 Septembre 1935* (Vienna, 1937), 624 f.
[24] Congrès Juif Mondial, *Protocole du premier congrès juif mondial, Genève, 8–15 août 1936* (Geneva, n.d.), 191.
[25] Some sources give the figure of 280 delegates present.

Stephen Wise thought it necessary, however, to declare on their behalf with equal force that the Congress neither 'sought [n]or purported to be a Parliament. A Parliament is a legal, national institution which is the legislative instrument of the State. Jews as Jews have no State and therefore can have no Parliament. . . .'[26] The Congress, he reminded his listeners, had no powers of compulsion. It had not been directly elected. It was not representative of the *entire* Jewish people. There neither would nor could be a Jewish congress that was representative of the people in its entirety. 'Surely one may say [therefore], that the so-called secret Protocols of the Elders of Zion could hardly be attributed with sanity to an assembly [such as this one that had been] openly called and publicly held'. Nevertheless, said Wise, the Congress would go far to express the 'will and purpose of a people' which 'wilful . . . small . . . group[s] of timorous or assimilationist Jews' known to beset it would not 'have it within [their] power . . . to annul'.[27] And there was more at the opening sessions of such anticipatory triumphalism.

None of this is possible any longer since our emancipation [Nahum Goldmann told the assembly] and it is futile to debate whether it would be better if matters were otherwise. No discussion is as unfruitful as one which poses the question 'if' about historical reality and actual contemporary conditions. We are no longer in the ghetto. The last remnants of the ghetto were destroyed in the World War. We have been involved in the evolution of Europe for more than a century. . . . There is for us no way back to the ghetto.[28]

The enemy, Goldmann went on to assure the delegates, was not nationalism, not nationalism in its proper, just, and organic form, that is to say. It was when it had taken on the immoral, illegitimate, and destructive form of 'state-nationalism', when it was engaged in brutalizing the world, and the weak of the world before all others, that it was evil and needed to be resisted. But it would fail,

Because it is an anachronism, because in the age of radio and aeroplanes the omnipotence of States, with their borders and tolls, their economic autarchy and their crazy monetary manipulations, presents a structure of absurdity that must be overcome and will be overcome.

As for the Jews themselves,

We shall survive the age. Only we must not crawl away and hide and we must not despair. Today we must organize, proclaim our rights to a world that hardly listens to us and concentrate our energies on self-help and co-operation in the great historic struggle that is to be sustained. With the right ideas we will carry through and tomorrow we shall triumph.[29]

Some speakers ventured to cut closer to the bone of the Jewish condition.

[26] *Protocole du premier congrès juif mondial*, 12–13.   [27] Ibid. 12–14.
[28] Ibid. 33.   [29] Ibid. 52–4.

Dr Samuel Singer, a member of the Romanian parliament and a prominent figure in that country's Jewish community, reminded the participants, that

Our masses and our intellectual and professional circles see the steady disappearance of possibilities of integration into the socio-economic machinery of the states in which we live and are terrified by it. Our places and functions are in the process of being taken over by forces that enjoy superior protection and against which we have insufficient means of resistance. All this takes place against the background of uproar in the press and savage street demonstrations against us Jews which the authorities upon whom we have to rely hardly ever put down.

None the less, said Singer, the Jews needed to attend not only to the violence and injustice inflicted upon them by others, but to the internal disorder that reigned among themselves. The general picture in Jewry was one of chaos: as had already been said in the course of the present Congress, the internal order of things, politically and socially, was better when the Jews were still enclosed within their ghettos. What was devastating the Jews at the present time was the fact that the attack mounted against them from without was coupled inexorably to deep disunity within.

Internal anarchy in Jewry combined with currents of political anti-Semitism released by those who have held or who now hold state power have reduced us to a condition, as in Romania, for example, in which substantial strata of our population have lost all socio-economic standing [*ont été complètement déclassés*].

And so, while

Berlin has extended powerful, visible and invisible tentacles that encompass the globe we have allowed the years to pass, perhaps the last years in which we might be able to prepare seriously to defend ourselves, but which we have devoted to discussions with the cautious Board of Deputies and the [B'nai B'rith] to see whether a World Jewish Congress ought or ought not to be established.

Jewry is in danger of foundering as region after region and state after state fall under Nazi influence and we remain as we are, crushed, busy discussing the legitimacy of an organization of worldwide defence—as worldwide and comprehensive as the attack to which we are subject.[30]

The problem for the Congress itself was not how and in what precise terms the internal ills and external enemies of Jewry were to be identified. These were all more than familiar. The pressing and more difficult question was what the Congress itself was now to *do*? A proposal that a general campaign against anti-Semitism be launched was easily agreed upon. A central bureau to collate, edit, and disseminate appropriate anti-anti-Semitic material to relevant centres and persons of influence and to

[30] Nahum Goldmann, *Protocole du premier congrès juif mondial*, 191–5.

the press would be established. And it was agreed too that wherever possible legal action would be taken against those who denigrated and persecuted the Jews.

These were not always entirely empty words. The World Jewish Congress managed to play a contributory role in the western powers' effort to get rid of the fascistically inclined and violently anti-Semitic Octavian Goga within weeks of his being appointed prime minister by King Carol (on 28 December 1937). France and Great Britain had strong political and strategic reasons of their own for wanting a Romanian leader who was less likely to move that country still further into the German-Italian orbit incidentally subjecting their Romanian investments to a threat of expropriation. But they found it helpful in their effort to persuade the king to find someone who was more to their liking when the WJC, rightly and hugely alarmed by Goga's National Christian Party's assumption of power, pressed them to invoke the relevant 1919 minorities treaty and to go so far as to support a full appeal against Romania at the Council of the League of Nations. Goga was only days in office when plans to divide the Jews once again into those who could prove their right to citizenship by standards the government would now lay down afresh and those who could not were being formulated. Those who failed to do so, Goga told the American minister in Bucharest, would have to leave the country.[31] The king, nothing loath, dismissed him on 10 February 1938, to form a non-party 'advisory government' which had the advantage of leaving effective power in his own hands. Goga declared dramatically upon his dismissal, 'Judah, you have vanquished me'; and the WJC, greatly tempted to agree with him, pursued its effort to bring Romania to court before the Council of the League despite the inevitable, disingenuous Romanian warning that the government—the new one in this case—would come down hard on the Jewish minority and follow what the Romanian foreign minister termed 'the Polish example',[32] namely threaten to withdraw from the League altogether if the matter was ever allowed to come up. But in any event, the WJC's victory, if victory it was, was only in the short term and was soon forgotten. The feelings and afterthoughts of the western diplomats involved[33] had been as mixed as were their motives. 'If we are not careful,' a senior official in London had commented on the morrow of Goga's dismissal, 'we will drift into the position where His Majesty's Government will be expected to make

[31] Gunther to Hull, 5 Jan. 1938, FRUS 1938, ii (Washington, 1955), 672.

[32] Reginald Hoare, the British minister in Bucharest, to Halifax, 14 Apr. 1938, PRO, FO 371/22454/3938.

[33] French and British alone in this instance, it needs to be stressed. Asked whether they would be willing to be associated with an action on behalf of Romanian Jewry, the Americans made clear that not being parties to the treaty there could be no question of their joining in any such action. Bullitt to Hull, 1 Feb. 1938, FRUS 1938, i. 6.

representations on behalf of the Jewish minority as though they had some
special duty and *locus standi* to do so, whereas of course our only *locus
standi* for any sort of intervention is the fact that we are one of the signatories of the Minorities Treaties and concerned to see that the procedure
adopted in order to implement them is being duly observed.'[34] And of
course there where it mattered most, in Germany, there was no treaty
guaranteeing the rights of minorities and therefore no corresponding
legal lever for the WJC to activate. When, a month or so later, Hitler's
Wehrmacht entered Vienna, Germany and Austria were joined together,
and the Jews of Austria were subjected to unprecedented ritual humiliation, the brief and purely marginal diplomatic triumph in Bucharest
paled far too rapidly before this new display of helplessness to retain lasting importance or even to be remembered.[35]

The greater problem remained. What was to be done where legal
action was futile or ruled out for formal reasons or where the enemy was
exceptionally powerful and dangerous and visibly impervious to such
small darts as the WJC or other Jewish groups or organizations were capable
of employing against it, where, in a word, Germany and its allies were
concerned. Here the Congress was apt, of necessity, to fall back on an
invitation to 'the Jews of the world to take up the challenge of National-
Socialism and to answer it with energetic resistance until full moral, legal
and civil quality is restored to German Jewry, and until the hatred and
defamation of Jewish history and the honour of the Jewish people
ceases'.[36] To the further, ineluctable question what this might mean in
actual practice, the best answer it could offer was that 'Jewish communities throughout the world' should, 'as a measure of defence of Jewish
honour', persevere with the boycott of German goods and services that
was already, independently, in train—subject (as the draftsmen of the
resolution were careful to add) to such legal conditions and regulations as
might obtain in any one of the relevant, individual countries.[37]

The call to carry on with the anti-Nazi economic boycott was a case
of leaders following the led, however, the WJC declaring approval of
what had started up spontaneously and in very nearly every part of the
Jewish world almost immediately upon the installation of the National
Socialists in power in Germany in 1933 and the promulgation of the first
of their major anti-Jewish decrees. Local initiative and the indignation of
private individuals had ensured that what seems to have been sparked off
earliest of all in Vilna spread rapidly to Warsaw and the rest of Poland,

[34] Minute by Orme Sargent, 12 Feb. 1938, PRO, FO 371/22453/251.
[35] I am grateful to Dr Gerhart Riegner for drawing the affair of Goga's enforced resignation to my attention and for very kindly allowing me to see relevant passages in his still
unpublished memoirs.
[36] *Résolutions adoptées par le premier congres juif mondial* (Geneva, [1936]), *passim* and 36.
[37] Ibid. 51.

from there to other parts of Europe, and then across the Atlantic. It was not long before a United Boycott Committee had been formed in Poland, an analogous council to co-ordinate activities had been set up in Great Britain, and a well-organized campaign was being run in the United States on a very large scale under the able leadership of Samuel Untermyer. Untermyer, a prominent lawyer and civic leader, vice-president of the American Jewish Congress, and soon to function as president of the Non Sectarian Anti-Nazi League, was known among other things for his considerable contribution to the drafting of the new Federal banking, trade, and anti-trust legislation inaugurated under Franklin D. Roosevelt's Democratic administration.

The boycott campaign in Poland came to an end two years later when the post-Pilsudski Polish regime resolved to enforce the relevant stipulations of the German–Polish non-aggression pact of 1934.[38] But elsewhere, especially in Great Britain and the United States, it gathered steam all the while and prospered. The means varied somewhat from country to country, but the spirit and intention were much the same everywhere: to demonstrate public sentiment and indignation—first and foremost among Jews, to be sure, but so far as possible in the non-Jewish public as well.[39] Where Jews were concerned, the appeal was before all else to loyalty underlined by an implicit threat that those who were deficient in it and put their business interests first would be stigmatized. In Britain committees were formed in all major centres of Jewish population, pamphlets were published, posters were printed for shopkeepers to put up in their shop windows to advertise the *non*-German origin of their goods, marches were held through the East End of London and along to the German embassy and on one occasion to a mass meeting in Hyde Park. There was no violence to speak of apart from occasional scuffles between militants and such Jewish traders as had been found, or were suspected of, violating the boycott. A Jewish community's traditional ability to ostracize members charged with what was thought to be impermissible behaviour still counted for something, but generally speaking the public co-operated willingly and the response was no less than massive: 530 delegates representing 360 Jewish organizations of various kinds with a total membership of 170,000 were present at the inaugural conference in London of the Jewish Representative Council for the Boycott of German Goods and Services held early in November 1933[40]—despite the fact that the formally representative body of British Jewry, the Board of Deputies, refused to play any part whatsoever. As in so many other

[38] Alfred Wislicki, 'The Jewish Boycott Campaign against Nazi Germany and its Culmination in the Halbersztadt Trial', *Polin: Studies in Polish Jewry*, 8 (London, 1994), 282–9.

[39] In the United States the powerful American Federation of Labor was helpful and sympathetic without going so far as to declare its support openly.

[40] Gewirtz, 'Anglo-Jewish Responses', *passim*.

matters of a political character, it stood shoulder to shoulder in this with the American Jewish Committee, a less strictly and formally representative body than the Board, but still the most senior and influential of the Jewish bodies in the United States at the time, its old associate the Alliance, and, on this occasion, with the semi-official Consistoire Central of France as well.

The grounds for the Board's refusal to place itself at the head of the campaign or at the very least offer it open support were of several kinds and changed over time. But all derived in one way or another from the extreme caution with which its leaders habitually approached public business, notably so where the prospect of finding themselves out of step with the government and with English public opinion was palpable. A strain of resistance to the pressures and emotions generated by the commonalty of Jewry ran through its performance in these years as well. This was never so powerful as to inhibit the Board from launching a continuous, devoted, and substantially if certainly incompletely successful effort to press the British government to relax its immigrant admissions policy. And it participated heavily and effectively in the mobilization of aid to such refugees from central Europe as had been allowed into the country. But the established, firmly oligarchic tendency of its then leaders to keep as much as possible of the public business of the Jews of Britain in their own safe hands—in contrast to those of the embarrassingly noisy and turbulent people who were constantly assailing them for their feebleness—continued to mark everything it did. It was 'axiomatic', the president of the Board, Neville Laski, told the Board in its assembly, when he was called upon in March 1933 to proclaim the boycott and sponsor a protest meeting, that Jews should feel sympathy for their German brethren. But, so long as there was a chance of improvement, 'We must do nothing and say nothing which can be misinterpreted and utilized by the left wing of the Nazi movement to crush the advice . . . which von Papen and the moderates in the German government have given to their followers.'[41] It was his view, he said on another occasion, that 'Every action designed to show the Nazi regime that persecution does not pay is commendable, but I would add, and as a loyal citizen it is essential that I should add, that such action as is taken must be conditioned by, and be subject to the overriding consideration of duty and loyalty to the country of which we are citizens.'[42]

[41] Cited in Gewirtz, 'Anglo-Jewish Responses', 259. It was borne in upon Laski in the course of time that Hitler was not a moderate. After *Kristallnacht* he and his colleagues concluded that the reinstitution of equality for the Jews of Germany was in fact a lost cause: 'The strongest utterances of indignation could not help the Jews of Germany who must be rescued as quickly as possible,' he told the Board on 16 Nov. 1938. 'There was nothing left among German Jewry but desperation and a very faint hope that they might find refuge in a kindlier country' (ibid. 265).

[42] *Jewish Chronicle*, 4 Oct. 1935. Cited in Gewirtz, 'Anglo-Jewish Responses', 258.

Laski knew that while the British government would not openly oppose or obstruct the anti-Nazi boycott, it disliked it. Officers of the Metropolitan Police had been sent to visit Jewish shopkeepers in the East End of London and advise them to remove boycott notices from their shop windows—on the grounds, the Home Secretary, Sir John Gilmour, explained to the House of Commons, that the display of such posters might cause 'feeling' that would, in turn, lead to 'breaches of the peace'.[43] When Laski met the Permanent Under-Secretary of State at the Foreign Office on 1 January 1934, Sir Robert Vansittart spoke to him in terms that were quite as fierce as (had either of them known it) those employed by the wartime British ambassador in Washington who had wanted the representatives of British Jewry warned of the consequences they might incur if the anti-Allied (more precisely, anti-Russian) activities of their cousins in the United States did not cease.[44] Vansittart, as Laski reported to his colleagues, said that

Information had come to him which justified him in saying that the aggressively Jewish, flamboyant and narrow character of the anti-German propaganda carried on by certain Jewish quarters in America was having results which were very nearly provocation of anti-semitism on a large scale. His advices were such as to justify him in saying that unless the soft pedal were put upon this type of propaganda and it approximated more to the type in which we [i.e. the Board of Deputies] had indulged . . ., there would soon be a serious outbreak of anti-semitism in the United States. People were fed up with Untermyer. . . . They are tired of having 'Jew' dinned in their ears. He referred to the JRC [the Jewish Representative Council for the Boycott of German Goods and Services] and the campaign they initiated. He said he disapproved as much as ever of their goings-on. He said that if it were not for the fact that a hint even of the most discreet character might be misinterpreted, a hint would have been given long ago to these people that their activities in the present form were distasteful to His Majesty's Government. He said that he approved of the use of an economic weapon against Germany, but he did not approve of a flamboyant user of such a weapon.[45]

Clearly, therefore, as a gesture of defiance, the boycott was making a mark of some kind. Thus outside Germany; but thus in Germany itself as well, having been noted, disliked, and been the cause of the government taking some not very serious countermeasures. Was it of any practical use, however? Was it likely to bring political results of any kind in its wake? At the World Jewish Congress in 1936 figures were adduced to show that the German economy was faltering and was (or ought to be) vulnerable to external pressure. Its export trade, the delegates were told, had fallen since the *Machtergreifung*: by 20.7 per cent worldwide, by 4.2 per cent in the United States alone. How far this was due to the boycott as opposed,

---

[43] Ibid. 268.   [44] See Chapter 7.
[45] BoD Archives, C11/6/4. Cited in Gewirtz, 'Anglo-Jewish Responses', 267.

for example, to American anti-dumping legislation no one could say.[46] But in any event, if the boycott was to have an impact that went beyond minor pinpricks and some small damage to German public relations in foreign parts two assumptions had to be realized. The economic power of the Jews would have to be shown to be truly formidable; and they themselves would have to be willing and able to employ such power effectively and coherently. But the former assumption had ceased to be tenable: the special circumstances that had allowed it to flourish briefly during the First World War had dissolved; and the latter, as was more than apparent, was baseless.

This had much to do in turn with the now deeply fragmented condition of Jewry. It was in part because, as Morris Myer, editor of the leading Yiddish-language newspaper in Great Britain and a leader of the boycott movement, put it at a session of the Board of Deputies in May 1933, 'the policy of the assimilationist Jews . . . is that Jews as Jews don't count, [that] we are to act as citizens of the country. We are to leave it to others, to the great men, to the Press to make protest. We are to do nothing ourselves.'[47] But it had at least as much to do with there having emerged from within the politically radical, nationalist wing of Jewish public life itself a countervailing policy founded on a very different view. Not only might it be right and proper for organized Jewry to meet the crisis precipitated by the Nazis' rise to power but efforts should be made to determine what should be done in the wider Jewish interest to most practical and palpable effect. This was an altogether more focused, more pragmatic, and very consciously hard-headed view of the matter than that which the boycott party had made its own. They shared the same craving for pride, dignity, and autonomy, but steered in practice in entirely different directions. One result was the Transfer Agreement between the World Zionist Organization and the German government, an agreement that no one denied was with the devil, that had begun as an entirely private venture proposed and entered into with the German authorities by a Palestinian-Jewish entrepreneur, but which the WZO, after some hesitation (and several rather mean and futile attempts first to deny involvement and then to claim the privilege of secrecy) had first agreed to support from the shadows, but had finally taken over as an act of major policy of its own.

The substance of the Transfer Agreement (entered into in its initial version on 22 August 1933) was simple enough. It was an arrangement whereby the German government, chiefly in the interests of expediting the evacuation of Germany by German Jews, but marginally too in the

---

[46] *Protocole du premier congrès juif mondial*, 288–93.

[47] *Jewish Telegraphic Agency*, 15 May 1933. Cited in Gewirtz, 'Anglo-Jewish Responses', 258.

interests of extending its markets, allowed those who were possessed of some capital to transfer part of it to Palestine in the form of German export goods. Money paid into a Jewish trust company established in Germany for the purpose would cover the cost of German goods shipped to Palestine for sale there. The proceeds of the sale would then be paid to the immigrants on or after their arrival. The arrangement was profitable to the Germans on other counts as well. It drove a wedge within Jewry—those within the National Socialist government who favoured the deal citing this as part of *their* justification for entering into an agreement with the race enemy. Only a fraction of the assets held by German Jews would be allowed to be transferred in this manner: the bulk of their property and material resources—rated at 6 billion RM at the time—being subject to confiscation. The heavy 'escape tax' (the *Reichsfluchtsteuer*)[48] had still to be paid by all leaving the country. And there were other charges which reduced the value of the capital emigrants were able to transfer by these means. From the National Socialist point of view the disadvantage of the scheme was that only a fraction—roughly a tenth—of German Jewry was able and willing to take advantage of the Agreement. In post-*Anschluss* Austria it was not allowed to be applied at all: Austrian Jews able and willing to leave were fated, overwhelmingly, to be extruded without a penny. But there was no dispute but that the Transfer Agreement offered a fair number of people the sole means whereby they might depart Germany without delay and in a condition that was better than destitution. Nor was there any question of it being the rule almost everywhere that the ability of a Jew from Germany or anywhere else to gain admittance to another country depended before all else on his economic condition and assets. This was famously the case even in Palestine. Migrants who could show that they were in possession of £1,000 were admitted freely as 'capitalists' in excess of the otherwise severe quotas laid down from time to time.

None the less, the commonest, most immediate, and, it may be said, most natural response of people both within and without the Zionist movement to news of the Transfer Agreement when it first leaked out was dismay at what was judged a scandalous transaction. That reputable businessmen, economists, bankers, but, more surprisingly and very much more distressingly, political leaders of the first rank too had identified a point at which the interests of the Jews coincided with those of the Germans and had acted upon it was almost beyond belief. They had made nonsense of the one small achievement that the Jews, collectively, had managed to notch up in the otherwise horrifyingly unequal struggle with National Socialist Germany. The boycott campaign might not have been supported by all, but that it should have been the one really well-established, markedly political, nationally minded, worldwide

---

[48] See Chapter 9.

Jewish movement—the Zionist Organization itself—that had taken an independent, dissident, not to say disloyal view of it was disgraceful. The public waters of Jewry had been muddied beyond repair. Admittedly, it was making it easier for German Jews to leave the country, although easier too for the Germans themselves to hurry Jews along the way. But even then it was the wealthy who were favoured. It did little or nothing for those of modest means and, ironically, it confronted the National Socialists (as they themselves were uncomfortably aware) with the prospect of the indigent staying on indefinitely.[49] In any event, the Transfer Agreement was an outrage. What, it was asked, remained of the Jews' grand attempt to stand on their dignity and, however limited the prospects of success, teach such free and liberal societies as were left a modest lesson in the confronting of evil. How was such a drastic, *public* departure from the vital rule of unity to be explained to ordinary folk? 'I am the president of the Jewish merchants of Poland and of the [Polish] Boycott Committee,' Waclaw Wislicki, a delegate to the WJC's preliminary conference in 1933, told his colleagues. 'What am I supposed to say to a little Polish Jew who comes to tell me that he wants to sell German goods too? "The Zionists do it," he tells me. "Why shouldn't I?"'[50]

Leo Motzkin, hugely unhappy, agreed. He had never favoured boycotts, he said. They struck at both the guilty and the innocent. There could be no question, of course, five months after the boycott had been launched, of opposing it. That would be to undermine a vital interest of the Jewish people. An evil government had turned upon the Jews. They, for their part, had responded by defensive action with the only weapon available to them, the people, as was always the case in such situations, preceding their leaders. As for the agreement that had been entered into with the Germans, so far as he knew (in September 1933), it was a private matter in which the Zionist Organization itself was not involved. Perhaps the WZO at its recent Congress should have been firmer on the subject. That had certainly been his view. Yes, he could see the logic of the arrangement: a matter of saving what could be saved. It was certainly not an act of betrayal. Still,

What good will it do us if some thousands of Jews be rescued in this way and their re-settlement in Palestine be made possible if it be seen as a breach of the [Jewish] front? The Jewish people is faced today by such catastrophes that it is capable of understanding only primitive [i.e. elemental] solutions. But I must ask you to understand that in none of these tendencies is there so much as a trace of betrayal of Jewry. What I said, from the very first moment, was that it was a great error; and that I shall endeavour to prevent it.[51]

---

[49] David Yisraeli, 'The Third Reich and the Transfer Agreement', *Journal of Contemporary History*, 6, 2 (1971), *passim*.
[50] *Protocole de la IIe conférence juive mondiale, Genève, 5–8 septembre 1933*, 70.
[51] Ibid. 82–3.

Stephen Wise, a fervent supporter of the boycott, was more circumspect when the issue came up. To be sure, the situation of German Jewry did now overshadow everything in Jewish life, he declared, and

the German Jewish problem is itself overshadowed and dominated by one question which must be answered by the [present] Executive in conference assembled. That question is: shall there be a world Jewish boycott of goods and wares and products manufactured in Germany? Put even more simply, shall Jews have any relation whatever, industrial or economic, with a nation which has declared war upon its own Jewish inhabitants, a nation which has declared war against the Jewish people everywhere by declaring that we Jews are an inferior, parasitic, empoisoning race of humanity?[52]

However, Wise did not condemn the Transfer Agreement outright, not even in the relatively mild terms Motzkin had chosen. Being most probably better informed about where the Zionist Executive actually stood on the matter and what precisely it was that it had sanctioned he was unwilling to quarrel with it openly. He limited himself to drawing a distinction between those who dealt with the Germans in the public interest and those who traded with them for private profit. Where the latter were concerned, he was firm: 'If it be proved to me that any Jew in or out of Palestine, or any representative of any group of Jews, has been so base as to attempt to do business with Germany for the sake of profit and gain, I attest,' he thundered, 'that life will not be bearable for any such man, in or out of Palestine.'[53] The distinction between public and private interest was a valid one, so far as it went. So was the argument that where the German Jews themselves and their ability to resettle elsewhere were concerned those whose lives and welfare were more secure had no choice but to agree that they must have a free hand to make the most of their limited possibilities. This left the question of the relevant moral imperatives open, as well as that of the actual *utility* of the Transfer Agreement itself.

V

The strength of the World Zionist Organization *vis-à-vis* the World Jewish Congress and, indeed, all other organizations whose concerns and membership were concentrated on and in the Diaspora went far beyond its being in important respects the model. Its strength lay in its excellent central organization, even though this was divided between London and Jerusalem, in its open membership, its fully parliamentary procedures, and in its ability to offer an implicit indictment of the manner in which virtually all other supra-Jewish communal organizations were formed and operated. It now had numbers too: its worldwide, paid-up membership

[52] Ibid. 23.   [53] Ibid. 63.

quadrupled after the First World War, dipped by about a third in the late 1920s, but from 1933 on picked up rapidly. It had firm party organizations, each a social and cultural indeed moral world unto itself. It had recognized leaders, youth organizations, and a network of agricultural training farms and schools for some of which it took direct responsibility while others were associated with it through their respective parent groups, the Zionist political parties themselves. Finally, under the terms of the Mandate and a host of *ad hoc* arrangements with the British Administration in Palestine, it held the central (although not exclusive) key to such Jewish immigration as the Mandatory regime was prepared to allow into the country at any given time. Most important of all, it was the preponderant influence on the lives of the Jewish population of Palestine, the *yishuv*.

TABLE 10.1. *Membership of the World Zionist Organization, 1911–1939*

Congress	Paid-up, voting members	Delegates
1911 (Basel)	175,894	387
1913 (Vienna)	217,231	539
1921 (Karlsbad)	855,590	512
1923 (Karslbad)	957,982	331
1925 (Vienna)	938,157	311
1927 (Basel)	631,151	281
1929 (Zurich)	604,616	310
1931 (Basel)	627,237	254
1933 (Prague)	843,607	318
1935 (Lucerne)	1,216,640	463
1937 (Zurich)	1,222,214	478
1939 (Geneva)	1,416,280	527

It was this latter factor before all else that put it in a class to which none of its rivals in contemporary Jewish public life could belong or even aspire. Its power base, uniquely, was political and territorial. It enjoyed a fixed and statutory status in the eyes of both the relevant imperial power and those of the League of Nations and the League's Permanent Mandates Commission.[54] Through the Jewish Agency Executive with which the Executive of the Zionist Organization itself was inextricably inter-

---

[54] The wording of the relevant articles of the Mandate was as follows: '*Article 2*: The Mandatory shall be responsible for placing the country under such political, administrative and economic conditions as will secure the establishment of the Jewish national home, as laid down in the preamble, and the development of self-governing institutions, and also for safeguarding the civil and religious rights of all the inhabitants of Palestine, irrespective of race and religion. . . . *Article 3*: The Mandatory shall, so far as circumstances permit, encourage local autonomy. . . . *Article 4*: An appropriate Jewish agency shall be recognized as a public body for the purpose of advising and co-operating with the Administration of

mingled, it formed what the members of the 1937 Royal Commission on Palestine in their *Report* judged to be nothing less than 'a Government existing side by side with the Mandatory Government'.[55] As the Commission's members had quickly discovered, the Jewish Agency/Zionist Executive stood at the peak of a pyramidal network of interlocking social, economic, financial, educational, and military institutions, chief of which were the elected Va'ad Le'umi (or Representative Council) of the Jewish population of the country (as opposed to the *world*wide Zionist Organization), the Histadrut workers' organization, and the semi-clandestine military arm of the *yishuv*, the Haganah.

To some or all of these each of the Jewish inhabitants of Mandatory Palestine adhered: supporting and reinforcing them, but also, in turn, being in some respects dependent upon them. Together with lesser, associated institutions, they provided the great majority of the Jews of Palestine with trade union protection and often with employment itself, with schooling for their children, with books and libraries, with high, middle, and to a limited extent low culture too, with housing, and with health care. Taxes were collected. Funds were budgeted and disbursed for public purposes. Armed defence was provided. And all this and more was carried on with minimal reference to the Mandatory government or none at all; and, in certain spheres, where necessary, in covert or even overt defiance of it. Thus within the *yishuv* internally. But the Jewish Agency/Zionist Executive functioned as its recognized external representative as well, serving therefore, in a manner analogous to that of a formally sovereign government, both as the central political motor force of the community over which it was placed—or, as its opponents, not entirely without justice, preferred to say, it had placed itself—*and* as that community's spokesman in its relations with the authentically sovereign

---

Palestine in such economic, social and other matters as may affect the establishment of the Jewish national home and the interests of the Jewish population in Palestine, and, subject always to the control of the Administration, to assist and take part in the development of the country. . . . The Zionist organisation, so long as its organization and constitution are in the opinion of the Mandatory appropriate, shall be recognized as such agency. It shall take steps in consultation with His Britannic Majesty's Government to secure the co-operation of all Jews who are willing to assist in the establishment of the Jewish national home.'

[55] Having written what remains to this day much the clearest and most penetrating analysis of the so-called Palestine Problem, the authors of the Peel Commission's *Report* deserve to be quoted in full on the role of the Jewish Agency: 'Allied as it is to the *Va'ad Le'umi*, and commanding the allegiance of the great majority of the Jews in Palestine, it unquestionably exercises, both in Jerusalem and in London, a considerable influence on the conduct of Government. Speaking generally, it may be said that the Jewish Agency has used to the fullest extent the position conferred on it by the Mandate. In the course of time it has created a complete administrative apparatus. This powerful and effective organization amounts, in fact, to a Government existing side by side with the Mandatory Government.' Palestine Royal Commission, *Report*, Cmd. 5479 (London, 1937), 174.

governments of the day, that of the United Kingdom, of course, before all others.

The cumulative effect over time was to reinforce its supremacy in the *yishuv* and to intensify the reliance of the Jews of Palestine upon it. But the Jewish Agency/Zionist Executive derived its special efficacy and authority no less from the fact that by the early 1930s it had come to be dominated by a single, remarkably well-organized, and potent political party. This was the moderately (in the course of time, no more than nominally) socialist Mapai[56] or Labour Party led by the equally remarkable David Ben-Gurion. Neither the political cohesiveness which was one of the distinguishing marks of the Palestinian Jewish community *despite* the deep party-political divisions periodically sundering it nor the sheer capacity for decisive action in hard circumstances that was the special mark of its elected leadership can be accounted for without due attention being paid to the efficacy of Mapai as a structured party. It is the case, too, that Mapai's internal strength and confidence and its undeviating, at times bitter, determination to rule the Palestinian-Jewish roost cannot be fully accounted for without equally close attention being paid to the role of David Ben-Gurion as, at one and the same time, its leader, principal founder, and in a profound sense its incarnation.

In its origins Mapai was an amalgam of two fairly distinct socialist-Zionist parties, one being roughly analogous in its (initial) outlook to the Marxist, would-be proletarian, Russian Social Democratic Workers' Party, the other closer in spirit to the more peasant-oriented Socialist Revolutionary Party. Union between them having been achieved, Mapai, was launched on its unremitting fight for a dominant presence in all the relevant institutions of the *yishuv* and of Zionism: in the Histadrut trade union federation and, by natural extension, in the *yishuv*'s major health and social services, in the statutory governing council of the Jewish community in Palestine, the Va'ad Le'umi, in the school system, in the central, semi-clandestine armed force the Haganah, and finally in the World Zionist Organization itself to which the Jewish Agency Executive and the movement's other central institutions were answerable. Much more clearly than any of their important rivals, the leaders of Mapai had perceived that the complex of separate and yet subtly interlocking and overlapping instruments of influence and autonomous internal government could be largely pulled together and set out to do so. The entire process, in which ideology in the form of fairly crude Marxist class argument, ordinary influence and interest peddling, and ferociously verbal if generally non-violent electoral campaigns sporadically peppered by street scuffles between followers of the relevant political parties were all

---

[56] An acronym for Mifleget Po'alei Erez-Yisrael—Palestine (literally: Land of Israel) Workers' Party.

brilliantly combined, came to its climax in 1933 in the course of the elections in all the Zionist movement's constituencies to the 18th Zionist
Congress.

The rise of Mapai under Ben-Gurion's leadership was an instance and
function of the general shift of emphasis, concern, and activity within the
Zionist movement from the Diaspora to Palestine, the beginnings of
which are traceable, as we have seen, to the natural desire of the chief militants to make the most of the long wished-for, dramatic, and at the same
time fundamentally unexpected political breakthrough encapsulated in
the Balfour Declaration. Other lines of division within the movement followed or were reinforced: between those who thought principally in
terms of the rehabilitation and transformation of the Jewish people and
those who thought all should be set aside in the interests of urgent rescue;
between those who believed that a continuous effort must be made to
keep the British alliance alive, even at the cost of a certain lowering of
sights and posture in their regard, and those who argued that a stiffer, more
independent, altogether more pugnacious line of conduct had a better
chance of keeping Anglo-Zionist relations on a dignified and even keel.
But there were doubts about the likely fate of the British alliance in all
quarters, a rapidly growing sense that it might not be long before it came
to a bitter end—if, in reality, it had not come to that already; and that it
would be necessary at some point in the future to fight it out both with the
British and with the Arabs if, that is to say, the *yishuv* was not to be crushed
and all expectations of independence buried for good. If that, or something like it were indeed the prospect, if, that is to say, all else failed, why
then, Mapai's bright young rising star, Chaim Arlosoroff, wrote privately
to Weizmann in mid-1932, it might be necessary to consider an 'organized, revolutionary' seizure of power in the country *before* a Jewish majority
of the population had been achieved. The effect might well be to

undermine the beliefs to which we have been attached for many years. It may be
a notion that is dangerously close to political and populist tendencies of a kind to
which we ourselves have never been drawn. It may seem unrealistic, even fantastic. It may be incompatible with our condition [status?] under the British mandate. All of this is in need of a discussion. . . . But there is one thing that I feel
exceedingly strongly—and that is, that I, for my part, shall never reconcile myself
to the downfall of Zionism before an effort [has been made] that is fully as serious as our struggle to renew our national existence and our commitment to the
Jewish people are earnest. Do not forget that there is in every turn of events in
the world, or in the Middle East itself, and in every emergency, the potential to
compel us to adopt a course of action of a kind that we would never choose of
our own free will. We must take this into consideration in all that we do and
plan, whether we like it or not.[57]

---

[57] Arlosoroff to Weizmann, 30 June 1932. Published posthumously as an appendix to
his diary: Chaim Arlosoroff, *Yoman Yerushalaim* (Tel Aviv, [1948]), 341. One of the few

Intercalated with these considerations were two other political pre-
occupations, on the practical implications of which the Zionists were
equally divided. How was the overarching issue of relations with the Arab
population likely to evolve? All tendencies in the movement, each in its
way, pined for a *modus vivendi*. But on what basis? And with whom ought
it to be concluded—if one could be concluded at all? Should an arrangement be sought with the so-called *effendi* class of notables, on the grounds
that it was they who held all relevant power in the Palestinian Arab world?
Should it be sought with the Arab peasantry on the grounds that a common, class-oriented front against notables, bourgeois, and imperialists of
all varieties and all nationalities, as well as all other real or imaginary 'class
enemies', was better suited to the purposes and outlook of the Jews themselves and more likely to succeed? If the country was to be shared with the
Arabs, as in one way or another it clearly had to be, how and on what
principles was it best to try to divide it? 'Parity' was the magic, ostensibly
worthy, and therefore attractive principle that Mapai chose to settle for in
the early 1930s. But what did 'parity' mean? If it meant equal representation for Arabs and Jews in a Palestinian Legislative Council, it had long
since proved to be a non-starter so far as the Arabs were concerned and it
would turn out, before long, to be unacceptable to the British as well.
And would 'parity' be acceptable to the Jews themselves when *they* had
had an opportunity to ponder it? Much the greatest of the imponderables

authentic intellectuals among the leaders of Mapai and a man of evident attainment,
Arlosoroff was commonly, and probably correctly, thought of as being of very great
promise. He came to a tragic end, however, when he was shot dead on the beach at Tel
Aviv in the summer of 1933. He had been under heavy attack by the extreme wing of the
Revisionist movement and the case against three members of a notably radical fringe
group seemed especially formidable when Arlosoroff's wife, who had been with him,
picked one of them out of a police line-up. The Zionist left wing led by Mapai then made
the most of the dismal affair politically, turning the 1933 Zionist Congress into a stage for
the denunciation of the Revisionist Party and the launching of a general (and very successful) campaign to bring about the political and social excommunication of the Revisionists generally. In the short term this helped to deflect the attack the Revisionists were
mounting upon the ruling coalition, not least on account of the Transfer Agreement of
which Arlosoroff himself had been one of the original architects. In the long term it helped
put an end to the Revisionists' chances, such as they were, of gaining a commanding position in the movement by electoral and parliamentary means. In the event, the judicial case
against two of the accused was dismissed by the court of first instance at their trial and the
conviction of the third man, the one who had been picked out of the line-up by Mrs
Arlosoroff, was overturned on appeal as unsafe. Evidence came to light subsequently to
suggest that Mrs Arlosoroff had been subject to a sexual assault by two young Arabs and
that Arlosoroff had been killed in his attempt to protect her. By then, however, the damage done to the social and political fabric of the *yishuv* was beyond repair. The 'left' could
not retract its charges without suffering a humiliating climb-down and divesting itself of
the political advantages it had reaped. The 'right', for its part, was too wounded by what
it regarded, not without justice, as a campaign that had partaken of some of the elements
of the classic anti-Jewish 'blood-libel' to be capable of reconciliation. Half a century
would pass before the Arlosoroff affair began to lose something of its bite.

confronting the movement was the question what it was precisely that the Zionist movement itself, here and now, in the real circumstances of the Land of Israel and of the contemporary Middle East generally, ought to be aiming for? What, in the still habitual German-language jargon of the movement, was Zionism's *Endziel*, the ultimate purpose or target to which it aspired?[58] And if it, the *Endziel*, could be agreed upon, should it be stated publicly for all to hear and for all opponents to make appropriate, necessarily hostile dispositions? Would that not be a case of a premature burning of boats and the collapse of that unending but necessary effort to keep some balance and a level head among the contending forces that the official Zionist leadership had been engaged upon incessantly since 1917: between the British in London as opposed to those in Jerusalem, between the British on the one hand and the various Arab forces on the other, between Zionists and non-Zionists within Jewry itself, between contradictory tendencies within the Zionist movement, between the tough-minded and the tender-minded of all schools?[59]

To none of these questions were there—nor, in the nature of things, could there be—clear, let alone agreed answers. From 1936 onwards, moreover, the *yishuv*'s own physical security was in question and the military aspects of its condition increasingly dominated its own collective mind and to a somewhat lesser extent, the Zionist movement generally.[60] Nevertheless, within the Zionist movement, steadily and inexorably, the *yishuv* was replacing the Jewish Diaspora as the effective centre of their world. It was thus among those who looked to Weizmann and his

---

[58] Discussed at length and with much passion, but to no practical effect, at the 17th Zionist Congress at Basel (30 June–17 July 1931).

[59] Chaim Weizmann was voted out of office and power in 1931. He was replaced by Naḥum Sokolov, a veteran but a weaker figure. Sokolov died in 1936 and Weizmann was restored to something like his former glory in 1937, playing a remarkable role behind the scenes of the Royal (Peel) Commission's investigation of the Problem of Palestine. Thereafter, however, he had to contend with the real rising star in the movement, Ben-Gurion, a much more formidable rival than any of those who had appeared before to challenge him.

[60] The long, originally triangular Anglo-Arab-Jewish conflict to determine the final disposition of what until 1917 had been the Ottoman backwater *sanjaks* of Acre and Nablus within the *vilayet* of Beirut and the semi-autonomous *muta-sarriflik* of Jerusalem has, quite naturally, been the subject of continuous examination from every conceivable scholarly and disputatious, honest and dishonest, wise and misguided point of view. It is not the purpose of this book, however, to contribute its mite to the accumulation. Nor could it be, without serious distortion of its structure. Nor have I thought it in the least necessary to comment upon it except, and then as briefly as possible, where it has been necessary to show the impact of events and developments in Palestine on the trends and patterns of the public life of the Jews in Europe, especially among the Zionists. Were this a history of the Zionist movement alone, a great deal more would, of course, have to be said about the subject. In a political history of European Jewry in which the Zionists played a part, one part among others, it has seemed to me to be sufficient if the interconnection between affairs in Palestine and affairs in Europe was referred to in very general, rather than detailed terms.

closest colleagues in London, thus among those who looked to Ben-Gurion and his people in Palestine, and thus too among the Revisionist radicals who looked to the dissident Jabotinsky. None doubted that it was the *yishuv* that required their unremitting attention, nor that it offered the one remaining, authentic source of hope for Jews in all parts. The Jews in their numbers had no choice but to evacuate Europe sooner or later because it was in Palestine alone that a life of physical and economic security as well as of dignity and personal and collective fulfilment could be sought. This, of course, was precisely the issue on which the Zionists had always been—and continued to be—most bitterly opposed: by the orthodox who rejected reform and reconstruction as a matter of first principle; by universalists of all creeds and varieties, but socialists especially; by out-and-out assimilationists on the grounds that the problems of the Jews were soluble only within the context of an effort to solve the ills of society as a whole; by those among secular Jewish nationalists who took what they believed was a more pragmatic view of what could and could not be done for the people in its entirety and argued that the afflictions of Jewry were of such magnitude that they could only be dealt with *in situ*; and finally, although a shade more mildly, by sympathizers with Zionism in the United States who argued that however proper and necessary Zionism might be as a programme for *European* Jews, it was irrelevant to the case of their American cousins. At all events, the darker the view taken by the Zionists of the immediate prospects for Jewry in Europe itself, the more compelling seemed the need to ensure that what could be saved from the anticipated wreckage should be saved and the less comprehensible the views of those in Europe who were determined to persist in what they considered to be the doomed enterprise of fighting for survival while staying put.

What rendered this current of thought less brutal and short-tempered, but also more legitimate than it would otherwise have appeared to be to those who were drawn to it, was that it was fed by many tributaries. It amounted, quite evidently, to a final breaking free from the old 'current tasks' (or *Gegenwartsarbeit*) dilemma that had bedevilled the movement since the Russian Revolution of 1905. It owed something too to a pattern of thinking that had become common among the Zionists during the years of relative obscurity that preceded their sudden advance to centre stage in Jewish public life in the latter stages of the First World War: the *anti*-Herzlian view that dwelled more on the multiple difficulties facing the Jews than on their multiple needs and sought, in what was hoped was a suitably sober and rational manner, to resolve the dilemmas facing the movement by a general lowering of sights. One such tendency, partly Aḥad Ha-'Amian[61] in inspiration, partly pragmatic, but also in a sense

---

[61] On Aḥad Ha-'Am see Chapter 6.

aesthetic, proposed to put quality before quantity. It regarded the Jews of eastern Europe *en masse* as largely beyond rehabilitation, as comprising human material out of which no new, fresh, frankly utopian society could ever be constructed. It looked therefore to the young and the fit, less worn and more malleable than their seniors, and therefore the one segment of Jewry to which really close attention should continually be paid because it alone could be relied upon in practice to build the new, socially, culturally, and morally brilliant society that was to rise upon the sands and rocks of Palestine. It was to this end that the dominant factions in the Jewish Agency/Zionist Executive held fast, or as fast as public counter-pressure allowed them, to a policy of selective immigration in the form of a distinct and heavy preference for *haluzim* (or pioneers), young people who had been carefully trained and were ready to assume the task of farming the Land and whatever other duties were demanded of them.

There was a clear duality, however, in the long-standing insistence on selective immigration. Intercalated with Mapai's well-articulated ideological and strategic considerations, there were, inevitably, the silent pleasures of power as well and that irrepressible compulsion to expand and consolidate it that besets all men who have once tasted it. Besides the contribution trained *haluzim* were to bring to the purposeful settlement of the country they would be natural and reliable recruits to the political forces of the left. Petty traders, self-employed artisans, *Lumpenproletarier*—all proto-typical eastern European Jews encumbered as likely as not with families and enfeebled by unproductive skills or wanting in any skill at all—would not be; and while there was no question of their actually being turned away at the gates, they were not at all, to Ben-Gurion's and his colleagues' minds, what were needed in what, in principle, was the last best refuge to which *all* who were afflicted by the miseries of Europe needed to escape.

There was no resolving these contradictory considerations. Entry into Palestine was never free or unimpeded and, while the Mandate lasted, there were obstacles to all classes of migrants that were not of the Jewish Agency's making anyway. But these considerations contributed much, subtly to be sure, to the long, slow, by no means always conscious or deliberate process by which Europe was mentally abandoned, the specific problems of the continent's Jewries dropping from sight, and virtually all thought and energy being funnelled into the Palestinian enterprise.

VI

Not surprisingly, the Zionists had been caught off balance by the crisis of German Jewry and had been no quicker than others to grasp the immensity of the threat posed by the National Socialists. A year before the appointment of Hitler to the Chancellorship, with the nature of his party already clear, Weizmann was pressing the case for 'correspondents' in Germany whose thesis it was that the Germans attached 'very great importance' to public opinion in Great Britain, so much so, that 'if a hint could be dropped in certain quarters that any outrages against Jews or any violent anti-Jewish propaganda would be regarded by the English Conservatives with grave dismay and would discredit the Hitler party in the eyes of leading British statesmen, such a hint would not be without effect'. He himself, he reported to a well-placed member of the English-Jewish establishment, had been in touch with the Conservative Member of Parliament Robert Boothby who was about to visit Germany, and was prepared 'to talk things over' with Hitler.[62] Ben-Gurion in the spring of 1933, several months after the National Socialist take-over in Berlin, was so absorbed in his party's race for power in the last bastion still to be fought for—the Zionist Congress itself—that he conducted his electoral campaign in Poland and elsewhere without any reference to events in Germany except, and then purely in passing, as an illustration of the validity of Zionism. 'One of the most difficult things the Zionist movement has had to face is how to uproot the notion that the matter of Zionism is fantastic,' he told a meeting of party activists in Warsaw on 19 April 1933. 'Now the public in England can see for itself: Palestine flourishes. It is not a miracle, it is Zionism's doing. Two facts: a bright light has been poured on the condition of the Jewish people, and a bright light has been poured on the state of affairs in Palestine as well.'[63]

This was a theme that was to be repeated endlessly once Hitler's regime was consolidated and its intrinsic nature and its inflexible hostility to the Jewish people became clear beyond all possible doubt. Leo Motzkin, always among the most immediately sensitive to the afflictions of the Jews in the Diaspora, spoke for all, one imagines, at the 18th Congress (Prague, 21 August–4 September 1933), the first to be held after the Nazi *Machtergreifung*, when he described the Congress itself as 'a tragic one . . . [because] its background was what had befallen German Jewry. . . . And what can be sadder than to be a prophet and see one's prophecy come true?'[64] What the Zionists were conscious of before all else, that is to say, was that the theses that defined their movement had been vindicated. They were conscious too of the irony of it being the Jews of Germany, those who, man for man, had always been firmest in rejecting them, who were now beating at the gates of the *yishuv* of which few among them had

---

[62] Weizmann to O. E. d'Avigdor-Goldsmid, 15 Jan. 1932, in Weizmann, *Letters*, xi, no. 244, p. 265.

[63] David Ben-Gurion, *Zikhronot* [*Memoirs*], i (Tel Aviv, 1971), 611.

[64] *Protocole de la IIe conférence juive mondiale*, 82.

previously known anything or cared much. *Satisfaction*, however, lay only in it now being evident that the movement had been granted an unparalleled opportunity to show what it could do in actual and immediate practice for the people it had long claimed to champion and in the interconnected fact that their enterprise in Palestine was in the process of being rapidly and radically strengthened.

The Jews of central Europe, those of the German *Kulturbereich* especially, were generally of high educational and cultural attainment. The young among them, it was expected, would duly be remade into *haluzim*. Their elders brought with them undeniable skills and qualifications—of the very highest order in some cases—in the arts, the sciences, the free professions, in banking, insurance, and in industry. A few possessed substantial economic resources. They differed, to be sure, from the common run of Palestinian Jews in outlook, conduct, language, experience, and, by and large, in their knowledge of, and attitude to, Jewish customs, history, and religious tradition. They tended to be vastly more formal and correct, not to say pedantic and meticulous, in their behaviour than was common among the dominant eastern European sector of the Jewish population of Palestine. But if, as a group, they were therefore given a hard time socially it was more because they struck the majority as somewhat alien and droll rather than as formidable. They offered a remarkable array of talent and experience. But they were not feared nor was their arrival resented. It was evident that they were a population in shock and that their disorientation was extreme. It was plain, too, that few among them, if any, were minded to assert themselves socially, fewer still politically. When all was said and done, none doubted that they were to be welcomed as an invaluable addition to the *yishuv*.

It was equally the case, to be sure, that the entry of central European Jews in unprecedented numbers raised the opposition of the Palestinian Arab political class to virtually everything the Jews in general and the Zionists in particular were about—or were thought to be about—to fever pitch. Jewish immigration was the issue that Arab nationalists of all varieties and all intensities regarded, with very good reason to be sure, as most threatening to them at every conceivable level: the social, the economic, above all the political. The fact that few among the central European immigrants were politically minded, let alone of a distinctly Zionist or Jewish nationalist persuasion, was not a factor that Arab activists, when they noted it at all, believed to be of any consequence, however. On the face of things, this was odd. Among the Jews of Palestine who favoured compromise solutions to the Arab–Jewish conflict, especially in those radical forms that the greater part of the Jewish population regarded as self-abnegatory, if not downright treasonable, the new central European component, the intellectuals among them especially, was soon prominent. But Palestinian Arab opposition to the Zionist enterprise, notably under the extraordinarily forceful leadership of the Mufti of Jerusalem, Haj Amin al-Husseini, tended towards the absolute.

The one basis on which the presence of Jews had been acceptable in the Islamic world in the past was the established one of *dhimmis*, namely as members of a caste consigned to total and permanent political inferiority. This, as all could see, was ruled out by the sheer size of the *yishuv* and its obvious tendency to grow, but even more by its intrinsic social and political quality. The arrival of so formidable a reinforcement was bound to produce a reaction. In the event it would serve as a major precipitant of what would later be termed the Arab Rebellion (1936–9). Armed and exceedingly violent, the Rebellion was directed against the Jews in the first place, but, probably unwisely on the whole from the Arab point of view, against the Mandatory Power as well. Doing so it impinged in new and contradictory ways on the Zionists' own, vital relationship with the British government. In the short term, notably in the security sphere, it brought them closer to the British. In the longer term it helped to drive a wedge between them that was never to be dislodged. In the longest term of all it propelled the *yishuv* inexorably towards an unanticipated and on the face of things improbable degree of military and economic self-sufficiency while Arab opposition to the original, central, stated purpose of the League of Nations Mandate came to be pitched at new and, so to speak, ever more palpable heights. For its part the Mandatory Power was launched afresh into what hitherto had been a still somewhat hesitant and desultory effort to escape from the toils of the now much regretted wartime decision to adopt the pro-Zionist 'Palestine Idea'. For the Jews themselves, in view of what had occurred in Europe, this could not have come at a worse time. What had begun by being a reasonable—and repeatedly promised—prospect of British support for Jewish ambitions in the country was now in the process of being replaced by ever firmer British opposition to them. A fresh, perhaps fatal arena of conflict had been opened up precisely when, as the Zionists saw it, they had been vindicated in everything they had stood for and when what they had always hoped to offer their people was in ever more desperate demand.

These were the circumstances in which the claim that the imperatives of Jewish unity and dignity as expressed in the anti-Nazi boycott campaign must be uppermost in all Jewish quarters collided with the counter-argument that practical achievement in Palestine and immediate reinforcement of the *yishuv* had to count for more. It was not a controversy of the kind that admits of resolution. To the argument that to trade with the enemy when the boycott was the sole weapon available to the Jews in Europe amounted to the pass being sold before the fight had properly begun and the city invested no explicit and authoritative answer was ever offered. Nor was there a direct response to the contention that it was to the mass of Jews in the Diaspora that the Zionists, the self-designated champions of their people, owed their primary duty of loyalty and concern. No one of public prominence proposed a satisfactory way of disentangling regard for moral and political propriety from considerations of strategic expediency. But nor was the thesis that both compassion and wisdom lay precisely in saving whomever could be saved and salvaging whatever could be salvaged ever effectively countered. The actual and immediate need of tens of thousands of men, women, and children of real flesh and blood to be admitted into Palestine remained the only wholly palpable datum. As National Socialist pressure mounted and the prospect of admission to other countries fell, the argument that their admission and settlement into Palestine needed to be eased and facilitated, not impeded, could not but seem increasingly unanswerable, at any rate among the Zionists.

The most common view was that these were times, as Gruenbaum would put it to the 19th Zionist Congress (in Lucerne in 1935), 'when the [Jewish] people were moving to Palestine in their numbers—not only, to be sure, because they were drawn to it, but because they are being forced out of the lands they had inhabited. [And that] it is for us to find room for them. After all, we had always prayed for mass immigration.'[65] That, the Transfer Agreement, whatever one thought of it, was an important means of finding that much wanted 'room' for German Jews was beyond question.[66] That, as a consequence of the workings of the Agreement, the country was enjoying a rare period of economic prosperity was equally evident, as was the link between the flow of immigrants and the country's economic capacity to absorb them on which the British administration had always set such store. Still this was not the only view. Even the most hard-headed of Palestino-centrics, those most inclined to the view that the destinies of Jewry hinged ultimately on the security and social quality of the *yishuv*, and the *yishuv* alone, found the issue an embarrassment; and, not unnaturally, there was a substantial minority within the movement that objected totally to the scheme. This was partly because it served some of them as a stick with which to beat the leadership, but chiefly because it cut across the grain of their deepest convictions. The sum of the quarrel was that there had been introduced into the public sphere of Jewry, in an odd and unexpected form, an instance of the ancient dilemmas of *raison d'état*: the very stuff of high politics in the histories of other peoples, but virtually unknown to the Jews themselves since the onset of the Exile and for that reason, perhaps, the more difficult for them to handle.[67]

[65] *Ha-kongres ha-zioni ha-XIX [1935]; Din ve-heshbon stenografi* (Jerusalem, 1937), 292.

[66] Some 60,000 Jews migrated from Germany to Palestine between 1933 and 1939. Payments under the Transfer Agreement while it was in force totalled 8 million pounds sterling (or approximately 40 million US dollars).

[67] The present issue was not one to which the ancient injunction on the duty to ransom captives (*pidyon shevuim*) was relevant. Nor, for example, was it an instance of the

The Transfer Agreement having been agreed upon with the Germans on the eve of the opening of the 18th Congress at Prague (21 August–4 September 1933), the Congress itself presented the first real opportunity for the subject to be brought up in an authoritative Zionist forum. Initially, there was not much more than a good deal of unhappy rumbling on the one hand and prevarication and circumlocution on the other. It was only when Meir Grossman, leader of the newly formed Jewish State Party,[68] employed the parliamentary tactic of 'interpellation' to demand a precise statement of the Executive's position on the subject that it became impossible wholly to avoid a row. Grossman used his right to intervene at the end of a debate on other matters to denounce the Agreement 'as shameful and inconsistent with the moral and material interests of the Jewish people'. He wanted the Congress to be told whether it had or had not been concluded with the knowledge and under the authority of the Executive and demanded a full-dress debate on the matter by the Congress itself before it dispersed.[69] When he was duly given a succession of dusty answers he continued to hammer away at his theme for several days—to no avail, however, technical parliamentary procedures keeping him and his friends at bay. The leadership, still unsure of itself and having no intention of exposing itself to more embarrassment than it felt it could handle, sought final refuge in a recommendation to the Congress that so delicate a matter was best discussed in the relative privacy of the Political Committee.

But that was not quite the end of the matter even after the Congress had dispersed. As the months passed and the Agreement held, its contribution to the demographic and economic growth of the *yishuv* was soon evident to all and beyond debate. On the other hand, the larger, or at any rate harder question of its propriety and legitimacy, and of the movement's own specific and declared responsibility for it, remained unsettled and unsettling until the next, the 19th Congress convened in Lucerne in 1935. There, after some moments of ferocious debate, it was resolved— quite openly on this occasion and by a series of votes in which the oppon-

---

need, terrible at times, to treat with tyrants and oppressors and contemplate the sacrifice of individuals to safeguard the entire community. (As discussed in David Daube, *Collaboration with Tyranny in Rabbinic Law* (London, 1965).)

[68] The Jewish State Party, initially named the Democratic Revisionists, more commonly 'the Grossmanists' (after their leader Meir Grossman), consisted of the substantial and influential segment of the Revisionist Party that refused to follow Vladimir Jabotinsky out of the established Zionist movement and into the 'New Zionist Organization' that he was forming, of which he would be the unquestioned, paramount leader. The Jewish State Party—its very name a challenge and provocation to all concerned, but first and foremost to Chaim Weizmann and his school—remained until its dissolution after the Second World War, in very lonely, and, when all was said and done, ineffective opposition—the only group of its kind within the movement proper.

[69] *Stenographisches Protokoll der Verhandlungen des XVIII Zionistenkongresses, Prague, 21. August bis 4 September 1933* (Vienna, 1934), 244.

ents of the scheme[70] were outnumbered by a factor of five—that the financial institution established to handle the mechanics of the transfer would be placed under the direct and formal authority of the Jewish Agency. It was only three years later, towards the end of 1938, notably after *Kristallnacht*, that the Agreement was allowed, more or less by common consent, to peter out—by which time much of the heat and the urgency of the questions it had evoked in such acute and passionate terms had been lost as ever more disheartening events crowded in.

VII

But the *questions* evoked by the Transfer Agreement remained unanswered and, in the extreme circumstance of Germany's onslaught on the Jews, were perhaps unanswerable. Where had the *interests* of the Jewish people actually lain, where *expediency*? Did the interests of the Jews lend themselves to definition? Who was entitled to define them, who to marshal such forces and resources as were available to their pursuit? Were they in fact of such a nature as to be pursued to good purpose? All that was certain, as we have seen repeatedly, was that on none of these matters was unity attainable and that the sharpest of all dividing lines within contemporary Jewry ran between those who (however they might formulate their arguments) saw no alternative to a strategy of patience and political self-abnegation and those *per contra* whose historical patience was exhausted, who wished to shake off all remaining bits and pieces of conventional public wisdom, and who were determined to strike out once and for all into the uncharted if no doubt equally dangerous waters of self-rule. All these two great, untidy and incoherent schools of public thought shared was a profound awareness of their people's vulnerability and isolation. For both, therefore, the paramount and most immediate question now as always was whether the Jews had allies—potential and contingent, if not actual and faithful—or whether they were alone. This question would be given its decisive answer on the highest possible political authority at an international conference convened *deus ex machina* by the President of the United States at Evian-les-Bains on 6 July 1938.

Ostensibly, the meeting of the Intergovernmental Committee, socalled, was to consider how the Jews of Germany (or Greater Germany after the *Anschluss* with Austria) might be granted a reprieve. In practice, it was the salient feature of the Evian assembly that no one of any consequence either among the participants or the onlookers expected it to lead

---

[70] The delegates of the Jewish State Party once again, joined on this occasion by some of the delegates of the middle-of-the-road General Zionists' Party. It is likely that as many as half the delegates present abstained entirely from casting a vote on this issue.

to anything of the kind. Nor had this been the seriously considered purpose of the American President and his advisers when they resolved (in March 1938) to convene it. Long before any of the delegates had arrived or even been appointed, the terms under which the meeting was to assemble sufficed in themselves to preclude any such possibility. It had been laid down as a preliminary condition, for example, that the question how the circumstances of the Jews *within* the lands of their birth and residence might be eased was not to be taken up at all. Each one of the leading delegations was under instruction to consider their affairs exclusively in terms of *re*settlement. Under no circumstances would reference to the *causes* of their distress be allowed; under no circumstances was Germany to be subject to criticism.[71] Nor was the plight of the rest—and much the greater part—of European Jewry, the natives of Poland and Romania in particular, to be discussed lest the Poles and the Romanians be encouraged to follow the German example, *increase* the pressure they were known to be exerting on their Jewish subjects to leave, and so, by establishing 'an inconvenient precedent',[72] compound the problem the Americans, the British, and the other participants were proposing to address.

The eventual fate of the Jews of Germany, Austria, and, rather more vaguely, Czechoslovakia was, to be sure, the declared matter of the conference. But it too would be subject to the proviso that they would not be referred to as Jews, but rather by the supposedly less charged term of 'political refugees'. 'The term "political refugees", for the purposes of the present meeting', it was firmly stated in the British delegation's memorandum of instructions, 'is intended to include persons who desire [*sic*] to leave Germany as well as those who have already done so', although, of course, no one doubted that at least 85 per cent of the people concerned were Jews and that few of these, if any, had actively desired to leave.[73] In the same vein of self-instructed inhibition, there was (at British behest, in this instance) to be no mention of Palestine, despite it being well known that the greatest single bloc of German Jews to have been able to resettle anywhere was that which had found refuge there,[74] and that the prospect

[71] Only the Colombian delegate (J. M. Yepes) ventured, in the event, to go somewhat beyond the rule when, at the third and last public meeting of delegates at Evian, 9 July 1938, he asked rhetorically whether a state, 'without upsetting the basis of our civilisation and, indeed, of all civilisation' could really be allowed 'arbitrarily [to] withdraw nationality from a whole class of its citizens?' Most of the other Latin American delegations were a great deal more reticent, telling the United States delegates that German economic pressure upon them was such that 'they did not dare join in any action which might seem to be even in the smallest respect critical'. Myron Taylor, chairman of the American delegation to Hull, 14 July 1938, *FRUS* 1938, i. 754.

[72] 'Memorandum of instructions for the United Kingdom Delegation', 5 July 1938, PRO, FO 371/22529.

[73] Ibid.

[74] By 1 July 1938 the distribution of Jews from Germany who had been admitted to other countries was (approximately) as follows: Palestine 44,000; European countries

of rapid and effective absorption of additional numbers, while anything but easy, was at least as good as those obtaining elsewhere.[75] But the defining and fatally limiting feature of the conference was that each and every one of the participants arrived armed with, and protected by, the firmest possible assurances that no delegation would be asked, much less expected, to modify such restrictive immigration and naturalization policies and regulations as their respective governments had been so carefully enforcing and which, taken together, formed the administrative fence within which the Jews of Europe, in their overwhelming majority, had now for some fifteen years been so effectively corralled. It followed that while the purposes of the participating governments were proclaimed to be of an irreproachably humanitarian nature, their intentions in all important cases were of a different order.

For all these reasons it is impossible to mark the point at which, in any particular case, political calculation ended and some residual if, in the event, empty good will was to the fore. No one doubted at the time that the conference at Evian had been designed at least in part to ease the burden of domestic pressure that had descended on the Roosevelt administration in the wake of the savagery of Germany's anti-Jewish campaign by initiating a large public gesture of some sort;[76] and that much the same could be said of some of the other western governments as well. But by no means all. The Canadian government's determination to prevent the admission of Jews in any number at all to any part of its vast territory was absolute and commanded widespread popular support. The prime minister himself, W. L. Mackenzie King, was positively undeviating in his personal view that Jews were a people who were bound to pollute Canada's 'bloodstream', undermine its unity, alienate great numbers of its citizens, strengthen the profoundly anti-Semitic forces of Quebec separatism, and end by bringing about bloodshed in the streets. His instructions to his delegate to Evian, Hume Wrong, were very frankly in this spirit. Mr Wrong was to bear in mind that he was there to 'listen, make notes and say as little as possible', that he was there for cosmetic purposes

37,000 (a number which includes repatriates); United States 27,000; Argentina 13,000; South Africa 7,600; Brazil 7,500. Several other countries had accepted smaller numbers. Most commonly, the rate of admission would be reduced later. In a few cases, Great Britain notably and Australia rather more moderately, it would be increased. *Sources*: Werner Rosenstock, 'Exodus 1933–1939: A Survey of Jewish Emigration from Germany', *LBIYB* 1 (London, 1956), 373–90; and Herbert A. Strauss, 'Jewish Emigration from Germany: Nazi Policies and Jewish Responses', *LBIYB* (2 articles) 25, 26 (London, 1980, 1981), 313–61; 343–409.

[75] When the absurdity of this evasion became embarrassing, the British delegate, at conference end, spoke that country's name after all—only to say, however, that since the entire question of Palestine was under discussion in London it was not a subject that the conference at Evian could have properly discussed.

[76] R. Breitman, and A. M. Kraut, *American Refugee Policy and European Jewry, 1933–1945* (Bloomington, Ind., 1987), 222–35.

only, and should any other delegate offer concrete proposals for a solution to the problem of the refugees he was to oppose them 'without seeming to be obstructionist'. Above all, the Canadian representative was under no circumstances to *promise* anything.[77] The line adopted by most governments, however, was milder in tone, falling midway between the sanctimoniousness of the Americans, the French, and the British, and the silent fear and deep disapproval of the entire enterprise evinced by the Canadians.

The consequences could not fail to be grotesque. The declared attempt to scour the world for lands that might, with luck, be prepared to accept more than a mere handful of Jews failed, as it was bound to do, the parade of reasons for shutting them out having taken up the greater part of the conference's time. The refusal to consider the *causes* of the problem of the refugees rendered the effort, such as it was, to assist the Jews to leave Germany and Austria indistinguishable in practice from an offer of assistance to National Socialist Germany in its continuing endeavour to extrude them. Alas for hypocrisy, but alas for the Jews of Germany as well, even in this latter respect the meeting at Evian proved to be a failure. The Germans were asked both before and after the conference whether they were 'prepared to cooperate with the other interested countries in the solution of the question of emigrants, particularly aiding the emigration of Jews of German nationality'. No country, the British ambassador in Berlin told the German foreign minister, 'was prepared to receive the emigrating German Jews, particularly [*sic*] if they were without means'. The question necessarily arose therefore whether the Reich government was 'prepared to cooperate in the transfer of capital in Jewish hands'. It was not, he was told.[78] When, after Evian, the American ambassador asked the State Secretary at the German Foreign Ministry (Weizsäcker) whether they 'would not lend [their] co-operation in some manner to the Evian Committee for emigrating Jews', he too was told that 'he should not entertain any hopes in that direction'.[79] Sounded on the likely attitude in Berlin to an attempt by George Rublee, the director of the new refugee organization set up at Evian, to arrange 'an orderly procedure . . . for the removal of the Jews from Germany' the response of the Germans was that the Americans, the British, and the French should put any such idea out of their minds. There was no evidence that there were any countries anywhere that were prepared to admit German Jews in significant numbers. The American quota of 27,000 persons a year was already, as all concerned knew, 'filled for a long time ahead.' '. . . [T]he

---

[77] I. Abella, and F. Bialystok, 'Canada', in David S. Wyman (ed.), *The World Reacts to the Holocaust* (Baltimore, 1996), 756.

[78] DGFP, D, v, 8 July 1938, no. 640, 894–5.

[79] Ibid. 27 July 1938, no. 641, 895.

Committee [established at Evian] had proved sterile,' Weizsäcker told the British ambassador (Henderson)—not unreasonably, in the circumstances. 'In order to justify its existence it now wanted to talk to the German Government.' Later, Weizsäcker took the opportunity to ask the British chargé d'affaires 'what the percentage of Rublee's Aryan descent was', noting, for distribution to his colleagues, that it was the chargé's belief that Rublee had no Jewish blood.[80]

But if, by prior intention, the performance of the participating governments at Evian was false and circumlocutory and the aftermath desultory and unserious, there was little in the conduct of those who had taken it upon themselves to represent the Jews themselves to command attention and respect. It is true that the conditions set the Jewish delegations were hard to the point of cruelty. It was not until the very eve of the conference that its precise form and nature were made clear to them, at which point considerable pains were taken to remove any illusions they may have had that they would in some sense or other be *participants* in the proceedings. A parallel effort was made to reduce their natural temptation to believe that they would be allowed to bring their case before the official delegates with appropriate force. Lord Winterton, the chief British delegate,

received us exceedingly coldly [Arthur Ruppin, in Evian for the Jewish Agency, recorded in his diary]; he rejected what we had to say and wished to know nothing at all of the problem of migration of Jews from Eastern Europe. The talk, which barely lasted a quarter of an hour and in which I served as spokesman, was a slap on the face for us. Winterton went out of his way to emphasize that it was not a conference (as I had called it) but an intergovernmental committee's consultation, his intention being to make it clear to us that in actual fact we had no business to be here at all.[81]

Only when it became plain that to allow the Jews no hearing at all would be not only visibly monstrous but absurd, was a subcommittee detailed off to listen to what they might have to say. Here too, however, the essential spirit in which the conference had been convened was made manifest. The subcommittee was chaired, as it happened, by the one official delegate who had been bold enough to state for all to hear that his own country's objection to an enlarged immigration of Jews was frankly racial and cultural rather than, as most found it more convenient to argue—wholly contrary to the facts in most cases—a necessary function of domestic employment policy and of the resources available for resettlement. Australia, Colonel T. W. White, minister for trade and customs,

---

[80] Ibid. 18, 20, and 24 Oct., 7 Nov. 1938, nos. 645–8, 900–3.

[81] Arthur Ruppin, *Pirkei Ḥayyai: be-vinyan ha-arez ve-ha'am*, iii (Tel Aviv, 1968), 302–3. Earl Winterton had recently entered the British cabinet as Chancellor of the Duchy of Lancaster.

explained, intended to stick to its policy of ensuring that immigrants were 'predominantly British'. 'Undue privileges' could not be granted 'one particular class of non-British subjects [i.e. Jews] without injustice to others'. His listeners should also appreciate, he said, that 'as we have no real racial problem we are not desirous of importing one by encouraging any scheme of large-scale foreign migration'.[82] The Colonel was equally forthright in his role as chairman of the subcommittee. He had the Jewish representatives marched in one at a time, like military defaulters brought up before their commanding officer. Each was allowed ten minutes (five, according to some testimonies) to say his piece and answer questions (if any) and was then dismissed. The entire business of listening to what the spokesmen had to say was therefore accomplished with exemplary efficiency and dispatch, the Jews, along with some non-Jewish delegates, having been effectively disposed of in the course of a single afternoon and the Colonel's feat being the more remarkable for his committee having no less than twenty-four different representatives of mostly Jewish organizations and institutions to listen to. All told, thirty-nine organizations, twenty of which were Jewish, were represented at Evian. While fifteen of the entire number agreed not to insist on appearing before Colonel White's subcommittee, all, including, naturally enough, the delegation of the Reichsvertretung der Juden in Deutschland that the German authorities had allowed both to emerge from Germany and to return to it, submitted written memoranda. None, however, not even members of the delegation that was directly and authentically representative of the people who were the stated subject of the conference, were allowed to address the plenum or do more than try to buttonhole the official delegates in the lobbies of the Hotel Royal.

That there should have been so very many delegations—meaning that it had proved impossible to band more than a fraction of them together to form a single more powerful delegation which would speak for all on all essentials with a single voice—was a great source of self-inflicted and long regretted shame and ridicule. So Goldmann, not a man to mince words, reported back to his principals when it was all over,[83] and not Goldmann alone. In truth, there could have been no plainer demonstration of the disunity and indecision that were rife in Jewry. But the worst of the miserable posture of the Jewish delegations and the equally miserable reception accorded them was not the impression others came away with. It was the contribution made to the frustration, bitterness, but above all anxiety—and therefore impotence—by which all who were active in Jewry's

[82] Cited in Michael Blakeney, 'Australia and the Jewish Refugees from Central Europe: Government Policy 1933–1939', *LBIYB* 29 (London, 1984), 115–16.

[83] Elisabeth Eppler, 'Pe'ulot hazala shel ha-kongres ha-yehudi ha-'olami bi-tekufat ha-shilton ha-nazi', in Y. Gutman (ed.), *Nisyonot u-fe'ulot hazala bi-tekufat ha-sho'ah* (Jerusalem, 1976), 42.

public arena were being steadily overwhelmed as they monitored events.

Once again, where the Zionists were concerned, this general consideration needs to be qualified somewhat. Zionist representatives were present at Evian. They had shared the anxiety that was the common lot of all Jewish delegations as the shape of the intergovernmental meeting was revealed to them and the distress which was their joint reward for having attended the proceedings to the end. But they had had from the first, as was so often the case in the past, a rather different outlook on the matter: the particular and to some extent contrary fear that if anything of substance did emerge from Evian it would almost surely be to their detriment. Whatever it was, they thought it was likely to serve the British government in what were its now visibly accelerating moves towards the final derailment of the Zionist enterprise in Palestine. The Royal Commission appointed in August 1936 to investigate the problem of Palestine and propose ways in which the 'legitimate grievances' of either the Arabs or Jews, if any, might be met had gone somewhat beyond its remit. It proposed that the Mandate be terminated and the country be divided into three: 'two sovereign independent States . . . one an Arab State, consisting of Trans-Jordan united with that part of Palestine which lies to the east and south of a frontier such as we suggest . . .; the other a Jewish State consisting of that part of Palestine which lies to the north and south of that frontier';[84] and Jerusalem where, as it happened, Jews constituted the majority of the population, which was to remain under British administration. The Jewish state was to be an affair of no more than some 2,000 square miles in area in all, the Arab–Jewish demographic balance within it would be barely in the Jews' favour, and its economic and military viability could not be other than exceedingly doubtful.

The Zionists were torn in their responses. The leadership was prepared to follow the Peel Commission's advice to bow to the validity of the 'peculiarly English proverb' that half a loaf is better than no bread[85] and accept the prospect of a mini-state as a good deal better than nothing: Weizmann with something approaching enthusiasm, having been party to the scheme from the first, Ben-Gurion more soberly because he saw it as at any rate holding out a promise of rapid and massive immigration— the sole basis on which a solid, sovereign Jewish presence in the country could ever be obtained and secured.[86] But a clutch of otherwise incompatible minority parties and influential individuals within and without the formal structure of the movement rejected it as a betrayal of the traditional aspirations of the Jews, or of Zionism's central purposes as they

---

[84] Palestine Royal Commission, *Report*, Cmd. 5479 (London, 1937), 381.

[85] Ibid. 394.

[86] On Ben-Gurion in this connection, see Yesha'yahu Friedman, 'Ben-Gurion ve-ha-britim: 1936–1940', *Kivunim*, 24 (Aug. 1984), 109–21.

themselves defined them, or of what they took to be Britain's long-standing undertakings, or of the Zionists' own Congress, negotiations with the British on the Peel plan having been entered into without its authority, or all these objections combined. The outcome was a fudge. The 20th Zionist Congress (Zurich, 3–17 August 1937) at one and the same time rejected the Royal Commission's recommendations and granted the Zionist Executive *ex post facto* authority to negotiate the terms on which a Jewish state (in what every one understood would be a severely limited stretch of territory) might be established after all.

However, in ways that had long since become (and would remain) characteristic of the history of the Mandate, nothing came of the Peel Commission's recommendations. The Arabs rejected them out of hand. The British government approved them, or seemed to have done, but then, thinking again, resolved in December 1937 to send a second commission to Palestine (under Sir John Woodhead), nominally to look at the problem once more, more particularly at the question of territorial boundaries, but essentially as a step towards disengagement from the Peel proposals altogether. The Woodhead Commission, by reducing the planned Jewish state to absurdly minute dimensions, duly dealt partition what was hoped to be a death-dealing blow. The Peel Commission's ideas were then formally buried in a preliminary statement of policy published in November 1938. And final government policy on Palestine was announced half a year later in the White Paper of May 1939. The Balfour Declaration was declared dead. The admission of Jews into the country was to be subject to additional restrictions and then brought to an end altogether. Further, exceptionally severe limitations were to be laid on the areas in which Jews might legitimately purchase land and settle. And Palestine itself was to be a unitary state more or less as it stood, namely as a country in which the Arab majority was permanently preponderant both demographically and politically. The two White Papers of November 1938 and May 1939 were still in the future—which is to say, under confidential discussion in Whitehall and Downing Street—when the Jewish Agency Executive met to consider who, if anyone at all, should travel to Evian to represent it. But there was little doubt about the direction in which the wind was blowing in London and that the fight for a foothold in Palestine had entered a new and exceedingly dangerous stage. 'Palestine,' Gruenbaum warned his colleagues,

might cease totally to be regarded as a country suitable for immigration. . . . There is a danger that in the course of the search for a country of refuge some other, new territory will be found to which, so it will be desired, Jewish migration will be directed. We for our part must defend the principle that it is only in Palestine that Jewish settlement can succeed and that there can be no question at all of an alternative to it.

Ben-Gurion doubted whether the meeting at Evian would lead to other countries being opened to Jewish immigration, but he agreed with Gruenbaum (and some others) that 'immense' dangers to the matter of Palestine and Zionism were in prospect.

From the Zionist point of view it might turn out to be the opposite of San Remo.[87] It might remove Palestine from international consideration as a factor relevant to the solution of the Jewish Question. . . . Members [of the Executive] who propose to offer a full exposé of the Jewish Question at Evian are mistaken. . . . The whole world is now acquainted with it and has the measure of its severity. What is in need of exposition is the *solution* to the Question—and for this the time is not ripe because in the eyes of the wider world Palestine is classed with Spain. You don't solve the problem of refugees [it will be said] in a country in which there are riots, in which bombs and murders are daily affairs, and in which there is unemployment and economic stagnation. The more we say about the terrible distress of the Jewish masses in Germany, Poland, and Romania the more damage we shall inflict [on our own position] in the current negotiations [on the future of Palestine].[88]

But perhaps the worst of the Jewish presence at Evian was its level. No person who could be deemed to be in the very first rank of contemporary Jewry was on hand at Evian. The major organized movements, communal and charitable institutions—the Zionist Organization, Agudat Yisrael, the Joint Distribution Committee, the Hebrew Immigrant Aid Society, the World Jewish Congress, the Board of Deputies of British Jews, the *yishuv* in Palestine, and the rest—were there in full force, represented by men and women of experience and competence, a few of whom were eventually to play roles of some importance in Jewish public life. Of none, however, at the time, save perhaps Arthur Ruppin, the great mandarin of organized Zionism, could it be said that he or she was a person of note. None of the real notables and magnates in Jewry was there: no Rothschilds, no latter-day Montefiores, no Warburgs, no successors to Crémieux or Bleichroeder, neither Brandeis nor Herbert Samuel, neither Einstein nor Freud. The leaders of Hasidic orthodoxy, men who in their old-fashioned way were closest of all to the ordinary, still traditionally minded, traditionally hard-pressed Jews of eastern Europe, stayed put. So did the Chief Rabbi of Great Britain and the Grand Rabbin of France and the leaders of Conservative and Reform Jewry in the United States. The chairman of the Jewish Agency, the presidents of the American Jewish Committee, the Board of Deputies of British Jews, and the American Jewish Congress all stayed away. So too, after some hesitation, did the one not implausible claimant to the role of contemporary Prince of the Jews, a man whose special strength lay

---

[87] The conference of the Allied powers in Apr. 1920 at which *inter alia* the Mandate for Palestine incorporating the Balfour Declaration was formally conferred on Great Britain.

[88] Jewish Agency Executive session in Jerusalem, 26 June 1938, Ben-Gurion in the chair, CZA, Ha-hanhala ha-ẓionit, *Protokol*, no. 55, vol. xxviii, fos. 6053–61.

precisely in his ability to command the respectful (if often, to be sure, somewhat resentful) attention of the great men of the day. In general, Weizmann believed that if any influence could be brought to bear on the proceedings it would be privately and separately, upon the various national delegations in their respective capital cities, not at Evian.[89] But what appears to have moved him to make up his mind finally, on the very eve of the conference, not to attend was the certain prospect that Palestine would not be touched upon and the high probability that he himself would not be given a serious hearing. It would be 'a waste of time', he decided, merely to go and try his luck. When it was all over a colleague told him that had he turned up he would only have 'swell[ed] the numbers of the Jewish representatives already filling the corridors of the conference'. Weizmann had guessed as much and stayed away.[90]

VIII

Of course, the meeting of the Intergovernmental Committee at Evian was one episode; and it may be judged, in retrospect, to have been a trivial one. But if trivial in substance, the performance at the Hotel Royal was none the less a singularly futile, dishonest, and to some extent cruel exercise. A great cast of actors had allowed themselves to be caught, as if by an especially gifted photographer: some, in their arrogance and complacency, some in especially awkward, even ugly positions, others in confusion, disarray, and humiliation. The meeting's accomplishments were only two: to have made manifest the universal refusal to allow a large-scale escape from Europe to occur; and—in some cases consciously (that of Lord Winterton for example), but for the most part indirectly and implicitly—to have confirmed the now general disposition to edge the Jews out of the international political arena into which they had so very

---

[89] Lord Samuel, Lord Bearsted, the Chief Rabbi, Neville Laski, Lionel de Rothschild, and Chaim Weizmann, in their capacity as members of the Council for German Jewry, did finally meet the Prime Minister (at the House of Commons on 15 Nov. 1938), but this was in the wake of *Kristallnacht* and chiefly in the interests of facilitating the entry and settlement of refugees in the United Kingdom. Nothing of a political nature was pressed on Chamberlain and the tone in which the deputation thought it necessary to approach the Prime Minister may be gauged by Samuel's telling him that 'the Council recognised the difficulties of the Government and they would not think of suggesting that the doors should be widely thrown open' (PRO, FO 371/22536).

[90] Weizmann to Jacobus Kann, 3 July 1938, no. 357, p. 409; Weizmann to Walter J. Baer, 11 July 1938, no. 365, p. 416; and Weizmann to Stephen S. Wise, 14 July 1938, no. 371, pp. 429–31, Weizmann, *Letters*, xviii. At Evian itself, the Zionist delegation issued a formal statement to the effect that as Weizmann, if he appeared, 'would only be one of the some fifty representatives appearing before the sub-committee there was insufficient cause to bother him [*le-hatriaḥ oto*]'. *Davar*, 14 July 1938, cited in S. B. Beit-Zevi, *Ha-ẓionut ha-post-ugandit be-mashber ha-sho'ah* (Tel Aviv, 1977), 171.

recently (historically speaking) gained admission. Evian, that is to say, signalled the onset of the final stage of the process by which the long march of the Jews of Europe to legal emancipation and social acceptance had first been arrested and was now, corners of the western world apart, being rapidly reversed. There was no knowing in July 1938 when and how the process would be complete, if ever, only that upon completion the Jews would be left politically emasculated and physically crushed. The larger certainty about the Jews of Europe at what we now know to have been the end of their day, was that they no longer had reason to believe that room could still be found for them in the continent of which they had been regular inhabitants since Roman times—*except* on the basis of repression and the continuous threat, here subdued, there undisguised, of decimation.

That Hitler's Reich was no more than the paradigm instance of a broader and deeper continent-wide phenomenon had become plain beyond denial. So was the fact that the phenomenon of repression, while almost infinitely varied in kind, detail, and intensity, was integral to much of what lent Europe—in its entirety, from the Urals to the Atlantic Ocean—such unity as it possessed. There had been reinsinuated into every one of the political, economic, social, and theological arguments against their continued presence in society as well as in the economy, and in political, intellectual, and artistic life—and most powerfully of all, into the *minds* of the majoritarian populations of the territories they inhabited—a tale of the burdens (actual or imaginary) that Europeans of other classes and other categories had incurred, century after century in consequence of having accepted the Jews in their midst. That this was the case in central and eastern Europe by dint of ever more systematic indoctrination and reformulation by state, party, and Church—by no means, therefore, merely through the efforts of eccentric publicists, preachers, and sundry ideological hysterics—was plain to the dullest eye. But in the liberal west too, through all the kind words and nodding of heads and, in certain cases, genuinely high-minded objection to what the Germans, the Poles, the Romanians, the Hungarians, and the rest were up to, there could be sensed the presence of two thin, continuous, unbreakable, and intertwined threads of ancient hostility and modern *schadenfreude*. Certainly, there was no institutionalized determination finally to punish a people that, besides other offences, had never properly disguised its contempt for the workings and infinitely elaborate and tortuous teachings of the Christian Church(es). But there was a distinct and detectable readiness none the less to see them brought to book at any rate for their social impudence, for having overreached themselves upon being accorded *droit de cité*, for being too visible, too independent, and—so it was commonly felt—insufficiently humble and grateful for what had been granted them. And then, the question that had begun to be asked with some frequency was had not the Jews in almost every possible way brought their current troubles upon themselves, the question more or less encapsulating the necessary answer.[91]

Seen in the long perspective offered by the history of the Jews themselves, there was, of course, a minor irony in it being the godless of Germany, not the God-fearing, who had put themselves in the forefront of the last of the campaigns to be mounted against them in Christian Europe. And the irony, such as it was, was only partly offset by it being one to which great numbers of churchmen, high and low, tended to rally. The chief doctrinal difficulty for them in this respect was that which was raised by the question how the Jewish apostates, 'non-Aryan' members of their own Churches, were to be treated.[92] But, in general, it was the sum of the spirit of the times in all European societies, classes, denominations, and influential institutions that there had been some retreat in mind and word, even if not everywhere in deed, from the terms in which the social and political emancipation of the Jews had originally been conceived. The steps actually taken in Germany, Hungary, Romania, Poland, and elsewhere to this end, along with the ever more strident calls throughout central and eastern Europe and the Balkans for the Jews' eventual but total extrusion, bag and baggage, had come to be met virtually everywhere with at the very least mixed feelings. And mixed feelings had led in turn to some toying with the idea of leaving the Jews in place after all provided only that some sort of forced reversion to their pre-emancipatory *status quo ante* was engineered.

Gerhard Kittel, an eminent New Testament scholar at Tübingen and an accepted authority on Ancient Israel, developed an argument along these lines when he joined the National Socialists and his attention

---

[91] An American Institute for Public Opinion poll found in 1938 that 48 per cent of those asked thought that the persecution of the Jews in Europe was 'partly' their own fault (Breitman and Kraut, *American Refugee Policy*, 228). Well after the war was over and the fate of the Jews of Europe was known to have been settled for all time, Sir Henry Gurney, an eminent British civil servant and a man who as Chief Secretary for Palestine knew a thing or two about the Jews and their recent history, remarked to Golda Meir (then Meyerson) in what he may have thought was friendly fashion: 'You know, Mrs. Meyerson, if Hitler persecuted Jews, there must be some reason for it.' Cited in Efraim Karsh, *Fabricating Israeli History* (London, 1997), 184.

[92] The favoured (temporary) solution in Protestant Germany was to arrange for Christians of Jewish origin, pastors as well as flock, to be shunted into a special division of the Church (Richard Gutteridge, *Open thy mouth to the dumb* (Oxford, 1976), *passim*). The Roman Catholics were rather more troubled by the clash between official racialism and their own doctrinal principle that properly baptized members of the Church might not be distinguished one from the other, being, in their view, indistinguishable in the eyes of God. Some not very energetic or successful efforts to go to the rescue of their own 'non-Aryan' Christians have been recorded, among them a promise extracted from the President of Brasil (but never honoured) to allow 3,000 such people to enter his country. On this see Pierre Blet, *et al.* (eds.), *Actes et documents du Saint Siège relatifs à la seconde guerre mondiale*, vi (City of the Vatican, 1972), 129–34, 216–17, and *passim*.

shifted to modern Israel.[93] A more interesting instance is that of Benito Mussolini whose ideas on the matter of the Jews, while vague, were for a time not ungenerous. It had occurred to the Duce after Hitler's rise to power to try to discover on what terms a form of social peace between the new German regime and its Jewish subjects might be achieved. To that end he sought to inquire of the leaders of organized Jewry, through the agency of Angelo-Raphael Sacerdoti, Chief Rabbi of Rome, what *their* minimal demands might be. When it was explained to him that the Jewish people, as such, had no established 'leaders', were not in any sense 'organized', and that the only visible candidate for the role of interlocutor, Weizmann, was preoccupied by Palestine, the inquiry was passed to Nahum Goldmann. Goldmann refused to bite, however. Sacerdoti was asked to tell the Duce, and Goldmann in due course (13 November 1934) told him himself, that the Jews of Germany were entitled to full equality of rights and that this was a matter on which no compromise was possible. One either enjoyed equality of rights or one did not. Were the Jews to agree to a compromise with Hitler, sacrificing the principle of 100 per cent equality, the Jews' equality of rights in all other countries would be in question.[94] But, in any case, in an age in which radical and sweeping solutions to ancient problems were most likely to gain a sympathetic hearing even an idea such as Mussolini's was likely be given short shrift—the more so as it would have required much more than common imagination to work out how the Jews of Frankfurt, for example, or of Venice, for that matter, could be conveniently and expeditiously returned to their ghettos. What was most in vogue was evacuation. Thus it was among the conscious and active enemies of Jewry who as a matter of central national policy pursued it with all possible vigour and urgency; and thus it grew as an idea among those who classed themselves as mere onlookers and who began to view it with understanding if not downright favour. But it was also present ever more firmly, ever more widely, among the Jews themselves: for what non-Jews saw as extrusion had become indistinguishable both in practice and in the minds of ever more numerous Jews from escape.

The nub of the matter for the Jews of Europe on the eve of the Second World War, however, was that there would be no escape. The eminent, the very wealthy, the exceptionally fortunate, the very far-sighted, the unusually energetic or adroit—these might, and in many cases did, succeed in getting through and out. For the Jews in the mass, for Jews in

[93] Gutteridge, *Open thy mouth*, 111–15.

[94] 'Incontro Mussolini–Goldmann', doc. no. 6, in Renzo De Felice, *Storia degli ebrei italiani sotto il fascismo*, 4th edn. (Turin, 1988), 515–24. Dr Gerhart Riegner, a long-time associate of Nahum Goldmann, recalls that after the war the thought that perhaps, on balance, it had been an error to have turned Mussolini's initiative down troubled Goldmann considerably.

general and as an overarching social category, the trap had fallen by 1938. There would be no fresh migratory wave, no new treks from one land to another of the kind with which their history was already sufficiently punctuated. And the consequence was that by then the long-delayed crucifixion of the Jews of Europe was already well in train.

Could they have resisted these great pressures more effectively? Could they have broken out of their captivity if they had tried harder, been more determined, if they had done this or done that, been less fearful—or, perhaps, contrariwise, more frightened? The questions stand: they stand even when the relevant scenarios remain undevised and the answers are not forthcoming. We can see that the shape and quality of the Jewish condition were being very radically and rapidly reset after the end of the First, the Great World War. We know that each one of the rushed and crowded international events between 1933 and 1939, notably those immediately preceding the conference at Evian and others subsequent to it, served to drain away a moral or political resource of some kind, demonstrating the intrinsic weakness of the Jews to others, concentrating the Jews' own minds on their vulnerability and isolation.

The spurt of close attention paid to the affairs of the Jews in such quarters of the world as could still be regarded as civilized in the wake of the brutalities inflicted upon them in Austria, not least in Vienna itself, on the occasion of the *Anschluss* a few months before Evian was not altogether specious and ungenerous. Nor was the additional wave of attention precipitated by the *Reichskristallnacht* launched some months after the Evian conference had dispersed. But in neither instance was attention other than limited and fleeting. In both it was swept away very rapidly by events in the larger political and strategic arena. This was true of the general public. It was doubly true of those limited circles of political influence and power which still counted for something in the context of imminent world war. But what was decisive in this context was that matters had come a long way since Lord Robert Cecil had observed—plausibly at the time, at any rate in the judgement of most of his colleagues and foreign analogues—that he did not 'think it is easy to exaggerate the international power of the Jews'.[95] Twenty-two years on, at Evian—or indeed anywhere else at the end of the 1930s—it would not have occurred to anyone of like standing, in Europe or the Americas to entertain so egregious an idea. It was the realization in the leadership circles of the Jews themselves that this was now the case that had been at the root of the refusal of anyone of the very first rank in Jewry to attend the meeting at Evian, namely that even if they were heard they would not be seriously listened to. Some months after Evian Neville Laski, as president of the representative body of the Anglo-Jewish community, asked for a small

[95] See above, p. 662.

deputation to be received by the British Prime Minister 'to put before
[him] their anxious hope that [he] will in the course of the negotiations
to be initiated [with Germany], bear in mind so far as may be possible the
need for the material and moral appeasement of the condition of our co-
religionists and others in Central Europe'. In the event, they were
received by the Foreign Secretary, Lord Halifax, instead. Halifax
explained to them with perfect courtesy that 'while he fully agreed with
the importance of . . . the question [they had raised], he did not think that
it necessarily affected or prevented the conduct of negotiations with the
German Government on matters involving peace or war'. The more precise response, devoid of velvet, to the Jews' approach to the Prime Minister was recorded in the relevant internal Foreign Office minute, of the
terms of which Laski and his colleagues were, of course, unaware.

It is . . . difficult to see what encouragement can be held out to such a deputation.
The increase of German power and prestige in Central and Southern Europe as
the result of the Munich Agreement is bound to lead to an increase in anti-
Semitism in that area. At the same time the outlets for Jewish immigration in
overseas countries have diminished and may shortly become non-existent. The
German Government are showing themselves unwilling even to discuss with
other countries proposals for a scheme of orderly emigration of Jews and other
refugees from Germany and it is not unlikely that other Governments will adopt
a similar attitude. Moreover, it is not at the moment possible to foresee the
opening of general negotiations, the subject matter of which would include the
Jewish question. Finally I think it is extremely doubtful whether it could be said
that the position of the Jews in Central Europe is in any way a British interest.[96]

   When, not many months later, the Czechoslovak republic was destroyed
totally and the balance of strategic power in Europe was reversed for all to
see, the 'position of the Jews in Central Europe' was decided for a
certainty. To be sure, the entry of the Wehrmacht and the Gestapo into
Bohemia and Moravia rendered others—Social Democrats, Communists,
ordinary citizens of the republic who for one reason or another had cause
to believe that they were in Germany's bad books—equally desperate for
shelter and escape. But it was the special fate of the Jews to constitute the
case which onlookers found easiest to shrug off and it is not hard to see
why this was so. It was partly, perhaps chiefly, because it had come to seem
a fixed, settled, and therefore expected element of a general pattern that
as the forces of National Socialism and its analogues and allies advanced

---

[96] Laski to Chamberlain, 4 Oct. 1938; Minute by R. M. Makins, 19 Oct. 1938, PRO,
FO 371/21636. Remnants of the older view of Jewry and its predicaments could still be
detected, however, among some members of the British official family. 'The Jews of Germany,' the British chargé d'affaires in Berlin thought it proper to warn London by way of
concluding an exceptionally vivid account of the brutalities, terrors, and logic of *Kristallnacht*, 'are indeed not a national but a world problem which if neglected contains the seeds
of terrible vengeance' (Ogilvie-Forbes to Halifax, 16 Nov. 1938, PRO, FO 371/21637).

so they were lost. But it was partly too because there was no longer anything that the Jews themselves in central Europe, or anywhere else, might do or say that seemed to matter a great deal one way or the other—except, faintly, as a nuisance.

George Kennan, then a member of the American Legation in Prague, recalls the atmosphere in his memoirs. 'A Jewish acquaintance came [to the Legation],' he writes. 'We told him that he was welcome to stay around there until he could calm his nerves. He paced wretchedly up and down in the ante-room, through the long morning hours. In the afternoon, he decided to face the music and went home.'[97] The conference at Evian had been that same little scene in the American Legation writ very large and in unintentional anticipation of what Kennan was so neatly and laconically to describe: written clearly enough, moreover, for its message to be grasped and registered by anyone who troubled to take notice of what had transpired there. What the Jews had been told somewhat implicitly at Evian, but thereafter in ever plainer language, was that they were now dismissed, that they would have to leave the stage on which really serious, practical political affairs were normally played out, but upon which they, so unreasonably, had imagined that they might perform with the others. How they would now proceed and at what cost to themselves, no one quite knew. But that was their affair. What was left to them, in Kennan's terms, was 'to face the music', namely to have the grace to go out into the night with minimal disturbance and unpleasantness to others.[98]

---

[97] George F. Kennan, *Memoirs 1925–1950* (Boston, 1967), 98.

[98] It would be well into the war before the significance of the process of exclusion was fully understood. Even then it would be mostly out of the mouths of officials of the middle rank—the babes and sucklings of modern government—that the truth, at all events the proximate truth of the matter, would emerge. It had become evident, wrote the draftsmen of a British *aide mémoire* to the State Department on 20 Jan. 1943, that something had to be done about 'the many thousands of refugees [who] continue to crowd into neutral countries in Europe', one reason being 'that the Germans or their satellites may change over from the policy of extermination to one of extrusion, and aim as they did before the war at embarrassing other countries by flooding them with alien immigrants' (*FRUS* 1943, i. 134).

Epilogue

THREE-FIFTHS of the civilian Jewish population of continental Europe[1] were done to death in the course of the Second World War by Germany and its allies. It was to be the solution for all time of what was conceived in Berlin as the Jewish Problem. Most victims were killed by firing squads or in gas chambers installed in camps

TABLE E.1. *The extirpation of European Jewry by the military and police forces of Germany and its allies, 1939–1945*

	Initial Jewish population	Low estimate of Jewish population losses		High estimate of Jewish population losses	
			%		%
Austria[a]	185,000	50,000	27.0	50,000	27.0
Belgium	65,700	28,900	44.0	28,900	44.0
Bohemia and Moravia	118,310	78,150	66.1	78,150	66.1
Bulgaria[b]	61,000	11,000	18.0	11,000	18.0
Denmark[c]	7,800	60	0.12	60	0.12
Estonia	4,500	1,500	33.3	2,000	44.4
Finland	2,000	7	0.35	7	0.35
France[d]	350,000	77,320	22.1	77,320	22.1
Germany[e]	185,000	134,500	72.4	141,500	76.5
Greece[f]	66,380	49,000	73.8	56,000	84.4
Hungary[g]	825,000	550,000	66.7	569,000	69.0
Italy	44,500	7,680	17.3	7,680	17.3
Latvia[h]	91,500	70,000	76.5	71,500	78.1
Lithuania[i]	168,000	140,000	83.3	143,000	85.1
Luxembourg	3,500	1,950	55.7	1,950	55.7
Netherlands[j]	140,000	100,000	71.4	100,000	71.4
Norway	1,700	762	44.8	762	44.8
Poland[k]	3,300,000	2,900,000	87.9	3,000,000	90.9
Romania[l]	609,000	271,000	44.5	287,000	47.1
Slovakia[m]	88,950	68,000	76.4	71,000	79.8
USSR	3,020,000	1,000,000	33.1	1,100,000	36.4
Yugoslavia[n]	78,000	56,200	72.1	63,300	81.2
TOTAL	9,415,840	5,596,029	59.4	5,860,129	62.2

[1] Exclusive therefore of the moderately sized Jewish community of the undefeated and unoccupied United Kingdom and, for simplicity's sake, of the very small communities of the three neutral countries, Sweden, Switzerland, and the Irish Republic as well.

for notes to table see p. 898

dedicated to the purpose. The rest were finished off by massive ill treatment and starvation in the ghettos and concentration camps into which they had been corralled or by subjection to homicidally intense slave labour and forced marches. The military defeat of Germany occurred before the programme could be completed, but National Socialist hegemony over Europe lasted long enough for the result to fall very little short of the intention—which was to deal the Jewish people, notably in its great east European heartland, a blow from which recovery would be impossible.

[a] 1938 figures.

[b] Inclusive of territories in Thrace and Macedonia annexed by Bulgaria in 1941.

[c] Inclusive of refugees from pre-war Germany, Austria, and Bohemia and Moravia.

[d] Inclusive of refugees from pre-war Germany, Austria, and Bohemia and Moravia.

[e] Exclusive of the some 65,000 ex-German Jews who were sent to their death from the countries in which they had found temporary asylum before the war.

[f] Exclusive of the Jewish inhabitants of Thrace and Macedonia ceded to Bulgaria in 1941.

[g] As enlarged by the annexation of Slovakian, Romanian, and Yugoslav territories in 1939, 1940, and 1941 respectively.

[h] Inclusive of refugees from pre-war Germany, Austria, and Bohemia and Moravia.

[i] Inclusive of refugees from pre-war Germany, Austria, and Bohemia and Moravia, but exclusive of the Vilna region annexed by Lithuania in October 1939.

[j] Inclusive of refugees from pre-war Germany, Austria, and Bohemia and Moravia.

[k] As of 31 Aug. 1939 and inclusive of Polish Jews who subsequently fled to the USSR but were caught up by the German war machine and liquidated.

[l] Exclusive of territory ceded to Hungary in 1940.

[m] Exclusive of territory ceded to Hungary in 1939.

[n] Exclusive of territory ceded to Hungary in 1941.

Principal source: Israel Gutman (ed.), *Ha-Enziklopediya shel ha-Sho'ah*, v (Tel Aviv, 1990), *passim*; but see Raul Hilberg, *The Destruction of the European Jews* (revised edn., New York, 1985), appendix B, 1201–20. The discrepancy between Hilberg's figures and those of Gutman and his team owes a good deal to Hilberg not having had access to Russian sources.

BIBLIOGRAPHY

ABRAMSKY, CHIMEN, *War, Revolution and the Jewish Dilemma* (London, 1975).

ADLER-RUDEL, S., *Ostjuden in Deutschland 1880–1940* (Tübingen, 1959).

—— 'The Evian Conference on the Refugee Question', *LBIYB* 13 (London, 1968), 235–73.

ALBERT, PHYLLIS COHEN, *The Jewish Oath in Nineteenth-Century France* (Tel Aviv, 1982).

ALDERMAN, GEOFFREY, *Modern British Jewry* (Oxford, 1992), 235.

ALSBERG, PAUL A., 'Documents on the Brussels Conference of 1906', *Michael*, 2 (Tel Aviv, 1973), 145–53.

ALTMANN, ALEXANDER, *Moses Mendelssohn* (London, 1973).

ALTSHULER, M., 'The Attitude of the Communist Party of Russia to Jewish National Survival, 1918–1930', *YIVO Annual*, 14 (1969).

—— *Ha-yevsektia bi-verit ha-mo'ezot (1918–1930): bein le'umiyut le-komunizm* (Tel Aviv, 1980).

ANCHEL, ROBERT, *Napoléon et les Juifs* (Paris, 1928).

—— *Les Juifs de France* (Paris, 1946).

ANCONA, ALESSANDRO D', *Scipione Piattoli e la Polonia* (Florence, 1915).

APTEKMAN, O. V., *Obshchestvo 'Zemlya i Volya' 70kh godov* (Petrograd, 1924).

Archives parlementaires de 1787 à 1860, première série (1787–1799) (Paris, 1878; repr. Lichtenstein, 1969), x. 752–60.

ARENDT, H., *Rahel Varnhagen* (London, 1957).

ARLOSOROFF, CHAIM, *Yoman Yerushalayim* (Tel Aviv, [1948]).

ARNSBERG, GAD, *Gabriel Riesser—Intelektual germani-yehudi ke-idiolog liberali* (Tel Aviv, 1990).

ARONSFELD, C. C., 'Jewish Bankers and the Tsar', *JSS* 35 (1973), 87–104.

ARONSON, I. M., 'The Attitudes of Russian Officials in the 1880s toward Jewish Assimilation and Emigration', *Slavic Review*, 84, 1 (1975).

—— 'The Prospects for the Emancipation of Russian Jewry during the 1880s', *Slavonic and East European Review*, 55, 3 (1977).

—— *Troubled Waters: The Origins of the 1881 Anti-Jewish Pogroms in Russia* (Pittsburgh, 1990).

ASCH, ADOLPH, and PHILIPPSON, JOHANNA, 'Self-defence at the Turn of the Century: The Emergence of the K.C.', *LBIYB* 3 (London, 1958), 122–39.

ASCHER, ABRAHAM, *Pavel Axelrod and the Development of Menshevism* (Cambridge, Mass., 1972).

—— *The Revolution of 1905*, 2 vols. (Stanford, Calif., 1988, 1992).

ASSAF, DAVID, *Derekh ha-malkhut: R. Yisrael me-Ruzhin u-mekomo be-toledot ha-ḥasidut* (Jerusalem, 1997).

AVINERI, SHLOMO, *Moses Hess: Prophet of Communism and Zionism* (New York, 1985).

BABEL, ISAAC, *1920 Diary*, trans. H. T. Willetts; ed. Carol J. Avins (New Haven, 1995).

BACON, GERSHON C., 'The Politics of Tradition: Agudat Israel in Polish Politics, 1916–1939', *Studies in Contemporary Jewry*, 2 (Bloomington, Ind., 1986), 144–63.

BALABAN, M., *Le-toldot ha-tenu'a ha-frankit* (Tel Aviv, 1934).

BANKIER, DAVID, 'Ha-miflaga ha-komunistit ha-germanit ve-yaḥasa le-antishemiyut ba-raikh ha-shelishi 1933–1938', *Yahadut Zemaneinu*, 2 (1985), 131–51.

BARNETT, R. D., 'A Diary That Survived: Damascus 1840', in Sonia and V. D. Lipman (eds.), *The Century of Moses Montefiore* (Oxford, 1985).

BARON, S. W., *The Russian Jew under Tsars and Soviets*, 2nd edn. (New York, 1976).

BARTAL, I., ' "Ha-model ha-mishni"—ẓarfat ke-mekor hashpa'a be-tahalikhei ha-modernizaẓiya shel yehudei mizraḥ eiropa (1772–1863)', in Y. Cohen, (ed.), *Ha-mahapekha ha-ẓarfatit ve-rishuma* (Jerusalem, 1991).

BARTOSZEWSKI, W. T., and POLONSKY, A. (eds.), *The Jews of Warsaw* (Oxford, 1991).

BARZILAI, YOSEF, 'Siḥot 'im Shim'on Dimanshtein', *He-'Avar*, 15 (1968), 216–39.

BAUER, BRUNO, *Die Judenfrage* (Braunschweig, 1843).

BAUER, YEHUDA, *Jews for Sale? Nazi-Jewish Negotiations, 1933–1945* (New Haven and London, 1994).

BEIN, A. (ed.), *Sefer Motzkin: Ketavim ve-ne'umim nivḥarim, biografiya ve-divrei ha'arakha* (Jerusalem, 1939).

BEIT-ZEVI, S. B., *Ha-ẓionut ha-post-ugandit be-mashber ha-sho'ah* (Tel Aviv, 1977).

BELOFF, MAX, *Lucien Wolf and the Anglo-Russian Entente 1907–1914* (London, 1951).

BEN-GURION, DAVID, *Zikhronot*, i (Tel Aviv, 1971).

BEN-SASSON, H. H., 'The Reformation in Contemporary Jewish Eyes', Israel Academy of Sciences and Humanities, *Proceedings*, 4, 12 (1970).

BERG, R., and URBAH-BORNSTEIN, M., *Les Juifs devant le droit français* (Paris, 1984).

BERGER-BARZILAI, Y., *Ha-tragediya shel ha-mahapekha ha-sovyetit* (Tel Aviv, 1968).

BERING, DIETZ, *The Stigma of Names: Antisemitism in German Daily Life, 1812–1933* (Cambridge, 1992).

BERLIN, ISAIAH, *The Life and Opinions of Moses Hess* (Cambridge, 1959).

—— 'Benjamin Disraeli, Karl Marx, and the Search for Identity', in Jewish Historical Society of England, *Transactions*, 22, 1968–9 (London, 1970), 1–20.

BIHL, WOLFDIETER, 'Die Juden', in *Die Habsburgermonarchie 1848–1918*, iii. *Die Völker des Reiches* (Vienna, 1980).

BIRNBAUM, PIERRE, and KATZNELSON, IRA (eds.), *Paths of Emancipation: Jews, States, and Citizenship* (Princeton, 1995).

BLACK, EDWIN, *The Transfer Agreement* (New York, 1984).

BLACK, EUGENE C., *The Social Politics of Anglo-Jewry 1880–1920* (Oxford, 1988).

BLACKBOURN, DAVID, and ELEY, GEOFF, *The Peculiarities of German History: Bourgeois Society and Politics in Nineteenth-Century Germany* (Oxford, 1987).

BLAKENEY, MICHAEL, 'Australia and the Jewish Refugees from Central Europe: Government Policy 1933–1939', *LBIYB* 29 (London, 1984), 103–33.

BLET, PIERRE, *et al.* (eds.), *Actes et documents du Saint Siége relatifs à la seconde guerre mondiale*, vi (City of the Vatican, 1972).

BLUMENKRANZ, B., and SOBOUL, A. (eds.), *Le Grand Sanhédrin de Napoléon* (Paris, 1979).

—— and —— (eds.), *Les Juifs et la révolution française* (Paris, 1989).

BOAS, JACOB, 'The Shrinking World of German Jewry', *LBIYB* 31 (London, 1986), 241–66.

BODIAN, MIRIAM, 'Ha-yazamim ha-yehudiim be-Berlin, ha-medina ha-absolutistit ve-"shipur mazavam ha-ezrahi shel ha-yehudim" ba-mahazit ha-sheniya shel ha-me'ah ha-18', *Zion*, 49, 2 (1984), 159–84.

BOEHLICH, WALTER (ed.), *Der Berliner Antisemitismusstreit* (Frankfurt-on-Main, 1965).

BRAHAM, RANDOLPH L. (ed.), *Hungarian-Jewish Studies* (New York, 1966).

BRANDES, GEORG, *Ferdinand Lassalle: eine kritische Darstellung seines Lebens und seiner Werke* (Leipzig and Berlin, 1900).

BREDIN, JEAN-DENIS, *The Affair: The Case of Alfred Dreyfus* (New York, 1986).

BREITMAN, R., and KRAUT, A. M., *American Refugee Policy and European Jewry, 1933–1945* (Bloomington, Ind., 1987).

BREUER, ISAAC, *The Jewish National Home* (Frankfurt-on-Main, 1926) trans. of *Das Jüdische Nationalheim* (Frankfurt-on-Main, 1925).

—— *Concepts of Judaism*, ed. Jacob S. Levinger (Jerusalem, 1974).

BREUER, MORDECHAI, *Modernity within Tradition: The Social History of Orthodox Jewry in Imperial Germany* [*Jüdische Orthodoxie im deutschen Reich 1871–1918*], trans. Elizabeth Petuchowski (New York, 1992).

BROVKIN, VLADIMIR N., *Behind the Front Lines of the Civil War: Political Parties and Social Movements in Russia, 1918–1922* (Princeton, 1994).

BRUMBERG, ABRAHAM, 'The Bund and the Polish Socialist Party in the late 1930s', in Yisrael Gutman, *et al.* (eds.), *The Jews of Poland between Two World Wars* (Hanover and London, 1989).

BRYM, ROBERT J., *The Jewish Intelligentsia and Russian Marxism* (London, 1978).

BUKHBINDER, N. A., *Istoriya evreiskogo rabochego dvizheniya v rossii* (Leningrad, 1925).

BUSI, FREDERICK, *The Pope of Antisemitism: The Career and Legacy of Edouard-Adolphe Drumont* (Lanham, Md., 1986).

CARLEBACH, ALEXANDER, 'A German Rabbi goes East', *LBIYB* 6 (London, 1961), 60–121.

CARON, VICKI, and HYMAN, PAULA, 'The Failed Alliance: Jewish Catholic Relations in Alsace-Lorraine 1871–1914', *LBIYB* 26 (1981), 3–21.

CESARANI, DAVID, *The Jewish Chronicle and Anglo-Jewry 1841–1991* (Cambridge, 1994).

CHARQUES, RICHARD, *The Twilight of Imperial Russia* (London, 1965).

CHASANOWITCH, L. (ed.), *Les Pogromes anti-juifs en Pologne et en Galicie en novembre et décembre 1918* (Stockholm, 1919).

CHERNIAVSKY, MICHAEL (ed.), *Prologue to Revolution* (Englewood Cliffs, NJ, 1967).

CHEYETTE, BRYAN, *Constructions of 'the Jew' in English Literature and Society* (Cambridge, 1995).

CHOURAQUI, ANDRÉ, *L'Alliance Israélite Universelle et la renaissance juive contemporaine* (Paris, 1965).

CLARDY, JESSE V., *G. R. Derzhavin: A Political Biography* (The Hague, 1967).

COBBETT, WILLIAM, *Good Friday; or, the Murder of Jesus Christ by the Jews* (London, 1830).

COHEN, NAOMI W., 'The Abrogation of the Russo-American Treaty of 1832', *JSS* 25 (1962), 3–41.

COHEN, STUART A., 'The Conquest of a Community? The Zionists and the Board of Deputies in 1917', *Jewish Journal of Sociology*, 19, 2 (1977).

COHEN, Y. (ed.), *Ha-mahapekha ha-zarfatit ve-rishuma* (Jerusalem, 1991).

COHN, NORMAN, *Warrant for Genocide* (London, 1967).

Comité des délégations juives auprès de la conférence de la paix, *Les Droits nationaux des Juifs en Europe orientale: Recueil d'études* (Paris, 1919).

Committee of the Jewish Delegations, ed. J. B. Schechtman, *The Pogroms in the Ukraine under the Ukrainian Governments (1917–1920)* (London, 1927).

Congrès Juif Mondial, Comité Exécutif, *Protocole du premier congrès juif mondial, Genève, 8–15 aout 1936* (Geneva, n.d.).

CORTI, Count EGON CAESAR, *The Rise of the House of Rothschild* (New York, 1928).

COWEN, ANNE and ROGER, *Victorian Jews through British Eyes* (Oxford, 1986).

DAUBE, DAVID, *Collaboration with Tyranny in Rabbinic Law* (London, 1965).

DAVIES, NORMAN, *God's Playground: A History of Poland*, 2 vols. (Oxford, 1981).

DEÁK, ISTVÁN, *Beyond Nationalism: A Social and Political History of the Habsburg Officer Corps, 1848–1918* (New York and Oxford, 1990).

DEUTSCHER, ISAAC, *The Prophet Armed. Trotsky: 1879–1921* (New York, 1954).

DIPPEL, JOHN V. H., *Bound Upon a Wheel of Fire* (New York, 1996).

DOBROSZYCKI, LUCJAN, 'The Fertility of Modern Polish Jewry', in Paul Ritterband (ed.), *Modern Jewish Fertility* (Leiden, 1981).

DODD, W. E., *Ambassador Dodd's Diary, 1933–1938* (New York, 1941).

DOHM, CHRISTIAN WILHELM VON, *Über die bürgerliche Verbesserung der Juden* (Berlin, 1781–83, repr. Hildesheim, 1973); trans. into English as *Concerning the Amelioration of the Civil Status of the Jews* (Cincinnati, 1957).

DOMB, I., *The Transformation* (London, 1957/8).

DRUMONT, ÉDOUARD, *La France juive* (Paris, 1886).

DUBNOV, S., 'Fun mein arkhiv', *YIVO Bletter*, 1 (Jan.–May, 1931), 405–7.

DUBNO[v], S. M., *History of the Jews in Russia and Poland*, 3 vols. (Philadelphia, 1916–20).

EISENBACH, ARTUR, *et al.* (eds.), for Institut Historii Polskiej Akademii Nauk, *Materialy do dziejów Sejmu Czteroletniego*, vi (Wroclaw, Warsaw, and Cracow, 1969).

—— *The Emancipation of the Jews in Poland, 1780–1870* (Oxford, 1991).

Eleh divrei ha-berit [*These are the words of the Covenant*] (Altona, AM 5579 [1818/19]).

ELIAV, M., *David Wolffsohn: ha-ish u-zemano* (Jerusalem, 1977).

Encyclopaedia Judaica, 16 vols. (Jerusalem, 1971).

ENDELMAN, T. M. (ed.), *Jewish Apostasy in the Modern World* (New York, 1987).

EREZ, YEHUDA, 'Aharon Zundelevich—yehudi 'amami be-zamaret ha-narodnikim', in E. Shaltiel (ed.), *Yehudim be-tenu'ot mahapkhaniot* (Jerusalem, 1982), 53–66.

ESCHWEGE, HELMUT, 'Resistance of German Jews against the Nazi Regime', *LBIYB* 15 (London, 1970), 143–80.

ETKES, E., 'Parashat ha-"haskalah mi-ta'am" ve-ha-temura be-ma'amad tenu'at ha-haskalah be-rusiya', *Zion*, 43, 3–4 (1978), 264–313.

—— 'Darko shel R. Shne'ur Zalman me-Lyady ke-manhig shel hasidim', *Zion*, 1 (Jubilee vol.) (1985).

—— (ed.), *Ha-dat ve-ha-hayyim* (Jerusalem, 1993).

ETTINGER, SHMU'EL, 'Medinat moskva be-yahasa el ha-yehudim', *Zion*, 18, 3–4 (1953).

—— 'Ha-rek'a ha-idiologi le-hofa'ata shel ha-sifrut ha-antishemit ha-hadasha be-rusiya', *Zion*, 35, 1–4 (1970).

—— 'Ha-yesodot ve-ha-megamot be-'izuv mediniyuto shel ha-shilton ha-rusi klapei ha-yehudim 'im halukat polin', *He-'Avar*, 19 (1972).

—— 'Takanat 1804', *He-'Avar*, 22 (1977), 87–110.

—— *Ha-antishemiyut ba-'et ha-hadasha* (Tel Aviv, 1978).

Evreiskaya Entsiklopediya, 16 vols. (St Petersburg, 1906–13).

FEDER, ERNST, *Politik und Humanität; Paul Nathan: Ein Lebensbild* (Berlin, 1929).

—— 'Paul Nathan and His Work for East-European and Palestinian Jewry', *Historia Judaica*, 14 (Apr. 1952).

FEINBERG, NATHAN, *La Question des minorités à la conférence de la paix de 1919–1920 et l'action juive en faveur de la protection internationale des minorités* (Paris, 1929).

—— 'Ha-mahloket 'im rusiya ha-zarit be-'inyan ha-haflaya le-ra'a shel yehudim zarim', *Zion*, 33, 1–2 (1968).

—— *Ha-agudot ha-yehudiot le-ma'an hever-ha-le'umim* (Jerusalem, 1968).

—— *Pirkei hayyim ve-zikhronot* (Jerusalem, 1985).

FELDMAN, E., 'Le-korot ha-irgun ha-kehilati ba-nesikhuyot ha-romaniot be-tekufat ha-takanon ha-organi (1832–57)', *Zion*, 22, 4 (1957), 214–38.

—— 'Ha-nisayon ha-rishon shel pe'ula amerikanit le-ma'an yehudei rusiya (1869/70)', *Zion*, 30, 3–4 (1965).

—— 'Pera'ot 1905 be-russiya ba-fe'ilut ha-diplomatit ha-britit', *He-'Avar*, 22 (1977), 59–83.

FIGES, ORLANDO, 'Ludwig Börne and the Formation of a Radical Critique of Judaism', *LBIYB* 29 (London, 1984).

FISHMAN, JOSHUA A. (ed.), *Shtudiés vegn yidn in Poiln 1919* (New York, 1974).

FOOTMAN, DAVID, *The Primrose Path: A Life of Ferdinand Lassalle* (London, 1961).

FOURIER, CHARLES, *Le Nouveau Monde industriel et sociétaire*, 2nd edn. (Paris, 1845, reprinted 1966).

FRANKEL, JONATHAN, *Prophecy and Politics: Socialism, Nationalism, and the Russian Jews, 1862–1917* (Cambridge, 1981).

—— *Jewish Politics and the Russian Revolution of 1905* (Tel Aviv, 1982).

FRIEDMAN, ISAIAH, *The Question of Palestine 1914–1918* (New York, 1973).

FRIEDMAN, YESHA'YAHU, 'Ben-Gurion ve-ha-britim: 1936–1940', *Kivunim*, 24 (Aug. 1984), 109–21.

FRISTER, ROMAN, *Lelo peshara* (Tel Aviv, 1987).

FUND, YOSEF, 'Agudat Yisrael mul ha-ẓionut u-medinat yisrael—idiologiya u-mediniyut', Ph.D. thesis, Bar-Ilan University, 1989.

GAINER, BERNARD, *The Alien Invasion: The Origins of the Aliens Act of 1905* (London, 1972).

GANS, M. H. (ed.), *Memorbook: History of Dutch Jewry from the Renaissance to 1940*, English trans. A. J. Pomerans (Baarn, 1977).

GARTNER, LLOYD P., *The Jewish Immigrant in England, 1870–1914* (London, 1960).

GELBER, N. M., 'She'elat ha-yehudim be-Polin be-shenot 1815–1830', *Zion*, 13–14 (1948–9).

—— 'The Intervention of German Jews at the Berlin Congress 1878', *LBIYB* 5 (London, 1960), 222–48.

—— 'La Question juive en Bulgarie et en Serbie devant le Congrès de Berlin de 1878', *Revue d'études juives*, 123 (1964), 83–4.

GERGEL, N., 'The Pogroms in the Ukraine in 1918–21', *YIVO Annual of Jewish Social Science*, 6 (1951).

GESSEN, YU. I., *Evrei v Rossii*, 2 vols. (St Petersburg, 1906).

—— *Istoriya evreiskogo naroda v Rossii* (revised edn., Moscow and Jerusalem, 1993).

GETZLER, ISRAEL, *Martov* (Cambridge and Melbourne, 1967).

—— 'Martov ve-Luksemburg', in Eli Shaltiel (ed.), *Yehudim be-tenu'ot mahapkhaniyot* (Jerusalem, 1982).

GEWIRTZ, SHARON, 'Anglo-Jewish Responses to Nazi Germany 1933–39: The Anti-nazi Boycott and the Board of Deputies of British Jews', *Journal of Contemporary History*, 26 (1991), 255–76.

GILLE, BERTRAND, *Histoire de la Maison Rothschild* (Geneva, 1965).

GINSBERG, ASHER ['Aḥad Ha-'Am'], *Kol Kitvei Aḥad Ha-'Am* (Tel Aviv, 1947).

—— *Igrot Aḥad Ha-'Am*, 2nd edn., ed. Arye [Leon] Simon with Y. Pograbinsky, 6 vols. (Tel Aviv, 1956–60).

GINZBURG, A., 'Emigratsia evreev iz Rossii', *Evreiskaya Entsiklopediya*, xvi, cols. 264–8.

GITELMAN, ZVI Y., *Jewish Nationality and Soviet Politics: The Jewish Sections of the CPSU, 1917–1930* (Princeton, 1972).

GLÜCKEL of HAMELN, *Memoirs*, trans. Marvin Lowenthal (New York, 1977).

GOLDHAGEN, D. J., *Hitler's Willing Executioners: Ordinary Germans and the Holocaust* (London, 1996).

GOLDSTEIN, JOSEPH, 'Some Sociological Aspects of the Russian Zionist Movement at its Inception', *JSS* 47, 2 (Spring 1985).

—— 'Jabotinsky and Jewish Autonomy in the Diaspora', *Studies in Zionism*, 7, 2 (1986), 29–232.

GOLDSTEIN, Y., *Manya Vilbusheviẓ-Shoḥat: perek ha-manhigut ha-mahapkhanit* (Haifa, 1991).

GRADOVSKY, N. D., *Torgoviye i drugiye prava evreev v Rossii* (St Petersburg, 1885).

—— *La Situation légale des Israélites en Russie*, i (Paris, 1890).

GRAETZ, MICHAEL, 'Le-"shivato" shel Moshe Hess la-yahadut—ha-rek'a la-ḥibur "Romi vi-Yerushalaim" ', *Zion*, 45, 2 (1980).

—— ''Aliyato vishki'ato shel sapak ha-ẓava ha-yehudi be-'itot milḥama', *Zion*, 56, 3 (1991), 255–73.

Great Britain, Parliamentary Papers, *Correspondence respecting the Persecution of Jews in Moldovia* (London, 1867).

—— *Correspondence respecting the Condition and Treatment of the Jews in Servia and Roumania 1867–76* (London, 1877).

—— *Correspondence relative to the Recognition of the Independence of Roumania* (London, 1880).

GREEN, NANCY L., 'Socialist Anti-Semitism, Defense of a Bourgeois Jew and Discovery of the Jewish Proletariat', *International Review of Social History*, 30, 3 (1985), 374–99.

GREENBERG, L., *The Jews in Russia: The Struggle for Emancipation*, 2 vols. (New York, 1976).

GRODZIENSKI, HAYYIM 'OZER, *Ahi'ezer: kovez igrot; pirkei hayyim*, 2 vols., ed. Aharon Suraski (Benei Berak, 1970).

GROSSMANN, KURT R., *Emigration: Geschichte der Hitler-Flüchtlinge 1933–1945* (Frankfurt-on-Main, 1969).

GROT, YA. (ed.), *Sochineniya Derzhavina*, vii (St Peterburg, 1878).

GRUENBAUM, Y., *Milḥamot yehudei Polin (1906–1912)* (Warsaw, 1922).

—— *Milḥamot yehudei polania, 1912/13–1939/40* (Jerusalem/Tel Aviv, 1941).

—— *Dor be-mivḥan* (Jerusalem, 1951).

GRUNWALD, MAX, *Vienna* (Philadelphia, 1936).

GUTMAN, YISRAEL, et al. (eds.), *The Jews of Poland between Two World Wars* (Hanover and London, 1989).

GUTTERIDGE, RICHARD, *Open thy mouth to the dumb! The German Evangelical Church and the Jews, 1879–1950* (Oxford, 1976).

GUTWEIN, DANIEL, 'Ya'akov Schiff u-mimun milḥemet rusiya-yapan: perek be-toldot "ha-diplomatiya ha-yehudit" ', *Zion*, 54, 3 (1989).

Ha-kongres ha-zioni ha-19: din-ve-ḥeshbon stenografi (Jerusalem, 1937).

HABER, ADOLF, 'Ha-pundakaim ha-yehudiim ba-publizistika ha-polanit shel "Ha-seim ha-gadol" (1788–1792)', *Gal-'Ed*, 2 (1975), 1–24.

HAGEN, WILLIAM H., 'Before the "Final Solution": Toward a Comparative Analysis of Political Anti-Semitism in Interwar Germany and Poland', *Journal of Modern History*, 58 (1966), 351–81.

HALPERN, I., 'Der va'ad arba aratsot in zeine batsiungen mit oisland', in Tscherikower (ed.), *Historishe shriftn* (Vilna, 1937), 68–79.

—— (ed.), *Pinkas va'ad arb'a ha-arazot* (Jerusalem, 1945–6).

—— (ed.), *Sefer ha-gevura: antologiya historit-sifrutit*, iii (Tel Aviv, 1950).

—— 'Gzeirat Woszczylo', *Zion*, 22, 1 (1957).

HALPHEN, ACHILLE-EDMOND (ed.), *Recueil des lois, décrets, ordonnances, avis du Conseil d'État, arrêtés et règlements concernant les Israélites depuis la révolution de 1789* (Paris, 1851).

HAMBURGER, ERNEST, 'Jews in the Public Service under the German Monarchy', *LBIYB* 9 (London, 1964).

—— 'One Hundred Years of Emancipation', *LBIYB* 14 (London, 1969).

HARCAVE, SIDNEY S., 'The Jewish Question in the First Russian Duma', *JSS* 6, 2 (1944), 155–76.

—— *First Blood: The Russian Revolution of 1905* (New York, 1964).

HEADLAM MORLEY, JAMES, *A Memoir of the Paris Peace Conference 1919* (London, 1972).

Hebrew Sheltering and Immigrant Aid Society, *Third Annual Report* (New York, 1911).

HEIFETZ, ELIAS, *The Slaughter of the Jews in the Ukraine in 1919* (New York, 1921).

HERSCH, L., *Le Juif errant d'aujourd'hui: étude sur l'émigration des Israélites de l'Europe orientale aux Etats-Unis de l'Amérique du Nord* (Paris, 1913).

HERTZ, Y. S., *et al.*, *Di Geshikhte fun Bund*, 3 vols. (New York, 1960–2).

HERTZBERG, ARTHUR, *The French Enlightenment and the Jews* (New York, 1970).

HERZEN, ALEXANDER, *The Russian People and Socialism: A Letter to M. Jules Michelet* (Coniston, Windermere, 1851).

—— *From the Other Shore* (Oxford, 1979).

HERZL, THEODOR, *Tagebücher*, 3 vols. (Berlin, 1922–3).

—— *The Complete Diaries*, ed. Raphael Patai, English trans. Harry Zohn, 5 vols. (New York, 1960).

HILBERG, RAUL, *The Destruction of the European Jews*, revised edn., 3 vols. (New York, 1985).

—— *Perpetrators, Victims, Bystanders: The Jewish Catastrophe 1933–1945* (London, 1995).

HINGLEY, RONALD, *The Russian Secret Police* (London, 1970).

HITCHINS, KEITH, *Rumania 1866–1947* (Oxford, 1994).

HOWE, I., *The Immigrant Jews of New York* (London, 1976).

HUNDERT, G. D., *The Jews in a Polish Private Town: The Case of Opatów in the Eighteenth Century* (Baltimore, 1992).

HYMAN, PAULA E., 'From Paternalism to Cooptation: The French Jewish Consistory and the Immigrants, 1906–1939', YIVO, *Annual of Jewish Social Science*, 17 (1978), 217–37.

—— *The Emancipation of the Jews of Alsace* (New Haven, 1991).

IANCU, CAROL, 'Adolphe Crémieux, l'Alliance Israélite Universelle et les Juifs de Roumanie', *Revue d'Études Juives*, 133, 3–4 (1974), 481–502.

—— 'Benjamin Franklin Peixotto, l'Alliance Israélite Universelle et les Juifs de Roumanie. Correspondance inédite (1871–1876), *Revue d'Études Juives*, 137, 1–2 (1978), 77–147.

—— *Les Juifs en Roumanie (1866–1919): de l'exclusion à l'émancipation* (Aix-en-Provence, 1978).

Ispolnitel'ny komitet Ukrains'komu narodu: Ob'yavlenie, Text and accompanying annotations in Y. Ma'or, 'Ha-keruz ha-antishemi shel "narodnaya volya" ', *Zion*, 15 (1950), 150–5.

ISRAEL, JONATHAN I., *European Jewry in the Age of Mercantilism 1550–1750* (Oxford, 1985).

JACOBS, LOUIS, *Theology in the Responsa* (London, 1975).

JANOWSKY, OSCAR I., *The Jews and Minority Rights 1898–1919* (New York, 1933; repr. New York, 1966).

Jewish Immigrants: Report of a Special Committee of the National Jewish Immigration Council, US Senate Document No. 611, 63rd Congress (Washington, 1914).

JOHNPOLL, BERNARD K., *The Politics of Futility: The General Jewish Workers Bund of Poland, 1917–1943* (Ithaca, NY, 1967).

JOLL, JAMES B., *Europe Since 1970* (Harmondsworth, 1976).

KAMPE, NORBERT (ed.), *Jewish Emigration from Germany 1933–1942: A Documentary History*, 2 vols. (Munich, 1992).

KATZ, D. S., *Philosemitism and the Readmission of the Jews into England 1603–1655* (Oxford, 1982).

KATZ, E., *He-Ḥatam Sofer: Rabbi Moshe Sofer, ḥayyav vi-yiẓirato* (Jerusalem, 1960).

KATZ, JACOB, 'Pera'ot hep-hep shel shenat 1819 be-germaniya 'al rik'an ha-histori', *Ẕion*, 38, 1–4 (1973), 62–115.

—— *Out of the Ghetto* (Cambridge, Mass., 1973).

—— *Goy shel Shabbat* (Jerusalem, 1983).

KATZBURG, N., *Antishemiyut be-hungariya, 1867–1914* (Tel Aviv, 1969).

——*Hungary and the Jews: Policy and Legislation 1920–1943* (Ramat-Gan, 1981).

KATZENELENBOGEN, S., *L'Émigration juive* (Brussels, 1918).

KAUFMAN, MENAHEM, 'The Daily Life of the Village and Country Jews in Hessen from Hitler's Ascent to Power to November 1938', *Yad Vashem Studies*, 22 (Jerusalem, 1992), 147–98.

KENNAN, GEORGE F., *The Marquis de Custine and his Russia in 1839* (Princeton, 1971).

KESSLER, HARRY, *Walther Rathenau: His Life and Work* (London, 1929).

Ketavim le-toldot Ḥibbat-Ẕion ve-yishuv Ereẕ-Yisrael, ed. Alter Druyanov, 3 vols. (Odessa, 1919; Tel Aviv, 1925–32); revised edition, ed. Shulamit Laskov, 7 vols. (Tel Aviv, 1982–93).

KISSMAN, JOSEPH, 'The Immigration of Rumanian Jews up to 1914', *Yivo Annual of Jewish Social Science*, 2–3 (1947/8), 160–79.

KLAUSNER, ISRAEL 'Tazkir 'al ba'ayat ha-yehudim be-rusiya me'et sar ha-pelekh ha-vilnai Pahlen', *He-'Avar*, 7 (1950), 91–122.

—— *Be-hit'orer 'am* (Jerusalem, 1962).

KLEIN, CHARLOTTE, 'Damascus to Kiev: *Civiltà Cattolica* on Ritual Murder', *Wiener Library Bulletin*, 28, 32 (1974), 18–25.

KLIER, J. D., *Russia Gathers her Jews: The Origins of the 'Jewish Question' in Russia* (DeKalb, 1986).

—— *Imperial Russia's Jewish Question 1855–1881* (Cambridge, 1995).

—— and LAMBROZA, S. (eds.), *Pogroms: Anti-Jewish Violence in Modern Russian History* (Cambridge, 1992).

KOCHAN, LIONEL (ed.), *The Jews in Soviet Russia since 1917*, 3rd edn. (Oxford, 1978).

KORZEC, PAWEL, *Juifs en Pologne: la question juive pendant l'entre-deux-guerres* (Paris, 1980).

KOSSOWSKY, WL., *Les Persécutions des Juifs en Russie* (Berne, 1915).

KRAKOWSKI, SHMU'EL, 'Yehudim ba-zava ha-polani be-ma'arekhet september 1939', in E. Mendelsohn, and Ch. Shmeruk (eds.), *Studies on Polish Jewry: Paul Glikson Memorial Volume* (Jerusalem, 1987), 149–70.

KREPPEL, J., *Juden und Judentum* (Vienna, 1925).

KULKA, O. D., ' "Da'at kahal" be-Germaniya ha-naẓional-sozialistit ve-"ha-be'aya ha-yehudit": ha-mekorot u-va'ayoteihem', *Ẕion*, 40, 3–4 (1975), 186–291.

KWIET, KONRAD, 'The Ultimate Refuge: Suicide in the Jewish Communities under the Nazis', *LBIYB* 19 (London, 1984), 135–67.

LANDA, MOSHE, ' "Gush ha-mi'utim" (1922)—makhshir beḥirot o etgar medini?', *Gal-'Ed*, 4–5 (1978), 365–96.

Lassalle, Ferdinand, *Nachgelassene Briefe und Schriften*, ed. Gustav Meyer, 6 vols. (Stuttgart-Berlin, 1921–5).

Lazare, Bernard, *L'Antisémitisme: son histoire et ses causes* (Paris, 1894; repr. 1982); English edn. with introd. by Robert S. Wistrich (Lincoln, Neb., 1995).

—— *L'Affaire Dreyfus: une erreur judiciaire* (Paris, 1897).

—— *Le Fumier de Job* (Paris, 1928); trans. into English as *Job's Dungheap* (New York, 1948).

—— *Contre l'antisémitisme: histoire d'une polémique* (Paris, 1983).

Le Prolétariat juif: Lettre des ouvriers juif de Paris au Partie Socialiste Français (Paris, 1898).

Lestschinsky, Jacob, *La Situation économique des juifs depuis la guerre mondiale (Europe orientale et centrale)* (Paris, 1934).

Levi, Franz, 'The Jews of Sachsen-Meiningen and the Edict of 1811', *LBIYB* 38 (London, 1993), 15–32.

Levin, Nora, *Jewish Socialist Movements, 1871–1917: While Messiah Tarried* (London, 1978).

—— *The Jews in the Soviet Union since 1917: Paradox of Survival*, 2 vols. (New York, 1988).

Levine, Herbert S., 'A Jewish Collaborator in Nazi Germany: The Strange Career of Georg Kareski, 1933–37', *Central European History*, 7 (1975), 251–81.

Levine, Hillel, *Economic Origins of Antisemitism: Poland and its Jews in the Early Modern Period* (New Haven, 1991).

Levitats, I., 'Le-bikoret "Sefer ha-kahal" shel Brafman', *Zion*, 3, 2 (1938), 170–8.

—— *The Jewish Community in Russia, 1772–1844* (New York, 1943).

—— *The Jewish Community in Russia, 1844–1917* (Jerusalem, 1981).

Levy, Richard S., *The Downfall of the Anti-Semitic Political Parties in Imperial Germany* (New Haven and London, 1975).

Lewin, Sabina, 'Batei-ha-sefer ha-elementariim ha-rishonim li-ladim benei dat Moshe be-Varsha, ba-shanim 1818–1830', *Gal-'Ed*, 1 (1973), 63–100.

Liebeschütz, Hans, 'Treitschke and Mommsen on Jewry and Judaism', *LBIYB* 7 (London, 1962), 153–82.

Lifschitz, Ya'akov ha-Levi, *Toldot Yizhak* (Warsaw, 1896).

—— *Sefer Mahzikei ha-dat* (Petrokov (Piotrków), 1903).

—— *Zikhron ya'akov*, 3 vols. (Kaunas, 1923–30; repr. Benei-Berak, 1968).

Lifshitz, E., ' 'Al shelihuto shel Binyamin Franklin Peixotto be-romaniya', *Zion*, 26, 2 (1961), 85–102.

Lilienblum, M. L., *Derekh la'avor golim* (Warsaw, 1899).

—— *Kol kitvei M. L. Lilienblum*, 4 vols. (Warsaw, 1910–13).

—— *Ketavim otobiografiim*, ed. S. Breiman, 3 vols. (Jerusalem, 1970).

Lipman, V. D., *Social History of the Jews in England 1850–1950* (London, 1954).

—— *A History of the Jews in Britain since 1858* (New York, 1990).

Livneh, Eli'ezer, *NILI: toldoteiha shel he'aza medinit* (Jerusalem, 1961).

Loeb, Isidore, *La Situation des Israélites en Turquie, en Serbie et en Roumanie* (Paris, 1877).

Loewe, Louis, *The Damascus Affair* (Ramsgate, 1940).

LOKSHIN, A., 'Formirovanie politiki (Tsarskaya administrastiya i sionizm v Rossii v kontse XIX–nachale XX v.)', *Vestnik evreiskogo universiteta v Moskve*, 1 (1992).

LOUGEE, ROBERT W., *Paul de Lagarde* (Cambridge, Mass., 1962).

LOW, ALFRED D., *Jews in the Eyes of the Gemans* (Philadelphia, 1979).

LÖWENBRÜCK, ANNA-RUTH, 'Zalkind Hourwitz—Ein jüdischer Aufklärer zur Zeit der Französischen Revolution', *Tel Aviver Jahrbuch für deutsche Geschichte*, 20 (1991).

LUKASHEVICH, STEPHEN, *Ivan Aksakov 1823–1886: A Study in Russian Thought and Politics* (Cambridge, Mass., 1965).

MACARTNEY, C. A., *National States and National Minorities* (London, 1934).

MCCAGG, WILLIAM O., *Jewish Nobles and Geniuses in Modern Hungary* (New York, 1972; 2nd edn. 1986).

—— *A History of Habsburg Jews, 1670–1918* (Bloomington, Ind., 1989).

MAHLER, RAPHAEL, 'Jews in Public Service and the Liberal Professions in Poland, 1918–39', *JSS* 6 (1944), 291–350.

—— *Divrei yemei yisrael: dorot aḥaronim*, i–vii, 2nd edn. (Merḥavia, 1952–80); vols. i–iv only abridged and trans. as *A History of Modern Jewry 1780–1815* (London, 1971).

—— *Yidn in Amuliken Poilen in licht fun zifern* (Warsaw, 1958).

—— *Yehudei Polin bein shetei milḥamot 'olam* (Tel Aviv, 1968).

MAIMON, SOLOMON, *An Autobiography* (Boston, 1888; repr. New York, 1967).

MAKHNO, NESTOR, *The Struggle Against the State and other Essays*, ed. A. Skirda (Edinburgh, 1996).

MALINO, FRANCES, *A Jew in the French Revolution: The Life of Zalkind Hourwitz* (Oxford, 1996).

MARGALIOT, ARAHAM, 'The Dispute over the Leadership of German Jewry (1933–1938)', *Yad Vashem Studies*, 10 (Jerusalem, 1974), 129–48.

MARR, WILHELM, *Der Sieg des Judenthums über das Germanenthum*, 4th edn. (Berne, 1879).

MARRUS, Michael R., *The Politics of Assimilation* (Oxford, 1971).

—— 'Le Comité de Défence Contre l'Antisémitisme', *Michael*, 4 (Tel Aviv, 1976).

—— *The Unwanted: European Refugees in the Twentieth Century* (New York, 1985).

MARX, KARL, *A World without Jews*, ed. D. D. Runes (New York, 1959).

MÉHÉE DE LA TOUCHE, J. C. H., *Histoire de la prétendue révolution de Pologne avec un examen de la nouvelle constitution* (Paris, 1792).

MELTZER, E., 'Mifleget ha-shilton OZON ve-ha-yehudim be-Polin (1937–1939)', *Gal-'Ed* (Tel Aviv), 4–5 (1978), 397–426.

MELVILLE, LEWIS, *The Life and Letters of William Cobbett in England and America*, 2 vols. (London, 1913).

MENDELSOHN, EZRA, 'The Politics of Agudas Yisroel in Inter-War Poland', *Soviet Jewish Affairs*, 2, 2 (1972), 47–60.

—— 'The Dilemma of Jewish Politics in Poland: Four Responses', in Bela Vago and George L. Mosse (eds.), *Jews and Non-Jews in Eastern Europe 1918–1945* (New York and Jerusalem, 1974).

—— *Zionism in Poland: The Formative Years, 1915–1926* (New Haven, 1981), 108.

MENDELSOHN, EZRA, *The Jews of East Central Europe between the World Wars* (Bloomington, Ind., 1987).

—— 'German and Jewish Minorities in the European Successor States between the World Wars', in E. Mendelsohn and Ch. Shmeruk (eds.), *Studies on Polish Jewry: Paul Glikson Memorial Volume* (Jerusalem, 1987).

MENDES-FLOHR, P. R., and REINHARZ, JEHUDA (eds.), *The Jew in the Modern World: A Documentary History* (New York and Oxford, 1980).

MEVORAH, B., ' 'Ikvoteiha shel 'alilat damesek be-hitpathuta shel ha-'itonut ha-yehudit ba-shanim 1840–1846', *Zion*, 23–4, 1–2 (1958–9), 46–65.

—— 'Ma'asei hishtadlut be-eiropa le-meni'at geirusham del yehudei bohemiya u-moraviya, 1744–1745', *Zion*, 28, 3–4 (1963), 125–64.

—— (ed.), *Napoleon u-tekufato* (Jerusalem, 1968).

MEYER, MICHAEL A., *Response to Modernity: A History of the Reform Movement in Judaism* (New York and Oxford, 1988).

MICHELET, JULES, *Bible de l'Humanité* (Paris, 1864).

—— *Journal*, i (1828–48), 2nd edn. (Paris, 1959).

MILTON, SYBIL, 'The Expulsion of Polish Jews from Germany October 1938 to July 1939', *LBIYB* 24 (1984).

MINCZELES, HENRI, *Histoire générale du Bund: un mouvement révolutionnaire juif* (Paris, 1995).

MINTZ, M., 'The Secretariat of Internationality Affairs (*Sekretariiat mizhnat-sional'nykh sprav*) of the Ukrainian General Secretariat (1917–1918)', *Harvard Ukrainian Studies*, 6, 1 (Mar. 1982).

—— 'Nesigat ha-Rotshildim me-milveh april 1891 le-rusiya min ha-heibet ha-yehudi', *Zion*, 54, 4 (1989).

MISHKINSKY, M., 'Ha-"Sozializm ha-mishtarti" u-megamot bi-mediniyut ha-shilton ha-zari le-gabei ha-yehudim (1900–1903)', *Zion*, 25, 3–4 (1960).

—— 'Mekoroteiha ha-ra'ayoniim shel tenu'at ha-po'alim ha-yehudit be-rusiya be-reishita', *Zion*, 31, 1–2 (1966), 87–115.

—— ' 'Al ha-de'ot ha-kedumot shel ha-sozialistim ha-mahapakhniim shelanu neged ha-yehudim', *He-'Avar*, 21 (1975), 20–34.

—— *Reishit tenu'at ha-po'alim ha-yehudit be-rusiya: megamot yesod* (Tel Aviv, 1981).

MONTEFIORE, C. G., *Race, Nation, Religion and the Jews* (Keighley, 1918).

MOSSE, WERNER E., PAUCKER, ARNOLD, and RÜRUP, REINHARD (eds.), *Revolution and Evolution: 1848 in German-Jewish History* (Tübingen, 1981).

MOTZKIN, LEO ('A. Linden'), *Die Judenpogrome in Russland*, 2 vols. (Cologne and Leipzig, 1910).

—— *La Campagne antisémite en Pologne* (Paris, 1932).

MUNDSCHEIN, YEHOSHU'A (ed.), *Kerem HaBaD: 'Iyun ve-Heker be-Mishnat HaBaD: Divrei Yemei ha-Hasidut ve-Darkei ha-Hasidim*, iv, 1 (Kefar Habad, 1992).

NA'AMAN, SHLOMO, 'Heinrich Marx, Karl Marx ve-Eleanor Marx: shelosha dorot nokhah etgar ha-shivyon ha-ezrahi', *Zion*, 57, 4 (1992), 395–427.

NADAV, M., 'R. Avigdor Ben Hayyim u-milhamto ba-hasidut be-pinsk u-be-lita', *Zion*, 36, 3–4 (1971).

NAMIER, LEWIS, *1848: The Revolution of the Intellectuals* (London, 1946; repr. 1992 with an introduction by James Joll).

NEHER-BERNHEIM, RINA, *Documents inédits sur l'entrée des Juifs dans la société française (1750–1850)*, 2 vols. (Tel Aviv, 1977).

NETTL, J. P., *Rosa Luxemburg*, ii (London, 1966).

NETZER, SHELOMO, *Ma'avak yehudei Polin 'al zekhuyoteihem ha-ezrahiyot ve-ha-le'umiyot (1918–1922)* (Tel Aviv, 1980).

—— 'Yizhak Gruenbaum ke-ish za'ir—zemihato shel manhig zioni be-folin', *Kivunim*, 10 (Feb. 1981).

NISSENBOIM, YIZHAK, *'Alei heldi* (Warsaw, 1929), 323.

OLLIVIER, GEORGES, *L'Alliance Israélite Universelle 1860–1960* (Paris, 1959).

ORBACH, ALEXANDER, *New Voices in Russian Jewry: A Study of the Russian-Jewish Press of Odessa in the Era of the Great Reforms 1860–1871* (Leiden, 1980).

—— 'Zionism and the Russian Revolution of 1905: The Commitment to Participate in Domestic Political Life', in *Bar-Ilan Studies in Judaica and the Humanities*, 24–5 (Ramat-Gan, 1989), 7–23.

PARFITT, TUDOR, ' "The Year of the Pride of Israel"—Montefiore and the Damascus Blood Libel of 1840', in Sonia and V. D. Lipman (eds.), *The Century of Moses Montefiore* (Oxford, 1985).

PATAI, RAPHAEL, *The Jews of Hungary: History, Culture, Psychology* (Detroit, 1996).

PÉGUY, CHARLES, 'L'Affaire Dreyfus et la crise du parti socialiste', *La Revue Blanche*, 20 (1899), 127–39.

—— 'Le Ravage et Réparation', *La Revue Blanche*, 20 (1899), 417–32.

—— *Notre Jeunesse* (Paris, 1933).

PELLI, MOSHE, *The Age of Haskalah* (Leiden, 1979).

PERETS, VL. N. and L. N., *Dekabrist Grigorii Abramovich Perets* (Leningrad, 1926).

PETIT, JACQUES, *Bernanos, Bloy, Claudel, Péguy: quatre écrivains catholiques face à Israël* (Paris, 1972).

PETRZIL, Y., *et al.* (eds.), *Yalkutei po'alei zion: Ha-mahapekha ha-rishona ve-ha-sheniya be-russiya*, i (Tel Aviv, 1947).

PHILIPPE, BÉATRICE, 'Les Archives Israélites de France de leur création en 1840 à février 1848; ou un journal juif sous Louis-Philippe: études de mentalité', Mémoire de maîtrise, University of Paris IV, 1974–5.

PILZER, JAY M., 'The League of Nations and the Jewish Question', Ph.D. thesis Duke University, 1976.

PINSKER, Y. L., *Autoemancipation! Mahnruf an seine Stammesgenossen von einem russischen Juden* (Berlin, 1882). Hebrew translation by Ahad-Ha-'Am in Y. Klausner (ed.), *Sefer Pinsker* (Jerusalem, 1921); English translation by D. S. Blondheim in B. Netanyahu (ed.), *Road to Freedom* (New York, 1944).

PIPES, RICHARD, *Russia under the Old Regime* (New York, 1974).

—— *Russia under the Bolshevik Regime* (New York, 1993).

PLAUT, W. GUNTHER, *The Rise of Reform Judaism: A Sourcebook of its European Origins* (New York, 1963).

POGGE VON STRANDMANN, H. (ed.), *Walther Rathenau: Industrialist, Banker, Intellectual and Politician: Notes and Diaries 1907–1922* (Oxford, 1985).

POLIAKOV, LÉON, *The History of Anti-Semitism*, iii. *From Voltaire to Wagner* (New York, 1975); iv. *Suicidal Europe, 1870–1933* (Oxford, 1985).

POLONSKY, ANTONY, *Politics in Independent Poland 1921–1939* (Oxford, 1972).

POLONSKY, ANTONY, BASISTA, JAKUB, and LINK-LENCZOWSKI, ANDRZEJ (eds.), *The Jews in Old Poland 1000–1795* (London, 1993).

―― *et al.* (eds.), *Jews in Independent Poland 1918–1939*, Polin: Studies in Polish Jewry, viii (London, 1994).

PORTNOY, S. A. (trans. and ed.), *Vladimir Medem: The Life and Soul of a Legendary Jewish Socialist* [English. trans. of V. D. Medem, *Fun mayn leben*] (New York, 1979).

POSENER, S., *Adolphe Crémieux*, 2 vols. (Paris, 1933).

PRAWER, S. S., *Heine's Jewish Comedy* (Oxford, 1985).

PRIBRAM, A. F. (ed.), *Urkunden und Akten zur Geschichte der Juden in Wien 1526–1847 (1849)*, 2 vols. (Vienna and Leipzig, 1918).

PROUDHON, P.-J., *Jésus et les origines du Christianisme*, 2nd edn. (Paris, 1896).

―― *Carnets*, ed. Pierre Haubtmann, ii (Paris, 1961).

PULZER, PETER, *The Rise of Political Anti-Semitism in Germany and Austria*, revised edn. (Cambridge, Mass., 1988).

―― *Jews and the German State* (Oxford, 1992).

RABINOWICZ, OSKAR K., *Fifty Years of Zionism* (London, 1952).

RADKEY, O. H., *The Election to the Russian Constituent Assembly of 1917* (Cambridge, Mass., 1950).

RAFAEL, Y., and SHRAGAI, S. Z. (eds.), *Sefer ha-zionut ha-datit*, 2 vols. (Jerusalem, 1977).

RAWSON, DON C., *Russian Rightists and the Revolution of 1905* (Cambridge, 1995).

Reichsvertretung der Juden in Deutschland, *Zur Konferenz in Evian* (Berlin, 1938; mimeograph).

REINACH, THÉODORE, *Histoire des Israélites depuis la ruine de leur indépendance nationale jusqu'à nos jours* (Paris, 1901).

REINHARZ, JEHUDA, *Chaim Weizmann: The Making of a Zionist Leader* (New York, 1985).

―― *Chaim Weizmann: The Making of a Statesman* (New York, 1992).

RENAN, ERNEST, *De la part des peuples sémitiques dans l'histoire de la civilisation*, 5th edn. (Paris, 1862).

―― *Histoire générale et système comparé des langues sémitiques*, part one, 5th edn. (Paris, 1878).

RHEINS, CARL J., 'Deutscher Vortrupp, Gefolgschaft deutscher Juden 1933–35', *LBIYB* 26 (London, 1981), 207–29.

RIASANOVSKY, N. V., *Nicholas I and Official Nationality in Russia, 1825–1855* (Berkeley, 1967).

RICHARZ, MONIKA (ed.), *Jüdisches Leben in Deutschland. Selbstzeugnisse zur Sozialgeschichte*, 3 vols. (Stuttgart, 1976–82). English edn. (abridged) *Jewish Life in Germany: Memoirs of Three Centuries* (Bloomington, Ind., 1991).

RINGELBLUM, EMANUEL, 'Shemu'el Zbitkower', *Zion*, 3, 3 (1938).

ROBINSON, JACOB, *et al.*, *Were the Minorities Treaties a Failure?* (New York, 1943).

ROBLIN, MICHEL, *Les Juifs de Paris: démographie-économie-culture* (Paris, 1952).

ROGGER, HANS, 'The Jewish Policy of Late Tsarism: A Reappraisal', *Wiener Library Bulletin*, 25, 1–2 (1971).

―― 'Government, Jews, Peasants, and Land in Post-emancipation Russia', *Cahiers du monde russe et soviétique*, 18, 1 and 2–3 (1976).

ROSE, P. L., *Revolutionary Antisemitism in Germany from Kant to Wagner* (Princeton, 1990).

ROSEN, ZEVI, 'Hashkafotav ha-anti-yehudiot shel Bruno Bauer (1838–1843), mekorot yenikatan u-mashma'utan', *Zion*, 33, 1–2 (1968), 57–76.

ROSENHEIM, JACOB, *Agudistische Schriften* (Frankfurt-on-Main, n.d.).

—— *Ausgewählte Aufsätze und Ansprachen*, 2 vols. (Frankfurt-on-Main, 1930).

—— *Zikhronot*, 2nd edn. (Benei Berak, 1979); German language edn. *Erinnerungen 1870–1920* (Frankfurt-on-Main, 1970).

ROSTWOROWSKI, EMMANUEL, 'La Grande Diète (1788–1792); réformes et perspectives', *Annales historiques de la révolution française*, 36 (July–Sept. 1964).

ROTENSTREICH, NATHAN, 'For and against Emancipation: The Bruno Bauer Controversy', *LBIYB* 4 (1959), 3–36.

ROZENBLIT, MARSHA L., *The Jews of Vienna, 1867–1914: Assimilation and Identity* (Albany, NY, 1983).

RUBINOW, I. M., *Economic Condition of the Jews in Russia* (Washington, 1907; repr. New York, 1975).

RUPPIN, ARTHUR, *Pirkei Ḥayyai: be-vinyan ha-areẓ ve-ha'am*, 3 vols. (Tel Aviv, 1968).

Russia, Census Office, *Pervaya Vseobshchaya Perepis' Naseleniia Rossiiskoi Imperii 1897 g., Obshchii Svod. i–ii* (St Petersburg, 1905).

—— Ministry of Interior, *Sbornik Uzakonenie Kasayushchikhsya evreev* (St Petersburg, 1872).

—— *Sionizm: istoricheskii ocherk ego razvitiya. Zapiska, sostavlennaya v departament politsii* (St Petersburg, 1903).

SALBSTEIN, M. C. N., *The Emancipation of the Jews in Britain: The Question of the Admission of the Jews to Parliament* (East Brunswick, NJ, 1982).

SALTMAN, AVROM, *The Jewish Question in 1655: Studies in Prynne's Demurrer* (Ramat-Gan, 1995).

SAMTER, N., *Judentaufen im neunzehnten Jahrhundert* (Berlin, 1906).

SAUER, PAUL, *Die Schicksale der jüdischen Bürger Baden-Württembergs während der nationalsozialistischen Verfolgungszeit 1933–1945* (Stuttgart, 1969).

SCHAPIRO, LEONARD, 'The Role of the Jews in the Russian Revolutionary Movements', *Slavonic and East European Review*, 40 (1961–2), 148–67.

SCHECHTMAN, JOSEPH B., 'The Jabotinsky–Slavinsky Agreement: A Chapter in Ukrainian–Jewish Relations', *JSS* 17 (1955).

SCHNEIDERMAN, JEREMIAH, *Sergei Zubatov and Revolutionary Marxism* (Ithaca, NY, 1976).

SCHOLEM, GERSHOM, *From Berlin to Jerusalem: Memories of my Youth*, English trans. Harry Zohn (New York, 1988).

SCHORSCH, ISMAR, *Jewish Reactions to German Anti-Semitism* (Philadelphia, 1972).

SCHUBERT, HERZL, *She'elat Evian 'al rek'a tekufata*, M.A. thesis, Tel Aviv University, 1990.

SCHWARTZ, SH., *Nordau be-Igrotav* (Jerusalem, 1944).

—— *Ussishkin be-igrotav* (Jerusalem, 1949).

SETON-WATSON, HUGH, *The Russian Empire 1801–1917* (Oxford, 1967).

SHAḤRAI, A. I., *Rabbi 'Akiva Yosef Schlesinger* (Jerusalem, 1942).

SHAKIRZYANOV, R. KH. (ed.), *Taina Izrailya* (St Petersburg, 1993).

SHAPIRA, ANITA, *Berl*, 2 vols. (Tel Aviv, 1980).

SHAPIRO, ROBERT M., *The Polish* Kehile *Elections of 1936: A Revolution Re-examined* (New York, 1988).

SHAZAR [Rubashov], SH. ZALMAN, *Orei Dorot* (Jerusalem, 1971).

SHEEHAN, JAMES J., *German History 1770–1866* (Oxford, 1989).

SHERMAN, A. J., *Island Refuge: Britain and Refugees from the Third Reich, 1933–1939* (London, 1973).

SHOḤAT, A., *Mossad ha-rabbanut mi-taʿam be-rusiya* (Haifa, 1975).

—— 'Ha-hanhaga bi-kehilot rusiya ʿim bitul ha-"kahal" ', *Z̧ion*, 43, 3–4 (1977), 143–233.

SHTIF, N. I., *Pogromy na ukraine (period dobrovol'cheskoi armii)* (Berlin, 1922).

SHURER, H., *et al.* (eds.), *Ha-pogrom be-kishinov* (Tel Aviv, 1963).

SILBERNER, EDMUND, 'Charles Fourier on the Jewish Question', *JSS* 8, 4 (1946).

—— 'Austrian Social Democracy and the Jewish Problem', *Historia Judaica*, 13 (1951).

—— 'Bernard Lazare ve-ha-z̧ionut', *Shivat Z̧ion*, 2–3 (1951–2).

—— 'British Socialism and the Jews', *Historia Judaica*, 14 (1952).

—— *Ha-soz̧ialism ha-maʿaravi u-she'elat ha-yehudim* (Jerusalem, 1955).

SIMPSON, JOHN HOPE, *Refugees: A Review of the Situation since September 1938* (London, 1939).

—— *The Refugee Problem: Report of a Survey* (London, Jan. 1939).

SLUTSKY, [Dov-] B[e]r, 'Ha-hagana ha-ʿaz̧maʿit be-ukraina', 1923, publ. in *He-ʿAvar*, 17 (1970).

SLUTSKY, Y., 'Zemiḥata shel ha-inteligenz̧ia ha-yehudit-rusit', *Z̧ion*, 25, 3–4 (1960).

—— 'Baʿayat ḥa-aḥrayut li-fraʿot ukrayna', *He-ʿAvar*, 17 (1970).

—— *Ha-ʿItonut ha-yehudit-rusit ba-me'ah ha-tesha'-ʿesre* (Jerusalem, 1970).

—— 'Le-toldot ha-yehudim be-rusiya be-sof ha-me'ah ha-18 (shalosh teʿudot)', *He-ʿAvar*, 19 (1972), 74–82.

—— and KAPLAN, M., *Ḥayyalim yehudiim be-z̧iv'ot eiropa* (Tel Aviv, 1967).

SMITH, PAUL, 'Disraeli's Politics', *Transactions of the Royal Historical Society*, 5th series, 37 (1987), 65–85.

SNEH, MOSHE, *Ketavim: 1928–1939*, i, ed. E. Meltzer (Tel Aviv, 1995).

SOFER, SHELOMO (ed.), *Sefer Igrot Sofrim* (Vienna, 1929).

SORKIN, DAVID, 'From Context to Comparison: The German Haskalah and Reform Catholicism', *Tel Aviver Jahrbuch für deutsche Geschichte*, 20 (1991), 23–58.

SPIRE, ANDRÉ, *Les Juifs et la guerre* (Paris, 1917).

—— *Poèmes Juifs* (Paris, 1959).

—— *Souvenirs à bâtons rompus* (Paris, 1962).

SPRINGER, A., 'Gavriil Derzhavin's Jewish Reform Project of 1800', *Canadian-American Slavic Studies*, 10 (Spring 1976), 1–24.

—— 'Enlightened Absolutism and Jewish Reform: Prussia, Austria, and Russia', *California Slavic Studies*, 11 (1980), 237–67.

STANISLAWSKI, M., *Tsar Nicholas I and the Jews: The Transformation of Jewish Society in Russia 1825–1855* (Philadelphia, 1983).

STANLEY, JOHN, 'The Politics of the Jewish Question in the Duchy of Warsaw, 1807–1813', *JSS* 44, 1 (1982), 47–62.

STEED, HENRY WICKHAM, *The Hapsburg Monarchy*, 3rd edn. (London, 1914).

STEIN, LEONARD, *The Balfour Declaration* (New York, 1961).

STEINBERG, BARUKH (ed.), *Sefer da'at ha-rabbanim* (Warsaw, 1902).

STERLING, ELEONORE O., 'Anti-Jewish Riots in Germany in 1819: A Displacement of Social Protest', *Historia Judaica*, 12 (1950), 105–42.

—— 'Jewish Reaction to Jew-Hatred in the First Half of the Nineteenth Century', *LBIYB* 3 (London, 1958).

STERN, FRITZ, *Gold and Iron: Bismarck, Bleichröder, and the Building of the German Empire* (New York, 1979).

STERNHELL, ZEEV, 'National Socialism and Antisemitism: The Case of Maurice Barrès', *Journal of Contemporary History*, 8, 4 (1973), 47–66.

STONE, JULIUS, *International Guarantees of Minority Rights* (London, 1932).

STONE, NORMAN, *The Eastern Front 1914–1917* (London, 1975).

STRAUSS, HERBERT, 'Pre-Emancipation Prussian Policies towards the Jews 1815–1847', *LBIYB* 11 (1966), 107–36.

—— 'Jewish Emigration from Germany: Nazi Policies and Jewish Responses', *LBIYB* (2 articles) 25, 26 (London, 1980, 1981), 313–61; 343–409.

SURASKI, AHARON, *Raban shel Yisrael: Perakim be-masekhet ḥayyav u-fo'alo shel . . . R. Ḥayyim 'Ozer Grodzienski* (Benei Berak, 1971).

SZAJKOWSKI, ZOSA, 'How the Mass Migration to America Began', *JSS* 4, 4 (Oct. 1942).

—— 'The Alliance Israélite Universelle and East-European Jewry in the '60s', *JSS* 4 (1942), 139–60.

—— 'The European Attitude to East European Jewish Immigration (1881–1891)', *Publications of the American Jewish Historical Society*, 41, 2 (Dec. 1951).

—— 'Mishlaḥoteihem shel yehudei bordo el va'adat malzerb (1788) ve-el ha-aseifa ha-le'umit (1790)', *Ẓion*, 18, 1–2 (1953).

—— 'Goral ha-tikim be-ministerion ha-ḥuẓ ha-zarfati ha-nog'im le-'alilat damesek', *Ẓion*, 19, 3–4 (1954).

—— 'Pera'ot be-alzas be'et ha-mahapekhot shel 1789, 1830, ve-1848', *Ẓion*, 20, 1–2 (1955).

—— 'Conflicts in the Alliance Israélite Universelle and the Founding of the Anglo-Jewish Association, the Vienna Allianz and the Hilfsverein', *JSS* 19 (1957), 29–50.

—— 'Jewish Diplomacy', *JSS* 22 (1960), 131–58.

—— 'Paul Nathan, Lucien Wolf, Jacob H. Schiff and the Jewish Revolutionary Movements in Eastern Europe 1903–1917', *JSS* 29 (1967), 75–91.

—— ' "A Reappraisal of Symon Petliura and Ukrainian–Jewish Relations, 1917–1921": A Rebuttal' [to Taras Hunczak, 'A Reappraisal of Symon Petliura and Ukrainian–Jewish Relations, 1917–1921', *JSS* 31 (1969), 163–84], ibid. 184–213.

TAL, URIEL, *Yahadut ve-naẓrut ba-'raykh ha-sheini'* (Jerusalem, 1969); English trans. *Christians and Jews in Germany* (Ithaca, NY, 1975).

—— *Structures of German 'Political Theology' in the Nazi Era* (Tel Aviv, 1979).

TAMA, DIOGENE (trans F. D. Kirwan), *Transactions of the Parisian Sanhedrin* (London, 1807; reprinted Farnborough, 1971).

TARTAKOWER, ARIEH, and GROSSMAN, KURT R., *The Jewish Refugee* (New York, 1944).

TCHERIKOWER, E., *Yehudim be-'itot mahapekha* (Tel Aviv, 1957).

TCHERNOFF, JEHUDA, *Dans le creuset des civilisations* (Paris, 1936–8).

TEMPERLEY, H. W. V. (ed.), *A History of the Peace Conference of Paris*, 6 vols. (London, 1920–4).

THEILHABER, FELIX A., *Der Untergang der deutschen Juden* (Munich, 1911).

TIMOFEEV, V. V., 'Evreiskaya emigratsiya iz Rossii v kontekste rossiisko-britanskikh otnoshenii kontsa xix veka', University of Kharkov thesis, 1993.

TOBIAS, HENRY J., *The Jewish Bund in Russia: From its Origins to 1905* (Stanford, Calif., 1972).

TOURY, JACOB, ' "The Jewish Question"—A Semantic Approach', *LBIYB* 11 (1966), 85–106.

—— 'Organizational Problems of German Jewry', *LBIYB* 13 (London, 1968).

—— *Kavim le-ḥeker knisat ha-yehudim la-ḥayyim ha-ezraḥiim be-germaniya* (Tel Aviv, 1972).

—— *Mekorot le-ḥeker knisat ha-yehudim la-ḥayyim ha-ezraḥiim be-germaniya* (Tel Aviv, 1972).

TROEN, S. I., and PINKUS, B. (eds.), *Organizing Rescue: National Jewish Solidarity in the Modern Period* (London, 1992).

TURTEL, H., 'Pulmus ha-hagira me-rusiya aharei "ha-sufot ba-negev" be-shenat 1881', *He-'Avar*, 21 (1975).

VAGO, BELA, and MOSSE, GEORGE L. (eds.), *Jews and Non-Jews in Eastern Europe 1918–1945* (New York and Jerusalem, 1974).

VAUTRIN, HUBERT, *La Pologne du XVIIIᵉ siècle vue par un précepteur français* (Paris, 1966).

VENTURI, FRANCO, *Roots of Revolution* (New York, 1966).

VERETÉ, MAYIR, 'Haẓa'ot polaniyot le-fitron teritoriali shel "she'elat ha-yehudim" ', *Ẓion*, 6, 3 (1941), 148–55.

—— 'The Balfour Declaration and its Makers', *Middle Eastern Studies*, 6, 1 (1970).

VITAL, DAVID, *The Origins of Zionism* (Oxford, 1975).

—— *Zionism: The Formative Years* (Oxford, 1982).

—— *Zionism: The Crucial Phase* (Oxford, 1987).

—— *The Future of the Jews: A People at the Crossroads?* (Cambridge, Mass., 1990).

VOLKOGONOV, DMITRI, *Lenin: Life and Legacy* (London, 1994).

WALDMANN, MARK, *Goethe and the Jews: A Challenge to Hitlerism* (New York, 1934).

WASSERSTEIN, BERNARD, *Britain and the Jews of Europe 1939–1945* (London and Oxford, 1979).

—— *Herbert Samuel: A Political Life* (Oxford, 1992).

WEILL, JULIEN, *Zadoc Kahn* (Paris, 1912).

WEIZMANN, CHAIM, *Trial and Error* (London, 1949).

—— *Letters and Papers*, Series A, 23 vols. (London and Jerusalem, 1968–80).

WERTHEIMER, JACK, ' "The Unwanted Element": East European Jews in Imperial Germany', *LBIYB* 26 (London, 1981), 23–46.

—— *Unwelcome Strangers: East European Jews in Imperial Germany* (New York, 1987).

—— *The Uses of Tradition* (New York, 1992).

WILSON, NELLY, *Bernard Lazare: Antisemitism and the Problem of Jewish Identity in Late Nineteenth-century France* (Cambridge, 1978).

WILSON, STEPHEN, *Ideology and Experience: Antisemitism in France at the Time of the Dreyfus Affair* (Rutherford and London, 1982).

WINAWER, H. M., *The Winawer Saga* (London, 1994).

WISE, STEPHEN S., *Challenging Years* (New York, 1949).

WISTRICH, ROBERT S., *Socialism and the Jews* (Rutherford and London, 1982).

WOLF, LUCIEN, *Sir Moses Montefiore* (New York, 1885), 218.

—— *The Legal Sufferings of the Jews in Russia* (London, 1912).

WOOLF, STUART, *Napoleon's Integration of Europe* (London, 1991).

World Jewish Congress, Institute of Jewish Affairs, *Unity in Dispersion: A History of the World Jewish Congress*, 2nd revised edn. (New York, 1948).

WYMAN, DAVID S. (ed.), *The World Reacts to the Holocaust* (Baltimore, 1996).

WYNOT, EDWARD D., ' "A Necessary Cruelty": The Emergence of Official Anti-Semitism in Poland, 1936–39', *American Historical Review*, 76 (1971), 1035–58.

—— 'The Catholic Church and the Polish State 1935–1939', *Journal of Church and State*, 15 (1973), 223–40.

YA'ARI, A. (ed.), *Mas'ot Erez-Yisrael* (Tel Aviv, 1946).

YAHIL, LENY, *Ha-sho'ah: goral yehudei eiropa 1932–1945*, 2 vols. (Jerusalem and Tel Aviv, 1987).

YAHUDA, A. S., *Dr. Weizmann's Errors on Trial: A Refutation* (New York, 1952).

YISRAELI, DAVID, 'The Third Reich and the Transfer Agreement', *Journal of Contemporary History*, 6, 2 (1971).

YO'ELI, M. (ed.), *Y. L. Pinsker* (Tel Aviv, 1960).

YODFAT, ARYE, 'Ha-dat ha-yehudit ba-shanim ha-rishonot shel ha-shilton ha-sovyeti (1917–1923)', *He-'Avar*, 19 (1972).

ZELDIN, THEODORE, *France 1848–1945*, 2 vols. (Oxford, 1973, 1977).

Zentralwohlfahrtsstelle der deutschen Juden, *Jüdische Bevölkerungspolitik* (Berlin, 1929).

ZIMMERMANN, M., 'Hashpa'at ha-le'umiyut ha-germanit 'al ha-le'umiyut ha-yehudit—irgunei ha-studentim ha-yehudiim be-germania be-reishit ha-me'ah ha-'esrim', *Zion*, 45, 4 (1980).

ZIPPERSTEIN, S. J., 'Jewish Enlightenment in Odessa: Cultural Characteristics, 1794–1871', *JSS* (Winter 1982).

ZITRON, S. L., *Toldot Hibbat Zion* (Odessa, 1914).

ZUR, YA'AKOV, 'Ha-ortodoksiya ha-yehudit be-germaniya ve-yahasa la-hit'argenut ha-yehudit ve-la-zionut', Ph.D. thesis, Tel Aviv University, 1982.

GLOSSARY

arendar	bailiff or leaseholder on a Polish estate
'askan	public activist or politico
doikeyt	determination to stay put (literally: 'hereness')
Endziel	ultimate purpose (of the Zionist movement)
gevir	communal oligarch
gzeira	punitive decree
ḥakham bashi	Sephardi chief rabbi (under the Ottomans)
halakha	the body of religious rules and injunctions governing behaviour
haskalah	enlightenment
ḥeder	traditional elementary school
Hofjude	'court Jew' (serving the ruler of an eighteenth-century German state)
Kadets	Constitutional Democrats in pre-revolutionary Russia
kahal	governing body of a Jewish community
katorga	penal servitude in pre-revolutionary Russia
kehilla	community
kelal Yisrael	the Jewish people in its entirety
kisufei ge'ula	the yearning for Redemption
kazyonny ravvin	crown (or state) rabbi in pre-revolutionary Russia
Machtergreifung	the seizure of power (by the German National Socialists in 1933)
malshin	sneak or delator
maskil	scholarly or intellectual participant in the *haskalah* movement
melamed	traditional elementary schoolteacher
millet	statutory ethno-religious group under the Ottomans
Mischling	person of mixed racial parentage under the National Socialists
narod	the Russian term for people or nation
parnas	communal worthy
pidyon shevuyim	ransoming of captives
pogromshchiki	perpetrators of pogroms
rashut	the ruling power in the land
rebbe	Hasidic leader
Rechtsstaat	a state governed by law
Sanhedrin	supreme rabbinical court in antiquity
Schutzjuden	protected (i.e. privileged) Jews

sheḥita	ritual slaughter
shtadlanut	intercession
shtetl	Jewish hamlet
uchĕnyi evrei	'learned Jew' (usually as adviser on Jewish affairs to a pre-revolutionary Russian provincial governor)
wojewoda	king's or prince's lieutenant in pre-partition Poland
yeshiva	rabbinical academy
yishuv	the Jewish population of Palestine
zemstvo	elected district or provincial council in pre-revolutionary Russia

INDEX